THE CAMBRIDGE HISTORY OF AFRICA

General Editors: J. D. FAGE and ROLAND OLIVER

Volume 3

from *c*. 1050 to *c*. 1600

THE CAMBRIDGE HISTORY OF AFRICA

1 **From the Earliest Times to *c.* 500 BC**
edited by J. Desmond Clark

2 **From *c.* 500 BC to AD 1050**
edited by J. D. Fage

3 **From *c.* 1050 to *c.* 1600**
edited by Roland Oliver

4 **From *c.* 1600 to *c.* 1790**
edited by Richard Gray

5 **From *c.* 1790 to *c.* 1870**
edited by John Flint

6 **From 1870 to 1920**
edited by G. N. Sanderson

7 **From 1920 to 1942**
edited by A. D. Roberts

8 **From 1943 to the 1970s**
edited by Michael Crowder

THE CAMBRIDGE HISTORY OF AFRICA

Volume 3

from *c.* 1050 to *c.* 1600

edited by

ROLAND OLIVER

CAMBRIDGE UNIVERSITY PRESS

CAMBRIDGE

LONDON · NEW YORK · MELBOURNE

Published by the Syndics of the Cambridge University Press
The Pitt Building, Trumpington Street, Cambridge CB2 1RP
Bentley House, 200 Euston Road, London NW1 2DB
32 East 57th Street, New York, NY 10022, USA
296 Beaconsfield Parade, Middle Park, Melbourne 3206, Australia

First published 1977

Printed in Great Britain
at the
University Printing House, Cambridge

Library of Congress Cataloguing in Publication Data
Main entry under title:
The Cambridge history of Africa
Bibliography: v. 3
Includes index.
CONTENTS:
v. 3. From *c.* 1050 to *c.* 1600, edited by R. Oliver.
1. Africa – History – Collected works. I. Fage, J. D.
II. Oliver, Roland Anthony.
DT 20.C 28 960 76–2261
ISBN: 0 521 20981 1 (v. 3)

CONTENTS

MAPS

PREFACE

In the English-speaking world, the Cambridge histories have since the beginning of the century set the pattern for multi-volume works of history, with chapters written by experts on a particular topic, and unified by the guiding hand of volume editors of senior standing. *The Cambridge Modern History*, planned by Lord Acton, appeared in sixteen volumes between 1902 and 1912. It was followed by *The Cambridge Ancient History*, *The Cambridge Medieval History*, *The Cambridge History of English Literature*, and Cambridge Histories of India, of Poland, and of the British Empire. The original *Modern History* has now been replaced by *The New Cambridge Modern History* in twelve volumes, and *The Cambridge Economic History of Europe* is now being completed. Other Cambridge Histories recently completed include a history of Islam and of the Bible treated as a central document of and influence on Western civilization; Histories in progress include a history of Arabic Literature, China, Inner Asia, Iran and Judaism.

It was during the later 1950s that the Syndics of the Cambridge University Press first began to explore the possibility of embarking on a Cambridge History of Africa. But they were then advised that the time was not yet ripe. The serious appraisal of the past of Africa by historians and archaeologists had hardly been undertaken before 1948, the year when universities first began to appear in increasing numbers in the vast reach of the African continent south of the Sahara and north of the Limpopo, and the time too when universities outside Africa first began to take some notice of its history. It was impressed upon the Syndics that the most urgent need of such a young, but also very rapidly advancing, branch of historical studies, was a journal of international standing through which the results of ongoing research might be disseminated. In 1960, therefore, the Cambridge University Press launched *The Journal of African History*, which gradually demonstrated the amount of work being undertaken to establish the past of Africa as an integrated whole rather than – as it had usually been viewed before – as the story of a series of incursions into the continent by peoples coming from outside, from the Mediterranean basin, the Near

East or western Europe. This movement will of course continue and develop further, but the increasing facilities available for its publication soon began to demonstrate a need to assess both what had been done, and what still needed to be done, in the light of some general historical perspective for the continent.

The Syndics therefore returned to their original charge, and in 1966 the founding editors of *The Journal of African History* accepted a commission to become the general editors of a *Cambridge History of Africa.* They found it a daunting task to draw up a plan for a co-operative work covering a history which was in active process of exploration by scholars of many nations, scattered over a fair part of the globe, and of many disciplines – linguists, anthropologists, geographers and botanists, for example, as well as historians and archaeologists.

It was thought that the greatest problems were likely to arise with the earliest and latest periods: the earliest, because so much would depend on the results of long-term archaeological investigation, and the latest, because of the rapid changes in historical perspective that were occurring as a consequence of the ending of colonial rule in Africa. Initially, therefore, only five volumes were planned, of which the first, Africa before *c.* 500 BC, based entirely upon archaeological sources (and edited by an archaeologist), would be the last to appear, while of the others – dealing with the periods of approximately 500 BC to AD 1050, 1050–1600, 1600–1790, and 1790–1875 – it was thought that the first to be published would probably be the last. (In the event, it has turned out to be Professor Richard Gray's volume 4, though Professor John E. Flint's volume 5 followed next in order.) Only after these volumes were well under way would an attempt be made to plan for the period after *c.* 1875. Nine years later, it can be said that three further volumes have been planned and editors appointed, and that it is hoped that these will appear at regular intervals following the publication of volume 1.

When they started their work, the general editors quickly came to the conclusion that the most practicable plan for getting out the first five volumes within a reasonable period of time was likely to be the simplest and most straightforward. The direction of each volume was therefore entrusted to a volume editor who, in addition to having made a substantial contribution to the understanding of the period in question, was a man with whom the general editors were in close touch. Within a volume, the aim was to keep the number of contributors to a minimum. Each of them was asked to essay a broad survey of a particular area or theme with which he was familiar for the whole of the period covered by the volume. In this survey, his purpose should be to take account not only of all relevant research done, or still in progress, but also of the gaps in knowledge. These he should try to fill by new thinking of his own, whether based on new work on the available sources or on interpolations from congruent research.

It should be remembered that the plan for these first five volumes was drawn up nearly a decade ago, when little or no research had been done on many important topics, and before many of today's younger scholars – not least those who now fill posts in the departments of history and archaeology in the universities and research institutes in Africa itself – had made their own deep penetrations into such areas of ignorance. Two things follow from this. If the general editors had drawn up their plan in the 1970s rather than the 1960s, the shape might well have been very different, perhaps with a larger number of more specialized, shorter chapters, each centred on a smaller area, period or theme, to the understanding of which the contributor would have made his own individual contribution. Indeed, the last three volumes seem likely to be composed more on such lines. Secondly, the sheer volume of new research that has been published since the contributors for the first five volumes accepted their commissions has often led them to undertake very substantial revisions in their work as it progressed from draft to draft, thus protracting the length of time originally envisaged for the preparation of these volumes.

But histories are meant to be read, and not simply to be continually rewritten and modified by their authors and editors. Volume 3 of *The Cambridge History of Africa* is therefore now launched for public use and appraisal, together with a promise that five further volumes should follow it at more or less regular intervals.

J. D. Fage
August 1975 Roland Oliver

INTRODUCTION: SOME INTERREGIONAL THEMES

There is obviously no scheme of periodization which is valid for Africa as a whole, and the opening and closing dates of this volume are not intended to be more than notional. In terms of political history, they fit best with events in North and West Africa, where the period opens with the great conquests of the Almoravids to the north and south of the western Sahara, and where it closes with the Moroccan conquest of the Niger bend, which destroyed the political unity of the western Sudan established during more than three centuries of strong rule by successive dynasties of Mali and Songhay. It is significant that these were the first and the last occasions on which conquering armies crossed the desert, and, taken together, they demarcate the high period of trans-Saharan communications, when the comings and goings of pious Muslims were reinforced by the golden trade of the Sudan, which fertilized the economic revival of all the Mediterranean lands. At its height, the Almoravid empire stretched from the Senegal to Saragossa, while that of the Almohads, which succeeded it, was narrower only in its lack of direct control over the desert routes. The golden trade, however, continued to flourish and to bind the two shores of the Mediterranean into a single network, which survived through medieval times. The Hafsid successors of the Almohads in Tunisia were trading, by the fifteenth century, as far afield as Norway in one direction and Bornu in the other.

In north-eastern Africa, the period almost coincides with that in which Egypt was the seat of an independent, sovereign power, controlled first by the Fatimids, then by the Ayyubids and finally by the Mamluks – a period during which Egypt enjoyed a special pre-eminence throughout the northern half of Africa on account of its central position across the pilgrimage routes both of African Muslims travelling to Mecca and of African Christians travelling to Jerusalem. During this period Egypt repelled both the Crusaders and the Mongols. It controlled the Red Sea and most of the eastern trade. It helped to overthrow the Christian kingdoms of Nubia, but continued to supply Ethiopia with its Christian bishops. Above all, Egypt provided both the Maghrib and sub-Saharan West Africa with a standard of civilization, learning, luxury and temporal power, which was emulated wherever in Africa Muslim rulers, scholars, pilgrims and merchants carried the tale of their long-distance travels.

Throughout the northern half of Africa, the period was one in which the religion of Islam made striking progress. To the north of the Sahara, and among the desert peoples, it was a period of consolidation, when the largely nominal adherence of Coptic and Berber populations already established during earlier centuries was built up through a peculiarly Islamic combination of revivalist propaganda and military action, whereby communities of active believers gathered around a reforming teacher would forcefully impose a stricter observance upon wider groups. The proliferation of these local movements was greatly assisted by the institution of the Pilgrimage and by the growing tradition of travel for study to schools in the Islamic heartlands. The parallel spread of Arabic as the language of theology and higher learning was helped forward by the progressive dispersion of bedouin Arabs through the arid pastoral lands on either side of the desert. It began with the penetration of northern Nubia by the Rabīʿa and Juhayna Arabs, and with what has been called the second Arab conquest of North Africa, initiated by the westward movement of the Banū Hilal and the Banū Sulaym into the southern borderlands of Ifrīqiya. It ended with the arabization of Mauritania by the Kunta tribes and with the penetration of southern Nubia, Kordofan, Darfur and Wadai by the Baqqāra and Shuwa pastoralists.

In the Negro lands of the sub-Saharan Sudan, the period saw the religion of the Prophet established as a potent factor in the political and trading systems of most of the major states. At the courts of Takrur, Ghana, Mali, Songhay, Kanem-Bornu and those of the Hausa city-states, Islam was recognized as the religion of men of cosmopolitan outlook, even though concessions had still to be made to the indigenous beliefs of the majority of the population. Kings processed in state to the Friday prayer, went on Pilgrimage and honoured those learned in Islamic law and theology. Muslim merchants held a near monopoly of long-distance trade, whether across the desert routes or southward through the savanna and the forest margins. Wherever two or three Muslim merchants settled with their dependants to found a warehouse compound, there a Muslim cleric of some description was likely soon to be found. South of the Sahara, there were as yet no mass movements such as had occurred to the north of the desert and in it, but the growing-points for future expansion were established. Not merely at the great capitals, but in scores of small towns and commercial settlements, there grew up a *noblesse de la robe* of preachers and teachers, lawyers and merchants, scribes and holy men, literate in Arabic, travelled, aware of a wider world, indispensable to rulers for a variety of worldly skills and thaumaturgical services, respected for their knowledge if not for their beliefs by the pagan people among whom they lived, growing steadily in numbers as the generations passed, and looking consciously towards a future when all women would go decently veiled and all men bow down together at the times of prayer.

In East Africa, too, Islam spread far to the south during this period, though in a rather different way. The conversion of the Danakil and the Somali corresponded rather closely with that of the Saharan nomads; but the penetration of the Ethiopian highlands, though attempted, was largely blocked by the southward expansion of a militant Christian kingdom, the dynamic vitality of which remains a source of wonder. South of the Juba, Islam reached as far as the Zambezi, but only along the palm-fringed coastline and on the offshore islands, where ocean shipping could keep open the lines of communication with the heartlands of the faith. There is no doubt that in this region Islam retained a more exotic flavour than in sub-Saharan West Africa. In racial composition the Muslim communities of the East African coast were no doubt predominantly African, but the nuclear elements of these societies were either foreign or at least claimed a foreign origin. These were not African societies which had been penetrated by Islam, but foreign settlements around which African elements had gathered. The difference was all important. In both religion and politics the leaders were from the immigrant communities. Though the material monuments were impressive, there was no basis here for Islamic expansion inland.

In those parts of Africa which were still largely beyond the range of Islamic influence, it was only during the last century or so of our period that the opening of the Atlantic sea-routes by the Portuguese began to provide regular, though even then hardly comparable, means of communication with the outside world. During the first four or five centuries of the period, therefore, the main themes of historical development were internal ones, and their discernment is made more difficult by the relatively thin and uneven nature of the surviving evidence. For many areas and for most of the period, the best potential source of evidence is archaeological; but this branch of inquiry is as yet little developed, partly through lack of research, but even more because it was only in the 1960s that the radiocarbon method began to provide a sufficiently accurate means of dating material from the first half of the present millennium. At the present time, therefore, most of our knowledge of these areas comes from the earlier and less chronologically structured layers of the oral traditions of the African peoples, which, even when taken together with the earliest reports by literate outsiders, hardly extend further backwards in time than about the middle of our period.

Nevertheless, certain broad themes can be dimly perceived. For example, the part of West Africa lying to the south of Hausaland – the country of the Jukun and the Nupe, the Yoruba and the Edo – was one area which, although as yet unpenetrated by Islamic influence, seems to have carried a particularly dense population, and to have been the scene of important developments in state formation. These states were based, like their Hausa counterparts, on walled towns, which were not only centres of government and religious cults but also supported a wide variety of local industries, such as iron-working and metallurgy, glass-making, weaving, tanning, leatherwork and dyeing. Agriculture was, of course, carried on in the surrounding countryside; but the fact that town walls enclosed considerable areas of unbuilt land suggests that these were cities of refuge into which rural populations could retreat in times of danger. It is probable that, then as now, many farming families had a city base. Wherever the country was open, horses were used for warfare and slave-raiding; and the fact that horses were kept for ceremonial purposes even in forest states to the south of the region suggests that cavalry power had originally been at the heart of the whole process of state formation. Archaeological investigation has shown that, as far south as Ife, which lies within the forest margin, the origins of urban settlement go back to the very beginning of our period. We thus see that the pattern of city-states, for so long associated by historians primarily with Hausaland, was in fact something much more widely spread, a pattern of settlement embodying a highly developed material and social culture, which owed little to Islamic or to any other trans-Saharan influences. And yet it was a pattern which conspicuously failed to penetrate some parts of the region, notably that occupied by the Ibo people of south-eastern Nigeria, which was certainly an area of dense population and, at least on the evidence of Igbo-Ukwu (see p. 501), one not without the stimulus of long-distance trade or a high order of technological skills.

West of the Volta, a different pattern prevailed. Here the terrain was more forested, the horse much less prominent, the walled city an exceptional feature. The most widespread social configuration was that of the Mande peoples, based upon groups of villages, each group ruled by a king, above whom there might at some times and in some cases be a king of kings, receiving tribute from lesser rulers. This region comprised the four main gold-producing areas of West Africa – those of Bambuk on the upper Senegal, of Bure on the upper Niger, of the Lobi country in the valley of the Black Volta, and the Akan forest of modern Ghana and the eastern Ivory Coast. It also comprised the main sources of the highly valued kola nut. Long-distance trade was therefore a much more important factor than in the part of Guinea to the east of the Volta, and it is tempting to ascribe a large role in political as well as economic development to the influence of the Mande merchant caste, the Dyula or Wangara, who operated over a wide region to the south of the Mali empire. Certainly the Dyula, in their ever-widening search for the materials of long-distance trade, and with their need for political protection along an extensive network of caravan routes, may have been the purveyors of a fund of common ideas, political and military, social and religious and economic. Nevertheless, the Dyula were few in number and were seldom in a position to use force. Although, here and there, they allied themselves with troops of horsemen, there was no real counterpart to the cavalry forces responsible for the pattern of settlement in so much of the territory to the east of the Volta.

It has to be remembered that, until the opening of the ocean trade by the Portuguese, the Atlantic seaboard represented to West Africans the end of the world. The sea was a source of fish and of salt, both of which could be traded profitably inland; but its shores held few other attractions for human settlement, and nor for the most part did the great forests of the coastal hinterland. Intensive settlement of the forest region proceeded gradually from its northern margin. As Samuel Johnson wrote of the Yoruba, 'The coast tribes were of much less importance then than now, both in population and in intelligence . . . The centre of life and activity, of large populations and industry . . . was in the interior . . . Light and civilization came from the north.'[1] In West Africa the intensive penetration of the forest region was probably a by-product of the growth of dense food-producing populations in the savanna. It was the opening of the sea-borne trade which, during

[1] Samuel Johnson, *The history of the Yorubas* (Lagos, 1921), 40.

the last century and a half of our period, began to shift the momentum of change from the northern to the southern margin of the forest.

Eastwards from the Bight of Biafra, the equatorial forest region broadens out to cover the whole northern half of the Congo basin, forming a natural barrier much more formidable than that between the West African savanna and the Atlantic coast. It was not, of course, an absolute barrier. In addition to the hunting bands of Pygmies, food-producing peoples lived strung out along the river lines. Canoes helped mobility. Migrations could occur and innovations could spread through the forest from one side to the other. For all that, it was not a terrain in which regular communications could be maintained as they could be in West Africa. Nor was there, in the Sudanic belt to the north of the Congo forest, a density of population or a state of social organization comparable to that existing further to the west, where the Hausa and the Dyula Mande spread their trading networks. The people inhabiting the territory of the modern Central African Republic appear, during our period, to have lived in chiefless, 'palaeonegritic' communities, still unaffected by the growth of states in Kanem and Darfur to the north, and exerting little pressure on the forest areas to the south. There was thus an immense and scantily populated region straddling the centre of the continent, and dividing the denser populations of Africa to the north of the equator from those to the south.

During our period at least, the main developments in Africa south of the equator occurred, not in the forest, but in the regions to the east and the south of it. In part, these were developments stemming naturally from the successful settlement of these regions by Bantu food-producers in an earlier period. The nuclei of comparatively dense farming populations emerged in the areas best suited to agriculture, which were in general the areas of high, but not excessive, rainfall. The interlacustrine region of East Africa was one such area. The Katanga/Kasai/Lower Congo region of southern Zaïre was another. The lands adjoining the middle and lower Zambezi were a third, and Iron Age archaeology is beginning to indicate that there may have been a fourth such area in the south-western Transvaal. In part, however, the developments of our period were a response to the advent of new population elements, bringing new farming techniques and a new concept of wealth and status based on the ownership and milking of cattle. This was, of course, something quite different from the first herding of cattle, which, as we know, was practised from the beginning of the Iron Age, and in some places earlier. Rather, it had to do with the interaction of pastoralism and agriculture in a way which gave a social and political advantage to the polygamous and patrilineal descent-group specializing in the ownership of cattle. (See pp. 626–8, 640, 643, 645–6, 650–1.) There can be little doubt that this was initially a result of the southward drift of Nilotic and Paranilotic peoples from the southern Sudan into northern Uganda and western Kenya, the impact of which is clearly marked in the archaeological record from about the beginning of the present millennium. The stages of its southward progress and diversification within the Bantu sphere are as yet imperfectly understood; but it would seem that here is a major theme linking the history of much of eastern, central and southern Africa.

On the whole it would seem that, in most of the sub-continent, influences passing overland from the north were more significant than those entering from the coasts to the east and the west. There is as yet no hard evidence of any sea traffic between West Africa and western Central Africa before the coming of the Portuguese. Along the Indian Ocean coast maritime trade with the Red Sea, the Persian Gulf and India grew steadily from the beginning of our period until it was interrupted by the Portuguese; but the only part of the interior to be seriously affected by it was the region between the Rovuma and the Limpopo, and more especially that between the Zambezi and the Limpopo. Here there were large resources in gold, the mining and trading of which invited political centralization. It is impossible accurately to locate the great kingdom of the Zanj reported by al-Mas'ūdī in the early tenth century; but there is no doubt that by about the eleventh century political organization on a scale unique in Bantu Africa was beginning to take shape around Zimbabwe Hill on the Rhodesian plateau. From all the evidence, it would appear that this organization bore a wholly African character, and one fairly strongly influenced by the pastoral revolution, but at the same time its growth in scale must have been largely a response to the external stimulus of the Indian Ocean trade.

On the western side of Bantu Africa the influence of the pastoral revolution and that of the Indian Ocean trade are equally nebulous. Developments in the mining and working of copper in what must have been a densely settled region in northern Katanga were already in progress on the eve of our period, and it is not yet clear from where the necessary skills were transmitted. On present evidence, coastal imports, though not quite absent, were very scarce. Here, as in the whole of the wooded savanna to the south of the Congo forest, where advanced metallurgical techniques were combined with a high level of domestic industries such as wood-carving and the weaving of palm fibres, a connection, however tenuous, with the forest region of West Africa must be suspected. In the region to the south of the Lower Congo we have firm evidence of the existence, by the time of the first Portuguese contact, of at least one large state, more considerable than any then existing in the interlacustrine region, and perhaps approaching the dimensions of the Mutapa kingdom to the south of the Zambezi. It may be, as Dr Birmingham suggests, that here the main incentive to political enlargement was the wealth of local trade and exchange within the region itself. Certainly, one lesson to be drawn from all the detailed studies of political growth in sub-Saharan Africa carried out in recent years is that larger states have always emerged as the result of a long period of piecemeal expansion, and never by means of the sudden conquest of large, previously stateless areas by migrants coming from a distance and imposing at a stroke the political institutions necessary to rule a large territory. It would in fact probably be true to say that larger states could only be founded on the backs of smaller ones, and that in most of Africa south of the equator the political units were, even by the end of our period, very small indeed.

On the whole, the chapters which follow lend little support to the idea that Africa, so long as it was developing independently, was showing a healthy progress, which came to an end with the establishment of the European connection in the mid fifteenth century. It is abundantly clear that the parts of the continent where development of all kinds had gone farthest before 1450 were precisely the parts which had long interacted with other cultures, including those outside Africa – first of all, Egypt and the Maghrib; next, the sub-Saharan, Sudanic belt from the Senegal to Somalia; next, the sub-Sudanic 'middle belt' of West Africa, which was in regular touch with the civilization of the Sudan. These parts of Africa were the remotest from the paths of the European expansion, which mainly affected peoples who were at a much simpler stage of development. The Portuguese opening of the Atlantic coast in fact resembled very closely the earlier opening of the Indian Ocean coast by Muslim traders and settlers. It was based on a monopoly of maritime shipping, and its local operations were conducted from coastal forts and offshore islands, where communities of slaves and mulattoes, corresponding to those of the Arab colonies of the east coast, soon supplied the intermediaries with the African peoples. The diplomatic and missionary contacts with the kingdoms of

Benin and Kongo were as exceptional for the Porguguese as those of the Arabs of Sofala with the fifteenth-century *mwenemutapas*. It was only with the conquering expedition of Paulo Dias de Novais to Luanda in 1575 that contact turned into colonization, and then only in a very limited area. The Portuguese settlements in East Africa within our period, even those at Sena and Tete on the Zambezi, were in every case taken over from those of the Swahili-Arabs. To the historian of Africa the activities of the fifteenth- and sixteenth-century Portuguese were more of a portent than a reality. The battle of Tondibi, at which the enormous host of Songhay turned and fled before a desert-weary force of 3,000 Moroccans, was a more important event than the building of Elmina Castle. In the history of Africa, as distinct from that of European exploration and discovery, the Portuguese pioneers were more significant as observers of the African scene than as agents of change in Africa.

CHAPTER 1

EGYPT, NUBIA AND THE EASTERN DESERTS

THE FATIMIDS

The Fatimid conquest of Egypt in AD 969 was accomplished without much difficulty, as the country had for some time already been in internal chaos and had suffered heavily from famines. The skilful political and religious propaganda of the Fatimids also prepared the ground for a ready acceptance of the new dynasty by the population. When the Fatimid general Jawhar (a former slave of Dalmatian origin), after overwhelming the last feeble resistance of the Ikhshidid army, entered al-Fusṭāṭ on 1 July 969 and formally proclaimed the new regime by introducing the *khuṭba* (Friday sermon) in the name of his master, the caliph al-Mu'izz (952–75), the event had a more profound significance and more far-reaching consequences than a simple change of dynasty so common in the annals of the Islamic world. The coming of the Fatimids marked a new epoch in the history of Egypt which, for the first time since the Ptolemies, became not only the seat of a completely sovereign dynasty, but also the centre of an empire that survived its original founders and lasted for more than five centuries.

The imperial idea was, indeed, inherent in the Ismā'īli ideology, of which the Fatimids were the most prominent champions, and only they, among all the Ismā'īli Shī'a branches, came within reach of attaining the ecumenical goal of the doctrine. They considered their North African period merely a preparatory stage, and the conquest of Egypt only one of the stepping-stones, on the road to the creation of the universal Ismā'īlī empire, ruled by the Prophet's descendants in accordance with the esoteric doctrine of the Ismā'īlīya. Nevertheless, they were realistic enough to see the strategic importance of Egypt as a bridge to the eastern parts of the Islamic world and as the economic basis for their political power.

Shortly after the conquest of al-Fusṭāṭ, Jawhar started to build a new capital, Cairo (in Arabic, *al-Qāhira*),[1] destined to overshadow the splendour of Baghdad, the seat of the rival 'Abbasids. Later he also

[1] So called, because on the day of its foundation the planet Mars (*al-Qāhir*, lit. 'the subduer') was in the ascendant.

laid there the foundations of the college mosque of al-Azhar, intended to be primarily a nursery for Ismāʿīlī missionary propaganda. The Fatimids assumed that the conquest of the Islamic world would be facilitated by a preliminary campaign of religious propaganda, and also by the collaboration of numerous Shīʿa dynasties and groups in the Near East. In this they were soon disappointed, as the Buwayhids, who controlled the ʿAbbasid caliphs, denied Fatimid claims to leadership, while other Shīʿa principalities (the Hamdanids of Aleppo and the Qarmatians of Bahrain), although prepared to recognize the spiritual suzerainty of the Fatimids, were unwilling to submit to their political domination. The Qarmatians, ideologically closest to the Fatimids and, until the conquest of Egypt, their military allies, became their fiercest enemies in Syria, and twice (in 971 and 974) launched attacks against Egypt.

The military and political efforts of the Fatimids to establish a firm foothold in the Fertile Crescent were not always crowned by success. The two holy cities of Mecca and Medina were won by lavishly distributed gifts, and in 970 readily recognized the Fatimid suzerainty, under which they remained until the second half of the eleventh century. The possession of these cities always conferred great prestige on a Muslim sovereign, and made it possible to influence the pilgrims who visited the holy places every year in great numbers. But in Syria and Palestine the Fatimids encountered many difficulties. In the course of the century following the conquest of Egypt, the dynasty was engaged in a prolonged and finally unsuccessful effort to establish control over these countries. By its end only Damascus and some coastal cities were firmly in the Fatimids' possession, the countryside being largely beyond the bounds of effective administration. In the long run it was their inability to solve the Syrian question that stopped the Fatimid advance eastward and led to the failure of the ecumenical ambitions of the dynasty.

The caliph al-Muʿizz, who moved in 973 from Tunisia to Cairo and died there two years later, was succeeded by his able and energetic son al-ʿAzīz (975–96), under whom the sovereignty of the Fatimids was recognized from Morocco to the Yemen, and for a short time even in Mosul in northern Mesopotamia. His reign was not marked by any great military operations, and only towards the end of his life did he prepare a sea and land campaign against Byzantine territory, victoriously completed under his successor.

During most of his reign the administration of Egypt was in the hands of a converted Jew, the vizier Yaʿqūb b. Killis, who had already served al-Muʿizz. He introduced a sound fiscal scheme, abolishing the abusive system of tax-farming and laying the foundations of an efficient civil service that remained in force until the end of the dynasty. Special attention was paid to the development of trade, both internal and international, as well as to industries and large-scale plantations. Soon Egypt eclipsed all other Near Eastern countries in wealth and prosperity. This was due, to some extent, to the fact that the revenues of Egypt ceased to be drained away to Iraq and were even increased by tribute from newly won provinces or from dependent rulers.

Whereas al-ʿAzīz was more than tolerant towards Christians and Jews, many of whom occupied high posts in administrative and economic life, he showed less leniency towards the Sunni, especially those of the Maliki legal school. The Ismāʿīlīya doctrine was proclaimed the state religion, and an elaborate propaganda organization, with the chief missioner (*dāʿī al-duʿāt*) at its head, made great efforts to implant the Shīʿa creed in Egypt and elsewhere. But the Shīʿa was never generally accepted in Egypt, the majority of the country's inhabitants remaining loyal to the Sunna throughout the Fatimid epoch.

Until his time, the main Egyptian military force had consisted of the free Berber tribesmen (mostly of the Kutama tribe) and to a lesser degree of the Slavonic (*Saqāliba*), Greek and Italian slave troops. These troops proved to be no match for the seasoned and disciplined Turks employed by the enemies of the dynasty. Al-ʿAzīz was the first to start the policy of recruiting great numbers of Turkish slave-soldiers (*mamlūk*, plural *mamālīk*) as cavalry, as well as of importing Sudanese slaves bought in Nubia for service as infantrymen. It was not long before these various troops started to quarrel, and their conflicts and insubordination later contributed much to the weakening of both the state and the dynasty.

With al-Ḥākim (996–1021), a ruler of highly unbalanced mind came to the throne. During the four years of his minority the eunuch Barjawān conducted the affairs of the state wisely as regent. In 1000 al-Ḥākim took over the rule personally, freeing himself from Barjawān's tutelage by assassination. His rule of more than twenty years was marked by such extravagant regulations, restrictions and prohibitions that there can be no doubt about his insanity, even if some of his actions were inspired by a genuine reforming zeal. About 1007 he started persecuting Christians and Jews to a degree never seen before or after in Islamic countries. They were forced to wear black robes, to ride only on donkeys and to display constantly, even in the baths, crosses or bells hanging from their necks. He then ordered all Christian churches in Egypt to be demolished, and the Christian population, which was still rather numerous in this period, was offered the alternatives of embracing Islam, of leaving the country or of being subjected to various forms of degradation and humiliation. Due to this pressure thousands of Copts, mostly *fellāḥīn*, changed their religion. In 1009 even the Holy Sepulchre in Jerusalem was destroyed, this act causing a general indignation throughout the Christian world; it also led to the breaking off of commercial relations with Egypt by the Byzantine emperor, Basil II, in 1015.

Nor were the Christians the only ones to suffer; the Muslim population, too, became victim of the caliph's caprices. Officials were tortured and killed in barbarous ways, and persons who transgressed some of the numerous prohibitions were scourged or beheaded. Among the regulations were those allowing shops to open only during the night, forbidding women to leave their homes (and shoemakers to make footwear for them), prohibiting all games, including chess. Many of these regulations were constantly repealed or reversed, so that finally no one knew what was wrong or right. In 1013 the caliph allowed the Christians and Jews to revert to their original faith, and even authorized the rebuilding of churches and the restoration of confiscated property.

One of the more enduring measures of al-Ḥākim's Ismāʿīlī zeal was the foundation, in 1005, of the *Dār al-ḥikma* or *Dār al-ʿilm*, an academy for teaching and propagating the extreme doctrines of the Shīʿa. In addition to specifically Islamic subjects, its curriculum included the teaching of many sciences and philosophy, and the institution played a significant role in making Egypt an important centre of learning.

In 1017 or 1018, accepting the theories of some Ismāʿīlī extremists, al-Ḥākim declared himself the incarnation of the Deity. This new doctrine was publicly preached and theoretically expounded by Hamza b. ʿAlī and Muḥammad al-Darāzī (killed in 1019), the founders of the Druze sect in Hawrān in Syria, which accepted the teaching of al-Ḥākim's incarnation as the main article of their creed. The caliph's end came in February 1021, when al-Ḥākim disappeared in the al-Muqattam hills, probably killed following a conspiracy of Turkish and Berber *amīrs* with the connivance of his sister Sitt al-Mulk, who was afraid of his increasing madness. As the corpse was never found, many refused to believe in his death, and in later years pretenders arose claiming to be the vanished caliph.

It is remarkable that the Fatimid empire did not disintegrate under this eccentric reign. It is true that the personal and religious authority of the caliph began to decline, but on the other hand there were some military and political successes under al-Ḥākim, such as the submission of Aleppo to Fatimid rule in 1016. The only serious revolt, that of the Kutama Berbers and nomadic Arabs in Barca (Cyrenaica), headed by a relative of the Spanish Umayyads, Abū Rakwa, was easily suppressed in 1005 and the remnant rebel army with its leader was finally crushed in Upper Egypt.

But under al-Ḥākim's son, al-Ẓāhir (1021–36), the first signs of the empire's fragile character began to appear. During his minority his aunt, Sitt al-Mulk, ruled competently, and after her death in 1027 the effective rule passed to the vizier al-Jarjarā'ī for almost twenty years. From this time on, the caliphs became little more than puppets in the hands of their prime ministers, at first civilians, but later military men, heads of various cliques who constantly fought among themselves.

In Syria the Fatimid government had to deal with the persistent revolts of Arab tribes, which for a time in 1024 occupied Aleppo and other cities. The Byzantines intervened, and hostilities started between them and the Fatimid army, but in 1038 a thirty-years' peace treaty was signed between the emperor and the caliph through which the Fatimids obtained the former Hamdanid territory in northern Syria. But the turbulent Arab tribes did not permit the Fatimids to enjoy their new gains for long. The Arab Mirdasid dynasty conquered Aleppo again in 1041, and in spite of many Fatimid attempts to retake it, it was irrevocably lost in 1060 together with all of northern Syria.

The reign of al-Mustanṣir (1036–94), one of the longest in Muslim history, covers a period full of important changes both internal and external. The early years of his caliphate witnessed the high-water mark of Fatimid power, and his initial successes in northern Syria aroused hopes that the time for the conquest of the east had finally come. Ismā'īlī propaganda and missions were revived, and countries in the east as far as Sind were infiltrated by Fatimid agents and missionaries (*dā'ī*), who made converts among all classes. In the Yemen, the Sulayhid dynasty of Sana (1038–1139), founded by a *dā'ī*, established a state that firmly and fervently supported Fatimid political and religious aims. Some years later a Turkish general of the Buwayhids, al-Basāsīrī, driven out of Iraq by the Seljuks in 1055, appealed to Cairo for support. With the aid of Fatimid money and arms, he conquered Mosul (1057) and in the following year entered Baghdad, forcing the 'Abbasid caliph to recognize the Fatimid suzerainty, and causing al-Mustanṣir's name to be recited in the mosques for forty consecutive Fridays. Many other towns in Iraq followed the example of the capital and some 'Abbasid insignia were sent triumphantly to Cairo as trophies.

But owing to internal disturbances in Egypt no military aid could be sent to al-Basāsīrī. A year later he was expelled by the Seljuk sultan Ṭughrul Beg, who restored the 'Abbasid caliph in Baghdad. Contrary to its being a starting point of new expansion, the al-Basāsīrī episode marked the final defeat of the Ismā'īlī Fatimid dream of hegemony by showing the inner weakness of the dynasty.

With the Seljuks there emerged in the Near East a fresh and dynamic force that shattered the former balance of power and inaugurated an era of profound political and economic changes. These Turkoman tribal warriors from Central Asia conquered the entire eastern part of the Islamic world in the first half of the eleventh century under the able leadership of Ṭughrul. They destroyed or subdued the local dynasties, and finally swept away the Buwayhids of western Iran and Iraq. They drove the Byzantines far into the interior of Asia Minor, and, by occupying Syria, inserted a wedge between the Fatimid and Byzantine empires. In terms of religion their rise brought triumph to orthodox Islam, since as zealous Sunni the Seljuks supported the 'Abbasid caliphate, with its claim on the loyalty of all Muslims. Arabia and the Holy Cities hastened to change their allegiance, and from 1070 onwards the *khuṭba* in Mecca was again pronounced in the name of the 'Abbasid caliph of Baghdad. The Fatimids were helpless before the new power, as their troops were no match for the invincible Seljuk army. All Syria was lost, apart from some coastal places in southern Palestine.

Nor was this loss the only one suffered by the dynasty at this time. The links with North Africa, the original base of the dynasty, had already begun to be loosened during the reign of al-'Azīz, under the governorship of the Zirid Manṣūr b. Bulūkkīn. In the first half of the eleventh century the Zirids grew gradually more independent, and Sicily, too, became attached more to Ifrīqiya than to Egypt; its Kalbite *amīrs* recognized the Zirid suzerainty in 1036. The final rupture with the Maghrib took place in 1051, when the Zirid Mu'izz b. Bādīs proclaimed himself independent of Fatimid rule and paid allegiance to the 'Abbasids in Baghdad. The response of the Fatimids to this affront was unusual: according to some sources, the vizier al-Yazūrī instigated the nomadic Arab tribes called the Banū Hilāl and the Banū Sulaym to move eastwards from Upper Egypt and to invade the dominions of the rebellious ex-governor. This reprisal produced the expected results – devastation and ravage in North Africa – but it did not bring it back under the Fatimid sway. On the other hand Egypt did thus rid itself of a turbulent element that had contributed seriously to anarchy in the countryside.

Despite the growing political difficulties in Syria and elsewhere, Egypt itself enjoyed a period of great prosperity until the mid eleventh century. As in all times, the wealth of the country depended largely on the Nile regime, and on the care given to the regulation and distribution of its waters. Thanks to the efficiency of the Fatimid administration, the dams and canals were regularly repaired and improved, and even an occasional period of low water did not greatly damage the general economic situation. Apart from food crops (wheat, barley, sugar-cane and other vegetables) many industrial crops such as flax, cotton and dye-plants were cultivated. In the lower Delta region a textile industry flourished, with manufacturing centres in Damietta (Dimyāt), Tinnīs and Dābiq, producing cotton, linen and silk cloth of various kinds and colours. Glass and crystal were manufactured in al-Fusṭāṭ and in Alexandria. Among other industries, those most flourishing were pottery, metal-working and paper-making. Shipbuilding, concentrated in Alexandria and Damietta, was dependent on the import of timber from Lebanon or Europe.

Internal trade was facilitated by cheap transport on the Nile. In Cairo there were over 20,000 shops owned by the caliph, who let them to shopkeepers for from two to ten dinars a month. Similarly most of the brick houses in the capital belonged to him, and rents were collected every month. The income from taxes, rents and custom duties, as well as from direct participation in trade, enabled the caliphs and their courtiers to lead a highly luxurious life; the ceremonial and pomp matched that of the Byzantine court, which was well known for its strict etiquette. Industry and trade, however, benefited from this luxury, as did the arts and sciences. The Persian traveller Nāṣir-i Khusraw, who visited Egypt between 1046 and 1049, was impressed by the general prosperity and security found there, and concluded his account: 'I could neither limit nor estimate its wealth and nowhere have I seen such prosperity as I saw here.'[1]

[1] *Sefer Nāme*, ed. and tr. C. Schefer (Paris, 1881), 53/tr. 155.

The internal security and tranquillity were disrupted some years after the Persian traveller's visit by the rivalry among the three main divisions of the Fatimid army – the free Berber tribesmen, the Turkish cavalry and the Sudanese infantry. This last group, favoured by al-Mustanṣir's mother, a Sudanese slave, grew larger and more influential (it is said that its strength reached over fifty thousand), thus causing the jealousy and envy of the others. Riots and initial street fighting grew gradually into regular battles, in which the Berbers sided with the Turks; after seven years of hard fighting (1062–9) the Turks, commanded by a Hamdanid prince, Nāṣir al-Dawla, drove the Sudanese into Upper Egypt. The victors then wrested all power from the caliph, and constantly increased their demands for payment and allowances, so that the caliph had to sell his treasures and farm out the taxes and customs to meet the insatiable demands of the troops. The Turks ravaged the whole country, looted in Cairo and terrorized the population. The situation was aggravated by the raids of the Lawāta Berbers from Cyrenaica, who overran the Delta and destroyed most of the dams and canals. This destruction, combined with the low flood of the Nile in 1065, led to a terrible famine lasting for many years and bringing the country to the verge of total disaster. As usual, the famine was accompanied by plague, the mortality rate increased and there were even some cases of cannibalism. Until 1073, when Nāṣir al-Dawla was assassinated by his rivals and a plentiful harvest put an end to the famine, Egypt lived in a state of growing anarchy, being devastated by the Turks in the interior, the Sudanese in the south and the Lawāta Berbers in the west and north. The authority of the state was paralysed and its economic resources exhausted.

At this juncture al-Mustanṣir summoned the governor of Acre, Badr al-Jamālī, a former Armenian slave, to restore order in Egypt. With his reliable Armenian and Kurdish troops he arrived by sea, took the Turks by surprise and entered Cairo without much opposition at the beginning of 1074. In a short time the Turkish troops were dispersed and disarmed and their officers put to death. In the course of the next three years the Arab and Berber tribesmen, as well as the Sudanese infantry, were brought under control, and peace and order were restored in Egypt.

Having been appointed by the caliph *amīr al-juyūsh* ('commander of the armies'), Badr al-Jamālī soon took over the civil vizierate, as well as the leadership of missions, and thus became the virtual ruler of the Fatimid realm. From this time onwards the caliphs, except for rare and brief occasions, no longer effectively controlled affairs, the power lying in the hands of military dictators. Badr al-Jamālī next devoted himself to the task of reorganizing the administration and restoring the prosperity of the country. The strongly centralized administration controlled all the finances, including tax revenues and payment of the troops, as well as the allocation of the military fiefs. The strict hierarchy of officials and the controlling powers of the vizier left room neither for the autonomous tendencies of provincial governors nor for the growth of widespread corruption. Many of the principles of Badr's reorganization remained in operation for centuries to come, thus witness to the sound grasp of their originator. It was due mainly to his efforts and those of his son, al-Malik al-Afḍal, who wielded supreme authority after his father's death in 1094, that the Fatimid regime was given a new vigour and another century of life.

The price of this prolonged life, as well as of Egypt's continuing prosperity, was the final abandonment of the former universal ambitions of the Ismā'īlī Fatimids. Whether this change in foreign policy was caused by a realistic assessment of Seljuk power, or by the fact that neither of the Armenian viziers shared the extremist Ismā'īlī faith, is difficult to decide. Nevertheless, their policy put an end to the propaganda and mission organizations, and the Fatimid caliphate ceased to be the ideological rallying-point for the Ismā'īlīs. A further heavy blow was dealt to the movement by al-Afḍal's decision, in 1094, to recognize al-Mustanṣir's youngest son al-Musta'lī (a boy of eight years) as his successor, instead of the eldest, al-Nizār, a man close upon fifty, who had already been nominated by his father. As a result of this act, the Ismā'īlī split into two rival branches: al-Nizār's cause was espoused by the more militant eastern section, already deeply shocked and disgusted by the changes in Egypt, where the Fatimids, who had started as leaders of a revolutionary movement with world-wide ambitions, ended as a local dynasty of puppets under military dictators. This branch, led by al-Ḥasan b. al-Ṣabbāḥ, refused to recognize al-Musta'lī or anyone of his line as *imām* of the Ismā'īlīya. The Nizārites, or, as they were soon commonly called, the Assassins (from Arabic *al-Ḥashīshīyyun*, 'eaters of hashish'),[1] soon developed a very effective organization in Persia and northern Syria, aiming at the overthrow of

[1] The name was given to the members of the sect by their contemporaries, both Muslim and Franks, in the belief that they used hashish to provoke ecstatic visions of paradise and thus be better prepared to face martyrdom; but Ismā'īlī sources do not confirm this theory. On the other hand, since the Nizārī branch employed murder as a political weapon, the proper name Assassin became in many Western languages a synonym for 'murderer'.

all established Muslim states and dynasties in order to fulfill the original revolutionary goal of the Ismāʻīlīya. For a time they played a vital role in Near Eastern history, but their influence on Egypt itself was indirect and rather marginal.

No large military expeditions were mounted outside Egypt. Most of Syria was firmly in the hands of the Seljuks or their vassals, and Badr contented himself with the reoccupation of some coastal towns (Acre, Ascalon, Tyre, Sidon) and with a bridgehead in southern Palestine. The Maghrib being already lost to the Zirids or to the Hilāli nomads, the western frontier of the Fatimid state did not extend beyond Cyrenaica. Only Yemen and southern Arabia remained in the Fatimid orbit, and both Badr al-Jamālī and his son showed a vivid interest in preserving the Egyptian position in this country, mainly for commercial reasons.

As already mentioned, Egypt had started to play an increasingly important role in international trade during the reign of al-ʻAzīz. Commerce was carried on with many countries to the west (Sicily, North Africa, Spain and Italian city-states), as well as with the Byzantine empire on the one hand and with Ethiopia, Nubia, Yemen and the Indian Ocean region on the other. In the middle of the eleventh century these relations took a new turn. The maritime trade of the Indian Ocean had hitherto been directed more to the Persian Gulf than to the Red Sea, but, as a result of the Seljuk wars in Iraq and Persia, it was now routed to Aden, and to the Egyptian ports on the Red Sea like Qulzum and ʻAydhāb. Thus Egypt became the most important link on this chief medieval trade-route during the rest of the Fatimid period and for many centuries to come. The eastern trade – that is to say, the commercial operations by the Arabs, Persians and other Muslim peoples in India, Indonesia, China and East Africa, where they bought spices, silk, ivory, precious stones and other luxury goods, and exported them via Egypt to the Mediterranean countries – was perhaps the single most lucrative economic enterprise in the Middle Ages. The European partners in this trade, mainly the Italian city-states of Venice and Amalfi, and later Genoa and Pisa, as well as some French and Spanish ports, such as Marseilles and Barcelona, exported to Egypt, in return, scarce commodities such as timber (for shipbuilding), iron, woollen cloth and wheat. The transit trade, in spite of the heavy customs and taxes levied by the Fatimid government, brought large profits to Egyptian merchants, among whom there were many Jews and Copts. At the same time it contributed much to the general economic prosperity and helped to sustain the country's self-sufficiency.

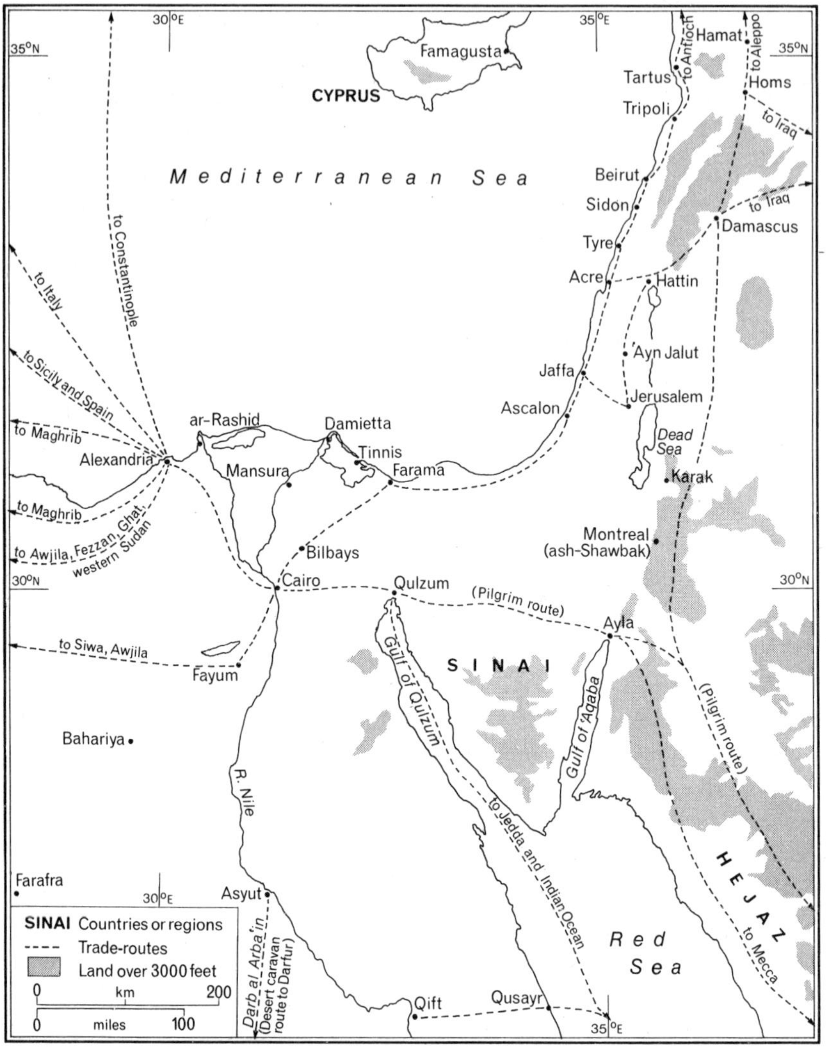

1 Egypt, Syria and the main trade-routes

It was concern about this trade that led to the establishment of close political ties between Fatimid Egypt and the Yemen (and even with some Indian states). The fear of harming commerce was perhaps another ground for the reluctance of the Armenian viziers to engage in military activities. It was sufficient to hold the eastern approaches to Egypt, of which the geographical position in itself enabled it virtually to monopolize the transit trade. Naturally enough the Europeans tried to destroy this monopoly, and the participation of the Italian maritime republics in the Crusades can be explained partly by their wish to reach the eastern trade directly, and thus dislodge the Muslims from their intermediary role.

The general prosperity of Egypt in the Fatimid epoch was not balanced by excellence in intellectual and cultural productivity, and the number of outstanding authors or works was surprisingly small. The caliphs patronized poets, writers and scholars, attracting them from all parts of the Islamic world, but these people rarely rose above the average. The mediocrity of the literary and scholarly output in Fatimid Egypt stands in sharp contrast to contemporary achievements in these fields in other Arab countries such as Syria, Iraq and Spain, as well as to the flourishing of Arabic culture in Egypt under the rule of succeeding dynasties. On the other hand Egypt at this time produced some brilliant scientific personalities, such as the astronomer ʿAlī b. Yūnus (died 1009), whose astronomic tables represent the most extensive known list of medieval astronomic observations, or the mathematician and physicist Ibn al-Haytham (Lat., Alhazen, died 1039). His optical studies belong to the fundamental works in this branch of physics, and his solutions to some mathematical and astronomic problems did not lose their validity until modern times. Similarly the art of medicine flourished, and Muslim, Christian and Jewish physicians competed for the favour of caliphs and nobles in their practices as well as in their scientific knowledge. One of these, Ibn Riḍwān (died 1061), is best known for his autobiography and his medical–philosophical polemic, written with his Christian colleague Ibn Buṭlān of Baghdad (died 1066), in which both displayed a large knowledge of Greek and Muslim philosophy and sciences.

Although the Ismāʿīlī doctrine was in general more favourable to the cultivation of philosophy than was orthodox Islam, and although many philosophical disciplines were taught at both Al-Azhar and the *Dār-al-Ḥikma*, the contribution of Fatimid Egypt in this field was negligible. On the other hand the literature expounding the tenets of the Ismāʿīlī theology and law was very rich; a positive aspect of this literature consisted in the fact that its works popularized general scientific knowledge among a wider public. But only during the early period of the Fatimid rule did these specific Ismāʿīlī branches of learning produce an original thinker, the *qāḍī* al-Nuʿmān (died 974), who attempted to reconcile the highly idealistic and esoteric Ismāʿīlī teaching with the political realities of a temporal empire, and who also laid the foundations of Ismā'īlī legal theory.

Not many historians were active at this period, and few of their works have survived: only Ibn Zulak (died 996), al-Muṣabbiḥī (died 1029), al-Quḍā'ī (died 1062) and Ibn al-Ṣayrafī (died 1147) are worthy of mention as chroniclers of their own times. Al-Shābushtī (died 1008) wrote a detailed history of Christian monasteries, and the Coptic bishop Severus b. al-Muqaffa' (died *c.* 1000) produced a history of the patriarchs which forms an important source for the internal history of Egypt as well as for Nubia and Ethiopia.

This dearth of literary and scholarly activity can be explained by the heretical character of the dynasty, since the orthodox Muslim authors were not attracted by it, and even the Ismā'īlī scholars were later reluctant to serve a dynasty that had abandoned most of the ideals of the original doctrine.

Quite a different picture is offered by Fatimid art and architecture, which reflect the material prosperity of the period in a more telling way than does the literary culture. Two main characteristics distinguish Fatimid art from that of other Arab countries: a rich interplay of local tradition with various foreign stylistic influences, and a wide use of figurative (human and animal) representation of objects. Among the surviving buildings the most famous are the al-Azhar mosque, rebuilt many times since its original construction, the al-Ḥākim mosque, in which North African elements are combined with those of Tulunid Egypt and Iraq, and the smaller al-Aqmar mosque (built in 1125), important for the ornamentation of its façade, which bears traces of Christian Armenian influence, and for the first appearance of the corbelled ('stalactite') niche that later became a general feature of Islamic architecture. From the twelfth century onwards, stone finally replaced brick as the main building material. Apart from the mosques, this period saw the construction of many mausoleums, some associated with mosques, others being separate buildings, each containing the tomb of its founder. Secular architecture is best represented by three massive gates of Cairo from the time of Badr al-Jamālī, built by Armenian builders on Byzantine plans. Just as Fatimid architecture was enriched by various sources, so in due time it influenced other parts of the Islamic world, notably North Africa, Spain and Sicily, where its traces can be found in many places.

Fatimid Egypt was also remarkably active in the decorative and industrial arts, combining highly developed techniques with refined artistic taste. This applies to bronzes, faience, glass and cut crystal, as well as to ceramic ware, wood-carving and textiles. It is mainly in these objects that realistic representations of human (musicians, dancers, hunters etc.) or animal motives are found, the Shīʿa being less strict in these matters than the Sunni. Many of these arts, such as the weaving of fine textiles, had a very long local tradition in Egypt, but even here Iranian influences are present in design and iconography, although there is no doubt that the artisans themselves were for the most part Copts or recently converted Muslims.

One of the most remarkable and positive aspects of Fatimid rule was its tolerance towards the Copts, who continued to occupy many important posts, mainly in the administration of finance. The situation of Jews was no less favourable: a number of them held the highest offices as viziers, and they were preponderant in commerce and banking. Apart from the comparatively short time under al-Ḥākim, the non-Muslim subjects of the Fatimids enjoyed a freedom of religion rarely seen in earlier or later periods. According to Gaston Wiet,[1] this tolerance, by bringing Muslims and Christians together, led to the gradual disappearance of the Coptic language from everyday use and to its supersession by Arabic. Whereas at the end of the tenth century the majority of Christians still spoke Coptic, in the twelfth century only the more educated clergy knew this language, and it became necessary to translate even liturgical books into Arabic to make them comprehensible to the majority of the lesser clergy and to the large masses of believers.

At the end of the eleventh century, when the Crusading armies approached the Holy Land, the Fatimids held there only Ascalon and some minor coastal towns. The Seljuks, whose conquests in Asia Minor had provided the immediate impulse to the Crusades, were already past their zenith, and the empire was divided among members of the dynasty and their governors, called generally *atābegs*. Neither these nor the Fatimids were able to offer any serious resistence to the invading Crusaders. Although the vizier al-Afḍal in August 1098 recaptured Jerusalem from a Turkoman *amīr* who had held it as a Seljuk fief, the city was lost to the Crusaders a year later (July 1099). The conquerors massacred the entire Muslim and Jewish population, as they had already done in Antioch and other occupied towns in Syria, thus inaugurating a kind of fanaticism and ferocity hitherto unknown in the Near East,

[1] *L'Égypte byzantine et musulmane*, vol. II of *Précis de l'histoire d'Égypte* (Cairo, 1932), 199.

where the relationship between peoples of different religions was in general tolerant. Shortly afterwards the Latin Kingdom of Jerusalem was proclaimed. Thus a new political power that was to influence the destiny of Egypt for the next two centuries was born.

The establishment of the Franks, as the crusading Europeans were called by the Muslims, in Syria and Palestine (apart from the Kingdom of Jerusalem, the Crusaders founded separate counties of Edessa and Tripoli and the principality of Antioch) did not arouse much apprehension in Egypt, which was not directly threatened. Al-Afḍal was concerned merely about the Syrian coastal towns, fearing that the Franks might gain direct access to the Red Sea and to the lucrative eastern trade. But his defensive measures were weak, and finally only Ascalon remained as a Fatimid outpost in southern Palestine. The loss of the Syrian ports was due to the intervention of Italian fleets; the Fatimid navy, the only one the Muslims could muster, proved to be ineffective or inactive. The Fatimids then acquiesced in a more or less passive attitude towards the Frankish states, and even entered into brisk trading relations with the Italian cities, concluding new treaties with Pisa, Amalfi and Genoa.

In 1116 the Crusaders extended their territory to the Gulf of Aqaba and built midway between it and the Dead Sea the formidable fortress of Montreal (al-Shawbak), which controlled the important caravan route from Egypt to Syria, and the pilgrim route to Mecca as well. For the next two or three hundred years pilgrims from the western Muslim world had to follow the route via Upper Egypt and ʻAydhāb, since the northern one was made dangerous by Crusaders' raids on caravans.

After the death of the caliph al-Mustaʻlī, his son al-ʻĀmir (1101–30), a child of five, succeeded to the throne. The vizier al-Afḍal's powers were absolute for another twenty years, during which Egypt continued to prosper under his generally mild and wise rule. In 1121 the caliph, dissatisfied by the passive role forced on him, had al-Afḍal assassinated; but he fared no better under al-Ma'mūn, the vizier of his own choice, who after a few years shared the fate of his predecessor. Al-ʻĀmir now decided to take all authority into his own hands and to rule without the aid of any vizier, but his direct rule, oppressive, capricious and inefficient, stood in sharp contrast to the benevolent times of the great viziers of the preceding half-century. He died violently – not, however, at the hands of discontented Egyptians, but at those of the Assassins, now bitter enemies of the Mustaʻlī branch of the Fatimids.

Al-ʿĀmir's cousin, al-Ḥāfiẓ, succeeded him, but was held prisoner for most of the first year of his reign by the vizier Kutayfat, a son of al-Afḍal. In 1131, however, al-Ḥāfiẓ freed himself from this tutelage and attempted to rule directly, but had no more success than his predecessor. With him began the final decline of the Fatimid dynasty and regime: the narrative of historians describing this period is a dull record of never-ending intrigues and struggles between the caliph and his viziers, and between the viziers and generals, each trying to seize the power and authority for himself.

All the remaining Fatimid caliphs were either children or adolescents at the time of their accession to the throne – al-Ẓāfir (1149–54, 17 years old), al-Fā'iẓ (1154–60, 5 years old) and al-ʿĀḍid (1160–71, 9 years old) – and the rule was therefore in the hands of their ministers or *amīrs*, remaining so even after the caliphs had reached maturity. The anarchy within the ruling class made any active policy vis-à-vis the Latin states in Syria and Palestine impossible, even had the Fatimid regime wished it. The task of fighting the Franks was left to the emerging dynasty of Zangid *atābegs* (regents or tutors) of the Seljuk princes in Mesopotamia and Syria. The founder, ʿImād al-Dīn Zangī, started to unify the northern part of the Fertile Crescent under his rule, and in 1144 he liquidated the Latin principality of Edessa. In the next years Zangī's son, Nūr al-Dīn Maḥmūd (1146–74), imposed his rule on southern Syria and Transjordan. Thus the Latin states were threatened from the north and east by a formidable enemy. Both sides faced one another on equal terms and neither of them was strong enough to overtake the other. At this juncture Egypt became the decisive factor in the power struggle between the Franks and Zangids.

After many years of Egyptian passivity towards the Latin states, the vizier Ibn al-Ṣallār inaugurated a new policy, and in 1151 launched the Fatimid fleet on raids against the Frankish ports. The Frankish counter-offensive, however, deprived the Egyptians in 1153 of their last foothold in Palestine at Ascalon. Until 1161 there were several battles on land as well as on sea between the Fatimid state, now headed by another energetic vizier, Ṭalā'iʿ b. Ruzzīk, and the Jerusalem kingdom, but the issue remained unsolved. In the meantime the internal strife in Egypt, among the pretenders to the vizierate, continued and it was apparent that the state was nearing collapse.

Both main protagonists, the Jerusalem king Amalric I and Nūr al-Dīn, master of Damascus since 1154, were watching these developments closely, and soon they entered into a struggle for Egypt, the control of which became vital for their ultimate victory. Twice, in 1163 and in 1167, Amalric intervened on behalf of an aspirant for the Fatimid vizierate, and twice Nūr al-Dīn sent the Kurdish general Shīrkūh (aided by the latter's nephew, Ṣalāḥ al-Dīn) to stop the Christian invasion. The issue ended with a compromise, both parties agreeing to evacuate their troops from Egypt, but the country became a virtual protectorate of the Jerusalem kingdom, having to pay a sum of 400,000 gold pieces in addition to the annual tribute, and with a Frankish high commissioner with a strong garrison installed in Cairo.

A year later Amalric, aware of the general weakness of Egypt, decided to conquer it completely. His army entered the country for the third time, in the autumn of 1168, massacred the Muslim and Coptic population of Bilbays and laid siege to Cairo. Nūr al-Dīn reacted swiftly and resolutely, realizing that the time for a final settlement of the Egyptian question had come. Again Shīrkūh and Ṣalāḥ al-Dīn marched into Egypt with a huge army; on hearing of their arrival, Amalric hastily abandoned his projects and retired to Jerusalem without offering battle. Shīrkūh and his troops were enthusiastically welcomed by the people and even by the Fatimid caliph. Shīrkūh became vizier (January 1169), but still remained in the service of Nūr al-Dīn. He did not long enjoy this office, for he died two months later, and Ṣalāḥ al-Dīn ibn Ayyub took over both the vizierate and the actual rule.

His position was full of difficulties: the troops resented the appointment of such a young commander and there were attempts at revolt in his army. Next, he had to subdue the Fatimid troops, mainly Armenians and Sudanese. There was also the curious situation of his being at the same time the vizier to a Shī'a caliph and the lieutenant of a Sunni ruler – he himself being a zealous Sunni. With tact and generosity on one hand, and an iron will and severity on the other, Ṣalāḥ al-Dīn successfully overcame all these obstacles, and was even able to repulse a combined Franko-Byzantine attack on Damietta. In September 1171 he ordered the name of the Fatimid caliph to be replaced by that of the 'Abbasid al-Mustaḍī' in the Friday sermon. The last Fatimid, al-'Āḍid, died shortly afterwards, and neither of these events caused any serious disturbances among the population. After two centuries of Shī'a rule, Egypt again became a member of the Sunni Muslim *oecumene*, with hardly any trace left of the former creed.

THE AYYUBIDS

The eighty years' rule of the Ayyubid dynasty was marked in Egypt, and to a lesser degree in Syria, by a political stability and material prosperity rarely achieved in earlier or later times. Artistic and intellectual activity, although not reaching the splendour of the 'Abbasid period, made Egypt – hitherto only a cultural periphery – into one of the main centres of Arabic and Islamic culture and learning. It was Ṣalāḥ al-Dīn who laid the firm foundations for the political, economic and cultural renaissance of Egypt and of some neighbouring countries.

Even stripped of the romantic aura given him by contemporary and later authors, Muslim and Christian alike, Ṣalāḥ al-Dīn (Saladin) remains an outstanding figure: a wise statesman and diplomat, a skilful warrior, and above all a man of character and purpose. A zealous and orthodox Muslim, yet always tolerant and chivalrous to his Frankish adversaries, he considered it his life duty to crush Christian power in the Near East. The acquisition of power and wealth was for him not an aim in itself but only a means of achieving the final triumph of Islam. His Muslim rivals, of course, did not see him in this light. They assumed he possessed the same self-interest and lust for power that animated their own policies, and they declined to ally themselves to his projects. This forced Ṣalāḥ al-Dīn to undertake a series of military campaigns and diplomatic actions directed againt his Muslim adversaries in Syria and Mesopotamia before he felt himself sufficiently strong to deal with the Franks.

Although the main theatre of operations was situated on Asian soil, Egypt became, and remained, the heartland of Ayyubid might. Ṣalāḥ al-Dīn was convinced that this country must become the chief centre of all political and military efforts, and must therefore be made able to defend itself against the Christians. The bitter experiences of Amalric's invasions and of the Franko-Byzantine attack on Damietta had clearly demonstrated the dangers of a weak Egypt for the whole cause of Islam. Until the death of Nūr al-Dīn (in 1174) Ṣalāḥ al-Dīn's position as his lieutenant did not permit him freedom of action outside Egypt, because the relationship between these two great men was somewhat strained, though it never came to open hostilities. Ṣalāḥ al-Dīn used this period (1169–74) to improve the economic position of Egypt; he accomplished it above all through two far-reaching measures, first by introducing the system of military fiefs and secondly by a new commercial policy.

Until his time the prevailing economic system as regards revenues and land-tenure in Egypt had been based on the ancient usage of leasing out the collection of taxes (*kharāj*) to rich and influential individuals. The Fatimid tax-farmers held their estates only for periods of from four to thirty years, but there were already cases of hereditary tenure of tax-farming rights in which the farmer paid a fixed yearly rent. The revenues went to the state treasury, and the troops were paid directly by the central government. Due to the internal strife, and the increase of corruption which went along with it in the last decades of the Fatimid regime, the financial resources from taxes were insufficient to maintain the army. At this time the *iqṭā*ʻ, or feudal rent, became the way of paying the higher officers, but it never took the place of the direct payment of salaries.

Ṣalāḥ al-Dīn introduced into Egypt a system that remained operative until the end of the Ayyubid dynasty: this system was modelled after the Seljuk one, but modified to suit the centralist and authoritarian tradition of Egypt. All the fiefs were reallocated and given to the Kurdish *amīrs*, officers and members of his own family. An Ayyubid fief-holder received two different kinds of fief; a special one for his personal needs (*khaṣṣa*), and another for the maintenance of his troops (*iqṭā*ʻ). The state protected the peasants against abuse and exploitation by their lords, by fixing the rents to be paid. A special ministry (*dīwān al-iqṭā*ʻ) controlled the disposition of the fiefs, their revenues and other matters connected with army organization and supplies. Not only members of the dynasty and the great *amīrs*, but also the lower ranks, were given fiefs: later, when the financial situation of the state improved, the troops – in addition to revenues from the fiefs – were paid in cash by the government. The bigger fiefs often passed over into hereditary ownership or at least into life tenure, whereas the smaller ones changed hands many times, mostly during the struggle for supremacy among Ṣalāḥ al-Dīn's successors. On the whole, this system of military feudalism marked a certain progress, for the productivity of agriculture increased and the Ayyubid army was established on a firm economic basis. But, even so, a prolonged campaign with its heavy expenditures meant that military lords got into debt, and Ṣalāḥ al-Dīn often had to stop his operations for this reason. An Ayyubid fief-holder in Egypt lacked the feudal rights and privileges of his counterparts in the Near East, especially in Syria, as he did not possess any administrative or jurisdictional functions, his holding being only a limited and revocable usufruct.

The Crusades and the establishment of Latin states in the Near East contributed decisively to the further development of Mediterranean trade. In spite of the state of war between Christians and Muslims, trade flourished, since both Egypt and the Italian city-states had an interest in this highly profitable venture. At the same time, neither the Italians nor the Frankish rulers lost sight of the economic and political advantages that a conquest of Egypt and direct access to the Red Sea could bring them. Ṣalāḥ al-Dīn, too, was aware of the importance of international trade, not only for Egypt but for the whole cause of Islam. After repulsing the attacks on Egypt, he inaugurated a new commercial policy that became standard for all Egyptian rulers of his own house, as well as for the Mamluks: he officially proclaimed that in future foreign merchants could not carry on their business in the interior of Egypt or in the Red Sea region. Non-Muslim merchants were allowed to be active only in Alexandria, where they established *funduqs*, i.e. storehouses with hostels. All the existing *funduqs* in Cairo and in other places in Egypt were closed and never opened again. Through these measures Ṣalāḥ al-Dīn further strengthened the monopolistic position of Egypt in eastern trade, and the great Egyptian merchants (the so-called *Kārimī*) were able to dictate their own prices to their European partners in Alexandria. The sultan was not at all averse to commercial exchange with the Christians. On the contrary, he encouraged it through treaties with the principal trading cities and made efforts to attract their merchants to Egypt. In a letter to the 'Abbasid caliph he stressed the advantage of trade with the 'infidels' because 'there is not one of them but supplies our land with the material of war'.[1]

It is therefore not surprising to find him pursuing a vigorous policy in relation to the Red Sea, the main artery of the eastern trade. That the fears of a Frankish intervention in these waters were not unfounded was demonstrated in 1182, when a Christian fleet sailed from Ayla and devastated a number of ports on both the African and Arabian shores. The Egyptians reacted swiftly, and their fleet destroyed every single one of the Frankish ships. Usually mild and chivalrous, Ṣalāḥ al-Dīn ordered the execution of all prisoners, which indicates how sensitive he was to the danger in this direction. In 1174 his brother Tūrān-Shāh had been sent to the Yemen, where he liquidated the Shī'a dynasties and established Ayyubid rule in the main cities including Aden, one of the most important points on the route to and from the east. Although

[1] Abū Shāma, *Kitāb al-Rawdatayn* (Cairo, 1956), 243.

the personal ambitions of Tūrān-Shāh played a role in this expedition, we can look on it also as a part of Ṣalāḥ al-Dīn's policy of making the maritime trade secure. As a result, the Yemen remained in the hands of the Ayyubids for more than half a century.

Having taken these steps for the improvement of the Egyptian economy, Ṣalāḥ al-Dīn turned his attention to the political problems facing the Near East after the death of Nūr al-Dīn. His general policy in the next twelve years was to subdue all the Muslim principalities of Syria and northern Mesopotamia, either by military operations or by diplomatic actions, while continuing more or less peaceful relations with the Franks until the moment when the balance of power would shift to his side. In 1174 Damascus, Hama and Homs had already fallen into his hands, and soon afterwards he received from the caliph the official investiture with the government of Syria and Egypt; only after this date (1175) did he consider himself to be an independent ruler (*sulṭān*), as can be seen from his coins. Between 1177 and 1179 he waged a war with the Crusaders and, although his army suffered some defeats, the general situation remained unchanged. To strengthen the defences of Egypt, he started the construction of the citadel and great walls in Cairo, and also directed his attention to reorganizing the navy. In 1179 his fleet harried the Frankish coastal towns and, when in the following year Ṣalāḥ al-Dīn initiated a combined advance by sea and land against the Jerusalem kingdom, King Baldwin quickly proposed a two-year truce, which was readily accepted.

The years between 1179 and 1186 witnessed the slow but steady increase of Ṣalāḥ al-Dīn's military and territorial power; he gained control successively over southern Asia Minor and northern Syria, where Aleppo at least submitted itself in 1183 to his suzerainty. The final crowning of his patient policy of unification came in 1186, when he was recognized by the Zangid prince of Mosul. No more enemies remained on his flanks, and his army was now larger than ever before, having been joined by contingents of seasoned Turkish soldiers of the Zangid princes.

In the meantime, in 1185, the truce with Jerusalem was renewed, despite the fact that Reginald of Karak, an undisciplined vassal of Baldwin, broke it by attacking the Meccan caravans and by his raids on the Red Sea in 1181 and 1182. Ṣalāḥ al-Dīn's attempts to retaliate by attacking Beirut by sea and land and by laying siege to the Karak fortress failed. In 1183, in face of a large army in Palestine, he had chosen to withdraw rather than to give open battle. When the new truce was broken again by the same Reginald in early 1187, Ṣalāḥ al-Dīn's power was at its height, and he seized the opportunity to launch his decisive campaign. In July the Muslim and Christian armies met at Ḥaṭṭīn in Palestine. Ṣalāḥ al-Dīn's victory was overwhelming. King Guy of Jerusalem, along with the flower of Frankish knights, fell into captivity, and in a lightning campaign that followed Jerusalem and numerous other Crusaders' cities were conquered. The Franks retained only the narrow coastal strip with the main ports of Tyre, Tripoli and Antioch.

The sultan then showed more magnanimity than prudence by allowing the garrisons of conquered towns, as well as King Guy and his knights, to gather in Tyre. The town soon became the rallying point of the Syrian Franks and the bridgehead of the Third Crusade. In fact, as soon as the news reached Europe that Jerusalem had fallen into Saracen hands, a fresh Crusade on a large scale was set in motion under the leadership of the three most powerful Christian monarchs, Frederick Barbarossa, Philip of France and Richard the Lionheart. The arrival of their main forces in 1191 enabled the Franks to launch an offensive in the course of which Ṣalāḥ al-Dīn's troops were defeated, Acre surrendered and the coast between Tyre and Jaffa was reconquered. It was a heavy setback for Ṣalāḥ al-Dīn, but the main goal of the Third Crusade – the taking of Jerusalem and of other holy places in Palestine – was not achieved. The exhaustion of the Muslim army on the one hand, and the imminent withdrawal of the royal leaders of the Crusade on the other, led to the conclusion of a three-year truce in September 1192. A few months later, in February 1193, Ṣalāḥ al-Dīn died in Damascus.

Notwithstanding the reverses of his last campaign, the achievement of Ṣalāḥ al-Dīn was unique. He unified the most populous and economically strong parts of the Near East into one empire, and he broke the strength of the Latin states, which were afterwards incapable of threatening the Muslims without aid from outside. Under his rule Egypt emerged as the principal political unit in the eastern Mediterranean, and as the head of the Muslim resistance against the Crusaders. Total victory was, however, denied to the great sultan because of the inherent instability of his feudal armies.

While he mounted the military jihad against the Franks, he paid no less attention to the ideological struggle in the name of orthodox Islam. The main instrument became the *madrasa* or religious college, an institution established by the Seljuks in the east in the eleventh century for the purpose of strengthening the Sunni teaching, as promulgated by the great theologian al-Ash'arī (died 935), and of fighting all heretical trends, especially the Ismā'īlīya and other Shī'a sects. Ṣalāḥ al-Dīn introduced the *madrasa* type of college into Jerusalem, Egypt and Hejaz. None of the Ayyubid *madrasas* in Egypt survived intact, but their influence, both doctrinal and architectural, on the following periods was manifest. The *madrasa* served not only as 'a fortress of theologians' but also as a centre of other branches of learning, and it is due to them that Egypt was able to continue the best traditions of Arabic scholarship and literature at a time when the eastern parts of the Islamic world succumbed to the Mongols. Although the Ismā'īlīya and some other Shī'a sects remained strong in parts of Syria, the struggle between Sunni and Shī'a Islam for the allegiance of the masses in Arabic lands was definitively decided in favour of the former by the ascension of Ṣalāḥ al-Dīn and his dynasty. After his time, Egypt and the majority of Fertile Crescent countries formed the bulwark of Islamic orthodoxy, and were free from any sectarian movements. Another feature of the Sunni revival was the introduction and growth of the Sufi (popularly known as *dervish*) brotherhoods and the establishment of many convents (sing. *zāwiya*, pl. *zawāyā*) all over the country. Most of the Sufi orders were introduced from Asia or North Africa, but in Egypt they developed special characteristics which in due course penetrated, through wandering scholars and saints, to other parts of Africa, and especially to the Sudanic region. Among the most famous brotherhoods (*ṭarīqa*) was the Aḥmadīyya, or Badāwīyya, order founded by a native of Morocco, Aḥmad al-Badāwī (died 1276), who nevertheless spent his whole adult life in Tanta, and is considered the greatest Egyptian saint. Although Sufism in Egypt did not play the same role in social and political life as it did in North Africa and the Sudan then and later, its influence on the masses of population was far from negligible.

Ṣalāḥ al-Dīn divided his realm among his sons and his younger brother al-'Ādil. At first Egypt was ruled by his son al-'Azīz, but Ṣalāḥ al-Dīn's sons soon fell into discord. Taking advantage of this situation, al-'Ādil gradually overcame all of them and in 1199 acquired for himself sovereignty over Egypt and the major part of Syria. During the next two decades his own sons superseded the descendants of Ṣalāḥ al-Dīn as rulers of the chief provinces under the general suzerainty of their father. Al-'Ādil was a true successor to his brother, with whom he shared many abilities and character traits: he continued the policy of restricted warfare, and employed as his chief weapons diplomacy and intrigue, at the same time paying much attention to economic and commercial matters and concluding new treaties with the Venetians and the Pisans.

Egypt retained its position as the centre of the empire and its rulers were considered to be the senior branch of the Ayyubid house. In 1200 al-ʿĀdil appointed his son al-Kāmil as governor of Egypt. It was a good choice, and the country was thus given a ruler who administered it for nearly forty years with intelligence, tolerance and an understanding of the needs of the population. Although the beginning of al-Kāmil's regency was marked by a famine and pestilence similar to those of 1066–72, his firm hand did not allow any disturbances, and his wise emergency measures soon restored the former prosperity.

Relations with the Crusading states still occupied first place in foreign policy, but none of Ṣalāḥ al-Dīn's successors showed the same dedication to the cause of Islam. The Ayyubid princes only very rarely took the offensive against the Franks, contenting themselves with remaining on the defensive, and seeking to negotiate a truce as soon as possible. This attitude, often criticized by contemporary Muslim authors, was dictated by their policy of expanding commerce with the Italian republics, as well as by the realization that the Latin states had ceased to represent any danger to the Ayyubid realm. Only when new Crusading armies from Europe appeared at infrequent intervals in the Near East were attempts made to overthrow the balance of forces, but these regularly failed, as will be discussed presently.

Al-ʿĀdil's chief concern was the defence of Egypt, since in the Christian camp the awareness of the strategic and economic importance of Egypt was gaining more and more ground. The raids on Rosetta in 1204 and on Damietta in 1211 were a forewarning of this new awareness, and the last two large-scale Crusading enterprises (in 1218 and 1249) were aimed at 'striking the head of the snake', while the Holy Land, with Jerusalem, was now considered a secondary objective. This shift in strategy was due not only to the recognition of Egypt's role as the paramount power of the Islamic world; its occupation would also permit direct access to the eastern trade and the breaking of the Muslim monopoly in it.

In the spring of 1218 a huge Crusading army, composed both of new arrivals from Europe and contingents from the Jerusalem kingdom, under the command of the papal legate, Pelagius, began to lay siege to Damietta, a very strong fortress and the key to Egypt. Although the

Ayyubid garrison there was reinforced, one of its most important defensive towers fell into Frankish hands in August; the news of its capture caused the death of al-ʻĀdil. Al-Kāmil was at once recognized by the members of the house as its head and as sultan of Egypt. In order to save the fortress of Damietta, the sultan offered to surrender to the Crusaders the whole kingdom of Jerusalem, as it was before Ṣalāḥ al-Dīn's conquest. The Crusaders haughtily refused to deal with the 'infidels', being sure of their victory and already visualizing the conquest not only of Damietta but of the whole of Egypt. The fortress fell by assault in November 1219, but further advance into the interior was delayed by interminable quarrels among the leaders of the Crusade.

In the meantime al-Kāmil had mobilized all the resources of Egypt and had summoned the Ayyubid princes to support him. It is remarkable that at this hour of supreme danger to Egypt his kinsmen laid aside their rivalries and rallied willingly round the head of the family. When in July 1221 the Crusaders, after two years of passivity, at last started their march southwards, the Ayyubid armies were ready for them. The Christians chose the season badly and their knowledge of the geography of the Delta was worse than lamentable. The river was rising, and soon the advancing army found itself surrounded by water and enemy on all sides. In the fiercely fought battle of Manṣūra (August 1221) the Crusaders were defeated and asked for terms of peace. Al-Kāmil acted generously and tolerantly, granting the enemy free withdrawal and the restoration of the Holy Cross (captured previously by Ṣalāḥ al-Dīn in Jerusalem) in exchange for Damietta and an eight-year truce. And so another attempt to conquer Egypt, and thus to eliminate the most dangerous foe of Christendom, ended ingloriously after so much hope and initial success.

Once the external threat was removed, the internal rivalry between the Ayyubid princes reasserted itself. Until 1227 al-Muʻaẓẓam of Damascus successfully opposed his brother al-Kāmil's claim to supremacy in the empire, and allied himself with, and later even recognized the suzerainty of, the Khwārazm-Shāh Jalāl al-Dīn, who had fled from his Central Asian realm before the advancing Mongols and was trying to carve out a new kingdom for himself in the Near East. Al-Kāmil, looking for allies, concluded a treaty of alliance with Emperor Frederick II, who resided in Sicily and was known for being exceptionally tolerant and liberal in religious matters.

In 1228 when Frederick set out on his Crusade, al-Kāmil honoured the terms of the treaty, although the situation in the meantime had changed radically to his advantage with al-Muʿaẓẓam's death in 1227. The new ten-year treaty signed in February 1229 was the most remarkable ever concluded between a Muslim and a Christian ruler. The sultan of Egypt ceded to the emperor Jerusalem and other holy places in Palestine, such as Bethlehem and Nazareth, together with the road to Jaffa and Acre, reserving only the ʿUmar Mosque (the so-called *Masjid al-aqṣā* or *Ḥaram*) to the Muslims, in exchange for the emperor's pledge to defend the sultan against all enemies be they Christian or Muslim. These terms aroused a wave of indignation on both sides. Both the Pope, who had previously cursed Frederick, and the whole Christian world stigmatized the emperor as a traitor who bargained with the infidels instead of fighting them, while zealous Muslims violently criticized the surrender of Muslim territory to the Christians as unnecessary. In fact, however, al-Kāmil gained more than he lost, since the territory itself was without much value, and the Muslim holy place remained in their hands. The alliance with the emperor increased his bargaining power vis-à-vis the other Ayyubids and deprived the Latin states of any military aid from Europe. Even from the point of view of Christendom the terms were advantageous, because by a stroke of the pen Frederick had achieved more than had the Third Crusade with its huge armies, and had restored the Holy City, the alleged goal of the entire Crusading enterprise, to Christian control. But at this time the genuine religious inspiration of the Crusades had become only a thin veil for the more mundane interests of the Italian maritime cities and of the Latin feudal lords. These interests were, of course, badly served by Frederick's treaty with al-Kāmil.

For the remaining nine years of al-Kāmil's life the treaty was in general observed by both sides. The sultan, free from Frankish interventions, dedicated these years to the attempt to unify the Ayyubid empire under his supreme rule. Realizing that the federal structure preferred by his uncle and father had repeatedly led to internal strife and friction, and that it had weakened the empire in every respect, he set the building of a strong centralized state as his goal. He died before achieving this aim and it fell to the Mamluks to make this idea a reality.

Under al-Kāmil Egypt continued to prosper economically and culturally. The sultan himself took a personal interest in the improvement of the irrigation and road system, completed the Cairo citadel and laid the foundations of the new *madrasas*. The truce with the Christians permitted several commercial treaties to be concluded with European nations, and internal and external trade flourished. Visitors from the outside world were surprised by the enormous number of Nile boats and ships plying between Cairo and Alexandria, loaded with trade goods coming from every part of the world. The administration became more efficient and less venal than it had been under the last Fatimids, and the general security of life and property attained a level not often encountered in medieval times. It is significant that from Ṣalāḥ al-Dīn's time until the end of the dynasty there are no records of the street fights that so plagued the cities in earlier and later periods.

Al-Kāmil's death, however, gave the signal for the renewal of rivalries among the Ayyubid princes. His son and immediate successor, al-ʿĀdil II, was deposed after two years' rule, and his brother al-Ṣāliḥ Najm al-Dīn Ayyūb (1240–9), the last of the efficient and outstanding sovereigns of the dynasty, ascended the throne. He too had to fight against rivals, mostly in Syria, and also against the Franks allied to his Muslim adversaries. In an attempt to increase his military might, al-Ṣāliḥ Ayyūb had recourse to the traditional but fatal expedient of enrolling Turkish mercenaries in his army, first a group of Khwarazmian warriors, and later Kipchak slaves bought in the south Russian steppes. The Khwarazmians soon became unruly, and one of their bands conquered Jerusalem on its own initiative in the summer of 1244, thus restoring the Holy City definitively to Muslim hands. The gradual increase of the *mamlūk* troops permitted the sultan to gain the upper hand over his rivals, and to attain the same dominating position as had his father and grandfather. His army won a great victory over the Franks in 1244, and then occupied and fortified Jerusalem; three years later Ascalon was captured and the Latin states were again in grave danger of being annihilated.

The loss of Jerusalem revived the crusading spirit in Europe, and it was the king of France, Louis IX, the Saint, who personally led the armies in his last attempt to call a halt to Muslim victories. The time seemed opportune, as the eastern parts of the Islamic world were inundated by a flood of Mongol invaders, and the Franks nursed exaggerated hopes for a military alliance that would enclose the Muslims from all sides and destroy them definitively.

The Crusade of Saint Louis that began in June 1249 was, in its strategy, tactics and final outcome, as nearly as possible the exact replica of that of 1218–21. The French army occupied Damietta without much effort, and then waited there idly for some time, marching towards Cairo only at the worst season and by the same difficult route through the maze of Nile branches and canals. The Egyptian army concentrated near Manṣūra, and the sultan offered to exchange Damietta for Jerusalem, but again the king refused to bargain with the infidels. At this juncture the sultan, al-Ṣāliḥ, died (November 1249). His death was concealed from the troops by his Turkish concubine, Shajar al-Durr, who took over the command and summoned the crown prince, Tūrān-Shāh, from Mesopotamia. In the battle at Manṣūra in February 1250 the Kurdish and Arab troops fled the field, but the disciplined Turkish *mamlūks* proved themselves the bulwark of the Ayyubid army. Two months later these same troops won an overwhelming victory at al-Fariskūr. King Louis and the flower of the French nobility were taken prisoner, and thousands of soldiers were killed or later executed. This battle destroyed for ever Christian hopes of conquering Egypt and the Holy Land, but at the same time it sounded the knell of the Ayyubid dynasty. The new sultan, Tūrān-Shāh, soon made himself unpopular with the leading *mamlūk* officers, arrogantly conscious of their part in the victory and fearing the competition of Tūrān-Shāh's own *mamlūks*. In May 1250 a group of *mamlūks* led by Baybars murdered Tūrān-Shāh, and in his place proclaimed Shajar al-Durr as sultan of Egypt and the queen of the Muslims, a rare case of a woman formally attaining sovereign status in Islamic lands. It is difficult to decide whether this queen was the last of the Ayyubids or the first of the Mamluks, as she was connected with both the vanishing and the oncoming dynasty.

In the Ayyubid epoch the rise of Egypt as the most important centre of Arabic culture became more apparent. A number of direct and indirect factors influenced this shift from the eastern parts of the Arabic world to its middle part. On the one hand Egypt prospered materially: whereas in 1090, under the Fatimids, the annual revenue of all Egyptian provinces was evaluated at about 3 million dinars, a century later under Ṣalāḥ al-Dīn (in 1189) the amount of more than 5 million dinars was attained. Such an increase in revenue made possible the vast building activities and the foundation of many *waqfs* (pious endowments) that traditionally formed the material base for the growth and prosperity of the Muslim intelligentsia. Another source of wealth was the profit from international trade promoted by all sultans through treaties with European states and cities, and by the control of all Red Sea ports on both shores.

The orthodox revival, as well as the generosity of Ayyubid rulers, attracted many scholars to Egypt at a time when the eastern portions of the Islamic world (Iraq, Iran and Central Asia), hitherto more important as cultural centres, were gradually sucked into the whirlwind of Mongol expansion. Later on, under the Mamluks, the cultural primacy of Egypt became more pronounced, and the country, together with Syria, continued to play the leading role in Arabic cultural and scholarly life.

The Ayyubid period was productive especially in poetry and historiography. Fresh life was given to Arabic poetry by the introduction of new strophic forms, called *muwashshaḥ* and *zajāl*, which originated in Muslim Spain but acquired a wide popularity in the Near Eastern Arabic countries too. This new style loosened the rigid metric formality of the ancient *qaṣīda*, and allowed the poet to express his individuality and feelings more freely. The first representative of the new school was Ibn Sanā' al-Mulk (1150–1211), an Egyptian judge who also wrote many panegyric poems. The most famous among the court poets was Bahā' al-Dīn Zuhayr (1186–1258), whose love lyrics were distinguished by simplicity and sincerity, and whose encomiums are free of exaggerated flattery. This epoch produced also 'Umar b. al-Fāriḍ (1182–1235), the greatest Arab mystic poet, and the only one on a par with the most famous Persian representatives of Sufi poetry. His poems, presented as traditional love or wine-songs, possess a second, mystic meaning; they are at the same time more abstract and passionate, but also less sensual, than the products of the great Persian Sufi poets. To a similar category belonged al-Buṣīrī (1211–95), the author of the famous 'Mantle Ode' (*Qaṣīdat al-Burda*), a praise-poem on the Prophet Muḥammad that won a quasi-sacred status and was widely used for magical purposes throughout the whole Islamic world.

The personality and exploits of Ṣalāh al-Dīn fascinated his Muslim contemporaries as much an they did the Franks, and it is no wonder that his biographies held a prominent place in the Arab historiography of the epoch. The best known are those written by 'Imād al-Dīn al-Iṣfahānī (1125–1201), by Ibn Shaddād Bahāl' al-Dīn (died 1234), who was chief secretary to Ṣalāḥ al-Dīn, and by Abū Shāma of Damascus (died 1268) who, contrary to his two predecessors, took a hostile attitude towards the great sultan. From among the Coptic minority came two universal histories describing events from the Creation until the mid thirteenth century, one by al-Makīn (died 1273), the other by Buṭrūs b. al-Rāḥib (*fl.* 1270). 'Alī al-Qifṭī (1172–1248) compiled a biographical dictionary of physicians and scientists, both Greek and Arab, thus giving a clear picture of the transmission of the Classical and Hellenistic heritage to the Islamic world.

The natural sciences and philosophy in Arabic countries were in this epoch past their zenith. The only outstanding figure was the Jewish philosopher Maimonides (died 1204), a native of Spain, who later became personal physician to Ṣalāḥ al-Dīn, and whose contributions to Jewish theology and philosophy marked a turning point.

The participation of Christians and Jews in the intellectual life of Ayyubid Egypt bears witness to the fact that the tolerant policy of the Fatimids continued under their successors. At the beginning of his reign, Ṣalāḥ al-Dīn forbade the employment of Copts in administrative and medical posts, but this restriction remained only formal, and the Copts continued to hold as many posts as before or after, since their services in fiscal and financial departments were indispensable for their smooth functioning. The thirteenth century is considered to be the golden age of Christian Arabic literature in Egypt, as the Coptic language disappeared almost completely from vernacular use, and the religious and profane literature of Christian Egyptians was written exclusively in Arabic. If the wars against the Crusaders did not particularly influence the tolerant attitude of the ruling classes towards their Christian subjects, the religious fervour stimulated by the fighting against foreign invaders led to increasing intolerance among the masses of the Muslim population that persisted for many centuries to come.

THE MAMLUKS

When Shajar al-Durr became queen after the death of Tūrān-Shāh, no one in the Muslim world relished the idea of a woman on the throne, not even the Mamluks who had proclaimed her monarch. For the military oligarchy now rising to power in Egypt it was rather a temporary expedient to master the situation they faced after the murder of the last Ayyubid. And so, after only eighty days of solitary rule, Shajar al-Durr married one of the great Mamluk *amīrs*, Aybeg (Aybak), who thus became the first Mamluk sultān of Egypt.

Muslim annals provide many examples of slave-soldiers as king-makers and holders of virtual control in the state, and record even some isolated cases of members of this group becoming nominal rulers, but the accession of Aybeg to the Egyptian throne was something unique. From his time until the Ottoman conquest Egypt knew no other rulers than those belonging to the military oligarchy consisting of former slaves of foreign origin, at first predominantly Turkish, later Circassian. It is usual to distinguish two Mamluk 'dynasties', the Baḥrī line that started with Aybeg and lasted until 1382, and the Burjī line that succeeded the former and was overthrown only in 1517 by the Ottoman sultan, Selim I. Among the Baḥris, the tendency to establish the hereditary system prevailed; fourteen rulers of the twenty-four were descendants of Sultan Qalā'ūn and three others were sons of sultans. In contrast, the Burjī Mamluks were averse to the dynastic system and preferred the system in which a freedman succeeded his former master on the throne.

The term *mamlūk* (lit. 'owned', 'slave') was applied chiefly to white slaves, and gradually came to designate those who were acquired by Muslim rulers to form the bulk of their standing armies. By the thirteenth century this institution had become an integral part of the political and social system in many Muslim countries, the soldier-slaves enjoying increasing powers. But only in Egypt, and in Muslim India, did they cross the gulf that separated them from the nominal kingship.

According to Islamic law, no person of slave status could officially hold a sovereign position in the Muslim state; therefore every Mamluk sultan was obliged to show his deed of manumission at the inaugural ceremony. The manumission of every *mamlūk* was performed after a certain time of military training and education, usually at the age of eighteen; the *mamlūks* were thus in reality freedmen, not slaves of their masters. On the other hand, the Mamluk oligarchy did not accept into their ranks anybody who was not brought up and trained as a slave-soldier; even their own children (called *awlād al-nās*, lit. 'sons of people') were barred from all higher military ranks and court offices. The self-perpetuation of the military oligarchy was assured by the arrival of new young slaves, and the emerging ruling military caste lived in complete social, cultural and even racial isolation from the other strata of Egyptian Arab society. Although the Egyptians had been used to rulers of foreign origin since Ptolemaic days, never before was the gulf between the masters (former slaves) and the subjects (theoretically free men) so wide and deep as under the Mamluk dynasty.

As is natural in a military society, even this exclusive caste was internally stratified. The Mamluk army was structured as follows. First, the royal *mamlūks*, who were further subdivided into the *mamlūks* of former sultans, the *mamlūks* of the reigning sultan, the *mamlūks* of the bodyguard and of the corps of pages selected among the latter, and the *mamlūks* of the *amīrs* who passed into the service of the sultan. Secondly, the *mamlūks* of the *amīrs*. Thirdly, the sons of *amīrs* (*awlād al-nās*) and soldiers recruited from the local population (*ajnād al-ḥalqa*). To this group, at the beginning, belonged knights of non-slave origin, but these gradually lost their importance and disappeared. The *amīrs* (generals and higher officers) were also divided into three categories: *amīrs* of ten, of forty, and of a hundred. Only the royal *mamlūks* could rise to the rank of *amīr*, and only the *mamlūks* who were freedmen of the reigning sultan could claim to be his successors. In their struggle for power the *amīrs* fought against each other, supported by their own regiments, thus provoking endless street fighting, descriptions of which monotonously fill the Mamluk annals. The tenure of the sultanate depended on the favour of the troops, the balance of power between rival *amīrs*, the political skill of the actual ruler, and, last but not least, on the strength of his royal *mamlūks*. Their number rarely exceeded ten thousand. Only the royal *mamlūks* were given proper military training in barrack schools and on the hippodrome, whereas the *mamlūks* of *amīrs* only mastered the rudiments of military skill. The *mamlūks*, as people from the steppes, were primarily mounted archers; the bow was the chief weapon, but the lance, sword, mace and shield were also a part of their equipment. All were excellent horsemen, and for more than two centuries the Mamluk army was one of the best in the world, achieving its superiority by its professional character and its tactical skill on the battlefield. Their victory over the Mongols, and over the remnants of the Latin Crusaders' states, contributed largely to the Mamluk reputation for invincibility that survived long after the army had lost much of its efficacy and entered a slow decline.

The reign of the Mamluks – or Turks, as they were generally called in the Muslim world, without regard to their various origins[1] – was the despotism of a small military oligarchy; its members were uncultured, rude, rapacious, tyrannical and treacherous former slaves, who were only superficially islamized and never arabized. But under this alien dynasty Egypt became the leading Arab country, both politically and economically as well as culturally, and enjoyed, at least during the first half of this period, a prosperity, stability and continuity of institutions shared by few other Muslim lands.

[1] The Mamluk state is known usually as *Dawlat al-Atrāk* ('Empire of the Turks') in contemporary sources.

'Izz al-Dīn Aybeg (1250–7) was thus the first Mamluk sultan of the Baḥrī line.[1] He was confronted with two urgent tasks: first, to bring the Crusade of Louis IX to an end, and secondly, to deal with the Ayyubid dynasty, still powerful in Syria. The French king's terms of surrender were faithfully observed, and after a month of captivity, Louis and the majority of his knights were released for a ransom of 800,000 French pounds, and the town of Damietta was reoccupied by the Mamluk army and its fortifications razed.

The Ayyubid princes in Syria were not prepared to let Egypt, the most precious part of the dynasty's realm, fall unopposed into the hands of a usurper and regicide. Their first invasion of Egypt was repulsed and, in view of the Mongol peril, a truce was then concluded between them and Aybeg. In order to legitimate his position, Aybeg proclaimed himself the caliph's viceroy, and contemplated a political marriage. This move was the immediate cause of his death, because Queen Shajar al-Durr had him murdered on hearing this news. But she herself met an equally brutal end only a few days later.

Aybeg's death was welcomed by the Baḥrī *mamlūks*, many of whom began to come back to Egypt from their Syrian exile. At first the sultan's young son was duly raised to the throne, but this was only a temporary measure of the *amīrs*, who were not yet in agreement about which of them should become sultan. This feature of mock primogeniture was repeated time and again after the death of many sultans. The young sons were installed with all ceremonies, but they were only shadow rulers without any real power. In the meantime the senior *amīrs* competed between themselves for the throne, and, as soon as the strongest seized power, he sent the puppet sultan into a luxurious retirement or exile.

At the beginning of 1258 the fall of Baghdad into the hands of the Mongol prince Hūlāgū, and the subsequent execution of the last 'Abbasid caliph, shattered the whole Islamic world. The danger to Egypt became more acute than ever because of the advance of Mongol armies into Syria, where, at the beginning of 1260, Aleppo and Damascus were sacked. The situation called for a strong person, and the regent Quṭuz, Aybeg's former deputy and commander of his *mamlūks*, was elected as sultan in November 1259. The Mamluk army led by Quṭuz and one of the senior *amīrs*, Baybars, marched from Egypt to Palestine and there in September 1260, near 'Ayn Jālūt, inflicted a heavy

[1] The name Baḥrī is derived either from their barracks on the island of Rawda in the River Nile (*Baḥr al-Nīl*), or, more probably, it indicates that they were imported from across the sea (in Arabic, *baḥr*).

defeat on the Mongol army and its Armenian and Georgian auxiliaries. The Mongol commander Kitbuga Noyon was captured and executed, while the rest of his army retreated hastily to Iraq, joined by the garrisons of occupied Syrian towns whose Muslim population had risen and expelled them.

For the first time the Mongols had been defeated in an open battle and their westward advance was definitively stopped. The Mamluk cavalry, employing tactics similar to those of their adversaries, had proved its worth, and from the time of this battle the aura of invincibility shifted from the Mongols to the Mamluks. While it is incontestable that this victory saved Egypt and parts of Syria from the devastations of the Mongol hordes, there is no ground for exaggerating its importance, as is sometimes done. The Mongols were already nearing the point of exhaustion in their expansive activity, and in many of the occupied countries were now more interested in consolidating their control than in further conquest. In the eastern part of the Muslim world, after an initial period of terrible destruction, conditions gradually returned to normal. The Mongols adopted Islam, and were soon assimilated into the local cultures in Iraq, Iran and Central Asia, to a higher degree than the Turkish Mamluks were in Egypt. For the indigenous population, both the Mamluks and the Mongols always remained a foreign ruling class, and differences between them were quantitative rather than qualitative. It should not be forgotten that the Mongol force at 'Ayn Jālūt was nothing but a detachment, which was vastly outnumbered by the Mamluk army, and that its rapid withdrawal from Syria was due to the fact that Hūlāgū was obliged to return to Mongolia owing to the death of the Great Khan. In the following years the Mongol rulers were occupied by the internal struggles between the various branches of the dynasty, and this greatly weakened their forces. They continued to threaten Syria from the east and north for some decades, and many times were involved in conflicts with the Mamluks, but they had already lost their initial drive.

Shortly after the battle Quṭuz was treacherously murdered by Baybars, who was proclaimed sultan on the spot. This former slave, who had distinguished himself at Manṣūra and 'Ayn Jālūt, and who came to power by means of two regicides, was the real founder of the Mamluk state, being not only an able general but also a far-sighted statesman and organizer. Like all his great predecessors, he grasped the necessity of defending Egypt in Syria and Palestine; this meant finishing off the remnants of the Latin states which were making common cause with the Mongols, and it also meant bringing the turbulent Ayyubid princes under control. His chief objective was, of course, to contain the Mongol threat for ever, and to rebuild the Egyptian empire on a new, strongly centralized base, finishing thus the unachieved work of al-Malik al-Kāmil. In a short time he made the Ayyubid principalities tributary, and the whole of Syria became an integral part of the Mamluk empire. For the next ten years, until 1271, Baybars undertook annual campaigns and raids against the Franks, conquering one stronghold after another, and crowning his work with the capture of Antioch in 1268. He then dealt a mortal blow to the power of the Assassins, who from his time on ceased to play any role in Middle East politics. A new defeat was inflicted on the Mongols in Asia Minor, where the sultan temporarily occupied Kayseri.

These military successes were more than matched by the political and diplomatic ones: a brilliant move was made by inviting one of the ʿAbbasids to Cairo and by installing him there as caliph. This inaugurated a new line of ʿAbbasid caliphs in Egypt, who, though mere figureheads at the mercy of the Mamluk sultans, nevertheless conferred legitimacy upon their virtual masters and benefactors. Although the total insignificance of these puppet caliphs was apparent, there were many rulers in the Islamic world, even as far as in India and West Africa, who deemed it important to seek official investiture from the ʿAbbasid residing in Cairo. This, of course, enhanced the prestige of Mamluk sultans even more. A corollary to this was the allegiance of Mecca and Medina, both of which now became dependencies of the Mamluk state; Baybars even adopted the title *khādim al-ḥaramayn* ('servant of the two Holy Cities'), which symbolized his primacy among Muslim rulers.

In foreign relations, a special place was given to the alliance with the Golden Horde, the Mongol state in the South Russian steppes, the ruler of which embraced Islam and became an enemy of the Persian Mongols, the Īl-Khāns. As the territory of the Golden Horde was the main source of supply of Turkish (Kipchak) slaves for the Mamluk army, friendly relations were of vital importance for the maintenance of military power. The same concern led to amicable relations with Constantinople, since the ships on which the slaves were brought to Egypt had to sail through the Bosphorus and Dardanelles.

Baybars's policy towards Christian Europe was equally successful. A couple of decades after the Crusade of Louis IX, the Christian powers, among them the emperors, vied with each other in establishing friendly relations and alliances with Egypt, now the most powerful force in the eastern Mediterranean. Commercial treaties were concluded with Italian republics, Sicily and Aragon, and the Mamluk empire became an important partner in European power politics, as well as in its economic policies. At the time of Baybars's death (1277) the Mamluk empire extended from Cyrenaica to the Euphrates, and from Little Armenia to Nubia; the Mongol danger no longer loomed over Syria and Egypt, and the final liquidation of the small Frankish enclaves was only a matter of time.

After a short interlude, in which two unimportant sons of Baybars held the nominal title of sultan, the then commander-in-chief, Sayf al-Dīn Qalā'ūn (1279–90), acceded to the throne. Only he, among all the Mamluks, was able to found a real dynasty that lasted until 1382, even if his numerous grandsons were mere puppets in the hands of powerful *amīrs*. It was during his reign and that of his son, al-Nāṣir Muḥammad, that the Mamluk state, and especially Egypt, enjoyed more than sixty years of internal tranquillity and general prosperity.

In the beginning Qalā'ūn continued the policies of Baybars: to check a new Mongol invasion into northern Syria, he concluded treaties with some Crusader cities, and sent embassies to the Byzantine and Roman emperors. In 1281 he inflicted a crushing defeat upon the Ilkhanid army at Hims, in a battle that once again confirmed the outstanding military prowess of the Mamluks. Although shortly afterwards the reigning Īl-Khān was converted to Islam, and the relations between the two states improved, Qalā'ūn continued to strengthen his alliances with the Golden Horde and other powers; his diplomatic activities reached as far as India and Ceylon. At the end of his reign he turned his attention to Little Armenia and the Franks, whom he accused of joining forces with the Mongols; his last feat of arms was the conquest of Tripoli (1289). Preparations for an expedition against Acre were completed at the moment of his death, and it fell to his son, al-Ashraf Khalīl (1290–3), to lead the campaign, in the course of which this last stronghold of the Crusaders was conquered (May 1291). Its capture precipitated the fall of the few remaining ports and castles, and in 1302 the island of Arwād, off the Syrian coast, where the Templars found their last refuge, surrendered. In contrast to the magnanimity of the Ayyubids, the garrisons and inhabitants of conquered or surrendered cities were mercilessly slaughtered or sold into slavery. Just as the Crusades began with horrible bloodshed committed by Christians, so they were ended in the same way by the Muslims.

After the assassination of al-Ashraf Khalīl, the royal *mamlūks* elevated his younger brother al-Malik al-Nāṣir Muḥammad to the throne. Even if his reign (1294–1341) was twice interrupted, first in 1294–9 by the sultans Kitbuga and Lājīn, and for the second time in 1309–10 by Baybars II, it was one of the longest in Egyptian history. During al-Nāṣir Muḥammad's second reign, as nominal as the first, the main event was the renewal of hostilities with the Mongol Īl-Khāns of Persia, who wished to recover what they had lost in 1282. At the end of 1299, Īl-Khān Ghāzān, a newly converted Muslim, crossed the Euphrates with a huge army, invaded northern Syria, and in the first battle routed the Mamluk army, afterwards occupying Damascus. But the Mongol losses were severe, and after Egypt launched a counter-offensive with fresh forces, the Īl-Khān gradually evacuated the conquered territory. After two years of uneasy truce, the Mongols again marched into Syria in the spring of 1303, and clashed with the Mamluks on the plain of Marj al-Ṣuffar near Damascus. For two days the issue was uncertain, but at last the Mamluk army won a decisive victory. For the fourth time the Mamluks had beaten the most dangerous foe Egypt had encountered, and never again did the Īl-Khāns risk a new campaign against the formidable Mamluk empire.

In 1310 the sultan al-Nāṣir Muḥammad took the reins into his own hands; bitter from the experience of the lean years of nominal sultanship, and twice deposed, he gradually got rid of potential rivals, and many leading *mamlūk amīrs* were executed or fled into exile. Not being a military leader, he avoided wars, as he feared entrusting a big army to a possible pretender. Indeed, there was now no need for any military campaigns, since the position of Egypt as the paramount power in the Near East was generally accepted by all other states, European and Muslim alike. Relations with the Īl-Khāns, whose rule was already nearing its end, were friendly, as were those with the old allies, the Golden Horde, Byzantium and a dozen other countries near and far. Among the numerous embassies sent to the Mamluk court we find envoys from Aragon, the Holy See, the Delhi Sultanate and Ethiopia. In 1325 Mansa Mūsā, the ruler of Mali, visited Cairo on his way to Mecca and spent such a large amount of gold there that the exchange rate of the gold dinar to the silver dirham fell by as much as six dirhams in the dinar, a depreciation of about 20 per cent.

The Mamluk empire did not expand very much beyond its normal frontiers formed by the Euphrates in the east, Tripoli in the west, Aswan in the south and the Pyramus mountains in the north. Only here did the Mamluk army find a field of activity. It frequently raided and pillaged the kingdom of Little Armenia, the last of the Christian states in this region.

The peaceful years of al-Nāṣir's reign brought both relative prosperity to the whole country and, at the same time, heavy expenditure for the maintenance of the sultan's court and for large-scale building activity. As always, it was the Egyptian peasant, the *fellaḥ*, on whom fell the main burden of supplying his feudal lord, as well as the state treasury, with the necessary income. Under al-Nāṣir Muḥammad, the system of military feudalism reached its most pronounced form: it found its formal expression in the cadastral survey of 1316, accompanied by new allocations of fiefs and redistribution of lands.

The Mamluk fief (*iqṭā'*) was a source of revenue temporarily conceded by the sultan to a military officer, bringing him an average yearly income corresponding to his military grade, in return for maintaining a certain number of men-at-arms. Most of the fiefs were landed estates, but some of them were allowances from taxes or customs. The basic unit of fief land consisted of a town or a village as a centre, and the surrounding cultivated lands. Each unit contained a surveyed number of acres (*faddān*), upon which a fixed number of dinars (*'ibra*) was assessed. The amount per acre differed according to its productivity, and represented in reality the land tax of the unit, whether paid directly to the individual landlord or to the state, i.e. the sultan's treasury. The fief units of any given individual did not form a contiguous tract of land, but were frequently situated in widely separated areas, so that the feudal lord could not become a holder of a large territory. It was also usual that the grantee did not reside in his fief, but in Cairo, or in the chief town of the district in which his fief was situated, leaving the management of his fief to a number of administrators and accountants, who were mostly Copts, like those employed by the sultan himself. The deed of grant normally specified that one-third of the income from the fief was destined for the personal use of the grantee, the remaining two-thirds for the maintenance of his subordinates according to their rank.

The assignment of fiefs was subject to change whenever the rank or office of the grantee changed, and also after his death. The natural tendency of the great *amīrs* to make their fiefs hereditary, as was possible under the Ayyubids and even under the first Mamluks, was checked under al-Nāṣir Muḥammad precisely by the redistribution of fiefs already mentioned, and by the strict prohibition of the sale of fiefs. Of the twenty-four parts of income-yielding territory in Egypt, the sultan allocated ten parts to himself, the remaining fourteen going to the *mamlūk amīrs* and officers. However, by the end of the thirteenth century only four parts belonged to the sultan. Some royal *mamlūks* below the rank of *amīr* were also given small fiefs, usually a village or half a village, sometimes even less, but the majority of Mamluk soldiers received direct salaries in cash and in kind.

This complicated system, with the incessant changes involved, required a huge administrative apparatus called the *dīwān al-jaysh* ('register of the army') or *dīwān al-iqṭā*ʿ ('register of fiefs'), with its seat in Cairo and branches in every province or large township. It supervised and surveyed the state of cultivation, kept the registers of all the fief-holders as well as of the fief units; calculations were made in a fictitious monetary unit denoted as *dīnar jayshī* (military dinar). This unit varied in value from ten to seven silver dirhams, according to the fief-holder's rank. Later, it had a fixed value of thirteen and one-half dirhams, and finally it lost all connection with the real monetary units. This makes a reconstruction of the value of the real income of fiefs, and thus of the financial situation in Egypt during the Mamluk epoch, a very complicated problem.[1] Later, especially after the financial crisis at the beginning of the fifteenth century, the value of fief revenues fell sharply, thus accelerating the decline of the military fief system as the main source of income for the maintenance of the army and state.

The majority of Egyptian peasants were hereditary holders of their land, which theoretically belonged to the state. With the expansion of the *iqṭā*ʿ system under the Ayyubids and the early Mamluks, the *fellāḥīn* became more and more exploited by their feudal lords. The main form of the feudal rent was the general land-tax (*kharāj*), fixed according to the productivity of the land and the products. This tax was paid either in kind or in money, or both, and an elaborate system of rates of exchange existed between the various kinds of products to be levied from one acre: the *kharāj* from a *faddān* of industrial crops or vegetables was higher than that of cereals. In addition to this, there were taxes on all domestic animals and poultry, honey and wax, and fruit trees. Sometimes a part of these taxes went directly to the state treasury, the rest being paid to the fief-holder. The state often claimed the labour of

[1] W. Popper, *Egypt and Syria under the Circassian sultans*, part 2 (Berkeley and Los Angeles, 1957), 108–9, attempted to summarize the income of the military class based on the data given by the cadastral survey of 1316 and to evaluate it in US dollars. According to his calculations the income of an '*amīr* of a hundred' varied between $109,000 and $126,000 yearly, that of a Royal *mamlūk* between $24 and $52.

peasants for public works, such as the building or maintenance of dams and canals; the *fellāḥīn* in neighbouring villages were then mobilized, and had to bring their working animals, tools and food with them, being paid nothing at all. Especially in the first half of the fourteenth century, the Mamluk government undertook many works of this kind; the lengthening of the Alexandria canal needed the labour of from 40,000 to 100,000 peasant workers yearly, but it brought more than 100,000 *faddān* under cultivation. A whole network of new canals and a dozen new dams made possible a further expansion of irrigated land and the establishment of many new villages.

The peasants were the serfs of their immediate landlord and were not allowed to leave their villages without permission. This was an innovation of the Mamluk regime, since under the preceding dynasties nothing similar had as yet existed. Although some sultans attempted to restrain the lords in their abuse of serfs, the general situation of the peasants as a totally dependent class was not improved. The share of produce which remained to the peasants after the payment of taxes and rents was very small, and they were permanently indebted; every year they received loans of grain (at interest of ten to eleven per cent) from their lords, who were provided with it in advance by the sultan from state granaries.

The system of military fiefs never led to the formation of independent economic units, as happened in medieval Europe and in some other parts of the Near East. Egypt remained a highly centralized country both economically and administratively. The Mamluk sultans tried to introduce a similar unity into Syria, where they succeeded politically in bringing it under the sway of the Cairo government in the form of six provinces headed by nominated governors, all of them *mamlūks*. On the other hand they did not basically change the economic position of the local hereditary feudal lords who became their vassals. Another distinctive feature was that the landlords in Egypt dwelt permanently in the cities, whereas in Syria they lived on the territory which formed their fiefs.

In spite of all previous technological progress, the productivity of crafts remained limited owing to the preponderance of handwork. The craftsmen worked and sold their products in workshops concentrated locally according to trades (*sūqs* and *bazārs*). Big enterprises capable of mass production – mainly cotton, silk, paper and sugar mills as well as glass factories – were either owned by the sultan, or by rich *mamlūks*, and in any case were under strict state control. Their products were intended either for export or for the personal use of the ruling and upper classes. The small craftsmen were loosely organized into guilds, voluntary organizations for mutual help and defence, headed by a warden (*'ārif*) nominated by the state and responsible to it for the organization and prices of his respective guild. The warden was thus an assistant to the state controller of markets (*muḥtasib*). Some crafts could be carried on freely, but many were regulated or under the control of the state, Egypt being throughout its history more *étatiste* than other countries. The Egyptian guilds were in many respects distinct from similar European organizations, which were largely independent bodies with self-government and large powers of monopolistic control over their members. The townspeople in Egypt, be they craftsmen or merchants, neither attained nor strove to form an autonomous political class, a bourgeoisie in the true sense of the word, that would rule the township freely and according to its own interests as distinct from those of the military feudal class. Thus an important socio-political factor of development was absent, and this situation enabled the perpetuation of the military despotism of the Mamluks, which finally led to the political and economic decay of the whole empire, and especially of Egypt.

Not even the *Kārimi* merchants and bankers – the wealthiest and most privileged group among the non-military classes – were allowed to play any role as an independent or self-governing body. The heyday of their trade coincided with the reign of al-Nāṣir Muḥammad and his immediate successors. The network of their commercial activities covered mainly the shores of the Indian Ocean as far as present-day Indonesia and southern China, but they were active as well in Ethiopia, Nubia and the western Sudan. The capital of the richest among them reached more than one million dinars, their fleets on the Red Sea and the Indian Ocean numbered hundreds of vessels, and their agents resided in every important town and port. In the fourteenth century some of the *Kārimi* merchants joined the sultans and *amīrs* as founders of *madrasas* and *waqfs* for charitable purposes, or as patrons of scholars and poets. The Mamluk government was well aware of their importance for the economic life of the empire, and protected their interests abroad in many ways, mainly through foreign policy. But inside the empire all their commercial activities were under the control of a special ministry (*dīwān al-matjar*), and they had to pay enormous taxes or lend money to the sultan without interest and without much hope of recovering it again. The sultans themselves to an increasing degree participated directly in international trade, and it often happened that they forced the merchants to buy their goods at high prices; the natural opposition against such forced buying (in Arabic, *ṭarḥ*) was broken by threats to confiscate the merchants' property. Although under al-Nāṣir Muḥammad these and similar practices were not infrequent, international trade as a whole was not yet seriously endangered, even if individual merchants suffered some losses.

The number of European trade partners increased in the fourteenth century with the arrival of merchants from Florence, Marseilles and Barcelona, who joined those of Venice and Genoa. All these city-states had their special hostels (*funduq*) in Alexandria, and were represented by consuls recognized by the Egyptian government. The modalities of relationship between the Franks and the Muslims were regulated in all respects by commercial treaties, and by special guarantees issued by the sultan for the safety of foreign merchants and their property. These generally friendly relations were from time to time disturbed by hostile activities caused by the revival of the Crusading idea on the part of some Frankish rulers. In 1365 the Cypriots, in alliance with the Venetians and Genoese, raided and plundered Alexandria, inflicting great damage on the town and its population. Some Egyptian chronicles declare this raid to be the most horrible catastrophe in the history of Alexandria. For a long time trade relations between Egypt and Europeans were strained, and it took many years before they were normalized and new treaties concluded.

After the income from agriculture, foreign trade represented the main source of the economic and financial might of Egypt. Customs duties on eastern goods were levied upon the arrival of a ship in a Red Sea port, and then again in Alexandria or Damietta, before the re-export; in addition to this, there were interior customs houses along the overland road and on the Nile. The calculation of customs duty, as well as other taxes, was done not only *ad valorem* but also according to the religion of the merchants. Sometimes the duties for goods imported by Christian ships reached thirty per cent of the value, whereas the Muslim merchants had to pay only ten per cent for the same. On the other hand, a Muslim merchant had to pay, in addition to the religious tax (*zakāt*), a number of other taxes (*maks*, pl. *mukūs*) that put him fiscally on the same level as his Christian counterpart. It is true that in 1316 al-Nāṣir Muḥammad undertook a large fiscal reform abolishing many non-canonical taxes, but this reform concerned agricultural products and their marketing rather than taxes from trade and crafts.

The best evidence of the continuous prosperity of Egypt at this time is its architectural monuments. In this respect the Mamluks did more than any other dynasty since the Ptolemaic era, and it was in this period that Egyptian (as well as Syrian) towns attained their typical aspect that was to survive into modern times. Mamluk architecture can be considered as a further development of the Ayyubid style, enriched by Syrian and Mesopotamian influences brought into Egypt by the flow of artists and artisans who fled from the east before the Mongol invasion. Bricks were definitively replaced by stone as the chief building material, and new features were added by using stones of various colours in interiors as well as on façades. Minarets were now designed as three-storey buildings: the base was square, then an octagonal part crowned by a balcony followed, while the cylindrical upper portion was topped by an octagonal lantern. For *madrasas* and big mosques (*jāmi*ʿ) a perfect cruciform interior plan became standard, but the exterior remained rectangular and massive. The highest achievement of medieval Egyptian architecture – in monumentality, solidity and elegance – is best represented by the mosques and *madrasas* of Baybars I, al-Nāṣir Muḥammad and al-Ḥasan, all of them in Cairo. The complex of Qalā'ūn is also a remarkable monument (built in 1284–5) that comprises a *madrasa*, a mausoleum and a hospital; its monumental façade is provided with double windows and rich stucco carvings, the interior with wood-carvings and marble cladding. The Mamluk style is further characterized by the development of the stalactite pendentive, the lavish use of geometrical arabesque ornaments and inscriptions in the decorative Kufic script. The sultans, *amīrs* and the richest merchants vied with each other in erecting mausoleums, usually attached to mosques or *madrasas*, but often constructed as independent buildings on the outskirts of Cairo.

Similarly, the epoch saw the foundation of numerous *khānakas* or *zāwiyas* – convents for Sufi brotherhoods, which were at the same time hostels for travellers and fulfilled many other religious and charitable functions. They were maintained by *waqfs* – pious endowments established in perpetuity, and drawing revenues on a parcel of land or other real estate exempted from taxation. The system of *waqfs*, encouraged by Islamic law, in many cases allowed the founder's posterity to be provided with a steady income, since they became supervisors or administrators of the *waqf*, with practically no state control over expenditures, and safeguarded by law from confiscation. An increasing number of those *waqfs* in the fourteenth and mainly in the fifteenth centuries indicates the tendency, on the part of *mamlūks* as well as other affluent men, to preserve wealth for their descendants and thus to escape from the strictly non-hereditary Mamluk feudal system.

Sultan al-Nāṣir Muḥammad did not leave any capable successor to the throne, although in the forty-odd years that elapsed between his death in 1341 and the end of the Baḥrī line in 1382 no less than twelve of his descendants (eight sons, two grandsons and two great-grandsons) were proclaimed sultan. Some of them were mere children and succeeded each other rapidly, even if some, like al-Ḥasan, sat on the throne for ten years in two periods (1347–51, 1354–61), or al-Ashraf Sha'bān, who retained the title for a whole fourteen years (1363–77). But effective rule was exercised by the powerful *mamlūk amīrs*, who plunged themselves into the age-old game of intrigue, and the formation and dissolution of alliances between various cliques, to attain the greatest share of power and wealth. The streets of Cairo again became a battlefield for the struggles of rival Mamluk regiments, and in consequence the economic life of the country suffered heavily.

In mid century the 'Black Death', the same that visited Europe after 1348, spread over the Mamluk empire in Asia and in Egypt, and took a heavy toll of life. According to some sources, in Cairo alone ten to twenty thousand people died every day, and the total number of deaths in the capital reached nearly 900,000. The Syrian provinces and the Egyptian countryside suffered in the same way, land was laid waste for lack of labourers, and cattle and fruit diseases aggravated the plague. As usual, famine broke out, and it took seven years before the situation returned to normal. It was the greatest catastrophe to befall Egypt during the whole Muslim period.

The plague diminished the number of Baḥrī *mamlūks* and, since the South Russian steppe was similarly depopulated by the 'Black Death' and civil wars, it ceased to supply Egypt with adequate numbers of young slaves, and the Turkish element in the Mamluk army dwindled away. Their place was taken more and more by slaves of Caucasian origin, commonly called Circassians (*al-Jarākisa*); the first regiment of Circassian *mamlūks* had already been founded by Qalā'ūn, and because it was garrisoned in the towers (*burj*) of the Cairo citadel, its soldiers received the name Burjīs to distinguish them from the Turkish Baḥrīs.

In 1382 the last of the Baḥrī line – the child-sultan al-Ṣāliḥ Ḥājjī – was deposed by the Circassian Barqūq, who thus inaugurated the second line of Mamluk sultans. With the exception of two rulers who were of Greek origin, all the remaining twenty were Circassians. In contrast to the Baḥrīs, the Burjīs were averse to the principle of hereditary succession, even if as a rule a son of a deceased sultan was at first raised to the throne, to be retired after the real succession was decided. This system gave rise to incessant intrigues and conflicts between rival factions of the Mamluk army and its powerful commanders. The only advantage of this system was that strong and energetic men became rulers and, indeed, this line provided Egypt with half a dozen competent sultans. But not even these were able to stop the general decline of the empire that started precisely at the end of the fourteenth century, after Barqūq's death in 1399.

The position of Egypt as the most powerful state in the Near East during the fourteenth century, and up to the middle of the next century, may be explained by the lack of any adequate rival; after the expulsion of the last Crusaders, and the decline of the Īl-Khāns in Iraq and Iran, no external enemy dared to challenge Mamluk political and military supremacy. But by the last quarter of the fourteenth century this situation had already begun to change slowly. To the north the new Ottoman state, after securing a firm basis on the Balkan peninsula, started to spread into Anatolia and to liquidate the numerous Turkoman principalities which had emerged there after the fall of the Seljuk sultanate and had survived the Mongol invasion. This eastern push brought the Ottomans near the Mamluk sphere of influence in south-east Asia Minor and conflict seemed inevitable.

It was postponed by the rise of a more deadly enemy in the east: a new wave of Central Asiatic warrior hordes of mixed Turkish and Mongol elements, led by a would-be world conqueror Tīmūr (or Tīmūr Lenk), began to pour into the eastern parts of the Islamic world. Like the Mongols, this new peril seemed invincible. In 1387 Tīmūr's armies invaded Asia Minor, and six years later Baghdad was captured, followed shortly afterwards by the whole of Mesopotamia. The threat to Syria was imminent, and Barqūq's position was weakened by a series of revolts by Mamluk governors in this country, instigated perhaps by Tīmūr. An alliance of the most threatened states, i.e. the Mamluk empire, the Golden Horde, the Ottoman state and the principality of Siwas, was hastily concluded, but since Tīmūr was wholly occupied by his campaigns in Transcaucasia, Russia and India, he did not attack the Mamluk realm.

The real danger arose after Barqūq's death in 1399; Mamluk *amīrs* in Syria revolted once more against his son and successor, Faraj, while their colleagues in Cairo rejected the offer of a renewed alliance by the Ottoman sultan Bayezid I, hoping thus to weaken a rival whom they dreaded most. They did not even make any preparations for a campaign, and were rather occupied with the struggle for the Egyptian throne. At the end of 1400 Tīmūr swept over northern Syria, and in a few months sacked and plundered all the chief towns, massacring thousands of inhabitants and afterwards building pyramids of their skulls. A hastily assembled Mamluk army led by Faraj was routed near Damascus, and the city itself capitulated after a short siege. It was during this siege that the famous historian Ibn Khaldūn met the great conqueror, who attempted in vain to draw him into his service; an account of this encounter is recorded in detail by the historian.

Fortunately for Egypt, the conquest of Syria by Tīmūr marked the last endeavour against the Mamluk empire. In the next two years the conqueror turned his attention towards the Ottomans, whom he heavily defeated in 1402, taking Sultan Bayezid prisoner. Later on, Tīmūr prepared a campaign against China, and in 1405 died in Central Asia. Although his presence in Syria was of short duration, its consequences were serious and irreparable. Syria was economically ruined, cities were destroyed and depopulated and many craftsmen were deported to Central Asia, thus diminishing the productive power of the Mamluk state. To cover the expenses of the war, the government in Cairo imposed new and heavy taxes that sometimes reached as high as thirty-to fifty per cent of capital; the taxes were levied on all property, even from the *waqfs*, which had hitherto been considered sacrosanct. Sultan Faraj even wanted to confiscate half of them, but the clergy declared it illegal. Another fatal measure was the steady debasement of the currency, which involved Egypt in financial inflation from which it never recovered. And, as usual, there were uprisings of bedouin tribes in the west and south, quarrels among rival *amirs*, street fighting and a general insecurity of life.

Contemporary sources agree that it was under the reign of al-Nāṣir Faraj (1399–1412, with a short interruption in 1405) that the Mamluk state was shaken by a heavy political and economic crisis, and they also consider that this period was the moment when the general decline started. The attempts of some of Faraj's successors to solve the crisis were unsuccessful, and their measures rather contributed to making it more profound and irreversible. From the second half of the fifteenth century onwards, the process of economic decay was greatly accelerated, affecting deeply the whole social and political structure.

Although Tīmūr's death removed the greatest menace, the Mamluk state was still confronted by external enemies: the Timurids in Iraq, the Turkoman states in Anatolia, and the Ottoman dynasty, which recovered its former strength and aggressive spirit in a surprisingly short time. The unsettled situation in Syria demanded numerous campaigns before order was restored, thus placing a further burden on the economic resources of Egypt. Under Sultan al-Mu'ayyad Shaykh (1412–21) the Mamluk armies were successful in bringing some of the Turkoman principalities in the north under control, but the profits of these conquests were doubtful, and they only worsened relations with the Ottomans. The Syrian and Egyptian coasts suffered from raids by European pirates, and the Mamluk navy was unable to put a stop to these attacks, which were ruinous to commerce.

It was under Sultan Barsbay (1422–38) that the government made energetic steps to protect Muslim shores against the repeated raids. Since the Christian kingdom of Cyprus, despite a peace treaty with Egypt, continued to allow pirates to use the island as a base, and Cypriot ships sometimes even took part in the raids, the sultan decided to launch a punitive expedition against them. After some preliminary attacks, the main campaign started in 1426. The Egyptian fleet transported the army, composed chiefly of volunteers and bedouin, to the island kingdom where, after a short siege, the capital and the king of Cyprus surrendered. The island was devastated and the Egyptian army returned triumphantly laden with rich booty and a large number of prisoners. King James of Lusignan was set free after becoming a vassal of Egypt and promising to pay an annual tribute. The island remained a tributary state of Egypt till the end of the Mamluk period; its conquest was the sole territorial addition made to the empire under the Burjī dynasty. In the 1440s the Mamluks also made several attempts to seize the island of Rhodes, then in possession of the Knights of St John, but their fleet was repulsed with severe losses.

The north-eastern frontier, with its numerous Turkoman principalities, assumed an important role, and the Cairo government, after its experiences with the Īl-Khāns and Tīmūr, was rather sensitive about this region. To consolidate the Mamluk position there, Barsbay sent an army to Mesopotamia and had some success. The war against the state of Aq-Qoyunlu ('white sheep'), which formed a buffer between the territories of the Mamluks, Ottomans and Timurids, resulted, however, in disorderly withdrawal of the Mamluk troops, which contributed much to the loss of their discipline and prestige.

But it was in the area of the economy that the measures taken by Barsbay in order to increase the revenues of the hard-pressed Egyptian treasury, as well as his own, proved in the long run to have fatal effects. His first moves in this respect were, however, promising: through a combination of military and political pressure, Egypt regained a firmer control in the Hejaz, at a time when eastern merchants were avoiding Yemeni ports, especially Aden, because of internal upheavals in this country. Instead of Aden, the merchants started to make more and more use of Jedda and other ports under Egyptian control, although the sultan imposed heavy customs there. From this time on, the bulk of the eastern trade flowed into Egypt without any intermediary; this led automatically to an increase in customs revenues and income from taxes.

Instead of supporting this trend and increasing the flow of merchandise to Egypt, Barsbay had chosen quite a different method, not being content with the income he was receiving. In 1423 he proclaimed a state monopoly on sugar, confiscated all private sugar plantations and closed sugar refineries, so that the consumers were forced to buy from the state at highly inflated prices. In response to the remonstrances of some Mamluks who were owners of sugar plantations, the sultan abolished the monopoly, but two years later, in 1429, he established it again both in Egypt and Syria, and the monopoly remained in effect until the end of the dynasty. Similar measures were applied to some other kinds of food, such as cereals and meat, but the monopoly on them was not so strict. In general, the monopolization of internal products and trade did not fulfil expectations; on the contrary it brought only soaring prices and a decline in the consumption of these goods.

Another step which had more far-reaching consequences was the declaration of a state monopoly in the trade in spices, in particular the trade in pepper. In 1429, a decree prohibited the sale of pepper to Frankish merchants by private individuals, i.e. the *Kārimi* merchants. The sultan then bought the stock already in Egypt very cheaply, as well as all pepper recently imported, and tried to sell it to European merchants at high prices. A load of pepper bought in Cairo for 50 dinars was resold in Alexandria for 130 dinars, although a year earlier its price was only 80 dinars. Later on the prices fell and often fluctuated, but in general remained comparatively high; in the 1450s Sultan Īnāl sold pepper for 100 dinars, Mu‘ayyad Aḥmad in 1462 for 85 and Qā'it Bay in 1480 again for 100 dinars. This monopoly definitively undermined the financial and commercial power of the *Kārimī* merchants, who began to leave Egypt, mostly for India, taking with them not only their capital but also their skill and experience. The European merchants who refused to buy at higher prices were sometimes imprisoned and held until they accepted the conditions dictated. Venice and Aragon protested vehemently against the monopoly and the misdeeds of Egyptian administration, but in vain. Only the demonstrations of Venetian fleets before Alexandria, and the raids of Catalan corsairs on the Syrian coasts, forced Barsbay to come to terms with the merchants, but even so he never abolished the monopoly. The conflicts arising between Mamluk sultans and European merchants backed by their governments continued with varying intensity until the beginning of the sixteenth century. During the second half of the fifteenth century trade relations worsened steadily, and were in no way improved by the activities of European pirates against Egyptian and Syrian ports. It is symptomatic for the decline of the Mamluk military system that the sultans were neither able to stop these raids nor to defend the coast effectively.

The monopolization of the spice trade by the Egyptian state, and the accompanying rise in prices, gave to some European nations an additional impulse in the search for direct access to the sources of these goods in the Far East and India. When at the end of the century these attempts met success with the Portuguese discovery of a direct sea-route to the Indian Ocean, Egypt, and with it the Muslim *oecumene*, lost the monopolistic control of the eastern trade. Even if the effects of this loss were not as decisive for the final collapse of Mamluk Egypt as formerly thought, the ensuing change in world trade-routes had a profound influence on the destiny of the whole Eastern Mediterranean and the Near East.

Besides introducing these monopolies, Barsbay interfered with the currency in many ways. In 1424 he forbade the circulation of European gold coins (Venetian ducats, Florentine florins, etc.) in his realm, where they were increasingly being used as units of currency because of the inferiority of Mamluk dinars. He then called these coins in, and issued his own dinars instead, which were of dubious value. Later he readmitted foreign currency, thus gaining great profits to the detriment of both Egyptian and European merchants. He also altered the relation of gold to silver to his own advantage. The silver and, above all, the copper coins that served as currency for the majority of the population were steadily debased, and the inflationary trend was further aggravated by Barsbay's successors, who repeatedly issued new copper coins. Although some sultans attempted to stop this dangerous trend, there was no remedy for the deep financial crisis: until the end of the dynasty the prices of food as well as of manufactured goods rose steadily, while the buying power of the people correspondingly fell. This led to the closing down of many factories and workshops and to a deterioration in quality; especially, the once-flourishing textile industry rapidly declined, and the markets were flooded with cheaper European cloth.

Barsbay's successors continued the policy of trade monopolies, as well as of currency debasement. At the end of the fifteenth century the economic decay of the Mamluk state was so far advanced that only drastic taxation, expropriation and other extreme measures allowed that state to continue its existence. The fifteenth century also witnessed profound changes in the system of land-tenure. As in the previous century, the general trend was characterized by the sultans' attempts to concentrate as much territory as possible in their own hands, and by the opposite tendency of the feudatories to pass on parts of their estates to their descendants as lands carrying no condition of military service. At the end of the fourteenth century the size of the royal estates was estimated at 518,000 *faddāns*, whereas a century later it rose to over 815,000 *faddāns*.[1] This increase was due to the confiscation of *iqṭā'* lands of deceased, imprisoned or disgraced Mamluk *amīrs*, as well as those who were no longer capable of military service. But at the same time it was necessary to parcel out these lands as new *iqṭā'* to the high-ranking officers, since the yield from their own estates was constantly diminishing. A high proportion of the royal estates was also given as *waqfs*, so that at the end of the period the *waqf* lands covered an acreage three times greater than they had done a century before. The sultans Barsbay, Īnāl and Qā'it Bay, in particular, granted large tracts of land to religious institutions and to public works they constructed. Nevertheless, a greater proportion of new *waqfs* were former *iqṭā'* lands, the overlords of which wanted to preserve the revenues for their heirs and also to escape taxation, since the *waqfs* were exempt from it.

The struggle of feudatories to make their temporary land-tenure permanent and hereditary was facilitated by the existence of a special category of estates, the so-called *rizq* (pl. *arzāq*) that were granted as pensions to old *mamlūks*, their widows and orphans. No services were

[1] These and the following figures are based on cadastral surveys recorded in Ibn al-Jī'ān's (d. 1497) book *Kitāb al-tuḥfa al-sānīyya*, ed. B. Moritz (Cairo, 1898).

attached to the holding of *rizq* lands and they could be considered as practically privately owned estates possessed hereditarily. It is not clear whether these lands were tax-free, since the sources give contradictory evidence; but even these contradictions indicate that at least some of them were exempt. Nor is there information about the total area of the *rizq* lands, but the number of Egyptian districts in which there were *rizq* estates increased by about one-third in the course of the fifteenth century. Another method used to convert the military fiefs into hereditary possession was to make them allodial lands (*mulk*, pl. *amlāk*). A fief-holder surrendered his fief voluntarily to the public treasury, and then purchased it as an allodial estate with full right of private ownership. At the end of the fourteenth century this category existed only in 160 Egyptian districts, whereas a century later it could be found in 616. Many of the *mulk* estates were then sold to townspeople, as was also done with the original *iqṭāʿ* lands. In spite of the fact that all Burjī sultans distributed fiefs lavishly to their *mamlūks*, the total size of *iqṭāʿ* estates constantly decreased, so that at the end of the century they represented only one million *faddāns*, as against more than 2.3 million *faddāns* a century before. The majority of districts which at the beginning of the fifteenth century had been exclusively military fiefs had become a mixture of *iqṭāʿ*, *rizq*, *mulk* and *waqf* estates towards its end. All this indicates that the system of military fiefs was in full decline and disintegration. Its final abolition, however, was brought about only by the Ottoman conquest in 1517 when most of the Egyptian lands became crown domains.

The main effect of this process was the diminishing of state revenues, since many categories of land were either tax-free or their Mamluk landlords found ways to cheat the treasury. According to many accounts, most of the *kharāj* tax taken from peasants in money or kind remained in the hands of their landlords and never reached the central treasury. The attempts of some sultans to introduce a stricter control of the revenues were of no avail. Egyptian agriculture in the course of the fifteenth century ceased to be the chief source of state income, as it had been before, and it was perhaps for this reason that Sultan Barsbay and his successors turned their attention to trade, hoping to improve their desperate financial situation through its monopolization. Other similar measures, like the drastic taxation of merchants and craftsmen, or currency manipulations, may be interpreted as a means of compensating for the losses in land revenues. A corollary of the process was also a general neglect of the irrigation works, the cleaning of canals and repairing of dams, since the central government was no longer willing or able to undertake them, and the Mamluk feudatories were interested in the direct exploitation of the peasants rather than in the methods of improving the yields of the land. The universal deterioration of the economy was accompanied by increasing corruption and inefficiency in the administration, and by the insecurity of life and property in the country and in towns. Many villages were abandoned by their inhabitants, who moved to large cities, while many townspeople left for Syria where the situation was better.

Natural calamities also contributed to Egypt's decline in the fifteenth century. There were many great droughts, prolonged periods of low water in the Nile, locusts, famines and plagues, all occurring with much greater frequency than in the preceding centuries. Since the economy as well as the administration were also in decline, it was impossible for the country to recover from these catastrophes, and their cumulative effects again accelerated the entire process. The chronic emptiness of the treasury also resulted in the deterioration of the Mamluk armed forces. Not only did the number of *mamlūks* diminish – in the second half of the fifteenth century it was estimated at between five and six thousand – but their fighting skill sharply declined for many reasons, such as the neglect of military training on the hippodromes, lack of discipline and the never-ending internal struggles between various factions and groups. As remarked above, more and more military fiefs were transformed into alloidial estates with no conditions of service, so that many former *mamlūks* ceased to be soldiers. The *dīwān al-jaysh* by the end of the century had completely lost track of the number of real soldiers, and was keeping many civilians, holders of military *iqṭāʿ*, on its muster-rolls.

All this was happening at a time when the former balance of power in the Near East was shifting to the disadvantage of the Mamluks. The Ottoman sultanate recovered swiftly after Tīmūr's withdrawal, and started on new expansive policy in the first half of the century. It won immense prestige and power by conquering Constantinople in 1453, whereupon the victorious sultan, Meḥmed, forbade the passage of slave-ships carrying young *mamlūks* to Egypt through the Straits, thus weakening further the Mamluk army. As long as the Ottomans were occupied in consolidating their conquests in the Balkans, the relations between them and the Mamluks were not hostile. The Mamluk sultans Jaqmaq (1438–53) and Īnāl (1453–61) followed a conciliatory policy towards their Turkoman vassals in eastern Anatolia, in spite of many rebellions and other instances of insubordination, in order to avoid giving the Ottomans any pretext for intervention. But by the 1460s the relations between both powers had worsened, owing to disputes over succession in the principalities of Karaman and Dhu'l-Qadr. For a time the ambiguous attitude of the ruler of the Aq-Qoyunlu Turkomans, a nominal vassal of Egypt, caused much anxiety in Cairo, and his defeat by the Ottomans was looked upon with satisfaction. The sultan Qā'it Bay, an energetic but cruel and exacting ruler, aggravated the already tense situation by foolishly giving hospitality to the fugitive Ottoman pretender prince, Jem, rival of the reigning sultan, Bayezid II. This support led in 1485 to open hostilities between the Mamluks and the Ottomans, who later invaded Cilicia and occupied some towns there. The war dragged on for five years and, although the Mamluk army in general had the upper hand, the issue was inconclusive; moreover, the campaign placed an even greater burden on the already strained financial situation of Egypt. Because the Ottomans then turned their attention to their European wars, the situation between them and the Mamluks improved, and both states remained on friendly terms until 1514.

In 1501, after brief reigns by four puppet-sultans, the Mamluks elected as sultan Qānṣawh al-Ghawrī (1501–16), one of the most capable rulers of the Burjī line. He at once restored internal order and vigorously tried to improve the lamentable situation in his realm. But the decay of Egypt and its provinces was already so far advanced that all his efforts were in vain. Like his predecessors, he took desperate measures, introduced heavy new taxes and customs duties, debased the currency and mercilessly squeezed all the inhabitants, not stopping even at exacting taxes from the *waqfs*. At the cost of the impoverishment and discontent of people of all classes, he raised the state revenue and was able to increase the number of his *mamlūk* soldiers by fresh purchases, while also improving their training. He built a navy in the Red Sea and equipped it with artillery and other fire-arms. There was also a revival of architectural activities, and many public buildings were erected in the whole realm.

The energetic defence measures were necessary, as a new and dangerous foe had appeared in the south. The Portuguese fleet under Vasco da Gama at last in 1498 reached India by navigating around Africa, and the Portuguese established themselves on the Malabar coast. Soon they started to seize Muslim ships trading in eastern goods between Indonesia, India and Egypt, and seriously attempted to gain naval supremacy in the Indian Ocean. The threat to the Egyptian monopoly in the spice trade was clear. The alarmed sultan, encouraged by a similarly alarmed Venice and asked by Muslim rulers of India and South Arabia to come to their help, took steps to check the Portuguese. At first he tried diplomatic methods, asking the Pope to intervene with the king of Portugal, and threatening to destroy Christian holy places in Palestine if the Portuguese depredations continued. When this appeal proved ineffective, Qānṣawh al-Ghawrī resolved on war. A new fleet was quickly built on the Red Sea and sent to India, where in 1508 it defeated the Portuguese squadron near Chaul, off the Malabar coast. But a year later the Portuguese had their revenge in the battle off Diu, where they almost completely destroyed the Egyptian fleet. In a short time a second fleet was built and equipped; it deserves mention that the Ottomans aided the Mamluks by sending war material and even some seasoned naval officers and gunners. In 1513 the Portuguese unsuccessfully attacked Aden and sailed into the Red Sea, but soon retreated. The Egyptian navy was thus able to maintain its supremacy in these waters, but contented itself with defending the approaches to the Red Sea and with conquering Yemen. It did not make any offensive moves against the Portuguese in the Indian Ocean. This defensive attitude did nothing to help Muslim trade, and the superior Portuguese ships embarked on a systematic destruction of Muslim shipping. At the same time some of the Indian rulers had surrendered to Portugal, and Egyptian merchants were expelled from Indian ports. Even pilgrim ships to Mecca were seized, and their passengers mercilessly killed. The Mamluk state thus never became a serious rival to the Portuguese in the Indian Ocean.

Until recently it was generally held that the Portuguese circumnavigation of the Cape of Good Hope, and the subsequent ravages which they inflicted on Muslim trade in the Indian Ocean, were responsible for the economic and political decline of Egypt. Recent research, however, has shown that in the first place the economic decay of Egypt had already started at the beginning of the fifteenth century; secondly, that it was due mainly to internal factors such as the state monopoly of trade, the continuous debasement of the currency and changes in the system of land-tenure; and thirdly, that the presence of the Portuguese in the Indian Ocean was too brief to have had such far-reaching effects on Egypt before its final collapse. Even the long-term effects of the Portuguese presence on the Mediterranean trade was not so disastrous, since under the Ottomans there was a revival of the spice trade between

Egypt and the Italian republics.[1] All that can be said about the effects of the breaking up of the Egyptian monopoly in the eastern trade is that it was merely an additional factor that came too late to be really decisive.

In the struggle with the Portuguese the technological inferiority of Mamluk Egypt became apparent. Egyptian ships, equipment and armaments were no match for the Europeans and the same can be said of the leadership and seamanship. This is not surprising, as the land-minded Mamluk horsemen were averse to everything connected with the navy, and the sea was not their element. Even more disastrous was the fact that the Mamluks missed the great fifteenth-century revolution in warfare, namely the introduction of fire-arms, handguns and cannons alike, and were inherently unable to draw any practical lessons from the changes brought about in tactics and strategy. There were, of course, some economic obstacles to a large-scale introduction of these arms, such as the lack of adequate sources of metals on Mamluk territory and the unfavourable financial situation of the state. But the decisive factor was the psychological and social attitude of the Mamluk ruling class to these innovations; they clung to the theory that only excellent horsemanship, personal bravery and cavalry tactics with bow and arrow, sword and lance were the best means for gaining victory. The introduction of fire-arms went against the very basis and structure of their military society. Since no Mamluk wanted to have anything to do with the new weapons, they had to be given to 'inferior peoples' such as the local levies, foreigners and black troops. At the same time the Mamluk élite was not prepared to allow these troops to become more numerous, since it would mean a total overthrow of the entire social and political system based on the fighting superiority of the Mamluk horsemen over the rest of the population. The infantry units equipped with arquebuses and cannons were purposely held at low numbers, and consequently were of little use on the battlefield.[2] On the other hand the Ottomans quickly adopted the new weapons and employed them very effectively in battle, without endangering their social and political structure in any way.

When the warlike and ambitious Sultan Selim I came to the Ottoman

[1] S. Y. Labib, *Handelsgeschichte Aegyptens im Spätmittelalter, 1171–1517* (Wiesbaden, 1965), 441–98; F. Braudel, *La Méditerranée et le monde méditerranéen à l'epoque de Phillipe II* (Paris, 1949), 423–37; F. C. Lane, 'The Mediterranean spice trade', *Amer. Hist. Review*, 1940, 45, 581ff.; cf. also J. van Leur, *Indonesian trade and society* (The Hague, 1955); M. A. P. Meilink-Roelofsz, *Asian trade and European influence in the Indonesian archipelago between 1500 and about 1630* (The Hague, 1962).

[2] Cf. D. Ayalon, *Gunpowder and firearms in the Mamluk Kingdom* (London, 1956).

throne in 1512, the relations with the Mamluk state quickly changed to open hostility. After defeating the founder of the new Safavid dynasty in Persia, Ismāʿīl, at the battle of Chaldirān (1514) Selim was prepared to strike a mortal blow at the last remaining rival to Ottoman power in the Near East. In 1516 he led his army into Asia Minor, while the old sultan, Qānṣawh al-Ghawrī, marched his troops to northern Syria. Although both rulers pretended that they had come to settle the Persian question, it was only a pretext and the two armies met in August at Marj Dābiq, a plain north of Aleppo. In the ensuing battle the Mamluk army suffered a heavy defeat, and their sultan fell. There was treason among the Mamluks, but the decisive factor was the Ottoman troops' masterly use of fire-arms; their concentrated fire wrought total destruction on the bravely charging Mamluk cavalry. Selim then occupied the whole of Syria, being welcomed by the population as a deliverer from Mamluk oppression.

In Cairo the Mamluks elected Ṭūmān Bay as sultan. Although he wanted to accept Selim's offer of the viceroyalty of Egypt if he would recognize Ottoman suzerainty, his *amīrs* forced him to refuse. Selim's army then advanced towards Egypt and on 23 January 1517 inflicted on the Mamluks another, and this time a final, defeat near Cairo. Ṭūmān Bay fled to the countryside, hoping to rally there a resistance movement, but he was soon betrayed, and hanged at one of Cairo's main gates. The Mamluk empire was destroyed for ever, and Egypt, Syria and other provinces became part of the Ottoman empire. With the collapse of the Mamluks, also, came the end of the ʿAbbasid shadow caliphate, as Selim sent the last of the line, al-Mutawakkil, to Istanbul, where he was held prisoner for some years.

In two fields the Mamluk period left durable monuments to posterity: in architecture and in historiography. Even at the time of the far-advanced decline under the Burjīs, the sultans of this line continued the building activity inaugurated by Baybars, and embellished the cities, mainly Cairo and Damascus, with numerous mosques, *madrasas*, *zāwiyas* and other public works. Especially the sultans Barqūq, Faraj, Barsbay, Īnāl, Qā'it Bay and Qānṣawh al-Ghawrī were founders of an important number of monumental edifices. They also repaired and restored the works of their predecessors, and did not neglect good roads, public baths, bridges, markets and caravanserais. No reign since that of al-Nāṣir Muḥammad was more prolific in architectural activity than that of the despotic Qā'it Bay, whose monuments are considered as marking the peak of Mamluk art. After the time of the last Mamluks no edifice of any importance was ever constructed in the central Arab lands.

In scholarship the historical writing of this Mamluk period deserves special attention, not only for its quantity but more so for the quality of some outstanding works, as well as for the wide horizon covered. The authors belonged partly to the Muslim clergy, in the wide sense of the word, and partly to the class of administrators. The majority of them were of Egyptian or Syrian origin, but we also find among them descendants of Turkish *mamlūks*. No other period of Egyptian history is better known in all its aspects than the Mamluk era; many historians extended their interest beyond the frontiers to countries as far away as India, Ethiopia, West Africa and Asia Minor. Noteworthy among the historians of the earlier epoch was Abu'l-Fidā' (1273–1332), an Ayyubid prince and governor of Hamat, who compiled a useful compendium of universal history and also a handbook of geography. The most eminent scholar of this time was without doubt the Egyptian al-Maqrīzī (1364–1442). Apart from a solid history of Egypt, he wrote a historical topography of Cairo and Egypt, a work of unique importance for archaeology and cultural history. He was also the author of a number of minor monographs on various subjects such as plagues, coins and coinage, Islam in Ethiopia, etc. Ibn Taghrībirdī (1411–69) left a monumental history of Egypt and of his own time, showing a rare insight into the political interplay inside the Mamluk oligarchy to which he belonged. The historian Ibn Iyās (1448–1524) recorded carefully and with astonishing detail the last days of the Mamluk dynasty and the beginning of the Ottoman domination. And it should not be forgotten that the great historian and sociologist, Ibn Khaldūn (1332–1406), spent the last twenty years of his life in Egypt, supplementing his famous *Al-Muqaddima* with the newly won experience of the Egyptian political and social scene.

Closely connected with historiography and geography were the encyclopaedias of general knowledge and manuals for civil servants. The works of al-Nuwayrī (1279–1332), al-'Umarī (1301–49) and al-Qalqashandī (1355–1418) represent the best of their kind ever produced in Muslim countries. Precious information on cultural history and life is furnished by numerous biographical dictionaries, the most noted being that written by Ibn Ḥajar al-'Asqalānī (1371–1449) and that by the historian Ibn Taghrībirdī.

The production in other fields of learning was abundant, but rarely do we find any original ideas or approaches; it was rather a period of learned compilations, epitomes, commentaries and glosses, as if the authors felt the urge to preserve all the knowledge accumulated by their predecessors, and to hand it down to posterity in the form of bulky encyclopaedias and works of synthesis. It is certainly not by accident that this era produced the famous universal historian al-Suyūṭī (1445–1505), the most prolific Arabic writer of all time, author of more than five hundred books, in which he covered the whole field of Islamic learning. There is little originality in his work, but until modern times he continued to enjoy the reputation of being one of the highest scholarly authorities in the Muslim world.

The Mamluks, as non-Arabs, were not interested in Arabic literature, which consequently withered and died out. Here, too, the activity of littérateurs exhausted itself in compiling anthologies and commentaries on the production of earlier times. The decline of classical literature was, however, more than balanced by the spectacular growth of many genres of folk literature. During this epoch the famous collection *The Arabian Nights' Entertainments*, an anthology of anecdotes, short stories, fairy tales and novels of various origins that had already circulated orally for many centuries in the Islamic East, was given the fixed written form in which it later became known to Europe. The professional story-tellers also entertained their audiences with prosaic folk romances centred around some historical or legendary person or event, such as the romance of ʿAntar, a pre-Islamic hero and poet, the cycle about the wanderings of the Banū Hilāl from Egypt to the Maghrib, and especially the romance about the wars against the Crusaders, where the central figure was the sultan Baybars, depicted as champion of Islam and a knight without fear and shame. At this time the shadow-plays, the first embryonic works of Arabic dramatic art, came from the Far East. The only known author of these pieces is the Egyptian physician and poet Ibn Daniyāl (died 1310), but this art did not find among the Arabic public the popularity it enjoyed chiefly in Turkey and elsewhere in the East.

The five and a half centuries covered by the three dynasties of the Fatimids, the Ayyubids and the Mamluks represent a decisive period in Egyptian history, its main trend being the gradual rise of Egypt from a dependent province of the ʿAbbasid caliphate to an entirely independent political unit, and later to the position of the paramount power in the Near East. With the political emancipation came the growth of economic prosperity and cultural activities in many fields, so that from the thirteenth century on Egypt supplanted Iraq as the centre of Islamic and Arabic learning. If the Fatimids definitively launched Egypt as an independent entity and provided it with a cordon of dependencies, the Ayyubids further confirmed its central role and made it the core of a large federation of Near Eastern states, thus creating the conditions for the final halt to the European offensive against the Arab lands. The historical role of the Mamluks is more controversial: a barbarous people from the steppe, alien to the indigenous population in the countries they ruled, they rose to power at a time of grave danger that menaced the central and western parts of the Muslim world. These circumstances made them champions of the old order, and of continuity amidst the disruptive forces of the Central Asiatic hordes, whose onslaught shattered the ancient social and political system in the eastern Islamic lands. The expulsion of the Crusader remnants from Palestine and Syria enabled the Mamluks to weld these countries, together with Egypt, into a unified and centralized empire recognized by Muslims and Christians alike as one of the big powers, whose hegemony in the eastern Mediterranean was not challenged for over two centuries. However, as soon as the external danger diminished, the Mamluk military regime lost its *raison d'être*, and its more negative aspects prevailed, overshadowing finally all its former positive contribution. The despotism, incapacity and rapacity of the later Mamluk oligarchy caused a general ruin of Egypt, undermined its economy and weakened it politically. Not even in their proper field of warfare were the Mamluks able to grasp the significance of the gunpowder revolution. That the regime survived so long, and did not collapse earlier, was due mainly to the lack of internal opposition and of powerful external foes. Its unregretted demise, however, marked the end of a definite epoch in the history of the Arab-speaking countries.

In the cultural sense the Mamluk period was one of conservation and preservation of the Islamic culture in its Arabic form. The eastern parts of the world of Islam witnessed at this time the rise of new cultures, the vehicles of which were the Persian and later the Turkish languages. In the West, the once flourishing Andalusian civilization was crumbling under the onslaught of the Christian reconquista. It thus fell to Egypt and Syria, unified under the Mamluk sultanate, to maintain and preserve the heritage of Arab civilization and culture. They fulfilled this task to the best of their ability under the difficult conditions of a foreign and despotic rule and of economic decay;

and it was this role of the custodian that enabled Egypt to emerge in the nineteenth century as the main centre of the Arab cultural revival.

EGYPT AND NUBIA

Throughout its entire history the core of Egypt was formed by the Nile delta, i.e. the triangle Cairo–Alexandria–Damietta. Here were concentrated the main towns and villages (their number remained constant for many centuries, at around 2,300) as well as the various economic activities, whereas Upper Egypt (Arabic, *al-Saʿīd*) played only a secondary, although not a negligible, role. On the fringes of the cultivated lands and beyond them roamed Arab nomad tribes not yet assimilated to a settled life. Some of these tribes, coming from Arabia or Syria, used Egypt only as a corridor to the west or the south; others remained for a shorter or longer time. Being notoriously anarchic, turbulent and always in opposition to any outside control, they represented an element of danger and unrest, too often causing disruption of economic life by their raids on villages or by holding up caravans. The policy of the Fatimids towards nomad Arabs, like that of all successive Egyptian dynasties, oscillated between pacification and attempts to use them as auxiliaries, or else to get rid of them permanently; the most famous case of this latter policy is that of the Banū Hilāl and the Banū Sulaym.

Already prior to the tenth century many Arab tribes, or parts of them, had migrated southwards to Upper Egypt and to the Eastern Desert between the Nile valley and the Red Sea littoral. Penetration further south along the Nile was for a long time made difficult by the relatively strong Christian kingdom of al-Maqurra in northern Nubia, but even there the Arabs were able to infiltrate gradually.

Towards the Nubian kingdoms the Fatimids followed the peaceful policy of their predecessors. Shortly after their conquest of Egypt in 975 they sent Ibn Sulaym al-Aswānī as an envoy to the king of al-Maqurra to get him to renew payment of the *baqṭ* (from Latin *pactum*, i.e. the symbolic tribute paid by 'allies' to the Byzantine emperors, and later, in many cases, to the Arabs) and to invite him and his subjects to embrace Islam. The first request was granted, the second refused, but neither then nor later did the Fatimids press the issue.

Ibn Sulaym's account, preserved by the fifteenth-century Egyptian historian al-Maqrīzī, forms one of the most valuable sources on the state of affairs in Nubia in the second half of the tenth century. At this time the Arabs from Egypt had already acquired lands in the extreme north of Nubia and were practically independent, whereas some of the Nubians to the north of the second cataract had been converted to Islam. It was thus here that were laid the foundations, at first hardly perceptible, of the process of arabization and islamization that later swept over the whole of Nubia and large parts of the eastern Sudan, and made these countries into an integral part of the Arab and Islamic world. The main towns of this northern province called al-Marīs (Coptic, 'the south') were Bajrāsh and Ibrim; the whole was under control of a powerful governor known as the 'Lord of the Mountain' (*Ṣāḥib al-jabal*), whose chief duty was to stop people – probably Arab bedouin – from entering Nubia without authorization. It seems, however, that the Nubian authorities were not able to prevent Arab penetration. Already in previous centuries many Arabs had bought lands from the natives, and Ibn Sulaym remarks that at his time the Arabs behaved in al-Marīs like landlords. Their settlement there is confirmed also by some tomb inscriptions, the dates of which demonstrate the continuous southward movement of Arab elements along the Nile.

The core of Nubia, the kingdom of al-Maqurra, was as yet hardly touched by Arab immigration, and this was even more the case in the southern Nubian state, 'Alwa. In the capitals of both, however, Muslim merchants were settled, inhabiting – in accordance with the pattern established in the whole Sudanic belt – separate quarters of the towns. Among the exports from Nubia to Arab countries, particularly to Egypt, we find cattle, ivory, ostrich feathers and slaves. These slaves were called *al-Nūba* or *al-Sūdān* ('blacks'); the slave-girls were favoured as concubines and nurses, the male slaves as domestic servants, but most of them were recruited into the army, where they served as foot-soldiers. Although previous Egyptian dynasties also had employed large numbers of black slaves in their armies, it was under the Fatimids that the demand for these slaves was at its height.

It does not seem that Nubia with its sparse population could itself have supplied Egypt with many of the slaves who were known as *al-Nūba*; the majority of them must have been brought from the countries still further to the south. This is confirmed by some Muslim authorities, who insist that black slaves in Egypt were obtained from a region south of Nubia with large pastures, plenty of cattle and animals, and inhabited by strong people. Although these indications are too general, it can be surmised that the main source was situated in the vast area stretching from the Ethiopian borders to Darfur and beyond.

The influence of the slave-trade on the destinies of Nubia was manifold. It was perhaps the concern for an undisturbed and steady flow of slave recruits that led the Fatimids to maintain friendly and peaceful relations with the Nubian kingdoms. The traders were the first Muslims to penetrate into the country and, although they do not seem to have actively propagated the Islamic religion, they brought the first elements of the new faith into the hitherto wholly Christian regions. In the course of their commercial activities they accumulated a large knowledge of the country, thus making the later penetration of Arab nomads easier. And, last but not least, they kept alive the contacts between Egypt and Nubia across the religious and cultural borderline.

Other relations, no less important, linked both countries. The patriarch of Alexandria was the head of the Monophysite Church, and so was recognized as the highest church dignitary for both Nubia and Ethiopia. On the other hand the king of al-Maqurra was regarded as protector of the patriarch; he used his excellent relations with the Fatimid government to intervene on the patriarch's behalf when the need for it arose, as happened many times in the course of the tenth and eleventh centuries. This period also marks the height of Nubian cultural influence, and it is not without interest that it spread also to Upper Egypt as far as Idfu, showing that even at this time the Christian Nubian culture had not yet lost all its dynamism. Although the religious links with Egypt were strong, Nubia cannot be considered to have been merely a cultural outpost of Coptic Egypt; its culture was an autochthonous and independent African civilization that continued in the traditions of ancient Kush and Meroe.

Nubia also played the role of a connecting link between Egypt and Ethiopia, and Nubian kings were sometimes asked by their Ethiopian colleagues to act as mediators between them and the patriarchs. And it was via the Nubian kingdoms that the Ethiopian church maintained its relationship with the outside Christian world. Although this relationship was never entirely severed, the decline of Christian Nubia from the thirteenth century on contributed largely to the growing isolation of Ethiopian Christianity, with all its consequences. As long as Nubia remained independent, it also fulfilled the role of a northern guardian of Christianity in north-eastern Africa against the waves of Islam and islamized peoples.

When the Arab nomads found their way southwards along the Nile barred by the still strong Nubian kingdom of al-Maqurra, they turned their attention to the Eastern Desert, which offered a special attraction to them. Between Aswan and the Red Sea existed gold and emerald mines centred around the Wādī al-'Allāqī. In the centuries following the 'gold rush' and the invasion of the Arab adventurer al-'Umarī during the second half of the ninth century, the situation in the mining districts became relatively settled. Most of the mines were owned by groups of Egyptian and Arab merchants, but some emerald mines belonged directly to the Fatimid treasury. The mining and digging was done mainly by imported Sudanese slaves or by free Beja labourers. The output of the Wādī al-'Allāqī mines was the chief source of gold for Egypt until the end of the thirteenth century, when the main deposits were exhausted and their further exploitation became unprofitable. Unfortunately, we have no indication about how much gold was produced in the heyday of the mining activities, so that it is impossible to assess even approximately the exact impact of the Nubian gold on the Egyptian economy. On the other hand the very existence of the mines markedly influenced the process of arabization and islamization of this region, since the influx of Arab nomads and merchants steadily increased.

Another factor in this process was the transfer of the eastern trade to the Red Sea in the second half of the eleventh century. The port of 'Aydhāb gradually became the main focal point at the Egyptian end of the maritime route. The abandonment of the pilgrim route via Sinai, due to the establishment of the Kingdom of Jerusalem, channelled pilgrim traffic into the route passing through Upper Egypt and 'Aydhāb to Jedda, and for more than three centuries it formed the artery of international trade. The Fatimids controlled the port of 'Aydhāb and levied duties there; the caravans then went to Aswan or Qus on the Nile, whence further transport was done on river boats. A fleet of warships was kept on the Red Sea by the Fatimids to protect the trade from pirates.

The native Beja tribes did not remain untouched by these events. Some of them entered into alliances with the penetrating Arab nomads, and together with them controlled the approaches to the mining districts. Many of the Beja tribesmen worked in the mines, while others were employed as caravan leaders and escorts. Their country was also well known for a fine breed of camels (*bukhtiya*), exported to many Muslim lands, particularly to Egypt. The demand for these animals increased more and more with the development of trade routes across the Eastern Desert, thus bringing a new impetus to the nomadic economy of the Beja.

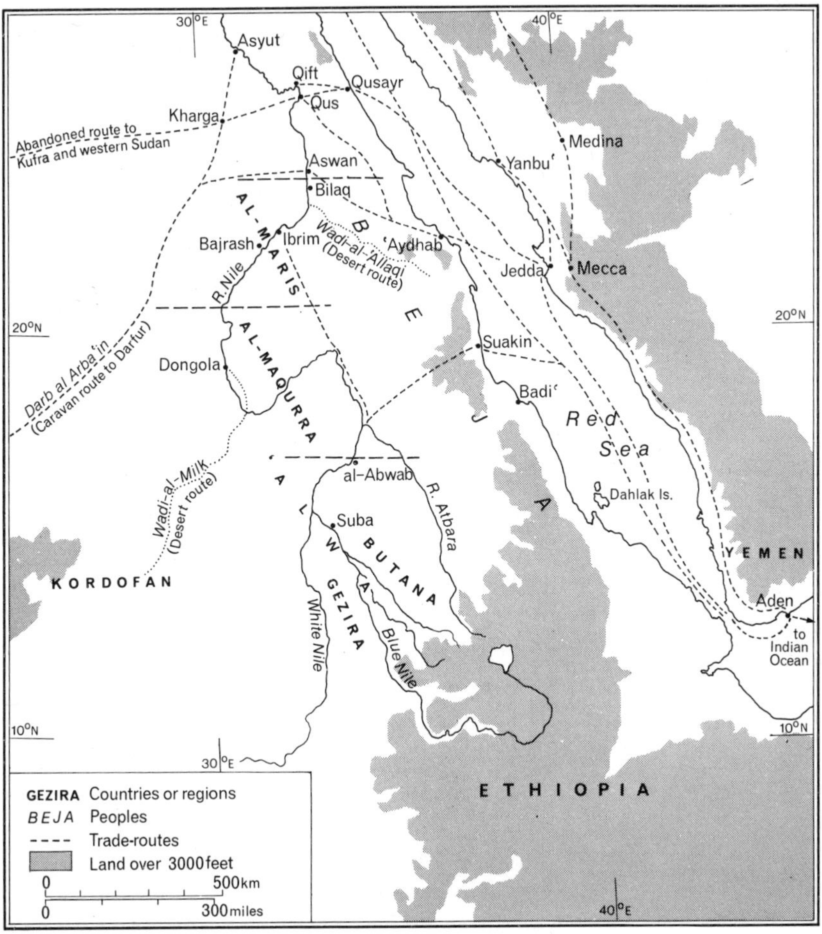

2 Nubia

The northernmost Beja groups, Hadariba and 'Ababda, gradually became arabized, even adopting fictitious Arab genealogies, but their ancient beliefs were only thinly disguised by Islam. For a long time the Arab tribes did not penetrate much further in the Eastern Desert than the latitude of the second cataract, being concentrated mainly in the Qus–Aswan region and in the gold mining districts. Among the Arab groups, the Rabī'a tribesmen gained during the tenth century the greatest power and prestige both in the country of the mines and in the Aswan region, and intermarried with the local Beja and Nubians.

The first Rabī'a principality emerged in the Aswan region in the mid tenth century. In 1004 the Caliph al-Ḥākim rewarded their chief with the honorific title *Kanz al-Dawla* for capturing the rebel Abū Rakwa, who retreated to Upper Egypt after being defeated in Egypt itself. The *Kanz al-Dawla* and his successors, called Banū Kanz for short, gradually became powerful rulers on the Nubian–Egyptian borders and an important factor in many respects until the Ottoman conquest. They do not often emerge in the rather scanty source material but, when they do, it is always at important moments of Nubian history; and each time they pushed further southwards the frontier of arabization and islamization. The Banū Kanz *amīrs* interspersed their loyalty to Cairo with open revolts, sometimes serving as spearheads of Egyptian influence in Nubia and sometimes assuming the role of mediators between Nubian kings and Egyptian sultans. But the accumulated effect of these shifting policies was always the strengthening of Arab and Muslim influence in Nubia. By a strange paradox the name of these agents of arabization was adopted to designate one of the main dialects of the Nubian language, the Kenuzi (Kunuzi).

The relative calm prevailing on the southern frontier of Egypt during the Fatimid epoch began to change with the advent of the Ayyubids. Already during the first years of the new dynasty we can discern in the relations between Egypt and Nubia harbingers of the more profound upheavals that were to come under the Mamluks. After the collapse of the Fatimid caliphate their black troops – estimated at 50,000 in number – remaining loyal to the cause of the defunct dynasty, revolted and retreated to Upper Egypt. In 1172 they launched an attack in alliance with some Nubians, and looted Aswan and some other places. An Ayyubid army crushed the revolt, and a couple of years later a strong punitive expedition led by Ṣalāḥ al-Dīn's brother, Tūrān-Shāh, conquered the province of al-Marīs with its capital, Ibrim, capturing many prisoners and converting local churches into mosques. The Ayyubid occupation did not last long, and after their army evacuated northern Nubia in 1174/5, the country was reoccupied by the Nubian king. It seems that apart from quelling the rebellion of black troops, the purpose of the expedition was to secure this region as a refuge in case Ṣalāḥ al-Dīn should not be able to hold Egypt against his suzerain Nūr al-Dīn. How far Ṣalāḥ al-Dīn's policy was influenced by the possibility of an alliance between Christian Nubia and the Crusaders is difficult to decide, since there is no evidence either way. In any case, the Christian states in Nubia were too weak to represent any real danger; this would have become clear to the sultan or his brother in the course of the punitive expedition. The early evacuation of Ibrim, and the loss of further interest in Nubia, tends to confirm this conclusion.

The southern borderland, however, remained turbulent during the whole Ayyubid period. The Banū Kanz attempted to re-establish their control over the Aswan region, given as fief to one of the Ayyubid *amīrs*, but in 1174 they were defeated by an Ayyubid army and forced to withdraw to al-Marīs; there they established their supremacy, intermarried in their usual way with the local inhabitants and contributed thus further to the process of arabization. Some of the nomadic and semi-nomadic Arabs from Upper Egypt were recruited into the Ayyubid army and later rewarded with lands, but many others opposed the introduction of state control and repeatedly rebelled until the end of the dynasty.

The slave-trade from Egypt to Nubia sharply decreased at this time, as the Ayyubids – in contrast to the Fatimids – were no longer interested in the recruitment of Sudanese or Nubian troops. This does not mean, of course, that the normal trade in slaves destined for domestic and other services did not continue as before. Nubian slaves were in demand not only in Egypt but in many other Muslim countries, mainly around the Red Sea.

The Red Sea littoral retained and even increased its importance for international trade and for pilgrimage. By establishing his suzerainty over Hejaz, Yemen and Aden, Ṣalāḥ al-Dīn and his successors got the entire Red Sea, and thus the Eastern trade, under their control. The port of ʻAydhāb was sacked and looted by the Franks during the naval raid of Reginald of Karak in 1183, but it was a solitary episode without any sequel and, until the Portuguese period, no Christian fleet appeared on the Red Sea. The protection of Muslim merchants on the land route from the coast to the Nile was achieved with the aid of the arabized Beja group, the Hadariba, the chief of whom exercised control over ʻAydhāb and shared its revenues with an Egyptian governor.

THE ARABIZATION OF THE SUDAN

The period between the thirteenth and the beginning of the sixteenth centuries brought profound political, ethnic and cultural changes to the region that constitutes the northern part of the present-day Republic of the Sudan. During this time Christian Nubia became gradually a subject state of Mamluk Egypt, and the Christian religion was superseded by Islam. The political decline of the Nubian states, mainly that of al-Maqurra in the north, opened the way for unhindered penetration of Arab tribes to the south, and this led in turn to the arabization of the whole country north of the tenth latitude. The process of arabization went hand in hand with that of islamization, and by the end of the fifteenth century both developments were almost completed.

Although under the Fatimids and Ayyubids the nomadic Arabs had already constituted a turbulent and troublesome element in Lower as well as in Upper Egypt, no period saw as many revolts of the Arabs against the central government as the Mamluk era. These uprisings were systematically put down by the better-equipped and trained *mamlūks*, with the result that the remnants of the defeated tribes migrated southwards. This flow was strengthened by tribes wanting to escape effective administrative control, and by Arab contingents which accompanied Mamluk punitive expeditions to Upper Egypt and Nubia and then settled in these regions. All this led to a relative over-population of Arab nomads and their herds in the borderland and created an explosive situation.

Under Baybars a new Egyptian policy towards Nubia was inaugurated. The impetus for this change came, surprisingly, not from the Mamluks but from the Nubians themselves, when in 1272 King David of al-Maqurra raided the important port of ʻAydhāb, thus touching a very sensitive spot. Four years later Baybars sent a punitive expedition to Nubia that penetrated as far as Dongola and defeated the Nubian army. The Mamluk victory was made easier by internal strife in the royal family, inside which a party emerged that sought Egyptian aid. From this time onwards, the Mamluk sultans frequently intervened in the internal affairs of Nubia, and gradually reduced its rulers to the role of their vassals or puppet kings. The northern part of Nubia, al-Marīs, was assigned to the sultan, and its revenues went to the Mamluk treasury, although the 'Lord of the Mountain' continued to be the governor. But the whole region had thus become even more islamized and part of the Muslim world.

Although Nubia proper was not directly annexed to Egypt, the continuous interventions and invasions of the Mamluk armies, as well as those of the Arab tribes, undermined the political and military power of the kingdom. When in 1315 the Mamluks chose as the Nubian king a prince who was already converted to Islam, this event signalled the beginning of the decline of Nubian Christianity. The conversion of the cathedral of Dongola into a mosque, recorded in an inscription of 1317, was the final act by which the former Christian kingdom became a Muslim state. Soon afterwards the throne of Nubia was seized by the wholly islamized and arabized Banū Kanz, who in the meantime had married into the Nubian royal family, and thus had some legitimate claims; beside this, they enjoyed the support of the Arabs and the Muslim Nubians. Although the relations of the Banū Kanz with the Mamluk sultans throughout the following century were strained and led often to armed clashes, the family retained effective control over the northern part of Nubia. We have only scanty information about what happened in the southern part of Nubia, at Dongola and in the kingdom of ʿAlwa. It seems that the Nubian kings of the ancient al-Maqurra dynasty, now Muslims, held a precarious control over Dongola, where the internal chaos was increased by frequent incursions of the Arabs to whom the region succumbed at a not precisely fixed date.

There is no better summary of the impact of the Arab nomadic tribes than that given by the great historian Ibn Khaldūn:

> With the Nubians' conversion to Islam the payment of the *jizya* (capital tax) ceased. Then several clans of the Juhayna Arabs spread over their country and settled in it; they assumed power and filled the land with rapine and disorder. At first the kings of Nubia tried to repulse them by force but they failed in it; so they changed their tactics and tried to win them over by offering their daughters in marriage. Thus was their kingdom disintegrated, for it passed to the sons of the Juhayna from their Nubian mothers according to the non-Arab practice of inheritance by the sister and her sons. So their kingdom fell to pieces and their country was inherited by the nomad Arabs of the Juhayna. But their rule presented none of the marks of statesmanship, because of the essential weakness of a system which is opposed to discipline and the subordination of one man to another. Consequently they have been divided until this day, and there is no vestige of central authority in their part of the country, but they remain nomads following the rainfall like the bedouin.[1]

The conversion of the kings to Islam, and the ascendance of the Banū Kanz, were the final blows suffered by the Christian religion in Nubia. With the islamization of the rulers came also the end of the *baqṭ*, an international agreement that had remained in force for nearly seven centuries – indeed, a unique case in the history of diplomacy. Additional factors were the growing isolation of Nubian Christianity from the outside world, and also the deterioration of the status of Christians in Egypt from where most of the higher clergy came. Christianity was not wiped out at once. It lingered on over a long period

[1] Ibn Khaldūn, *Kitāb al-ʿibar*, vol. v (Beirut, 1956–61), 922–3.

and died out by internal feebleness and a lack of any external stimulus. In the more southerly state of ʿAlwa it remained alive until the beginning of the sixteenth century, when it came to an end together with the kingdom, through a joint action of Arab tribesmen and the Funj.

The disintegration of the northern Nubian kingdom, to which the earlier penetration of Arab tribesmen substantially contributed, facilitated the great Arab breakthrough to the rich pasture lands beyond the Nubian desert. In general this movement followed two main routes, one easterly and one westerly. It is difficult if not impossible to discern the numerous migratory moves and to fix them chronologically, since the Arabs who penetrated into the Sudan came mainly in small groups of different tribal origin rather than in large tribal entities, and because their immigration was more akin to infiltration over centuries than a sudden invasion.

The Beja country in the east did not absorb many Arabs, as it did not offer rich pastures; the majority therefore only passed through it to the interior. The nomadic tribes, commonly called Juhayna, reached the region between the Atbara river and the Blue Nile (the Butana) in the fourteenth century, and thence crossed to the Gezira (the land between the Blue and White Niles) in the course of the fifteenth century. There they settled in the metropolitan area of ʿAlwa and in Sennar, and progressed to the south as far as the island of Aba on the White Nile. Although the core of these tribes came from Upper Egypt, there was also some migration from Arabia proper, across the Red Sea.

Comparatively few Arabs remained to the north of Dongola and they were soon absorbed socially and linguistically by the local Nubians, even if Islam superseded the Christian faith of the latter. The intermixing of the Arabs and the Nubians was also in progress in the middle Nile valley between the Fourth and Sixth Cataracts, but here the Nubians adopted the Arabic language and fictitious Arab genealogies. These arabized Nubians, known as Jaʿaliyyūn, consisted of a settled population of farmers, craftsmen and merchants. Many of them started in the course of the fourteenth century to migrate to other parts of the Sudan, mainly to Kordofan and further westward.

The second main stream of the Arab nomads penetrated into the interior by a westerly route, either directly from Upper Egypt or from Dongola. It seems that this migration took place earlier than that in the east. In the course of the thirteenth and fourteenth centuries the Arabs occupied the belt of grazing lands stretching from the Nile to northern Darfur, continuing there to rear camels and sheep, and forming a large group known as the Kabābīsh (from *kabsh*, 'ram'), but consisting of clans of various tribes. The later arrivals from the north or east did not find enough room for themselves in the northern belt, and had to continue their migrations further southward into southern Kordofan, and thence along the horizontal axis to the west, to southern Darfur, Wadai and the Lake Chad region. Finding these regions unsuitable for either camel or sheep, they were forced to adopt cattle-breeding as their main activity, taking it over from the autochthonous populations of Negroid stock. These tribes then became known as the Baqqāra (from *baqara*, 'cow'). Although these preserved their nomadic way of life and their tribal system intact, they intermarried with the local peoples, inaugurating thus another process, that of the gradual Africanization of the Sudanese Arabs.

Once the barrier formed by the Nubian kingdom had been broken, there was no other centralized state all the way between the Nile valley and Lake Chad to hinder the free penetration of the nomadic Arabs. The region known later as Darfur was inhabited by a conglomeration of small ethnic groups, both sedentary and nomadic, which until the coming of the Arabs did not seem to have been much in contact with the neighbouring countries, even if there are some slight traces of Christian Nubian civilization on their territory. The whole area of the Nilo-Chadic Sahel lay until the thirteenth century outside the commercial interests of Egypt, or for that matter of any other Arab state, and thus the information about it is correspondingly meagre if not entirely lacking.

In the thirteenth century Darfur was known to be in the hands of the Daju (Dajo), who are traditionally considered to have produced the first local dynasty. Arkell's theory[1] about the strong political and cultural influence of Kanem exercised during the Daju period and later is not substantiated by any trustworthy evidence. However, taking into account the migratory movements of the semi-nomadic Zaghawa of Arabic sources,[2] a certain influence coming from the more western regions is not impossible. In the mid fourteenth century the Daju hegemony in the northern part of Darfur was superseded by that of the Tunjur, who are believed to have come from Nubia and to have been of Arab origin; but since the traditions of so many islamized peoples

[1] A. J. Arkell, 'The History of Darfur, AD 1200–1700', *Sudan Notes and Records*, 1951, **32** and 1952, **33**.

[2] Although Arab sources localize these Zaghawa in the region to the north and north-east of Lake Chad, and thus allow us to identify their core with modern Teda-Daza, it seems that the name had a wider connotation, namely that of all nomadic and semi-nomadic tribes between the Nile and the Chad.

in the Sudan have the tendency to glorify their past by claiming kinship with famous dynasties or nations of the East, the historicity of such claims is dubious. As the coming of the Tunjur to Darfur was roughly contemporary with the Arab breakthrough, it is not impossible that some groups of mixed Nubian–Arab origin were drawn into the great westward movement and settled then in northern Darfur, pushing the Daju more to the south. It may well be that a temporary alliance of the Tunjur with the vigorous Arab nomads helped them to achieve the leading position in northern Darfur, where the symbiosis with the Arabs led also to their adoption of the Arabic language. On the other hand they are also regarded as having had some connection with the Banū Hilāl and Tunisia, or with North Africa in general, although this may only be an echo of the tradition of the Kayra, the next Darfur ruling family. Darfur was at this time losing its former isolation, and opening itself to migrations and influence coming from the north and north-east along the well-known route of the *Darb al-Arbaʿīn* (lit. 'forty days' route') and also along the Wādī al-Milk. Even then the trade seems to have been rather insignificant. From the Tunjur era only small quantities of Venetian and Indian beads found at Uri are witness to commercial relations with Egypt and the Red Sea ports. The chief cultural changes came with the infiltration of the nomadic Arabs, with their new breeds of cattle and pastoral techniques and, perhaps, with new weapons.

But, as everywhere in the Sudan, only a part of the incoming Arabs settled in Darfur proper, other groups moving further westward to Wadai and to the Lake Chad region. Although we may presume that the nomadic tribes had been present in this region since the mid fourteenth century, the first documented evidence stems from the year 1391, when the then *mai* of Bornu, Abū ʿAmr ʿUthmān b. Idrīs, wrote to the Mamluk sultan, Barqūq, complaining of the raids committed by the Judham and other Arabs against the population of Kanem. The main complaint concerned the sale of Bornu subjects, among them a number of the king's relatives, as slaves to Egyptian merchants, who brought them to their country's markets. The *mai* asked the sultan to help in the return of the enslaved people from Egypt and requested the punishment of the Arabs for their unlawful action.[1]

[1] Al-Qalqashandī, *Ṣubḥ al-Aʿshā* (Cairo, 1913–19), vol. V, 279–81, vol. VIII, 116–18.

RELATIONS WITH NORTH-EAST AND EAST AFRICA

The history of the Red Sea littoral region has been more closely connected with the fortunes of Egypt than with other parts of the Sudan. The Mamluk sultans paid increasing attention to the Red Sea ports and to the safety of trade routes between its shores and Upper Egypt. In 1267 an Egyptian army conquered as far as the port of Suakin and brought it under Mamluk suzerainty. At the beginning of the fourteenth century, when the penetration of the Arab nomads made this region unsafe, a Mamluk punitive expedition reached as far as the Atbara river and the Taka region near the Ethiopian border, but there was no attempt to occupy this country permanently. After the expulsion of the Crusaders and the reopening of the more convenient pilgrim route across Sinai, the port of ʿAydhāb lost its former importance and, although this route remained in use until the mid fourteenth century, the number of pilgrims going there steadily decreased. ʿAydhāb suffered further heavily by the economic decline of Upper Egypt under the last Baḥrī sultans, and by the frequent clashes between the Hadariba chieftains and the Mamluk governors over the custom revenues. The safety of the land routes could not be maintained when the Mamluk state was in decline, and the Beja and the Arab tribes often attacked the caravans. The rise of Jedda as the main port for the spice trade in the first quarter of the fifteenth century sealed the fate of ʿAydhāb. Sultan Barsbay prohibited the merchants from calling at this port and when the Hadariba chiefs retaliated with attacks on Egyptian caravans, a punitive expedition destroyed the town almost completely. The more southerly port at Suakin was not able to take over the role of ʿAydhāb in the international trade, because it lacked easy communications with the navigable Nile: it served, however, as the outlet for the export of camels, ivory, slaves and other products from the interior of the Sudan, and played also a minor part as a gateway for the Arab economic penetration and arabization of these eastern regions.

The momentum gained by the Arab penetration of the Sudan in the fourteenth and fifteenth centuries led to a total overrunning of the northern Sudan by Arab-speaking nomads. At the end of this period there emerged a cultural and linguistic pattern totally different from the previous one. Islam drove out Christianity, and the majority of the inhabitants adopted Arabic; but many groups such as the Nubians and the Beja retained their original languages. The incoming Arabs mixed widely with the indigenous population, thus causing the emergence of the new stock, culturally Arab and Muslim, that forms the bulk of the northern Sudanic population up to the present day.

The disappearance of Nubian Christianity under the combined impact of the Mamluk army and Arab nomads meant a further step in the islamization of north and north-eastern Africa. Compared with the situation at the beginning of the seventh century, when a continuous belt of predominantly Christian countries stretched all the way from the Mediterranean to Ethiopia, the beginning of the sixteenth century offered a profoundly changed picture, for at this time Ethiopia remained the last surviving Christian outpost in Africa. Although the fall of Christian Nubia might have increased the religious isolation of Ethiopian Christianity, it severed neither the contacts with the Coptic church of Egypt, whose patriarch remained still the formal head of the Ethiopian Christians, nor the mundane relations with the outside world, notably with Egypt.

It even seems that, with the rise of the Solomonid dynasty in Ethiopia and that of the Mamluks in Egypt, these contacts became more regular and lively. The political relations between both states were in general correct, troubled only occasionally by Ethiopian protests against the persecutions of the Christians in Egypt. According to al-ʿUmarī,[1] the Ethiopians considered themselves guardians of the Nile for its descent to Egypt, and pretended that they permitted the regular flow of its waters as a sign of their homage to the Egyptian sultan. In Ethiopian as well as in Egyptian sources the story is often repeated that occasionally the Egyptians attributed the low Nile to a diversion of its upper course by the Ethiopians, or that the *negus* threatened to deprive Egypt of the Nile waters by deflecting its course to the desert if the sultan would not yield to some demands concerning the position of Christians or of the patriarch. Even if many Egyptians did believe in the reality of such a danger to their country, the rulers were well aware of the unreality of it. When in 1325/6 Amda-Siyon sent an embassy to al-Malik al-Nāṣir with a similar threat, the Sultan only laughed and sent the envoys back.

The Cairo government was more touchy in the face of other threats. In the middle of the fourteenth century, when the patriarch of Alexandria was arrested for refusing to pay excessive taxes, the Negus Newaya Krestos seized all the Muslims in the country and drove away all the Egyptian caravans, thus causing great damage to the trading

[1] Ibn Fadl Allāh al-ʿOmarī [al-ʿUmarī], *Masālik al-abṣār fī mamālik al amṣār* (*L'Afrique moins l'Égypte*), tr. Gaudefroy-Demombynes (Paris, 1927), 30.

interests of the *Kārimi* merchants. The Mamluks hastened to release the patriarch and the trade was opened again.

Ethiopian territory represented one of the most important markets for the *Kārimi* merchants, whose commercial operations covered alike its Christian parts and the Muslim states in the south. The main Egyptian commodities were linen, cotton and silk textiles of both Egyptian and European provenance, and weapons; among the export goods we find ivory, spices and, above all, slaves. According to al-ʿUmarī, Hadya in south-west Ethiopia was the main centre for the export of eunuchs who, however, were castrated farther in the interior of the country. Ethiopian slaves were in general highly esteemed in all Muslim countries from Egypt to India, and considered to be the most loyal and reliable guardians as well as commercial agents.

Already some time before the disintegration of the Nubian kingdoms heralded the gradual disappearance of Christianity in the Nile valley, a number of Muslim states had come into existence to the south of the Ethiopian highlands (see pp. 139–43). In eastern and southern Shoa there emerged the states of Ifat, Adal and some smaller principalities that controlled the main trade-routes from Zeila, the most important port for those parts of the Horn of Africa. Farther to the west, on the upper Awash and beyond it, both among settled Sidama and nomadic Cushitic groups, Islam was adopted by the ruling classes in the states of Dawaro, Fetegar, Hadya and Bali. This belt of Muslim states (fittingly called by al-Maqrīzī *al-ṭirāz al-islamī*, lit. 'the Muslim fringe') contributed largely to the encirclement of Christian Ethiopia by Islam, and became an effective barrier against the expansion of the Ethiopian state towards the south and south-east. Although the Muslim states were not very strong and never able to form a united front, the Solomonid rulers were well aware of the potential danger arising from their existence, and from the time of Amda-Siyon (1329) there was for more than two centuries a series of Ethiopian–Muslim wars, only rarely interrupted by short periods of peace. Eventually, in the first half of the fifteenth century, the *negus* was recognized as overlord and the majority of Muslim rulers became his vassals.

This state of affairs did not fail to affect in various ways the relations between Egypt and Ethiopia during the Mamluk period. As the most powerful Muslim power of the time, Egypt claimed the role of protector of Ethiopian Muslims, and on some occasions the Cairo government intervened through the Coptic patriarch on behalf of their coreligionists, who were persecuted by Ethiopian kings. But on the other hand the interest in trade with Christian Ethiopia, and not least the inability to help the Muslim states effectively, forced Egypt to adopt a conciliatory policy. The religious contacts were kept alive, and the students from Ifat (Zeila) had their own hostel at al-Azhar; but no diplomatic relations were maintained between Cairo and the Muslim states, in contrast to the frequent exchanges of embassies under the Christian kings. Only in the year 1452 do we hear about an embassy of the ruler of Jabart (presumably Ifat), who came to Cairo probably to ask help after the defeats inflicted by Zara Ya'qob, but without any tangible result.

Surprisingly enough, it was Christian Ethiopia that profited from Egyptian technical aid, even if it did not come from the official side. Al-Maqrīzī's testimony about this contribution is sufficiently eloquent:

The power of king Isḥāq ibn Dāwūd (e.g. Yeshaq, 1412–27) grew thanks to a Circassian *mamlūk*, formerly an armourer of Cairo, who came to his court and established there an important arsenal, in which were stored weapons such as sabres, lances, armoured coats etc., whereas formerly they knew only spears and other throwing weapons. The king welcomed also a high personality from the Cairo court, an *amīr* named Altunbughā who had been governor of Upper Egypt and then fled to his court. Being well versed in the use of arms and in cavalry tactics, he gained a strong influence over the king, teaching his soldiers archery, and fighting with lances and sabres. He even produced for him some fire-arms, so that they all learned the art of war from him. Finally the king received at his court a Jacobite Christian from Egypt, Fakhr al-Dawla, who organized his empire and created the financial administration. Through all this Ethiopia became a state with a [real] sovereign and an [effective] administration, whereas in former times the king's realm, like that of his fathers, was only an anarchy without offices, organization and laws . . . When his empire was thus organized and the king felt powerful, he wanted to take hold of the Muslim states, and started long and terrible campaigns against these states, his vassals . . . and he thus put an end to the Muslim dynasties there.[1]

Zeila seems to have been the southernmost port frequented by Egyptian merchants, whose chief centre for these regions, however, was Aden, where the commercial, and also the climatic conditions were more favourable. Through Zeila, and to a lesser degree Berbera, there passed the main stream of slaves from the Ethiopian hinterland, and both were also the starting points for caravans to the interior. In the Muslim states of southern Ethiopia, Egyptian economic influence was

[1] al-Maqrīzī, *Historia regnum islamiticorum in Abissinia*, ed. and tr. F. T. Rinck (Leiden, 1790), 21; cf. also al-'Omarī, *Masālik*, 36–7.

paramount, and the only currency in circulation was Mamluk dirhams and dinars.[1]

Direct Egyptian contacts with the rest of the Horn of Africa, and south of it, were slight or non-existent. The numismatic evidence is tenuous and, surprisingly, only very small numbers of Mamluk, or, as a matter of fact, of any other Muslim Egyptian coins, have so far been found. With the exception of some glass, hardly any objects of Egyptian or Syrian origin have been found on the East African coast. Trade between these parts and Egypt, or the Red Sea ports in general, seems to have been almost entirely lacking. The exchange of goods went on through the intermediary of South Arabian ports and/or Zeila.[2]

The pilgrims from East Africa, unlike those from the west, did not pass through Egypt and Cairo on their way to the Holy Cities, and so even the cultural and religious links were missing. An echo of Egyptian influence – but only as far south as Mogadishu – could be seen in some elements of the regalia, such as the use by rulers of a canopy or parasol surmounted by effigies of birds; similar emblems of royal dignity were at this time widely diffused in many islamized African states, and are generally recognized as going back to the Fatimid ceremonial. In later centuries similar regalia were used by rulers of Malindi, Mombasa, Kilwa and other coastal cities, who probably took them over from Mogadishu.

Egypt was neither politically nor economically interested in the East African coast, and the lack of any useful information about these regions in contemporary Egyptian literature, so rich in regard to other parts of Africa, tends to confirm this. According to some Portuguese sources, the local rulers of Mombasa and Ozi recognized at the beginning of the sixteenth century the suzerainty of the Mamluk dynasty (or that of the caliph).[3] But, as there is as yet no corroborative evidence from the Egyptian side about any direct political contacts with these distant countries, this information must be evaluated with caution; it

[1] Tomé Pires says explicitly in his *Suma Oriental* (*c.* 1515) that Zeila and Berbera are outlets for the whole of Abyssinia, but adds that very little goes to Cairo; it seems that he had in mind the direct overland route from Ethiopia to Egypt; cf. G. S. P. Freeman-Grenville, *The East African coast – selected documents from the first to the earlier nineteenth century* (Oxford, 1962), 125.

[2] Gervase Mathew's assertion that in the fourteenth and fifteenth centuries 'Somalia and the North Kenya coast down to the Tana river can be considered as part of an Egyptian sphere' is not substantiated by any evidence; cf. R. Oliver and G. Mathew, eds., *History of East Africa*, vol. 1 (Oxford, 1963), 111. When the coastal chronicles mention relations with the outside world at this period they speak always about India, South Arabia or Persia, never about Egypt.

[3] Cf. J. S. Trimingham, *Islam in East Africa* (Oxford, 1964), 19, note 1.

nevertheless witnesses to the fame enjoyed by Egypt in the Indian Ocean area.

The region as a whole, and the East African coast in particular, must have felt in these centuries the effects of the growing role of Egypt in international trade in many ways. This commerce was, of course, dependent on a complicated network of trade relations, with ramifications towards India, Indonesia, Malaya, China, Persia, Arabian countries and East Africa, so that a number of various factors, local as well as international, were constantly affecting it. On the other hand, the changes in trade influenced in varying degrees the prosperity of the participating regions. It is natural that the communities whose chief economic activity was turned to this trade, as was the case of the coastal cities in East Africa, would be especially affected by any new trends in it. Bearing this in mind, it is surely not by pure chance that the spectacular growth of material prosperity on the East African coast from the thirteenth and fourteenth centuries on coincided with the great expansion of Egypt's international trade and growing participation in the carrying commerce between the east and Europe. The larger capital investment and organizational skill of the *Kārimī* group had given the Indian Ocean trade a powerful new stimulus, and, together with the increasing European demands for spices and other eastern wares, brought about a growing prosperity to all participants. Not only the material welfare of the coastal cities benefited from this process, but indirectly so did Islam as a religion and culture. It was in these centuries that the coast became definitively an integral part of the Islamic world. Though Egypt's share in this general development was important, the contribution of other countries like Arabia, Persia and Muslim India should not be forgotten.

RELATIONS WITH THE MAGHRIB AND WEST AFRICA

With the gradual ascendance of Egypt to the centre of the Arab and Islamic world, its relations with, and influence in, other parts of Africa were undergoing many changes. Various manifestations of Egypt's impact in north-eastern Africa have already been described, and it has been found that it was naturally strongest in Nubia, but less so in Ethiopia and farther to the south; there were also differences in the degree of this impact under successive Egyptian dynasties. The same evolution can be observed also in the relations between Egypt on one hand and the Maghrib and the central and western Sudan on the other.

Under the Fatimids, Egypt and the Maghrib for nearly a century formed a unified empire. Although these two parts differed in their ethnic backgrounds, they shared many cultural traits, due on the one hand to their ancient Mediterranean heritage and on the other to their more recent but very real adherence to Islam as a religion and culture. It was during the Fatimid epoch that the mutual influence reached its peak. The Fatimid caliphs were able to conquer Egypt only with the aid of their Berber (Kutama) army, and for a certain time these warriors from the Maghrib played a significant role in the internal as well as external policy of the dynasty. The Fatimids also brought from the west their whole fleet, manned by experienced Tunisian seamen, thus founding Egypt's naval preponderance in the eastern Mediterranean on skill and material of Maghribi origin. The same period witnessed the coming of many magico-religious practices of Berber origin to Egypt (and farther eastwards), wrapped, of course, in Islamic clothing, and thus influencing the popular religion. Egypt at this time did not have much that was original to offer, being only one of many cultural provinces of the Islamic world, the centre of which was situated further to the east, in Iraq and Iran. Nevertheless, the country on the Nile fulfilled the very useful role of a channel through which manifold oriental influences penetrated to the Maghrib. It has already been mentioned that Fatimid art and architecture – the products of various influences – exercised a certain impact in the western Islamic countries, chiefly in Ifrīqiya under the Zirid dynasty at a time when the political links were loosening.

It is somewhat paradoxical that the greatest contribution of Egypt to the history of the Maghrib was the sending the Banū Hilāl and Banū Sulaym to the west. The immediate as well as the remote consequences of the invasion of these nomadic Arab tribes are discussed elsewhere (see pp. 243–5); here some of the effects this event have had on relations between Egypt and the Maghrib will only be pointed out. The Hilalian invasion led – together with the rise of the purely Berber dynasties of the Almoravids and Almohads – to the severing of all political and cultural links between the Islamic Orient and Occident. From the end of the eleventh century the political frontier and influence of Egypt did not reach beyond Cyrenaica. In later centuries the Maghribi dynasties did not even recognize the spiritual authority of the 'Abbasid caliphs in Cairo, and some of them even pretended to the caliphal title. For various reasons neither the Ayyubids and Mamluks looked westwards, nor did the Berber dynasties look eastwards.

Although the political organizations and the economic systems in the Maghrib and Egypt show some similarity, there is no reason to consider them as borrowing or imitation. In the cultural sphere, the Maghrib liberated itself from the tutelage of Egypt and the east, and became independent. The discernible foreign influences came now predominantly from Muslim Spain, stressing thus again the separation of the Maghrib from the east.

But even during the period of full Maghribi political and cultural autonomy there were continuing flows of men and goods from the west to the east and vice versa. Egypt, and especially Cairo, exercised in the Ayyubid, and more so in the Mamluk, era a strong attractive power for the Westerners, not only as the necessary transit stage on the pilgrimage, but also as the centre of Arabic and Islamic learning. Some of these scholars remained permanently in Egypt, like the famous historian Ibn Khaldūn, enticed by the greater opportunities offered by this cosmopolitan metropolis, but the majority returned to their home countries.

No less intensive was the exchange of products: the Maghrib exported to Egypt mainly oil, woollen cloth, coral, hides, salt fish and black slaves (occasionally as many as 2,000 yearly) and even, in periods of low Nile floods, corn. The principal goods going from Egypt to the west were glass and metal wares, weapons, spices, perfumes, silk, linen and cotton cloth and, again, corn. The commerce reached its peak at the beginning of the fifteenth century, and it is said that it was Ibn Khaldūn who drew the attention of the Mamluk sultan to the importance of the trade with the Maghrib. The commerce was partly sea-borne but, owing to the threat from European pirates, the traders preferred the caravan route going along the coast. This unbroken interchange helped to maintain the fundamental cultural unity of Muslim North Africa, notwithstanding the separate ways followed by both the main regions in their development.

After the abandonment at the end of the ninth century of the direct route from the Egyptian oases to Ghana via Kufra, Kawar and Asben, due to its dangerous character, the contacts between Egypt and the central and western Sudan remained for many centuries insignificant compared with the fully developed commercial, cultural and political relations existing between this part of the Sudan and the Maghrib. It is true that at the end of the eleventh and in the course of the next two centuries some rulers of Kanem and Mali undertook the Pilgrimage and on these occasions visited Egypt, too, but these visits aroused only mild interest in Cairo, and no contemporary Egyptian chronicles considered them worthy of record. The religious contacts were in these centuries more intense. Already in the Fatimid period groups of Maliki scholars (but it is not clear whether they came from Egypt or Ifrīqiya) used to travel to Kanem to propagate Islam among the local population. In the middle of the thirteenth century a hostel (*riwāq*) was founded in Fusṭāṭ for Kanemi students. This indicates that, at the beginning of the Mamluk period, direct contacts with the Sudan began to improve. In the field of commerce the Egyptian merchants formed only a minority among the well-established colonies of Muslim traders in the Sudan, who were mostly of Maghribi origin. Before the fourteenth century Egyptian products were imported into the Sudan not directly, but via North Africa, and mostly by non-Egyptians.

It is therefore not surprising that the amount of information about the Sudan to be found in Egyptian Arabic literature before the Mamluk period is not abundant, and is drawn to a large extent from earlier, Maghribi sources. But from the beginning of the fourteenth century we can observe in Egypt an increasing interest in these parts of Africa, as witnessed by copious accounts written by authors like al-ʿUmarī, al-Qalqashandī and al-Maqrīzī. Even Ibn Khaldūn, who had acquired much of his material about Mali already in the Maghrib, found some valuable sources of information in Egypt itself. The reasons for this renewed interest were manifold, but commercial relations stood incontestably in the foreground. The central and western Sudan represented for Egypt valuable markets as well as the source of various commodities – in the first place, gold. After the exhaustion of the Nubian gold mines in al-ʿAllāqī, the western Sudanese gold from Bambuk and Bure had found its way to Egypt in increasing quantities, and Mamluk coins were minted from it. It has already been mentioned how the influx of this metal brought by Mansa Mūsā affected the exchange rate between gold and silver in the first quarter of the fourteenth century. This was, of course, exceptional, but that a steady flow of Sudanese gold was reaching Egypt is confirmed by numerous stories about the wealth of merchants, and by the highly instructive remark by al-Qalqashandī that Egyptian traders in the Sudan were selling their goods only for gold. This lucrative commerce did not last for long, however, as in the course of the fifteenth century the import of gold began to decrease, owing to the competition of Italian (chiefly Genoese) and Catalan merchants, who deflected it to Europe through their trade with North Africa. Until the end of the Mamluk dynasty, the Portuguese factories along the West African coast contributed further to the diminishing of the gold export to Egypt.

Equally important for Egypt were the Sudanese markets: textiles always figured as the first on the list of Egyptian exports. According to Ibn Baṭṭūṭa, the inhabitants of Walata only wore garments of fine Egyptian fabrics, and in the copper-mining centre of Takedda the people gained their livelihood solely by trade with Egypt, importing quantities of fine cloth as well as other wares from Egypt. This importance of the Sudan as a market is stressed also by Ibn Khaldūn, who indicates that every year big caravans with as many as 12,000 camels were travelling from Egypt to Mali.[1]

Although we can find traces of earlier contacts, it seems that it was Mansa Mūsā's pilgrimage and visit to Cairo that inaugurated a new chapter in the history of relations between Egypt and the Sudan (see also pp. 394–5). Until that time the western Sudan had been under the commercial and cultural influence of Morocco or Ifrīqiya; from then on the Sudanese states looked more towards Egypt. Mansa Mūsā's visit also opened the eyes of the Egyptian authorities and merchants to new horizons of commercial possibilities. Though he arrived in Egypt with large quantities of gold, he returned back heavily indebted: his creditors nevertheless recovered their money in Mali, discovering thus a new field for financial investment. Apart from regular commercial transactions, Egyptian merchants took advantage of the natural curiosity of the Sudanese who came to Cairo with Mansa Mūsā or later, to supply them at exorbitant prices with less valuable goods. It is interesting to note also the great demand of the Mali people for Turkish, Ethiopian and other slave-girls, and also for eunuchs and Turkish boys. The slave-trade thus went in both directions. For the presence of slaves originating in the western parts of the Sudan in Egypt there are no concrete data in the contemporary sources, but we can surmise that they were not much valued, especially in comparison with those coming from Nubia or Ethiopia. In the whole of Mamluk history hardly ever is there a mention of black slaves; only at the very end of the fifteenth century do we hear about a corps of black arquebusiers in the Mamluk army, and it seems that the black Africans served also in the artillery, but no indication is given about their original home. The silence of the sources is, of course, no proof for the absence in Egypt of western Sudanese slaves. It cannot be forgotten that black

[1] *Kitāb al-ʿibar*, vol. VII, 52.

slaves as a whole belonged to the lowest stratum of Egyptian society, being employed in the most despised kinds of menial work, and thus escaping the attention of historians and other writers. It remains nevertheless likely that the slaves continuously formed a part of the Egyptian import from the countries situated to the west of Lake Chad, even if this region delivered far smaller numbers than the more easily accessible sources in the Nilotic Sudan and Ethiopia. Some of the slaves from the west reached Egypt as re-exports from the Maghrib.

Egypt was connected with these parts by the route going by Awjila, an important slave-market, and the Fezzan. There the road bifurcated: one route led southwards via the Kawar oasis (Bilma), where the famous alum mine was exploited and its product exported to Egypt, to Kanem and Bornu; the other route continued in a general westerly direction to Ghat and Tuat and thence to the Niger. The route via Tuat seems to have been the preferred one at the time of Mali's heyday, whereas after the fifteenth century the principal route went via Aïr (Asben). These routes across the Sahara were employed by merchants as well as by pilgrims, be they of royal blood or commoners. Nowhere do we find any mention of the southern route leading from the Chad region via Wadai and Darfur to the Nile and the Red Sea; it seems that this *ṭarīq al-Sūdān* came into increased use only much later. The reasons for the neglect of this shortest line of communication connecting the central and western parts of the Sudan with the Red Sea littoral for such a long time are not difficult to discern; until the thirteenth century the existence of Christian Nubian states did not attract Muslims to cross their territories on their way to the Holy Cities, whereas after their decline the presence of Arab nomadic tribes along the eastern half of the trip made it highly insecure. Only with the growth and consolidation of Wadai, Darfur and the Funj state was it possible to consider this route as relatively safe.

In the context of commercial relations between Egypt and the Sudan, it must be pointed out that no mention at all is to be found in Arabic sources about the routes by which cowrie shells were imported, although they were in use from the eleventh century. Judging by the number of cowries circulating in the Sudan, they must have been imported for many centuries and in considerable quantities. It is the more surprising, in that they figure only exceptionally among the wares from Egypt, the most likely transit stage on the way from their place of origin in the Indian Ocean to West Africa. A few passing references to cowrie shells being exported from Egypt to the Maghrib as material for ornaments and trinkets are to be found in the Jewish *Geriza* documents,[1] whereas the Muslim sources are quite silent about them. This meagre evidence does not justify the conclusion that the main flow of cowries to the Sudan in the period before the fifteenth century passed through Egypt.

In parallel with the development of trade went also the strengthening of cultural and ideological links. This process was conditioned not only by Egypt's leading position in the Muslim world, but also by the gradual spread of Islam and Islamic learning in the sub-Saharan belt, mainly in towns such as Timbuktu, Jenne and Gao (see pp. 416–20). More and more Muslims, recruited mostly among the '*ulamā*', were performing the Pilgrimage, and it became a custom to spend some time in Cairo to refine theological and juridical knowledge. Aḥmad Bābā's biographical dictionary and the Sudanese chronicles are full of names of learned men who bore the honorific title of *al-ḥājj*, or who had studied in Egypt. To their home countries they brought, apart from the acquired knowledge, also many Arabic books; al-'Umarī mentions that Mansa Mūsā bought in Cairo several books on Maliki law, and from the beginning of the sixteenth century we have the testimony of Leo Africanus, who found in Timbuktu a great number of doctors, judges, priests and other learned men, who were bountifully maintained at the king's cost and charges. And thither were brought various manuscripts and written books from Barbary which were sold for more money than any other merchandise.[2]

And there were many Egyptian clerics who went to the Sudan and settled there permanently, enticed by the wealth of the country and the generosity of its rulers; in Kano in the fifteenth and in Songhay in the sixteenth century there were among them even a few Sharifs (see pp. 313–16).

The prestige of Egypt as the chief source of genuine Islamic learning is demonstrated also by the correspondence between some western Sudanese rulers such as Askiya Muḥammad of Songhay, Ibrāhīm Sura of Katsina and Muḥammad Settefen of Agades with the celebrated Egyptian polyhistor Jalāl al-Dīn al-Suyūṭī (d. 1505) concerning the problems of Islamic faith and practice in societies permeated with

[1] Cf. S. D. Goitein, *A Mediterranean society*, vol. I, *Economic foundations* (Berkeley and Los Angeles, 1967), 154, 275, 373.

[2] Jean-Léon l'Africain, *Description de l'Afrique*, tr. A. Épaulard and ed. with others (Paris, 1956), vol. II, 468–9.

strong pagan survivals. Askiya Muḥammad personally met this scholar in 1496 and was advised by him on juridical matters.[1]

How far these continuous contacts with Egypt affected Sudanese Islam in general is uncertain, owing to the difficulty of distinguishing what was specifically Egyptian and what came from other Muslim countries, chiefly from the Maghrib. It can, however, be assumed that the pilgrimages, and the subsequent prolonged stays in Cairo, contributed to the widening of Sudanese scholars' horizons, to their acquisition of a larger and deeper knowledge of Islamic learning, thus enabling Sudanese urban civilization to be more closely integrated with the wider context of the Muslim world. It is only from the fourteenth century, a period that coincided both with the rise of Mali and with increasing contacts with Egypt, that we can speak about the *Bilād al-Takrūr* – as these regions of the Sudan were known in the Near East – as a cultural province of the Islamic *oecumene*.

It was highly unfortunate that the growth of Islamic learning in the Sudan was contemporaneous with the decline of creative thinking in Arabic countries, and that the Takruri Muslims encountered in Egypt a rather fossilized kind of learning, which left its mark on Sudanese Islam. This Islam was characterized for a long time by its prevalently conservative, passive and bookish form. This was undoubtedly due to the influence Egyptian scholars exercised on the passing pilgrims, on Sudanese students at al-Azhar, and also through correspondence with the rulers. For nothing was more alien to Egyptian *'ulamā'* of the Mamluk period than the idea of reform or concern for practical, political or social matters. As long as the rulers recognized the place of the *fuqahā'* in the framework of the state, and so long as the *sharī'a* law was theoretically in force, the clerical class accepted any form of government, be it exercised by the Mamluks or Askiyas. Such an attitude was, of course, more acceptable to the ruling class than to the uncompromising ideas of men like al-Maghīlī. On the other hand the Maghribi tradition of reform proved to be of far greater importance for the future of Sudanese Islam than were the official Islamic theories reaching the Sudan through Egypt.

The adherence to this Islam of the Egyptian *fuqahā'*, destined only for the upper urban classes, helps to explain why the more popular forms of Islam like the saint-worshipping Sufi brotherhoods did not find their way into the western and central Sudan until the very end of this period.

[1] Cf. John Hunwick, 'Notes on a late-fifteenth-century document concerning "al-Takrur"', in C. Allen and R. W. Johnson, eds., *African Perspectives* (Cambridge, 1970), 7–33.

In this aspect the eastern Sudan represents a sharp contrast. Here Egypt's influence was also strong but, Islam being professed by the totality of nomadic and settled arabized population, the field was open for all forms of popular religion as developed in medieval Egypt, especially the proliferation of Sufi orders. On the other hand the impact of 'learned' Islam was much more restricted.[1]

In the field of political and administrative institutions, it is surprising to see how small has been the Islamic or, for that matter, Egyptian contribution. Neither in the empires of Mali and Songhay nor in Kanem-Bornu can we discover any significant feature that could point to Egypt or the Maghrib as its model. When al-'Umarī spoke about military *iqṭā'* and other benefices in Mali, he was applying mechanically a known terminology to an alien system; and even if there really was any similarity to the Egyptian *iqṭā'*, it is hard to see how it could have been influenced from the north. The administrative systems in Mali, Songhay and Kanem-Bornu evolved from local conditions and were correlated to these, so that the adoption of foreign models would be without meaning. Not even in the most developed Sudanese state, the Songhay empire – about which we are also best informed – can anything approaching the Near Eastern administrative method be detected. The only exception represents the system of *qāḍī* courts which evolved in all the great states, but this was tied up exclusively with the activities of expatriate merchants and small Muslim communities in urban centres. Even the very pious ruler Askiya Muḥammad held his own courts fully in the tradition of African rulers.

In two lesser fields there were undoubtedly innovations due to Egyptian or at least Muslim influence. The first concerns regalia; as in Ethiopia and some parts of East Africa, the emblems of rulers were enriched by ornamented parasols, the display of coloured standards and drums.[2] It has already been pointed out that this custom was introduced by the Fatimids; but it was under the Mamluks that it reached the greatest extension, and was diffused into many African countries which came in contact with Egypt. The second innovation concerns the military. According to the Kano Chronicle, Sarki Kanajeji (1390–1410) of Kano was the first to introduce quilted armour (*lifidi*,

[1] It is significant that Muslims in the eastern Sudan use as plural of the word *faqī* (correctly *faqīh*) the form *fuqarā'*, derived from *faqīr*, meaning a Muslim mystic, member of a Sufi order, dervish; this indicates the close link between religious teaching and membership of an order, cf. P. M. Holt, *The Mahdist state in the Sudan* (Oxford, 1958), 17–18.

[2] The drums as regalia were, however, inherited probably from pre-Islamic tradition, but their use together with the two other items is typically Mamluk.

from Arabic *libda*, *lubbāda*), coats of mail and iron helmets as part of the soldiers' equipment.[1] The origin of these items points without any doubt to Mamluk Egypt. Although it came into general use only later, the quilted armour formed one of the distinguishing features of warfare in many parts of the central Sudan until modern times. It contributed to the development of Sudanese horsemanship along the lines set up in the Near East during the Middle Ages.

It is noteworthy that during the Mamluk period Egypt maintained far more important contacts with the western than with the central Sudan. While Mali and Songhay were connected with Egypt through many commercial and cultural links, and merchants and scholars from both sides kept them alive with incessant travels, the relations with Kanem-Bornu, a country geographically much nearer to Egypt, were on a much smaller scale. Some of the *mais* continued the practice of Pilgrimage until the mid fourteenth century, and there were occasional embassies like that mentioned by al-Qalqashandī, but on the whole this region did not have the same interest for Egypt as did the more western parts of the Sudan. This was due partly to the lack of suitable export commodities such as gold, and partly, of course, to the anarchic situation in which Kanem found itself from the second half of the fourteenth century onwards (see pp. 290–2). Only after the consolidation of the empire at the beginning of the sixteenth century did the mutual contacts become more active, and with them came also a stronger influence from the north. But this did not occur until Egypt and Tripolitania had been incorporated in the Ottoman empire.

EGYPT'S ROLE IN AFRICA

If one tries to sum up the role Egypt played in regard to other parts of Africa during the period under discussion, four main points seem to be noteworthy. First, Egypt was the starting-place for later Arab migrations both to the west and to the south. In both cases these movements led to profound ethnic, cultural and linguistic changes in the invaded regions, a process that has continued steadily until the present. In the Maghrib it concerned mainly a degree of arabization – islamization having been practically complete before the coming of the Banū Hilāl – which left only enclaves of Berber-speaking groups. To the south of Egypt, arabization lagged somewhat behind islamization,

[1] Cf. 'The Kano Chronicle', in R. Palmer, ed. and tr., *Sudanese Memoirs* (Lagos, 1928), 107.

but on the other hand vast territories previously untouched by Islamic conquest were permanently occupied by the Arabs. The result was the emergence of a continuous Arabic belt between the Nile and Lake Chad.

Secondly, closely connected with these movements was also the process of the disintegration of the compact Christian area in north-east Africa. The rise of Egypt as the leading Muslim country was accompanied by a steady diminution of the number of Copts in the country itself. In spite of this, the patriarch of Alexandria retained his authority as the supreme head of the Nubian and Ethiopian churches. This position enabled the Coptic church to play a not negligible role in the cultural life of these countries, and to serve as a channel even for diplomatic relations between Ethiopia, Nubia and Egypt. At the beginning of the thirteenth century an irreparable blow was inflicted on African Christendom by the islamization of the Nubian kingdom, followed by the dying out of Christianity among the northern Nubians. The breaking up of this connecting link left Ethiopia as the only remaining Christian state on the whole continent, and as an isolated outpost surrounded on all sides by Muslim countries. Although Egypt cannot be considered to have been the sole originator of this state of affairs, since the islamization of southern Ethiopia and Somalia was the work of peoples from south Arabia, it was nevertheless the Mamluk intervention in Nubia that set the whole process in motion, and was in the last resort decisive.

Thirdly, the contacts with the central and western Sudan became intensive only relatively late, from the thirteenth and fourteenth centuries on, when Egypt's interests were chiefly economic; for a time Sudanese gold was the main source for Cairo mints, and the sub-Saharan regions offered a highly profitable market for Egyptian exports. The pilgrimages of rulers and clerics strengthened religious and cultural links, and intensified Islamic consciousness and learning among the urban classes. The character of Egyptian Islam of the period supported rather the conservative formalistic and legalistic outlook of Takruri *'ulamā'* and their masters, with the consequence that the spread of Islam among other strata of society was not encouraged. A durable heritage of this close contact is represented by the huge bulk of information about the Sudan in the historical and geographical literature of Mamluk Egypt. In the central Sudan as well as in Ethiopia, Egyptian influence was felt to some degree also in the field of military technology, e.g. the introduction of quilted armour and other knightly equipment and the new cavalry tactics.

Fourthly, in the Fatimid, Ayyubid and Mamluk periods Egypt absorbed huge numbers of black slaves from various parts of Africa, chiefly from Nubia, Ethiopia and the Horn of Africa, partly also from the central and western Sudan. Under the Fatimids the black guards of the caliph played a significant though diminishing role in the political and military life of the country, and for shorter spans of time gained, thanks to their numerical strength, a decisive influence. In no other medieval Muslim state did the black troops reach a comparable status; only the subsequent changes in warfare and tactics under the late Fatimids, and especially under Ṣalāḥ al-Dīn, brought about the downfall of the African infantry. The lot of other imported African slaves in Egypt was not different from that in the rest of Muslim countries; they were mostly to be found in towns as menial workers and servants, whereas their employment in agriculture seems to have been limited. Although standing on the lowest rung of the social ladder, even among the slaves, interbreeding with the local inhabitants must have been quite frequent, especially among the second and third generations which were already culturally assimilated.

CHAPTER 2

ETHIOPIA, THE RED SEA AND THE HORN*

The second half of the ninth century seems to have been a period of revival for the Christian kingdom of Ethiopia. The damage done to its economic life by the rapid expansion of Islamic power in the Near and the Middle East had not destroyed Aksum altogether. It had only weakened it. Unable to maintain its usually strong frontier garrisons, Aksum had lost extensive territories on the Red Sea coast as well as along the Beja borderlands in the north. Furthermore, the areas which had long been conquered and incorporated into the empire beyond the Tekeze river in the west – notably the Walqayt and probably also the ancient Samanoi – had apparently broken off and regained their independence. These calamities had befallen the Christian empire of Aksum in rather rapid succession, following upon the rise of Islam and the eventual control of the Red Sea trade by Muslim powers and merchants. All this seems to have brought about a certain degree of political disintegration and a decisive weakening of the central institutions of the state for a period of over two centuries. But when, in the last quarter of the ninth century, we begin to have a few literary and traditional references to the Ethiopian region, it becomes very clear that the Christian state had definitely survived all these vicissitudes in the highland areas of southern Eritrea, Tigre, Lasta and Angot. These areas form the high ridge which separates the basins of the numerous rivers flowing in the direction of the Nile and the Red Sea, and as such they constitute a compact geographical unit. It was also in the northern half of this area that Sabean settlers had intermingled with the Cushitic inhabitants of the land, out of which grew the distinctive civilization of Aksum. Here, in its ancient cradle, the Aksumite state continued to exist throughout the troubled years of the seventh and eighth centuries.

* A rigorous transcription of Ethiopian names has been discarded in favour of a simple system which should be readily comprehensible to English readers. It has proved impossible to eliminate all inconsistencies. [Ed.]

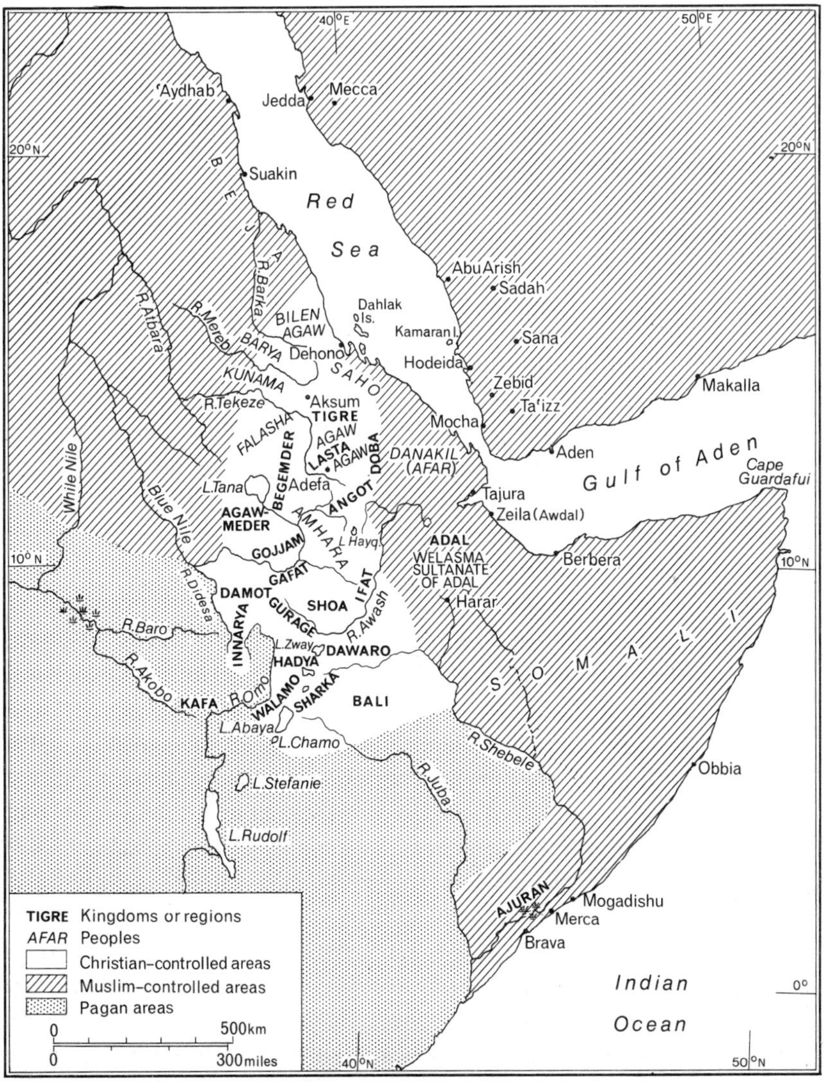

3 Ethiopia, the Red Sea and the Horn

THE NINTH AND TENTH CENTURIES

The earliest and most useful historical reference to the Ethiopian region in the period under review is given by the Arab geographer and historian, al-Ya'qūbī (*fl.* 872–89). Besides indicating the continued existence of the Christian state after the rise of Islam, al-Ya'qūbī's brief description of the kingdom of the 'Habasha' also shows that the characteristic organization and imperial traditions of Aksum were still intact in the ninth century. The Habasha were ruled by a Jacobite Christian monarch bearing the title of *nejashi*, a title which had been used by Aksumite rulers since pre-Christian times. In much the same way as his predecessors such as King Ezana, the *nejashi* also had under him many tributary local rulers who obeyed his orders and paid taxes to him. The territories which he ruled also seem to have been quite extensive, although mainly limited to the highland areas of central Ethiopia. Al-Ya'qūbī tells us that, southwards, Habasha territory extended to the land of the 'Zanj', a term usually applied by Arab geographers to the indefinite and unknown hinterland of the East African seaboard. To the north, the Beja were organized into a number of small mutually independent kingdoms which had apparently encroached on the frontier provinces of ancient Aksum. Even in this direction, however, it seems that the southernmost tribes of the Beja were still Christian by religion and that they still paid allegiance to the *nejashi* of the Habasha. The descendants of these Christian Beja tribes are remembered by local traditions as the Belew and, under the remote overlordship of the Christian kings of Ethiopia, they continued to dominate the region of southern Eritrea until the beginning of the fourteenth century.

Perhaps the most interesting development since the rise of Islam was the close commercial contacts that seem to have been re-established between the Ethiopian interior and the neighbouring Muslim areas. Al-Ya'qūbī relates that the Habasha had 'mighty cities', to which Arab merchants came for trading. In his first work, written in AD 872, he mentions Dahlak as the major outlet for this trade. Some years later, in another treatise written in AD 889, he also mentions Zeila, particularly in connection with Arab merchants coming from Baghdad, the capital of the 'Abbasid caliphate. Thus, by the last quarter of the ninth century, two major highways connected the Ethiopian interior with the Muslim world. Although Dahlak seems to have often been controlled by the Christian Habasha, Zeila was almost certainly far beyond their territorial limits.

According to al-Ya'qūbī, a place called Kubar was the capital of the *nejashi*. This place is also mentioned later on by the tenth-century Arab traveller, al-Mas'ūdī, as the centre of the Christian kingdom. Some years ago Conti Rossini proposed that 'Kubar' was a calligraphic error in the original manuscripts for 'Ksum', or Aksum.[1] Trimingham supports

[1] C. Conti Rossini, 'Les listes des rois d'Aksum', *Journal Asiatique*, 1909, 263, note 1.

this with a quotation from the astronomer al-Battānī (d. AD 929).[1] However, it seems to be very doubtful whether Aksum was still the centre of the Christian kingdom in the ninth and tenth centuries. Both Muslim and Christian traditions strongly indicate that the centre of equilibrium of the Christian state had already shifted further south by the middle of the ninth century. A historical tradition about the island monastery of Lake Hayq in Angot relates that it was founded in the ninth century by a king who is also said to have moved his capital from Aksum in the direction of the lake.[2] The chronicler of Aḥmad b. Ibrāhīm was also told that a nearby church was built 720 years before the Muslim army destroyed it in 1532. Sites of apparently important royal settlements have also been discovered recently not very far from Lake Hayq. It therefore seems that al-Ya'qūbī and al-Mas'ūdī's Kubar was far to the south of Aksum, probably somewhere between southern Tigre and Angot.

Other traditions also indicate the slow southward movement of Christian families from Tigre to Amhara and northern Shoa in the period beginning with the ninth century. The ancestors of Tekla-Haymanot (*c.* 1215–1313), who later became an outstanding monastic leader in Shoa, apparently first left Tigre in that period. This family is said to have first settled in Amhara, from where it moved by stages to northern Shoa. The movement started with Tekla-Haymanot's ancestor eighteen generations before him, which takes us to the beginning of the ninth century. Most probably, the migration of this family represents a slow population movement from the old provinces in the north to the much richer areas in the south. The process also seems to be connected with the southward shift of the centre of the Christian kingdom. We also have the dominant traditions about a powerful Christian king called Dignajan, who led a strong army into the Ethiopian interior, and whose exploits are said to have reached beyond Shoa in the south. These traditions do not give any particular dates to the activities of this king. But since some versions of the story connect the king's exploits with the migration of Tekla-Haymanot's family, it is most likely that both belong to the ninth century. Together with the general picture of political and military strength transmitted by al-Ya'qūbī's description of the Christian Habasha, it appears that all these traditions add up to show that, by the second half of the ninth century, the Christian kingdom of Ethiopia had entered a new period

[1] J. S. Trimingham, *Islam in Ethiopia*, 2nd ed. (London, 1955), 51, note 1.

[2] Taddesse Tamrat, 'The Abbots of Debre Hayq, 1248–1535', *Journal of Ethiopian Studies*, 1970, **8**, 1, 87–8.

of conquest and expansion. It is most probable also that, in this period, the frontiers of the kingdom began to extend further south and they apparently reached the northern parts of the Shoan plateau.

The Christian rulers apparently continued to claim control over the areas further south during the last part of the ninth and the first years of the tenth century. This clearly brought them into conflict with the inhabitants of those areas, and some valuable contemporary references show that they were fighting desperately along the new frontier lines in the south. The tenth-century Arab writer, Ibn Ḥawqal, tells us that these wars had assumed serious proportions. A notorious queen, whose name and origins are not given, led the revolt or resistance against the Christians. On one occasion she even defeated and killed the Christian king, and she ruled 'with complete independence in her own country and the frontier areas of the territory of the *Hadani*, in the southern part of the land of the Habasha'.[1] Ibn Ḥawqal wrote his book in about AD 977, when the above-mentioned queen was still active, and he tells us elsewhere that she had assumed power about thirty years earlier.[2] This takes the period of intensive conflict back to the early 940s, the date which seems to be confirmed by another equally important and contemporary historical reference to Ethiopia.

The biographers of the Alexandrian patriarchs, Cosmas (933–42) and Filatewos (979–1003), make a reference to those troubled days in Ethiopia.[3] An Ethiopian monarch had displeased Patriarch Cosmas, who retaliated by refusing to consecrate and send Egyptian bishops for Ethiopia. As a result the seat of the metropolitan in Ethiopia had been vacant for about seventy years. The effect of the continued absence of a metropolitan in Ethiopia began to show in the decline of the number of ordained priests, and many churches were being closed down. The Egyptian hagiographer also goes on to tell us that the perfidy of the Ethiopians in defying the spiritual leadership of Alexandria brought about the wrath of God on the country, which became a victim of drought, famine and all sorts of pestilence. Moreover, a powerful and apparently non-Christian queen raised a serious revolt and led very successful campaigns against the Ethiopians, burning down churches and devastating the country. Finally, in the reign of Patriarch Filatewos, the Ethiopians repented and obtained a new Egyptian bishop through the good offices of King George of Nubia, and all was well once again.

[1] Ibn Ḥauḳal [Ḥawqal], *Configuration de la terre*, tr. J. H. Kramers and G. Wiet (Paris, 1964), I, 56.

[2] Ibid. 16.

[3] Sawirus b. al-Mukaffa, *History of the patriarchs of the Egyptian Church*, vol. II, tr. Yassa 'abd al-Masih, Aziz Suryal Atiya, and O. H. E. Burmester (Cairo, 1943–59), II, 118–20, 170–2.

The queen who led these anti-Christian wars is called the queen of the *banū al-hamwīyya*, and there seems to be no doubt that both Ibn Ḥawqal and the biographer of Filatewos are referring to the same female monarch. More than forty years ago, Conti Rossini proposed that the word *al-hamwīyya* in the title of the queen should read *al-damuta*,[1] which he suggested refers to the origins of the queen in the vast territory called Damot which extended south and south-eastwards from the Blue Nile gorge. Conti Rossini's guess is now supported by Ibn Ḥawqal's geographical treatise, recently translated by Gaston Wiet, where the queen's territories are specifically located 'in the southern part of the land of Habasha', which fits in perfectly with the general pattern of development in the medieval history of Ethiopia. The Christian kingdom, which had been reviving and re-establishing its power in the interior during the ninth century, was now confronted in the tenth by very strong resistance movements. These resistance movements were apparently led by the pagan inhabitants of the Shoan plateau, and they decisively arrested the conquest and expansion of the Christian state. This was further complicated by the renewed pressures of Islam, which began to take deeper root not only in the coastal settlements but also in the rich areas of the Ethiopian interior.

Although Aksum had been in direct communication with the Muslim religion since the days of the Prophet, it was only after the tenth century that Islam began to make a major breakthrough in the Ethiopian region. The Dahlak islands had already become Muslim at the beginning of the eighth century. Most probably, many of the other coastal settlements of the Red Sea and the Gulf of Aden also began to have their earliest Muslims at the same time. It is probable that in all these places the earliest Muslims were mainly of Arab or other non-African origin. It can also be safely assumed that, from the eighth century onwards, these coastal settlements increasingly developed their Muslim characteristics, and that they also propagated Islam among the predominantly nomadic peoples in the lowlands who were their immediate neighbours. But clearly the impact of all this proselytizing effort was minimal until the tenth century, and the immediate hinterlands of both the Red Sea and the Gulf of Aden remained pagan for a long period of time.

Trade and trade routes seem to have been the most important channels for the penetration of Islam into the Ethiopian region. After the Muslim victories over Persia and Byzantium, Muslim merchants

[1] C. Conti Rossini, *Storia d'Etiopia* (Bergamo, 1928), I, 286.

controlled the eastern trade both along the land routes and the Red Sea. And wherever these merchants operated in the Ethiopian region, Islam was gradually introduced. The Arab merchants who, according to al-Ya'qūbī, came to Habasha for trade paved the way for Islam, which they must have propagated in the market villages and particularly among their local servants and partners. Most probably, this was the origin of the early Muslim communities of which some traces have been found even in the Christian province of Tigre.[1] The Muslim communities which would later become important in the eastern foothills of the Shoan plateau also have traditions of specifically Arab origin going as far back as the ninth century. While the Dahlak islands were certainly the gateway for the founders of the Muslim families in northern Ethiopia, those of the Shoan region must have received their inspiration from Zeila, which is also mentioned by al-Ya'qūbī as an important port in the Gulf of Aden. We can thus envisage the early establishment of a number of Muslim communities along the two major trade routes leading into the interior from Dahlak and Zeila. Nevertheless, these early communities were still very weak, and did not constitute a serious danger either to the Christian kingdom or to the pagan interior of southern Ethiopia. As late as the middle of the tenth century al-Mas'ūdī tells us that 'the Muslim families who live [in the land of the Habasha] are tributary to the indigenous people'.[2] After the second half of the tenth century, however, a combination of crucial factors increased the religious and political significance of Islam in the whole of the Ethiopian region.

After the conflict with the pagan queen of the *banū al-hamwīyya*, the power of the Christian kingdom seriously declined in the interior; and certainly this was one of the important factors in the intensive movement of expansion of Islam. But, more important still, the rise of an independent Muslim power in Egypt under the Fatimids, and the subsequent revival of the Red Sea as a major channel of the eastern trade, gave an additional impetus to the growing influence of Islam in the whole region. The importance of the Red Sea as a line of communication between the Mediterranean region and the Far East had developed since Ptolemaic times. The Romans and their Byzantine successors had done their best to divert the eastern trade from going through the territories of their Persian enemies. This conflict between east and west had given the Red Sea particular importance. But after

[1] M. Schneider, 'Stèles funéraires arabes de Quiha', *Annales d'Ethiopie*, 1967, 7, 107–22.

[2] Al-Mas'ūdī, *Les prairies d'or*, ed. and tr. C. Barbier de Meynard and P. de Courteille (Paris, 1864–77), III, 34.

the Muslim conquest in the seventh century much of the area which originally belonged to Byzantium and Persia was united under Islam. From the middle of the eighth century onwards, Baghdad was the centre of this extensive Muslim empire, and all the trade routes from the east naturally tended to converge on it. The Red Sea gradually became one of the backwaters of the eastern trade. With the rise of Fatimid power in Egypt, however, the old commercial and political rivalries began to be replayed between the Fatimids in the west and the 'Abbasids in the east. The new rulers of Egypt did everything to make the Red Sea a Fatimid lake and to attract trade in their direction (see p. 19). They made sure that the governments ruling in the South Arabian peninsula were all friendly towards them. They established the new port of 'Aydhāb, where they organized naval units to police the Red Sea which now became busier and safer. As a result, the Red Sea and the Gulf of Aden began to regain their former importance and Muslim merchants started to make a much more intensive exploitation of the Ethiopian interior.

As masters of Egypt, the Fatimids could also exert considerable influence on Christian Ethiopia, which continued to import its bishops from the Alexandrian Church. There are some specific indications that they put pressure on the patriarch of Alexandria to see to it that the interests of Islam and the Muslim merchants were safeguarded in Ethiopia. They even tended to interfere in the selection of the Egyptian metropolitans sent to Ethiopia. On one occasion, in the reign of Caliph al-Mustanṣir (1035–94), an Egyptian bishop newly appointed for Ethiopia had to promise that he would build mosques on arrival in his Ethiopian diocese.[1] It is apparent, however, that this pressure was applied partly because of the reluctance of the Ethiopian kings to give freedom of public worship to the increasing number of local Muslims who naturally appealed for Fatimid intervention. This background of Fatimid protection, as well as the revival of trade in the Red Sea, seems to have enhanced the process of expansion of Islam in the Ethiopian region.

Of the two major routes into the Ethiopian interior coming from Dahlak and Zeila, the latter assumed a much greater importance, and it was in this direction that Islam was destined to play a most significant role in the history of the Ethiopian region. There seems to be no doubt that Zeila began to serve as a launching pad for Muslim influence into the interior as early as the ninth century, when it is first mentioned

[1] Sawirus, *History*, II, 347–51.

by al-Ya'qūbī. This is also clearly reflected in the traditions of origin of the earliest Muslim states in the area. A local Arabic chronicle, edited and translated by Enrico Cerulli in 1941, preserves the tradition that the first Mahzumite prince of the so-called 'sultanate of Shoa' began to rule in the last decade of the ninth century.[1] The sultanate of Shoa is the earliest Muslim political unit reported by local traditions known to us so far. The exact location of this state is impossible to define; but it seems that it included the eastern foothills of the present-day Shoan plateau, and it probably extended also east of the Awash river into the south-western reaches of the Chercher massif. Despite the above tradition of the chronicle, it is improbable that the state was actually formed as early as the ninth century. Neither al-Ya'qūbī in the same century, nor even al-Mas'ūdī and Ibn Ḥawqal in the tenth, imply the existence of such a viable Muslim community, let alone a state, in the area as far inland as the Awash valley during that early period. As we have seen above, al-Mas'ūdī actually indicates that even at the time of his visit to Zeila, the Muslims were living as the protégés of the local Habasha. What seems to be quite certain is only that some Muslim traders, probably of Arab origin, had already started visiting and probably also settling in the area by the ninth century. We have already seen above that al-Ya'qūbī describes quite an active commercial intercourse between Habasha and the neighbouring Arab countries. The same thing is reflected, about a century later, by both al-Mas'ūdī and Ibn Ḥawqal.

It can safely be imagined that the number of Arab merchants who penetrated the interior gradually increased from the tenth century onwards. An ever-increasing number of these merchants also seem to have settled along the major trade-routes. These Muslims certainly did not have their own political units as yet. Rather, they seem to have lived under the old pagan rulers of the region, with whom they had very close associations and over whom they gradually acquired considerable influence. It is interesting to note here that the above-mentioned chronicle of the sultanate of Shoa begins its narrative by reporting the death of a local ruler, 'Queen Badit, daughter of Maya in the year [AD 1063]'.[2] It is most probable that 'Queen Badit, daughter of Maya' had established some relations with the Arab world through the Muslim merchants settled in her territory. Among these Muslim settlers in the Ethiopian interior, there may have been some Muslim preachers

[1] Enrico Cerulli, 'Il sultanato dello Scioa nel secolo XIII secondo un nuovo documento storico', *Rassegna di studi Etiopici*, 1947, 1, 5–14.

[2] Ibid. 10.

who started to convert more and more of the local people to Islam. However, even the chronicle of the sultanate of Shoa does not report any major conversions in the interior until the beginning of the twelfth century. Then, in the year 1108, it is reported that there took place 'the conversion of *Gbbah* to Islam, in the reign of Sultan Harba'ir'.[1] It has not been possible to give a secure identification of the area (or people) called *Gbbah*. But Trimingham has recently made an interesting suggestion that the term may refer to a people who were probably ancestral to those later known as Argobba.[2] This is a very tempting suggestion and, geographically, it makes very good sense. The Argobba were a Semitic-speaking group who lived in the eastern foothills of the Shoan plateau and in the Harar area. Their Semitic language also makes them a very good candidate for the proposed identification, because an analysis of the names of the princes in the chronicle has also convinced Cerulli that an Ethiopian Semitic language was spoken in the sultanate of Shoa. In the fourteenth century, the Arab historian al-'Umarī also tells us that a local Semitic language was spoken in the kingdom of Ifat, which, as we shall see, later replaced the sultanate of Shoa. Thus, until a better solution is available, Trimingham's proposal to identify the *Gbbah* with Argobba seems to be satisfactory. Immediately after the conversion of *Gbbah*, the chronicle mentions another significant event, namely a conflict between the Amhara and a state which was most probably the sultanate of Shoa. This is the earliest record of a conflict between the Christian Amhara and the expanding Muslim communities in the area, and the chronicle reports that 'the Amhara fled from the land of *Werjih* in 1128'.[3] The *Werjih* were a pastoral people, and in the fourteenth century they occupied the Awash valley east of the Shoan plateau. But what is particularly important at this juncture is to underline the rapid succession of three very crucial events in the history of the region. First, we have here a report of the definite formation of a Muslim sultanate of Shoa, certainly at the beginning of the twelfth century. Secondly, this sultanate is clearly seen actively promoting the expansion of Islam, as in the conversion of the *Gbbah* 'in the reign of Sultan Harbair', as reported by the chronicle. And finally, we see here the beginnings, in the second quarter of the twelfth century, of the long struggle between Islam and Christianity in the Ethiopian region.

[1] Ibid. 10.
[2] Trimingham, *Islam in Ethiopia*, 62.
[3] Cerulli, 'Il Sultanato', 10.

CHRISTIAN ETHIOPIA, *c.* 1000–1150

It has already been shown how the Christian kingdom again started to decline after a brief period of revival in the ninth and early tenth centuries. After the military reverses which they suffered in their conflict with the queen of the *banū al-hamwīyya* (*c.* 940–80), the Christians apparently withdrew from the territories they had acquired in the south during the ninth century. Their capital city was no longer Aksum but Kubar, which was located further south, probably in the region of southern Tigre and Angot. No contemporary historical records have survived in Ethiopia about the period before the rise of the Zagwe dynasty in the middle of the twelfth century. There are, however, some invaluable references to the country in the history of the patriarchate of Alexandria, which gives short glimpses into the life of the Ethiopians at that time. The Ethiopians clung to the Christian legacy which they had inherited from Aksum. They preserved their spiritual connections with the Alexandrian patriarchate and continued to import Egyptian bishops from Cairo. The old monasteries and churches established in southern Eritrea, throughout Tigre, and in the Agaw districts of Wag, Lasta and Angot continued to be the spiritual powerhouses of Ethiopian Christianity. These monasteries and churches provided the country with a firm Christian leadership, and their influence on the lives of the people was considerable. The Ethiopian Church became the most important symbol of the identity and independence of the Ethiopians, and it developed a biblical and Christian ideology which kept the indomitable spirit of the Christians still intact throughout the long history of the country. This ideology consisted in the gradual self-identification of the Ethiopian Christian nation with the ancient Israel of the Old Testament. The beleaguered state of the Christian highlands, surrounded by hostile pagan and Muslim neighbours, made the identification a relatively easy process. Here, in the broken valleys and on the inaccessible mountains of northern Ethiopia, were the chosen people of God, the 'second Israel'. By virtue of its ready acceptance of Christ, the Messiah, this 'second Israel' had replaced the 'first Israel', which had forfeited its favoured position in the eyes of God because of its rejection of His only Son. The almost complete isolation of Ethiopia from the Christian world made the society highly introspective, and it drew all its cultural and political inspiration from the early Christian and biblical traditions which it had inherited and which it tenaciously kept intact. The Ethiopians then began deliberately to imitate religious, cultural, social and political institutions from the Old Testament. It is most probable that many of the biblical elements in Ethiopian Christian life and worship owe their origin to such deliberate imitations during the early medieval period, and not to any as yet unsubstantiated pre-Christian Judaic influences on the early history of Aksum.

The development of Old Testament practices and the identification with Israel is reflected in a number of interesting references from the ninth century onwards. In the first half of that century, the Ethiopians forced an Egyptian bishop, Yohannes, to return to Cairo because he was suspected of not having been circumcised. He incurred the suspicion when he was merely trying to explain St Paul's teaching on circumcision.[1] The Egyptian bishops also had difficulty in imposing monogamy on the Ethiopians, who kept many wives and concubines in the best tradition of the patriarchs and kings of ancient Israel. Whereas both circumcision and polygamy could be traced to pre-Christian practices in Cushitic Ethiopia itself, the tenacity with which Ethiopian kings and their Christian subjects clung to them was largely due to the existence of these practices in the Old Testament, which they had received as an integral part of the Christian tradition. This is in fact very clear from a letter which an Egyptian bishop, Sawiros, solicited the Alexandrian patriarch to write to Ethiopia. Sawiros had worked very hard to persuade his Ethiopian congregation to be monogamous, and to facilitate his work in Ethiopia he requested the patriarch to write to the Ethiopians 'forbidding them from observing the customs of the Old Testament'.[2] These customs to which Sawiros alluded probably also included dietary prohibitions, ritual cleanliness, as well as the strict observance of the Sabbath, which was to remain the basis for endless disputations between the Ethiopian Church and the Alexandrian patriarchate for many centuries.[3] In much the same way as the more recent development of Zionist movements in many local African churches, the Ethiopian Church had, by the ninth century, drawn considerable inspiration from the Old Testament, which it always used as a strong bulwark for preserving its independence from Alexandria. This permeated the liturgy of the church as well as the daily life of the individual Ethiopian. The music of the church and its ritual dancing in front of the Ark, for instance, are clearly reminiscent of many similar scenes in the books of the Old Testament. All these seem

[1] Sawirus, 'History of the patriarchs of the Egyptian Church', vol. I, tr. B. T. A. Evetts, in *Patrologia Orientalis*, 1915, **10**, 508–11. [2] Sawirus, *History*, II, 330.

[3] Taddesse Tamrat, *Church and state in Ethiopia, 1270–1527* (Oxford, 1972), 207–31.

to have developed in this crucial period when Christian Ethiopia was cut off from other Christian areas and left alone to its own devices. But the highest expression of this dependence on the Old Testament is the gradual identification of the various peoples of Christian Ethiopia with the twelve tribes of ancient Israel. As part of the same process, the family of the monarchs was also identified with that of kings David and Solomon; and the priestly families in Ethiopia also began to trace their origin from the High Priests of Israel. It is most interesting that it is also in the early tenth century that we begin to have the earliest references to these traditions which are the first versions of the legend of the queen of Sheba, and which later developed into the well-known *Kebra Nagast*.[1] The hagiographer of Patriarch Cosmas (920–32) describes Christian Ethiopia on one occasion as 'Abyssinia which is a vast country, namely, the kingdom of Saba from which the queen of the South came to Solomon, the Son of David the King'.[2] These traditional connections between Ethiopia and Israel gradually became more and more elaborate until we reach the final versions of Abū Ṣāliḥ and the Ethiopic *Kebra Nagast*. According to Abū Ṣāliḥ, who wrote at the beginning of the thirteenth century,

> The Abyssinians possess also the Ark of the Covenant, in which are the two tables of stone, inscribed by the finger of God with the commandments which he ordained for the children of Israel . . . And the Ark is attended and carried by a large number of Israelites descended from the family of the prophet David.[3]

The possession of the Ark of the Covenant is also one of the most basic claims made in the *Kebra Nagast* which, however, further embellishes the story and derives the very origin of the Aksumite state from the legendary union between King Solomon and the queen of Sheba. By the fourteenth century, when the *Kebra Nagast* was finally translated into Ethiopic, the equation with Israel had already been made, and the term *Siyon* began to be used in reference to the Christian kingdom,[4] just as the term Mount Zion was used in ancient Israel.[5] This biblical identity has characterized Christian Ethiopia throughout the ages, and it is the result of a vital cultural process which started in the early medieval period of Ethiopian history.

[1] C. Bezold, *Kebra Nagast* (Munich, 1909). [2] Sawirus, *History*, II, 118.

[3] Abū Ṣaliḥ, *The churches and monasteries of Egypt and some neighbouring countries*, tr. B. T. A. Evetts (Oxford, 1895), 287–8.

[4] J. Perruchon, 'Histoire des guerres d'Amda Seyon, roi d'Ethiopie', *Journal Asiatique*, 1889, **14**, 281, 287, 301.

[5] A. R. Johnson, *Sacral kingship in ancient Israel* (Cardiff, 1955), 27–9, 61–4.

Thus, the picture that emerges of Christian Ethiopia during the whole of the eleventh and the first half of the twelfth centuries is one of a religiously homogeneous state of which the territories included only the central and southern highlands of what is today Eritrea, the whole of Tigre, and the mountainous areas of Wag, Lasta, Angot and Amhara. Its eastern limits were conterminous with the edge of the Ethiopian plateau which drops steeply into the Danakil lowlands. The Tekeze river in the north, and the upper waters of the eastern tributaries of the Blue Nile further south, formed its western boundary. In the south, Christian hegemony probably reached in that period only as far as the headwaters of the river Wenchit. Within this compact highland area ruled the Christian monarchs of Ethiopia, who claimed direct descent from the ancient kings of Aksum, and whom the legend of the queen of Sheba had lately characterized as the distant offspring of King Solomon of Israel. The kingdom was probably divided into a number of smaller principalities headed by hereditary rulers who paid homage to the *negus* who kept his court at Kubar. This is precisely how al-Yaʿqūbī described the kingdom of the *nejashi* in the ninth century, and there is no doubt that the same structure was maintained, even if on a much smaller scale, during the tenth, eleventh and twelfth centuries. Ever since the court had moved from Aksum to Kubar, the areas in the immediate neighbourhood of the new royal settlement seem to have assumed particular importance. Among these, the nearby Agaw districts were probably an important source of manpower for the kingdom in that period, and the inhabitants of these districts were soon to become the most dominant section of the Christian population.

The Agaw constitute a major part of the speakers of Cushitic languages. The exact position of their language in relation to the other branches of this family is defined by linguists as Central Cushitic. And the Agaw language group is itself divided into a number of dialects of which the distribution extends from as far north as Bogos in central Eritrea to as far south-west as *Agawmeder* in north-western Gojjam. It is apparent that the Agaw language area originally included the whole of the Ethiopian plateau north of present-day Shoa. But even after the long period of semitization, which started at least in the first millennium BC, the Agaw language continued to be spoken in the districts of Avergele, Bur, Wag, Lasta and beyond the rivers Tekeze and the Blue Nile in the west. The whole Agaw area east of the Tekeze river was converted to Christianity during the Aksumite period; but, except for the use of the Ethiopic language in the liturgy and worship of the church, the inhabitants of this area remained predominantly Agaw in their linguistic affiliations. Semitic expansion southwards to Amhara (and probably also to the areas further south where other Semitic languages were spoken) bypassed the Agaw stronghold between the Selleri and the Tekeze rivers. This expansion was apparently effected through a narrow corridor which formed the high ridge separating the basins of the Tekeze and the Awash. But when the capital of the Christian monarchs shifted south of Aksum to Kubar, the ancient Agaw stronghold in the upper basin in the Tekeze suddenly became the very centre of the kingdom. Large numbers of the Agaw were probably recruited for military and other services in the royal court, and the process of assimilation and partial semitization was further intensified. Inter-marriages between the family of the *negus* and those of the Agaw hereditary rulers probably took place, and the Agaw were thus brought into the political and military power structure of the Christian kingdom. Through such slow developments, for the historical reconstruction of which we only have very meagre traditions, the Agaw finally took control of the Christian state and established a new dynasty of their own, which has been known in Ethiopian history as the Zagwe dynasty, which only means the 'dynasty of the Agaw'.

THE ZAGWE DYNASTY, *c.* 1150–1270

From a very close investigation of the few references to the period immediately before the rise of the new dynasty, one can clearly detect a definite revival in the power of the Christian state. It seems that, by the second half of the eleventh century, the Christian kingdom had not only outlived the disastrous effects of its conflicts with the queen of the *banū al-hamwīyya*, referred to above, but it had also entered a new period of conquest and expansion. References in the *History of the Patriarchs of Alexandria* indicate that the Ethiopian monarchs successfully defied Fatimid attempts to reduce Christian Ethiopia into a distant sphere of influence. In about 1080, the Egyptian bishop, Sawiros, secured nomination as metropolitan of Ethiopia by promising the Fatimid caliph that he would pursue and encourage pro-Muslim policies in Ethiopia and that he would also send large tributes to Cairo every year. When he attempted to implement these promises in Ethiopia, the bishop was humiliated and put in jail for some time. When the Fatimids threatened to destroy the churches of Egypt as a reprisal for this insult, the Ethiopian monarch is said to have replied that, if any church in Egypt was molested, he would himself dismantle the Ka'aba in Mecca. Regardless of whether this report is a mere legend or a historical fact, its inclusion in the biography of an Alexandrian patriarch certainly indicates that Christian Egyptians had started to look upon Ethiopia as a champion of their church. In fact, the patriarchate was to continue to use Christian Ethiopia as a trump card in its relations with the Muslim sultans of Egypt throughout the fourteenth and fifteenth centuries. But since this is first reported towards the end of the eleventh century, it certainly indicates a definite revival in the power of the kingdom at the time. There are also tantalizing reports which seem to show that the frontiers of both church and state had once again started to expand during the beginning of the twelfth century. An interesting passage in the Arabic chronicle of the sultanate of Shoa, which reports that there was a conflict between the Amhara (Christians) and the Muslims in the area of the eastern foothills of the Shoan plateau in the year 1128, has already been referred to. This seems to be an indication of a new Christian attempt to expand southwards during that period. We also have other traditions of a slow movement of isolated Christian families towards the Shoan plateau. One such tradition has it that the family of Tekla-Haymanot (*c.* 1215–1313) settled in north-eastern Shoa ten generations before him. This takes us back to the second half of the eleventh and the first years of the twelfth centuries. The *History of the Patriarchs of Alexandria* also seems to imply a period of Christian expansion in an invaluable reference to the rather strained relations between Ethiopia and Patriarch Gabri'el (1131–45).[1] It is reported there that the Ethiopian monarch first asked the Egyptian metropolitan in Ethiopia to appoint an additional bishop for the country. When this was refused, the king wrote to both Patriarch Gabri'el and the Egyptian sultan asking for the appointment of more bishops for his kingdom. The Egyptian chronicles show that the request was eventually denied, but the desperate attempt of the Ethiopians clearly indicates that they had begun to acquire more extensive territory, for the evangelization of which they needed additional bishops and clerics. This interpretation fits in with the general historical context of the period, and we have other references to Ethiopian monarchs addressing similar requests to Cairo when their growing empire became too unwieldy for a single metropolitan. Thus, it seems very clear that the end of the eleventh and the beginning of the

[1] E. Renaudot, *Historia patriarcharum Alexandronum* (Paris, 1717), 510–13.

twelfth centuries saw a definite movement of revival and Christian expansion. This was further enhanced by the rise to power of the new and very energetic 'dynasty of the Agaw'.

We will perhaps never know for certain the exact circumstances under which the new dynasty arose. But it seems very clear now that it came to power towards the middle of the twelfth century and lasted for about one hundred and fifty years.[1] The founder of the dynasty was a local prince of Bugna, in Lasta, perhaps related by marriage to the preceding ruling house as some traditions have it. The first definite result of the dynastic change was the establishment of yet another capital at Adefa in Bugna, not very far from the present-day site of the town of Lalibela. This was located at the heart of Agaw country and it was from here that the new rulers set about rebuilding the Christian kingdom of Ethiopia. Because of lack of contemporary sources, the early history of this period is rather obscure. But the increasing amount of traditional material which has recently come to light and the few references in the *History of the Patriarchs of Alexandria*, as well as the rich architectural remains of the period, enable us to provide a skeletal history of the dynasty.

A crucial development, which was to be of utmost importance in the subsequent history of Ethiopia, was the great enthusiasm with which the Zagwe kings began to look outwards and to strengthen their communications with Egypt and the Holy Land. In the hagiographical traditions about his life, the third Zagwe king, Yimrihane-Kristos, is said to have written to the Egyptian sultan asking for building materials in return for Ethiopian gold, and the request is said to have been granted. The same Zagwe king is said to have built the beautiful church of Yimrihane-Kristos, not very far from his capital Adefa, and which has been named after him. Many foreign ecclesiastics described as 'Romans' are said to have come to his kingdom, and their traditional tombs in this church and in the neighbouring districts are still treated with much awe and respect. Another interesting tradition is that in the year 1189, the famous Egyptian ruler, Ṣalāḥ al-Dīn, gave the Ethiopians a number of churches in Jerusalem when he expelled the Latins from the Holy City. This seems to have increased the number of Ethiopian pilgrims to Palestine along the old caravan routes from northern Ethiopia to the Nile Valley, which were apparently used very frequently at the time. Between the years 1205 and 1209, for instance, a number of official delegations were exchanged between Cairo

[1] Taddesse Tamrat, *Church and state*, 53–7.

and Adefa, during the patriarchate of Abba Yohannes (1189–1216).[1] The zeal with which the Zagwe began to strengthen their ties with Egypt and with the Holy Land seems to have left permanent imprints in the literary and architectural history of the period. Cerulli has suggested that the close contacts which the Zagwe inaugurated with the eastern Mediterranean region may have resulted in some literary activities in the form of translations and original compositions.[2] Conti Rossini also thought that the literary developments of the fourteenth and fifteenth centuries must have started during the Zagwe era, which he called 'the dawn of a new period in Ethiopian literature'.[3] But the extent of the Zagwe fascination with the Holy Land is particularly seen in the building of a series of underground churches at a site near the capital city of Adefa.

All of these churches have traditionally been attributed to the greatest Zagwe king, Lalibela, and the site has later been called after him. Although we do not know the dates of the beginning and the end of his reign, it is certain that Lalibela was on the throne in 1205 and 1225. A hagiographical tradition about his life reports that, before he acceded to the throne, Lalibela was miraculously flown to Jerusalem, where Christ appeared to him and guided him in his tour of the Holy City. At the same time, the Saviour intimated to the Zagwe prince that he would soon reign over his people, and instructed him to build a second Jerusalem in Ethiopia. On his return to Ethiopia, Lalibela became king, and tried to carry out his divine instructions with the help of the 'Angels of God', who served him as masons and ordinary labourers. Whatever the circumstances under which they were built, we now have a set of eleven subterranean churches artistically carved out of the living rock at the site of Lalibela. Ten of the churches are built in two groups, consisting of six and four churches, respectively. A small stream runs between the two hills under which these two groups of churches were built, and it has been named *Yordanos*, after the river Jordan in the Holy Land. The eleventh church is built as a separate unit on its own. The deliberate attempt by the builders of these churches to emulate the Holy City of Jerusalem is very clear from the names given to some of the major sites and churches. At one end of the first group of churches is a high spot called 'Calvary', under which the 'tomb of Adam' is said to be located. Directly below this spot, beautifully chiselled out of

[1] J. Perruchon, 'Extrait de la vie d'Abba Jean, 74e patriarche d'Alexandrie, relatif à l'Abyssinie', *Revue Sémitique*, 1898, **6**, 267–71, 365–72; 1899, **7**, 76–85.

[2] Enrico Cerulli, *Storia della letteratura etiopica* (Rome, 1956), 35–7.

[3] Conti Rossini, *Storia d'Etiopia*, I, 306.

the rock, is the church of 'Golgotha', in which there is a crypt at one of the corners representing the 'tomb of Christ'. The Zagwe king had reproduced a second Jerusalem in the highlands of Ethiopia, and traditional celebrations were held annually on these sites re-enacting the baptism, the passion and crucifixion of Christ.

Regarding the architects and builders of these churches, various theories have been offered, most of them favouring non-Ethiopian workmanship. The traditions referred to above about the presence of foreign Christians in Ethiopia at the time have tended to be used as confirmation of this conclusion. It must be remembered, however, that the architectural forms and artistic details of all these churches are based on those which are seen on the Aksumite steles, and on the palaces and churches which have been dug out in the Aksumite region. The architectural continuity between the Aksumite and the Zagwe monuments is so close and obvious that only architects deeply imbued with the building traditions of Aksum could have engineered the rock churches of the Zagwe period. A major factor which encouraged the conclusion that non-Ethiopians were responsible for the Lalibela churches was the fact that, until very recently, little or nothing was known about other rock-hewn churches in the area between Aksum and Lalibela. Now, however, literally hundreds of such churches, tucked into inaccessible cliffs and mountain tops, have been discovered throughout central Tigre.[1] Since 1966 attention has been focused on these rock-hewn churches of Tigre, and, although the chronology of these monuments is not yet well defined, it appears that the monolithic churches of the Zagwe period may have been the last phase of a long architectural tradition in Christian Ethiopia itself.

Besides their obvious patronage of Ethiopic literature and Christian arts, the Zagwe kings also seem to have started to expand the territories of the Christian kingdom. There is an eyewitness report that the Zagwe had a large army, estimated in 1209 as consisting of more than 60,000 soldiers.[2] The same document also indicates that the Zagwe monarch who reigned in 1209 led successful expeditions outside his domains. Local traditions about the same period seem to show that the Zagwe had launched a policy of expansion into the pagan areas to the west and south. They apparently made an attempt to control Gojjam, with the local Agaw rulers of which they seem to have had a number of armed conflicts. The extent of the Zagwe success in Gojjam is not

[1] Tewolde Medhin Joseph, 'Introduction générale aux églises monolithes du Tigrai', *Proceedings of the Third International Congress of Ethiopian Studies* (Addis Ababa, 1969), I, 83–98.

[2] Perruchon, 'Extrait', 83.

known. But Beke recorded in the 1840s local traditions among the Agaw of northern Gojjam that their ancestors came from Lasta. Although there are no chronological indications in these traditions, it may be that they refer to the earliest Zagwe attempts to expand into the area. From a close look at the traditions of the church, it is also apparent that the earliest Christian breakthrough into the region between the upper Tekeze and Lake Tana was made during the Zagwe period, to which, for instance, the foundation of the island monastery of Tana Qirqos seems to belong. We also have an important tradition of a larger Zagwe expedition into medieval Damot, south of the Shoan region. It is in this southerly direction, particularly in Shoa, that persistent allusions are made to the establishment of Zagwe political power. We have seen above that some isolated family genealogies indicate early Christian settlement in Shoa in the late eleventh and early twelfth centuries. It seems that this southward movement was further enhanced by the reviving power of the Christian kingdom under the Zagwe monarchs. Traces of early Christian settlements in northern Shoa, extending as far south as the river Muger in the west and Kesem in the east, are numerous in the local Christian traditions about that period. The most significant of all these traditions is the story of the Egyptian monk, known in Ethiopia as Gebre-Menfas-Qeddus ('the servant of the Holy Ghost'). He is said to have come from his country during the reign of King Lalibela (early thirteenth century), and settled on the top of Ziqwala, a crater mountain which is located about thirty miles (approx. fifty km) south-east of Addis Ababa. His still unpublished hagiography clearly indicates that the area was at that time the common frontier of Christianity, Islam and paganism, and that Gebre-Menfas-Qeddus preached the gospel among the local inhabitants. The places where this Egyptian monk is believed to have preached probably constituted the southernmost area reached by the Christians in the early thirteenth century.

There seems to be no doubt that the territories of the Zagwe kingdom were more extensive than those of the immediately preceding period. Zagwe control of northern Ethiopia was very firm; the land between the upper Tekeze, the Bashilo and Lake Tana had been brought under Christian rule as part of Amharaland; and all the Christian communities as far south as the sources of the rivers Awash and Kesem paid homage to the Zagwe kings in Adefa. Moreover, what were essentially Agaw, but definitely non-Christian, territories of Simien, Dembya and Gojjam had also come under the Zagwe sphere of influence. What is more important is that the Zagwe kingdom had, by the middle of the thirteenth century, begun to share the benefits of the lucrative trade which was handled by predominantly Muslim merchants along the caravan routes running from the Gulf of Aden into the rich Ethiopian region.

It is most probable that, during the whole period until the middle of the thirteenth century, the Christian kingdom depended entirely on the caravan routes coming from the north, which followed two major branches. The first of these was the long and arduous route which left northern Ethiopia, passed through the Beja country to ʿAydhāb and joined the main pilgrim road, which ran to Qus on the Nile. This route is attested by a number of Arabic and local sources, and it was mainly used by royal envoys to Egypt and by Ethiopian pilgrims going to the Holy Land. The second major road came from the mainland opposite the Dahlak islands and constituted the most vital line of communication which Christian Ethiopia had with the surrounding Muslim world. Dahlak had become Muslim in the beginning of the eighth century, and it was an important outpost of the Muslim empire, and one used by both Umayyad and ʿAbbasid rulers as a place of exile for delinquent officials. But, at the beginning of the tenth century, Dahlak seems to have rebelled against ʿAbbasid rule, and al-Yaʿqūbī later describes it as 'the island of the *nejashi*', a title which he gave to the Christian ruler of Ethiopia.[1] It is impossible to define in precise terms what actually the relations were between Dahlak and its Christian Ethiopian overlord. Other historical references from the tenth to the middle of the twelfth centuries indicate, however, that there were special relations between the Dahlak islands and the turbulent kingdom of the Yemen on the other side of the Red Sea.

The Yemen had declared its independence from the ʿAbbasid caliphate under a new local dynasty founded by a certain Muḥammad b. Ziyād (818–59), who was originally sent by Caliph al-Ma'mūn (813–33) to rule the region on his behalf. Ziyād built the city of Zebid, where he made his capital, and he was at first able to rule over both the highland and the coastal (Tihama) districts of south Arabia, including Hadhramaut and Aden. Already in his own lifetime, however, the mountainous districts, of which Sana was the most important centre, had slipped out of his control, and endless conflicts took place between his descendants and the many successive dynasties which emerged in highland Yemen.

[1] Al-Yaʿqūbī, *Historiae*, ed. T. Houtsma (Leiden, 1883), 1, 219.

But, for our own purposes, it will suffice to focus attention on the rulers of Zebid, whose influence, except for some brief periods, was limited to the Tihama on the coast including Aden. It is apparent that, ever since its emergence, the Ziyād dynasty had established special relations with Dahlak. Al-Ya'qūbī gives Dahlak as the only port on the Ethiopian coast of the Red Sea, and most of the Arab merchants he mentions in the area probably came from the Yemeni kingdom. Later, al-Mas'ūdī tells us that there were special arrangements between the Ziyadid rulers of the Yemen and the Habasha, and that Dahlak was regularly visited by Yemeni boats carrying merchants and rich merchandise.[1] Ibn Ḥawqal is more precise about the relations between Dahlak and the Ziyadid princes, who received 'from the ruler of the Dahlak islands presents consisting of black slaves, amber, panther skins of the best quality, and other objects'.[2] For the same period of the tenth century, a local Yemeni historian, Umarā (d. 1174), reports that the Ziyadid princes collected 'a tribute imposed upon the ruler of the city of Dahlak, comprising, among others, 1000 head of slaves whereof 500 were Abyssinian and Nubian female slaves'.[3]

It is not certain if one can deduce from these notes a direct Yemeni hegemony over the Dahlak islands. Except for the Yemeni historian Umarā, who says that the tributes were 'imposed', al-Mas'ūdī only mentions the existence of special 'treaty relationships' between the two countries, and Ibn Ḥawqal states simply that Dahlak sent its presents to Zebid 'on the basis of an [old] custom'. It is apparent that the attitude of Dahlak was one of deference to the much richer and stronger kingdom of the Ziyadids, which it furnished with a regular supply of the highly priced Habasha slaves. It seems very clear that it was the considerable volume of the slave trade which tended to give an impression of a particularly close relationship between the two countries. This becomes very clear in the eleventh and early twelfth centuries, when the Habasha slaves disposed of their Ziyadid masters and established their own dynasty at Zebid for a very uneasy period of over a century.[4] The Habasha rulers of Zebid fought endless wars among themselves and against other Arab princes, who sometimes defeated and expelled them from the Tihama. On such occasions, they retreated to the Dahlak islands, which they used as a strong base against their Arab rivals. Large numbers of Ethiopian slaves were exported through Dahlak to the Yemen. This was reflected in the generally dark complexion

[1] Al-Mas'ūdī, *Les prairies d'or*, III, 34–5.
[2] Ibn Ḥauḳal, *Configuration*, I, 22.
[3] Umarā, *Yaman, its early medieval history*, tr. H. C. Kay (London, 1892), 8.
[4] Ibid. 14–117.

of the Tihama population, as Umarā commented in the twelfth century: 'The Arabs of Tihama beget children by black concubines, and . . . a black skin was common to both slave and free.'[1] Although it is often impossible to tell the exact area of origin of these slaves, some are explicitly said to have been taken from as far inland as the leading Christian provinces of Tigre and Amhara. Some of these later assumed considerable importance as religious and political leaders in the Yemeni kingdom. This regular traffic between the Ethiopian and Yemeni coasts always made the relationship between the two very close.

The uneasy and interrupted Habasha slave dynasty of Zebid came to an end in 1131 when the last Habasha ruler died. A major factor in the downfall of this dynasty was the increasing Egyptian presence in the Red Sea, which was to be dominated by the successive Fatimid and Ayyubid rulers of Egypt until the middle of the thirteenth century. Highland Yemen had always been the home of dissidents, and it was particularly infested with 'Alids. The governors sent from Baghdad by the caliphs never succeeded in establishing orthodoxy there, and when the Fatimid dynasty established itself in Egypt, the particularly 'Alid sympathies of the region tended to favour Egyptian hegemony. The meticulous organization of the Fatimid propaganda machine further enhanced this development. The most serious and open declaration in favour of Fatimid rule over the Yemen came from 'Alī b. Muḥammad Sulaihi, who had created a dynasty of his own in highland Yemen in the 1030s. Sulaihi and his successors entered into a protracted conflict with the Habasha slave dynasty, a conflict which lasted until the advent of the Ayyubids, who effectively brought to an end both the pro-Fatimid Sulaihi dynasty and the last elements of the Habasha rulers of Zebid. It is apparent that, throughout the period of increasing Fatimid influence in the Red Sea, the inhabitants of Dahlak followed a careful policy of non-alignment. There is no doubt that they gave shelter to the Habasha princes of Zebid, who were fighting against the pro-Fatimid Sulaihi. They continued to do this right down to the end of the Fatimid period, even though some of the Habasha princes sometimes misused their hospitality and were 'practising treachery against the Prince of Dahlak'.[2] At the same time Dahlak also showed enough deference to the Fatimid rulers of Egypt, about which there are some specific references. In the reign of Caliph al-Mustanṣir (1035–94), we have a report that the ruler of Dahlak deported to Egypt a Coptic monk, Abdun, who had created a serious misunderstanding between

[1] Ibid. 36. [2] Ibid. 82.

the caliph and the Patriarch Cyril (1077–92). Abdun was first relieved of all his valuable belongings and then deported to Cairo, where he was executed in 1086. Some thirty years later, in 1119/20, Dahlak even entertained important Fatimid envoys sent from Cairo to Yemen on official business. This cautious policy always characterized the attitude of the rulers of Dahlak, and it seems to have precluded direct Egyptian hostilities against the islands throughout the Fatimid, Ayyubid and Mamluk periods.

The large number of Arabic inscriptions collected on the Dahlak islands indicates that their Muslim inhabitants led a rich cultural life, and that they were organized into an effective sultanate, which had its most glorious period between the eleventh and the middle of the thirteenth centuries. This was precisely the period during which the Dahlak islands were perhaps the only commercial outlet for the Christian kingdom of Ethiopia, which always constituted their most vital hinterland. There are no contemporary historical references which help us to determine the full extent of the commercial activities going on between the Dahlak islands and the interior of northern Ethiopia. The most important items of trade, which are profusely attested to in the sources, are the Nubian and Habasha slaves for which Dahlak was a major entrepôt. Ibn Ḥawqal mentions the importance of hides and skins in the trade of the area with the Yemen.[1] Perhaps some foodstuffs consisting of fruit, grain and cattle were also supplied to the Yemeni ports. But there is no doubt that the vitality which the sultanate of Dahlak had until the middle of the thirteenth century depended to a very large extent on its monopoly of all the external trade of the Ethiopian interior. When, in the second half of the thirteenth century, the centre of the Christian kingdom began to shift further south, where more prosperous Muslim sultanates had emerged in the hinterland of Zeila, the Dahlak islands drifted to a sudden and increasing insignificance.

Throughout the long period since the early eighth century, the Dahlak islands do not seem to have been of much importance for the propagation of Islam in the Ethiopian interior. The Christian Church in northern Ethiopia was very well established, and it made the preaching of Islam a difficult, if not an impossible, task. Muslim merchants were no doubt tolerated, and they probably moved about freely throughout the Christian kingdom on commercial affairs. They were also apparently allowed to establish communities of their own along

[1] Ibn Ḥauḳal, *Configuration*, I, 54.

the major trade-routes and in some vital centres of commerce. There are traces of such communities, for instance, near Qiha, in Enderta, where ruins and Arabic inscriptions have been found.[1] Of the sixteen inscriptions from the Qiha region which have been studied, ten bear specific dates which range between the beginning of the eleventh and the middle of the twelfth centuries. This was precisely the period in which, as has been seen above, contacts with the Yemen were close and regular, and it is particularly interesting to note that many of the persons named in the inscriptions seem to have had Yemeni origins. But, unlike the areas further south in Shoa, Ifat, Dawaro and Bali, the existence of such early Muslim communities did not result in the formation of later Muslim political units. This was certainly because of the strength of the Christian Church in northern Ethiopia. In fact, it seems very clear that the presence of Muslims in the area was tolerated only because of their vital role as long distance merchants, and they were actively persecuted whenever they attempted to proselytize. In comparison to its great importance as the only commercial outlet of the Christian interior for many centuries, the role of Dahlak in the expansion of Islam was minimal indeed. And, in about the middle of the thirteenth century, when the Zagwe kingdom began to use the caravan routes from Zeila through its southern provinces of Amhara and Shoa, Dahlak lost even the old commercial monopoly it had long had over the interior of northern Ethiopia.

The earliest documentary evidence we have for the direct use of the Zeila routes during the Zagwe period comes from the library of the island monastery in Lake Hayq. In a late-fifteenth-century manuscript there is a colophon which relates the emigration of a wealthy Jew called Yosef from Aden 'during the reign of the Zagwe (kings)'. Yosef settled in Amhara, and his descendants of the ninth generation presented the manuscript to the monastery of Hayq towards the beginning of the sixteenth century.[2] This takes us back to the second half of the thirteenth century, when Yosef came from Aden, most probably via Zeila. From that period onwards the Zeila route was certainly the most important channel of communication for Christian Ethiopia, of which the centre had moved further south to Amhara and Shoa under the new 'Solomonic' dynasty which emerged in 1270.

[1] C. Pansera, 'Quattro stele musulmane presso Uogher Hariba nell Enderta', in C. Conti Rossini, ed., *Studi Etiopici* (Rome, 1945). Schneider, 'Stèles funéraires', 107–22.

[2] Taddesse Tamrat, 'The Abbots', 112–14.

THE RISE OF THE 'SOLOMONIC' DYNASTY

It seems that, throughout the period of its existence, the Zagwe dynasty was overshadowed by the general belief that its power had been first acquired through an illegitimate act of usurpation. This belief that the Zagwe monarchs were 'usurpers' is first echoed in an interesting reference in the hagiographical accounts about the reign of Patriarch Yohannes (1146–67). The patriarch received a letter from an Ethiopian king requesting him to replace the aged metropolitan, Mika'el, with a younger Egyptian bishop. The patriarch declined the request on the grounds that a metropolitan could not be replaced while he was still alive. The hagiographer also adds that the old age of Metropolitan Mika'el was *not the real reason* for the Ethiopian request. The real reason was that the king ruling Christian Ethiopia at that time had acquired power through illegitimate means and the metropolitan had refused to recognize him.[1] Since the letter of the Ethiopian king was also addressed to the Egyptian vizier 'Alī b. al-Ṣallār, who died in 1153, it must have been written sometime between 1146, the year of Yohannes's accession to the patriarchal seat, and 1153. Conti Rossini has used this important incident for his dating of the Zagwe rise to power. This dating fits in very well with the local tradition, which reports that the Zagwe ruled for a total of 133 years before they were deposed in 1270, as well as with the short list of only seven monarchs who actually reigned during the whole period.[2]

Thus, there is convincing evidence that the Zagwe were at first believed to have 'usurped' power from an earlier, 'legitimate' dynasty. It may also be true that there was 'a strong resistance . . . at first offered to the new dynasty by the clergy under Abuna Mika'el', as Trimingham puts it.[3] It is in fact apparent that some elements of such resistance were kept alive until the very end of Zagwe rule. The gradual identification of the ruling house of Christian Ethiopia with the family of King Solomon of Israel has been considered above. The evidence seems to be very strong that this identification was already well established in the early years of the tenth century, so that the dynasty deposed by the Zagwe in about 1150 was widely considered in Ethiopia to be a 'Solomonic' dynasty. Because of the close union between church and state embedded in the whole legend of the queen of Sheba, it can be assumed that the hard core of the resistance to the Zagwe dynasty

[1] Renaudot, *Historia Patriarcharum*, 525.
[2] Taddesse Tamrat, *Church and state*, 55 (note 3).
[3] Trimingham, *Islam in Ethiopia*, 56.

came from the ecclesiastical hierarchy of the Ethiopian Church. Most probably, even after the Zagwe were well in the saddle of power, and despite their obviously genuine patronage of the Christian Church, anti-Zagwe feelings were kept alive in various parts of the country. There are in fact some isolated pieces of evidence to show that such anti-Zagwe political movements were harboured, particularly in the ancient monastic centres of Aksum and Debre Damo, of which the long history is closely related with the ancient kings of Askum. Whereas these important centres of the church had been specially favoured by the ancient rulers of Christian Ethiopia, the Zagwe monarchs seem to have rather neglected them, and they do not figure even in important land grants attributed to King Lalibela in northern Ethiopia. In fact, the Zagwe monarchs seem to have patronized the monastery of Debre Libanos of Shimezana in southern Eritrea, so much so that it tended to overshadow the ancient and originally more powerful communities of Aksum and Debre Damo. The founder of Debre Libanos, Abba Meta'i, became the patron saint of the Zagwe monarchs, and Lalibela's wife, Masqal Kebra, is believed to have specially promoted the building of the rock church dedicated to him at Adefa.[1] In Shimezana extensive land-grants were made to his monastery and it clearly seems that, under a group of hand-picked Agaw monastic officials, Debre Libanos was given considerable ecclesiastical power in the region of northern Ethiopia. All this seems to have created much discontent and opposition among the older monastic communities. Perhaps these communities were in secret alliance with some local families who claimed direct or indirect descent from the ancient kings of Aksum. The most militant elements of such an anti-Zagwe alliance seem to have always fanned trouble and discontent wherever possible. The most important object of these people was to underscore the 'illegitimacy' of Agaw political power, and to 'restore' the old ruling family. It is ironic that this political movement seems to have been most active during the reign of Lalibela, also known as Gebre-Masqal, who was certainly the strongest and most glorious of the Zagwe kings. This is reflected from the story about the final Ethiopic edition of the legend of the queen of Sheba, which later became the book of the *Kebra-Nagast*. We are told that the original version of the *Kebra-Nagast* was in Arabic, and that it was brought to Ethiopia by apparently Coptic clerics in 1225, in the reign of King Gebre-Masqal (Lalibela). The document immediately generated considerable interest, and there

[1] G. Simon, *L'Éthiopie* (Paris, 1885), 315–16.

were probably some attempts to translate it into Ethiopic. However, it could not be translated because 'it came in the days of the Zagwe; and they did not translate it because it says that those who reign, not being Israelites, are transgressors of the Law'.[1] The obvious implication of this is that the anti-Zagwe elements had gone to great lengths in obtaining a copy of this document, which the reigning monarchs considered subversive and the translation of which they probably forbade. And the protagonists of 'Solomonic' legitimacy at the time seem to have been local princely families and ecclesiastical officials in the region of Aksum. This becomes clear because it was the chief priest of Aksum and a pro-Solomonic local chief of Enderta, Ya'ibike-Igzi, who preserved the document until after the fall of the Zagwe, and who had it translated into Ge'ez in the second decade of the fourteenth century. But the individual who benefited most from the whole propaganda was Yekunno-Amlak, a young man who seems to have belonged to a chiefly family in Amhara.

The Amhara were a Semitic-speaking people who apparently occupied the rich highlands between Lasta and Tigre in the north and the northern fringes of Shoa in the south. The foothills of the plateau which drop suddenly into the Blue Nile gorge and the Danakil lowlands formed the frontiers of Amharaland in the west and east, respectively. Like many of the other Semitic-speaking peoples, the precise origins of the Amhara are still very obscure. Linguistically, they constitute part of what has recently been called South Ethio-Semitic, of which the other major sub-groups are Argobba, Harari, Gafat (now apparently extinct) and the languages and dialect-clusters which have traditionally been given the collective name of Gurage. South Ethio-Semitic and North Ethio-Semitic (which consits of Ge'ez, Tigre and Tigrigna) are two sub-groups of what is called 'Ancient Ethio-Semitic', which, together with South Arabian, descended from South Semitic. The most up-to-date attempts to classify the modern Semitic languages of Ethiopia give some useful insight into the relative chronology of the separation of these languages, and they have tended to provide a much greater time depth for the history of these languages and their speakers. According to these new studies,[2] Ancient Ethio-Semitic was already

[1] Bezold, *Kebra Nagast*, 140–1.

[2] Harold C. Fleming, 'Ethiopic language history: testing linguistic hypotheses in an archaeological and documentary context', *Ethno-History*, 1968, **15**, 353–88. M. L. Bender, 'The languages of Ethiopia: a new lexico-statistical classification and some problems of diffusion', *Anthropological Linguistics*, 1971, **13**, 5, 165–288. Robert Hetzron, *Ethiopian Semitic: studies in classification* (London, 1972).

distinct from South Arabian, and began to be spoken in northern Ethiopia, at a time much earlier than what had hitherto been suggested by archaeologists, who date the earliest Sabean migration to about 700–500 BC. In fact, these glottochronological comparisons indicate that the split between South Arabian and ancient Ethio-Semitic probably took place not later than 2000 BC; that the divergence between North Ethio-Semitic and South Ethio-Semitic began before 300 BC; and that the diversification among the various constituents of South Ethio-Semitic may have occurred between 300 BC and AD 100. If linguistically accurate, all these conclusions have far-reaching implications for Ethiopian history. But it is particularly the estimated dates for the split between North Ethio-Semitic and South Ethio-Semitic, and for the diversification of the South Ethio-Semitic languages, which are most relevant to the purposes of this chapter.

While the above indications are of considerable assistance in reaching a more lucid reconstruction of the history of central Ethiopia, there are no tangible historical reasons which preclude our tentative acceptance of these no doubt controversial linguistic conclusions. What they tend to show is simply that the ancestors of the various peoples now speaking the modern South Ethio-Semitic languages probably started moving out of northern Ethiopia more than three centuries before the Christian era; and that their languages had already been diversified when Aksum was only beginning to emerge as a focal point in the history of the Ethiopian region. The few isolated early references to some of the speakers of the South Ethio-Semitic languages also seem to confirm precisely this point, that they moved out of northern Ethiopia before the establishment of the Christian Church in Aksum. The earliest traditional reminiscences we have about Christian settlement in Amhara, for example, indicate clearly that, by about the ninth century, there was a distinct tribal (or linguistic) group known by the name of Amhara in the area between the Tekeze river and the valleys of the eastern tributaries of the Blue Nile. This invaluable note is preserved for us in the traditions of the genealogy of Saint Tekla-Haymanot (1215–1313) which report that a very early ancestor of the saint settled in Dawint, in Amharaland, eighteen generations earlier. The tradition also relates that the Amhara were still pagan at that time, and the first establishment of the church in the area is attributed to Tekla-Haymanot's ancestor, who settled among the local people. Successive generations of the same family are reported as having continued the work of evangelizing in the area, which still had pockets of viable pagan communities as late as the fourteenth century.

The southward migration of speakers of South Ethio-Semitic in pre-Christian days, which is so usefully suggested by the above linguistic conclusions, also helps to elucidate the rather contradictory and confused traditional accounts we have hitherto had about the Gafat and the Gurage. To start with the Gurage, they were supposed to have first occupied their present-day habitat in the fourteenth century when the well-known Emperor Amda-Siyon (1313–44) settled their ancestors, whom he had recruited from *Gur'a* (hence the name Gurage) in northern Ethiopia. This tradition had been particularly ennobled by Professor Ullendorff's adoption of it as reported in the work of an early-twentieth-century Ethiopian scholar, Aleqa Tayye.[1] It is indeed possible that Amda-Siyon established Christian military colonies in the area, as we shall see; but these cannot have been the ancestors of speakers of Gurage. The Gurage are clearly reported as having been still pagan in the fourteenth century, when a leading disciple of Tekla-Haymanot, Zena-Marqos, preached among the *Mihur*, who are particularly mentioned in his still unpublished hagiography. The same picture emerges from the many other traditions we have about the early attempts to evangelize the area between the Awash and Lake Zway. In fact, Alvarez indicates that they were still pagan in the sixteenth century, and William Shack's more recent study of the Gurage is a revealing description of an essentially pagan society. All these go to show the pre-Christian origins of the speakers of the languages and dialect-clusters known by the now imprecise term Gurage. The origins of the Gafat were almost certainly pre-Christian as well.

The first tradition we have about the Gafat is that they were a particularly notorious pagan people. A fifteenth-century monastic leader, Meba-Siyon, is reported to have once wondered and said, 'When will [the Gafat] believe; and when will they be baptized . . .?' This man lived during the reign of Zara-Ya'qob (1434–68), when some of the Gafat were apparently converted to the church.[2] In the sixteenth century, Alvarez tells us, 'they are pagans and great warriors, and they always carry on war with the Prester'.[3] Bermudez, and even Almeida in the seventeenth century, characterize them as fierce pagan people.

[1] E. Ullendorff, 'Gurage notes', *Africa*, 1950, **20**, 336–7; *The Semitic languages of Ethiopia* (London, 1955), 228.

[2] E. A. W. Budge, *The lives of Meba-Siyon and Gabra-Kristos* (London, 1898), 25, 79.

[3] F. Alvarez, *The Prester John of the Indies*, tr. C. F. Beckingham and G. W. B. Huntingford (Cambridge, 1961), 458.

Moreover, all the early references we have to the Gafat locate them between the headwaters of the Awash river and the Blue Nile gorge. The chronicler of Emperor Susenyos (1607–32) mentions some Gafat tribal groups even further north, in the area between the lower basin of the Jema and Muger rivers. Thus, it can be assumed that, throughout the sixteenth century, the Gafat occupied the extensive area which has the form of a crescent running between the lower basin of the Jema to as far west as the Gudru river in medieval Damot. Perhaps this area was much more extensive in the centuries before the sixteenth, and the Gafat and the western fringes of the Gurage may have occupied contiguous territories before the Gafat were finally pushed across the Blue Nile to southern Gojjam. This certainly corroborates, or is confirmed by, the linguistic classification of the area, in which, according to Hetzron for example, Gafat is a sister language of the Northern and Western Gurage languages and dialect-clusters, all descending from what he calls Outer South Ethio-Semitic.

Outer South Ethio-Semitic is one of the two major branches of South Ethio-Semitic, the other being Transversal South Ethio-Semitic. This last branch consists of Amharic, Argobba, Harari and the dialect-cluster known as Eastern Gurage. The speakers of Outer South Ethio-Semitic and Transversal South Ethio-Semitic most probably started occupying parts of central Ethiopia already before the establishment of the church in Aksum. The first to reach the area may have been the speakers of Outer South Ethio-Semitic, whom Hetzron calls the 'vanguard', and whose descendants later spoke Northern Gurage, Gafat and Western Gurage. They apparently moved in a generally southerly and south-westerly direction, and it is precisely in the area between the Blue Nile gorge and the upper basin of the Awash river that early traditional and historical references seem to locate the habitats of these people. Following on the steps of their Outer South Ethio-Semitic brethren, the speakers of Transversal South Ethio-Semitic moved in a generally south-easterly direction, with the speakers of 'Harari and Eastern Gurage at the extremity, Argobba in the middle and Amharic in the north. The Amhara migrated the least and remained in close contact with the northern Aksumite civilization.'[1]

As we have seen, the earliest Christian settlement in Amhara is said to have been established in the ninth century. The traditions about the foundation of the churches in and around Lake Hayq also seem to belong to the same period. It can be assumed that evangelizing pressure

[1] Hetzron, *Ethiopian Semitic*, 124.

on the Amhara was redoubled during the time when Kubar was the centre of the Christian kingdom, between the ninth and the middle of the twelfth centuries. By the time the Amhara are reported to have been in conflict with the Muslim sultanate of Shoa, as has been shown, there seems to be no doubt that they had already started to play their historic role as the spearhead of Christian expansion in the Ethiopian region. The period of Zagwe ascendancy apparently strengthened the particularly Christian identity of the Amhara. In about 1248, a famous monastic school was established on the island of Lake Hayq by an Agaw monk, Iyesus-Mo'a (d. 1292), who attracted many pupils from the local Christian families in Amhara and northern Shoa. When they left his school, many of Iyesus-Mo'a's pupils established their own monastic centres in their native districts, and an intensive process of Christianization was inaugurated, thus making Amharaland in particular a more integral part of the Christian kingdom. The increasing importance of the trade-routes from Zeila also enhanced the significance of this region. By the last quarter of the thirteenth century, Amharaland had become so important in the political life of the Christian state that it was the centre of the vital struggle to depose the Zagwe kings.

The man whose name tradition has preserved as the leader of the struggle is Yekunno-Amlak. We do not know precisely what were his origins. In one account he is said to have been born to a chiefly family in Amhara where he was brought up very well by his parents, who sent him to the monastic school of Lake Hayq for religious education. Without clearly underlining the real background to his career, the traditions simply place him in the centre of events which brought about the end of the Zagwe dynasty. But the most important theme in all the stories about him is his very close association with the theory of 'Solomonic' legitimacy. The earliest versions of the traditions about his conflict with the Zagwe make him a descendant of the last 'Solomonic' prince, Dilna'od, who had been deposed by the Zagwe seven generations earlier. With local clerical support in Amhara, Yekunno-Amlak is said to have raised the standard of rebellion against the last Zagwe king, who at first captured and detained him, but who was later killed at the hands of Yekunno-Amlak himself. There are, however, some indications of other more tangible factors which contributed to the gradual shift of political power from the Agaw north to Amhara in the south.

Amhara apparently constituted one of the administrative units of the

Zagwe kingdom. Most probably, the few isolated Christian communities in northern Shoa were also distant sub-districts of the Amhara province. Zagwe power in the region had been growing since the early days of the dynasty and, as we have seen, important Christian centres had been founded as far south as the Ziqwala mountain and the upper basin of the Awash river in the early part of the thirteenth century. Amhara was the point of departure for all this. Moreover, the province was the only channel of communication with the fast-developing Muslim commercial states in the hinterland of Zeila, from where long distance trade routes went into the Ethiopian interior in various directions. One of these routes passed through the Harar region, crossed the Awash river and turned northwards when it reached the south-eastern foothills of the Shoan plateau, and passed into Amhara through the Muslim sultanate of Ifat. The importance of this sultanate and the network of trade routes which were under its control for quite a long time will be considered below. But it can be said here that the growth of a chain of Muslim states along the trade-routes from Zeila led to intensive commercial activities in the Ethiopian interior in the south, and this tended to overshadow the importance of the Zagwe north. The only way open for the Christian kingdom to survive and to preserve its ancient dominance in the area was to pursue an aggressive policy, in order to participate actively in the economic exploitation of the rich interior of southern Ethiopia. And as a frontier province where these vital developments could be followed at close range, Amhara assumed a key position within the Zagwe Christian kingdom.

But the Zagwe had begun to lose their former vitality by the middle of the thirteenth century. A leading factor in the decline of Zagwe power seems to have been the chronic succession problem among the members of the ruling family. Almost throughout the Zagwe period, the death of a monarch was marked by an intensive struggle for power among the Zagwe princes. Apparently, even the glorious reign of Lalibela was not spared these difficulties. It seems that Lalibela was once deposed by his nephew, Ne'akweto-Le'ab, who was later stripped of his ill-gotten powers and placed under confinement. When Lalibela died, there was again a conflict between his own son Yitbarek and Ne'akweto-Le'ab. Persistent traditions about the amicable relations between Yekunno-Amlak and Ne'akweto-Le'ab seem to indicate that the Amhara, and particularly Yekunno-Amlak, supported Ne'akweto-Le'ab in his dynastic conflict with Lalibela's son, Yitbarek. But Yitbarek was the victor in the end, and it may have been on this occasion that he arrested Yekunno-Amlak and probably also other supporters of his cousin. Yekunno-Amlak broke out of his jail, however, and apparently led an open revolt against Yitbarek in Amhara and northern Shoa. He enlisted the support of many local chiefs in Shoa, and he even claimed in a subsequent letter to Egypt that he had many Muslims in his following. His early messengers to Egypt went via Zeila and Aden under the auspices of the kingdom of the Yemen, thus avoiding the old northern route (via 'Aydhāb and Dahlak), where his Zagwe, opponent was apparently still strong. The general picture that emerges is one in which there was a rather protracted armed conflict between the Zagwe king Yitbarek and Yekunno-Amlak, who had established a virtually independent Christian kingdom of his own, consisting of Amhara and northern Shoa. Through his direct and amicable relations with the Muslim commercial sultanates in the hinterland of Zeila, Yekunno-Amlak opened an alternative line of communication with the Red Sea, and with Egypt via Aden in the Yemen, and completely isolated the Zagwe from participating in the vital commercial activities in southern Ethiopia. This successful defiance weakened the Zagwe considerably and, in the end, in one of the frontier skirmishes the Zagwe king, Yitbarek, was killed, and Yekunno-Amlak set out to reunify the Christian kingdom.

Zagwe power had always been strong in northern Ethiopia, and it was there that the new king had his most serious difficulties. It is apparent that when their king, Yitbarek, lost his life in the battle of Gayent Qirqos, as tradition has it, his forces retreated northwards to northern Tigre and organized a very tough resistance centred around their monastic stronghold, Debre Libanos of Shimezana. The abbot of the monastery, Yirdi'anne-Kristos, was an Agaw from Bugna, the native district of the Zagwe monarchs, and he had held the office for more than forty years. His influence in the area was apparently considerable, and many other Agaw officials from Bugna are mentioned with him in the land charters of the monastery. When Yitbarek was defeated and killed by Yekunno-Amlak in the south, Yirdi'anne-Kristos and the other Zagwe officials apparently mobilized all their resources to resist the Amhara conqueror. It in fact appears that they had crowned a new Zagwe king called Dilanda, who was donating land to Debre Libanos and its dependants in the year 1268. Dilanda was probably trying to enlist the support of the monastery in his struggle with his Amhara rival in the south. But two years later, in 1270, the same monastery was the recipient of similar land grants donated by Yekunno-Amlak, who had apparently taken full control of northern Ethiopia as well. The dynastic change brought about a complete transformation in the political hierarchy of northern Ethiopia. Yekunno-Amlak appointed a completely new cadre of local officials for the region, and many of them are listed with him in his land grants. Perhaps the most interesting change effected in these new appointments was the combination of the monastery of Debre Libanos and the cathedral of Aksum under the joint leadership of one man, Tekeste-Birhan. It is obvious that the intention of the new king was gradually to subordinate the position of Debre Libanos, which had been favoured by the Zagwe, to the power of Aksum which, as has been seen above, always led the anti-Zagwe movement in northern Ethiopia. Also mentioned among the new dignitaries of Yekunno-Amlak is a leading local chief of Enderta, near Aksum, who had also been in alliance with Aksum in its persistent opposition to the Zagwe.[1] The most striking success of Yekunno-Amlak was precisely in that he managed to establish very close associations with the traditional enemies of the Zagwe, and to be able to lead effectively the anti-Zagwe opposition throughout Christian Ethiopia. Most probably, it was at that time, when he had already scored a number of military successes against Yitbarek, that Yekunno-Amlak sought to use the theory of 'Solomonic legitimacy'. He may or may not have been a descendant of the last 'Solomonic' king deposed by the Zagwe. But the considerable military power he had acquired by 1270, and the brilliant successes he had scored against his Zagwe rivals, were quite sufficient in themselves to enable him to make the historic claim that he was a direct descendant of the ancient 'Solomonic' kings of Ethiopia. His position of strength and the apparently enthusiastic support he received from the church tended to make his claims very convincing to his own contemporaries; and the stereotyped re-editions of these early claims by successive royal chroniclers have made them look almost real to posterity. Thus, the Amhara dynasty founded by Yekunno-Amlak has been known as 'Solomonic', and his advent to power in 1270, a 'restoration'.

It seems that by the time he was making land grants to Debre Libanos of Shimezana in 1270, Yekunno-Amlak's territories included the whole of northern Ethiopia. However, some pockets of resistance apparently survived even after that date, particularly in Tigre. This emerges from

[1] C. Conti Rossini, 'L'evangelo d'oro di Dabra Libanos', *Rendiconti della Reale Accademia dei Lincei* (Classe di scienze morali, storiche e filologiche), 1901, 10, 177–219.

an interesting reference where it is reported that Yekunno-Amlak had sent an ambassador to Sultan Baybars (1260–77) 'with gifts and presents among which there were lions, as dark as night. The ambassador arrived in the country of Sahart [Tigre] whose prince rebelled against the king of Abyssinia and held the ambassador together with the objects he had with him.'[1] This prince may have very well been an old sympathizer of the Zagwe dynasty, and his rebellion seems to have been effectively suppressed.

We know very little about Yekunno-Amlak (1270–85), except that he deposed the Zagwe and that he ruled for fifteen years. One traditional account tells us that he was forty years old when he effected the dynastic change, and when he died he left a large family, many of them sons. During the period of his rule, he apparently pursued a mature and careful policy both towards the church and the various local chieftaincies. He distributed generous land grants to some of the key monasteries and, as if to overshadow the fame of the Zagwe as devout church-builders, he is believed to have commissioned the construction of the beautiful rock-hewn church of Genete Maryam, not very far from the site of Lalibela's churches. On his death in 1285, one of his sons, Yagba-Siyon (1285–94), succeeded him. It is clear, however, that Yekunno-Amlak's descendants were seriously divided among themselves, and there are persistent historical traditions about prolonged civil wars, particularly between 1293 and 1299. These years were a very crucial formative period, and one lasting result of the desperate struggle was the conception and institution of the royal prison at Mount Gishen. This was a remarkable constitutional device, particularly designed to ensure the stability of the new dynasty. From the end of the thirteenth century onwards, it became a standing rule for all the male descendants of Yekunno-Amlak, except the reigning monarch and his own offspring, to be detained on the top of Mount Gishen. Access to this could be had only from one side, since all the other sides consisted of perpendicular cliffs falling into the gorges and valleys with which the mountain is surrounded. On the slopes of the Ambassel range, of which Gishen forms one of the pinnacles, were settled very loyal guards, whose commander was under the direct orders of the royal court that no one should have access to the detained princes without the express instructions of the reigning monarch himself. When a monarch died, he was succeeded by one of his sons according to seniority. The other sons were immediately rounded up

[1] Mufazzal, 'Histoire des sultans mamlouks', *Patrologia Orientalis*, 1920, **14**, 387.

and taken to the top of Gishen for permanent detention. If, however, the king had no sons who could succeed him, then consultations were made among the dignitaries of the court, and an army was sent to Gishen to bring down a close relative of the deceased monarch, usually one of his brothers, according to seniority. This rule was kept generally intact throughout the fourteenth, fifteenth, and the first half of the sixteenth centuries, until Aḥmad b. Ibrāhim destroyed the royal prison during the jihad. Even if there were cases of faction-fighting among the supporters of the princes, the loyalty which the Christian officials had to the above rule was almost absolute, and the strength and stability of the kingdom during that period was mainly derived from this.

Thus, the period immediately after Yekunno-Amlak's death was one of intensive internal struggle among his sons and grandsons. This lasted for almost thirty years, and it was not until the accession of Amda-Siyon (1314–44), one of the grandsons of Yekunno-Amlak, that the Christian kingdom began, once again, to make a strong impact on the history of the whole of the Ethiopian region. But Amda-Siyon's special achievements as a great warrior-king cannot be fully understood without a recapitulation of the history of Islam in Ethiopia and the Horn.

ISLAM IN ETHIOPIA AND THE HORN, *c.* 1100–1376

The early traces of Muslim penetration into the Ethiopian interior up to the beginning of the twelfth century have been briefly considered above. As has been seen, the most important gateway for this early Muslim expansion was Zeila on the Gulf of Aden. The hinterland of Zeila was vast, and it extended as far west as southern Amhara and Shoa in the north and the rich areas beyond the Rift Valley lakes in the south. It was on the long-distance caravan routes to these regions that the most viable Muslim communities were established. We do not know exactly who the native inhabitants of these regions were at the time of the first advent of Islam in the area. The Arab geographers generally used terms such as Habasha for the people of the Ethiopian interior regardless of whether they were Christian, Muslim or pagan; Berber for the inhabitants of the Horn, whom they sometimes qualified as 'black Berbers', to distinguish them from the Berbers of the Maghrib; and Zanj, for the various peoples of darker complexion whom they located beyond the Habasha and the 'black Berbers'. Special names for specific peoples were very rarely employed, and even the use of the above terms was not always standardized. It is, however, very clear that, throughout the period with which this chapter is concerned, the vast hinterland of Zeila was predominantly occupied by people belonging to the same stock but speaking diverse languages. This basic situation is most carefully brought out by al-'Umarī in his fourteenth-century description of the people of the Ethiopian interior. Characterizing the Ethiopians as 'the strongest of the sons of Ham', he went on to say that, 'Although they belong to the same race, they speak different languages, at least fifty.'[1] Today, the largest section of the population of this area consists of speakers of Eastern Cushitic, and most probably their ancestors have been in occupation of the region at least for the last ten centuries. According to the most up-to-date linguistic classification, Eastern Cushitic is made up of Burji-Sidamo and a group of related languages collectively referred to as Lowland Cushitic and consisting of Saho-Afar, Macro-Somali and Macro-Oromo (with Galla forming the largest section).[2] Early speakers of Burji-Sidamo, which consists of Alaba, Burji, Darasa, Gudella, Kambata and Sidamo, most probably occupied the whole area on both sides of the Ethiopian Rift Valley, extending between the upper waters of the Awash in the north, the Gibe-Omo in the west and south and the Shebele in the east. And since there are Alaba traditions of migration from the Harar area, the early habitat of Burji-Sidamo speakers may have been even more extensive towards the east. But the vast lowland which runs in the form of a crescent from what is today south-eastern Eritrea down to Borana country in southern Ethiopia, was apparently occupied by the ancestors of Saho-Afar speakers in the Danakil depression, the Somali in the Horn, and the Galla, whose presence in the whole region became increasingly dominant only from the sixteenth century onwards.

The traditional view that the Galla preceded the Somali in the Horn is no longer valid.[3] It is rather the Somali who are referred to in the accounts of early Arab geographers. In fact, there was a basic continuity in the use of the term Berber since the first century of the Christian era, to describe the land and the people of the Horn. The *Periplus*, Claudius Ptolemy, and Cosmas Indicopleustes employed it in much the same way as the Arab geographers did after the ninth century. There

[1] Al-'Umarī, *Masālik al-abṣār fi mamālik al-amṣār: l'Afrique moins l'Égypte*, tr. M. Gaudefroy-Demombynes (Paris, 1927), 20–2.

[2] Harold C. Fleming, 'Baiso and Rendille: Somali outliers', *Rassegna di studi Etiopici*, 1964, **20**, 82–3.

[3] Ibid. 84–93. H. S. Lewis, 'The origins of the Galla and Somali', *Journal of African History*, 1966, **7**, 27–46.

seems to be no doubt now that the Arab geographers had particularly the Somali in mind when they spoke of the 'black Berbers' of the Horn; and the earlier use of the term by Greek writers may very well indicate a more ancient occupancy of the Horn by the same stock of people. The contacts between the Near and the Middle East on the one hand, and the African side of the Gulf of Aden on the other, were very old and regular; and the earliest advent of Islam in these regions must have certainly occurred within the first century of the Muslim era. During the eighth and ninth centuries Islam had struck very deep roots in the coastal regions of the Gulf, and, as was shown above, the impact of this had already begun to be felt in the interior of central Ethiopia.

The inhabitants of the Horn at that time seem to have been the ancestors of the present-day Somali. Their most important coastal settlements were Zeila and Berbera on the Gulf of Aden, and Mogadishu, Merca and Brava on the Benadir coast. Each of these settlements apparently owed its growth and development to the regular stream of merchants from Arabia, and from the countries around the Persian Gulf, who visited these places and who later started to live in them. These foreign elements of predominantly Arab origin no doubt intermarried with the local natives, which is clearly shown in the rich genealogical traditions of the Somali people. There are some traditional historical references to these separate settlements, of which Mogadishu seems to have been the most prominent after the tenth century. Some traditional accounts about Mogadishu date the first Arab settlement on the site to the second half of the eighth century, to which period two Arabic inscriptions in the town are clearly attributed. According to more reliable indications, however, the most important early migration to the area took place in the first years of the tenth century, when some Arab individuals from al-Aḥsā on the Persian Gulf left there for religious reasons and established the first viable Arab colony at Mogadishu. These early settlers were later followed by many successive Arab and also Persian immigrants, who later gave origin to the many tribal groups in the town. It is apparent that until the second half of the thirteenth century, Mogadishu was essentially a confederation of these different tribes, who were unable to evolve a united sultanate for about three hundred years. The thirteenth century was clearly a crucial period for Mogadishu, in which many vital developments were taking place. Many Arabic inscriptions published by Enrico Cerulli indicate that the citizens of the town included some prominent individuals of Arab and Persian origin. The most ancient surviving mosque in

Mogadishu, the Jāmiʿ, was also apparently built in that century, according to the inscription on the tower gate, which bears the date 1238.[1] The other two old mosques, Arbaʿ Rukun and Fakhr al-Dīn, also belong to the same period. Perhaps the most important development at that time was the establishment of the first sultanate of Mogadishu by Abū Bakr b. Fakhr al-Dīn, sometime before 1269. Mogadishu had certainly acquired its prominent position on the Benadir coast by that time, and al-Dimashqī (1256–1327) described it as a leading commercial port, where merchants from Arabia, Persia and India came regularly and did business with the local traders, who also seem to have established vital lines of communication with the interior of the Horn.[2]

The two other important towns on the Benadir coast, Brava and Merca, had also taken shape in about the same period. Cerulli reports an Arabic inscription from Brava, commemorating the death of a Muslim resident in 1104/5, which certainly indicates the existence of a highly developed Muslim community there in the eleventh century. Merca was also an important settlement in the same period. Al-Idrīsī (1100–62) gives a fairly accurate description of its location in his geographical treatise written in about 1150. It was a coastal town and two stages away from it in the interior there was a river of which the rich valley produced much corn. This was certainly the Webe Shebele, to which al-Idrīsī also seems to make another reference when he locates fifty villages of the Hawiya along the bank of an unnamed river.[3] The Hawiya still form one of the most important tribes of the Somali, and at the time when al-Idrīsī was writing his book they occupied the coastal area between Ras Hafun and Merca, as well as the lower basin of the Webe Shebele. Al-Idrīsī's mention of the Hawiya is the first documentary reference to a specific Somali group in the Horn, and it constitutes a very important testimony to the early Somali occupancy of the whole region. Later Arab writers also make references to the Hawiya in connection with both Merca and the lower valley of the Webe Shebele. Ibn Saʿīd (1214–74), for instance, considered Merca to be the capital of the Hawiya, who lived in fifty villages on the bank of a river which he called 'the Nile of Mogadishu', a clear reference to the Webe Shebele.[4] Yāqūt, another thirteenth-century Arab geographer, also mentions Merca, which he says belonged to the 'black Berbers':[5]

[1] Enrico Cerulli, *Somalia, scritti vari editi ed inediti* (Rome, 1967), I, 8.
[2] Ibid. I, 41–2.
[3] Ibid. I, 45.
[4] Aboulfeda [Abū'l-Fidāʿ], *Géographie*, tr. M. Reinaud (Paris, 1848), II, I, 232.
[5] Cerulli, *Somalia*, I, 92.

this is certainly a reference to the Somali. By the thirteenth century Mogadishu, Merca and Brava had become important Muslim and commercial centres on the eastern seaboard of the Horn. Many Muslim merchants of Arab, Persian and probably Indian origin lived in these towns. The local people in the coastal areas and in the interior were predominantly Somali and, most probably, they had already embraced Islam as their religion.

An exactly similar development seems to have taken place in the coastal areas and in the immediate hinterland of the Gulf of Aden further north. There is no controversy about the early occupation of this region by the Somali. The earliest tribal group known to have inhabited this region were the Dir, a major section of which, the Isa, still occupy the adjoining areas of former French Somalia and Ethiopia. According to local traditions, the Dir constitute an important ancestral tribe of all the modern Somali. As the most ancient inhabitants of the region between Tajura and Cape Guardafui, it seems the Dir had established very old connections with Arabia, whence had come a regular stream of Muslim merchants and preachers, most probably ever since the beginnings of Islam. But it was only after the tenth and eleventh centuries that the impact of these Muslim Arabs left a permanent imprint on the historical traditions of the area, particularly with the creation of the big clan families of Darod and Ishaq. Somali traditions have it that Shaykh Darod Ismāʿīl came from Arabia, settled among the Dir, married a local Dir woman, and later became the ancestor of the huge clan family called after him, Darod. There are exactly similar traditions about another Arab, Shaykh Ishāq, who gave rise to the second major clan family, the Ishaq.[1] Comparative genealogies seem to indicate that the advent of the Darod and Ishaq in the area took place between the tenth and thirteenth centuries. There is no doubt that these traditions about the two Arab shaykhs reflect a period of intensive islamization among the Somali. But it is also apparent that the creation of these viable clan families released dynamic internal forces which later brought about fresh waves of Somali expansion throughout the coastal areas and in the interior of the Horn. What is more interesting for the history of the whole region is, however, that the period of these vital developments in Somali country exactly coincides with the period in which Zeila and to a smaller degree Berbera also began to be the most important outlets for the Ethiopian

[1] Ibid. 1, 60–1. I. M. Lewis, 'The Galla in northern Somaliland', *Rassegna di studi Etiopici*, 1959, 15, 32–6.

interior. The Arab geographers make references to these two settlements on the coast of the Gulf of Aden from the ninth century onwards. For al-Ya'qūbī, Zeila was an island 'dans les parages de Mandel'. Less than a hundred years later, the famous tenth-century traveller, al-Mas'ūdī, mentioned Zeila among other ports through which regular commercial and diplomatic intercourse was maintained between the Yemen and the country of the Habasha. In the same century, Ibn Ḥawqal gives the relative locations of the 'island of Zeila – and the town of Berbera' in his maps and geographical descriptions of the region. The next valuable mention of Zeila comes from al-Idrīsī's twelfth-century work where it is described as

> a town of small size but highly populated. Many foreign travellers are found in it, because most of the ships from Kolzum disembark there with different types of merchandise, which come to the land of the Habasha. The export [of Zeila] consists of slaves and silver. As for gold, it is very rare. The people drink water [drawn] from wells.[1]

In the following century Ibn Sa'īd (1214–74) also refers to both Zeila and Berbera. Zeila was, he tells us, a town of considerable size and its inhabitants were completely Muslim. Berbera was the capital of the Berbers, who had mostly embraced Islam, and who were therefore no longer sold in the slave markets of the neighbouring Muslim countries.[2] Ibn Sa'īd's description gives the impression that Berbera was of much more localized importance, mainly serving the immediate Somali hinterland, while Zeila was clearly serving more extensive areas. But there is no doubt that Zeila was also predominantly Somali, and al-Dimashqī, another thirteenth-century Arab writer, gives the town its Somali name *Awdal* (Adal), still known among the local Somali.[3] By the fourteenth century the significance of this Somali port for the Ethiopian interior had increased so much so that all the Muslim communities established along the trade routes into central and south-eastern Ethiopia were commonly known in Egypt and Syria by the collective term of 'the country of Zeila'.[4]

Zeila was certainly the point of departure for the numerous Muslim communities and political units in the Ethiopian region, most of which, just like the Somali clan families of Darod and Ishaq, had persistent traditions of Arab origin. We have seen above the early formation of the sultanate of Shoa, which was already established by the first years

[1] Al-Idrīsī, *Géographie*, tr. A. Jaubert (Paris, 1837), 28–30.
[2] Aboulfeda, *Géographie*, II, 1, 231–2.
[3] Cerulli, *Somalia*, I, 46.
[4] Al-'Umarī, *Masālik*, 4.

of the twelfth century. This sultanate derived its origin from the well-known Mahzumite family of Mecca, and it lasted until the last quarter of the thirteenth century. Its Arabic chronicle, published by Enrico Cerulli, gives the impression that, towards the end of its history at any rate, the so-called 'sultanate of Shoa' was merely a loose confederation of petty Muslim principalities. These principalities were ruled by individuals, who apparently had close family relations, and who fought endless wars against one another. Most probably, all of them were essentially merchant-princes, with very sharp commercial rivalries which precluded the development of a strong Mahzumite state. This was particularly because, it appears, there were also other non-Mahzumite principalities of Arab origin already established in the Ethiopian region. One of these was the kingdom of Ifat, whose thirteenth-century ruler, 'Umar Walasma, claimed descent from the family of the Prophet Muḥammad through Abū Ṭālib. The territories of Ifat and Mahzumite Shoa had common frontiers, and in 1271 'Umar Walasma gave a daughter in marriage to one of the quarrelsome Mahzumite princes of Shoa. The marriage alliance did not last for long, and Ifat and Shoa plunged into a series of armed conflicts which resulted in the complete annexation of the sultanate of Shoa by 'Umar Walasma in 1285. Thus, the old sultanate was no longer in existence, and its leading position as the Muslim vanguard was taken by the more viable kingdom of Ifat.

By the end of the thirteenth century, there seem to have already existed many other Muslim principalities besides Ifat in the Ethiopian region. Most of these only emerge into significance in the documents we have about the fourteenth century. However, it really seems clear that their first formation and early development belong to the preceding period of two hundred years. Some of the Arabic inscriptions on tombstones collected between the modern towns of Harar and Dire Dawa bear thirteenth-century dates,[1] and they show the existence of fairly well-developed Muslim communities in the region of Harar, which probably was an important centre of dispersal for many of the founders of other Muslim settlements further inland. Both Arabic and Ethiopic documents indicate the existence of three Muslim kingdoms in the interior, other than Ifat. The first of these was Dawaro, immediately to the west of the Harar region, and comprising parts of the area between the upper waters of the Webe Shebele and the Awash,

[1] R. P. Azaïs and R. Chambord, *Cinq années de recherches archéologiques en Ethiopie* (Paris, 1931), I, 125–9.

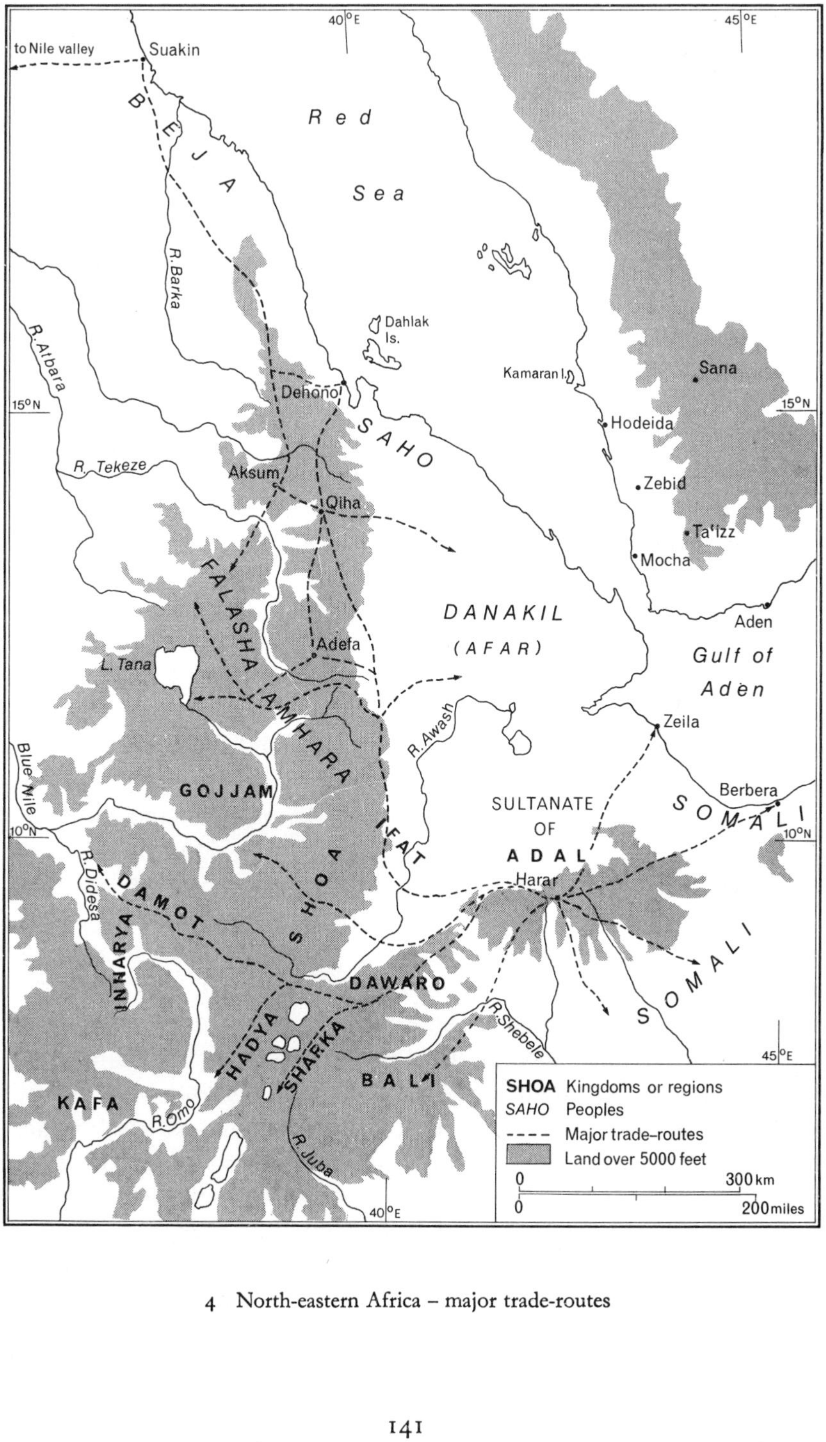

4 North-eastern Africa – major trade-routes

extending perhaps as far east as the present-day district of Chercher in the Harar plateau. The second was called Sharka, a small Muslim settlement organized into an independent state in what is today the province of Arusi. The third was Bali, a much more extensive kingdom, occupying the high plateau separating the basins of the Webe Shebele and the Rift Valley lakes. Muslim influence had penetrated further inland in this direction, and by the first half of the fourteenth century al-'Umarī included three other areas – Arababni, Darah, and Hadya – among the Muslim states of Ethiopia. It has not been possible to offer satisfactory identification for Arababni and Darah, which are only mentioned by al-'Umarī, who was later copied by al-Maqrīzī. But Hadya was a very important area, most probably located immediately to the west of Sharka and Bali. Its early significance as the centre of the slave trade is referred to by Ibn Sa'īd already in the thirteenth century, and al-'Umarī's description makes it an extensive and prosperous territory in the fourteenth. References to Hadya in later (fifteenth-century) Ethiopian documents provide us with the general picture that it was a strong Muslim principality, tributary to the Christian kingdom of Ethiopia and occupying the area between the upper course of the Awash river in the north and the Rift Valley lakes in the south. The Muslim identity of the local rulers of Hadya in the fifteenth and sixteenth centuries is very well established. But it is only al-'Umarī who characterizes it as a definitely Muslim kingdom already in the fourteenth century. Local Ethiopian indications are at best equivocal on this point and, although Muslim merchants and preachers had no doubt been established in the area even before the fourteenth century, most probably Hadya was still a pagan area in the days of al-'Umarī, who may have exaggerated the historical notes he collected from his Ethiopian informants about the early establishment of Muslim communities in the area, and about the commercial importance of Hadya. Besides the 'seven Muslim states of Ethiopia' enumerated by al-'Umarī, there were perhaps many other, much smaller, shaykhdoms throughout the region between the Awash river and the Gulf of Aden. It seems that these numerous shaykhdoms were mutually independent and that there were intensive commercial and political rivalries among them. This clearly emerges from the fourteenth-century chronicle of the Ethiopian Emperor Amda-Siyon (1314–44), in which are actually listed many such 'kingdoms' and 'principalities' which had very little sense of unity even in their struggle against the common threat of Christian domination over the whole area.

Of all these Muslim principalities, Ifat was undoubtedly the leading one. It derived this position of strength mainly from its geographical location in the north-eastern foothills of the Shoan plateau, an area through which the most important route from Zeila passed to the central Christian provinces of Amhara and Lasta. After 1285, its annexation of the former 'sultanate of Shoa' increased its territories and political importance. And, as a very powerful Muslim principality in the interior, Ifat seems to have exercised much control on the major trade routes of Zeila. It was perhaps only in this sense that al-'Umarī could say in the fourteenth century that the king of Ifat 'reigned over Zeila'. Otherwise, given the long distance between Ifat and the Gulf of Aden as well as the existence of many mutually independent shaykhdoms in the intervening area, the king of Ifat could not have ruled directly over Zeila, which, as we shall soon see, had a completely different political development of its own. Nevertheless, Ifat's pre-eminence in the long-distance trade of the Ethiopian interior, in which Zeila throve, certainly tended to give the rulers of Ifat a special influence in the whole Muslim region, including the ports of the Gulf of Aden. When Ifat began to use this great influence it had in the area against the interests of the reviving Christian kingdom, there ensued a long period of armed conflict between the two, which resulted towards the end of the century in the effective annexation of the territory of Ifat by the Christian kings and the almost complete elimination of Ifat as an independent Muslim power in Ethiopia.

We have already seen that Christian Ethiopia had started to make use of the caravan routes to Zeila by the middle of the thirteenth century. The rise of the 'Solomonic dynasty', and the resultant shift of the centre to southern Amhara and Shoa, gave a particular significance to the Zeila routes in which the Christian kings began to show an ever increasing interest. Apparently motivated by these considerations, we see the first Solomonic king, Yekunno-Amlak, interfering actively in the internal conflicts of the Mahzumite princes of the sultanate of Shoa as well as in the final show-down between the latter and the kingdom of Ifat. However, in 1285, the year in which Yekunno-Amlak died, Ifat succeeded in conquering and occupying the territories of the sultanate of Shoa. The following three decades saw a rapid growth in the territories and military strength of Ifat in the Shoan region. In the meantime, the sons and grandsons of Yekunno-Amlak were deeply involved in bitter wars of succession, and a valuable Arabic document for 1299 reports what seems to have been a considerable territorial concession to an Ifat leader by one of the sons of Yekunno-Amlak.[1] All this certainly gave much of self-confidence to the rulers of Ifat, who continued to encroach on the vital interests of the Christian kingdom. An important aspect of this was the almost complete and jealous control which Ifat began to exercise on the long-distance routes to the coast. This development was essentially the most immediate reason for the protracted Muslim–Christian wars in the region after the second decade of the fourteenth century. The ruler of Christian Ethiopia at that time was Yekunno-Amlak's grandson Amda-Siyon (1314–44), who had already re-established peace and unity within the Christian kingdom itself, and had also acquired extensive new territories by conquering the rich areas of Gojjam, Damot and Hadya. With all these newly acquired provinces, which soon became inexhaustible sources of manpower and material weath, Amda-Siyon launched a series of campaigns against Ifat and the outlying Muslim areas. Hostilities started in the early 1320s, with Amda-Siyon accusing the then king of Ifat, Haqedin I, of unlawfully detaining one of his envoys who was apparently on a mission to the coast. In retaliation for this act, Amda-Siyon invaded Ifat, and he was at first successful in defeating and killing Haqedin, whose territories were sacked by the Christian troops. The war continued, however, with Haqedin's son putting up a very effective resistance for some time. Many of the pastoral Muslims living in the adjoining lowlands beyond the eastern foothills of the Shoan plateau staunchly supported Ifat in its struggle against the Christian army. Two important peoples mentioned in this connection are the Werjih and the Gebel. We have already seen the Werjih in conflict with the Christian Amhara towards the beginning of the twelfth century, and both the Werjih and the Gebel continued to come to the assistance of Ifat, together with other Muslim groups, throughout its long struggle with the Christians in the first half of the fourteenth century. But Haqedin's son and his allies were finally overwhelmed by the Christian forces of Amda-Siyon, who occupied Ifat and established garrisons at a number of important sites. For the first time in its long history, Muslim Ifat was effectively reduced to a tributary state.

Ifat did not accept easily its new subordinate position, and it continued to wage frequent wars of resistance and rebellion against its Christian conquerors. One of the most serious of these revolts occurred in 1332, about ten years after Amda-Siyon's first conquest and occupa-

[1] Enrico Cerulli, 'L'Etiopia medievale in alcuni brani di scrittori arabi', *Rassegna di Studi etiopici*, 1943, **3**, 281–4.

tion of Ifat. Sabredin, who was probably a grandson of 'Umar Walasma, organized the rebellion. At first he discontinued sending tribute to Amda-Siyon, who had apparently given him the governorship of Ifat. Then he attacked the Christian garrisons established in the ancient territories of his Muslim ancestors; he burnt down the churches in the frontier districts, enslaving the clergy, who were also forced to embrace Islam as their religion. Moreover, he arrested all Muslim and Christian merchants who did business for Amda-Siyon, confiscating all the precious goods which had been entrusted to them by the Christian king. In addition, Sabredin set up a huge Muslim league against Amda-Siyon, in which all the Muslim-inhabited areas between the coast and the Ethiopian interior seem to have participated, at least in the earliest stages of the conflict. Thus, Sabredin's rising was a very serious one, and it threatened to reverse the hard-won military superiority which the Christians had begun to enjoy since the beginning of the fourteenth century. But, the energetic Amda-Siyon stood up to the test, and sent out a series of surprise attacks against Ifat and its allies. He himself led a major part of the Christian army in a protracted campaign which lasted for a whole period of eight months. Many of the nomadic Muslims between the Shoan plateau and the coast, as well as the sedentary Muslim principalities like Dawaro, Sharka and Adal, fought on the side of the Ifat rebel. Amda-Siyon marched through Most of these areas along the major trade routes between Shoa and the Harar plateau, and he was finally victorious over all his Muslim opponents. Sabredin was soon captured in Dawaro, the king of Adal was killed in action, the local princes of Dawaro and Sharka were also arrested, and many of the adjoining Muslim principalities submitted to Amda-Siyon. This unqualified victory, which is narrated in the Christian chronicles, is essentially confirmed also by the contemporary Arab historian, al-'Umarī, who wrote his account of Ethiopia immediately after the Muslim revolt of 1332.

The basic reason for Amda-Siyon's remarkable success lay in the lack of a united front among the Muslims themselves. The Muslim states described by al-'Umarī consisted only of the sedentary, commercial and agricultural communities long established in the Ethiopian interior. The pastoral people like the Werjih, the Gebel and the Doba, inhabiting the vast lowland area between the edge of the Ethiopian plateau and the coast, who had apparently accepted Islam by the eleventh century, fell entirely outside the narrative of the Arab historian. These lowland peoples, who were most probably the ancestors of the Afar, apparently had their own small, mutually independent shaykhdoms and principalities. Although they are often seen to have entertained strong sympathies towards their neighbouring and better-organized Muslim states like Ifat, Dawaro and Adal, they were never under the direct rule of these states. In times of war between the Christians and the Muslim states, these nomadic Muslims attacked the Christian forces in a completely uncoordinated manner and usually caused much destruction and havoc among the Christian troops. In times of general peace in the whole area, however, the fierce inhabitants of the semi-desert lowlands often waylaid the long-distance merchants, and they were of great concern to the sedentary Muslims and Christians alike.

Outside the highland Muslim principalities of Ifat, Dawaro, Bali, and later Adal, and beyond the isolated settlements along the caravan routes, these Ethiopian bedouin lived in a world entirely of their own. Military alliances contracted with them were always fickle and completely unreliable. The long and impressive list of allies which Ifat is believed to have had during the struggle against Amda-Siyon most probably consisted of such people, whose loyalties to Ifat did not outlast the earliest stages of the bitter conflict. Neither was the alliance among the better-organized Muslim states particularly strong in 1332. The Christian chronicler describes many cases of mutual suspicions and treachery, between the kingdom of Ifat and Adal in particular, and even among the brothers and relatives of Sabredin there was much internal rivalry for local power, which certainly facilitated Amda-Siyon's victories against them. This lack of unity among the Muslims of Ethiopia was keenly observed and bemoaned by both al-'Umarī and al-Maqrīzī, who considered it to be the most important reason for the relative weakness of Islam in Ethiopia.

There was also another important factor which contributed to the rather unstable relations between the Muslims of Ifat and those of the hot lowland areas immediately to the east. It is most probable that the rulers of Ifat and their sedentary subjects inhabiting the eastern foothills of Shoa spoke Ethio-Semitic. This seems to be clear from al-'Umarī's description of Ifat, whose language he tells us was 'Abyssinian and Arabic'.[1] Following this, al-'Umarī not only gives a list of words some of which are still identifiable, but he also provides us with the earliest Arabic description of the Ethiopian alphabet. Again, the names of the princes in the Arabic documents published by Enrico Cerulli

[1] Al-'Umarī, *Masālik*, 7–13, 21.

regarding the early sultanate of Shoa and the Walasma dynasty of both Ifat and Adal, indicate that some sort of Ethio-Semitic was spoken by the early Muslims in these areas. The implication of all this is that early Islam, in the Shoan region at least, had its first roots among the Ethio-Semitic speakers of the area, who later formed and ran the sultanate of Shoa and consequently the Walasma kingdoms of Ifat and Adal. Perhaps the picture was also the same in the Muslim communities immediately to the south of Ifat, particularly in Dawaro, Sharka and Hadya, where Ethio-Semitic speakers similarly may have taken a leading role. Thus, it is apparent that, in the major Muslim states of the region, Ethio-Semitic speakers formed the dominant section of the population. This linguistic factor may have provided another dimension for the basic cleavage between the sedentary Muslim communities in the Ethiopian interior and the nomadic peoples of the vast lowlands between the plateau and the coast, who were predominantly speakers of Eastern Cushitic.

This basic lack of unity among the Muslims, as well as the superiority of the Christian army in both manpower and internal organization, ensured the continued success of Amda-Siyon and his immediate successors against the Muslim areas. From the war of 1332 onwards, the principalities of Ifat, Dawaro, Sharka and Bali had completely submitted, and it is apparent that the local administration of these places was at first entrusted to loyal members of the ancient ruling families. These governorships tended to be hereditary for some time even after the Christian conquest; but the Christian emperors always preserved the right to confirm the local successions. Al-'Umarī describes how every time a local Muslim ruler died, his contending sons and relatives went in haste to the court of the Christian emperor, each with his own presents, asking for his support and official confirmation to become the next ruler of the land of his ancestors. The emperors granted such confirmation to the most influential descendant of the deceased, as long as his continued allegiance was not in question. But, as the years went by, the Christian court started to interfere more and more directly in the local politics of the Muslim provinces. As the leading Muslim area, Ifat was a particular target for a new Christian policy of 'divide and rule' energetically applied among the Muslims in general. Maqrīzī describes how the son and successor of Amda-Siyon, Sayfa-Ar'ad (1344–70), began to play one member of the Walasma family of Ifat against another, sometimes even a son against his father. This eventually led to two important developments. First, the continuous political strife generated in Ifat considerably weakened the old Muslim state. Secondly, the internal political forces in Ifat divided into two parties: one side advocating peaceful coexistence and continued submission to the Christian court, and the other completely opposed to Christian rule and fully committed to a movement of resistance and armed conflict against the Christian army.

The leaders of the militant anti-Christian party were Haqedin II and his younger brother Se'adedin, both great-grandsons of Sabredin, who had rebelled against Amda-Siyon in 1332. Their father, Aḥmad b. 'Alī b. Sabredin, was a very good friend of Emperor Sayfa-Ar'ad. On one occasion when 'Alī, his father, was suspected of rebellious motives, Aḥmad was appointed governor of Ifat in place of his father, who was immediately placed under detention. Some years later, 'Alī was released and reinstituted as governor of Ifat, and because of an apparent quarrel between father and son, Aḥmad left Ifat and began to live with Emperor Sayfa-Ar'ad in the Christian court. His sons Haqedin II and Se'adedin accompanied him during this self-imposed exile. Aḥmad was considered a traitor by his Walasma relatives in Ifat, and when he died his sons continued to be regarded by Ifat with similar suspicion. But the two sons of Aḥmad, Haqedin II and Se'adedin, broke off from both the Christian court of Sayfa-Ar'ad and their grandfather, 'Alī, who was Sayfa-Ar'ad's governor of Ifat. They went into the wilderness gathered an increasing number of followers from among the Muslim areas of the interior, and raised the standard of open revolt against both Sayfa-Ar'ad and their grandfather, 'Alī, whom they branded as a Christian puppet. They declared their sacred aim as being complete freedom for the Muslims from Christian domination, and this apparently attracted many religious leaders and military adventurers into their following. They first attacked Ifat, where 'Alī was forced to ask his overlord Sayfa-Ar'ad for Christian reinforcements. The rebels were victorious over the combined forces of 'Alī and Sayfa-Ar'ad, and they even occupied Ifat for some time.

But Ifat was too vulnerable, and Christian counteractions could easily reach the area from the Shoan plateau, which had now become the centre of the expanding Christian empire. Thus, Haqedin II and his followers moved their headquarters to an unidentifiable place which Maqrīzī calls *Wahal*. This movement was most probably in the general direction of the Harar plateau, because it is precisely from that area that we later find Se'adedin, Haqedin's younger brother and immediate successor, continuing the war against the Christian emperors. In the last quarter of the fifteenth century Se'adedin's descendants ruled from a town called Dakkar, a little to the south of the present site of Harar. Later still, in about 1520, another descendant transferred his seat of government from Dakkar to Harar itself. Thus, there seems to be no doubt at all that it was in the area around Harar that Haqedin II first established himself, when he finally abandoned Ifat as a centre of Muslim resistance against the Christians. The strategic position of the Harar plateau, through which all the important trade routes from Zeila passed into the Ethiopian interior, must have also played a decisive role in the choice of the area as a focal point for continued warfare against Christian Ethiopia. But the end result of Haqedin's decision was the effective revival of Muslim resistance against further Christian expansion towards the east, and the rise of a better organized and highly united Muslim kingdom in the Harar plateau, which is often called in the Christian documents the kingdom of Adal.

The origins of the name Adal are obscure. But al-'Umarī mentions it with Shoa and Zeila as being an integral part of the Muslim confederation led by Ifat. Amda-Siyon's chronicler, who was also al-'Umari's contemporary, lists 'the king of Adal' among the numerous Muslim principalities who fought against the Christian forces in 1332. Although none of these points to any precise location of Adal, it is clear that the place bearing that name was already Muslim, and that it had an organized kingdom of its own by the first half of the fourteenth century. The chronicler of Amda-Siyon relates the story that 'the king of Adal' was killed in action in 1332, and that his 'sons' submitted to the Christian conqueror. But we have no more mention of the area until after the careers of Haqedin II and Se'adedin, whose descendants are clearly referred to as 'kings of Adal'. It seems from this that when Haqedin and Se'adedin abandoned Ifat, they established themselves in an area which had formerly been called Adal. As militant leaders of a new anti-Christian movement in the whole area, the two Walasma princes probably overshadowed in importance the descendants of the original 'king of Adal', who may have abandoned the title in favour of their more successful Muslim brethren either by agreement or even by force. But there is no doubt that a new Walasma dynasty was then established in Adal by the great-great-grandsons of 'Umar Walasma of Ifat. From the last quarter of the fourteenth century onwards, this dynasty dominated the whole area between the Harar plateau and the Gulf of Aden until the end of the period with which we are concerned in this chapter.

Haqedin's transfer of his political centre from Ifat to the Harar area was also important in another sense. We have seen above that the dominant section of the population in the Muslim principalities of Shoa and Ifat were speakers of Ethio-Semitic languages. Linguistic research since the end of the nineteenth century has brought to light the existence of speakers of an Ethio-Semitic language called Argobba near the present site of the modern town of Harar. Speakers of the same language were also to be found until very recently in the environs of the location of ancient Ifat. Many miles separate the two localities where Argobba is probably still spoken. It is quite possible that this could be accounted for if one envisaged an age-old commercial intercourse between the two areas both before and after the fourteenth century. But the fourteenth-century rise of a Walasma dynasty in the Harar region, led by large numbers of people who were clearly of Ifat origin, must have had a considerable role to play in the planting and development, in and around Harar, of the communities speaking Harari and Argobba – both of which belong, with Amharic, as we have seen earlier, to what is currently called Transversal South Ethio-Semitic.

FURTHER CHRISTIAN EXPANSION, *c.* 1376–1468

The political significance of the rise of the kingdom of Adal on the Harar plateau lay especially in its tendency to unify all the forces of Islam throughout the Ethiopian region. After the Christian conquest of the old Muslim states of Ifat, Dawaro and Bali in the fourteenth century, only a loose confederation of political and religious interests existed among the numerous Muslim communities and petty shaykhdoms between the Gulf and the eastern frontiers of the Christian empire. Following upon the success of Haqedin II and the establishment of the Walasma dynasty in the Harar area, however, dynamic movements of Muslim unification seem to have been effected. The impact of this was apparently felt not only along the frontiers of conflict between the two Christian and Muslim states, but also throughout the Somali interior of the Horn. Despite the continuous hostility between them, the Christian empire of Ethiopia and the new Walasma kingdom of Adal were characterized by the same outward movement of conquest and expansion. The expansion and consolidation of Adal had two major implications in particular. First, it constituted a serious threat to the peace and security of the predominantly Muslim-inhabited provinces of the Christian empire along its eastern frontiers. Secondly, it is apparent that ever since the establishment of their power around Harar, the Walasma princes of Adal set out on a series of campaigns to bring the Somali interior of the Horn under their effective sphere of influence. More than anything else, it seems that this process of Adali expansion into the Horn provides a reasonable background for the southward movement of many Somali tribes which is narrated in the traditions collected by Enrico Cerulli.[1] It is also clear that the absence of any organized state in the Somali hinterland of the Gulf of Aden clearly facilitated the rapid ascendance of Walasma power in the area.

The process of state formation was apparently very slow among the Somali who occupied the immediate hinterland of the Gulf of Aden. This seems to be clear from Mufazzal's fourteenth-century description of political life in Zeila: 'As for [the people of] Zeila and their tribes, they have no kings. But they are divided into seven tribes. These people are Muslim and their preachers recite the public prayers in the name of their seven chiefs.'[2] The general picture transmitted by this passage is very similar to the story told in the *Periplus*, that the coastal settlements beyond the limits of Aksum and along the coast of the Gulf of Aden were not organized into a united state, but that each lived under its own local chief.[3] This long tradition of political decentralization had been kept intact for more than ten centuries until the days of Mufazzal, when very serious attempts were being made to incorporate the area into an empire. Mufazzal himself tells us about one of the earliest moves to build an empire in the area, which was undertaken by the kingdom of the Yemen:

> The king of Yemen sent some people to build a big mosque in Zeila so that they would hold public prayers in his name. He sent all the pieces of stone as well as the other items required for the construction from Aden. But a number of the tribes of Zeila collected the stones and threw them into the sea. In retaliation for this insult, the king of Yemen imposed an embargo on their ships sailing to the port of Aden for a period of a whole year.[4]

The Yemen was ruled at that time by the Rasulid dynasty, which had been established in 1228 by a former ally and an agent of the Egyptian Ayyubid occupation forces in the country. Thus, the Rasulids started by having strained relations with Egypt, against whom they conducted a prolonged struggle for the control of the Hejaz and the profitable

[1] Cerulli, *Somalia*, I, 60–7.
[2] Mufazzal, 'Histoire', 387.
[3] *The periplus of the Erythrean Sea*, tr. W. H. Schoff (London, 1912), paragraph 14.
[4] Mufazzal, 'Histoire', 387.

trade of the Red Sea. However, the Yemen never constituted an effective threat to Egyptian interests in the area, and Mamluk control over both the Red Sea trade and the Holy Cities of Islam became increasingly powerful. The African ports of 'Aydhāb and Suakin, and to some extent also the islands of Dahlak, were gradually brought into the widening Egyptian sphere of influence, and, by the first half of the fifteenth century, the Mamluks encouraged the merchants of the east to bypass Aden, to navigate directly through the straits of Bab-el-Mandeb and land their merchandise at Jedda for direct shipment to Egypt. Thus, Mamluk ascendancy, particularly over the Arabian and African coasts of the northern part of the Red Sea, was firmly established until the advent of the Ottomans in the second decade of the sixteenth century. Nevertheless, largely because of its physical contiguity, the Rasulid kingdom of the Yemen exercised considerable influence in the southern part of the Red Sea, in the Gulf of Aden and to a lesser degree on the Arabian coast of the Persian Gulf. Most of the Rasulid princes were noted for their cultural refinement and for their pursuit of knowledge. Throughout the period of their rule (1228–1454), the Yemen had certainly become a vital centre for Muslim culture and for the propagation of Islam.

It has already been observed that there were close ties between the Yemen and the Ethiopian region before the middle of the thirteenth century, particularly through the Dahlak islands. These relations were continued even after Zeila replaced Dahlak as the most important outlet for the Ethiopian interior. There are many historical references which testify to the survival of these traditional connections between the two areas. Yekunno-Amlak (1270–85), who founded the Solomonic dynasty, once used the good offices of King Muẓaffar (1250–95) of the Yemen in asking for a new Egyptian bishop from Cairo. Muẓaffar was a very strong monarch. His forces conquered and occupied Zaffar, and the whole of the Hadhramaut and Bahrain submitted to his power. His son, Mu'ayyad Dāwūd (1297–1321), also had very good connections among Ethiopian Muslims, who once presented him with the well-known *chat* plant, of which the leaves have a narcotic effect. Other presents were also exchanged between local Ethiopian princes and the Rasulid monarchs of the Yemen.[1] It is very clear, however, that the Rasulids considered themselves as having superior powers to their Ethiopian friends, and there are some passages in Khazraji's historical

[1] Al-Khazraji, *History of the Resuli dynasty of Yemen*, tr. J. W. Redhouse (E. J. W. Gibb Memorial Series, III, pt. 2; London, 1907), 119–20, 161, 171. Al-'Umarī, *Masālik*, 12–13.

writing where actual suzerainty over Ethiopian coastal areas is explicitly claimed. On one occasion, the Yemeni governor of Zebid is said to have exercised direct control 'over the peoples of Awan (Massawa) and of Zeila and of other remote regions'. This last reference belongs to about the second half of the fourteenth century, and it is most probably connected with Mufazzal's story, quoted above, that the Rasulids had made a definite attempt to annex the coastal region around Zeila. As Mufazzal tells us, however, this was strongly resisted by the local tribes of Zeila, and it was almost certainly a complete failure. Throughout the next period of two hundred years, it was the local Walasma dynasty of Adal, and not Rasulid Yemen, which was to establish much more effective military and political control over Zeila and the neighbouring areas.

There seems to be no doubt now that the new Walasma rulers of the Harar plateau began to annex extensive Somali tribal areas to the east and south-east. The Somali interior of the Horn was used by them as an inexhaustible source of manpower for their growing army, which was always kept active in the perennial frontier clashes with the Christian empire. The armed conflict between the two states was particularly active between the end of the fourteenth and the middle of the fifteenth centuries; and there are isolated references which show that the Somali had definitely begun to be directly involved in them. I. M. Lewis gives an invaluable reference to an Arabic manuscript on the history of the Gadabursi Somali, who, together with the Isa, form the largest group of the ancient Dir clan-family. 'This Chronicle opens', Lewis tells us, 'with an account of the wars of Imam 'Ali Si'id (d. 1392) from whom the Gadabursi today trace their descent, and who is described as the only Muslim leader fighting on the western flank in the armies of Se'ad ad-Din, ruler of Zeila.'[1] Se'adedin, as we have seen above, was the joint founder of the Walasma kingdom of Adal with his brother Haqedin II. When the latter died, he assumed full powers in Adal and revived the struggle with the Christian army, against which he was successful on many occasions. This brought him considerable renown throughout the Muslim world, and a number of Arabic historical works refer to him with complimentary notes. Se'adedin (1373–1403) furiously attacked the frontier Christian provinces of Dawaro and Bali in particular, and drove away large numbers of cattle and slaves, which he collected as booty. The successes of his forces continued to disrupt

[1] Lewis, 'The Galla', 31.

the security of the eastern frontier provinces throughout the last quarter of the fourteenth century, and it was not until his final confrontation with Emperor Dawit (1380–1412) that Se'adedin began to suffer very crucial military reverses. Finally, in 1403, Dawit led a series of energetic campaigns into the very heart of the Harar plateau and repeatedly defeated Se'adedin, whom he pursued as far as Zeila, where the Walasma prince was captured and executed.

Dawit's son and immediate successors, Tewodros (1412–13) and Yishaq (1413–30), carried on the Christian military pressure on the Harar plateau. The Walasma family of Se'adedin actually left for Arabia in a self-imposed exile which lasted, according to Maqrīzī, for a number of years. In the meantime, the Christian forces made serious attempts to occupy the Harar region, in which they seem to have scored many temporary successes:

By the death of Sa'ad ad-Din the strength of the Muslims was abated. For the *Hati* and the Amhara having acquired this country settled in it, and from the ravaged mosques they made Churches. The Muslims they harassed for the space of 20 years, during which the faithful suffered so many defeats and losses that no one is equal to recounting them.[1]

Maqrīzī singles out Emperor Yishaq for his zeal in uprooting Islam from the Ethiopian region and for his crusading campaigns against the kingdom of Adal. It is also in reference to Yishaq's reign that we have the earliest historical mention of the Somali in Ethiopian documents. The Somali and the *Simur* are said to have submitted and paid tribute to him. Dr Enrico Cerulli has shown that *Simur* was an old Harari name for the Somali, who are still known by them as Tumur.[2] Hence, it is most probable that the mention of the Somali and the Simur in relation to Yishaq refers to the king's military campaigns against Adal, where the Somali seem to have constituted a major section of the population.

The ten sons of Se'adedin were welcomed and entertained in Arabia by the Rasulid king of the Yemen, Nāṣir Aḥmad b. Ash'arī Ismā'īl (1400–24). When they returned home, he sent with them some Arab auxiliaries and there was again a revival of Walasma power in Adal. Sabredin (1409–18), Mansur (1418–25), Jemaldin (1425–32) and Badlay (1432–45) successively took over their father's throne in Adal, and they all conducted energetic campaigns against the occupation forces of the Christian empire. It appears that they were increasingly successful in

[1] A.-Maqrīzī, *Historia regnum islamiticorum in Abyssinia*, ed. and tr. F. T. Rinck (Leiden, 1790), 27.

[2] Cerulli, *Somalia*, I, 111–12.

forcing the Christians to evacuate their settlements within Adali territory. The conflict had become so desperate that, in their hopeless attempts to hold on to the Adali territories acquired since Se'adedin's death, both Tewodros (1412–13) and Yishaq (1413–30) seem to have lost their lives while fighting against the Walasma princes. For a period of four years after Yishaq's death, the political situation in the Christian empire was very chaotic, and Jemaldin (1425–32) took advantage of this to score a number of easy victories on the frontier. His brother, Aḥmad Badlay (1432–45), continued the successes of his brother. Maqrīzī tells us that he actually recovered Bali, a Muslim province which had been under Christian rule since the days of Amda-Siyon (1314–44). Some Christian documents attribute to him very ambitious plans of not only recovering the frontier Muslim provinces but also of leading a major jihad against the whole of the Christian highlands, over which he is said to have actually nominated prospective governors. In the early years of the reign of Emperor Zara-Ya'qob (1434–68), Badlay led many raids, which were always successful and which created much havoc within the frontier provinces of the Christian empire. Finally, however, a renewed invasion of Dawaro by him was repulsed by the Christian army in 1445. Zara-Ya'qob himself led the defences of Dawaro, Badlay was killed in action, and the Muslim army suffered considerable casualties.

An interesting passage in *Meshafe Milad*, attributed to Zara-Ya'qob himself, relates the story that for his campaigns of 1445, Badlay collected numerous levies, beginning 'from the house of *Me'ala* to *Meqdush* [all of whom] were allied with the people of Adal'.[1] The 'house of *Me'ala*' no doubt means the *Bait Mala* of northern Eritrea, and *Meqdush* is certainly a reference to the Somalo-Arab sultanate of Mogadishu. It has already been seen that a local leader of Arab origin, Abū Bakr b. Fakhr ad-Dīn, had founded the sultanate of Mogadishu in the second half of the thirteenth century. The sultanate continued to thrive and when Ibn Baṭṭūṭa visited the city in 1330 it had become an important centre for Muslim culture as well as an active commercial port on the Benadir coast.[2] The general picture which emerges is that Mogadishu was essentially a city-state, though with considerable influence on the neighbouring coastal and inland districts. Further south, the Hawiya controlled Merca, and apparently in the fifteenth century a fairly strong state was established by the Ajuran, who were of a mixed

[1] Zara-Ya'qob, *Meshafe-Milad*, ed. and tr. K. Wendt (Corpus Scriptorum Christianorum Orientalium: Scriptores Aethiopici, Louvain, 1962), **42**, 19.

[2] Ibn Baṭṭūṭa, *Travels of Ibn Baṭṭūṭa*, tr. H. A. R. Gibb (London, 1962), II, 374–8.

Arab and Hawiya origin. The Ajuran state expanded into the interior along the lower valley of the Webe Shebele and was in control of the immediate hinterland of Mogadishu with which it had amicable relations, particularly in the days of the so-called Muẓaffar dynasty which ruled the sultanate of Mogadishu during the sixteenth century. Mogadishu was still at the height of its cultural and commercial power when some Portuguese documentary references are made to it in the end of the fifteenth and the beginning of the sixteenth centuries. On the return trip from his first voyage to India, Vasco da Gama simply passed by Mogadishu in 1499 without making any attempt to control it. And the Portuguese descriptions show that it was still in a very strong and prosperous condition. Rich commercial ships were anchored in its harbour, and it was in regular and active contact with India and Arabia. A list of its exports, given in the account of a Portuguese writer within the second decade of the sixteenth century, includes 'much gold, ivory, wax, cereals, rice, horses, and fruits'.[1] Cerulli has rightly concluded that the traffic in gold and horses particularly indicates the possible trade relations between Mogadishu and the interior of Africa. Perhaps this also included the Ethiopian interior, where Muslim merchants had been involved in long-distance trade for many centuries.

But there is no doubt that, by the middle of the fifteenth century, the sultanate of Mogadishu was considered in Christian Ethiopia to be an important Muslim area which inspired and actively supported the militant campaigns of Adal against the Christian empire. Together with the earlier mention of the Somali and Simur having been in conflict with the Emperor Yishaq, Zara-Ya'qob's mention of Mogadishu as an ally of Adal is an important confirmation of the early Somali involvement in the protracted frontier struggle. This was to be even more significant, as will be shown, during the Muslim invasion of the Ethiopian highlands in the sixteenth century. For the moment, however, Zara-Ya'qob's victory over Badlay in Dawaro relaxed the military pressure from Adal for about forty years. Yet, the only thing Zara-Ya'qob could do was to maintain his power in the frontier provinces of Ifat, Dawaro and Bali, which had been in Christian hands since the fourteenth century. Even after his victory of 1445, Zara-Ya'qob could never recover the territories which had been acquired by Dawit (1380–1412), Tewodros (1412–13) and Yishaq (1413–30) in the Harar plateau, which was to remain completely outside the

[1] Cerulli, *Somalia*, I, 118–19.

limits of the Christian empire of Ethiopia until the end of the nineteenth century. But Zara-Ya'qob consolidated his power along the frontier, and strengthened the old system of defence by establishing new and loyal military colonies in the whole area.

Besides his pacification of the Muslim frontier provinces, Zara-Ya'qob is particularly noted for the personal commitment he had towards the further expansion and effective reorganization of the Ethiopian Church, which had already been extending its frontier throughout the period covered by this chapter. Just as in the organization of the state, the legacy of Aksum was also reflected in the basic structure of the medieval church of Ethiopia. The bishop continued to be an Egyptian, selected and appointed by the Coptic patriarch in Cairo. He was appointed for life, and when he died, requests for his replacement were sent to Egypt by the Ethiopian kings, together with rich presents both to the Muslim rulers of Egypt and to the patriarchs. When he came, he was usually accompanied by a number of Egyptian clerics and relatives who often remained in Ethiopia for the rest of their lives. In Ethiopia, the bishop and his companions were very well provided for. There were extensive pieces of land in convenient parts of the Christian kingdom which traditionally belonged to the Egyptian bishop. He was attended by many clerical and secular officials, who were permanently attached to his episcopal residence and to the traditional fiefs which went with the office. As the highest official in the Ethiopian Christian hierarchy, the Egyptian bishop was an integral part of the imperial court, where he was almost always physically present. But as a foreigner who very often did not speak the local languages, he was a rather isolated figure. His major responsibility was to ordain priests and deacons, and, whenever the bishop was a man of strong personality, he also provided an overall spiritual leadership to the Ethiopian Church. On the whole, however, the position of the bishop suffered considerably from the obvious inconvenience of his coming from Muslim-dominated Egypt. Because of the political implications for the Coptic Church in Egypt, the bishops shied away from openly encouraging Christian militancy against Islam in Ethiopia, even during the protracted wars throughout the period between the thirteenth and sixteenth centuries. They rather tended to be champions of peaceful coexistence and, while this had a considerable impact on the policies of the Ethiopian emperors towards Islam in Ethiopia and the Horn, the Ethiopian clergy and the Christian peasantry as a whole could not understand the reluctance of the Egyptian bishop to give full support to their religious sentiments against Islam. This undermined the image of the episcopal office among the Ethiopian Christian population in general, and it gave much opportunity to the more militant hermits and monks to cast a heavy shadow of doubt on the purity of even the religious life of the Egyptian bishop himself. Of the long list of bishops who served Ethiopia during the period covered by this chapter only Ya'qob (1337–44), Salama (1348–88), Bartelomewos (1399–1436), Mika'el and Gabri'el (1438–68), and Yishaq and Marqos (1481–1530) are vividly remembered in the traditional records of the country as having left permanent imprints on the history of the Ethiopian Church, to which they gave relatively more effective leadership.

Besides the Egyptian bishops, the local hierarchy consisted of large numbers of Ethiopian clerics. These were of two different kinds, namely, those attached to the imperial court and those serving in the distant, self-administering monasteries and other local churches. The former were called *kahenate debtera* (lit. 'the clergy of the tent'), and they wielded much power and influence by virtue of their close association with the monarch, whom they served as experts and advisers, particularly on religious matters. They staffed all the richly endowed chapels of the imperial court as well as the other Royal Treasure churches in the central provinces of Amhara and Shoa. They also controlled the work and movements of the Egyptian bishop, who was, like them, an integral part of the imperial entourage. Acting as the natural intermediaries between the bishop and the rest of the Ethiopian Church, the *kahenate debtera* supervised the ordination of priests and deacons and, as a result, they possessed a vast patronage throughout the Christian kingdom. The position of the bishop especially depended on them, and whenever there was a serious breach between them and the Egyptian prelate, the latter almost always lost the struggle, and he was often disgraced and sometimes even sent back to Egypt. Thus, because of their vulnerable position, most of the Egyptian bishops entirely depended on the *kahenate debtera* with whom it was always politic to live in peace and harmony. It is apparent that the close alliance between the bishop and the *kahenate debtera* was most effective until the first half of the fourteenth century, when a series of vital developments in Ethiopian monasticism were beginning to revolutionize the life of the ordinary clergy in Ethiopia.

The largest section of the Ethiopian clergy consisted of those who staffed the distant monasteries and the numerous local churches all over the Christian highlands. Unlike the *kahenate debtera*, these rarely visited the imperial or episcopal courts except perhaps when they received Holy Orders. For practical purposes they may be divided into two groups, namely the secular and the monastic clergy. The secular clergy included the married priests who had families of their own and who served in what may be called the secular churches. Priesthood was essentially a part-time profession for them, since much of their time was spent in cultivating the land which they received in return for their church services. They were thus part and parcel of the ordinary Christian peasantry. Apart from their ability to recite and sing a specified number of prayers required by the liturgy, such as those for the celebration of Mass, the secular clergy were not particularly noted for their high educational attainments. The monastic clergy, on the other hand, devoted the whole of their lives to religious pursuits, and they tended to be more highly educated and better versed in the religious and literary traditions of the Ethiopian Church. They lived in their respective monastic communities, which were often located in isolated areas, which made them more spiritually oriented. Ever since the introduction of monasticism into northern Ethiopia by the Nine Saints in the sixth century, the monastic communities thus established had provided the country with its only educational facilities, and the cultural and the literary leadership of the Ethiopian Church continued to be in the hands of the monastic clergy. This was further enhanced after the middle of the thirteenth century, when more and more monastic centres were being established in the central highlands of Ethiopia.

The revival of the Christian state under the 'Solomonic' emperors, as well as the expansion of its frontiers throughout the Ethiopian plateau, had opened up new and vast areas for Christian settlement. Together with the southward shift of the centre of the Christian empire, dynamic monastic schools were emerging on the Amharan and Shoan plateau. The earliest and most notable of these was the island monastery of Lake Hayq, where a former inmate of Debre Damo in Tigre, Abba Iyesus-Mo'a (d. 1292), settled in 1248 and opened a new school. Many young men from Amhara and northern Shoa rushed to join the Hayq school, and in a matter of three decades Iyesus-Mo'a had produced a large number of disciples, most of whom returned to their respective native areas and established their own monastic communities. Thus, by the beginning of the fourteenth century many such communities had been founded on many of the islands of Lake

Tana, in the region between the Tekeze river and the uppermost course of the Abbay, in Amharaland, and in the northern part of Shoa. The process continued throughout the fourteenth and early fifteenth centuries, when the graduates of the relatively older monastic schools moved out to new areas and started their own communities. This movement of expansion by the church got much support from the military expansion of the Christian state, which had already strengthened its powers throughout the interior of the Ethiopian region. By the first half of the fifteenth century, Christian churches and monasteries were firmly established in Falashaland, eastern Gojjam, Damot, and as far south as Lake Zway in the Rift Valley.

Monasticism was the most effective vehicle for the expansion of the church into the Ethiopian interior. By the middle of the fourteenth century, two important monastic groups had emerged, and both of them worked hard to extend the frontiers of the church in their respective areas. The 'House of Tekla-Haymanot' was the older of the two and, because it was active in the central provinces, it was also the stronger. It consisted of the followers of Tekla-Haymanot (1215–1313) from Shoa, who had his religious training at the Hayq monastic school referred to above, as well as at the ancient monastery of Debre Damo, which had been founded by one of the Nine Saints in the sixth century. After completing his studies, Tekla-Haymanot returned to his native land and established his own school in the still predominantly pagan district of Shoa. He was joined by many young men who studied under him, and by the time he died, at the beginning of the fourteenth century, the monastic community of Asbo founded by him had become a strong religious and cultural centre. Its location in Shoa, whither the centre of the Christian state had shifted, made it increasingly important. Like all monastic communities in Ethiopia, it had very humble beginnings. But the second generation of its leaders was already very famous in the first half of the fourteenth century. Both the Egyptian bishop, Abba Ya'qob (1337–44), and the Ethiopian emperor, Amda-Siyon (1314–44), held the monastery and its leaders in high esteem. It was in fact from the monastery of Tekla-Haymanot at Asbo that Bishop Ya'qob and the emperor recruited priests and deacons to establish new churches in the territories recently conquered by the Christian army to the south and west of Shoa. Most of these were monks who had studied under Tekla-Haymanot himself, and the new communities they organized were formally subordinated to their original monastery of Asbo. Thus, the House of Tekla-Haymanot won complete control over the churches in and south of Shoa. This growing influence of Asbo gave its abbot, Filippos (1314–41), such a position of strength that he led a daring attack on emperors Amda-Siyon and Sayfa-Ar'ad (1344–70) for their adherence to the traditional polygamy of their royal ancestors. In this, Filippos was actively supported by Bishop Ya'qob and the monasteries in the north, and it seems that the movement had also won at least the sympathy of a large section of the palace guards and other court officials. Deeply offended by Filippos and his supporters, who pried into their private lives, Amda-Siyon and Sayfa-Ar'ad reacted by exiling the most militant leaders into the peripheral areas of their empire. Filippos and some of his close associates were publicly flogged, and exiled, first, to a frontier district in Tigre, and then to the area of Lake Zway south of the river Awash. Bishop Ya'qob was humiliated and disgraced by Amda-Siyon, and he was finally sent back to Egypt when he refused to change his mind. But the House of Tekla-Haymanot eventually derived many benefits out of this temporary adversity. With Filippos disgraced and exiled, there was a great exodus of the more militant members of the order from Shoa to other regions. They went and settled in such remote areas as Begemder, Falashaland, the islands of Tana, and eastern Gojjam. Wherever they went they continued their spiritual connections with Asbo. This led to the expansion of the order throughout the central highlands. In the northern province of Tigre, there were also many monastic leaders who were apparently associated with Tekla-Haymanot during his stay at Debre Damo. Later, we see a number of monasteries cropping up throughout Tigre, and deriving their ultimate origin from Tekla-Haymanot. Thus, in the period under discussion, the 'House of Tekla-Haymanot' was certainly the larger and stronger of the two monastic groups.

The second group was founded by Abba Ewostatewos. He was originally from Ger'alta in Tigre, but he later moved to Sera'e, in what is today Eritrea, and established a strong base there. The districts of Marya, Bogos, Hamasien, Sera'e, and Akele Guzay were predominantly Christian at that time, and Ewostatewos provided a new and dynamic religious leadership in the area. His monastic school attracted many young men from Sera'e and the neighbouring districts and the local chiefs gradually came to know about him. Just as in the case of Filippos in Shoa, he was apparently on very good terms at first with Bishop Ya'qob and Emperor Amda-Siyon, both of whom he is said to have met on different occasions in Eritrea. Ewostatewos won fame for his militant order which was highly committed to the principle of monastic life.

He taught his pupils not to depend on the secular world for their livelihood, but rather to produce enough food for their own maintenance. He formally forbade them to receive any presents from the rich or from people in authority, so that they could maintain their spiritual independence. He publicly denounced the slave trade, in which the Christian chiefs were also involved, and he took the local people to task for their failure to live according to the teachings of Christ. On some occasions he even publicly excommunicated the local chiefs for their failure to follow his teachings, and refused to have any dealings with them until they did so. He accused many of his fellow priests and monks in northern Ethiopia of a lack of basic commitment and courage in admonishing their congregations to live according to the teachings of the church. All this gradually brought him into a double-edged conflict with the local chiefs, and with the clergy, who were sensitive to his outspoken criticisms. He became more and more isolated, and his almost complete alienation from the majority of the clergy was further enhanced by his attempt to revive some Old Testament practices. He specially insisted on the strict observance of the Sabbath, which had long been banned as a 'Jewish' practice by the Alexandrian patriarchate. The majority of the Ethiopian Church had apparently followed Alexandria on this at the time, and Ewostatewos and his still small community in Eritrea were actively persecuted. In the end, Ewostatewos had to leave Ethiopia altogether, accompanied by many of his disciples, on a self-imposed exile to the Holy Land. He later moved to Cyprus and Armenia, where he died in about 1352. Some of his followers returned to Ethiopia and, with a handful of their old schoolfellows who had been left behind, they started to revive their master's teachings. In time they organized themselves into a very effective monastic order, which was particularly active in what is today Eritrea. Because they were still under the official excommunication of the Egyptian bishops in Ethiopia, the followers of Ewostatewos were persecuted wherever they went, and the earliest monastic centres established by them tended to be in peripheral, frontier areas. Apparently because of this, we have vivid traditions of their evangelizing efforts among the Barya and Kunama, among the pastoral nomads between the coast and the Eritrean plateau, and among the Falasha, the so-called 'black Jews of Ethiopia', who lived in the region north of Lake Tana with their ancient traditions of biblical origin. After about a century of such dedicated mission work, towards the middle of the fifteenth century, the 'House of Ewostatewos' emerged as a very powerful monastic group. The leading monastery of this order was Debre Bizen, founded in 1390, and it had a large number of both dependent and allied communities throughout the Eritrean plateau. Despite the continued excommunication by the Egyptian bishop, this order had clearly acquired a majority status in the area where it had also gained great popularity among the local people, by whom the name of Ewostatewos was regarded with much awe and respect.

The situation in the first half of the fifteenth century was that the Ethiopian Church had been polarized between the two monastic groups. The House of Tekla-Haymanot was numerically the larger of the two, and its relations with the royal court had also considerably improved since the days of Amda-Siyon and Sayfa-Arad. Its complete obedience to, and close co-operation with, the Egyptian bishops had also made it the more official and more established order in central Ethiopia. In Eritrea, however, the House of Ewostatewos continued its defiance of the bishop, and continued to gain ground in the moral, social and even political leadership of northern Ethiopia. Besides the ecclesiastical schism which this process engendered, the regional and political undertones of the situation increasingly forced the emperors of the period to intervene and bring an end to the problem. Finally, Emperor Zara-Ya'qob (1434–68) took the initiative by calling a council at his court in 1450 and, by twisting the arms both of his Egyptian bishops and the House of Tekla-Haymanot, rehabilitated the followers of Ewostatewos by accepting, among other things, their insistence on the observance of the Sabbath. Zara-Ya'qob did this as part of an overall programme of revitalizing the Ethiopian Church. His attention was drawn not only towards the elimination of internal conflicts (doctrinal or otherwise), but he also made a serious attempt to reorganize the monastic and ecclesiastical resources of the country for the basic purpose of strengthening the church. He generously endowed the monasteries all over the highlands, and ordered them to extend and consolidate the teachings of the church in their respective spheres of influence. This programme was quite successful within the period of his reign. Indeed, all the evidence points to those years as the period when the Ethiopian Church reached the pinnacle of its cultural, literary and spiritual attainments. But the period of general decline in Christian military power which followed soon afterwards tended to undo much of what had been achieved earlier. Local religious opposition to the expansion of the church was strong and persistent, even in the more glorious days of Christian conquest which started in Amda-

Siyon's reign.[1] Although the presence of the church had increasingly been felt throughout the Falasha, the pagan and Muslim areas since the fourteenth century, it had essentially failed to acquire a permanent foothold in most of these places. The position of the Ethiopian Church was firmly established only among the predominantly Semiticized peoples of northern and central Ethiopia. As regards the much wider Christian empire of the fourteenth and fifteenth centuries, the church had certainly failed to serve as a unifying factor, a role which the Ethiopian emperors had obviously intended it to play.

THE REVIVAL OF MUSLIM POWER, *c.* 1468–1543

The end of Zara-Ya'qob's reign was a landmark in the history of late medieval Ethiopia. Throughout his thirty-four years as emperor, he had established a firm, if despotic, rule in his empire and he had initiated a number of radical social, religious and political reforms which he energetically implemented through a combination of coercion and persuasion. When he died, none of his successors was competent enough to maintain a similar control over the extensive Christian empire. It is apparent that this decline of central power was mainly due to the increasingly serious conflict over the succession to the imperial throne which characterized the second half of the fifteenth century. As we have seen above, wars of succession had already started to shake the foundations of the Solomonic dynasty following the death of its founder, Yekunno-Amlak. Apparently because of this, the institution of the royal prison of Mount Gishen had been established. Nevertheless, it is possible to notice serious political tension under the general façade of legitimacy throughout the period covered by this chapter. Tension usually rose to a head towards the end of a long and effective reign, and the death of the monarch almost always occasioned considerable uncertainty about his succession. A major reason for this was that the Ethiopian emperors continued to be polygamous and formally kept at least three queens in their court. Each of these queens had her extensive contacts and pressure groups throughout the empire, and she naturally tended to use this patronage to make sure that her own offspring got the succession. The succession struggle often started in the closing years of the reign of the monarch, and could explode into prolonged civil wars following his death. So long as the mon-

[1] Taddesse Tamrat, 'A short note on the traditions of pagan resistance to the Ethiopian Church (14th and 15th centuries)', *Journal of Ethiopian Studies*, 1972, **10**, 137–50.

arch himself continued to exercise an effective control over his realm, he could always suppress all attempts to force his hand over the succession, and his loyal and powerful officials could thwart civil wars by immediately crowning his eldest son when he died. Naturally, this could be done more easily if the monarch was survived by a son old enough to provide effective leadership for the Christian empire. On almost all the occasions where this was not the case, wars of succession could not be avoided, and peace and order were restored only after the accession to power of a relatively strong prince who could personally handle the affairs of the state.

The last decade of Zara-Ya'qob's reign saw a number of attempts to depose the emperor, who tells us himself that his queens and their sons were implicated in this defiance to his rule. However, he managed to suppress all these movements and, when he died, he was succeeded by his son Ba'da-Maryam (1468–78), whose mother had been one of those queens who were accused of plotting against the emperor, for which she had been flogged to death. Ba'da-Maryam was old enough to rule on his own, but, in an apparent attempt to dissociate himself from his father's repressive rule, he decreed a total amnesty for all his father's prisoners and considerably decentralized the administration of the empire which his father had jealously guarded in his own hands. It is apparent that this act immediately brought the young emperor much popularity: but in the long run, it led to the resurgence of the elements which had opposed Zara-Ya'qob's reforms. It also tended to relax the firm control which the court had imposed throughout the empire. The effect of all this was hardly noticeable in the days of Ba'da-Maryam himself, who, even if he was much weaker than his father, had a relatively easy time until he began to suffer disastrous military reverses in his conflicts with the kingdom of Adal towards the end of his reign. In the ensuing period of the reign of his sons and grandsons, however, the Christian empire was to come to the lowest ebb of its power in the region.

Ba'da-Maryam was survived by two sons who were only four and six years old. The ideal arrangement on such an occasion would have been to take these minor princes to Mount Gishen, from where an older relative of the deceased monarch would be brought down and be crowned king of kings of Ethiopia. But their mother, Queen Romna, was apparently powerful, and had strong allies among the royal officials. These crowned the elder son of Ba'da-Maryam, Eskender (1478–94), who was only six years old at the time. A council of regents was appointed to administer the empire on his behalf, and this meant that for much of Eskender's reign the young monarch himself had no effective control over his own empire. The absence of this effective leadership from the person of the monarch was particularly felt when divergencies of political interests began to develop among the members of the council of regents, who soon started to intrigue for each other's elimination. By the time Eskender was old enough to exercise power on his own, his Christian army had been rent into so many unruly factions that his single military venture against Adal ended in complete failure. Moreover, when he died in 1494, one section of his army raised to the throne his infant son, Amda-Siyon II, who was less than six years old. Another section of the army marched to Mount Gishen, brought down Na'od, Eskender's brother, who was about twenty at the time, and declared him emperor. The two factions divided the country, and fought a series of desperate wars which claimed the lives of some of the elderly officials of the court. At first, the supporters of the infant prince were successful, but when he died, only six months later, Na'od (1494–1508) was brought to power and he proceeded to punish those members of the army who had opposed his accession six months earlier. Once again civil war broke out in the central provinces of Amhara and Shoa, and many leading officials of the Christian army lost their lives.

Throughout this period of the decline of Christian power, the kingdom of Adal revived once again and stepped up the frontier struggle. Precisely at the time when the Ethiopian throne was occupied by a series of under-aged princes, Adal was in the most capable hands of a powerful general called Maḥfūẓ, who had dominated the political scene in Adal since the 1480s and who is variously given the title of *imām*, *amīr* and *garad*.[1] It appears that at that stage there were two contending political factions in Adal, with different views about relations with Christian Ethiopia. The Walasma king Muḥammad (*c.* 1488–1518) led the moderate party, which apparently favoured a policy of coexistence. This was strongly opposed by the militant group led by his general, Maḥfūẓ, who preferred to continue the old tradition of conflict, and who actually aimed at the effective restoration of Muslim control over the eastern frontier provinces of Ifat, Fetegar, Dawaro and Bali. It is apparent that this militant faction had a much larger following in Adal

[1] Arab-Faqih, *Histoire de la conquête de l'Abyssinie*, tr. René Basset (Paris, 1897–1901), 10, 61, 74, 98, 395.

at the time. The relative ease with which Maḥfūẓ and his followers scored their repeated successes against the internally divided Christian empire also tended to make this policy of confrontation a very popular one. Throughout the reigns of Eskender (1478–94) and Na'od (1494–1508), Maḥfūẓ successfully attacked the frontier provinces. Large numbers of the Christian military colonists were either killed or taken into slavery, and the Muslims always returned to Adal with huge spoils in slaves and cattle. The emperor, Na'od, himself died in 1508 while trying to defend the province of Ifat from one of the regular forays of Imam Maḥfūẓ. Maḥfūẓ continued his aggressive policy until 1516, when Na'od's son and successor, Lebna-Dengel (1508–40), led a surprise attack against him in Fetegar, where he was apparently ambushed and killed. While this brought about a temporary relief in Christian Ethiopia, it sparked off a bitter struggle for power between the two political factions in Adal, and it was eventually the militant followers of Maḥfūẓ who took control of the Muslim state.

King Muḥammad was assassinated not long after Maḥfūẓ was ambushed and killed by the Christians. The king had fled from the battlefield, where his famous general had fallen, and he had apparently lost popularity in Adal, which probably led to his assassination. It is quite clear, however, that his kingdom was soon reduced to a confused political state. For the two years immediately following the king's death, the throne was successively occupied by five usurpers who are merely mentioned in the *Futūḥ al-Ḥabasha*, which is decidedly in favour of Maḥfūẓ. The official Walasma king-list ignores them, and only mentions two members of the royal family as having succeeded Muḥammad. Cerulli has rightly interpreted this to mean that in the struggle for power after the king's assassination, a number of military officials unrelated to the Walasma had exercised effective power, overshadowing the more legitimate princes, who nevertheless continued to claim the Adali throne for themselves.[1]

Thus, the picture that emerges is one of a continuous civil war in Adal, in which power was contested among the legitimate Walasma princes on the one hand and a number of rival military officials on the other. Two of the men who usurped power at the time seem to have been close associates of the fallen general Maḥfūẓ. The first of these is called 'Ousani, slave of *Garad* Maḥfūẓ', and his rule apparently lasted for only three months, after which he was killed by another rival. The

[1] Enrico Cerulli, 'Documenti arabi per la storia dell'Etiopia', *Memoria della Reale Accademia dei Lincei* (Classe di scienze morali, storiche e filologiche), 1931, 4, 49, notes 5 and 6.

second was Garad Abun, who fought for five months against the killer of 'Ousani', and assumed power which he seems to have exercised until 1525, when he was defeated and killed by Muḥammad's son Abū Bakr, with whom he had been fighting since 1520. Garad Abun had a large following, which he had apparently inherited from his predecessor, Maḥfūẓ. Even after he was killed, his followers organized themselves under a new leader, 'Umardin, and continued to defy Abū Bakr. Other than the apparent struggle for mere power, the reasons behind the disturbances do not come out very clearly even from the *Futūḥ al-Ḥabasha*. However, some of the basic issues seem to be reflected from the accusations levelled against the legitimate king Abū Bakr:

Il ruina ses États; les coupeurs de routes se montrèrent, les cabarets firent leur apparition; les gens de sa cour s'attachaient aux voyageurs pour les dépouiller; le vice s'étalait et personne, à cette époque, ne recevait satisfaction d'une injustice; les nobles, les jurisconsultes et les cheikhs réprouvaient la conduite du prince.[1]

Abū Bakr and his government are also implicitly accused for their failure to defend the western frontier of Adal, which was once again being overrun by the Christians after the death of Maḥfūẓ. On one occasion, the Christian governor of neighbouring Dawaro invaded Adal and deeply penetrated its territories, which his army devastated and looted heavily. Abū Bakr could not apparently put up effective resistance against this attack, and the Christians took with them large numbers of prisoners and cattle. At this juncture, the followers of Garad Abun pursued the Christian army, defeated them, and returned the Muslim prisoners as well as the spoils collected by the Christians back to Adal. Abū Bakr was deeply humiliated by this success of his enemies, who made considerable capital out of the incident. Armed conflicts between Abū Bakr and Garad Abun's followers continued with even greater vigour. On one occasion, the latter actually forced Abū Bakr to evacuate the new town of Harar, which had replaced Dakkar as the royal capital of Adal in 1520.

Among the defiant troops who fought against Abū Bakr, there was a young man, Aḥmad b. Ibrāhīm al-Ghāzī, who was originally a knight in the service of Garad Abun. This young man later assumed the leadership of the opposition army on the death of 'Umardin in one of the battles. After a short period of uneasy truce, which had apparently been concluded between the two contending parties, Aḥmad accused Abū

[1] Arab-Faqih, *Histoire de la conquête*, 15.

Bakr of bad faith, and he resumed hostilities with an increasingly powerful army. Aḥmad's followers scored a series of military successes and finally forced the king to come to terms with them and, in effect, to share power with their leader. Under the new arrangement, the king was allowed to return to Harar and occupy the throne of his ancestors, while Aḥmad b. Ibrāhīm was to be in full control of the affairs of state under the nominal orders of the king. Aḥmad's prestige and influence grew throughout Adal, and he seems to have gained the co-operation of most of the religious leaders of the area. In fact, from this time onwards many legends and mystical traditions began to develop around his name, and the lofty title of *imām* is said to have been supernaturally given to him. Fully equipped with these religious sanctions, which enhanced his leadership, Imam Aḥmad conducted his first attack on the Christian frontier province of Dawaro, apparently in 1526. But this was not a complete success, so that the Muslims lost many of their leading officials, who were either killed or captured by the Christians. Although Imam Aḥmad returned to Adal with much booty, this partial failure brought about an important setback in his leadership, and his old rival, King Abū Bakr, apparently tried to use the incident to regain his lost power. A final military struggle took place between the king and the *imām*, in which Abū Bakr was killed and his younger brother 'Umardin crowned in his place by Imam Aḥmad, who was now the only effective ruler of the country.

Aḥmad went on strengthening his position within Harar, and extending his power and influence over the Somali, with whom he seems to have generally been in conflict at the beginning of his career. In its narrative of the internal struggle for power in the years between 1520 and 1526, the *Futūḥ al-Ḥabasha* consistently mentions the Somali as the supporters of Aḥmad's rival, Abū Bakr, who is often accused for his unholy alliance with them. Whenever Aḥmad and his comrades-at-arms scored a victory against him, Abū Bakr fled into Somali country and returned soon with fresh recruits for the next round of hostilities. Whereas he certainly disapproved of their alliance with his rival, Aḥmad seems to have realized the immense possibilities of raising a large army from the Somali interior. And, now that he had successfully eliminated Abū Bakr, Imam Aḥmad began to pacify the Somali. He is first seen in the role of an arbiter in the local conflicts among some Somali tribes. Then he is seen making attempts gradually to integrate the Somali into the Adali state structure. The *Futūḥ al-Ḥabasha* clearly indicates that Aḥmad had considerable difficulties in this. Reference has been made above to traditions which show that Adal had already made alliances with some Somali tribes, who sometimes served in the Adali army. It is apparent, however, that although he had enjoyed great prestige among them, Adal had not been able to establish effective control over the numerous Somali tribes between the Harar region and the Gulf, except perhaps in the narrow corridor through which the major trade routes came from Zeila and Berbera. On either side of this corridor lay the country of Somali tribes who led their traditional nomadic lives in complete independence from any external powers. The general safety of the caravan roads probably depended on the relative strength of the king in Adal, as well as on the political equilibrium he was able to create in the area through his relations with the tribal chiefs. Otherwise the trade-routes were apparently never free from the menace of possible attacks by disgruntled tribes of the Somali. This emerges very clearly from the accounts of Somali resistance to the policy of integration which Imam Aḥmad energetically pursued among them prior to his declaration of a jihad against Christian Ethiopia. He led a series of effective expeditions into a number of Somali tribal areas, forcing them to pay tribute as well as to maintain law and order in the whole area. More important still, he invited the Somali chiefs of the area to participate in his projected holy war against Ethiopia. Although it is impossible here to delimit the extent of the Somali interior affected by Imam Aḥmad's propaganda, the *Futūḥ al-Ḥabasha* gives among his followers a long list of Somali tribes who can still be identified as members of the Darod or Ishaq clan-families. Even the Hawiya seem to have been represented in Aḥmad's crusading army.[1] Besides the Somali, Aḥmad had also incorporated into his army other peoples in the area who had been in continuous conflict with the Christian empire ever since the fourteenth century, such as the Harla, the Hargay, the Shoa and Geday. By about 1527–9, the *imam* was at the head of a strong state, with an ever-increasing sphere of influence in the interior of the Horn, and ready to lead crucial military offensives against the Christian empire.

It is apparent that the Christian empire did not fully realize the extent of the new Adali menace under the leadership of Imam Aḥmad. Lebna-Dengel and his officials seem to have looked at their relations with Adal under the old traditional terms of occasional raids and

[1] Ibid. 34–6, 44–6, 67–70, 118–19, 152, 169, 171. I. M. Lewis, *A pastoral democracy* (London, 1965), 14, 15, 145, 157, 263–4.

counter-raids along the frontiers. That Imam Aḥmad was building up a strong power base for an eventual holy war against his empire did not apparently cross the emperor's mind. Even his chroniclers essentially misunderstood and distorted the dynamics of Aḥmad's advent to power:

At the end of his [Lebna-Dengel's] eighteenth regnal year, there arose in Adal Aḥmad, son of Abrahim. He became obnoxious from childhood and troublous in all his doings. Because of his considerable restlessness he became a highway robber. And then lowly men gathered around him and he began to have a large following, and he devastated the country. When some of the leaders of the *Geraja* rose against him he excelled them and defeated them. Thenceforth, the whole country was agitated by his greatness and his fame spread in all countries.[1]

Aḥmad's early military confrontation with the Christians essentially followed the traditional methods of raiding the frontier districts and returning to Adal with large booty; and this may have also encouraged the apparent lack of seriousness displayed at first towards the new Adali ruler at the court of the emperor. But more important still, it was Lebna-Dengel's successes against Maḥfūẓ in 1516 which still tended to give the Christians an exaggerated sense of security. None of the first armed conflicts between the two states since 1516 was sufficiently disastrous to dispel the false notion of military superiority which Lebna-Dengel and his officials continued to have in their relation with Adal. Nevertheless, the growing ineptitude of the Christian military leadership in the frontier provinces is quite obvious from both Muslim and Christian sources. Reference has already been made to the campaigns of Fanu'el in Adal which ended up in the Christian army's being routed by the followers of Garad Abun, among whom Aḥmad was still a junior cavalry officer. Soon afterwards, in 1525/6, Aḥmad led his maiden expedition against the Christian army, successfully raided the province of Dawaro and, although his followers suffered many casualties on the way back to Adal, he brought back with him much booty, which seems to have been the major purpose of the expedition. In the following year, the Christian emperor sent a large army under Degelhan, his governor of Bali, to raid and invade Adali territory. Aḥmad was preoccupied with Somali affairs at the time, and the Christians scored an initial success in their campaigns, collecting much spoil in slaves and cattle. Both the Christian and Muslim sources

[1] C. Conti Rossini, 'La storia di Lebna Dengel re d'Etiopia', *Rendiconti della Reale Accademia dei Lincei* (Classe di scienze morali, storiche e filologiche), 1894, 3, 624, 635.

agree, however, that Degelhan's venture in 1527 ended up in complete disaster. Aḥmad postponed his Somali expeditions, and pursued the Christian troops on their way back to the highlands. Many of Degelhan's followers were either killed or captured and all the booty and prisoners they had collected were returned intact to Adal. For a long time until after the death of Imam Aḥmad, this expedition by Degelhan was to be the last offensive undertaken by the Christian empire, which henceforth could only afford to be engaged in purely defensive tactics. Indeed, the impact of Aḥmad's victory over Degelhan was so traumatic that the Christian troops in the frontier provinces tended to avoid any direct confrontations with the *imām*'s forces. In the following two years, Aḥmad and his soldiers continuously invaded and devastated the provinces of Fetegar, Dawaro and Ifat. The Muslim army penetrated deep into Christian territories, looted and burned down churches, took large numbers of prisoners and collected considerable booty from the rural areas as well as from market places. On all these occasions, Imam Aḥmad met with little or no organized resistance on the part of the Christian army. While this deeply shook the general sense of security in Christian Ethiopia, it increased the confidence of the *imām* and his army and led to the final showdown of 1529.

The battle of Shimbra-Kure in 1529 marked a major turning-point, in which Imam Aḥmad broke the backbone of Christian resistance against his offensives. The emperor had apparently expected this confrontation, and had mobilized a large army to defend his realms. The troops were recruited from all over the empire and the list of Christian generals who participated in the battle includes the *Baher-Negash* and other officials from the Eritrean plateau, many district governors from Tigre, Amhara, the Agaw territories, Begemder, Gojjam, Shoa, as well as from the frontier provinces of Ifat, Fetegar, Dawaro, Bali and Damot. Although they differ in the corresponding figures which they give, both Christian and Muslim sources are unanimous about the superiority of the emperor's army in terms of the numbers of soldiers. Lebna-Dengel concentrated his defensive army on the central Shoan plateau where he and his ancestors often resided, and there was no attempt to engage the Muslim army beyond or at the frontiers. Imam Aḥmad and his invading army met no major resistance until they reached the Semarma, apparently a tributary of the Kesem, in the province of Fetegar. The first stages of the fighting took place on the banks of the Semarma, where the Christians were initially successful and pushed the Muslims towards Shimbra-Kure, which was further east. There again the Christian army was better off at the beginning, but it was finally overpowered by the Muslim troops' courageous fighting around their *imām*, who spurred them on with his cries of 'Victory or paradise!' The fighting lasted for much of the day and, late in the afternoon, the Muslims scored a resounding victory over the Christians, who lost a very large number of men in the rank and file and a great many of their generals. The *imām*'s chronicler later estimated the Christian casualties as follows:

Le nombre des patrices du Tigré qui furent tués s'éleva à 86, tous des choums d'archers (?) parmi les grands. On tua 10,000 et plus des gens de marque du Tigré; 125, des autres patrices . . . Dans la mêlée, les Musulmans coupèrent les jarrets à 600 chevaux des infidels.[1]

This chronicler actually lists by name the leading Christian generals who fell on the battlefield, and the Christian sources essentially agree with the picture painted by the Muslim writer. But Aḥmad could not pursue his success at Shimbra-Kure by leading further offensives against the retreating Christian forces. He had himself lost over five thousand men; the surviving troops opposed his intentions to continue hostilities, and they asked to be taken back to Adal. The *imām* accepted these protestations of his followers and marched back to Harar for the time being. Before he did so, however, he had completely shattered the traditional strength of the Christian state and essentially broken the unity of its army.

Never again could Emperor Lebna-Dengel raise such a large army as on the day of the battle of Shimbra-Kure in a united command against Imam Aḥmad. From then onwards, Christian strategy tended to change into one of a series of local resistance movements. The emperor himself retreated to the upper waters of the Awash river from where he exhorted his provincial and district governors to put up effective resistance against Muslim advances. The result was that each of these local armies succumbed under the pressure of the much more united army of the *imām*, who resumed the frontier invasions only a few months after his victory at Shimbra-Kure. Thus, in the remaining months of 1529 and in 1530 Aḥmad led his forces into Dawaro and Bali respectively, and destroyed the Christian system of frontier defence in these provinces. In 1531 he returned to the Shoan plateau by way of Dawaro, where he crushed the isolated resistance movements, and marched on to the upper waters of the Awash in pursuit of the emperor. The emperor himself withdrew further west to Damot, but

[1] Arab-Faqih, *Histoire de la conquête*, 130.

his leading officials put up courageous but desperate resistance against the *imām*'s army, which they engaged at different points on both sides of the upper Awash. Here, in these series of bloody confrontations, fell some of the most senior advisers and generals of Lebna-Dengel. Aḥmad's army spread out across the rich plateau of Shoa north of the Awash in full force and devastated the major Christian centres in the area. The leading monastery of Debra Libanos was burned down with a large number of its inmates, and this is graphically described by the Muslim chronicler as follows:

> Les moines qui l'habitaient s'enfuirent dans une montagne inaccessible. Puis une partie s'en revint à l'église, en disant: 'S'ils brûlent notre église qui est pour nous un lieu de pélerinage, il nous y brûleront aussi.' Ils y entrèrent et s'assirent au milieu, en attendant qu'on y mit le feu . . . Un Musulman . . . y mit le feu . . . A cette vue . . . les moines allèrent à l'envie se jetter dans le feu comme le papillon contre une lampe, à l'exception d'un petit nombre d'entre eux.[1]

The old Egyptian bishop Abuna Marqos had died a year earlier, and the emperor, who was only thirty-five years old at the time, had suffered the loss of a great many senior advisers and officials, most of whom were his own relatives. Thus, the quality of the Christian leadership was getting considerably poorer as the *imām*'s occupation army pushed on towards the heart of the empire in northern Shoa, Amhara and Tigre.

The next round of defensive actions taken by the emperor was aimed mainly at preventing the *imām* from gaining an easy breakthrough into these northern areas. To this end, Lebna-Dengel moved from western Shoa to Amhara, and stationed the leading officials of his dwindling army at the difficult mountain passes between northern Shoa and Amhara. These measures were fairly effective in themselves, but the *imām* led his followers into Amharaland along the easternmost route through Ifat and Gidim. Once he reached the Amhara plateau, he sent contingents of his army in all directions to devastate the countryside. Ever since the rise of the Solomonic dynasty in 1270, Amhara had been the centre of the expanding Christian empire. The emperors had built a large number of richly endowed churches and monasteries in the area, and it was also here that many of them had their most treasured country houses. All these were now overrun one by one, their rich treasures were looted, and they were all burnt down to the ground. From this time onwards the emperor fled from one

[1] Ibid. 254–5.

part of the country to another, and the Christian resistance increasingly assumed a picture of guerrilla warfare, which was very strong in the mountainous areas of Lasta and Tigre. In the meantime, Imam Aḥmad pushed on to Tigre and southern Eritrea, opened up contacts with Muslim communities in the region of present-day Galabat, crossed the Tekeze, raided Begemder as far as Lake Tana and even penetrated deep into northern Gojjam, always burning and looting the countryside. The royal prison of Gishen in Amhara, the ancient cathedral of Aksum and numerous other monasteries in Tigre, the island monastery of Gelila in Lake Tana, and a number of churches in north-eastern Gojjam, were some of the leading establishments which were burned to ashes, together with invaluable illuminated manuscripts and art objects. Even the rock churches of Lalibela and central Tigre were assaulted and still bear the permanent imprints of the violence which left the wall paintings charred and damaged.

The character of the *imām*'s campaigns had completely changed since his return to the Shoan plateau in 1531. He had now come to occupy the conquered lands, and to administer them together with his Adali territories. As his army swept over the provinces of Bali, Dawaro, Shoa, Ifat and Amhara, he forced Lebna-Dengel to move the centre of his resistance further northwards. The overall effect of this was to leave the rich territories of the Christian empire south of Shoa entirely at the mercy of the Muslim army. Thus, the *imām* gradually consolidated his control of these realms, either by nominating his own Muslim governor over each district or by confirming the old local hereditary chiefs to administer the area on his behalf. He extended the same administrative system wherever he conquered additional territories from the Christians, so that by 1535 he had appointed Muslim governors over all the provinces of the former Christian empire. According to the Christian chronicler, Aḥmad's power 'consolidated from this time onwards, and he ruled from the sea of Aftel to the sea of Deheno'.[1] *Aftel* is a Christian corruption of *Awdal*, which is the local Somali word for Zeila, and *Deheno* was a Christian settlement on the mainland opposite the island of Massawa. Thus, Imam Aḥmad had succeeded in carving out a vast empire extending from Zeila to Massawa on the coast and including what once used to be the interior of the Christian empire of Ethiopia. It is very hard to explain the rapidity or the magnitude of his successes against Christian Ethiopia, which had looked quite invincible only fifty years earlier. There is no doubt that the

[1] Conti Rossini, 'La storia de Lebna Dengel', 629, 639.

civil wars and succession problems which had troubled the Christian state since the 1470s had contributed to its weakness in the face of the *imām*'s army. But this can hardly provide the whole explanation, since there was a clear revival of Christian power in the reigns of Na'od (1494–1508) and his son Lebna-Dengel (1508–40), particularly after 1516. It has also been traditional in Ethiopia to explain Aḥmad's success in terms of the human and material support he is believed to have received from the Ottomans, into whose sphere of influence the Red Sea had already come. Here again the evidence is slight and, although there are some references to this effect in the contemporary sources, Ottoman assistance does not seem to have been a major factor in the remarkable successes of Imam Aḥmad. The vast Christian empire, which had overextended itself since the middle of the fourteenth century, was not yet sufficiently integrated to withstand sustained external aggression by a highly united army such as Aḥmad had mobilized under his own charismatic leadership within the fifteen years of his effective career. Islam was still the religion of most of the people in the frontier provinces of Ifat, Dawaro and Bali, and they paid homage to the *imām* at the earliest sign of his effective victory over the Christian army. The various Semitic-speaking and Cushitic communities south of the Blue Nile and the Awash, which had been brought under Christian rule in the fourteenth and fifteenth centuries, had little or nothing to lose from the defeat of their Christian overlords; and they soon made their peace with the new Muslim conqueror. The Falasha of Begemder had always fought for their freedom since the fourteenth century, and they now enthusiastically made an alliance with Imam Aḥmad, for whose army they served as invaluable guides. The Agaw-speaking inhabitants of the region south of Lake Tana were still predominantly pagan, and they supported the Muslim army in harassing the Christians who had conquered and increasingly settled their ancient homeland in eastern Gojjam. The basis for the unity of the empire in its wider connotations was mere force continuously displayed and exercised by the Christian monarchs and their local representatives. When this was completely shattered by the youthful Muslim army, Lebna-Dengel was left enjoying the loyalty of only a small section of his empire in northern Ethiopia.

Nevertheless, Imam Aḥmad had not been able to capture the emperor, nor completely to suppress the profound Christian loyalties of the ancient provinces of southern Eritrea, the whole of Tigre, the Agaw areas of Wag and Lasta, and some islands of resistance unevenly spread throughout northern Shoa, Amhara and eastern Gojjam. There are clear indications that his otherwise firm control over much of the area was continuously frustrated by this, and he was beginning to evolve very radical means to pacify the emperor and his patriotic supporters. This seems to emerge in one of the Christian chronicles from the invaluable reference to the fact that the *imām* proposed in 1539 a marriage alliance between himself and the emperor's family:

> And in the thirty-first year of his [Lebna-Dengel's] reign, this Muslim [Aḥmad] sent to the king saying, 'Give me your daughter so that she becomes my wife and let us make peace. But if you do not accept this, there is no place where you can escape from me.' And the king replied to him saying, 'I shall not give you [my daughter], for you are a heathen.'[1]

There is another reference elsewhere that the *imām*'s wife, Dil-Wambera, had given her daughter to one of the emperor's sons, Minas, who was taken prisoner by the Muslims in 1538 or 1539. The officials of the *imām* were highly divided over the issue, and it was later decided that the Christian prince be sent as a present to the Ottoman governor of Zebid. However, both these references seem to indicate that, ten years after his initial victory at the battle of Shimbra Kure in 1529, the *imām* had reached a high degree of political maturity and that he was prepared to make a realistic pact with his Christian foe. Lebna-Dengel would not compromise on this point, and he continued the resistance until he died in 1540, when he was succeeded by one of his sons, Galawdewos (1540–59). About five years before he died, however, Lebna-Dengel had decided to appeal for Christian assistance from Europe and had sent a Portuguese envoy to Rome and to Lisbon.

EUROPE AND CHRISTIAN ETHIOPIA, *c.* 1400–1543

Only a brief outline need be given here of the early contacts between Ethiopia and Christian Europe.[2] These contacts hinged on two important historical phenomena: the first was the profound devotion which many Ethiopian religious leaders had towards making the hazardous Pilgrimage to the Holy Land; and the second was the development of the literary legend about the Prester John of the Indies and its various proliferations. There is no doubt that Ethiopian pilgrims started to visit Jerusalem and other holy places in the Aksumite period.

[1] R. Basset, 'Études sur l'histoire d'Ethiopie', *Journal Asiatique*, 1881, **17**, 329; **18**, 100.
[2] They are discussed in greater detail in Taddesse Tamrat, *Church and state*, 248–67.

But it was only from Ṣalāḥ al-Dīn's triumphant occupation of the Holy City in 1187 that the Ethiopian Church seems to have received a permanent site where the pilgrims could reside and worship. In 1189 the Egyptian ruler is said to have granted some places of worship in Jerusalem and Bethlehem to the Ethiopians, who still use this donation as a basis for their continued possession of these sites. From then onwards a regular flow of Ethiopian pilgrims seems to have visited the Holy Land. The most frequent road followed by them was the land route through northern Eritrea to Suakin, then across the desert to Qus on the Nile; they went by boat down to Cairo, from where they took the land route again across the Sinai peninsula. The pilgrimage was often undertaken in large groups and the casualties on both the outward and the return trips were very high. A very small fraction of the pilgrims returned home, while a small number of them remained either in the Holy Land or at various points along the route. Thus by the middle of the fourteenth century small Ethiopian communities were found in some Egyptian monasteries in the Nile Valley, at the monastery of St Catherine on Mount Sinai, in Jerusalem and other places in the Holy Land, as well as in Armenia and the island of Cyprus further north. Towards the end of the fifteenth century it seems very clear that Ethiopian monks could be found not only in the Nile Valley and in the Levant, but also on the island of Rhodes, in some of the Italian city-states, particularly Venice and Florence, and increasingly in Rome. For the beginning of the sixteenth century we actually have a number of itineraries of Ethiopian monks who travelled to Europe through the Holy Land. These early pioneers set the tone of the relations between Europe and Ethiopia until the middle of the sixteenth century. Wherever they met fellow Christians from other countries, they transmitted vivid traditions about their church and its distinctive liturgical practices, about the Christian kingdom and its continuous conflicts with the neighbouring Muslim areas, and about the Ethiopian interest in breaking their age-old isolation from the rest of the Christian world. Very often these monks were too patriotic, and the stories they related about their country seem to have exaggerated the power and wealth of the Christian monarchs. After the revival of the Christian state under the Solomonic rulers in the fourteenth and fifteenth centuries, such stories were a true reflection of the sense of power and self-confidence which the Christians felt throughout Ethiopia. The reports of Muslim merchants in Egypt and Syria also corroborated the essential truth of the conquests and expansion of the Christian empire in the

African hinterland of the southern Red Sea. Thus, the image which Europe began to have regarding Christian Ethiopia from the early Crusades onwards was one of a very powerful and wealthy state. It seems to be very far fetched now to suggest that this had anything to do with the early development of the European legend about the Prester John of the Indies. But it is true that from the last years of the thirteenth century onwards, there was a gradual identification of the legendary Prester John with the increasingly powerful Solomonic monarchs of Ethiopia.

The legend of the Prester John developed in an atmosphere of Christian despair and despondency in the middle of the twelfth century, when the balance of power in the wars of the Crusades had tipped decidedly in favour of the Muslims throughout the east Mediterranean region. Essentially, the legend had the practical effect of reinforcing the religious stamina of the Crusaders by holding out the promise that a fabulously rich and mighty oriental king-priest was due to march against Islam from the east in support of his fellow Christians. But despite the force with which the legend seems to have kindled the imagination of Europe at the time, nothing came out of it for over a hundred years. Once the identification with Ethiopia was made, however, very clear attempts were made to see the legend come true. The Dominican Archbishop of Sulṭāniyya, William Adam, who visited the island of Socotra in the second decade of the fourteenth century, repeatedly proposed that the Crusaders should blockade the Red Sea trade with the help of the Ethiopians. Other strategists resorted to the ancient legend that the Ethiopians had it in their power to divert the direction of the Nile, and it was proposed that this power should be used by the Crusaders to strangle Mamluk Egypt. The Solomonic kings of Ethiopia had begun to pose as the protectors of the Coptic Christians in Egypt, and this brought about occasional conflicts between the rulers of the two countries. On the home front, we have already seen the protracted wars between the Christian rulers and the Muslim areas in the Ethiopian interior. All these conflicts were interpreted in Europe as making part and parcel of the wars of the Crusaders, and the Ethiopian kings were hailed as Christian heroes. The first message of congratulation on record was sent in 1400 by King Henry IV of England, who addressed his letter to the 'King of Abyssinia Prester John'.[1] From that time onwards we have isolated

[1] *Royal and historical letters during the reign of Henry IV, King of England and of France, and Lord of Ireland*, ed. F. C. Hingeston (London, 1860), I, 419–22.

references to Europeans in Ethiopia, some of whom seem to have come as official envoys. In 1427 and 1450 we have reliable reports of Ethiopian delegations sent to Europe to establish friendly relations and to ask for European technicians and artisans. It is probable that some of the artisans requested in 1450 had reached Ethiopia, where some Europeans are reported as having been in the emperor's court in the early 1480s. It was, however, the Portuguese, with their remarkable success in navigating the eastern seas, who took most seriously the search for Prester John, with whom they established contact before the end of the fifteenth century.

The first two Portuguese envoys assigned to discover the location of the Prester John's empire left Lisbon in 1487, only three months before Bartholomew Diaz set out on his famous voyage round the Cape of Good Hope. For the following seven years, one of these envoys, Pero de Covilhã, travelled widely in the Levant, the Indian Ocean, the Persian Gulf, the Red Sea, and the Gulf of Aden actively collecting information regarding the land of the Prester John of the Indies. All the reports he gathered pointed towards the Christian empire of Ethiopia, where he finally arrived, apparently in 1494, using the route from Zeila. He was not permitted by the Ethiopians to realize his plans to return home and report his findings; and he was to remain in Ethiopia and die there more than thirty years later. A Portuguese priest, João Gomez, was later assigned to travel to the land of the Prester John. Apparently, he first tried to penetrate the interior from Malindi, and failed, but he is reported to have reached the country soon after the Portuguese took Socotra in 1507. He also seems to have been unable to return to his country, and probably died on his way back. These early Portuguese initiatives were apparently received with many uncertainties by the Ethiopians, who procrastinated in their response. As we have already seen, however, this advent of the Portuguese coincided with the troubled days when Emir Maḥfūẓ of Adal was continuously and successfully harassing the frontier provinces. The benefits of a close alliance with the Portuguese seem to have slowly dawned upon the Ethiopian rulers, and they sent their first official response in 1512. The king at the time, Lebna-Dengel (1508–40), had acceded to the throne when he was only twelve, and the empire was being administered on his behalf by Empress Eleni, who was the regent. Empress Eleni sent her envoys with rich gifts and a letter to King Manuel (1495–1521), who received them with considerable warmth in 1513. Her letter included very high hopes about the grand alliance with the Prester John, which the Portuguese monarch had always had in mind. The empress wrote to him:

We can supply mountains of provisions and men like unto the sands of the sea . . . We have news that the Lord of Cairo is building ships to fight your fleet, and we shall give you so many men . . . as to wipe the Moors from the face of the earth. We by land, and you, brothers, by the sea.[1]

Thus, the Ethiopian response to Portugal started on a very high note, but the delegation Manuel sent in return did not reach Ethiopia until 1520. By that time the young emperor Lebna-Dengel had assumed full powers and the empress was too old and completely powerless. The exultations of his victory over Emir Maḥfūẓ in 1516 were still fresh in the emperor's mind, and his reception of the Portuguese delegation was at best only lukewarm. He disclaimed responsibility for the Ethiopian mission sent out by the empress, and the Portuguese delegates merely trotted up and down the country until they left for home in 1526 without concluding an effective alliance.

Two of the Portuguese had remained in Ethiopia when their countrymen left for Europe. It was to one of these, João Bermudez, that Lebna-Dengel entrusted his appeal for European assistance at the time of his great need in 1535. Bermudez later returned to the Red Sea with the Portuguese fleet under the new Governor of India, Estavão da Gama, who conducted an expedition against Suakin, Kosseir and Suez in 1541. On his return trip from Suez, Estavão stopped at Massawa, where he received fresh appeals from the Ethiopians to help them against Imam Aḥmad. The Portuguese governor selected a small force of four hundred men, and sent them into the Ethiopian interior under the command of his own brother, Christovão da Gama. The newly crowned emperor of Ethiopia, Galawdewos (1540–59), was at that time in northern Shoa, where he had been leading a small resistance movement againt the Muslim occupation. His camp was elated at the news of the Portuguese military assistance and began marching northwards to join his allies. But the Portuguese had already started hostilities with the *imām*, who was in the northern province of Tigre. At first they were very successful and, although they were greatly outnumbered by the *imām*'s forces, they effectively used their artillery and scored repeated victories against him. In the summer of 1542, however, Imam Aḥmad received substantial reinforcements from Zebid, consisting of a few hundred well-armed Turks, ten field guns, and some Arab horsemen. With these additional forces, the Muslims

[1] E. Sanceau, *Portugal in quest of Prester John* (London, 1943), 18.

attacked the Portuguese, who were easily defeated and their commander held and executed by the *imām*. The number of the Portuguese soldiers was now reduced to about two hundred, and the only hope for them was to avoid any direct confrontations with the Muslim army until they joined forces with Emperor Galawdewos. In the meantime, the *imām* had sent most of the Turkish matchlockmen back to Zebid, keeping only two hundred with whom he camped in the vicinity of Lake Tana. Towards the end of the year, the emperor joined the Portuguese and they spent the whole of January reorganizing their forces and preparing to attack the *imām*. Finally, on 22 February 1543, the two armies met at a site called Woina-Dega and fought a desperate battle, in which Imam Aḥmad was defeated and killed.

Ever since his victory at the battle of Shimbra-Kure in 1529, Imam Aḥmad had dominated the scene throughout the Ethiopian interior and the Horn. Nevertheless, the huge empire he had begun to build for himself was in a constant state of emergency throughout this period. Although he had nominated Muslim governors over all the districts of the Christian empire, he did not have enough time to consolidate his power in his newly conquered territories. Moreover, it was mainly the charisma of his personal leadership which gave his army the internal unity and discipline which it displayed, particularly after 1531. When he lost his life at Woina-Dega, his army disintegrated and his followers rushed back to the Harar plateau in various directions. Only in the frontier provinces of Dawaro, Fetegar and Bali did some of his close associates hold on until the Christians advanced once again towards those areas. Imam Aḥmad b. Ibrāhīm left a legacy of complete destruction for the highland Christians of Ethiopia, and they have immortalized his career with numerous legends and with the name *Gragn*, 'the left-handed'.

CHAPTER 3

THE EAST COAST, MADAGASCAR AND THE INDIAN OCEAN

The eastern coast of Africa looks out over the Indian Ocean, which, though vast, is comparatively easily navigated. Consequently there has been much contact over the past two thousand years among the peoples who inhabit its shores. This, coupled with similar climatic and ecological conditions in most of the surrounding coastal lands, has resulted in a considerable degree of cultural homogeneity, particularly marked in the western part of the ocean. Communication between the African coast and the interior was, on the other hand, difficult.

Voyages in this part of the Indian Ocean would have been facilitated by the pattern of the monsoon regime, the winds blowing from a north-easterly direction towards East Africa for half the year, and from the south-west for the other half. This renders voyages by sailing ship from the Persian Gulf and north-western India particularly easy; those from Aden and the Yemen are rather more difficult. To the south, the South Equatorial Current facilitates voyages from the Far East to Africa, and the return is assisted by the monsoonal drift setting to the east between that current and India, together with predominantly westerly winds in this region.

The main motive for voyages to East Africa was trade, but the pressure of population in the arid lands bordering the northern margin of the Indian Ocean provided a stimulus to migration. In the traditions of the coast, religious persecution figures as the reason for migrants leaving their homelands in the Persian Gulf, but it is probable that the attractions of well-watered lands, coupled with the prospect of wealth and a comfortable life in an agreeable environment, played at least as great a part. Such was certainly the case with more recent migrants. These migrations can be compared also with the settlement of Arabs from South Arabia in Indonesia.

The chief articles of commerce sought in East Africa were its natural products. In the north these were mainly frankincense and myrrh. Gum resins of these classes, mainly used for incense in the ancient world, as today in Muslim regions, were gathered in the form of exudations from shrubs native to what is now Ethiopia and Somalia;

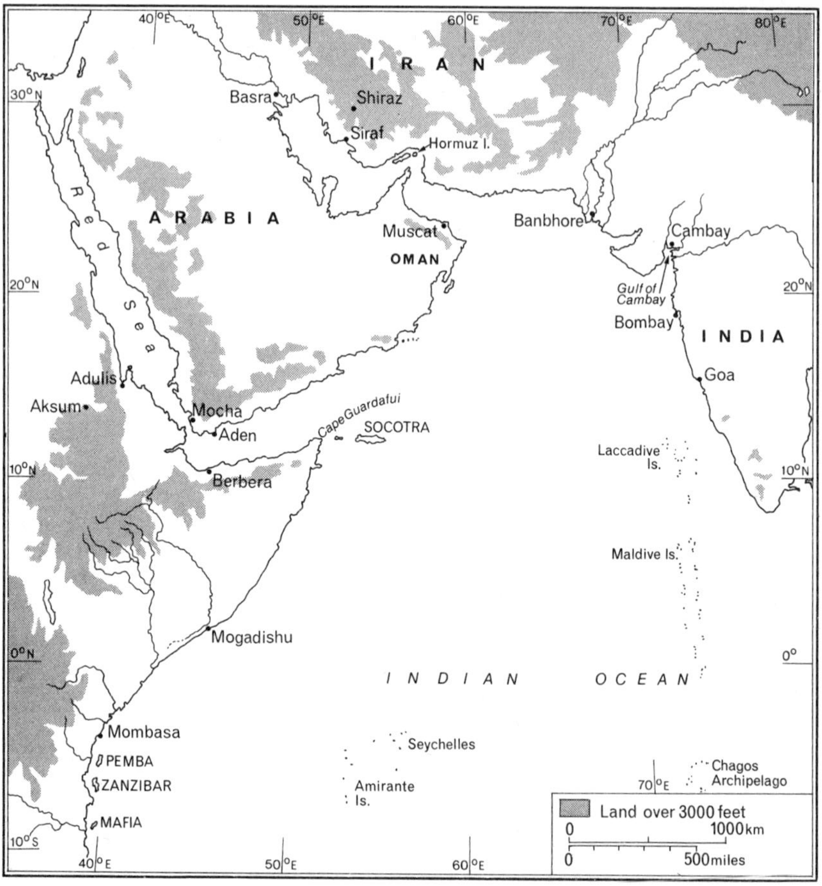

5 The Indian Ocean lands

the myrrh from the region was reckoned to be better than that from Arabia. Further to the south, ivory was the most important export. This product was much in demand in China, as well as in India, where it was esteemed as being of more suitable quality for working than the local product, which was in any case insufficient for the demand. Gold was to attain a prominent place in the trade of the coast. Mined in what is now Rhodesia, it was brought down to the coast and shipped to the ports which grew up to the north. Timber, cut from the mangrove forests found from the Lamu region southwards, and especially in the delta of the Rufiji river, was probably always an important export; poles from these sources provided material for roofing in the Gulf region, and probably also southern Arabia. Slaves were probably exported on a significant scale from the north, at least from the time of the *Periplus* onwards, but there is little evidence of their having been shipped from the southern part of the region until the eighteenth century. In addition, iron is mentioned in the twelfth century as an export both from what is now the Kenya and the Mozambique coast. The focus of this trade was, for most of the period considered here, the Persian Gulf. Here were situated the entrepôts, not only for commerce to the great centres of civilization in Iraq and Iran, but also for trade with the Far East, which was the final destination of many of the goods from East Africa, especially ivory.

The eastern coast of Africa can be considered as divided into two climatic regions unequal in size. The first corresponds roughly to modern Somalia, the most natural division being at Kismayu; the second extends from thence to the Zambezi. The island of Madagascar has a character of its own.

The Somali coast lacks the more or less plentiful rainfall found in the rest of Africa in the same latitudes. Most of it is very arid, though rainfall increases towards the south. The coast is lined with sand-dunes, unstable close to the shore, consolidated and carrying some vegetation to the rear. Inland are plains which are arid, but capable of supporting a pastoral, nomadic population. The plains are traversed by the Webe Shebele and the Juba, both in the southern half of the country. The coast is almost entirely bereft of harbours, those of the main ('harbour') towns, Mogadishu, Merca and Brava being very poor. These are situated on what is called the Benadir coast, presumably because they are the first tolerable anchorages to be reached when sailing southwards along the even more inhospitable northern coast.

The overwhelming majority of the population of this region today are nomadic Somali, who extend also over a large part of eastern Ethiopia and into the north-eastern interior of Kenya. Only about one-eighth of these people, almost all of whom live in the southern part of the country, practise agriculture. Negroid people form a small minority; they are in part remnants of the Bantu-speaking people who were living in the southern part of the area before the southward spread of the Galla and Somali, and partly the descendants of slaves brought from the south in more recent times. They are settled along the two rivers and the hinterland between them. The curious dialect of Swahili spoken in the port of Brava is also associated with these early Bantu peoples.

The littoral of the southern sector of the coast consists in general of a narrow, sandy plain, fertile for certain crops, with fresh water to be had in many places. Behind this is a gently rising belt of bushland, around 100–200 kilometres in width. While a few more favoured parts have attracted cultivation, most of it consists of scrubby bushland of *Brachystegia* and *Acacia commiphora* type, hard to penetrate and deficient in ground-water. While this belt of bush, the northern part of which is termed *nyika* in Swahili, can hardly be held to be such a barrier to penetration of the interior as it has often been presented, it is a fact that it was little traversed in the past. Its general unattractiveness, compared with the coast, together with the presence of tsetse, have no doubt been deterrents to its development. There are very few permanent rivers, and none of these except the Zambezi is navigable for any distance. There was, therefore, little to attract maritime people to penetrate the interior.

The coast enjoys a good and fairly reliable rainfall, of the order of 100 centimetres per annum. Coconuts, cassava and, in the low-lying depressions, rice, are the chief crops cultivated. The warm, shallow off-shore waters are rich in fish of the smaller sorts, which form an important part of the diet of the people.

The shore is fringed by coral reefs, which provide a considerable degree of protection from the ocean waves. In addition to the reefs, protection is afforded by the large islands of Pemba, Zanzibar and Mafia, facilitating coastal traffic. Much of the shore is lined with mangroves, but these stretches are broken here and there by sandy beaches. The configuration of the shore, consisting of a steep upper part and a very gently sloping lower section, is well suited to use by the smaller ships of the region, which sail in at high tide and anchor a little off shore. As the tide recedes the boat comes to rest on the muddy foreshore, where it can easily be unloaded by hand. Thus any protected part of the shore free of mangroves is suitable as a harbour.

The coast is broken by a number of deep inlets which provide even better shelter. These inlets are 'drowned valleys', old estuaries now submerged by a rising sea-level. The northernmost of them is Bur Gao, a little north of the Kenya border; the harbours of Dar-es-Salaam and Mombasa are other examples. They often contain extensive mangrove forests, with timber of commercial value. The greatest such forests of the coast are found in the wide delta of the Rufiji river, which is consequently the main goal of the dhows seeking timber for export to the Persian Gulf and Arabia. Some of the inlets have islands within or associated with them; such is the case with the Lamu archipelago,

Mombasa and the great harbour of Kilwa. These islands provided the preferred sites for early towns, protected from possible enemies by the water between them and the mainland.

The larger off-shore islands, Pemba, Zanzibar and Mafia, offer similar advantages: their ecology is similar to that of the coast, but they enjoy an even greater rainfall. Not only these, but the smaller isolated islands, such as Koma and Songo Songo, attracted settlement, as did the string of Bajun islands extending parallel to the southern Somali coast. The east coast of all these islands is exposed, and consequently the settlements were nearly all on the landward side. The Comoro islands are similar in character to the off-shore islands, save that they are volcanic.

The population of the coast from Brava southwards, as well as that of the islands, is Swahili-speaking (in various dialects), Swahili being a Bantu language incorporating a very large number of words of Arabic origin. In the main, the people gain their living from agriculture and fishing. In the hinterland of the north of Kenya and south of Somalia are a few hunting and gathering people who speak a Cushitic language; otherwise, the languages neighbouring to Swahili are all of the Bantu family. The inhabitants of the towns and villages from Kismayu in the north to the Kerimba island and Ibo in Mozambique can be considered as belonging to a single 'Swahili' civilization, composed of two elements, one African and one Arab or Muslim. The African tribal loyalties, and to some extent African customs, have been abandoned for the wider loyalty and culture of Islam; the Arab element has to a greater or lesser extent merged with the African, so that there is no clear line between the two.[1]

The Swahili-speaking people distinguish themselves sharply from the *watu wa bara*, the people of the hinterland, whether or not the latter have adopted (usually in a rather superficial fashion) the Islamic faith. These people retain their tribal organization and loyalty as well as their language; hardly any of them have survived on the coast itself without being incorporated in the 'Swahili'. The Rufiji people, who live in the delta of that name, whither they descended from the Matumbi highlands, are an exception.

The island of Madagascar can almost be considered to be a continent

[1] The term *mswahili* (also, in Zanzibar and Pemba recently, *shirazi*) is often used to designate one of primarily African, often slave, origin, but the term is an imprecise one, and often used in a wider sense. *Mwarabu* is used of those Swahili speakers who are to a greater or lesser degree of Arab origin. It is interesting that this word, despite its derivation, does not indicate a true Arab; such recent immigrants are called *wamanga* (from Oman) or *washihiri* (from southern Arabia).

of its own: its distinctiveness is indicated by the disinclination of its people to be considered part of Africa. It can be divided into three zones. In the centre, running the length of the island, is a plateau region four to six thousand feet above sea-level. East of this, and divided from it by precipitous scarps, is a comparatively narrow plain with a coastline fringed with dunes and lagoons, exposed to fierce winds and occasional cyclones. To the west is a wider but more arid plain, with good harbours and off-shore islands at its northern end. All except its northern extremity lies south of the area of the monsoon regime. The south-east trade winds give to the eastern side of the island a warm and humid climate with plentiful rainfall. The west on the other hand is comparatively dry, and indeed arid at its southern end. The plateau has a cooler climate with moderate rainfall; its former forests have been destroyed by man in recent centuries, resulting in bare lateritic hills covered with poor pasture.

The inhabitants of Madagascar virtually all speak dialects of a language of Indonesian origin, and many of their cultural traits and crops are derived from the same region. Morphologically, however, the people appear to divide into two racial groups, one of Asian and one of African origin, with an intermediate mixed type. An African element is evident in the language and in certain traits. The number of the original immigrants to Madagascar appears to have been small. The early population seems to have lived scattered around the coastline, especially near the mouths of rivers. The penetration of the interior highlands seems to have occurred mainly within the last four or five centuries.

The earliest information we have from the Arabs concerning the African coast and its population, known to them as Zanj, dates from the ninth and tenth centuries. Al-Mas'ūdī writes of a cattle-keeping (and cattle-riding) people who, he indicates, were of Ethiopian (Cushitic) stock. The Zanj had kings who were in some fashion elected, and who had troops under their command. Their society was one in which formal religion played a considerable part, holy men preaching to the people in the presence of the king, according to al-Jāḥiẓ (ninth century). They are described also as agriculturalists, their staple diet being sorghum and an aroid which seems to be *Colocasia esculenta* (a type of cocoyam). They cultivated coconuts and bananas too, and honey and meat also formed part of their diet.

There is, on the other hand, linguistic evidence that Bantu-speaking people had settled on the coast and in its hinterland before the beginning of the period with which we are concerned (see Volume 2, chapter 6). This is confirmed by Mas'ūdī, who records one word used by the Zanj people which is almost certainly Bantu, and another which may be so. How these apparently Cushitic and Bantu elements related to each other is uncertain. The Cushitic, pastoral element may have constituted a ruling class in Zanj society, or the two peoples may have lived alongside one another.

Archaeologically speaking, there are no settlements known on the coast which antedate for certain the ninth or tenth century; nor any which were not already importing goods directly or indirectly from the Islamic world. In the hinterland, however, numbers of settlements of iron-using agricultural people have been found dating from the early centuries AD onwards; culturally these show little or no coastal influence.

From a circumstantial statement in a Chinese source of the mid ninth century, which must be based on hearsay from Muslim traders, it seems clear that the inhabitants of Berbera, or the Horn, were pastoralists; an interesting detail is that they lived on blood as well as meat and milk, traits found today among the Cushitic Galla and the Paranilotic Masai. However, the Somali were in occupation of the area, or parts of it, at an early date; the Hawiya clan-family were in the Merca area in the thirteenth century (Ibn Sa'īd) and almost certainly a hundred years earlier, at the time of al-Idrīsī. The Galla were expanding into southern Somalia in the sixteenth century, in which area they displaced the Bantu *Kashūr* population, who appear to have been living alongside the Somali. These *Kashūr*, pressed southwards by the Galla, were the ancestors of the Miji Kenda (Nyika) peoples now living in the hinterland of the Kenya coast.

The great traveller Ibn Baṭṭūṭa, who visited Kilwa in 1332 or thereabouts, describes the Africans of the place as very black; they tattooed their faces, a trait characteristic of the Makonde and related Bantu-speaking peoples of the present day. In Mogadishu, he tells us, they conversed in *Maqdishī*; it is not clear whether this was a Bantu language, like the present dialect of Swahili spoken in Brava, or Somali. The former, however, seems more probable, the name of one of the two old quarters of the town being of Bantu origin, though no Bantu language is now spoken there. Ibn Baṭṭūṭa makes no mention of anything that would indicate the presence of hunting or pastoral peoples on the coast, but this is probably due to the fact that he saw nothing outside the ports; the presence of such people two centuries later is indicated by Barros.

THE EARLIEST MUSLIM SETTLEMENTS

The Arab geographers viewed the eastern coast as divided into four regions (see p. 191). The Barbar region (*Bilād al-Barbar*) covered the Horn of Africa, down to a point rather north of the Webe Shebele (the *Nīl Maqdishū*); the country of the Zanj (*Arḍ al-Zanj*) extended from there to about the latitude of Tanga or the southern end of Pemba island. There, according to al-Idrīsī, who completed his description of the world in 1154, began the Sofala country (*Arḍ Sufāla*), whose southern limit is uncertain but is likely to have been in the region of the Limpopo river.[1] Beyond this was the shadowy land of *Wāq-Wāq*. In addition, al-Idrīsī divides off a small stretch of coast between the lands of Berdera and the Zanj, which he terms the country of the black pagans (*Arḍ Kafarat al-Sūdān*). From the time of this author onwards Madagascar is referred to as *al-Qumr*; earlier geographers did not distinguish the island, including it in the general term *Wāq-Wāq*.[2]

Al-Mas'ūdī, writing of the first half of the tenth century, refers to voyages on the sea of Zanj from Oman and Siraf; the latter, situated on the eastern side of the Persian Gulf and serving Shiraz and other towns in the interior, was the greatest port of its age. Al-Mas'ūdī himself sailed across this sea with shipowners and captains from Siraf, embarking at Suhar in Oman. The last occasion he voyaged across it, returning from the island of *Qanbalū* to Oman, was in AD 916/17.[3] He describes the goal of these voyages to have been this island, estimated as around 500 *farsakhs* (approx. 1,400 nautical miles) from Oman, and the country of *Sufāla* and the *Wāq-Wāq*. Buzurg (a contemporary of Mas'ūdī) states that the place where ships normally went on to in the Zanj country was 800 *farsakhs* from *Qanbalū* (here 'Zanj' seems to be used in the general sense), but sometimes ships were carried down to the cannibal country 1,500 *farsakhs* from *Qanbalū*. This indicates that trade was carried on as far south as the lower Mozambique coast.

Al-Mas'ūdī is particularly concerned with the island of *Qanbalū*; he mentions no town by name either there or on the mainland, but Buzurg writes of what is evidently a town surrounded by a strong wall,

[1] None of the earlier geographers, with the doubtful exception of the anonymous author of the Hudūd al 'Ālam, mentions a town of *Sufāla*: the misinterpretation of *Arḍ Sufāla* as indicating the settlement of that name has led to much misunderstanding. *Sufāla* is used to mean shoal water [al-Mas'ūdī, *Murūj al-Dhahab*, I, 332; ed. and tr. C. Pellat, *Les prairies d'or* (Paris, 1962), I, 135], though it can also mean low-lying land.

[2] One should also be aware of the danger of confusion between [Jazīrat] al-Qumr, the island of Madagascar, and Qimār or Qumair, equated with Khmer or Cambodia.

[3] Al-Mas'ūdī, *Murūj al-Dhahab*, I, 233; Pellat, *Les prairies*, I, 94.

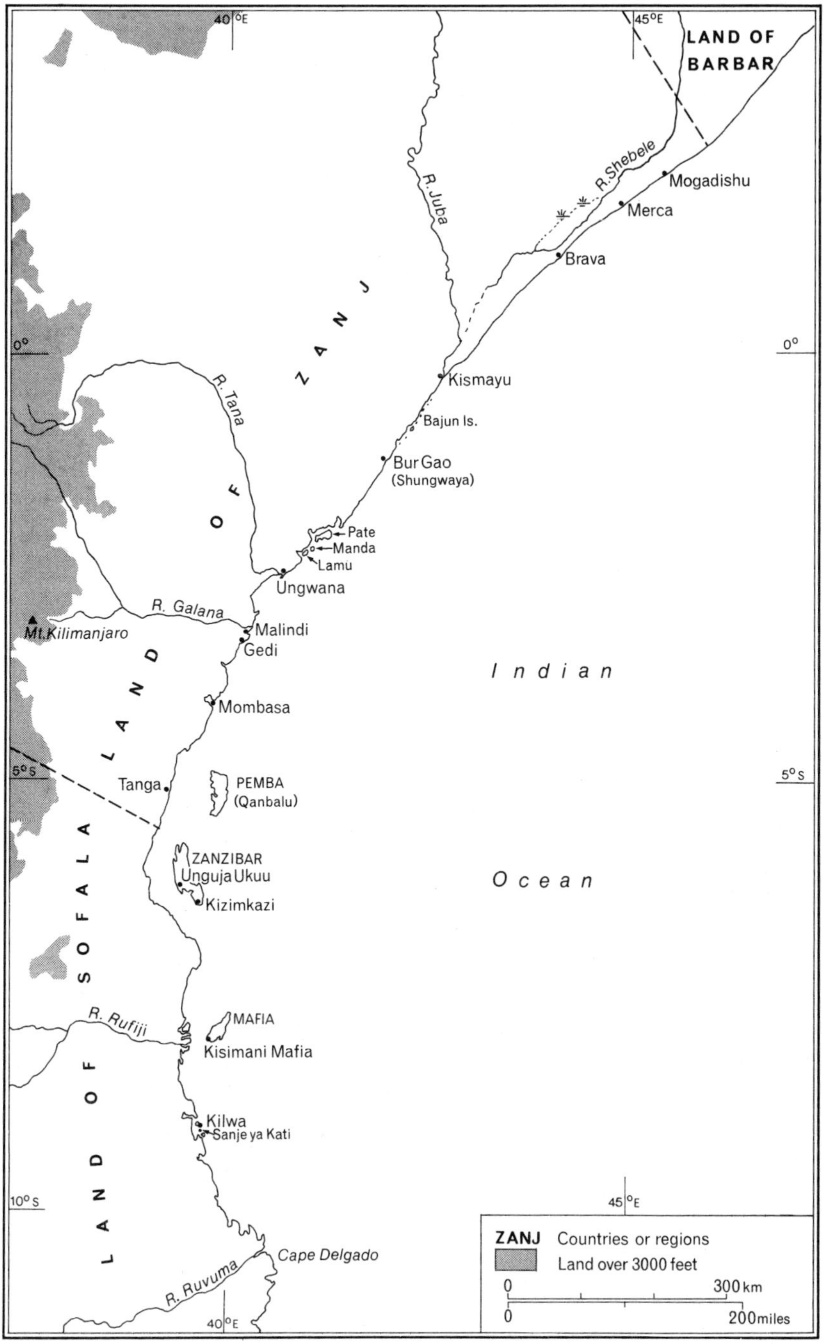

6 The East Coast settlements

with an estuary about it. To both of these authors *Qanbalū* is the most important place in the region and presumably a centre of trade. The island is almost certainly to be identified with Pemba (Jazīrat al-Khaḍrā', 'the green island'), mainly on the evidence of Yāqūt, who mentions M.k.n.b.l.ū., presumably *Mkanbalū*, as one of two cities on the island. It in turn is likely to be the modern Mkumbuu, though nothing as old as the tenth century has been found there. (The other city, M.t.n.b.y., may be Mtambwe Kuu.)

Al-Mas'ūdī tells us that *Qanbalū* had a partly Muslim population with a ruling family; the Muslims, however, spoke the Zanj language.[1] The implication that they had been there for some time is supported by his statement that the Muslims conquered the Zanj of the island around the time of the change from the Umayyad to the 'Abbasid dynasty, that is, around AD 750. This is the only evidence we have of immigration at this early date.

Al-Mas'ūdī lays great emphasis on the export of ivory, and in a not very convincing passage describes how the Zanj killed the elephants. He also dwells on the evocative product ambergris, again with a rather muddled account of how it was obtained. There is some emphasis on leopard skins. Tortoise-shell suitable for making combs is mentioned. So too is gold: 'the land of *Sufāla* and the *Wāq-Wāq* which produces gold in abundance and a thousand wonderful things';[2] the casual way in which this is mentioned suggests that the gold trade was little developed at this time. The statement that the Zanj 'use iron for ornament instead of gold and silver just as they use oxen . . . both for beasts of burden and for war'[3] may be interpreted as meaning that they set a high value on iron, or that it was the main metal used for trade. We know also from two other sources, al-Istakhrī (also tenth century) and Ibn Ḥawqal, that a type of timber was imported from the country of the Zanj; such was used in the construction of houses in Siraf. This timber was almost certainly mangrove poles, which up to the present day form an important part of the cargoes of the dhows from the Gulf on their return voyage. Ibn Ḥawqal, writing *c.* 970, tells of the ships of a certain man of Siraf voyaging to the country of the Zanj. Otherwise he has little information to give us; he considers the country

[1] Ibid. I, 124/tr. I, 93. Elsewhere he writes as if the whole population were Muslim in his time.

[2] Ibid. III, 6/tr. II [1965], 322–3. Buzurg b. Shahriyar, *Kitāb 'ajā'ib al-Hind*, XXXVII [ed. P. van der Lith, tr. L. M. Devic, *Livre des merveilles de l'Inde* (Leiden, 1883–6) ,65]. states that in the high regions of the Zanj country are gold mines in sandy soil, in which they dig. The account is mixed with legend; those digging, we are told, sometimes encounter ants as big as cats, which devour them. [3] Al-Mas'ūdī, *Murūj*, III, 27.

miserable, sparsely settled and little cultivated, except near the residence of the king. He also states that part of the Zanj country is cold (perhaps based on vague information of the snow-covered mountains of the interior) and inhabited by white Zanj.

Chinese documents from the ninth century onwards mention a country called Muâ-liĕn whose location is related to a region called B'uâ-sât-lâ. Muâ-liĕn ('Ma-lin') has usually been identified with Malindi, despite the inappropriateness of the Chinese account. It has recently much more convincingly been proposed that Muâ-liĕn should be identified with Meroe, and B'uâ-sât-lâ with the ethnonym Besharīya (Bisharin).[1]

Archaeology has some evidence to offer for this period, though no site of the ninth to tenth century is known in Pemba. There were, however, other trading settlements of this period: those known are at Gezira, south of Mogadishu, Manda on an island north of Lamu, and Unguja Ukuu on Zanzibar island. On the mainland north of Bagamoyo is the site of a small settlement which appears to have been engaged in the production of salt. The earliest strata at Kilwa date back to this period, too, but it was then a poor place, probably without a Muslim community. A few imports, however, attest that it engaged in trade. At Ungwana on the river Tana the lowest archaeological level probably goes back to around AD 1000.

Kilwa apart, among these settlements only Manda has been investigated. Here at some time in the ninth century, without any apparent period of development, there came into existence a town of quite remarkable wealth, though of no great extent – it appears to cover some twenty hectares – within which may have lived, on the analogy of modern Lamu, four or five thousand people. Though some buildings were of mud and wattle, in the area investigated the structures exposed were well built of coral stone, such as was to remain almost the sole building material for permanent edifices until modern times. The stone was usually set in lime mortar, though mud was sometimes employed. Two techniques were employed that were never used subsequently. First, we find walls built of large blocks of 'terrestrial' coral, weighing up to a ton each and laid without mortar; these are found in positions where they appear to have been designed to resist the incursions of the sea. Secondly, some buildings are constructed of burnt brick set in mud mortar. There is a higher proportion of imported goods at Manda than at any other known site on the coast at any period. Besides the Islamic

[1] P. Wheatley (following Velgus), 'Analecta Sino-Africana Recensa', in H. N. Chittick and R. I. Rotberg, eds., *East Africa and the Orient* (New York and London, 1975).

pottery, these goods included some Chinese stoneware and porcelain, and large quantities of Islamic glass. It is remarkable that the proportion of the more expensive glazed wares to the unglazed, both local and imported, is greater than at Siraf itself.[1]

No period of development can be distinguished at Manda; it was as wealthy at its inception as it ever was subsequently. This fact, coupled with evidence of foreign techniques found there, suggests that it was the creation of colonists from overseas. This being the case, it is probable that the population was, in the main at least, Muslim, though no mosque of this early period has been found there, nor was there any local coin mint (though a few Islamic coins from abroad were used, including some small Fatimid types, one minted in Sicily).

The imported pottery at Manda bears remarkable resemblance to that found at Siraf, on the eastern side of the Persian Gulf. In particular, some of the unglazed jars are identical to pottery manufactured in the vicinity of Siraf. It seems clear, therefore, that Manda was trading with the Gulf, and probably with Siraf itself, which of course accords well with the pattern indicated by Masʿūdī. Ivory is likely to have been a major export; elephants are common on the mainland to this day. Mangrove poles were probably also an important export, there being extensive areas of mangrove forest in the region. Local industries included the manufacture of beads of marine shell, probably used for trading with people on the mainland. Spindle-whorls attest spinning and presumably weaving, probably of cotton, but this was only on a small scale. Much iron was smelted; whether for export or for trade with the interior is uncertain. It is interesting that in the twelfth century Idrīsī emphasizes that iron was produced and traded at Mombasa and 'Mulanda', usually identified with Malindi, but possibly Manda. It is probable that Manda, like *Qanbalū*, traded with regions further to the south; such trade, rather than direct long-distance commerce across the Indian Ocean, would account for the few imports of this period found at Kilwa, and a single sherd of Sasanian-Islamic ware in northern Madagascar.

The site of the early town at Unguja Ukuu in Zanzibar has not been investigated, but the find of a hoard of gold coins a century ago, probably at this site, coupled with the amount of imported pottery (Islamic ware of the ninth to tenth centuries) visible on the surface, indicates that it was an important place. A gold dinar which is likely to have been part of this hoard is dated the equivalent of AD 798/9, and

[1] D. Whitehouse, 'Excavations at Siraf', interim reports in *Iran*, 1968–72, **6–10**.

was struck by the vizier of Harūn al-Rashīd. Though we have no useful information from external sources about Zanzibar (assuming *Qanbalū* to be correctly identified with Pemba) in the ninth to eleventh centuries, we may remark that the earliest dated inscription from East Africa is at Kizimkazi on this island. This inscription, unique also for its fine floriated Kufic style, is dated the equivalent of AD 1106/7. Idrīsī (mid twelfth century) tells us that the inhabitants of what is probably Zanzibar island were predominantly Muslim. That island is described by Yāqūt (*c.* 1220) as 'the seat of the King of the Zanj, and a converging point for ships from all quarters. Its people have now transferred themselves to another island called Tumbatu whose people are Muslims.'[1] It is hard to believe that all Muslims had gone from the mainland; the passage may rather mean that Tumbatu, a small island off the north-west coast of Zanzibar, where there are substantial ruins, had become the chief settlement. There were 'kings' of the Zanj in other places, according to other authors.

Idrīsī's account (1154) gives a wealth of detail, but it is difficult to know how much of it is accurate. *Qanbalū* for example, now clearly of less importance, he places, certainly wrongly, in the vicinity of Socotra. The whole of the mainland coast from the Horn southwards is portrayed as being pagan; south of Ras Hafun he mentions some fifty villages of the (Somali) Hawiya. Of the identifiable places, Merca is mentioned but not Mogadishu (or at least not under that name); the people of what is probably Brava anoint stones with fish oil. At Mulanda (usually identified with Malindi) he mentions a *maqanqa* who charms snakes, clearly the Bantu *mganga*, a medicine-man. *Munfasa* or *Manīsa* appears south of this. This name is probably muddled with Manfia, otherwise Manfisa (Mafia), not otherwise mentioned. Ibn Sa'īd (*c.* 1250) has Mombasa in this position, one degree south of Malindi, and stated to be the capital of the kings of the Zanj. He mentions Mogadishu, but places it south of Merca. No towns south of Mombasa can be identified; *Ṣayūna*, perhaps as far south as the Zambezi, is described by Ibn Sa'īd as being the chief town of the Sofalans. Idrīsī lays emphasis on the production of iron in the middle part of the Sofala coast; according to him people of Java transported it to India, where it was esteemed to be of the highest quality, and used for the manufacture of swords of unequalled excellence. The last town of the Sofala country, *Dāghūta* (=Danghuta? – possibly to be identified with Angoche), and its territory, was that in which most gold was found.

[1] Yāqūt, *Mu'jam al-buldān*, ed. F. Wustenfeld (Leipzig, 1866), IV, 366.

The period after Idrīsī is marked by the rapid rise of Mogadishu. Ibn al-Mujāwir tells that after the Banū Mājid people were driven from the Mundhiriyya region of the Yemen in 1159 a section of them settled in Mogadishu; merchants from Abyan and Haram also settled there after the destruction of those ports.[1] Yāqūt (*c.* 1220) describes Mogadishu as being the most important place on the coast, and a little later Ibn Sa'īd writes of it as a famous place of which all would have heard, and a centre of Islam. Both these authors tell us that Merca was Muslim by this time. Yāqūt describes the town as being in the country of the Barbar, at the beginning of the country of the Zanj. The Barbar themselves were intermediate in type between the Habash and the Zanj; the inhabitants of Mogadishu, however, were foreigners, divided into clans each with their own shaykh; they had no single ruler. A visiting merchant had to stay with one of the elders, who would sponsor him in his dealings. The chief goods exported were sandalwood, ebony, ambergris, and ivory. Ibn al-Mujāwir a few years later gives Mogadishu and Kilwa as the stages on the voyage from Aden to al-Qumr, Kilwa having been briefly mentioned by Yāqūt simply as a town in the land of Zanj. The former author also has interesting information on al-Qumr and the trade of the Sofala country, as well as about a raid apparently from the Far East which will be considered below. Al-Dimashqī mentions the Laccadive and Maldive islands as a stage on the voyage to 'Mogadishu of the Zanj' amongst other places, presumably from the Indies. No other town in the Zanj country is here named. Yāqūt's information about Zanzibar island has been mentioned above. In addition, he tells us, citing his source, that the two towns on what is evidently Pemba island each had its own sultan, one professing to be an Arab from Kufa.[2]

There is archaeological evidence for the existence of a considerable number of trading towns or settlements on the coast and islands in the eleventh to thirteenth century. All those previously mentioned continued in existence, with the exception of Unguja Ukuu. None of the sites lies south of the Kilwa region, save for two in Madagascar. With the exception of *Qanbalū* and Manda, none can be shown to have been Muslim before about 1200. After that date, and perhaps slightly before, there were substantial mosques at (Kisimani) Mafia, at Kilwa, and at Sanje ya Kati near Kilwa. The architecture of these mosques is *sui generis*, but two thirteenth-century monuments at Mogadishu,

[1] *Tārīkh al-Mustabṣīr*, I, 130.
[2] Yāqūt, *Mu'jam*, II, 75.

apparently minarets (which, with a similar tower at Merca, are the only ancient examples of such structures on the coast), are held to be of Persian inspiration.[1]

To the writer's knowledge the only inscriptions relevant to Muslim immigration, other than that at Kizimkazi mentioned above, are from Mogadishu. The earliest is the gravestone of a man with the *nisba* ('surname') al-Khurāsanjī, dated the equivalent of AD 1217. Another gives the date of the building of the minaret of the Friday Mosque (Juma') at Mogadishu as the equivalent of AD 1269. A third, dated to the same year, is in the mosque of Arba' Rukun and mentions one Khusrau b. Muḥammad al-Shirāzī. This is the only epigraphic mention of the Shirazi, and the only such Persian name known to the writer. The Shirazi are nowhere mentioned in the external sources in connection with East Africa; we may, however, note in this connection the presence of a clan calling itself Sirafi at Merca,[2] and of a family with the *nisba* al-Sīrāfī at Mogadishu.[3] Siraf suffered grave damage at the end of the tenth century, but recent excavations have shown that it continued to exist until the fifteenth century, though in a much reduced state. The suggestion that these families must have come from Siraf to the Somali coast before the eleventh century must therefore be regarded as unproven.

To summarize the foregoing very briefly, it can be said that there is emphasis in the early sources on Islamic trade and settlements on the islands of Pemba and Zanzibar. In the twelfth century sources of lesser reliability emphasize the pagan nature of the mainland coast. Archaeological evidence makes it almost certain that as early as the ninth century there was an important Islamic town on Manda island, which is very close inshore, but as yet there is no certain evidence of mainland settlements of any size until three centuries later.

The information set out above will now be compared with the accounts given in the internal sources recorded later. These sources are documents written on the East African coast itself. The only one of any antiquity is the version of the Chronicle of Kilwa originally set down about 1520 or 1530. The others are accounts of the history of towns mostly on the Kenya coast, none of which can be shown to date from before the nineteenth century. The account in the *Book of the*

[1] E. Cerulli, *Somalia, scritti vari editi ed inediti*, vol. II (Rome, 1959), 239, citing the view of Monneret de Villard.

[2] Cerulli, *Somalia*, vol. I (Rome, 1957), 25–6.

[3] Ibid. I, 98. This family, and another, has a genealogy going back to the mid eighth century, but without other evidence this must be treated with great reservation.

Zanj[1] of pre-Islamic immigration of Arabs from Himyar in southern Arabia, their founding of most of the more important towns of the coast from Mogadishu to Mombasa, and also Kilwa, together with their subsequent conversion to Islam, is uncorroborated by other sources and unsupported by the archaeological evidence, and must be dismissed as unhistorical. At best it preserves the memory of traders from south Arabia who, as in the time of the *Periplus*, may have continued to come to these coasts. The same may be said of the Syrians, who, according to the chronicles of Pate and Lamu (island towns on the northern Kenya coast), were sent by the Umayyad caliph ʻAbd al-Malik (AD 685–705), and of the towns they are supposed to have founded on the coast. Mythical too are the stories of the expedition sent by the caliph al-Manṣūr (AD 754–75) against the disloyal towns of the coast, the account in the *Book of the Zanj* of the despatch of governors by Harūn al-Rashīd, and the Persians whom the Pate Chronicle says he sent to colonize the coast. At best, these accounts may have some connection with the conquest and colonization of *Qanbalū*, but even this is unlikely, since neither that place, nor indeed any other in Pemba and Zanzibar, finds mention in these chronicles in connection with this period.

It is convenient to note here the story of the emigration from Oman to the land of Zanj of the two joint rulers of the Julanda family, the brothers Saʻīd and Sulaymān b. ʻAbbād, together with their families and followers. Though this derives from an external source, the *Annals of Oman*, it is as we have seen of so late a date (the early eighteenth century) that it is better considered with the other traditions. The emigration is stated to have taken place after the defeat of the two brothers by Umayyad forces in the reign of ʻAbd al-Malik b. Marwān (AD 685–705).[2] It might appear to receive some confirmation from a passage in the *Book of the Zanj*, where the Kilindini of Mombasa are stated to have been originally of the Julanda tribe. But this tradition is otherwise uncorroborated, and other derivations given in the same passage are very doubtful. The most we can say is that these traditions may enshrine the memory of an early migration from Oman, which is not in itself unlikely. Many settlers are of course known to have come from this region in later times.

The sixteenth-century Portuguese historian Barros, basing his

[1] A conflation from two or more sources, published by Cerulli in *Somalia*, I.

[2] See S. B. Miles, *The country and tribes of the Persian Gulf*, 2nd ed. (London, 1966), 16. The account is published in *History of the Imams and Seyyids of Oman by Salīl ibn Razīk*, ed. G. P. Badger (London, 1871), 5. J. Schacht expresses scornful doubt of the reliability of the story in his review of G. S. P. Freeman-Grenville, *The medieval history of the coast of Tanganyika*, in *Bibliotheca Orientalis*, 1964, **21**, 111.

account on a local source of his period, tells of the next supposed immigration to the coast. This is a movement of people to whom Barros refers as *Emozaydij*, by which he evidently means followers of the Shīʿa Zayd. The event, if historical, probably occurred after Zayd's rising and death in AD 740. Barros tells us that the heretical Zaydites spread 'like a slow plague' down the coast. Being the first settlers from abroad, he says, they did not find any celebrated towns, but settled in places where they could live in security from the pagan inhabitants. Subsequently there arrived a fresh party of Arabs (considered below) who were, Barros tells us, of a different sort of Islam. The Zaydites, unwilling to submit to them, retreated to the interior, where they intermarried with the pagans and became known as *Baduys*. This name suggests the Arabic *badawī* (bedouin, nomad). In another passage,[1] ignored by previous writers, after describing the food of the Zanj as consisting mainly of wild fruit and game together with the milk of such cattle as they possess, Barros states that milk is the principal food of the Moors they call *Baduys*, who frequent the interior and have some intercourse with the Kaffirs, but who in comparison with those that live in the civilized cities and towns are considered to be barbarians. In the same paragraph he refers to cattle being common on the coast northwards from Mogadishu. The *Baduys* are thus pastoral Muslims, probably Cushitic-speaking people (of mixed origin in Barros' view) in contact with the Bantu-speaking people of southern Somalia.[2] This circumstantial account sounds plausible so far as the religious background goes. The Zaydites would probably have sailed from the Persian Gulf as they were, it seems, prominent in adjacent regions. On the other hand, if the only reason for their emigration was religious persecution, they could have found a haven with co-religionists much nearer home.[3]

The new immigrants who displaced the *Emozaydij* were, we are told by Barros, from near al-Aḥsā, not far inland from Bahrain. The account of the emigration of these people (from al-Aḥsā) bears such similarities to that of the emigration from Shiraz to Kilwa which succeeded it, that it is likely that they represent two facets of a legend which refers to emigration from the Persian Gulf, probably extending over a considerable period. The al-Aḥsā people are said to have founded first Mogadishu and then Brava, these being the first towns of the coast;

[1] G. M. Theal, ed., *Records of south-eastern Africa* (reprinted Cape Town, 1964), VI, 232.

[2] J. H. Linschoten's map of AD 1596 places the *Baduis* well north of Mogadishu. A connection is also possible, but I think unlikely, with the Baidoa plateau in south Somalia.

[3] Barros also says that they were attracted by the fame of the gold of Zanzibar (Theal, *Records*, VI, 233), but this reads as if it may be a gloss.

the town of Mogadishu gained such power and state that it became 'the sovereign and head of all the Moors of this coast'. Kilwa is stated to have been 'founded' rather more than seventy years after Mogadishu.[1] This refers to the establishment of the 'Shirazi' dynasty there, to which event the discussion will shortly return.

The sect of the new immigrants appears from the account of Barros to have been different from the *Emozaydij*. Until the end of the tenth century al-Aḥsā had been the capital of the fearsome, revolutionary and 'communistic' Qarmatian sect; Bahrain, its port, probably played an important part in the commerce of the Gulf. If such an immigration took place at a sufficiently early date, it can be maintained that the people concerned were of this persuasion. But there is no sign of Qarmatian influence in East Africa, which except for recent immigrants is almost entirely orthodox Sunnī.[2]

The primacy accorded by Barros to Mogadishu entirely accords with the external evidence. The epigraphic evidence for the presence of a person from Shiraz in the thirteenth century, and of another Persian there, has already been mentioned. Barros does not, however, mention the immigration of people from the Yemen, which seems certainly to have taken place. We may note here traditions recorded by Cerulli at Mogadishu that the 'Shirazi' were the first settlers at that place; they were followed by Arabs called *Madagān*, and these by other Arabs called *Ḥalawānī*. The identity of both these groups is uncertain.[3] The disparate origin of the population of Mogadishu is probably indicated by the government by elders of the various tribes at this time. Barros emphasizes that Mogadishu was the first town to develop the gold trade with the land (also referred to as the mine) of Sofala, and it is likely in view of Mogadishu's rapid rise to prosperity that this was the case. Barros states that the relationship was established peaceably, the king and people of the country welcoming the traders for the cloth and the goods which they brought to exchange for the gold and ivory, which until that time had never been exported from that part of the coast of Sofala.

In addition to the written sources we must take some account of the oral traditions of the Mrima coast and the islands concerning the pres-

[1] De Barros, Dec. I, bk. VIII, ch. 4.

[2] R. L. Pouwells, in a recent article ['Tenth-century settlement of the East African coast: the case for Qarmatian/Isma'ili connections', *Azania*, 1974, IX, 65–74], maintains, however, that Qarmatians of Bahrain probably were involved in the settlement of the northern portion of the coast.

[3] Cerulli, *Somalia*, II, 238–44. The Halawān were succeeded by the Muẓaffar, who are known to have been the ruling family in the sixteenth century.

ence of people referred to as (Wa)Debuli, who in these traditions are generally maintained to have come before the 'Shirazi' and who are claimed to have been responsible for some of the early ruined buildings. It seems likely that 'Debuli' should be connected with the great port of al-Daybūl on the Indus, which flourished up to the thirteenth century. In view of the lack of mention in the written sources, it seems unlikely that they settled in any great number, though a person with the *nisba* al-Daybūlī is mentioned in the Arabic Chronicle of Kilwa as a prominent person at that place early in the fifteenth century. Probably the traditions preserve the memory of a period in the twelfth century and perhaps early thirteenth century when merchants from the Indus region were active on the coast.

Taking the evidence all together, it seems probable that from the middle of the eighth century onwards there was some immigration from time to time from the Persian Gulf, especially Siraf, from lower Iraq (remembering the ruler in Pemba from Kufa) and perhaps from Oman. Most of the immigrants during the time before the twelfth century settled in Pemba and Zanzibar; Manda, so close to the mainland, appears anomalous.

THE SHIRAZI DYNASTY

In the twelfth century more foreigners emigrated from diverse parts of the Persian Gulf and settled in Mogadishu, Brava and probably elsewhere on the Benadir and the coast of the Shungwaya country, the southern hinterland of Somalia remembered as the homeland of the *Kashūr*. These foreigners developed the trade of Mogadishu, which rapidly rose to a position of pre-eminence. In particular, they opened up the gold trade with the Sofala country, which until then can only have been on a minor scale.[1] In furtherance of the trade with the south some of these merchants, ancestors of whom came from the Persian Gulf and who were remembered as of 'Shirazi' origin, settled on the islands of Mafia and Kilwa, rapidly, it appears, achieving a position of dominance. By about AD 1200 they had established themselves as rulers.[2]

[1] Mas'ūdī, as has been shown, mentions the production of gold in the south, and Idrīsī a place (unidentified) from which it was exported; yet the metal was not of sufficient importance in the trade of the coast to merit mention as an article of commerce, though ivory, sandalwood, ebony and ambergris were.

[2] H. N. Chittick, 'The "Shirazi" colonization of East Africa', *Journal of African History*, 1965, **6**, 3, *passim*. Two late traditions seem to indicate that the Shirazi dynasty originated in Shungwaya, but there is doubt whether a town of that name existed at so early a date [see footnote, p. 230].

It is related in the Arabic Kilwa Chronicle that other Shirazi settled at other places: Mandakha, Shaughu (or Shaungu), Yanbu, the Green Island (Pemba), and Hanzuan (Anjouan in the Comoros). In interpreting this, we must bear in mind that the account may represent the conflation of memories of movements at various times. Mandakha is likely to be Manda (either by elimination of the last syllable, or by a miswriting of Manda Kuu, old or great Manda); here there may be the survival of a tradition of the immigration to that place of people coming directly from the Persian Gulf, or of the involvement of its merchants, together perhaps with fresh ones from the mainland, in the trade focused on Mogadishu. The inhabitants of Manda were remembered in the Pate Chronicle as 'the wearers of gold'. This may enshrine the memory of such trade, or simply signify the wealth of Manda. On archaeological evidence Manda was flourishing in the twelfth century, though perhaps not so wealthy as before, and soon to decline. Much the same may be said of Pemba (*Qanbalū*), which around this time disappears from the prominent place it had in the accounts of the Arab geographers. Shaughu/Shaungu may be Shanga on Pate island, which appears, again on archaeological evidence, to have been prosperous at this time. A settlement of immigrants from the north in the Comoro islands around this time or later is probable, a similar tradition to that in the Kilwa Chronicle being found there.

The beginning of the 'Shirazi' dynasty at Kilwa and Mafia is marked by the appearance of coins inscribed in an angular style of a Kufic flavour and bearing the name 'Alī b. al-Ḥasan,[1] and the construction of mosques built of stone. On the archaeological evidence Mafia was at least as important as Kilwa during the thirteenth century. The two places are closely linked in the accounts given of this period in the Kilwa Chronicle, and a critical consideration of these sources, especially the Arabic, indicates that it is likely that the sultans of this first dynasty ruled from Mafia, no doubt the town that stood at its western tip now known as Kisimani Mafia.[2] If this deduction is correct, Kilwa was ruled by a governor, usually the son of the ruling sultan. We lack any chronicle of Mafia, save a very late and almost valueless tradition mainly concerning the town of Kua, on an adjacent island, and consequently know hardly anything of events in that area.

The establishment of the 'Shirazi' at Kilwa is presented in the Kilwa

[1] A very few minute silver coins at the very beginning of this period appear to bear the name 'al-Ḥasan' alone; this was probably the father of 'Alī.

[2] Against this view is the fact that Kilwa is mentioned in the external sources of the early thirteenth century, but not Mafia.

Chronicle as a peaceable event, associated with commerce, symbolized by the purchase of the island by the first sultan ʻAlī b. al-Ḥasan (or b. al-Ḥusayn) from the pagan ruler, who resided on the mainland, in exchange for cloth. A family of Muslims resident on the island is mentioned, and there were probably others, for there was a mosque. Barros states that there were other Muslims on the islands of Songo and Shanga who had conquered the mainland for a distance of twenty leagues from Kilwa. Songo is probably Songo Mnara, where, however, relics of this period are lacking: but at Sanje ya Kati, another island just to the south of Kilwa, and almost certainly to be identified with this Shanga, there are remains of thirteenth-century date and perhaps rather earlier. In any case it is clear from the Arabic Chronicle, reinforced by surviving traditions, that there was a substantial town on Sanje ya Kati, since some time after the reign of ʻAlī b. al-Ḥasan/Ḥusayn there began an extended struggle between its people and Kilwa. These people twice succeeded in placing their own nominees on the throne of Kilwa (or in subjecting Kilwa to their own rulers). One of these had the *nisba* al-Mandhirī, or al-Mundhirī. This suggests that he may be connected with the Banū Mājid from the Mundhirīyya district of the Yemen, a section of whom, it will be recalled, settled in Mogadishu.

Kilwa was, as has been remarked, known by the 1230s to the outside world as a stage between Mogadishu and al-Qumr (and evidently also, in view of the control by Mogadishu of the gold trade, with the Sofala country). This connection with al-Qumr (Madagascar) is attested also by the presence at Kilwa in the thirteenth century of steatite vessels evidently imported from that island, being similar to those dating from the same period excavated by Pierre Vérin at Mahilaka and at Nosy-Bé. The expansion of Kilwa in this period is marked also by the import of Chinese porcelain, and by a great increase in the amount of glass beads, especially of the wound variety, shipped probably from India; the trade in this commodity had hitherto been insignificant. Such beads were finding their way into the interior to such places as Ingombe Ilede (see pp. 528–30) where those found in the burials are precisely of types found in the thirteenth century, and into the fourteenth, at Kilwa. Commerce would mostly have been carried out by barter, or by the exchange of gold. The very large number of coins minted are all of copper, except the very few minute early silver issues (see footnote 1, p. 202); they are of low intrinsic value and can only have served as small change.

The area directly controlled by Mafia and Kilwa was very restricted, probably extending little beyond the islands. The fact that Shanga is said to have conquered the coast for a distance of twenty leagues from Kilwa may indicate that Kilwa in like fashion exercised some sort of dominion over a stretch of the mainland. But the mainland is presented as the abode of hostile pagans, both under this and the succeeding dynasty, and the object of periodic raids. Mafia island is large enough to provide food for a substantial population; Kilwa, however, is not. While it is notable that there is no known early settlement on the mainland opposite Kilwa, it seems probable that Kilwa would have controlled the coast in the immediate vicinity, and the fertile area a little to the south, for the purposes of cultivation; at the present time people from Kilwa island sail across to the mainland for this purpose. Zanzibar was certainly independent of Kilwa, both in this period and, it seems, up to the time of the coming of the Portuguese.[1] Kizimkazi in the south of that island we know on archaeological grounds to have flourished through the thirteenth century, and it appears that there was a fairly close relationship between Kilwa and Zanzibar, the second of the rulers deposed by the people of Shanga having taken refuge there. He appears to have received support from Zanzibar when he returned to regain his position at Kilwa.

The settlements which are known from archaeology to have flourished on the coast from the region of Dar-es-Salaam up to that of Lamu were certainly independent of Kilwa and probably independent of each other. They imported Islamic pottery, glass and beads similar to those brought to the big cities, and probably served as collecting centres for goods, especially ivory, to be shipped to Zanzibar and Kilwa. That there was considerable coastwise trade is attested by the occasional occurrence, as far away as Manda, of pottery apparently made in Kilwa. The comparative isolation of these other settlements, as well as their independence, is indicated by the almost total lack of the coins which from this time on are so common at Mafia and Kilwa.

THE MAHDALĪ DYNASTY AT KILWA

The prominence so far given to Kilwa and Mafia is a reflection of our greater historical and archaeological knowledge of those places than of Mogadishu. It must be remembered that throughout the thirteenth

[1] Barros alone records a conquest of Zanzibar by Kilwa, but Zanzibar was clearly independent in the fifteenth century.

century Mogadishu (with which we may associate the lesser ports of Merca and Brava) was the more important town, and that the trade of Kilwa was probably primarily directed towards it. This position was, however, to be reversed.

The change in the balance hinges round the control of the gold trade, although how it came about is somewhat uncertain. It is probably to be linked to a change of dynasty which took place at Kilwa towards or at the end of the thirteenth century. The new rulers were of the Mahdalī or Mahādila family, the name of a clan of *sayyids* which around the time concerned was living in the south-west of the Yemen. The dynasty was also known as that of Abū'l-Mawāhib, 'the father of gifts', the sobriquet of its most famous ruler.

While we are told that the first of this dynasty, al-Ḥasan b. Ṭālūt, seized the kingdom by force, it was 'with the help of his people'. It seems clear that there were Mahdalī already resident at Kilwa and that there was no invasion. Al-Ḥasan's assumption of power appears to have been accompanied by a repudiation of the dominance of Mafia, which from this time onwards ceased to have a prominent place in the account given in the chronicle, and, from the archaeological evidence, seems to have been less wealthy. His son, Sulaymān b. al-Ḥasan, appears to have been killed when he in turn was sultan, apparently by the Mafia faction at Kilwa, for we are told that the son of this man, al-Ḥasan b. Sulaymān, 'revenged his father upon the people of Mafia and fought and overcame them'.

The early fourteenth century was, according to the archaeological evidence, a period of great prosperity at Kilwa. Building in stone increased markedly, and a new architectural style appeared including the introduction of vaults and domes. This style is exemplified by a large extension to the Great Mosque (more than doubling its area) which was built at this time, and by the construction of the remarkable palace and emporium known as Husuni Kubwa. In this building an inscription has been found giving the name of a king (*malik*), al-Ḥasan b. Sulaymān, probably to be identified with the grandson of the founder of the dynasty mentioned above, and probably the Abu'l-Muẓaffar Ḥasan surnamed Abu'l-Mawāhib visited by Ibn Baṭṭūṭa in about 1332.

These sultans all issued coins, of a style slightly different from those of the previous dynasty. Those of the founder, al-Ḥasan b. Ṭālūt, are very rare, perhaps indicating a short reign, but those of his successors, Sulaymān b. Ḥasan and al-Ḥasan b. Sulaymān, are common; indeed those of the latter sultan are (along with those of 'Alī b. al-Ḥasan) the commonest of all. Imports of Chinese wares increased greatly in this period: Islamic wares on the other hand are uncommon, being almost confined to a type of pottery believed to have been made in the region of Aden. This agrees well with the connection with south-western Arabia implied by the Yemeni origin of the dynasty. This may have had its beginnings at an earlier date, in view of the route Aden–Mogadishu–Kilwa–Madagascar mentioned by Ibn al-Mujāwir. The relationship seems to have been quite close in the fourteenth century; according to the Arabic Chronicle, al-Ḥasan b. Sulaymān spent two years of his youth studying in Aden, during which period his brother Dā'ūd was regent. A century later a deposed sultan of Aden took refuge at Kilwa, so it seems relations remained close.

We now return to the matter of the gold trade. Barros gives an account of Dā'ūd b. Sulaymān's being summoned from Sofala where he had grown rich in the gold trade (evidently with regions of what is now Rhodesia), to take over the kingdom of Kilwa. Dā'ūd and his son, incongruously named Sulaymān Ḥasan (which implies that his father was named Ḥasan), controlled this trade, and from this time on the kings of Kilwa 'always sent governors to Sofala, that all business might be transacted through their factors'. The son, Sulaymān Ḥasan, Barros goes on to say, conquered a great part of the coast, and made himself lord of the islands of Pemba, Mafia and Zanzibar. He also 'beautified the town of Kilwa, building a stone fortress there and walls, towers and noble houses, for until his time the town was constructed of wood'.[1]

The events of this period may be tentatively set out in brief as follows. Al-Ḥasan b. Ṭālūt, a leading member of the Mahdalī family at Kilwa, with interests in Sofala, displaced the 'Shirazi' ruler, with assistance from the anti-Mafia faction among the people of Kilwa. In the reign of his grandson, al-Ḥasan b. Sulaymān, Mafia (where 'Shirazis' had continued to rule) was finally defeated. With the defeat of the 'Shirazis', the connection with Mogadishu was severed, or largely so, this leading to a decline in the importance of that town from about 1330 onwards. The way was now open for Kilwa to channel her commerce directly to her friends in Aden. In the meanwhile, relatives of the king of Kilwa had obtained control of the Sofala region and Kilwa was able to monopolize commerce with the south. In the latter

[1] Theal, *Records*, VI, 242. The reference to the conquest of Pemba and Zanzibar by Kilwa is the only record of such action at any period, and, uncorroborated, must be considered dubious. Barros refers the events described in this paragraph to a period long before the Mahdalī dynasty; the account, however, is almost certainly misplaced, and probably refers to the early kings of that dynasty. See Chittick, 'Shirazi colonization', 280.

part of the fourteenth century Kilwa appears to have declined somewhat. This is indicated both by the lack of information in the barren accounts of the sultans given to us by the Kilwa Chronicle, and by the archaeological evidence; few stone buildings were erected, and the minting of coins ceased. The reasons for this decline are quite obscure. In the first half of the fifteenth century, however, there was a renewal of building activity, and a new and quite extensive town, with houses almost entirely in stone, was built on the adjacent island of Songo Mnara. To judge by the imported pottery, trade with the Persian Gulf was the most important, but the visit of the king of Aden, deposed in AD 1454, indicates that the connection with that place was maintained.

In the middle of the fifteenth century occurred the first of many disputes about the succession. The ruling family of Zanzibar was able to interfere in this dispute, and it seems that that island held a position of considerable influence at this time. Her sultans issued their own coinage – the only place other than Kilwa and Mogadishu to do so. By the end of the century there were almost constant intrigues at Kilwa, usually by those holding the next offices below the sultan, the *amīrs* and viziers. These dissensions and the resultant weakness were such as to lessen Kilwa's hold over her southern possessions and the trade therefrom; this is also reflected in a decline in building activity and of the standard of masonry. By the time the Portuguese arrived, the governor of Sofala, frustrated by, or taking advantage of, the state of disorganization at home, had in effect declared himself independent. We can assume that the control of the mother city over Angoche and other towns north of Sofala (if indeed they had ever been subject to Kilwa) was also affected.[1]

Meanwhile in the fourteenth century, and to a greater degree in the fifteenth, other towns were achieving a modest, and sometimes considerable, prosperity. All, by the fifteenth century, were Muslim, as is attested by mosques and graves; their inhabitants probably spoke an ancestral form of Swahili. Each town appears to have been ruled by an independent shaykh or sultan. These communities, which we can now speak of as 'Swahili', were sharply differentiated from the people of the hinterland and those inhabiting the intervening bush. These people were probably still pagan; Barros tells us they lived largely by hunting and food collecting, though some (in the Usambara mountains at least)

[1] The sites of these towns have not been archaeologically investigated, but it seems likely that their development goes back to the early reigns of the Mahdalī dynasty; Angoche may be identifiable with Da[n]ghuta of Idrīsī.

were, on the archaeological evidence, agricultural. Between the ruler of each coastal town and the chiefs of the tribes in the vicinity there were probably agreements as to rights and obligations, similar to those described in the *Book of the Zanj* with reference to the Shungwaya region. There is no evidence that the people of the coastal towns attempted either to penetrate the interior or to convert its inhabitants to Islam, except in the far south. With regard to the latter region it is clear that at the time of the arrival of the Portuguese there were substantial numbers of Muslim traders on the Zambezi river at Sena and Tete. According to one authority, their presence there goes back to not later than the early thirteenth century.[1] The evidence for penetration at such an early date appears to be inadequate, and since there is no evidence of Muslim towns on the coast south of Kilwa before the fourteenth century (following the view set out above), it is very unlikely that such penetration took place before that period.

While a number of these new towns grew up on the coast of Tanzania north of the Rufiji, the more important of them were in the region of Mombasa and Malindi, and from the north bank of the Tana to the Lamu archipelago. There were lesser settlements probably dating back to this period on the mainland up to Kismayu and on the Bajun islands off the Somali coast. Apart from Mombasa and her rival Malindi, the most notable of these towns were those in the Lamu archipelago. Lamu itself was mentioned by an Arab author, Abu'l-Maḥāsin, in the fifteenth century, and had existed for some time before, as is corroborated by the archaeological evidence. In the time of Abu'l-Maḥāsin it was being engulfed by sand; at the present day the site, east of the present town, is covered by a great hill of sand. The most prominent place in the histories is, however, given to Pate. According to the chronicle of that town, it began to be an important place as early as the thirteenth century and in the first half of the fourteenth century is said to have conquered the whole of the coast, including Kilwa. However, a critical examination of the sources coupled with the archaeological evidence has led to the conclusion that this part of the account is without historical foundation.[2] Pate does not appear to have been a place of any consequence before the latter part of the fifteenth century, and was not a place of major importance until the seventeenth century.

[1] D. P. Abraham, 'The ethno-history of the empire of Mutapa: problems and methods', in J. Vansina and others, eds., *The historian in tropical Africa* (Oxford, 1964), 114.

[2] H. N. Chittick, 'A new look at the history of Pate', *Journal of African History*, 1969, 10, 3, 375–91.

Mombasa, as has been observed, has a long history. Like Kilwa, it has traditions of a 'Shirazi' dynasty, taking over it seems from pagan rulers, but practically nothing is remembered of this period. The account of Ibn Baṭṭūṭa, who called there about 1332 on his way between Mogadishu and Kilwa, indicates that it was considerably less important than either of those towns. By the end of the fifteenth century, however, this was no longer the case, and it seems that by then a considerable amount of the trade of the coast passed through that port. Henceforth Mombasa was to play a prominent role through the time of the Portuguese to the present day.

THE TOWNS OF THE COAST

The following account of the nature of the Muslim towns of the coast, of their inhabitants and of their way of life is based on the evidence afforded by excavations, chiefly at Kilwa, and on the eyewitness accounts of Ibn Baṭṭūṭa and the Portuguese, and refers mainly to the fourteenth and fifteenth centuries, the period of greatest prosperity.

The inhabitants of the towns can be considered as falling into three groups. The ruling class was usually of mixed Arab and African ancestry (the 'dark Moors' of the Portuguese); such also were probably the landowners, merchants, most of the religious functionaries and the artisans. Inferior to them in status were the pure-blooded Africans, probably mostly captured in raids on the mainland and in a state of slavery, who cultivated the fields and no doubt carried out other menial tasks. Distinct from both these classes were the transient or recently settled Arabs, and perhaps Persians, still incompletely assimilated into the society.

Population figures are difficult to estimate; that of Kilwa was put by an eyewitness with d'Almeida's expedition in 1505 as 4,000; a contemporary Portuguese historian, G. Correa, has 12,000, while the population of Mombasa was estimated at 10,000. The total area of the town site as deduced from the visible remains is about double that of Lamu, a town on an island off the northern coast of Kenya. The population of Lamu at the present day is probably 6,000-odd, but is likely to have been much greater when all the houses (many of which are now in ruins or partly empty) were fully occupied.[1] On the other

[1] J. de V. Allen, in 'Swahili culture reconsidered', *Azania*, 1974, IX, 105–38, puts the maximum population of Lamu in the past as at least 18,000, but this seems exaggerated, not taking account of the fact that there were probably always areas occupied by collapsed or ruined buildings.

hand the whole of the area of Kilwa town may not have been occupied at the same time; its maximum population may be put at between 11,000 and 20,000 souls.

Most of the city-states of the coast probably had single rulers. Though Mogadishu was originally a republic, by the 1330s it was ruled by a shaykh with officials and a council assisting him. There was probably a council at Kilwa also. The sultan there was always from one family, apart from usurpations, but it is not clear how individual rulers were selected; sometimes at least a sultan seems to have designated his own successor. The ruler was assisted by a number of officials, notably a *qāḍī* (judge), an *amīr* and a vizier; the division of functions between the last two ministers is not clear. These officials were appointed by the sultan from, it seems, particular families. The royal family, at least at Mogadishu, had eunuchs in their service. The shaykh at that place moved in considerable state; Ibn Baṭṭūṭa describes him as walking in procession beneath a silk canopy or parasol topped with a golden bird. In front of him was a band of drums, trumpets and fifes. He was preceded by the *amīrs* of the army and followed by the *qāḍī* and the lawyers and the Sharifs.

The *Book of the Zanj* describes a form of association between the immigrant Arabs and the Zanj on what is now the southern Somali coast. Each Arab, or group of Arabs, had a Zanj who acted as his patron (*ṣāḥib*), and who with his tribe would support him if he had a dispute with another Zanj; the Arabs on their side gave military protection. If an Arab absconded with the goods of a Zanj, the Zanj were entitled to take the goods of another Arab until the debt was settled. In Mombasa, evidently at a later date, there was an association between the individual Miji Kenda tribes and Arab tribal groups. These accounts indicate a symbiotic alliance between the towns and the African peoples nearest to them; it is interesting to note that the latter do not seem from this account to have been in an inferior position. There is no evidence for such relationships south of Mombasa; the mention of raids by Kilwa on the mainland tribes gives an indication of enmity. But it is hard to believe that in most places for most of the time there was not a reasonably amicable relationship between the townsmen and the countrymen, for otherwise trade would hardly have been possible. Moreover, none of the towns on the mainland, except Gedi, appear to have been defended by walls before the sixteenth century; such rather flimsy defences as are found on the northern part of the coast appear to have been put up against the Galla and, later, the Masai. For the island towns the sea provided an adequate defence.[1] One has the impression, indeed, that the townsmen were peaceable, and there is no evidence of permanently organized military or naval forces. The arms of the people when mustered for a fight were bows and arrows, and spears, with light shields. They do not appear to have used gunpowder.

As to the religion of the coastal cities, they appear, throughout the period for which we have information, to have adhered to Sunni (orthodox) Islam, and in general to the Shāfī'i school. Ibn al-Mujāwir tells us that Kilwa was of the Khariji school in his day, having previously been of the Shāfī'i school. But by the time of Ibn Baṭṭūṭa (1332) it had reverted to the Shāfī'i persuasion; the people of Mombasa, described as devout, chaste and virtuous, were of the same school, as indeed are the majority of the inhabitants of the coast at the present day. Ibn Baṭṭūṭa was impressed with the piety, generosity and humility of the ruling sultan, al-Ḥasan Abu'l-Mawāhib. He found at Kilwa several Sharifs (descendants of the Prophet's family) from the Hejaz; they seem rather to have been attracted to the place by the prospect of getting money for nothing rather than for love of learning or other cause. For we are told that the sultan was very particular about setting aside one-fifth of the booty acquired in raids against the pagans of the mainland, for distribution to the Sharifs, as prescribed in the Koran. He met a further Sharif at Mogadishu who was anxious to descend on the Kilwa sultan.

The larger towns of five centuries ago must have looked much like the older cities of the coast, such as Lamu, at the present day. There was no overall planning in these towns; they were rather agglomerations of buildings, the streets being the spaces left over, so to speak, after their construction. The towns had no focus; the *jāmi'*, or Friday Mosque, which can be considered the centre of the community in so far as it had one, is hemmed in by buildings in these towns, though a small space nearby may be occupied by graves. So too, it seems, with the dwelling of the shaykh or sultan: a house like the others, only larger (Husuni Kubwa at Kilwa is an exception; but this unique palace stands outside the town). No public buildings other than the mosques have been identified, though at Mogadishu the *qāḍī* had a special, and apparently very comfortable, house for his pupils, in which Ibn Baṭṭūṭa lodged.

[1] There is a rather unclear reference to walls at Kilwa in a Portuguese source, but none can now be seen, nor have any defensive walls been found in excavations.

The smallest settlements were of rectangular mud-and-wattle houses, probably with gabled roofs of *makuti* (made of coconut-palm leaves bound round a split palm rib) or simply of fronds of the *mwaa* (*Hyphaene*) palm, as at the present day. The lower strata at Kilwa, believed to date from before the coming of Islam, have yielded traces of such rectangular houses. The only stone buildings in the smaller towns of the fifteenth century were the mosque, perhaps one or two houses and a number of tombs. These tombs on the coast from around Dar-es-Salaam northwards are very large enclosures with panelled decoration at the eastern end, and, in the case of tombs of men, large pillars, commonly decorated with inset bowls of porcelain. They very seldom carry inscriptions.

In the larger towns the better houses were of stone, built very close to one another, often sharing a party wall and sometimes communicating with each other in a fashion which suggests a family relationship between the occupants. The blocks of buildings were separated by very narrow lanes which had only to accommodate people on foot, for there was no wheeled traffic. On the fringes of the town the houses would have been of mud and wattle; as late as the early fourteenth century most of Kilwa seems to have consisted of such buildings, for Ibn Baṭṭūṭa remembered it as a town of wood and thatch.

The stone houses were of one storey, except in the largest towns, up to three floors being found at Kilwa. The standard of masonry was high; coral stone was used almost exclusively, set in a very hard lime mortar, though mud mortar was sometimes used, as at the well-preserved town of Gedi, situated south of Malindi. Lime plaster was used for the paving of floors, and also of the lanes. The durability of the work is shown by the fact that most of the Great Mosque at Kilwa has survived intact for more than five centuries. This building, although smaller than the large mosques of the Arab homelands, nevertheless covered a large area, some forty by twenty metres in the fourteenth century; in the previous century, however, before it was enlarged, it was only about one-third of this size. The palace and emporium of Husuni Kubwa is even larger, covering nearly a hectare and containing over a hundred rooms.

This building and the adjacent Husuni Ndogo show perplexing affinities with much earlier Umayyad and ʿAbbasid buildings in the homelands of Islam; this connection has yet to be explained. In general, however, the architecture is *sui generis*, its particular style having been evolved on the coast itself. The absence of any mosques of the type commonest in Persia and elsewhere, with a central courtyard, is remarkable. Certain features of ornament and elements of the buildings are aesthetically pleasing and designed with sensitivity, but it cannot be said that the architect approached the design of a building with any imaginative concept of the structure as a whole. The buildings are rather sets of well-designed elements grouped together.

The houses follow a fairly uniform plan. They were entered by a doorway leading to a sunken courtyard, surrounded by terraces and ranges of steps or benches. Facing onto this was usually a reception room and verandah, with the main living room behind, and bedrooms to the rear of this. Such a basic arrangement was often elaborated by the addition of other rooms, including latrines, which were well constructed of cut stone, with an adjoining 'bidet' for ablutions. In larger houses there was a separate 'domestic' courtyard, with adjoining kitchens and servants' rooms. At Gedi some houses were also provided with a special alcove in which jars for cooling water were installed. The rooms were somewhat narrow, and often long, their width being restricted by the weight of the heavy flat stone roofs supported on mangrove poles. Only the rooms facing onto the courtyards were provided with windows, so that those to the rear, lit only through doorways, must have been dark, though the thickness of their walls and their considerable height would have rendered them cool. Domes and vaults (also of rather small span) were on occasion also used for roofing, though these are rarely found outside the Kilwa region. In the fifteenth century they were often ornamented with Chinese porcelain bowls and decorated Islamic pottery set into their under surfaces.

Decoration in carved coral stone was of its highest standard in the fourteenth century; it was used principally to ornament the mihrabs of mosques and the main entrances to houses. These had recessed frames of cut stone, fitted closely together without mortar in their faces, often with carved cable-like or, later, herring-bone ornament. The decorative motifs found – roundels, plaques and, rarely, friezes – are all geometric. There was no representational art in this or any other medium, no doubt for religious reasons. Inscriptions are rare, but the epigraphic art on occasion reached a very high standard. The stone used for this work was fine-grained coral, also employed for arched doorways and their jambs, and for ornamental niches which were often built into the walls of houses. Walls were also probably decorated with carved wooden friezes, and perhaps also carpets, as is suggested by the survival of rows of holes for suspension pegs.

Such evidence as we have concerning modes of trade in the period before 1500 can, in general, only be inferred. Nearly half of the total area of the fourteenth-century palace of Husuni Kubwa at Kilwa is occupied by what appears to be an emporium. A large number of store-rooms are disposed around a huge courtyard, with, in one corner, far from the palace proper, a building of unusual plan, interpreted as the house or offices of the factor in charge of the place.[1] It is concluded that the sultan of the period concerned traded on a very large scale, and it may be that he monopolized the foreign commerce. The building did not remain long in use, and indeed may never have been completed, and it may be that the sultan's direct participation in the trade decreased. But his indirect interest remained very great, although the figures we are given for the duties levied are almost unbelievably high. According to one Portuguese source the sultan, in addition to raising a tax of one *mithqāl* (about five grams of gold) on every five hundred pieces of cotton cloth imported for the Sofala trade, kept two-thirds of the articles for himself. On top of this the merchants had to hand over a further one-seventh of the goods to his representative in Sofala when they got there. On their return to Kilwa they had to pay a five per cent tax on the gold they had acquired; if they passed by Kilwa and went on to Mombasa, the five per cent was levied there on behalf of the sultan of Kilwa.[2] At Mombasa the ruler also acted on his own behalf and took one *mithqāl* of gold on each thousand pieces of cloth, and kept half of the cloth for himself, using it to trade on his own account to Sofala and Kilwa. At Mogadishu, as we learn from Ibn Baṭṭūṭa, one of the numerous rich merchants would take a visitor under his wing and entertain him. The visiting merchant, however, was compelled to conduct all his business through his host, who presumably took a commission or a reward.

It has already been noted that except in the region of the Zambezi there was no significant Muslim penetration of the interior. Elsewhere trade must have been carried on with the adjacent peoples, to whom such goods as came from the further interior probably passed from village to village; by the early seventeenth century the Yao were to make long-distance trading expeditions to the coast. Trade with the mainland must have been carried on by barter; the export trade, both by the same method and probably also by payment in bullion. In

[1] It is possible that the large adjacent enclosure known as Husuni Ndogo was also built for commercial purposes, although the writer considers it more likely that it is an unfinished mosque.

[2] This is interesting evidence that Mombasa was in some degree subject to Kilwa.

regard to the goods traded, we can usefully distinguish four categories: those sought for export, those imported for trade with the mainland, those imported for use in the coastal towns, and those produced in those towns for trade with the interior.

The development of the gold trade has already been described. This was probably of little importance before the latter part of the twelfth century, and only the larger towns, and latterly Kilwa and her dependent ports in the south, appear to have been seriously involved. Even making allowances for the fascination that gold had for the Portuguese, it is clear that at the time they arrived, and no doubt from the fourteenth century onwards, the trade in this was on a very large scale, exports in times of peace from Sofala and other ports in the region being reported in 1506 to have averaged over a million *mithqāls* – approximately 5,000 kilograms a year – a figure which appears to refer to the period before the arrival of the Portuguese. On the other hand, in the years 1512–15 the Portuguese secured an average of only 12,500 *mithqāls* a year, a decrease so drastic as to make one think the earlier figure may be exaggerated. Much gold, however, was undoubtedly escaping the control of the Portuguese, being exported through Angoche and other towns further north. A considerable quantity of copper was also exported from Sofala.

Ivory was the principal export in the period before the twelfth century, and probably remained so for the smaller towns in all periods. Though the trade was mostly with the Persian Gulf, it was reaching China (though trans-shipped en route) as early as the ninth century; so too was ambergris, a product which figures prominently in the accounts of external sources. This mysterious substance commanded a high price, but in view of its extreme rarity the total value can hardly have been very great. Frankincense and myrrh were the chief products of the Horn; these too were being imported by China in the thirteenth century. Mangrove poles, and perhaps other timber, were probably always an important commodity. Iron appears to have been exported in substantial quantities in the twelfth century, and perhaps from Manda at an even earlier date.

The question of slaves is puzzling. Accounts of the massive revolts by Zanj slaves engaged in irrigation projects in southern Iraq during the ninth century suggest that an active slave-trade from East Africa was already in existence by this time. But there is very little evidence for their export from East Africa except in the north, though the capture of a number by a ship from overseas is mentioned in a tale of

Buzurg's, and they are reported to have been sought by the people of Java (or perhaps Sumatra). Even in the *Periplus* they are notable by their absence in the list of commodities, except in reference to what is now the Somali coast. It seems most likely that the Horn continued to be the main source of slaves; human beings are comparatively expensive to transport and subject to loss by disease, so that the shorter voyage from the Horn would have been advantageous.

The principal and perhaps only goods imported for trade with the mainland were cloth, especially of the finer and coloured sorts, and glass beads, the latter mainly from the thirteenth century onwards. Most of this merchandise came from India, though much of it would have been trans-shipped in the Persian Gulf and Oman. These goods were also used in the coastal towns themselves, as was silk, but the main commodity imported for the use of the citizens was pottery, porcelain and, in lesser quantities, glassware. Neither glazed pottery nor glass appears to have been made at any period on the coast. The taste for Chinese porcelain developed in the fourteenth century (though a little was imported before then) and at Kilwa greater quantities of this than of Islamic wares were imported from that time on. Much was traded to northern Madagascar from the fifteenth century on, perhaps largely re-exported from Kilwa. A little of this porcelain was traded on the southern mainland; very small quantities of celadon were reaching Zimbabwe in the fourteenth century, and later Chinese wares occur at other sites on and south of the Zambezi. In the rest of eastern Africa, such imports are unknown in the interior.

Among the local products used for trade to the interior in the period before the thirteenth century, beads made of marine shell must have been important; large numbers of the grooved stone implements used for making these have been found both at Kilwa and Manda. Later, their place seems to have been taken by the imported glass beads. At Kilwa, too, in the same early strata, many cowrie shells occur. These become uncommon after the increase in imports of beads and after the introduction of coinage; it seems likely that they were used for trade with the interior rather than as local currency, in view of the fact that they were so easily obtainable. Such was probably also the significance of a hoard of cowries of later date at Gedi.

Much cotton was grown, spun and no doubt woven from the thirteenth century onwards. Mogadishu produced cloth of high quality, as we are informed by Ibn Baṭṭūṭa; this is an industry which has survived until the present day. On the other hand, when writing about the clothes of the people, he mentions garments of Egyptian origin; this is almost the only evidence we have of trade with Egypt in this period. Silk is stated in a Portuguese source to have been produced at Pate, and traded thence to other places. Cloth made at Kilwa was probably both for local consumption and for trade with the interior; later, in the sixteenth century, a coarse cloth for local consumption was produced in the Sofala area.

We know from the records of Aden that rice was imported to that place from Kilwa. The region of Kilwa is not particularly well suited to the production of rice and it is probable that much of it came from Madagascar, where we know that a surplus was produced. We might expect that salt would have been exported to the interior; the production of this commodity as practised at the coast leaves few traces other than broken pots, and there is only evidence of production on a small scale at Kilwa and in the area of Pate. An earlier, but otherwise insignificant, settlement of around the tenth century north of Bagamoyo on the other hand appears to have produced substantial quantities of this commodity. Other crafts carried out at Kilwa included the carving of ivory and bone, the minting of copper coins and perhaps other copper work, and possibly the manufacture of beads of semi-precious stone. Most if not all of the products of these industries were for use in the towns, rather than for trade with the interior, though some of them were probably exported to northern Madagascar.

The boats of the coast were built with planks sewn with coir twine and having matting sails. These vessels were evidently of the *mtepe* type in use until recently, the ancestry of which goes back to the time of the *Periplus*. They were probably used mainly or entirely for coastal trade, the long-distance commerce being carried out by larger ships from the Arab lands.

The Portuguese when they first arrived were much struck by the luxury of the clothes, of silk as well as cotton, of the upper classes. They were also impressed by the amount of gold and silver jewellery, including earrings and bangles for both arms and legs, none of which has survived. The slaves are described as wearing only loin-cloths. Millet and rice appear to have been the staple crops; according to Ibn Baṭṭūṭa bananas were an important food of the people of Mombasa. For meat, fat-tailed sheep, goats, cattle and hens were raised; then as now fish formed a large part of the diet. The Portuguese were much impressed by the quantities of fruit grown; there were often fruit trees in gardens to the rear of houses. Onions and other vegetables were grown in gardens watered from wells; cisterns apparently designed to hold water for such irrigation have been found at Kilwa.

At Mogadishu Ibn Baṭṭūṭa was struck by the obesity of the people; 'one of them', he says, 'eats as much as several of us'. The staple food of the people was rice, which was cooked with ghee and served on large wooden platters. With it were served side-dishes of chicken, meat, fish and vegetables. Pickled lemons, mangoes and peppers were eaten with curdled milk, also as an accompaniment to the rice. Ripe mangoes were also eaten as fruit; unripe bananas were cooked in fresh milk. The cooking arrangements were very simple. Normally, a portable earthenware stove was used, with three horns on the top of which the cooking vessel was placed, with charcoal beneath. In addition, a sort of cylindrical oven set in the floor was used for the baking of small loaves of rice or millet flour. Probably, as at the present day, fish would have been part-grilled, part-smoked, round open fires. Betel leaves enclosing lime and areca nut were chewed as a stimulant.

The upper classes would have eaten off imported Islamic or Chinese ware. Up to the fourteenth century, the poorer people would seem to have eaten from communal eating bowls but from the fifteenth century small locally made vessels become common and may have been used as individual food bowls; they may alternatively indicate a greater number of side dishes. Their food was sweetened with honey, bees being kept in cylindrical hives hanging from trees, as at the present day.

When considering cultural regions, it is often as useful to think in terms of oceans as it is in terms of continents. There has been much dispute as to whether the coastal civilization should be described as African or Arab. This dispute has been largely unprofitable, for just as the northern part of the continent belongs primarily to the Mediterranean cultural orbit, so the eastern belongs to that of the Indian Ocean; both belong also to the wider world of Islam. These cities of the coast were primarily Islamic, and their way of life mercantile. The springs of their civilization are to be found on the northern seaboard of the Indian Ocean. But it cannot be said to have been Arab; the immigrants were probably few in number, and there would have been far fewer women than men among them. Though, as at the present day, they may have shown a preference for women mainly of Arab extraction, most Arab men must have married Africans or women of mixed blood, and their stock was rapidly integrated with the local people. As to language, a form of Swahili was certainly being spoken in the sixteenth century, and probably much earlier. It has been observed that the ruler of Mogadishu spoke the local language in the early fourteenth century (though he knew Arabic); this was in a region where one would expect Arab (and Persian) influence to be greater than it was further south. Arabic was, however, retained for writing.[1] The poor Arabic of the Kilwa Chronicle (*c.* 1530) would seen to indicate that this was the writer's second language. Though the civilization of these merchant cities was, within the common framework of Islam, peculiar to itself, particularly in its architecture, one can detect little in it that appears to have been derived from the indigenous peoples of the continent. On the hinterland of the coast this civilization had little impact, except for the stimulus to trade. The local pottery of the coast is unrelated to that of the interior; even such skills as building in stone and the use of lime mortar were unknown except in the immediate vicinity of the littoral. Only in the region of the Zambezi, and in Madagascar, did this civilization have any influence on the interior.

The society of the coast was bourgeois, comfortable; sometimes, for the most fortunate, life approached the luxurious. From the point of view of the homelands of Islam, from which they drew their spiritual inspiration, these cities represented a frontier of the civilized world. Their citizens lived isolated from the mainstream of events of the time, preoccupied with their own affairs, and chiefly with the making of money. We have no evidence of any interest in the advancement of science; of their literature and music we know nothing, though we can presume that they would have entertained themselves with these arts. The people of the cities of the coast evolved a society and a culture which in many respects was peculiar to themselves and which we may term a Swahili civilization: to the heart of Africa, however, this civilization contributed little.

MADAGASCAR

The island which the Arabs call al-Qumr has become known as Madagascar as the result of a corruption of the name Mogadishu, which Marco Polo understood to be a large island. Madagascar is considered by its inhabitants as wholly distinct from the continent, and its history reflects this distinction though there are certain African connections.

The Malagasy language is believed to be derived from a language also ancestral to Maanyan of Borneo.[2] The general opinion is that

[1] The earliest extant manuscript in Swahili dates from the early eighteenth century; the Arabic script appears to have been adapted for writing Malagasy at an earlier date.

[2] O. C. Dahl, *Malgache et Maanjan, une comparaison linguistique* (Oslo, 1951).

immigrants from Indonesia were the first inhabitants of Madagascar. Although it is maintained by some that there were people living on the island before the arrival of those from the Far East, the evidence for this is unsatisfactory, it being doubtful whether the one or two supposed stone tools found are of human workmanship. There is uncertainty over the chronology of the Indonesian immigrations, and the extent and nature of the African influence, the presence of which is clear from linguistic and other evidence, is much disputed. The discussion here will be confined to a general outline, paying particular attention to the question of African influence.

By the tenth century, the Indonesians, practising slash-and-burn agriculture, were settled here and there on the coast, and some of them had probably penetrated to the plateau of the interior. At this time the external sources begin to offer a little but valuable information. Buzurg, quoting one Ibn Lākis, gives an account of a prolonged raid on the East African coast by people from the (Far Eastern) islands of Waq-Waq in the year AD 945/6, only ten years or so before the time at which he was writing. They came, we are told, to seek the products of the coast – ivory, tortoise-shell, panther skins, ambergris and Zanj slaves, which were in demand in their country and in China. Whatever the accuracy of the account of the raid (the Waq-Waq are said to have come in a thousand ships, which must be exaggerated), and whichever the islands of Waq-Waq may be,[1] it seems reasonable to conclude that the voyage from the Far East to eastern Africa, and presumably Madagascar, followed a known route and was on occasion made by numbers of ships.

Comment has already been made on Ibn al-Mujāwir's remark about the voyage from Aden to al-Qumr with stages at Mogadishu and Kilwa. He goes on to say that a ship from al-Qumr sailed to Aden in a single voyage in 1228/9; it had intended to stop at Kilwa but reached Aden in error. He also indicates that the boats of the people of al-Qumr had outriggers, and tells us of a tradition he had heard in Arabia that people of al-Qumr at an earlier date had attacked and expelled the fishermen inhabitants of Aden. There they settled, erecting buildings on the mountains. The invaders, however, died out and there were no

[1] M. J. de Goeje, in *Livre des merveilles* (Leiden, 1883), tr. L. M. Devic, believes them to be Japan, but this does not appear to have been generally accepted. It seems best to regard them as the islands of the Orient in general. Waka is one of the names for an outrigger canoe in Indonesia and elsewhere, and it seems possible that the name of this characteristic vessel has become connected with the people (H. Deschamps, *Histoire de Madagascar* (Paris, 1961), 40).

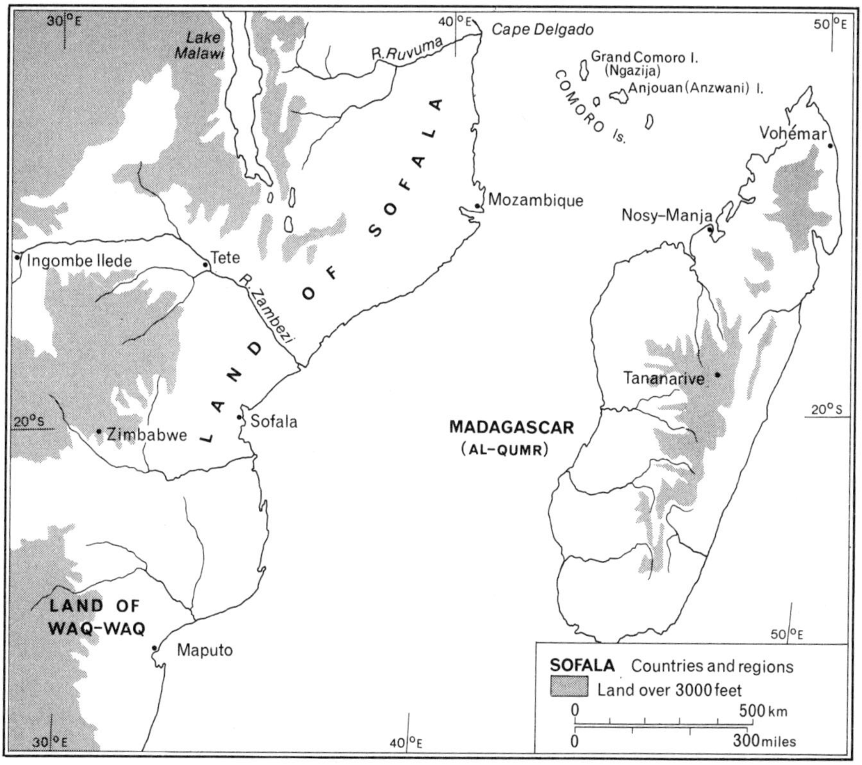

7 Sofala and Madagascar

more migrations. This voyage too is said to have been carried out in one stage, or monsoon (*mawsim*). When it is supposed to have taken place is not clear, but it appears to have been long before the writer's time. The story sounds improbable as it stands, but indicates that voyages were made from Madagascar at an early date.[1]

Idrīsī indicates that voyages from the Far East towards Africa were being made in the twelfth century: the inhabitants of the islands of Zalej (Java, or perhaps Sumatra), he tells us, sail to the Zanj country in large and small ships to trade, and speak each other's language. This seems to indicate that an Indonesian tongue was spoken on the mainland. On the other hand, as we have seen, the mainland appears to have

[1] Ibn al-Mujāwir's information is here taken from the version set out by G. Ferrand, 'Le k'ouen-louen et les anciennes navigations inter-océaniques dans les mers du sud', *Journal Asiatique*, 1919, **13**, 473–9. Ferrand interprets the account of the occupation of Aden as a memory of the successive migrations of western Indonesians of which Ibn Saʿīd gives an account. This interpretation is possible; but the voyage of 1228/9 can only have been from Madagascar.

been occupied by Bantu and Cushitic speakers at the period concerned. It may be that Idrīsī is referring to the commerce and language of Madagascar; he gives no description of al-Qumr. As observed below, there are no Indonesian elements in the languages of the mainland.

The fact that Idrīsī states that the Zanj have no ships in which they can voyage has been taken as showing that they would not have been able to cross from the mainland to Madagascar. But in the relevant passage of Idrīsī his information is contrasted with the statement that ships from Oman and elsewhere 'destined for the islands of Zalej which belong to the Indies' go to the Zanj country to trade there. The account should surely be taken as indicating only that the Zanj had no ships which they used for long-distance voyages, the foreign trade being in the hands of others. We should not regard the statement as inconsistent with their having smaller boats in which the traverse of the Mozambique channel would have been possible. Indeed an account by Buzurg of the kidnapping of a king of the Sofalan Zanj mentions their having small boats.

Ibn Sa'īd, writing about 1250, tells us that some of the Khmer (Qumr) expelled by the Chinese eventually reached Madagascar. Communication between the Far East and Madagascar evidently presented no insuperable difficulties. While there is likely to have been sporadic immigration to the island throughout the period, it seems that it was particularly marked in the early part of the second millennium. The new arrivals settled on the east coast, and perhaps on the north-west, and brought with them, or acquired from India, a knowledge of wet-rice cultivation. In the plateau of the interior at this time were living the Vazimba people. Their name suggests an African origin, but their language appears to have been purely Malagasy, and the general opinion is that they represent earlier, Indonesian settlers, though there is evidence that they were mixed with people of African ancestry. These legendary Vazimba people of the plateau, remnants of whom survive on the west side of Madagascar, lacked chiefs. They soon came under pressure from the new arrivals in the east, among whom were the ancestors of the Hova. These peoples gradually moved into the interior, displacing or absorbing the Vazimba, and fortifying their villages with ditches in an Indonesian fashion (in contrast to the African-type palisades found in the western part of the island). The Hova occupation of the Merina plateau, accompanied by an extension of irrigated rice cultivation, was to develop into the great Imerina kingdom of this region.

The central part of the west coast was occupied in the first half of the second millennium by people speaking a Bantu ('Cafre') language, as opposed to the Malagasy language ('Bouqi' – the island is still known as Buki, or Bukini, in Swahili) of most of the remainder. These people were evidently immigrants from Africa; it seems unlikely that they came as slaves, for at the time of their contact with the Portuguese they were organized in riverine chiefdoms. They were eventually to be absorbed into the kingdom of the Sakalava, whose culture has important African elements. There is also evidence that the Bara of the southern plateau were of African origin; though formerly held to be late arrivals, it has recently been maintained that they came at least as early as the sixteenth century. There is evidence which may suggest some connections with the area of the Zimbabwe culture.[1]

There are various words of African derivation in Malagasy and cultural traits among the people which are evidently of African origin, notably the keeping of cattle, and the Zebu breed of the cattle themselves, as well as the names of other animals from the mainland. Deschamps has explained this, and the presence of Africans, by suggesting that the first Indonesian immigrants settled first on the African coast, migrating later to Madagascar.[2] An objection to this view is the absence of words of Indonesian origin in the languages of the mainland; the undoubted Indonesian traits on the Swahili coast, such as the house-forms, the use of the outrigger canoe (*ngalawa*), and the presence of the banana can as well be explained as having been transmitted from Madagascar itself. The African elements in the island could equally be explained by immigration (including that of captured slaves) from the mainland.

Turning now to the question of trade with the lands of the north, a find of 'Sasanian–Islamic' pottery in the region of Irodo on the north-eastern coast indicates that there was some slight trading contact with such places as *Qanbalū* and Manda in the ninth and tenth centuries. Finds of sgraffiato pottery on both the north-west and north-east coasts indicate that such trading continued, probably on a rather greater (but still minor) scale, during the following two or three centuries. Ibn al-Mujāwir's reference to the trade route from Aden via Mogadishu and Kilwa to al-Qumr has already been mentioned. These

[1] R. K. Kent, *Early kingdoms in Madagascar, 1500–1700* (New York, 1970), ch. 4.

[2] Deschamps, *Histoire*, 28. Kent, in *Early kingdoms*, maintains that an Afro-Malagasy race was formed on the mainland before the arrival of the Bantu in eastern Africa, and sees a greater African element in Madagascar than others allow – e.g. Aidan Southall, 'The problem of Malagasy origins', in *East Africa and the Orient*, ed. H. N. Chittick and R. I. Rotberg (New York, 1975), a balanced assessment of the problem.

finds of imported Islamic goods cannot be said to be evidence of any weight that there were Muslims (East African or Arab) settled at the places concerned; it is noteworthy that Ibn al-Mujāwir in his accounts of the voyages of the people of al-Qumr to Aden gives no indication that they were, or included, Muslims.

The earliest Muslim settlements in this southern region appear to have been in the Comoro islands.[1] The Kilwa legend of the coming of the 'Shirazi' tells us that one of the seven ships (interestingly, that of the father, supposedly the sultan of Shiraz) sailed to Anjouan in the Comoro islands, the party settling there. A similar legend is also remembered in the islands themselves and on the north-western coast of Madagascar. If this immigration is in fact roughly contemporary with the Islamic settlement at Kilwa, we should assign a date around the turn of the twelfth–thirteenth century and connect it also with Mogadishu and the Benadir coast. The Comorian traditions, however, are somewhat confused as to the course of events and as to dates, and in any case, being only recently recorded, no great reliance can be placed on them. Archaeological evidence for this early period is lacking, but virtually no work has been done in this field.

It will be recalled that at Kilwa the Mahdalī (or Ahdalī) dynasty succeeded that of the Shirazi. The fact that a family of the name of Ahdalī is remembered in the Comoros as having arrived after the 'Shirazis', and that this family was among those from which the kings of Anjouan were drawn, suggests that the 'Shirazi' did reach the Comoros before the establishment of the later dynasty at Kilwa at the end of the thirteenth century.[2]

The Muslim settlers in the Comoros, with whom one should probably join slaves brought with them, mixed with Malagasy and perhaps with non-Muslim Africans on the islands. Their descendants were

[1] These, known in Arabic as the islands of al-Qamar, are likely in the minds of Arab authors to have been confused with, or sometimes included with, al-Qumr, except where individual islands are named.

[2] The tradition is also perhaps an indication that the Mahdalī dynasty of Kilwa had influence or control over Anjouan. The traditions are set out by Claude Robineau in 'L'Islam aux Comores, une étude d'histoire culturelle de l'île d'Anjouan', in P. Vérin, ed., *Arabes et Islamisés à Madagascar et dans l'Océan Indien* (Tananarive, 1967), 39–56; Robineau is inclined to date the final islamization of the Comoros to the fifteenth century. In these traditions Ḥasan al-Shirazi (otherwise Ḥasan b. Sa'īd Isa) lands at Anjouan and marries the daughter of an earlier ruler, 'Alī. A brother of Ḥasan lands on Ngazija and another on Mayotte. M. Fontoynont and E. Raomandahy, 'La Grande Comore', *Mémoires de l'Académie malgache*, 1937, **23**, 12, give yet another version of the legend of the seven brothers in seven ships from Shiraz; according to which one landed at Ngazija, one on Anjouan, and one on Madagascar, 'where he was the origin of the Antalaotra'. 'The Comorians' are given as the source of this legend.

known as Antalaotra, or people of the sea, speaking a form of Swahili with a large admixture of Malagasy words.

On the island of Madagascar itself the earliest Muslim settlements were probably on the north-west coast. In this region the Portuguese at the beginning of the sixteenth century found a number of flourishing towns, each under its own shaykh, which were trading with Mombasa and Malindi; a later record of 1617 tells of vessels from Lamu and Pate at the most important of the towns, Nosy Manja. The people of these towns were known as Antalaotra, and probably derive from the people of the same name in the Comoro islands. While, on the archaeological evidence, at least one of these towns was trading with the north as early as the thirteenth century, we cannot be sure that they were Muslim before the fifteenth century, and have only the testimony of the Portuguese that the Muslims had been long established when they arrived. The towns were on islands, or defended by massive walls, which indicates that they kept themselves separate from, and may have been sometimes at enmity with, the Malagasy of the region, a state of affairs similar to that found on the mainland coast.

On the north-eastern coast there were other towns which were at least linked with Islam; of these the most important was at the modern Vohémar. Excavation of graves at this place, known anciently as Iharana, has brought to light a rich collection of grave-goods, with imported pottery, much of it Chinese, glass beads and vessels, bronze mirrors, etc. The most characteristic objects are vessels made from chlorite-schist, most of them with three legs. Similar vessels have been found at Kilwa and attest trade with that region. Other sites of the people concerned, remembered as the Rasikaji, are known in the same region of the island. The graves at Vohémar are arranged in the usual Muslim fashion, with the head to the east, facing north towards Mecca. But the inclusion of grave-goods in their burials is of course entirely opposed to the tenets of Islam, and indicates a large incorporation of pagan elements. Though only meagre remains of masonry now are to be found at the site of Iharana, the people are known to have constructed permanent buildings, two having been recorded in the eighteenth century. It seems that these places were not settled before the fifteenth or possibly the later fourteenth century; the date originally ascribed to these graves by the excavators can now be shown to be much too early. On the evidence of imported Chinese porcelain, the settlements continued to exist for some three centuries. Little is known of the origin of the Iharanians, though traditions, particularly of a people living at the present day north of Vohémar, suggest that some of their ancestors came from the Comoros and the East African coast.

It appears that certain of the Iharanians migrated southwards along the coast. This is probably the origin of two remarkable groups of people who live in the south-eastern part of the island, and are known as the Zafi-Raminia and the Anteimoro. Among both are found confused traditions of an 'Arab' and Muslim origin, and the common people (but not the nobles) among the Anteimoro appear to have settled in their present homes, among earlier inhabitants, roughly around AD 1500, and the Zafi-Raminia rather earlier. If they in fact derive from Iharana, the movement southwards must have occurred early in the development of that place. In any case, an origin involving foreign elements from northern Madagascar, the Comoros, and ultimately from the East African coast is probable.

These peoples retained very little of Islam (though this element appears to have been greater in the past than it is at the present), or of the civilization of the towns of the north of the island and of the African coast. They did, however, preserve the knowledge of writing in Arabic script, which they employed for their own language. This skill and the knowledge of how to manufacture a type of paper was particularly well developed among the Anteimoro. These people were, according to tradition, originally organized in one kingdom, which by the sixteenth century was divided into four. Their seers (*ombiasa*), versed in magical sciences, and having a knowledge of writing, came to exercise much influence among adjacent peoples. These seers, the centralized polity of the Anteimoro, and their expansionist tendencies, were all to play a part in the development of the kingdoms in the interior in the seventeenth and following centuries.

The Portuguese displayed hardly any interest in Madagascar, seeing little of value in the resources of the island, and preferring to establish their bases on the mainland; there was, however, some commercial contact, notably in Mahajamba Bay on the north-west coast. There appears on the archaeological evidence to have been little or no diminution in the amounts of imports reaching northern Madagascar by the traditional routes in the sixteenth century, though the Portuguese presence in the Indian Ocean must have made this trade more difficult.

THE PORTUGUESE

The Portuguese expansion into the Indian Ocean was prompted by both religious and commercial motives. A great block of Muslim countries lay across the trade-routes to the east; through them all the exotic products of the Orient had to pass. A prime object of the Portuguese was to gain access to the sources of these goods and to control trade in the products, of which pepper was the most important. But their prodigious exploits must also be viewed against the background of the confrontation between Christianity and Islam which had dominated the western world for centuries. For the Christians to have direct access to the Orient was harmful to the Muslims in a commercial way; to control a route round Africa was strategically to outflank Islam. The aim of linking up with the legendary Christian kingdom of Prester John in the Orient was prominent among the aims of the earlier expeditions; although it was known by the end of the fifteenth century that this kingdom was in Africa, it was believed to be much larger than in fact was the case.

Vasco da Gama's voyage to India in 1498 marks the turn of an era, for during the next two centuries Portugal was the dominant power on the East African coast and in the Indian Ocean generally. It is, however, easy to over-emphasize the importance of the coast in this region. For the Portuguese, there was nothing in East Africa of commercial or other interest, with the exception of the fabled gold of Sofala, and to a lesser extent ivory. Their chief purpose was to maintain a base on the way to the East. East Africa was entirely inferior to the interests of India and indeed of the further Orient. This is signified by the fact that for almost the entire period of Portuguese ascendancy, officials in East Africa received their orders from the viceroy at Goa.

No significant attempts were made to colonize the northern region of the coast, and it has been estimated that towards the end of the sixteenth century, after a long period of peace, there were hardly fifty Portuguese living north of Cape Delgado. The Portuguese displayed very little interest in the local peoples, apart from those in the towns with which they were concerned. They tell us nothing of the great movement of people from the Shungwaya area of southern Somalia which was taking place in this period (see p. 189). Only in the south did the Portuguese attempt to penetrate, and to some extent colonize, the interior in their quest for gold; numbers of them also settled on the coast and in the Kerimba islands. From Sofala the traders penetrated into the regions of Uteve and Manyika to the north-west, by agreement with the rulers. Further north, they moved up the Zambezi in an attempt to gain direct control of the gold trade and eventually of some of the mines themselves. Their initial penetration and settlement was carried out by permission of the *mwene mutapa*, the ruler of the region (see chapter 8), to whom they paid a substantial tax. During the first half of the sixteenth century they established settlements at Sena and Tete, approximately 260 and 515 kilometres from the sea, respectively. Small stone forts were built at each, and by the end of the century there were forty or fifty Portuguese at each place with some hundreds of other inhabitants, mostly Christian converts. From these towns traders peacefully travelled to, and settled in, other places south of the Zambezi. Soon they were clearing and establishing plantations, and later, supported by their local followers, were to challenge the authority of the *mwene mutapa*.

In the course of this expansion on the Zambezi there was bitter rivalry between the Portuguese and the Muslim traders from the coast already established there. In this rivalry the Portuguese came off best; on the other hand their somewhat heavy-handed attempts to gain control of the mines resulted in a lesser, not greater, amount of gold reaching the coast than before their first arrival. Portuguese policy on the coast was founded on playing off one city-state against another. It should not be thought that despite their frequently repressive and cruel actions, they were without friends: the shaykh of Malindi, north of Mombasa, was a loyal ally, no doubt through a combination of fear and hope of gain; Zanzibar too was at times a friend of Portugal. No attempt was ever made to conquer the coast in an organized fashion; nor, given the slim resources of the Portuguese, would any such conquest have been possible. Rather they attempted to obtain the co-operation of the local rulers by the imposition of treaties. But after the first visits of the Portuguese, the rulers did not honour the arrangements for the payment of tribute that had been negotiated with or extorted from them, and in 1505 a fleet under d'Almeida attacked Kilwa and Mombasa, sacking both, as well as towns further north. It was proposed to use Kilwa as a base, and a fort was built there in the astonishingly short time of some twenty days by the crews of the ships, with the forced assistance of the inhabitants. But it was occupied for only seven years; thereafter the Portuguese fell back on the towns of Mozambique and Malindi as their bases. Fortifications had been constructed at the former, to be replaced by the fort which survives to the present day;

there was also a castle at Sofala. Of these places Mozambique was the most important, though until about 1550 the captain of the place divided his time between there and Sofala. There was a captain also in Malindi; in both places they arrogated to themselves, so far as they could, the profits and revenues of trade.

Through the greater part of the period of Portuguese domination there was intermittent defiance of the Portuguese by the individual towns of the coast, with consequent reprisals. It would be unprofitable here to go into the details of these, but one should remark that for most of the time the little states continued their existence without direct interference except for the payment of tribute. Most of the sixteenth century appears to have been a period of peace, though not of prosperity, as will be shown. Pate, and to a lesser extent other towns in the Lamu region, were exceptions to the general decline of the settlements. Reason to disbelieve the account of the rise and expansion of Pate as reported in its chronicle has been given (see p. 208). At the time of the arrival of the Portuguese it was a town of secondary importance, meriting a brief mention, together with Lamu, in one account. By the end of the century it was a force to be reckoned with, and during the succeeding two centuries it became, after Mombasa, the most prominent town on the coast north of Mozambique. The reasons for its prosperity are uncertain, but are most probably due to its ready access to ivory, which would have been sold to Mombasa, elephants being common in its hinterland.

A new factor, the Turks, came into play in the latter part of the sixteenth century. From about 1550 there were minor raids down the coast from the Red Sea, and they soon began to cause trouble for the Portuguese in the Persian Gulf. In 1585 Amir 'Alī Bey reached as far as Mombasa, and prompted the populations of numbers of towns to rise in revolt against their hated overlords; he made a further visitation in 1588 when the people of the island of Pemba rose, massacring the Portuguese. At the same time from the south came a fearful incursion by the cannibal Zimba, whose origins in the region to the north of the Zambezi are described in Volume 4, chapter 7. They overcame the settlements at Sena and Tete on the Zambezi; others of them pushed along the coast, killing and eating every living thing, according to the Portuguese; in 1587 they overran Kilwa, killing 3,000 of the inhabitants. Soon they reached Mombasa, where with the connivance of the Portuguese commander, who was investing the place, they slaughtered the Muslim inhabitants. At Malindi they were halted, chiefly by the intervention of the Segeju, Bantu-speaking people who had migrated from the north. Returning to their homes in the south, the Zimba disappeared from the coastal scene north of Cape Delgado.

The Portuguese, having defeated 'Alī Bey and occupied Mombasa island, now decided to make a permanent base for their captain there, and in 1593 began the construction of the great Fort Jesus. This was built on the most up-to-date lines, to the design of an Italian architect, and occupied by a substantial garrison. About this time there died the last of the 'Shirazi' rulers of Mombasa; the Portuguese brought in the ruler of Malindi as sultan in his place. Thus they rewarded nearly a century's loyalty to themselves on the part of that town, and so hoped to secure their position in Mombasa. With the construction of Fort Jesus began a period during which the Portuguese attempted to exercise greater control over their dominions on the northern coast. Their power, however, was soon to be challenged not only by revolts but also by powers from overseas.

During the fifteenth and sixteenth centuries large movements of population were taking place in the hinterland of the northern coast. The Galla were pressing upon the Bantu-speaking people in southern Somalia, who were known to the Arabs as *Kashūr*. In turn the Somali were bringing pressure to bear on the Galla. In the late fifteenth or early sixteenth century a Muzaffarid dynasty, apparently related to the Somali Ajuran, who by then controlled the lower Shebele basin, was established at Mogadishu. Later the Ajuran succumbed to Hawiya immigrants, and the Muzaffarid dynasty collapsed about 1624.

Pressure by the Galla on the *Kashūr* in the Shungwaya region caused the latter people to start to move south in the early to middle fifteenth century; a few groups may have departed before this date. By about 1700 the greater part of the Shungwaya region, from the Juba to the Tana rivers, together with the town of Shungwaya,[1] which had a Muslim, 'Shirazi' population, had been abandoned. These displaced *Kashūr* were the ancestors of the Miji Kenda ('Nyika') and other tribes who inhabit the hinterland of the coast from the Tana river to a little

[1] Certain traditions of the coast indicate that Shungwaya town was among the earlier Muslim settlements, and imply that it was the place of origin of the first of the Shirazi dynasty at Kilwa. These traditions are all late and otherwise uncorroborated. The site of the town, usually held to be at Bur Gabo (Bur Gao), a little north of the present Kenya border, does not, on archaeological evidence, appear to have been occupied before the mid fifteenth century. Another site apparently associated with the name lies opposite Pate island, and is dated primarily to the fourteenth century. The *Book of the Zanj* states that the town of Shungwaya was on the Juba river, but no site has been found there. Because of the doubt about the antiquity of the town of Shungwaya, it has been omitted from the account of the early Muslim towns given above.

north of Tanga, and perhaps of other tribes of the north-eastern Bantu group. In the case of one tribe, the Segeju, we have precise indications of its progress from Portuguese sources: they were in the region of Malindi in 1571, near Mombasa a little later, and by 1659 were at Vanga near the present southern Kenya border where Digo (also derived from the *Kashūr*) were already living.

Because the scale of Portuguese operations in the Indian Ocean was small – over an extended period an average of only six ships a year went to India – their attempts to control commerce in the Indian Ocean succeeded in doing little more than disrupt the pattern of trade. The consequence of this, and of their occupation of Sofala, was that the city-states of the coast declined rapidly. This is particularly true of Kilwa and the other coastal towns of what is now Tanzania, which were more or less dependent on that city, and on the gold trade. Short-sighted as well as rapacious sackings of towns added to this decline, which was compounded by the irruption of the Zimba. Nor did Portugal's interest in East Africa afford any profit to herself. For a small country, estimated to have had a population of just over a million and a quarter, to send out fleets to the Orient and to maintain garrisons over such enormously long lines of communication, constituted an almost intolerable burden. Had their efforts resulted in some profit to the state they might have been deemed worthwhile, but it is doubtful whether they ever did so. Their commercial policy in East Africa was one of exploitation in the crudest sense: take what you can, and give nothing. To an inept commercial policy was added a corrupt and inefficient administration. High posts were allotted, years in advance, to Portuguese of high birth or influence. The chief object of these persons, as of their inferiors, was to accumulate as much wealth as possible in the short period of their tenure, and the amount of corruption and sometimes outright theft was astonishingly great.

From the point of view of East Africa north of Cape Delgado, the only lasting legacy of the Portuguese was the decline of prosperity; they might otherwise hardly have existed. The few converts to Christianity must soon have returned to Islam; no trace of them exists at the present day. Similarly, we can detect no vestige of Portuguese culture among the people of the coast, save a very few words incorporated in the Swahili language, and perhaps the bull-baiting in which the people of Pemba still engage. On the coast north of Mozambique, only Fort Jesus stands as a monument to the costly, misguided, but nevertheless astounding enterprise of a tiny nation.

CHAPTER 4

THE EASTERN MAGHRIB AND THE CENTRAL SUDAN

A principal underlying theme for the central Sahara and Sudan in this chapter, in the period roughly from AD 1050 to 1600, is supplied by the basic pattern of penetration. New people, new ideas, new goods were crossing, or sometimes emerging from, the Sahara, and becoming established in the Sudan. There was considerable mobility, too, within the central Sudan itself, most dramatically illustrated by the exodus of the court of Kanem into Bornu about 1400. In the corresponding chapter in the next volume, concerned with the seventeenth and eighteenth centuries, it is more the tendency towards consolidation of states and societies which runs through the whole story.

The countries of the Sudan were by no means inactive partners in the trans-Saharan relationship. Sudanese gold was of critical importance for the Mediterranean economy; Sudanese slaves coloured the societies into which they were received. Even Islam, that most outstanding of all the gifts of the outside world to the Sudan in this early period, was influenced in its North African base by the beliefs and observances which these same slaves brought with them. Nevertheless, what was received in the Sudan countries had, on balance, a more profound historical influence than what was exported thence. Just what form this influence took in the Sudan depended upon the strengths and weaknesses, the needs and ambitions and preferences, of the receiving societies. And it is by rivetting our attention upon the local contribution that the new school of the historiography of black Africa has performed its most signal service.

The Sahara lies like a great ocean, shielding the Sudan. The caravan towns scattered along its borders, north and south, were the ports and harbours from which the desert ocean was navigated; for during the five and a half centuries with which this volume is concerned the Sahara was crossed regularly, year by year. This communication was mainly between the settled peoples on either side of the desert, but it was the sparse desert population which provided both the mariners and the pirates. That is to say, they bred the camels and operated the carrying industry, but on occasion they were also the predators. The achievements of those who ventured upon trans-Saharan communication, and of those who helped to maintain it, were considerable. Yet the desert remained essentially a barrier, isolating the Sudan countries from much of the development of the Mediterranean world. There is even evidence that the barrier became broader during the period covered by this chapter or shortly before: numerous Iron Age sites, for example, in and near the Kerki region, 19°E and 16°N, some dated to the tenth century AD, show how recently the desert has encroached there.[1] Muslims in the Sudan felt this isolation particularly keenly: even as late as the middle of the nineteenth century, the leading scholar of Timbuktu could write, 'This our land is the tail of the world, and our people are the tail of mankind.'

Sometimes nomadic groups erupted from the desert lands into the sown, and it is a curious fact that until recently these episodes have been differently interpreted according to whether they occurred to the north of the desert or to the south. For the eastern Maghrib, approximately modern Libya and Tunisia, the influx of the Banū Hilāl in the eleventh century has usually been regarded as disastrous, the devastation of a horde of locusts. For the central Sudan, by contrast, the encroachment of nomads, in this area particularly the Zaghawa, has sometimes been presented as fundamentally constructive. Urvoy, in a vivid simile, compared this intrusion to Belot's astronomical theory, of a small star, dense and rapidly rotating, hurled with great speed into a diffuse, immobile and inert nebula. From this collision there resulted the new pattern of the solar system, the perfect image, according to Urvoy, of the origins of many Sudanic states and empires.[2]

Radical alternatives for both locusts and hurtling stars have now been suggested. It was first argued that the decline of the eastern Maghrib had begun earlier, and for other reasons, and that the invading Banū Hilāl merely took advantage of this. Later, the hypothesis was advanced that, rather than decline, there had been a centrifugal shift of economic emphasis, both before and after the arrival of the Banū Hilāl. In the Sudanic belt, the influence of nomads is increasingly discounted. In Kanem, a nomadic contribution of a sort is admitted, from Teda/Daza-speaking peoples, but the settled life is seen as having absorbed and assimilated the nomads, rather than as having been trans-

[1] J. L. Schneider, 'Evolution du dernier lacustre et peuplements préhistoriques aux Pays-Bas du Tchad', *Bulletin de Liaison* (Association sénégalaise pour l'étude du Quaternaire de l'ouest africain, 1967, 18–23).

[2] Y. Urvoy, *Histoire de l'empire du Bornou*, no. 7 of *Mémoires de l'IFAN* (Paris, 1949; reprinted Amsterdam, 1968), 21.

formed by them. In Hausaland, the idea of a nomadic contribution has practically vanished.

The nomad, in the traditional view, was a horseman. He introduced the horse to the Sudan countries, and cavalry was an essential element in establishing the new statecraft. Here too reconsideration is possible: horses may have come into the Sudan a good deal earlier, perhaps in the days of the horse-drawn chariots of Saharan rock art, and survived among various local peoples. It may even be that the nomads, arriving later, switched from camels to horses as part of their acclimatization to Sudanic conditions.

The merchant and the Muslim, much better than the nomad, have maintained their reputations as important contributors to Sudanic development. The relationship between trade and Islam has been so often postulated that economic determinism threatens to swallow up the religious element; it is particularly this relationship which needs a fresh look. In trans-Saharan traffic many items, as will be seen, were luxury goods of little direct practical use to government. But all commerce was valuable to the local authorities because of customs duties, and this was as true of the oasis islands and archipelagos amid the desert sea, such as the Fezzan, and of the Sudanic cities, as it was of the governments north of the Sahara. The slave-trade dominated the commerce of the central Sahara and Sudan, much as did that in gold to the west. The slave staple had important implications for the emerging states south of the desert, placing a premium upon military strength, and upon local tribute and exchange arrangements, while providing at the same time – for only a minority of the newly acquired slaves were exported – a valuable accession of population. The Muslim contribution, apart from its commercial overtones, should be explored not only in those respects, such as literacy and education, which in addition to their religious desirability were also of obvious utility to society, but in more strictly spiritual matters also, such as prayer, for these too had profound practical significance.

In all this it is quite clear, whether or not we go as far as the radical sceptics in their doubts about the importance of nomad intruders, that there are two elements to be considered: the foreign contribution and its impact on the one hand, the local heritage and its resilience on the other. In some cases, the local situation seems to have overcome and absorbed the new arrivals, for example in the evolution of the Kanembu and subsequently still more in that of the Kanuri. In other cases, particularly among traders, this was less likely to happen, for individuals naturally hoped to return home after their travels. The position of Islam was less clear: there was a strong tendency for it to be absorbed into the local setting, amalgamated with local patterns of belief. The process of acculturation is aptly, though presumably unintentionally, illustrated by the traditions, known at Kano and elsewhere, of a copy of the Koran wrapped in many hides of sacrificed animals, and treated as an almost pagan cult object. Islam might be forgotten altogether: one tradition among the Jukun (the most prominent group today tracing descent from the Kwararafa) asserts that the chiefs of the Kanuri, the Shuwa, the Sulebawa Fulani and the Jukun all came of the same stock, and that each was given, by the Prophet Muḥammad himself, a copy of the Koran. But the Jukun chiefs gradually lost the reading habit, and eventually adopted the traditional faith of their neighbours. Historically implausible, indeed fantastic, as some of these details are, the danger to Islam in remote areas was real. Hence the extreme importance of widely acknowledged obligations and links, such as those centring upon the Pilgrimage, and of highly mobile groups, like the Sharifs (Arabic *sharīf*, pl. *shurafā'*, descendants of the Prophet). This dual theme, of penetration – whether nomadic, commercial, Islamic, or of whatever kind – and of local reaction to it, of contributions from the outside and derivations from the local heritage, underpins all that follows.

The geography of Africa, in so far as that continent was penetrated by Muslims up to the end of the sixteenth century, suggested a picture of latitudinal belts, of which five may be broadly distinguished: the Mediterranean, the Saharan, the Sahelian, the Sudanic and finally the equatorial forest. The Arabs call North Africa, apart from Egypt, *al-maghrib*, 'the west'; Tunisia and northern Libya are *al-maghrib al-adnā*, 'the near west', or the eastern Maghrib. Coastal Libya consists of two narrow fertile strips, one in Cyrenaica and the other further west in Tripolitania. Between these, the desert thrusts through to the Mediterranean on a front three hundred miles broad. The country lacks geographical unity: apart from the coastal strips, it is mainly desert, often of a most forbidding character. It was easier to travel from Cyrenaica to Egypt, or from Tripolitania to Tunisia, than to move about within Libya. This cleavage helps to explain why, about the beginning of the period covered by this chapter, Fatimid control over the eastern Maghrib declined so quickly once the centre of Fatimid authority had been transferred to Cairo. It was also a factor in directing the

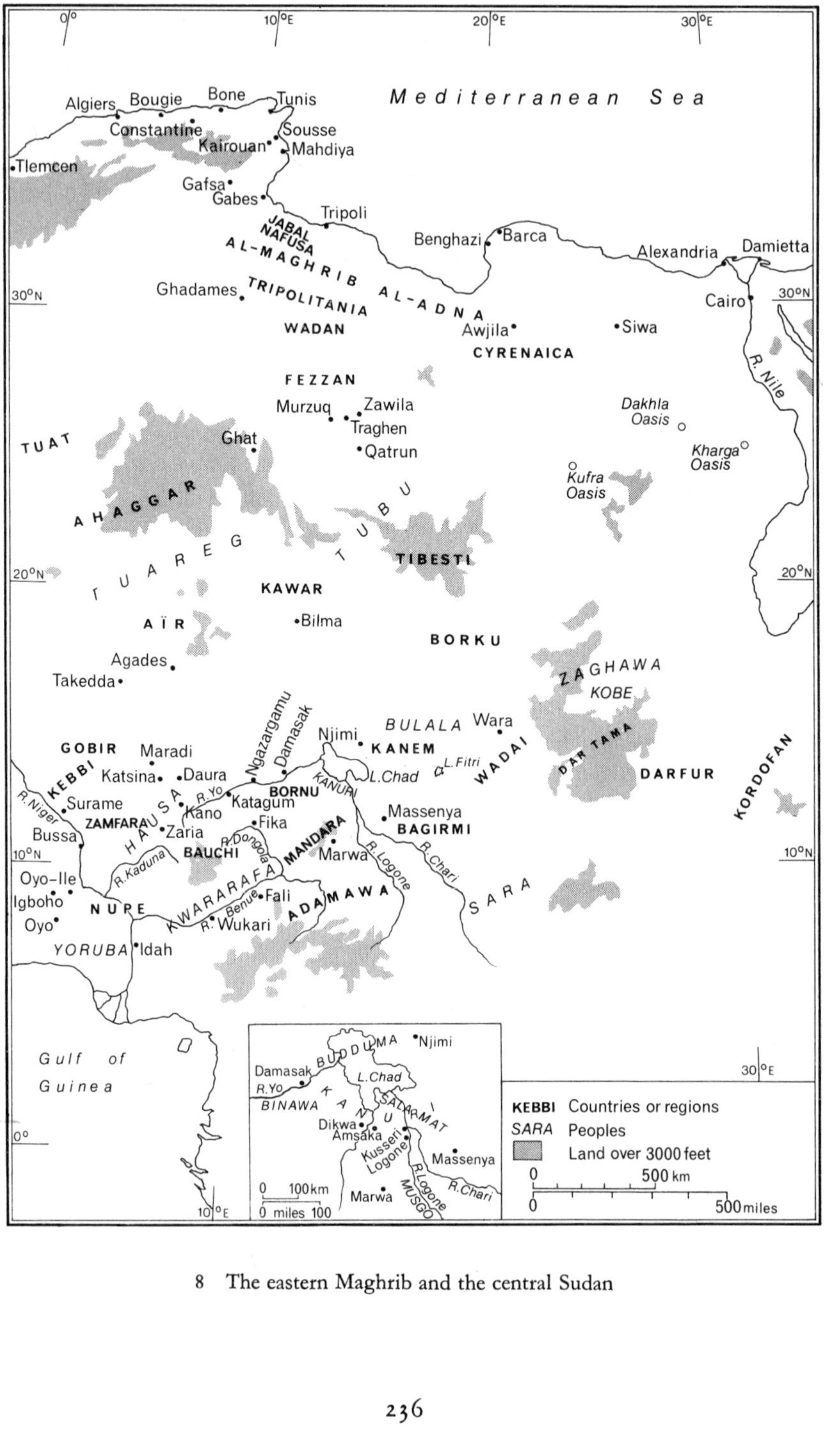

8 The eastern Maghrib and the central Sudan

attention of the coastal cities of the eastern Maghrib towards participation in the growing complex of Mediterranean trade. Even the Ottomans, whose arrival in the eastern Maghrib marks the beginning of the close of this period, came by sea, and bypassed Cyrenaica, which effectively acknowledged their authority only in the mid seventeenth century. Nonetheless, the Libyan desert was passable: routes ran east and west, not only near the coast, but in the hinterland through Siwa and Awjila, or further south again through al-Wāḥāt and Kufra, as well as north and south, from Cyrenaica through Kufra and, most important of all for this period, from Tripolitania through the Fezzan to Bornu and Hausaland.

If Libya was the least favoured country of the Maghrib in climate and agricultural resources, Tunisia was the most blessed. The long eastern coast, flat and well watered, the distinguishing feature of the country, made the territory not only inviting to invaders, but easy of approach. This circumstance was reinforced by Tunisia's position in the Mediterranean, reaching towards Sicily and Sardinia. Tunisia has been a central meeting place, a pivot in the rise and fall of empires, ever since the time of the Roman overthrow of Carthage. In our period, it was the springboard for the last attempt, by the Banū Ghāniya coming from the Balearic islands, at the restoration of Almoravid power.

Events in Tunisia have sometimes exercised profound influence over countries to the south. In the thirteenth century, for example, important links grew up between the Tunisian Hafsids and the rulers of Kanem. Yet Tunisia never possessed an extensive hinterland; the modern state does not stretch even as far south as Ghadames. It was Tripoli, with its fluctuating direct or indirect influence over the Fezzan, which was more actively involved in Saharan affairs. The Sahara itself was thinly populated, though probably less so than today. Only very rarely did it foster a movement of primary importance: the Almoravid explosion in the far west in the eleventh century formed a dramatic but isolated exception. The main significance of the Sahara has been as an avenue of approach between North Africa and the Sudan, rugged enough to bar the passage of many innovations, some valuable, some harmful, yet open to the brave, the ambitious, the greedy, and to the fugitive and to the slave under compulsion – open, too, to the ideas which these brought with them. The principal route throughout our period was the highway from Tripoli through the network of oases which made up the Fezzan, leading on to Kawar, which was an important stage both for its water and oases and for its salt industry, and thus to Lake Chad. From Egypt a south-westerly route crossed the Libyan desert via Kufra, and past Tibesti to Borku and Lake Chad. This was the shorter road from Egypt to the central Sudan, but because of its harshness, and its vulnerability to the predatory Tubu, it was little used. To the west a road passed through Ghat and the habitable massif of Aïr towards Hausaland. The very early development of the road through Fezzan to Lake Chad, already flourishing in the ninth century, may partly explain why political and religious development in the Chad region, where Kanem was already a recognized state when our period opens, was so much more rapid than in Hausaland. The road north from Hausaland, through Aïr, came into its own only later in our period, and formative foreign influences came into Hausaland first from west and east, rather than from the north. Even more striking is the case of Wadai to the east, which remained sunk in profound obscurity throughout our period. Bagirmi likewise had no outlet northwards of its own.

For those for whom the Sahara was home, rather than the road into or out of the Sudan, several factors were needed to make possible a tolerable life. Nomadic skills and hardiness were essential, illustrated by such peoples as the Tubu, the Tuareg and the Zaghawa. Equally indispensable was the life of the oases, and here a settled population did most of the necessary work. The oasis dwellers were perhaps in part the remnants of Sudanic peoples who had, long before our period, inhabited a wetter Sahara in larger numbers; but they were also constantly replenished during the period by slaves and freedmen. The third requirement in the equation was trade: without caravans passing through, paying tolls, hiring guides, selling and buying, open to extortion and even plunder, Saharan society would have been poor indeed – as it is today.

Sāḥil (Sahel) is an Arabic word meaning 'coast', and if the desert itself resembles an ocean, it is reasonable to speak of its edges as coasts and their caravan towns as harbours. The term 'Sahel' is fairly common in Muslim Africa. The fortunate plain of Tunisia, already mentioned, is called the Sahel; in east Africa, the name 'Swahili' derives from the plural, *sawāḥil*. The limits of the sub-Saharan Sahel are not easy to define exactly; it is that band where the nomadic and settled, the white and black, meet and mingle, without either having clear predominance. The *bilād al-sūdān*, often shortened to 'Sudan', is another Arabic term, meaning 'the land of the blacks'. The Sudan, in this wide sense, comprises the relatively well-watered, yet still fairly open country, the savanna lands lying between the Sahel and the forest. The country changes imperceptibly: in the north, sand and scrub with wells and scattered oases; then light grazing lands, without enough rainfall for regular cultivation; then cultivable land with denser plant life gradually reducing stock-keeping to an accessory occupation. Staple crops were millet nearest the Sahel, then sorghum, and yams furthest south. In Hausaland particularly, cereals and cattle throve, animal transport was efficient, and although the economy was mainly agricultural, the long dry season encouraged crafts, trade and travel.

Within the Sudan belt, there are few natural barriers to the mobility of men and ideas between east and west. From Lake Chad to the west, the sand and clay plains extend as far as Kano and beyond without any natural feature interrupting them; to the east, likewise, no natural boundary appears between Kanem and Wadai, or still further east. Only the lake itself is an obstacle, shallow and marshy, difficult to cross even today, and treacherously subject to sudden fluctuations in size. Particularly on the western (Bornu) side, villages were built several miles from the usual shore, since the *harmattan* wind might easily drive the water over the land. Boyd Alexander, visiting the lake in 1904, one morning retraced his passage across part of the lake the evening before, and found the water gone, leaving numbers of fish stranded, some as much as four feet long. It is not altogether fanciful to take this changeable lake as symbolic of the political empires of the central Sudan: fairly stable in their home territories, and on the fringes sweeping out with punitive expeditions, the imposition of tribute, slave-raids, the employment of nomad auxiliaries in harassing tactics, or whatever other means might be available, but receding as suddenly, often to leave little lasting result. Northwards, the lake adjoins the desert, which, though crossed by the Tripoli road, was sufficiently harsh to prevent any extensive east–west exchange of populations and languages. Southwards the lake abuts on the flood-plains of the Chari and Logone rivers, which have had the same effect. Within the east–west network of the Sudan belt, various major developments occurred. The Fulani, spreading slowly and over centuries from the lower Senegal, were a potentially highly charged strand in the central Sudan. Moving in somewhat the same fashion, but in the opposite direction, from the east, were the Shuwa Arabs. When the final crucial military confrontation took place between the two peoples, at the beginning of the nineteenth century, it was just a little to the west of Lake Chad, although many individuals and groups had passed further in their respective directions. It was a little to the west, because the exodus of the *mai*, or ruler, from Kanem to Bornu at the end of the fourteenth century had burst through the bottleneck south of the lake. The exodus had led at the time to the growth of fruitful associations between Bornu and Hausaland.

A linguistic map of the area, superimposed upon the natural physical features, reveals further patterns. To the east of Lake Chad are the languages of the Teda/Daza group, including those two languages (spoken respectively by the northern and southern branches of the Tubu people) as well as Kanembu, Zaghawa and, apparently, Kanuri. To the west of the lake are the Chadic languages, the most important of which is Hausa. Linguistic and archaeological evidence suggests that the present linguistic boundary has been in place since long before the mid eleventh century without mass population movement. Kanuri is the exception, a Teda/Daza language spoken to the west of the lake, its presence there a memorial to the exodus which came to a climax at the end of the fourteenth century. The linguistic affiliation of Kanuri with the Teda/Daza group is somewhat unclear; it may be a form of Kanembu, modified through amalgamation with Chadic languages west of the lake, just as the Kanembu immigrants themselves evolved into the Kanuri people partly through the absorption of those peoples, loosely called the So or Sao, already living in the Bornu area. The underlying stability of population and language here is indicated by the fact that many of the earliest settled sites are still today inhabited by the Kotoko, speaking a Chadic tongue, and apparently descended from the original So.

Language defines another boundary, between north and south. The central Nigerian highlands, where now the Chadic languages from the north meet with those of the Niger–Congo family to the south, may in the past have served as a refuge for the northernmost speakers of Niger-Congo languages gradually driven southwards by encroaching Chadic groups, themselves pressed by increasing desiccation of the Sahara. This trend can be seen also in the replacement of the Hausa by the Tuareg as inhabitants of Aïr.

The Sudan was the first fully Negro area in the heart of Africa which Arabic speakers came to know: hence the name. The Arabs were much less concerned with the forest dwellers, those still more numerous Negro peoples living south of the savanna. The Arabs knew little about these people, whom they called by names such as Lamlam; they told strange stories about them, even attributing cannibalism to them.

Thus the growth of our knowledge about these regions and their inhabitants is handicapped by the lack of documentation; for it is primarily to Muslims, visiting strangers and local scribes both, that we owe much of our knowledge of the central Sudan. It remains to be seen how far oral tradition, linguistic and anthropological researches, and other means of penetrating the past of these unlettered realms to which no visitor (or very few) came, will eventually supply us with information comparable to that available for the Sudan and the Sahel. In the meanwhile, we have to work with the materials at hand.

THE EASTERN MAGHRIB

The history of North Africa contains several of the most striking illustrations in African history of nomadic intrusion. The initial Muslim conquest, sweeping through in the seventh century but only very gradually consolidating, brought with it the Arabic language and the Islamic religion. In Tunisia, an already established civilization assimilated these elements relatively rapidly, pointing again to the importance of the local base for, and contribution to, any new amalgam. In Morocco, on the other hand, with a slighter foundation to build upon the corresponding evolution took much longer. This incursion augurated the first main period of the Islamic history of North Africa, the period of Islamic expansion, which continued until the eleventh century. Not only North Africa, but most of Spain, as well as Malta and Sicily, fell to the Crescent.

The second period, from the eleventh century until the early sixteenth, was marked by an intermittent, and ultimately quite threatening, Christian response to this challenge. Malta, Sicily and Spain were restored to the Christian fold, and the war was carried even to North Africa. This period, like the preceding one, was ushered in by nomadic invasion: this time both in the west, where in the mid eleventh century the Almoravids marched out of the Sahara to overrun north-west Africa, and were invited into Spain as champions against the growing Christian power there; and in the east, where at the same time occurred the celebrated incursion of the nomadic Banū Hilāl and Banū Sulaym – Ibn Khaldūn's plague of locusts.

The opening of our period, in the mid eleventh century, corresponds almost exactly with the demise of Fatimid rule in Ifrīqiya – the region corresponding roughly to modern Tunisia, but extended eastwards to include Tripolitania and west to Bougie and Constantine.

This area had been the seat of Fatimid power, with a new capital at Mahdiya, in the tenth century. Some scholars stress the instability of the Fatimid position in Ifrīqiya. Armed resistance to the Fatimids had been led by the Kharijites: in AD 944 their leader, Abū Yazīd, besieged Mahdiya. He died in 947; some scholars have suggested that his followers, fleeing south, were the seed of the Bayajidda legend (see pp. 307–8).[1] But his movement was only one, although the most threatening, of a host of troubles, which seemed to show that the Fatimids had either to enlarge and consolidate their control locally, or move on.[2] According to this line of argument, the Fatimids, in advancing against Egypt in 969, were in a sense being pushed out of Ifrīqiya.

Other recent analysis, on the contrary, points out that historians may have been misled by the anti-Fatimid tone of most of the surviving written records. Rather than an infinitesimal minority of heretics, the caliph and his tribal guards, exploiting a staunchly orthodox population, there is evidence of the growth of an often comfortable *modus vivendi* between rulers and ruled. Particularly after the Abū Yazīd affair, the Fatimids replaced force by persuasion, and where necessary restrained their own too zealous partisans. It seems very probable that more local people actually adopted the Fatimid faith than has been thought. More careful study of architectural evidence indicates that many buildings, hitherto dated to the latter part of the eleventh century, that is to say after the return to orthodoxy, are in fact from the Fatimid period. Extensions to the great mosque at Sousse, for example, once thought to have been the result of an influx of refugees from the depredations of the Banū Hilāl, are now placed at least half a century earlier, and may even have predated the Fatimid move to Egypt. To illustrate the details of evidence and its interpretation, there is among the extensions to the Sousse mosque a defaced stone, which almost certainly carried originally some Fatimid inscription.[3]

From this point of view, it was more the attraction of Egypt than difficulties in Ifrīqiya, which lay behind the Fatimid migration. The conquest of Egypt had been an early Fatimid ambition, and in the mid tenth century the temptation was especially enticing. The Ikhshidid dynasty had degenerated into a puppet affair, with real power resting in the hands of a black eunuch, Abū'l-Misk Kāfūr – the name means 'dusky

[1] See, for example, W. K. R. Hallam, 'The Bayajida legend in Hausa folklore', *Journal of African History*, 1966, 7, 1, esp. 49–50.

[2] A. Laroui, *L'histoire du Maghreb: un essai de synthèse* (Paris, 1970), 126–7.

[3] A. Lézine, *Deux villes d'Ifriqiya: études d'archéologie, d'urbanisme, de démographie: Sousse, Tunis* (Paris, 1971), 13–16, 115–18.

camphor' – who from 966 to 968 was the sole ruler of Egypt. In 969 the Fatimid army, commanded by Jawhar the Sicilian – originally a Christian, who had been brought as a slave to Kairouan – conquered Egypt. The building of Cairo began almost at once, and in 972 Jawhar completed the great mosque of al-Azhar ('the fair' or 'the bright', from a title of Fāṭima). Soon after, this was made into an academy by the caliph, who had in 973 followed his soldiers and transferred his capital to Cairo. Although the mosque later suffered a period of official disfavour because of its original association with Fatimid proselytizing, it recovered and has ever since served a profoundly important educational role throughout the Muslim world. Among the *riwāqs*, or special sections for students from various areas, the central Sudan was represented from an early date.

Ifrīqiya, meanwhile, had been left under the administration of a tributary dynasty of Sanhaja Berbers, the Zirids, who had helped save the Fatimids from Abū Yazīd. Zirid loyalty to Cairo waned. Religion played a part in this, for even when full allowance is made for the revisionist views already mentioned, the Zirids had still to weigh the advantages of a Cairene alliance sustained by their continuing adherence to the Fatimid, Ismā'īlī faith, against the dangers of a sectarian government imposed upon a generally orthodox, Sunni population. In 1005 a revolt in Barca, by Arabs and Berbers, was easily suppressed by al-Ḥākim, the Fatimid caliph at that time (see p. 12). In 1017–18 popular disturbances broke out in several centres, culminating in the massacre of Ismā'īlī officials. Economic contraction may have been a more important aggravation. As the centre of Fatimid political gravity settled ever more firmly at Cairo, so trading interests were drawn thither, and away from Ifrīqiya. Control over the routes between Ifrīqiya and Egypt became increasingly precarious: Arabs seized Barca, Zanata Berbers took over in Tripoli. In 1051, the Zirids formalized their *de facto* independence by acknowledging the suzerainty of the 'Abbasid caliph in Baghdad. This was, in the immediate circumstances, an attempt to win greater local support, to restore Zirid influence in Tripolitania and extend it to Cyrenaica, and to woo the loyalty of the Arab tribes of the Banū Hilāl, already infiltrating westwards. The plan misfired. Exactly how has been the subject of much recent dispute.

According to the traditional view, the Fatimid caliph in Cairo, by way of retaliation against the defecting Zirids, authorized the passage into North Africa of the Banū Hilāl and Banū Sulaym, at that time in Upper Egypt. Some scholars have attributed to these immigrants an important part in the arabization of North Africa, arguing that the nomads' Arabic has been the source of most rural dialects there today. Others have minimized the positive cultural contribution of the newcomers, pointing out that, at least in Tunisia, the process of arabization was already well advanced, and that the immigrants, who in any case lacked the religious enthusiasm of their predecessors, hardly numbered more than 150,000. That they gravely harmed North Africa has been more generally agreed: they are accused of having caused immense destruction in the Ifriqiyan regions, provoking disturbances, serving as mercenaries in any local quarrel, causing the ruin of the holy city of Kairouan – which to this day has never fully recovered. The arrival of the nomads inaugurated a period of anarchy, which spilt also backwards into Egypt, where the Lawata Berbers from Cyrenaica ravaged the west and north, overrunning the Delta and destroying much of the irrigation system there. In the eastern Maghrib, confusion was increased by Christian encroachment. Pisa, with Genoese support, sacked Mahdiya in 1086. More significantly, the Normans of Sicily captured a number of coastal towns during the twelfth century. Only with the arrival of the Almohads in the thirteenth century was order restored, and from the Almohad viceroys emerged the Hafsids, who were to rule Ifrīqiya for over a quarter of a millennium.

Recently, the hypothesis of the Hilalian catastrophe has undergone considerable critical scrutiny, arising in part from more careful study of the sources, and in part as a reaction against French historiography. This last, elaborated during the French colonial period, laid much stress upon the Banū Hilāl as a cause of North African decline, and as an illustration of the irreconcilable conflict of Arab and Berber interests. The new analysis is part of a broader attempt, by North African scholars and others, to 'de-colonize' history. It is now suggested that the nomads may have entered North Africa from Egypt as part of a general movement of peoples in the eleventh century; and that they were welcomed as prospective allies both by the Zirids and by the Hammadids of Bougie further west. The Fatimid intervention is reduced to a successful bid to persuade the Banū Hilāl to abandon their new-found allegiance to the Zirids, and to offer instead their loyalty to the Fatimids. This was the more easily achieved as Zirids and Banū Hilāl had quickly quarrelled. The decline of Kairouan, so the revisionist argument continues, was less the result of Hilalian blows, and more a part of a general pattern of decentralization, the Ifriqiyan state disintegrating as trade and economic activity in general deserted the capital in favour of provincial centres. The Banū Hilāl merely accelerated this process. Ibn Khaldūn, the prime source for the old view, comes under suspicion as too late an observer – he died in 1406 – and one too closely associated with the Andalusian refugees in North Africa, who were often antagonistic to the nomads. As for al-Idrīsī, writing much closer to the events, in Sicily in the twelfth century, his descriptions of the interior do not appear to confirm any widespread dislocation in Ifrīqiya beyond the coasts. The behaviour of nomadic immigrants in general, whether they plundered farmers and merchants, or accepted more conciliatory roles as partners or even employees, is seen to have depended on opportunity. In a declining state nomads would have had a freer hand to pillage, whereas a strong one would have kept them in rein.

According to the new view, it was the Zirid monarchy which was the chief casualty of the unrest exacerbated by the nomads, and of the period of fragmentation in Ifrīqiya which followed. The Banū'l-Rand dynasty became independent at Gafsa, an Hilāli dynasty at Gabes, and other towns likewise developed into separate principalities. Bougie, the new capital of the Hammadids, flourished, and al-Idrīsī described its trading connections to the east, west and south, and its local shipbuilding and iron mines. Nevertheless, the displacement of Ifriqiyan primacy in North Africa continued on a wider stage. The Fatimid headquarters had moved east from Ifrīqiya to Egypt. In the west, the Almoravids had given a new unity to Morocco and Spain, before being ousted in their turn by the Almohads. And northwards the power of Christian Europe was waxing. The Norman raids just mentioned were a direct impingement upon Ifriqiyan soil of this third trend, and led to the fleeting establishment of Norman authority, encompassing both Tripoli and Mahdiyya, on the North African coast. The idea of a political unity bridging the Mediterranean here was by no means fantastic. Sicily had earlier been a Fatimid domain, though independent since the caliph moved to Cairo; and in the 1060s the Zirids attempted, without success, to reoccupy the island, which had then just been invaded by the Normans. The Muslim capital of Palermo fell to the Normans as late as 1072. But the Norman Ifriqiyan empire was the creation of one Sicilian king, Roger II, and of his leading minister, and nowhere lasted more than fifteen years.

More important than this Christian sally was the Muslim riposte which it drew forth – the Almohad conquest of Ifrīqiya in two campaigns, of 1151/2 and 1159/60 (see pp. 342–3). The recapture of Mahdiya, after severe siege action, in 1160 marked the end of the precocious Norman adventure in North Africa. The Almohads eliminated also the last surviving vestiges of local Christianity. Earlier in the century, the future *mahdi*, Ibn Tūmart, had paused to teach and exhort in various parts of the eastern Maghrib on his way back from the Middle East, and it was indeed in Mallala, near Bougie, that he first met 'Abd al-Mu'min, who was later to succeed him and to lead the conquest of Ifrīqiya. Almohad authority in Ifrīqiya was divided between two capitals, Bougie and Tunis. The main theatre of Almohad activity, however, was in the western Maghrib and in Spain, Seville becoming the preferred residence of some of the Almohad caliphs. Ifrīqiya lay, comparatively unattended to, on the periphery.

The processes of distintegration of centralized government in Ifrīqiya, despite Almohad remedies, were stimulated by two formidable figures. One was Qarāqūsh, an Armenian and perhaps also a Sharif. Soon after Ṣalāḥ al-Dīn had, in 1171, displaced the Fatimid dynasty in Egypt, he contemplated establishing a refuge for himself, in case of need, in Ifrīqiya. This project came to nothing, but Qarāqūsh, with a party of Turkish troops, did move west. Advancing through Awjila to Zawila, he mastered the Fezzan and Wadan, and then turning north took Tripoli. Encouraged by Qarāqūsh, Gafsa revolted against the Almohads, and was brought once more to heel only in 1180, by the armed intervention of the Almohad caliph.

The other disturbing arrival was 'Alī b. Ghāniya. Almohad success in the west had overturned Almoravid authority in the western Maghrib and in Spain, but a remnant, the Banū Ghāniya, still survived in the Balearic islands. Strengthened by the arrival of refugees from the Almohad conquests, and spurred on by the continuing theological confrontation between Almoravid and Almohad, the Banū Ghāniya decided that the best defence against Almohad invasion of the islands was to launch an offensive in North Africa. In 1184 'Alī b. Ghāniya landed at Bougie, which fell without a blow. The Almohad garrison was absent, and the population, surprised during the Friday prayer, were captured in the mosque – thereafter it became the prudent habit of the people of Bougie to shut the town gates during the Friday prayer. In Ifrīqiya, support for the final Almoravid fling came from the surviving stalwarts of the Berber Hammadid dynasty, which had submitted to the Almohads in 1152, as well as from other Berber groups, and even from the Arab tribes recently arrived from the east.

The Almohad caliph, hearing of the initial success of ʻAlī b. Ghāniya in the eastern Maghrib, sent an army against him. Bougie and other strong points which had so shortly before succumbed to the Almoravids now welcomed again the Almohads. ʻAlī b. Ghāniya, surprised while laying siege to Constantine, fled to the region of southern Tunisia. Thence he made contact with Qarāqūsh, and an incongruous alliance emerged, perhaps linked by some common orthodox loyalty against what was regarded as Almohad heterodoxy, of Hilāli and other Arab bands, Almoravid loyalists and other Berbers, and Turkish soldiers under an Armenian commander. The allies drove the Almohads back, only Mahdiyya and Tunis remaining in their hands. ʻAlī b. Ghāniya solicited the moral support of the ʻAbbasid caliph at Baghdad, echoing the earlier orthodox aspirations of the Zirids, and the caliph ordered Ṣalāḥ al-Dīn to succour the Almoravids, which he did by instructing Qarāqūsh to collaborate with them. In 1187 the Almohad caliph al-Manṣūr marched to the relief of Tunis and the re-establishment of Almohad authority in Ifrīqiya. The expedition was in the main successful, though ʻAlī b. Ghāniya and Qarāqūsh escaped into the desert. An Almohad governor of Ifrīqiya was installed at Tunis. Tunis, nicknamed the burnous, or mantle, of the Prophet, was to be the capital of the Hafsids, in succession to Kairouan of the Aghlabids, and Mahdiya of the Fatimids. ʻAlī died soon after.

Contrary to al-Manṣūr's expectations, the situation in Ifrīqiya became more complex and disordered than before. Yaḥyā b. Ghāniya succeeded his brother, and recouped many of the Almoravid losses. Qarāqūsh fell out with Yaḥyā, and the forces of the two former partners clashed several times. Ṣalāḥ al-Dīn, in need of strong Muslim support in his struggle against the Frankish kingdoms of Palestine, developed friendly relations with the Almohads. And, within the ranks of the Almohads, insurrection broke out against the Almohad governor of Ifrīqiya. In the maze of shifting fortunes and allegiances which followed, we find such curious alignments as the co-operation of the Almohad governor with Yaḥyā b. Ghāniya the Almoravid, against the rebellious Almohad prince of Mahdiyya. At the end of 1203, Tunis itself fell to the victorious Yaḥyā. Almohad influence in Ifrīqiya was at its nadir.

By a twist of fate, this triumph of Yaḥyā b. Ghāniya marked the end of any Almoravid hopes of recovery against the Almohads. Just at the time that he overcame Tunis, the Balearics submitted to the new Almohad caliph, al-Nāṣir, who immediately afterwards turned to the east. Yaḥyā abandoned Tunis, and withdrew south. The retreating Almoravid forces were severely defeated, and in 1207 al-Nāṣir was able to return westwards, leaving eastern Ifrīqiya in the hands of 'Abd al-Wāḥid b. Abī Ḥafṣ (d. 1221), nicknamed *sayf Allāh* ('the sword of God'), a governor of unusually unshakeable loyalty to the Almohad leadership, but with almost autonomous powers, and whose son Abū Zakariyā (1228–49) was to be the effective founder of the independent Hafsid dynasty. Yaḥyā b. Ghāniya, the indefatigable rebel, finding Ifrīqiya now closed against him, continued operations on the fringes of the desert. He ranged far to the west, sacked Sijilmasa, and in 1212/13 besieged Qarāqūsh in Wadan. Faced with famine, Qarāqūsh yielded on the sole condition that he should die before his beloved son was killed; this was done, both perishing crucified. Another son of Qarāqūsh submitted to the Almohads, and served as an officer in their army. Later he attempted to follow his father's turbulent and independent example, in this same region of Wadan, but was himself captured and killed in 1258, not by any North African authority but by the agents of the ruler of Kanem.

Yaḥyā b. Ghāniya, the last representative of the Almoravids, died in obscurity in 1233–4, having by his leadership sustained the cause for half a century. The Almohads could draw but little satisfaction from the demise of their ancient enemy: in the west their own government was collapsing in factionalism, and in the east, in 1236/7, Abū Zakariyā proclaimed the independence of Hafsid Ifrīqiya from Almohad sovereignty.

Taking up again the theme of the nomadic contribution, there is abundant evidence during the episode of the Banū Ghāniya that the nomadic tribes were not in themselves a decisive factor. Their influence depended upon their being marshalled by one or other of the principal political protagonists. Yaḥyā b. Ghāniya was peculiarly effective in rallying their support during his largely destructive career; but Abū Zakariyā, the first Hafsid, likewise carefully cultivated the friendship of the tribes, turning their influence to the cause of stable government. Three further points may be borne in mind about the nomads. First, they were expensive: a strong state, drawing revenue from taxes and customs, might more easily find the means to buy the nomads' support, whereas a wandering adventurer such as Yaḥyā b. Ghāniya had to rely mainly on prospects of booty and looting as bribes, with lamentable results for many towns and regions overrun by his supporters. Secondly, they were unreliable, and moved easily from one side to the other according to the changing fortunes of war and power. And thirdly, their mobility, particularly on the shores of the desert, made effective military action against them difficult, as the Almohads found to their exasperation, watching Yaḥyā b. Ghāniya disappear again and again towards the south, beyond the reach of retribution.

Abū Zakariyā, despite casting off the political authority of the caliphs in the west, had not renounced Almohad beliefs; indeed, his very loyalty to them was one reason for his separation from the back-sliding caliph, al-Ma'mūn. For a time the Friday prayers in Ifrīqiya continued to be said in the Mahdi's name, and when in 1236 Abū Zakariyā substituted his own, he found himself acknowledged as rightful caliph in various centres in Morocco and in Muslim Spain. His son and successor, al-Mustanṣir (1249–77), assumed the title of *amīr al-mu'minīn* in 1253, and was recognized as caliph by the Sharifs of Mecca in 1259, and also by the Mamluks of Egypt in 1260. But this was by default: the last 'Abbasid caliph had been killed by the Mongols, who captured Baghdad in 1258, and for the moment the caliphal office was vacant. In 1261, however, Sultan Baybars, architect of the Mamluk state, and perhaps anxious about the growing pretensions of his western neighbour, installed a puppet 'Abbasid caliph at Cairo. He thus inaugurated a new line, without political power but of considerable prestige value even as far away as West Africa (see pp. 43–5).

Al-Mustanṣir, deprived of the homage of the east so soon after it was accorded him, was able nonetheless to enhance his reputation in the Muslim world a few years later, when St Louis of France, in 1270, led a Crusade against Tunis. Perhaps the prosperity of Ifrīqiya lured the French; perhaps commercial interests were a contributory cause, for Ibn Khaldūn tells us that certain merchants of Provence, having failed to get restitution for monies owed to them in Tunis, had encouraged the expedition. But religious fervour on the French side was also important, particularly the quite misguided expectation of St Louis that al-Mustanṣir wished to become a Christian. The Crusading army landed by Carthage. Within a few weeks illness ravaged the camp, and St Louis himself died, his final military initiative having had even less effect than his unsuccessful attempt on Egypt in 1249/50. His brother, Charles of Anjou, king of Sicily, quickly concluded a peace treaty with al-Mustanṣir, who was himself worried by the impending withdrawal of his nomad contingents towards the southern pastures for the winter.

The Hafsid dynasty, so patiently and effectively established by Abū Zakariyā and his son al-Mustanṣir, was one of several which, as successors to the Almohads, shared North Africa amongst themselves, continuing in power until the sixteenth century. In the far west, it was the Marinids who took over, their power based on twin capitals, Fez and Marrakesh, parallel to the Ifriqiyan situation with Tunis and Bougie. Between west and east, the Zayyanid dynasty emerged at Tlemcen, despite attempts by its neighbours on either side to extend their authority over it. Abū Zakariyā, for instance, even before declaring his independence, had conquered as far as Algiers; but Hafsid control over western Ifrīqiya and beyond was never secure, and Abū Zakariyā's son had to retake Algiers in 1274/5. Julien has gloomily described the post-Almohad period as one 'of a vain attempt to revive the past, of a long stagnation and a slow decadence'.[1] For the Hafsids of Ifrīqiya, this summary seems to partake a little of the common tendency of earlier historians, who confused military activity and political pretensions with sound government. It is in the time of the Hafsids, with their major capital at Tunis, that we may begin to trace the outlines of what was eventually to become the modern Tunisian nationality, and the Tunisian state. In Libya, on the contrary, Tripolitania continued under western influence, first Almohad and then Hafsid, while Cyrenaica looked east.

Government rested upon the manipulation of alliances and conflicts among the various elements of society, such as the tribes and the towns, and their chiefs and lords. Al-Mustanṣir's own succession had been imperilled when local and Almohad resentment against the privileges of Andalusian refugees and immigrants disturbed the state for a time after Abū Zakariyā's death. The Hafsids, direct heirs of the Almohad administrative hierarchy, were less dependent upon the skills and services of the Andalusians than were the Zayyanids; nevertheless, this refugee group, establishing standards of etiquette and diplomacy, did exercise considerable influence. Muslims were not the only refugees from Spain who enriched North Africa: Jews suffered persecution in Spain in 1391, and after the fall of Granada their expulsion was ordered. These Spanish victims reinforced indigenous Jewish communities in North Africa. In Morocco, Jews came to play a role both political and economic: in Tunisia their contribution was more purely financial. The immigrants brought appreciable benefits to their host countries,

[1] C.-A. Julien, *History of North Africa: Tunisia, Algeria, Morocco: from the Arab conquest to 1830*, tr. J. Petrie, ed. C. C. Stewart (London, 1970), 139.

though their very success often generated hostility and envy among local people. A few Christians were also tolerated, both foreigners who came to trade and mercenaries, mostly of Catalan origin, recruited to the royal bodyguard.

The Arabs, the Banū Hilāl and Banū Sulaym, constituted another sometimes intractable component of the state. Earlier Hafsid rulers had been careful not to cede land to them, giving them only grants of money; but in 1284 they received their first charter of *iqṭā‘* over several districts. This arrangement gave the Arab chiefs the right to levy agricultural and municipal taxes, sometimes even the right to use the land, in return for military service and perhaps the collection of extra taxes on behalf of the sovereign. The pattern of fiefs in land exchanged for levies of tribal troops continued to be characteristic throughout our period. The Arabs regained much of their original independence and influence by supporting now one, now another, of contending claimants to the throne, or of local governors seeking autonomy in Constantine, Bougie, Tripoli and elsewhere.

Political power tended to concentrate in the hands of a small number of persons, including individuals who were important as local leaders (such as the Hilāli chiefs), strangers presenting no direct danger to the throne (such as the Andalusians), or, a group which has not been mentioned but which was of considerable importance, slaves and freedmen, in whom the ruler might hope to find strong personal loyalty.

Stability was not a prime virtue of this complex system of checks and balances, and for nearly a century following the death of al-Mustanṣir b. Abī Zakariyā in 1277, there were recurrent difficulties. Pressure and intervention from abroad might also distract the state. Very soon after 1277, Tunis became entangled with European quarrels, particularly between Aragon and the Angevins in Sicily, and a little later between Venice and Genoa. The pendulum of North African power swung west, to the Marinids of Morocco. Marinid armies took Tunis and Constantine, but were defeated at Kairouan in 1348 by the Hilālis. Ifrīqiya in the mid fourteenth century was wracked with disorder.

In 1370, however, Abū'l-‘Abbās succeeded in reuniting and reorganizing the country, rescinding land grants and checking local insubordination. After him his son, Abū Fāris (1394–1434), ruled successfully for forty years, balancing the main sections of the population in the kingdom – Almohads, Arabs and Andalusians. Abū Fāris tolerated Jews and Christians, and with tolerance he combined devotion to Islam. Sharifs frequented his court, the pomp and circumstance of

Muslim festivals adorned the state, and acknowledgements of his piety came in from east and west, even from the holy cities. Abū Fāris was succeeded, after a brief interruption, by his grandson Abū 'Amr 'Uthmān (1435–88), whose reign of over half a century compared in length with the tireless and active career of Yaḥyā b. Ghāniya; but whereas the Almoravid had little to contribute save war and bloodshed, the Hafsid in the main peacefully ruled a peaceful realm.

Meanwhile, although the waves advanced and retired with myriad variations in local fortune, the tide of Christian recovery in the western and central Mediterranean continued to flow, until the Ottoman intrusion forced a stalemate, and set the stage for three centuries of uneasy confrontation. Trade, in these circumstances of recurrent violence, was frequently hampered and interrupted. The practice of corsairing, which was to become so notorious in the seventeenth and eighteenth centuries, stretches back even before our period. Practised by both Muslims and Christians, it was in itself destructive of friendly relations, and through the common pattern of reprisals even small incidents were often multiplied and magnified. An extraordinary document of 1358, in which a Venetian merchant wrote to the ruler of Tripoli, announcing the reprisals which the merchant intended to take against the commerce of Tripoli, well illustrates this. Or again, just at the end of the twelfth century, some Pisans having behaved piratically towards Tunis, the ruler decided to recoup himself at the expense of the Pisan traders and their associates in Tunis. The alarmed traders fled, and were followed by a spate of letters from Tunisian merchants, complaining of debts left unpaid, but also warmly stressing the possibility of a return to former harmony.

Peaceful Muslim–Christian relations across the Mediterranean did often obtain, and in this respect the situation in the eastern Maghrib paralleled that in Egypt under the Fatimids and later, where Sicily and the Italian city-states were important trading partners. Egypt was at a great advantage in the vast network of eastern trade on the other side of the continent, trade which from the middle of the eleventh century shifted more and more from the Persian Gulf to the Red Sea. The Saharan and Sudanic hinterland of the eastern Maghrib, despite its importance for slaves, could not compare with the wealth of the Orient. Indeed, trade with the interior of Africa, and trade with western Europe, seem to have been two fairly distinct patterns in the eastern Maghrib. Tunis was deeply engaged with Europe, but relatively little passed from the African interior to Europe by this route: a little ivory, for example, and some ostrich plumes – Louis XII of France in 1484 sought ostriches and falcons from North Africa. Tripoli, on the other hand, was a main centre of trans-Saharan commerce, but it was a pivot for trade with the Muslim Middle East more than with Europe. The two patterns may be distinguished in another way also: in trans-Saharan trade, Ifrīqiya was exporting its own manufactures, especially cloth, while from the European point of view North Africa was increasingly a source of primary products only. Maritime trade may have loomed disproportionately large in the eyes of the local governments, because customs duties levied upon it formed one of the most accessible sources of revenue, others being duties on land trade, rural taxes and the income from government farms and from monopolies. A recent and very stimulating study of North African history condemns the trade of the Mediterranean, which enriched only the ruling élite, and divided society:

> il était par là d'une nature complètement différente du commerce saharien car celui-ci était un commerce intérieur et intéressait tout le pays.[1]

The Saharan trade, according to this argument, united society. But the reasoning seems forced. Much that came across the Sahara constituted luxury items, and it is difficult to see how slave-soldiers, for instance, recruited to the government forces, helped to unify society in any very satisfying way.

The Almoravids of the Balearic islands, finding Spain closed against them after ʻAlī b. Ghāniya had launched his crusade in Ifrīqiya, turned to the Christians for the trade goods they needed – arms, munitions, even vessels, in exchange for the grain and other produce of the islands. Trade in war materials was always a problem: the Christian powers prohibited it with Muslims, but Christian merchants were often less particular. The letters of the Tunisian merchants to the Pisans, mentioned above, include a reference to contraband trade in steel, though hides were evidently by far the main export from Tunis at that time. In 1188/9 a twenty-year treaty of peace and commerce was signed between the Balearic Almoravids and the Genoese, the Genoese ambassador to the islands acting as intermediary. Even before this, in 1157, the Pisans had signed a rudimentary treaty with Tunis.

The basic purpose of such treaties – and many more were to follow, between various Mediterranean trading partners – was threefold: to

[1] Laroui, *L'histoire*, 201.

restrict piracy, to guarantee security for persons and property, and to facilitate trade. Treaties became steadily more complex. Another between Pisa and Tunis, in 1353, is an elaborate affair, promising that Pisans should have equal rights with Genoese, that traders should be held individually responsible for their defaults, and so on. These treaties often provide for a consul and a *funduq*. The *funduq*, or hostel/warehouse, supplied the necessary setting for foreign trade in Tunis as elsewhere, for example in Alexandria where Ṣalāḥ al-Dīn had, for the sake of firmer centralized control, concentrated all the *funduqs* of Egypt. Within such a walled enclosure – which might be defended, in time of popular tumult and mob violence – were the residences, whether temporary or permanent, of foreign merchants, together with stores for their goods. Buying and selling might take place at the *funduq*. It had a certain extraterritorial quality, offering the right of asylum, and freedom of worship. A well-equipped *funduq* might include a church, and perhaps a public bath. Wine might be sold in a *funduq* – one fervent Hafsid, in 1283, built a mosque on the site of such a bibulous establishment. Even the Jews of Tunis had their own *funduq*, as well as their own quarter. In times of security, merchants tended to move both their homes and their shops outside the *funduq*; and, particularly at the end of our period, the importance of the *funduq*, except as a shopping centre, had declined considerably. Foreign traders had little freedom or opportunity to move into the interior; local Jews often performed this function. Trade at Tunis might be conducted under the supervision of the customs authority, and thus to a certain extent with government backing, or it might be done privately. It was the standard practice for foreigners to rely upon a local representative or agent. Auctions were a means of trading particularly favoured by the Muslims. In the absence of extensive capital, trade often depended on credit and trust. Co-operative ventures showed a high degree of sophistication. At the beginning of our period, it was Muslim models which showed the way, but by the end the initiative in devising new forms of credit, insurance, co-operation and the like had passed into European hands: the agreement of 1585, prolonging the life of the coral company based at Marseilles, has been published, and shows the complexity of such arrangements. Corsairing, too, was of course a complicated financial venture, requiring capital. Even ransom might depend upon credit facilities of a kind – we have contracts of this sort, with individuals guaranteeing to reimburse traders for ransom money paid, from Genoa as early as 1156.

The Hafsid period was particularly favourable for trans-Mediterranean trade. Just at the time that Abū Zakariyā was asserting Hafsid independence in Ifrīqiya, there was a flurry of treaty activity: he signed one with Venice in 1231, one with Pisa in 1234, one with Genoa in 1236. Sicily sent a consul, and diplomatic relations were established with Aragon. Al-Mustanṣir b. Abū Zakariyā received embassies from the Italian cities and from almost all the states of the western Mediterranean, even from countries as distant as Norway (1262/3) and Kanem (1257). The abortive invasion by St Louis in 1270 only temporarily disturbed relations: al-Mustanṣir was soon in renewed commercial contact with Aragon, Pisa, Venice and Genoa. The relative importance of the various trading partners of Tunis shifted very gradually during our period. In the twelfth and thirteenth centuries, Genoa and Pisa were outstanding, together with Marseilles. In the fourteenth and early fifteenth century, Venice and Florence (trading through Porto Pisano) joined the front rank. In the middle of the fourteenth century, Tunis was trading with all five, and with Alexandria, Constantinople, Cyprus, Rhodes, Calabria, Sicily, Seville, Cette and Nîmes. The last independent Hafsid ruler was in correspondence with Genoa in 1517.

A complete list of exports and imports would be long indeed. Among the goods coming into the eastern Maghrib were grain, alum, perfumes, wine, falcons and other hunting birds, haberdashery, glass, paper, dyes, woodwork, metal, a little hardware, gold, silver and jewellery. Exports included dried fruit, dates, olive oil, salt fish, salt, sugar, some horses, wool, leather, hides, carpets, coral, tan-bark and some slaves. Amongst these the staples were grain as an import, and wool, hides and leather as exports. Vagaries of supply might reverse normal currents: in good years grain was exported, and in 1234/5 we have mention even of silk and coral sent from Marseilles to Tunis – unless these are unsold goods being returned. Various commodities – such as cloth, spices, arms – moved in both directions.

The intellectual history of the eastern Maghrib during our period is dominated by Ibn Khaldūn (1332–1406), who during his career of high office served various of the North African dynasties, but who began his studies of grammar, philosophy, law and poetry in Tunis. Ibn Khaldūn was fascinated by the contrast between the nomadic and settled, the desert and the sown, and argued that nomads alone possess *ʿasabiyya*, that group loyalty which is essential to statecraft. Nomads, motivated by *ʿasabiyya*, and hardened in the harsh school of the desert, are able to overrun and conquer settled realms: but this new setting then corrupts the immigrants, and the whole cycle is eventually repeated. Ibn Khaldūn was thus the first to explore in detail the problem of the nomadic contribution in African history. He shows the Andalusian viewpoint, against the Hilālis, though his analysis at many points transcends such ideology.

Another writer, Abū Muḥammad 'Abd Allāh al-Tijānī, was secretary to one of the Hafsid princes, and with him travelled through both parts of the eastern Maghrib, Tripolitania and Ifrīqiya in the period from 1306 to 1309. His *Riḥla* ('journey') has come down to us, and supplies a wealth of information; it was also one of the sources used by Ibn Khaldūn. A later chronicler, if the attribution of the *Tarīkh al-dawlatayn* ('history of the two empires' – Almohad and Hafsid) to him is correct, was al-Zarkashī, who lived in the time of Abū 'Amr 'Uthmān, in the later fifteenth century.

Although the Hafsids maintained many of the outward signs, the emblems and formulas, of the Almohads, and justified themselves by religion as much as their predecessors, yet at the same time the Andalusians in particular encouraged the autonomy of politics, leading to a certain laicization of power. The Andalusians, having learnt to regard religion as a more personal affair, thus helped prepare the way for Sufism, or Islamic mysticism, the growth of which at a popular level was the outstanding feature of the post-Almohad period. The *ṭarīqa*, or Sufi brotherhood, provided an all-inclusive social organization, catering alike for saints, hermits and other individuals totally committed to the religious life, as well as for ordinary men and women who continued their ordinary secular and domestic lives though with certain additional devotional duties required by their *ṭarīqa* – an arrangement rather like that of the tertiaries, or third orders, within the Roman Catholic Church. Saints replaced prophets, orthodoxy mystically interpreted overcame explicit sectarianism. The organization of the brotherhoods laid great stress upon the derivation of spiritual authority, the spiritual genealogy from one holy figure to another stretching back ultimately to the Prophet. In many cases a physical derivation was also traced, through the Prophet's daughter Fāṭima, such descendants having the title Sharifs. This emphasis may reflect a residual orientation from the days of Fatimid rule. It is curious to note that Sufism and the cult of saints, so early and so deeply embedded in North Africa, spread only later, and with relatively marginal effect, to the central and western Sudan – Senegambia, far to the west, is almost the only exception. Sharifs, however, are to be found in every corner of Muslim black Africa, and their travels, tribulations and triumphs have contributed substantially to the planting and maintenance of Islam on even the most distant frontiers.

Just as, in the middle of the twelfth century, a Sicilian Norman offensive along the coasts of the eastern Maghrib led to a Moroccan Almohad response, so as the sixteenth century dawned the expanding ambitions of Christian Spain summoned the Ottoman Turks into this same area. In Spain, Christian enthusiasm had been enhanced by the fall of Granada in 1492, while Christian consciousness of the Muslim peril had been rekindled by the revolt of Moorish mountaineers there in 1501, and anxiety was felt about possible retaliation being planned by Moorish refugees in North Africa. Refugees, whose arrival in the host state has meant a precious increment of skill, or wealth, or manpower, have often appeared from the point of view of the expelling power as a dangerous source of retributive action. It may have been to forestall precisely this kind of danger that the Bornu authorities, in the fifteenth century, endeavoured to bring Hausaland under some tributary obligation, after Bornu emigrants, apparently refugees, had established themselves in Kano. In fact, the refugees in North Africa had taken an appreciable part in the growth of corsairing at the expense of Christian shipping during the fifteenth century. Corsair attacks on the Spanish coast in the spring of 1505 provided the final spur to Christian invasion. A succession of the main ports of the central and eastern Maghrib fell into Spanish hands, including Bougie and Tripoli both in 1510. Tripoli was subsequently given to the Knights of St John.

Towns which had not been conquered were awed into the payment of tribute. Two Muslim champions, 'Arūj and his brother Khayr al-Dīn Barbarossa, emerged to stem the Christian advance. 'Arūj was killed in 1518, but Khayr al-Dīn went on to become the real founder of the Algiers Regency. After the death of 'Arūj had left him in an exposed and difficult position, he decided to solicit the help of the Ottomans. Sultan Selim, who had only just conquered Egypt, in 1517, bestowed titles and appointments upon Khayr al-Dīn, and supplied him with troops and arms. Algiers was at the heart of Khayr al-Dīn's African operations; once secure there, he intervened in Tunis, deposing the now shattered Hafsid dynasty, but within a year the Spaniards had themselves taken Tunis and restored the Hafsids. Soon after,

Khayr al-Dīn was called to Constantinople to direct Ottoman operations at a higher level.

The eastern Maghrib limped on, distracted by Christian encroachment – by the Spaniards, by the Neapolitans, by the Knights of Malta – rescued by Muslim warriors, such as Dragut, working under a loose Ottoman rein, and all the while rent by internal divisions. In 1551 Tripoli returned to Muslim hands. Two vital Christian victories were won, at the sea battle of Lepanto in 1571, and in the Spanish conquest of Tunis in 1573. These jarred the Ottomans into definitive action in the eastern Maghrib. In 1574 Tunis was reconquered. In 1581, Philip II of Spain abandoned his hopes of an African empire, and accepted a truce with the Ottomans. These subsequently brought their African possessions within the framework of normal Ottoman organization, making them into three regencies, administered by pashas. Tripolitania,[1] Tunisia and Algeria ceased to be the frontier of the holy war against the Christians, and became rather remote provinces of a mighty empire. From this time, the modern North African units of Libya, Tunisia, Algeria and Morocco begin to emerge clearly. Effective centralized Ottoman authority, never strong, gradually waned further during the seventeenth century, and by the eighteenth both the regencies of the eastern Maghrib were under hereditary dynasties – the Karamanlis in Tripoli, and in Tunisia the Husaynids, who continued until the country was declared a republic in 1957.

The rise of the Ottomans had important implications for Mediterranean commerce, as well as in the political sphere. During the early growth of Ottoman power, in the fifteenth century, Tunisia and the other North African states may have profited from a diversion of the commercial activity of the Italian maritime republics away from the Middle East. There was also the fact that the Egyptian Mamluks, pressed by the Ottomans and other challengers, resorted to increased financial exactions levied upon trade, to the eventual discouragement of local and foreign merchants alike. The French and the Ottomans signed a treaty in 1535, the provisions of which were completed in 1569 – thus inaugurating the famous Capitulations. When Ottoman rule was extended to the eastern Maghrib, the French benefited accordingly. They became the ranking foreign community in Tunis, they alone having a consul there at this time. The consul was also responsible for French trade at Tripoli. The French possessed, however, no *funduq*. Corsairing was now of the greatest importance; it had increased follow-

[1] Cyrenaica did not even acknowledge the authority of Istanbul until 1640.

ing the resurgence of Muslim confidence with the conquest of Constantinople in 1453, forcing Christian merchant vessels to begin sailing in convoy for protection. With the Ottomans established in Tunis, the main preoccupation of the French consuls there was with ransom affairs: ransoms were paid mainly in foreign coin, particularly the gold crowns of Spain, this proving a useful means of attracting the precious metal at a time when trade with Spain was severely restricted by religious feelings on both sides.

Looking back over the five and a half centuries of the history of the eastern Maghrib, and in particular of the Tunisian area, which are our concern in this volume, one can distinguish a slowly repeating pattern of dynasties established with strong foreign connections, which were gradually assimilated to a Tunisian political character and a firmly orthodox (though also Sufi) Sunni form of Islam. The period opens with the Zirids, representatives of the Shīʿa Fatimid dynasty in Egypt, declaring in favour of local autonomy and the Maliki school of the Sunni faith. Even while the Fatimids were still centred in the eastern Maghrib, it is unlikely that they had disturbed the tradition of appointing a Maliki *qāḍī* for Kairouan. To them succeeded the Almohads, whose political centre of gravity lay far to the west, and whose doctrines bore the peculiar stamp of confrontation with the Almoravids. In due course the Almohad governors of Tunisia became the Hafsid dynasty, and although there was no sudden symbolic break such as had marked Zirid relations with the Fatimids, the end result was complete political independence and an increasing identification with traditional Maliki orthodoxy. Following the Hafsids, another foreign power, the Ottomans, took over; but in Tunisia these evolved into a local dynasty, the Husaynids, just as in Tripolitania the Karamanlis emerged. The Ottomans brought their own Sunni rite, the Ḥanafī, but this never displaced North African Malikism, and remained the eccentric badge of the Turkish immigrants and of their direct descendants.

THE DESERT AND ITS TRADE

The eastern Maghrib was, for the most part, confined to the Mediterranean coast. Only rarely and intermittently did effective control extend from the coastal area into the hinterland behind, to the centres of the northern Sahara. The impossibility of pinning down the Almoravid leader, Yaḥyā b. Ghāniya, in this region illustrates its independence. In this area a ring of petty principalities, oases and cities, protected by the desert, enjoyed, because of their position upon various trading routes towards the Sudan or across North Africa, a prosperity generally quite out of proportion to the natural resources.

First, in the desert east of Egypt, was the region known simply as al-Wāḥāt, 'the oases'. Ibn al-Faqīh al-Hamadhānī, writing about 900 and drawing largely on ninth-century works, traces a route linking Egypt with Ghana and its famous gold in the west. This ran from Ghana to Kūkū or Kawkaw, that is to say Gao, the capital of Songhay, on the Niger bend; thence it went to another Sudanic people, perhaps the Arinda or Arna, a Tubu group of uncertain origin apparently living in Aïr at this early date; from there again perhaps to Tibesti, though it must be borne in mind that both the Tibesti and the Aïr identifications here are rather speculative; and finally to Kufra, the westernmost oasis, and on through the others to Egypt. Ibn Ḥawqal, writing about 967–77, also refers to this route, but adds that, owing to winds and bandits in the desert, it had been abandoned about a century earlier. The region of al-Wāḥāt, he said, still bore signs of its former activity, in the abundance of vegetation and livestock, which had reverted to a wild state. Al-Muqaddasī, in the later tenth century, gave a similar picture of decline: the oases, he said, which lie between the Maghrib and the Sudan, and which are joined by some writers to the Maghrib, had been in former times a rich district, but while fruit, sheep and cattle were still plentiful there, these had, as in Ibn Ḥawqal's report, become wild. Ibn Ḥawqal stressed the hospitality of the people of al-Wāḥāt, and their desire to attract merchants. Al-Mas'ūdī, on the other hand, writing in 943, emphasized rather the self-sufficiency of the oases, and their isolation from nearby countries. So great had this isolation become that, according to al-Bakrī and the *Kitāb al-istibṣār*, in the eleventh and twelfth centuries, knowledge of the way to Kufra whether from the north or from the east had been entirely lost, although individuals who stumbled upon Kufra by chance returned to paint its prosperity in glowing colours. Quite different is the description given by al-Idrīsī, in the mid twelfth century, of a desolate Kufra, its houses destroyed, its water supply silted up, its livestock become savage, nothing but ruins remaining. Very little is known of the actual course of events in Kufra during our period: it was apparently a Tubu region, and indeed the last traces of Tubu control survived until the Karamanli conquest early in the nineteenth century. Arabs may have been responsible for the destruction pictured by al-Idrīsī; he did state that they went there frequently on their forays.

The evidence for grave decline along this diagonal trans-Saharan route is thus very strong, although it is perhaps possible that the inhabitants of the oases closer to the Nile, when questioned about the location of Kufra by potentially warlike intruders, professed a false ignorance in order to protect still useful trading partners. The Egyptian end of the route, at least, enjoyed some prosperity: al-Idrīsī tells of the highly esteemed indigo grown and exported by the eastern oases. The period of decline seems to have been followed by some recovery. We learn from al-'Umarī, in the fourteenth century, of a route from Upper Egypt to Mali, passing through the oases. Of Awjila, earlier mentioned by al-Idrīsī as one of the approaches to the Sudan countries, Leo Africanus said that it lay on the highway from Mauritania to Egypt through the Libyan desert. Giovanni Anania offered similar commentary later in the sixteenth century, adding that gold was plentiful, this being the route which merchants followed between Cairo and Timbuktu. Of al-Wāḥāt, Leo said that the inhabitants there were wealthy, profiting from the trade between Egypt and Gaogao, presumably the Gao of Songhay. Leo described the people of the oases as black in colour, perhaps a reflection of the slave-trade. However, in the absence of information about staging points further west in the sixteenth century, it is difficult to determine how far the diagonal traverse had been maintained or restored. Awjila certainly, and even al-Wāḥāt perhaps, might have been on alternative routes from the eastern Maghrib, or on branches from the Chad/Tripoli highway: by the eighteenth century, we know from Hornemann that commerce between Cairo and the Fezzan was in Awjilan hands. Leo's account of Kufra – if this identification of his Berdeua is correct – stressed, as had some earlier records, the extreme isolation of this oasis, rediscovered by accident by a lost caravan very early in the sixteenth century. The people of Kufra were so stupefied by the arrival of strangers that they had to be compelled by force even to supply the visitors with water.

Further west again, where the eastern Maghrib is already merging with the central, lay Ghadames, another important Saharan city, playing a significant role in trans-Saharan commerce. It was a typical oasis city, with palm trees, but no growth of cereals except in the shade of palms; thus it depended heavily on trade. As with many other north-central Saharan places, the main axis of its interest lay south-west, through Tadmekka to Timbuktu. It was in the quarter of the Ghadamsi merchants that the Moroccan invaders, at the end of the sixteenth century, built their citadel at Timbuktu. Ghadames boasted that it had never paid tax to any sultan until the time of the Hafsids. The Almohads had sent a column to Ghadames during their operations against Yaḥyā the Almoravid, but without lasting effect. Abū 'Abdullāh, the Fatimid agent who solicited the support of Mansa Mūsā of Mali while the latter was on pilgrimage in the early fourteenth century, was active in Ghadames and its neighbourhood, so that the town was evidently still pursuing an independent policy then. Abū Fāris, the Hafsid (1394–1434), was the first to impose the burden of regular tax or tribute; several Hafsid expeditions against Ghadames are mentioned in the later fifteenth century, but during the Hafsid period no oppressor entered to pillage the town save one, the *qā'id* Ibrāhīm. In Leo's time, Ghadames was a rich place, trading to the Sudan, but paying tribute or protection money to the Arabs. The Ottomans stepped into the shoes of the Hafsids as distant, but occasionally demanding, overlords of Ghadames. The expedition of Ramaḍān Bey, in 1610, when Ghadames had failed to meet certain requests for Negro concubines, eunuchs and other goods, is mentioned below (p. 271). The language of Ghadames, following the pattern of its commerce, was a Berber dialect standing between that of the Jebel Nefusa and the Tuareg speech.

Further south lie two Saharan centres which were of crucial importance in determining the character and pattern of trans-Saharan contacts: in the east (and for our purposes much the more influential), the Fezzan complex of oases, and westwards, the Aïr massif. Fezzan, into which 'Uqba b. Nafi' had penetrated in the seventh century, was well known in the Muslim world by the ninth, and it is significant that much of the renown attaching to Fezzan arose from its trade in slaves. Al-Ya'qūbī, late in the ninth century, spoke of Zawīla as an Ibāḍī stronghold, important in the slave-trade. Ibāḍī Berbers were also trading further south, in Kawar, in slaves drawn from the Zaghawa and other peoples. 'Uqba himself is said, perhaps apocryphally, to have imposed an annual tribute of 360 slaves on the Kawar region, cutting off one of the fingers of the local ruler as a lasting reminder. In the mid tenth century, al-Iṣṭakhrī contrasted Nuba, Zanj, Habash and Beja slaves, all from the Nile countries and eastern Africa, with those passing north through Zawīla from the central Sudan, whom he found blacker and better than any others. The slave revolt in Iraq, late in the ninth century, particularly associated with Zanj slaves, may have given all those from eastern Africa a bad name, and correspondingly heightened the demand for those from the central Sudan. The interest of the central Sudan authorities in such developments appears in the Bornu records, which describe Mai Arki of Kanem, about the second quarter of the eleventh century. He possessed many slaves, of whom he settled 300 in each of three places in Kawar and the Fezzan, where he himself died. Al-Bakrī, just as our period opens, wrote of slaves sent from Zawīla to Ifrīqiya and adjoining countries. The central Saharan routes maintained their importance, and the extension of Turkish control to Ghat, Murzuq and Ghadames in the mid sixteenth century very probably reflects the Ottoman newcomers' own interest in the trade.

The prestige of Zawīla, which became an important centre under the Berber Banū Khaṭṭāb, was enhanced by its reputation as the town of the Sharifs, and long after it had ceased to be the capital of the Fezzan, it was customary for the chief wife of the sultan of Fezzan to be a Sharif from Zawīla or from Wadan. Late in the twelfth century the Banū Khaṭṭāb dynasty had collapsed under the blows of Qarāqūsh. Early in the thirteenth, Kanem was expanding, and its ruler, Dunama Dibbalemi, marched north to restore stability on his kingdom's vital life-line to the north. It seems likely that commercial and religious considerations were reinforced by ties of kinship between the ruling house of Kanem and the Tubu people, whose main sanctuary of Tibesti lay just to the east of the Fezzan, upon which it was heavily dependent for all the luxuries and some of the necessities of life. Mai Dunama founded a new capital, Traghen, and installed a lieutenant there, probably Tubu. Effective control over the Fezzan from Kanem was not a practicable proposition in the long term; from the lieutenant evolved a new independent dynasty, the Banū Naṣūr, which remained until the early fourteenth (or perhaps sixteenth) century, when a Sharif from Fez made Murzuq his capital, and inaugurated yet another dynasty, the Awlād Muḥammad. These gradually reduced the Tubu influence and presence in the Fezzan.

It has been usual, even in quite recent historical writing, to sketch this great Kanem of the thirteenth century on a grand scale, for example from the Fezzan in the north to Adamawa in the south, from Kano in the west to Wadai or even beyond in the east. Such dimensions are considerably inflated. But that Kanemi intervention in the Fezzan did have lasting effects seems indicated by the survival, even into the nineteenth century, of Bornu titles in the administration of the Fezzan, for example *galadima* for the first minister and *kaigama* for the general. A similar Bornu influence may be traced in some Fezzan place-names. It is possible that Mai Dunama's political and military initiative was able to build upon a northward penetration of people and influence going back much further. As early as the first half of the ninth century, the political centre of the Jebel Nefusa was for a time the ancient town of Ignawun, the Berber word for black – just as Ghadames had a Tin Ignawun, 'the Negroes' well' – and the Jebel Nefusa once had a governor able to speak the language of Kanem.

The Aïr massif, in Hausa called Abzin (often incorrectly written Asben), lying to the west of the Fezzan/Tibesti/Kawar complex, was of less central importance throughout most of our period. The local inhabitants in the eleventh century were Hausa-speakers, later to become the Gobirawa. Their centre was Asode. Some Tuareg may have arrived before AD 1000, others followed in the eleventh century; Awjila was one of the places from which they were said to have come. Among the first attempts of the Tuareg at supratribal organization was the formation of a confederacy, the Itesan. Al-ʿUmarī, in the fourteenth century, spoke of the sultan of Aïr as being more powerful than his two counterparts of Takedda and Tadmekka. The main income of the desert-dwellers, al-ʿUmarī continued, was from their beasts of burden, indicating again the importance of the Tuareg and others in the carrying trade. They had no horses, he said, and rode camels. It is likely that the copper trade from Takedda, which flourished particularly during this period (see pp. 277–9), may have benefited Aïr, lying not far to the east. Ibn Baṭṭūṭa travelled from Gao to Takedda with a large caravan of Ghadamsi merchants. The sultan of Takedda came riding on a horse to receive Ibn Baṭṭūṭa: we may speculate that this was a sign of special local prosperity, based on the commerce in copper. But the Agades sources appear not to mention this trade specifically.

Ibn Baṭṭūṭa probably went home from Takedda through Aïr; he speaks of a sultan there, and of good grazing – more than a century later, al-Suyūṭī sent to Aïr a ruling about grazing rights. Late local chronicles put the appointment of the first sultan, Yūnus, only in the first decade of the fifteenth century. Whence he came is uncertain: perhaps from Asode, which even today has strong ties with Hausaland; or from Fezzan, or some area south of Aïr. He was of servile origin, even, according to one implausible tradition, the son of a concubine of the sultan of Istanbul – which was, of course, still Christian Constantinople at this time. Only the children of mothers of servile origin might become sultans of Aïr; one, Muḥammad, ruling in the last quarter of the fifteenth century, was nicknamed Settefen ('black'). Barth was told, in the nineteenth century, that the sultans were Sharifs, but this seems incorrect. The sultan was intended to serve as a neutral arbitrator amongst the disputatious Tuareg factions; he never became the keystone of a strong centralized state. Leo Africanus observed that the sultan had to please his subjects, or he would be deposed. After some uncertainty – one location proved too inaccessible for oxen bringing the essential imports of grain from the Sudan – a new capital emerged, at Agades. This may have been a town of the local Hausa-speakers, with whom fighting followed. Tuareg pressure on these original inhabitants had, by the end of our period, driven them southwards into their new home of Gobir.

One factor prompting the Tuareg to instal even so much as a figurehead sultan may have been the need to organize better control of the trade-routes. The third sultan, about the second quarter of the fifteenth century, secured a *fatwā*, or legal opinion, confirming the propriety of levying tolls of horses and cloth upon passing caravans, though later advice, including that of al-Maghīlī, was against this. The salt trade from Bilma, later a celebrated Tuareg monopoly, may also have been taking shape in this period, and early in the second half of the fifteenth century we hear of the 'Asbenawa' coming to Gobir, and of salt becoming common in Hausaland. The emergence of the sultanate may also have owed something to political developments. It now seems unlikely that Mali ever extended its authority as far east as Takedda, contrary to the opinion of Ibn Khaldūn (who was probably speaking in fact of Tadmekka, though he mistakenly used the name Takedda); but in the second quarter of the fifteenth century Kano, strongly under Bornu influence by this time, did march against Aïr. Its army had to turn back for lack of water, but a more united front may well have appeared desirable to the Tuareg there.

In 1493 a list of questions arrived in Egypt for the celebrated jurist al-Suyūṭī. Its provenance is not clear: it is labelled simply as coming from Takrur, i.e. from West Africa in the most general sense. From internal evidence, however, it seems likely that the questions are based on experience in Aïr, although a case may also be made out for Tadmekka. The questions throw much light on the condition of society at the time. A variety of taxes and imposts were levied. Groups came asking for land, and among the requirements made of such a group was that it should have one or more leaders – perhaps a hint of the transition from nomadic life to settled chieftaincy. Disputes arose over slave or free status, as will be shown (pp. 274–5). There were difficulties about spirit-possession, particularly among women, who in general enjoyed a degree of freedom reprehensible in orthodox eyes. And so on.

In the sixteenth century, external political interference became decidedly burdensome. The Timbuktu chronicles refer to an expedition by the *askiya* in 1500/1, almost certainly against Aïr. The text is apparently corrupt, but may refer to the imposition of tribute. The ruler at that time, Muḥammad, son of the sister of Muḥammad Settefen, died a violent death in 1502/3; it is possible that this was vengeance wreaked by his own subjects, who perhaps found the tribute he had agreed to pay too burdensome. Leo, who gives us a description of Agades a little later, does not mention this invasion, though his remark that Agades paid tribute to Songhay of about 150,000 ducats may refer to such troubles. Leo said that the town was walled, and that its population included many foreign merchants, who kept large numbers of slaves especially for caravan work between Kano and Bornu. It appears that the move to Agades as capital occurred just at this time, after and perhaps as a result of the first Songhay invasion, although the foundation of Agades seems to have been in the first half of the fifteenth century. The second Songhay invasion took place in 1516. This is remembered in the chronicles of Aïr, when the 'accursed *askiya*' came and ate up all the land, remaining for a year north of Agades. The *askiya* may have installed his own garrison in Agades; in any case, the Songhay connection was evidently of lasting significance, for a dialect of Songhay was still spoken in Agades in the nineteenth century. The claim that subsequent rulers of Aïr descended from the slaves of the *askiya*, whom he settled there, seems unlikely. This second Songhay intervention had profound implications for Hausaland also, for it was in a quarrel over the booty gained in the expedition that Kebbi broke with its erstwhile ally, Songhay, and henceforth served as a bulwark between Hausaland and the Niger bend (see pp. 298–9). After the rule of the first *askiya* had come to an end, Bornu took a hand in the area, conquering Agades perhaps in 1532, making treaties with several tribes and installing a slave representative – from whom, two centuries later, it was claimed in Bornu that the chiefs of Agades descended, presumably another false assertion. Later in the century Aïr appealed to Bornu for help against Kebbi, but Kebbi defeated the Bornu army sent in response. At the end of the sixteenth century the rule of Agades was disputed between rival claimants – Kano and Katsina (backed by Bornu) supporting one, Kebbi the other – and the naturally precarious sultanate seemed weaker than ever. Yet some prestige it had: after the 1500/1 invasion, the *askiyas* of Songhay adopted the copper trumpets of the sultans of Aïr, and in the mid sixteenth century Aïr was still regarded, at the Songhay court, as a state in some respects comparable to Songhay itself.

Aïr, the Fezzan, every Saharan centre which enjoyed a degree of prosperity above mere subsistence, depended upon trade, whether trans-Saharan or, as with Takedda copper sent to Bornu, or Bilma salt to Hausaland, at closer range. Trade was carried by caravans, as important for our period and area as were railways for the opening up of the North American west in the nineteenth century. We have little detailed information about the organization of Saharan caravans in the period before 1600, indeed even before 1800, but it is unlikely that this changed radically over the centuries. Each caravan had a duly appointed leader, generally called the *khabīr*. His installation was a formal affair, sealed with recitation of the *fātiḥa* – the opening chapter of the Koran, somewhat like the Lord's Prayer among Christians – and he might receive payment in money and clothes before the caravan set out. The *khabīr* had full authority over the caravan, but at the same time he was responsible for any accidents and losses except through misfortunes beyond his control. He paid the blood-money for any member of the caravan lost in the desert through his, the *khabīr*'s, negligence. An unscrupulous *khabīr*, on the other hand, might sell an entire caravan to the Tuareg marauders, and divide the spoil with them, but such deceit was rare. The ideal *khabīr* was a man of many parts. He knew the desert routes and watering places, and was able to find his way by the stars at night, or if need be by the scent and touch of the sand and vegetation. He had to understand the proper rules of desert hygiene, remedies against scorpions and snakes, how to heal sickness and mend fractures. He had to know the various chiefs of towns and tribes with which the caravan had to deal along the way, and in this respect a responsible *khabīr* might consolidate his position by strategic marriages in several localities, or into several tribes.

Beneath the *khabīr* were a number of other caravan officials – in a small group one man might combine several offices or functions, while for a larger caravan there might be more than one person for each subordinate job. The muezzin called to prayer, and the *imām* led the prayer, just as in any other congregation of the faithful. The regular daily prayers might be said individually, and not always at the fixed hours, for such variation is the normal privilege of those who journey. The *imām* had also to bury the dead, and resolve questions of inheritance.

Another important official was the scribe. In a small caravan, his might be the only formal appointment beside the *khabīr*. His duty was to record and regularize all major transactions within the caravan, and in particular to supervise the disposition of the property of any caravan member dying along the way. In some cases it was apparently he rather than the *imām* who dealt with inheritance matters. If a merchant died without heirs at hand, his property was auctioned. For such work, a large caravan might even have had its own auctioneer, while the scribe recorded the sales and the *khabīr* was entrusted with the proceeds until these could be handed over to the proper beneficiaries. There was sometimes a public crier, and the *khabīr* might have had one or more messengers to carry out his orders. Special guides, called *takshīf*, were sometimes needed; it was one of these, nearly blind, who helped Ibn Baṭṭūṭa's caravan to a safe arrival in the Sudan. Everyone beneath the caravan officials in the hierarchy was expected to play his or her part in the daily work. At each campsite, some would go to pasture the camels – a rough standard was four camels for a merchant, three carrying merchandise and one food and water – others to fetch water, to cut wood, or to put things in order and to cook. Often slaves performed the more menial of these tasks.

Religious and other solemnity marked the caravan's progress. Wives and children left behind in North Africa sometimes gathered up the earth trodden by the departing travellers, and treasured it in amulets, trusting thus to protect their menfolk and bring them home once more. Members of a caravan might take vows of chastity, the better to invoke divine defence – though many did not, or were manifestly unobservant. Music – the *khabīr* often had kettledrums, or horns or trumpets – called the caravan at dawn. If there were pilgrims in the group, as was frequently the case, they marched to the sound of hymns and prayers, perhaps bearing before them the green standard of the Prophet. Koran recitation while travelling is approved in the religious law, though not (except perhaps for students) while walking to market. The arrival of a large caravan was the signal for rejoicing among the townspeople; in Ghadames, for example, everyone put on holiday clothes for this occasion. Some halts were at holy places, such as the *zāwiya* of Sīdī Aḥmad in Aïr, belonging to Tuareg clerics, where people might stop to read the sacred books, and to which pilgrims came from afar. Such a place was a sanctuary, and thus caravans liked to camp there, some leaving part of their goods there to be picked up again on the return journey from the Sudan, and giving also presents to the clerics. When the caravan arrived safely at its destination in the Sudan, its camp outside the city walls exchanged its bustling market appearance for the likeness of a mosque, and many prayed then more fervently, in thanksgiving, than they ever had before. Many difficulties and dangers beset the trans-Saharan caravans. But at the same time these caravans surely presented as brave and splendid a spectacle as any medieval pageant, and their passing has left the desert bare.

Despite the variety of commodities which were carried in this way to and from the central Sudan, the area was in danger of remaining a commercial backwater. The main sources of ivory lay further east, those of gold to the west. One item, however, rescued the central Sudan from economic oblivion: slaves were this black ivory, this black gold. It has already been shown, in talking of Zawīla, how early its reputation as a slaving entrepôt was established. This trade continued throughout our period. Ibn Baṭṭūṭa, to take one example of many, remarked that Bornu was celebrated for its exports of excellent female slaves, eunuchs (or servants? – *fityān*), and saffron-dyed fabrics. It has been suggested that, just at the end of our period, the trans-Saharan trade in slaves slackened a little, owing to rising opportunities for Atlantic export. Similarly it has been argued that a main cause for the raiding which the Kwararafa, from the Benue region, carried out as far afield as Bornu and Kano, and which came to a climax in the seventeenth century, may have been the attractive possibility of selling slaves to the Europeans on the Niger delta. It seems unlikely, however, that at so early a date the Atlantic trade had any significant influence on the Saharan: on the contrary, it is at least a plausible hypothesis that the Ottoman presence, arriving in North Africa in the sixteenth century, boosted trans-Saharan commerce.

A principal purpose of the black slaves brought from the central, as from the eastern, Sudan was to supply army recruits in North Africa. Black soldiers had varied fortunes, sometimes enjoying privilege and power verging upon licence, at other times becoming the victims of repression. The ʻAbbasids, early in the tenth century, had massacred the black troops of the Tulunids in Cairo. Early in the eleventh century, black troops had helped to put down protests against the increasingly heretical claims of the ruler al-Ḥākim; for a time under al-Mustanṣir, who ruled from 1036 to 1094, and whose mother was Sudanese, they had unusual influence. Nāṣir-i-Khusraw, visiting Egypt in mid-century, judged that there were 30,000 black troops at Cairo, the largest single group in an army of over 100,000. But before the end of al-Mustanṣir's long reign, the Turkish and Berber soldiers had driven the Sudanese out of Cairo, and they withdrew to upper Egypt, terrifying the people and interrupting cultivation. Under the last of the Fatimids, al-ʻĀdid, who died in 1171, there was a formidable rising of black troops, abetted by the sultan himself, and Ṣalāḥ al-Dīn, already the chief power in the land, had hard work to put them down. He banished them from Cairo, and razed their barracks outside the Zuwayla gate, turning the quarter into a garden.

Military service was not the only stimulus to the demand for black slaves. Eunuchs, fewer and far more expensive than ordinary slaves, were also in demand for special purposes, as in the harem or in certain government offices. Al-Muqaddasī distinguished three principal varieties of black eunuch, the best going to Egypt, the worst to Aden, but he did not indicate exactly where these came from.

Ibn Baṭṭūṭa, who also praised the Bornu eunuchs, commented favourably upon the slave-girls of Bornu, and thus reminds us of another very important element in the trans-Saharan traffic – an element almost without parallel in the Atlantic counterpart – the supply of concubines. Indeed, it is arguable that a considerable majority of the slaves crossing the Sahara were destined to become concubines in North Africa, the Middle East, and occasionally even further afield. And it may be this, in turn, which helps to explain why a flow of slaves possibly greater in total than that across the Atlantic has not led to any comparably dramatic racial confrontation in North African society, although distinctions there of course are. Certain groups were particularly favoured for their appeal. The Abyssinians usually ranked high. Al-Idrīsī, writing in the mid twelfth century, placed the Nubian girls above those of Ghana, Kanem, Zanj, even Abyssinia, and elsewhere, telling how the princes of Egypt bought them at extravagant prices, charmed by their sweet company and their extraordinary grace. Al-Tūnusī particularly signalled the charms of the Kuka, south-east of Wadai, more enticing than even the most attractive Abyssinians:

> Ils ont de jeunes esclaves qui sont belles à ravir, et d'une grâce à soulever toutes les émotions du cœur; leurs charmes troublent et bouleversent l'âme, tournent la tête aux plus dévots ascètes, et les plongent dans des désirs voluptueux.[1]

Soldiers, eunuchs and concubines were only three principal categories of slave opportunity in North Africa: many slaves, less gifted, went into less adventurous or less intimate professions. Nor, of course, were black slaves exclusively in demand for these tasks. White and black slaves formed separate army corps; white and black attended the rulers; white and black suffered the indignity of castration; and white

[1] Muḥammad b. 'Umar al-Tūnusī, *Voyage au Ouadây*, tr. Dr Perron (Paris, 1851), 247.

and black fanned the fires of love – al-Idrīsī, for example, praised the concubines of North Africa and of Europe as well as the Nubians.

Slaves circulated as tribute, alms and gifts, as well as commercially. They formed a regular feature of tribute, such as that which the Hausa principalities began paying to Bornu not long after the exodus. Tribute, or tax, in slaves might also be demanded north of the Sahara. In 1609/10, Ramaḍān Bey, the Ottoman commander in Tunis, marched as we have seen against Ghadames. He had asked the town to send him five handsome eunuchs, of fifteen years of age, to serve as palace attendants, eight pretty Negresses of the same age, and 200 skins, and the people of Ghadames had returned only a polite answer. After withstanding a siege, Ghadames, fearful lest its palms be destroyed – 500 had already been cut down – paid 5,000 *mithqāls* instead.

Alms and gifts may similarly be described through a few examples: the first Muslim missionary in Kanem, Muḥammad Mani, received in the eleventh century alms from Mai Humai, comprising 100 slaves, 100 camels, 100 gold coins and 100 silver coins, in gratitude for instruction in the Koran. A wicked ruler of Katsina is said to have given, for a charm which would assure him of immortality, a hundred each of slave boys and slave girls, horses and mares, bulls and cows, as well as sheep, goats, clothes and other items. A Bornu song recalls how the *mai* once gave his *kashella*, or military commander, fifty male slaves and fifty female, fifty cows, eighty horses and twenty donkeys. The *kashella* redistributed most of the slaves, ten to each of his three musicians – no doubt it was musicians who later sang the song – five to each of his four wives, two to each of his ten household servants, ten to the *imām*, and two to the *imām*'s wife. Surely there is a large element of bravado and exaggeration in these tales, as in the remark of Mai al-Ḥājj 'Alī b. 'Umar in the mid seventeenth century that, if he captured fewer than 4,000 slaves in a raid, he gave them at once to his clerics and set out again. Presents of slaves from the Sudan to rulers in the eastern Maghrib are reported from time to time, for example in 1257 to a Hafsid ruler from 'the king of Kanem and the lord of Bornu', and apparently with increasing frequency after the Ottoman arrival in North Africa in the sixteenth century.

The processes of tax and tribute payment, and of offerings, gifts and alms, like the ordinary transactions of trade, do not explain the initial recruitment of slaves. Kidnapping was a constant method, having the advantage of low overheads, and allowing almost anyone to join in. Al-Idrīsī, describing the Zaghawa, told how the townspeople, though of the same race as the nomads round about, used to steal the nomads' children by night, and then hide them until they could be sold to foreign merchants at cut rates. The custom of child-stealing, he thought, was widespread in the Sudan, where no stigma attached to it. Al-Idrīsī's view was, no doubt, biased; yet the importance of kidnapping as a source of slaves may have been generally underestimated by scholars. Records of slaves freed in Sierra Leone in the nineteenth century show nearly as many originally enslaved by kidnappers as by raiders, and recent research suggests that the same was true in East Africa.

There were also more organized raids, ranging from village affrays to regular expeditions of state. Members of an unsuccessful village raiding party might slip back, ashamed, to their homes by night; the return of successful raiders, with captives, was on the contrary an occasion of general rejoicing. The purpose of village raids was sometimes to extort ransom, and people were particularly pleased when they found that they had taken the children of chiefs. The pattern of ransom did not always reduce the flow of slaves: relatives sometimes pawned themselves to secure the captives' release, or the ransom itself might be fixed in slaves. A Hausa story tells how a Muslim cleric and a pagan, whose village had been raided in their absence, went to ransom their children. The captor chief, in deference to the cleric's status, reduced the normal ransom of two slaves to one; the cleric went at once to the market and bought a girl to exchange for his daughter. The pagan, happily, was a witty fellow, and by a stratagem got his child back for nothing. State expeditions are exemplified by Leo's description, in the sixteenth century, of the ruler of Bornu setting out once a year to acquire the means to pay his foreign merchant creditors, who waited, living at his expense, for his return. If the raid was insufficiently productive to clear all the *mai*'s outstanding debts, some of the unfortunate merchants had to wait a twelvemonth. In the nineteenth century, we have an eyewitness account of the utility of tree-houses among the pagan Kimre in the Bagirmi region as a refuge against slave-raiders, and it is at least a likely guess that some similar purpose lay behind the tree-dwellings of Kanem which al-Marwazī, writing in the twelfth century but drawing on earlier information, mentioned. Slaving was an essential economic enterprise, for without it the central Sudan had little with which to balance its payments in foreign trade; rulers would have had to forgo accustomed luxuries, and the state its customs revenue. But it would be too narrow a view to exclude the evident excitement and adventure of slave-raiding, the opportunity near at hand for a young man to make his fortune, the thrill of the gamble of it, and the chance, rare as it may have been (particularly for the rank and file, who had to surrender a proportion of their captives), of picking up a beautiful slave for oneself, or of being able with the profits to buy one. A praise-song, said to honour Humai, *mai* in the eleventh century, breathes the exultation of slaving:

> You put to flight a warrior, Dalla, son of Mukka, chief of the land of Mobber, during the freshness of the rainy season:
> Again and again you put him to flight:
> Then forced him onto a raft of papyrus grass:
> Then you returned to your camp:
> And came back and again forced him onto his raft:
> And captured (from his following) a thousand slaves:
> And took them and scattered them in the open places of Bagirmi:
> The best you took (and sent home) as the first fruits of battle:
> The children crying on their mothers you snatched away from their mothers:
> You took the slave wife from a slave, and set them in lands far removed from one another.[1]

The passage is interesting in several respects. Water was evidently a refuge, and not infrequently the boatmen took their revenge, the Budduma of Lake Chad for example coming by canoe at floodtime to kidnap wading or stranded individuals. The song suggests that slaves were already being used as colonists. There are references to the same sort of thing in North Africa, particularly on marginal land, often unhealthy, where black slaves settled as colonists or squatters. In the central Sudan it seems likely that slave settlements were much more important, helping to remedy underpopulation by forced migrations, generally from further south, and to enlarge, for the ambitious ruler, the essential human foundation of his state and power. The song's separation of mother and child, husband and wife, is contrary to Islamic law, and suggests what is indeed obvious at many points in this story – that the scrupulous application of the strict letter of the law was exceedingly difficult.

Enslavement as punishment, fairly often remarked elsewhere in Africa, seems to have been more common to pagan than to Muslim areas of the central Sudan. The Jukun king, for example, is said to have had the right to sell into slavery all the uterine relatives of any person convicted of witchcraft. He also took slaves as fines – seven, for instance, from the household of anyone wrongly making a virgin

[1] J. R. Patterson, *Kanuri songs* (Lagos, 1926), 2–3.

pregnant. Pagan slavery was sometimes linked with human sacrifice: there are references to this among the Jukun, to mark the death of the king, the confirmation of a new king, or to bring rain withheld by a previous king. The So may have done the same, and traces of such practices may be found in the recollections of peoples today, for example among the Moundang, south of Marwa, who kept the death of the chief secret for a year, burying him in a jar, and then holding a formal funeral, at which a sheep or perhaps one or two slaves were sacrificed. Usuman dan Fodio had heard that some Gobirawa used, when ill, to sacrifice a male or female slave to encourage recovery. Not only slaves were liable: Anania reported that in 'Logone' – perhaps to be identified with the city-state of Logone-Birni on the Logone river – the best friends of the king should, at his death, accompany him into the hereafter.

Transactions in slaves varied as much in extent as did recruitment activities. Some vaunts of huge numbers, running into thousands, have already been mentioned. At the other end of the scale, a Hausa story tells of a man with two wives: one spent ten cowries daily in the market, for tobacco, and the other asked for five only, which she saved. Finally the economical one had sufficient cowries to buy a slave-girl. The other wife then gave up smoking, but so great was her irritation that she left the family home.

Large organized slave-raids tended to operate at some distance, and to move beyond the limits of the Muslim community; as some newly captured slaves probably always remained with their immediate captors, such raiding contributed substantially to the melting-pot of central Sudanese society. A few favoured slaves might re-establish contact with their original homes, even acting as intermediaries between the erstwhile aggressor and victim communities. On the other hand, casual kidnapping, and many other methods of enslavement, might entangle even free Muslims, theoretically immune. A complaint recorded in the questions already mentioned (p. 265), probably from Aïr in the late fifteenth century, indicates some of the complications:

> Some men dispute over [the status of] free men and call them slaves. If one such person dies, they do not divide [his estate] among his inheritors and those who survive him are then called slaves. If you tell them that these are free men, they almost kill you and reply: 'These people are slaves, "followers of the sword".' . . . Some sell them in the teeth of controversy and dispute.[1]

The Hausa Chronicle recalls it as a most serious offence of Rumfa, Sarkin Kano – in other sources quite a venerated figure – that he sold

[1] J. O. Hunwick, 'Notes on a late-fifteenth-century document concerning "al-Takrūr"', in C. Allen and R. W. Johnson, eds., *African perspectives* (Cambridge, 1970), 13.

children, presumably Kano children, who were properly ineligible for enslavement.[1]

What the people being enslaved and exported thought of it all is, though perhaps easy to guess in general terms, difficult to discern in detail. The song of the Bornu slave-girl, lamenting that her slave lover has been sent to Zawīla, where he will have difficulty in finding kola, reflects a degree of sophisticated resignation which was no doubt part of the picture. The Hausa folk story of Kani, a sixteen-year-old girl of Maradi, captured by Kano raiders, perhaps more accurately reflects the alarm and uncertainty of simple people. She was carried north by Hausa slavers, in a party of fourteen female slaves. Two were sold to marry dogs in a city along the way – this might be an echo of Agades where, at least later, roving dogs made the streets unsafe at night. In the next city, inhabited by tailed Muslims, four were given to be eaten. The survivors, on discovering this, begged the slavers to save them, as they were Muslims: the chief of the town reluctantly agreed that those knowing how to pray should be spared – four passed the test, the other four were eaten the same day. These are very much the kinds of fantastic fears which we know haunted the minds of many who sailed into slavery from the West African coast.

Slaves being the principal export, they were found in barter transactions for every kind of import. Horses were particularly valued, and instances of the exchange of slaves for horses occurred almost everywhere. In the legends of Abū Zayd the Hilāli, it is told how he offered 99 slaves of five spans, 99 of six, and 99 old women with heads white as cotton, for a white mare belonging to Mallam al-Tiftif of Tunis: Abū Zayd later acquired the mare by the cheaper method of killing the *mallam*. Leo told how the ruler of Bornu exchanged fifteen or even twenty slaves for one horse. His account of the horse-trade in Gaoga is discussed later (pp. 304, 311–12). Deeper into the Sudan, we are told that in the fourteenth century Kano began trading regularly with the Kwararafa, horses from Kano going south and slaves coming north.

Many slaves never moved out of the central Sudan at all, but remained there to enlarge, or simply to replenish, the local population. It seems likely that much of the central Sudan suffered from chronic underpopulation: the natural growth rate, slowed down by disease and infant mortality, and perhaps also by social institutions such as polygamy and concubinage, was hardly sufficient to repair, even in the long

[1] R. S. Rattray, *Hausa folk-lore, customs, proverbs* (Oxford, 1913), I, 22. This account appears also in A. Mischlich and J. Lippert, 'Beiträge zur Geschichte der Haussastaaten', *Mitt. des Seminars für Orientalische Sprachen zu Berlin*, 1903, 6, *Afrikanische Studien* (see 204, 228).

run, the intermittent ravages of drought, epidemic and war which threatened an absolute decline in numbers. Slave imports were a valuable remedy.[1] Slaves, whether kept or re-exported, were vital to the central Sudan. As a nineteenth-century Hausa remarked, himself having been a slave in Bornu, 'The country of Bornu – I am telling the truth – is a country of slaves.'[2]

Although slaves were the principal export, both the other staples of black Africa, ivory and gold, found a place in the history of the central Sudan. Early legends of the So (or Sao) people, around Lake Chad, speak of a hunter carrying two elephants slung on a stick like two small 'beef' – reflecting the successful hunting of elephants at an early date, and suggesting perhaps that this may have been more for meat than for ivory. Elephant-hunting may have played a part in the very preliminary stages of state formation: traditions recall that Abdullah Boru, ancestor of the Kobe Zaghawa sultans in Wadai, first established himself as an elephant-hunter able to supply meat. Explicit evidence for the central Sudan is lacking, but it may be that such scattered hunting references as these point to a role here for the hunting associations, well-armed and fortified with an esoteric cult, transcending clan and other divisions, similar to that which they played in early Malinke state-building (see p. 353). As trading links with the north expanded, so did the demand for ivory. The Crusades stimulated European interest in gold and ivory, particularly the soft ivory of Africa. Ivory exports from the central Sudan were apparently maintained: Leo told of the ruler of Gaoga giving an Egyptian trader one hundred wonderfully large tusks.

Legends abound concerning gold, and Ghana was known as the land of gold well before the year 1000. But this strange, gilded garden lay always to the west of our area. The central Sudan boasted of no comparable mineral wealth, though it was reported that the Kwararafa possessed a gold mine. Some gold went north from Bornu – we are told of several instances in the seventeenth century – but it was described in terms of curiosity, such as a gilt saddle, or a golden tortoise, rather than of bulk. Regalia and ornaments – such as the maces of the chief praise-singers of the *mai*, horse-trappings, decorations for the

[1] The preceding discussion has concentrated chiefly upon the export theme; in the corresponding chapter in volume 4, more attention is given to the internal employment of slaves.

[2] J. F. Schön, *Magana Hausa: native literature, or proverbs, tales, fables and historical fragments in the Hausa language, to which is added a translation in English* (London, 1885), 52.

head – tended to be of silver rather than gold. Travellers in the nineteenth century remarked the comparative absence of gold in Bornu, and were sometimes asked to bring some. In view of all this, Leo's description of the *mai* seems curious:

The king seemeth to be marvellous rich; for his spurs, his bridles, platters, dishes, pots, and other vessels wherein his meat and drink are brought to the table, are all of pure gold; yea, and the chains of his dogs and hounds are of gold also.

Leo's recent French editors do their best to make this credible, pointing out that the metal plates of horse-trappings may be very thin.[1] But the passage remains puzzling, and constitutes perhaps another cause for doubt about the reliability of Leo as a reporter for this region. Leo went on to add that the king, despite this wealth, preferred to pay only in slaves.

Against the unique attraction of gold as the most valued metal then known, there weighed, not very heavily it seems, certain Islamic legal restrictions on the uses of gold. Although these are fairly numerous – men, for example, should not wear gold – they seem generally to have been given little more than token acknowledgement: Tuareg princes, it is said, never actually touched with their hands the gold which they industriously extorted from Songhay. In North Africa the actual work of goldsmithing was done by Jewish craftsmen (see p. 449).

Gold was also convenient to handle. An early Ibāḍī source describes an episode which occurred about AD 1050, when two traders travelled back from the Sudan together. One carried gold; he journeyed comfortably on a riding camel, and in camp sat quietly in the shade, his wealth in sealed bags. The other brought slave women, who caused him endless trouble, continually falling ill, or complaining of hunger or weariness, sometimes running away. Ease or difficulty of transport was always a factor to be taken into account by the provident merchant. Slaves were not the only highly perishable commodity: horses were another, and ostrich feathers and kola. Much skill and experience were needed to prepare and preserve all these over the enormous distances which they covered. Articles such as ivory, salt and natron, and cowries in bulk, were more resistant, but sometimes awkward to carry. Coral, perfumes, copper, perhaps cloth, were, like gold, relatively easy to manage.

While gold was in short supply, copper, relatively abundant in the

[1] Jean-Léon l'Africain, *Description de l'Afrique*, tr. A. Épaulard, with notes by Épaulard, T. Monod, H. Lhote and R. Mauny (Paris, 1956), II, 481.

central Sahara, to some extent took its place. Hornemann, indeed, about 1800 remarked that copper was for Bornu what gold was for Timbuktu and Hausaland. Copper has a long history as a metal of special esteem in black Africa. Probably as early as the mid tenth century, it was reported in Muslim Spain that in black Africa gold and copper were exchanged weight for weight. Varieties of copper were generally recognized, and that of a dark rich red colour was particularly prized. This may well be the origin of the 'living gold' which the So are said to have introduced into the central Sudan, a luminous metal of mysterious qualities, surrounded by myth. In the early eighteenth century, Labat reported stories on the west coast of Africa of unusual red copper, a ring of which would give light equal to that of two candles. Strange properties continued to be associated with copper, and the practice of wearing a red copper ring for protection against *jinns* was one of many pagan accretions later condemned by Muslim reformers in Hausaland.

The early and widespread use of copper among the So is revealed by the many bronze ornaments, and the waste and remains of forges, which survive among other archaeological artifacts; in contrast, no gold ornament has been found. Tradition among the Kotoko, however, the most likely modern descendants of the So, is explicit that the Kotoko themselves have never worked in metal, this being the skill of foreigners. The earliest reference to copper currency in the central Sudan comes from the fourteenth century, when al-Maqrīzī reported that cloth, cowries, and pieces of gold or copper valued in cloth, were all circulating in the region. A copper weight, the *raṭl*, long continued as a principal form of currency in Bornu, and even when it ceased to circulate it continued as a standard accounting device.

The main source of copper for the region in the early days was Takedda, where al-Maghīlī taught for a time, situated to the north-west of Agades, and now fairly confidently identified with Azelik spring – *Teguidda* is the Tuareg word for a spring. Here are to be found the ruins of mosques, of cemeteries and of houses, together with blocks containing native copper, pieces of worked copper, pottery and beads. The site of the mine is nearly thirteen kilometres distant. Ibn Saʿīd perhaps refers to Takedda as an important centre for trade with the Sudan countries as early as the thirteenth century.[1] Mansa Mūsā, early in the fourteenth century, profited from import duties on copper, which was

[1] J. M. Cuoq, *Recueil des sources arabes concernant l'Afrique occidentale du VIIIe au XVIe siècle* (Paris, 1975), 218n; see also 280n, 284n.

then re-exported to the non-Muslim Sudan for two-thirds of its weight in gold, but we do not know if this was from Takedda.

Ibn Baṭṭūṭa visited Takedda in the mid fourteenth century, and it is to him that we owe our best picture of this thriving mining centre. The houses were built of red stone; the water supply passed by the copper mine, and both its colour and its taste were thus affected. The mine was on the outskirts of the town: the casting of the metal was done in the houses. This was the work of slaves, men and women. The copper was fashioned into bars, thin and thick, valued at 600 or 700 and 400 to the gold *mithqāl*, respectively. The thin bars served as currency for minor purchases, of meat or wood, for example, the thick for more important things, such as grain, butter and slaves. Takedda copper was exported to Bornu, Gobir, the Zaghawa and elsewhere. The inhabitants of Takedda lived in luxury, vying with one another in the number of slaves each possessed, and never selling an educated female slave, or only at a very high price. Ibn Baṭṭūṭa himself tried twice to purchase such a woman, but each time the contract was cancelled at the last moment. The Takeddans, he said, had no occupation but trade, going each year to Egypt and importing quantities of all the fine fabrics to be had there. Ibn Baṭṭūṭa travelled north from Takedda with a caravan including 600 slave women.

The later history of Takedda is more difficult to trace. Essentially a town of the Massufa Berbers, it was reinforced by scholars from Walata, refugees fleeing the rancour of Sonni ʿAlī.[1] But eventually Takedda was abandoned. The celebrated mine Hofrat en Nahas, south of Darfur, began supplying copper to the central Sudan; exactly when we do not know, but Barth's account in the mid nineteenth century almost certainly reflects a much older tradition. In Darfur, he wrote, the *kantar* of copper sold for an equal weight of ivory, or for one six-span slave; in Bornu or Kano, the copper *kantar* fetched double its weight in ivory. In Barth's time, copper was also coming across the Sahara from Tripoli.

Coral was another commodity of worth, combining high value, lively demand in the Sudan and ease of carrying. It was so much desired that, when the local people in the sixteenth century were unable to exploit a good site for it near Bone, the ruler of Tunis licensed certain Genoese merchants to fish for it there. Several strings of coral were among the gifts which a merchant of Damietta presented to the ruler of Gaoga in Leo's presence. In the coastal areas of West Africa, coral

[1] H. T. Norris, *The Tuaregs* (London, 1975), 38.

was often an item of royal regalia, and the king's subjects might, for example, be debarred from wearing coral before him. Even in Timbuktu, at least in the seventeenth century, coral was part of the insignia of the ruling pasha. In the central Sudan, it seems to have been more a woman's ornament, worn in necklaces, nose decorations, bands around the head and so on. This different usage may derive from the stronger Islamic heritage of the central Sudan contrasted with that of West Africa, for the Koran twice includes among the signs and mercies of God ornaments which are taken from the sea, and the commentaries explain that these are such things as pearls and coral, suitable for the adornment of women. The Kanuri word for coral is *murjan*, from the Arabic.

Salt was another precious commodity with which, like copper, the central Sudan region was relatively well endowed. Excellent white salt was available from Bilma, in Kawar. We do not know exactly when this Bilma salt became widely available in the area of Lake Chad, but it is likely to have been early in our period, for al-Idrīsī in the twelfth century wrote of another mineral product of good quality coming from this region: alum, popularly called Kawari alum. The availability of Bilma salt in Hausaland, as has been shown, seems to date from about the mid fifteenth century, and to have derived from the activity of Aïr merchants.

Natron was another commodity popular in Sudan trade. Bornu was well supplied with it, particularly from the Muniyo region, though the highest quality natron was brought from the desert by Tubu. Bornu exported natron to Hausaland, and even as far afield as Nupe. Natron had many uses: in various kinds of cooking – to curdle milk, for example; mixed with animal food, sometimes as a medicine; and in tanning leather. A Bornu song, the lament of a girl abandoned by her lover, mentions that some thought natron might be used to induce abortion; there is even a reference, rather improbable, to natron as a building material; and it was used to enhance the flavour of chewing tobacco – this last function being of considerable importance.

Another item, of perhaps unexpected importance, was perfume. In the absence of detailed study of terms and translations, it is sometimes difficult to know in each case just which aromatic substance is in question: but the broad outlines are clear enough. Civet cats, *Viverra civetta*, are reported throughout black Africa from Liberia to Mombasa, wild animals but hunted for capture, the males being kept in cages for the sake of their civet. Females were released, and there does not appear to have been sufficient domestication to allow rearing the animals in captivity. The civet was once believed to be simply the sweat of the cat, collected from various parts of its body. Heating was certainly used to encourage secretion, but the civet came only from the cuticle of the strong-smelling posterior gland. Various areas were of special repute as exporters of civet, among them Hausaland, Bornu and the lands to the south of Christian Ethiopia. Some prices, quoted by Leo Africanus in the sixteenth century for Fez, suggest the luxury value of civet: a slave might fetch twenty ducats, a eunuch forty, a camel fifty, a pound of civet sixty, and the cat itself two hundred. Other exports included a type of *bakhur*, or frankincense, a gum gathered from trees in the Aïr region. The upper classes in North Africa rejoiced in such fragrant luxury: in the British Museum today is a splendid perfume burner belonging to a Mamluk *amīr* of the thirteenth century. Camphor and attar of roses were favoured imports into black Africa; ambergris was carried inland from the coasts. Myrrh, sandalwood and a variety of scented roots, gums and so forth, circulated. The Pilgrimage provided an excellent opportunity for the exchange of perfumes, even though the use of these is prohibited during the performance of the central rites of the Pilgrimage, and aromatics might thus pass from one end of the Muslim world to the other. Even today, the Pilgrimage months are still a peak period for perfume sales in Arabia.

Various factors combined to make perfumes so popular. From a purely practical point of view, they were relatively easy to carry and, in case of need, to conceal and smuggle – like gold, but unlike, say, cloth, ivory, kola and slaves. Ibn Baṭṭūṭa, entering Mali in the fourteenth century, remarked that the traveller needed nothing more than a little salt, some glass beads and perfume, in order to purchase his every want. Aromatics, following beliefs widespread in the Muslim world, were also thought to have significant curative properties: camphor was especially esteemed as a preventive and cure, both in North Africa and the Sudan – and indeed was recommended in the treatment of cholera among Bangladesh refugees even in 1971. But at the same time it was held that some perfumes might propagate diseases, for example a bunch of flowers transmitting the plague; and there are instances in North Africa of specially prepared perfumes used as a deliberate and lethal poison. Aromatics were also valued as aphrodisiacs, a quality naturally of enhanced appeal in a society of polygamy and concubinage; it was for this, rather than for its scent alone, that ambergris, for example, was so much desired.

More solemnly, perfume was closely interwoven with Islamic

religious imagery and practice. *Ma shamma rā'iḥat al-islām*, 'It has not smelt the scent of Islam', is a common way of describing a pagan area. Descriptions of paradise and the dwellers therein often elaborate upon the marvellous aroma. In Islamic towns, the sellers of candles, incense and perfumes are those nearest the mosque; one set of annual accounts for the al-Azhar mosque during the Fatimid period includes fifteen dinars for incense from India, camphor, musk and the like. As part of the religious pattern, perfumes were also often used in burials: this was certainly the case in North Africa, and though it cannot be documented for the central Sudan during this period, it is reported on either side, for example in Ethiopia and Senegambia. In a somewhat different symbolism, the resumed use of perfume might indicate the end of a period of mourning.

With so many recommendations, it is not surprising to find that perfumes, in addition to being principal commodities in trade, were often a part of the tribute which a lesser dignitary might pay to his superior, or of those regal presents which the great lords exchanged among themselves, as well as being sometimes employed in kingly ceremonial. Perfumes were among those elements of the royal magnificence the use of which al-Maghīlī recommended to Rumfa, ruler of Kano late in the fifteenth century.

Ostrich feathers were also a part of Rumfa's splendour, but we do not know whether this was with al-Maghīlī's approval or not. Rumfa was the first to introduce this usage into Hausaland; it may well have been one of his several borrowings from Bornu court ceremonial. Ostrich feathers were also among the traditional regalia of the Zaghawa sultans; and warriors all across black Africa, from the Somali, Galla and Amhara in the east to Hausaland and beyond, wore ostrich feathers as a token of martial or hunting prowess. After our period, ostrich feathers were a principal export from the Sahara and Sudan. It is difficult to determine how early this trade began. One authority has suggested about 1500 for early feather exports from Hausaland to North Africa; but, although ostrich feathers were in wide demand in many parts of the Muslim world, the distribution of ostriches throughout much of North Africa may have made much long-distance trade from the Sudan at an early date unnecessary.

This survey of some principal trade goods may be completed with the description of two which, by their delayed arrival in the central Sudan, one in the fifteenth century and the other still later, remind us of the remoteness of the region despite its trading contacts. These are kola and cowries. Considering that kola became 'the coffee of the Sudan', and was the object of addiction there (very much as coffee and tobacco elsewhere), it is curious to recall that at the beginning of our period it was totally unknown in our area. The first to introduce kola into Hausaland was Amina, queen of Zaria, probably in the first half of the fifteenth century.[1] She traded with Nupe, but Nupe had then only a middleman's role. The main source of kola was the forest region beyond Gonja, in the north of modern Ghana, and in the third quarter of the fifteenth century the arrival of the first merchants from Gonja at Katsina is signalled. The road to Gonja became one of the most celebrated trade-routes from Hausa: a Hausa proverb, equivalent to 'long journeys making heavy purses', speaks of the road to Gonja, 'far away and profitable'. Tolls might be assessed in kola; an early-nineteenth-century report speaks of ten nuts per load being levied on caravans passing through Bornu towards the central Sudan. Quite unlike coral or gold or other such items, kola is not easy to transport: very perishable, it is a matter of skill and experience to know how to pack and preserve it over the enormous distances which it often travelled. Nevertheless, its popularity as a mild stimulant, uncondemned by Islamic regulations, assured it a steadily expanding market, which reached finally as far as Wadai, the Fezzan and Tripoli. Kola was part of many social courtesies: both the arriving guest and the welcoming host might be expected to offer it; Islamic festivals, as well as private ones such as weddings, might be adorned with the distribution of kola; it was an acceptable offering from a junior official to his superior, or from a disciple to a shaykh; and so on. Parties to an agreement sometimes ate the same kola, each taking half. Some of these observances perhaps derived from older, non-Islamic traditions, evolved in the forest regions. They also roughly paralleled the use of other stimulants elsewhere in the Muslim world, betel for example in India, and the more powerful *qat* of East Africa.

Despite transport difficulties, for some of the sources of cowrie shells were very far away, cowries are reported in wide use in the western Sudan at an early date. In Mansa Mūsā's day they were already employed as currency, and merchants whose principal imports these were made a substantial profit. In Timbuktu, early in the sixteenth century, cowries were employed for small transactions. According to Leo, they were brought from Persia, and were exchanged at 400 to the

[1] The Kano Chronicle dates Amina thus; Hassan and Shu'aibu recommend a mid-sixteenth-century date, but modern scholarship prefers the older.

ducat. Later in the same century, the supply of cowries to the empire of Songhay was one of the issues entangled with the Moroccan invasion. A contemporary Spanish observer noted that Songhay had been buying cowries from Morocco, and had then switched to suppliers in Cairo and Mecca because they offered better prices – another hint of the revival of the diagonal north-east/south-west route. One concession which the *askiya* may have offered to the Moroccans after their first victory was the right to carry salt and cowries to Songhay without import duties. But the first mention of cowries in Hausaland is not until the early eighteenth century, though they rapidly became very popular, and later in the century there were reports, presumably exaggerated, of gifts of as many as ten million cowries from the ruler of Nupe to that of Gobir. It was not until the mid nineteenth century that they began to circulate in Bornu, where the method of counting by fours, rather than by fives as elsewhere in West Africa, may derive from the old copper currency units there.

The partnership of trade and Islam in Africa south of the Sahara has been so often affirmed as to seem almost a truism. As far as the propriety, and piety, of trade are concerned, Muslim opinion is not unanimous, but has fluctuated between distant poles. Muḥammad al-Tūnusī, almost the only one of innumerable North African traders to have left us a detailed account of his travels in the Sudan countries, exclaimed:

> Noble industry, honoured by the most virtuous of men, the holy Prophet of God, Muḥammad! Who does not know, among the nations of Islam, the revered traditions which tell of the Prophet's travels in Syria, serving the commercial interests of Khadījah, Mother of true believers? Who does not know how many times he praised the dealings of men honest and sincere in their transactions, moderate in their gains . . . Following the example of the Prophet, a multitude of men, in various regions, have devoted themselves to commercial enterprises.[1]

Among many traditions attributed to the Prophet which support such a point of view is one, almost certainly apocryphal, which holds: 'Pitch is the remedy for scab in camels, the Sudan is the remedy for poverty in men.'

Over against this, Maliki law states explicitly that it is blameworthy to go trading to the country of the enemy, or to the *bilād al-sūdān*; this recommendation was evidently well known in the central Sudan,

[1] al-Tūnusī, *Voyage au Ouadây*, 332.

for Usuman dan Fodio discussed it at length. There is, however, no legal objection to non-Muslims coming to Muslim countries to trade. Had these provisions been generally applied in the Sudan, trade would have been at a standstill, for it was an almost invariable characteristic of every part of the Sudan that, while Muslims might travel with relative security in many non-Muslim areas, for a non-Muslim to venture into Muslim centres was difficult, often perilous. It is possible that these provisions, to which ardent Muslim reformers might be less willing to turn a blind eye, were a contributory factor encouraging military raids rather than peaceful commerce during periods of heightened religious enthusiasm.

Looking at the Muslim trader from the point of view of the non-Muslim Sudanese, it has sometimes been assumed that the economic prosperity of the trader contributed to the prestige, in Sudanese eyes, of his religion. While this was, and is, probably true as a general rule, there was the further possibility that visitors exclusively interested in trade might generate as much resentment as emulation. And there are instances suggesting that the non-Muslim might sense at least a potential discrepancy between religious conviction and commercial action. In the later ninth century two merchants from the Jebel Nefusa in Tunisia, learned and pious men, went trading to the Sudan. There they met a king who was ill, and fearful of death. They spoke earnestly with him of God, and of paradise and hell. The king called them liars: 'If you really believed all this', he argued, 'you would not come to us looking for this world's goods.' Nevertheless, according to the story, he did convert, and he recovered. The anecdote of the Jebel Nefusa travellers suggests that Muslim traders did sometimes combine hortatory and healing activities, and others, with their commerce. But many a busy trader would have had little time, or inclination, for such things; it is worth recalling that, while Ibāḍī merchants were for centuries pre-eminent in trans-Saharan commerce, there is little to suggest that converts in the central Sudan adopted this rite. They seem from the beginning to have been orthodox Muslims. More important, the pioneer Muslim presence in the non-Muslim Sudan was often represented as well by clerics, men forwhom religious activities were generally more important than were commercial ones. The hypothesis of an independent religious penetration in the Sudan, only loosely associated with trade, seems strengthened by the evidence of Mediterranean commerce, which led to little religious interaction, and hardly any conversion.

Another commonly asserted association is that between trade and the processes of state formation. In the economic and commercial sense, this appears to have functioned in two ways. First, the growth of long-distance trade may have brought into the developing state various commodities of practical value to the government, such as arms. However, even if the definition of practical value is extended as widely as possible, including perhaps ostrich feathers as part of the royal regalia, it is still clear that a large proportion of the goods involved in long-distance trade were either luxury items, or (like cloth) things for general consumption, with little direct utility in government. The second, and more important, way in which trade made an economic contribution to state development was through taxes and tolls. The opportunity to levy tolls on any substantial volume of trade might be a highly significant source of income for a government, which would be thus enabled to undertake many projects otherwise impossible. The importance of duties on copper in Mali in the time of Mansa Mūsā has already been mentioned. Leo said that traders bringing merchandise from other places had to pay heavy duties to the sultan of Agades, who in his turn paid tribute to Songhay of nearly 150,000 ducats. If this scale of transaction is at all closely related to the facts, then the traditional picture of the sultan as a man almost without authority, except for his receipt of tolls, seems in need of revision.

The building of city walls, one of the principal themes in the emergence of the states of Hausaland, had various purposes, such as military defence, and the corresponding ability to protect refugees and other visitors who sought shelter. But it is likely that walls and gates also greatly facilitated the levying of tolls, and discouraged smuggling. The establishment of a market is a further step towards the regular collection of taxes and tolls. According to the Kano Chronicle, the first market in Kano was founded in the fifteenth century, by refugees from Bornu and presumably modelled on Bornu practice. At the very end of that century, Rumfa appeared as founder of another great Kano market, as well as one who built or extended the city walls. In its elaborate provisions for market management, and in its insistence on fair dealing, correct weights and the like, Muslim law lent itself easily to the encouragement of these tendencies. But, in these as in all other economic activities, there were limits to what the traffic would bear. Too extortionate charges might choke off the flow of trade. In this respect, Muslim law might be invoked again. In the questions sent to Egypt late in the fifteenth century, probably from Agades, there is mention of rulers who took part of their revenue from taxes on travelling Muslims, from market dues on all who brought livestock, slaves, clothes, food, even firewood, and from tolls levied at the city gates on entering and on leaving. Just a little later the *askiya* was complaining to al-Maghīlī about unjust sultans who interfered with caravans, opening and valuing loads, taking what they wished and calling it *zakāt*, the basic Islamic tax. The supply of important materials, and revenue from tolls, were economic benefits which local governments derived from trade. Less tangible, but at least equally influential, were the results of the mobility, interwoven with the patterns of trade, of men and ideas.

STATES OF THE CENTRAL SUDAN

The emergence of Kanem as an organized state – or more accurately perhaps at this early stage, as a unified people – first occurred probably in the ninth or tenth century. The Zaghawa, black nomads like the Tubu, were very early distinguished in this area by the Arab geographers. Perhaps the first reference is from the early eighth century, and speaks of Zaghawa and Tubu together.[1] Several authors in the ninth century wrote of the Zaghawa, and al-Ya'qūbī elaborated to say that the Zaghawa inhabited Kanem, the region north-east of Lake Chad; they lived in huts, having no permanent towns. If Ḥ.w.ḍ.n may be read as Hausa, then the Zaghawa ruled them also. A century later, al-Muhallabī wrote of the Zaghawan realm as being greater than that of Songhay, though less populated. Agriculture and stock-raising were practised. The divine kingship seems to have played a central part in drawing together the diverse fragments of society. Al-Muhallabī tells us that the king was worshipped, the people believing that from him came life and death and sickness and health. They imagined that the king did not eat food, and anyone chancing to meet the camels carrying the king's food was immediately killed, though the king did drink in the presence of his chiefs.[2] Long-distance trade was also developing, though whether it was more the needs of the traders which prompted

[1] This is al-Khuwārizmī, writing probably between AD 836 and 847. He uses the name Qurān, which survives in contemporary usage as Goran, and which indicates the southern Tubu, or Daza. Curiously, the printed text gives not Qurān but Fazzān, the difference in Arabic being a slight shift sidewards of one diacritical point. See T. Lewicki, *Arabic external sources for the history of Africa to the south of Sahara* (Wroclaw, 1969), 15–16, and H. v. Mžik, ed., *Das Kitāb ṣūrat al-arḍ des Abū Ga'far . . . al-Huwārizmī* (Leipzig, 1926), 6, 107.

[2] The distinction between eating and drinking somewhat parallels the experience of Joseph's companions in prison, of whom the baker was killed, while the butler was restored to give again the wine cup into Pharaoh's hand.

the emergence of the state, or the development of the state which attracted commerce, may never be known. Al-Ya'qūbī, writing in AD 872, remarked that among the slaves exported north through Zawīla were those from the Zaghawa. The active interest of Mai Arki, ruler of Kanem about the turn of the millennium, in the northern outlet of the slave-trade has already been mentioned (p. 263). Al-Muhallabī's 'divine king', although he ruled over subjects clad in skins, himself wore elaborate clothing of wool and silk, evidently imported. Before long, Islam too had found a foothold: although several of the Banū Kūkū rulers of Kanem had read the Koran, it is Humai who is remembered as the pioneer of Islam in Kanem, whether as a convert or as a Muslim by birth. About 1075 he seized power, and established the Saifawa dynasty.

According to al-Muhallabī's information, one of the principal Zaghawan towns was Mānān. Various other tenth-century authors refer to the Zaghawa, and in al-Mas'ūdī we find the Zaghawa and Kanem as two distinct entities. Al-Idrīsī's work, in the twelfth century, is unfortunately difficult to interpret, but it seems clear that Kanem and the Zaghawa were more separate, the latter closely linked with Kawar and nomadism. Their chief lived in Mānān, described as a town in Kanem. Most of the chief's troops went naked and the Zaghawa in general were scantily clad in skins, hints of non-Muslim tendencies. Ibn Sa'īd, in the thirteenth century, said that Mātān (? = Mānān) had been the capital of Kanem until the conversion of the Saifawa rulers, when Njimi replaced it; Mātān was still associated with the Zaghawa, now under Kanem and mostly Muslim.

We have thus four elements of the classical Sudanic state-formation situation: the nomadic intruder, the divine king, long-distance trade, and Islam. Until recently, most scholars concerned with the central Sudan regarded the birth of Kanem as an outstanding instance of nomadic intervention, in this case, so it was believed, by the Zaghawa. It was with Kanem and the Zaghawa particularly in mind that Urvoy formulated his celebrated simile of Belot's dualist theory of the origin of the universe. The Zaghawa thus appeared to have been the original founders of Kanem, and the ancestors of the Kanembu – and through them later of the Kanuri – people. Now this view has been sharply challenged,[1] partly on the grounds that local sources for the history of Kanem do not mention the Zaghawa, and pay little attention to Mānān.

[1] See, for example, Abdullahi Smith in J. F. A. Ajayi and M. Crowder, eds., *History of West Africa*, I (London, 1971), 168–70.

The Zaghawa, therefore, were perhaps driven out of Kanem by the emergent Kanembu, and never incorporated into the latter. The picture painted by local traditions, which vary a good deal amongst themselves, is of the legendary Arab figure, Sayf b. Dhū Yazan, who assumed the leadership of the Magumi nomads, living north-east of Lake Chad. His descendants, the Saifawa, were to become the ruling dynasty of Kanem and later of Bornu, a dynasty extinguished only in 1846. At first, they were perhaps little more than the heads of the Saifawa lineage of the Magumi clan. Gradually other groups were incorporated, and Kanem began to take shape. The nomadic tradition was still strong, and a parallel for the emergence of a united polity amongst nomads may be drawn with the Aïr sultanate; though Aïr, as we have seen, was far from an effectively centralized state. Side by side with the nomadic ideal, sedentary life was growing up: towns were mentioned even in the tenth century, and agriculture as well as stockkeeping was already a major occupation. Military conquest, of nomad groups as well as settled, also played a part in the development of Kanem. The Saifawa seem also to have preferred intertribal marriages, marrying outside the Magumi clan; as the sons of these marriages succeeded, so the peoples of their mothers were knit more closely into the developing fabric. Both the Tubu and the Zaghawa were later reported to be staunch advocates of exogamous marriage. Finally the 'divine king', so vividly described by al-Muhallabī, survived in modified form into the Muslim period, and probably contributed to social unity.

It is, however, precisely this survival, in whole or in part, of the Zaghawa kingship in Kanem which makes the expulsion and exclusion of the Zaghawa seem implausible. Yet a third hypothesis may be advanced, although very tentatively in view of the sketchy evidence. This is that the pattern of early evolution under the Magumi did include Zaghawa as well as other groups. The name Zaghawa may have disappeared from local memory of these events, but it may even at the time have been used loosely to cover many disparate elements, rather as Takrur was applied in West Africa, or Zanj to the east. The central point at this stage was Mānān. With the accession, in the later eleventh century, of Humai the Muslim usurper, Njimi replaced Mānān as the capital, rather as Gao replaced Kukiya after the conversion of the rulers of Songhay. Those of the Zaghawa who resisted the process of assimilation with its Islamic overtones, and who maintained their ancient loyalty to Mānān, formed now a pagan rearguard action, which was gradually forced eastwards. They could not, however, altogether escape either the suzerainty of Kanem, or islamization; although those who went furthest, and who are still today a distinct group in Wadai and Darfur, have preserved unusually rich pre-Islamic survivals connected with the kingship and other rites, and the major group amongst them, the Kobe Zaghawa of Wadai, link their conversion to the arrival from the east of Abdullah Boru, as late as the beginning of the seventeenth century. Some Zaghawa still look back to a 'Bornu' origin. This seems at least a possible interpretation of a sequence of events about which we cannot be at all certain.

The growth of Kanem, encouraged now by the rulers' remarkable devotion to Islam, and the establishment of the clerics' privileged position, came to its climax in the early thirteenth century, under Mai Dunama Dibbalemi. His principal political achievement appears to have been the conquest of Fezzan, where, as we have seen, he established a new capital at Traghen, replacing the Berber Banū Khaṭṭāb by a lieutenant of his own. This imperial action probably reflected the great importance to Kanem of security for trade and travel on the road northwards; it may also be linked with the rise of the Hafsids in Tunisia. About the same time a Kanemi hostel was established in Cairo. Trouble was, however, brewing at home. Dibbalemi destroyed the *mune*, or sacred pre-Islamic talisman of Kanem, and from this sacrilegious act, according to the local accounts, sprang all the troubles that followed. It is very tempting to see this act of Dibbalemi's as an attempt to make a clean break with the past, to rid local Islam of the accretion of local compromise accumulated over the previous two centuries; and such an interpretation seems confirmed by al-Maqrīzī's report that Dibbalemi himself was the first Muslim ruler. Not all Muslims in Kanem would have supported such hard-line action, for some would have been moderate men, appropriate forerunners of Muḥammad al-Amīn al-Kanemī and his rejection of Fulani extremism in the nineteenth century. If the preceding argument has any truth in it, then the Muslim presence twice divided early Kanemi society, first in the expulsion of recalcitrant Zaghawa, later in controversies initiated by Dibbalemi. But it must be stressed again that the evidence is scanty and tentative.

Already in Dibbalemi's time divisions had occurred amongst his sons, and after his death civil dissension became endemic. Fezzan slipped from Kanemi control, the *mai*'s representative declaring himself independent and founding the Banū Naṣūr dynasty. Four *mais* in succession, all great-grandsons of Dibbalemi, fell fighting the So to the south of Lake Chad. Most serious of all, the Bulala wars began in earnest in the mid fourteenth century. The Bulala were apparently a cadet branch of the Saifawa line, descended from a Saifawa mother and thus excluded from the normal succession. Encroachment by Arabs from the east, who enslaved and sold the Muslim citizens of Kanem, and killed a brother of the *mai*, proved the straw that broke the camel's back. These Arabs, who arrived in so unfriendly a style, may have been a link between the notorious Banū Hilāl from Egypt and the Shuwa, who later played such an important and generally constructive part in Bornu. In the 1390s the harassed *mai*, 'Umar b. Idrīs, abandoned Kanem, and with his court and followers fled into Bornu, whither some prior immigration from Kanem had somewhat prepared the way. This was the exodus, the act of conception for the new state of Bornu, which was to be, until Rābiḥ's conquest late in the nineteenth century, a leading power of the central Sudan. It was also the opening of the eastern door of Hausaland.

As far as the establishment of Bornu was concerned, these hopeful prospects were very far from being realized in the early days. Dynastic feuding continued to wrack the Saifawa even in their refuge; and, although the sources are not explicit about this, it seems almost indubitable that warfare with the So continued, having been so fierce in the fourteenth century, and still proving a major stumbling-block to Aloma in the sixteenth. There was yet another hazard: violent confrontation occurred in the reign of 'Uthmān b. Idrīs between him and the *kaigama*, Muḥammad b. Dalatu. This continued through several reigns, and involved several *kaigamas*. Two *mais* were deposed. We do not know the origin of the title *kaiga-ma*, 'the master of Kaiga', but it probably refers to a district south-west of Lake Chad, in the Bornu region. Al-Qalqashandī (d. 1418) in Egypt gives Kākā as the capital of Bornu. Later reports say that the office of *kaigama* was always held by a slave. In the nineteenth century, Dala was remembered as a Hausa slave to whom responsibility for the defence of the eastern marches of Bornu had been entrusted not long after the exodus, and his descendants, the Dalatoa, still enjoyed an hereditary authority in the region. It seems very likely that Ibn Dalatu and Dalatoa are two names sharing a common source, although the early records do not tell us why the office was created, while the nineteenth-century report has forgotten its perversion through revolt. If this identification is correct, perhaps one may carry it further, and see in these events the source of Leo's account of Gaoga (? = Kaiga) and the rebellious slave who seized power there. This possibility is discussed later, in connection with Darfur and Wadai (pp. 304–5).

Not until ʿAlī Gaji b. Dunama came to the throne in the last quarter of the fifteenth century did Bornu begin to emerge from the time of troubles. ʿAlī eliminated his dynastic rivals, and founded a permanent capital at Ngasargamu. Clerical advisers at court seem to have acquired a new and still greater significance in his time. And it was apparently now that the title *khalīfa*, or caliph, came into common use for the *mai*, perhaps as a counterweight to the growing pretensions, nurtured on the Pilgrimage, of the *askiya* of Songhay, dubbed *khalīfa* of Takrur. ʿAlī's son and successor, Idrīs Katagarmabe, carried the ancient war with the Bulala into Kanem so successfully that he was twice able to reoccupy Njimi. It is indicative of the extent to which a new society, the Kanuri, and a new state, Bornu, had evolved since the exodus, that the Saifawa seem to have felt no temptation to return permanently to Njimi. Raids, such as those carried out by Idrīs Katagarmabe, or by Idrīs Aloma at the end of the sixteenth century, were not intended to be a prelude to definitive conquest. Contacts with the north, which had been so important during the great days of the first empire in Kanem, were renewed from Bornu in the sixteenth century. Aïr was brought into a tributary relationship, in 1532 according to one report, and this seems to have been sustained, for Bornu later went, though quite ineffectively, to the aid of Aïr, then suffering depredations at the hands of Kebbi. Diplomatic relations were established with Tripoli, possibly even during the period when the Knights of St John were in control there, much more certainly with the Ottoman Turks after they had expelled the Knights. In 1569/70 Idrīs Aloma became *mai* of Bornu, by far the best known – through the work of his indefatigable chronicler, Ibn Fartuwa – of all the Saifawa dynasty before the nineteenth century.

The traditional picture of the origins of Hausa society, through the imposition of Berber immigrants upon a Negro population, perhaps about the beginning of our period, is even more than the corresponding view of Kanem in need of revision. Linguistic evidence does not support the idea of such a recent mixture; on the contrary, the relationships among the various Chadic languages, of which Hausa is by far the most important, suggest that these languages have been in the area, though isolated from one another, for a much longer period. The theme here is thus not the origin of a people, but the way in which a society already in place developed new forms and institutions. About the very early stages of this process we know little, though we may surmise a pattern of agricultural village life, with here and there a larger settlement emerging as a *gari*, or town. Some of these towns grew further, becoming walled cities (*birane*; singular, *birni*). The siting of a *birni* might be influenced by various factors: the proximity of some place of religious reputation, the residence perhaps of powerful spirits; the junction of important trade routes; the availability of natural resources, such as the abundant iron in the Kano area. The *birni* was also a fortified place, its walls embracing a large plot into which people from the surrounding countryside might flock in times of emergency, and where also some farming might be carried on, if the *birni* were subjected to a long siege. Such protection might also attract people from further away, for the arrival and eventual absorption of immigrants and refugees from diverse regions seems to have been a basic feature in the development of these states.

If the report in the Kano Chronicle is correct, town walls were first developed in Hausaland on a substantial scale by Queen Amina of Zaria, in the fifteenth century; but archaeological work on this interesting problem is yet to be undertaken. Some evidence suggests that fortifications of a sort had begun earlier in Kano, although the Bornu records notice these only late in the sixteenth century. The *birane* encompassed a more cosmopolitan population than did the preceding settlements, which were much more exclusively based on kinship; and, in this more diversified society, government changed from a family affair of lineage heads to a delicately poised balance between the *sarki*, or hereditary ruler, on the one hand, and his officials and fiefholders on the other.

Although there is a very widespread tradition that there were seven original Hausa states, among which Daura seems to have had some antique primacy – being, for example, the one through which the tribute of Hausaland to Bornu sometimes passed – only four seem to have been of substantial proportions in our period: Gobir, Katsina, Zaria (originally Zazzau), and Kano. The people of Gobir, as has been noticed above, lived in the Aïr region early on, whence they were driven by encroaching Tuareg, the fifteenth century being perhaps the time of major Gobirawa movement. Of the development of Katsina and Zazzau during this time little is known. The Kano Chronicle allows us to form a somewhat fuller picture of the fourth of these states. The region had become a centre of political power and religious influence, based in particular upon Tsumburburai, the spirit of Dala hill.

Into this sphere came an immigrant group, led by Bagauda, from the north-east. Bagauda is remembered as a founder of the Kano state: he built a new *birni*, surrounding Dala hill. But Bagauda did not overthrow or displace the authority of Tsumburburai, and tension between the newcomers and the old religion continued through several reigns, until the ninth *sarki* destroyed the spirit's shrine. Not long after, under Yaji dan Tsamiya, the eleventh *sarki*, Islam was introduced into Kano, by a party of Wangarawa, probably immigrants from the Mali region, perhaps in the second quarter of the fourteenth century. It is significant that this vital innovation should have come to Hausaland not from the north, as to Ghana or Kanem, but from the west; similarly, after the exodus of the *mai* into Bornu, Hausaland was deeply affected by new ideas from that quarter also.

The second half of the fifteenth century was a watershed. Three major rulers, perhaps contemporaries, Muḥammad Rabbo in Zaria, Ibrāhīm Sura in Katsina, and Muḥammad Rumfa in Kano, altered the character of Hausa development, by introducing or confirming Islam and weaving it into the fabric of statecraft. Of Muḥammad Rabbo we know least, little more than that he was the first Muslim ruler of Zaria. In Katsina, Ibrāhīm was a severe master, requiring, as had Yaji of Kano, his subjects to pray, but going further and imprisoning those who refused. It was to him, together with Muḥammad Settefen of Agades, that al-Suyūṭī addressed by name his tract for the rulers of Takrur. Ibrāhīm succeeded Muḥammad Korau, remembered as the first Muslim ruler, and also apparently the founder of a new dynasty.[1] 'Alī, who followed Ibrāhīm and whose long reign covered the first quarter of the sixteenth century, was called the *murābiṭ*, 'man of the *ribāṭ*', perhaps in honour of his having fortified the city. Of Muḥammad Rumfa, we know a great deal more, to a large extent because it was in his time that the forbidding cleric, al-Maghīlī, visited Kano. These two men, king and cleric, important in themselves, are particularly so because of the detailed information available about them. We may therefore consider them more closely.

Among the many clerics whose travels in the central Sudan illustrate the theme of mobility within the Islamic world, and in some cases also beyond the Islamic frontiers, and whose influence demonstrates the importance of that mobility, the best known and most significant of all

[1] Early Katsina chronology, as is true of most of Hausaland, is confused. The writer has followed the opinion presently preferred by scholars. It is, however, possible that Korau and Ibrāhīm Sura ruled early in the fourteenth century, and that Ibrāhīm Maje was the strict reformer in al-Suyūṭī's day.

within our period is Muḥammad b. ʻAbd al-Karīm al-Maghīlī, from Tuat. Celebrated in the earlier, North African stage of his career as a scholar, controversialist and persecutor of Jews, he travelled south in the 1490s to visit Agades, Takedda, Kano, Katsina and Gao. It was in the affairs of the Songhay empire that he made his most substantial contribution, justifying the *askiya*'s revolt against the legitimate dynasty on the grounds that Sonni ʻAlī had offended more by mixing Islam and paganism than he would have done had he been an outright pagan.

Al-Maghīlī's part in Hausaland, though less far reaching in its consequences, was nonetheless of substantial importance. His work in Katsina is remembered only in vague outline: according to some reports, he himself converted the *sarki* there, while other sources say it was the commoners, more than the rulers, who in Katsina responded favourably to him. Al-Maghīlī may have influenced Katsina indirectly as well, for one of his pupils, Muḥammad al-Tazakhti, a Timbuktu cleric who had studied with him at Takedda, became *qāḍī* at Katsina. He had stopped there on his way back from Pilgrimage, and remained there until his death in 1529/30.

For al-Maghīlī in Kano, evidence is relatively abundant, but confused. The Kano Chronicle reports the arrival of Islam in the time of Yaji, in the fourteenth century. Then, late in the fifteenth century, under Rumfa, the arrival of another Muslim group is described in some detail:

> The Sherifs came to Kano. They were Abdu Rahaman and his people. There is a story that the Prophet appeared to Abdu Rahaman in a dream and said to him, 'get up and go west and establish Islam' . . . So he journeyed [from Madina] until he came to Kano . . . Abdu Rahaman lived in Kano and established Islam. He brought with him many books. He ordered Rimfa to build a mosque for the Friday prayer, and to cut down the sacred tree and build a minaret on the site. And when he had established the Faith of Islam, and learned men had grown numerous in Kano, and all the country round had accepted the Faith, Abdu Karimi [*sic*] returned to Massar [Egypt], leaving Sidi Fari as his deputy to carry on his work.[1]

This passage, although the names are puzzling, is generally taken to refer to al-Maghīlī. Abdu Karimi may be his own name, Ibn ʻAbd al-Karīm; Abdu Rahaman may be a mistake for this, or it may refer to a colleague of his. Sidi Fari is apparently an assistant, but some authorities say that the title, meaning 'the white Sayyid', is a nickname for al-Maghīlī himself.

In contrast, the Wangarawa Chronicle, recently published from a

[1] H. R. Palmer, ed. and tr., *Sudanese memoirs: being mainly translations of a number of Arabic manuscripts relating to the central and western Sudan* (Lagos, 1928; reprinted London, 1967), III, p. 111.

copy dated 1650/1,[1] describes in detail the arrival of the Wangarawa Muslims in Kano, and of al-Maghīlī, but separates these by three days only, placing both in the fifteenth century. That this is not a second, different Wangarawa migration is suggested by the fact that both here and in the Kano Chronicle the first Muslims to arrive are confronted by opponents who regularly defile the new mosque. The Wangarawa Chronicle has, apparently, elided two events which in fact happened more than a century apart, placing both in Rumfa's time. A similar elision may have taken place in another version, the Hausa Chronicle.[2] In this case, it is al-Maghīlī who is moved to an earlier period, but the Wangarawa are not mentioned. As in the Kano Chronicle, al-Maghīlī comes from the east, and returns thither when his pioneering work is done, leaving behind a majority of his followers, who later pass (wrongly, in the chronicler's view) as Sharifs. Time went on, according to the Hausa Chronicle, and eventually the rulers of Kano began to turn away from Islam, a retrograde tendency which reached its nadir under none other than Rumfa himself, who followed 'crooked ways'.

Of the three chronologies, the third is obviously wrong: we know that al-Maghīlī was active in Rumfa's time, or at the very least just after. Since the Wangarawa Chronicle seems to involve unjustified telescoping, we may prefer, though tentatively, the Kano Chronicle. But the third account, the Hausa Chronicle, may nonetheless have some accuracy in its presentation of Rumfa as a ruler who seriously overstepped the bounds of orthodoxy.

The 'crooked ways' mentioned by the Hausa Chronicle include building up a harem of 1,000 women, requiring that subjects approaching their king pour dust upon their heads, forbidding anyone else to use the names by which Rumfa's own children were known and selling children. He scorned Islam, the Chronicle continues, and did what he wished. Most people followed his evil example, and of the clerics who ventured to preach against him, one, Mohamma b. Zāra, was murdered on his way to the mosque, and another was frightened away from the town and subsequently died while under arrest. The Kano Chronicle, though generally very much more favourable to Rumfa, confirms some of these actions, saying that he was the first *sarki* to have a thousand wives, reserving all first-born virgins from the royal slave settlements for himself. He also introduced *kame*, the right of the ruler to requisition the property of his subjects.

[1] M. A. al-Hajj, 'A seventeenth century chronicle on the origins and missionary activities of the Wangarawa', *Kano Studies*, 1968, 1, 4, 7–16.

[2] Given at the beginning of Rattray, *Hausa folk-lore*, 1.

The Kano Chronicle dwells on other more constructive elements in Rumfa's statecraft. He established another market, extended the city walls, built a new palace, initiated new military tactics, set up the *Tara-ta-Kano* or Kano Nine, a council of state, began giving important state offices to eunuchs, and adorned the kingship with new pomp, such as royal music (including copper trumpets from Aïr) and ostrich feather insignia. The influence of Bornu in much of this seems fairly clear.

Al-Maghīlī wrote a Mirror for Princes for Rumfa, as well as another letter, both of which happily have survived, and which set out al-Maghīlī's concept of ideal government at some length. Only in certain points is it possible to trace a correspondence between al-Maghīlī's advice and Rumfa's practice. Al-Maghīlī recommends a comely presence for the king, including the use of perfume, but not extravagance in either style or cost. He underlines the need for trusty advisers and officials, but it is not clear that eunuchs are what he has in mind. He prefers a militant foreign policy:

> The sojourn of a prince in the city breeds all manner of trouble and harm. The bird of prey abides in open and wild places.[1]

This advice Rumfa fulfilled. In his time there occurred the first war with Katsina, which went on for eleven years without either side gaining the upper hand. Rumfa's extension of the city walls was also in accord with al-Maghīlī's stress upon the value of these for defence. Al-Maghīlī's careful provisions for taxation include such methods as *kame* as a very last resort only, when calamity has befallen the state and the treasury is empty. Only in one matter, but a very interesting one, does al-Maghīlī apparently sanction some local compromise: he allows an oppressor, *ẓālim*, to exercise judicial functions, if there is no alternative – but such a one may be called only *ḥākim*, and never *qāḍī*, or judge proper.

In view of the conflicting evidence, it is difficult at this stage to arrive at a definite opinion about al-Maghīlī's relations with Rumfa. It seems, nevertheless, that the fairly widely accepted view, of Rumfa as a dutiful disciple of al-Maghīlī, applying Islamic principles for the benefit of the state, is not fully proven, and that there is at least a chance that the two men parted on more distant terms, al-Maghīlī's writings for Rumfa being perhaps better understood as reproach for shortcomings than as agreed policy statements. For the unbending cleric to

[1] T. H. Baldwin, tr., *The obligations of princes: an essay on Moslem kingship by Shekh Mohammed al-Maghili of Tlemsen* (Beirut, 1932), 10.

have thus clashed with his royal patron would not have been out of place in al-Maghīlī's career: he had been accused before the authorities of sedition in Morocco: he seems to have left Aïr after the lax Muslims there rejected his uncompromising attitude; and there is some suggestion that his relations with Katsina and even with Songhay subsequently cooled (see pp. 418–19). A clash would certainly fit in with a recurrent pattern in the Sudan countries, a pattern which became ever more intense until it culminated in the theocratic revolutions of the early nineteenth century.

It was in the time of 'Alī, the *murābiṭ* of Katsina, early in the sixteenth century, that hostilities broke out between Songhay and Hausaland, particularly Kano and Katsina. Leo vividly describes the Songhay invasion: marriage alliances and crippling tribute were imposed, the grandsons of the Gobir king were castrated for the Songhay court. As frequently happens with Leo's evidence, however, it is difficult to fit this dramatic scenario into what we know from other sources. The Hausa chronicles apparently neglect the catastrophe; and this cannot be explained simply as embarrassment at a humiliating debacle, because the Kano Chronicle, for example, does not hesitate to portray the Sarkin Kano in a variety of undignified postures, defeated on various occasions by Katsina, by Zaria, by the Kwararafa. The Timbuktu chronicles, telling the story from the Songhay side, refer only very briefly to a minor expedition against Katsina, just after Leo's visit.

The period of direct Songhay domination in Hausaland was short, whether its impact was peripheral or profound on the evolution of the Hausa states.[1] In 1517, the erstwhile allies, Songhay and Kebbi, quarrelled about the distribution of booty after a joint expedition against Aïr. The first *kanta* (ruler) of Kebbi, Kuta, was able to defy Songhay, and thus effectively to cut communications between that empire and its vassals, if vassals they had been, in Hausaland. In the 1530s another Songhay attempt against Kebbi was repulsed decisively; in 1553 a peace was arranged. The Bornu attack on Kebbi, perhaps in 1561, arising from Aïr's appeal for Bornu help against Kebbawa harassment, has already been mentioned. The army of Bornu, at first successful, proved unable to take Surame, the capital, another fortified city of the Hausa region. In the 1590s, al-Manṣūr, sultan of Morocco, wrote to Kanta Dā'ūd of Kebbi, accusing him of harbouring Songhay refugees. This, together with al-Manṣūr's demand that Kebbi should

[1] The evidence for Songhay influence on Hausaland is further discussed in the bibliographical essay for this chapter.

give him the boats and other equipment which had formerly been paid to Songhay, suggests that Kebbi might have returned to some sort of tributary status. Al-Manṣūr also claimed that Kebbi was preventing people from Kano and Katsina from passing through Kebbi to make their submission to him. These claims over Kebbi, coupled with Morocco's contacts with Bornu a decade earlier, leading to Bornu's declaration of *bayʿa* (homage) to Morocco, indicate again the broad scope of al-Manṣūr's ambition in the Sudan, certainly extending well beyond the boundaries of Songhay proper. But such ambition went unfulfilled; even Songhay alone was too big a prey for the Moroccan serpent to swallow.

On the margins of Hausaland lay the seven Banza Bakwai, or 'bastard Hausa' states, contrasted with the Hausa Bakwai, the genuine seven, such as Gobir, Katsina, Zaria and Kano, the states just discussed. Some of the Banza Bakwai were of relatively slight importance during our period; one at least, the Yoruba, lies outside our area – and in fact the Hausa connection of many is uncertain. Two deserve special attention: Nupe and the Kwararafa, the former on the lower Niger, the latter on the Benue.

Beyond Hausaland proper, Nupe stands as the south-eastern bastion of the central Sudan. The geography of the country is dominated by its low relief and abundant rivers; yet crops from the drier north may still be grown here. Linguistic evidence and the Yoruba traditions, better preserved than those of Nupe, suggest that the earliest significant links were with the south, rather than northwards. The founding father of the Nupe nation was Tsoede. He was born of a Bini mother, near the confluence of the Niger and Kaduna rivers; his father, a prince from Idah, had been visiting there. Later Tsoede was sent to Idah, amongst the slave tribute which Benin owed; the ruler of Idah recognized him as his son. On the ruler's death, Tsoede fled back to Benin, and gradually succeeded in unifying the greater part of what was to become the Nupe state, bringing together people already there. By about 1530, according to this account, he had established an independent dynasty in Nupe. Tsoede, although apparently a local boy returning home rather than a foreign intruder, again illustrates the difficulty of interpreting stories about a perhaps legendary pioneer statesman. Some recent scholarly analysis suggests that he was no more than the personification of that chain of events which led to the founding of a supratribal state; but it is as difficult to disprove as to prove his individual existence, and the question is better left open. The power of the *etsu*, or ruler, of Nupe was probably slight in most periods, perhaps limited to attempts to collect taxes and to preserve the loyalty of local subordinate leaders. He was hedged with divinity, wearing only white, allowing no stranger to see him eat, permitting no one to be killed in the presence of the king or even in the same town; magic, ritual and taboo were important.

A connection between Nupe and Yoruba can be discerned even in the mythical past, when Oranyan, grandson of Oduduwa, married the daughter of a Nupe king; their son, Shango, who was later deified, was thus half Nupe, and is said to have been born in Nupe, although at this time it is unlikely that the emergence of the Nupe state had progressed far. Fuller Yoruba traditions relate how the Yoruba ruler, the *alafin*, later abandoned his capital of Oyo-Ile because of Nupe attacks, and how his successors maintained a capital-in-exile at Igboho. The approximate dates of the exile are 1535 to 1610. Some name Tsoede as the original antagonist of the Yoruba; whether or not he played such a part, and as we have seen even his very existence is in some doubt, the dates seem about right for the emergence of Nupe as a powerful force. There is some evidence that the success of Tsoede, or of the trend which he personifies, both in uniting Nupe and in challenging the Yoruba, was related to cavalry power, but this remains somewhat hypothetical.

While these traditions of state formation, and political and military activity, point to the importance of Nupe relations with powerful southern neighbours, other evidence indicates that contacts of various kinds were developing also to the west and north. Ibn Baṭṭūṭa may echo such contacts, in speaking of a great kingdom of the blacks, further down the Niger, in the country of the Līmiyyīn. This kingdom he called Yūfī, or Yūwī, or Nūfī, and the name has often been taken as a variant of Nupe, which the Hausa call Nyffe. Doubt has recently been cast on this identification, since Ibn Baṭṭūṭa used the same name, and the same location, for an area supplying the gold trade of Sofala, on the east coast. However, since his information about West Africa is fuller and fresher than that on East Africa, the mistake, if mistake it is, is more likely to have been on the latter side. The Katsina chronicles record that Muḥammad Korau waged war against Nupe, which then shared a common frontier with Katsina. If we accept an early fourteenth-century date for Korau, then Ibn Baṭṭūṭa's visit to the Sudan may even have fallen within his reign. But, as we have seen, Korau is more likely to have ruled in the later fifteenth century, when his wars with Nupe perhaps arose from that same nascent Nupe expansion which precipitated conflict with Yoruba.

More certain – though the dating is still vague, probably early in the fifteenth century – is the beginning of significant trade with Hausaland. Under Queen Amina of Zaria, kola was introduced into Hausaland, coming from Nupe; it is likely that this kola was merely in transit, from the producing areas in Gonja to the west, for kola-growing seems to have been introduced into Nupe itself, again from Gonja, only later. Queen Amina also introduced eunuchs, another innovation in Hausaland, and these too came from Nupe; they may perhaps show a Yoruba influence, for eunuchs played an important part in government there. Indeed, all the products of the west came into Hausaland at this time, according to the Kano Chronicle, thus underlining Nupe's role in entrepôt trade. Among the goods going south to or through Nupe were horses. Nupe's resources in iron and silicates may also have contributed to the political power and to the economic attractiveness of the state.

Nupe was affected by the struggle for spheres of influence in Hausaland which flared up in the sixteenth century between Bornu to the east and Songhay, replaced before long in this role by Kebbi, to the west. Bussa, an important centre on the western frontier of Nupe, was seized by Songhay in 1505, and had apparently been receiving Muslim Wangara immigrants earlier than this. There is some indication that, as Kebbi successfully sustained its break with Songhay a little later in the sixteenth century, so it took over north-western influence in Nupe, for Muḥammad Kanta of Kebbi is said to have summoned all Hausaland to help build him a town, and to have punished the Nupe contingent for delay by requiring them to make their section of the wall of shea-butter and mud.

Religious interpenetration went on as well. Opinions differ as to whether the Yoruba *egungun* rituals are borrowed from the Nupe *gugu*, or were its origin. The Wangarawa from the west would certainly have brought Islam. A Nupe Muslim cleric is said to have advised one of the exiled *alafins*, in about the 1580s. The cleric acted in a typical role, that of mediator, in this case between the *alafin* and his temporarily estranged chiefs. We may ask, though the question cannot yet be answered with confidence, whether this sign of Islamic clerical influence even in Yoruba is part of that spread of Islamic intervention, zeal and unrest which may be traced, from the Niger to Wadai, in the closing stages of the sixteenth century, and which may be related to that unprecedented intrusion, the Moroccan conquest of Songhay in 1591 (see Volume 4, pp. 137–8). An important Islamic infusion came to Nupe in the middle of the seventeenth century, when Koyam refugees from Bornu fled even as far as Nupe, where the town of Kutigi, later to become one of the largest in Nupe and a powerful Islamic centre, is said to have been founded by them. Curiously enough, the Bornu immigrants are said to have introduced an elaborate ritual and pageant, the *gani*, observed once a year, which is still maintained today, and which is only with some difficulty to be understood within a serious Islamic context.

While emphasizing that the evidence, briefly summarized in the foregoing discussion, is extremely fragmentary, one may hazard the general impression that, by the sixteenth century, Nupe was emerging as a powerful state, strengthened by natural resources and still more by its strategic commercial location, guided by one or more able kings who were able both to elaborate their traditionally divine role by southern exemplars, and to begin supplementing that role with the resources of Islam. The affairs of Nupe so prospered that it was successful in its challenge to the power of the Yoruba.

The second main power on the southern borders of the central Sudan, the Kwararafa, are less well known than the Nupe, although they came to play a much more prominent and troublesome role in the military affairs of the region than the Nupe ever did. There is no Kwararafa figure corresponding to the Nupe Tsoede. The Kwararafa appear to have been a loose confederacy of ethnic groups. Some unity was provided by the Jukun, or priestly caste, living in the Benue valley, but many other peoples were associated, such as the Bolewa of Fika. Traditions suggest that Kwararafa elements were moving into the area from further east about the end of the first millennium. From Lake Chad, some moved on to the middle Gongola and to the Benue, others to the upper Gongola. By the middle of the thirteenth century, the Kwararafa apparently dominated the Gongola/Benue complex: they may even have been fighting with Katsina by this time. The first recorded conflict with Kano was in the time of Yaji, the later fourteenth century: it seems to have been Yaji who was the aggressor, and the Kwararafa bought him off with slaves. The combination of armed confrontation and the slave-trade may be significant, the search for black ivory leading to recurrent raiding and retaliation. In contrast to the

Nupe, there are for the Kwararafa rather few references to trade, although tribute might be paid, one way or the other, in the intervals between hostilities. Yaji's son also demanded slave tribute from the Kwararafa, but went on to exchange horses regularly with them for slaves. Queen Amina's conquests in the earlier fifteenth century are said to have extended as far as Kwararafa and Nupe. Muḥammad Rumfa's son waged war upon Kalam, one of the Kwararafa principalities. In most of these engagements, the Kwararafa seem to have been the victims of Hausa prowess, and perhaps Hausa expansion. In the next century, however, the heyday of Kwararafa military ascendancy in the central Sudan, the boot was on the other foot.

The history of Wadai, the easternmost area within the strict compass of this chapter, is very largely subordinate during these centuries to that of Darfur, which seems to have been Kanem/Bornu's dominant neighbour to the east. The first remembered rulers of Darfur were the Daju, living in the Jebel Marra massif, and collecting tribute from the tribes round about. The Daju claim to have come from the east, and most of their rulers had Arab names; tradition does not, however, attribute an Arab origin to them. Another people, the Tunjur, tracing their origin to the Arabian peninsula through Tunis and in particular through Abū Zayd, the legendary Hilāli hero, followed the Daju into Darfur, and eventually the central power passed peacefully from the Daju to the Tunjur. The Tunjur introduced the Arabic language and customs. It is not clear whether they were entirely pagan, or themselves Muslim but without the power to impose Islam upon their tributaries and neighbours, unable indeed to maintain the faith adequately even amongst themselves in their isolated position. About the middle of the fifteenth century, the legitimate Tunjur ruler, Shau or Sau, was overthrown by his half-brother, Dali, founder of the Kayra dynasty, which continued in Darfur until the Mahdist conquest of the nineteenth century. Dali, the son of Aḥmad al-Ma'qūr, extended the range of organized government, dividing the country into five principal provinces; and he established a system of criminal law, which in due time was written down as the Book of Dali, the Kitab Dali. The basis of the law was not Islam, but rather the need for adequate revenue for the government. Instead of capital or corporal punishment and imprisonment, for all crimes both serious and trivial Dali prescribed fines, payable in cattle or cloth. Wadai had also fallen into the hands of immigrant Tunjur Arabs, who apparently maintained themselves more effectively than did their brothers in Darfur, for it was only with ‘Abd al-Karīm's successful revolution in the earlier seventeenth century that Tunjur rule over Wadai came to an end.

Recently the suggestion has been advanced that Gaoga, mentioned by Leo Africanus, corresponds to Darfur, or to a greater Darfur. According to Leo, about a hundred years before (i.e. early in the fifteenth century), a rich merchant had taken a Negro slave to Gaoga. The slave, finding himself near his former home, murdered his unsuspecting master and returned to his relations. Amongst his master's plundered possessions were arms and trade goods. The rebellious slave secured some horses from white merchants, and embarked on a series of raids which eventually established him as a powerful lord. He was followed by his son, who ruled for forty years; after him came his brother, Mose (?Mūsā), to whom succeeded his grandson Homara (?‘Umar), who was ruling at the time of Leo's second visit to the Sudan countries, probably 1512–14. Leo also claims to have been present when a visitor from Damietta presented to the ruler of Gaoga a very fine horse, a Turkish sabre, a mail shirt and other items, receiving in return five slaves, five camels, five hundred ducats of the local currency and nearly a hundred tusks of ivory. Leo refers more than once to the wealth of those to the north fortunate enough to trade with Gaoga. At the time of Leo's visit, the *askiya* of Songhay – whom Leo calls king of Timbuktu – was the most powerful of the three principal rulers of the Sudan countries, the *mai* of Bornu was the least, and the king of Gaoga occupied the intermediate rank. The army of Bornu had to hurry back from a proposed expedition into Hausaland when it was reported that invasion threatened from Gaoga.

Leo's Gaoga has never been satisfactorily identified. Some scholars have dismissed the whole account as one of garbled hearsay; others have sought to associate it with a Bulala dynasty centred round Lake Fitri, or with Kanem more generally, or with Daju or Nubian refugee groups. The latest hypothesis, developed by Pierre Kalck, is that Gaoga was more probably a state of great extent centred upon Darfur, and including also Wadai. If this is correct, then it would seem likely that Dali, or perhaps his father Aḥmad al-Ma‘qūr, may have been the usurping slave in Leo's account. There are, however, many difficulties remaining in the evidence, and already grave objections have been raised to the new view. Another alternative, but also speculative, is the one already mentioned (pp. 291–2), identifying Gaoga with Kaga in Bornu, where the *kaigama*, initially an important figure in the defences of the fledgling kingdom of Bornu, embarked soon after the exodus upon a decidedly rebellious and recalcitrant policy.

Towards the end of the sixteenth century, or possibly early in the seventeenth, Tunsam, the Kayra sultan of Darfur, was overthrown by his nephew or great-nephew Sulaymān, nicknamed Solong (meaning 'redface' or Arab, his mother being of the Massalit tribe to whom an Arab origin is generally ascribed). Sulaymān Solong, both by his military enterprise and by his introduction or reintroduction of Islam, gave the kingdom a new foundation. Material culture, however, was still but little developed. Sulaymān's talismanic drum and shield were held in great awe, but there is no mention of fire-arms, which were by this time in use both in Bornu and (among the invading Moroccans) in Songhay. People wore clothes of skins, the king's robe of honour was of red leather, and when a carpet was brought from Egypt to Sulaymān's successor he was uncertain what to do with it, trying to wrap it round himself as a garment.

IRON, HORSES AND GUNS

Three innovations have helped to change the face of the central Sudan: metal, horses and guns. Of these, the first is more a problem of the first millennium, and is considered in detail in the previous volume. Received archaeological opinion is now that iron reached Daima mound in Bornu, site of some of the most significant excavations in the central Sudan, in the fifth or sixth century AD, although its arrival in the Chad region as a whole may perhaps antedate this by several centuries. As the iron-working of the Nok culture in Nigeria, to the west, began considerably earlier, it seems likely that this craft derived, not from Meroe, but from North Africa, perhaps from Carthage. The appearance of iron at Daima was apparently not linked to any overall cultural dislocation; metallurgy seems to have spread gradually from one established village to another. In the Benue region the first iron-workers appear to have been immigrants, but even here the salient feature of those settlements which have been excavated is continuity. It may even be possible to generalize, as in the following quotation, from the archaeological evidence about iron in a way that is relevant also for the problem of nomadic intrusion, discussed earlier:

> Rather than far-flung migrations of discrete, tightly-knit tribes, there is widespread diffusion and transfer of ideas, presumably also of people in small

numbers, between related groups . . . The continuous flow of culture as recorded in its material items contrasts most vividly with the hectic peregrinations claimed by some oral traditions.[1]

Sources of iron continued to influence patterns of development throughout our period. The availability of iron-ore in Tibesti may have contributed to the emergence of the Magumi and other groups as the ancestors of the Kanembu and Kanuri peoples. After the exodus, a contributory factor in the decision of the *mais* to stay in their new home of Bornu, rather than returning to Kanem, may have been greater proximity to the sources of iron in the Mandara region; an early reference to the trade in Mandara iron, at Quamoco, a town south of Lake Chad, occurs in a late-sixteenth-century work by Anania. The iron of Dala hill was almost certainly a major element in drawing together the settlement that was to become Kano. Guns, the third innovation, appear only at the very end of our period, and are discussed in more detail in the following volume. It is likely that there has been a tendency for scholars to overemphasize the impact of fire-arms, for even in those armies of the central Sudan which possessed guns, other developments in tactics were of equal or greater significance. In addition, grave problems of maintenance and replacement may have led to a cyclical pattern in which guns were introduced and then gradually petered out, to be reintroduced again later.

Horses, however, 'swallowing the ground with fierceness and rage', occupy the centre of our stage. The standard argument has been that immigrants, particularly nomads, bringing the horse with them, employed the animal with such military and political effect as to create new forms of statecraft in the central Sudan. For the area around Lake Chad, the Zaghawa are cast in this role. For Hausaland, the Bayajidda legend seems to reflect the same development – by introducing the horse, slaying the sacred snake, revolutionizing the water supply, and marrying the queen, Bayajidda clearly appears as herald of a new era.

As we have seen in other respects, there are difficulties about this picture of nomadic or other foreign intrusion; moreover, just as the contribution of fire-arms needs to be reconsidered, so also does the impact of the horse. First, it is evident from the numerous pictures of horses and horse-drawn chariots in Saharan rock art that, during the period before the camel became common in North Africa about the

[1] N. David, 'The archaeological background of Cameroonian history', mimeo. to the Colloque Internationale du CNRS, *Contribution de la recherche ethnologique à l'histoire des civilisations du Cameroun* (Paris, September 1972), 16.

fourth century AD, horses were fairly widely used in the Sahara. Just what purpose they served – fighting, racing, hunting, transport – is not certain; but, whatever their function, there is no reason to doubt that horses reached the Sudan countries in those far-off pre-cameline days. And there is some evidence to suggest that horses established and maintained themselves in the Sudan, quite independently of the wealth and technology of the great medieval states and empires. The scattered references, admittedly few, to wild horses in both the Sahara and the Sudan point to this. More numerous are the accounts of horses in the possession of rather remote Sudanic peoples, some at least of whom were quite divorced from any pattern of nomadic immigration and trans-Saharan communication, quite unmoved by ambition for any elaborate state formation. Some even lived in swampy regions which appear thoroughly unsuitable for horses. Indeed, the central Sudan is ringed to the south with horse-owning peoples – the Yoruba, the Angass and others of the Bauchi plateau, the Bedde of the swamps on the marches between Hausa and Bornu, the Jukun near the Benue, the Ankwe in the same region, the Musgo on the Logone river, the Bagirmi and neighbouring peoples such as the Somrai and the Bua, the inhabitants of Dar Tama east of Wadai. Some, though obviously not all, of these fulfil the conditions of isolation and undeveloped political organization mentioned above. Common characteristics of these horses were that they were small, often of sorry appearance, but sometimes also of special qualities of speed, endurance, resistance and sure-footedness. We have no great time-depth for horses in any of these regions, certainly no evidence to prove that they were already there when the first recorded nomadic encroachments began in the latter part of the first millennium of the Christian era. It is, therefore, possible that these horses derived initially from the stables and herds of the immigrants – stolen perhaps, or bought (about 1400, for example, Kano was engaged in brisk traffic with the Kwararafa, horses going south and slaves north), or having simply run away. Then, in the somewhat unfavourable conditions of their new environment, their size decreased over generations. On the other hand, however, it is equally possible that the small horses of the more southerly Sudanic lands were already there when the nomads arrived, and that they descended from still more ancient progenitors which were themselves small. This seems the more likely of the two alternatives.

If we examine the Bayajidda legend keeping the possibility in mind that horses were already known in Hausaland, we see that the implications of the story are by no means as clear-cut as is sometimes assumed. Briefly, the sequence of events is this: Bayajidda came from the Middle East to Bornu; later, he fled westward, almost alone, coming to Daura in Hausaland; there, an old woman received him, but told him that water could not be drawn until a later day in the week; Bayajidda, despite this, went to the well, killed the snake which guarded it, and drew water; finally he married the queen of Daura. Some versions of the legend say that Bayajidda fled from Bornu on a horse, others that he rode a mule. In all versions, the old woman professed not to know his mount – in some she said it was like an ox, but not an ox, suggesting that (if it was in fact a horse) horses were unknown; but in others she said it was like a horse but not a horse, indicating that she knew quite well what a horse was and that this was not one; or yet again she said that she did not know whether it was a horse or an ox. Her uncertainty may conceivably have arisen simply because Bayajidda arrived at night, and she could not see his mount. In some accounts, the queen comes riding on her own horse; in some, the snake's head resembles that of a horse. Finally, even if Bayajidda is accepted as the pioneer of horses in Hausaland, this does not necessarily help us with the problem of the arrival of the horse in the Sudan generally, since he may have done no more than bring the animal westwards from the Chad region. In the midst of so many uncertainties, a degree of prudent wariness seems called for in interpreting the contribution of Bayajidda to the history of the horse in the central Sudan.

Turning to the Chad region, Yāqūt, writing in the thirteenth century but drawing for his Zaghawa material on al-Muhallabī over two hundred years earlier, said that the Zaghawa had camels and horses. Various details suggest that of the two, camels may have had a special prestige. It was a camel, for instance, that carried the king's food to his dwelling, so sacred a task that, as has been noted, immediate death was the punishment for anyone chancing to meet the animal on its way. The first Muslim missionary in Kanem, Muḥammad b. Mani, received from successive *mais*, with each of whom he read portions of the Koran, gifts of fifty, sixty, eighty and finally a hundred camels. This last number came from Mai Humai, who added also a hundred each of gold coins, silver coins and slaves, the slaves in particular perhaps indicating the growth of trade or tribute relations between the nomads and the settled people further south. In the twelfth century a queen is remembered for her special gift of a hundred camels to each of two princes. Horses also appear, as in this praise-song:

Yours the market of the finest horses, Ume Jilmi [Humai] . . .
Head of a troop of horse today you are the greatest of all horsemen.[1]

The mention of the market may mean that Humai was busy buying horses. If so, did these come from North African suppliers, or possibly from people to the south, or both? Dunama, Ume Jilmi's son and successor, is said to have had 100,000 horses, a number which, even allowing for marked exaggeration, it is unlikely that he or his immediate predecessors brought with them, though some recent secondary sources have dated the arrival of the horse in the region to his reign, about the first half of the twelfth century. In the earlier thirteenth century, Dunama Dibbalemi, conqueror of the Fezzan and opener of the *mune*, had 41,000 horses. He is also known as Dunama b. Salmama, 'Dunama the son of the black', another sign of the immigrants' increasing assimilation to their new setting in the Sudan. Al-Maqrīzī, in the fifteenth century, said this Dunama was a nomad, with an army of 100,000 riders, footmen and carriers together. Dunama, he added, ruled five kings; their (apparently the five kings') horses were small. Among the clay artefacts left by the So, misty predecessors of the Kanuri in the Bornu region, are models of horses and horsemen, but to date these intriguing fragments of evidence is very difficult. The vast disparity in numbers of camels and horses in the reports mentioned above may indicate not that horses predominated but that camels were owned, and known in detail, by the *mais* and their immediate followers, while horses were, at least in part, possessed in numbers by local people, subjects, tributaries or allies, and were counted in the round numbers of hearsay. Fragmentary though the evidence is, we may be glimpsing here not the intrusion of nomadic horsemen, overwhelming local resistance, but the gradual metamorphosis of immigrant cameleers into a cavalry power, drawing partly upon local animals, and, perhaps, modelled on local example. Climate and environment may have contributed to the change, for camels throve much less well in Bornu. Only those actually bred in Kanem could remain in Bornu for long, and then only if they could find special dune-grazing. Military exigency also dictated the change. Camels were essential in near-desert conditions: even in this century, the French had to abandon their post at Djado, near Bilma, having failed with horses alone to check raids by the Tubu and others, the raiders travelling by camel, with led horses whose water and fodder might, if need be, be carried by the camels. The horses were mounted only for the actual raid, being then still fresh. But in more normal

[1] Patterson, *Kanuri songs*, 1.

conditions, the horse was faster and more nimble, and in every way – excluding only its deep natural fear of the camel, which may, however, be overcome by training – superior in battle. Al-Maqrīzī, writing in the fifteenth century of Kanem, said that the army there might reach 100,000 men, including foot, carriers and horse, and he added that the horses were small. This may indicate that they were of some local breed.

A somewhat similar transition, from traditional camels to Sudan-derived horses, seems to have occurred in Aïr. Al-'Umarī, writing in the fourteenth century, said that there were no horses there, the people riding camels only. By the seventeenth century, however, there were evidently some horses in Aïr, for horsemen from the sultan of Aïr came raiding cattle belonging to Fulani who were under the protection of Bornu. About the same time – whether or not as cause and effect is not clear from the sources – a punitive expedition of a thousand horsemen was mounted from Bornu against Aïr. This was successful, and the *mai* of Bornu left behind in Aïr one of his own slaves, four clerics and a thousand horses. This suggests the flow of horses from Bornu to Aïr, just as, perhaps, to Hausaland. In fact, so celebrated did Bornu become for horses that the central Sudanic equivalent of 'carrying coals to Newcastle' is 'to increase the number of horses in Bornu'.

The French scholar, Henri Lhote, wrote: 'The camel is the perfect instrument of the raider, but not that of the conquering warrior, founder of empires. It is the mount of a brigand not a soldier.'[1] The Muslim Arabs in the seventh century, he continued, realized this, and abandoned their camels for horses. The choice, as we have seen, is not so free: terrain, climate, tactics and cost may all help to determine it. Nonetheless, a change of this kind does seem to have come about in the case of the nomads entering the central Sudan. Exactly how it came about is unclear, but we are left again wondering whether the nomadic immigrant or the settled Sudanese contributed more substantially to that central Sudanic civilization the first growth of which it is the purpose of this chapter to describe.

Two further points, size and equipment, deserve mention before the discussion about horses is completed. The best size for a fighting horse depended upon local conditions: it is reported, for example, that the Tubu preferred small ponies, as being much more easily manoeuv-

[1] H. Lhote, 'Le cheval et le chameau dans les peintures et gravures rupestres du Sahara', *Bulletin de l'IFAN*, 1953 (sér. B), 1224.

rable in thick scrub country. In particularly mountainous country, the small, sure-footed local horses were presumably more suitable than larger, clumsier breeds, though the only explicit reference of this kind in a military context concerns the people of Siwa oasis, who used asses on their military expeditions in order to be able to follow otherwise inaccessible paths. On the whole, however, such cases as these are likely to have been exceptions, and the general rule would favour the larger horses. Armoured warriors needed big horses. In nineteenth-century Hausaland, and very probably earlier, such men had to be lifted into the saddle, just as the medieval knights of western Europe. We have a most interesting account of a confrontation between large and small horses, taken from the annals of the Bulala. A Bulala sultan, perhaps he who fought, with varying success, against Aloma of Bornu at the end of our period, waged a campaign against Sultan ʻAlī Dīnār, a local prince ruling north of Lake Fitri. After some inconclusive fighting, the Bulala proposed that the battle be postponed to another day, and waged then on small horses. ʻAlī Dīnār agreed, equipping himself accordingly. But the Bulala, deceitful, came on larger horses after all; and this, coupled evidently with some treachery among ʻAlī Dīnār's own people, enabled the Bulala to drive him out.

For cavalry charges, the small local horses were obviously inadequate: indeed, it has been suggested that animals commemorated in the Saharan rock art, from which Sudanic horses – if the foregoing argument be correct – descended, drew light chariots because they were too small to carry a rider at all. Larger varieties of horse subsequently became established in the Sudan. Bornu and Mandara/Marwa, for example, were outstanding breeding centres. To launch these varieties, and thereafter to renew them from time to time, imports of horses from the north were necessary. Control of such import opportunities may have been a main factor explaining the initial success of the Bulala, in the fourteenth century, against the legitimate dynasty in Kanem:

> they had three hundred and thirty-three markets, and became very powerful: they had many horses whereas the Saifawa had few.[1]

Leo Africanus's account of Gaoga, in the sixteenth century, may confirm this, if the identification of Gaoga with the Bulala is correct. But even if it is not – and we have seen that there is more than one other alternative – Leo's description of imported horses bought from white

[1] Palmer, *Sudanese memoirs*, II, 39.

merchants remains significant. Of Bornu itself, Leo said that the king had 3,000 horse in continual readiness, and a huge number of foot. His realm having once been wasted by an invading infantry army, he had sent for the merchants of Barbary to bring him a great store of horses, for which he paid fifteen or even twenty slaves per head. Leo, however, told no heroic tale of the knights of Bornu then leading an army of vengeance: instead there were annual slave-raids, for the rather pedestrian purpose of paying the Barbary merchants. In the nineteenth century, when more detailed information becomes available about the fate of horses imported into the Sudan, it is lamentably evident that the risks of serious illness and death were great. Health conditions can hardly have been better in earlier centuries, and we may imagine that the trans-Saharan horse trade was an expensive, luxury affair, contributing a good deal less to the maintenance of the horse population of the Sudan countries than has sometimes been imagined.

Secondly, equipment was also needed. It was characteristic of some of the local horse-owning peoples with the small breeds, that they had little or no harness for their horses. Such people rode bareback, perhaps with a bridle but with no bit. In order to give themselves a firmer seat, as before a raid, they cut their horses' backs until the blood flowed, and thus cemented themselves on. Absence of harness did not necessarily reduce the rider's control over his mount: some recent descriptions speak of horses being as obedient as dogs. But it would leave him at a serious disadvantage in the shock of mounted mêlée.

THE PENETRATION OF ISLAM

The first establishment of Islam in the central Sudan occurred at the beginning of our period, with the conversion of the *mais* of Kanem. Thereafter the faith spread gradually, very slowly and with periods of retraction, but on the whole with remarkable persistence. The exodus carried Islam from Kanem to Bornu. The Bulala, who drove the royal court from Kanem, may in the fourteenth century perhaps have been at first the champions of pagan reaction againt encroaching Islam, but, whether or not this is correct, they were evidently serious Muslims by the time Aloma waged war upon them at the end of our period. The arrival of the royal court in Bornu prepared the way for the penetration of Islam into Hausaland from the east. It had already reached Kano and Katsina, at least, from the west earlier in the fourteenth century. Aïr became a Muslim state somewhat later. Bagirmi was one in the sixteenth century, and it was partly through inspiration drawn from Bagirmi that 'Abd al-Karīm, towards the end of that century or early in the next, was able to weld Wadai into a state with at least a Muslim government. In Mandara, at the end of our period, Aloma intervened to place a protégé of his, from the Mandaran ruling family, upon the throne, and it is likely that adoption of Islam was part of the price for such support. It may be that it was also in the time of Aloma that the Tubu adopted Islam.

This wide expansion raises many interesting questions. Who was it that brought Islam to the central Sudan, implementing the missionary function? What was it that the peoples of the central Sudan found most attractive in the new religion? What was it – at least in the sphere of secular history, though not of theology – that was fundamentally new in the contribution of Islam to the central Sudan? And how was the faith maintained upon such an out-of-the-way frontier of the Muslim world?

It has already been suggested, in the earlier discussion of trade, that the simple equation of the North African or Saharan merchant with the pioneer Muslim, the *de facto* missionary, fills in only a part of the total picture. There was also a clerical contribution, provided by men for whom their faith was also their calling, their vocation. The greatest of these for the central Sudan during our period was al-Maghīlī, who has already been discussed in the context of Hausaland and more particularly Kano. In order further to elaborate the clerical half of the picture, consideration should be given to the role of the Sharifs.

The Sharif, or descendant of the Prophet Muḥammad through his daughter Fāṭima, has from the earliest times been an active figure in the expansion of Islam in Africa. His religious authority, as guardian of Islamic orthodoxy, was indubitable. Al-Maghīlī was perhaps the first to introduce the theme of apocalyptic expectancy into the central and western Sudan; some traditions say that the *mujaddid* ('renewer'), who would appear once in each century, must be a Sharif. The Sharif performed a variety of clerical functions, such as healing, divining and praying; and quite naturally some of his special qualities came to parallel, in the untutored popular mind, traditional local functions. Among the *bori* spirits of the Hausa, for example, the barber Wanzaamii is called 'unacknowledged Sharif', because like a Sharif the barber, though he is less expert, practises magic.

The financial position of the Sharif was strengthened by the provision in the Koran (viii. 41) that, of booty taken by the Muslims,

> the fifth of it is God's, and the Messenger's,
> and the near kinsman's, and the orphans',
> and for the needy, and the traveller,
> if you believe in God.

The possible beneficiaries listed here are understood to include Sharifs, and, since booty was often an important element of state revenue, a Sharif – who might also qualify as a needy traveller – might hope to be hospitably received and rewarded by any pious ruler. Al-Maghīlī, in his advice to Rumfa of Kano, stressed the state's obligation of generosity to Sharifs.

Such economic privileges and religious authority greatly enhanced the mobility of the Sharifs, who, distinguished by their green turbans, honoured on special occasions by the green banner of the Prophet, might travel with relative impunity over long distances, and sometimes through otherwise inhospitable regions. Coming often as men of religion, though some Sharifs were also traders in the ordinary way, protected by the wrath of God, supported by the alms of God-fearing men, the Sharifs helped to confirm the faith on even the furthest limits of the Muslim world. Their entry into the ranks of the influential and privileged in Muslim societies in Africa was assured. Leo, speaking of Gaoga, observed that while all learned men were respected there, Sharifs were particularly highly esteemed. There are many references, from many different areas – for example, in sixteenth-century Songhay under the *askiyas* – to the Sharifs as a group comparable to the '*ulamā*' or clerics, to the pilgrims, and to the judges and lawyers. Several tribes in the central Sudan area claim a corporate Sharifian character: the Awlād Sara and the Awlād Muharib, two of the wealthiest and most influential nomad Shuwa groups in Bornu, are counted as Sharifs. Abū Zayd, the legendary folk-hero of the Shuwa and others, who may perhaps be traced back to the Banū Hilāl in the eleventh century, boasted that his mother was a Sharif. In several cases, Sharifian descent was part of a dynasty's title to rule. This was so with the Fatimid dynasty, ruling in North Africa just as our period opened; they indeed sought to extend the Koranic provision for Sharifs, and to make it one of the foundations of their tax system. The Awlād Muḥammad, ruling the Fezzan from the sixteenth century until the nineteenth, were descended from a Sharif of Fez who stopped there while on pilgrimage, and established a new capital there, Murzuq. Zawīla, the leading town of the Fezzan when our period began, had also had important Sharifian connections: it was known as the 'town of the Sharifs'; ancient, lofty edifices nearby were remembered in the nineteenth century as the tombs of Sharifs who had fallen in battle against the infidel. And it was customary for the chief wife of the sultan of the Fezzan to be a Sharif from Zawīla or Wadan. Other Sharifs from north-west Africa are said to have settled in Qatrun, the southernmost oasis of the Fezzan, in the sixteenth century; and some Tripolitanian Sharifs may have moved on to Tibesti from Murzuq – but these did not become rulers. Even the Saifawa dynasty of Bornu boasted, if not precisely a Sharifian origin, at least one from the Quraysh, the tribe of the Prophet. When the *mai* of Bornu wrote to Cairo late in the fourteenth century complaining about the depredations and slave-raiding of certain Arabs from the eastern Sudan, he spoke of his Quraysh derivation from Sayf b. Dhī Yazan. In fact, as scholars in Cairo remarked, this derivation is not Quraysh, but Himyar. The same confusion continued at the end of our period, when Ibn Fartuwa exclaimed of Aloma,

Truly his descent is traced back to the Kuraish and such is not the case with many people . . . Alas! every ruler is inferior to these chiefs since they are of the tribe of Kuraish descended from Himyar.[1]

Most important of all for the history of Africa south of the Sahara were the Sharifian pretensions of the 'Alawī dynasty of Morocco, which were used at the end of our period to justify the Moroccan conquest of Songhay. The sultan, al-Manṣūr, wrote to the notables – Sharifs among them – of Fez in 1591, rejoicing in the conquest:

Praise God . . . who had made illustrious the Qurayshite dynasty among all the dynasties and in a fashion still more special this generous, holy, prophetic, Fatimid and 'Alawī family! By Him has triumphed the brilliant sword of Hashim, who has conquered the yellow infidel as the black infidel of the Sudan. By the prophetic lights of the caliphate which radiate from this dynasty, He has brought out of the night peoples where the crow has croaked since the epoch of Ham, He has fulfilled the noble prayer which this dynasty addressed to Him in uniting the race of Shem to the race of Ham.[2]

With so many advantages associated with the status of Sharif, it is not surprising that, while many were born to this greatness, others achieved it, or had it thrust upon them. When al-Maghīlī left Kano about 1502, most of his followers remained behind, and they and their descendants came to be regarded as Sharifs, though they were, in one chronicler's opinion at least, only ordinary Arabs. An early English

[1] Palmer, *Sudanese memoirs*, I, 16, 69.

[2] H. de Castries, 'La conquête du Soudan par El-Mansour, 1591', *Hespéris*, 1923, 3, 483.

translation of this story is faulty, but the fault may perhaps accurately reflect someone's earnest endeavour to explain the meaning of the Hausa *sharifai* to the translator:

The rest remained and continued to perform great deeds in Kano. Their descendants are found [and] known in Kano until to-day, till people called them seraphs, but surely they were not seraphs, they were just Arabs.[1]

It has been observed that the religious activities of Sharifs were often assimilated, in public opinion, to those of traditional practitioners of supernatural arts. This side of the Muslim cleric's image in the Sudan is too often overlooked in studies of the history of Islam in black Africa, in favour of such matters as literacy. But neglect of more purely religious elements, whether these verge towards magic and superstition, or aspire to the most fervent piety, obscures the fact that it was precisely these elements which, in many cases, constituted the main initial appeal of Islam in non-Muslim eyes in the Sudan countries. Many skills may be traced – in the interpretation of dreams, in healing by faith, in divining the future – but underpinning all was, quite simply, belief in the power of prayer. It is here that we must first seek an understanding of how the religion took root in black Africa, influencing its new surroundings and being influenced by them.

Muslim prayer comprises two major forms: *ṣalāt*, formally regulated, often with great strictness, in the law; and *du'a*, spontaneous prayer offered when and how the worshipper chooses. The special litanies and recitations of the brotherhoods lie somewhat between the two, but had hardly become important in the central Sudan before the end of our period. Some accounts associate the arrival of organized Sufism, and of the Qādiriyya brotherhood in particular, with the work of al-Maghīlī, about 1500, but the most recent studies of his writings have revealed little sign of his explicit concern with such matters.

The principal varieties of the *ṣalāt* are the five daily prayers, required of every believer, and the major congregational prayers – the Friday prayer, and the festival prayers at the end of Ramadan and at the time of the Pilgrimage sacrifice. The contribution of prayer to social discipline is particularly evident here. In Maliki law, the dominant rite throughout the central and western Sudan, even the daily prayers are twenty-seven times better if said in congregation, and the Friday and festival prayers are by definition congregational. The impact of such prayer, bringing even the newest converts under a strict routine, has

[1] Rattray, *Hausa folk-lore*, I, 14.

been remarked since the earliest days of Islam, and the experience of the Arabians in the seventh century was reflected again and again, though often in muted tones, in the Sudan countries as elsewhere. One main reason for the suspicion which settled Muslims felt about the religion of nomads was the irregularity of the latter in their prayers: the overuse of *tayammum* (ablution with sand), even when water was available; the absence of cathedral-mosques suitable for the Friday prayer; the interruptions of the stock-keeper's responsibilities – the pastoral Fulani, for example, might have to miss the dawn prayer. Among settled people, the times and practices of the required prayers determined the shape of the day. Congregational prayer, as well as reinforcing social discipline, early became a significant part of the pomp and circumstance of the state. Aisa, the woman who, according to some accounts, ruled Bornu for seven years before Aloma ascended the throne, had in two ways signified her authority: by going to war, and by attending the Friday prayers with the court officials. In some areas, such prayers were the only occasions on which the ruler appeared to his subjects, most especially on the festivals when the prayers were said in the open, outside the town, and worshippers went and returned in sometimes splendid processions. Should the ruler, perhaps through illness, be unable to take his normal part in these ceremonies, public anxiety might find his absence an evil omen. The sermon of the Friday prayer was given in the name of the locally recognized rulers. Ceremonial prayer also played a more practical part in politics. The ruler might receive important visitors on these occasions; proclamations were read; matters of general policy, for instance plans for an expedition, might be discussed and resolved; private citizens might petition the ruler. Such gatherings allowed the ruler to keep an eye on his subordinate officers, for even those in relatively distant places might be expected, unless disobedient, to visit the capital for the festivals. Elections sometimes took place, and revolutions, too.

In times of special emergency, variations were allowed. The seriously ill, for example, might pray by signs; or those in grave danger might observe the shortened *ṣalāt al-khawf*, the prayer in time of fear. Special forms of *ṣalāt* were available for communal crises, such as the *ṣalāt al-istisqā'*, the prayer for rain; while yet others, such as the unusually pious prayers of the night, and the *ṣalat al-istikhāra*, the prayer for divine guidance, served more individual needs. *Ṣalāt* of this kind was very close to *du'a*. Here prayer performed, not so much a disciplinary or a ceremonial function, as an instrumental one: it was directed towards the accomplishment of a specific purpose, bringing rain, healing the sick, overthrowing enemies, or whatever might have been the matter in hand. Such prayer, beseeching God's protection for travellers, was of special relevance in the light of the dependence of the central Sudan, and not in religious affairs only, on trans-Saharan links for the maintenance of its characteristic civilization. Legends of the demon-haunted desert on the highway from Tripoli to Bornu, which have survived until this century and which earlier travellers such as Ibn Baṭṭūṭa reported, point to a vivid awareness of the practical dangers of the desert, and to the need for supernatural support on the crossing. The prayers of pilgrims were regarded as particularly potent, and even caravans on purely secular errands were often glad to welcome such companions. It has already been noticed how a larger caravan numbered both muezzin and *imām* amongst its officials, and how the caravan camp, having so often along the way resembled a bustling market, or in moments of peril an embattled laager, might at the end become a great mosque of grateful people. Within the Sudan countries also, prayer protected travellers, and thus contributed everywhere to the extraordinary mobility of Muslims. Folklore has preserved the memory of such things. A Hausa tale, to give but one illustration, tells of a man renowned in prayer who prostrated himself, spat on his staff, and struck the waters of a river, which then parted for him to cross.

Prayers for rain, also, had an obvious local relevance throughout the central Sahara and Sudan. Prayer for purposes of divination was widely employed. Once in the sixteenth century a prince of the blood royal in Bornu – there is doubt whether the fugitive was Aloma, or his grandfather Idrīs Katagarmabe – had to flee for a time into Kanem, after such enquiry had revealed him as a threat to the throne. The reigning *mai*

> assembled the learned men of Birni Gazargamu, and sent them apart for contemplation and divination. They sought guidance, and finally all told Ali Gaji Zeinami what they saw. They said, 'In this city there is a Sultan's son, who will one day become our Sultan.'[1]

Prayer of this kind, for divination or other specific purposes, often involved going into spiritual retreat and isolation (*khalwa*), perhaps for as long as forty days. Instrumental prayer, though provided by Muslims, needed not always to be for Muslims, and was sometimes the reason for a pagan community's accepting or even inviting a Muslim cleric. Successful prayer, whether for rain or healing or victory or any other

[1] Palmer, *Sudanese memoirs*, II, 42.

specific need, might open the door for conversion and further Muslim penetration of a new area.

Maḥrams, or letters of privilege, show how highly the local rulers valued the service of prayer. One *maḥram* exempts the descendants of the *imām*, 'Abdullāh Dili, from military service and jihad, from the responsibility for entertaining chiefs and from other customary tasks, and from fines – a useful list of some of the duties which an ordinary citizen might owe the state – having only the obligation to pray. Imam 'Abdullāh probably lived about 1200, in Kanem. Another suggestive *maḥram*, in favour of the Fulani *gabidâma* and his descendants, was originally issued by 'Alī Gaji Dunamami, towards the end of the fifteenth century. The beneficiaries of this *maḥram* were exempt from taxation and other customary obligations, for the sake of their *du'a*. The title *gabidâma* may point to some connection with Kebbi, which was at this time on the eve of its rise to great-power status, first in conjunction with the expansion of Songhay towards the east, and later as a bulwark against that expansion. Fulani may have been moving eastwards from Kebbi into Bornu, and the Bornu authorities were perhaps using these people as a lever to enhance their own influence in Hausaland. Anania, at the end of our period, observed how North Africans served as *dottori* (clerics) in Bornu, and were very well paid, as was the case, he added, everywhere in the Sudan, where clerics were rare. Clerics have sometimes shown, at least according to later reports, a certain reluctance to accept local wives, since these would entitle the new in-laws to free prayers and other religious services. Economic and other benefits in return for religious support, in the Sudan context, is paralleled in medieval Europe by *frankalmoign*; an important difference, however, is that in the central Sudan grants of land as such seem to have been much less important than tax and other benefits.

While such instrumental prayer was clearly a valuable adjunct to any ruler's armoury, the fact that it might occasionally be turned against him illustrates the two-edged nature of Islam, as a weapon of statecraft, of immense practical significance, but at the same time introducing at least the possibility of an appeal beyond the king to God. The disastrous defeats which attended the first efforts of the *mais* of Kanem to move into Bornu in the later fourteenth century were attributed to the curse of a woman – apparently not a cleric – whom a *mai* had wronged. The fall of Songhay, and the consequent rise of Katsina, were derived according to some accounts from the curse of al-Maghīlī, aggrieved at Songhay's lack of support for him. An admirably terse example is the passage about the Sharif 'Abd al-Karīm, a Muslim revolutionary in Wadai in the early seventeenth century:

> Then the Sultan of the Tunjur gave him his daughter to wed, and said 'pray God for me'.
> But he prayed on his own behalf, and so the Sultan died, but the Sharifs rule Wadai till now.[1]

The final climax of the inherent confrontation between Islam and Sudanic kingship came with the jihad of Usuman dan Fodio, in the nineteenth century, but the seeds of tension were already becoming visible in our period.

There were, of course, innumerable examples of prayer as an act of piety and humble devotion. The preceding discussion has concentrated on the more utilitarian aspects of prayer, its disciplinary, ceremonial and most of all its instrumental functions, not because these are intrinsically the more important, but because they did have a greater significance in the practical, outward evolution of statecraft and society in the central Sudan.

Islam was itself an innovation of the most profound importance in the central Sudan. In some respects this newness appeared in connection with prayer, although the possible assimilation of such Muslim religious observances to local ways of understanding has already been remarked upon. Another aspect of Islam was of indubitable strangeness, and was to have far-reaching consequences. This was literacy. A pair of anthropologists, looking recently at the effects of literacy, and basing their generalizations chiefly upon evidence drawn from ancient Greece, suggest that writing down some of the main elements in the cultural tradition of a particular society

> brought about an awareness of two things: of the past as different from the present; and of the inherent inconsistencies in the picture of life as it was inherited by the individual from the cultural tradition in its recorded form.[2]

Such tension had not arisen in a society employing only oral tradition, for there 'structural amnesia' operated to bring the past more closely into line with the present: that is to say, those elements of the past which ceased to be relevant for an understanding of contemporary society were forgotten; the record of the past, as preserved in living memory, being constantly remodelled in order to keep it closely meshed with the present. The double awareness aroused by literacy, on the

[1] Ibid. II, 32.

[2] J. Goody, ed., *Literacy in traditional societies* (Cambridge, 1968), 56.

contrary, led to 'scepticism, not only about the legendary past, but about received ideas about the universe as a whole'. Individuals were 'impelled to a much more conscious, comparative and critical, attitude to the accepted world picture, and notably to the notions of God, the universe and the past'. These particular aspects of the Greek experience are markedly absent from Muslim development in the central Sudan, and indeed throughout all black Africa. Several reasons, according to the anthropologists' argument, explain why the effect of Muslim literacy has been different: its relatively narrower distribution, the continuation of teaching methods more suited to an oral than to a literary tradition, concentration upon a holy book in a foreign language (as Arabic was for most, though admittedly not all, in the central Sudan), but most of all the close association between literacy and Islam as an exclusive, all-embracing religion. 'It is above all the predominantly religious character of literacy that, here as elsewhere, prevented the medium from fulfilling its promise.'[1]

This is perhaps an unnecessarily gloomy conclusion. The central Sudan in the period from 1050 to 1600 was not situated, as ancient Greece had been, at a crossroads of the civilized world. Rather it was perched, somewhat precariously, at the far end of perilous routes. The primary theme of the area and period is, as has been suggested throughout this chapter, the pattern of penetration, carrying ideas, organizations and people across the Sahara and further and further afield, but always with one eye over the shoulder lest the lines of communication become overextended and break. Literacy made its most important contribution just at this point, a guarantee that essential lifelines with the heritage of the Muslim heartlands would not be severed. A kind of holding operation took priority.

The anthropologists lamented that Muslim black Africa, hog-tied by religion, restricted the 'explosive potentialities' of literacy to results far 'less radical' than obtained elsewhere. Yet, taking a longer view, it is clear that Muslim literacy did have a dramatic impact. Aloma, at the very end of our period, was one of the first rulers in the central Sudan to show the double awareness of which the anthropologists speak: he seems to have known well enough that the past, of the great days of Islam, was vastly different from the present, of corrupt and mixed Muslim practice, which he saw around him; and, similarly, he knew that any individual's experience in the central Sudan in his day would have been largely inconsistent with the recorded cultural

[1] Ibid. 241.

traditions of Islam. Turning to still later periods, awareness of these tensions between past and present became even more compelling for men such as Usuman dan Fodio. The reaction of the concerned Muslim of the central Sudan, however, was in a sense the mirror image of that found in ancient Greece: the Greeks used the present to refine their understanding of the past, while in the central Sudan it was the past – and the ideals of Islam there enshrined – that was used to reform and re-order the present.

One further point may be made about literacy before education in the narrower sense is discussed. The anthropologists stress its association with 'the notion of the world of knowledge as transcending political units'. This was of critical importance in black Africa, though Muslims there would have spoken of the authority of God and His law – equally given universality of application by its expression in written form – rather than of 'the world of knowledge'. The 'transcending of political units' is also reproduced in black Africa, where it has taken two forms: one, and usually first, the creation of larger states incorporating various smaller traditional units, all of which recognize, more or less, even if only in the payment of tax or tribute, that Islam has superior claims; and secondly, the appeal, often revolutionary, of the reformers to the obedience demanded by God, overriding that of even these larger states, even of those among them that patronized these very reformers.

Muslim education, throughout black Africa, began with the simple Koranic school, often no more than a group of children on the porch of their teacher's house during the rainy season, or around a bonfire at dawn and dusk during the dry one. The pupil's essential equipment was his writing board, on which were written portions of the Koran for him to memorize, or, as it might be in the case of longer passages, simply to learn to read fluently. A song about Humai, the eleventh-century ruler of Kanem, describes him thus:

> Whose writing slate is made of 'kabwi' wood:
> At night [a warrior] on a coal-black horse;
> but when day dawns he [is to be seen] with his Koran in his hand.[1]

The board became a popular simile: a Shuwa love-song likens the shoulders of a pretty girl to the board of the Prophet Moses, from which he said his prayers. The standard of education might be very low, pupils learning to recite, in barbaric accent and without understanding,

[1] Patterson, *Kanuri songs*, 3.

a few snatches of the Koran. The water with which the writing was washed from the slates might be drunk – perhaps a literal fulfilment of the verse of the Prophet Jeremiah, 'Thy words were found, and I did eat them' – or used otherwise as medicine.

Pupils often performed menial tasks, domestic or on the farm, for their teacher. The story of the Tubu schoolboy Issa shows what this might involve. Issa feared to go away, even to a more celebrated teacher, lest he should have to guard the well at watering-time, draw water, fill the waterskins, water the calves, take the animals to pasture and have no time to study all the rainy season and part of the dry. Persuaded at last to go, Issa stayed only a week; then he stole a camel, covered two days' journey in a single night, and came home. Although the system was open to occasional abuse, as Issa evidently thought, it often worked well, and had the advantages that even a student from a poor family could, so to speak, earn his way, and that pupils were prepared for that peasant or pastoral life which, for most, was the only opportunity open to them. The Koranic schools were closely integrated with the local communities, and often served purposes much like those of the initiation schools of traditional pagan societies. A glimpse of the Koranic school's place in society comes from Ghadames in 1610. The Ottoman commander from Tunis was advancing upon the city, which had refused his request for slaves and other tribute. The Ghadamsi children, while their parents prepared to resist, paraded through the streets and mosques, carrying their slates and calling upon God to help them.

Beyond memorization of the Koran was the second main sphere of the traditional Islamic curriculum, in which the student learnt the Arabic language, and went on to work with subjects such as grammar, rhetoric, jurisprudence, logic, Koranic commentary, the traditions of the Prophet and the sources of the law. Such studies were usually centred on particular books. Each book would be read, sometimes even memorized; commentaries on the book would be examined; and the chain of authorities, from the original author or first commentator down to the student's present teacher, would be learnt. After mastering each book, or subject, the student received from his teacher an *ijāẓa*, or licence, indicating that the student himself was now competent to teach that subject to others.

The basic pattern in both stages, the memorization of the Koran and advanced studies, was one of master-seeking, the pupil moving from one teacher to another, from one place to another. Particularly for younger pupils, teachers might be their own relatives – a father, an uncle, an elder brother. But even for the young it was generally felt better to leave home. A Bornu song tells of a mother sending her son away to study, for even though his father is a cleric, a child with its mother cannot study. Teachers also moved about, sometimes with their pupils. In many cases, the pioneer Muslim missionary in any particular area is remembered primarily as a teacher. One account of al-Maghīlī's visit to Hausaland, for example, tells how he wrote out the Koran for them himself from memory, having brought no books with him, and how he taught them the rules of the faith. He then went on to Katsina, to perform a similar function, though in this case it was not he himself who did the writing. Because of this, Katsina was ever after – so the account runs – inferior to Kano in religious scholarship, just as the fact that al-Maghīlī – according again to this tradition – came from Bornu bringing no books with him meant that anyone from Kano wishing to acquire the best education should go to Bornu, where he might remain or whence he might return. These tales, semi-legendary as they clearly are, do point to an early dependence of Hausaland upon Bornu in matters of religious learning, and it is interesting that the Hausa words for 'reading' and 'writing' both derive from Kanuri. The Pilgrimage helped immensely by providing a framework for pupil and teacher mobility over a vast area.

Loyalties established betweeen teacher and pupil were often close and lasting, and where the individuals on both sides were, or became, persons of authority, such connections might be very influential. A Hausa folktale tells of a teacher who prayed for the special wishes of his four pupils: one for a lovely wife, one for wealth, one for high office and one for wisdom. Later, the teacher visited them all, and found the pupil who had been blessed with wisdom surrounded by clerics learning from him. When the visitor arrived, these students left, and the visitor and his former pupil talked all through the night. This simple story accurately illustrates a strong social bond between Muslims in the central Sudan.

The exchange between the heartlands of the Muslim world and its outlying Sudanic provinces was always two-way: not only did pioneers venture from the heartlands outwards, but Sudanese themselves visited the Holy Lands. The Pilgrimage was the chief magnet drawing men and women towards the central shrines of the faith. The Pilgrimage is, like the prayer, one of the five pillars of Islam, required of every Muslim provided that certain conditions of road safety, health and the like are fulfilled. There is a remarkable tradition of royal pilgrimages from the Lake Chad region. The first Muslim king of the Saifawa line, Humai, apparently died in Egypt in the eleventh century, and the likely presumption is that he was on Pilgrimage. His son and successor, Dunama b. Humai, ruling probably in the early twelfth century, went three times on Pilgrimage. According to the *Diwan*, on each of the first two occasions he left 300 slaves in Egypt; and, when he came a third time, the people of Egypt began to fear lest he take their country from them. So they opened a sea-cock in his ship, and he drowned. This strange story is not so implausible as at first it seems. We have a number of similar instances of the establishment, by travelling rulers, of slave colonies along the way (see Volume 4, pp. 94–5), and some of these may well have had political implications, if not a directly political intent. And in Egypt the political situation, in those days of late Fatimid decline and disorder, in which Sudanese slave troops often played some grim part, was such as to engender suspicion and violence (see p. 74). The ill-fated ship may have been making from ʿAydhāb to Jedda, for this was the major Pilgrimage route at that time and until the mid thirteenth century, when the recession of the Crusades and the decline of the gold-mining in the ʿAydhāb region made the overland route through Sinai preferable. In the mid thirteenth century, people from Kanem passing through Cairo on their way to Mecca gave money to a judge, Ibn Rashiq, who established a school and taught in it. This establishment was also a hostel where Kanemi travellers might stay. There is no indication, however, that the *mai* was directly involved in this project. The letter which the *mai*, late in the fourteenth century, addressed to the Mamluk sultan in Cairo, refers to two preceding *mais* in that century as pilgrims. Aloma renewed the tradition, which flourished particularly in the seventeenth and eighteenth centuries. Bello of Sokoto, in the nineteenth century a severe critic of the way in which Islam was practised in Bornu, nevertheless admitted that the earlier rulers had been good and devout Muslims, many among them pilgrims.

Al-Yaʿqūbī, in the ninth century, mentioned Zawīlan pilgrims. Al-Gharnāṭī, in the twelfth – reading Zawīla for his Zaylaʿ, a seaport and not in the Sudan – lauds the Zawīlans as the most virtuous of the Sudan peoples, praying, fasting, making the Pilgrimage each year on foot. Several rulers of Aïr in our period bore the title *al-ḥājj* ('the pilgrim'), including one unfortunate who ruled for twenty years and was then killed by his subjects. Hausaland stands in curious contrast, for scarcely a ruler there went on Pilgrimage. The Kano Chronicle mentions one *sarki*, al-Hajji, in the mid seventeenth century, who may have been a pilgrim. The Chronicle adds drily that he was deposed in under nine months, for reasons which the chronicler has forgotten. Conceivably he then sought consolation in Pilgrimage. Further west again, in Mali, we come once more upon a strong sequence of royal pilgrimages, but these lie outside our area.

It is difficult to see why Hausa rulers should have been so much more reluctant to set out for Mecca than were their contemporaries in Kanem, Bornu, Aïr, Mali or elsewhere. Perhaps part of the explanation lies in the fact that Islam in Hausaland was from the beginning represented essentially by foreigners – Fulani, Wangarawa, Kanembu and Kanuri – and thus never achieved that degree of identification with the kingship which was realized in Bornu/Kanem and in the medieval Mande world.

Many clerics also went on the Pilgrimage, and these men were of particular importance in maintaining Islamic connections throughout the Sudan, since they often visited, and sometimes settled in, towns away from their home districts. The Timbuktu chronicles mention several learned men from the west who travelled from town to town in Hausaland on their way home. One, a pupil of al-Maghīlī, became *qāḍī* in Katsina, and stayed there until his death. But, whereas rulers very rarely set out for Arabia without the intention of returning home, clerics sometimes did: for them, the religious attractions of life in the Hejaz, or the scholarly intensity of Cairo, might be more powerful than the ties of home. Hence we find sometimes that the local authorities took measures to prevent the loss of valuable and skilled personnel. One account of the Wangarawa pioneers of Islam in Kano says that they intended to perform the Pilgrimage, but were enabled to leave Mali only by a miracle, so determined was the ruler there to keep them. And again, repeated appeals by the Sarkin Kano were needed to prevent them from going on from his city. We are even told that the *qāḍī* of Timbuktu once prevented another cleric from taking his family with him on Pilgrimage, knowing that if he did he would never come back. Many commoners went also, swept up in the wake of the great, or by their own choosing. Hornemann, approaching the Fezzan, met such a pilgrim; and, though this encounter occurred about 1800, the circumstances are almost timeless within the Muslim era in Africa:

> This man (as he himself told me), was above sixty years old; and this was his third voyage from Fez to Mecca, without possessing the least means of

accommodation for the journey; without preparation of food for his subsistence; nay even without water, excepting what commiseration and the esteem in which his pilgrimage was held, might procure for him, from the charity and regard of travellers better provided in the caravan.[1]

The establishment of slave colonies or settlements by passing pilgrims, and the way in which clerical pilgrims might stop here or there along the way to study, to teach, even to accept official appointments, have already been mentioned. People sometimes stopped also for weariness. The town of Damasak in Bornu is said to take its name from a phrase meaning 'we are tired', and to have been founded by pilgrims returning from Mecca. The etymology is dubious, but the event which it purports to represent is likely to have happened frequently. In the mid fifteenth century, when some Fulani passed through Hausaland towards Bornu, introducing some religious sciences previously unknown in Hausaland, they left behind a few men in Hausaland, 'together with some slaves and people who were tired of journeying'. We are not told, however, whether those who went on were on Pilgrimage.

Sometimes such pilgrim settlements were involved in the early stages of state formation. This occurred in Bagirmi, where, according to one account, a Fulani cleric, Ould Dédé, set off on Pilgrimage, following his father who had preceded him some years before. Coming to the Bagirmi region, he found that his father, already on his way home, had died there and been buried. The son decided to go no further, but stopped and founded Bidderi, which soon became an important religious centre. This may have been round about 1500, and the Fulani, thus established, joined with other groups as founders of Bagirmi. Another story, which links the Pilgrimage with developments in statecraft in a different way, concerns 'Abd al-Karīm (sometimes called Ṣāliḥ), who early in the seventeenth century took power in the Wadai region. It is said that he met some Muslims from Sennar while they were on Pilgrimage, and returned with them to their country. Distressed by the wickedness which he found there, he journeyed further, and thus came to Wadai. It is difficult, in the Sudan countries at this early time, to be sure how far these details are historically accurate. That they are not intrinsically improbable, at least in so far as the significance of the Pilgrimage is concerned, is suggested by the way in which the Fatimid movement was launched in North Africa in the tenth century. Abū Abdullāh, who had come to Mecca with some Yemeni pilgrims, met

[1] F. Hornemann, 'Journal', *Proceedings of the Association for promoting the discovery of the interior parts of Africa* (London, 1810; reprinted London, 1967), II, 108.

there notables from the Kutama tribe; he returned with them to North Africa, and won them over to the Fatimid cause, with incalculable consequences for the subsequent history of the Muslim world.

The Pilgrimage, together with contact particularly in Cairo, enhanced the authority and reputation of all who undertook it. This was true in terms of political prestige, of serious scholarship and of the popular practice of Islam. In Hausaland, every pilgrim was believed to have the power to prepare charms, whether to cure or to curse, and repeated pilgrimages enhanced the potency of these preparations. A curious legend of the *mai* of Bornu illustrates the importance of sanction or approval from the Islamic heartlands: when the propriety of a certain act was disputed at the court of Bornu, the *mai* stretched out his hand in the direction of Cairo, and miraculously clutched exactly the book from the al-Azhar mosque which resolved the controversy. The point at issue was whether it was right to exhume a corpse in order to cut off the hand, suggesting perhaps a rather macabre side to some of the supernatural procedures of the Bornu clerics at that time, in the mid seventeenth century. The al-Azhar volume disapproved.

The benefits of Pilgrimage were not obtained without a high price in danger and discomfort. Several rulers who died on Pilgrimage have already been mentioned; many more were those lesser men who fell and have no memorial. Illness, particularly epidemics, was much dreaded. Perhaps the Pilgrimage figure, Malam Alhaji, in the *bori* or spirit-possession dances of the Hausa, illustrate the danger to health:

> Learned man and pilgrim. Pretends to be old and shaky, and to be counting beads with his right hand while reading a book in his left. He walks bent double, and with a crutch, coughing weakly all the time.[1]

Pilgrims, particularly in desert country, might stray and die. Waldede, an outstanding Fulani cleric active in Bornu and Bagirmi about 1600, is said to have been born when his mother was on Pilgrimage; she lost her way, and dying of thirst, gave birth to the child, who was found soon after.[2] The sanctity of the pilgrim, often a safeguard, did not entirely protect him from violence and molestation, even – or perhaps particularly – within Arabia. In 1453, the Pilgrimage caravan returning to Cairo suffered great losses through floods, the death of camels, theft

[1] A. J. N. Tremearne, *Hausa superstitions and customs* (London, 1913), 534; he goes on to say that Malam Alhaji is present at all marriages within the *bori* group.

[2] E. J. Arnett, *The rise of the Sokoto Fulani: being a paraphrase and in some parts a translation of the Infaku'l Maisuri of Sultan Mohammed Bello* (n.p., n.d. [1922]), 5. Waldede is perhaps to be identified with the Ould Dédé mentioned above, though the dates appear to conflict. [See also vol. 4, ch. 2, 108–9.]

and kidnapping. The entire Takrur section – people from the western Sudan, and perhaps also from our area – was captured by the Arabs, being taken by surprise and unorganized, and none returned. The North African pilgrims, on the other hand, fought back, and took some Arab prisoners. On this same journey, Mansa Mūsā a century earlier had lost a third of his camels and of his followers.

Even for those who survived the temptations of piety and the dangers of the road, and returned safely home, the journey was likely to be a long one, perhaps taking years for those without wealth and privileges in transport. This is reflected in a legend of the origin of the Budduma. Bulu was a Kanembu; his brother, going on Pilgrimage, entrusted his wife to Bulu's care. The brother's return was so long delayed that Bulu, thinking him dead, took his wife in levirate marriage. When the brother did after all appear, Bulu fled ashamed to the islands of Lake Chad where, after further adventures, he became progenitor of the Budduma people.

Many pilgrims traded as they went along. The profits of trade helped the pilgrims, while by the same token the Pilgrimage gave an added impetus to the economic life of the regions through which the pilgrims passed. Most of the detailed reports of commodities sold by the pilgrims come from later than our period, but the goods are not, with a few exceptions like powder and shot, likely to have altered much over the centuries. Religious mementos were popular: rosaries, little packets of earth from Mecca and Medina, water from the sacred well of Zemzem (a well which some believed linked underground with the well of Kairouan, so that a pilgrim's platter dropped in the one might appear in the other), wax from the candles of the Holy Land mosques, and so on. Books were another religious commodity; and from North Africa shrouds and turbans were sent for blessing to Mecca, so that there was a considerable trade in these garments. Personal ornaments, from gems and coral to cheap rings of lead or glass, were sold. Perfumes came into Mecca, and flowed out again with the returning pilgrims, from and to widely separated parts of the Muslim world. Weapons and munitions were sold, and slaves – among those in greatest demand were the companionable concubines of Ethiopia. All these, and many other things, would be carried by a returning *ḥajj* caravan, the camp of which sometimes resembled a market.

This chapter has been arranged around the theme of penetration – of people, techniques, goods and beliefs – principally across the Sahara from north to south, but also into North Africa, and within the Sudan itself. The essential corollary of this theme is the endeavour to discover also what kind of societies were at the receiving end of these influences, what contributions the receiving societies made to the new mix and what kind of change the penetrating elements suffered in their new environment. Both elements, penetration and reception, are essential to our understanding. Both have had their own particular champions amongst those who record or relate, and those who study, the history of the area. More stress was, in general, given to the idea of penetration during the period of European colonialism, partly because that period was itself one of remarkable penetration, and scholars scanning the past found many ready parallels in their contemporary situation, amidst the arrival of new commercial, military, religious and other factors. It would, however, be too narrow a view to associate the stress on penetration only with the scholarship of the nineteenth and early twentieth centuries. There is a strand of local Muslim scholarship of far more respectable antiquity which equally emphasizes the importance of religion, learning and other aspects of civilization brought from outside, and the crucial role of heroic, and foreign, ancestors. Nor is this school of thought exclusively Islamic, for many local Muslims locate the earliest stages of such penetration in pre-Islamic days, or attribute it to non-Muslim or even anti-Muslim heroes early in the Islamic era. In some cases similar non-African origins, in the east, are claimed by those who are not themselves Muslim even today. It is in very recent years that primary attention has swung markedly away from penetration, and has focused upon the receiving society. This new vantage-point allows us to appreciate much more fully the strength and importance of the local contribution, and to trace the largely spontaneous evolution of many forms which hitherto have been regarded as basically derived from outside. Here, too, the scholar has the opportunity to make comparisons between what he sees in the past, and what is going on all around him in the era of national independence, with old local heritages reviving, and new local prospects being forged. Such marriages between current circumstances and aspirations, and our understanding of the past, have been, and may be, fruitful. But current circumstances sometimes fluctuate wildly, as indeed has happened in our area within as brief a period as fifty years, and perhaps in the long run the most acceptable historical analysis will be that which seeks a middle way, recognizing both the refreshment and stimulus of penetration, and the richness and growth of the local heritage.

CHAPTER 5

THE WESTERN MAGHRIB AND SUDAN

ALMORAVIDS AND ALMOHADS TO *c.* 1250

During the second half of the eleventh century the Almoravids, who had emerged from the south-western Sahara, extended their conquests from Ghana in the south, and over the Maghrib to Spain in the north. Morocco, which had previously been divided among rival dynasties, was united and began to assume its own political identity. Muslim Spain, which had previously attempted to exert political influence over Morocco, now came under the rule of a Berber dynasty. It was under this union that the Muslim civilization of Spain made its greatest impact on Morocco. The western Sudan, which had previously been connected with the Maghrib by enterprising traders only, became more closely attached to the Maghrib, and not only for the relatively short period of the Almoravid occupation. Greater intensity of Islamic activity south of the Sahara and the ever-increasing trade fostered relations between the Maghrib and the western Sudan. A good illustration of the greater integration of the Muslim Occident, from the Sudan to Spain, is the group of Muslim royal tombstones dated between 1100 and 1110, which in all probability had been sculptured and inscribed in Spain, and then carried across the Sahara to be erected on the graves of two kings and a queen of Gao, who were recent converts to Islam.[1]

About 1055, after they had forced the Sanhaja of the southern Sahara into the Almoravid movement, the spiritual leader ʿAbdullāh b. Yāsīn and the military commander Yaḥyā b. ʿUmar led these nomads northwards to conquer Sijilmasa from the Maghrawa dynasty of the Zanata (for the earlier history of the Almoravids, see Volume 2). There were, perhaps, three principal reasons for the Almoravid advance towards the Maghrib. First, inspired by a militant Islamic dynasty, they came to fight for the cause of a pure and rigorous Malikism against Islamic heresy which had infested southern Morocco. Secondly, as a sequel to the long struggle in the Maghrib between Sanhaja and Zanata, the Almoravids sought to destroy the power of the Zanata dynasty, which had established itself in Morocco during the tenth

[1] J. Sauvaget, 'Les épitaphes royales de Gao', *Bulletin de l'IFAN*, 1950, **12**, 419–29.

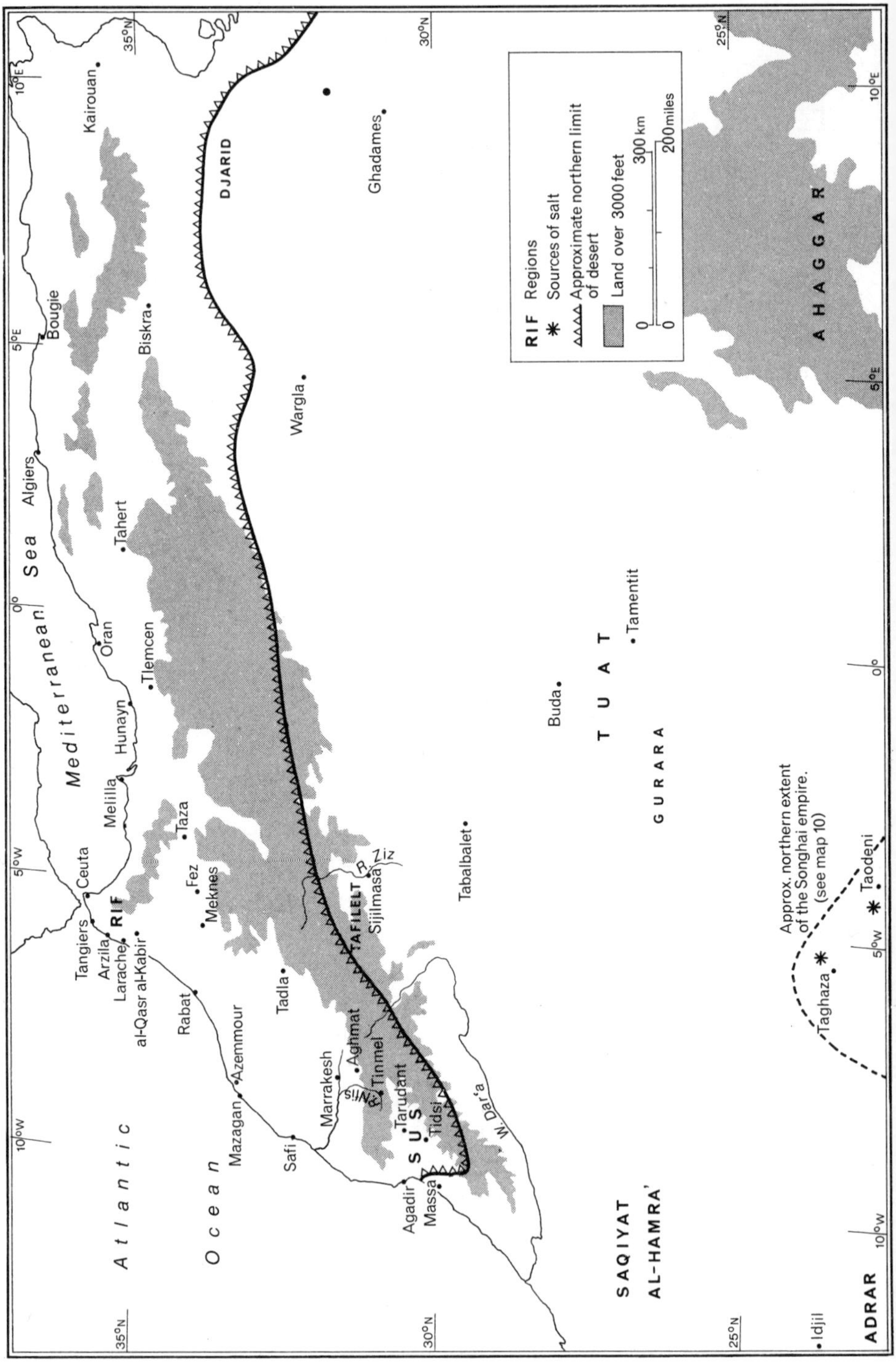

RIF Regions
Sources of salt
Approximate northern limit of desert
Land over 3000 feet
0 300 km
0 200 miles
Mediterranean Sea
Atlantic Ocean
DJARID
TAFILELT
RIF
SUS
TUAT
GURARA
SAQIYAT AL-HAMRA'
ADRAR
AHAGGAR
Kairouan
Bougie
Biskra
Algiers
Tahert
Oran
Tlemcen
Hunayn
Melilla
Taza
Ceuta
Fez
Meknes
Tangiers
Arzila
Larache
al-Qasr al-Kabir
Rabat
Azemmour
Mazagan
Safi
Tadla
Marrakesh
Aghmat
Tinmel
Tarudant
Tidsi
Agadir
Massa
Sijilmasa
R. Ziz
W. Dar'a
Ghadames
Wargla
Buda
Tamentit
Tabalbalet
Taghaza
Taodeni
Idjil
Approx. northern extent of the Songhai empire. (see map 10)
35°N
30°N
25°N
10°E
5°E
0°
5°W
10°W

century. Thirdly, the domination of the Zanata over Sijilmasa and Aghmat, two of the more important centres for the trade with the Sudan, threatened the control of the Sanhaja over the trans-Saharan trade. Zanata from Ifrīqiya were also prominent among the foreign traders of Awdaghast, at the southern end of the Saharan route, which about that time was conquered by Ghana.

Indeed, soon after they had conquered Sijilmasa, the main Almoravid force drove back to the south, across the Sahara, and captured Awdaghust from Ghana. Within a year, they had regained control over the trans-Saharan routes and over its two termini on both shores of the desert. Their authority, however, was seriously challenged. While the Almoravids were fighting in Awdaghust, Sijilmasa was recaptured by the Zanata, and the garrison, which the Almoravids had left behind, was massacred. When Ibn Yāsīn called the Almoravids for a second expedition to Sijilmasa against the Zanata, he faced a revolt of the Juddala, who had been reluctant and had had to be coerced into the Almoravid movement. Yaḥyā b. ʿUmar was defeated and killed in fighting against the Juddala, who seceded, at least for a while, from the movement. Yaḥyā was succeeded as emir, or supreme military commander, by his brother, Abū Bakr, who reconquered Sijilmasa.

Between 1056 and 1059 the Almoravids conquered southern Morocco from Darʿa and Sus in the south to Tadla in the north, dispossessing the Zanata. In 1059 they faced the heretic Barghawata Berbers, whose state and heresy had survived since the eighth century in the Atlantic plains. Ibn Yāsīn was killed in the fighting against these heretics, but Abū Bakr b. ʿUmar continued the war until the Barghawata were defeated and their power was destroyed.

The Almoravid movement reached a moment of crisis with the death of its leader, Ibn Yāsīn, and after the main objectives had been achieved – with the sweeping away of heresy, with the overthrow of the Zanata domination in southern Morocco and with the establishment of a secure control over the Saharan trade. Continued resistance by the Zanata from their bases in Fez and Tlemcen compelled the extension of military expeditions. But the Almoravids were sons of the desert, and the attachment of Abū Bakr b. ʿUmar to the nomadic way of life and to the Sahara is a recurrent theme in the sources. Details of the events of the 1060s are obscure, and it is possible that at that period the Almoravids shifted to and fro between the Sus and the Sahara.

The Almoravids preferred to avoid settling in the urban milieu of Aghmat, capital of the Sus, which as a commercial centre for the trade with the Sudan attracted many foreign merchants. In 1070, therefore, Abū Bakr initiated the establishment of the new capital of Marrakesh, which retained for a long time the appearance of a Saharan town. But before much progress had been made in the construction of the new capital, Abū Bakr received news of a dispute between the Lamtuna and the Massufa in the desert, 'where their [the Almoravids'] stock, their roots and the source of their reinforcement lay. He feared dissension and the severance of the bonds of unity, and returned [to the desert] to restore his authority.'[1] Abū Bakr appointed his cousin Yūsuf b. Tāshfīn as his deputy in Morocco to continue the war against the Zanata. Before leaving for the desert Abū Bakr divorced Zaynab, whom he had married after defeating her former husband Laqqūt, the Zanata ruler of Aghmat; she was accustomed to urban luxury and Abū Bakr wanted to spare her the hardship of the desert. This beautiful, intelligent, cunning and ambitious woman next married Yūsuf b. Tāshfīn, soon after the legally prescribed period of waiting had elapsed.

Zaynab brought Yūsuf a large fortune, to which he added levies from his tributaries. He bought slaves from the Sudan and Christian captives from Spain, and so built up his army. He introduced drums and flags, and changed the character of the Almoravid army from that of a force of nomadic tribesmen to that of a heterogeneous imperial army corps. This step also marked the beginning of the process of alienation from the desert. In fortifying his personal position vis-à-vis his leader, Ibn Tāshfīn also tempted some of the Lamtuna chiefs in Abū Bakr's camp, by the promise of rewards, to join him. Yet, he still acknowledged Abū Bakr as his superior and reported to him on events in the Maghrib.

In the meantime Abū Bakr accomplished the pacification of the Sahara, and may have also led some raids towards the Sudan. He then turned back to the Maghrib, but on encountering the respectful defiance of his lieutenant, this humble shaykh of the desert, who was probably reluctant to settle permanently in the Maghrib, gracefully conceded to his ambitious cousin Ibn Tāshfīn: 'I cannot live out of the desert, and I came only to hand over authority to you . . . I will soon be back in the desert, the residence of our brothers and the seat of our sultans.'[2]

[1] Ibn Khaldūn, *Kitāb ta'rīkh al-duwal al-Islāmiya bi'l-Maghrib min Kitāb al-'Ibar*, ed. M. G. de Slane (Paris, 1847), I, 239; tr. M. G. de Slane, *Histoire des Berbères et des dynasties musulmanes de l'Afrique septentrionale* (Paris, 1925–56), II, 72.

[2] *Al-Hulal al-mawshiyya fī dhikr al-akhbār al-Marrākushiyya*, ed. I. S. Allouche (Rabat, 1936), 15.

The crisis was over. Abū Bakr returned to the Sahara and Ibn Tāshfīn remained at the head of the northern wing of the Almoravids; he now set out to establish an empire. Fez was conquered in 1075, and by 1082 Tlemcen and Oran had fallen to the Almoravids. In 1083 Ibn Tāshfīn conquered Ceuta and secured control of the straits of Gibraltar. Across the straits, in Spain, the Muslim 'party kings' (*mulūk al-Ṭawā'if*) were at war with each other over the debris of the Umayyad caliphate. The growing weakness of the Muslims encouraged the Christian reconquista. The *fuqahā'* (jurists) in Spain, who witnessed the self-destruction of Islam, became attracted by the religious vigour of the Almoravids and inclined to seek their military aid, but the Muslim rulers of Spain hesitated. It required the shock of the fall of Toledo to the Christians in 1085 to convince those rulers that only the Almoravids could stop the Christians' advance. In 1086 Ibn Tāshfīn, dedicated to the ideal of the jihad, crossed to Spain and scored a spectacular victory over the Christians at Zallāqa. But following this victory he returned to Morocco, and a year later be became, in name as well as in practice, the sole authority over the Almoravids following the death of Abū Bakr b. 'Umar in 1087.

However, until 1087 Ibn Tāshfīn had continued to pay nominal allegiance to Abū Bakr. This is proved by the fact that until that date the golden dinars of the Almoravids were struck in the name of the emir Abū Bakr b. 'Umar. Ibn Tāshfīn's name appeared on coins only after 1087. In 1076, eleven years before his death, Abū Bakr b. 'Umar had led the southern wing of the Almoravids to the conquest of Ghana and part of the western Sudan. The fourteenth-century chronicler Ibn Abī Zar' states that Ibn Tāshfīn's dominions extended over the Sahara and reached as far as 'the mountains of gold' in *Bilād al-Sūdān*. The conquests of Abū Bakr b. 'Umar in the Sudan were, therefore, regarded as part of the Almoravid empire, and Ibn Tāshfīn, like the former leader Abū Bakr, was acknowledged to be the head of the two wings of the Almoravids – of those in the Maghrib as well as those of the desert. Perhaps there was not at that stage a complete break between these two wings of the movement.

Political domination of the Almoravids over parts of the Sudan, it will later be shown, only lasted a few decades. Yet references in the Arabic sources indicate continuous political relations between the Almoravids in the Maghrib and some rulers of the Sudan. A letter from Ghana to Ibn Tāshfīn is mentioned in the *Kitāb al-Istibṣār*, written in the twelfth century. Yāqūt (1179–1229) described the visit of the king of Diafunu, an enigmatic but evidently powerful monarch of the Sudan, to the veiled king of the Maghrib, perhaps in the first half of the twelfth century. Reference has already been made to the royal tombstones, which were sent from Spain to Gao between 1100 and 1110. Abū Yaḥyā al-Massūfī, brother-in-law of the Almoravid ruler 'Alī b. Yūsuf b. Tāshfīn (1106–72), is reported to have had authority over several tribes of the Sahara. Marrakesh, the capital of the Almoravids in southern Morocco, was close enough to the desert to maintain contacts with the Sanhaja of the Sahara.

Both in Morocco (in the mints of Sijilmasa, Aghmat, Marrakesh and Fez) and in Spain (in the mints of Seville, Cordova, Malaga and Almeria) the Almoravids produced rich and varied coinage. Their dinars were made of pure gold and were in great demand outside their empire. These highly valued gold coins were later imitated by Alfonso VIII of Toledo, whose dinars, struck from 1173 onwards, became known as *le morabeti alfonsi*. The Almoravid empire seems to have thrived on Sudanese gold, as the trans-Saharan trade reached a new peak.

Aghmat, the commercial town near the capital of Marrakesh, flourished, and according to al-Idrīsī (writing in 1153–7), 'no one was wealthier and in better condition [than those] under the rule of the *Mulaththamūn* [the veiled people, the Almoravids] . . . Their slaves and agents go [to the Sudan] in caravans of seventy to a hundred camels, all loaded.'[1] Perhaps more than any other dynasty in Moroccan history, the Almoravids, with their camelry, were able to guarantee the security of the Saharan trade.

The Almoravid link with the Sahara, however, gradually weakened with their growing involvement in the Maghrib and in Spain. Ibn Tāshfīn's victory in Spain in 1086 had arrested the advance of the Christians, but soon after his return to Morocco internal disputes among rival Muslim emirs invited the renewal of Christian pressure. Ibn Tāshfīn was called in again, and in 1088 scored another victory in the Battle of Aledo. Yet, because of the enmity of the Muslim emirs in Spain, whose fear of their deliverer was hardly less than their hostility to their Christian enemies, Ibn Tāshfīn again retreated from Spain. In 1090 he crossed the straits for the third time, and supported by *fatwās* – legal opinions of leading jurists – he turned against the Muslim emirs, whom he charged with corruption, negligence, illegal

[1] al-Idrīsī, *Nuzhat al-mushtāq fī ikhtirāq al-āfāq*, ed. R. Dozy and M. J. de Goeje (Leiden, 1866), 66–7; tr. R. Dozy and M. J. de Goeje, *Description de l'Afrique et de l'Espagne* (Leiden, 1866), 76–7.

taxation and collaboration with the Christians. By 1094 he had deposed all the Muslim emirs and re-established Muslim unity in Spain under his authority.

The uncouth, austere nomads of the desert, who were committed to a formal, legalistic and puritan Islam, came to rule over Andalusia, where a sophisticated, refined, urban Muslim civilization flourished. This dichotomy was never resolved, and was among the factors that eventually led to the revolt of Muslim Spain against the Almoravids. Yet there were significant reciprocal influences; just as Spanish Islam was hardened under the impact of the Almoravids, so the latter were softened by the Andalusian civilization.

Paradoxical as it may seem, these nomads of the desert opened the Maghrib to Andalusian influences. In previous centuries there had been intermittent communication between Muslim Spain and the Maghrib, but the Almoravids brought about a cultural symbiosis. Spanish scholars were recruited to the Almoravid administration, where they held influential bureaucratic posts. Ibn Tāshfīn's successors grew up in this cultural milieu, and enjoyed the company of poets and other artists. Under the Almoravids there was an impressive growth of urban life in Morocco, and these rulers were dedicated to the construction of buildings, mostly by Andalusian architects. Henri Terrasse, a leading authority on Moroccan art and architecture, claims that, by introducing Andalusian civilization to Morocco, the Almoravids prepared the ground for the absorption of Andalusian refugees in the following centuries.

Both in Spain and in the Maghrib the Almoravid conquest was viewed by large sections of the population as a foreign invasion. In fact, the Sanhaja maintained their distinct habits, and forbade their subjects to imitate them in adopting the *lithām* (veil), which remained a conspicuous mark of the ruling privileged class. The Sanhaja received most of the benefits of the Almoravid government, and they clearly formed the aristocracy. As commanders of the army they were also territorial governors in the provinces. Andalusian secretaries had considerable influence, but the combination of the political traditions of the Sahara and Spain failed to produce a cohesive government. Nevertheless, the Almoravids bequeathed the notion of a united Morocco, coerced through conquest.

Continued ethnic superiority dictated the exclusion of other ethnic groups from service in the army, and from the privileges attached to it. But at the same time the Almoravids could not rely on the flow of new

Sanhaja reinforcements from the Sahara. They therefore resorted to employing Christian mercenaries, following the example of the Muslim emirs of Spain in the period of the *mulūk al-Tawā'if*. These Christians were given freedom of worship, and the Almoravids found themselves with a Christian ward and a church in their new capital of Marrakesh.

In his relentless jihad against negligence and laxity in the Sahara, and heresy in southern Morocco, Ibn Yāsīn had endeavoured to implement the *sharī'a*, the law of Islam, in all its ramifications and at all levels, both in personal conduct and in the organization of the Islamic state. Following the death of the spiritual leader, the emir (Abū Bakr b. 'Umar and later Yūsuf b. Tāshfīn) became the sole authority. Both these emirs, however, had been disciples and close associates of Ibn Yāsīn, and are described as having been men of piety and virtue. In pursuing the practice and teaching of Ibn Yāsīn, Ibn Tāshfīn abolished all illegal taxes in his vast kingdom, and levied only those taxes stipulated in the *sharī'a*. He favoured the *fuqahā'* (the jurists), sought their legal opinions and acted on their advice.

Under the Almoravids the *fuqahā'* emphasized the formal legalistic aspects of Islam, based on the Maliki school. Even personal investigation of the sources of the law – the Koran and the Prophetic traditions (*ḥadīth*) – were proscribed, and jurists were directed to refer only to the Maliki manuals that dealt with the numerous details of Islamic jurisprudence. The *fuqahā'* stifled any intellectual activity and restricted theological studies. No allegorical exegesis of the Koran was allowed, which implied that the attributes of God should be explained in a strictly literal way that led to anthropomorphism.

The abolition of illegal taxes and the religious dedication of the Almoravids aroused an initial response, even enthusiasm, among Muslims in the Maghrib and in Spain. But the imposition of narrow-minded Malikism collided with the emerging trend towards Sufism, which developed in Andalusia from the end of the eleventh century onwards. Abu Ḥāmid al-Ghazālī, who led the way to the integration of Sufism into the mainstream of Islamic orthodoxy, supported Ibn Tāshfīn in 1090, when he turned against the Muslim emirs of Spain. But al-Ghazālī also vigorously condemned the *fuqahā'* who sought the salvation of the soul through legalistic exercises, and he preached that religion was above all a matter touching the heart. The *fuqahā'* prevailed upon 'Alī, the son of Yūsuf b. Tāshfīn, to burn al-Ghazālī's books.

'Alī was twenty-three when he succeeded his father Yūsuf b. Tāshfīn in 1106. He had grown up in the urban civilization of Spain, and lacked the vigour and statesmanship of his father. But he was even more pious than his father, and was completely dominated by the *fuqahā'*. From 1118 onwards 'Alī's weakness was exploited by the Christian kings of Castile, Aragon and Barcelona to renew the reconquista of Spain. By 1143, when 'Alī died, the Muslims had been driven from Cordova and Seville. A year later the Muslims of Spain revolted against the Almoravids, when the religious opposition of the growing mystical movement combined with the political ambitions of the local Muslim aristocracy. By that time the Almoravids had lost the greatest part of Morocco to the Almohads, whose religious and ethnic opposition aggravated the alienation of the Almoravids.

Muḥammad b. Tūmart, the founder of the Almohad movement (Arabic: *al-Muwaḥḥidūn*) belonged to one of the Masmuda tribes of the Anti-Atlas. He was born about 1080, and between 1100 and 1105 – still in the lifetime of Ibn Tāshfīn – he set out to study in the east, mainly in Baghdad. Perhaps he had already suffered from the decline of free intellectual activity under the Almoravids. In the east, Islamic orthodoxy was then consolidating two of its greatest theological achievements, those of al-Ash'arī and al-Ghazālī. Al-Ash'arī (died 935) showed the way to solve the discrepancy between the belief in the spiritual and immaterial character of divinity and the anthropomorphic language of the Koran. Al-Ghazālī, as already mentioned, bridged the gap between the legalism of the *fuqahā'* and the mysticism of the Sufis. Ibn Tūmart adopted the teaching of both al-Ash'arī and al-Ghazālī, but these were transformed in the process of evolving a doctrinal basis for a religious reform in the Maghrib.

In Islamic jurisprudence Ibn Tūmart repudiated the four established schools of law (*madhāhib*) and sought to reassert the right of personal interpretation (*ijtihād*) of the Koran and the Prophetic traditions. Against the Almoravid obsession for the minutest details of the elaborate system of the canonical law, Ibn Tūmart emphasized morality. Actually, it was as a reformer of bad morals, which presumably were current in some circles of society, that Ibn Tūmart first appeared on his return to the Maghrib from the East. In blaming the Almoravids for anthropomorphism, Ibn Tūmart resorted to allegorical interpretation of the attributes of God in the Koran. The indivisibility of these attributes was necessary for the affirmation of God's unity (*tawḥīd*), and the movement assumed the name of *al-muwaḥḥidūn*, 'those who proclaim the unity of God'. Ibn Tūmart's reform encouraged the revival of individual investigation in all the religious sciences, which had been suppressed by the monopoly claimed for jurisprudence at the time of the Almoravids.

Abstract theological notions, however, are inadequate for a popular movement. The idea of the *mahdī*, the inspired leader, was current among the Berbers of the Maghrib, a residue of the Fatimid propaganda. In establishing his authority among the Masmuda tribesmen, Ibn Tūmart was proclaimed *mahdī*, the one who was sent to re-establish the true faith. He even invented a fictitious genealogy to show that he was a descendant of the Prophet. Ibn Tūmart pursued an intensive programme of indoctrination among his adherents, using the Berber language for that purpose.

On his way back from the east, Ibn Tūmart stayed for some time near Bougie, in the central Maghrib, where he was joined by a group of disciples, among whom was his future successor, ʻAbd al-Mu'min. In 1120–1 Ibn Tūmart entered Marrakesh, the capital of the Almoravids, and soon began to criticize moral practices. He rebuked the reigning emir, ʻAlī b. Yūsuf b. Tāshfīn, for wearing the traditional veil of the desert Sanhaja, and attacked the emir's sister for going about in public unveiled. The emir was impressed by Ibn Tūmart's piety and learning, but the latter was soon in conflict with the Maliki *fuqahā'*. By the time the *fuqahā'* convinced the emir that Ibn Tūmart represented a serious danger, the reformer was safe among his tribesmen in the mountains of the Anti-Atlas.

The Almoravids, former nomads of the desert, never had effective control of the mountains, and when Ibn Tūmart rejoined the Masmuda, he was able to mobilize the resentment of the Berbers and their dislike of central authority. He also managed to exploit the perennial enmity between Masmuda and Sanhaja, the agriculturalists of the mountains against the nomads of the plains and the Sahara. He turned it into a jihad, couched in the religious terms of his new doctrine. For three years after his return to his village in 1121–8, Ibn Tūmart preached among the Masmuda tribes, until his leadership was recognized by their representatives. In 1125 he established his headquarters in Tinmel, in the very centre of the Masmuda country and in a well-defended strategic place.

Ibn Tūmart was well acquainted with Berber society, and he endeavoured to maintain as much as possible of the Berber traditions. He established a consultative assembly of fifty tribal representatives, and allowed the different groups to preserve their identity within the community. Yet his own tribe – the Ḥarga – was given precedence, and a privy council, which included ten of his closest disciples, directed the affairs of the movement. In promoting the cohesion of the community Ibn Tūmart imposed severe discipline, made spiritual exercises compulsory and punished those who failed to observe the precepts of Islam. This culminated in 1128 with a violent purge to forestall internal dissension before the confrontation with the Almoravids.

In the same year the Almoravids failed in an attempt to destroy the Almohads. The latter moved onto the offensive, only to be defeated at the gates of Marrakesh. Shortly afterwards Ibn Tūmart died, but his death was kept secret for about two years, until the authority of his successor ʻAbd al-Mu'min had been established. ʻAbd al-Mu'min was a Zanata from the region of Tlemcen, and his succession to the leadership of the movement was in recognition of his learning, piety and devotion to Ibn Tūmart's doctrine. Though he was formally adopted into the Ḥarga, Ibn Tūmart's tribe, he remained somewhat alien to the Masmuda. Whereas Ibn Tūmart was the spiritual originator of the Almohad movement, ʻAbd al-Mu'min proved to be the real founder of the Almohad empire and of its ruling dynasty.

Following the defeat at the gates of Marrakesh in 1128, ʻAbd al-Mu'min avoided the plains, which were securely dominated by the Almoravids. Instead, he advanced along the Atlas range, where the Almohads hardly encountered any resistance. When ʻAbd al-Mu'min reached the Rif, the Almoravids were encircled, and the final confrontation became inevitable. In 1145 the Almohads defeated the Christian mercenaries of the Almoravids, and in the same year the Almoravid ruler Tāshfīn b. ʻAlī (1143–5) was captured; in 1146–7 the capital Marrakesh was conquered. There followed a general massacre of the Lamtuna, the backbone of the Almoravid empire. But resistance to the Almohads continued among the Berber tribes of the Atlantic plains, and for about two years ʻAbd al-Mu'min ruthlessly suppressed the revolt with much bloodshed and destruction.

Like that of their predecessors, the power base of the Almohads was in southern Morocco. ʻAbd al-Mu'min, therefore, wanted to keep Marrakesh as the capital. Yet the city had to be purified of the sanctuaries of the 'infidels', and many of the religious buildings of the Almoravids were destroyed as well as their palace. The Kutubiyya mosque was later built on the site of the palace.

The official title of the Almoravid ruler had been *amīr al-muslimīn*, or 'commander of the Muslims'. The title *amīr al-mu'minīn*, 'commander of the faithful', was avoided, and remained the prerogative of the 'Abbasid caliph of Baghdad, whose supreme (but remote) authority the Almoravids acknowledged. 'Abd al-Mu'min went further, and as *khalīfa* (successor) of the *mahdī*, who was ranked next to the Prophet, he assumed the title *amīr al-mu'minīn*. Once again – as in the time of the Fatimids – the Maghrib seceded from the 'Abbasid caliphate. But it was the first time that the ruler of Morocco came to be regarded as a caliph, a tradition which has seldom been abandoned since. It had far-reaching political implications, with the repeated attempts of successive Moroccan dynasties to establish a 'Caliphate of the Muslim Occident'. At different periods this caliphate claimed to include the whole Maghrib, Andalusia, the Sahara and the western and central Sudan.

The Almoravid Sanhaja had not expanded their conquests eastwards to the central Maghrib (Algeria), perhaps because it was then ruled by the Sanhaja dynasty of the Banū Ḥammād. The latter consolidated their authority over that region after the collapse of the Fatimid empire in the Maghrib, and established their capital in the inland fort of Qal'a. In 1062–3 they built the town of Bougie (Bijāya) on the coast, which soon became a flourishing port, enjoying widespread commercial connections with Europe, the Middle East, the Sahara and the western Sudan. In 1090, under the increasing pressure of the Arab nomads, the Banū Hilāl and related tribes, the Banū Ḥammād abandoned Qal'a and moved their capital to Bougie. When Ibn Tūmart visited Bougie on his way back from Mecca, about 1120, it was an intellectual centre, where men and women mixed together, indulging themselves in wine and music. It was there that Ibn Tūmart first appeared as a censor of morals. It was also in Bougie that 'Abd al-Mu'min joined the small circle of Ibn Tūmart's disciples.

In 1145, two years before the fall of Marrakesh, the Banū Ḥammād joined hands with the Almoravids against the Almohads, only to be defeated near Tlemcen. As soon as his authority over Morocco was secured, 'Abd al-Mu'min turned against the Banū Ḥammād in a first step towards the conquest of the whole Maghrib. In 1151/2 he conquered Algiers and Bougie, and a year later, in Setif, he won a fierce battle against the Arab nomads of the central Maghrib. The Almohad army was smaller in numbers, but better disciplined than the Arab tribesmen. In 1160, 'Abd al-Mu'min conquered Mahdiya (the former capital of the Fatimids), which had been in the hands of the Normans of Sicily since 1134. This was followed by the subjugation of the small principalities that had succeeded the Zirids in Ifrīqiya, and for the first time the whole Maghrib was united under a local Berber dynasty.

The newly extended empire stretched the resources of the Almohads, who still relied mainly on the Masmuda. Moreover, in the twelfth century the imposition of a central authority over Ifrīqiya and the central Maghrib was an almost impossible task because of the Arab nomads. They were constantly in overt or latent dissent, and seized every opportunity to revolt. In 1184 the Banū Ghāniya invaded Ifrīqiya from the last bastion of the Almoravids, in the Balearic Islands. They were joined by the Arabs and by the Sanhaja, as well as by a band of Turkomen led by Qarāqūsh (see pp. 246–8). After repeated attempts the Almohads finally succeeded in restoring their authority in Ifrīqiya, though at the price of the establishment of a powerful Almohad family, the Banū Ḥafṣ, as autonomous governors, who eventually broke off to proclaim an independent caliphate (see pp. 248–9).

In order to weaken the Arab resistance in the east, 'Abd al-Mu'min transferred the more turbulent elements to Morocco, and settled them in the Atlantic plains. This was the region of the Barghawata, an area which had first been destroyed by the Almoravids in their war on those heretics. It was depopulated again in 1197–8, when the Almohads cruelly suppressed the revolts in these regions. The Almohad government thus helped the Arabs to overcome the barriers of the Atlas mountains, and accelerated their expansion into Morocco to complete the nomads' predominance over the lowlands of the Maghrib as far as the Atlantic. The appearance of the Arabs added to the complexity of the ethnic composition of Morocco, and introduced a significant non-Berber element to the population. The Arabs also increased pasture lands at the expense of agriculture, which gradually became confined to the mountains.

The Arabs were soon to play an increasing role in the politics of the Almohad empire. In his efforts to establish a hereditary dynasty, 'Abd al-Mu'min expected the opposition of the Masmuda, to whom he was still a stranger. He therefore sought the support of the Arabs in order to secure the succession of his son. Towards the end of the Almohad period, when succession disputes became more frequent, leaders of the Arab tribes supported one candidate against the other. With the decline of the Almohad army, the Arabs became the most powerful force in the Moroccan plains, and no ruler could have held authority without their support. Arab nomads, who were often joined by arabized Zanata, were given lands free of tax in return for military service, and became the tribes of the *makhzin*. By this time the Almohad army had lost its original spirit, which had lent it cohesion and inspired it in battle.

The Almohads, like their predecessors the Almoravids, waged jihad against fellow Muslims whom they regarded as heretics, and more dangerous than infidels. Once they had overcome these adversaries, the Almohads, again like the Almoravids, crossed the straits into Spain to help to arrest the advance of the Christians. For the first time since the eighth century the whole Maghrib and Spain were united, but fighting at both ends – in Ifrīqiya and in Spain – strained Almohad resources. Abū Ya'qūb Yūsuf (1163–84), the son and successor of 'Abd al-Mu'min, was dedicated to the jihad in Spain, where he died in battle in 1184. His own son and successor, Abū Yūsuf Ya'qūb (1184–99), scored an important victory over the Christian armies in 1195 at Alarcos. It was perhaps after this victory that he adopted the title al-Manṣūr. His army was then based on mercenaries – Arabs, Zanata and even some Turkoman units. The Christians were forced to retreat, but their defeat was skilfully exploited by the Bishop of Toledo to inspire a crusading spirit, and to bring about a co-ordinated effort of the Christian kingdoms of the Peninsula. In 1212 they defeated the Almohads in the battle of Las Navas de Tolosa. This defeat marked the decline of the Almohads, and not only in Spain.

The growing pressure of the Christians in Spain, revolts in Ifrīqiya and the succession of weak caliphs disrupted the fragile structure of the Almohad empire. This empire had been the creation of the Masmuda tribes, who remained the conquering aristocracy, and sought to retain exclusive privileges. They even restricted the diffusion of the Almohad doctrine, which served as a lever for their fiscal policy. The non-Almohad Muslims were regarded as infidels, and therefore lost rights over their lands, which became subject to heavy taxation.

It was only in 1162, one year before his death, that 'Abd al-Mu'min succeeded in overcoming the opposition of the Masmuda to integrate his own tribe, the Kumya (a branch of the Zanata), into the Almohad community. He soon employed them as his trusted bodyguard. He relied on the support of his tribe and that of the Arabs in securing the succession of his son and in the establishment of a ruling dynasty. Hence, almost from the beginning, there was a cleavage within the aristocracy between 'Abd al-Mu'min's descendants, who became known as *sayyids*, and the Masmuda Almohads, both the tribal headmen and the religious shaykhs. Leaders of the Masmuda Almohads held important positions in the army and as provincial governors. Abū Ḥafṣ ʻUmar had played a leading role in rallying the Masmuda around Ibn Tūmart, and supported ʻAbd al-Mu'min after Ibn Tūmart's death. His descendants remained influential, and some of them became viziers under ʻAbd al-Mu'min's successors. Tensions developed also between the Almohad shaykhs and the bureaucracy, mainly Andalusians, whose allegiance was exclusively to the caliph.

The delicate balance between the caliph and the Almohad shaykhs was seriously disrupted when al-Mustanṣir (son of al-Nāṣir, son of al-Manṣūr) became caliph at the age of sixteen in 1213. The shaykhs took control of the *makhzin*, and after al-Mustanṣir's death in 1224 they sought to put on the throne another caliph who would be amenable to their influence. Rivalry within the ranks of the Almohad shaykhs and the intervention of the Arabs reduced the country to internal strife. This situation was exploited by al-Ma'mūn, another son of al-Manṣūr, who came from Spain with Christian cavalry given to him by the king of Castile. In 1230 he defeated the Almohad shaykhs and made himself caliph. For two years, until his death in 1232, al-Ma'mun led a violent reaction against the political and religious traditions of the Almohads, killed many shaykhs, and went as far as repudiating the doctrine of the *mahdī*. He deprived the dynasty of its religious legitimacy.

Al-Rashīd (1232–42), son of al-Manṣūr, restored the Almohad doctrine and reached agreement with the shaykhs, because the only alternative allies were the undisciplined tribal mercenaries. But the *makhzin* did not recover, and the empire disintegrated. In 1236 the Hafsid governor of Ifrīqiya proclaimed himself caliph as the true custodian of the doctrine of the *mahdī*. In 1239 the governor of Tlemcen, Yaghmorasen b. Zayyān of the Banū ʻAbd al-Wād, declared himself independent of the Almohads. The Muslims in Spain also revolted against the Almohads, and fell an easy prey to Ferdinand III. By 1276 this Christian king had conquered all the Muslim possessions in Spain save Granada. In Morocco itself the Banū Marīn of the Zanata gradually expanded to become, from 1248 onwards, the virtual rulers, although they nominally acknowledged the sovereignty of the caliph, until the latter was deposed in 1269.

By the middle of the thirteenth century, Morocco had developed a religious heritage of its own, and though neither the doctrines of the Almoravids nor those of the Almohads survived in their entirety, both had a profound impact. Both dynasties eradicated heresies which had played an important role in introducing the Berbers to Islam. The Maliki school, without the severity of the Almoravid tenets, remained predominant in spite of the attempts of the Almohads to overrule it by deriving the *sharīʿa* directly from the Koran and the Prophetic traditions. The subtle rationality of the Almohad doctrine could not satisfy more than a limited circle of disciples. But Ibn Tūmart's programme of moral reform perhaps contributed to the rigorism of Moroccan Islam, in which the precepts of Islam are strictly observed.

The reign of al-Manṣūr (1184–99) is regarded in Moroccan historiography as the peak of the Almohad empire. This was also the only period when an Almohad caliph attempted to implement the Almohad reform. He imposed discriminatory restrictions on the Jews, persecuted the Maliki *fuqahā'*, and in his piety even questioned the adoration of Ibn Tūmart as the impeccable *mahdī*. Nevertheless, he was keenly interested in philosophy, and maintained Ibn Rushd (Averroes) at his court. Indeed, the influence of Andalusian civilization tempered the puritan austerity of the Almohads, though they were more concerned with philosophy than with poetry, and built more forts and mosques than palaces and gardens.

By far the most important development in the religious life of Morocco under the Almohads did not emerge directly from their doctrines and reforms. Yet, it is significant that almost all the prominent mystics of the Maghrib, who became – in their lifetime or after their death – founders of Sufi *ṭarīqas*, lived in the latter half of the twelfth century under the Almohads. This was indeed the culmination of a long process in which the ascetic tradition of the Maghrib in its encounter with the intellectual and popular mysticism of Andalusia was fertilized by the new formulas of orthodox Sufism coming from the east. The Almoravids, as has been shown, had attempted to nip Sufism in the bud and had burnt al-Ghazālī's books. Ibn Tūmart, on the other hand, incorporated elements of al-Ghazālī's teaching in his doctrine. So, when popular piety was attracted by the mystics and made them holy men, the Almohad caliphs sought to increase their own prestige by extending their patronage to the saints. It was perhaps in their official support of the founders of Moroccan Sufism, rather than in their own reform, that the Almohads contributed to the evolution of the patterns of religious life in Morocco.

The progress of the Christian reconquista of Spain in the eleventh and twelfth centuries was one of many other symptoms of the changing character of relations between the Maghrib and Europe. European fleets became dominant in the western Mediterranean, and between 1134 and 1160 the Normans of Sicily occupied Mahdiya. Europe was then recovering from a long economic recession, and the commercial enterprise of the Italian cities was supported by a nascent industry. When, in the middle of the twelfth century, Italian merchants were interested in the development of trade with North Africa, the Almohads were in the process of uniting the whole Maghrib under their authority. The advantage of controlling all the ports of the North African coast could well have been among the factors that motivated the costly eastward expansion of the Almohads. Tripoli, Tunis and Bougie were the more important trading ports.

In 1153 ʻAbd al-Mu'min signed a treaty with Genoa, which was renewed in 1161. In 1168 Pisa signed a treaty with his son Abū Ya'qūb Yūsuf, which was renewed by al-Manṣūr in 1186, and again by al-Nāṣir in 1211. The treaties accorded the Italian merchants free access to the principal ports and security in return for agreed tolls and duties. In the twelfth and thirteenth centuries merchants from Genoa, Pisa, Venice and Marseilles established factories (*fundūqs*) in coastal towns from Tripoli to Ceuta on the Mediterranean, and as far as Massa on the Atlantic coast of Morocco. By the end of the Almohad period Christian traders settled also in the capital Marrakesh, and lived in the same quarter with the Christian mercenaries who were in the service of the caliph. They supplied wine to the Christian militia, whose commander exerted his influence in favour of the merchants. Jews became prominent as middlemen in the growing Muslim–Christian trade.

The main imports to the Maghrib were varieties of European cloth, but also grain, spices, copper, beads, precious stones and perfumes. These were products of Europe, as well as oriental wares which the Italians shipped across the Mediterranean. Exports from the Maghrib included skins, leather goods, alum (needed for the dyeing of textiles) and wax. Though references to exports of gold from the Maghrib are few, it is very likely that its importance increased as the balance of trade between the Maghrib and Europe became more favourable to the latter. It was also about this time that the long process of the reintroduction of gold into the monetary system of Europe began.

The growth of the maritime trade contributed to the prosperity of the Almohad empire, though in perspective it marked the beginning of the uneasy partnership in which European traders held the initiative and exchanged manufactured goods for agricultural products and raw materials, both of local origin or in transit from the Sudan. Still, in the twelfth and thirteenth centuries the cities of Morocco – Marrakesh and Fez – flourished and their artisans thrived. The Almohads maintained security along the internal routes and encouraged trade. New caravanserais for the caravan trade were established in Marrakesh and Fez, both on important crossroads. Marrakesh developed at the expense of Aghmat, and presumably took over much of its trade with the Sudan.

Whereas inside Morocco, and along the mountain passes, the Almohad army was in better control than the Almoravids had been, the Masmuda could not do so well in securing the Saharan routes. At the end of the twelfth century the Almohad governor of Sijilmasa executed some highway robbers who had disturbed the route between Sijilmasa and Ghana. In the thirteenth century the Arab nomads, together with the Zanata, moved along the pre-Saharan steppes to threaten the caravan trade across the desert.

The trans-Saharan trade, however, continued, and Sudanese gold reached the Almohad caliphs, who produced gold dinars of excellent quality. These dinars, like those of the Almoravids, were highly appreciated in Europe, even after the decline of the dynasty. Arab geographers of the period continued to record reports about the fabulous gold resources of the Sudan. Also, Sudanese slaves were numerous in Morocco, both as domestics and in military service. Indeed, if one goes by the repeated accounts of slave raids in the Sudan and of the arrival of Sudanese slaves in the Maghrib, it is possible that the export of slaves from the Sudan increased in the twelfth and thirteenth centuries. The Sus, Sijilmasa and Wargla are most often referred to as the northern entrepôts of the trans-Saharan trade.

GHANA AND ITS SUCCESSOR STATES

The period of the Almoravids and the Almohads in the Maghrib coincided with a transitory period in the western Sudan, between the decline of Ghana and the rise of Mali. Because of the political upheaval following the disintegration of Ghana, Arab geographers failed to present a clear picture of the Sudan at that period, and oral traditions fill in the gaps only partially.

In 1072, back in the desert after he had conceded the leadership of the Almoravids in the Maghrib to Ibn Tāshfīn, Abū Bakr b. ʻUmar led the southern wing of the Almoravids in a jihad against the Sudanese, both those who were then living in the desert and those of the Sahel. Whereas al-Bakrī, in 1067–8, refers to several Sudanese groups deep in the Sahara as far as Adrar, al-Idrīsī, writing in 1154, records the expulsion of Sudanese from the desert. Indeed, oral traditions in Mauritania claim that it was Abū Bakr b. ʻUmar who drove the Sudanese away from the Sahara. It was, in fact, the outcome of the longer confrontation between Berber nomads and the Sudanese.

As the Almoravid pressure increased, Ghana was conquered. The 'veiled people' (*al-mulaththamūn*) overcame the Sudanese, plundered their territories, imposed tribute upon them, and converted many of them to Islam. According to al-Zuhrī, writing in the middle of the twelfth century, the people of Ghana were converted to Islam by the Lamtuna (the Almoravids) in 1076. Seven years later, according to the same authority, the Almoravids supported the newly converted Ghana in enforcing Islamic orthodoxy in Tadmekka. The latter, an important commercial town in the southern Sahara, north-east of the Niger bend, traded with Tahert and Wargla. Tadmekka had been visited by Ibāḍī traders from North Africa since the ninth century, and had become an outpost of the sect in their missionary efforts among the Sudanese. These early Ibāḍī influences in the southern Sahara and the western Sudan were eradicated under the impact of the Almoravids, who, in the Sudan as in the Maghrib, secured the victory of orthodoxy and the predominance of Malikism. On the northern fringes of the Sahara the Hilalian nomads contributed to the final decline of the Ibāḍī communities, and the influence of these heretics in the Sudan dwindled.

We know nothing about the Almoravid occupation of Ghana, beyond the fact that its king and people were Muslims from then on. In 1087, ten or eleven years after the conquest of Ghana, Abū Bakr b. ʻUmar died. According to Saharan traditions, he was succeeded as leader of the southern wing of the Almoravids by six rulers, his descendants and those of his brother Yaḥyā, before the community was divided. By the beginning of the twelfth century the Almoravids had lost whatever control they had over parts of the Sudan, and Ghana had reasserted its independence. In 1154 al-Idrīsī described Ghana as 'the greatest country in the land of the Sudan, the most populous, and having the most extensive trade'.[1] For al-Zuhrī it was the capital of Gnāwa (i.e. Guinea, 'the country of the black people'). According to these sources, Ghana still attracted trade, and this is perhaps confirmed

[1] al-Idrīsī, *Nuzhat al-mushtāq*, 6/tr. 7.

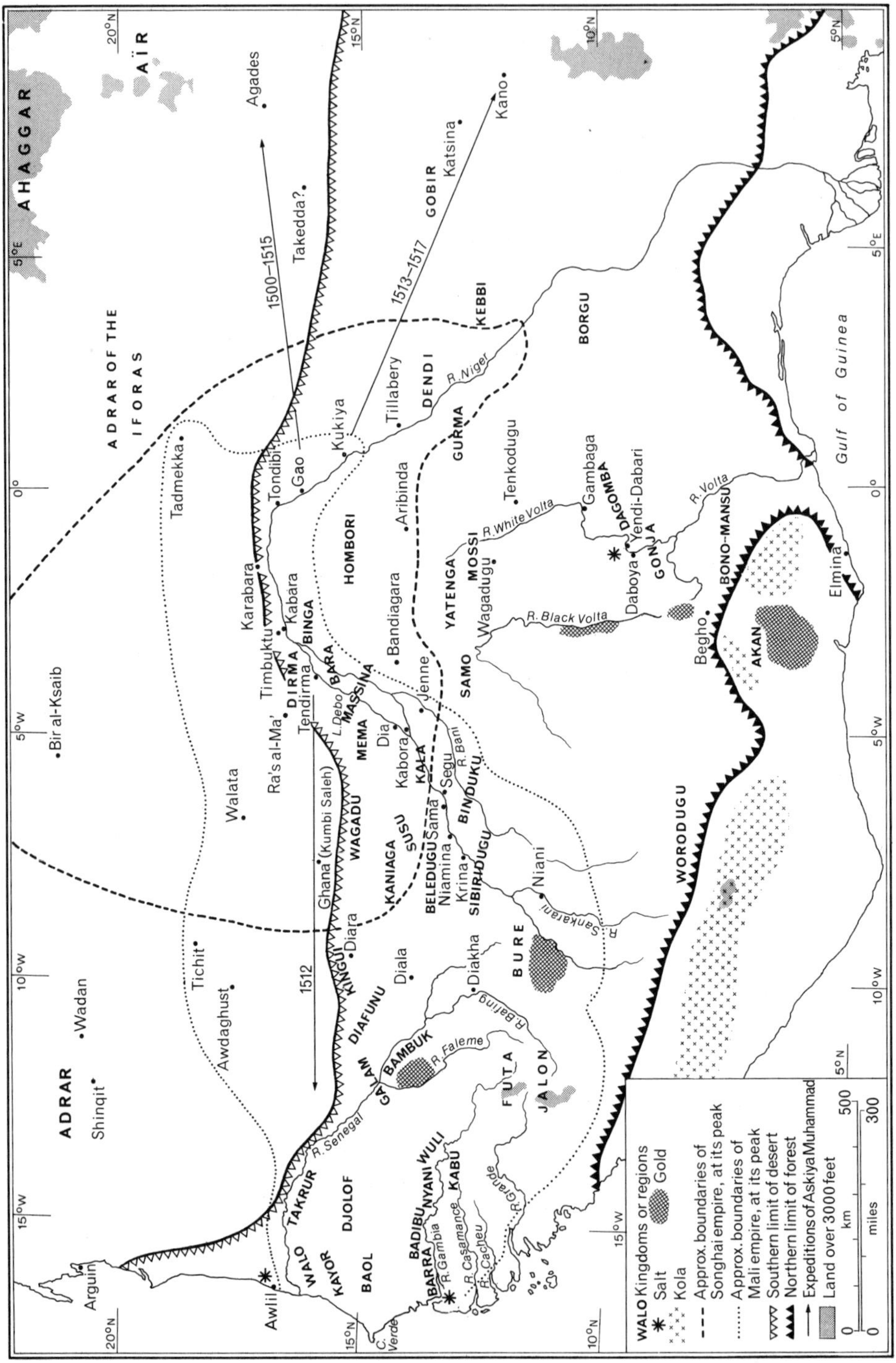
AHAGGAR
AÏR
ADRAR OF THE IFORAS
ADRAR
Agades
Takedda?
Katsina
Kano
GOBIR
KEBBI
BORGU
DENDI
GURMA
1500–1515
1513–1517
1512
Tadmekka
Tondibi
Gao
Kukiya
Tillabery
Aribinda
Tenkodugu
Gambaga
DAGOMBA
Yendi-Dabari
GONJA
Daboya
BONO-MANSU
Begho
AKAN
Elmina
Gulf of Guinea
R. White Volta
R. Volta
R. Black Volta
MOSSI
YATENGA
Wagadugu
SAMO
HOMBORI
Bandiagara
Karabara
Kabara
BINGA
Timbuktu
DIRMA
BARA
Tendirma
MASSINA
L. Debo
Jenne
Dia
Kabora
MEMA
KALA
Segu
R. Bani
BINDUKU
Sama
SUSU
WAGADU
Ra's al-Ma'
Bir al-Ksaib
Walata
Ghana (Kumbi Saleh)
KANIAGA
BELEDUGU
Niamina
Krina
SIBIRIDUGU
Niani
R. Sankarani
WORODUGU
Diara
KINGUI
DIAFUNU
Diala
Diakha
BURE
R. Bafing
R. Faleme
BAMBUK
GALAM
FUTA JALON
Tichit
Awdaghust
Wadan
Shinqit
R. Senegal
TAKRUR
DJOLOF
WALO
KAYOR
BAOL
WULI
NYANI
BADIBU
BARRA
KABU
R. Gambia
R. Casamance
R. Cacheu
R. Grande
C. Verde
Awlil
Arguin
R. Niger
20°N
15°N
10°N
5°N
15°W
10°W
5°W
0°
5°E
WALO Kingdoms or regions
Salt
Gold
Kola
Approx. boundaries of Songhai empire, at its peak
Approx. boundaries of Mali empire, at its peak
Southern limit of desert
Northern limit of forest
Expeditions of Askiya Muhammad
Land over 3000 feet
km
0
500
miles
0
300

by the archaeological excavations at Kumbi Saleh, which may suggest that the town – believed to have been the Muslim twin-town of the royal town of Ghana – was flourishing in the twelfth century.

Ghana, however, did not regain its former power, and ceased to be the all-embracing kingdom of the Soninke. Also, it lost exclusive control over the gold and the Saharan trade. The Diafunke, a section of the Soninke west of Kingui, in the Sahel, established an important state. In the middle of the twelfth century Diafunu extended its authority over the Sanhaja of the southern Sahara, who had been seriously weakened by the migration of their contingents to the Maghrib and Spain. The capital of Diafunu developed into a commercial centre to which traders came from the Sus, Tafilelt and even from Ghadames. On a visit to Marrakesh towards the end of the Almoravid period, the king of Diafunu was accorded a stately reception. He himself was described as black, semi-nomad, wrapped in the Sanhaja veil. Soninke rulers in the Sahel came under the cultural influence of the Saharan nomads. Diafunu, however, did not survive long and gave way to the rise of the Niakhate dynasty in Diara.

Among other Soninke states that emerged as a result of the political fragmentation of Ghana, Mema, situated in the lacustrine region of the Niger south of Timbuktu, seems to have been the closest heir to Ghana. Mema, according to some traditions, was founded by a chief of the crown slaves of Wagadu (Ghana). As the northern Soninke of the Sahel had been weakened through the long confrontation with the Sanhaja, which reached its climax in the Almoravid conquest of Ghana, a southern group of the Soninke, the Susu, rose to hegemony. From their homeland in Kaniaga, the Susu extended their authority over their neighbours, and reached the height of their power early in the thirteenth century, under the rule of Sumanguru Kante. He took over the former territories of Ghana in the north and the rising Malinke chiefdoms in the south. By that time many of the northern Soninke were Muslims, but the Susu, who had not been exposed in the same degree to the influence of the Sahara and the Maghrib, faithfully adhered to their ancestral religion. An interpretation of oral traditions may represent the Susu as an indigenous African reaction to the disintegrating effects of the northern impact.

Some traditions say that when Sumanguru conquered Ghana he persecuted the Muslim traders there. This harassment of traders from the Maghrib may have prompted the Almohad governor of Sijilmasa, shortly before 1199, to send a letter 'to the king of the Sudan in Ghana', reproaching him for detaining traders: 'We may live as good neighbours though we differ in [our] religions.'[1] The destruction of Ghana and its trade is ascribed to Sumanguru, from whose oppression the principal Muslim families – Arab and Berber traders along with their Soninke associates – escaped to settle in Biru, a small Soninke village. Biru became known by its Berber name of Walata, and attracted the neighbouring Massufa nomads, who had already been involved in the Saharan trade as guides and as the owners of the Taghaza salt mine in the heart of the desert. As the principal terminus of the caravan trade, Walata replaced both Awdaghust and Ghana, the Berber and the Sudanese towns, respectively. Walata had a mixed population of Berbers and Sudanese, reflecting the *rapprochement* between the two ethnic groups as a result of the intensification of the trade and the advance of Islam. Ghana had twin towns to allow the coexistence of a royal capital and a commercial entrepôt, but Walata was devoid of a political role, being a cosmopolitan Muslim town. This change was also associated with the shift of the political centre of gravity from the Sahel south into the interior, with the rise of Susu, and later that of Mali.

When Ghana was the leading power in the western Sudan, the main source of gold was Bambuk, the district between the Senegal and the Faleme rivers. Centuries of exploitation had reduced the productivity of the goldfields of Bambuk, while demand in the Maghrib for the gold of the Sudan was increasing. In the eleventh and twelfth centuries new goldfields were opened up in Bure on the upper Niger. As trade routes extended southwards to the new sources of gold, a wider section of the Sudan came within the orbit of an extensive commercial network. Al-Bakrī's account of the chiefdoms of Malal and Do must refer to the beginning of a more elaborated political organization, and to the emergence of chiefdoms among the Malinke of the upper Niger, who earlier in the eleventh century were still referred to as Lamlam, one of the names given to the 'primitive', loosely organized peoples. In Malal, one of these early chiefdoms of the Malinke, the ruler is reported by al-Bakrī to have been converted to Islam by a Muslim who was resident in the country. The evidence points to the interaction between the development of trade, the emergence of chiefdoms, and later also the spread of Islam.

Oral traditions of the Malinke refer to early chiefdoms which preceded the rise of the empire of Mali. These chiefdoms, each a regroup-

[1] al-Maqqarī, *Kitāb nafḥ al-ṭīb* [*Analectes sur l'histoire et la littérature des Arabes d'Espagne*], tr. R. Dozy, G. Dugat, L. Krehl and W. Wright (Leiden, 1855–61), II, 72.

ing of neighbouring villages, spread between the upper Senegal and the upper Niger valleys. They were ruled over by different Malinke clans. Hunters' associations seem to have played an important role in the process of state-building. Hunters had an esoteric cult, were well armed and their associations cut across clan, status and caste boundaries. The future kings of Mali belonged to the Keita clan, and they began as rulers of a Malinke chiefdom on the Sankarani. The Keita chiefs are described in the traditions with the attributes of hunter-kings. At a period when the Malinke country was brought into the orbit of the continental trading system, the Keita chiefs recruited hunters' associations to further their own interests. They sought to increase their power and to gain control of the benefits accruing from the new trading activities. This evolutionary process was, however, disturbed at the end of the twelfth or beginning of the thirteenth century, when the Malinke were subjugated by Sumanguru, the powerful king of Susu. The empire of Mali emerged a few decades later from a war of independence in which the great Sundiata succeeded in uniting the Malinke clans and chiefdoms.

The successive hegemonies of Ghana, Susu and Mali tell the story of the central part of the western Sudan, between the Sahel and the upper Niger, where the Almoravid aftermath caused disruption, re-orientation and restructuring. West of this area was Takrur, on the lower Senegal. On the evidence of al-Bakrī, Takrur had become a Muslim kingdom before Ibn Yāsīn came to preach among the Sanhaja. With the rise of the Almoravids, the king of Takrur became their ally. In 1056 Labi, son of War Dyabe, king of Takrur, joined Yaḥyā b. 'Umar in fighting the rebellious Juddala. The Almoravid victory over Ghana may have added to the strength and wealth of Takrur. If al-Idrīsī's account is correct and well interpreted, it may indicate that in the twelfth century the authority of the king of Takrur expanded up the Senegal river to Barisa, which was an entrepôt for the gold trade of Bambuk. A century earlier, according to al-Bakrī, this place was clearly within the sphere of influence of Ghana, the ruler of which controlled the overland routes to Barisa (or Yaresna) and the supply of salt. In the twelfth century Barisa received salt from Awlil by way of Takrur and the Senegal river. Writing in 1240, Ibn Sa'īd described the association of the ruler of Takrur and its aristocracy with the white traders from the Maghrib, whom they imitated in their dress and in their food. Ibn Sa'īd was also the first Arab author to notice the distinction between two sections of the population of Takrur: the sedentaries, or the ancestors of the present Tukolor and the nomads, the ancestors of the present Fulani.

East of the Niger bend, the Songhay state remained sheltered from the direct intervention of the Almoravids. But, as has already been mentioned, marble tombstones from Andalusia dating from 1100 to 1110 indicate closer relations with the Almoravid empire across the desert. The kings of Songhay had been Muslims since the tenth century; yet in the available king lists of Songhay, none of the kings before the thirteenth century had a Muslim name. Sauvaget, who analysed the inscriptions on the tombstones, suggests that the Muslim names of the successive kings who died between 1100 and 1120 were those of recent converts. According to al-Bakrī, only Muslims could succeed to the kingship of Songhay, and Sauvaget suggests that in fact the kings may have converted to Islam only on their election. Nominal and partial acceptance of Islam by the king of Songhay is suggested also by the pre-Islamic customs which persisted at his court, as described by al-Bakrī.

In the twelfth century, as in preceding centuries, most of the trade of Gao was with the central Maghrib, by way of Wargla. Only a few caravans came to Gao from Sijilmasa. Until this time the Songhay still kept apart from events on the other side of the Niger bend. It was only with the expansion of Mali that the Songhay were brought into the ambit of the western Sudanese imperial system, first as vassals, and then, from the fifteenth century on, as the rulers of a vast empire.

MARINIDS IN MOROCCO AND ʿABD AL-WADIDS IN TLEMCEN, *c.* 1250–*c.* 1430

The defeat of the Almohads in 1212 at the battle of Las Navas de Tolosa in Spain (see p. 344) exposed their vulnerability not only in the Iberian peninsula but also in the Maghrib. The Banū Marīn, a nomadic and warlike sub-tribe of the Zanata, who had lived in the pre-Saharan steppes between Tafilelt and Figguig, exploited the weakness of the caliph and invaded the cultivated lands of north-eastern Morocco. It is unlikely that the Banū Marīn had any political motives at first, other than the normal desire of nomads to increase their resources at the expense of the peasant population. Gradually, however, they established their hegemony over the local people, who were forced to pay contributions. Towns like Taza, Fez and Qasr al-Kabir were also made to pay tribute.

In 1240, when they were laying siege to Meknes, the Banū Marīn were defeated by the Almohad caliph, Saʿīd. They retreated to the Sahara, but by that time the taste of authority and the struggle against the Almohads had stimulated their political ambitions. In 1245, under the leadership of Abū Yaḥyā Abū Bakr, son of Abd al-Ḥaqq, the Banū Marīn invaded Morocco once again, where their advance was temporarily halted by the last attempt of the caliph Saʿīd to restore the Almohad empire. But following the death of Saʿīd in 1248, Abū Yaḥyā conquered Fez, Taza, Meknes, Sale and Rabat. Fez became the centre of a new *makhzin*, rival to that of the Almohads in Marrakesh. When Abū Yaḥyā died in 1258, the Almohads held only the High Atlas, the Sus and the region of Marrakesh. Weak as they were, the Almohads could still threaten the Marinids by exploiting internal divisions within the new dynasty. The new Marinid ruler, Abū Yūsuf Yaʿqūb (1258–86), consolidated his power in a final assault, which led to the conquest of Marrakesh in 1269 and to the end of the Almohad empire.

The Marinids succeeded the Almohads in Morocco. In Ifrīqiya the Hafsids were already established as heirs to the Almohads. Since 1236 the Hafsid rulers had assumed the title of caliph as the true guardians of the Almohad doctrine. The Marinids, who had no religious legitimacy of their own, deemed it prudent to pay nominal allegiance to the remote Hafsid caliph. The name of the Hafsid caliph, however, was omitted from the Friday sermon (*khuṭba*) in Morocco within thirty years, when the Marinid sultans felt secure enough.

The Hafsids and the Marinids were territorially separated by the rise of a third dynasty, that of the ʿAbd al-Wadids, or the Zayyanids, with their centre at Tlemcen. Their kingdom was always weaker than either of its neighbours, and its boundaries were fluid. Though it was for long periods under the patronage of the Marinids, the Hafsids or the Christian king of Aragon, this dynasty survived for three centuries until the Ottoman conquest in 1554. The main asset of Tlemcen was its commercial prosperity as the focal point for the trade of Europe with the Maghrib and the western Sudan. Tlemcen had replaced Tahert as the commercial entrepôt of the central Maghrib. In the middle of the eleventh century al-Bakrī described it as the destination of traders from all directions. A century later al-Idrīsī regarded Tlemcen as the third richest town in the Maghrib, after Fez and Aghmat. By the thirteenth century Aghmat had declined, while Fez and Tlemcen, as the capitals of rival dynasties, competed for their shares in the growing trade with Europe.

In its location Tlemcen had a certain advantage over Fez. The port of Oran had been established in the tenth century by the Andalusians, to trade first with Tahert and then with Tlemcen. Oran and, from the latter part of the fourteenth century, Hunayn were well situated for the trade with Europe, and diverted a substantial part of the trade to Tlemcen. During that period Sijilmasa was the principal terminus at the northern end of the trans-Saharan route. Though Fez was closer in distance to Sijilmasa, caravans preferred the route to Tlemcen, which avoided the passage of the Atlas range. The artisans of Fez, however, developed a thriving craft industry of weaving and leather products for export to the Sudan, to the Orient and to Europe. The enterprising merchants of Fez endeavoured to establish a lucrative commercial network. But in order to support their traders, and to offset the geographical advantages of Tlemcen, the Marinid sultans of Fez had to gain control of Sijilmasa.

In the middle of the thirteenth century, when the two dynasties were still in their formative stage, the Marinids and the ʿAbd al-Wadids fought over Sijilmasa. In 1257 Abū Yaḥyā, the Marinid, conquered Sijilmasa and the Wādī Darʿa, and forestalled an attempt by Yaghmorasen, ruler of Tlemcen, to take over the town. But in 1264, when Abū Yūsuf Yaʿqūb, the Marinid, was engaged in fighting the Almohads, Yaghmorasen took possession of Sijilmasa. Following the conquest of Marrakesh in 1269, Abū Yūsuf attacked Tlemcen in 1272. The capital of the ʿAbd al-Wadids survived, but Sijilmasa was reconquered by Abū Yūsuf. From then on Tlemcen was unable to challenge the military superiority of Fez, though its rulers often allied themselves with the adversaries of the Marinids, both the internal Muslim ones and the external Christian ones. In 1287, a rebellious son of the Marinid Abū Yaʿqūb Yūsuf (1286–1307) sought refuge in Tlemcen.

Tlemcen was a thorn in the flesh of the Marinids, both commercially and politically. In 1299, Abū-Yaʿqūb conquered the central Maghrib as far as Algiers and besieged Tlemcen for a period of eight years. During the siege Abū Yaʿqūb built a new town, al-Manṣūra, opposite Tlemcen. This town, sometimes referred to also as 'New Tlemcen', soon developed as a commercial entrepôt with markets and caravanserais, where merchants – Muslims, Christians and Jews – assembled from many lands. Though the bulk of the trade was diverted to al-Manṣūra, Christian merchants secretly supplied provisions to the besieged town. In 1307 Abū Yaʿqūb was murdered by one of his eunuchs, the army retreated and Tlemcen was relieved. The rival town of al-Manṣūra was destroyed.

For about thirty years, from 1308 to 1337, Tlemcen regained not only its commercial prosperity but also greater political independence vis-à-vis Aragon and in its relations with its neighbours in the Maghrib. The Hafsids were then involved in an internal dynastic dispute and their state was temporarily split into four principalities.

In Fez, the murder of Abū Yaʿqūb was followed by the short reigns (1307–10) of his two sons Abū Thābit and Abū Rabīʿ. They were succeeded by Abū Saʿīd ʿUthmān, brother of Abū Yaʿqūb. His relatively long reign (1310–31) was troubled by the recurrent revolts of his son Abū ʿAlī, who was made governor of Sijilmasa. From this strategic position Abū ʿAli conquered the oases of Tuat, Gurara, Wādī Darʿa, the Sus and Marrakesh. There was a real danger of a split, and the rise of a rival Marinid state in southern Morocco in control of the termini of the trans-Saharan trade. These prospects must have pleased the rulers of Tlemcen. Twice Abū Saʿīd had defeated his rebellious son, and twice he had left him as a governor of Sijilmasa, perhaps because of local support he had there. In 1331, Abū Saʿīd was succeeded by his son Abu'l-Ḥasan, and it was left to him to defeat his brother Abū ʿAlī and to reassert the authority of Fez in Sijilmasa. Abu'l-Ḥasan, the greatest of the Marinid sultans, put an end to internal dissent and resumed an offensive policy.

Ever since the rise of their dynasty, the Marinids had cultivated cordial relations with the Hafsids in Tunis, and Abu'l-Ḥasan's marriage to a Hafsid princess cemented this alliance. When Abū Tāshfīn, ruler of Tlemcen, arrogantly harassed the weakened Hafsids, the latter invoked the aid of Abu'l-Ḥasan. This was an excellent pretext for the Marinid sultan to fight his erstwhile enemies in Tlemcen. In 1335 he invaded the central Maghrib and laid siege to Tlemcen, while rebuilding the rival town of al-Manṣūra. In May 1337 Tlemcen was conquered, and Abu'l-Ḥasan announced his victory to the principal Muslim kings of the day. Delegations reached him to convey greetings from the kings of Egypt, Granada, Tunis and Mali. For Mali the Moroccan conquest of Tlemcen had a special significance. For the first time all the outlets of the trans-Saharan trade in the western and central Maghrib – including Sijilmasa and Tlemcen – were under one authority. This, as shall be shown later on (see pp. 395–6), was the occasion for the beginning of a series of diplomatic exchanges between the kings of Mali and Fez.

The Hafsids became in reality clients of the Marinid sultan. In 1346, Abū Bakr, the Hafsid, an ally and an in-law of Abu'l-Ḥasan, died, and once again the kingdom was in the throes of a succession dispute. Abu'l-Ḥasan could not resist the temptation – perhaps he was even invited by some Hafsid dignitaries – and in 1347 he annexed Ifrīqiya. Abu'l-Ḥasan reached the height of his power, and reunited the western and central Maghrib as it had been in the days of the Almohads. But, like the Almohads, he was engaged at the same time in a war in Spain which put an enormous strain on his resources, and, again like the Almohads, he encountered the opposition of the Arab tribes in Ifrīqiya.

The Hafsid rulers of Ifrīqiya had pursued a liberal policy towards the Arab tribes, and avoided direct interference in their internal affairs. Abu'l-Ḥasan sought to impose a more direct rule, abolishing the rights of Arab chiefs to collect tribute from peasants under their protection, and establishing garrison posts to watch over their movements. The Arabs revolted, and in April 1348, less than a year after he had conquered Ifrīqiya, Abu'l-Ḥasan's army was defeated by the Arabs near Kairouan.

While Abu'l-Ḥasan was fighting in Ifrīqiya to reassert his authority, his own son, Abu 'Inān, governor of Tlemcen, hastened to Fez and declared himself sultan. He claimed that he had to forestall the assumption of power by al Manṣūr, who was governor of Fez. Tlemcen threw off Moroccan rule and the central Maghrib was in revolt. As the overland route was blocked, Abu'l-Ḥasan returned by sea only to have his fleet wrecked in a storm. With the remnants of his army, Abu'l-Ḥasan failed in an attempt to subdue Tlemcen, and retreated to Sijilmasa in January 1350. His son, Abu 'Inān, refused to give up the throne and in May 1350 he defeated his father in battle. Pursued by his son, Abu'l-Ḥasan sought refuge in the High Atlas, where he died in May 1351 among the Hintata. Ironically, it was in the land of a leading Almohad tribe that the greatest of the Marinid sultans ended his life, beaten and deposed.

Abū 'Inān was as ambitious as his father, perhaps even more so, as he assumed the caliphal title of *amīr al-mu'minīn*. In 1352 he reconquered Tlemcen and the central Maghrib. In 1353 he annexed Bougie, and in 1357 he accomplished the conquest of Ifrīqiya when he entered Tunis. But the next year, in 1358, he was forced to retreat in the face of the growing opposition of the Arabs. He was, one may say, re-enacting the career of his father. Back in Fez, he fell sick and was murdered by one of his ministers. His death marked the beginning of a period of anarchy, which lasted until the extinction of the dynasty in the fifteenth century. We shall come back to this period after analysing some of the main features of Moroccan history under the Marinids.

As successors to the Almohads, the Marinids regarded themselves as guardians of Islam in the Iberian peninsula. Indeed, the Marinids could hardly ignore Spain, because as early as 1260, while they were still fighting both the Almohads and Tlemcen, a Spanish force landed in Sale. Abū Yūsuf Yaʿqūb drove this force away, but he must have realized the significance of this intervention. After he had exterminated the Almohads (1269) and had taken over Sijilmasa (1274), he crossed the straits and scored a victory over the Christians in 1275. A series of Moroccan interventions in Spain, continuing until 1285, resulted in the conclusion of an agreement in which the king of Castile undertook not to intervene in the affairs of the Muslim territories in the peninsula. The Marinids proclaimed it a victory to enhance their prestige. In 1291, the cessation of hostilities between Aragon and Castile increased the pressure from the Christians.

Though the Muslim emir of Granada often allied himself with the enemies of the Marinids, Abu'l-Ḥasan regarded it as his duty to come to this emir's aid when called. In 1333 he crossed the straits and conquered Algeciras, and in 1340 (after his successful exploits in the central Maghrib) Abu'l-Ḥasan's fleet gained control of the straits and laid siege to Tarifa. Soon afterwards the odds turned against him, the siege of Tarifa ended with the defeat of the Muslims and in 1344 Algeciras was reconquered by the Christians. This, followed by the disaster in Ifrīqiya, was the last time the Marinids, or any Moroccan dynasty, actively intervened in Spain. As the Christians established their military and economic superiority, the Maghrib moved onto the defensive.

The history of the Maghrib may be related in terms of the succession to hegemony of rival Berber confederations. The Sanhaja of the Sahara (the Almoravids) had been replaced by the Masmuda of the High Atlas mountains (the Almohads), who in their turn were overthrown by the Zanata of the sub-Saharan steppes (the Banū Marīn). Whereas both the Sanhaja and the Masmuda sought to retain exclusive privileges and prerogatives of authority, the Banū Marīn Zanata were better disposed to integrate other groups into the *makhzin* – and mainly the Arabs. Three factors may have contributed to this trend: first, the Banū Marīn and related Zanata clans were not numerous enough to secure ethnic military support for the dynasty; secondly, the Zanata of the steppes and the lower plains had already begun to be assimilated with the Arab nomads with whom they shared a similar way of life; thirdly, by the second half of the thirteenth century the Arabs had increased their influence and power in Morocco, and no one could have ruled there without their co-operation. The Marinids, therefore, established a *makhzin* based on Zanata and Arabs. When riding in state, the Marinid sultan was flanked on either side by an Arab and a Zanata chief as a symbol of the dual character of the *makhzin*.

Under the Almohads the intrusion of the Arab nomads into Morocco had contaminated the exclusive Berber character of the country. Under the Marinids, as the Arabs expanded their domains and assimilated many of the Zanata and other Berbers of the plains, Morocco experienced an intensive process of arabization. Whereas in the *mahkzin* and in the army of the Almoravids and the Almohads, Berber was spoken, under the Marinids Arabic became the common and official language.

The expansion of the Arabs increased the domains of the nomads at the expense of the cultivated lands. Many gardens and forests were destroyed, peasants in the plains were exposed to depredations and to unofficial taxation by the nomads. It seems as if the decline in the population of Morocco, for which there is some evidence in the thirteenth and fourteenth centuries, was connected with the growth of nomadism. With the changing character of the countryside, the population of Morocco became divided into three types: nomads, increasingly isolated townsmen and dissident mountaineers.

The Marinids hardly attempted, and never succeeded, in imposing their authority over the Berbers of the mountains. Large parts of the Atlas, the Rif and the Jibal were virtually autonomous. Though the mountain Berbers sometimes recognized the sovereignty of the sultan, they were outside the effective government of the *makhzin*. In the latter half of the fourteenth century, when the dynasty was torn by internal rivalry, Marrakesh came under the patronage of the tribal chiefs of the High Atlas. This was, in fact, the first sign of a change from the old passive role of the mountain peoples to a more active intervention in the lands of the *makhzin*.

Villages and small towns seem to have been submerged by the nomad expansion. The larger towns survived as isolated oases of urban civilization and commercial activity. Marrakesh, the capital of the two previous dynasties, declined, while Fez, which had already been the leading cultural centre, now became the capital. The sultan Abū Yūsuf built the 'New Fez', as the seat of the sultan and his *makhzin*, a twin-town to the 'Old Fez'. Andalusian immigrants settled in Fez and introduced a more refined urban style in building, in the arts, in literature and philosophy. But this influence was restricted to the towns, and more particularly to Fez, and it contributed even further to the mutual alienation of urban and rural life, and to the lack of interaction between the capital and the provinces.

The dichotomy between Fez and the countryside was even more emphasized in religious life. Fez was adorned with *madrasas*, while the rural population drifted towards the *zāwiyas*. Unlike the two preceding dynasties, the Marinids had no doctrinal message of their own and no religious legitimacy. During their early formative period they sought to derive their legitimacy from the Hafsid caliph in whose name the public prayer was said. After they had established their power in Morocco they abandoned this fiction, and acquired recognition as patrons of the *ʿulamāʾ* and as restorers and guardians of Islamic orthodoxy. Against all political odds, they paid dearly for their interventions in Spain, which were greatly motivated by the desire to be worthy successors to former dynasties in fighting for the Faith. Almost all the Marinid sultans are described as being pious and devoted Muslims, and some of them, such as Abu'l-Ḥasan and his son Abū 'Inān, even attained some distinction as scholars.

Before Abu'l-Ḥasan, the sultans held the title of *amīr al-muslimīn*, formerly used by the Almoravids, which implied no claim to the status of a caliph or *amīr al-muʾminīn*. Abu'l-Ḥasan, who led a jihad against the Christians of Spain and brought the whole Maghrib under his authority, aspired to be caliph. In the fashion of caliphs, he added to his name the honorific title Nāṣir al-Dīn. An inscription written towards the end of his reign, at the height of his success after 1346, refers to him as *khalīfa*. Indeed, his ambition to be recognized as a caliph goes some way to explain Ibn Khaldūn's account of a deputation from Mansa Sulaymān of Mali to Abu'l-Ḥasan, some time before 1348:

> They lauded the authority of the sultan, acknowledged his prerogative, conveyed the submission of their king and his willingness to pay the sultan his dues, and to act according to his wish and advice . . . The sultan [thus] achieved his aim of setting himself above other kings and making them submit to his authority. He thanked Allah for his favours.[1]

Abu'l-Ḥasan is presented here as being a true predecessor to the Saʿdids of the sixteenth century, who as caliphs claimed sovereignty over the Sahara and the Sudan beyond it.

[1] Ibn Khaldūn, *Taʾrīkh al-duwal*, II, 394–5/tr. IV, 243–4.

Though the political ambitions of Abu'l-Ḥasan were defeated, his son Abū 'Inān clung even more assiduously to the title of caliph. In all his inscriptions Abū 'Inān is called *amīr al-mu'minīn*. An inscription in the Andalusian mosque of Fez indicates that even a later ruler, like Abū Sa'īd 'Uthmān, at the time of the dynasty's decline, boasted the title of caliph.

It was under the Almohads, as has been shown, that the founding saints of Moroccan Sufism lived. But it was in the period of the Marinids that their spiritual successors institutionalized mysticism by the establishment of the Sufi orders (*ṭarīqas*), which were mostly ramifications of the Qādiriyya. Heads of the *ṭarīqas* were believed to have supernatural power and a sacred emanation (*baraka*) which could be transferred by physical contact with the man or his grave. In this way Moroccan Sufism became closely associated with the cult of saints, who performed miracles and who could act as mediators and intercessors between men and God.

The cult of saints absorbed pre-Islamic beliefs and customs, and Sufi centres, or *zāwiyas*, were sometimes established in the place of traditional pre-Islamic shrines or holy stones. This new type of Berber Islam, with its more popular aspects, contributed to the islamization of the countryside because the religious message reached the remotest Berber tribes of the mountains, who had had little to do with the more formal aspects of Islam in past centuries. Though the expansion of this brand of Islam was made easier by the incorporation of Berber traditions, Sufi leaders are reported to have striven against pagan or Christian survivals and to have instructed the people to observe the precepts of Islam more strictly.

The old institution of the *ribāṭ* developed from an outpost for a jihad into a centre of devotion, which by the fourteenth century was mainly concerned with the exercise of mystical rituals. Whereas the Almoravids (*al-murābiṭūn*) derived their name from the concept of the *ribāṭ* as a preparation for jihad, a saint and a leader of the Sufi orders was often referred to as *murābiṭ*, associated with the *ribāṭ* as a place of devotion. Through Maghribi dialects and French usage, the *murābiṭ* is better known as *marabout*, and that type of Islam as 'maraboutism'.

Under the Marinids the *ṭarīqas* became intimately involved in the life of the Berber tribes, and though the marabouts did not exercise direct political power they were very much in the centre of village life. They acted not only as religious guides and a source of blessing but also as arbiters in private and public disputes. Maraboutism proved adaptable to the political and social traditions of the Berbers. With the growing alienation between the urban *makhzin* and the countryside, maraboutism developed largely as an extra-*makhzin* phenomenon.

The Marinid sultans were themselves attracted by the mysticism of the Sufis, and they admired some saints, who were invited to stay at the court. But these were the urban mystics, who operated well within the boundaries of Islamic orthodoxy, and were themselves somewhat divorced from the rural marabouts. Also, the institution of the *mawlid* (the Prophet's birthday) as an official festival, by the sultan Abū Yaʿqūb in 1292, was another attempt at adjustment to the popular trends of Islam and at the development of a common culture. In Tlemcen Abu'l-Ḥasan built the sanctuary of the great saint Sīdī Abū Madyān, while Abū ʿInān established another in honour of Sīdī al-Ḥalawī.

But the sultans were unable to control the growing popular movement, the charismatic leaders of which were in direct communication with the rural population. Prudently, without insulting the religious feeling of the people, the sultans sought to strengthen Islamic orthodoxy and its representatives, the *fuqahā'*. They established *madrasas* as institutions of religious education in which the tenets of the Maliki school of law were taught. The sultans encouraged young men from the rural areas to join the *madrasas* in Fez, as a way to limit the influence of the marabouts. The students lived in the *madrasas*, which developed as residential colleges. These institutions, with their emphasis on conformity, shaped the élite of Morocco, among whom members of the bureaucracy were also recruited.

The Marinids established a rudimentary *makhzin* only, which was decentralized in nature. Marinid princes and influential Zanata and Arab chiefs ruled over provinces with little interference from Fez, while at the level of local communities headmen needed the confirmation of the sultan, which was often rather theoretical. Taxes, even when levied, rarely reached the treasury of the *makhzin* in Fez, and the only secure and direct sources of income were duties and concession fees paid by foreign European traders. The sultans, therefore, encouraged the activities of foreign traders and were disposed to grant concessions to them, often to the disapproval of both local traders and the *ʿulamā'*.

In Fez itself the chancellery employed not only graduates of the *madrasas* but also Andalusian immigrants and bureaucrats who had acquired experience in the service of other dynasties. Most famous of the latter was Ibn Khaldūn. The chamberlains, who formed the inner circle of the sultan's advisers and often screened him from the influence of others, were mostly persons with no outside connections or independent power, such as slaves, eunuchs, freedmen and Jews. The senior political official was the vizier, who was appointed from outside the royal family, though often he was a Zanata. Eventually these formed clans of viziers such as the Banū-Waṭṭās, and, as weaker sultans succeeded each other rather rapidly, the power of the viziers increased considerably, though not their own security.

At the higher levels of the provincial administration there was little differentiation between the military and civilian functions. The great Zanata and Arab chiefs were also in command of their warriors, who did not form a regular army but were called up in time of war. Both Zanata and Arabs were nomad horsemen and the Marinids, unlike the Almohads, never had an infantry of their own people. Their infantry, who formed also the standing army, were mercenaries – some Turkomen, but mainly Christians or renegades. Christian mercenaries, as has been shown (see pp. 337–8), had been employed also by the Almoravids and the Almohads. They were of even greater importance in the service of the ʿAbd al-Wadids in Tlemcen, where they wielded considerable power. Whereas in previous centuries most of these Christian mercenaries were recruited individually from among captives or adventurers, in the thirteenth and fourteenth centuries they were often officially dispatched by the kings of Castile or Aragon. The latter, for example, had the right to appoint the commander of the Christian unit in Tlemcen, though perhaps not in Morocco. This way of recruiting had political implications, and the presence of those Christians who had the right to worship freely was an affront to orthodox *ʿulamā*'. Still, their efficiency in war made them indispensable.

An effective army was needed not only for external wars but also for the maintenance of government. The lack of religious ideology as a source of legitimacy and for mobilizing popular support, as well as the cleavage within the society between the *makhzin* and the countryside, left sheer force as the principal means of achieving political authority. Also, the Marinid dynasty had little internal cohesion. Rival claimants to the throne appeared as early as 1258, after the death of Abū Yaḥyā and before their rule over Morocco had been consolidated. Soon after Abū Yūsuf had secured the throne, he faced revolts from members of his family who held offices in the provincial government. This, in fact, became a recurrent theme in the history of the Marinids.

Not only brothers and cousins challenged the reigning sultan, but also sons revolted against fathers: Abū ʿAlī, as governor of Sijilmasa, against his father the sultan Abū Saʿīd ʿUthman; and Abū ʿInān, who took advantage of his father's disastrous defeat in Ifrīqiya to proclaim himself sultan. In common with other dynasties, succession became complicated because of the great number of royal princes and the lack of established rules of succession.

Seventeen Marinid sultans reigned after Abū ʿInān, between 1358 and 1465, three of whom succeeded as children, at the ages of four, five and ten. Seven of the sultans were murdered, five were deposed and only five died in office. During this troubled period the viziers had more power than did their sultans, but they were exposed to constant threat from other ambitious politicians, and viziers held office for periods which were almost as short as those of the sultans' reigns. Political competition was conducted by intrigues, but determined by force. Military force was in the hands of the commander of the Christian mercenaries, the head of the (Muslim) guard, and the great Arab shaykhs. All these, therefore, were drawn into succession disputes, coups and counter-coups. The Marinids, one may say, carried the seeds of their own destruction within their dynasty and their system of government.

The more illustrious periods in the history of Morocco under the Marinids were those during the reigns of kings like Abū-Yaʿqūb (1286–1307) and Abu'l-Ḥasan (1331–48), who pursued an aggressive policy in Spain and against the neighbouring kingdoms of the Maghrib. Morocco, it seems, had not yet settled its own affairs; nor had its neighbours. Even in the second half of the fourteenth century, when the three kingdoms of Morocco, Granada and Tlemcen were all weak, their rulers interfered in each other's affairs. Whenever a resourceful king came to the throne in Fez, like Abū Fāris ʿAbd al-ʿAzīz (1366–72) or Abu'l-ʿAbbās (during his second reign 1387–93), he set out to conquer Tlemcen. The ruler of Tlemcen reciprocated when in 1421 he put his own protégé on the throne of Fez. In the last quarter of the fourteenth century the Naṣrid king of Granada repeatedly interfered in the succession disputes in Fez, and he seems always to have had a Marinid candidate in Granada as a threat to the reigning sultan.

Towards the close of the century the growing Christian pressure diverted the rulers of Granada from indulging in interference in Morocco. In 1415, a screen was drawn between Morocco and Granada when the Portuguese occupied Ceuta. This may be regarded as a landmark in the history of north-west Africa, as it augured Christian aggression on the African coasts. In Morocco, the Marinid period came to its end in 1420, though sultans of that dynasty reigned until 1465 under the tutelage of the Banū Waṭṭās.

The predominance that the Italian merchants established over trade with the Maghrib in the twelfth century was challenged in the thirteenth century by the Catalans. Though Catalan ships had visited the ports of the Maghrib for some time, their effective entry into trade with Africa may be dated at the conquest of Majorca by King James I of Aragon in 1229. Majorca had been for a long time under Muslim rule and had close connections with the Maghrib. The Catalans were determined to use Majorca as a springboard to the Maghrib, and in particular to Tlemcen and its ports which were situated opposite the Balearic Islands.

Aragon's relations with the Maghrib were both commercial and political. Jews played an important role in the Catalan trade. There were Jewish communities with commercial interests in Barcelona, Majorca, Tlemcen, Sijilmasa and Tuat – that is, in strategic centres along the route of the gold trade from the Sudan to Europe. Family, religious and commercial relations between those Jewish communities facilitated the flow of the trade, with Majorca as the linchpin of this system. In the fourteenth century the existing information about the Sahara and the Sudan stored in Majorca was exhibited in the portulans and planispheres. Jews played a leading role in Majorcan cartography.

Jews helped to bridge the Christian and Muslim worlds, and Spanish kings used to send Jews as ambassadors to Muslim rulers. In 1274, less than twenty years after he had conquered Majorca, James I extended his patronage to two Jewish families in Sijilmasa. Jews from the Maghrib were accorded favourable conditions in his kingdom, and the period is regarded as having been the golden age of the Jews in Aragon. Indeed, conditions for the Jews improved also in the Maghrib where, after the persecutions by the Almohads, they enjoyed the patronage of the Marinids in Morocco and of the ʻAbd al-Wadids in Tlemcen.

In order to develop relations with the Maghrib, Peter III, the son of King James I of Aragon, encouraged the Muslims of Valencia to trade with Tlemcen and to emigrate there. Jews, Muslims and Christians therefore took part in the trade on both shores of the Mediterranean. Christian Catalan traders formed an important community in Tlemcen, where they enjoyed special privileges. They came under the leadership of the commander of the Christian militia in the service of the ruler of Tlemcen. From 1254 onwards this commander, known as *alcayt*, was appointed by the king of Aragon. The latter attached great importance to this office and in the years 1277–9 Jaume Pérez, the bastard son of King Peter III, was at the head of the Christian community of Tlemcen. Besides his official tasks he was engaged also in the gold trade. By this time, indeed, the commercial relations of Catalan Spain with Tlemcen must be viewed in the wider context of the aggressive policy pursued by the kings of Aragon in the Maghrib.

When Yaghmorasen established the independent emirate of Tlemcen on the débris of the Almohad empire, some 2,000 of the Christian mercenaries of the Almohads came to serve the ruler of Tlemcen. Most of them had been Castilians, but in 1254 the Christian militia led a mutiny and was disbanded. The Castilians were replaced by Catalans, despatched by James I. Because of their military weakness, and their vulnerability to attacks from their Muslim neighbours, the Marinids and the Hafsids, the ʿAbd al-Wadids were exposed to the pressure of Aragon. They gave favourable conditions to the Catalan traders, including a rebate of part of the duties they had paid. Aragon even claimed an annual payment of 2,000 golden dinars from Tlemcen for the services of the militia as well as in order to 'buy peace' and to win the favours of the king of Aragon. In 1285 Castile, Granada and Morocco formed an alliance, which brought Aragon and Tlemcen closer to each other. A treaty signed in 1286 marked the peak of Aragon's influence over Tlemcen, which amounted almost to a protectorate. Aragon, however, failed to support Tlemcen when such aid was desperately needed. With the shifting alliances between Muslim and Christian kingdoms in Spain and in the Maghrib, a rapprochement between Morocco and Aragon at the end of the thirteenth century opened the way for the Marinid sultan Abū Yaʿqūb to conquer the central Maghrib and to lay siege to Tlemcen from 1299 to 1307. During the siege Catalans traded in al-Manṣūra, under the auspices of the Marinids. After the siege had been lifted, and during the period of Tlemcen's recovery, between 1308 and 1337, its rulers courageously defied attempts by Aragon to reassert their domination. Cordial political relations were not restored, because of the growing religious tensions and because of the growth of piracy, both Christian and Muslim, in the Mediterranean. Yet, in spite of worse political relations and insecurity on the sea, trade continued, though under greater strains.

While Catalan traders held much of the trade of Tlemcen, Italian traders, mainly from Genoa, maintained their predominance in Ceuta and in the Atlantic ports of Morocco, such as Sale. The competition among Christian traders of different nations and cities made commercial sanctions against the Muslim authorities almost impossible. The political ambitions of the Spaniards in the Maghrib caused their traders to be treated with suspicion, and the Muslim rulers seem to have had more easy relations with the Italians, whose interests were purely commercial.[1]

European traders, as has already been mentioned (p. 363), provided the Marinid sultans with a direct, independent source of income. Indeed, the Mediterranean trade contributed to the isolation of the *makhzin* from the society. Some enterprising European traders developed personal relations with the sultans. Cristiano de Spinola of Genoa stayed with Abū-Ya'qūb for some time during the siege of Tlemcen very early in the fourteenth century. Under the Marinids some European traders were given permission to penetrate inland, as did the Genoan trader who lived in Tafilelt at the end of the thirteenth century, and who furnished information to Giovanni de Carignan for his portulan. In the 1280s the Majorcan Franciscan Ramon Lull attempted missionary activities in the interior of the Marinid sultanate.

By the fourteenth century a complex trading system had developed between Europe and the Maghrib, in which the two regions exchanged their own products and at the same time carried the transit trade of other regions. The Europeans brought to the Maghrib products of the Orient, while the Maghrib channelled products of the western Sudan. Imports to the Maghrib included metals (iron, copper, tin) and hardware, timber, silk, cowries, precious stones, glass beads, glassware, spices, perfumes, paper and hunting birds. Textiles of different descriptions (cotton, linen and woollen cloth, and in particular dyed cloth) were often a major part of the consignments, but it is significant that the Maghrib also exported textile products (cotton and woollen cloth), though of different quality. Similarly, the excellent oil of the Maghrib was exported, and oil of lower quality was imported. Various dried fruits were sent in both directions, whereas the shipping of grain from one side of the Mediterranean or the other depended on the fortunes of the harvest in the different regions. Among its own pro-

[1] Though in 1234, before the rise of the Marinids, Genoan traders in Ceuta were massacred after their plot to take over the town had been exposed. In retaliation, about a hundred warships from Genoa blockaded Ceuta, until a peace treaty was signed and good relations restored.

ducts the Maghrib exported hides and leather products, wool, carpets, corals, wax, sugar, salted fish, dyeing materials and horses. From the western Sudan and the Sahara caravans brought to the ports of the Maghrib slaves, ostrich feathers, ivory, gum Arabic and the much desired yellow metal.

The flow of gold from the Maghrib to Europe levelled off a balance of trade which was otherwise greatly in favour of Europe. In Europe, the gold lubricated an expanding economy, and the Italian cities showed the way in introducing gold currency. Genoa and Florence minted gold coins from 1252 and Venice from 1284. In the first half of the fourteenth century the northern European states returned to the gold standard. As a result, the demand for gold increased considerably and its value went up, reaching a peak between 1305 and 1339. This stimulated an ever-growing trade between the two shores of the Mediterranean with repercussions further into the interior of Africa, across the Sahara. At the other end, the empire of Mali throve on this trade, and its traders, the Wangara or Dyula, extended the trade routes south to open new goldfields in the Akan forest.

The ascendancy of the Italian merchants in the trade in African gold was well established, and it had hardly been compromised by the intrusion of the Catalan traders. Much of the gold which the traders of Majorca and Barcelona obtained at the ports of Tlemcen – Oran and Hunayn – eventually reached Italy. Records of the 1360s mentioned the shipping of gold from 'Yspania' to Genoa. The Italians had a more direct access to gold in Ceuta. But the Genoans, who had cultivated propitious relations with the Muslim authorities in Ceuta, found it difficult to continue their trade after the Portuguese had conquered Ceuta in 1415.

At the beginning of the fourteenth century, when the trade of Tlemcen was at its peak, its ruler Abū Ḥammu (1308–18) said that he would have liked to have sent all traders away save those who traded with the Sudan. The latter brought in the precious gold needed all over the world. Other traders, on the contrary, sent this gold out to pay for perishable goods. We are fortunate to have an excellent account of a great commercial firm that carried on an extensive trade between Tlemcen and the western Sudan about the middle of the thirteenth century. It was the enterprise of five brothers of the Maqqarī family of Tlemcen, a very successful firm, whose 'wealth increased to the extent that it could hardly be computed'.[1]

Two of the brothers, Abū Bakr and Muḥammad, lived in Tlemcen,

[1] al-Maqqarī, *Kitāb nafḥ al-ṭīb*, ed. M. M. ʿAbd al-Ḥamīd (Cairo, 1949), VII, 129–32.

where they exchanged European merchandise for goods from the Sudan. The two youngest brothers, ʿAbd al-Wāḥid and ʿAlī, lived in Walata, which was then the terminus of the caravans in Mali. There they distributed the merchandise received from the north to local traders, and collected from them goods to be sent with the north-bound caravans to their brothers in Tlemcen. The eldest brother, ʿAbd al-Raḥmān, who was perhaps the head of the firm, lived in Sijilmasa. There he obtained information about goods and prices in the markets at both ends of the Sahara, in North Africa and the Sudan, and could therefore regulate the flow of goods to secure the largest profits. In Sijilmasa he was responsible also for the organization of the caravans. The Maqqarī firm invested in the maintenance of the principal trans-Saharan route from Sijilmasa to Walata via Taghaza; they dug wells and paid the guides and the nomads on that route, in order to provide maximum security for the traders.

This was evidently a relatively new route, because geographers of the eleventh and twelfth centuries described routes which passed farther to the west, where watering places were available at shorter intervals. Three factors contributed to the eastward shift of the main route. First, at the northern end of the Sahara, the Arab nomads of the Maʿqil became masters of the Sus and Wādī Darʿa from the beginning of the thirteenth century onwards. Security deteriorated and the caravans from Sijilmasa, which had previously travelled to the Wādī Darʿa to take a westerly route, now set out directly towards the desert to avoid the Arabs. Secondly, in the middle of the Sahara, this route reached the salt mine of Taghaza, which by the fourteenth century had become the major source of salt for the western Sudan. Thirdly, at the southern end of the Sahara, Walata replaced both the Berber commercial entrepôt at Awdaghust, and Kumbi, the capital of Ghana, as the main terminus of the caravans.

In 1352 Ibn Baṭṭūṭa made his way to Mali by this trans-Saharan route, and left a detailed first-hand account of the journey. Traders assembled in Sijilmasa to join the caravan, which set out under the leadership of a man of the Massufa. For centuries members of this tribe had served as guides of the caravans. These were essential, because no routes were visible on the sand, and one of the traders in Ibn-Baṭṭūṭa's caravan who had lagged behind was lost in the desert.

After twenty-five days the caravan reached Taghaza, where the houses were built of salt. Salt was dug there under the ground and cut into large slabs, two of which made a camel's load. No food was produced at Taghaza, and the labourers, all slaves of the Massufa, lived on dates from the Maghrib, millet from the Sudan and camel meat supplied by the nomads. It was a miserable and unhealthy place, but 'in spite of its wretchedness, transactions in tremendous sums of gold took place there'.[1]

In Taghaza, Ibn Baṭṭūṭa's caravan had to take on water for the ten days' journey to Tasarahla, because there was no water on that part of the route, except some ponds left over by the rain. Tasarahla is perhaps Bir al-Ksaib, the only important watering place between Taghaza and Walata. There the caravan took a longer rest before entering the most difficult part of the desert, where shortage of water was made worse by the danger of the moving sands. Caravans used to set out for the daily march at dawn and continued until the sun was high up in the sky. They rested till the afternoon prayer and then marched again until well after dark, when the night prayer was said. But on the last and most dangerous stage of the route to Walata, Ibn Baṭṭūṭa's caravan set out only after the afternoon prayer and travelled throughout the night until sunrise, and then stopped for the rest of the day. Even so, a caravan could not cover the distance between Tasarahla (Bir al-Ksaib) and Walata with its own water supply only. From Tasarahla one of the Massufa was sent forward as a scout to Walata to inform the people there of the approaching caravan. People from Walata then went out with water a distance of four days' travel to meet the tired and thirsty caravan. If the scout did not reach Walata, the whole caravan might perish.

The same scout also carried letters from the traders to their friends and associates in Walata, asking them to hire lodgings for them. In Walata, as in other commercial towns in West Africa, the residents served as hosts to foreign traders, introduced them to the local chief, informed them of current prices and acted as brokers in commercial transactions. In 1352 Walata was within the empire of Mali, and the caravan traders first paid their respects to the governor, a representative of the king of Mali, and then to another official, who was perhaps inspector of the market and the king's commercial agent. He had the right to buy from foreign traders before they disposed of their merchandise in other ways.

In Walata, Ibn Baṭṭūṭa reported, most of the inhabitants were Massufa. These Berbers were the leading traders and the *ʻulamāʼ*,

[1] Ibn Baṭṭūṭa, *Tuḥfat al-nuẓẓār fī gharāʼib al-amṣār wa-ʻajāʼib al-asfār* [*Voyages*], ed. and tr. C. Defrémery and B. R. Sanguinetti (Paris, 1922), IV, 378.

whereas the black Soninke rendered services to local and foreign traders. There were also traders from the Maghrib as residents in Walata, such as Ibn Baddā' of Sale, with whom Ibn Baṭṭūṭa lodged. A century earlier, in the middle of the thirteenth century, two brothers of the Maqqarī family had lived there. They built stone houses and married local women. Soon afterwards Walata was conquered by Mali, and the Maqqarī brothers suffered big losses. They even hired warriors to guard their property. One brother then sought audience with the king of Mali. He was well received and the king confirmed their position as leading traders in his country. The king of Mali even corresponded directly with the brothers in Tlemcen, sending them instructions to buy goods for him. The brothers' business prospered, but our sources tell us that their sons in Tlemcen lost all the assets because of local disturbances and the oppression of the rulers. Nothing, however, is known about the fate of the branch of the family in the Sudan, the descendants of 'Abd al-Wāḥid and 'Alī. Perhaps one of their descendants moved from Walata to the capital of Mali, where in 1352 Ibn Baṭṭūṭa met 'Abd al-Wāḥid al-Maqqarī.

'Abd al-Wāḥid al-Maqqarī was related by marriage to Muḥammad b. al-Faqīh of the Jazula tribe in southern Morocco. The latter was the head of the Maghribi community, which had its own ward in the capital of Mali. He was married to the king's cousin, and had easy access to the court. Together with the local *qāḍī* and *khaṭīb* (preacher), he introduced Ibn Baṭṭūṭa to the king of Mali, fulfilling the traditional role of the resident Muslim community as intermediaries with the local authorities. In the second half of the fourteenth century, according to Ibn Khaldūn, the capital of Mali was 'an extensive place, well watered, cultivated and populated. It had brisk markets, and was a stopping place for trading caravans from the Maghrib, Ifrīqiya and Egypt.'[1]

Justice administered by the authorities of Mali gave security to foreign traders and to their property. If a man from North Africa died in Mali, his property was given in trust to one of his compatriots until it was claimed by his heirs. If pestered by officials, foreign merchants could appeal to the king. In one case, reported by Ibn Baṭṭūṭa, the king's commercial agent in Walata was dismissed following a complaint that he had underpaid a trader for his merchandise. Indeed, the official was also made to pay the full price of the goods. In Mali, and elsewhere in the western Sudan, theft was regarded as a capital crime which was punished by death or enslavement. Trade routes

[1] Ibn Khaldūn, *Ta'rīkh al-duwal*, I, 267/tr. II, 116.

across the length and breadth of Mali were safe, and, as Ibn Baṭṭūṭa experienced, it was not necessary to go in a caravan. In these circumstances trade flourished and traders from all parts of North Africa, from Morocco to Egypt, were attracted to settle in the commercial towns of Mali.

North African traders, together with their Sudanese agents, formed the floating population of the great commercial centres of the Sahel, which were the termini of the trans-Saharan trade. Throughout the centuries they moved from one centre to another, according to the changing patterns of the trade. One may even discern a general shift of both the Saharan routes and the termini from west to east. Early in the thirteenth century, as has already been indicated, Awdaghust had been replaced by Walata, which remained the principal entrepôt during most of the period of Mali's hegemony until the second half of the fourteenth century. Timbuktu, further to the east, was first mentioned by Ibn Baṭṭūṭa, who visited this place in 1363 on his way back from the capital of Mali. Timbuktu was then still a small town, inhabited mainly by Massufa Berbers.

In 1339, a map drawn by Angelino Dulcert indicated a route from Sijilmasa via Buda (in Tuat) to Walata and Mali. But the Catalan map of Abraham Cresques done in 1375 showed the route running from Sijilmasa, through Tuat and Taghaza, to Timbuktu. This is a clear demonstration (which will be corroborated below with evidence from the Sudan) that by the third quarter of the fourteenth century Timbuktu had replaced Walata as the principal terminus of the Saharan trade. Indeed, it was about that time that Ibn Khaldūn reported that the Maʿqil Arabs, who by then had evaded any control by the Marinid sultans, attacked caravans on their way to Walata from Buda, the most western of the oases of Tuat. Caravans, therefore, took another route and made Tamentit, at the eastern end of Tuat, their rendezvous.

'The prosperity of Timbuktu', as the seventeenth-century al-Saʿdī, author of the *Ta'rīkh al-Sūdān*, said,

> was the ruin of Biru [Walata] . . . The market had previously been at Biru. Caravans used to come there from all points of the horizon. The pick of scholars, pious, and rich men from every tribe and country [of the Maghrib and Egypt] lived there . . . Then, all those gradually moved to Timbuktu where they were joined by different Sanhāja groups.[1]

Awdaghust and Walata, the market towns which preceded Timbuktu, were land-locked towns, and merchandise was carried from them

[1] al-Saʿdī, *Taʿrīkh al-Sūdān*, ed. and tr. O. Houdas (Paris, 1900), 20–2/tr. 36–8.

to the south on donkeys or on porters' heads. Timbuktu was open to the desert caravans coming from the north, but at the same time had a port on the Niger, a dozen miles away. It was, in the words of al-Sa'dī, 'a rendezvous for those coming by boat and by land'.[1] The growth of Timbuktu as a commercial centre, from the second half of the fourteenth century, was closely associated with the development of the Niger waterway as a trade artery, linking Timbuktu with Jenne.

The best accounts of the trade on the river between Timbuktu and Jenne are from the beginning of the sixteenth century. Leo Africanus, who visited the region about 1512, described the merchants of Timbuktu as carrying goods to their agents in Jenne in small boats on the Niger. Some years earlier Fernandes, a Portuguese compiler of accounts from West Africa, reported that salt was transported by boats from Timbuktu to Jenne. There the salt bars were divided into smaller pieces to be taken on porters' heads to the gold mines. Located in the south-eastern end of the inner delta of the Niger, Jenne was the farthest point on the waterway in the direction of the goldfields on the fringes of the Akan forest. It was in the fourteenth century, with the increasing demand for gold in Europe, that the message was sent across the Sahara and enterprising Sudanese traders opened routes to these new goldfields. Jenne developed as an entrepôt for the trade in this direction, whereas Begho, which perhaps may be identified with Bitou (see pp. 489–90), emerged as the southern outpost of this trade complex. It may be best to quote al-Sa'dī:

> Jenne is one of the greatest Muslim markets, where traders carrying salt from the mines of Taghaza meet traders with the gold of Bitou . . . It is because of this blessed town [Jenne] that caravans come to Timbuktu from all points of the horizon.[2]

In the northern centres of the Sahel, such as Walata and Timbuktu, the proportion of Berbers from the Sahara and Arab-Berbers from North Africa was high among the leading merchants. In the market towns which developed further inland, such as Jenne, trade was mainly in the hands of Sudanese traders, most of them of Soninke origin. Soninke traders of the Sahel communicated with the foreign traders from the Maghrib and became Muslims themselves. They developed a trading network to carry the gold from its sources to the termini of the Saharan caravans. Until the twelfth century most of the gold came

[1] al-Sa'dī, *T. al-Sūdān*, 21/tr. 36.
[2] Ibid. 11–12/tr. 22–3.

from Bambuk, at the confluence of the Senegal and the Faleme rivers. Then the goldfields of Bure, on the upper Niger, were exploited, and contributed to the rise of Mali to hegemony. In the latter part of the fourteenth century, as has been stated, they opened routes even further south to the Akan forest.

Beyond the Sahel, the Soninke traders operated among the Malinke and Bambara, whose language they adopted, and became known as Marka in the middle Niger among the Bambara, or Dyula in the upper Niger among the Malinke. In the Arabic sources all the Mande-speaking traders are referred to as Wangara. Al-Idrīsī also called the gold-bearing country of the Mande by this name. A seventeenth-century Sudanese scholar explained the term Wangara in relation to the Malinke: the Wangara and the Malinke are of the same origin, but whereas the Malinke are the warriors, the Wangara are those traders who travel from one end of the world to the other.[1]

In the middle Niger area Jenne was preceded as a commercial (and Islamic) centre by Dia. Dia itself may have been founded in the eleventh or twelfth century by the Soninke as part of their political and commercial expansion. Significantly, Wangara families far and wide remember Dia as the town of their ancestors. It was from Dia that Wangara came to Jenne and made it a flourishing town, and a centre for their ever-increasing commercial network.

Until the middle of the fourteenth century, the Wangara operated within the dominions of Mali, the first Sudanese empire which gave effective political unity to the Sahel and the savannah, between the desert and the upper Niger. For the second half of the fourteenth century there is accumulating evidence that the Wangara ventured beyond the political frontiers of the empire. They reached the Akan goldfields, they opened routes to 'the land of kola' (Worodugu in the Ivory Coast), made contact with peoples of the western Atlantic coast and, more significantly still, they built up trade with Hausaland to the east. During the reign of Yaji, king of Kano (dated to the second half of the fourteenth century), 'the Wangarawa came from Mele, bringing with them the Mohammedan religion'.[2]

Most of the trade across the Sahara was between the Sudan and the Maghrib, but part of the trade of the Sudan turned also to Egypt. An older route between Ghana and Egypt, via Gao, Aïr, Tibesti and

[1] Ibn al-Mukhtār, *Ta'rīkh al-Fattāsh*, ed. and tr. O. Houdas and M. Delafosse (Paris, 1913), 38/tr. 65.

[2] H. R. Palmer, 'The Kano Chronicle', *Journal of the Anthropological Institute*, 1909, **38**, 70.

al-Wāḥāt (the oases of Kharga and Dakhla), is reported to have been abandoned in the ninth century. This route, however, seems to have been revived in the thirteenth or fourteenth century (see pp. 260–1). Al-'Umarī described a route from Upper Egypt through the oases and the desert to Mali. This was confirmed by Leo Africanus early in the sixteenth century, who said that the people of al-Wāḥāt as well as those of Manfalūṭ (near Asyut in Upper Egypt) were wealthy because of their trade with the Sudan. Both Ibn Baṭṭūṭā and Ibn Khaldūn reported active trade with Egypt, perhaps over alternative routes. In the middle of the fifteenth century Egyptian traders came to Tuat to meet traders from the Sudan. Part of the gold of Mali reached Egypt by way of Gao. A revival of the trade between Egypt and Mali could have been stimulated by the impressive visit of Mansa Mūsā to Cairo, on his way to Mecca, in 1324. Mansa Mūsā and his companions spent much gold in Egypt, where they bought goods of all kinds. Turkish slaves, bought in Cairo, attended the king of Mali, while the richer people in Walata wore Egyptian clothes. Egyptian traders frequented the towns of Mali. It was because of these many connections of Mali with the Muslim world across the Sahara that there is more information in the external Arabic sources about Mali of the fourteenth century than about any other period.

THE HEGEMONY OF MALI IN THE WESTERN SUDAN

The Arabic sources offer glimpses of the western Sudan at different periods from the ninth to the fourteenth centuries. It is only by piecing together this information that one may reconstruct something of the dynamics of the history of the region as a whole. Of all the external Arabic sources, Ibn Khaldūn alone produced a chronicle of a dynasty, because he was aware of the value of oral traditions. He recorded such traditions from people of the Sudan whom he met in Egypt and in the Maghrib, and added information from people of the Maghrib who had lived in the Sudan. His introduction to the history of Mali is an excellent précis of about five hundred years of history until the beginning of the thirteenth century:

When Ifrīqiya and the Maghrib were conquered [by the Arabs] merchants penetrated the western part of *Bilād al-Sūdān*, and found among them no one greater than the king of Ghana . . .

Later the authority of Ghana waned and its power declined whilst that of the veiled people, their neighbours on the north next to the lands of the Berbers, increased. The latter overcame the Sudanese, plundered their territories, imposed upon them tribute, and converted many of them to Islam. As a result, the authority of the rulers of Ghana dwindled away, and they were overcome by the Susu, their Sudanese neighbours, who subdued and crushed them completely.

Later, the people of Mali outnumbered the Sudanese peoples in their neighbourhood and expanded over the whole region. They conquered the Susu and took over all their possessions, both their original territory and that of Ghana, as far as the Ocean to the west.

Their greatest king who overcame the Susu, conquered their country and seized power from their hands, was Mari-Jata. He ruled for twenty-five years, according to what they relate.[1]

Ibn Khaldūn's chronicle is a valuable link between the written sources and the oral traditions. Mari-Jata is undoubtedly to be identified with Sundiata, whose epos is central to the historical traditions of the Malinke. He was the son of a Malinke chief of the Keita clan, ruling an area on the Sankarani affluent of the upper Niger. Miraculously cured from the crippledom he had suffered from birth, Sundiata became a great hunter and warrior. He attracted many followers but aroused the jealousy and fear of his half-brother, Dankaran-Tuma, who was then the reigning chief. After some attempts had been made on his life, Sundiata went into exile outside the Malinke country. According to some versions of the tradition, he was warmly received at the court of the king of Mema. He proved a distinguished warrior and was given important positions of command.

At that time the Malinke came under the domination of Sumanguru, king of Susu. Sundiata's brother Dankaran-Tuma was defeated and the country was devastated. Sumanguru, it seems, was determined to crush the political and military power of the Malinke. But a descendant of the royal family survived, and envoys were sent in secret to find Sundiata and call him back to lead his people. The king of Mema gave Sundiata cavalry to help in defeating Sumanguru, who was a symbol of pagan reaction and threatened Mema and its interests. As Sundiata circuitously approached his native country, he was joined by Malinke warriors. Perhaps he relied on hunters' associations, which were able to unite different Malinke clans and chiefdoms.

A series of victories over the Susu marked the retreat of Sumanguru back to his own country and the advance of Sundiata to the heart of the Malinke country. The decisive battle at Krina on the Niger is drama-

[1] Ibn Khaldūn, *Ta'rīkh al-duwal*, I, 263/tr. II, 109–10.

tized in the traditions as a struggle between two powerful magicians, Sumanguru and Sundiata. The latter was victorious only after he had discovered, by treachery, the Achilles heel of Sumanguru. Following the victory at Krina, the commanders of Sundiata's army conquered territories in all directions, though we are not certain how far they reached.

The consolidation of the kingdom was achieved, according to Niane's version of the epos,[1] in two stages. Before the battle of Krina the Malinke chiefs assembled to confirm Sundiata as their war leader. The unity of the Malinke was therefore forged in their war of liberation. After the war they gathered again, this time at Kaba (Kangaba), where the Malinke chiefs swore fealty to Sundiata as their sovereign. Each chief then accepted his own chiefdom from the hands of Sundiata. The country of the Malinke ceased to be an alliance of independent chiefdoms to become one empire with dependent provinces, and with the Keita as the ruling clan.

After the great assembly at Kaba, Sundiata returned to Niani, which was then in ruins, and made the small ancestral village into the capital of a growing empire. Oral traditions seem to support the location of the imperial capital of Mali between the thirteenth and the sixteenth centuries at Niani on the Sankarani river. Indeed, the traditions insist that the kings of Mali never settled outside the Malinke country. This, in fact, is the assumption that will be made in this chapter. Admittedly, references to the capital of Mali in the Arabic sources may yield different interpretations, and the recent excavations at Niani have not confirmed beyond doubt that this was the site of the capital. Suggestions for alternative sites are even less convincing, however, and if conflicting interpretations of the written records and the archaeological evidence seem to cancel each other, the oral traditions must remain the safest guide. It is therefore assumed that it was from Niani on the Sankarani, far in the south, that the kings of Mali ruled their extensive empire. By the fourteenth century they even made it, as we have already seen (p. 372), an important commercial centre.

During his exile Sundiata is said to have stayed at the court of the king of Mema, whose title was Tunkara. This king even supported Sundiata with troops, and after his victory Sundiata sent rich presents to Mema. An alliance was contracted between Sundiata and the king of Mema, according to which this Soninke state was incorporated into the empire of Mali as an autonomous kingdom. In the oral traditions

[1] D. T. Niane, *Sundiata: an epic of old Mali*, tr. G. D. Pickett (London, 1965), 58.

Mema is closely associated with Wagadu, which was very likely the 'Ghana' of the Arabs. Ghana had ceased to exist as a political entity at the beginning of the thirteenth century, and one may suggest that vague references to Ghana in the Arabic sources after that may in fact refer to Mema, as its most direct successor. This may help explain an obscure passage of al-'Umarī, which says: 'No one in the vast empire of this ruler [of Mali] is designated king except the ruler of Ghana, who, though a king himself, is like his deputy.'[1] This could well refer to the greater measure of autonomy granted to Mema, whose ruler enjoyed a higher status among the vassal kings and the provincial chiefs.

Sundiata, or Mari-Jata, as he is called by Ibn Khaldūn, was succeeded by his son Mansa Uli, who made the Pilgrimage, and passed through Egypt on his way to Mecca during the reign of the Mamluk sultan Baybars. The latter ruled from 1260 to 1277, and thus we have, for the first time, an approximate date for the reign of a king of Mali. 'This Mansa Uli', says Ibn Khaldūn, 'was one of their greatest kings.'[2] One may therefore assume that he continued the conquests of his father. Elsewhere I have argued that it is likely that under his rule Mali expanded over the Sahel and took control of the trading centres of Walata, Timbuktu and Gao.[3] There he came into direct contact with Muslims of the Maghrib, and became aware of the importance of contacts with the Muslim world. This could have led him to his pilgrimage to Mecca.

Mansa Uli was succeeded by his brother Wati, and after him authority passed to Khalīfa, another brother. 'Khalīfa was weak minded and used to shoot arrows at his people and to kill them for sport. So they rose against him and killed him.'[4] Weak kings undermined the authority of the state. It was perhaps during the reign of the weak-minded Khalīfa that Songhay threw off the rule of Mali for the first time. 'Alī Kolon and Salman Nari, who were, according to one version of the tradition, princes of Songhay, lived as hostages at the court of Mali. When the opportunity suggested itself, 'Alī Kolon left Mali with his brother, perhaps at the head of troops he had commanded in the service of the king of Mali. During his flight he fought against troops sent by the king of Mali to stop him. But he reached his homeland,

[1] al-'Umarī, *Masālik al-abṣār fī mamālik al-amṣār* [*L'Afrique moins l'Egypte*], tr. Gaudfroy-Demombynes (Paris, 1927), 59.

[2] Ibn Khaldūn, *T. al-duwal*, I, 264/tr. II, 111.

[3] See N. Levtzion, *Ancient Ghana and Mali* (London, 1973), 95–6, 162.

[4] Ibn Khaldūn, *T. al-duwal*, I, 264/tr. II, 111.

made himself king and 'liberated his people from the rule of Mali'.[1] The independence of Songhay, however, did not last for long, because the next resourceful ruler of Mali, Sakura, brought Songhay back into the fold.

After the deposition of Khalīfa, the kingship was given to Abū Bakr, who was a grandson of Sundiata by one of his daughters. According to one oral tradition, he was adopted by his grandfather as son, and was therefore eligible. It is likely that Abū Bakr was made king by officers of the court, those who had deposed Khalīfa, and among whom slaves and freed slaves were prominent. They preferred to install Abū Bakr, who would be more amenable to their policy, because his claim to the throne was dubious. Such an interpretation may be supported by the fact that the kingship was then usurped by Sakura, a freed slave of the royal family.

With Sakura, Mali again had a powerful ruler, and reached a new climax after its first glory under Sundiata and Mansa Uli. 'During his powerful government their dominions expanded, and they overcame the neighbouring peoples . . . Their authority became mighty and all the nations of the Sudan stood in awe of them. Merchants from the Maghrib and Ifrīqiya travelled to their country.'[2]

Sakura is reported to have conquered Gao, but this was probably a reconquest, after Songhay had revolted in the days of Khalīfa. In the tradition of powerful kings of Mali, whose authority was secured, Sakura went on the Pilgrimage. He visited Cairo in the reign of the Mamluk sultan al-Malik al-Nāṣir b. Qalā'ūn, perhaps sometime after 1298. Sakura was killed on his way back from Mecca, and the throne reverted to the legitimate heirs.

The next king was Mansa Qu, son of Mansa Uli, and he was succeeded by his own son Mansa Muḥammad. After him 'the kingship passed from the descendants of Mari-Jata to those of his brother Abū Bakr. Mansa Mūsā, son of Abū Bakr, became king.'[3] Abū Bakr, or, in the local form of the name, Bakari, was according to oral traditions the brother of Sundiata and his closest associate both in exile and in the creation of the empire. Mansa Mūsā was in fact a grandson, not a son, of Abū Bakr.

The twenty-five years of Mansa Mūsā's reign, perhaps 1312–37, were 'the golden age' of the empire of Mali. Sundiata and Mansa Mūsā were the two greatest kings of Mali, but whereas the former was

[1] al-Sa'dī, *T. al-Sūdān*, 5–6/tr. 10–12.
[2] Ibn Khaldūn, *T. al-duwal*, I, 264/tr. II, 111.
[3] Ibid. I, 264/tr. II, 112.

the god-hero of the oral traditions, the latter was the favourite of the Muslim writers. Indeed, each category of sources attributes to the king of its choice so many deeds and achievements, that the credit for some of these must be due to other less celebrated rulers. In a more general way, one may say that Sundiata made a small chiefdom into an empire and Mansa Mūsā accomplished the work of his predecessor in shaping the Islamic outlook of the empire and in giving it universal fame. In 1324 he made the Pilgrimage to Mecca and on his way left a deep impression in Egypt. He encouraged the building of mosques and the development of Islamic learning, and initiated closer diplomatic relations with Morocco.

Under Mansa Mūsā, Mali reached its farthest territorial expansion. To the west, Mali's rule reached as far as the Gambia and the lower Senegal valley, and the emerging Djolof (Wolof) kingdom seems to have acknowledged its authority. To the north, Ibn Khaldūn says, 'Mansa Mūsā's power was highly regarded in the desert adjacent to the territory of Wargla.' Mali did not expand so far, but some of the veiled Sanhaja of the southern Sahara were 'in subjection to the king of the Sudan, paid him tribute and were recruited to his armies'. An envoy of the ruler of Tadmekka, in Adrar of the Iforas, told Ibn Khaldūn in 1353 that the town was answerable to Mali. Mansa Mūsā reasserted the authority of Mali over Gao, a remote and rebellious tributary. Muli, downstream of Gao on the Niger, was regarded as the last province of Mali to the east. In the south, Mansa Mūsā preferred an indirect control of the gold-bearing region of Bure, because whenever conquest was attempted and direct rule imposed, the production of gold decreased considerably. The authority of Mali probably did not extend southward beyond the Malinke country, although it was about that time, as has already been mentioned, that the Wangara traders, perhaps with the encouragement of the king of Mali, penetrated as far as the Akan forest, to the sources of gold and kola (see pp. 488–91).

During his absence on pilgrimage Mansa Mūsā appointed his son Muḥammad as deputy, and it was very likely this same son who succeeded his father as Mansa Magha. The succession of a son deprived Sulaymān, brother of Mansa Mūsā, of his right to the kingship as the eldest male in the royal family. Mansa Magha died in the fourth year of his reign, and one may suspect the hand of his uncle Sulaymān, who now became the king. Subsequent events confirm such an interpretation of a crisis within the ruling dynasty.

Mansa Sulaymān was a powerful ruler, and held together the vast empire his brother had consolidated. He continued the Islamic policy of Mansa Mūsā, as well as the diplomatic relations with Morocco. It was during the reign of Mansa Sulaymān, in 1352–3, that Ibn Baṭṭūṭa visited Mali, and described the security which prevailed throughout the empire. But Ibn Baṭṭūṭa was also an eyewitness to an episode which throws light on a rupture inside the royal family:

It happened during my sojourn in Mali that the Sultan was angry with his chief wife, the daughter of his paternal uncle. She was called Qasa, which means with them 'the Queen'. She is his partner in kingship, according to the custom of the Sudanese, and her name is mentioned together with that of the king from above the pulpit. He imprisoned her with one of the chiefs, and put in her place another wife, Banju, who was not a king's daughter. The people talked about it, and disapproved of his actions . . . The chiefs [also] spoke in Qasa's favour, and so the king assembled them in the audience chamber, and Dugha [the linguist] said on his behalf: 'You have said much in favour of Qasa, but she committed a capital crime.' Then a female slave of Qasa was brought in with chains on her hands and legs. She was told: 'Say what you know.' She told them that Qasa had sent her to Jata, the king's cousin, who had fled from the king to Kanburni. Qasa invited him to overthrow the king, informing him that she herself and all the armies were ready to accept his authority. When the chiefs heard this, they said: 'Verily, this is a capital crime, and she deserves death.'[1]

Mansa Sulaymān succeeded in averting the coup d'état of 1352 or 1353. But only seven years later, immediately after Sulaymān's death in 1360, a civil war broke out between his house and that of his brother Mansa Mūsā. Qasa, Sulaymān's son, had succeeded his father, but died after nine months in the throes of a succession struggle:

Dissension broke out among the people of Mali. Authority over them became divided and their [rival] rulers contested the kingship. They killed each other and were preoccupied with civil war until finally Mansa Jata came out [victorious] and consolidated power in his hands.[2]

This Mansa Jata (elsewhere called Mari-Jata) was son of Mansa Magha, Mansa Mūsā's son. He may be identified with the rebellious prince Jata of Ibn Baṭṭūṭa. Jata, whose father Mansa Magha had been overthrown by Mansa Sulaymān, was in hiding, waiting for an opportunity to avenge his father and to restore the kingship to the house of Mansa Mūsā. He failed once when the plot with the queen Qasa was unveiled by Sulaymān. But after the latter's death Jata came forward, stirred up a civil war and emerged victorious.

[1] Ibn Baṭṭūṭa, *Tuḥfat*, IV, 417–19.
[2] al-Sa'dī, *T. al-Sūdān*, 9/tr. 17.

Mari-Jata II is described by Ibn Khaldūn as 'the most wicked ruler [the people of Mali] had', corrupted and tyrannic, who 'depleted the treasury and nearly pulled down the structure of government'. He died of sleeping sickness in 1373–4. Mūsā, his son, was appointed to succeed him. He had good intentions, and 'abandoned the ways of his father', but he was a weak king and took no part in the government, which was exclusively held by his minister (vizier), Mari-Jata. For fourteen years, until his death in 1387, Mūsā was only a nominal king. His minister, however, successfully restored the empire, which had deteriorated during the civil war and through the irresponsibility of the former king, Mari-Jata. Once again, as in the case of the usurper Sakura, a court official came forward to save the empire where the legitimate kings had failed. The vizier mobilized the army to subdue the eastern provinces, which presumably were in open revolt. He advanced beyond Gao to lay siege to Tadmekka. He did not conquer that town, which remained from then on outside the rule of Mali. With a continuous struggle for the throne in Mali, it is likely that Gao also finally achieved complete independence.

Mūsā, the nominal king, was succeeded by his brother Magha in 1387, and he was probably also a puppet in the hands of the court officials. After one year he was deposed, and the throne was usurped by another vizier, who married the widow of Mari-Jata II, Mūsā's mother. After a few months he was avenged by a member of the house of the same Mari-Jata. In 1390, in the middle of this ferment, the throne was seized by a man who 'came out from the land of the pagans [to the south] . . . and claimed descent from Mansa Qu son of Mansi Uli son of Mari-Jata the Great'. The wheel came full circle with the return to power of the old branch of the dynasty.

Troubles at the court left the empire without an effective government. From within the Niger bend the pagan Mossi, who had been till then in the process of creating their own states, were attracted to the middle Niger valley, which was almost defenceless. It was at that time that Timbuktu developed into a flourishing commercial centre, sprawling in open country, and exposed to attack. The Mossi invaded Timbuktu, and forced the horrified representatives of Mali to flee. The Mossi wrought destruction to the town, killed many people, seized booty and retreated. When all was safe, the people of Mali returned to take up the reins again.

The Tuareg of the region of Timbuktu had acknowledged the authority of Mali until they realized that the empire had exhausted its military power. The nomads then began to harass the city of Timbuktu, and its citizens complained that 'a king who is unable to defend a town has no right to be its sovereign'. In 1433–9 the last vestiges of Mali's rule in Timbuktu were removed and the town was taken over by the Tuareg. Jenne, itself defended by the surrounding water, seems to have become independent of Mali about the same time, and, until its conquest by Sonni 'Alī in 1473, the king of Jenne extended his authority over an important section of the Niger waterway leading to Timbuktu. There is evidence to suggest that other provinces of the Sahel, like Mema and Diara, also broke away from Mali in the first decades of the fifteenth century. So Mali had lost its rule over the Sahel even before the Songhay began their expansion in the middle of the fifteenth century.

For a better understanding of the disintegration of Mali, the empire is to be viewed as divided into two distinct parts: the Malinke country of the savannah to the south and the non-Malinke regions of the Sahel to the north. The former was the nucleus of the empire, united by Sundiata during the war of liberation. Following the victory over the Susu, Mali expanded into territories which had formerly been part of the kingdom of Ghana, and were later to come under the rule of Songhay. In the Sahel, Mali ruled over alien peoples who had been incorporated into the empire mostly by force, and who accepted its domination as long as the kings of Mali maintained security to encourage trade, the main economic asset of the Sahel. But, once the empire failed to defend the country and security deteriorated, those peoples exploited the weakness of Mali to reassert their independence.

Significantly, where the imperial expansion of Mali was accompanied by Malinke colonization – as on the upper Gambia – the authority of the kings of Mali survived much longer, well into the fifteenth and sixteenth centuries. North of the Malinke country, the authority of Mali was reduced to the three provinces mentioned by al-Sa'dī: Kala, Binduku and Sibiridugu. There, on the banks of the Niger and the Bani rivers south of Jenne, was the country of the Bambara, who were related to the Malinke. Under the imperial authority of Mali small chiefdoms developed there, the subjects of which were Bambara peasants and the rulers perhaps Malinke and Bambarized Soninke. Some of them held the title of *mansa*, and the fact that they owed their existence to Mali may explain why they maintained allegiance to Mali longer than did others.

Mali prospered under powerful kings and was shaken to its foundations when weak kings occupied the throne. This is an indication of the strong personal role played by the king in the government of the empire. The king was personally active in exercising authority and was the final appeal in the administration of justice. Complaints against ill-treatment by officials were investigated and the wrongdoers were severely punished.

A basic weakness of the ruling dynasty was the lack of defined rules of succession in view of the numerous contenders. There were signs of conflict between the brother and the son of a former king. This conflict brought about a devastating civil war between the house of Mansa Mūsā and that of his brother Mansa Sulaymān. Another division within the Keita dynasty was between the descendants of Sundiata and those of his brother Abū Bakr. When in the fourth generation Sundiata's descendants were unable to hold authority, the kingship passed to Mansa Mūsā, grandson of Abū Bakr. The first ruling generation of this new branch – Mūsā and Sulaymān – brought the empire to its peak, but succeeding generations again proved incompetent. It resulted in what seems to have been yet another transfer, back to the line of Sundiata, whose descendant seized power in 1390.

Among fourteen kings of royal descent (excluding usurpers) only four were described as great kings, but their rule extended over more than half the period under review (*c.* 1230–1390). Twice, kings were deposed by royal rivals, twice by non-royal usurpers, and in at least two other cases kings were merely puppets under the patronage of the court officials. The latter intervened, either as patrons or usurpers, to ensure the survival of the empire when its existence was in danger because of the irresponsible conduct of the kings. In other Sudanic kingdoms (such as Diara and Songhay) dynasties were overthrown, but in Mali, in spite of recurrent crises, the kingship eventually returned to the Keita, and remained with them until the final liquidation of the empire.

In Mali, as in other Sudanic kingdoms, there is some evidence of the traits of divine kingship – of elevating the king far above commoners, nobility and even members of his own lineage. No one was permitted to be present when the king took his meal. Rules concerning ceremonial submission were strictly observed. Those who came into the royal presence had to fall prostrate before the king and to place dust or ashes upon their head. No one was allowed to enter with his sandals on nor to sneeze before the king. In public, the king spoke through a spokesman, who repeated the words of the king in a loud voice. The king was richly dressed and his audience was a display of gold, silver and ivory. He was surrounded by a decorated bodyguard of slaves with the dignitaries of the state seated before him. These were, according to Ibn Baṭṭūṭa, the Muslim *qāḍī* and *khaṭīb*, the *nā'ib* (lit. 'deputy') and the *farariya* or emirs.

The *farariya* were commanders of the cavalry, and the king cultivated their goodwill by gifts of gold, horses and luxurious clothes. For distinction they were decorated with gold anklets and were honoured with the privilege of wearing wider trousers. Horsemen were the striking force of the army of Mali, and it was in the possession of cavalry that kings of large centralized states had a decisive military superiority over other peoples of the Sudan. The king had to spend considerable sums in purchasing horses for his cavalry, because the price of imported Arab horses was very high. Horses bred locally are reported to have been small in size. The cost of horses must have limited the possibility of maintaining private cavalry forces, and the development of a feudal type army.

The power of the king in relation to the hereditary nobility was enhanced also by the employment of slaves, who owed exclusive loyalty to the king. Slaves and freed slaves formed the inner circle of the king's retinue and were entrusted with delicate and responsible tasks at the court and in the administration of the empire. Under strong kings they executed the policy of the monarch, but when weak kings came to the throne, these officials took control to save the monarchy and the empire.

The court official who appears most prominently in the historical sources is the *dyeli*, who was both a bard (*griot*) and a spokesman. He was master of ceremonies as well as the king's counsellor and his intimate friend; the only man who could see the king in his wrath. The *dyelis* led the recitation of the history of the kingdom, and, as custodians of the oral traditions, they were experienced in constitutional procedures. They also settled disputes between clans and tribes.

The *dyelis* were among the *nyamakala*, or the occupational castes. They were considered inferior by the freemen, but at the same time were feared because they could both praise and slander. Smiths, who were *nyamakala* as well, were also close to the king as manufacturers of arms and as masters of magic and divination. Like the *dyeli*, they were despised and feared at the same time. It seems, therefore, that the king's confidants were either slaves or people of caste. Because of their low status they needed a patron, and because they had no kin among the nobility or the freemen they were reckoned to be more reliable. Indeed, Muslim scribes and divines whose services were needed at the court also had no immediate links with those who could have challenged the king's authority.

We know little about the provincial administration of Mali. It appears that local rulers of regions incorporated into the empire were left as vassals. In order to ensure their loyalty, sons of vassal chiefs were sent to the capital as hostages, where they served the king, perhaps as military commanders. Vassal chiefs were supervised by a resident representative of the king. Important towns such as Walata had governors appointed by the king, and the monarch also appointed governors of provinces. According to scattered references in the sources, it seems that these governors were either members of the royal family or the king's slaves.

Trade was one of the factors that contributed to a territorial organization on a larger scale and also to the growing power of the monarch. The latter was conscious of the need to maintain direct communication with foreign traders throughout his empire. In Walata, we have seen, he had his commercial agent.

The king also held monopolistic control over imports of strategic importance, such as horses and metals. Duties were levied on imports of salt, copper and other merchandise, but there is no mention of tax on exported gold. Rare nuggets of gold, however, were reserved for the king. The kings of Mali probably did not control the gold-bearing region directly, and were satisfied with the tribute paid in gold by the inhabitants there, and with the control of the trade routes leading to the goldfields. This was enough for the kings of Mali to accumulate vast quantities of gold, as Mansa Mūsā clearly demonstrated when he distributed gold lavishly in Cairo.

Trade, though vital for the central government, concerned a small segment of the population only. The greater majority of the inhabitants of Mali were engaged in agriculture, cultivating millet, sorghum and rice, in fishing and in cattle breeding. The diversity of primary products stimulated local trade and broadened the economic basis of the empire. Some agricultural products were also traded over longer distances. Rice was transported from the Gambia to the interior, whereas millet and sorghum were sent from the inner delta of the Niger to Timbuktu, Walata and as far as Taghaza.

Agriculture in the Sudanic savanna was and is one of the better developed in West Africa, because of adequate rainfall. Agricultural technology, however, was based on the hoe as the principal tool. Still, farmers produced some surplus, part of which was exchanged in the local trade network, while part was channelled through taxation to feed the army and the administration. There seems to have been no shortage of land, and rulers increased agricultural production by organizing the exploitation of labour. They settled slaves in new villages to till the land and to fill the royal granaries.

The *nyamakala* artisans – workers in iron, hide and wood – maintained a rudimentary industry and contributed to the diversity of saleable goods. One industry, however, perhaps the most developed of all, was not restricted to the *nyamakala*, and did not result in the creation of an occupational caste: weaving and other branches of the textile industry seem to have expanded in the western Sudan along with Islam. Converts dressed themselves more fully than pagans. Muslim towns, like Timbuktu and Jenne, boasted many workshops of weavers and tailors, who were often part of the Muslim élite.

Barter was the elementary mode of exchange. Later, essential commodities of trade, like salt, copper or pieces of cloth, became recognized media of exchange. The next development was the introduction of currency in the form of cowries. Cowries as currency in the western Sudan were first mentioned about the middle of the fourteenth century, first by al-ʿUmārī and then by Ibn Baṭṭūṭa – before that time, cowries were imported only as ornaments. It is very likely that this development took place when Mali attained its greatest territorial expansion and elaborated forms of economic and administrative organization. For the first time the Sahel and the Sudanic savanna were integrated, bringing regions of diverse economic resources into one political unit. Greater social and economic differentiation – with a court, an army, peasants, occupational castes and slaves – encouraged the beginnings of a market economy. Evidence from other parts of West Africa also points to the link between state building and the introduction of cowrie currency. Cowries were brought with great profit from the Maldive Islands via Egypt to North Africa and across the Sahara. With recognizable units of minute value, cowries were most suitable for buying and selling food and other commodities at the level of local and district markets. Large-scale transactions and long-distance trade, with North African connections, were conducted on the basis of the golden *mithqāl* (weighing 4.25 to 4.75 grams) and its equivalent coin, the golden dinar.

In the empire of Mali, one may say, political, social and economic institutions were elaborated and later bequeathed in various forms to other states of West Africa. Such a view of the place of Mali in West African history needs the vindication of more research. But the present writer feels ever more confident in suggesting that the experience of Mali in the integration of Islam and Muslims into its religious, social and political texture set a pattern which may be observed in many parts of West Africa and at different periods.

Ghana, as we have seen (p. 349), was converted by the Almoravids after the ground had already been prepared through the long and peaceful influence of Muslim traders from North Africa. The latter communicated with the Sudanese traders, the Wangara, who plied between the commercial centres of the Sahel and the sources of the gold. Through their commercial occupation these Sudanese traders became detached from the agricultural and tribal ways of life, in which the traditional African religions are rooted. Hence, they adopted Islam more easily, and in their wanderings found hospitality as well as a sense of community among fellow Muslims in the trading centres which developed along the routes to the goldfields, and which were described by al-Bakrī as early as the middle of the eleventh century.

Al-Bakrī also recorded an account of the conversion to Islam of the king of Malal, an early Malinke chiefdom. His country was afflicted by drought from one year to the other. All the prayers and sacrifices of the local priests were in vain. Then a Muslim, who happened to stay there, promised that if the king accepted Islam he would pray for his relief. When the king agreed, the Muslim 'taught him to recite some easy passages from the Koran and instructed him in those religious obligations and practices [the minimum] which one ought to know'. On the following Friday, after the king had purified himself, the two set out to a nearby hill. All that night the Muslim prayed, emulated by the king. 'The dawn had just begun to break, when God brought down abundant rain. The king ordered that the idols be broken and the sorcerers expelled from his country. He, together with his sons and the nobility, sincerely embraced Islam, but the common people of his kingdom remained pagans.'[1]

This Muslim succeeded in winning over the chief by demonstrating the omnipotence of God; praying to Him saved the kingdom after all sacrifices performed by the local priests had failed. The king's conversion, according to this account, was rather rudimentary, and the

[1] al-Bakrī, *Kitāb al-masālik wa'l-mamālik*, ed. M. G. de Slane (Algiers, 1911), 178; tr. M. G. de Slane, *Description de l'Afrique septentrionale* (Paris, 1913), 333–4.

majority of his subjects remained pagans. Oral traditions also assert that chiefs among the Malinke came under Islamic influence long before the time of Sundiata, founder of the empire. But in the epos Sundiata appears as a great hunter and a magician, with little or no reference to Islam. This may be a typical bias of the traditions, but it must have had some historical significance. Though he himself could have been an islamized king, Sundiata had to lead a people the overwhelming majority of whom were pagans. In mobilizing the national resources of the Malinke he turned to the traditional religion for support, to the particularistic spirit of his people, rather than to the universalistic appeal of Islam.

From its centre on the upper Niger, Mali expanded into the Sahel, to incorporate old centres of Islam like Dia and Walata. Muslim traders operated over routes across the empire, and some of them even came to live in the capital, near the court. Through the trans-Saharan trade Mali came closer to the Muslim world beyond the desert, and more so for those of its kings who went on pilgrimage to Mecca. As the small Malinke chiefdom turned into a vast multi-ethnic empire, with influential Muslim elements inside and extensive Islamic relations with the outside, its kings changed their orientation from closer attachment to their ancestral religion towards an Islamic outlook.

The bulk of the evidence about Islam in Mali relates to the fourteenth century, to the reign of Mansa Mūsā and his brother Mansa Sulaymān. Mansa Mūsā is described as a 'pious and righteous man',[1] who 'made his empire a part of the land of Islam, built mosques . . . and instituted the public prayer on Friday . . . He attracted Maliki scholars . . . and was devoted [himself] to Islamic studies.'[2] Mali had the appearance of an Islamic state and was accepted as such in the Muslim world. Yet a more critical and attentive reading of the Arabic sources would reveal strong traditional survivals beneath a layer of Islam.

Ibn Baṭṭūṭa was present in Mali at the two Islamic festivals when the king came to take part in the public prayer. The royal presence made an Islamic festival into an official ceremony, to which non-Muslims may also have been attracted. In return, the prestige of Islam was recruited to exhorting loyalty to the king, as revealed by the contents of the sermon delivered by the *khaṭīb*. As the Islamic festival became a national feast, it had to accommodate pre-Islamic rites, which were among the sources of the legitimacy of the kingship. Ibn Baṭṭūṭa described a

[1] al-Sa'dī, *T. al-Sūdān*, 7/tr. 13.
[2] al-Umarī, *Masālik*, tr. 53.

dance of masks and a recital of the traditional history by the *griots* on the afternoon of the festival day.

Ibn Baṭṭūṭa, the pious Muslim of another civilization, regarded 'this ridiculous reciting of the poets' among 'the vile practices' of the people of Mali, along with other pre-Islamic customs, such as the rule that 'all women must come before the king naked'.[1] He was also critical of the practice of sprinkling dust or ashes on the head when greeting the king. Significantly, in Ghana of the eleventh century, under a pagan king, Muslims were exempted from this practice, and greeted the king, instead, by clapping hands. But in Mali all subjects, Muslim and non-Muslim, had to follow the custom. In other words, as long as Islam stood in opposition to the kingship, as in Ghana, Muslims were not obliged to follow a traditional custom. But, under islamized kings, who themselves combined Islamic and traditional elements, pre-Islamic customs had to be accommodated.

Among 'the commendable practices' of the people of Mali, Ibn Baṭṭūṭa praised their devotion to prayer, in particular their observance of the Friday prayer, and their concern to study the Koran by heart. These are among the ritual aspects of Islam, which were more closely observed than the provisions of the Islamic law. Shortcomings in the application of the *sharī'a* were most apparent in marriage customs and sexual behaviour. The precepts of Islam, however, were observed in different degrees by the various social groups in the kingdom. There were the commoners, whose only link to Islam was their membership in an islamized empire; then, the king and the nobility, whose greater adherence to Islam was compromised by the survival of some traditional customs and beliefs; finally, those Muslims – traders and clerics – who were fully committed to Islam.

Muslims who lived in the capital or near the courts of lesser chiefs rendered religious services to islamized rulers. These Muslims were pious and observant believers themselves, but had to tolerate the more diluted forms of Islam as practised by their chiefs, and even to take part in ceremonies where pre-Islamic rites were performed. Such was the position of the *qāḍī* and the *khaṭīb* in the capital of Mali described by Ibn Baṭṭūṭa. In purely Muslim towns, centred around the market, and not around a chief's court, Islam was more vigorous and exclusive, and the Muslim *'ulamā'* held authority.

The seventeenth-century author of the *Ta'rīkh al-Fattāsh* described the autonomy of 'Diaba, a town of *fuqahā*', in the middle of the land of

[1] Ibn Baṭṭūṭa, *Tuḥfat*, IV, 423–4.

Mali. The sultan did not enter it and no one had authority there but its *qāḍi*'.[1] In the sixteenth century, under the *askiyas* of Songhay, the *qāḍī* was regarded as being the sole authority in Timbuktu. But, this was the culmination of a longer process in which Timbuktu developed to become the metropolis of Islam in West Africa.

'Timbuktu', al-Sa'dī says, 'has never been sullied by the worship of idols.'[2] The town was founded by Muslim Tuareg, and kept its Islamic appearance ever after. In the fourteenth century, when it began to develop as a commercial centre, Timbuktu also became a cultural centre of Islam. Traditions say that the great mosque of Timbuktu was first built by the order of Mansa Mūsā, and Leo Africanus (who visited the town in 1512) suggests that the mosque was built by an Andalusian architect, referring very likely to Mansa Mūsā's companion, the poet and architect Abū Isḥāq al-Sāḥilī.[3] The latter died in Timbuktu in 1346, and was buried there. Timbuktu must have been an intellectual centre of some importance for al-Sāḥilī to settle there.

The development of Islamic learning in Timbuktu was officially encouraged by Mansa Mūsā, who is reported to have sent Sudanese '*ulamā*' to study in Fez. This was continued at least until the end of Mali's rule in Timbuktu in 1433, because Kātib Mūsā, the last *imām* of the great Friday mosque in Timbuktu under the rule of Mali, was among those who went to study in Fez. In Fez, as we have seen (p. 363), the Marinid sultans established *madrasas* and encouraged the study of the Maliki *fiqh*. Mansa Mūsā, who cultivated relations with the Marinid sultans of his time, perhaps followed the Moroccan example by establishing *madrasas* in Timbuktu. Students and teachers were sent to Fez for further education in order to maintain a high level of scholarship.

This aim was achieved, and a *faqīh* who came to Timbuktu from the Hejaz (perhaps at the beginning of the fifteenth century) found the city 'full of Sudanese *fiqahā*', who surpassed him in [the knowledge of] *fiqh*'.[4] So, he himself decided to travel to Fez to study *fiqh* there before he settled in Timbuktu. Among the leading scholars of Timbuktu at that time was Modibo Muḥammad of Kabora, and around him were 'Sudanese students who diligently pursued science and piety'.[5] His native town Kabora (Diafarabe), on the Niger, was mentioned by Ibn Baṭṭūṭa, together with the neighbouring city of Diagha (Dia):

[1] Ibn al-Mukhtār, *T. al-Fattāsh*, 176/tr. 314.

[2] al-Sa'dī, *T. al Sūdān*, 21/tr. 36.

[3] Leo Africanus, *Description de l'Afrique*, ed. and tr. A. Épaulard and others (Paris, 1956), II, 467.

[4] al-Sa'di, *T. al-Sudān*, 51/tr. 83–4.

[5] Ibid. 47–8/tr. 78.

'the people of Diagha', he says, 'were Muslims of old, and are distinguished by their piety and their quest for knowledge'.[1] Kabora remained an important centre of Islamic learning well into the fifteenth century.

By the sixteenth century, during its golden age, most of the leading scholars of Timbuktu were 'white' Sanhaja and other migrants from the Sahara and North Africa. But all the evidence suggests that this was a later development, associated with the migration of scholars from Walata to Timbuktu in the first half of the fifteenth century. Under the rule of the Tuareg those 'white' scholars took over also the senior religious offices. Before that, under the rule of Mali, black Muslims, who had come to Timbuktu from different regions of the interior, upheld the scholarly reputation of Timbuktu and held such offices as *qāḍī*, Friday *imām* and *khaṭīb*.

Pilgrimage, besides Islamic scholarship, was an important factor which enhanced the unity and universality of Islam. The Pilgrimage also inspired reform of the Islamic milieu of the Sudan to bring it closer to what pilgrims observed in the principal centres of the Muslim world, be it Mecca, Cairo, Kairouan or Fez. The pilgrimages of Muslim rulers often had more immediate consequences. Hence, the Almoravid movement had its origin in the pilgrimage of the Sanhaja chief, Yaḥyā b. Ibrāhīm, and Askiya al-ḥājj Muḥammad of Songhay consulted great scholars in Egypt about the affairs of his kingdom, and his Islamic policy gained new impetus after the pilgrimage.

Pilgrimage is in the first place an act of religious observance, and it is very likely that rulers followed a religious impulse when they decided to undertake the Pilgrimage. But this act has always had its political connotation, which must have added to the motivation of rulers of the Sudan. Externally, it was the opportunity to get to know the outside world, to display the greatness of the empire before this world, and to make the western Sudan an integral part of the Muslim world. Internally, the Pilgrimage increased the king's prestige in the eyes of the Muslims in the empire and bestowed on him an emanating blessing (*baraka*) which was respected by Muslims and non-Muslims alike.

The Pilgrimage across the Sahara, through the Maghrib and Egypt to Mecca, took more than a year, and it was also an expensive adventure. Only kings whose authority was well established could be absent for such a long period, and only those whose kingdom prospered could undertake the cost. Indeed, the three rulers of Mali who went to Mecca

[1] Ibn Baṭṭūṭa, *Tuḥfat*, IV, 395.

in the thirteenth and fourteenth centuries – Mansa Uli, Sakura and Mansa Mūsā – were all described as powerful kings.

Mansa Mūsā was the most famous of the pilgrim kings of the Sudan. His visit to Cairo in 1324 left a deep impression in Egypt, and was recorded in chronicles there (even until the sixteenth century) as one of the principal events of that year. In preparing for his pilgrimage Mansa Mūsā collected provisions from all over his country as a special contribution from his subjects. He was accompanied by a retinue of thousands: slaves to serve him and his wife, and to carry provisions, soldiers to guard the caravan, and state dignitaries. He reached Egypt after his caravan had suffered a good deal from the hardships of the desert.

He sent a rich present of fifty thousand dinars to al-Malik al-Nāṣir b. Qalā'ūn, the Egyptian sultan, to announce his arrival and to herald his greatness. But the meeting with the Egyptian sultan caused embarrassment to Mansa Mūsā. The most powerful king of the Sudan, in whose presence people prostrated and put dust on their heads, was made to kiss the ground before the Egyptian sultan. In other respects, however, Mūsā was given royal treatment and was lent a palace in which to reside during his three months' stay in Cairo before the *ḥajj*. Mansa Mūsā joined the Egyptian pilgrims' caravan to Mecca.

Mansa Mūsā brought with him gold to pay for his expenses and to display his wealth and generosity by distributing presents and alms. So much gold was spent or given away, in fact, that the value of gold in Cairo decreased considerably. The merchants of Egypt made great profits in their dealings with the Sudanese, whose simplicity and naïvety they exploited. The vast quantities of gold that Mansa Mūsā had brought were all exhausted and he had to borrow from Egyptian merchants at an exorbitant rate of interest. This evidence about Mansa Mūsā's visit to Cairo is from Egyptian sources. Al-'Umarī adds that when the people of Mali realized how they had been deceived in Cairo, they changed their attitude towards Egyptian merchants who visited Mali, and handled them roughly. Nevertheless, it seems that Mūsā's visit stimulated trade relations between Egypt and Mali.

The pilgrimage of Mansa Mūsā is sometimes viewed as a landmark in the history of Mali. Sources of different nature and origin echoed its significance: Muslim and non-Muslim traditions in the western Sudan, Egyptian chronicles, and perhaps also Jewish and Christian cartographers, who from the 1330s onwards put Mali and Mansa Mūsā on their maps. The decorated umbrella and Turkish slaves from

Egypt, which are described at the audience of the king of Mali, may be some of the innovations introduced into the court following his visit to Cairo. Perhaps even Mansa Mūsā's Islamic policy was more ardently pursued after his pilgrimage, and in particular the building of mosques and the promotion of Islamic learning. But, how much are historians allowed to hang on this individual episode, spectacular as it was? Certainly Cairo was stunned by the splendours of an exotic king, but in the fourteenth century it was with Morocco that Mali had the more significant connections. The trans-Saharan trade reached new dimensions with the European demand for the gold. Following the establishment of the economic and the religious links between Morocco and the Sudan, diplomatic relations evolved.

According to Ibn Khaldūn, the exchange of embassies began after Abu'l-Ḥasan had conquered Tlemcen in 1337. This confirmed Abu'l-Ḥasan as the greatest ruler in the Maghrib and gave him complete control over the North African section of the gold trade. So, 'the sultan Mansa Mūsā greatly desired to address him'. Abu'l-Ḥasan treated the Malian emissaries with deference, and reciprocated by sending a deputation with rich presents to the king of Mali.

Mansa Mūsā had died before his embassy returned from Morocco and Abu'l-Ḥasan's presents reached Mansa Sulaymān. This was probably shortly after Sulaymān had wrested the kingship from the hands of his nephew Magha, son of Mansa Mūsā (see p. 381). It was before Sulaymān had consolidated his authority, and he may have taken the opportunity to gain support from the Moroccan sultan for his own personal position. This may explain why the deputation that Sulaymān sent to Abu'l-Ḥasan 'lauded the authority of the [Moroccan] sultan, acknowledged his prerogative, conveyed the submission of their king and his willingness to pay the sultan his dues, and to act according to his wish and advice'.[1] The reader may remember that this passage has already been quoted (see p. 361) to suggest an alternative explanation – namely, that this was the subjective view of Abu'l-Ḥasan, then at the height of his power, and aspiring to be recognized as caliph.

Whatever explanation one chooses, the situation soon changed again. In 1348 an official deputation from Mansa Sulaymān was eyewitness to one of the greatest disasters that befell Abu'l-Ḥasan. The deputation came to greet Abu'l-Ḥasan on his conquest of Ifrīqiya (in 1347), but when they were in Constantine news of the defeat of the Marinid army by the Arabs of Ifrīqiya reached that town. The people of

[1] Ibn Khaldūn, *T. al-duwal*, II, 394–5/tr. IV, 243–4.

Constantine revolted in their turn and the emissaries of Mali narrowly escaped with their lives. Abu'l-Ḥasan was beaten and deposed by his son Abū 'Inan.

Abu'l-Ḥasan died in 1351, and a year later Ibn Baṭṭūṭa was present at a memorial ceremony for him held at the court of Mansa Sulaymān. This is another indication of the close relations between the two kingdoms. Even Ibn Baṭṭūṭa's visit may have had latent political significance. He had been received by the sultan Abū 'Inān before his departure and came to see him again immediately after his return to Fez. In fact, Ibn Baṭṭūṭa was called back from Takedda by the sultan, who must have had some idea of Ibn Baṭṭūṭa's itinerary and whereabouts.

A deputation sent from Mali to Fez in 1360 is the last one recorded by Ibn Khaldūn. During the rest of the fourteenth century, as we have already seen (pp. 365, 383), both kingdoms – Mali and Morocco – were in decline and a prey to dynastic rivalries. Courtiers on both sides of the Sahara wielded real power at the expense of the kings. Diplomatic activity, which had developed when the two kingdoms were at their peak, must have diminished.

SHARIFS AND OTTOMANS IN THE MAGHRIB, c. 1430–1591

The Portuguese conquest of Ceuta in 1415 was a serious blow to the prestige of the Marinids, whose power had already been in decline for half a century. But the sultanate of Fez was given a new lease of life by the intervention of the Banū Waṭṭās, a clan of the Zanata related to the Banū Marīn. Their stronghold was in northern Morocco, and they held important offices in the administration of the Marinids. After the death of the Sultan Abū Sa'īd 'Uthmān in 1420, the disputed succession was resolved by the governor of Sale, Abū Zakariyā' Yaḥyā al-Waṭṭāsī. He proclaimed 'Abd al-Ḥaqq, the one-year-old son of the deceased sultan, as king. Abū Zakariyā' himself acted as a regent until 'Abd al-Ḥaqq came of age in 1437. Abū Zakariyā' continued to hold real power as vizier until his death, and was succeeded in this office by two other members of his family.

In his bid to get rid of his patrons, the sultan 'Abd al-Ḥaqq diverted popular resentment against the Wattasid viziers. But, when in 1458 the sultan was unable to prevent the conquest of al-Qaṣr al-Kabīr (between Ceuta and Tangier) by the Portuguese, the agitation of the religious circles was directed against him. He was even more severely criticized for employing Jews in the administration of his finances. His closest adviser, the Jew Hārūn, directed the reorganization of the fiscal system and abolished the exemption of marabouts and Sharifs from taxation. The religious opposition gained strength and erupted in 1465, when a massacre of the Jews in Fez preceded the murder of ʿAbd al-Ḥaqq, the last Marinid sultan.

The insurrection was led by the head (*Naqīb*) of the Sharifs in Fez, Abū ʿAbdallāh Muḥammad b. ʿAlī al-Jūṭī. He held authority in Fez with the title of *imām* for about seven years, until 1472. This was the first overt political action of the Sharifs, the descendants of the Prophet, in Morocco since the eclipse of the Idrisid dynasty in the ninth century. The rise of the Sharifs was associated with the cult of saints or maraboutism, which had gained strength and intensity ever since the twelfth and thirteenth centuries. If a sacred emanation (*baraka*) can be bestowed by God on selected persons, none is more worthy of that beneficent force than the descendants of the Prophet. In 1437, the year ʿAbd al Ḥaqq came of age, the grave of Idrīs II (791–828), the founder of Fez, was miraculously rediscovered and became a popular shrine. The Sharifs, who claimed descent from Idrīs, exploited the new cult for political aims. They were successful in leading the religious opposition and in inciting the fanatical mob of Fez against the Jews, but their military resources were almost nil. In 1472 Fez was conquered by Muḥammad al-Shaykh, son of Abū Zakariyāʾ and the Banū Waṭṭās, former patrons and viziers, returned as sultans.

In 1471, while Muḥammad al-Shaykh was laying siege to Fez, the Portuguese conquered Tangier and Arzila. Neither Muḥammad al-Shakyh, the first Wattasid sultan (1472–1505), nor his son Muḥammad al-Burtuqalī (1505–24) succeeded in arresting the expansion of the Portuguese along the Atlantic coast of Morocco. The effective authority of the Wattasids was restricted to Fez and its environs. They had a limited control over the Atlantic plains, and it was only by force that they could exact some tribute from tribes of the Middle Atlas. Marrakesh was virtually autonomous, and the High Atlas, the Sus and the pre-Saharan oases were completely outside their authority. Even the mountainous Rif in the north was held by a Sharif who defied the authority of the Wattasids.

The decline of the central authority caused political fragmentation. Local chiefs, Berbers and Arabs, who fought each other, wrought destruction and undermined their own authority. Maraboutism, however, throve upon the debris of the state, deriving strength from regional particularism. Insecurity in the countryside led people to seek the protection of the *zāwiyas*, local centres of the Sufi *ṭarīqas* and seats of the great marabouts. These latter mobilized the population to counter the Portuguese offensive and led the jihad against the Christian infidels. They promoted fanaticism and xenophobia, which became inherent in Moroccan Islam. The jihad added strength to local powers at the expense of the sultanate. Indeed, the end of the sultanate came when such a regional power, the Sa'dids, or the Sharifs of the Sus, employed against the sultan that same military power they had built up during the jihad against the Portuguese.

The name Banū Sa'd is a late appellation, and was given to the first Sharifian dynasty in the seventeenth century only by the supporters of their successors, the 'Alawid Sharifs. They were so called, pejoratively, to indicate that they were not true descendants of the Prophet but rather those of the Prophet's foster-mother Ḥalīma al-Sa'diyya. Whatever their real genealogy, it was as Sharif that their ancestor came from the Hejaz at the beginning of the fourteenth century. He was invited by the people of the valley of the Dar'a to bless their crop of dates, the harvest of which had failed for some years before.[1]

During the last two decades of the fifteenth century the Portuguese established commercial factories in the principal Atlantic ports of Morocco, in Azemmour, Safi and Massa, where they gained the cooperation of some coastal tribes. In 1505 they built the fort of Agadir (Santa Cruz de Aguer) to support their intervention in the trade of the Sus. This was followed by the conquest of Safi (1508) and Azemmour (1513), and by the building of another fort at Mazagan (1514). The Portuguese became more aggressive and began to raid adjacent tribes for supplies as well as for slaves, and added to the insecurity which had already prevailed in that region.

The people of the Sus sought the protection of their marabouts, who in turn invited the Sharif of Dar'a, Abū 'Abdallāh Muḥammad, to lead them in jihad against the Portuguese. In 1510/11 the Sharif came to Tidsi, near Tarudant in the Sus, where the Masmuda and other tribes swore allegiance to him. The Sharif's first attack on Agadir failed and many Berbers were killed. Shortly afterwards the Sharif retired to his *zāwiya* in Dar'a. It is likely that he encountered the opposition of the merchants of Tidsi and Tarudant who feared that the jihad might interfere with their trade to the Portuguese forts.

[1] al-Ifrānī, *Nuzhat al-ḥādī bi-akhbār mulūk al-qarn-ḥādī* [*Histoire de la dynastie Sa'adienne au Maroc, 1511–1760*], ed. and tr. O. Houdas (Paris, 1888), 6/tr. 12.

When he had first been invested with the direction of the jihad, the Sharif Abū 'Abdallāh Muḥammad added to his name the honorific title of *al-qā'im bi'llāh* ('he who rises by the aid of Allāh'). It was a clear indication that his political ambitions extended well beyond the scope of the region. But he was prudent enough not to raise the suspicion of the Wattasid sultan of Fez, Muḥammad al-Burtuqalī. He therefore sent his two sons, Aḥmad and Muḥammad, to Fez, where they became distinguished for their learning, austerity, religious intransigence and zeal for the jihad. Aḥmad, the elder, was appointed to teach in the famous mosque of al-Qarāwīn, while Muḥammad, the younger son, was made tutor to the sultan's sons. The two brothers also participated in military expeditions against the Portuguese in Arzila, Larache and Tangier. In 1512/13 they sought permission to rejoin their father in the Sus and the sultan gave them each a drum, a standard and twenty horsemen with the authority to carry on the jihad in the name of the sultan.

In the meantime the marabouts succeeded in reconciling the Sharif with the people of the Sus. In 1512/13 Abū 'Abdallāh Muḥammad al-Qā'im returned to Tidsi, where he was joined by his two sons. By 1514 Tarudant, the principal town of the Sus, accepted his authority, and he had then about three thousand horsemen and an infinite number of infantry at his disposal, according to the evidence of Leo Africanus, who visited his court.[1]

In 1514/15, the Portuguese garrisons of Safi and Azemmour, in alliance with nomad tribes, raided the province of Ḥāḥā (north of the Sus) and reached the gates of Marrakesh. The people of Ḥāḥā sought the protection of the Sharif, who shifted his residence to Afughal in Ḥāḥā.

The choice of Afughal was by no means accidental. It was the site of the tomb of the most venerated saint of the Sus, Abū 'Abdallāh Muḥammad b. Sulaymān al-Jazūlī, the founder of the Jazūliyya branch of the Shādhiliyya brotherhood. The Shādhiliyya spread in the Maghrib in competition with the other brotherhood, the Qādiriyya. Whereas the strongholds of the Qādiriyya were in Algiers, Bougie, Tuat and Fez, the Shādhiliyya was influential in Tlemcen, the Rif and the Sus. The two brotherhoods differed in their relations with the political authorities, and while leaders of the Qādiriyya were co-operative, the Shādhilīs were in opposition; they criticized the government and represented Islamic intransigence. Al-Shādhilī, the founder, was a

[1] Leo Africanus, *Description*, I, 92.

Sharif, a descendant of the Idrisids. Many Sharifs from all over Morocco joined the brotherhood, and al-Jazūlī himself claimed descent from the Prophet. His principal work *Dalā'il al-Khayrāt* is a collection of prayers for the Prophet. He established new *zāwiyas*, mainly in southern Morocco, which, together with the older centres of the Shādhiliyya, formed a widely spread network. In the middle of the fifteenth century when the central authority was disintegrating, this religious organization assumed political significance. Al-Jazulī and his disciples took part in the religious agitation which threatened 'Abd al-Ḥaqq, the last Marinid sultan, and when al-Jazūlī died in 1465, rumours spread that he had been poisoned by the order of 'Abd al-Ḥaqq.

The impact of this alleged martyrdom of al-Jazūlī was at least as great as that of his words and deeds. A group of disciples, led by 'Umar b. Sulaymān al-Shayaẓmī, known as al-Sayyāf, sought to avenge their master. For twenty years al-Sayyāf burned and sacked parts of the Sus, carrying with him the body of al-Jazūlī. In 1485/6, after al-Sayyāf had been killed, the body of the saint came to rest and was buried at Afughal. When the Sharif Muḥammad al-Qā'im died, he was buried beside this saint, and following the conquest of Marrakesh by his son Aḥmad al-A'raj both the saint and the Sharif were reburied in that town, and an impressive mausoleum was built as a shrine.

The sanctity of al-Jazūlī enhanced the prestige of the Sharif, just as the military force built up by the Sharif was blessed by the marabouts, many of whom were affiliated with the Jazūliyya. The Sharifian dynasty, which lacked a tribal basis for its power, needed the marabouts and the brotherhood to recruit mass support. In their decisive struggle against the Wattasids the Sharifs were aided by a coalition of marabouts and *shaykhs* of the Atlas and the Rif, which was cemented by the Jazūliyya brotherhood.

At Afughal the Sharif Muḥammad al-Qā'im confirmed his elder son Aḥmad al-A'raj as his heir. The younger son, Muḥammad al-Mahdī, was appointed governor of the Sus and made Tarudant his residence. The energetic Muḥammad al-Mahdī dedicated himself to a programme of economic reconstruction in order to increase the resources of the nascent Sharifian state. He encouraged the production of sugar cane, which became the principal export commodity of the Sus. He sought a greater control over the gold trade from the Sudan, in order to have free access for trade with European merchants other than the Portuguese, so as to procure fire-arms and gunpowder, which the Portuguese were reluctant to sell. The urgent need to break the Portuguese commercial monopoly on the coast added economic motivation to the jihad. Muḥammad avoided a frontal attack on Agadir, and preferred a blockade which considerably reduced the trade of that port.

The Sharif Abū ʿAbdallāh Muḥammad al-Qā'im died in 1517/18. Aḥmad al-Aʿraj succeeded him at Afughal, while Muḥammad al-Mahdī remained in charge of the Sus. In 1520/1 central Morocco was afflicted with severe famine and epidemic. Thousands from the provinces of Dukkāla and Tamasna sold themselves into slavery in the Portuguese port of Azemmour. The two brothers Aḥmad al-Aʿraj and Muhuammad al-Mahdī initiated a programme of relief and supplied food at reasonable prices. The concern of the Sharifs for the welfare of the population, even outside the territory under their direct rule, increased their prestige. At the same time they continued to harass the Portuguese who, after 1520, were on the defensive. Berber tribes who had been allies of the Portuguese were called to join the jihad against the infidels. Consequently, the Portuguese garrisons remained within their fortifications, relying on their superior artillery. After they had lost the co-operation of the Berbers in their immediate hinterland, they could get supplies only by force, and turned brigands.

The first phase in the rise of the Sharifian dynasty was accomplished in 1524, when Aḥmad al-Aʿraj entered Marrakesh at the invitation of its people and ruler. Marrakesh was then under the protection of the powerful Hintata tribe of the Masmuda. But the Sharif had no intention of sharing power with others, and he killed his host, the emir of Marrakesh. The people of Marrakesh soon rallied around the Sharif and swore him allegiance. They were followed by the tribesmen.

As leaders of the jihad, the Sharifs were able to amass great quantities of arms and mobilize many troops without arousing the suspicion of the sultan of Fez. Though Aḥmad al-Aʿraj acted as an independent ruler, he prudently continued to send presents to Fez as a token of his subordination to the sultan. But as soon as he became more confident of his own strength and popular support, Aḥmad al-Aʿraj made it clear that as a Sharif he could not be a tributary.

The conquest of Marrakesh by the Sharif almost coincided with the death of the sultan Muḥammad al-Burtuqalī, and the accession of his son Aḥmad al-Waṭṭāsī (1524–48). In 1528/9 the new sultan made a truce with the Portuguese in northern Morocco and turned his troops against the Sharif. Troubles in Fez and the intercession of the marabouts obliged the sultan to abandon the siege of Marrakesh. When the two armies met again in 1537, the sultan was defeated, and this time the intervention of the marabouts halted the advance of the Sharif on Fez. In return, the sultan recognized the Sharif's authority over the country south of Tadla and the division of Morocco into two, with Fez and Marrakesh as rival capitals, was confirmed. Such a situation had existed almost three centuries earlier, during the disintegration of the Almohad empire. In the thirteenth century Marrakesh was eclipsed by Fez, whereas in the sixteenth century the southern capital triumphed.

Aḥmad al-Aʿraj established himself as sultan in Marrakesh, but his authority was compromised by the role of his brother, Muḥammad al-Mahdī. As governor of the Sus, the latter controlled much of the economic resources of the new dynasty, and led most of the military operations against the Christians. Mutual envy between the two brothers developed into an open conflict in 1539/40. Aḥmad al-Aʿraj was deposed by his brother Muḥammad al-Mahdī, who became the head of the Sharifian dynasty.

In 1541 Muḥammad al-Mahdī achieved his greatest victory over the Portuguese with the conquest of Agadir. From the beginning of the sixteenth century the small garrisons of the Portuguese forts had stood firm against numerous attacks. They were short of supplies and, with the growing hostility of the population, trade diminished. John III, king of Portugal, decided to evacuate the forts of Safi, Azemmour and Arzila. By 1550 only Mazagan was left in the hands of the Portuguese on the Atlantic coast of Morocco. The success of the jihad against the Christians was the springboard for the extension of the Sharifian state over the rest of Morocco. The sultanate of Fez was no match for the Sharif, but west of Morocco a new Muslim power was about to intervene in the politics of Morocco. In 1527/8, the year in which the Sharif Muḥammad al-Qā'im died, Algeria became part of the Ottoman empire.

The Christian reconquest of Spain increased religious fanaticism on both sides of the straits, in the Maghrib and in the Iberian peninsula. Piracy in the Mediterranean, which may have begun for worldly gains, was carried on during the fifteenth century under the banner of jihad, especially as Muslim exiles from Spain joined the corsairs. Many other corsairs were renegades, captives who had converted to Islam. The principal Mediterranean ports of North Africa developed as independent 'republics' of corsairs. The official Muslim authorities of Fez oscillated between support of the corsairs and attempts to appease the Europeans, in particular the kings of Aragon and Castile, to avert punitive expeditions. The corsairs attacked Christian ships and raided the coasts of Spain. The Spaniards retaliated, and the need to bring privateering to an end was one reason for their large-scale offensive on the North African coast.

In 1399 Tetuan was attacked by a Castilian fleet in retaliation for the corsairs' attacks. But Spain was still divided, and war against Islam still continued in the Iberian peninsula itself. Spanish initiatives in the Maghrib had been delayed until the union of Castile and Aragon and the liquidation of Granada (1492). By then the Portuguese offensive in Morocco was in full swing, and the intrusion of Spain had to be preceded in 1494 by an agreement, sanctioned by the Pope, which divided the Maghrib between the two Christian kingdoms. Portugal was given a free hand on the Atlantic coast, whereas the Mediterranean coast east of Ceuta was left for Spain, which had had important commercial interests there for almost two centuries.

Spain exploited the weakness of the rulers of Tunisia and Tlemcen and between 1496 and 1510 took possession of the principal ports of the Mediterranean coast: Melilla, Mers al-Kabīr, Oran, Bougie and Tripoli. The Spanish *presidios* remained restricted to the ports and dependent on supplies from the sea alone. Only in Oran did the Spaniards create a wider base by gaining the co-operation of some local tribes.

By the end of the fifteenth century the kingdom of the 'Abd al-Wadids had disintegrated into its many components. The authority of the emir was restricted to Tlemcen and its environs, and even there his power was undermined by recurring conflicts over succession. The emir was unable to arrest the Spanish aggression, and he soon came under the Christians' patronage. As in Morocco, the jihad against the invading infidels was led by marabouts. But the latter were divided among themselves and failed to halt the Spaniards. One of them therefore called in the aid of Turkish corsairs who, under the leadership of the two brothers 'Arūj and Khayr al-Dīn Barbarossa, had operated from Tunis since the beginning of the sixteenth century. The corsairs themselves were committed to jihad against the Christians. They landed in Algiers in 1516 and started by eliminating local rulers, including those who had invited them. 'Arūj gained control over the coastline east and west of Algiers, though he was unable to subdue a Spanish garrison in a fortress on an islet off the harbour of Algiers.

In 1517, at the invitation of its people, 'Arūj conquered Tlemcen. But he had no more than 1,500 men with him, and a year later he was defeated and killed by a large Spanish force under the command of the governor of Oran. His brother Khayr al-Dīn, who had stayed behind in

Algiers, reorganized their forces and conquered key positions like Bone and Constantine. His offer to place the newly conquered land under the protection of the Ottoman sultan was accepted, and he himself was made governor of the Maghrib with the title of *beylerbey*. Infantry units of janissaries were sent from Anatolia to support the corsairs. In 1529 the fortress of Algiers, which had been held by a Spanish garrison, was conquered. Khayr al-Dīn improved the harbour of Algiers, which functioned both as a base for piracy and as a commercial entrepôt.

In 1533 Khayr al-Dīn was called to Istanbul to become admiral of the Ottoman fleet. In Algiers *beylerbeys* held office successively until 1587, when the Ottoman Maghrib was divided into three separate provinces, each headed by a pasha. The governor of Algiers (whether the *beylerbey* or the pasha) could exercise his authority only with the consent of two rival factions: the corporation of corsair captains (*tā'ifat al-ru'asā'*) and the militia of the janissaries under their *agha*.

The janissaries were responsible for establishing Turkish authority in the country, while the corsairs provided the means from the spoils of their privateering. From the latter part of the sixteenth century onwards, politics in Algiers evolved around the conflicts between corsairs and janissaries.

The *beylerbeys* of Algiers posted garrisons in the principal towns and organized the collection of taxes from all sections of the population: city dwellers, peasants and nomad tribesmen. In Algiers, most of the marabouts, who combined religious and political influence, were affiliated with the Qādiriyya.

The close relations between the Qādiriyya and the Ottoman sultans in the central parts of the empire helped the *beylerbeys* to secure the tacit co-operation of the marabouts. There were no formal links, but the Ottoman authorities treated the marabouts with great respect and rewarded them generously for their services in communicating with the local population.

The distribution of the two rival brotherhoods, the Qādiriyya (in Algeria and in Fez) and the Shādhiliyya-Jazūliyya (in southern Morocco and in Tlemcen) tallied with the political alignments in the Maghrib. The Ottomans of Algiers and the Wattasids of Fez, with the blessing of the Qādiriyya, were in alliance against the rising Sharifian dynasty of Marrakesh, which had the support of the Shādhiliyya-Jazūliyya. The Shādhilīs of Tlemcen sympathized with the Sharif and later sought his aid against the Ottomans.

According to the tradition of the Wattasids, the last sultan of that dynasty, Aḥmad al-Waṭṭāsī, made tactical agreements with the Portuguese, which discredited him in the eyes of the religious leaders. On the other hand, the successful jihad of the Sharif Muḥammad al-Mahdī enhanced his prestige. The Sharif's military power increased after he had acquired modern artillery from Europeans. These arms, which he had employed in the conquest of Agadir from the Portuguese, were later turned against the sultan of Fez. In 1544/5 he defeated the Wattasid army and captured the sultan Aḥmad al-Waṭṭāsī. Many Turks and renegades who had served the Wattasids then joined the Sharif.

In Fez the strong man of the Wattasids, Abū Ḥassūn, mobilized the support of the Qādirī marabouts. He recognized the sovereignty of the Ottoman sultan, Sulaymān the Magnificent, and solicited his support. An envoy of the Ottoman sultan came to Marrakesh, demanding that the sultan of Fez should be set free and that the *kuhṭba* of the Friday prayer should be said in the name of the Ottoman sultan. Muḥammad al-Mahdī rejected the Ottoman intervention and ordered the execution of the envoy. In 1548/9 Meknes was captured by Muḥammad al-Mahdī, and in the next year, 1549/50, he laid siege to Fez. Inside the city marabouts of the Qādiriyya encouraged opposition to the Sharif. Their leader al-Wansharīshī was killed when Muḥammad al-Mahdī broke into the city.

Shortly after the conquest of Fez, a deputation from Tlemcen invited Muḥammad al-Mahdī to deliver their city from the Turks. Since 1517 the rulers of Tlemcen had oscillated between the Spaniards in Oran and the Ottomans in Algiers, changing alliances and patrons. The rise of the Sharifs, with whom they shared affiliation to the Shādhiliyya, suggested an alternative for the political orientation of Tlemcen. Al-Ḥarran, son of Muḥammad al-Mahdī, conquered Tlemcen in June 1550. Against the instructions of his father, al-Ḥarran advanced east, to Mustaghnam and the Chelif valley. The Ottomans with their Berber allies counter-attacked, defeated the Sharifian army and re-conquered Tlemcen.

News about the defeat of the Sharifian army gave rise to widespread revolts of the Berbers in the Atlas mountains and in the Sus. Ottomans and the supporters of the Wattasids incited the Berbers, exploiting resentment against the heavy taxation imposed by Muḥammad al-Mahdī. The jihad of the Sharif against the Portuguese had been fought by zealous volunteers and had been financed by the Sharif with revenues from the monopoly over the sugar industry, the control of the gold trade and from voluntary contributions. But for the struggle for power inside Morocco Muḥammad al-Mahdī employed mercenaries. For this purpose and for the maintenance of a large court, the Sharif needed new sources of revenue. He therefore levied taxes from the tribes of the Atlas and the Sus, who for generations before had evaded taxation. He even pressed marabouts, who had been traditionally exempted from any fiscal obligations. In their indignation the marabouts protested that the tax, which became known as *al-nā'iba* ('the affliction'), was illegal according to the religious law of Islam.

Muḥammad al-Mahdī thus antagonized those same marabouts who had supported him in the past. He set out from Fez to crush the rebellion, and executed those marabouts who refused to pay the tax. The predatory habits of the troops, Turkish and renegade mercenaries, added to the distress of the population. The rebels retreated and dispersed before the troops, but returned and reorganized when the Sharifian army moved away. Muḥammad al-Mahdī had not yet accomplished the pacification of the south when he was informed that an Ottoman army was about to attack Fez to reinstate Abū Ḥassūn the Wattasid.

In 1550, after the conquest of Fez by the Sharif, Abū Ḥassūn crossed the straits to seek the support of Spain and Portugal against the Sharif. Eventually he reached Algiers, where the *beylerbey* Ṣālih Ra'īs regarded the cause of Abū Ḥassūn as a convenient pretext to attack the Sharif. In October 1553 the Ottoman troops moved towards Fez. Muḥammad al-Mahdī, who had hastened from the south, came out to meet the Ottomans near Taza, but retreated without giving battle when he realized the superiority of the Ottoman artillery. The *beylerbey* entered Fez in January 1554, and Abū Ḥassūn was declared ruler as vassal of the Ottoman Sultan.

For four months the Ottoman troops, Turks and Berbers from Kabylia, stayed in Fez and harassed its population. Abū Ḥassūn then bought the withdrawal of the Turks for four hundred *mithqāls*, which he had collected from the Muslim merchants as a loan and from Jewish and Christian merchants as contributions. The people of Fez, led by the religious establishment, supported Abū Ḥassūn and the restoration of the Wattasīd. Abū Ḥassūn had a formidable task to rebuild both the army and the administration. He recruited Turks and renegades as mercenaries, and set free Christian captives who produced fire-arms and gunpowder for him. He reappointed to the administration those supporters of his dynasty who had been deposed by Muḥammad al-Mahdī. Finally, he reached an agreement with Aḥmad al-Aʿraj, the deposed brother of Muḥammad al-Mahdī, who was then in Tafilelt. Abū Ḥassūn and Aḥmad al-Aʿraj advanced from two directions, from north and south, on Marrakesh.

Muḥammad al-Mahdī first dealt with his brother and then turned against Abū Ḥassūn. The battle was drawn, but an agent of the Sharif murdered Abū Ḥassūn, whose army dispersed. In September 1554 the Sharif reconquered Fez.

The former dynasty was exterminated, but the opposition to the Sharif continued. The pro-Wattasid 'party', mainly marabouts affiliated with the Qādiriyya, became the pro-Ottoman 'party'. In consolidating his authority Muḥammad al-Mahdī did not hesitate to order the execution even of the *qāḍī* of Fez and the *khaṭīb* (preacher) of Meknes. More than two hundred of the wealthier and more influential people of Fez were killed and their property was confiscated. Religious endowments (*ḥabūs*) were also taken over by the Sharif in order to improve his finances and to deprive the religious establishment in Fez of an independent source of income.

Muḥammad al-Mahdī felt rather uncomfortable in Fez, a sophisticated urban centre, which remained in opposition to the uncouth Sharif of the south. He therefore moved the capital to Marrakesh, where he was closer to his former allies, the turbulent tribes of the Atlas and the Sus, and away from the Ottoman frontier.

By assuming the caliphal title of *amīr al-mu'minīn*, the Sharif challenged the Ottoman sultan. He was apprehensive of the latter's ambition to incorporate the whole Maghrib into the Ottoman empire. He therefore negotiated secretly with the Spaniards and reached an agreement about a common action against Algiers. Reasons of state came before religious considerations. The Sharifian dynasty, it should be recalled, had come to power on the wave of a jihad against the Christian invaders. Along with other marabouts, the Sharif agitated against the sultans of Fez because of their co-operation with the Christian invaders. By relinquishing the jihad and by acting in collusion with the Christians against another Muslim power, the Sharif exposed himself to the criticism of the marabouts, who had already been alienated by his taxation.

In 1556, following the death of the *beylerbey* Ṣāliḥ Ra'īs, Algiers was thrown into an internal struggle between the corsairs and the janissaries. The latter supported local commanders to the vacant office, whereas the corsairs were willing to accept nominees from Istanbul.

The Spanish governors of Oran wished to exploit this situation, and urged Muḥammad al-Mahdī to attack Tlemcen. The city was easily conquered with the aid of the Shādhilī marabouts. But with the appointment of a new *beylerbey*, Ḥasan, son of Khayr al-Dīn Barbarosa, Tlemcen was recaptured. This was made easier because of the turmoil in Morocco following the death of Muḥammad al-Mahdī in October 1557. He was murdered by the commander of his Turkish mercenaries, who was in fact an agent of the new *beylerbey*, Ḥasan.

Abū Muḥammad ʿAbdallāh al-Ghālib bi'llāh, son of Muḥammad al-Mahdī, was proclaimed sultan to succeed his father. He immediately appealed to the marabouts of the Jazūliyya in the Sus to support the dynasty that they had brought to power. In spite of the recent antagonism with the Sharifian authorities, the marabouts mobilized their followers and defeated the Turkish mercenaries who had held Tarudant. The *beylerbey* Ḥasan b. Khayr al-Dīn advanced on Fez, but failed to score a decisive victory in the first battle. He feared that the Spaniards of Oran might cut off his line of communications and supplies, and returned to Algiers.

The sultan ʿAbdallāh al-Ghālib eliminated potential rivals by murder, prison and exile. Three of his brothers – ʿAbd al-Mu'min, ʿAbd al-Malik and Aḥmad – sought refuge with the Ottomans in Tlemcen. ʿAbd al-Mu'min remained in Tlemcen, where he was later murdered by an agent of ʿAbdāllah al-Ghālib. ʿAbd al-Malik and Aḥmad were sent to Istanbul, where the former entreated the Ottoman sultan Murād to support his claim to the sultanate of Morocco.

In 1559/60, in alliance with the Spaniards, ʿAbdallāh al-Ghālib captured Tlemcen, but once again he was soon forced to evacuate that city. The following year some of the dignitaries of Tlemcen, supporters of the Sharifian dynasty, moved to Fez. Their departure weakened the fifth column of the Sharif in Tlemcen, which had lured both Muḥammad al-Mahdī and his son to adventurous attacks on that city.

The sultan ʿAbdallāh al-Ghālib died in January 1574, after a reign of seventeen years. He was succeeded by his son Muḥammad *al-Mutawakkil ʿalā'llāh*. Two years later, in January 1576, an Ottoman force left Algiers to install ʿAbd al-Malik, son of Muḥammad al-Mahdī, as ruler of Morocco and a vassal to the Ottoman sultan. Spain was then seeking reconciliation with the Ottomans of Algiers and did not intervene to support the sultan Muḥammad al-Mutawakkil. The latter was defeated and retreated to Marrakesh.

In March 1576 ʿAbd al-Malik entered Fez, and the *khuṭba* of the

Friday prayer was said in the name of the Ottoman sultan Murād. Shortly afterwards ʿAbd al-Malik gave rich presents of gold to the Turks on condition that they should leave Fez and return to Algiers. ʿAbd al-Malik then began to build up an army of his own, composed of Andalusians, Turks, Berbers and Arabs, which he organized, equipped and trained according to the Ottoman model. Years of exile among the Turks had left their impact. The new sultan spoke Turkish and adopted Turkish costume and manners. But he could also speak Spanish and Italian, and shortly after he had been freed from the Ottoman troops he re-established contacts with Spain.

The deposed sultan Muḥammad al-Mutawakkil was hunted by his uncle's troops and left for Portugal. There he tempted the young king Don Sebastian to invade Morocco. The landing of the Portuguese force was exploited by ʿAbd al-Malik to renew the spirit of jihad. He assembled a large army to meet a smaller Portuguese force in the Wādī al-Makhāzin near al-Qasr al-Kabīr (Alcazar) at the beginning of August 1578. The Portuguese were defeated, and both Don Sebastian and al-Mutawakkil died. This battle became known as 'the battle of the three kings', because the third king, ʿAbd al-Malik himself, died a natural death at the beginning of the battle and the victory was accomplished by his brother and successor Abu'l ʿAbbās Aḥmad.

Mawlay Aḥmad marked this glorious victory by adopting the honorific title al-Manṣūr ('the victorious'). The victory over a European nation like Portugal projected the image of Morocco as a mighty power. Ambassadors reported to their monarchs about the luxury of the court, where the sultan imitated the ʿAbbasid caliphs of Baghdad and used to talk to people from behind a curtain. Morocco was not, in fact, as powerful as it appeared, and the sultan successfully avoided another test of his military power by exploiting the rivalry of his two neighbours, the Ottomans and Spain.

The Ottomans were the more dangerous of the two neighbours, because there was always a pro-Turkish 'party' in Fez. Also, any aggression by Spain against Morocco would be resisted with the spirit of a jihad, which had already been rekindled by the great victory over the Christian invaders. More than any of his predecessors, Mawlay Aḥmad emphasized the caliphal titles and prerogatives. It was, as we shall see, in stressing his status as caliph and leader of the jihad that he set forth his demands to the *askiya* of Songhay.

Turkish mercenaries had been employed by the Moroccan sultans – Wattasids and Saʿdids – at least since the Ottoman occupation of

Algiers. Mawlay Aḥmad al-Manṣūr strengthened the Turkish element among his troops even further and reorganized his army with the aid of Turkish instructors. Under their influence more fire-arms were introduced, and were handled more effectively. He needed a standing professional army for this purpose and recruited Andalusians (Muslim refugees from Spain) and renegades (Christian captives or adventurers who converted to Islam by force or voluntarily). He also paid due attention to military logistics and created units responsible for supplies, fortifications and communications. The modernization of the army, however, was restricted to the élite corps of foreign origin. The auxiliary troops, of Arab and Berber tribesmen, had outmoded traditional weapons. For the first time the standing army at the service of the sultan had an overwhelming military superiority over the tribesmen, but the sultan was careful not to send it against his Berber subjects. Yet the alienation between the state and the society became more acute.

Excessive taxation caused misery for the local population, but was not enough to defray the cost of the extravagant expenses at the court and the maintenance of a professional army of mercenaries armed with expensive fire-arms. Al-Manṣūr sought other sources of income, which he hoped to derive from a tighter control over the trade across the Sahara with the Sudan

As governor of the Sus, Muḥammad al-Mahdī wished to control the trans-Saharan trade, as a source of income to support the Sharifian jihad. In 1537 Aḥmad al-Aʿraj conquered Tafilelt, through which much of the gold of Timbuktu reached the Maghrib. Two years later (and shortly before he was deposed by his brother), 'Mawlay Aḥmad al-Akbar Sultan of Marrakesh' sent a letter to Askiya Isḥāq demanding that the Songhay ruler should hand over to him the salt mines of Taghaza. The *askiya*, sure of his power, sent an insulting reply and made this defiance clearer by dispatching a raiding party of two thousand Tuareg to attack the fringes of the province of Darʿa. The Tuareg raided the market-place of Banū Sabīḥ and took booty, but followed closely the *askiya*'s instructions not to kill anyone.[1]

In the 1540s, according to Marmol-Carvajal (a Spaniard who was prisoner in Morocco for over seven years), the authority of Muḥammad al-Mahdī reached as far as Sāqiyat al-Ḥamrā'. He attempted to extend it further into the desert, and organized a military expedition to reach

[1] al-Saʿdī, *T. al-Sūdān*, 99/tr. 163–4.

Wadan, then an important commercial town close to the Portuguese factory in Arguin. But the Sharif gave up his plans, when he was informed of a large Sudanese force which had moved up to defend Wadan.

Since the fourteenth century the oases of Tuat had developed into a pivot of the trade with the Sudan. After the conquest of Tafilelt, Aḥmad al-Aʿraj, and then his brother, Muḥammad al-Mahdī, sent *qāʾids* to govern Tuat in their name. Because of pressing problems in the north – the conquest of Fez, the confrontation with the Ottomans and the Berber revolts in the Atlas and the Sus – Muḥammad al-Mahdī was unable to defend Tuat when the people of the oases were harassed by the Kunta, a tribe of mixed Arab and Berber descent.

The interest in the salt mines of Taghaza remained as strong as ever, but because Muḥammad al-Mahdī was unable to employ military force in the desert, he reverted to clandestine intrigues. He induced al-Zubayr, a native of Tafilelt, to kill the governor of Taghaza, who was a nominee of Askiya Dāwūd. Some of the leading salt traders, all of them Tuareg, were also killed. Those who survived came to Askiya Dāwūd, and promised to abandon the salt mines of Taghaza. The same year they brought salt from a new mine called Taghaza al-Ghizlān. The Tuareg returned for some time to Taghaza, but these mines had already been exhausted. There is accumulating evidence that the size and weight of the salt bars were considerably reduced, and at the beginning of the sixteenth century – according to Fernandes – it was very difficult to load the salt bars of Taghaza because these were too thin and tended to crumble.[1]

In Morocco Taghaza was still thought of as an inexhaustible source of revenue. Mawlay Aḥmad al-Manṣūr demanded from Askiya Dāwūd to be given one year's revenue from Taghaza as a contribution to the jihad. Askiya Dāwūd sent him a contribution of ten thousand *mithqāls* of gold in recognition of al-Manṣūr's achievement for the sake of Islam. It is clear that Askiya Dāwūd made his contribution voluntarily and from a position of strength. Al-Manṣūr appreciated the *askiya*'s generosity, and friendly relations continued between the two monarchs. The death of Askiya Dāwūd in August 1582 was the occasion for official mourning at the court of al-Manṣūr. Presents were exchanged between al-Manṣūr and Askiya Al-Ḥājj soon after the latter's accession.[2] But shortly afterwards the Moroccan sultan initiated a more aggressive policy towards his southern neighbours.

[1] V. Fernandes, *Description de la côte occidentale d'Afrique*, tr. P. de Cenival and T. Monod (Paris, 1938), 9.

[2] al-Saʿdī, *T. al-Sūdān*, 111, 120/tr. 180, 193.

In the 1580s Morocco was relieved from the pressure of both its neighbours. Spain was exhausted by the revolt in the Netherlands and its international repercussions, while the Ottomans were engaged in war with Persia. Also, the pashas, who had replaced the *beylerbeys* of Algiers since 1587, served for short periods of three years and discontinued the aggressive policy of their predecessors against Morocco. For the first time for more than three decades the Moroccan sultan was able to send strong military expeditions to the south. In 1578, following raids of tribesmen on Tuat, the dignitaries of the oases sought the protection of the Ottomans. In 1579 and again in 1582, Ottoman troops from Algiers and Tunisia visited Tuat. In 1583, in order to forestall the establishment of Ottoman authority there, al-Manṣūr sent an expedition to occupy Tuat and Gurara. Fighting against nomad tribesmen went on until 1589.

Al-Manṣūr followed the example of his father Muḥammad al-Mahdī in attempting to extend his authority over the Saharan trade both along the Atlantic coast and the central route via Tuat and Taghaza. In 1584 he sent an expedition from the Sus which, after ninety days' marching across the desert, made contact with the Sudanese. The latter soon realized that they could not fight the Moroccan musketeers and offered their surrender. The authority of the Moroccan sultan was recognized by the Arabs of the western Sahara and by the Sudanese on the lower Senegal. This account by al-Fishtālī, the secretary and the official historian of al-Manṣūr, is contradicted by two other (more hostile) sources – the anonymous chronicle of the Sa'dids and the *Ta'rikh al-Sūdān* – which say that this expedition ended in a disaster, when most of the army died of thirst and hunger.[1]

In 1586 the offensive on the central route to Songhay began with the seizure of Taghaza by a force of two hundred musketeers. They found the mine deserted, because its occupants had been warned in time and had run away. On the advice of the Tuareg salt traders, Askiya Al-Ḥājj of Songhay officially forbade people to trade with Taghaza. The Tuareg searched for new sources of salt and opened the mines of Taodeni. The Moroccan *qā'id* who had seized Taghaza returned empty-handed to Marrakesh. Al-Manṣūr, furious because of the loss of the revenue from Taghaza, put pressure on the *askiya* to lift the ban. As a lever for applying the pressure, al-Manṣūr exploited the presence at his court of a man from Gao, who claimed to be a brother of the reigning

[1] al-Fishtālī, *Manāhil al-Safā*, ed. A. Ganun (Rabat, 1964), 59–61; al-Sa'dī, *T. al-Sūdān*, 120/tr. 193; *Chronique anonyme de la dynastie Sa'adienne*, ed. G. S. Colin (Rabat, 1934), 68.

askiya. Songhay was at that time in the midst of the worst civil war in its history (see pp. 439–41).

In January 1590 al-Manṣūr sent a letter to the *askiya* saying that according to the opinion of the *fuqahā'* the revenue from the salt mines of Taghaza should be given exclusively to the treasury of the *imām*, the caliph. He announced his decision to impose a toll of one *mithqāl* on every camel which came to Taghaza. The revenue accrued would be devoted to the jihad and to provide provisions for the troops, whose protection against the infidels extended to the Sudan. Al-Manṣūr then referred to a letter he enclosed from the alleged brother of the *askiya*, who asked for military support to overthrow the *askiya*. The Moroccan sultan concluded: 'We have delayed our reply to him until we shall see what comes to light from you.'[1]

Askiya Isḥāq sent back an insulting reply, and al-Manṣūr resolved to send an expedition to Songhay. He disclosed his ambitious plans to members of his council, who were rather sceptical. How, they asked, would the army be able to cross the waterless desert? Why, they added, did the present sultan aspire to do what none of the former dynasties had ever done? Al-Manṣūr had a ready and well-argued reply, saying that the desert, which was crossed by traders' caravans, should not be an obstacle to an army with good supplies. Former dynasties of Morocco had been engaged in fighting (for conquest or defence) in Spain and in North Africa east of Morocco. These wars were now over, because the Muslims had no longer any foothold in Spain, whereas the rest of the Maghrib was part of the Ottoman empire. In the past, the sultan added, the sultans' troops had similar weapons to those possessed by the kingdoms of the Sudan – namely, cavalry and bowmen. But now a small force of musketeers could beat an enormous army of Sudanese, who knew nothing of those dreadful fire-arms. Finally, the sultan reminded his councillors of the riches of the Sudan, and the prospect of gold and slaves. The council then unanimously approved the sultan's plans.[2]

The sultan assigned some of his best troops for the expedition to the Sudan under the command of a young renegade, Jūdār. This force counted one thousand renegade musketeers, one thousand Andalusian musketeers and five hundred *spahis* or mounted musketeers (most of

[1] *Rasa'il Sa'diyya*, ed. A. Ganun (Tetuan, 1954), 132–5; for other versions see al-Fishtālī, *Manāhil*, 56; al-Sa'dī, *T. al-Sūdān*, 137/tr. 215–16; *Chronique anonyme*, 456; 'Relation de l'anonyme Espagnol', in H. de Castries, 'La conquête du Soudan par El-Mansour, 1591', *Hespéris*, 1923, 3, 468.

[2] al-Fishtālī, *Manāhil*, 65–6; al-Ifrānī, *Nuzhat al-hādī*, 91–2/tr. 160–2.

whom were also renegades). Those were joined by one thousand five hundred recruits armed with lances; four thousand warriors all together. Careful preparations were undertaken to provide sufficient water and food provisions as well as other supplies, including large quantities of ammunition. Ten thousand camels were assembled in Dar'a to carry the supplies and the equipment. About one thousand auxiliaries, artisans of all kinds and doctors accompanied the expedition to care for the fighting troops and their needs.[1]

The expedition left Marrakesh in October 1590 and reached the Niger river at Karabara at the end of February 1591. About half of the troops perished in the desert, but the rest were in position to fight a decisive battle at Tondibi against the Songhay army less than a fortnight later. Al-Manṣūr was proved right in relying on the superiority of fire-arms, because a force of less than two thousand musketeers was enough to defeat a Sudanese army of over one hundred thousand bowmen. The battle of Tondibi will be discussed further later in this chapter, as the final phase in the history of the Songhay empire. In Morocco news of the victory was received with great jubilation. The sultan boasted that he had accomplished the unity of the Muslim West under his sovereignty as caliph.[2]

The politico-religious element was of great importance in al-Manṣūr's policy towards the Sahara and the Sudan. After the defiant reply of Askiya Isḥāq and the final resolution to dispatch the expedition, al-Manṣūr sought to turn the '*ulamā*' of Timbuktu away from the *askiya*. In August 1590 he sent a letter to the *qāḍī* 'Umar of Timbuktu explaining the legal obligation of the Muslims to pledge allegiance (*bay'a*) to him as the caliph.[3]

'Abd al-Malik, the brother and predecessor of al-Manṣūr, had come to power with the support of the Ottomans and began his rule as vassal of the Ottoman sultan, Murād. Al-Manṣūr, crowned with the victory at the battle of Alcazar, wanted to fortify the independence of Morocco vis-à-vis the Ottomans. As Sharif he regarded himself as being more worthy the caliphal title than the Ottoman sultan. His recognition as a caliph in the Sahara and the Sudan could add substance to his claim. In 1582, almost a decade before the expedition to the Sudan, an envoy of the king of Bornu Mai Idris (1569/70 – *c.* 1619) had come to Marra-

[1] al-Sa'dī, *T. al-Sūdān*, 138/tr. 217; 'Anonyme Espagnol' in de Castries, 'La conquête', 468–9.

[2] 'Lettre de Moulay Admed El-Mansour aux Chérifs, aux jurisconsultes et à tous les notables de Fez', in de Castries, 'La conquête', 478–88.

[3] al-Fishtālī, *Manāhil*, 67.

kesh to seek military aid from al-Manṣūr for a jihad against his infidel neighbours. It is likely that the king of Bornu turned to the Moroccan sultan after a clash with an Ottoman force that had crossed the desert, and after he had realized that the Ottomans in Tripoli were unwilling to strengthen their southern neighbours by the supply of advanced fire-arms. Al-Manṣūr sent back to Bornu the text of a *bay'a* (deed of homage), which the king of Bornu agreed to sign.[1] Al-Manṣūr thus achieved at least a nominal sovereignty over Bornu, far on the southern flank of the Ottomans. After the conquest of Songhay, al-Manṣūr blamed the ruler of Kebbi for preventing the arrival of embassies from Katsina and Kano, who wanted to come to pay allegiance to him through the commanders of his army in the Sudan.[2] So, whether by military conquest or through nominal allegiance, al-Manṣūr claimed sovereignty over the whole width of the northern belt of the Sudan, from Wolof to Bornu, from the lower Senegal river to Lake Chad.

Yet, in the midst of the great jubilation to mark this unprecedented glory of Morocco, there were voices of scepticism, as reported by a contemporary Spanish observer. Over two thousand of the best musketeers of Morocco had been sent to the Sudan, and more of these élite troops would be needed as reinforcements to secure the domination of the occupied land. These troops of renegades and Andalusians might later be badly needed at home, because these were the main support of the regime. Also, the cost of maintaining the army in the Sudan might drain much of the revenue from the Sudan. This shrewd observer realized that the goldfields themselves could not be conquered, and that the flow of gold would decrease because of the political turmoil caused by the conquest.[3] This report was written before the end of 1591, only six months after the battle of Tondibi, and some of its predictions became true a few years later. In Morocco the glory of the conquest of Songhay faded away after a short while, but it was a turning point in the history of the Sudan.

THE HEGEMONY OF SONGHAY

The Moroccan conquerors established their residence in Timbuktu, and the city became the official capital of the pashalik. The Moroccan conquest, however, marked the beginning of the gradual decline of Timbuktu, after it had reached its peak of commercial prosperity and

[1] Ibid. 62–3; 'Anonyme Espagnol', in De Castries, 'La conquête', 475.
[2] *Rasā'il al-Sa'diyya*, 129.
[3] 'Anonyme Espagnol', in de Castries, 'La conquête', 476–7.

in Islamic learning under the *askiyas* of Songhay during the sixteenth century.

Though the royal capital was in Gao, Timbuktu had then been the real metropolis of the western Sudan. Tension between Gao and Timbuktu, royal traditions and Islam, *askiyas* and *qāḍīs*, were of great significance in the politics of Songhay.

Timbuktu, we have seen, developed as the principal terminus of the caravan trade from the second half of the fourteenth century onwards. The city soon attracted Muslim scholars. Under the rule of Mali the leading scholars were Sudanese, who came down to Timbuktu from towns and villages of the Niger valley. In 1433 the city was lost to Mali and came under the protection of the Tuareg, the white nomads of the southern Sahara. Under their rule, as a result of the influx of Arab and Berber merchants and scholars from the northern Sahara and the Maghrib, the office of *imām* of the Friday mosque of Timbuktu passed from black to white incumbents. Sīdī 'Abdallāh al-Balbālī (of Tabalbalet in the oases of Tuat) held office during the later period of the Tuareg and at the beginning of Sonni 'Alī's reign. His successors were Abu'l-Qāsim al-Tuwātī (of Tuat), Manṣūr al-Fazānī (of Fezzan), and Sīdī 'Ali al-Jazūlī (a Moroccan), whose deputy was 'Uthmān al-Tishītī (of Tichit). These scholars lived, along with the older community of Sudanese scholars, in Jingerber, the quarter of the Friday mosque in Timbuktu.

About that time a new quarter developed around the Sankore mosque by the settlement of Sanhaja scholars. Most of them had come from (or via) Walata, which had preceded Timbuktu as a market and a centre of learning. Walata was the city of the Massufa Sanhaja, and following its decline some of its leading merchants and scholars moved to Timbuktu. Shortly before the end of Mali's rule in Timbuktu, the *faqīh* Al-Ḥājj came from Walata to become *qāḍī* of Timbuktu. He was succeeded in this office, under the rule of the Tuareg, by Abū 'Abdallāh And-ag-Muḥammad, who had also lived earlier at Walata. The emerging Sankore community was reinforced with the arrival of Muḥammad Aqīt, the head of an important clan of Massufa Sanhaja. This clan had migrated from Tichit to Massina, but when Fulani migrated to Massina in great numbers, Muḥammad Aqīt moved to Walata. From Walata he moved to Timbuktu, but only after an old enmity with Akilu, the Tuareg chief, had been settled. Muḥammad Aqīt came to Timbuktu with his many dependants. His son 'Umar married the daughter of Abū 'Abdallāh And-ag-Muḥammad, and the two families formed the nucleus of the new aristocracy of Timbuktu. Maḥmūd, the grandson of Muḥammad Aqīt, and his three sons – Muḥammad, al-'Aqib and 'Umar – were *qāḍīs* of Timbuktu in succession for the whole sixteenth century under the *askiyas* of Songhay.

Throughout the sixteenth century the authority of the *qāḍī* in Timbuktu was uncontested and the *askiyas* rarely intervened in the internal affairs of the city. Moreover, the Muslim scholars of Timbuktu exerted influence over the imperial policy of the *askiyas*. At that time Timbuktu came to the level of some of the great Muslim cities in the intensity of its intellectual life.

There were one hundred and fifty or one hundred and eighty schools for the teaching of the Koran in Timbuktu in the middle of the sixteenth century. In one of them one hundred and twenty-three writing boards were counted.[1] These numerous schools for beginners formed the broad basis for the higher levels of education. In the three principal mosques and in the private homes of the leading scholars, circles of students gathered to hear their lessons and to read texts in all the branches of the Islamic sciences: Koranic exegesis (*tafsīr*), the Prophetic traditions (*ḥadīth*), jurisprudence (*fiqh*), logic (*manṭiq*), syntax (*naḥw*), rhetoric (*bayān*), etc. Even without an official institution of higher education, Timbuktu looked like a university city. Scholars were known for their specialized subjects and students went to learn a subject from the foremost authority. After he had completed the reading of a text, the student received from his master a certificate (*ijāza*), which gave him permission to teach that text to others. Chains for the transmission of learning developed and through them one can discern several traditions of scholarship which contributed to the flourishing of education in Timbuktu.

The old Malian tradition in Timbuktu, which had been encouraged by Mansa Mūsā (see p. 392), proved vital as one of the sources for Sanhaja scholarship in Timbuktu. Modibo Muḥammad al-Kābori, the doyen of the Sudanese scholars in the first half of the fifteenth century, was the teacher of Abū-'Abdallah And-ag-Muḥammad. Aḥmad Bābā said of And-ag-Muḥammad that he was the first of his ancestors who had dedicated himself to learning. His daughter's son, the *qāḍī* Maḥmud b. 'Umar b. Muḥammad Aqīt, was a student of the *qāḍī* Ḥabīb, a descendant of the fourteenth-century scholar 'Abd al-Raḥmān al-Tamīmī.

During the rule of Sonni 'Alī in Timbuktu members of the Aqīt and And-ag-Muḥammad families sought refuge at Walata, which they had

[1] Ibn al-Mukhtār, *T. al-Fattāsh*, 180/tr. 315–16.

left a few decades earlier. Some time before 1483 an important scholar from Morocco, 'Abdallāh b. Aḥmad al-Zammūrī, visited Walata, taught there and praised its scholars. It was perhaps also at Walata that Maḥmud b. 'Umar Aqīt read the *Mukhtaṣar* of Khalīl with the *faqīh* 'Uthmān al-Maghribī.

But in the sixteenth century scholars of Morocco had little to offer to their colleagues in the western Sudan. Towards the end of the century Aḥmad Bābā complained that the *fuqahā'* of the Maghrib were limited to the study of the *Risāla* of Abū Zayd and the *Mukhtaṣar* of Khalīl, two very basic manuals of the Maliki school.[1] During his exile in Marrakesh (1594–1607), Aḥmad Bābā taught in the central mosque and students from all over the Maghrib came to hear his lessons. The scholar from Timbuktu thus demonstrated the superiority of Sudanic scholarship over that of the Maghrib.

Intellectual life in Timbuktu at this time was stimulated by Egyptian influence. Many of the scholars of Timbuktu went on the Pilgrimage and stayed in Cairo on their way. In the fifteenth and sixteenth centuries Cairo produced some eminent scholars, such as al-Suyūṭī (d. 1505), Ibrāhīm al-Qalqashandī (d. 1516), Muḥammad al-Bakrī (d. 1545) and al-Laqānī (d. 1551). It is significant that al-Laqānī was the only Maliki among these scholars; the others were Shāfi'īs. From them the scholars of Timbuktu learned *ḥadīth*, mysticism, language and literature. This is a clear indication that Timbuktu had succeeded in breaking out of the narrow parochialism of the Maliki school.

The sophistication of the scholars of Timbuktu mitigated the influence of the zealous Maliki reformer Muḥammad b. 'Abd al-Karīm al-Maghīlī. When he was in Gao, al-Maghīlī received the news that his son had been killed by the Jews in Tuat. He urged the *askiya* to put in jail all the people of Tuat who happened to be in Gao at that time. But the *qāḍī* of Timbuktu, Maḥmud b. 'Umar, objected on the ground that these persons were innocent. The *askiya* complied and released the merchants. This *qāḍī* of Timbuktu was known for his impartial pursuit of justice, but it is likely that he took this line also in opposition to al-Maghīlī. The Muslims of Timbuktu seem to have favoured the milder approach of al-Suyūṭī rather than the extremism of al-Maghīlī. The divergence of opinions between the two is evident from their replies to questions from the Sudan. Whereas al-Suyūṭī saw no harm in the manufacture of amulets provided there was nothing

[1] Aḥmad Bābā, *Nayl al-ibtihāj bi-taṭrīz al-dibāj* (Cairo, 1596), 114. Cf. J. O. Hunwick, 'Further light on Aḥmad Bābā al-Tinbuktī', *Research Bulletin*, Centre of Arabic Documentation, Ibadan, 1966, **2**, 2, 19–31.

reprehensible in them, al-Maghīlī was categorically against the trade in amulets. Whereas al-Suyūṭī gave licence to some forms of association between Muslims and infidels, al-Maghīlī insisted that jihad was the only way to deal with infidels.[1]

The Sufi brotherhood of the Qādiriyya became widespread in the western Sudan through the influence of the Kunta marabouts during the second half of the eighteenth century. Kunta traditions claim that their ancestor Sīdī 'Umar al-Shaykh (d. 1552) was initiated into the Qādiriyya by al-Maghīlī who, in turn, had been initiated by al-Suyūṭī. This tradition is not supported by any other source and there is not even the slightest positive evidence that al-Maghīlī met either al-Suyūṭī or Sīdī 'Umar al-Shaykh.

Though Sufi brotherhoods had been of great importance in the Maghrib since the fourteenth century, there is no evidence in any of the chronicles of Timbuktu that Sufi brotherhoods had been introduced to Timbuktu and into the western Sudan, at least until the middle of the seventeenth century. On the other hand, there are clear references to some important aspects of Sufism, such as mysticism and ascetism, as well as references to miracles performed by saints and to the visitation of the saints' tombs.

Among those who had brought Sufism to Timbuktu was Sīdī Yaḥyā al-Tādilsī. He came to Timbuktu sometime after 1433 and died there in 1461/2. Remembered for his miracles and sanctity, he became the patron saint of Timbuktu. The first white *imām* of the Friday mosque, Sidi 'Abdallāh al-Balbālī, a contemporary of Sīdī Yaḥyā, is also described with the attributes of a Sufi. So was his successor in the post, Abu'l-Qāsim al-Tuwātī. These and others came to Timbuktu from the Maghrib, and their mystical way of life, their sanctity and emanating blessing (*baraka*) go some way to explain why they were given the office of the *imām* of the Friday mosque.

Sufi influences undoubtedly had first come from the Maghrib. But the mystic experience was later enriched when the '*ulamā*' of Timbuktu met some eminent Sufis in Mecca and in Cairo, among them 'the pole' (*al-quṭb*) Muḥammad al-Bakrī (died 1545), a great poet and mystic.

Al-ḥājj Aḥmad, father of Aḥmad Bābā, met Muḥammad al-Bakrī, adhered to him, sought his blessing and learned useful lessons from him. When al-ḥājj Aḥmad asked him to suggest a saint (*walī*) through whom he could gain favour, Muḥammad al-Bakrī pointed to al-ḥājj

[1] J. O. Hunwick, 'Notes on a late fifteenth-century document concerning "al-Takrūr"' in C. H. Allen and R. W. Johnson, eds., *African perspectives* (Cambridge, 1970), 29–30.

Aḥmad's own brother Abū Bakr. Al-Bakrī also regarded the *qāḍī* Maḥmud b. 'Umar as a saint (*walī*). It is clear, therefore, that some members of the Aqīt clan, as well as other '*ulamā*' of Timbuktu, were practising Sufis. One may perhaps identify them, as they are referred to in their biographies with such attributes as the saint (*walī*), the ascetic (*zāhid*), the godfearing (*wāri'*), the pious (*taqī*), the gnostic (*'ārif*), the one who sees the invisible (*mukāshif*) and performs miracles (*ṣāḥib karamāt*).[1] Saints (*walīs*) of that description were not restricted to Timbuktu, and could be found among the Sudanese '*ulamā*', in such men as the *faqīh* Muḥammad Saghanogho, the first *qāḍī* of Jenne, and Ṣāliḥ Jawara, a close associate of Askiya Muḥammad.

Many of the scholars of Timbuktu are described as being ascetics who renounced pleasure in worldly things. At the same time, they are known to have been quite wealthy. They received grants of land and slaves, money and clothes from the *askiyas* and other dignitaries of Songhay. The merchants bestowed presents on the scholars to solicit their blessing.

Timbuktu was an affluent city, and beyond the atmosphere of learning, piety and justice, its people – including scholars – had their own human vices. Gossip, sometimes vicious, was current in Timbuktu. Even an *askiya* was worried lest his recent military defeat would be a subject for gossip among the people of Timbuktu when they met behind the Sankore mosque.[2] Slanderers caused friction and conflicts even among the '*ulamā*' themselves. Timbuktu was not a city of piety and scholarship only, because its scholars formed a leadership which became involved in imperial politics. It is better to deal with these aspects, however, as the discussion of the history of the Songhay empire proceeds.

Towards the end of the fourteenth century, after internal conflicts over the succession had weakened the empire of Mali and undermined its authority, Songhay became independent. Songhay was ruled by the Sonni dynasty which had come to power about a century earlier. The political vacuum created by the decline of Mali encouraged the expansion of Songhay in the area west of the Niger bend. Sonni Silman Dandi (died 1464) conquered Mema, which had become independent of Mali, along with other provinces of the Sahel, in the first decades of the fifteenth century.

[1] For references to mystics, see Aḥmad Bābā, *Nayl*, 93–5, 102, 161; al-Sa'dī, *T. al-Sūdān*, 16–19, 29–34, 42, 48, 50–2, 58, 72/tr. 30–3, 48–57, 68–9, 78–9, 81–4, 93–4, 119.

[2] al-Sa'dī, *T. al-Sūdān*, 88/tr. 146.

About the same time, in 1433/4, Akilu-ag-Malwal, chief of the Tuareg, became the ruler of Timbuktu. Instead of raiding this flourishing city, as they had done in the last period of Mali's rule, the Tuareg now protected the city and levied tribute in return. Muḥammad-n-Adda, a Sanhaja from Shinqit, and one of the dignitaries of Timbuktu, was appointed governor of the city (*Timbuktu-koi*). He administered the city in the name of Akilu, who preferred to stay in the desert among his tribesmen.

The governor Muḥammad-n-Adda seems to have pursued an independent policy as he watched the growing power of Songhay on the right bank of the Niger river, opposite Timbuktu. In 1464, when Sonni 'Alī became king of Songhay, Muḥammad-n-Adda prudently sent a letter of greetings and good wishes to the new king, begging him to count him as one of his household.

Muḥammad-n-Adda died shortly afterwards, and his son 'Umar was appointed by Akilu to succeed him. Where his father had tried to avert an attack on Timbuktu by cultivating the good will of Sonni 'Alī, the young 'Umar sent an insulting letter to Sonni 'Alī, boasting of his power to ward off any aggression. 'Umar did not anticipate that within two or three years he himself would call Sonni 'Alī to deliver the city from the Tuareg, who turned oppressors. They forced people out of their homes and violated the women. The governor himself was deprived of his share, one third of the revenue. Timbuktu-koi 'Umar sent secretly to Sonni 'Alī and offered the submission of the city.

Sonni 'Alī appeared with his troops opposite Timbuktu, across the river. While Akilu fled to Walata, Timbuktu-koi 'Umar sent boats to help the Songhay army in crossing the river. But, fearing Sonni 'Alī's revenge for the insulting letter 'Umar had sent him, the young governor of Timbuktu escaped to Walata and left his brother al-Mukhtār to meet Sonni 'Alī. Indeed, Sonni 'Alī confirmed al-Mukhtār as governor of Timbuktu. As al-Sa'dī describes it:

> In January 1496, Sonni 'Alī entered Timbuktu, committed gross iniquity, burned and destroyed the town, and killed many people there. When Akilu heard of the coming of Sonni 'Alī he brought a thousand camels to carry the *fuqahā'* of Sankore, and went with them to Birū [Walata] . . . The godless tyrant [Sonni 'Alī] was engaged in slaughtering those [of the people of the Sankore] who remained in Timbuktu and humiliated them.[1]

Those persecuted by Sonni 'Alī, the people of the Sankore, were members of three clans, the descendants of Muḥammad Aqīt, And-ag-

[1] Ibid. 65–6/tr. 105–8.

Muḥammad and *al-qāḍī* Al-Ḥājj. These Sanhaja scholars developed intimate relations with the Tuareg. 'They are of greater importance to me than anything else', Akilu said when, in his flight to Walata, he took with him 'Umar ibn Muḥammad Aqīt, his three sons and his in-laws of the And-ag-Muḥammad clan.

Sonni 'Alī claimed that he persecuted the people of the Sankore because 'they were sympathizers of the Tuareg and their protégés'. The Tuareg had withdrawn from Timbuktu but continued to threaten the new possessions of Songhay from the desert. Sonni 'Alī seems to have treated the people of the Sankore as collaborators of his enemies rather than simply as Muslims and scholars. Such an interpretation is supported by al-Sa'dī:

> Notwithstanding all the wrong and pains Sonni 'Alī inflicted upon the '*ulamā*', he acknowledged their eminence and used to say: 'Without the '*ulamā*' the world would be of no good.' He did favours for other '*ulamā*' and respected them.[1]

These other '*ulamā*' were members of the older group of scholars of Timbuktu, who had been prominent under the rule of Mali. Sonni 'Alī appointed a new *qāḍī* from among them, Ḥabīb, a descendant of Sīdī 'Abd al-Raḥmān al-Tamīmī, and had the greatest respect also for al-Ma'mūn, Ḥabīb's cousin. Sonni 'Alī was also sympathetic towards people from the Maghrib and the northern Sahara, who had no close connections with his Tuareg enemies. He honoured Sīdī 'Abdallāh al-Balbālī, *imām* of the Friday mosque, and made Ibrāhīm al-Khadar al-Fāsī (from Fez) his secretary. It is also clear that Sonni 'Alī did no harm to the Muslims of Jenne, who fitted more closely the patterns of Islam in the western Sudan than the '*ulamā*' of the Sankore.

The detailed account of the persecution of the people of the Sankore appears only in the *Ta'rīkh al-Sūdān*. The *Ta'rīkh al-Fattāsh* has another report about the hardships inflicted by Sonni 'Alī. When Sonni 'Alī laid siege to Jenne (probably in 1473, or about four years after the conquest of Timbuktu),[2] he was informed that the people of Timbuktu were deserting the city to their places of origin, to Walata, Futa and Tichit. Sonni 'Alī sent a messenger to Timbuktu to announce that all those who were loyal to him should spend the night at Hawkī, across the river. He threatened to kill those who remained in the city. The messenger reached Timbuktu about noon-time, and as he

[1] Ibid. 67/tr. 109.

[2] Ibn al-Mukhtār, *T. al-Fattāsh*, 48–9/tr. 93–5; but see al-Sa'di, *T. al-Sūdān* 70/tr. 116, where it is said that the people of Timbuktu came out to Hawkī in 1448.

made his announcement, people panicked and rushed out of the city, without even taking the basic necessities. By sunset only the sick and the blind were left in Timbuktu.

In this case, as in the case of the people of the Sankore, Sonni 'Alī was ruthless in pursuing political ends. Other examples of Sonni 'Alī's decisiveness were the decimation of the Fulani, whom he hated, and the project of digging a canal to Walata. Sonni 'Alī was undoubtedly an outstanding personality, but his treatment of the Muslims was without precedent in the western Sudan, where Muslims were usually treated with deference, and were somewhat immune from political vicissitudes.

The privileged position of Muslims in the kingdoms of the western Sudan was attained because of their role as representatives of a powerful religion, able to recruit supernatural aid through prayers, charms or amulets. Their literacy was employed in the service of the state, while their commerce contributed to its economy. They injected Islamic elements into the spiritual, social and political systems. Yet, in the empire of Mali, and in Songhay until the middle of the fifteenth century, the Muslims became accommodated to the existing socio-political system without challenging it. Being politically neutral, Muslims moved freely across frontiers and were given the role of peace-makers. Their homes and places of worship became sanctuaries.

The Sanhaja scholars of Timbuktu did not fit into this pattern of West African Islam. In their relations with the world-wide scholarly community of Islam, they became aware of the political undercurrents of Islam. Their involvement in the political affairs of Songhay under the *askiyas* is an indication of what political aspirations they might have had at the time of Sonni 'Alī. Politicized Islam could not have been integrated smoothly into a Sudanic state, and could not have been tolerated by a ruler like Sonni 'Alī.

Perhaps the most detailed account of Sonni 'Alī's attitude to Islam is provided in the answers to a series of questions put to al-Maghīlī by Askiya al-Ḥājj Muḥammad. The questions must have been phrased by one of the Muslim scholars in the service of Askiya Muḥammad. This nearly contemporary source can be supplemented by the seventeenth-century chronicle and by oral traditions.[1]

[1] El-Hadj Rawane M'Baye, 'Un Aperçu de l'Islam Songhai ou réponses d'al-Maghīlī aux questions posées par Askiya El-Hadj Muḥammad, Empereur de Gao', *Bulletin de l'IFAN*, 1972, 34, 237–67; J. O. Hunwick, 'Religion and state in the Songhay empire, 1464–1591', in I. M. Lewis, ed., *Islam in Tropical Africa* (London, 1966), 298–301. For the oral traditions, see J. Rouch, *Contribution à l'histoire des Songhay* [*Memoires de l'IFAN*] (Dakar, 1953), 181.

Sonni ʿAlī's mother was from Fara, where the people worshipped idols, sacrificed to them and supplicated them. The cult of these idols was in the hands of priests, diviners and sorcerers. Sonni ʿAlī grew up in this atmosphere among his maternal uncles. These beliefs and practices he combined with the knowledge of magic which he had inherited from his father, Sonni Muḥammad Daʿo, in the tradition of the magician-kings of Songhay. (Indeed, even after they had lost temporal power, the Sohantye, descendants of Sonni ʿAlī, retained their prestige as powerful magicians.) Yet, for about four centuries the kings of Songhay were also (at least nominally) Muslims, and Islam was integrated into the royal religious cult. As part of his education Sonni ʿAlī, as a Songhay prince, had a rudimentary Islamic education.

Sonni ʿAlī observed the fast of Ramadan and gave abundant contributions to mosques, but at the same time he used to worship idols, to give presents to diviners, sought the help of sorcerers and sacrificed animals to trees and stones. He pronounced the *shahāda* and other formulas without understanding their meaning. He used to pray, but was careless in observing the correct time, and he often postponed a prayer until the night or the next day, then instead of performing the prescribed ritual of the prayer he only indicated it by slight inclinations, and merely repeated the name of the prayer, instead of reciting the *fātiḥa* and other *sūras*, which he did not care to learn.

Al-Maghīlī's verdict that Sonni ʿAlī was undoubtedly a pagan may have applied to many of Sonni ʿAlī's ancestors, and indeed to other kings and dynasties in the western and central Sudan. These kings and dynasties maintained a middle position between Islam and paganism. They supported the Muslims, and came themselves under Islamic influence, but they did not become unqualified Muslims because they derived their legitimacy from the traditional religion and its values.

Sonni ʿAlī was no exception to this rule – in his casual way of performing Islamic ritual, in referring also to the custodians of the traditional Songhay religion, as well as in supporting *ʿulamāʾ* who were willing to serve the court. But when he suspected that a group of Muslims presented a political threat, he persecuted them unscrupulously and cruelly.

Sonni ʿAlī was an energetic and relentless ruler; he won all his wars and conquered every country he attacked. He turned the small Songhay state into an empire when he conquered Timbuktu, the lacustrine region, Massina, the inner delta of the Niger and Jenne. Most of his conquests were along the Niger waterway, as he depended largely on the support of the fleet manned by the Sorko fishermen. Sonni 'Alī laid siege to Jenne with four hundred boats during the period of high water, and the town was conquered only after it had been reduced to starvation. When he contemplated the conquest of the landlocked town of Walata, where Akilu the Tuareg had found refuge, Sonni 'Alī wanted to secure the support of his fleet and began the digging of a canal from Ra's al-Mā' to Walata. He was engaged in this ambitious project with great assiduity when news reached him about an invasion of the Mossi.

The Mossi, of whom more will be said towards the end of this chapter, invaded the lacustrine region of the Niger around 1430, and it was probably about the same period that they sacked the city of Timbuktu.[1] In 1477/8 the Mossi renewed their pressure when they appeared near Sama, in the Bambara country. They avoided the Niger waterway, which was securely held by the Songhay fleet, and advanced across the Sahel to lay siege to Walata in July–August 1480. They forced their way into the town, and retreated with booty and prisoners, but were pursued by the people of Walata (under the command of 'Umar b. Muḥammad-n-Adda, the former governor of Timbuktu), who succeeded in rescuing their captured kinsmen from the Mossi. In 1483 Sonni 'Alī stopped the digging of the projected canal, in order to put an end to the military exploits of the Mossi on the fringes of his growing empire. The two armies met on the right bank of the Niger, south of Lake Debo, where the Mossi were defeated and pursued by Sonni 'Alī back into their own country. The Mossi had been warded off by Sonni 'Alī, but were not subjected, and both Askiya al-Ḥājj Muḥammad and his son Askiya Dāwūd had to send more expeditions into the land of the Mossi.

In order to protect his new empire along the Niger, Sonni 'Alī fought not only the Mossi to the south but also the nomads in the north. These were mainly the Tuareg, but it is likely that the Songhay already had encountered the first Arab (Ḥassani) groups who had then been penetrating into the Sahara. Within the conquered territory, in Massina, on the vital Niger waterway, he fought the Fulani: 'There were none among his enemies that Sonni 'Alī hated more than the Fulani . . . he massacred the Sanqare clan [so ferociously] that only a small group survived that could gather under the shade of one tree.'[2]

These Fulani had migrated from the Sahel to Massina about the begin-

[1] For a revised chronology of the Mossi invasions, see N. Levtzion, *Ancient Ghana and Mali* (London, 1973), 232, note 44.

[2] Ibn al-Mukhtār, *T. al-Fattāsh*, 44/tr. 83–4; for the date of the Fulani migration to Massina, see Levtzion, *Ancient Ghana and Mali*, 233, note 10.

ning of the fifteenth century. It was probably not simply aversion towards the Fulani, prevalent among many of their Sudanese neighbours, which was the reason for Sonni 'Alī's attitude. It is more likely that these nomads caused trouble to the imperial authorities even at that early stage, as they did later in the sixteenth century, when the *askiyas* preferred to avoid direct intervention in Massina. The *askiyas* ruled the Fulani through their own chief, or *ardo*, whose appointment needed the confirmation of the *askiya*. Significantly, when two cousins disputed the succession to the office of *ardo*, Askiya Isḥāq (1539–49) preferred to leave the candidates to seek popular support and fight each other. The more popular candidate, however, was regarded as dangerous to the imperial authorities and was murdered. His rival had failed to gain public approval and was forced to abdicate. Only then did the *askiya* appoint a man of his own choice. Whenever the imperial army invaded Massina, as in the punitive expedition of 1582, the *ardo* retreated into the open Sahel and came back soon after the Songhay troops had left. The *askiya* could lay his hands on the Fulani chief only by ruse. In the process of the building of his empire, the impulsive Sonni 'Alī had no time for such subtle stratagems, and used brute force to suppress all signs of Fulani irredentism.

On the south-eastern frontiers of the empire Sonni 'Alī failed to subdue the Bariba of Borgu (in northern Dahomey), who remained (together with the Mossi) formidable enemies of Songhay until the end of the empire. The expansion of the new empire along the Niger, from Kebbi and Dendi in the south-east to Sibiridugu beyond Jenne in the south-west, created a territory in the shape of a crescent following the Niger bend. Inside the crescent, on the Gurma (right) side of the river, Sonni 'Alī led many expeditions to the mountainous country of Hombori and Bandiagara against the Dogon, the Tombo and the Gurma to secure the 'soft under-belly' of his empire.

Sonni 'Ali established royal residences along the Niger in Kukiya, Gao, Kabara and Dirma (a province north of Lake Debo). But he stayed in none of them, because he spent all his days warring. The conquest of the territory along the Niger does not seem to have taken much time and effort. Around 1473, after the conquest of Jenne and the two unsuccessful attempts on the defended frontiers of Mali, most of the country he later bequeathed to his successors was already in his hands. In the following two decades he fought with highly mobile forces in different parts of the empire, to contain hostile neighbours along the frontiers and to nip in the bud subversions and insurrections.

Sonni 'Alī died suddenly, as he was leading his army home from a campaign in Gurma, in November 1492. He had held power for twenty-eight years. The commanders of the Songhay army immediately declared Sonni Baro, son of Sonni 'Alī, king of Songhay.

News of Sonni 'Alī's death and the succession of his son reached Muḥammad b. Abī Bakr Ture, one of the senior commanders of the Songhay army. With troops loyal to him, Muḥammad Ture declared war on Sonni Baro and defeated him in two battles, once in February and again in April 1493. Sonni Baro retreated down the Niger river to Ayonu near Tillabery. He was followed by the Sohantye, members of the Sonni dynasty. Some of them, however, stayed behind as magicians to serve the new ruler of Songhay, Askiya Muḥammad.

In the oral traditions of Songhay, Mamari (as Muḥammad Ture was called) is said to have been the son of Sonni 'Alī's sister, who killed his maternal uncle to seize power.[1] A measure of continuity between the Sonni and the Askiya dynasties is therefore implied. But, in the Arabic chronicles, Muḥammad the future *askiya* is referred to as Ture, which may indicate that he was related to the Ture clan of the Soninke. The Ture were closely associated with trade and Islam. One could perhaps develop the argument one step further in suggesting that the origin of Muḥammad Ture may explain his relations with Sonni 'Alī and later his policy as *askiya*.

Muḥammad Ture was a brave man of strong character and he often quarrelled with Sonni 'Alī. Perhaps Muḥammad Ture opposed the ruthless treatment of the Muslims by Sonni 'Alī. Indeed, whenever Muḥammad Ture's life was in danger because of Sonni 'Alī's rage, his mother is said to have hurried to implore the prayers of a woman from the house of al-*qāḍī* Al-Ḥājj, one of the Muslim families most severely persecuted by Sonni 'Alī. Muḥammad's closest supporter in his revolt was Mansa Kura, chief of Bara (a province north of Lake Debo). Mansa Kura, who later accompanied Askiya Muḥammad to Mecca, must have been an islamized chief. On the other hand, one of the principal supporters of Sonni Baro was the *Dendi-fari*, commander of the eastern frontier of Songhay.[2] In a way, Muḥammad Ture's revolt may be viewed as a confrontation between the provinces west of the Niger bend and Songhay proper.

The Sonni dynasty derived its legitimacy from the socio-religious

[1] J. Rouch, *Contribution*, 187; see also Ibn al-Mukhtār, *T. al-Fattāsh* 48/tr. 93–4.
[2] *T. al-Fattāsh*, 53, 59/tr. 102, 132–3.

system of Songhay, with Kukiya as its ritual centre. Muḥammad, who had come to power as a reaction to the particularistic spirit of Songhay, wished to promote the integration of the western provinces and to broaden the basis of his authority. He therefore sought to revive the imperial heritage bequeathed by Mali, of which Islam was an essential component. Gao remained the royal capital, but Timbuktu, the largest and most prosperous city in the empire, developed as a rival centre of power, a kind of second capital (and Leo Africanus refers to 'King Askiya of Timbuktu').[1] The same '*ulamā'*' of Timbuktu and Walata who had been persecuted by Sonni 'Alī, turned under Askiya Muḥammad from opposition to co-operation with a regime that sought their blessing and their advice in the administration of the empire.

Askiya Muḥammad seized power in April 1493. Some three years later, in October or November 1496, he set out on the Pilgrimage and returned in August 1498. He was absent for almost two years, and his authority must have been well established if he could stay away for such a long period so early in his reign. At the same time, his motivation for the Pilgrimage must have been quite strong if he was ready to take the risk of this long absence, over and above the toil of the journey.

Sonni 'Alī was the 'magician-king' versed in the traditional occultism of Songhay. Askiya Muḥammad, a usurper, was deprived of this vital power to manipulate the supernatural. The pilgrimage to Mecca bestowed on him the *baraka*, an emanating blessing, which was respected by both Muslims and non-Muslims. The 'pilgrim-king' replaced the 'magician-king'.

Askiya Muḥammad brought back from the pilgrimage not only the title of *al-ḥājj*, but also that of a caliph (*khalīfa*). As a caliph, he became the acknowledged head of the community of believers in the western Sudan, including the scholars of Timbuktu. Sonni 'Alī had resorted to fierce persecution to curb the power of an independent body of scholars in Timbuktu. Askiya Muḥammad as *amīr al-mu'minīn* ('commander of the faithful') brought them into the imperial system, and mobilized their support.

There is no direct evidence about Askiya Muḥammad's commitment to Islam before his accession or even before his pilgrimage, but it is clear that he returned as a sincere and devoted Muslim. In his desire to administer the empire according to the Islamic law, he sought the advice of distinguished scholars such as Jalāl al-Dīn al-Suyūṭī, whom

[1] Leo Africanus, *Description*, II, 473.

he met in Cairo, and Muḥammad b. 'Abd al-Karīm al-Maghīlī from Tuat, who visited Gao. We know enough, however, about the organization of the Songhay empire under Askiya Muḥammad and his successors to assert that he did little in practice to reform the empire in line with the ideals of Islamic political theory. Any attempt in this direction would have provoked the reaction of the Songhay nobility, many of whom still adhered more strongly to the Songhay traditions than to Islam.

Al-Maghīlī, who advocated radical reforms, was a foreigner, and a passing visitor. The local '*ulamā*' of Timbuktu, Gao and other towns were less demanding. They were gratified that Askiya Muḥammad put an end to the iniquities committed by Sonni 'Alī, and praised him for his love for scholars and godly men, his humility before the scholars and his generosity to them. The court ceremonies and the protocol, which continued according to the old Songhay traditions, were adjusted to accommodate the new class of Muslim dignitaries. The Sharifs were permitted to sit with the *askiya* on his dais. Only they and other scholars could eat with the *askiya*, who used to rise from his seat to greet scholars and pilgrims.

Askiya Muḥammad encouraged the administration of the Islamic law by the appointment of *qāḍīs*. He appointed the first *qāḍī* of Jenne, and established courts in other towns. In 1497/8, after the death of the *qāḍī* Ḥabīb, who had been appointed by Sonni 'Alī, Askiya Muḥammad appointed Maḥmūd b. 'Umar b. Muḥammad Aqīt as *qāḍī* of Timbuktu.

Under Askiyā Muḥammad and his successors the *qāḍīs* held real authority in Timbuktu and seem to have been more influential than the governor of Timbuktu (*Timbuktu-koi*). The *qāḍī* acted independently, and even prevented messengers of the *askiya* from carrying out their duties in the city. The limitations which the *qāḍī* imposed on the *askiya*'s authority in Timbuktu found expression in the following dialogue between Askiya Muḥammad and the *qāḍī* Maḥmūd b. 'Umar: 'Are you ruling in my place?' the *askiya* asked in indignation. In reply the *qāḍī* recalled that the *askiya* had made the *qāḍī* his mentor to guide him in his deeds, that he might be saved from hell.[1] There was an element of tension between these two strong personalities, who represented religious and political authority.

The scholars of Timbuktu, as has already been said, introduced a new brand of Islam into the western Sudan, marked by vigour, severity

[1] *T. al-Fattāsh*, 60–1/tr. 115–17.

and political motivation. There were, however, other *'ulamā'* who fitted better into the traditional role of the Muslim divines in the Sudanic states: that of intimate advisers, who prayed for their rulers and recruited supernatural aid for their welfare and that of their state. Two of these *'ulamā'* – *mori* Ṣāliḥ Jawara (a Soninke) and *alfā* Muḥammad Toli – escorted Askiya Muḥammad to Mecca and are reported to have performed miracles on the way.

Mori Ṣaliḥ Jawara was particularly attached to 'Umar Komdiagha, brother of Askiya Muḥammad, and when 'Umar died, Ṣāliḥ secluded himself for three days. As *Kurmina-fari*, governor of the western provinces, 'Umar Komdiagha was in charge of that part of the empire where Islamic influence was strongest. He cultivated friendly relations with Muslims, and sent his own son (the future *askiya*) Muḥammad Benkan to study with the Sankore scholars of Timbuktu.[1]

Askiya Muḥammad consolidated the empire created by Sonni 'Alī and expanded it even further. The shape and the extent of the empire under Sonni 'Alī had been determined largely by the Niger river, because of his dependence on the Sorko fleet. Sonni 'Alī had what may be called an army of popular levies into which all elements of the Songhay population had been mobilized. Askiya Muḥammad introduced the distinction between civilian subjects and soldiers. He created a professional army, which was recruited from among the conquered peoples, and the legal status of its soldiers was that of slaves.[2] Such an army he was able to send on military expeditions overland, away from the Niger waterway, as far as the Sengalese Futa in the west, as well as to Agades and Hausaland in the east.

Traditionally, most of the military expeditions to the west were under the command of the *Kurmina-fari*. He fought the *Baghana-fari*, who ruled over the Sahel just west of the Niger, formerly in the name of the king of Mali, but for most of the fifteenth century as an independent ruler. It was under the auspices of the *Baghana-fari* that the Fulani settled in Massina early in the fifteenth century, and they remained allied to him for the rest of the century. A son of the Fulani chief of Massina came to the aid of the *Baghana-fari* against the Songhay and was killed in the battle. It seems, therefore, that 'Umar Komdiagha's victory over the *Baghana-fari* was essential for confirming the authority of Songhay over the Fulani of Massina and for the security of the western wing of the vital Niger waterway.

[1] al Sa'di, *T. al-Sūdān*, 88/tr. 147.
[2] Ibid. 72/tr. 118; *T. al-Fattāsh*, 116/tr. 211.

In 1500/1 Diala (in Kaarta) was conquered, and a royal residence of Mali was pillaged there. In 1506/7 Askiya Muḥammad raided Galam on the Senegal, which is said than to have been still under the rule of Mali. Thus Askiya Muḥammad wiped away the last vestiges of Mali's rule in the Sahel. Subsequently, the frontier between Songhay and Mali followed the course of the upper Senegal river. On the Niger river, Sibiridugu (south of Niamina and Segu) was mentioned by Askiya Muḥammad as the province which 'separates us from the Sultan of Mali'.[1]

The most powerful state in the Sahel, following the disintegration of Mali's rule there, was centred on Diara in Kingui (the present *cercle* of Nioro). About the beginning of the fifteenth century the Niakhate dynasty, which had ruled Diara as vassals of Mali, was overthrown by the Diawara clan. The Diawara killed the representative of Mali at Diara and asserted their independence. Their state grew stronger and its capital became an important entrepôt linking the caravan trade of the desert with the overland routes to the goldfields of the upper Senegal and the upper Niger.

In 1511/12 Diara was attacked by Tengella, who had made himself ruler of the Senegalese Futa (see pp. 457–8). The Diawara called in the aid of *Kurmina-fari* 'Umar, who led a Songhay army to defeat Tengella. This overland expedition was remembered as one of the most outstanding military exploits of Songhay, when 'a huge army crossed the remote desolate wilderness, over two months journey, from Tendirma to the Futa'.[2] The Diawara then probably acknowledged the sovereignty of Songhay.

Inside the Niger bend the Mossi remained a threat to the empire. In 1497/8 Askiya Muḥammad led his troops against the Mossi. It was shortly after he had returned from Mecca, and Askiya Muḥammad must have been still under the influence of what he had learned on the pilgrimage. It was, therefore, according to the testimony of the *Ta'rīkh al-Sūdān*, the only war in that region which was conducted as a jihad.[3] According to the rules of a jihad, the attack began only after the Mossi had rejected the summons to accept Islam. Askiya Muḥammad advanced into the Mossi country, wrought destruction and took many prisoners. Those captured were converted to Islam. The Mossi, however, were not subjugated, and over half a century later Askiya Dāwūd led yet another expedition into the land of the Mossi (see p. 437).

[1] Ibid. 73/tr. 140.

[2] *T. al-Fattāsh*, 77/tr. 146; see also *T. al-Sudan*, 77/tr. 127.

[3] *T. al-Sūdān*, 74/tr. 123.

Until the end of the empire the king of Mossi and the king of Bussa (Borgu) were regarded as the worst enemies of Songhay.[1] Sonni 'Alī had failed to subdue the Bariba of Borgu, and in 1504 Askiya Muḥammad was badly defeated in another attempt against Borgu. The *askiya*'s concubine, mother of the future Askiya Mūsā, fell prisoner in the hands of the king of Bussa and the *askiya* himself barely escaped death or captivity. Songhay's expansion to the south was therefore stopped at the frontiers of Mali, Mossi and Borgu.

Walata, where Akilu the Tuareg chief and some of the scholars of Timbuktu had found refuge, was not conquered by Sonni 'Alī. The two chronicles of Timbuktu do not mention an expedition of Askiya Muḥammad to Walata. But Leo Africanus was told (about 1512) that when the king of Timbuktu, very likely Askiya Muḥammad or his lieutenant 'Umar Komdiagha, had come with his army to Walata, the ruler of that town retreated to his people in the desert and harassed the Songhay garrison of Walata. The Songhay king soon realized that he could not hold Walata under the constant pressure of the nomads and agreed to evacuate it in return for a tribute from the ruler of Walata.[2]

There is no record that the Tuareg had ever been defeated by Songhay, but they seem to have accepted the sovereignty of the *askiyas*, as allies rather than as subjects. The *askiya* ruled over Timbuktu and the other markets of the Sahel, and it suited the commercial interests of the Tuareg to be part of that imperial system. As an ally, the *Maghsharen-koi*, chief of the Tuareg in the environs of Timbuktu, was given a daughter of Askiya Muḥammad in marriage. A generation later the *Maghsharen-koi* was married to a daughter of Askiya Dāwūd. These Tuareg chiefs became involved in the internal conflicts of the royal family when, around 1528, one of them gave asylum to Ismā'īl from his brother Askiya Mūsā. Sixty years later the *Maghsharen-koi* joined other chiefs of the western provinces in support of Balma' Ṣādiq against two successive *askiyas*. Units of Tuareg camelry, in the service of the *askiyas*, operated in the Sahara, mainly against Arab tribesmen. Tuareg merchants loyally co-operated with the *askiyas* against the sultan of Morocco in the long dispute over the salt mines of Taghaza. In fact, Songhay control of Taghaza for most of the sixteenth century could only have been achieved through the agency of the Tuareg allies.[3]

In the fifteenth century there was a marked growth of trade across

[1] Ibid. 119/tr. 192.
[2] Leo Africanus, *Description*, II, 464.
[3] *T. al-Sūdān*, 83, 106–7, 109, 125/tr. 138, 174, 178, 200.

the Sahara to Hausaland. Agades was then established as a political centre for the Tuareg of Aïr and as a rendezvous for caravans from Gao, Hausaland and Bornu to Tripoli and Egypt. The king of Agades, according to Leo Africanus, derived considerable revenue from duties paid by the foreign merchants who formed the majority of the population. But he had to pay part of his revenue, to the tune of about 150,000 ducats, to the *askiya*. This tribute was imposed on Agades after Askiya Muḥammad had raided Aïr and deposed its ruler in 1499/1500. It has been suggested that Askiya Muḥammad launched this expedition because the sultans of Agades were unable to control the predatory inclinations of the Tuareg.[1] In 1515 Askiya Muḥammad again attacked Agades, perhaps in order to reinforce his authority there.

In between the two expeditions against Agades, Askiya Muḥammad invaded Hausaland. He conquered Katsina and Zaria and killed the rulers of these city-states. He then proceeded against the more powerful king of Kano. After a long siege the latter sued for peace, offered the *askiya* one of his daughters in marriage and promised to deliver to the *askiya* a third of his revenue. The *askiya* left some of his people behind to collect this tribute and he himself turned against Gobir, which was then a prosperous kingdom. He killed the king of Gobir and castrated his grandsons to serve as eunuchs in his palace. He appointed a governor over Gobir and impoverished its people by exacting heavy taxes. The population of cities like Gobir and Katsina was reduced by half, because the *askiya* had taken away a great number of men, some to work for him and others to sell as slaves.[2]

Songhay lost its hold over Hausaland after the revolt of Kuta Kanta, the ruler of Kebbi, in 1515. Kebbi lies between the territories of the Songhay and the Hausa-speaking people. As a vassal of the *askiya*, Kuta Kanta jointed the Songhay expedition to Agades, but was deeply disappointed when the *Dendi-fari*, the senior Songhay official on that front, refused to give him a fair share of the booty. Kuta Kanta broke off relations with Songhay and recurrent attempts to force Kebbi back into the fold were defeated. Independent Kebbi formed a new eastern frontier for Songhay, leaving the Hausa states completely within the Bornu sphere of influence. The first and only attempt to unite the western and central Sudan in one empire did not last more than a decade.

[1] J. O. Hunwick, 'Songhay, Bornu and Hausaland in the sixteenth century', in J. F. A. Ajayi and M. Crowder, eds., *History of West Africa*, vol. I (London, 1971), 220–1, 230–1.
[2] Leo Africanus, *Description*, II, 472–8.

By 1515 Askiya Muḥammad had reached the peak of his power, which was about to decline. The loss of his eastern conquests in Hausaland indicated that he had overstretched the military and organizational potential of the empire. The more serious danger, however, came from within, in his own home and palace. In 1519 Askiya Muḥammad lost his closest adviser and supporter with the death of his brother ʿUmar Komdiagha. Another brother, Yaḥyā, was appointed in his place as *Kurmina-fari*.

Askiya Muḥammad himself was then about seventy years old, and he was losing control over his numerous sons. Thirty-four names appear in the list of Askiya Muḥammad's sons as recorded in the chronicles of Timbuktu.[1] Most of them were born in the large harem of concubines which the *askiya* maintained. In their fierce competition over titles and offices, they could not rely on the support of maternal relatives (as often happened in African kingdoms), but they had formed instead cliques and alignments which made the *askiya*'s court into a den of jealous and ambitious princes.

Some time after 1519 the office of *Binga-farma* became vacant. This was the governorship of Binga, a province in the lacustrine region south of Timbuktu. *Binga-farma* was among the more prestigious offices held by the royal princes. The holder of this office had a drum beaten before him, and the army commanders, including princes, were expected to come out to meet him and to dismount when they saw him. As governor of a province in the west, the *Binga-farma* was among the followers of the *Kurmina-fari*, who was consulted about the appointment to this office. *Kurmina-fari* Yaḥyā recommended Bala, one of the youngest sons of Askiya Muḥammad, who was famous for his courage. The objection of the jealous princes was overruled by the *askiya*, but their resentment and enmity persisted.

The senior among Askiya Muḥammad's sons in Gao was the *farimondyo* Musa, who led the agitation against his father. He claimed that Askiya Muḥammad had come completely under the influence of ʿAlī Folon, 'master of the royal household' (*hu kokarai-koi*), who prevented others from approaching the *askiya*. In fact, he did it because Askiya Muḥammad had lost his eyesight, and ʿAlī Folon concealed this from others. Mūsā threatened ʿAlī Folon with death, and the latter sought asylum with *Kurmina-fari* Yaḥyā in Tendirma in 1526/7.

Without ʿAlī Folon near him, the old and blind Askiya Muḥammad could have done little to restrain his sons. In 1527/8 Mūsā led his

[1] *T. al-Sūdān*, 133/tr. 211–12; *T. al-Fattāsh*, 78–9, 149–50.

brothers in revolt against their father. *Kurmina-fari* Yaḥyā was called from Tendirma and attempted to appease his nephews, but the rebellious princes killed even their uncle. During the public prayer of *'īd al-aḍḥā* in August 1528 Mūsā declared the deposition of his father, and would not let the congregation pray before they had paid allegiance to him. Askiya Muḥammad abdicated and his son Mūsā became *askiya*.

The princes, Askiya Muḥammad's sons, were divided among themselves. Some of them supported their brother Askiya Mūsā, but others escaped to Tendirma and rallied around another brother, 'Uthman Yūbābu, who had been appointed *Kurmina-fari* by Askiya Muḥammad shortly before his abdication. Askiya Mūsā defeated them in battle, some were killed, while others sought refuge among the Tuareg (as did the future Askiya Ismā'īl) or outside the empire.

On his way to fight his brothers, Askiya Mūsā was met by Maḥmūd b. 'Umar, the *qāḍī* of Timbuktu, who wanted to bring about a reconciliation between Mūsā and his brothers. But he soon realized that Askiya Mūsā would not lend his ear to pleading and was determined to fight. Following the battle, *Binga-farma* Bala sought the sanctuary of the *qāḍī*'s home in Timbuktu. But Askiya Mūsā refused to respect the sanctuary, and made *Binga-farma* come out and killed him. He rejected also the plea by a delegation from Jinja (in the lacustrine region), famous for its pious and saintly Muslims, to spare the life of the chiefs of Bara and Dirma who had joined *Kurmina-fari* 'Uthmān against Askiya Mūsā.

In all three cases the Muslims acted according to their traditional role as peace-makers, who advocate clemency and whose mosques and homes become sanctuaries for wrongdoers. Askiya Mūsā's consistent defiance of the Muslims' intercession was a departure not only from his father's policy, but also from the accepted norms of political conduct in the western Sudan. It was among the signs of an unmitigated rule of terror, seemingly unconcerned even for its own legitimacy. Back in Gao, Askiya Mūsā eliminated his brothers, who disappeared one after the other. Those who survived joined together and killed him in battle in April 1531. He reigned for two years and nine months.

It was perhaps because he mistrusted his brothers that Askiya Mūsā had appointed his cousin Muḥammad Benkan, son of 'Umar Komdiagha, to the highest office of *Kurmina-fari*. When news about Askiya Mūsā's death reached Muḥammad Benkan, who happened to be in Gao, he took the seat of the *askiya*. When those princes who had revolted and killed Askiya Mūsā returned to declare the senior among them as the new *askiya*, they discovered that someone else had presented them with a *fait accompli*. Their attempt to force their way to the throne had failed and the dignitaries of Songhay swore allegiance to the new *askiya*, Muḥammad Benkan.

It is said of Askiya Muḥammad that he was austere and that he was afraid of the evil eye. His son Askiya Mūsā had few hours of rest during his reign. It was therefore left to Askiya Muḥammad Benkan to add lustre to the kingship. He clothed his courtiers with magnificent costumes and introduced musical instruments (trumpets and drums) into the court. A brave soldier himself, he reinforced the Songhay army, which he led on so many expeditions that the people of Songhay became tired of him and grew to hate him. He scored a victory over the pagan Gurma, but was badly defeated in the last attempt of Songhay to subdue Kebbi.

Muḥammad Benkan was the only *askiya* who was not a son or a grandson of Askiya Muḥammad. He maltreated his old uncle, the deposed Askiya Muḥammad, whom he forced out of the royal residence and confined to an island in the Niger, where he suffered from biting bugs and jumping frogs. At the same time, Muḥammad Benkan brought back his childhood friend Ismā'īl, son of Askiya Muḥammad, who had been in hiding with the Tuareg. Muḥammad Benkan gave his daughter in marriage to Ismā'īl and made him swear that he would never betray him.

One day when Ismā'īl visited his father on the island, Askiya Muḥammad induced him to establish contact with a eunuch confidant, who would collaborate in conspiring against Askiya Muḥammad Benkan. Ismā'īl was also moved by the humiliation which his own sisters suffered at the hands of Muḥammad Benkan, who made them appear in his audience with their faces uncovered. Collaborators at the court succeeded in turning the powerful *Dendi-fari* against the *askiya* and it was he who deposed Muḥammad Benkan in April 1537. The deposed *askiya* escaped to his brother 'Uthmān, the *Kurmina fari*, at Tendrina and both went into exile in Mali.

The *Dendi-fari*, who had deposed Muḥammad Benkan, swore allegiance to Ismā'īl as *askiya*. The new *askiya* immediately set his father Askiya Muḥammad, free and gave him rooms in the royal residence. In gratitude Askiya Muḥammad ceremonially robed his son with the green gown, the green cap, the white turban and the Arabian sword, which were the insignia given to Askiya Muḥammad when he had been made caliph. This ceremony marked the restoration of legitimacy to the office of the *askiya*, after the rule of two usurpers. Askiya Ismāʿīl reigned for two years and nine months, until his death in November 1539. For the first time an *askiya* died a natural death while on the throne.

The succession after Askiya Ismāʿīl was without a crisis as the dignitaries of Songhay, very likely with the consent of the princes, elected Isḥāq, son of Askiya Muḥammad, as the new *askiya*. But this peaceful succession was followed by an agitated reign full of fears and suspicion. Askiya Isḥāq killed or dismissed anyone whom he suspected of showing the slightest sign of opposition. In this way he appointed three *Kurmina-faris* in succession; he executed the first, foiled the conspiracy of the second, and only the third – Dāwūd – survived to succeed him as *askiya*.

Both *askiyas* – Isḥāq and Dāwūd – received a good Islamic education. It is said of Askiya Dāwūd that he committed the Koran to memory, and that he studied the *Risāla*, a work of Islamic jurisprudence, in its entirety. Askiya Isḥāq was a devoted Muslim, who gave alms generously and observed prayer in congregation quite strictly. But even in religious affairs he behaved with little moderation. Twice he forced scholars, against their will, to be *qāḍīs*, one in Jenne and the other in Tendirma. His religious piety did not prevent him from extracting as much as he could from the merchants of Timbuktu; seventy thousand *mithqāls* were found in the hands of his servant who had been going to and fro between Gao and Timbuktu.

When Askiya Isḥāq was on his deathbed, some faithful friends called *Kurmina-fari* Dāwūd from Tendirma, so that he could be in Gao or Kukiya in time to secure his accession. The only other claimant was *Arbinda-farma* Bokar, a son of Askiya Muḥammad's daughter, a handsome prince who was loved by the people of Songhay. Dāwūd called in a Muslim divine, who killed *Arbinda-farma*, it was said, by a magical spell.

Dāwūd was the greatest of the *askiyas* after Askiya Muḥammad, and his long reign of over thirty-three years (1549–82) was one of renewed vigour for the empire. 'He reaped what his father and brothers had laboured and sown . . . no one raised his hand against him, and all were obedient subjects.'[1]

He reorganized the Songhay army, and scored victories over the Mossi and Borgu. He fought the people of Gurma, Hombori and Bandiagara, and led a successful expedition to Mali. He defeated the Fulani of the Sahel as well as the Arabs of the desert. The only military defeat recorded was a raid on Katsina by an élite corps of horsemen. Perhaps

[1] *T. al-Fattāsh*, 93/tr. 176.

these expeditions consolidated the frontiers of the empire, which had been violated by peoples on the periphery during periods of internal unrest in Songhay.

During the reign of Askiya Dāwūd, Timbuktu reached the peak of its prosperity as well as Islamic erudition. Askiya Dāwūd himself was versed in the Koran and in the Islamic law, and during his reign he continued to study with a shaykh who came to the palace every morning. Askiya Dāwūd even exceeded his father in his generosity to Muslim scholars. He gave them gifts of land, slaves, grain, cattle and clothes. He contributed generously to the reconstruction of the Friday mosque of Timbuktu.

Whenever he passed Timbuktu on his military expeditions, Askiya Dāwūd used to pay visits to the *qāḍī*, to meet the '*ulamā*', to pray at the mosque and to give audience to the merchants and notables of the city. But, just as in the time of his father, his relations with the *qāḍī* and the leading scholars of Timbuktu were rather tense. When, once, slanderers caused the exchange of unworthy words between Askiya Dāwūd and the *qāḍī* al-'Āqib, the latter at first refused to see the *askiya* when he passed Timbuktu on his expedition to Mali. The *askiya* was made to wait outside the *qāḍī*'s home for a long time before he was given permission to enter, and the *askiya* humiliated himself before the *qāḍī* until the latter was reconciled. The *qāḍī* proudly maintained his moral authority.

On his visits to Timbuktu, Askiya Dāwūd was the humble Muslim disciple. In Gao he was the Songhay king, surrounded by ceremony and guided by a protocol of old traditions. The disparity between the two settings become apparent when one of the leading scholars of Timbuktu came to visit the *askiya* in his palace. He was shocked by the persistence of pre-Islamic practices and said to the *askiya*: 'I was amazed when I came in, and I thought you were mad, despicable and a fool when I saw you spitting into the sleeves [of the eunuchs] and the people [around] carrying dust on their heads.' The *askiya* smiled and said: 'I was not mad myself, and I am reasonable, but I am the head of sinful and haughty madmen and I therefore made myself mad.'[1] Even a devoted Muslim like Askiya Dāwūd could not relieve the monarchy of its pre-Islamic basis, and had to compromise in reconciling the two sources of his legitimacy, the traditional and the Islamic.

The long and powerful reign of Askiya Dāwūd was a turning point in the history of the dynasty. Before his accession all the *askiyas*,

[1] Ibid. 114/tr. 209–10.

except Muḥammad Benkan, had been sons of Askiya Muḥammad. Other sons of the founder of the dynasty held senior offices and titles. Askiya Dāwūd appointed his own sons to senior positions as these became vacant. From then on, all the *askiyas* were sons (and later grandsons) of Askiya Dāwūd. In practice this implied the elimination from accession to high office of all the other descendants of the founder, Askiya Muḥammad. This process of elimination did not, however, bring about the easing of succession disputes. Competition and intrigues among Askiya Dāwūd's sons proved even more cruel and destructive than those which had divided the sons of Askiya Muḥammad.

When Askiya Dāwūd died in 1582, his senior son, *Kurmina-fari* Muḥammad Benkan, was in Tendirma. Askiya Dāwūd wanted this son to succeed him, but because he was away, another son, Al-Ḥājj, who was then the senior prince in Gao, was elected *askiya* by his brothers and the dignitaries of Songhay. Muḥammad Benkan, who was about to lead his army against the new *askiya*, finally decided to resign and to reside in Timbuktu as a student of Islamic sciences. The *qāḍī* wrote on his behalf to Askiya Al-Ḥājj, who was inclined to agree, but the commanders of the army pointed out that as long as Muḥammad Benkan was in Timbuktu every official or prince on a visit to Timbuktu would be suspected of intriguing with him. Askiya Al-Ḥājj therefore ordered that Muḥammad Benkan should be detained.

Askiya Al-Ḥājj appointed his brother al-Hādī to replace Muḥammad Benkan as *Kurmina-fari*. But just over a year later al-Hādī set out from Tendirma to Gao against Al-Ḥājj. His brothers in Gao had intimated that the *askiya* was sick (as he was indeed) and powerless. But these same brothers later betrayed him, and on his arrival in Gao in March 1584 al-Hādī was arrested. Less than three years later, in December 1586, Askiya Al-Ḥājj was deposed by his brothers.

Askiya Dāwūd's sons then made their brother, Muḥammad Bāni, *askiya*. When this news reached al-Hādī in his prison he remarked, 'The most foolish of those born to our father has become king.'[1] Askiya Muḥammad Bāni was despised by his brothers, who conspired to depose him. The plot was discovered, and those in league were severely punished. At this stage events in the west led to the worst ever civil strife in Songhay, which was regarded as being among the causes for the self-destruction of the empire on the eve of the Moroccan invasion.[2]

[1] *T. al-Sūdān*, 121/tr. 195.
[2] *T. al-Fattāsh*, 126/tr. 220.

It all began in Kabara, the river port of Timbuktu, where two senior officials had their residence. One of them, the *Kabara-farma*, was in charge of the port and levied tolls from the boats on the river. The other was the *balma*, commander of the Songhay troops in the western provinces. Whereas the *balma* was a member of the royal family, a son or a grandson of the *askiya*, the *Kabara-farma* was a slave or a eunuch of the *askiya*'s household. Each of the two was expected to attend to his own affairs.

The *Kabara-farma* Alu was an oppressive, insolent eunuch, who was hated by the Muslims of Timbuktu. On one occasion he molested Maḥmūd Ka'ti, when he wrested from him a field which had been granted to Maḥmūd Ka'ti by Askiya Dāwūd. But when in March 1588 the same *Kabara-farma* flogged and jailed a slave of Balma Muḥammad Ṣādiq (a son of Askiya Dāwūd), the *balma* killed the *askiya*'s eunuch. The *balma* feared the *askiya*'s revenge and called his brother, the *Kurmina-fari* Ṣāliḥ, to march on Gao. They agreed that Askiya Muḥammad Bāni would be deposed and that *Karmina-fari* Ṣāliḥ would become *askiya*. Mutual suspicions instigated by slanderers resulted in an open conflict between the two brothers, and *Kurmina-fari* Ṣāliḥ was killed. His troops, however, joined the *balma*, who proceeded to Gao at the head of both armies.

During his residence in Kabara, Balma Ṣādiq had cultivated friendly relations with the scholars and merchants of Timbuktu. He then relieved them from the oppression of the *Kabara-farma* Alu. Balma Ṣādiq won the support of the people of Timbuktu; the merchants gave gold, the *imāms* prayed for him in the mosque, and even the tailors joined together to make garments for him. The *askiya*'s officials in the city and the Tuareg chief also pledged their support. All the chiefs of the western provinces, both local rulers and royal princes, joined Balma Ṣādiq. (Only the *Binga-farma* supported the *askiya* and ran away to Gao.)

Once again, as in the revolt of Askiya Muḥammad against Sonni Baro almost a century earlier, there was a confrontation between the western and eastern parts of the empire. The western provinces and the 'Muslim party' of Timbuktu supported Balma Ṣādiq, while the eastern provinces, the Songhay dignitaries and officials as well as the royal princes in Gao, remained loyal to the reigning *askiya*. It appears that, while Timbuktu and the western provinces were in revolt, the custodians of Songhay traditions, who had resisted the encroachment of Islamic influence, became prominent in Gao.

Askiya Muḥammad Bāni died on the day the Songhay army set out from Gao to meet Balma Sādiq. After some hesitation among the officers of the court, Isḥāq, son of Askiya Dāwūd, prevailed and was made *askiyā*. As soon as news about the death of Askiya Muḥammad Bāni reached the western provinces, Balma Ṣādiq was declared *askiya* by his army. Messengers were sent to announce this in Timbuktu, which celebrated the occasion by beating the drums on the roofs. A week later a fierce battle was fought between the two rival *askiyas* and the two Songhay armies.

Balma Ṣādiq was defeated, hunted down and killed. All the chiefs of the western provinces were deposed and jailed. Askiya Ishāq immediately appointed new chiefs, but he could not replace the heavy losses among the troops. Only a few of those who had joined Balma Ṣādiq returned from the civil war. Tendirma, the seat of the governor of the western provinces, was destroyed. Hence, only three years before the Moroccan invasion, the Songhay empire was maimed. It had lost about half of its army and the western provinces were emasculated.

The Moroccans exploited the internal dissension among the Songhay. A contemporary source reports that about 1583 the Moroccan sultan al-Manṣūr sent an Arab shaykh of the desert to Gao as his agent. This man, Manṣūr b. al-Filālī, shaykh of the Banū Sālim, was chosen because as a merchant he had paid frequent visits to Gao, he knew the country and had connections with the Songhay kings. This shaykh stayed in Gao for three years and gained the confidence of the rulers in Gao. During the civil war, after the death of Askiya Al-Ḥājj (December 1586), he persuaded one of the rebellious brothers of Askiya Muḥammad Bāni (1586–8) and Askiya Isḥāq II to retire to the Maghrib until the end of the civil war. In Taghaza this prince was seized by the Moroccan governor and was sent in chains to Marrakesh, where he arrived in March or April 1589. This prince was later made to write a letter to the Moroccan sultan seeking his military aid to overthrow the reigning *askiya*. This letter was sent to Askiya Ishāq along with the sultan's ultimatum in January 1590.[1]

Askiya Isḥāq had defeated his rebellious brothers in April 1588, and felt secure enough to reject the Moroccan ultimatum. He seems to have been so little concerned with the threat of the Moroccan sultan that he set out on a campaign to the remote province of Kala. He was there when news reached him of the Moroccan expedition.

[1] al-Fishtālī, *Manāhil*, 55; according to *T. al-Sūdān* (137/tr. 215) it was a slave of the *askiya* who presented himself as a brother of the *askiya*.

The warning came when the Moroccans were still in the desert, far enough away for the Balma Muḥammad Gao to suggest that he should go out to fill in all the water holes and expose the approaching invaders to thirst. This advice was rejected and, instead, messengers were sent with letters from the *askiya* to the tribal shaykhs on the route of the expedition, asking them to fill in the water holes. Attacked and wounded by the Tuareg, these messengers were found by the advancing Moroccan troops.[1]

The Songhay army was assembled rather hastily, and was not in a position to attack the exhausted Moroccans immediately as they emerged from the desert. Sporadic attacks by Songhay archers from the river were easily repulsed. The Moroccans arrived in Karabara (near Bamba) and just over a week later they advanced towards Gao. Askiya Isḥāq came out with his army to meet them at Tondibi, and the decisive battle took place.

The size of the Songhay army at Tondibi was variously estimated at 10,000, 12,500 and 18,000 cavalry and 30,000, 80,000 and 100,000 infantry.[2] The *askiya* ordered a herd of cattle to be driven in front of his army. This, he hoped, would cause disorder in the Moroccan ranks. But at the first volley of fire the cattle turned back and caused confusion in the Songhay army. According to another version the Moroccans opened a way for the cattle to pass through and then closed their ranks again. The battle was decided within a short time, and most of the Songhay army was routed by the heavy fire. Only the rearguard' a unit of brave and resolute warriors, who tied themselves together, did not retreat and continued to shoot arrows at the Moroccans until they were overcome in hand-to-hand fighting.

The Moroccans did not pursue the defeated Songhay, who crossed the river to the Gurma side. Jūdār, the commander of the Moroccan force, entered Gao, which was almost deserted, and his disappointment at the Songhay capital found expression in the often-quoted remark that 'The house of the shaykh of the donkey-drivers in the Maghrib is superior to the *askiya*'s palace.'[3]

The Songhay army suffered heavy losses at Tondibi. Many people, including civilians, lost their lives while crossing the river in panic and confusion. Askiya Isḥāq offered his submission to the Moroccan sultan and offered to pay a tribute of a hundred thousand pieces of

[1] *T. al-Fattāsh*, 150/tr. 268–9; 'Anonyme Espagnol' in de Castries, 'La conquête', 470.

[2] *T. al-Fattāsh*, 146/tr. 264; *T. al-Sūdān*, 140/tr. 219; al-Fishtali, *Manāhil*, 70; 'Anonyme Espagnol' in de Castries, 'La conquête', 471.

[3] *T. al-Sūdān*, 141/tr. 221.

gold and a thousand slaves. The Moroccan troops were extremely tired, and they had already contracted tropical diseases. Jūdār was, therefore, inclined to accept the *askiya*'s offer and to retreat from the Sudan. But by then the Moroccan sultan was resolved to keep control of the Sudan. He rejected the conditions and sent another pasha to replace Jūdār, with clear instructions to accomplish the conquest of Songhay and to make an attempt to reach the gold mines.

In their retreat the Songhay cavalry deposed Askiya Isḥāq and proclaimed the *balma*, Muḥammad Gao, the new *askiya*. Shortly afterwards, Askiya Muḥammad Gao was lured to his own destruction, when he accepted an invitation of the Pasha Manṣūr. He was seized, chained and killed. Two brothers, sons of Askiya Dāwūd, then became *askiyas*, one in Timbuktu as a protégé of the Moroccans and the other in Dendi, where he continued the resistance of Songhay to the foreign occupation.

An analysis of the political system of the Songhay empire must begin with its basic weakness – namely, the lack of cohesion within the royal dynasty. Succession disputes were not uncommon in African kingdoms, but in Songhay kings were not safe even after they had secured their accession. Only three out of nine *askiyas* died a natural death in office; all the others were deposed or murdered by their own brothers.

Revolts, plots, conspiracies and intrigues may be viewed as delayed succession disputes. Because a new *askiya* was invariably proclaimed soon after the death or the deposition of his precedessor, other claimants were not campaigning as alternative candidates, but found themselves in rebellion against a legitimate *askiya*. Of all the potential candidates, the one who happened to be in Gao when the throne became vacant was always successful. The one elected by the royal princes, then in Gao, was endorsed without any delay by the dignitaries of Songhay and the officers of the court. He had immediately at his disposal the élite corps of the army, under the command of the *Dendi-fari* or the *hi-koi*, to meet any challenge.

Such a policy of avoiding any delay in the succession could have added to the stability of the throne but for one important reason: some of the better candidates were always outside the capital, as provincial governors. Such was, for example, the position of the *Kurmina-fari*. In the hierarchy of Songhay the *Kurmina-fari* was second only to the *askiya*, and this powerful office was given to a senior member of the royal family, a brother or a son of the *askiya*. He was, therefore, also a most likely candidate for the kingship. But only two *Kurmina-faris* (Muḥammad Benkan and Dāwūd) came to Gao in time to be elected *askiya*. Others were far away in Tendirma, and to their disappointment saw one of their brothers, who had happened to be in Gao, made *askiya*. One *Kurmina-fari* conceded graciously, but three others led their armies to Gao in their attempt to seize power. In all cases the *askiya*'s troops in Gao proved superior to the troops which the *Kurmina-fari* was able to raise in the western provinces.

Whereas only two of the nine *askiyas* succeeded from the office of *Kurmina-fari*, four had held the office of *fari-mondyo* before their accession. It appears that the holder of this office was the senior prince in Gao, and had therefore a good chance of succession to the throne. Muḥammad Benkan, the favourite son of Askiya Dāwūd, was promoted by his father from the office of *fari-mondyo* to that of *Kurmina-fari*. Because of this promotion he was away from Gao when his father died and lost the kingship.

The *balma*, commander of the regular Songhay troops in the west, was among the *Kurmina-fari*'s lieutenants. Three *balmas* were actually promoted to become *Kurmina-faris*. Both the *Kurmina-fari* and the *balma* were greeted as *tunkara*, which was among the royal titles of old Soninke states, such as Ghana/Wagadu and Mema. They were indeed ruling, in the name of the *askiya*, over the territories of these old Soninke states. The office of *balma* was reserved for royal princes, though three of those who held this office were related to the *askiya* through their mothers. Royal princes held also two territorial governorships in the western provinces, those of *Binga-farma* and *Bana-farma*. Together with the *balma*, they seem to have formed an advisory council for the *Kurmina-fari*.

Other chieftaincies in the western provinces were held by local hereditary rulers, such as *Bara-koi*, *Dirma-koi*, *Hombori-koi* and *Jenne-koi*. All these rulers were given daughters of the *askiya* or of the *Kurmina-fari* in marriage. They also became involved in the internal conflicts of the dynasty, mostly as supporters of their immediate lord, the *Kurmina-fari*. At least twice, such local rulers were severely punished for aligning themselves against the *askiya*, after the latter had defeated the rebellious *Kurmina-fari*.

Local hereditary chiefs in the western provinces were granted ceremonial and other privileges. Only the *Jenne-koi* was entitled to spread his carpet in the *askiya*'s audience, and to put flour, instead of dust, on his head. Only the *Dirma-koi* was allowed to enter the *askiya*'s palace mounted on a horse, and only the *Bara-koi* could tell the *askiya* what he ought not to do and the latter was obliged to adhere to his advice. When the *Bara-koi* Mansa Kura was alone with Askiya Muḥammad in the Prophet's tomb at Medina, the former made the *askiya* swear that he would take the *Bara-koi*'s daughters only in marriage (and never as concubines), that the *askiya* would obey him in guiding him as to what was permitted and what was forbidden, and that the *Bara-koi*'s house would be a sanctuary for those fleeing from the *askiya*'s rage.[1] It is significant that these were privileges which were traditionally enjoyed by Muslim elders in Sudanic kingdoms.

The chronicles of Timbuktu often refer to *ahl Songhay*, i.e. 'people of Songhay', which should be interpreted as the dignitaries or notables of the kingdom. These were members of the traditional Songhay aristocracy. Even after the expansion of Songhay under Sonni 'Alī and Askiya Muḥammad, it seems that the traditional aristocracy was concerned mostly with the eastern part of the empire, or with Songhay proper. Senior officials in the western provinces like the *Kurmina-fari* and the *balma* were royal princes, whereas their counterparts in the east, the *Dendi-fari* (governor of the eastern front) and the *hi-koi* (commander of the fleet), were non-royal dignitaries.

Under the command of non-royals, the eastern part of the empire was more stable and loyal to the *askiya*. The office of the *Dendi-fari* could be regarded as terminal, because there was no higher office to be promoted to, and as a non-royal he could not aspire to become *askiya*. Hence, most of the *Dendi-faris* died in office, whereas the same is true of only four out of the fourteen *Kurmina-faris*. (Eight *Kurmina-faris* were deposed or murdered in connection with attempts to seize power at the centre; two others were made *askiyas*.) Only once did the *Dendi-fari* take part in a coup, when in 1537 he helped Ismā'īl against Askiya Muḥammad Benkan. In that case the *Dendi-fari* could have been moved by his loyalty to the great Askiya Muḥammad. As the most senior official among the dignitaries of Songhay, the *Dendi-fari* was the only one who could reproach the *askiya* with frankness.[2]

The *hi-koi* was second in the hierarchy of the non-royal dignitaries, and he could expect promotion to *Dendi-fari*. While the latter was away from the capital most of the time, the *hi-koi* was always close to the *askiya*, both in the palace and on military expeditions. He was therefore one of the most powerful officials in the empire, but his personal position was by no means secure. In a court full of intrigues, the

[1] *T. al-Fattāsh*, 69/tr. 132–3.

[2] Ibid. 11/tr. 13.

incumbent *hi-koi* – the military chief in Gao – was often suspected by a new *askiya*. One *hi-koi* was deposed and another was murdered because of sheer suspicion. A third *hi-koi* was jailed after he had been caught red-handed in a plot. On the other hand, at least two *hi-kois* proved their loyalty to the *askiya* by foiling coups.

Many of the royal princes in the capital held titles about which little is known. Most of them, however, seem to have been commanders of cavalry units. Together the royal princes could impose their will, and the candidate they had agreed upon invariably succeeded to the throne. Indeed, on one occasion there was a confrontation between the royal princes, the sons of Askiya Dāwūd and the officers of the court (the *hi-koi*, the *hu-kokorai-koi* or 'master of the royal household', the *sha'a-farma*, and the *barei-koi* or 'chief of protocol'). It was in 1588 when, after bloody disputes among the sons of Askiya Dāwūd, the officers of the court decided that in the interests of the empire the kingship should be wrested from those brothers who kept killing each other. The officers therefore concealed the death of Askiya Muḥammad Bāni and planned to present the people with a *fait accompli* by secretly enthroning a son of Askiya Ismā'īl. But as soon as the sons of Askiya Dāwūd had been informed of this, they joined together, encircled the royal tent and forced the officers of the court to pay allegiance to the candidate of their own choice, one of their number – namely, Askiya Isḥāq II.

Among those closest to the *askiya* was the *wanadu*, the linguist 'who repeats the *askiya*'s words to the people'.[1] In Songhay, as in other Sudanic kingdoms, this official was among the custodians of the traditional heritage. When a slave of the *askiya* who came back from Mecca with a group of pilgrims shook hands with the *askiya*, the *wanadu* threatened to cut off the slave's hand. This *wanadu* was immediately deposed, but the incident indicated that traditional rather than Islamic values were dearer to him. Besides the linguist, who orally made public the *askiya*'s orders, there was also a Muslim scribe in the *askiya*'s retinue, who wrote official documents.

In Mali, slaves and freed slaves had been prominent among the officers of the court and in the provincial administration. As confidants of the kings they enjoyed political influence, intervened in succession disputes, and even seized the throne when impotent royals risked the very existence of the empire (see pp. 386–7). In Songhay, the court and the

[1] *T. al-Sūdān*, 101/tr. 167.

provincial administration were dominated by the numerous royal princes and the Songhay nobility. Slaves seem to have had little or no political influence.

Slaves assumed greater importance in the economy of the empire. Royal farms were spread all over the empire from Dendi in the east to the Sahel west of the Niger bend, with a heavier concentration in the lacustrine region south of Timbuktu. Slaves under the supervision of a headman, who himself was a slave, produced large quantities of grain, mainly rice, for the royal granaries. Seeds were supplied by the *askiya*, and the headman of each farm was responsible for the delivery of a yearly quota. He often kept the surplus for himself and some prominent slaves had their own stores of grain. They could even own slaves, cattle and horses, but the wealth they had accumulated eventually returned to the *askiya*, who inherited the property left by his slaves. The *askiyas* granted gifts of land and slaves to their favourites among the Muslims, which provided the scholars with a regular source of income.

Askiya Muḥammad increased the number of slaves. As in earlier wars of conquest by Sonni 'Alī, the land of Gurma, within the Niger bend, remained a reservoir for slaves not far from the capital. A son of Askiya Dāwūd boasted that within one day a royal prince could bring back a thousand slaves by raiding the land of the pagans. So many slaves were put onto the market after a raid on the pagans of Gurma, in fact, that the price of slaves was considerably reduced.[1] Gao had a busy slave market, which was visited by traders from the Maghrib.

In the fifteenth century slaves were in great demand in southern Morocco for the expanding sugar cane plantations. The bourgeoisie of Fez bought slaves of both sexes for domestic service. Black slaves reached Barca and Tripoli in great numbers, to be distributed to Egypt and Turkey on the one hand, and to Sicily and Italy on the other. In Sicily they were employed in agriculture. Naples, Genoa and Venice had black slaves in the fifteenth century, perhaps because of the scarcity of labour in Europe in that period.[2] Most of the black slaves came to Tripoli and Barca from Bornu, but quite a few were taken to these places from the western Sudan, as attested by Portuguese sources of the mid fifteenth century, and by the presence of a slave trader from

[1] *T. al-Fattāsh*, 105/tr. 195; *T. al-Sūdān*, 95/tr. 157.

[2] C. Verlinden, 'Esclavage noir en France méridionale et courants de traite en Afrique', *Annales du Midi*, 1966, **78**, 335–43; M. Malowist, 'Les fondaments de l'expansion européenne en Afrique au 15e siècle: Europe, Maghrib et Soudan Occidental', *Acta Poloniae Historica*, 1968, **18**, 174–6.

Mesarata (near Tripoli) at the court of Askiya Dāwūd a century later.[1]

There seems to have been economic prosperity in Songhay, at least during the reign of Askiya Muḥammad. Leo Africanus reported an abundant supply of food, which was produced in the southern savanna and was shipped to Timbuktu by the Niger river. Sudanese traders came to Gao with so much gold that they could not find enough commodities to buy, and spent only about half of their gold. There was great demand in the western Sudan for goods imported from the Maghrib and from Europe: clothes of various descriptions, copper and copper wares, glass and stone beads, perfumes and horses. The Sudanese were ready to pay high prices for these most luxurious commodities.[2]

From the fourteenth century onwards cowries became the most widely spread currency within the boundaries of the Sudanic empires. Ibn Baṭṭūṭa reported that traders from the Maghrib derived large profits from the import of cowries. Later on, one of the *askiyas* discovered that cowries imported directly from Cairo were much cheaper, and he banned the import of cowries from Morocco. In 1591, as part of his offer of submission to the sultan Mawlay Aḥmad al-Manṣūr, Askiya Isḥāq suggested lifting this ban and renewing the lucrative trade in cowries from Morocco.[3]

The fifteenth and sixteenth centuries saw the development of an urban culture. In Walata, the oldest commercial town, people lived in much the same way as their kinsmen, the nomads of the desert.[4] But in Timbuktu merchants, artisans (mainly weavers) and '*ulamā*' formed a distinctive bourgeoisie. They were joined by foreign merchants, who added lustre to the city. In Timbuktu the merchants of Ghadames built the most beautiful quarter. Under the leadership of the '*ulamā*', Islam was used to reinforce the autonomy of the city vis-à-vis the *askiya*.

Leo Africanus contrasted the sophisticated city dwellers of Songhay with the peasants and herdsmen of the countryside. In the winter the latter were dressed in sheepskins, but in the summer they went naked, covering their private parts only. These people were completely ignorant, and one could travel a hundred miles without meeting a man who could read and write. They were heavily taxed by the king.[5] The

[1] Zurara, *Chronique de Guinée*, tr. L. Bourdon (Dakar, 1960), 216–17; Cadamosto, *Relations des voyages à la côte occidentale d'Afrique*, tr. C. Schefer (Paris, 1895), 48; *T. al-Fattāsh*, 104/tr. 193.

[2] Leo Africanus, *Description*, II, 465–71.

[3] 'Anonyme Espagnol' in de Castries, 'La conquête', 473.

[4] Leo Africanus, *Description*, II, 464; see also Ibn Baṭṭūṭa, *Tuḥfat*, IV, 386.

[5] Leo Africanus, *Description*, II, 471–2.

rustic commoners and the bourgeoisie are represented here as being worlds apart, but more research is needed about the different impact of trade, Islam and imperial government on villages and on the nomads' camps according to their proximity to cities and routes. This, in turn, is closely related to the degree of integration and cohesiveness of Songhay and of other states in the western Sudan.

Songhay was the first Sudanic empire the power of which extended into the Sahara as far as the salt mines of Taghaza. The southern half of the trans-Saharan routes were patrolled by the Tuareg in the service of the *askiya*. The northern section of the Sahara came increasingly under the domination of Arab nomads. They imposed their 'protection' over the pre-Saharan oases and extracted tribute from the inhabitants and traders there. Leo Africanus described the poverty of the indigenous population of the oases as being a result of the pressure of the Arabs.[1]

Many of the oases on the northern fringes of the Sahara were at that time entrepôts for the trade with the Sudan. Sijilmasa, which had been the principal gate for the Sudan, declined after the middle of the fourteenth century. At the beginning of the sixteenth century, the town itself was in ruins and its people lived in the *qṣūr* around. The oases of Tuat (Buda, Tamentit and Tabalbalet) and Gurara were the rendezvous for traders and caravans from Morocco, Tlemcen and Tunis before they entered the desert. In 1447 the Italian Malfante stayed at Tamentit and described an active trade with the Sudan, in which the people of Tuat acted as brokers, for a very high commission. Malfante's host, a wealthy merchant, had lived for some thirty years in Timbuktu and travelled extensively in the Sudan.[2]

Jewish goldsmiths were conspicuous in almost every town and oasis which developed commercial relations with the Sudan. Jews almost monopolized the working of gold, as Muslims shunned it because of a religious injunction. The royal mints at Fez and Tadla, for example, were run by Jews. Both in Morocco and in Tlemcen Jews aided the rulers in the economic reconstruction of their countries. Jewish refugees from Spain joined their Moroccan co-religionists and became active both in the trade with the Europeans on the coast and in the trade with the Sudan.

In the fifteenth century, with the growth of commerce in Tuat, the number of Jews increased considerably. This period is sometimes

[1] Ibid. I, 31, 40; II, 419, 429, 432, 434–5, 455.

[2] Ibid. II, 430, 432, 436; C. de la Roncière, *La découverte de l'Afrique au moyen âge* (Cairo, 1925), I, 151–7.

referred to in the oral traditions of Tuat as the 'Jewish period'.[1] Malfante reported that the numerous Jews of Tuat were secure under the protection of local chiefs and that they acted as intermediaries in the flourishing trade. Rabbinical *responsa* indicate that Jews joined caravans which crossed the desert to the Sudan. In 1440, the Jews excited the rage of the population of Tamentit when they invited the intervention of the ruler of Tlemcen in their quarrel with the Arabs of the oasis.

In 1479 the militant *'ālim* al-Maghīlī came to Tuat and deplored the situation in which Jews evaded the discriminatory regulations which should have governed their conduct. He complained that Jews rode horses, dressed like Muslims and were dominant over the ignorant population of Tuat. With the approval of a few scholars, but against the advice of many others, including the *qāḍī* of Tuat, al-Maghīlī incited the people of Tuat against the Jews and caused their massacre in 1492. Soon after these events al-Maghīlī travelled to the Sudan and seems to have imparted his hostility towards the Jews to Askiya Al-Ḥājj Muḥammad. The latter is described as being an enemy of the Jews; he declared that he would allow none of them to settle in Timbuktu, and even threatened traders from the Maghrib that he would confiscate the property of any of them who had commercial relations with Jews.[2]

The most westerly route across the Sahara, leading from the Wādī Dar'a through Adrar, which had declined since the twelfth century, was revived in the fifteenth century. The revival of this route is connected with the growing importance of the salt mine of Idjil (between Rio de Oro and Fort Gouraud). This mine had been vaguely referred to by Cadamosto in 1455, but its trade was described in detail by Fernandes about half a century later.[3] Traders from Wadan, then the principal town of Adrar, carried the salt from Idjil to Tichit, where it was taken over by the merchants of Walata, who sent it to Timbuktu. In return for the salt of Idjil, part of the gold of the Sudan reached Wadan, where it was distributed to Oran, Huynan, Fez, Marrakesh, Safi and Massa, and sold to Italian merchants there. It was in Arguin, on the coast opposite Adrar, that the Portuguese established their factory in 1455. In their attempt to divert part of the gold that was transported via the western Saharan route, the Portuguese even built

[1] A. G. P. Martin, *Les oases sahariennes* (Algiers, 1908), 40; J. W. Hirschberg, *A history of the Jews in North Africa* [in Hebrew] (Jerusalem, 1965), II, 18–19; La Roncière, *La découverte*, I, 146–7, 152.

[2] Leo Africanus, *Description*, II, 468.

[3] Cadamosto, *Relations*, 54–5; V. Fernandes, *Description*, 79–85.

an advanced post in Wadan. They abandoned this post after a short time because of the hardship of the desert and the hostility of the population. The Portuguese, however, partly succeeded in securing a link with the Saharan trade from their base in Arguin, which was their first rewarding achievement in the hazardous navigation along the barren Saharan coast.

For about fifty years (between 1383 and 1435), Portugal did not produce gold coins, because of the scarcity of the yellow metal. The resumption of gold minting in 1436 was made possible when, following the conquest of Ceuta in 1415, the Portuguese began to occupy the Moroccan ports on the Atlantic coast, and were able to secure control of the gold-trade from the Genoese merchants. However, from the middle of the sixteenth century, Genoese merchants began to co-operate with the Muslim rulers in developing Larache, Sale, Tarakouron and Massa as rival ports to those held by the Portuguese. Genoese merchants were favoured because their presence did not expose Morocco to the danger of foreign political and military intervention. Also, they helped in breaking the monopoly Portugal had attempted to establish over the external trade of Morocco. Finally, they were willing to sell fire-arms which the Portuguese declared to be contraband.

The sympathy of the Muslim authorities towards Italian merchants allowed representatives of Genoese and Florentine firms to venture into the interior. In 1447 Antonio Malfante reached Tuat, and in 1469 Bendetto Dei is said to have visited Timbuktu. Both were expected to explore the prospects for the revitalization of the overland trade in gold as a counter-measure to the menacing maritime exploits of the Portuguese.

Following the introduction of a newly designed caravel in 1440, the Portuguese began their advance along the Atlantic coast of the Sahara. From their ships the Portuguese raided nomad encampments of the 'Azenegues' (Sanhaja) on the coast and took prisoners. Later on, these captives were exchanged for black slaves, and gradually the mutual suspicion was mitigated by the development of commercial relations. The nomads brought skins, hides, civet and gum, slaves and gold to Arguin to exchange for cereals, clothes of various kinds, silk, silver and horses.

In 1444 the Portuguese finally passed the arid coast of the Sahara and reached Cape Verde. There, in the land of the black people, the country was more densely populated and the Portuguese encountered a more organized resistance. Communications with the coastal peoples had at first been somewhat difficult, but in 1455 the Venetian Cadamosto and the Portuguese Diogo Gomes established commercial relations with the rulers of the Wolof on the coast south of the Senegal river and with the Malinke states on the Gambia river. From the Wolof only slaves could be obtained, but the Gambia river offered a waterway for penetrating the interior. The Portuguese reached Cantor on the upper Gambia, where they met the Diakhanke traders. The latter brought slaves, gold and local cotton cloth from the interior, which they exchanged for various textiles, copper rings and wares, cowries as well as horses. On the Gambia the Portuguese created yet another link with the trade system of the western Sudan. Trade had already been carried on between the centre of the Mali empire and the Gambia, and on the river itself; the arrival of the Portuguese made it international.

The amount of gold procured by the Portuguese in Arguin and on the Gambia was rather modest, because they diverted only a small fraction of the northbound gold-trade to the Maghrib. But even that limited trade contributed to financing the exploration of the coast south of the Gambia.

The real reward for the unrelenting efforts of the Portuguese navigators came when, in 1471, they reached the place which later became known as Elmina. Within a few years the Portuguese obtained there gold in quantities larger than they had ever seen before. In Elmina they came close to the goldfields of the Akan forest, which had already been developed by the Dyula traders since the middle of the fourteenth century. For over a century that gold had been carried by the Dyula, through the commercial network of the western Sudan and the Sahara, to quench the thirst of Europe for that precious metal. With the arrival of the Portuguese at Elmina, a growing part of the gold was directed south to reach the Christians more directly.

The Portuguese soon realized that both on the Gambia and at Elmina they had established contacts with a very sophisticated and elaborate commercial system operated by the Manding-speaking traders – Dyula and Diakhanke. In 1513 the governor of Elmina complained that much gold was still taken north by the 'Mandinga' (Dyula). Had there been a sufficient supply of slaves and other merchandise, the governor added, he could have obtained any amount of gold the king of Portugal demanded. Another document indicates that the flooding of the Gambia with commodities of value attracted to Cantor those Dyula traders who used to come to Elmina with their gold.[1]

[1] A. Teixeira da Mota, 'The Mande trade in Costa da Mina according to Portuguese documents until the mid-sixteenth century', unpubl. paper, *Conference on Manding Studies*, London, 1972.

For about half a century after 1482, Lisbon received over 400 kilograms of gold annually from Elmina. But in the second half of the sixteenth century the supply of gold to Lisbon declined, because Portugal had lost its monopoly over the trade with Guinea. English, French and Dutch ships visited Elmina, and the competition between traders of different nations offered better terms for the African partners in the gold trade. Though Lisbon saw less gold, the supply of the precious metal to traders of other European nations increased considerably. By that time, however, American silver had begun its flow to Europe, and the western Sudan gradually lost its role as the principal source of precious metal for Europe.

The commercial interests of Portugal on the Atlantic coast of Morocco should be viewed as part of their imperial commercial economy. It was indeed in the 1450s, after the Portuguese had established a factory in Arguin, that they also developed trade in Safi. Their intervention in the ports of Morocco (such as Azemmour and Mazagan) escalated in the 1480s after the discovery of Elmina. In the Sahara and in Guinea the Portuguese intruded into a trading system which had been linked to Morocco, and they soon discovered that their African trading partners demanded Moroccan goods in exchange for the gold. These goods, which had been carried across the Sahara and over the routes of the Sudan, were now taken by Portuguese ships from the Moroccan ports. In Safi the Portuguese bought wheat, which they sold to the nomads in Arguin. Moroccan horses were sold by the Portuguese in the Senegambia. In Elmina Moroccan textiles were in demand, and the Portuguese had to comply.[1]

Significantly, the withdrawal of Portugal from the Atlantic coast of Morocco in the middle of the sixteenth century coincided with the loss of its monopoly in the Gulf of Guinea and the decline of its trade there. In Morocco, the rise of the Sharifian dynasty, which led the jihad against the Portuguese, was connected with the revival of the Muslim Saharan trade after it had been threatened by the Christian maritime commerce.

By the beginning of the sixteenth century the Portuguese dominated the economy of southern Morocco from their fort at Agadir. They discouraged the sugar industry in order to avoid competition with the sugar plantations on the Portuguese islands of Madeira, the Azores and the Cape Verde isles. At the same time, the Portuguese monopolized

[1] R. Ricard, 'Le commerce de Berbérie et l'organisation économique de l'empire portugais aux 15e et 16e siècles', *Annales de l'Institut d'Études Orientales*, 1936, **2**, 266–85.

the trade in indigo and cotton. The towns of Wādī Dar'a and the Sus traded with both the Sudan and the Portuguese, diverting to the latter much of the trade which before had reached Marrakesh or Tlemcen.

From about 1515 the Sharif Muḥammad al-Mahdī, as governor of the Sus, pursued an economic policy to free the country from Portuguese tutelage (see pp. 400–1). He encouraged the production of sugar, gained control of the gold-trade and sought to establish commercial relations with traders of different European nations. It was this combined effort – an economic and military jihad – which brought about the conquest of Agadir and the subsequent withdrawal of the Portuguese from the other Moroccan ports. From the middle of the sixteenth century English traders carried much of the external trade of Morocco, though they were not allowed a monopolistic control.

The reconquest of Tafilelt, the expansion to Tuat and Gurara, and the expedition to Wadan were part of an overall policy of the new Sharifian dynasty to revive the Saharan trade and to recover the flow of the gold through Morocco, against Christian attempts to divert it to the coast. The desire to have a firmer control of the Taghaza salt mines, and, finally, the conquest of the Sudan by Mawlay Aḥmad al-Manṣūr, might also be viewed as extensions of this policy.

In West Africa, the European presence along the coasts contributed to a gradual reorientation from the north to the west (in the Senegambia) and to the south (in the Gulf of Guinea). West African history which, until the middle of the fifteenth century, had been viewed almost exclusively from the north, gained new perspectives. The Portuguese sources offer information not only about the peoples closer to the coast, but also new insights, from a different angle, about developments farther in the interior, in the declining empire of Mali.

Leo Africanus described Mali, about 1512, as extending along a branch of the Niger, south of Jenne. The king of Mali was then under heavy attacks from the *askiya*, which reduced him to extreme poverty.[1] Songhay's attacks on Mali, which were a feature of the period 1500–10, ceased for about thirty years. The revolt of Kebbi, the weakness of the old and blind Askiya Muḥammad, the series of disputes, assassinations and depositions in the dynasty gave Mali this respite. Mali even became partly involved in the internal politics of Songhay when the deposed Askiya Muḥammad Benkan found asylum in one of its provinces.

The accession of Askiya Ismā'īl in 1537 marked the recovery of

[1] Leo Africanus, *Description*, II, 466.

Songhay, and his two successors resumed the pressure on Mali. During the first phase of its expansion, under Sonni 'Alī, Songhay conquered territories which had already become independent of Mali. Askiya Muḥammad and his lieutenant 'Umar Komdiagha attacked the north-western provinces of Mali beyond the upper Senegal. From the 1540s onwards, Askiya Isḥāq and Askiya Dāwūd directed their attacks against the provinces of Mali on the Bani and Niger rivers, which defended the access to the central part of Mali. In 1545/6 the *Kurmina-fari* Dāwūd entered the capital of Mali. The king of Mali escaped and his town was occupied by the Songhay army for seven days.

The king of Mali could not resist a direct assault by the more formidable army of Songhay, but the Songhay would have found it extremely difficult to establish their rule over the heartland of the Malinke country, which was hilly with dense vegetation. Askiya Muḥammad had warned that 'any one who does not keep away from fighting in the mountains and in the forest exposes his army to ruin and casualties'.[1] In addition, because of the Sotouba falls (upstream of Bamako), the Songhay could not employ their powerful fleet against the centre of Mali. Indeed, these falls marked the south-western limits of Songhay expansion.

Rather than conquering Mali, the *askiyas* preferred to whittle away its power by repeated attacks. The provinces of Kala and Binduku, which formed a buffer zone between Mali and Songhay, were subject to interventions from Songhay, but were not integrated into the Songhay empire. Political adversaries of the *askiyas* found asylum in towns in Kala as late as the 1580s. Askiya Isḥāq II led an expedition against Kala in 1591, when the invading Moroccan force was already close to the Sudan.

The collapse of the Songhay empire released Mali from the century-old pressure on its northern frontier. In place of the formerly vigorous Songhay, there succeeded a much weaker authority on the middle Niger separated from Mali by a disintegrating country of warring chiefs. Maḥmūd, the king of Mali, even saw new prospects for reviving something of the power of the old empire. In 1599 he attacked Jenne, but was defeated by Moroccan reinforcements sent in boats from Timbuktu. Mali ceased to be a political factor on the middle Niger, and is mentioned no further in the Arabic records of that region.

As seen from the north, through the Arabic and Muslim records, Mali was reduced to a kingdom of local importance during the fifteenth and sixteenth centuries. But during that same period, as the Portuguese

[1] *T. al-Sūdān*, 105/tr. 172.

reached the Senegal and the Gambia rivers, they became aware of the powerful inland empire of Mali, whose influence reached the Atlantic coast. As they sailed up the navigable sections of the Gambia, the Casamance, Rio Cacheu and Rio Grande, the Portuguese encountered representatives of the imperial authority of Mali.[1] By the middle of the fifteenth century Mali had vassal kingdoms between the Gambia and Rio Grande, which formed an imperial sub-system known in traditional accounts as Kabu.

The extension of the authority of Mali to this region was accompanied by a westward migration of Malinke traders, peasants and warriors. The traders came in search of maritime salt, which was extracted near the estuary of the Gambia, and of gold from the gold-fields of Kabu. The arrival of the warriors is associated with the exploits of Tiramakhan Traore, one of the generals of Sundiata. Many chiefly houses in the area trace their origin to Tiramakhan and to the kingdom of Kabu, which he is said to have established. Even the Guelowar royal clan of the Serer states, north of the Gambia, claim descent from Malinke warriors who hailed from Kabu.

The political situation which may be inferred from Portuguese records and traditional accounts is that the *farim* (ruler) of Kabu represented the authority of Mali in the west. Other Malinke chiefs were subordinate to him, though they had considerable autonomy. The arrival of the Portuguese and the growth of trade on the Gambia brought about significant changes. As a result of their share in the trade and their contacts with the Portuguese, local Malinke rulers gradually increased their power at the expense of their remote overlord, the king of Mali. But even as late as the end of the sixteenth century, when the authority of Mali on the Gambia must have been only nominal, the *farim* of Kabu still used to go to the capital of Mali to be ceremonially installed.

North of the Gambia, the Wolof and Futa Toro had been within Mali's sphere of influence, perhaps until the second half of the fourteenth century, when the Wolof became independent under Ndiadiane N'diaye, the first *burba* (king) of the Djolof empire. For about two centuries this empire held together the different states of the Wolof (Kayor, Walo and Baol) and the Serer.

Between 1444 and 1510 the Wolof country was visited by the Portuguese, whose accounts throw some light on the political organization

[1] Cadamosto, *Relations*, 158–9; D. Gomes, *De la première découverte de la Guinée*, tr. T. Monod, R. Mauny and G. Duval (Bissau, 1959), 38, 40; V. Fernandes, *Description de la côte occidentale d'Afrique* (Sénégal au Cap de Monte, Archipels), tr. P. de Cenival and T. Monod, ed. T. Monod, A. Teixeira da Mota and R. Mauny (Bissau, 1951), 37, 43, 55, 59, 69, 75.

of the Djolof empire.[1] The *burba* was elected by a college of electors which included also the rulers of the component states. These rulers sent annual presents to the *burba*, but were virtually autonomous. Indeed, it is likely that they often elected a weak *burba*, whom they expected not to interfere in their own internal affairs.

After an early hostile encounter with the Portuguese, the latter established commercial relations with the Wolof. In the middle of the fifteenth century the *burba* extended his authority over the Malinke states on the northern bank of the Gambia (Nyumi, Badibu, Nyani and Wuli) in order to have his share of the growing trade on the Gambia. In the 1480s Prince Bemoi, who ruled the empire in the name of his brother Burba Birao, shifted the seat of the government from its traditional place in the interior to a site closer to the coast, and sought to intensify trade with the Portuguese. He exchanged gifts with the Portuguese King John II and agreed to receive missionaries. Princes who opposed this policy revolted in 1489 and killed Burba Birao. Bemoi himself escaped to seek refuge with his Portuguese allies. He was taken to Lisbon, where he was received with great pomp by King John II, and was baptized. The king of Portugal sent a military expedition to help Bemoi to regain power in his country. The commander of this expedition was ordered to build a fort at the mouth of the Senegal river. This fort and an alliance with a Christian king of Djolof should have added strength to the Portuguese presence in the Senegambia. But the project failed because of a dispute between Bemoi and the Portuguese commander. The latter accused Bemoi of treachery and killed him.

Bemoi's was a brave attempt to secure the benfits of the trade with the Portuguese for the *burba*, and his failure precipitated the disintegration of the Djolof empire. The rulers of the vassal states who were closer to the coast derived wealth and strength from the trade and became more powerful than the *burba*, their overlord. The *damel* of Kayor broke away in the middle of the sixteenth century and was soon followed by the *brak* of Walo and the other vassals. Subsequently Djolof remained only one of several independent states of the Wolof.

The Djolof empire was also shaken by the violent rise, at its expense, of a Fulani empire in Futa Toro. The origins of this empire go back to waves of Fulani migrants who had left the region of Termes (in the south-eastern part of present-day Mauritania) in the fourteenth and

[1] Zurara, who wrote in 1448; Cadamosto, who stayed at the court of the *damel* of Kayor for twenty-eight days in 1455; Diogo Gomes, who visited the coast in 1456; V. Fernandes and D. Pacheco Pereira, who recorded information in the first decade of the sixteenth century.

fifteenth centuries. One wave resulted in the formation of the Fulani communities in Massina. Another wave of Fulani migrants reached the Futa Jalon, where they came under the leadership of Tengella (or Temala of the Portuguese records). Futa Jalon was then within the ambit of Mali and, in challenging the authority of Mali, Tengella brought together the different ethnic groups of Futa Jalon. About 1490 Tengella descended from Futa Jalon into the upper Gambia where he threatened the lines of trade and communication with the heartland of Mali. Sometime between 1493 and 1495 an embassy of King John II of Portugal visited the king of Mali, Mansa Mamudu, and reported that he had been fighting at that time against 'the king of the Fulos, called Temala'.[1]

From the upper Gambia Tengella continued his advance northwards into Futa Toro, which he made the basis for his military operations. In 1512, according to the *Ta'rīkhs* of Timbuktu, Tengella 'king of the Futa' invaded Diara in the Sahel. The chief of Diara had sought the aid of the *askiya* and a strong Songhay expedition was sent under the command of the *Kurmina-fari* 'Umar Komdiagla. Tengella was defeated and killed but his son Koli led the defeated army back to Futa Toro.

In Futa, Koli's power increased at the expense of his neighbours, in particular the Djolof empire. About 1534 he attacked the Bambuk goldfields but was defeated by Mali, perhaps with the support of Portugal. Koli died in 1537, but his successors – known in tradition as the Denianke – continued his expansionist policy. By 1600 the 'empire of the Grand Foul' extended from the Sahel to Futa Jallon and over the upper Senegal, where they controlled both the Bambuk goldfields and the important commercial town of Diakha on the Bafing river.[2]

The loss of Bambuk to Mali at the end of the sixteenth century almost coincided with the defeat of Mansa Maḥmūd at the gates of Jenne by the Moroccans. It is to this period that one may date the collapse of Mali and its final disintegration. In 1620–1 Richard Jobson travelled up the Gambia river and noticed that all the 'petty kings on the south side [of the river] . . . had all reference to the great king of Cantore [Kabu]'.[3] Jobson probably heard nothing of Mali in the interior, which by then had lost all authority on the Gambia (see also pp. 455–6).

The Malinke expansion to the Gambia had taken place during the period of Mali's hegemony, but their migration to the south, as far as the fringes of the forest, occurred during the period of its decline, and

[1] De Barros, *Die Asia* (Nurenberg, 1844), I, 22.

[2] This interpretation is based on the unpublished Ph.D. thesis of J. Boulègue, *La Sénégambie du milieu du 15e siècle au début du 17e siècle* (University of Paris, 1968).

[3] R. Jobson, *The golden trade* (London, 1932), 64–5.

may be viewed as part of the disintegration of the empire. Though little is known about the extent of Mali's authority south of the upper Niger, it is likely that the kings of Mali were concerned with the trade that their subjects, the Dyula traders, had carried on with the kola-producing forest and the Akan goldfields since the middle of the fifteenth century.

Dyula traders had settled in the commercial town of Begho just north of the Akan forest before the arrival of the Portuguese at Elmina in 1471. Other Dyula settlements were established along the routes which linked Jenne with the southern goldfields. By 1500 the Dyula of Begho had penetrated the forest and were trading on the coast to trade with the Portuguese. Indeed, the Portuguese soon realized that the Mande-speaking traders whom they met both on the Gambia and at Elmina were part of an all-embracing commercial system, associated with the empire of Mali. Caravans which reached the Gambia travelled under the orders of the king of Mali and were escorted by Malinke warriors. Mande-speaking warriors moved also along the southbound route to Begho. Towards the end of the sixteenth century such warriors in alliance with Muslim Dyula from Begho conquered the country north of the Black Volta river and created the Gonja state.

The founders of Gonja, known as Gbanya, fought against the two older states in the region, Bono Mansu and Dagomba, which, between them, had dominated the access to the goldfields. A revised chronology of both states suggests that they were not founded before about the middle of the fifteenth century. The fact that their emergence coincided with the development of the gold trade between the forest and the middle Niger, suggests that the two events must have been connected. Bono Mansu had direct control over some of the sources of gold and kola of the forest. A central theme in the traditions of Bono is the trade with the western Sudan on which 'its prosperity and advanced civilization depended'.[1] According to these traditions Muslim traders visited Bono, established their own ward in the capital and had social intercourse with the rulers of the state.

Bono was the southern terminus of trade routes from the middle Niger through the kingdoms of Mossi, Mamprusi and Dagomba. The early existence of these routes may be inferred from scattered evidence about old, pre-seventeenth-century Muslim groups. The first group of Yarse, Muslim traders of Mande origin, settled among the Mossi about the beginning of the sixteenth century. Farther to the south, the old Dagomba capital Yendi-Dabari, near the White Volta river, had a large

[1] E. L. R. Meyerowitz, *The sacred state of the Akan* (London, 1951), 198.

rectangular and possibly two-storeyed building, and a walled and carefully floored enclosure, which, the archaeologists suggest, may well have been a kind of a caravanserai for passing traders.[1] South of Dagomba, in the vicinity of the Black Volta river, one finds Muslim groups who claim to have lived there before the Gonja invasion at the end of the sixteenth century.

The traditions of Mamprusi and Dagomba suggest that these states were the creation of groups of invaders, horsemen from the north-east. There are different versions about their itinerary and the cultural influences which they could have absorbed during their migration. One may, however, view their arrival and the formation of their states as a southward extension of the process of state-building which had begun some centuries before in the Sahel and the northern savanna. Because of their military superiority, based on cavalry, these invaders imposed their authority over the indigenous acephalous societies. They created centralized and stratified chiefdoms in place of the former politico-religious organization where the authority of the earth-priests depended not on physical but on moral and religious sanctions. The invaders, who were inferior in numbers, adopted the Mole-Dagbane dialects of the peoples among whom they had settled.

The encounter, which involved both violence and acculturation, is represented in the traditions as a marriage between the chiefs' ancestor and the daughter of the *tengdana*, the earth-priest. The former murdered his father-in-law and imposed himself as a ruler over the people of the land. Na Gbewa, the son of this usurper, is remembered as the founder of both the Mamprusi and the Dagomba kingdoms. His residence was at Pusiga, in the north-eastern corner of present-day Ghana. Na Gbewa's sons quarrelled over the chieftaincy and separated. Tusogu continued the senior line as king of Mamprusi, while his brother Sitobu descended from the Gambaga scarp to lay the foundations of the Dagomba state.

The history of Mamprusi before the eighteenth century is rather obscure. The kingdom comprised four territorial divisions, one of which was under the direct rule of the *nayiri*, king of all the Mamprusi. Chiefs of the other three divisions enjoyed a large measure of autonomy. The *nayiri*'s suzerainty was acknowledged by neighbouring peoples such as the Tallensi and the Kussasi, but Mamprusi's authority over them

[1] P. L. Shinnie and P. Ozanne, 'Excavations at Yendi-Dabari', *Transactions of the Historical Society of Ghana*, 1963, **6**, 118. But more recently it has been remarked that the quarter excavated is firmly believed by local Dagomba chiefs to have been part of the Ya Na's residence. See I. Wilks, 'The Mossi and Akan states, 1500–1800', in J. F. A. Ajayi and M. Crowder, eds., *History of West Africa* (London, 1971), 352, note 32.

was seldom effective. Mamprusi was less unified and more heterogeneous than Dagomba, its sister state to the south.

The real founder of the Dagomba kingdom was Na Nyaghse, son of Sitobu, whose reign is dated to the middle of the fifteenth century. He established his authority over the country which now forms the western part of Dagomba near the White Volta river. The conquest of this area, according to traditional accounts, was rather brutal. He achieved the subjugation of the indigenous peoples and their complete integration into the new kingdom by slaughtering all *tengdana* (earth-priests) and by appointing his own men as village chiefs in their place. The capital Yendi-Dabari was on the route leading to Bono-Mansu, and the Dagomba extended their authority along that route as far as the Black Volta river. The invasion of the founders of Gonja at the end of the sixteenth century broke the hegemony of Dagomba in that area. About a century later the Gonja even forced the Dagomba to abandon their old capital and to shift the centre of their kingdom eastwards.

Traditional accounts of the history of the Mossi kingdoms trace the origin of their rulers to Nedega, 'king of Gambaga' (Mamprusi). The *moro naba*, king of the Mossi, refers to the *nayiri* of Mamprusi as 'father' and as an acknowledgement of his seniority, annual gifts of a horse, slaves and cloth were sent to Gambaga. There are different versions of the oral traditions, but the main theme is that Nedega's daughter ran away from her father northwards to the region of Tenkodugu, where she met a Busanga hunter and give birth to a son, Widraogo. Widraogo's descendants established chiefdoms which later crystallized to form the two rival kingdoms of Wagadugu, in the south, and Yatenga, in the north.

Widraogo's descendants are known in Mossi as the *nakomse*, or holders of the political authority (the *nam*). Their subjects, the conquered indigenous peoples, are called *tegbisi*, or 'sons of the land'. Their headmen still hold the office of *tegsoba* ('master of the land') and are responsible for the ritual relationship with the land. The peoples conquered by the *nakomse* were of two main groups: peoples speaking Voltaic languages (who were akin to those who came under the domination of the Mamprusi and the Dagomba), and peoples speaking dialects of the southern Mande sub-family. The latter, whose political organization was based on village communities, offered greater resistance to the *nakomse* than did the Voltaic people, with their segmentary system.

Naba Rawa, Widraogo's son, led his warriors northwards as far as the Bandiagara cliffs. It was an expansionist thrust which was not yet accompanied by the creation of a stable political structure. It was probably about that time, between the 1430s and the 1480s, that the Mossi raided the middle Niger, as recorded by the *Ta'rīkhs* of Timbuktu. In their expansionist mood the Mossi were lured by the political vacuum in that region following the decline of Mali. In 1483 Sonni 'Alī defeated the Mossi warriors and drove them away from the middle Niger.[1] The jihad of Askiya Muḥammad in 1498 was probably directed against the successors of Naba Rawa in the northern chiefdom of Zandoma. Zandoma was later integrated into the Mossi kingdom of Yatenga.

It was only in the third generation after Widraogo that the *nakomse* established their authority over the central part of their kingdom. Naba Wubri was a son of Zungrana (son of Widraogo) from a wife given to him by the Nyonyose, the indigenous people. Naba Wubri represents the alliance between *nakomse* and *nyonyose*, and the transformation of the *nakomse* from war chiefs to sovereigns who rule with the consent of their subjects. Gradually, Naba Wubri and his successors extended their authority over dispersed *nakomse* chiefdoms, which had been created during the first phase of the Mossi expansion. They were recognized as overall rulers or *moro nabas*.

Sometime in the first half of the sixteenth century, the succession of Naba Kundumie, grandson of Naba Wubri, was contested by his brother Yedega, who ran away with the official regalia. Naba Kundumie failed in his attempt to prevent the breakaway of Yedega. The latter, in possession of the regalia of Widraogo, imposed his authority over the *nakomse* of the north, who before had been independent of the *moro naba*. By the end of the sixteenth century Mossi was divided into two states: that of Wagadugu under the *moro naba* and that of Yatenga under Yedega's descendants. Each state had a central core of chiefdoms which were more directly controlled by the paramount and peripheral chiefdoms, which, though they recognized the sovereignty of their paramount, were virtually independent.

In the process of the conquest the *nakomse* integrated as subjects some of the indigenous peoples (the Nyonyose in the south and the Kurumba in the north). Other peoples evaded the rule of the *nakomse* by either retreating to the shelter of the cliffs of Bandiagara – as did the Dogon – or by fierce resistance – as did the Samo. The Dogon and the Samo formed a kind of '*cordon sanitaire*' between the Mossi states and the middle Niger.

[1] The best analysis of Mossi history is M. Izard, *Introduction à l'histoire des royaumes Mossi* (Paris, 1970). His hypothesis about the proto-Mossi to explain the origins of the Mossi kingdoms and the Mossi eruption to the middle Niger is not convincing.

CHAPTER 6

UPPER AND LOWER GUINEA

PROLEGOMENA AND ORIENTATIONS

The sources available for the history of Guinea before the seventeenth century are not good. The Arabic writers whose works enable historians with some confidence to reconstruct the main political outlines of the West African Sudan from about the eleventh century onwards, and even to gain some insight into aspects of its economic and social history, were in general uninformed about developments further south. Literacy in Arabic did spread to some of the peoples of Guinea, but it did not do so significantly before about the seventeenth century, and there are few if any surviving documents of historical value whose origins relate to earlier than the eighteenth century. With the advent of European traders to the Guinea coasts in the fifteenth century, a considerable corpus of documentation in European languages did begin to build up. But centuries were to pass before Europeans began to penetrate significantly into the interior. Their direct knowledge, and that of the Africans who acquired literary skills from them, was therefore confined to the coastlands. Even here there must have been much which escaped their notice, and even more that was at best imperfectly understood, while what they had to say about what was going on further than a few miles from the coast was essentially hearsay.

Some of the historical traditions maintained orally by the peoples of Guinea themselves certainly relate to times before 1600. In lower Guinea, for example, there are some traditions, such as those of the Yoruba, the Edo of Benin, and the Akan, which have something to say about events which may have occurred as far back as the thirteenth century – in extreme cases, perhaps even to as far as about the eleventh century. But traditions with this sort of time-depth are in general characteristic only of a minority of Guinean peoples, those who were early to develop sophisticated political institutions, and who were able to maintain them more or less intact into modern times. But their politicization, and therefore their need of history and their use of it, were not static. Thus, during the 700 or so years in which it may be supposed that the Yoruba, the Edo and the Akan have maintained a sense of their political identity, it is known that new dynasties have arisen, new states and kingdoms have been created. Much of their earlier history, if not altogether forgotten, thus became less relevant to current political reality. What was retained was cast into heroic and mythical terms designed to meet the needs of later rulers. Thus the mainstream of Yoruba tradition as it is known today is the tradition of the kingdom of Oyo, a kingdom which before its seventeenth- and eighteenth-century rise to predominance seems likely to have been only of peripheral significance in Yoruba history. Similarly, Akan traditions today are dominated by those of the Asante, whose kingdom, by their own account, was a new creation of the seventeenth century.

The historicity and, still more, the chronology of the earliest surviving stages of the historical traditions of the Guinean peoples are necessarily difficult to ascertain in the absence of independent corroborative data. Some historians have therefore concluded that they are not the stuff of which history can be made. But it is not impossible to find supporting evidence in, for example, sociological, cultural and linguistic data. It is probably true to say, for example, that the historical traditions of the Yoruba need to be viewed in conjunction with the vast mass of information comprised in less overtly historical kinds of oral literature, such as the Yoruba *oriki* or Ifa divination poems. Certainly the *kple* and *klama* songs that survive among the Ga and Adangbe of the south-east of modern Ghana, and some of the traditional formal dances of Ife (which historical tradition asserts was the place where Yoruba monarchy was first developed), throw light on the past of the Akan and the Yoruba, respectively, which seem scarcely to have been recorded by the specifically historical traditions.[1]

But the exploration of oral literature, dance forms or linguistic evidence in search of historical information is something which is still in its infancy (and also something which few historians can embark on with any confidence without expert assistance). Moreover, the results are likely more to compound than to clarify the questions on which the historian is seeking enlightenment. The historicity and the dating of evidence from these kinds of sources, which are not themselves overtly historical in intention, are likely to be even more difficult to establish than are those of purportedly historical traditions. In these circum-

[1] Some idea of what may be involved here may be gathered from the chapters on the Ifa cult by W. Abimbola, on *Oriki* by Chief J. A. Ayorinde, on proverbs, songs and dances by Chief I. O. Delano, and on ceremonies by O. Ogunba, in *Sources of Yoruba history*, ed. S. O. Biobaku (Oxford, 1973). For *kple* and *klama* see the chapter by J. H. Nketia in *The historian in tropical Africa*, ed. J. Vansina, R. Mauny and L. V. Thomas (London, International African Institute, 1964).

stances, and in default of written evidence, the obvious recourse of the historian seeking corroboration for or explanation of the surviving historical traditions of the Guinean peoples must be to the evidence of archaeology. At present, however, archaeology does not give very much help to the historian concerned with the history of Guinea from the eleventh to the sixteenth centuries.

Apart from a handful of pioneer excavations, the application of scientific archaeology to the exploration of the Guinean past is a very recent development, essentially one of the last two decades. The number of professional archaeologists in the field is small – hardly one-tenth the number of trained historians. They are very unevenly distributed; while, for example, there have been some impressive excavations in the Guinea zones of Nigeria and Ghana, Liberia and the Ivory Coast have hardly been subjected even to exploration by archaeologists. The high forest and the high annual rainfall impede systematic archaeological exploration and pose any number of practical and methodological problems for the excavator. Above all, it must be recognized that the relatively recent period from the eleventh century AD onwards is not the one which most naturally interests those archaeologists who are attracted to West Africa. The most challenging problems for archaeologists in West Africa – and, by and large, their most significant achievements – relate to very much earlier times. Despite all the pressures brought to bear by historians on their archaeological colleagues, this balance is unlikely to be significantly altered, nor indeed is there any reason why it should be.

Nevertheless, where archaeologists have addressed themselves to problems relevant to the period of Guinean history covered in this chapter, the results have uniformly been in one direction. The excavations that have been undertaken in recent years in the southern regions of Nigeria and of modern Ghana – for example by Willett and others at Ife, by Connah at Benin, by Willett at Old Oyo, by Thurstan Shaw at Igbo-Ukwu, and by Posnansky and his colleagues at Begho – have done nothing to deny the evidence of extant historical traditions. If anything, they have tended to confirm their general indications, and to suggest, moreover, that the historians and anthropologists who have worked on these traditions in the past have inclined to be conservative in their assessments of their time-depths.

Whether future archaeological work will substantiate this conclusion, based as it is on a very small number of sites, most of which were already known to be of critical importance in the historical period, and whether it will apply outside the rather small areas in southern Nigeria and southern Ghana where the relevant work has been done, of course, remain open questions. But a similar conclusion might also be reached from the results which have so far been published of the excavations undertaken by Filipowiak and others at Niani in the Republic of Guinea. These are taken as relating to a kingdom, ancient Mali, which historians think of as 'Sudanic' rather than as 'Guinean'. But they do relate to the period in question, and if the geographical context of lower Guinea can be stretched to as far as Old Oyo, perhaps Niani, little further from the sea than the site of Old Oyo, can equally be thought to be relevant to upper Guinea.

For the time being, at least, it would seem to be an implication from the available archaeological evidence that historians should not discount the earlier traditions of the Guinean peoples on the grounds that their historicity cannot be established or that they imply unreasonably long time-scales. Obviously it is important to maintain an open mind on these traditions where they are not reinforced by any other kind of evidence. But where such evidence is lacking, and especially where the later stages of tradition are not contradicted by the European documentation as it becomes available, it would seem foolish not to work on the assumption that the earlier stages of the Guinean traditions are in fact attempts, in whatever fashion, to express historical realities of some kind.

If this is the working assumption, the historian is then faced with the fact – and it is a fact, whatever interpretation may be placed on it – that the earliest stages of historical traditions among Guinean peoples are commonly concerned with a claim that the founding ancestors were immigrants, usually indeed coming to their present homeland from somewhere further in the interior.

In recent years, many historians have been sceptical of this concept, deservedly so perhaps in view of the uncritical use made of it by some writers who were not originally trained as historians: Meyerowitz and Lucas, for example, have elaborated schemes which trace the ancestry of the Akan and the Yoruba, respectively, back to the shores of the Mediterranean.[1] In fact it is hardly a matter of dispute that all the peoples of the Guinea zone today belong essentially to one Negro stock which is autochthonous to western Africa. On the other hand, it is clear enough that in Africa – as elsewhere in the world – early man was a creature of the savannas rather than of the forests. It was in the

[1] E. L. R. Meyerowitz, *The Akan of Ghana: their ancient beliefs* (London, 1958), esp. Introduction and ch. 6, and her *The divine kingship in Ghana and ancient Egypt* (London, 1960); J. O. Lucas, *The religion of the Yorubas* (Lagos, 1948).

savannas that he developed cereal agriculture and animal husbandry, and so provided himself with the base from which his stock could multiply and could evolve ever more sophisticated forms of society. But much of the Guinean landscape was covered – as it is still – by dense rain forest that provided a frighteningly difficult environment for pre-industrial human society. Even hunting–gathering societies could not develop as they did on the savannas, for the forest contained little large game. For much the same reasons, lack of grazing and the presence of tsetse, animal husbandry could not become a basic means of subsistence, and the use of animals for transport was also ruled out. The close-packed forest trees and creepers made any kind of communication difficult away from the rivers. The conditions made it impossible to cultivate the staple millets and other grain crops of the Sudan and, other than some species of African yams, which were laborious to cultivate, and which in any case were more suited to the forest fringes than to the forestlands themselves, there were few alternative starchy staples before the introduction of cultigens of south-east Asian or of American origin, such as cocoyam and plantains, cassava and maize. Despite some who would argue to the contrary, it is improbable that the latter were available in West Africa before the sixteenth century. The date of the arrival of south-east Asian foodcrops is much more open, but if, as seems likely, their acceptance in East Africa is to be associated with an Indonesian colonization of Madagascar between about the fourth and the eighth centuries, then it would seem reasonable to suppose that it was probably only about the beginning of the period covered in the present chapter that they might have begun to be significant for farmers on the western side of the continent.

There is archaeological evidence to show that the problems of coping with the forest environment were not so great that it was ever totally uninhabited. Indeed, one of the earliest known skeletons of the Negro type, dated to about 9000 BC, comes from a site in the forest zone of West Africa, at Iwo Eleru in south-western Nigeria. But it seems obvious that the conditions of life in the forest must have handicapped the development of human society there compared with what was possible in the Sudanic savannas. The food-producing revolution, the evolution of metal-using and other advanced technologies, the growth of organized trade and states, must all have begun earlier and proceeded faster in the Sudan than they did in the Guinea forestlands. With the resultant increase in the Sudanic population, and with its more advanced technologies and economic and political organization, the peoples of the Sudan would have developed both a need to expand into the forest, and there to explore and exploit such resources as it might offer, and the means with which to do these things. It seems likely then that there would have been a general tendency for people from the Sudan to move towards and into the Guinea forests from about the time that the south-east Asian food crops became available, and as soon as they possessed adequate modes of economic and political organization. It has already been suggested that the south-east Asian crops are likely to have reached West Africa by about AD 1000, and by about this time also it is known from the Arabic accounts of kingdoms such as ancient Ghana and Kanem that the Sudanic peoples had made substantial advances in political and economic mobilization. There is thus reason to believe that there is some substance in the Guinean traditions of migrations from the north which resulted in the foundation of their kingdoms.

It is unlikely, however, that these migrations were invariably the mass movements of whole peoples that they are commonly presented to be, either in the traditions themselves or in some of the interpretations placed upon them. As the forest was opened up by the new crops and technologies, so there may have been some general drift of population in West Africa from north to south. But in general it would seem that the first pioneers of economic and political development in the forestlands would have been small parties of enterprising traders or political adventurers (or, perhaps, refugees from political turmoils in the Sudanic states). These would have settled among the original forest dwellers, developed their production and trade, married their women and adopted their languages. The forest communities would in consequence have increased in size and in their social stratification, and would either have themselves begun to organize monarchical governments and trading systems on the Sudanic model, or would have been subjected to such organization by the immigrants. The earliest Guinean traditions rarely provide unequivocal evidence that this is what actually did happen, presumably because in most cases the beginnings of the process are chronologically very remote indeed. There is, for example, archaeological evidence from Ife which suggests that urbanization among the Yoruba – and presumably, therefore, the relevant economic and political sophistication – goes back to at least the eleventh century. But, as will be seen, early Akan traditions can certainly be interpreted in accordance with this model, and there seem to be two adequately attested examples of its operation on the chronological or geographical fringes of the subject matter of this chapter. Thus the kingdom of Gonja (in central modern Ghana) emerged in the sixteenth and seventeenth centuries following upon, first, the settlement of Sudanic traders in the area, and, secondly, the arrival of soldiers from the Sudan. North of Gonja, in the southern Sudan, the creation of the various Mossi-Dagomba kingdoms during the fourteenth and fifteenth centuries may be attributed clearly enough to the arrival of conquering immigrants from the east or north-east.

The migrations remembered in the Guinean traditions of origins really need to be considered and interpreted in relation to three factors: the known historical patterns in the western and central Sudan from about AD 1000 onwards; the possible motives for exploration and exploitation of the forestlands by Sudanic traders and adventurers; and the actual geographical and climatological conditions in Guinea – for hitherto no more has been said about these than that much of its landscape was and is covered by dense rain forest.

The early Arabic accounts suggest that there were two main foci for political and economic growth in the West African Sudan, one among the Mande-speaking peoples of the western Sudan, and the other among the peoples speaking Nilo-Saharan languages, such as the Kanuri, or Afro-Asiatic languages, such as the Hausa, to the north and west of Lake Chad. In the first of these areas, ancient Ghana was in full tide by the tenth and eleventh centuries, and its political and commercial traditions were maintained without significant interruption (though with some shift towards the south and east) in the subsequent empires of ancient Mali and of the Songhay. In the second area, the political strength of the kingdom of Kanem was evident from about the eleventh century and reached a peak about the thirteenth century. It is not clear from the evidence whether it ever developed a commercial interest to match that of the western Sudanic states, especially in trade towards the south (as opposed to trade northwards across the Sahara). But by about the fifteenth century, when the Kanem monarchy had retreated southwards into Bornu, its Hausa neighbours in the south-west had developed smaller kingdoms which were to evince a lively interest in the commercial exploration of lands even further to the south and west. In both foci, therefore, the political organization and strength needed to promote adventures into Guinea were in evidence from about the eleventh century onwards. In the western Sudan, the necessary economic motivation and organization for southern ventures were also early in evidence.

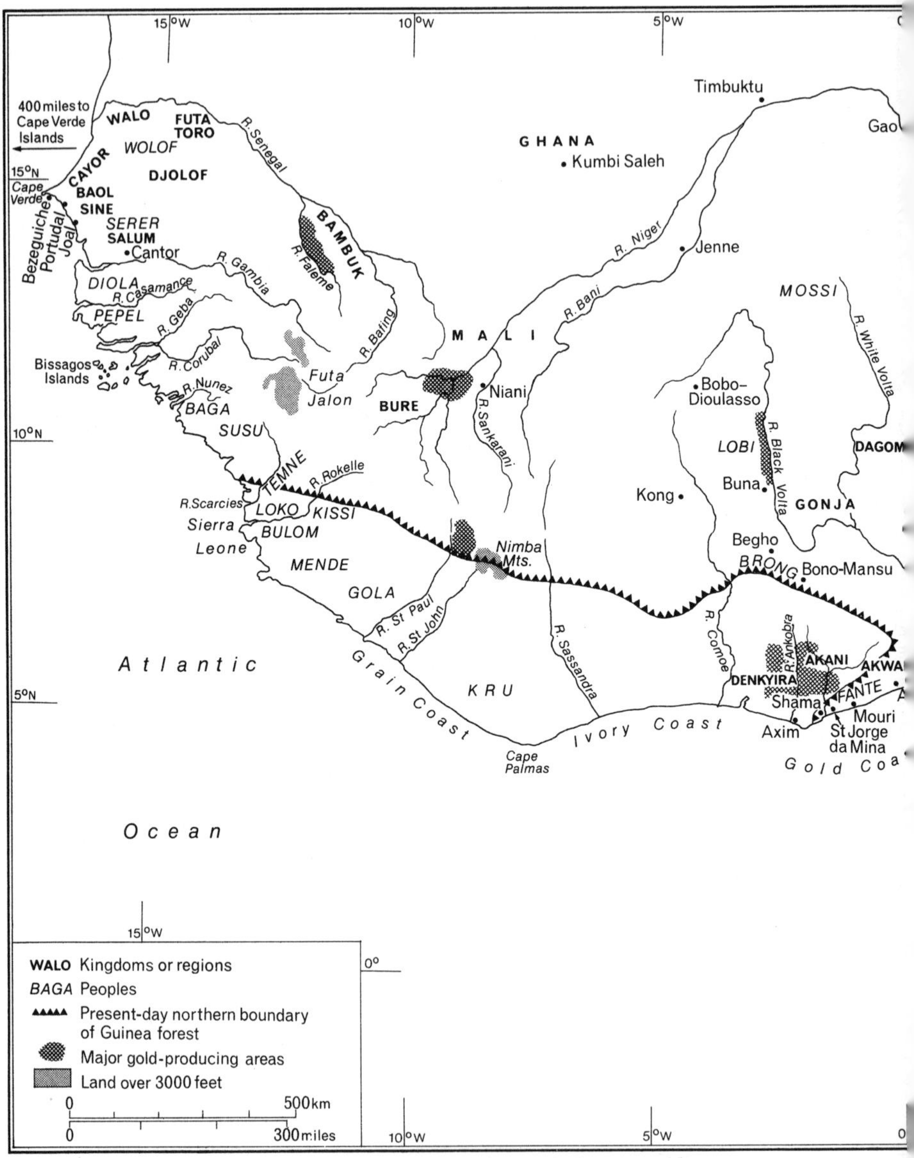

11 Upper and Lower Guinea

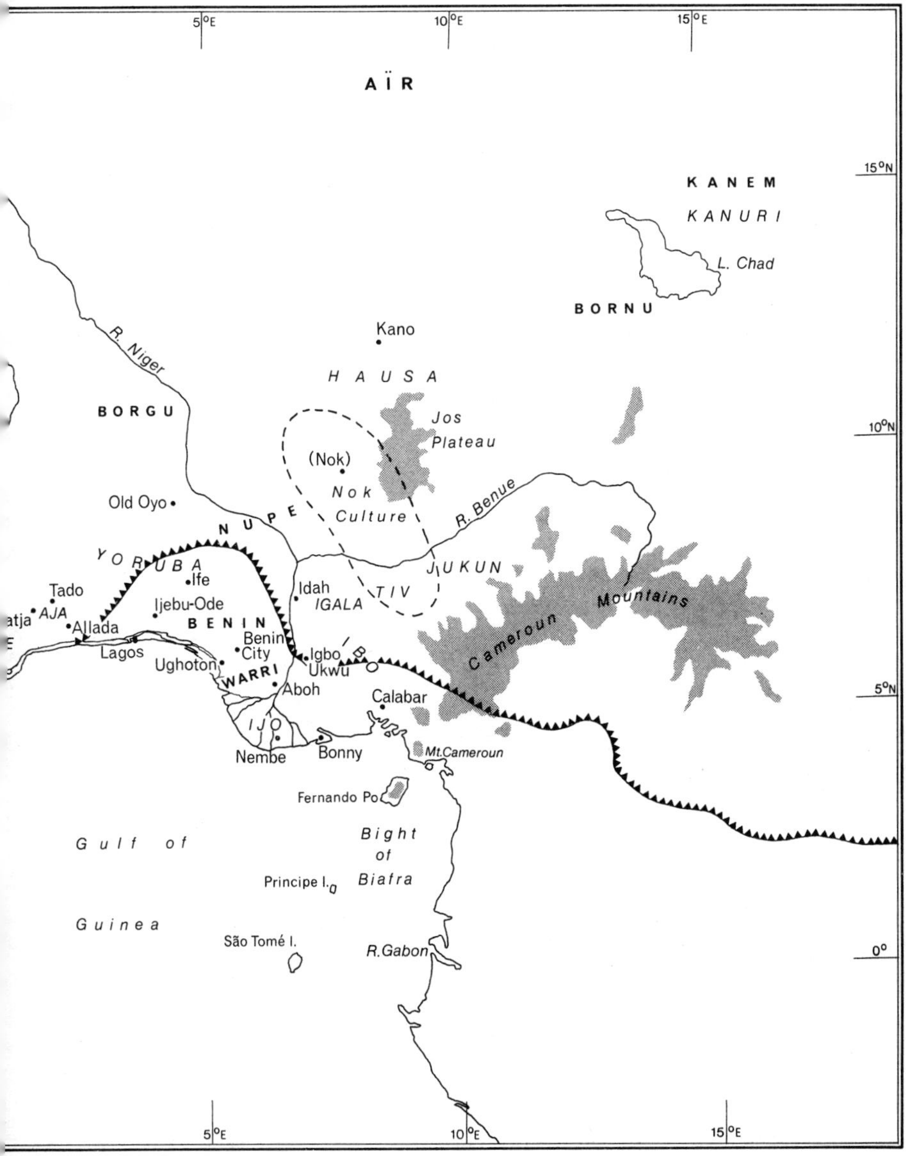
5°E
10°E
15°E
AÏR
15°N
KANEM
KANURI
L. Chad
BORNU
Kano
R. Niger
HAUSA
BORGU
Jos Plateau
10°N
(Nok)
Nok Culture
Old Oyo
NUPE
R. Benue
YORUBA
Ife
Tado
AJA
Allada
Ijebu-Ode
BENIN
Idah
IGALA
TIV
JUKUN
Cameroun Mountains
Benin City
Lagos
Ughoton
WARRI
Igbo Ukwu
IBO
Aboh
Calabar
5°N
IJO
Nembe
Bonny
Mt.Cameroun
Fernando Po
Gulf of Guinea
Bight of Biafra
Principe I.
São Tomé I.
R.Gabon
0°

It is thus possible to project into Guinea much the same sort of framework that is commonly used for writing the history of the West African Sudan. It may be suggested that the Guinean peoples were subjected to two distinct streams of influences from the north, stemming respectively from the Mande centres of political and economic power in the north-west and from the Kanuri/Hausa centres in the north-east, in the latter of which economic mobilization may have lagged behind the development of political power. As far as the influences from the north-west are concerned, there is evidence both from the Sudan and from Guinea of the importance of economic motives for expansion towards the south. Ghana, Mali and Songhay were all states which strove to profit from the control of trade between West Africa and the Sahara and North Africa. A number of commodities featured prominently in this trade: from the north, West Africa received brass and copper, cloth and spices, manufactured goods and horses, and Saharan salt; and in return it exported gold, slaves, skins and leather, and ivory. But the lucrative heart of the trade was the exchange of gold and salt. Originally the main sources of gold were the alluvial deposits of Bambuk and Bure in the Mande-occupied valleys of the upper Senegal and Niger rivers. But the Mediterranean world's demand for gold was continually increasing, while the demand for salt in West Africa was practically insatiable: there were few good sources of it anywhere away from the coasts, while it was readily obtainable from old lake beds at a number of points in the Sahara. Thus as a specifically Mande merchant class, the Dyula or Wangara, began to evolve, its members must naturally have begun to venture further afield in search of new sources of gold which might be secured in exchange for the salt and other goods they received from the north.

In this way Dyula merchants came to the gold fields of the Lobi country astride the upper Black Volta valley, and then were led beyond these to the richest gold deposits in all West Africa, in the forestlands of the territories later to be known as Ashanti and the Gold Coast. Trade routes thus developed which also served for a general exchange of the produce of the Sudan, and of the more northerly lands with which it traded, for the very different products of the forests. Commercially the most important of these seems to have been the kola nut. *Cola nitida* was native to the forests from Ashanti to Liberia, and provided a variety of nut which was highly valued in the Sudan and which could also to some extent be exported across the Sahara.

Gold and kola thus provided good motives for commercial expansion into Guinea from the major states and empires of the western Sudan. There is evidence that by about the beginning of the thirteenth century, if not earlier, some Mande merchants were establishing themselves in or alongside the major Guinean settlements reached by this trade, and through these Mande colonies all kinds of influences – political, religious and cultural as well as economic – could flow to the Guinean peoples. There is no comparably attested evidence for commercial expansion towards the south from the other main focus of Sudanic development in the central Sudan before the rise of the Hausa trading network. Large-scale and long-distance Hausa trading would seem to be a relatively late development, sparked off – as was major Akan economic activity – by the arrival of Mande merchants. The evidence of the Kano Chronicle suggests that Wangarawa may have first reached Hausaland about the middle of the fourteenth century. But their commercial (and islamizing) influence there may not have been very significant until the middle of the following century, and the same source suggests that the opening of what was to become one of the major trade-routes for Hausa merchants, to Gonja for kola, may also have been about the middle of the fifteenth century.[1]

Thus the development by Hausa traders from the central Sudan of a trading network reaching to eastern or lower Guinea seems likely to have taken place at least two hundred years later than the development of its prototype by Mande traders in the west. There is, however, some suggestion that there may have been an earlier stage or stages of central Sudanic influences reaching into eastern Guinea. As will be seen, the evidence for this, such as it is, is defined essentially by legends such as those of Kisra, and these suggest that such influences had a political or military, rather than an economic, complexion. If so, their starting point can hardly have been Hausaland, for it seems likely that the effective development of the small Hausa kingdoms was more or less contemporary with the commercial expansion which has already been discussed. Conceivably the source could have been the so-called So (or Sao) civilization based on the plains immediately south of Lake Chad and in the lower valleys of the rivers, such as the Chari, which flow into the lake.

Archaeological work here has perhaps produced as many questions as it has answers. It is clear, however, that human development was at once encouraged and restricted by the heavy black clay soils of the

[1] The Kano Chronicle references may be found in the translation by H. R. Palmer, *Sudanese Memoirs* (reprinted London, 1967), 104, 109, 111.

region which, during the rainy season, are at once unusually productive and also virtually impassable. Farming peoples therefore concentrated their settlements on occasional low eminences rising above the plain, which in course of time developed into the habitation mounds which archaeologists call *tells*. Radiocarbon dates for the So mounds excavated by J.-P. Lebeuf in the lower Chari valley suggest that for the most part these were occupied between about AD 500 and 1300; these mounds have revealed an impressive assemblage of terracotta figurines of men, horsemen and cattle, and of ornaments of stone, copper and brass. Similar mounds further to the west that have been excavated by Graham Connah, especially that at Daima, have provided evidence of continuous habitation from Stone Age times (about 500 BC), with metal, in the form of iron, first appearing about a thousand years later, onwards to about AD 1000.

Whether such a culture or cultures could have provided a starting point for politico-military movements of the kind indicated by the Kisra legend is clearly very much an open question. The terminal dates for the So culture explored by Lebeuf would seem to fit with the movement of the kingdom of Kanem into Bornu and the region south of Lake Chad, and this could have had repercussions further south, perhaps by way of the Benue valley. But, of course, this could not have been earlier than about AD 1300, and there is some evidence that there must have been at least some *trading* connection between the central Sudan and eastern Guinea long before this, especially if the radiocarbon dates obtained by Thurstan Shaw for his remarkable discoveries at Igbo-Ukwu prove to be acceptable in the light of subsequent finds.[1]

At Igbo-Ukwu, to the south-east of Onitsha in eastern Nigeria, in the country of the Ibo, who provide almost a paradigm of stateless society, Shaw's excavations revealed a marvellous assembly of elaborate and beautiful copper and bronze work, pottery, beads, textiles and objects made of wood and ivory. Part of this seems to have been deliberately hidden away, but part was certainly associated with the interment of a man who must have been a priest-king of some magnitude. Four out of five associated radiocarbon measurements gave dates approximating to the ninth century AD. The inference is therefore that ninth-century Iboland had already evolved a high degree of economic and craft specialization, and also that it must have been in trading contact with

[1] T. Shaw, *Igbo-Ukwu* (London, 1970); for discussion on the dating and its implications, see, for example, D. Northrup, 'The growth of trade among the Igbo before 1800', *Journal of African History*, 1972, **13**, 2, 217–36, and B. Lawal, 'Dating problems at Igbo-Ukwu', ibid. 1973, **14**, 1, 1–8.

the outside world. Shaw thinks that many of the beads were imports, while the metal for the copper and bronze work must certainly have been imported, for, leaving out of account the questions of where and how the bronze alloys (for the most part of copper and lead) were made, or how the *cire-perdue* casting technique may have come to Igbo-Ukwu, the plain fact is that the nearest possible source of copper ore is many hundreds of miles away. (Shaw himself only considered possible sources to the north, the nearest of which would have been in Aïr, about 1,125 kilometres north of Igbo-Ukwu. But there would also be possible sources of copper to the south, in the Congo, the nearest being little further away than Aïr.) If the ninth-century date is accepted, it is therefore necessary to think of the people of Igbo-Ukwu at this early period as being in contact with some kind of trading system extending at least 1,125 kilometres. Furthermore, if there were trade over such a distance, it would be reasonable to suppose that there may also have been more local commercial activity, no doubt based on the exchange of salt and other produce, such as fish, from the Niger delta region (which certainly had a lively commercial life, including the use of currency, when Europeans arrived there in the sixteenth century) for the produce of cultivable lands further north.

The problem of the source of Igbo-Ukwu's metals, and of its commercial implications, is not new. A considerable corpus of magnificent bronze or brass sculpture and ornaments, often made by the *cire-perdue* process, but in a style and tradition which differ somewhat from those which seem to have operated at Igbo-Ukwu, has long been associated with a wide area of modern Nigeria further to the west, with particular centres at Ife and Benin, and north-eastwards towards the Niger and Benue valleys and the Bauchi plateau. It is generally accepted that this art, together with work of comparable excellence in terracotta and ivory and, doubtless also, wood, was a product of the court life of the peoples of this extensive region, the Yoruba and their neighbours in Benin, Nupe and Igala country, which was centred around their supposedly divine monarchs. It is also now generally accepted that its style was in all probability derived from the art of the Nok culture which flourished in the Bauchi–Benue region between about 900 BC and AD 200. But relatively little of this art has been found in archaeological contexts, and its dating was for long a very open question. There was in fact very little chronological evidence of any kind beyond Yoruba and Benin traditions that the latter's royal dynasty was an offshoot from the monarchy of Ife, and the Benin tradition that the art of brass-casting by the *cire-perdue* process was introduced from Ife to Benin during the reign of its fifth king, who was thought to have lived about the later thirteenth century. However, recent excavations at both Ife and Benin show that such a dating is by no means improbable. Ife was existing on its present site, and certainly producing terracottas, by the tenth or the eleventh century, and excavations at the site at Ife to which the heads of Benin kings were traditionally sent to be buried have provided two radiocarbon dates of which the later is approximately tenth century. Similarly excavations at Benin giving material suitable for radiocarbon dating indicate that this city was already flourishing by about AD 1200–1300.

It is therefore not unreasonable to suppose that the court arts of casting sculpture in copper and its alloys may have been quite widely spread throughout the southern half of modern Nigeria by about the ninth century, the time suggested by the Igbo-Ukwu radiocarbon dates. Thus the whole of this region must have had trading contact with the outside world by this time, as otherwise the craftsmen at the courts would not have been able to secure their metal. However, there is much to suggest that copper and its alloys were originally rare and expensive metals, perhaps equivalent to gold in other contexts. Only great potentates – divine kings or priest-kings – could afford to commission work in them, and brass-workers remained closely associated with courts until recent times. At Ife, supplies of metal seem at first to have been so scarce that the casts were often made with thicknesses of metal that European bronze-casters would have regarded as impossibly thin. (This, incidentally, is a considerable tribute to the technical skill of the Ife casters.) Regular supplies of copper and its alloys on any scale seem only to have begun with the coming of European sea trade to Benin at the end of the fifteenth century; the quantity of relatively late Benin castings, which are generally very much thicker, is considerably greater than the work associated with the earlier period centred on Ife.

Both in Yorubaland and at Benin, strong monarchical governments were maintained into the nineteenth century, and a monarchical tradition of very similar type was also characteristic of the Nupe and Igala (already mentioned in connection with the distribution of bronze art), and also of the Jukun (or Kwararafa), further to the north-east in the Benue valley, and of the Borgawa (or Bariba) further to the north-west. The latter two peoples, of course, were close neighbours of the Sudanic kingdoms which developed in Kanem, Bornu and Hausaland from about the eleventh century onwards. There seems no reason to doubt the Benin and Yoruba traditions that the centralized monarchy of Benin resulted from the arrival of a Yoruba prince, Oranyan, and his interaction with existing Benin society, possibly with a number of competing smaller monarchies. Ife, from which the new Benin dynasty was founded, is traditionally the centre from which all the Yoruba kingdoms were also derived, possibly by not dissimilar processes. Some surviving Yoruba traditions of origin are creation myths, but others assert that their monarchical system was the work of immigrants from the north, who were also associated with the foundation of the Hausa and Kanem kingdoms. The same concept can be found in the Kisra legend found among the Nupe, Igala, Jukun and Borgawa. In other words, the centralized monarchies of central and western Nigeria tend to link their origins with the emergence of organized monarchy in the central Sudan. In so far as the legends indicate any date for this, it is done by reference to known events in the history of the Nile Valley and the Red Sea area in the seventh century, specifically the Persian conquest of Egypt in 616 in the reign of the Sasanid king Chosroes II (Kosrau in Persian, i.e. Kisra) and the rise of Muḥammad in the Hejaz in 622–30.

Such chronological references are very likely, of course, to have been imported with the expansion of Islam in Nigeria following the Fulani jihad of the early years of the nineteenth century. On the other hand, it should be noted that the Kisra legend, especially in Borgu, is maintained in a pagan folk-culture which does not meet with the approval of Muslim society. It is certainly permissible to believe that the centralized monarchies of central and western Nigeria did result from interaction between their autochthonous peoples and emigrants from the north or north-east from at least Hausaland and Bornu, where similar state-forming processes were beginning about the tenth and eleventh centuries. However, there are few clues as to what the motive and nature of the emigration might have been, or as to the nature of the interaction with the recipient local peoples. On the whole, as has been said, the traditions seem to suggest that the process had a political or military rather than a commercial flavour. The immigrants are presented as horsemen – even in Benin, a country in which horses can hardly live, but where the king and aristocracy commonly paraded in public on horseback. This leads to the inference that they were conquerors, and this was certainly the case with the founders of the Mossi-Dagomba states, which are the western neighbours of the Borgawa, and which were probably formed by the same movement as led to the emergence of the

Borgu kingdoms. They also tend to be presented, for example in Yorubaland, as the founders of the towns which here, as in Hausaland, are the vital centres of the kingdoms and are walled, which suggests that they could either have begun as the encampments of the invaders or as the refuges of the invaded. (Some major nineteenth-century urban foundations certainly began in these ways, for example, Ibadan as an invaders' camp and Abeokuta as a place of refuge.)

In all probability the legends are providing simplistic rationalizations for a complicated process – or series of processes; there is no reason to suppose that formative influences from the north were felt only once – which may well have extended over many centuries, and of which the earlier stages may have been completely overlaid by later developments. The military and creative political roles of the incomers from the north, which seem to be stressed in the legends of origin, were probably only one aspect of the process of political and economic centralization. The evidence of the Nok culture suggests that the autochthonous peoples may already have reached a considerable degree of sophistication in many aspects of life, and the subsequent high degree of wealth and sophistication in the organized society of Yorubaland and Benin – as well as the evidence from the excavations at Igbo-Ukwu, in an area which subsequently had little centralized political authority – suggest too that growing trading connections with the outside world must also have been significant.

But this concept of backward forest peoples having their social development fertilized and accelerated by influences stemming from the more fortunate inhabitants of the Sudanic savannas should now be tempered by the observation that not all Guinea is covered by dense rain-forest inimical to human progress. The position today is that there is really no dense forest in the Guinea coastlands north of Conakry, and that eastwards from about longitude 2° W (which runs through the middle of modern Ghana) and westwards from about longitude 5° E (about half-way between Benin and Ibadan), the width of the forest begins to taper, and there is a total gap in it between about longitudes 0° and 3° E, a distance of approximately 320 kilometres. A thousand years ago, when agriculture was still essentially a savanna-bound practice, the area of thick forest may well have been more extensive than this, perhaps reaching to as far as about 10° N, i.e. up to approximately 160 kilometres further north than it now does. Even so, the savannas of the Sudan would still have extended to the coast from somewhere not very far north of modern Conakry. However, north of about the present limits of the forest generally, and also between about the middle of modern Ghana and easternmost Dahomey in particular, annual rainfall, relative humidity and the length of the dry season are such that the forest could not regenerate itself if subjected to the activities of a growing population of farmers. Thus not only was the forest gradually eroded along the whole length of its northern frontier (thus incidentally increasing the area of the upper Guinea coastlands which was open to the Sudan), but a significant wedge would also have been opened into it in the centre through which Sudanic influences could penetrate to the Guinea peoples.

Thus, while the area corresponding to modern Liberia and the western Ivory Coast remained thickly forested, and to this day is very thinly peopled, the region from southern modern Ghana eastwards into Nigeria, which is also penetrated by the two major waterways of lower Guinea, the Niger and the Volta, became the scene of lively political and economic developments and is today one of the most densely populated in all West Africa. The waterways must already have facilitated communication in this region; the expansion of the savanna, with the possibilities that were thus opened up for the use of horses for military purposes and of donkeys for the carriage of goods, made possible a universal widening of economic, social and political horizons. Indeed, the common concept of the Akan and Yoruba kingdoms as 'forest states' rather than 'savanna states' needs some modification. It is true that the main centres of Akan power, above all the Asante kingdom of the eighteenth and nineteenth centuries, did come to be centred in the forest lands. But the first major Akan political and commercial centres, such as Bono and Banda, were either in the savannas just north of the forest or in the northern fringes of the forest itself. Ife, the traditional first centre of Yoruba authority and development, is in the forest, but it is very close to its northern limits, and the dominant Yoruba power of the seventeenth and eighteenth centuries, Oyo, had its capital (Old Oyo, or Katunga) in the savannas not far from the Niger.

The point here seems to be twofold. The Togo–Dahomey gap in the forest provided a rich ground for agricultural experimentation and adaptation (some authorities think that it was here that the West African yams were domesticated and developed), and so for population growth leading to increased pressure to prospect in the forest, to settle and clear it, and to exploit its products. It also, as has just been remarked, became a zone which was not only very open to influences from the Sudan, but also one in which there could be a free flow and mixing of the Guinean peoples, their economies and their ideas. On the other hand, however, there was still a forest–savanna boundary, and a longer and more open and traversable one than probably anywhere else in West Africa. Thus there would be more fruitful opportunities here than elsewhere for the exploitation of this boundary, for example for the interchange of forest and savanna produce, and for the exchange and mixing of ideas between the Sudanese and Guinean peoples. This region therefore became a powerhouse for all kinds of experimentation and purposeful development, a powerhouse too in which currents from the Sudan could both generate and flow together with indigenous Guinean currents, thus producing a quite remarkable potential.

It is probably best to attempt to reconstruct the history of the Guinean peoples in the period from the eleventh to the sixteenth centuries in two stages, divided by the arrival by sea on the West African coasts of European explorers, traders and missionaries. This is not primarily because the advent of the Europeans immediately brought about a very sudden or significant change in Guinean history. They settled at only a few selected points on the coast, and on the coast only, and even here their political and economic strength tended not to be significantly greater than that of the local African communities. Thus their direct influence on the course of events even a few miles away from the coast remained slight until the seventeenth century, when the development of an insatiable demand for African slaves to meet the labour needs of their plantations in the Americas began to generate pressures which led in some areas to a considerable transformation of Guinean society. However, there are two reasons why the coming of the Europeans is significant. It meant that for the first time it was possible for at least some Guinean peoples to have dealings with the outside world which were not filtered through the peoples of the Sudan and the Sahara. Secondly, the presence of the Europeans on the coast meant the beginning of the production of contemporary documentary evidence for the history of Guinea. It is true that the amount of contemporary documentation before the seventeenth century is slight, and that it bears directly on only a few relatively small areas of coastland. But at least from the time of the coming of the first Europeans onwards, the historian is not totally dependent on speculative reconstructions from oral traditions and their reconciliation with fragmentary archaeological evidence, and above all he has material with which to begin to construct an objective chronology.

However, the coming of the Europeans was itself something of a fragmentary process. It began with Diniz Dias's discovery of the mouth of the Senegal and Cape Verde for the crown of Portugal in 1444–5. But it was not until the 1470s that the Portuguese (or any other European adventurers for that matter) began to venture much further afield than about Sierra Leone. The first voyage to Mina, the Gold Coast (the coast of modern Ghana), was in 1470–1; the Bight of Biafra and the island of Fernando Po (named after its discoverer) were reached probably in the following year; and by the end of the decade the Portuguese were probably familiar with most of the coast from Mina to about the Cameroun, though there is some doubt whether their first contacts with the kingdom of Benin were at this time or in the early 1480s. The first surviving coherent account of the whole West African coast is that of Pacheco Pereira, written about 1505, and it is apparent from this that even at this late date the Portuguese were little acquainted with two sizeable stretches of the coastlands, between Sierra Leone and Mina (i.e. the coast of modern Liberia and the Ivory Coast), and between Mina and about Lagos (i.e. the coasts of modern Togo and Dahomey). Thus the coming of the Europeans was a piecemeal and, indeed, selective process, which occupied a period of nearly forty years from 1444 onwards. Until 1460, they were significantly concerned only with the coast from the Senegal to Sierra Leone, and then in the 1470s and 1480s they began to turn their attention to and become involved on the Gold Coast and what is now the coast of Nigeria.

The first of these regions, which is also that which geographically is the westernmost Sudan, will be called 'Upper Guinea'; the second, which is also that lying astride the Togo–Dahomey gap in the forest, will be called 'Lower Guinea'. This is to borrow, and also to adapt, terms which came into general European usage in the seventeenth and eighteenth centuries. The adaptation is necessary because, as originally conceived, these terms had nothing to do with the history of West Africa, but resulted from the conditions governing the operation of sailing ships to and from its coasts. In this sense, Upper Guinea included the coast beyond Sierra Leone to Cape Palmas, close by the modern boundary between Liberia and the Ivory Coast, for up to this point it was not too difficult for a sailing ship to return to Europe more or less directly. Beyond Cape Palmas, however, the set of the winds and currents was such that the best sailing route to return to Europe began by continuing eastwards along the coast of Lower Guinea to as far as the Gabon or São Tomé, where winds and currents began once again to favour a voyage to the west. In fact, as is suggested by Pacheco Pereira's work, early Europeans paid little attention to the coasts of modern Liberia and the Ivory Coast. These coasts were regarded as dangerous for sailing ships. There was no shelter to compare with that provided by the creeks and river mouths of the coast to the north or in the Niger delta region, and ships ran the risk of being driven onto an open shore by treacherous winds or currents. Furthermore, as has been seen, the forests here seem to have been thinly populated, by peoples who had less political and economic organization than those to the north or east of them, and therefore there was less incentive here for European trade. Historically, then, there is a case for regarding Liberia and the southern Ivory Coast as an intermediary area for which the term 'Middle Guinea' might be coined.

DEVELOPMENTS BEFORE THE ARRIVAL OF EUROPEANS ON THE COAST

The coastlands of Upper Guinea (in the narrower sense adopted here) lay relatively close to the centres of political and economic power of the great empires of the western Sudan. The upper reaches of the Gambia river are only approximately 560 kilometres from Kumbi Saleh, the presumed site of the capital of ancient Ghana, while, wherever the capital of ancient Mali was situated at the height of its power in the fourteenth century,[1] it cannot have been more than about the same distance from the coast of Sierra Leone. Moreover most of this region was open savanna, relatively easily traversable by animal transport or by cavalry, and it is also provided with good natural waterways such as the Senegal and Gambia and the rivers of Guinea. The conceptual framework for the history of Upper Guinea prior to about 1450 must inevitably therefore be one in which this region lay wide open to the receipt of influences from the great Mande and Muslim powers in its hinterland.

The indigenous peoples of Upper Guinea seem undoubtedly to have been ancestors of the peoples who today speak languages belonging to what linguists have universally agreed to call the West Atlantic sub-family of the Niger-Congo (i.e. Negro) language family. Ignoring for the moment the Tukolor and Fulani, whose history requires separate treatment, the distribution of these 'West Atlantic' peoples today is

[1] This issue has been debated since about the beginning of the present century. A recent contribution, which also gives the earlier references, is J. O. Hunwick, 'The mid-fourteenth century capital of Mali', *Journal of African History*, 1973, **14**, 2, 195–208.

essentially as follows. In the north, between the lower Senegal and the lower Gambia, are the two large groups of the Wolof and the Serer. South of the Gambia, for the most part hugging the coastline and the tidal reaches of the creeks and rivers (and also on the Bissagos islands) south to Sierra Leone, are a congeries of much smaller ethnic groups such as the Diola, the Pepel, the Balante and the Baga. In the south-western Guinea Republic, and in much of Sierra Leone and north-western Liberia, Mande-speaking peoples are today dominant, but these are interspersed with such major West Atlantic groups as the Temne, Bulom, Kissi and Gola.

The general assumption among anthropologists and geographers[1] seems to be that the West Atlantic peoples shared in the growth of civilization in the western Sudan to the extent that they developed animal husbandry, considerable agricultural skills (including sometimes systems of crop rotation and the swampland cultivation of rice), and a high degree of village society and industry (including iron-working), but not to the extent that they developed much in the way of sizeable and positive politico-economic structures involving social stratification. The explanation for this could well be that they were not touched by the stimulus of trans-Saharan trade as were their Mande-speaking neighbours to the east and north, and that the subsequent development of the Mande empires of Ghana and Mali meant that the use of advanced techniques of political and economic exploitation became more or less a Mande monopoly, leading to an expansion of Mande-speaking peoples to the west and south at the expense of the West Atlantic peoples. By and large, demographic and anthropological evidence supports this view, and the available historical evidence does not contradict it, even if it throws rather less light than one would like on the historical processes that may have been involved.

Certainly in the central area from the Gambia river to the Scarcies river on the northern frontier of Sierra Leone, the West Atlantic peoples very much give the appearance of being 'refoulés littoraux'.[2] Their landward boundary corresponds very closely with the limits of the tidewater, the canoe was a basic element in social, religious and political, as well as economic life, and the people depended on the produce of the coastal waters and rivers almost as much as they did on that of their fields. The large shell-mounds characteristic of these

[1] See, for example, A. Mendes Correia, *Raças do Imperio* (Lisbon, 1943); J. Richard-Molard, *Afrique Occidentale Française*, 2nd ed. (Paris, 1952); A. Teixeira da Mota, *Guiné Portuguesa* (Lisbon, 1954).

[2] The term is Richard-Molard's, in *Afrique Occidentale*, 108–11.

coastlands suggest, however, that this was a very ancient practice, doubtless antedating any historic expansion of the Mande-speaking peoples. But both to the north and south of the Gambia–Scarcies region, the situation is different, and there is evidence of expansion from the Sudan, especially by Mande-speaking groups, during the period covered by this chapter.

The rather dry savanna country from the Gambia northwards to a little south of the mouth of the Senegal, is inhabited by the Wolof and the Serer, whose domain today reaches inland for about 150 kilometres. When Europeans first made their acquaintance in the fifteenth century, these people had a hierarchical social system involving distinct classes of royal and non-royal nobles, free men, occupational castes such as blacksmiths, jewellers, tanners, tailors, musicians and griots, and slaves. There was also a complex political structure of five coastal kingdoms, from north to south – Walo, Kayor, Baol, Sine and Salum, which were themselves tributary to the king or emperor of Djolof (i.e. Wolof), whose capital lay over 300 kilometres inland and about half-way between the Senegal and the Gambia.

According to tradition, the founder of this Wolof empire was Ndiadiane N'Diaye, a king (*burba*) for whose reign dates in the early thirteenth century are conventionally assigned. It seems more probable, however, that the rise of the empire was associated with the growth of Wolof power at the expense of the ancient Sudanese state of Takrur, and that this was essentially a fourteenth-century development. Takrur, astride the middle Senegal valley, was contemporary with ancient Ghana, and the history of the two kingdoms has a common pattern, albeit that of Takrur, which seems to have been appreciably smaller, is somewhat less well known. Both seem to have been formed by the interaction between Saharan Berbers and Negro agricultural peoples. In the case of Ghana, the latter were Soninke (i.e. northern Mande); in the case of Takrur, they seem to have been essentially Serer, though it is possible that the kings of Takrur from about AD 1000 onwards may have been of Soninke origin. Takrur, like ancient Ghana, flourished as a market for trans-Saharan traders, and both were thus open to a growing Islamic influence. The Soninke kings of Ghana seem to have been converted as a consequence of their conquest by the Almoravids *c.* 1076; in Takrur, the conversion would seem to have been a more peaceful process occurring about a generation earlier. While it had been politically independent of Ghana, Takrur seems undoubtedly to have come within the sphere of its larger Mande successor empire, Mali, created by Sundiata (*c.* 1230–60), with the consequence that Mande commercial and political influence in Takrur must have been considerable for about the next hundred years.

The result of all this was that Takrur became an area in which there was as long a tradition of both centralized, hierarchical government and organized commerce as there was anywhere else in the western Sudan, in which Islam became earlier and more deeply implanted than elsewhere, and in which there was a considerable mixing and reshuffling of ethnic groups, immigrant Soninke and Saharan Berber and local agricultural Serer. In particular, two new cultural and ethnic identities seem to have emerged. One was the Tukolor (i.e. 'people of Takrur'), presumably Serer at base, and with a language akin to one of the branches of the Serer tongue, who were sedentary and islamized. The other was the Fulani (or Peuls or Fulbe), whose language is virtually identical with that of the Tukolor, but who at this stage remained steadfastly pagan. The Fulani were cattle-herders, perhaps originally of Saharan stock, who tended to resist assimilation within the growing orbit of sedentary civilizations such as those of Ghana or Takrur. They may well have escaped the former by settling in Futa Toro, south of the bend of the middle Senegal, where they must have pastured their cattle between the cultivated fields of Serer peoples with whom – if the linguistic evidence is any guide – they must have struck up a close relationship. But then the growth of the organized government of Takrur caused the Fulani from about the eleventh century to begin the great dispersion throughout the grasslands of the Sudan which was ultimately to take them as far east as Adamawa.

The Fulani need not be followed so far in this present chapter, but it is relevant to it to note that by the fifteenth century considerable numbers of them had settled in the Futa Jalon uplands in which most of the rivers of Upper Guinea rise. Indeed, the Fulani dispersion must be considered along with the Mande expansion as one of the factors tending to push the West Atlantic peoples towards the coast. In fact there seems likely to have been a symbiotic relationship between the growth of Mande imperial and commercial power and the Fulani dispersion. It was the Mande towns and trading system which provided the best markets for the Fulani to dispose of their dairy produce and hides, and sometimes cattle themselves, and to acquire what little they required in the way of goods and services from settled society. In Futa Jalon as elsewhere, close relations developed between the Fulani and the islamized Mande urban and commercial communities.

The establishment of the kingdom of Takrur thus had considerable repercussions for the West Atlantic peoples, and perhaps for the Serer in particular. Those Serer who escaped absorbtion in the emergent Tukolor and Fulani groups appear to have done so by sheltering behind the Wolof who, perhaps simply because they were initially more remote from the growth of Takrur power, seem to have retained their ethnic integrity. Nevertheless the Wolof also experienced, at a second remove, the powerful new influences being generated in the westernmost Sudan by Berber penetration, by the growth of Islam and of Mande trade, and by the emergence of the Tukolor and Fulani. The Wolof developed a class hierarchy, with a nobility which was at least nominally Islamic, and, together with Mande and Tukolor elements, began to exert a dominating influence on the trade and government of their Serer neighbours. As the imperial power of Mali declined from about 1360 onwards, it was possible for the dynasty established by Ndiadiane N'Diaye to gain control of the old kingdom of Takrur in the region just south of the middle Senegal now known as Futa Toro, and also to extend its imperial control over the congeries of Serer communities further to the south (see also pp. 457–8).

Further south still, Sudanic pressures and influences on the West Atlantic peoples at this early stage seem to have been more expressly Mande. There appears to be one instance in which a whole Mande-speaking people emigrated from the upper Niger valley to settle close by the coast in West Atlantic lands. This was the Susu, who, under their king Sumanguru (*c.* 1200–35 ?), had striven for the mastery of ancient Ghana after the decline of Almoravid power there, but who were ultimately worsted by the Keita under Sundiata, the creator of the new Mali empire. Certainly the modern Susu inhabit a solid block of territory astride the Scarcies river. More generally, however, what seems to have happened was that the West Atlantic lands were penetrated on a wide front between the Gambia and the west of modern Liberia by numerous small bands of Mande-speaking traders or adventurers.

In the case of the traders, an obvious motive was to gain access to the supplies of salt manufactured by the West Atlantic peoples in the tidelands. In at least two areas, the valleys of the rivers Geba and Corubal in Guinea-Bissau, and the headwaters of the rivers St Paul and St John close by the modern Liberia–Guinea Republic boundary, there is evidence also that alluvial gold deposits were being worked. Both salt and gold acted as powerful magnets for traders. Where there was little indigenous centralized political organization – as seems to have been the general rule among West Atlantic peoples at this time – there must have been a natural tendency for traders, with the help of soldier-adventurers from the Mali empire, to seek political control. This would have been beneficial to them in two respects: it would have provided a system of law and order permitting the free and economic movement of trade goods and traders, and it would also, by way of tribute, lead to accumulations of produce which could be used either as trade goods or for the sustenance of merchants and their porters or pack-animals. The result was the emergence of a number of petty states in the Mande style ruled by potentates bearing the title *farim*. This would seem to be equivalent to the title *farma* borne by the officials sent out by the Mali *mansa*, or emperor, to represent his power at the traditional centres of subject peoples within his empire. There is evidence indeed that originally the *farim* owed allegiance to the Mali *mansa*, though with the decline of Mali imperial power from the later fourteenth century onwards, the *farim* obviously became increasingly independent.

Few details of the processes by which the *farim* established their power now seem to be available, but some light on them may be thrown by the better authenticated changes associated with the growth of a major Mande-Dyula trade system further east, in the western half of Lower Guinea, in modern Ghana and the adjacent western lands of the Ivory Coast Republic. The headquarters of this trade system was the Sudanese town of Jenne. The date of Jenne's foundation is uncertain. Local sources trace the city back to the eighth century, and assert that its people were converted to Islam at the beginning of the twelfth century. Whatever the truth in this, the significant points seem to be that by about the end of the thirteenth century, Jenne was becoming important as a place where Muslim Mande merchants, Dyula probably of Soninke origin, were settling in some numbers, and that their interest in this town is largely to be explained by its geographical situation.

The major artery both for trade and for political control in the Mali empire was the river Niger, leading from the Mande heartlands and the Bure and Bambuk goldfields eastwards to the Niger bend, with its trading entrepôts of Timbuktu and Gao at the southern end of the short central trans-Saharan caravan routes, and on towards the growing agricultural, manufacturing and commercial wealth of Hausaland. However, Jenne is not situated on the Niger, but occupies an easily defensible site in marshland adjacent to its southern tributary, the Bani river, which joins the main river just south of Timbuktu. Thus, while not very readily accessible from the Mande homelands around the upper Niger, Jenne is a very suitable base from which to develop trade to the south, and to link this with the trans-Saharan trade at Timbuktu or Gao. As has already been pointed out, the Black Volta valley and the forest lands around modern Asante were rich in gold resources, while *Cola nitida* grew in the forest from Liberia in the west to modern Ghana in the east.

From Sudanese and North African sources, such as the Timbuktu *ta'rīkhs* and Leo Africanus, and from the gold-hungry Portuguese explorers of the fifteenth century, it is possible to build up quite a comprehensive picture of the trading system operated by the Dyula merchants of Jenne. It is worth noting, incidentally, that much of the Portuguese information on this subject, for example in the writings of Cadamosto, Pacheco Pereira and Valentim Fernandes, was gathered in the Senegambian region far away to the west, a fact which gives some idea of the extent and sophistication of the Mande trading system, at least by the fifteenth century.

The mainspring of Jenne's trade, as of that of ancient Ghana, was the exchange of Saharan salt for West African gold-dust. The salt was brought to Timbuktu by caravans of camels, each camel carrying two large blocks of salt weighing up to as much as 90 kilograms apiece. At Timbuktu, the salt was trans-shipped into canoes and transported up the Niger and Bani to Jenne. Here a 90-kilogram block of salt was worth some 454 grams of gold-dust (i.e. 64 gold £s), which seems to have been about twice its value at Timbuktu. If Fernandes is to be trusted, the Timbuktu–Jenne exchange of salt for gold was not only profitable, but also conducted on an appreciable scale, for he indicates that the turnover of a Jenne-based merchant engaged in this trade could be of the order of about 30,000 gold £s a year. At Jenne, the salt was broken down into head-loads and taken south at the beginning of the dry season by caravans of porters. At the end of the season, these would return with loads of gold-dust. Some of this gold would be absorbed in the Sudan, but much of it was remitted back to Timbuktu for the trans-Saharan trade.

The Arabic and Portuguese sources stress the importance of gold and salt in the trade of the Dyula merchants based on Jenne, doubtless because this exchange was its most spectacular and lucrative aspect and also because, so far as the Portuguese were concerned, the gold trade was their major interest in West Africa. But in addition to salt, Jenne is also reported as importing from the north brass and copper, silks and cloth (blue and red cloths are specifically mentioned), and spices, and presumably some of these goods were also re-exported to the south. However, since the Jenne trade-routes were linking the very different ecological zones of the savannas and the forest, it is likely that there was also a growing trade in local produce, with cattle and other products of the savannas being exchanged for those of the forest lands. But it should be noted that transport south of Jenne seems to have been essentially by head-loading, a very expensive means of transport except for goods of high value in relation to their weight and bulk, and, apart from gold, the forest product best fitting this description is most likely to have been kola nuts. In fact the only commodity besides gold specifically mentioned as reaching Jenne from the south is slaves. Like cattle going south, these of course transported themselves, and perhaps one of their main values to the merchants was as porters.

The *Ta'rīkh al-Sūdān* says that the gold brought to Jenne came from 'Bitou', while Pacheco Pereira writes of Mande merchants going to buy gold from the land of 'Toom', specifically from the markets of 'Beetuu, Banbarranaa and Bahaa'. There seems little doubt that 'Toom' corresponds to the modern region of Asante, for the Akan are called *Ton* by the modern Dyula (and *Tonawa* by the Hausa). It is also commonly assumed that 'Bitou' or 'Beetuu' is a reference to Begho (or Bi'u or Bew), which, though now ruined and deserted, was once a major commercial centre on the edge of Akan territory, and just east of a gap in the Banda hills through which merchants from Jenne would have passed on their way to secure gold from the Asante region immediately to the south-east. ('Bahaa' might also be a version of Banda, the name for the kingdom which arose with Begho as its major town.) In fact this identification is not certain. The *Ta'rīkh al-Fattāsh* says that the power of the emperor of Mali extended to Bitou, and it is tolerably certain that Begho was beyond its reach. Secondly, Pacheco Pereira actually has two references to Beetuu, Banbarranaa and Bahaa; in the other, it is *from* them that the Mande merchants went to Toom. Thirdly, as has recently been pointed out, the name used by contemporary Arabic authors for the capital of Mali is B.t. or B.n., with some indication that the first vowel may be a long 'i' and the second a long 'i' or 'a'; these forms are remarkably close to 'Beetuu' and 'Bahaa'. 'Beetuu, Banbarranaa and Bahaa' are therefore perhaps just as likely to have been names of places (or peoples) in Mandeland itself (which had its own goldfields in Bure and Bambuk) as they are to have been in or near the Akan country, the more so perhaps as Bambara (cf. 'Banbarranaa') is today a name for a major branch of the Mande-speaking peoples who, in eighteenth-century sources, are also said to have been fighting with a people called 'Beetoo'.[1]

There is, however, no doubt that Dyula merchants did establish significant trade-routes southwards from Jenne, and that the most important of these did reach Begho and, beyond it, Asante and the Gold Coast (on which, indeed, as has already been observed, the Portuguese recognized the presence of Mande merchants very shortly after their own arrival on the coast in the 1470s). The Dyula practice was to establish settlements of their own alongside the major political centres of the local peoples, and some of these developed into sizeable communities which were themselves of political as well as of commercial significance. One such major settlement, approximately 300 kilometres due south of Jenne itself, is Bobo-Dioulasso, a name which might loosely be translated as 'the Dyula settlement in the country of the Bobo' (who are one of the Gur-speaking peoples of the upper Volta basin). Approximately 225 kilometres further south, there was another important Dyula settlement at Kong, from which a wide arc of gold and kola-producing forest-lands could be reached by caravans of porters in little more than a week's journey. But to the south-west, the forest lands of the western Ivory Coast and Liberia are still today very thinly peopled and little developed commercially, and in any case they were within equally easy reach of towns in the Mande homeland on the upper Niger. On the other hand, by far the most significant sources of gold lay to the south-east of Kong. Some gold was worked close by Begho itself, while beyond it lay the major deposits of Asante and the Gold Coast. Today there is a significant line of Dyula settlement south-east from Kong to the modern town of Bonduku, just east of the gap in the Banda hills, and to the site of Begho itself. There also seems to have been another Dyula trade-route from Jenne to this same area running a little to the east of the Bobo-Dioulasso-Kong route close by the Black Volta, and passing through the Lobi goldfields on the way.

Begho and Bono-Mansu, located about 65 kilometres to the south-east of Begho, close by modern Tekyiman, together with Buna (Bouna, Bona) just west of the Black Volta and approximately 130 kilometres north of Bonduku, figure in tradition as the seats of the earliest Akan monarchies, and it seems clear that their rise is

[1] See postscript to Hunwick, 'The mid-fourteenth century capital of Mali', 204–5.

associated with the growth of trade from Jenne. Both Begho and Bono-Mansu seem in fact to have had separate Dyula and Muslim quarters alongside the traditional pagan town where the king lived. In Begho it is said to have been tensions between these in the seventeenth century which led to civil war, the eventual abandonment of the site and the removal of the Dyula westwards across the Banda hills to a new trading centre at Bonduku. What is not so clear is the date when the Dyula became a significant force in the country on the fringes of the forests of modern Asante, and the exact nature of their interaction with the local Akan peoples.

In the area where Begho once stood, there are today many square kilometres of mounds representing abandoned and ruined habitation sites, and one of these mounds can be as large as to cover half a square kilometre. So far archaeologists have been able to do no more than make a few trial excavations, and the most that can at present be said is that there was organized settlement here, though not necessarily trade, by the eleventh century, and that there is some evidence of a prosperous trading community from about the middle of the fifteenth century to the early eighteenth century. The Bono kingdom was conquered by Asante in 1722 or 1723, following which its kings became subordinate to the kings of Asante and moved to Tekyiman. Meyerowitz has argued that the Tekyiman dynasty has retained solid evidence that it became established at Bono-Mansu in 1295, and also that it was about half a century later that gold was discovered in the vicinity and that relations were opened up with the Sudan. Both the existence of this evidence and its chronological implications have been challenged, and dates around the beginning of the fourteenth century for the establishment of organized government in Bono, and the beginnings of its gold-mining and of significant trade with the Sudan, do seem to be on the early side in relation to what is thought to be the probable chronology of Jenne's commercial development. Wilks and Flight prefer to interpret the evidence as indicating that the foundation of the Bono monarchy that was conquered by Asante probably occurred no earlier than the early years of the fifteenth century.[1] (A date later than this, incidentally, would not square well with the observed presence of Mande merchants on the Gold Coast by the end of that century.)

[1] E. L. R. Meyerowitz, *Akan traditions of origin* (London, 1952), 32–3; *Akan of Ghana*, 103–27. For criticism and reassessment, see, among others, C. Flight, 'The chronology of the kings and queen-mothers of Bono-Manso: a revaluation of the evidence', *Journal of African History*, 1970, **11**, 2, 259–68; D. M. Warren, 'A re-appraisal of Mrs Eva Meyerowitz's work on the Brong', *Research Review* (Legon), 1970, **7**, 1, esp. 60ff; I. Wilks in J. F. A. Ajayi and M. Crowder, eds., *History of West Africa* (London, 1971), **1**, 356–8.

Little is known of the early history of Buna, for in the seventeenth century its wealth and prosperity incited its conquest by Dagomba or Mamprusi cavaliers from the east, and a change of dynasty seems to have been one of the results. The territory of Banda was probably fairly small, and its significance is likely to have been as a frontier zone, the furthest point along the route from Jenne at which the immigrant Dyula had a reasonable chance of controlling the political situation in their own interest. Bono lay beyond this point, firmly in the territory of the Brong, the northernmost Akan group. Whether immigrant Dyula took an active part in its political as well as its economic development is far from clear. It seems more probable that their coming, and the wealth generated through the new trading opportunities they presented, stimulated the traditional leaders of the Brong kinship groups to develop a hierarchical monarchical system of government, and to impose this on the surrounding peoples ever more firmly and extensively. Muslim Dyula leaders may often have been useful to them as administrators and advisers, and sometimes the two sides may have become allied or united through marriage. But essentially what emerged was an Akan power, in which, for example, the great annual 'festival of the nation' was associated with the successful harvesting of the yam crop, and inheritance and succession to office followed the matrilineal line. Matrilinealism indeed may have served to help Bono and later Akan states absorb and benefit from alien and Muslim influences without losing their essential identity.[1]

Bono is renowned in Akan tradition for the wealth and splendour of its kings, and this was based on their control of the gold-trade and of gold-mining, both of which seem to have been essentially royal monopolies conducted by their agents and slaves. As the strength of the monarchy grew, it seems to have extended its power to the south-east, parallel with the northern edge of the forest as it slopes away towards the Volta and the Togo-Dahomey gap. In this way, more and more of the trade-paths leading from the gold-producing areas in the forest would have come under Bono's control. In this way too, concepts of kingship and political organization may have passed round the forest to its southern edges fronting the coast. Certainly by the time of the Portuguese arrival in the 1470s and 1480s, the coastal peoples seem to have been organized in a number of small kingdoms – about a dozen in all along approximately 320 kilometres of coast eastwards from

[1] This follows upon the suggestion of I. Wilks in Ajayi and Crowder, *History of West Africa*, I, 364.

the Ankobra river – which had their capitals a little way inland, and which were quickly able to organize to sell gold to the Portuguese. Some of these kingdoms today have traditions which trace their origins to emigrants from Tekyiman (i.e. Bono).[1] Some of the coastal people, e.g. the Afutu and Gomoa, speak – or once spoke – Akan dialects which the linguists place together with Brong, the dialect of Bono, in the same 'Guan dialect-cluster'. But the ethnic history of the coastlands of modern Ghana is one of considerable complexity which may never be satisfactorily unravelled.

The gradually widening strip of savanna which extends along the coast east of about modern Sekondi seems to have been open to settlement or influence not only by people coming along the edge of the forest and through the gap in the Akwapim-Togo hills through which the Volta reaches the sea, but also by peoples arriving directly from the east or from the north through the forest itself. In the extreme south-east of modern Ghana, the Ewe have traditions of migration from the east; so too do the Ga and Adangbe monarchies on the Accra plains (though here there is evidence, for example in the *klama* and *kple* songs, of a submerged Guan population). Further west, in south-central Ghana, the dominant cultural influence today is that of the Fante, whose Akan speech differs little from the Twi spoken in the forest, and who may therefore be thought to have come directly through it – an idea for which there may be support in some of their traditions. In all probability, the coastal population of modern Ghana is the result of layer upon layer of settlement and acculturation. This could possibly help to explain its political fragmentation, though this was certainly perpetuated and indeed accentuated by the competing European influences present on the coast in later times.

Despite the apparent importance of the Volta gap for the diffusion of early Akan concepts of political and economic organization, obviously the forest-lands directly south of Bono cannot have been untouched by its influence in its period of splendour, because otherwise gold could not have been brought out from it to adorn its court life and to feed the Dyula traders. But it was probably initially thinly peopled, and perhaps initially gold-mining in it was something of a seasonal occupation for servants and slaves sent out by the Bono kings. However, with the ever-increasing appreciation of the wealth to be won from mining and

[1] Note, however, that the historicity of traditions among coastal peoples who have a long contact with Europeans and a long history of literacy is open to question; see D. P. Henige, 'The problem of feedback in oral tradition: four examples from the Fante coastlands', *Journal of African History*, 1973, 14, 2, 223–35.

trading in gold, there must have been ever more incentive for northern Akan to settle permanently in the forest, and for its indigenous inhabitants to grow in number and in wealth. By the time of the Portuguese arrival on the coast, it is evident that there was an important nucleus of Akan activity centred around the rich gold-bearing area of the Ofin and upper Ankobra valleys.

People from this area coming to the coast to sell gold were known by the early Europeans mainly by variants of the name Akan. Pacheco Pereira, the earliest authority, writing *c.* 1505, calls them 'Hacanys'; later European variants include 'Accany' for the area and 'Acanistians' for the people. Slightly later, a closely adjacent area and its people are called by names such as 'Quiforo', 'Cufferue', 'Juffer' etc. These are European attempts to render 'Twifo', which means simply 'the Twi (or Twi-speaking) people'. The most important characteristics of these Akans and Twifo in European eyes was that they were skilled traders and that they sold the best gold that was available at the coast. An African state called Twifu survived into colonial times, albeit apparently somewhat south of its original home, but there is now no trace of a kingdom called Akani, the name surviving only as the generic term for the speakers of the major group of languages encompassing Twi, Fante, Guan etc. However, it is clear that the region which the early Europeans called Akany was equivalent to Adansi, which from the early eighteenth century onwards was a southern province of the Asante empire. But some years previous to this, Adansi had been conquered by the earlier Akan empire of Denkyira. As a result of these two conquests, it is now difficult, if not impossible, to reconstruct the earlier history of this region with any certitude.

Nevertheless it is apparent that political and economic developments in this rich gold-bearing region in the heart of the forest were of the utmost importance for the subsequent history of the Akan. The nineteenth-century Ghanaian historian Reindorf expressed this when he wrote: 'Adansi was the first seat of the Akan nation; there God, according to tradition, first began the creation of the world. They were the most enlightened tribe among the Twi nation from whom the others acquired knowledge and wisdom.'[1] Essentially what was happening in the area known to the Europeans as Akani and Twifo was twofold. First, the hitherto unparalleled wealth made possible by the growth of gold-mining and trading was leading to a great build-up

[1] C. C. Reindorf, *The history of the Gold Coast and Asante*, 2nd ed. (Basel, n.d. [1951?]), 48–9.

of population in the heart of the forest. Secondly, any number of able and ambitious traditional leaders of Akan kinship groups were endeavouring to control this growth of population and wealth to their own advantage by attracting or forcing into their service more clients, slaves, soldiers and traders than were their rivals. The end result of this process was the emergence in the early years of the eighteenth century of the empire of Asante which ultimately was to control virtually all the territory of modern Ghana. Before this, in the seventeenth century, the stage had been reached at which there were three major Akan forest powers competing to control the exploitation and exportation of gold. These were Denkyira in the west, Akwamu in the east, and, squeezed between these two, and less united and successful, the kings of Akyem. While, as is shown by its conquest of Bono, Asante looked north as well as south (its capital, Kumasi, lay at the strategic junction of the trade-routes to the north-west that were dominated by the Dyula, those to the north-east operated by Hausa traders, and those leading south towards the coast), the growth of its three predecessors was mainly conditioned by the desire to control as many as possible of the trade-paths leading to the new markets established on the coast by the European traders.

Akani and Twifo represent the nuclear area in the forest in which these major essays in Akan economic and political imperialism all had their birth, and there is scarcely a ruling family among the Akan which does not trace its ancestry back to this area, and sometimes indeed back beyond it to the earlier period of political and economic experimentation that resulted from the coming of the Dyula to the northern edge of the forest and the emergence of states like Bono and Banda. Thus, although since *c.* 1730 Akwamu has been no more than one of a number of petty states in south-eastern Ghana, its chiefs still preserve the tradition that their ancestors came from Twifo, before that from Dormaa – an area just south of Begho, with whose chiefs they still preserve ritual links – and before that from Kong. Similarly, the group of chiefs who ultimately created the Asante monarchy regard themselves as descended from men who left Adansi, probably in the early seventeenth century. It would seem likely that this was because they had not been successful in the struggles that were going on there for the control of men and the new sources of wealth. But the subsequent rise to power and fame of states like Asante, Denkyira and Akwamu has now totally obscured the historical details of the political and economic processes that were taking place in the Akani/Twifu region in the fifteenth and sixteenth centuries. Some commentators would have us believe in the existence here at this time of a centralized Bono-style state, ruled from a capital called Akyerekyere (not far from the modern Akrokeri in northern Adansi); others that there was some kind of federation of chiefs, possibly similar to the federation out of which the Asante monarchy emerged; and yet others that there was little more than a jostling, competitive society of enterprising trading entrepreneurs seeking to exploit the new gold wealth.[1] But whatever the political shape of the old Akani/Twifu area, it is certain that it was torn apart by the rivalries that were engendered by the new wealth and the growth of population, and that the end result was the birth of the major Akan forest states, Denkyira, Akwamu and Asante, that were to dominate the history of the Gold Coast from the seventeenth century onwards.

Much of what is known, or may reasonably be surmised, of the history of the Akan area before the arrival of the Europeans on its coast derives from the fact that its gold-trade was of international importance. East of the Volta, in what are now the republics of Togo and Dahomey and the southern half of Nigeria, there was no gold trade, and any attempt at historical reconstruction must be even less precise. The starting points must be the precious few pieces of archaeological evidence, namely that the rich urban and court life of the Yoruba was already evident at Ife by the tenth or eleventh century, that Benin city was already flourishing by the thirteenth century, and the rich finds at Igbo-Ukwu, suggesting that Iboland, if it did not perhaps have a political system to match those that seem to have existed in Yorubaland and Benin, could rival them in social and economic sophistication apparently as early as the ninth century. To these may be added a number of inferences. Examples of court art in the best Ife style are also known from Nupe, north-east across the Niger from Yorubaland, and from Igala, north-east across the Niger from Benin; it is therefore possible to infer that these countries also had developed state systems before the fifteenth century. Secondly, when first discovered by the Portuguese, the Benin kingdom was already of considerable extent, and this seems to have involved it in both political and commercial relations with a number of other areas.

Pacheco Pereira says that the kingdom of Benin was 'about eighty leagues long and forty wide'. In the Portuguese context, 'long' must

[1] See, for example, Reindorf, *History*, 48–9; Meyerowitz, *Akan traditions*, 89–98; W. E. F. Ward, *A history of the Gold Coast* (London, 1948), 47–9; K. Y. Daaku, *Trade and politics on the Gold Coast* (Oxford, 1970), 145–8; and articles in *Ghana Notes and Queries*, 1966, 9.

mean coastwise; thus the extent of the kingdom from east to west would have been something on the order of 385 kilometres, and from north to south about half this. The latter distance would bring it to the borders of modern Yoruba country; the former is equivalent to the distance between the lower Niger and about modern Lagos. These correspond broadly with the accepted limits of power of the Benin kingdom in subsequent centuries. Thus, if Pacheco Pereira's information is correct, the Benin monarchy was near the peak of its power at the end of the fifteenth century, and an appreciable period of growth would have been necessary to reach this stage. However, Benin royal authority was not exerted directly throughout this area. In the east, the Ibo communities living west of the Niger had developed chiefly governments which looked to Benin for their inspiration, while the sizeable Itsekiri kingdom which the Portuguese called Ugueri (Oere or Warri) had a dynasty which would seem to have sprung from Benin in the mid fifteenth century. In the west, a formal government for the island of Lagos seems to have been established in the same sort of way about a century later; it certainly does not seem to have existed when the Portuguese first entered the Lagos lagoon – perhaps it was their interest in the trade of this region which led Benin to act in this way.

Direct Portuguese contact with Yorubaland was minimal. Just north of the Lagos lagoon, Pacheco Pereira knew of a 'very large city called Geebuu, surrounded by a great moat', and he reported that the 'river of this country' was called 'Agusale'. This must be Ijebu-Ode, the capital of the southernmost Yoruba kingdom of Ijebu, and presumably 'river' (*rio* in Portuguese) is an error of some kind for 'king' (*rey*), for the Ijebu king's title is *awujale*. More than this, the Portuguese knew only that the kings of Benin paid some sort of homage to a powerful interior potentate 'who among the Negroes is as the Pope among us'. Despite the misleading geographical indication that this king lived to the east of Benin, the name given to him, 'Hooguanee' or 'Ogané', together with some other details, suggest very strongly that this was the *oni* (king) of Ife, for whom the modern Benin name is *oghene*.[1]

[1] The Pacheco Pereira references are in his *Esmeraldo de situ orbis*, ed. and tr. R. Mauny (Bissau, 1956), 130–5; see also João de Barros, *Decadas da India*, Dec. 1, bk. 3, ch. 4, in G. R. Crone, ed. and tr., *The voyages of Cadamosto, and other documents* (London, 1937), which adds further detail, including that the Ogané lived to the *east* of Benin. For comment on this point, and both passages generally, see A. F. C. Ryder, 'A reconsideration of the Ife–Benin relationship', *Journal of African History*, 1965, 6, 1, 25–37, and the same author's *Benin and the Europeans, 1485–1897* (London, 1969), 24–32.

The fact that for half a century or more the Portuguese concentrated their interest in what is now southern Nigeria on trying to cultivate commercial and political relations with the organized monarchy of Benin may well provide important clues to the earlier history of this region. It suggests, for example, that the early Yoruba kingdoms, like the early Akan kingdoms such as Bono and Banda, may have looked primarily northwards, towards the Sudan, for their external trade and other relations. But this is not to say that there was nothing of importance towards the south, because otherwise there would have not been the important offshoot of the Ife-centred Yoruba monarchical system at Benin. But the Benin system, with its own offshoots at Warri, among the western Ibo and at Lagos, seems to have developed a momentum of its own, and a structure which seems to have been more centralized and powerful within its sphere than was the Yoruba system in its sphere, even if it was still of some importance for Benin to maintain relations with Ife.

The Portuguese could trade at Benin only with the *oba* (king) and his accredited agents, and on terms laid down by him and his administration, which ultimately became so onerous that they withdrew altogether from the Benin market. But initially this highly centralized system afforded them a much more sizeable and important market for their goods – of which the most important was probably brassware – than was available anywhere else in the region. In exchange the Portuguese took slaves, cloth and peppers. But only for the last of these was there any European demand, and as soon as the Portuguese had succeeded in establishing their spice trade with Asia, they ceased trading in Benin peppers. The importance of Benin's exports of beads and cloth and, initially, of slaves also, to the Portuguese was that they were readily exchangeable on the Gold Coast for gold, which was the West African product which they wanted above all others. Now if beads and cloth from Benin were marketable on the Gold Coast, and bearing in mind the traditional conservatism of West African consumers, there is at least an inference that the southern Akan had already developed a taste for these particular varieties of beads and cloth, i.e. that there was a coastwise trade in them before the advent of the Portuguese. (The Akan demand for slaves is readily explicable on the grounds that more porters would be needed to carry these goods into the interior than would be needed to bring an equivalent value of gold-dust out from it, and that there was also a growing demand for labour to open up and operate the more southerly gold-mines.)

Now the peculiarity of this situation is that, except for slaves, which were a natural enough outcome of the military processes by which the Benin kings extended and maintained their authority, these Benin exports do not seem to have been locally produced. Benin itself has virtually no weaving tradition, and its soils are not suited to the cultivation of cotton or, really, to much productive agriculture (today much of its food is imported from better agricultural lands further north). Descriptions of the cloth purchased at Benin by the Portuguese suggest most strongly that most of it must have been produced either in the northern reaches of its empire or in adjacent Yoruba and other lands to the north-west or Ibo or other lands to the north-east. Similarly, the beads exported also seem to have come from these directions; there is some suggestion that the blue *akori* beads which were highly prized on the Gold Coast and in southern Togo and Dahomey may have derived from the production of glass (or perhaps of iron slag) at Ife, while stone beads, of the carnelian type, seem to have been primarily exports from the upper Benue valley region. In the seventeenth century, at least, it seems certain that some of Benin's beads reached it via a market called 'Gaboe', which may well be identified with the Ibo town of Aboh at the head of the Delta.[1]

There thus seem to be grounds for believing that the motive behind the establishment of a centralized and extensive system of monarchical government in Benin may have been, at least in some measure, to control and to profit from an important junction between east–west and north–south routes of trade. A north–south trade between the coastlands of the Niger delta and their hinterland would be virtually inherent in the situation. The Delta and its coastal mangrove swamps are either unsuitable or impossible country for farming. On the other hand, they were a highly rewarding environment for fisherfolk and salt-makers, who would need to exchange their produce for the foodstuffs and other products of the farming communities accessible northwards by the Niger and its distributaries. The traditions of the Ijo and other peoples of the Delta suggest that by about 1400 these had already established petty kingdoms at suitable points on the sand-bar fronting the coast to exploit this situation. Pacheco Pereira is presumably referring to one of these when he wrote of 'a very large village comprising more than 2,000 households' at the mouth of the Real river; in all probability, indeed, this is Bonny. Here 'much salt is made' and

[1] Northrup, 'The growth of trade among the Igbo', 220–1, re Benin's trade in beads via 'Gaboe'; F. Willett, *Ife in the history of West African sculpture* (London, 1967), esp. 105–8, re beads and their manufacture at Ife.

there were dugout canoes as large as any found in Guinea, some capable of holding 80 men. The salt was traded some 100 leagues up river in exchange for yams, cows, goats and sheep. Another passage in Pacheco's work suggests that the people at the other end of this trade were the 'Opuu', a name which may with some confidence be identified as referring to the northern Ibo close by the Igala.[1]

An east–west trade could hardly be in primary produce, but must rather have been in luxury goods such as the cloth and beads that are suggested by the Benin exports (although it must not be forgotten that these seem originally to have been imports from the north). Its emergence may well be explained by the fact that, westwards from the Niger delta behind the sand-bar to the mouth of the Volta and just beyond it, there is a practically continuous system of coastal lagoons providing a ready-made highway for canoe cultures such as those of the peoples of the Niger delta. It is also not wholly beyond the bounds of possibility that Niger canoemen could have ventured an equivalent distance to the south, albeit in less favourable conditions, so as to reach copper-producing lands close by the Congo mouth: at least, Fante fishermen from the Gold Coast are reported to have reached so far in the seventeenth century.

Benin's presumed role in exploiting this situation seems to have been essentially a parasitic one. Its Edo people are land- and not water-dwellers; they could only trade with the Portuguese via Ijo and Itsekiri intermediaries. There are some traces of Benin influence on the western Ijo, but essentially the Delta kingdoms seem to have been spontaneous creations. But it is surely significant that two of the major directions of Benin imperial advance were north-east towards the lower Niger, where the significant Ibo market centres of Aboh and Onitsha evolved, and beyond this towards Igala and the Benue river, and west towards Lagos and beyond. There are even traditions which suggest that the Ga kingdoms just across the Volta on the south-eastern Gold Coast originated with emigrants from Benin or the Niger delta. Subsequent Benin political action at Lagos could have been designed to prevent Yoruba interference with the lagoon trading route and, after the Portuguese arrival, to ensure that all European trade with the productive Yoruba kingdoms was done via Benin. However, it is notable that Benin political power never seems to have effectively crossed the Niger to the east or south-east, perhaps essentially because

[1] Pacheco Pereira, *Esmeraldo*, 136–7, 146–7; E. J. Alagoa, 'Oral tradition among the Ijo of the Niger delta', *Journal of African History*, 1966, 7, 3, 405–19; Northrup, 'The growth of trade', 223–4.

it was land based. But obviously the eastern Ibo, north of fish- and salt-producing kingdoms on the coast such as Bonny, Nembe (Brass) and Old Calabar, east of Benin, and south of the Igala kingdom and the Benue, are likely to have been affected by the trading system on which the Benin kingdom fed, and this presumably provides the context for such wealth as that revealed by the excavations at Igbo-Ukwu, close by the Niger and modern Onitsha.

It should be noted that both Benin and – despite some anthropologists' beliefs to the contrary – the Delta peoples, the Ibo and probably also their northern neighbours, the Tiv, seem to have had regular currencies by the time of the arrival of the Portuguese. This seems a clear indication of the sophistication of their commercial systems engaged in the exchange, often over considerable distances, of goods such as salt, cloth, metals, beads and fish (as well as rather more local exchanges of foodstuffs, such as yams, cattle and, presumably, palm oil). Some of the coastal peoples, some of the Ibo, and probably also the Tiv, had metal currencies either in the form of lengths of copper or copper-based (i.e. brass or bronze) rods and wires, or of manillas, horseshoe-shaped bracelets made of the same metals. Benin, and possibly some of the peoples along the lower Niger, used manillas and cowrie shells. Another early currency of which little is known, and to which the first reference is in the seventeenth century, took the form of arrow-shaped pieces of iron. These have been found not only among the Ibo, but also appreciably further to the north, for example in the Benue valley, in the Jos plateau and in Hausaland.

The Portuguese exploited this situation by themselves importing manillas (by about 1500) and cowries (by about 1515). Cowrie shells, of course, originate in the Indian Ocean, whence the Portuguese brought them in their ships. It is obviously of the greatest significance that they must have previously come to Benin (and also to Yorubaland, though there they seem to have been used more for ritual than for currency purposes) by overland routes, and it is interesting to note that Ibn Baṭṭūṭa noted their use as currency in Mali and Gao in 1352/3. The distribution of the arrow-shaped iron currency is also an indication of southern Nigeria's trade-links with the central Sudan.

Although there is evidence of the trade which the kingdoms of Benin and of Yorubaland, and the Niger delta peoples also, had with more northerly territories, there is little that can be said about the history of these before the sixteenth century other than that some of them had kingdoms with whom the more southerly kings maintained relations.

Of the Igala kingdom, with its capital at Idah on the Niger adjacent to the most north-easterly point of Benin power, little can be said other than that there is traditional and cultural evidence that at various times its history and constitution was much influenced both by Benin and the Yoruba, and also by the Jukun or Kwararafa, the ruling group of a kingdom along the middle Benue who also played their part in the history of Hausaland and Bornu. But it has been demonstrated that it is practically impossible to assemble this evidence in any meaningful chronological frame.[1]

Across the Benue north-west from Igala lay the kingdom of Nupe, but here again meaningful historical reconstruction is fraught with problems (see pp. 299–302). At a time which in all probability was early in the sixteenth century, Nupe seems to have received a new dynasty founded by a legendary hero, Tsoede, who is said to have come from Igala. This event must have caused the disappearance of much of its earlier historical tradition: the subsequent concept of the earlier situation is one only of a loose confederation of petty kings who paid tribute to the *atta* of Igala. Whether this is a true picture, it is impossible to say. Even the subsequent history of the Nupe kingdom is now difficult to reconstruct, because in the nineteenth century it was conquered by Fulani who eventually established their own line of rulers.

It does seem clear, however, that with the arrival of the Tsoede dynasty, Nupe embarked on a career of military aggression. This may have been directed particularly across the Niger into northern Yoruba territory; at least Yoruba traditions suggest that from the early sixteenth century onwards there were continual wars with Nupe, and it would seem too that these had an important effect on the subsequent course of Yoruba history. At a time which has been calculated to be around 1535, Nupe invaded the northern Yoruba kingdom of Oyo, and forced its kings to abandon their capital, and to embark on something like eighty years of exile. According to Oyo tradition, the Yoruba king at the time of the invasion had a Borgu wife, and it was with her kinsmen in Borgu to the north-west of Oyo that he took refuge. Subsequently his successors were able to return to Oyo territory, and ultimately (*c.* 1610?) to reoccupy their traditional capital. A point of particular interest is that it was very shortly after this that Oyo embarked on its own career of military conquest, with cavalry as its principal arm, which was to extend its power down to the Aja states on the coast to the south-west,

[1] J. S. Boston, 'Oral tradition and the history of Igala', *Journal of African History*, 1969, 10, 1, 29–43.

and was to establish its dominance over all the more southerly Yoruba states for a period of practically two centuries. One explanation for this is simply that Oyo had to build up a military strength to resist Nupe pressure, and that once this had been successfully done, it was free to embark on aggression of its own (and chose to do this towards the south and south-west, where commercial activities were increasing as a result of the European trade on the coast). But it seems probable that Borgu may have played an important role in this new build-up of military and royal power in Oyo, that it was in Borgu that the Oyo kings learnt their military tactics and secured the horses required for their cavalry. It is even possible at a pinch to interpret Oyo tradition at this point as indicating something approaching a change of dynasty, the subsequent royal line being initially as much Borgawa as it was Yoruba.[1] It is also possible to speculate that the subsequent course of events in Yorubaland involved a shift in its history, comparable to that suggested in Benin tradition for the arrival of Oranyan and in Nupe tradition for the arrival of Tsoede. If this was so, then the previous political pattern in Yorubaland might have been one of a congeries of petty kingdoms owing only nominal allegiance to the ritual leadership of the kings of Ife, and it would not be until the Oyo conquests that any attempt was made to establish a unitary state.

THE PERIOD OF EUROPEAN INVOLVEMENT

The only Europeans consistently involved with West Africa before the very end of the sixteenth century were the Portuguese. In the early years of coastal exploration, they faced competition – probably more than may be apparent in the surviving documentation – from seamen and merchants from nearby Castilian ports, and there were also a considerable number of foreigners, particularly Italians, in the Portuguese service. But after Columbus's first voyage in 1492 and the Treaty of Tordesillas in the following year, Castilian enterprise was diverted to America. Twenty years before this, Portuguese pioneers had reached the Gold Coast, and the Portuguese crown's appreciation of the great wealth to be won there by trade led it by the 1480s to develop a policy of endeavouring to ensure that European sea trade with the Guinea coasts would be a Portuguese monopoly under strict royal control. This

[1] Leo Frobenius, *The voice of Africa*, tr. R. Blind (London, 1913), I, 177, 210–12; II, 269. This problem is discussed by R. C. C. Law in his Ph.D. thesis, 'The Oyo empire: the history of a Yoruba state, principally in the period *c.* 1600–*c.* 1836' (University of Birmingham, 1971), 37–9.

policy was by and large successful. Individual foreign merchants, principally French and English, did make occasional voyages to Guinea between about 1480 and the 1570s, but these sporadic ventures were in general unsupported by their home governments, and so made little headway against the state power which Portugal maintained on the Guinean coasts and seas. It was only with the first Dutch voyages to Guinea in the 1590s that there appeared a competitor who was eventually willing to mobilize national resources in sufficient strength to affect the Portuguese position there.

However, the aims of the Portuguese in Guinea were limited, and so too were the resources available to implement them. The general Portuguese purpose was to combat the position of strength which Muslim power had achieved in the Near East, on the southern shore of the Mediterranean, and – for a time – in the Iberian peninsula itself, by breaking out into the oceans and securing direct access to the peoples and resources of the lands beyond the Islamic world. But the richest economic prizes, and the most powerful allies against Islam, were seen as lying around and beyond the Indian Ocean. Once direct access to these had been secured, as it was after Vasco da Gama's voyage to India and back in 1497–9, Africa became only of secondary interest. In general its peoples and resources were thought less well organized or developed to provide useful trade and allies in the struggle against Islam. Portuguese interest in Africa became focussed only on those areas which could produce in quantity goods of special value to their trading system, or which seemed to offer sufficient evidence of political organization over a sufficiently large area to make it worth while for the Portuguese to seek to infiltrate them and to develop them as satellites of its commercial empire.

This policy was conditioned by the fact that Portugal was a small and economically poorly endowed nation to seek to control an empire which, however much she chose to concentrate on commercial rather than territorial exploitation, still stretched halfway round the world, from Brazil to the Moluccas. Her sixteenth-century population numbered no more than about 1,500,000, inadequate to develop all her agricultural resources, with which she was not unduly endowed, and she had little in the way of minerals or industry. To operate her empire at all, she needed to make sufficient profit from the sale of Asian or African produce to be able to buy elsewhere the goods which the Asian or African peoples required in exchange. Her strength lay in the skill of her seamen and in the strength and sophistication of the national resolve which she had developed to combat, and to advance at the expense of the Muslim world. But these were increasingly sapped by the losses of trained seamen and of reliable and efficient officials that were inherent in the months of voyaging and the years of residence in the tropics that were involved in the maintenance of her empire.

The early Portuguese interest in Benin provides a good example of their African policy as it had developed by the beginning of the sixteenth century. Benin provided one of the few examples of both organized trade and an effective centralized government extending over a large area within easy reach of the coast. Therefore, if the Portuguese could ally themselves with its administration, they could see a chance of spreading their influence widely at minimum cost to themselves in men and money. Secondly, of course, in the Benin region it was possible to buy goods which could profitably be exchanged for the gold of the Gold Coast. This too was important if the Portuguese were to make the maximum use of their limited resources, especially as, once they had opened up their Indian Ocean trade, gold and slaves were the only two African exports for which they had a strong and consistent need.

Gold came first and foremost in Portugal's demands on Africa because it was in short supply to meet the needs of the expanding governments and economies of the new western European nation-states, and also because the producers of Asian goods, such as spices, drugs, sugar and silks, for which there was a profitable and ever-growing European demand, were much less interested in taking in exchange the European exports of the time than they were in acquiring bullion. The Portuguese interest in acquiring African slaves grew steadily throughout the fifteenth and sixteenth centuries. Initially their main use was to supplement the labour force in Portugal itself, especially in the thinly populated southern provinces recently reconquered from the Muslims. Then the Portuguese appreciated that, instead of spending scarce bullion on purchasing Asian sugar, they could grow it themselves on their recently discovered Atlantic islands. Plantations began to be developed in Madeira and the Azores in the first half of the fifteenth century, and by the 1460s the Cape Verde islands also began to be used in this way. Africa was the obvious source to which the planters looked for the large quantities of labour they needed.

In the 1490s, the Portuguese also began to settle Fernando Po, São Tomé and the other islands in the Gulf of Guinea. Initially this was because the islands were ideally situated to serve as calling points where their Guinea ships could be revictualled and overhauled before returning home (or, later, crossing to America), and from which trade could be conducted with the coasts from Benin to the Congo for slaves to make up the cargoes of these ships. But within a few years the settlers had appreciated that the islands' volcanic soils and high rainfall made them very suitable for tropical plantation agriculture. Thus the islands themselves became major markets for African slaves, so much so in fact that by the 1570s their slave population had become so large that serious difficulties were arising in trying to keep control of it. This led many of the planters to transfer their activities to Brazil, with the result that there was a great intensification of the trans-Atlantic trade in African slaves, which had begun on a relatively small scale some half a century earlier to help meet the labour shortages of the Spanish colonies in the New World.

But it took some time before the Portuguese government could work out and begin to implement a fully comprehensive and rational policy for their nation's Guinea interest. Although it was quick to realize the particular importance of both the Gold Coast and Benin, the Portuguese pioneers did not get so far along the Guinea coast until the 1470s and 1480s, and it was not until after the proving of the sea route to India at the turn of the century, followed shortly afterwards by the discovery of Brazil, that it could really think out the best way to fit the African trade into an overall imperial scheme. But Portugal's trade with Upper Guinea had begun more than half a century earlier, and in part, when formulating its later African policy, its government was drawing on lessons learnt there through hard experience.

Prior to the discovery of the Gold Coast, although the Portuguese crown and its agents had sponsored and undertaken most of the work of African discovery, the actual work of exploiting the discoveries had been largely left to individual Portuguese entrepreneurs or settlers operating under particular or general royal licences. The value of the Cape Verde islands, especially of Santiago, which had a good natural harbour, as a safe base from which to conduct trade with Upper Guinea was quickly appreciated, and their colonization was encouraged by granting the settlers freedom to trade on the coast from the Senegal to Sierra Leone. As has been seen, the coastlands south of the Gambia had been penetrated by merchants, and to some extent politically organized also by princelings, who were offshoots from the Mali empire, while north of the Gambia the coastal lands were under the jurisdiction of the Wolof empire, which itself had its links with Mali and its trade.

There were thus opportunities for trade here for commodities such as gold, slaves, gum, ivory, dyewoods and peppers. The Cape Verde islanders began to establish a number of trading settlements on the mainland. North of the Gambia, these were perforce largely on the coast, for example at Beziguiche, Portudal and Joal, which were on the coasts of the Wolof sub-kingdoms of Kayor, Baol and Sine, respectively. From the Gambia southwards, however, there were rivers such as the Casamance, the Geba, the Nunez, the Scarcies and the Rokelle, which could be used by small boats to penetrate inland for roughly thirty to fifty kilometres, thus enabling the Portuguese largely to bypass the local West Atlantic communities, and to establish their settlements inland alongside those of merchants from Mandeland. In the exceptional case of the Gambia, which is navigable by ocean-going ships for a distance of approximately 240 kilometres, it was possible for the Portuguese to gain direct access to the major trading centre of Cantor (Kuntaur).

Since there was no shortage of land in Portugal itself, settlement in the Cape Verde islands (or elsewhere in Africa) initially had few attractions for its more sober and industrious citizens; hence in part the need to encourage it by granting the islanders freedom to trade with the mainland. Many of the original settlers, and especially those who went to the mainland, were therefore what Blake has called 'a not very choice collection of unprincipled adventurers, slave dealers, political exiles and fugitives from justice',[1] quite a few of whom were not Portuguese at all, and most of whom had little care for the interests of the Portuguese government. As they moved to the coasts and up the rivers of Upper Guinea, so these men largely passed beyond the effective jurisdiction of the authorities at Santiago and entered that of various African authorities. They settled down in their new environments, took African wives, and entered into a variety of alliances, agreements and understandings with the local African traders and rulers. Thus there was born a new society of *lançados*, private European or half-caste traders living in or alongside African communities, and *grumetes*, their African associates, originally for the most part their slaves, whose outlook and interests were as much or more African as they were Portuguese or European.

By the time that the discovery of the Gold Coast and of Benin had convinced King John II (1481–95) and his government that the Guinea trade should be brought under strict royal control, the situation in

[1] J. W. Blake, *Europeans in West Africa, 1450–1560* (London, 1941), I, 28.

Upper Guinea was totally out of hand. Administrative measures designed to check or to control from Santiago the activities of the *lançados* were ineffective, and official embassies sent inland to establish formal relations between the kings of Portugal and Mali were totally fruitless. So too were attempts to build a royal fort on the Sierra Leone coast and to place a puppet, Christianized prince on the Wolof throne. Indeed, official and unofficial Portuguese activities in Upper Guinea were combining to reduce the power of African rulers to maintain the systems of order needed for the flourishing of peaceful trade. The competition between competing European traders and trading interests seems likely to have been a factor in the decline of the Wolof empire, and in the emergence of its subordinate rulers as independent, but not very effective, petty kings. It is possible that the increasing emphasis placed by the Europeans on the slave-trade was an important factor in this and similar processes; certainly the disruption and diminution of political authority produced a situation of increasing warfare, and hence of increasing numbers of war captives available for sale to the Europeans. The beneficiaries of this situation on the African side were for the most part not local men but immigrant Mande or Fulani. An early and outstanding example was Koli Tengella (*c.* 1512–37), who, after his father had been defeated in a revolt against the Songhay empire in Massina, led a mixed band of Fulani and Mande followers westwards to Futa Toro, where they established an essentially pagan kingdom at the expense of Wolof power. It was essentially from Fulani or Mande adventurers that the Europeans secured the slaves that by the end of the sixteenth century were their main commercial interest.

Tengella's arrival in the coastlands from the Sudan shows that, however much the old political and social orders may have been weakened by the *lançados*, they were by no means the only disruptive influence. About 1545 the Europeans on the coast became aware that the Upper Guinea coastlands were being invaded from the south-east by warrior bands called the Mane. These Mane advanced parallel to the coast, attacking and almost invariably overcoming each small West Atlantic community they came up against. On each occasion, some of them settled down to become overlords of a new small kingdom, while the remainder, sweeping up in their train some of the local people as auxiliaries (called Sumba), would continue their advance and repeat the process further to the north-west. From the evidence of their dress and weapons, and also that of their language, there is really no room for doubt that the Mane were in origin Mande warriors, and it was only when they came up against the Susu, another Mande people with a military tradition, that their advance petered out. But south of the Susu, their coming brought about a radical rearrangement of the ethnic pattern. The Mande-speaking Mende became established as one of the dominant stocks of modern Sierra Leone. North of the Mende, the modern Loko people also today speak a Mande language, but there is reason to believe that their ethnic base is essentially 'West Atlantic'. Their neighbours, the Temne, have a West Atlantic language, but it would seem that their chiefly families may be of Mane origin. Throughout modern Sierra Leone, and in adjacent Liberia too to some extent, the coming of the Mane resulted in the establishment of more positive kingdoms than had hitherto existed. If these were usually on a small geographical scale, there was henceforward a sharper division between rulers and ruled than before, and this too was to the advantage of the European slave-traders as they began to increase their demands on Africa.

The Mane were first observed about the middle of the modern Liberian coastline, but they seem to have possessed a tradition (which was recorded by a European writer in 1625) that they first came to the coast from Mandeland close by a place where the Portuguese had a fortress. If this was indeed the case, this can only be on the Gold Coast, where the castle of São Jorge da Mina (the modern Elmina Castle) was begun in 1482. This was followed by other forts at Axim (1503–8?) and Shama (*c.* 1560) to the west, and at Accra to the east (when this fort was built is unclear; it was probably after 1557, and obviously prior to 1576, when the local Ga seem to have destroyed it). Since the Mane tradition apparently remembered only one Portuguese fort, and the second one, at Axim, is west of the first, at Elmina, it seems reasonable to suppose that they must have arrived on the Gold Coast somewhere near Elmina between 1482 and *c.* 1508. It would be conceivable that the Mane might have reached the coast near Axim after *c.* 1508, but this would give them less time to pursue their career of conquest westwards to Liberia, so this seems a less credible alternative. It also seems more likely that they should have arrived in the very early days of the Portuguese presence on the Gold Coast, before they were very familiar with its affairs; otherwise, despite the fragmentary nature of the surviving Portuguese documentation concerning the Gold Coast, it is difficult to see why some record of their passing should not have been preserved.

If the Mane did indeed set out towards Liberia and Sierra Leone from the Gold Coast, it would not be unreasonable to suppose that their arrival there was associated with the same circumstances that led King John II to command the building of Elmina Castle – namely, the desire to establish control over the flourishing gold exports of the Akan territories that had followed upon the opening up of the Mande-Dyula trade-route from Jenne. It has already been seen, with respect to Begho, that this could lead to Dyula merchants' attempting to take new political and military initiatives, involving their enlisting the services of Mande warriors, small parties of whom were doubtless already employed to guard their caravans. The Dyula intervention in Begho may well have been associated with a general worsening of their trading situation which became apparent in the sixteenth century. Wilks has suggested that the prime cause of this was that, following the establishment of the Portuguese on the Gold Coast, there was a significant decline in the amount of gold reaching Jenne. It is impossible to be sure of this for, though the amount of gold secured by the Portuguese was soon impressive – it was up to at least 570 kilograms a year by the 1500s – it might be supposed that much of this came from southerly Akan resources which had recently been opened up, in part in response to the European demand, and which had never contributed much to the northern trade. Elsewhere, indeed, Wilks has suggested that the northern trade continued to dominate in the northern Akan territories until the nineteenth century.[1]

In fact it is not too difficult to see more local factors combining to force new initiatives on the Mande north of the forest. One was simply the growth of Bono power; by controlling more and more of the trade-paths out of the forest, its kings would be in an ever stronger position to dictate the terms on which the Dyula could buy gold. Secondly, there was the rise of the relatively new kingdom of Dagomba, which was soon to interfere with the Dyula trade by conquering Buna, and which may already have affected it adversely by securing, at Daboya, the only good source of salt in the interior of modern Ghana. Thirdly, of course, the Dyula were now no longer the only long-distance merchants trading with the Akan; as has been seen, they had been faced with competition from Hausa traders from about the middle of the fifteenth century. This threefold threat to their original domination of the trade between the Akan and the Sudan seems almost certainly to have suggested to the Dyula that they should try and secure political control of

[1] The first opinion may be found in Ajayi and Crowder, *History of West Africa*, I, 362; the second in the earlier article, I. Wilks, 'A medieval trade route from the Niger to the Gulf of Guinea', *Journal of African History*, 1962, 3, 2, 340–1.

Gonja. This was a territory of little intrinsic significance, indeed it was largely barren and consequently thinly inhabited, but of considerable strategic importance, lying north of Bono, east of Begho and Banda, and south-west of Dagomba, and with all the important trade-routes leading south to the Akan forest and gold-bearing lands either crossing it or passing close by its borders.

In fact, because of its lack of resources and population, establishing and maintaining a political and military power in Gonja was a matter of some difficulty. Defeats were inflicted on both Bono and Dagomba which restricted their ability to interfere in Gonja, but it was not until the seventeenth century that the Mande completed the erection there of a central government, and this quickly fell apart, so that in the following century Gonja became an easy prey for Asante. But the first Dyula moves to control Gonja through the use of military forces brought or sent from Mandeland seem undoubtedly to have been taken in the sixteenth century. Perhaps then the origin of the Mane lies here, with a band of Mande warriors who had met with some reverse, had been cut off from the north, and so had chosen to fight their way out to the south and west.

The first Portuguese sailors reached the Gold Coast in 1471, during a period (1469–74) when the Portuguese crown had sub-contracted the work of maritime exploration and of trading with new discoveries to a Lisbon merchant, Fernão Gomes, whose captains in fact took it as far as the islands in the Gulf of Guinea. The richness of the gold resources of the Gold Coast, and the trade that could be done there, were quickly apparent and attracted the notice of adventurers from many seafaring western European nations. The Portuguese crown therefore decided that Portugal's interests here could not be left to a private individual, that trade with Lower Guinea should be a state enterprise, and that royal power should be established on the Gold Coast to ensure that only the Portuguese crown could have access to its gold trade. Portugal in fact decided to act on the coast very much as Bono was acting on the northern edge of the Akan forestlands. This was the genesis of the decision to establish a royal fort at the best available site on the central section of the Gold Coast between Cape Three Points and Cabo das Redes (the modern Fetta Point), and, later, to extend this system of control over virtually the whole length of the coast from which gold could be bought, from Axim, close by the mouth of the Ankobra in the west, to Accra in the east.

D'Azambuja, the commander of the expedition sent out from Lisbon in December 1481 to build the first fort, chose the site at Elmina for a number of reasons. In the first place, it was central. Secondly, it was technically a very good site. Virtually all the many forts built by Europeans on the Gold Coast occupy small rocky outcrops, which provide good foundations and building material, and project a short distance out from the coast, thus providing landing places immediately to the east which offer some shelter from the prevailing south-westerly wind and current. Elmina, with the little river Benja entering the sea immediately east of the rocky outcrop, is one of the best of these. Thirdly, this river was the boundary between the two coastal Akan states of Komenda and Fetu, thus providing a chink into which the Portuguese could hope to insert their political power with hope of it taking firm root.

They were in fact remarkably successful in this. D'Azambuja engaged in negotiations for permission to build his fort with a man whom the Portuguese sources call Caramansa. It is not clear who Caramansa was, whether he was the king of Komenda (whose capital lay a little way inland) or merely some local chief. At any rate, he at first objected to the Portuguese building a permanent on-shore base. In the words of one Portuguese historian, he asked d'Azambuja 'to be pleased to depart, and to allow the ships to come in the future as they had in the past, so that there would always be peace and concord between them. Friends who met occasionally remained better friends than if they were neighbours.'[1] But presumably d'Azambuja could reply that if Caramansa refused his permission, the Portuguese would take their fort and, therefore, their trade to Fetu or elsewhere, and eventually the fort was built. During the building, there was some kind of a brawl with the local people in which the Portuguese demonstrated their superior force, but obviously d'Azambuja and Caramansa had reached some kind of agreement. There is no record of its terms, but it can be presumed that it was not unlike later agreements between Europeans and African rulers concerning forts on the Gold Coast, in which 'Notes' were exchanged by which permission to build and use the fort was granted in return for specific annual payments from the Europeans to the African king. The Portuguese in 1482, and other Europeans on subsequent occasions, seem to have interpreted a Note as a cession to them of the land on which the fort was built (in 1486, Elmina was in fact formally given the status of a Portuguese city), and the payments to African kings were regarded rather as presents to facilitate trade and

[1] Quoted from Crone, *Voyages of Cadamosto*, 121.

good relations. On the African side, however, it may be doubted whether any king had power to cede land, and the payments were probably regarded as an acknowledgement by the Europeans of African sovereignty, that technically they had become subjects of the king.

In fact what happened at Elmina, Axim and Shama was that the forts, and the settlements of African and half-caste merchants, artisans, soldiers, servants and slaves that developed under their walls to serve them, became detached from the local African polities and became tied to the alien interest. This must have been a constant source of annoyance and friction for the kings of the coastal states, but on balance it seems to have been an evil which they were prepared to suffer in order to trade with the foreigners. This they wanted to do because both directly and indirectly the trade brought them revenue and profit. Equally the Europeans on their side needed at least the tacit goodwill of the local people and authorities if they were to trade successfully. The Portuguese both could and did mount punitive expeditions against coastal peoples who traded with their European rivals. But their forts and their soldiers and ships were intended more to protect their position on the Gold Coast from European competitors than they were to impose any control on the Africans. Their strength lay in the fact that, if other Europeans could be kept away, then the Africans had to come to them if they wanted to exchange their gold for useful imports like cloth and metals. Their garrisons were not a military threat on land beyond gunshot of their ships and forts; indeed the latter were hardly defensible without the co-operation of the local Africans. A purely European military force, dependent entirely on imported foodstuffs and stored rainwater, would have its efficiency increasingly sapped by disease and by claustrophobic ennui unless it were continually reinforced and replenished by a frequent service of ships from home, and this Portugal lacked the resources to provide. Thus they came to depend on the local Africans for military support, fresh water and provisions, as well as for trade. Each side was therefore bound to the other by self-interest and, if the two got at cross-purposes, ultimately the Africans were in the stronger position. They could withdraw their trade, blockade a fort, or even capture and destroy it.

But this clearly was a drastic last resort. It was never undertaken against the Portuguese by the Akan states on the coast, but only by the Ga of Accra in 1576. It is not known why the Ga acted in this way, but their position seems to have differed from that of the Akans in at least two respects. While the power and wealth of the Akan rulers and merchants were intimately bound up with the gold industry and trading, the Ga did not themselves possess gold-bearing land; the most they could do was to act as hosts for Akan gold-traders coming to the coast. Secondly, their kingdoms must have been relatively recent foundations, so that perhaps their kings were more jealous of their sovereignty, especially since many of their subjects may have not been Ga in origin but came from Guan-speaking Akan stock. They may thus well have thought that it was better to do without trade with Europeans than to let the latter consolidate on their shores *imperia in imperiis* of the type that the Portuguese had established at Elmina, Axim and Shama.

While the Portuguese consolidated their position at these forts (and thus established a pattern which later Europeans were to multiply almost tenfold after the Dutch had gained their first foothold at Mori in 1598), there was virtually no European trade on the coasts of the Ga states for more than fifty years after the destruction of the fort at Accra. On the other hand, it cannot be said that this Portuguese monopoly of the southern trading outlets of the Akan had much effect on the latter's history; certainly it could not bear comparison with the effect on this history of the rise of Bono to control their northern trading outlets. The Portuguese were foreigners, who were effectively confined to their forts and did not penetrate themselves into the interior. The most their presence could do was to exacerbate and perpetuate the competition between, and the divisions among, the coastal Akan states and, no doubt, by providing additional and competitive markets, accelerate the power struggles that were building up in the forest in and around Akani and Twifu. But the mainsprings of political and economic action here remained intrinsically African, deriving indeed from the original growth of states like Bono, Banda and Buna following the stimulus from the Dyula.

The Portuguese took no interest in the coast between the Volta and Benin, for some of the same reasons that they also neglected Middle Guinea. Since there was no gold to be had here, there was no point in landing on its open and dangerously surf-bound beaches. Behind these, and behind the lagoons that lay between the beaches and terra firma, however, things were stirring. It was probably in the fifteenth and sixteenth centuries that the Aja peoples were beginning to erect the kingdoms that became some of the most fruitful suppliers of slaves to European traders from the mid seventeenth century onwards.

Indigenous traditions depict this process as resulting from a migration from western Yorubaland to Tado (about 95 kilometres from the sea, near the modern Togo–Dahomey frontier), whence there was a dispersion in all directions. Some people went further west to Nuatja, which is the traditional dispersal point for the Ewe of southern Togo and of the trans-Volta region of southern modern Ghana, rather as Ife is the traditional dispersal point for the Yoruba. Others went south-east from Tado towards the coast, where the kingdom of Allada (Great Ardra) and a number of smaller, satellite kingdoms were developed, at a time which is commonly supposed to be about 1575. Some confirmation of these traditions may be found in the considerable (but unfortunately unexcavated) earthworks still to be seen at Tado and Nuatja. The most plausible explanation of what was happening would be that the ancestors of the Aja and the Ewe (or perhaps only of their ruling clans) were refugees of some kind from the state-building operations that were taking place in Yorubaland. This is perhaps more likely than that they were active offshoots of this process. The Ewe and the Aja form today a single linguistic entity even if there is considerable fragmentation between the dialects of their various groups. It is really only the Aja (and their offshoot, the Fon) who have developed monarchical state institutions; indeed the Aja and the Fon might be called 'Ewe who have kingdoms'. The Ewe, as has been seen, were those who claim to have travelled furthest from Yorubaland; conversely the Aja would have been those most affected by trade and other influences stemming from the growth of political and economic power in Yorubaland and Benin.

But all this was in the dark as far as the early Europeans were concerned. It was only at Benin that the Portuguese made direct contact with a major Lower Guinea kingdom and sought to convert it to their own purposes. In this, they were completely unsuccessful. In about 1487, they secured a footing at Ughoton (Gwato), which was as near as their ships could get to the capital, Benin City, about 30 kilometres to the north-east. However, after about thirty years, the Portuguese abandoned their official post at Ughoton, and such relations as they subsequently had with Benin were conducted mainly by individual merchants from São Tomé and the other Gulf of Guinea islands. The establishment at Ughoton was clearly not producing the results the Portuguese government had expected of it.

As has been seen, even on the Gold Coast, where Portuguese royal power in Guinea was most strongly established, there were limitations to it. But there at least they could if need be seek to bend things their way by using their ships to bombard the coast or to land punitive expeditions. At Benin, however, the Portuguese power was entirely peripheral. The people of the coastlands were not subjects of its king, so there was no point in demonstrating against them. At Ughoton, the Portuguese were about 65 kilometres from the sea up a treacherous river system, yet they were still remote from the seat of government, which could only be reached overland. Power here depended on the possession of soldiers, of which Benin had many and the Portuguese few, and on the control of trade-routes by land or by canoe with which the Portuguese could not interfere. For Benin, trade with the Portuguese was not the near necessity which it became for the coastal Akan kings and merchants, but a marginal luxury in which the Benin king could choose whether or not he and his people should engage. Initially, however, the Portuguese thought it worth their while accepting the king's conditions for trade. If Benin could deliver goods that they wanted, then relations with it might develop so that the king and his court would be converted into Christian allies and might ultimately become their dependants.

Further south, in the Kongo kingdom, things did work out in this way. In Benin they did not, partly because the king was in a much stronger position than the Kongo king, partly because the Portuguese trade there did not develop as had been hoped. The Portuguese had no need of Benin peppers once their Indian Ocean trade had been established. After an initial period during which Benin's recent wars of expansion seem to have provided a useful stock of slaves from which Portuguese purchases might be drawn, the slave-trade proved disappointing. By 1516, indeed, the king must have decided that the kingdom's manpower should not be further depleted; thereafter only female slaves were readily offered for sale to the Portuguese. By this time, of course, the Portuguese trade with Benin was being conducted from São Tomé and the other Gulf of Guinea islands, and the settlers there had appreciated that slaves – and other useful commodities – could be purchased without restriction from Itsekiri, Ijo and other peoples of the Niger delta region who were beyond or on the fringes of Benin authority.

However, Portuguese relations with Benin did not end with the withdrawal from Ughoton or its restriction on the export of male slaves. In 1514, the *oba* of Benin sent an embassy to Portugal, complaining about the slaving activities of her king's subjects who had settled on the Gulf of Guinea islands, but also asking for a Christian mission and fire-arms to be sent to him. This seemed to be the opportunity for which the Portuguese had been waiting, for hitherto the Benin kings had shown little or no sign of wishing to depart from the traditional ancestral religion which was central to the position of their monarchy. In fact it is apparent that the king (probably Oba Ozuola) was far less interested in Christianity than he was in getting fire-arms. This was a time in which he was hard-pressed in wars which were making him unpopular with his soldiers and subjects. He was thus prepared, at least for the moment, to countenance Christianity if this was the price that had to be paid to get guns to bring his wars to a successful conclusion and to re-establish his powers over his people. But it was Portuguese policy to supply arms only to firmly Christian allies, and though the king allowed one of his sons and some of his officials to be baptized, he did not submit to baptism himself. Benin tradition says that Ozuola was ultimately poisoned by his war-weary soldiers.[1] The Portuguese and Christian interest was now associated with a dead and discredited king, and the traditional national beliefs regained the ascendancy. The Portuguese sent another mission to Benin in 1538, possibly because they were alarmed by the fact that French merchants had begun to send ships there, as English merchants were to do from the 1550s. But the fact that the Portuguese could not stop these voyages shows that they had no power to control or even to influence the Benin monarchy.

Richard Eden's account of Thomas Windham's visit to Benin in 1553 provides, indeed, some of the earliest independent testimony of the power and majesty of this monarchy. The Englishmen were conducted to the court 'where the king sate in a great huge hall', with his noblemen sitting 'cowring . . . upon their buttocks with their elbows upon their knees and their hands before their faces, not looking up until the king command them'.[2] Trade was possible only after negotiation with the king (in Portuguese), and apparently only from his stores, where a great stock of peppers had been built up.

By this time, the Portuguese had virtually no contact with Benin. Its monarchy had rebuffed them and the interest of the Portuguese traders in the Delta had shifted increasingly elsewhere, in particular perhaps to the Itsekiri kingdom of Warri. The kings here, as has been

[1] On the question of who was *oba* when the Portuguese arrived, and on the circumstances of Ozuola's reign and death, see Ryder, *Benin and the Europeans*, esp. 30, 46 and 50; J. U. Egharevba, *A short history of Benin*, 3rd ed. (Ibadan, 1960), esp. 26–7; and R. E. Bradbury, 'Chronological problems in the study of Benin history', *Journal of the Historical Society of Nigeria*, 1959, I, 4, esp. 277–81.

[2] Blake, *Europeans*, II, 317.

seen, claimed to originate from Benin, but they followed a very different policy. They seem to have welcomed the Portuguese as providing both new trading opportunities and a useful political counter-weight to Benin. They placed no restrictions on the sale of slaves, accepted Christian missionaries, and in due course became converts themselves. But Warri was a very much smaller kingdom than Benin, and much more on the fringe of the major political and commercial systems of the region. It could not provide the Portuguese with the entry to these systems for which they had hoped, and soon, with the arrival of Dutch merchants in Guinea, the period of Portuguese dominance in Europe's maritime trade with Guinea was itself about to collapse.

Indeed the appearance of the Dutch on the scene in the 1590s, followed by their destruction of the Portuguese position by about 1640, marks the beginning of a new era in the history of the Guinea coastlands. These became involved in the all-out struggle between the new capitalist societies of western Europe for access to and control of world trade, which was a major theme of European, indeed of world history, in the seventeenth, eighteenth and nineteenth centuries. West Africa's place in this struggle was formally at first rather a secondary one, the major areas of conflict outside Europe itself lying rather in Asia and the Americas, and with no significant European penetration into the interior of the continent before the nineteenth century. Nevertheless the European competition for world trade gradually began to exert a major influence on the course of Guinean history. The Europeans believed that they could not exploit the resources of tropical America without recourse to African labour. The ever-increasing demands they placed on Guinean societies for the supply of slaves for the Americas meant that for the first time Europeans were helping to shape the course of their history. Although Guinean societies were sometimes remarkably successful in adapting themselves to these new demands, new strains were being created which they could not wholly control, and the initiative in their own development was beginning to slip into foreign hands. By the beginning of the nineteenth century, when Europeans ceased to require slaves from Africa, large areas of Guinea were themselves becoming enslaved by a European-controlled world trading system. A crisis emerged in West Africa's relations with Europe in which Europeans were only too ready to seize the initiative, and to use their economic and technological strengths to erect there a formal colonial system.

CHAPTER 7

CENTRAL AFRICA FROM CAMEROUN TO THE ZAMBEZI

The history of Central Africa[1] between AD 1000 and 1600 can be broadly divided into three parts on the basis of the historical evidence so far available. In the south-east the territory of Zambia is primarily known in this period through archaeological research. The main theme is the transition from Early Iron Age cultures to Later Iron Age cultures. This transition concerned the spread of more advanced technologies, the evolution of new pottery styles, and the exchange of rare commodities over increasingly long distances. The second region, in the savannas of south-western Zaïre and Angola, saw the emergence in the late medieval period of several important political leaders. Their exploits have been recorded in oral evidence which can be supplemented, in the sixteenth century, by the writings of early European visitors to the region. Finally, the third and largest part of Central Africa covers the equatorial forest and the woodland margin to the north of it. Here historical evidence is extremely sparse, and historical speculation depends largely on ethnographic and linguistic data. The results are so far unsatisfactory, but further work should gradually enable us to understand the two main themes of the history of the north. One is the interaction between forest cultures and savanna cultures both north and south of the equator. The other is the changing relationships between gathering and farming peoples within the forest.

The most important geographical feature of Central Africa during the Later Iron Age and subsequently was its extreme sparsity of population. Nowhere in either the forest or the savanna did population densities approach those of West Africa or the interlacustrine region. Only along the southern forest margin did a slightly greater clustering of villages occur. It was in this belt also that in the later years states began actively to encourage the concentration of population to intensify agricultural production. The sparse Central African populations

[1] 'Central Africa' is here defined as the area bounded by the south Atlantic in the west, the lakes of the western rift valley in the east, the Cameroun highlands and Ubangi-Chari watershed in the north and the lower Kunene and middle Zambezi in the south, thereby covering Zambia, Angola, Zaïre and the southern half of former French Equatorial Africa.

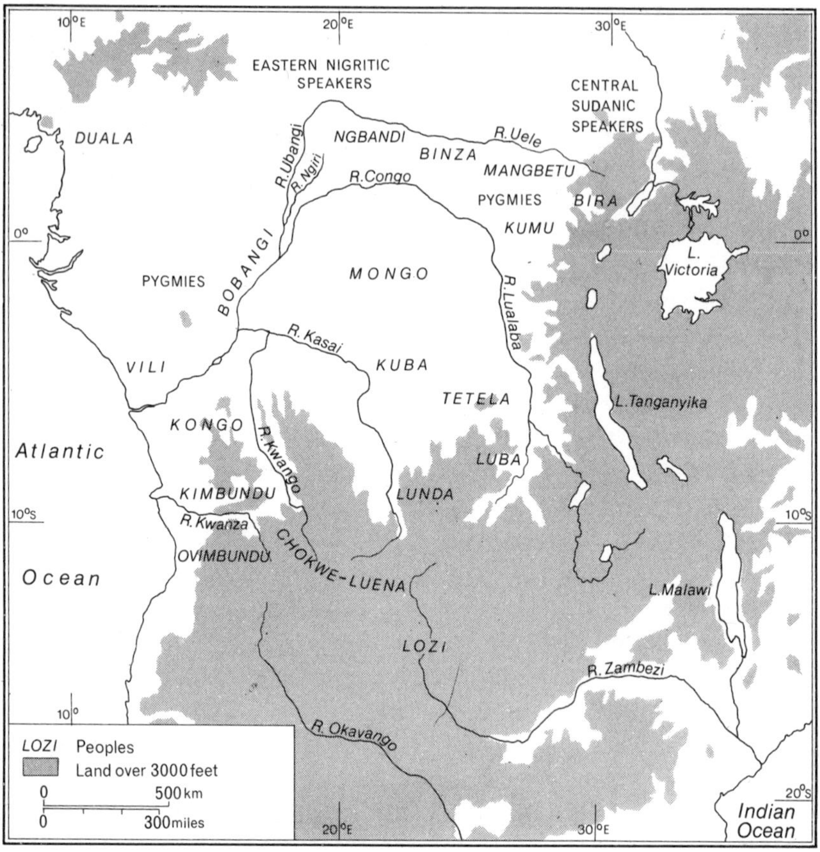

12 Central Africa

belonged to five different categories of peoples. In the north-west peoples ethnically and linguistically related to the populations of West Africa spoke languages of the Eastern Nigritic group of the Niger-Congo family. In the north-east the languages spoken were Central Sudanic. In the forest the Pygmy hunter-gatherers differed from their food-producing neighbours in culture and economy but spoke the same languages as the food-producers. The fishing and planting economies of the forest were practised mainly by Bantu-speaking peoples. Bantu speakers also occupied most parts of the southern savanna during the Later Iron Age, together with some communities of non-agricultural Khoisan-speaking peoples. These five roughly defined groups constantly interacted with each other, thereby changing the cultures of individual villages. There were not, however, any major trade arteries or other lines of long-distance communication through Central Africa comparable to the coastal traffic of East Africa or the caravan routes of West Africa. Nothing facilitated the rapid spread of political and economic innovations. The long distances and sparse population also tended to militate against the establishment of domestic markets or the growth of specialized local industries. When foreign contacts between Central Africa and the outside world were established, from the middle of the second millennium, they tended to foster a predatory traffic.

SOUTHERN CENTRAL AFRICA

At the beginning of the second millennium AD the southern savanna of Central Africa was particularly sparsely populated. The changes of the previous thousand years, dramatic though they had been, related to a small number of thinly scattered homesteads, villages and rock-shelters. In many places Late Stone Age peoples survived alongside the Iron Age farmers. Their kits of quartz blades, scrapers, arrowheads and other cutting tools were still being manufactured and retouched with techniques already several thousand years old. By the second millennium, however, these hunter-gatherer communities had become subject to more persistent outside influences than ever before. Some of them managed to obtain clay pots and other Iron Age material possessions by trading with, or possibly by raiding, their new agricultural neighbours. Others probably established a more permanent symbiotic relationship with Iron Age communities. They may have exchanged meat and hides for tools, pots and grain, in a manner still practised between hunters and farmers in the forest regions of equatorial Central Africa. Such a relationship, however, commonly caused the hunters to become absorbed by marriage, by clientship and by assimilation.

Despite the pressure of more advanced Iron Age cultures, many Late Stone Age societies survived in the southern savanna. At Nakapapula rock-shelter in northern Zambia, stone materials have been found on floor levels occupied after the eleventh century AD, and the local Lala people have oral traditions in which they describe the hunting and gathering peoples with whom they associated in the past. At Nachikufu, in the same region, and Kandanda in western Zambia, radiocarbon dating tentatively suggests that lithic technology survived until at least the middle of this millennium. As yet there is unfortunately no evidence to indicate what connection there might be between the Late Stone Age hunter-gatherers of the early second millennium, and the Khoisan hunter-gatherers of the later second millennium. No study of recent hunter-gatherer technology forms an adequate basis for comparison, and linguistic or biological comparisons are even more difficult to make.

Although hunter-gatherer communities survived in Central African rock-shelters until well into the second millennium, they had by then been outnumbered in many areas by the growing communities of iron-working agriculturalists. (This process is extensively described in Volume 2 of this series.) The farmers settled especially in the wetter, more fertile, pockets of highland, river valley or forest margin. Where the soil and rainfall permitted, many of them added Asian bananas to their cycle of crops, thus increasing food yields, and stimulating population growth. In Zambia and southern Zaïre, still the only part of the region which is archaeologically known in any detail, the pottery tradition of the Early Iron Age has been classified into several regional styles. The Dambwa and Kalundu groups of southern Zambia did not survive into the present millennium, but were superseded by the 'Middle' Iron Age Kalomo culture which grew out of the Dambwa culture. The Chondwe and Kapwirimbwe groups of the Copperbelt and Lusaka district probably continued to flourish until the early centuries of this millennium, when they were supplanted by Later Iron Age cultures. In eastern Zambia the Kamnama group bore greater similarities to the Early Iron Age cultures in Tanzania, Malawi and Rhodesia than to other Zambian groups. Finally, two related Iron Age traditions at Kalambo Falls, in northern Zambia, and Sanga, in southern Zaïre, flourished around the turn of the millennium and deserve special attention for the light they shed on the later history of Central Africa.

Early Iron Age peoples settled periodically at Kalambo Falls between about the fourth and the twelfth centuries AD. Related peoples spread over the woodland of northern Zambia, often living in rock-shelters rather than open villages. The land was mostly of poor fertility, and people had frequently to move in search of new sites. Villages were probably smaller than in the fertile southern areas of Zambia. Although the Kalambo villages used iron, there is no sign that they were familiar with copper. This is perhaps an indication of their poverty, since related people at Sanga, in southern Zaïre, had developed the richest of the late-first-millennium Iron Age cultures yet known in Central Africa.[1]

[1] D. W. Phillipson, 'The Early Iron Age in Zambia', *Journal of African History*, 1968, **9** 191–211, and his 'Notes on the later prehistoric radiocarbon chronology of eastern and southern Africa', ibid. 1970, **11**, 1–15, and 'The prehistoric succession in eastern Zambia', *Azania*, 1973, **8**, 3–24. J. E. G. Sutton, 'New radiocarbon dates for eastern and southern Africa', *Journal of African History*, 1972, **13**, 1–24.

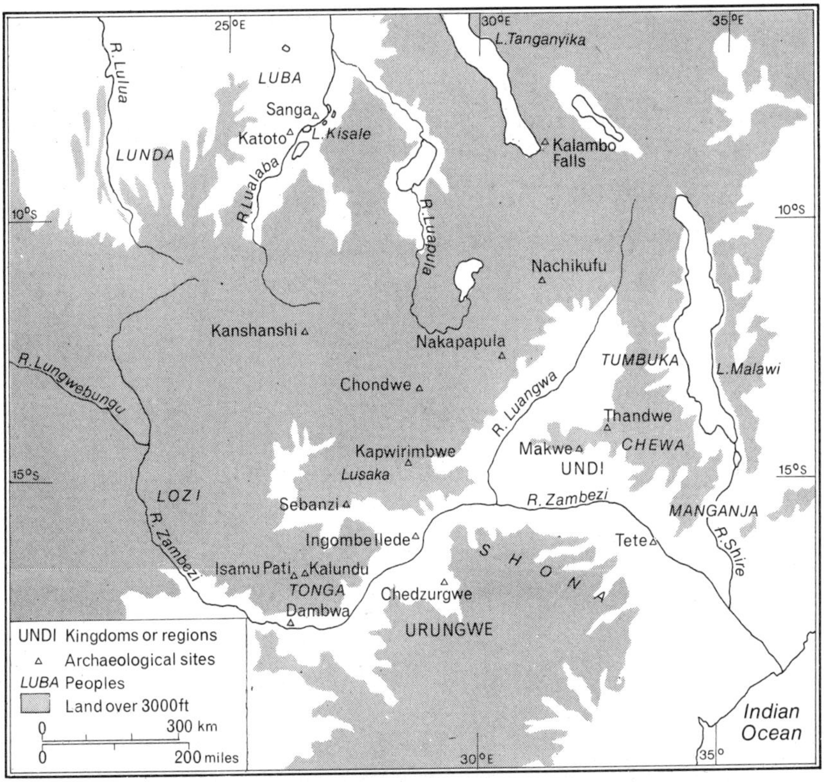

13 Southern Central Africa

Sanga, by Lake Kisale on the upper Lualaba, is approximately 480 kilometres west of the Kalambo region. Its earliest pottery tradition, with elaborately bevelled pot rims, and horizontal grooving on the necks of vessels, is similar to the Kalambo wares. In contrast to Kalambo, however, Sanga had developed a rich metal-working tradition by the end of the first millennium. The area surrounding the upper Lualaba valley appears to have been particularly attractive to Iron Age peoples. Both the river itself and the numerous small lakes were rich in fish. The vegetation was comparatively light and the woodland good for hunting game. The rainfall would have been adequate for cereals such as sorghum and millet, and where the ground retained its moisture well, bananas could have been grown with little labour. At some stage oil palms had been successfully introduced into this region and provided an item of agricultural wealth and trade. So far we can only speculate about the degree of agricultural development at Sanga. The archaeological finds do not show farming to have been a prestige activity, like hunting and fishing, which had to be commemorated with grave goods. Yet it need not be doubted that a society enjoying such a variety of material possessions and employing such advanced metal-working techniques practised agriculture. Once their hunting, fishing and agricultural prosperity was established, the Lualaba communities were able to diversify their economy beyond the narrow limits of subsistence. Their iron tools, ornaments, needles and bells show a proficient level of workmanship. The most spectacular manufactures, however, were of copper.

The people of Sanga probably obtained their copper from mines at places such as Tenke along the upper reaches of the Lualaba about 320 kilometres away to the south-east. Although none of these mines has yet been investigated, they may have resembled a mine at Kansanshi, near the source of the Lualaba, which has been exploited since the mid first millennium AD. This mine penetrates a hill roughly thirty metres high, into which hand-dug shafts were sunk. The shafts followed narrow seams of malachite about six to nine metres in depth. The richest ore was probably hand-sorted and then melted in small charcoal furnaces activated by several sets of bellows. The molten copper was cast either into cross-shaped ingots of different sizes, or into long bars. The extent to which the copper was traded at the earliest period is not at all clear. The lake-dwellers of Sanga may have bought their copper from traders by offering dried fish, grain, salt, palm oil or sorghum beer in payment. Alternatively they might have sent expeditions southwards to extract and smelt the copper on their own account. During the dry off-season, when agricultural work was in abeyance, it would have been possible to dispatch teams of labourers and craftsmen. Either way, however, they obtained enough copper to adorn some of their deceased with fitting tributes to their wealth and status. Arms and legs were weighed down with bracelets and anklets of fine copper wire tightly bound round a fibre core. Necklaces were made of copper beads cut from sections of heavy, square wire.

At some period in Sanga history, large numbers of cruciform copper ingots were placed in a few of the graves. The accumulation was so great that one may assume that they had been stockpiled for commercial reasons. The chronology of this development is still obscure. No living floors have yet been found in the Sanga region from which to create a sequence. Although three separate pottery traditions have been found in the graveyard, the stratigraphy of the burials is almost inevitably disturbed. The copper crosses are usually in graves containing Mulongo and 'red slip' pottery styles rather than associated with common Kisalian wares. A further handicap is the limited radiocarbon evidence, which consists only of two isolated late first millennium dates. We cannot therefore yet judge whether the copper users were a wealthy minority, or immigrant traders, or perhaps even later occupants of the site. We also have no indication of how far back into the first millennium or forward into the second millennium the Sanga cultures might have stretched. Despite these limitations, the Sanga necropolis does reveal that an advanced copper-using culture had developed by the late Early Iron Age in south-eastern Zaïre.[1]

While the people of Sanga were perfecting their specialized industries, farming communities were continuing to expand over the more attractive, tsetse-free areas of Central Africa. One of the most attractive of these areas seems to have been the fertile plateau of southern Zambia. By the end of the first millennium the Early Iron Age peoples of southern Zambia had not only assimilated most of the old hunting and gathering population, but had evolved a new culture called Kalomo, which grew out of the Dambwa group and superseded the Kalundu group. This Kalomo culture was marked by advances in both industry and agriculture. Its people lived on village settlement mounds. Each mound gradually increased in height as old buildings were flattened to make way for new ones, and as domestic refuse piled up around the huts. The height of each mound may even have been deliberately increased to raise the site above the floor of the surrounding, marshy plateau. Each mound could have accommodated up to a hundred or so people at a time. The Kalomo mounds, although used over several hundred years, were probably not continuously occupied. After a few years they were probably abandoned, and only reoccupied when the surrounding land had had a chance to recover its fertility. This pattern of spasmodic occupation appears to differ from the continuous occupation of mounds practised further west by the Lozi, though at a much later date. The Lozi mounds were situated on the upper Zambezi plain where annual flooding brought new fertility. The wealth and permanence of Lozi villages may also have been increased by a fishing industry.

[1] J. Nenquin, 'Notes on some early pottery cultures in northern Katanga', *Journal of African History*, 1963, 4, 19–32; J. Hiernaux, E. de Longrée and J. de Buyst, *Fouilles archéologiques dans la vallée du Haut-Lualaba: I Sanga (1958)* (Tervuren, 1971).

The material possessions of the Kalomo people, although more diverse than those of their predecessors, were still limited. Iron was predominantly used for small tools such as arrowheads, spearheads, razors, chisels, knives, needles and bracelets. Some hoes and axes were in use, but it is likely that much agriculture still relied on wooden digging-sticks weighted with bored stones. Occasional ornaments of copper were known, and clay figurines were fashioned to represent human beings and cattle. Relay trade with neighbouring peoples brought a few foreign objects such as conus shells, cowries, and glass beads. More commonly beads were made of local shell of ostrich egg. Ornaments, however, were comparatively scarce, and some people were buried with but a single iron bangle to commemorate their lives.

The development of the Kalomo economy can be traced from material remains. In the early period people were still heavily dependent on wild game for meat. Bones from twenty-odd species of animal were found at the lower levels of Isamu Pati mound. By the end of the Isamu Pati occupation, however, up to eighty per cent of the meat supply may have been derived from domestic animals. Oxen, sheep, goats, dogs and small hens were kept. A similar change in emphasis from gathered vegetable foods to domesticated crops may have occurred. One should, however, be careful not to exaggerate the decline of gathering as an economic pursuit. Even the modern population of the Kalomo region make use of over a hundred wild tubers, green leaves, shoots, fruits, nuts, and even grass seeds, for culinary purposes. The only grain crop surely identified as present in Kalomo mounds is sorghum, though it is likely that eleusine millet was also grown. Grain porridge probably formed a staple part of the diet, and grain beer may have been brewed for feasts, weddings and funerals.[1]

The north-west of Zambia is an area still only sparsely known to archaeology. Because it is an area of Kalahari Sands, clays are rather scarce and pots are not extensively used. This means that it is hard to trace changes in history and culture through ceramic styles. Where pots are used in place of gourds and wooden vessels, they are made by men rather than by women, and commonly have cross-hatched incisions in place of comb-stamped decorations. The style of the north-western pottery, tentatively known as the Lungwebungu tradition, appears to derive directly from local variants of the Early Iron Age pottery tradition. It covers much of the upper Zambezi basin, and spreads into

[1] B. M. Fagan and others, *Iron age cultures in Zambia*, 1 (London, 1967); T. Scudder, *Gathering among African woodland savanna cultivators* (Lusaka, 1971).

Angola and Zaïre as well as across north-western Zambia. This area of apparently unbroken Iron Age cultural evolution contrasts quite markedly with the changes which occurred in the rest of Zambia from the twelfth century AD.

In the north-east and centre of Zambia the Early Iron Age tradition was dramatically replaced in about the eleventh to thirteenth centuries by the Later Iron Age Luangwa tradition, whose style of pottery is still used by the Chewa, Bisa, Bemba, Lala, Eastern Lunda and other peoples. One example of the new culture was found at Twickenham Road in Lusaka. An old hillside village of the Kapwirimbwe Early Iron Age tradition was reoccupied, probably from about the twelfth century. The new occupants built houses of upright poles lashed closely together, and caulked with laterite clay. Their grindstones suggest that they were cereal farmers, and the bones which they threw out belonged to both domestic cattle and hunted game. They had a much more plentiful supply of iron than their predecessors, probably obtained from nearby smelting sites on the Lusaka plateau. This iron was used not only for small razors, needles and bracelets, but for large agricultural and wood-working implements. The people of Twickenham Road used ivory bracelets and copper necklaces. The copper might have come from small ore deposits south of Lusaka, but it might also be evidence of early trade. The possible sources of supply are the copper-mining region of southern Katanga, around 400 kilometres to the north, or, more probably, the somewhat less distant copper-producing region of Urungwe, south of the Zambezi. Similarities between the pottery of Muyove and that of Kapwirimbwe suggest that links between the Lusaka plateau and the Urungwe district of Rhodesia may have existed even earlier than this. Further evidence that the Later Iron Age occupants of the Lusaka plateau were in trading contact with their neighbours consists of occasional finds of cowrie shells and glass beads. These must have come ultimately from the eastern coast of Africa, however devious the route of transmission may have been. In addition to bangles, bracelets and beads, the occupants of the Twickenham Road village embellished their personal appearance by filing their front upper teeth into points. This custom became common among many peoples of Central and south-eastern Africa in the Later Iron Age.[1]

The sketchy outline of the domestic economy and material culture of the Later Iron Age in the southern savanna will in due course be

[1] D. W. Phillipson, 'Excavations at Twickenham Road, Lusaka', *Azania*, 1970, 5, 77–118.

amplified, or modified, by new archaeological research. So far material comparable to that from Twickenham Road has been found on the Copperbelt, where the Chondwe site was reoccupied in the twelfth century by Later Iron Age settlers. Further north, the long Early Iron Age sequence of Kalambo Falls gave way to a Later Iron Age culture by the fourteenth century. In the east of Zambia, Later Iron Age pottery has been noted at Thandwe and Makwe. Whereas the Early Iron Age pottery of the east was quite distinct from the other Zambian styles of the period, the pottery of the second millennium is clearly of the single Luangwa tradition which stretches from the Lusaka plateau to Mozambique, Malawi, the border of Tanzania, and into Zaïre. It is dated to very early in the second millennium in Zambia and to a few centuries later in sites so far investigated in Malawi. The tradition appears to have spread rather rapidly to all pot-makers in the region. Although it appears to derive from the Early Iron Age styles in the area, and has definite parallels with, for instance, the Chondwe Early Iron Age pottery, no transitional wares have yet been found to illuminate the wholesale change of pot-making over such a wide area. Such rapid and widespread change does suggest that influential communities, sufficiently large to include women specialized in pot-making, must have spread over much of Zambia and Malawi. Immigrant raiders would not have had such a profound cultural influence.[1]

In southern Zambia the Iron Age sequence in the second millennium is a little more complex than in the east. It would, however, appear that the Kalomo culture was gradually replaced by new Iron Age cultures from about the twelfth century – that is, at the same period that the Luangwa Later Iron Age tradition was becoming established in eastern Zambia. The earliest of the Later Iron Age potteries of the south are probably to be found in the Kafue valley or at the lower levels of the Sebanzi Hill site. They do not derive from the preceding Kalomo wares, but from some other Early Iron Age pottery, probably within the Zambian Early Iron Age tradition. From the twelfth century the evolution of Later Iron Age pottery styles is continuous, and leads without a break to the modern potteries of the Ila-Tonga peoples.

One Later Iron Age site in Zambia has attracted considerable attention. This is Ingombe Ilede, on the lower reaches of the middle Zambezi. The riverside hillock on which Ingombe Ilede stands was first occupied for a while just before, or in the early part of, this millennium. The

[1] D. W. Phillipson, 'Iron Age history and archaeology in Zambia', *Journal of African History*, 1974, **15**, 1–25.

pottery then used there resembled the Later Iron Age pottery of Sebanzi, in southern Zambia, and had certain resemblances to the styles which evolved into the modern Tonga pottery of the region. This early occupation did not last long, and the site was then abandoned for several centuries. In about the fourteenth century the hill was reoccupied by people of a different cultural group whose pottery was more akin to the northern Luangwa wares. Among these new settlers were traders who established a small town or camp. For a few years around AD 1400 Ingombe Ilede flourished, either as a permanent settlement or as a trading emporium occupied each year during the trading season. The traders who used Ingombe Ilede were wealthy by Central African standards. They were lavishly supplied with glass bead necklaces. They used gold, both for their bangles, and to mount their conus-shell pendants. They wrapped their dead in shrouds of woven cotton or in bark cloth. Their graves were richly furnished.

The basis of Ingombe Ilede's wealth was primarily trade, and the major item was probably copper. This copper was mined in Urungwe, 112 kilometres south of the river (see pp. 589–90). The site of Chedzurgwe, at the heart of the copper-mining region, was occupied in the fifteenth and sixteenth centuries by people whose pottery was identical to that of Ingombe Ilede. Their shallow bowls and delicate beakers were far finer than the Tonga or Shona wares of their neighbours. The decoration was a beautiful comb-stamping with skilful graphite burnishing. The copper was cast into H-shaped ingots with a particularly characteristic trapezoidal cross-section. The ingots usually weighed between three and four kilograms. The miners were probably the Mbara people, known to early-sixteenth-century Portuguese visitors as 'the people of Mobara'. Later in the sixteenth century they were apparently conquered by the Mutapa confederacy and the north-western trade-route to the Zambezi dried up.

When Urungwe copper reached Ingombe Ilede, it was probably sold both to the peoples north of the Zambezi and to peoples of the lower valley. One commodity with which peoples of the north may have paid for their copper was ivory, and some evidence of ivory-working is found at Ingombe Ilede. Such ivory could have been sold down river to the coast. The main imports from the coast were probably cloth and beads. The importation of cloth into south-eastern Africa at this time apparently began to stimulate a local weaving industry, and Ingombe Ilede used large numbers of spindle whorls. Although beads were plentiful at Ingombe Ilede, they seem rarely to have reached

Chedzurgwe. One might perhaps surmise that political and economic power rested at Ingombe Ilede and other similar sites, while the sites in the southern hills represented mining outposts under the control of the riverside magnates. Ingombe Ilede did not, however, only represent a flourishing market centre, where copper and ivory were accumulated by wealthy merchants before being sold for exotic luxuries of Asian origin. It was also a manufacturing site. The copper ingots were not merely retailed, but were converted into fashionable jewellery. The tools of the Ingombe Ilede coppersmiths included, in particular, wire-drawing equipment. The wire was either made into fibre-core bangles at once, or wound onto reels for sale. The whole industry was very short-lived on this particular site, however, and by the late fifteenth century Ingombe Ilede had been abandoned.[1]

The archaeological researches undertaken in Zambia have, as yet, provided only rather slight information about the political and social history of the southern savanna. Even the wealthy entrepreneurship at Ingombe Ilede only indicates limited craft specialization and localized class distinction, rather than a growing scale of political organization. No empires emerged comparable to those of south-eastern Africa. The majority of early second millennium peoples continued to live in small isolated villages. Their only institutionalized social contacts were with immediate neighbours. Even the smallest societies, however, required some outside contacts. Marriage, for instance, would be impossible in a small village unit consisting of a single lineage. Procedures for exchanging brides must, therefore, have existed between distinct communities. In some cases warfare may have dominated inter-community relations. Captives became clients or pawns, and young women brought new blood and vigour to the victors. More frequently the transfer, or exchange, of wives was peaceably achieved in long-drawn-out ceremonies, often beginning in childhood. Marriage often required payment by the husband's lineage to the wife's lineage for services lost. This compensation could take the form of livestock or material possessions. The payment of bridewealth was probably the major occasion when exotic or prized possessions were expended. Material wealth was accumulated to acquire enough wealth and status to marry. It is likely that the glass beads and shells which spread from the Zambezi trading camps to the Later Iron Age villages of Central Africa commonly changed hands as bridewealth. Elsewhere copper bracelets,

[1] P. S. Garlake, 'Iron Age sites in the Urungwe district of Rhodesia', *South African Archaeological Bulletin*, 1971, **25**, 25–43.

iron bangles or raffia cloths were probably hoarded for a similar purpose.

Marriage was an important institution not only in the economic and social life of Later Iron Age societies, but also in political life. The lineage, whether patrilineal, matrilineal or unilineal, formed a tightly knit, and exclusive, group. Under some circumstances several lineages were brought together under a political overlord. So far very little is known about the development of chieftainship in Zambia. Many areas were undoubtedly too poor to make centralized control possible or worth while. The Bemba, for instance, only began to expand the scale of their kingship in the eighteenth century, and the Tonga never developed large-scale chiefdoms. Elsewhere, however, a few early clues about political organization have come to light in the form of chiefly insignia. At Ingombe Ilede, and at Katoto in Katanga, iron bells have been found which closely resemble those used in more recent centuries to symbolize military leadership. The Lunda kings, for instance, were accompanied by a royal bell when they went to war. It is likely that the bells used in earlier times may have served similar political functions.

As one advances into the second millennium, the archaeological data connected with political development can be effectively supplemented by oral tradition. This oral data, in which existing societies give a rationalized explanation of their political and religious institutions, may yield clues to actual historical developments. In Zambia oral sources have so far revealed few political traditions earlier than the eighteenth century. Much more oral data has been uncovered in Malawi, Zaïre and Angola. It may be that peoples in the valleys of the southern Congo basin created more durable institutions at an earlier period. There are hints in Angola, for instance, that chiefs whose influence transcended lineage boundaries may have begun to develop well before the middle of this millennium. But the earliest layer of oral history so far recovered comes from Malawi.

The traditional political history of modern Malawi began among the Chewa-speaking peoples. In this area the Phiri clan, which attached great symbolic significance to fire, created several kingdoms known by the name Maravi or Malawi. The earliest documentary reference to a Maravi kingdom occurs south-west of Lake Malawi in a Portuguese document of the early seventeenth century.[1] This state, governed by a ruler called the *kalonga*, began to emerge much earlier, perhaps from

[1] Gaspar Bocarro stayed with the great chief Muzura at his town of Maravy in March 1616. Cited in G. M. Theal, ed., *Records of south-eastern Africa* (Cape Town, 1899), III, 416.

the fourteenth or fifteenth century. By the sixteenth century it had spawned a second Maravi kingdom among the Manganja of the Shire river. Another offshoot created the Maravi kingdom ruled by the *undi* in the Tete district of Mozambique. Although the *undi* kingdom was probably founded in the sixteenth century, it was not until much later that it began to derive economic strength from the ivory trade of the Zambezi basin. But although the political and economic power of the Maravi kingdoms belong to a late period in their history, the religious roots of the kingdoms properly belong to an earlier period, during the Later Iron Age.[1]

The earliest forms of organization among the Chewa seem to be connected with shrines. The shrine cults related to areas of land, rather than to lineages and cults of ancestor worship. They somewhat resembled modern territorial cults and were quite distinct from movements of spirit possession concerned with medical and psychological healing. These Maravi cults, like the *malunga* of Angola (see p. 536), were responsible for calling forth the rains, for limiting the floods, for granting success to the huntsman and fertility to the farmer. Each one cared for the well-being of all the inhabitants of its zone of influence, and cut across social boundaries. The cult was managed by an élite of priests and officials. Among the Chewa, as among their Tumbuka and Manganja neighbours, the cults long preceded the development of the Maravi kingdoms of the Phiri clan.

The early Tumbuka of central Malawi claimed that the world was dominated by a high god whose representative on earth was a snake called Chikangombe. This snake lived on hilltops and travelled with the wind. Chikangombe 'married' priestesses whose families guarded his hilltop shrines. These beliefs probably evolved slowly among local Late Stone Age and Early Iron Age ancestors of the Tumbuka, Chewa and Manganja. The early cults were undoubtedly very localized, although they recognized the same type of god. By the Later Iron Age two different trends were emerging. One was a growing regional differentiation. The religion of the southern Tumbuka, for instance, was becoming distinct from that of both the northern Tumbuka and the neighbouring Chewa. A second trend was the development of a hierarchical relationship among some Chewa shrines. 'Mother shrines' became senior to their associates. When this happened, shrine guardians took on political functions, and sometimes became owners of

[1] See B. Pachai, ed., *The early history of Malawi* (London, 1972), chs. 6 by J. M. Schoffeleers and 7 by H. W. Langworthy.

land-holdings. It was onto this basis of incipient political growth that the Maravi concepts of chiefship and kingship were gradually grafted, perhaps from about the fourteenth century. Political power began to pass from the hands of the wives of the 'snake-god' to those of male chiefs. The old shrines faced competition from new shrines around royal graves. Conflict between rival priestly traditions continued for centuries. Only among the southern Manganja, where the old cults had been weak, did the new chiefs of the Phiri clan emerge with unchallenged authority. In this area the Lundu kingdom became a great power on the Shire river. Once its kings were firmly established they had the authority and confidence to reincorporate some of the old cult practices into their new political system.[1]

In addition to absorbing the religious ideas from the old, localized communities of the Chewa, the Maravi kings developed their own royal rituals centred round the chief's perpetual fire. This fire was fed with reed mats, used during puberty ceremonies, in order to symbolize life and fertility. The fire was only quenched when the king died. Royal fire was also designed to assist rain-calling at the end of the dry season.[2] The importance of fire as a royal symbol was also very marked among the southern neighbours of the Maravi, the Shona, on the southern side of the Zambezi valley. There, however, the periodic royal fire ceremonies were perhaps used less to mark a transition of reign or season, and more as a means of uniting diverse people in common loyalty to a king (see p. 587).

WESTERN CENTRAL AFRICA

From the shrines and kingdoms of Malawi, the discussion moves far to the west, to Angola, at the opposite end of the Central African savanna. Our knowledge of the history of Angola has recently been enhanced by fresh work on the oral tradition of the Kimbundu-speaking peoples.[3] These Kimbundu[4] occupy a large slice of western Central Africa along the lower Kwanza and middle Kwango rivers. They are

[1] T. O. Ranger, 'Territorial cults in the history of Central Africa', *Journal of African History*, 1973, **14**, 581–97.

[2] J. M. Schoffeleers, 'The meaning and use of the name Malawi', in Pachai, *Early history of Malawi*, 91–103.

[3] J. C. Miller, *Kings and kinsmen: early Mbundu states in Angola* (Oxford, 1976). I am grateful to Dr Miller both for allowing me to cite his work prior to publication by the Clarendon Press, Oxford, and for commenting on my own interpretations presented here.

[4] It would be more conventional to refer to the Kimbundu-speaking peoples as Mbundu, but this can lead to confusion with the neighbouring Ovimbundu.

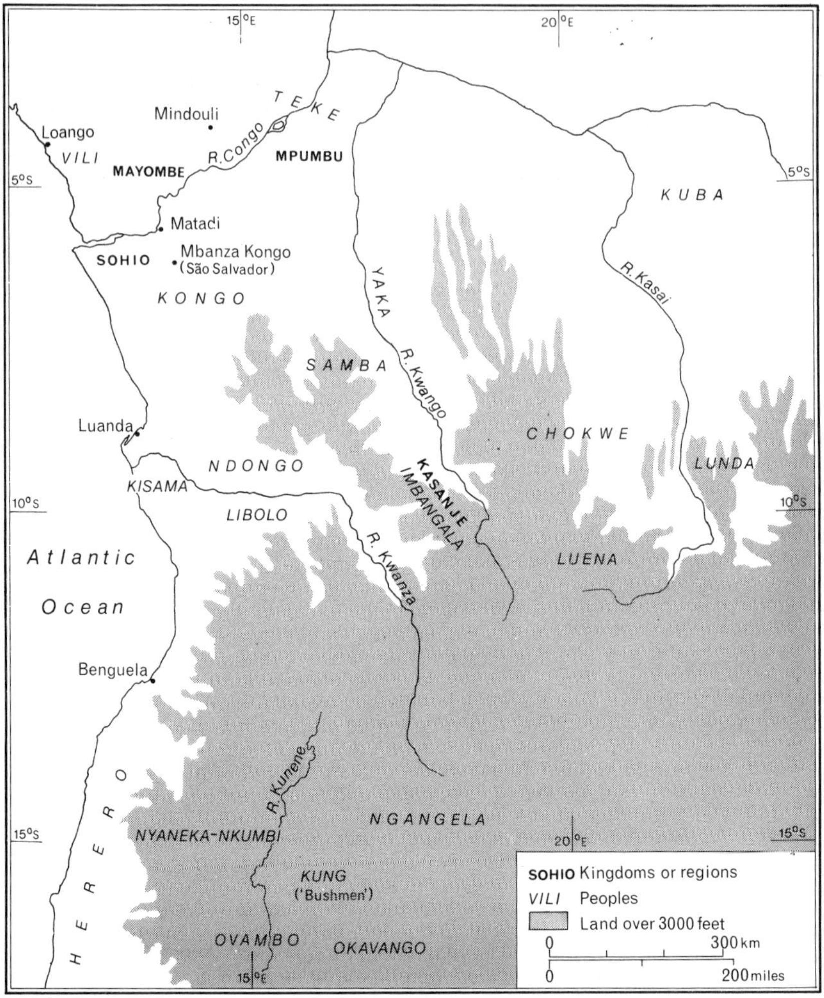

14 Western Central Africa

bordered in the north by the Kongo, in the south by the Ovimbundu, and in the east by the Chokwe-Lwena peoples of the upper Kasai and upper Zambezi. The history of the Kimbundu peoples in the early centuries of this millennium was probably similar to the history of other Later Iron Age peoples of the woodland savanna. In particular it reveals the early importance of religion as a source of wider political influence. Economic ties between the Kimbundu peoples appear to occupy a later and more modest place in the growth of political power than do lineages and shrines.

The central Kimbundu, known as the Ndongo, may have been settled on the Luanda plateau since Early Iron Age times. This open country was moderately suitable for both agriculture and pastoralism, though it occasionally suffered from inadequate rainfall, and from the depredations of the tsetse fly. The best land was in the north-west, where a pocket of rain-forest separated the plateau from the semi-barren coastal plain. The early Ndongo had few contacts with the coast. Although shoreline villages specialized in salt-drying, in fishing, and in shell-collecting, their trade seems to have been primarily directed northwards towards the Kongo peoples, rather than eastwards to the Kimbundu. On the landward side the Ndongo were surrounded by two other Kimbundu groups. In the north-east the deep Kasanje depression was occupied by the Pende, who later developed links with the interior of the Congo basin. In the south the Kwanza valley was occupied by the Libolo, whose territory stretched towards the Ovimbundu highlands of southern Angola. At one time or another each of the three groups played a dominant role in the history of the Kimbundu, and each created institutions which sought to dominate the autonomous lineages.

The early Kimbundu all lived in small villages controlled by the male members of a single kin-group. The village was the home, and spiritual focus, of all members of the lineage, even those who were permanently or temporarily absent. Its theoretical structure consisted of a set of full brothers, together with the older sons of their sisters. Wives belonged to their own kin-groups, but resided with their husbands. Young children stayed with their mothers until they were old enough to join their uncles in their own kin-villages. Rituals destined to ensure good harvests and healthy progeny had to be performed amongst one's own kin. Spiritual well-being was preserved by an elder who had custody of ritual kaolin and red-wood powders. Most of the Kimbundu lineages continued to function until the end of the sixteenth century. Over the previous three hundred years, however, many of them had been temporarily subjected by chiefs who sought to make their influence paramount in central Angola.

The first attempt at political consolidation among the Kimbundu was connected with the all-important function of rain-making. The Pende, in particular, came to believe that power to intercede with the weather gods was vested in wooden figurines located in small river-beds. These *malunga* figurines were carefully guarded by their custodians. The *malunga* cults resembled the early 'territorial' cults of Malawi. The shrine custodians used their spiritual authority to exact tribute and loyalty from the Pende. By concentrating both wealth and power into their own hands, some *malunga*-holders came to resemble small kings. A few of the titles of these shrine guardians, together with traditions retelling their great feats, have survived and been incorporated into more recent political institutions. The majority of *malunga* cults were rather narrowly circumscribed by a single valley or stream. They were gradually replaced by a more powerful, and more mobile, form of political authority which spread southwards among the Kimbundu.

The second cult to become politically important was associated with new ritual symbols, made this time of iron, called *ngola*. The *ngola* idea was introduced to the Ndongo from the Samba area in the north. The fact that the *ngola* symbols were made of iron may have been related to the increasing economic importance of iron. It is at this time that idealized smith-kings emerged among the Kimbundu as guardians of the sacred objects. Until further Iron Age archaeology has been undertaken in Angola, the extent of the technological and economic innovations which may have begun in the fourteenth century cannot be gauged. The emergence of the new *ngola* chiefs is often interpreted in oral tradition in the guise of a conquest by Samba migrants equipped with superior battle-axes and arrowheads. Similar themes of migration and conquest are frequently found in oral tradition to account for the emergence of new policies or institutions. In practice a peaceful diffusion of *ngola* symbols may have occurred. In the ongoing struggle between political centralization and lineage autonomy, the *ngola* were initially mobilized on the side of autonomy. Ndongo lineages found them very effective in resisting alien encroachment, for instance by southern kings from Libolo. Each Ndongo village sought to acquire a protective *ngola*. Its guardian became a Samba by virtue of his function, if not by his ethnic origin, and shrine guardians with Samba titles proliferated. Oral traditions in each village were modified to excise the old records and give legitimacy to the new titles. A newly appointed Ndongo office-holder adopted the genealogy, the history and the prestige of his *ngola*.

Although the *ngolas* were at first local figures, compatible with lineage autonomy, there gradually began to develop among them a hierarchy of authority. As the forces of centralization increased, the holder of the *ngola a kiluanje* title, in particular, began to acquire political and military influence. Although the chronology of this development is still obscure, a recognizable form of *ngola*-kingship may have been emerging several generations before the first sixteenth-century documentary records of it became available. By the mid sixteenth century the kingdom of the *ngola a kiluanje* was rapidly expanding. Spiritual and political authority may have been reinforced by royal control of market-oriented trade. The royal capital was apparently built close to the lower Lukala iron mines and the kingdom also came to control the Kisama salt mines and to receive tribute from them.

In the south the *ngola*-kings came into conflict with another, rather different tradition of Kimbundu political centralization. The political methods of the Libolo may have had their roots in an old and shadowy kingdom called Kulembe, where government involved a more fluid and mobile method of control than the fixed shrines used by the northern agriculturalists. The Libolo king appointed regional governors who could visit his subjects and who were personally responsible for their loyalty and support. The Libolo also developed important initiation rites associated with the training of their warriors. For a brief period, probably in the early sixteenth century, the Libolo kingdom succeeded in expanding northwards across the Kwanza. Its governors dominated part of the Luanda plateau. One chief even crossed the plateau to settle on the northern escarpment, where his title is still used by local people. This northern thrust was short-lived, however, and by the mid sixteenth century the *ngola a kiluanje* had succeeded in confining the Libolo to the south side of the river.

In the south the peoples of Libolo were connected rather loosely with the peoples of the southern half of modern Angola. The history of this region in the Later Iron Age is still almost completely unknown. The main Benguela plateau was already occupied by Ovimbundu peoples, but they were not yet organized into the familiar kingdoms of Bihe, Wambu, Bailundu and others. The domestic economy was a mixed one, and it is possible that the Ovimbundu gained their cattle and cattle customs from peoples yet further south. Beyond the central plateau our knowledge is even less adequate. The Herero were probably mainly pastoral, but the Nyaneka-Nkumbi and the Ovambo had mixed planting and herding economies. Along the rivers of south-eastern Angola fishing was an old and important element in the economy of the Okavango and neighbouring peoples. The disunited Ngangela farmers lived in very sparsely populated regions. All of these southern peoples probably had occasional contacts with Kung (Bushman) hunter-gatherers, but nothing specific is known about their history until the nineteenth century.

Returning to the northern part of the southern savanna, one finds a rather more thickly peopled region on the borders of the great equatorial forest. This lush belt of forest borderland was occupied by a very large number of distinct ethnic groups. Although the vegetation probably made hunting a little more difficult than it was in the open country, the extra rainfall made agriculture more secure. The ethnic fragmentation among the lower Kasai peoples can be interpreted in different ways. Perhaps an old population was organized into small Early Iron Age societies that were so entrenched that they absorbed all new arrivals. Or perhaps the disruptions associated with the later slave-trade caused small groups of refugees to settle in the forest as independent, embattled villages. Either or both of these explanations are possible. By the end of the sixteenth century some societies living around the forest margin, for instance the Bushong, or Kuba, had begun to experiment with original forms of state-building which later resulted in the emergence of powerful kingdoms. More important experiments in managing growing societies occurred, however, not along the forest border, but in the open savanna. Ultimately the most successful political techniques were devised among the Lunda peoples.

South of the forest fringes the inland savanna was covered by light sandy soils which supported a very sparse population. In the favoured riverside areas where denser populations could be supported, struggles developed between local lineages and centralized chiefs which were entirely comparable to events already described among the Kimbundu. In the early centuries of this millennium, the Lunda were probably very like other peoples of the savanna. They farmed, hunted, trapped fish and gathered fruit, drank palm wine and danced at initiation festivals. The old men stayed at home to weave raffia cloth with which to purchase young brides. The young men went to war in order to gain status in the community. The women, young and old, cared for the routine, grew the crops, cooked the food, carved the kitchen utensils and made the great clay pots used for storage and cooking and brewing. The children probably tended goats, collected termites for roasting, scared birds off the sorghum and baboons away from the bananas.

The Lunda were governed by elders known as *tubungu* who commanded respect by their seniority, their experience, and above all their spiritual powers. These elders were known not by their personal names, but by the titles of the offices which they held. Relations between the Lunda title-holders were governed by fictitious geneologies. One title would be deemed to be the brother, son, wife, sister or father of another title, and its holders would treat each accordingly, regardless of their family relationship. Alliances were recorded in oral tradition as marriages, with the senior title described as the husband, the junior title, although held by a male chief, described as the wife. The titles belonged to heads of lineages. The lineages, however, were never of equal strength, and constant rivalry took place between them. Conflict occurred not only over such important lineage questions as matrimony, but also over fundamental economic considerations such as land use and fishing rights. Competition over hunting grounds may have been less important. According to tradition, these early Lunda were not skilled hunters, and did not use bows or possess powerful hunting charms, but relied on simple traps and snares. Personal combat was settled with wooden clubs rather than iron spears, and the scarcity of iron suggests that the Lunda may have belonged at this time to the Early Iron Age tradition of Central Africa.

Among the Lunda lineages, three seem to have played a particularly significant role in the struggle for hegemony. The earliest to achieve a recorded superiority over its rivals was that of the *yala mwaku*. In time, however, it was challenged by the leader of the junior *kinguri* lineage. In the ensuing conflict, which oral traditions remember as a fight between father and son over palm wine, the senior lineage title was suppressed. All lineage headships which had been subservient to it were released from their obligations. There followed a long period of conflict and realignment. A third lineage, called *lueji*, attempted to drive the supporters of the *kinguri* out of Lunda. The rivalry may have lasted a long time, but eventually, perhaps by the fourteenth or fifteenth century, the balance of power was resolved in favour of the *lueji* by the intervention of outside influences.

The new power which emerged in Lunda is orally remembered in the form of exploits by a great hunter called Chibinda Ilunga.[1] This fictional folk-hero represented centralized, chiefly political power, as against the social power of the lineages; he imposed his domination by symbolically 'marrying' the *lueji* lineage. The advent of Chibinda Ilunga provided an outside influence of sufficient prestige and power to arbitrate in the civil wars of the Lunda. This prestige was gained, according

[1] Some accounts of Chibinda Ilunga have been collected by M.-L. Bastin in *Tshibinda Ilunga: héros civilisateur* (Mimeograph, Brussels, 1966, 2 vols.).

to the legends, by his effective use of hunting charms, both to track down his quarry and to protect his master-huntsmen from evil spiritual influences embodied in snakes and predators. His physical power derived from a skilful use of iron, and a much wider range of weapons than had previously been known to the Lunda. The advent of Chibinda Ilunga might be conceived to represent the growth among the Lunda of the technical traditions of the Later Iron Age. It has already been suggested from archaeological evidence that Later Iron Age traditions were spreading in northern Zambia at about this time. A Lunda transition to a more advanced material culture midway through the first half of the present millennium would therefore have nothing surprising about it. The source of these cultural influences is not yet known. In northern Zambia there is a tendency to look across into Zaïre for archaeological antecedents. They may have come from wealthy inhabitants of the Lualaba valley where advanced metallurgical techniques had developed in copper-working by early in the present millennium. Recent versions of Lunda tradition, recorded within the last hundred years, claim that the ideas personified by Chibinda Ilunga were associated with the Luba peoples. This Lunda attribution of their 'civilizing hero' to a particular ethnic group could be an anachronism inserted into the tradition at a later date. Yet the Luba do share several political practices with the Lunda, and later, like them, formed a large and powerful nation. Perhaps the complex and sophisticated political methods which evolved among both the Lunda and the Luba could have common roots in the Later Iron Age societies of southern Zaïre.

Among the Lunda, some political stability was apparently achieved by about the fifteenth century. An alliance was formed between a centralizing foreign chief, independent of the Lunda lineages, and an old lineage title of long-standing respectability. The dissident lineages allied to the holders of the *kinguri*, and to its brother-title the *kinyama*, were defeated and driven out. The *kinyama* title was carried southwards and eventually became the senior title among the Luena chiefs of the upper Zambezi. The *kinguri* title was taken westwards, along with Lunda traditional symbols such as the drum, the double bell and the royal bracelet. The supporters of the *kinguri* also carried charms which had been acquired by contact with the new hunter-king of the Lunda.

From being a small isolated farming and fishing people on the forest margin during the early second millennium, the Lunda spread their ideas and symbols by stages into the southern savanna. The earliest diffusion of Lunda influence, albeit of very indirect influence, was probably carried by short-range relays of refugees, rather than by any purposeful colonizing movement. Small numbers of Lunda migrants were absorbed into surrounding societies. They probably lost their language and many of their customs quite quickly, but they preserved and transmitted a striking political legacy. Their system of perpetual titles spread westwards to become grafted onto the institutions of many different peoples. The new title-holders retained few links with Lunda, although occasional attempts were allegedly made to enlist their support by conflicting factions in the Lunda homeland. The old Lunda lineages took fright at the rapidly increasing power of the new kingship, but were unable to resist. They became absorbed into a centralized Lunda state whose ruler eventually acquired the title of *mwata yamvo*.

Meanwhile the *kinguri* title of the west was gaining increased military power. Its awesomeness was enhanced by ritual acts of great cruelty. At this time, perhaps early in the sixteenth century, the new chiefs of the Lunda-Chokwe political culture came into contact with the easternmost Kimbundu peoples of the upper Kwanza valley. In the process an even more tightly organized martial culture emerged which focussed on war camps called *kilombo*. Camp followers were regimented on strict military lines. Recruitment into the *kinguri*'s war camps was exclusively by initiation and not by birth. This effectively destroyed the influence of the old lineages, and enhanced the power of the war-leader. Such a radical break with traditional practice repelled many of the *kinguri*'s followers. They rejected the fierce Spartan life of the camps, and moved away to adopt a sedentary, married life with conventional lineage loyalties. In their search for new recruits to replace those lost, the war camps became even more mobile among new peoples. Even the Chokwe began to reject the *kinguri* and its military dictatorship. In its stead the Chokwe began to adopt Chibinda Ilunga as their folk-hero. The great master-huntsman became the human symbol depicted on beautiful Chokwe wood-carvings. Eventually a revolution occurred which rejected the leadership of the *kinguri*, the most senior Lunda title, and supremacy passed to the *kasanje* title. By the mid sixteenth century, the supporters of the *kasanje* had created a military force known as the Imbangala, with which they rapidly conquered their way right through the southern Kimbundu territory as far as the Atlantic.

The Imbangala of the lower Kwanza had lost all their individual ethnic affiliations, and many of their old customs. They had no legitimate offspring and therefore no lineages which might arouse factional loyalty. All Imbangala became so named by initiation. The initiation, and the military training, involved severe forms of anti-social behaviour, including ritual cannibalism, which cut the initiate off from traditional society, and bound him irrevocably to his classmates. Although the Imbangala were united through isolation from their former tribal families, their camps tended to segment frequently, as new war-leaders hived off from the old regiments. One of the camps was described in 1601 by Andrew Battell, a captive English seaman who spent some months with the Imbangala. The camp he lived in was well fortified against attack. Each section was organized as a fighting unit, with its arms always at the ready. At the centre the war-chief was surrounded by a retinue of admiring wives who accompanied him on his ceremonial inspections of the camp, carrying his arrows and his wine cups. The chief decked himself out with elaborate hair styles made of shells, and anointed his many ornamental scars with magical ointments. His followers were particularly fond of palm wine, and their progress was marked by an extravagant felling of palm trees. When the Imbangala reached the Atlantic coast, in the late sixteenth century, they discovered an entirely new economic phenomenon: the overseas slave-trade. This discovery soon led them to invade, and virtually to destroy, the populous kingdom of Ndongo (see Volume 4, pp. 351–8).[1]

THE OPENING OF THE ATLANTIC

The history of Central Africa presented so far is mainly one of isolated communities responding to local influences from their neighbours. In the south-east we have some evidence relating to the way in which Early Iron Age societies gradually acquired the technology of the Later Iron Age. In the south-west we have an oral record of the interaction of chiefship and priesthood among neighbouring peoples. All these contacts, however, were predominantly local ones. New ideas seem by and large to have spread without creating lasting, institutionalized links between distant communities. The institutions of Central Africa were in this respect very different from the growing empires and trading systems of western and eastern Africa. In the early second millennium West Africa was becoming linked by regular trade ties to the Mediterranean world. The northern face of Central Africa, between

[1] E. G. Ravenstein, ed., *The strange adventures of Andrew Battell* (London, 1901), contains the most vivid primary account of the Imbangala. Their history is to be found in Miller, *Kings and kinsmen*, which seriously modifies this author's own earlier account in *Trade and conflict in Angola* (Oxford, 1966).

the Benue and the Bahr al-Ghazal, had no mineral resources comparable to those of the western Sudan to attract long-distance traders. The copper mines of Darfur may already have been in operation, but nothing brought regular caravans further south, or stimulated the growth of commercially oriented kingdoms. In eastern Africa the early second millennium also saw an expansion of trading horizons. But the wealthy cities of Manda, Kilwa and Sofala derived their profits from the tropical lowlands and from the high interior of south-eastern Africa, not from the remote lands of Central Africa beyond the great lakes. Even in the south, external trade had only a limited effect as a few shells and beads were carried north-westwards across the middle Zambezi. On all fronts therefore Central Africa remained effectively cut off from the growth of world commerce until the second half of the present millennium.

Central Africa's isolation was broken in the late fifteenth century by the opening of the Atlantic Ocean. Until then the Atlantic had remained a closed sea, and Africa's western front, unlike its northern and eastern fronts, had enjoyed no active communication with the outside world. A local sea-borne traffic in textiles or salt may have existed along the coast, as it did in West Africa. Dugout canoes and coastal fishing may have predated the arrival of Portuguese caravels. The odd foreign vessel might have drifted through, after being swept round the Cape and up the Benguela current, with no means of returning to the familiar monsoon lanes of the Indian Ocean. Such occasional, one-way traffic from Asia could have been responsible for introducing innovations of economic importance to western Central Africa. Banana cultivation in the lower Congo might have spread from the coast rather than across the continent. Other Asian cultural influences, such as xylophone-playing, certainly reached the area at an early date, though by a route as yet unknown. However plausible occasional visits by storm-driven seamen may seem, the fact remains that no regular ocean-going traffic existed in the South Atlantic until the 1480s.

When maritime trade to the west coast of Central Africa was opened by the Portuguese, its scale initially was small. The primary objective of the Portuguese was to find mineral wealth comparable to the gold of the West African mines. Instead, they had to content themselves with ivory, palm cloth, dyewood and exotic curiosities. Soon, however, they developed a second and more significant interest. This was to supply unskilled labour to the small island-colony which they had created on São Tomé. São Tomé was colonized in the 1490s by sugar-planters sent out from Portugal, partly in order to rid the mother country of convicts and of racial and religious minorities, and partly to foster tropical agriculture. The settlers brought few women with them and not enough men to cut the cane and turn the sugar presses. So they began to buy slave labourers and wives on the mainland. Very soon they were running a surplus of slaves which they could resell, either to the Gold Coast mines, or in Portugal to meet the shortage of agricultural labour. By the 1530s, when Brazil began to be opened up, the slave-trade was becoming good business.

When the Portuguese were seeking trading bases on the Central African mainland, they naturally sought wide estuaries with safe anchorages. These were scarce in the north, along the forest coastline, owing to sand banks and choked deltas, but they found one really good harbour at the mouth of the Congo river, which they called the Zaïre. There they established contact with the important kingdom of the Kongo people. During the next hundred years the Kongo became the best known of all the Central African peoples. Their king even tried to establish his own embassy at the court of Saint Peter in Rome. Numerous reports by Portuguese missionaries, merchants, and chroniclers, and occasional correspondence by western-educated Kongo, shed considerable light on the social culture, the economic development, and the political statecraft of the north-western savanna. It should be remembered, however, that the witnesses who described the scene also represented an intense foreign influence, which brought radical changes to Kongo society.

The origin of the dynasty which ruled the Kongo kingdom probably goes back to the fourteenth century. Oral chroniclers of the seventeenth century indicated that about half a dozen kings had reigned before the first Portuguese merchant adventurers witnessed the scene in 1483. The scope of the early kingdom is but vaguely defined. Essentially, the rulers were kings of Mbanza Kongo, a settlement surrounded by a well-watered plateau of rich soils with numerous villages. There is no sign that Kongo owed its foundation to any spectacular wealth in minerals, or other marketable produce of a specialized kind. It was, above all, a quietly prosperous farming community. The factors governing the kingdom's growth from this central farmland were probably ecological. Mbanza Kongo, apart from enjoying local prosperity, was strategically placed within striking distance of both forest and grassland environments. This access to contrasting, and complementary, sources of wealth probably stimulated the growth of the Mbanza Kongo chiefdom. The central power was apparently based on a modified type of trade conducted through a system of tribute and reward.[1]

The main administrative function of the Kongo king, and of his vassal chiefs, was the collection of taxes at the different levels of society. At the lowest level, the village chief received tribute from his people. Higher up the pyramid, provincial governors received tribute from the chiefs. Finally, at the top, a portion of each governor's receipts was sent to the capital for the king. The system worked, because it was in everyone's interest that it should do so. The flow of goods was not all in one direction. Those who paid could expect return benefits. On the material plane, each tax-collector, chief, or governor would expect to reward those who paid him, with counter-gifts. At the royal court a governor who faithfully paid his taxes in regional produce such as forest palm-cloth, coastal salt or cattle hides might expect to be rewarded with beer or clothing or perhaps dried fish and roast venison. Only a part of the goods paid in tribute were consumed by the court, the remainder being used to reward loyal subjects. This redistribution gave the kings an influential power of material patronage. The increased exchange of goods probably also fostered greater specialization in craft production.

The payment of tribute was undertaken not only for purely material gain. There were also political and spiritual rewards of a kind less visible, but no less real. In homesteads which were poor, isolated and beset by insecurity, it was important to belong to a larger, safer community. The way to belong was to pay tribute to a strong chief in the most public and visible way. Tax-paying was an occasion of great public rejoicing. This visible show of loyalty was rewarded by the chief with feasting and beer-drinking. Even at court the king symbolically handed out edible delicacies to his governors at the annual or biannual tribute presentation. Failure to pay suitable tribute could have drastic consequences. Even the greatest provincial governor could lose his position and become a commoner if he failed to live up to the expectations of his office. The payment of tribute thus fulfilled an important role in determining one's standing in society and in the political hierarchy.

The religious role of tribute-paying is less clearly described than the political or economic ones, but it is nevertheless likely that the payment of tribute, like the payment of church tithes in Europe, was believed to

[1] The following account of the Kongo kingdom is based on the secondary sources discussed in the bibliography. These works themselves are founded on Portuguese writings, modern ethnography, and a very small amount of oral tradition.

ensure against supernatural calamities. The function of a king certainly contained a sacral element. The uncertainties of disease, death and famine could be more effectively countered by divine intervention than by any agency of government. Kings therefore attempted to gain acceptance as the spiritual spokesmen of gods or god-like ancestors. Before the establishment of the kingdom at Mbanza Kongo, the area was controlled by an influential shrine guardian, the *mani kabunga*. The new kings enlisted the support of this shrine, and each king 'married' the lineage of the *mani kabunga*.

The kings and provincial aristocracies which dominated this Kongo system of economic exchange, of political influence, and of religious power, claimed to belong to an intrusive foreign caste which established its overlordship by virtue of conquest. Although some element of foreign influence might have existed in the Kongo kingdom, it is unlikely to have been the sole factor of positive growth. The dynasty's alleged migration from Bungu is probably no more than a symbolic representation of their loyalty to the tribal ancestors. The prestige of the early Kongo rulers undoubtedly owes more to their success in the management of their heritage than to any exotically acquired strain of political genius.

The growth of the Kongo kingdom began as an expansion from the Mbanza Kongo plateau in order to bring it into regular two-way communication with a growing sphere of adjacent communities. By the late fifteenth century, the peoples of the Soyo coast, approximately 160 kilometres away, were linked with Mbanza Kongo. So too were the riverside and island peoples of the lower Congo river. Some links were well-regulated tributary ties, but others were more military. The relationship with the estuary peoples appears to have been one of raiding and counter-raiding in which the Kongo king readily welcomed maritime assistance; in 1491 a few Portuguese ships were induced to sail upstream to the Matadi rapids in support of an expedition by the Kongo king.[1] In the north-east of the kingdom the fishing and pot-making villages of the Nkisi river described their links with Mbanza Kongo in the form of real or fictional migrations, each led by a chief carrying the ancestor's basket of religious paraphernalia.[2] The most distant region to establish links with the Kongo kings was the off-shore island of Luanda, located more than 240 kilometres south of the capital. It was there that the king obtained his small, spiralled, *nzimbu*

[1] Francisco Leite de Faria, ed., *Uma relacão de Rui de Pina sobre o Congo escrita em 1492* (Lisbon, 1966).

[2] Van Wing, *Études Bakongo*, 2nd ed. (Brussels, 1959).

shells which served as currency in many parts of the kingdom. These shells formed a significant part of the royal treasure-hoard, and could be issued in carefully controlled numbers to favoured supporters. When Portuguese priests first visited Mbanza Kongo, they received alms in *nzimbu* shells. Once in the hands of Europeans, the shells took on the functions of coinage and were used for the previously unfamiliar purposes of wage-payment and marketing. Their traditional role as a token of measurement, for gifts and exchanges, or as a store of permanent wealth, was now enhanced by the third concept of currency as a specie for purposes of trade.

Little can be said about the chronology of the growth of this complex Kongo kingdom. All that we can be sure of is that in 1600, after a century of overseas contact, it dominated a region more than half the size of England which stretched from the Atlantic to the Kwango. Within that area a relatively high level of craft specialization had developed among potters, weavers, salt-makers, fishermen, blacksmiths and coppersmiths, all of whom traded part of their output, either by the traditional flow of goods through the tribute network, or by the increasing use of regular market-places. In the late sixteenth century, six provincial rulers overshadowed the rest of the king's governors, but their position was not a fixed constitutional one, and other territorial commanders came and went as the balance of power shifted. One force behind the kingdom's development was probably population growth. As villages developed increasingly close together, isolation and independence ceased to be possible. Since favoured parts of Kongo had a rich soil and a good climate, new households did not have to move very far away in search of settlement sites. By remaining close to their neighbours, however, they were faced with the need to create a pattern of government which would regulate inter-village relations. Thus by 1600 Kongo had grown mainly from its own roots on its own soil with its own traditions of loyalty and behaviour. It should not, however, be overlooked that by 1600 Kongo had also been in regular contact for over a century with the Portuguese, who brought a whole new set of ideas and influences. The impact of these influences on Kongo society needs careful assessment.

It has been argued that Kongo was neither a conquest-state, with a ruling élite which belonged to a distinct culture, nor a long-distance trading empire, based on a market network. By the sixteenth century, however, the kingdom was beginning to take on both these aspects. Rulers became increasingly separated from their subjects, and traders became an increasingly powerful middle class. These changes were closely connected with the arrival of the Portuguese.

The Portuguese interest in Kongo, and in the neighbouring territories of Central Africa, was primarily commercial. Strategic and evangelistic considerations played a secondary, though often related role. Before the Portuguese reached Central Africa their early trade in West Africa had been of two kinds. Their skills in cabotage trade had enabled them to carry bulk goods such as cloth, beads, iron, slaves and food efficiently from one part of the coast to another. Their profits were then converted into gold, ivory and pepper for remittance to Lisbon. This cabotage trade, however, could make little contribution to Kongo, which already had a varied economy, and one little able to benefit from coastal navigation. A second form of Portuguese trade therefore became more important. This was the carrying to Africa of Mediterranean manufactures, especially North African textiles. In West Africa this trade enabled the Portuguese to cut into existing markets accustomed to trans-Saharan trade. No such long-distance trade had existed previously in Kongo, but European goods nevertheless gave the Portuguese an effective and original entrée there. By offering expensive and exotic gifts of clothing to the Kongo kings, traders were able to claim counter-gifts from the tribute received at court. They bought raffia cloth, ivory, dyewood and copper, while the court developed a taste for colourful cloaks of wool, cotton and even silk. The redistribution of these textiles, together with iron knives, glass mirrors, Venetian beads and glazed china was carefully controlled and limited by the court. The exotic and ostentatious imports created a new court culture, distinct from the material culture of the common people. Although some foreign trade-goods were probably used to reward provincial governors and even chosen chiefs, the downward percolation of foreign wealth was carefully restricted. Thus men and women of influence began to take on the appearance of a separate, privileged class of rulers. The introduction of a new material prosperity enhanced the prestige of the king and gave new incentives to chiefs to remain loyal to the system. The power of the king in the early sixteenth century appears to have been on the increase. This growth was accompanied by new Portuguese contributions to the ruling group in the form not only of goods but also of services by teachers, artisans, lawyers and priests. The king's spiritual authority was enhanced by new Christian rituals of glittering novelty performed in churches built by expatriate stone-masons. In their search for spiritual security the Kongo kings had found a new source of religious reassurance. They may also have inspired a new kind of awe among their followers.

The first consequence of Kongo's growing connection with world trade was to raise the prestige, authority and wealth of the king and his closest supporters. The second was to involve the new élite in an increasingly frenetic search for resources with which to pay for the goods and services received from outside. The traditional material prosperity of most Central African societies was, as has been seen, rather limited. Even kings had few durable possessions of distinctly greater quality or number than their subjects which could be stored as a permanent form of wealth. Shells, textiles, tools and personal ornaments of copper or ivory were the main symbols of wealth. Central African societies also had very little investment in productive capital. A farmer required only simple tools. A hunter may have invested in a somewhat greater range of equipment, bows, arrows, spears, clubs, game nets, but even his capital resources were limited and probably co-operatively used. The most developed capital investment may have been in fishing communities, where canoes, nets, lines, traps and drying ovens all required an outlay. The traditional capital reserve of early modern Europe was, of course, land, which was gradually being enclosed and brought into private ownership. No such development occurred in the sparsely populated conditions of Central Africa, where common land, of greater or lesser quality, was normally readily available to anyone with the manpower to exploit it. Manpower was indeed the key to all true wealth in these communities. A society with enough able-bodied men and women to clear and plant the land around was a prosperous society by Central African standards.

The kings of Kongo and the merchants of Europe were each aware that the greatest productive resource of the southern savanna was human labour. As a result the sixteenth-century history of the Kongo peoples is tragically bound up with the growth of the Atlantic slave-trade. To the kings, in whom a taste for luxuries had been fostered, slave-trading became an unavoidable solution to their need for foreign exchange. In so far as they also required foreign luxuries to reward their vassals, the trade had also become necessary to their political survival. Yet the longer-term effect of slave-trading was both economically and politically harmful. The loss of labour was not matched by the importation of producer goods. Even the consumer goods acquired became less durable, as the Brazilian trade in tobacco and alcohol partially superseded the more valuable trade in textiles, ceramics and metal wares.

The politics of the slave-trade required very careful management on the African side. A king who succumbed to the inducements to trade could easily split his society and cause uncontrollable rebellions to break out. The initially successful participation of Kongo in the trade raises the important question as to whether the country had an existing class of slaves who could be readily sold without causing severe political stress. The answer is probably that there was no such thing as a 'class' of slaves in Kongo, but that many individuals belonged to a transitory group of servile subjects. These were people of foreign origin, people who had been outlawed for criminal acts, people who had lost the protection of their kinsfolk, or become irredeemably indebted to others. They differed from slaves in European ownership in that under normal conditions they were likely to be reabsorbed into society. Families and clans probably welcomed foreign accessions to their numbers. Women were particularly easy to integrate, but even male strangers probably did not remain the 'slaves' of society for very long.

Since slaves were not readily available inside Kongo, the kings began at an early stage to seek captives from outside. Border raids became a regular feature of the kingdom, and may have led to territorial expansion. In the 1510s and 1520s Kimbundu prisoners from the south were on sale at the capital. Portuguese traders also frequented the north, where they bought slaves from the Mpumbu region south of Kinshasa. Traders to Mpumbu, or Pombo, were called *pombeiros*, and this title was subsequently applied to all slavers, both white and later black. The attempt to confine slaving to the periphery of the kingdom was not wholly successful. Local chiefs soon found that neighbourhood feuds were a quick source of captives. The king attempted to institute a system of checks, to ensure that kidnapped Kongo were not sold as slaves, but such controls became difficult to administer as the number of Portuguese traders in the kingdom rose. As a result tensions inside the kingdom increased further.

The king was not alone in finding slave-trading hard to control. The Portuguese also discovered that the traffic was not amenable to discipline. There were two distinct Portuguese policies towards Kongo in the early years of contact. The first policy, devised by kings João II and Manuel I of Portugal, attempted to Christianize and develop Kongo, to make it a prosperous trading partner, and a base for future expansion into Africa. This policy led to the sending of craftsmen, teachers and priests who could westernize the kingdom's institutions. A number of Kongo were also taken to Europe for further education, and one was even elevated to the rank of bishop. In contrast to this policy of modernization, there was a second policy favoured by the governors of São Tomé island. This involved the removal of the wealth of Kongo, largely represented by manpower, and its investment in other spheres of Portuguese activity, notably São Tomé, Mina and later Brazil. When pursued with vigour, such a trade policy rapidly undermined the policy of investment and development inside Kongo. Furthermore, the agents of development, including many of the priests and missionaries, soon became caught up in the slave-trade, and assisted in the exploitation of the kingdom, rather than in its economic growth. The change must be partly attributed not just to corruption and venality among individual colonists, but to a wholesale shift in Portuguese overseas policy. Once India had been discovered, Kongo was no longer so attractive a goal. It accordingly received less capital and human investment from Portugal than it had come to expect in the first flush of enthusiasm. The Lisbon monarchy began to acquiesce in the policy of exploitation.

The government of Kongo during the opening decades of the slave-trade, and during the period of attempted westernization, was in the hands of Afonso I. He reigned from about 1506 to 1543. Although undoubtedly an able and powerful man, he had constant difficulty both in curbing the excesses of the traders, and in persuading Lisbon to maintain the scope and quality of its aid programme. He nevertheless persisted in a policy of co-operation with the Portuguese, and by the time of his death a modified form of Catholic Christianity had become entrenched as part of the court culture. His failure to win more tangible benefits, however, led to the growth of new and severe stresses. The first threat to the kingdom in the latter years of Afonso's reign came from provincial rulers. These were anxious to establish their own direct contacts with foreign merchants. The ones most affected were, of course, those nearest the coast, and the king had constant difficulty in maintaining their loyalty. Other governors challenged his power not by breaking away, but by attempting to capture the kingship for themselves, with its increasing profits and prestige. The fact that the throne was an elective office may have increased the tensions and disputes over succession; it sometimes ensured also that when a ruler was finally installed he had already proved his political acumen and military ability. The succession to Afonso I, for instance, was in dispute for some time, but when Diogo I finally consolidated his hold on the state he was able to govern successfully for sixteen years. After his reign, in the 1560s, another period of fragmentation and disputed succession occurred. This period of turbulence, however, was overtaken by a second and quite different threat to the kingdom. This was the Jaga disruption.

The Jaga wars, which all but destroyed the Kongo kingdom in 1569, have been the subject of much speculation among historians. Because contemporaries thought of the Jaga as ferocious and entirely alien warriors, who must have come from far away, the speculation has been primarily concerned with their migrant origins. Even serious anthropologists have tended to treat their cannibalism as a fixed cultural trait which might be traced to source. More sober comment has suggested that their militancy might have been influenced by the new Imbangala war culture which was evolving at a comparable date in the regions far to the south of Kongo. A more plausible explanation of the Jaga wars ought surely to be sought within the immediate framework of Kongo and its near neighbours. For over eighty years the region had been subjected to increasing strains. Any slave-trading society was liable to become oppressive and fractious. There is no reason to suppose that Kongo chiefs were any more considerate of their subjects than others caught up in the slavers' spiral. The Jaga wars might, therefore, be interpreted as a virulent rebellion against authority, wealth and privilege. The main victims were chiefs, traders, Portuguese and the king. The factionalism which had developed between provinces and in ruling clans may have prevented any concerted action from being taken to protect the capital from looting and destruction. Support for war in Kongo, and even leadership of it, may also have come from border peoples, perhaps in Matamba or among the Teke, who suffered from the king's raiding policy. The evidence, however, is altogether too thin to judge, and the layers of horror-laden myth which began to accumulate immediately after the event are too thick to penetrate.[1]

The consequence of the Jaga disruption for Kongo was fundamental. It brought a Portuguese military invasion which affected not only the kingdom itself but a wide section of western Central Africa. In the 1560s Portugal was beginning to take a renewed interest in Africa after a period of comparative neglect following the discovery of Asia. This revived interest led to substantial, though ultimately catastrophic, Portuguese military adventures in both south-eastern and

[1] M. Plancquaert, *Les Yaka: essai d'histoire* (Tervuren, 1971); J. C. Miller, 'Requiem for the Jaga', *Cahiers d'Études Africaines*, 1973, **49**.

north-western Africa. During this phase of militant expansionism the loss of Kongo as a trading base immediately led to a military counter-offensive. Some 600 white troops were sent to restore Alvaro I to his throne at Mbanza Kongo. This restoration brought with it a new class of self-reliant traders, adventurers and rogues, who established themselves in a kingdom which, in their eyes, now owed them a debt of gratitude. Their presence severely modified the traditional Kongo system of trade through the political hierarchy. From 1571 a commercial middle class developed around small nuclei of traders and former soldiers. They built compounds, bought slave retainers, and sired large mulatto families. Their *pombeiro* agents were either sons or trusted slaves, whom they sent on long trading expeditions to the growing slave-markets a hundred and more miles inland. These large trading families maintained close contacts with the king, whom they tried to control and exploit. The king became dependent on the traders for an important part of his revenue of gifts, tolls, tributes and fines. The traders, on the other hand, were dependent on the king for security, freedom of movement, and a supply of war captives and convicts which could supplement the slaves gained by long-distance caravanning. In between the rival, but interdependent, groups of the traders and the princes, the priests acted as intermediaries. The court and the merchant community each vied with the other for control of the church, and each sought to have influential priests in its pay. Factions developed on either side and frequent accusations of treason and threats of excommunication were exchanged between the king's secular canons and the expatriate missionaries.

From the 1570s the kings of Kongo enjoyed a renewed period of stability. Both Alvaro I and Alvaro II reigned for a full generation, successfully manipulating the diverse political and economic interest-groups at work in their kingdom. They kept at bay the forces of the new Portuguese colony of Angola, which had been created on their southern border. They attempted, though unsuccessfully, to diversify their diplomatic connections by entering into direct relationship with the papacy. They claimed sovereignty over a wider stretch of the southern savanna than ever before. This period of stability came to an end with the growth of rival trading groups on the coast. Early in the seventeenth century the Dutch began to frequent the Atlantic seaboard and to offer alternative business openings and competitive prices. The effect was to heighten once again the rivalry between princely factions and so cause renewed political fragmentation in Kongo.

Despite the alternating forces of unity and division, however, the Kongo kingdom remained a major state during the early seventeenth century.

To the south of Kongo, among the Kimbundu peoples, the *ngola* kingdom of the Ndongo continued to expand during the sixteenth century. The royal capital, on the plateau some 160 kilometres behind the coast, grew into a small town with fine compounds and royal chambers richly decorated with wall hangings. In 1564 a Jesuit visitor regarded it as comparable in size to the university town of Evora, from whence he came. Distinguished visitors were received at court in regal style and allowed to share palm wine with the king. As a mark of particular esteem kola nuts were handed round. The king, though perhaps not his subjects, kept cattle on his lands. His personal wealth was measured by foreigners in ivory and copper. His association with iron-working continued to be of ritual, if not also of economic, significance.

The king of Ndongo soon emulated his Kongo neighbour in developing commercial relations with the Atlantic trading fraternity. Portuguese prospectors visited the country in search of minerals, and traders camped around the capital with displays of cloth which they brought on credit from ships anchored along the Luanda coast. From the Portuguese point of view, however, trade developed very slowly. It was, moreover, in the hands of private merchants from São Tomé, and not adequately controlled by the royal treasury in Lisbon. In 1571 it was therefore decided to offer Ndongo to a private developer from Lisbon as a proprietary colony of the Brazilian or Virginian type. The 'lord proprietor' was to be Paulo Dias de Novais, grandson of Bartholemeu Dias, who had sailed through Angolan waters eighty years earlier on his great voyage to the Cape.

The creation of Angola as tropical Africa's first conquest colony was not initially a success. It failed disastrously in the terms in which it was conceived, and no other comparable colonizing venture was attempted in Africa until modern times. There were five clearly formulated objectives in the project, but all were abortive. The first was to establish white agricultural settlements on the coast, but the soils proved too poor and the rainfall too precarious. The second aim was to conquer open spaces in the interior as landed estates for European colonists. But the Kimbundu were too hostile, and the kings of Ndongo soon showed how limited the effectiveness of muskets was when confronted by massed armies of bowmen with a much faster rate of fire. The Portuguese also found guerrilla warfare beyond them and spent long, cramped months in small earthen redoubts unable to make even short-range sorties until new supplies of powder and lead came from Lisbon. Their third objective was a mythical silver mine, one hundred miles up the Kwanza, but although they spent thirty years opening up the river route and fortifying it with three garrisons, they found no minerals. Their fourth objective was to capture the Ndongo salt-trade, and from it the lord proprietor hoped to recover his costs in the form of tithes. Here again, however, their aim was frustrated, and the salt mines of Kisama, a bare 80 kilometres south of Luanda, permanently eluded the Portuguese grasp. The fifth and final objective of the conquest was the creation of a Christian commonwealth, in which missions would have state support for their proselytizing endeavours. The newly founded Jesuits had been the most ardent lobbyists in favour of the Angolan conquest. They argued that without government support all converts would inevitably return to their own faith and kin. Although the Jesuits remained powerful in Angola, and eventually became large landowners and slave-holders, their missionary achievements were slight.

Although the declared objectives of the colonizing charter of 1571 were not achieved in Angola, the project did meet with success in another direction. The colonizers succeeded in establishing a small state among the western Kimbundu. In it tribute was paid not to a traditional chief, but to a Portuguese army officer. This process proved highly effective in accumulating slaves and provided the new state with export revenues. By the end of the sixteenth century the success of the system was so phenomenal that the export of slaves through Luanda was creeping towards 10,000 persons a year. The demographic impact on the Kimbundu must have been severe. In addition to slaves exported, many victims died in war or in transit, and whole communities moved away from the slaving frontier towards the north, east and south. In the seventeenth century Capuchins reported that Ndongo, the richly peopled country which had so attracted the Jesuits, had rapidly become a waste land. In less than a hundred years the Luanda hinterland had been raided out and slaves could no longer be recruited by imposing levies on subjected Kimbundu chiefs. Long-range raiding campaigns had to be mounted, for which men had to be recruited and supplies bought. The Portuguese crown, now in the hands of the Spanish Habsburgs, intervened in 1591 to rescind the donation charter, and undertake direct conquest, financed by tax-farming. Still the wars proved costly, and in 1603 the alleged silver mountains were reached and the myth of mineral wealth exploded. By the early seventeenth century two new lines of policy were being considered. The first involved the creation of a new colony in Benguela, 320 kilometres down the coast, where mineral prospecting and slaving might prove more profitable. The second involved a gradual return to trade, instead of warfare, as the major means of gaining slaves. This latter policy was stimulated first by the rising prosperity of Brazil, which became increasingly capable of paying for its labour imports, and secondly by the growing competition of the Dutch, who could not be excluded from the slave-trade by the imposition of military monopolies, but had to be met on competitive economic terms. Meanwhile the Ndongo kingdom maintained a policy of retreat and resistance. Unlike Kongo, and some of the West African states, it had difficulty in absorbing, controlling and using to its own benefit a foreign commercial community. It was increasingly forced to resist foreign activity. And when, inch by inch, resistance failed, the Kimbundu were absorbed into the semi-colonial, Luso-African community of Angola, with its cultural synthesis of white and black, free and slave, artisan and farmer, trader and soldier. The culture of Portugal often gave way to Kimbundu culture in language and custom, and even in religion and medicine, but the links with Portugal were occasionally renewed by the arrival of new governors, judges or tax-collectors, and by the reinforcement of the army with convicts or immigrants from the Atlantic Islands and Brazil.[1]

Although the advent of the Portuguese, and the creation of black Africa's first white colony, was the most important theme in the sixteenth-century history of the western Kimbundu, other significant developments were also taking place in the east. New links between the Ndongo and their neighbours probably reached, and crossed, the Kwango river at this time. Salt probably formed an important item in the growing trade of the region. The carefully fashioned blocks of rock-salt were sometimes woven into bamboo cases to make a more durable form of currency. They were fetched by people who came from far away to the east. The long-distance footpaths used by the salt traders probably became avenues for the dissemination of European goods and influences.[2] The material goods obtained at the trade fair were probably not the most important factor of change among the

[1] D. Birmingham, *Trade and conflict in Angola* (Oxford, 1966).

[2] D. Birmingham, 'Early African trade in Angola and its hinterland', in J. R. Gray and Birmingham, eds., *Pre-colonial African trade* (London, 1970), 162–73.

peoples of the inland savannas. Far more important were the American food-crops which had been adopted around the trading settlements, and in the vegetable gardens of the Angolan garrisons. At first, from about 1600, maize and cassava spread along the main trading axes to the savanna markets. In later centuries they spread further, to become staple crops among many subsistence farmers. Their diffusion was accompanied by other important plants including tomatoes and tobacco. The latter, however, was never grown on a sufficient scale to meet the demand which had been created for it, and imported Brazilian tobacco remained a key commodity in the slave-trading system. The inland spread of tobacco will one day be plotted through an archaeological study of smoking pipes. The scientific recovery of other imported objects, like glass schnapps bottles, glazed bowls, brass pans, bronze anklets, Asian shells and European beads, will give specific information about the speed with which the new commercial frontier moved into the continent. Traditional evidence from the Kuba region suggests that even the most rapid spread of coastal culture, carried by fast-moving bands of refugees, only reached the middle Kasai after the mid seventeenth century. On the upper Kasai the first influences appear to have been felt at a comparable date. Once new commercial influences did penetrate the area, however, leaders such as the *mwata yamvo* of Lunda used every political device to channel trade to their courts, and to monopolize the benefits to be gained from it. The seventeenth century saw a period of considerable political growth along the new savanna trade-routes.

NORTHERN CENTRAL AFRICA

The history of the southern half of Central Africa, encompassing the woodland savanna of the Atlantic plateaux and those astride the Congo–Zambezi watershed, already contains enough pieces to outline some major trends. In the northern half of Central Africa, filled by the great equatorial forest, with its northern woodland fringe, the situation is still much less clear. The tempo of historical change was probably rather slower than in the south. The terrain made communications difficult except by water and hindered the spread of economic and cultural innovations. One effect of this was that the region had a very varied and fragmented ethnic composition. Isolation was further emphasized by an extreme sparseness of population. In the south the different cultural traditions appear to have been drawing together during the present millennium; nearly all the peoples were matrilineal, Bantu-speaking, cereal farmers who possessed some livestock; most of them had progressed from an earlier to a later tradition of Iron Age technology. The north, in contrast, had four major and quite distinct populations which rivalled each other throughout the second millennium AD. Among these four no dated evidence for early iron-working is yet available. Some of them, both in the forest and in the northern savanna, may have remained unfamiliar with metals until late in the present millennium. Agriculture, on the other hand, was probably well established north of the forest at an early date. Hunting and gathering nevertheless remained important economic activities, especially in the forest.

The most important hunter-gatherer groups of northern Central Africa were the Pygmies. Their history can only be surmised from evidence relating to the bands which survived into the nineteenth and twentieth centuries. To the earliest ethnographic observers, Pygmy society seemed conservative and timeless. Each band roamed its ancestral hunting-grounds, camped beside its own streams, and intermarried with familiar neighbours. Despite this appearance of timelessness, important changes had occurred among the forest peoples. Some of the more fertile parts of Pygmy territory had been gradually infiltrated by food-producing peoples. Their economic activities had given the food-gathering peoples a new vision of life. The earliest food-producers may have been ancestral Bantu-speaking cultivators and fishermen, who may have begun to penetrate the forest region from the north as long ago as the first millennium BC. Later, and probably more influential, groups of woodland peoples have penetrated the forest from both north and south in more recent times. These new communities of Negro peoples, who specialized in fishing, intensive vegetable cropping and forest agriculture, may at first have had but slight effect on the Pygmy gathering economies. Nevertheless a kind of symbiotic relationship, or even an interdependence, did develop between some of the Pygmy bands and their food-producing neighbours. Many Pygmies who became aware of the new opportunities presented by a food-producing way of life seem to have defected from their own societies and joined the agricultural communities around them. They became fully absorbed into the new way of life, though physical evidence of the Pygmy heritage is found among many farming societies of the central forest. In some areas identifiable Pygmy groups have disappeared altogether in recent times. Other Pygmy communities retained their cultural identity, but nevertheless maintained regular contacts with their neighbours. These enabled them to exchange hunted game and skins for agricultural produce and artisan wares. Even in the remotest and densest parts of the forest, trading contacts caused Pygmies to acquire cultural features from their neighbours. They acquired some new social customs, such as tribal initiation, and some foreign technological skills, but above all they adopted Bantu and Central Sudanic languages at the expense of their own speech, which has been entirely lost. Thus although by 1600 the Pygmies were the least changed of the Central African peoples, even they had been deeply influenced by agricultural neighbours.

The new forest societies which influenced the Pygmies over the broadest front were those of the Bantu-speaking farmers and fishermen. A few of these Bantu societies have been visited by amateur historians who have collected fragments of oral traditions. Others have had long-established contacts with literate outsiders. Among the latter the best known are the peoples living between the western fringes of the Mayombe forest and the Atlantic coast. Even before the opening of the Atlantic to long-distance shipping, the Vili people had begun to thrive. From a base solidly grounded on subsistence agriculture, they developed an economy increasingly geared to market production. Their foremost achievement was in the field of cloth-weaving. Living on the edge of the forest, the Vili had access to ample supplies of palm raffia. From this they wove cloths which became so refined and so colourful that they could be traded to many neighbouring peoples. By the sixteenth century the Vili showed signs of the advanced mercantile skills which were later to carry them far to the south along the long-distance caravan routes of the savanna. A second important industry among the Vili of Loango was salt-making. Because the Loango coast had a relatively low rainfall and a pronounced dry season, it was possible to collect brine from the coastal lagoons and boil it over wood fires until it had caked into salt blocks. These could be profitably sold to the coastal peoples of Gabon, where high rainfall and coastal swamps made salt-drying difficult. Salt was probably also used to trade with inland forest neighbours. The earliest European traders found that ivory was plentiful in Loango. It is likely that the Vili bought part of the supply from neighbouring Pygmy hunters to whom salt would have been a valuable exchange commodity. The Vili also conducted an early trade in copper which they obtained, either directly or indirectly, from mines on the Teke plateau, north of the lower Congo river.

The growth of trade between the forest and the coast had important effects on the Vili systems of government at Loango during the latter part of the sixteenth century. The king of Loango, as seen by the traditions of his people, was primarily a figure of ritual significance. His authority was represented by a royal fire which burnt throughout his reign and was extinguished on his death. Each new king kindled his own sacred fire, in the manner of some other Central African rulers. Envoys from the provinces came to light torches from the new fire and bear them home as a sign of political allegiance. The king also partook in rain-making ceremonies, to give thanks for the cycle of the seasons and the bounty of the harvest, or to plead with the deity for more favourable conditions. Rain-making was usually associated with a priesthood which stemmed from the oldest recognized level of population. The position of priests was powerful but hazardous, as seen in Ndongo, where the rain-makers were executed during one particularly harsh season. The king of Loango also demonstrated his supernatural attributes by carefully disguising his ordinary human needs. Thus, if he was thirsty, he would order his attendant to ring a bell, and all present, even European guests, would fall flat on their faces so as not to behold the king drinking. At mealtimes, he retired alone to a special closed chamber lest any witness of his eating should cause him to die. It was important, also, that the king should be in good health and without physical defect.

The ritual activities of the Vili king were matched by his political functions as chief judge and legislator, as co-ordinator of foreign and military policy, and as ceremonial host to foreign embassies. His councillors and kinsmen received delegated authority as provincial governors, as commanders of the guard, wardens of the wives' compound, watch-dogs against sorcery, administrators of ordeal trials, and king's messengers. A striking feature of Loango government was the existence of a second court, parallel to that of the king. It was ruled by a woman, variously described as the king's sister, his wife, and the mother to his heir. Her key function was a symbolic representation of the women of the kingdom and of their rights.[1] Such women chiefs, or chiefly titles with female attributes, were common among the savanna Bantu, and matrilineal characteristics occurred in many of the diverse and otherwise unrelated political systems of the savanna and southern forest. The northern neighbours of the Vili, as far as the Ogowe, were all matrilineal in their inheritance. In this they contrasted

[1] P. M. Martin, *The external trade of the Loango coast, 1576–1870* (Oxford, 1972), ch. 1.

sharply with the north-western Bantu, and with the nineteenth-century Fang immigrants into the Gabon and Cameroun forests, among whom the male line was the more important.[1]

In the hinterland of Loango, beyond the Mayombe forest, were the dominions of the Teke peoples. The Teke, also known as Tyo and Ansiku, occupied a sandy savanna plateau stretching across the Congo river just where it emerges from the equatorial forest. The river system of the middle Congo has been likened to an hour-glass which widens out into the Ubangi network in the north, and into the Kasai-Lower Congo network in the south. It is joined in the middle by the single, broad, island-spattered stretch of navigable river which crosses approximately 800 kilometres of forest. In modern times the link between north and south has become an important channel of regular two-way communication. Bobangi fishing people have been large-scale traders, relaying manufactures, raw materials and staple foods, from village to village up and down the water corridor. In earlier centuries this corridor was probably important as a line along which Iron Age, food-producing populations could span the forest barrier. Fishing communities could flourish along the Congo, and, without being composed of long-distance immigrants or traders, could act as agents for the transmission northwards or southwards of new cultural influences. The Teke at the southern end of this corridor may, therefore, sometimes have been the first recipients of new impulses from the north. One of these impulses may have been political, and it is thought that the Teke may have contributed important elements to the western savanna systems of government. Certainly by 1535 the Teke kingdom, or kingdoms, were known to the Portuguese, although their size and influence may have been magnified by sixteenth-century chroniclers in proportion to their remoteness. By the mid sixteenth century the fortunes of the Teke had begun to decline, despite their alleged political prowess. They found themselves caught on the fringe of an expanding Kongo society which was increasingly turning its energies to slave-trading. The greatest slave-markets were found among the Mpumbu peoples of the southern Teke borders. More northerly Teke peoples, under the name Ansiku or Yansi, began to move eastwards into the lower Kasai forest mosaic. They moved either in flight, or in quest of victims of their own, which they sought with increasing intensity as they became caught up in the Atlantic trading complex.

In the southern forest, as elsewhere, contact with the growing

[1] A. Jacobson, *Marriage and money* (Lund, 1967).

long-distance trading economies of the Atlantic zone brought benefits as well as hardship and insecurity. In the sixteenth century the Teke probably controlled or worked the Mindouli copper mines, and benefited from increased sales of copper to the Vili of Loango. Like other savanna peoples, the Teke and their forest neighbours also profited from the introduction along trade-routes of cassava and maize. As these crops supplemented or even superseded millet as the staple crop, levels of agricultural productivity rose. In theory this should have led to rising standards of living and to increased manpower investment in more advanced economic activities. In practice, however, it may have done little more than compensate for the labour loss caused by the slave-trade, and the conversion of human resources into items of conspicuous consumption such as foreign tobacco and alcohol.

The changes associated with Atlantic trade probably only influenced the south-western corner of the forest, and perhaps a few main waterways, in the period before 1600. Elsewhere the forest farming of the north and east remained untouched by American food-plants. In many areas Pygmy gatherers probably remained relatively more numerous than Bantu farmers, although both were very thinly scattered. In the north-west the patrilineal forest farmers were even more divided and fragmented among themselves than other forest peoples. They formed a large number of small, isolated and divergent Bantu language groups. Only in very recent times has some degree of cultural uniformity been created by the Fang. One explanation of the great cultural and linguistic diversity may be historical. The north-west forest may contain the oldest Bantu-speaking peoples of Central Africa. Without archaeological evidence we cannot even speculate on the date or cause of the penetration of the forest by food-producers, whether as vegeculturalists, or as neolithic farmers, or as fully-equipped Iron Age agriculturalists. Some of the early people, however, seem to have adapted themselves very successfully to the waterlogged environment of large parts of the northern forest. Their descendants, known generally as *les gens d'eau* – 'the water peoples' – practise highly successful fishing in the perpetual swamps of the Ngiri, the Ubangi, and the middle Congo. Even deeper in the forest groups such as the Ngangulu and the Mbochi, sometimes known as *Zwischenvölker*, seem to exhibit cultural characteristics of both the northern and southern forest peoples. A study of their customs and languages might give new clues as to the relative importance of different levels of cultural influence from either north or south among the forest peoples.

The coastal peoples of the north-western Bantu area became cut off from their previous inland neighbours by the Fang conquests of the nineteenth century. Even before this, however, their culture had been somewhat modified by outside contacts. In the sixteenth century they were well-known as fishermen, and had begun to trade spasmodically with the Portuguese slavers. The growth of trading economies in the late sixteenth century led to the shift of small numbers of people from the hinterland to the coast. This shift was large neither in scale nor in distance, but the emphasis changed from riverside settlements a few miles inland to settlements on the river estuaries. North of Cameroun mountain, the Balundu and Bakole began to press in on the old Efik coast-dwellers. In the Cameroun estuary the Duala took up positions where they could trade freely with visiting ships for iron and copper bars. The number of coastal people probably remained small, to be reckoned in hundreds rather than thousands, and their trade was in no way comparable to that of Benin in the west. They nevertheless laid the foundations of a society which grew into the trading states of the nineteenth century. By 1600 an embryonic dynasty of princes had been established among the Duala.[1]

The central part of the equatorial forest presents historical problems which are little better understood than those of the north-west. There does, however, seem to be some slight unity among the numerous Mongo peoples who occupy much of the territory enclosed by the great bend of the Congo. The Mongo are patrilineal peoples, like their northern neighbours, and share with them a number of customs associated with marriage, divorce and inheritance. They also show signs of intermarriage with Pygmy stock, suggesting to many observers that this was once a Pygmy territory which has been penetrated by Negro outsiders within comparatively recent times. Some of these influences may have come from the north-western Bantu; others from the Eastern Nigritic peoples of the northern savanna. Even the Tetela, at the southern edge of the forest, have traditions which might be attributable to a southward migration, though a detailed judgement will have to await the finds of properly controlled fieldwork. Although the unity of the Mongo group is not very marked, it does seem to require some explanation other than a remote common ancestry, or a series of parallel developments in a uniform environment. The clues may well lie outside the forest, in the central Sudan.

[1] E. Ardener, 'Documentary and linguistic evidence for the rise of trading polities between Rio de Rey and the Cameroons, 1500–1650', in I. M. Lewis, ed., *History and social anthropology* (London, 1968), 81–126.

To the north of the forest, the woodlands which stretch from central Cameroun to the Sudan Republic are occupied by two major groups of peoples. The oldest appear to be the Central Sudanic peoples, whose territory forms a horseshoe round the Uele region of northern Zaïre. Inside the horseshoe, and stretching as far back as the Cameroun Highlands, are the Eastern Nigritic peoples, who appear to have intruded eastwards along the forest fringe into Central Sudanic territory. The date of this intrusion by a distinct branch of the Niger-Congo language family is unknown. Both savanna populations are assumed to have an old history of Stone Age agriculture. In recent centuries, at least, this history has also been much affected by the adjacent forest. Although the Central Sudanic peoples generally lost ground to their Eastern Nigritic neighbours in the west, and latterly perhaps also to Arabs in the north and Nilotes in the east, some of them appear to have expanded successfully southwards into the forest. Their ability to do so, and to acquire client peoples among Pygmy hunter-gatherers, must have depended on their agricultural skills. The simplest basis of agriculture would have been an indigenous adaptation of food-producing to the many available forest tubers. In a more ingenious theory, Murdock would have liked to believe that Asian cultivars were introduced to the Central Sudanic peoples at a very early date. There is, however, no evidence that banana cultivation spread across Ethiopia and the upper Nile before reaching the forest via the central Sudan. An alternative to the theory of indigenous forest agriculture suggests that Asian food-plants had already reached the north-eastern forest, from the west, south or east, before the Central Sudanic peoples began to colonize it from the north. Whatever the causes of the Central Sudanic expansion, the impact was felt deep into the forest. In the north the Mangbetu and a cluster of related peoples imposed their culture. Further south, the traces of Sudanic influence are less distinct, and Bantu languages are currently spoken, but several peoples of north-eastern Zaïre have traditions referring to northern influences. These include the Bira, the Kumu and the Lengola.

The impact of savanna cultures on forest peoples – and perhaps also of forest cultures on savanna peoples – was not felt only along the eastern forest margin of the Uele area. A similar oscillating interaction took place along the Ubangi on the central border of the forest. Here the savanna cultures and languages were Eastern Nigritic. According to one hypothesis, the Ngbandi were the largest formerly Bantu-speaking group to be overrun, while others, such as the Babwa and

Binza, although retaining their Bantu languages, were nevertheless influenced in other ways which are still remembered. Alternatively, it is possible to argue, in the present state of our ignorance, that the selective change of culture moved in the opposite direction, from south to north. On this showing, the Babwa and Binza would appear to be Eastern Nigritic peoples of the Ngbandi group who have been Bantuized to the extent of losing their old speech, as did neighbouring communities of Pygmies.

The major feature of the history of the northern savanna is the continuation into the second millennium of local change among very diverse but interacting farming and hunting peoples. By the sixteenth century, however, there may have been a new factor as the northern savanna came into contact with the long-distance exchange economies of the eastern Sudan and Sahara. In the early sixteenth century, a Spanish Arab, al-Ḥasan b. Muḥammad, later known as Leo Africanus, travelled from Bornu to Egypt via 'Gaoga', a kingdom probably centred on the Wadai–Darfur area, and connected to Egypt by the forty-day *Darb al-Arbaʿīn* route (cf. pp. 304–5). The reigning dynasty of Gaoga appears to have been founded in the fifteenth century, and to have governed a wide, but variable, confederation of ethnic groups. Bornu was a major enemy of Gaoga, but intermittent warfare did not stop trade along the thirteenth parallel, nor the rise in prosperity of the northern oases along the route to Egypt. Egyptian traders sent the king of Gaoga weapons, textiles and horses, for all of which he paid generously in slaves. There is no reason to suppose that the slaves were anything other than local captives. The slaving methods were presumably typical of the Sudanic latitudes, where fast horsemen with modern swords overcame villagers on foot with wooden bows. In time, though perhaps not before 1600, the slave catchment area may have spread southwards towards the Ubangi basin, bringing increasing numbers of the northern woodland peoples into the destructive orbit of the trans-Saharan traffic. The ivory trade was probably based initially on elephant-hunting in the northern woodland, and only later spread southwards. One commodity which may have stimulated real new wealth was the copper of Hofrat en Nahas in southern Darfur, but this was not mentioned by Leo Africanus.[1]

For the time being historical research in both the savanna and forest regions of northern Central Africa will continue to concentrate on the

[1] P. Kalck, 'Pour une localisation du royaume de Gaoga', *Journal of African History*, 1972, **13**, 529–48.

question of economic innovation among subsistence communities with a high degree of independent self-reliance. It is unlikely that evidence will reveal the emergence of any large-scale political organization before the seventeenth century. One feature which is of interest, however, is the emergence of trader-fishermen operating over long distances on the great river systems. These seem to have evolved institutionalized friendships, which enabled them to travel safely among remote peoples to whom they were only distantly related. Apart from this instance of external contacts, the focus of all activity seems to have remained the homestead and the village. Outsiders represented a threat to security, rather than an opportunity for wider co-operation and development. This timid isolationism was only reinforced in later centuries, as foreigners began to encroach on the forest margins in search of captive slaves.

The achievements of the later Central African Iron Age can be much more clearly witnessed in the open savanna regions to the south of the forest. There inter-community relations became more important. The diffusion of more advanced technology, the exploitation of scarce mineral resources like salt, iron and copper, the redistribution of raw and worked materials, all took on new importance. Religion became more organized, peoples became more closely united, states became more expansive in attempts to improve the quality of life and resist the threats of famine and war. Success was primarily marked by a growth of population, and an extension of territory to new agricultural lands. Distinctions of wealth and class rarely became important, and few material possessions were of a durable, ostentatious kind. Land never became so scarce as to become a matter of private ownership, with its concomitant centralization of wealth and influence. Within societies, distinctions between freemen and slaves were probably temporary rather than perpetual. Those who lost their kin or clan-fellows became the servants of those who had wider family support around them. Those with the greatest support acquired powers of chieftainship, to which religious functions were commonly attached.

The most important change to occur at the end of this half millennium during the sixteenth century was the gradual opening of Central Africa to outside influences. By 1600 these had only affected the south-western area. During the next 300 years they were to spread, first through the savanna and later deep into the forest, where many of the changes which they caused were of a highly disruptive kind.

CHAPTER 8

SOUTHERN AFRICA

Southern Africa can be divided into two ecological regions with sharply contrasting historical evolutions. The huge western zone consisting of South-West Africa, Botswana and the western Cape remained until 1600 a predominantly non-agricultural area. The peoples who occupied sparsely the vast expanses of acacia scrubland at the centre of the Kalahari were necessarily hunter-gatherers. At its fringes, however, pastoralism was possible, and in the far north, the pastoralists had become iron-using and Bantu-speaking by the end of the period. It seems likely that Iron Age pastoralists such as the Herero had spread in a westerly direction towards the plateau of southern Angola. Elsewhere pastoralists remained Late Stone Age peoples, who were very different in language, culture and appearance from their Bantu-speaking neighbours. They lived in association with closely related hunter-gatherers, and their contacts ranged from open conflict over waterholes, grazing lands and game, to various forms of clientship and trade.

The eastern half of southern Africa, comprising Rhodesia, southern Mozambique and eastern South Africa, has a rather more complex history than the south-west. With richer soils and vegetation, heavier rainfall and more abundant mineral resources, it has been able to support a far larger population. In modern times, this population has been classified into two broad cultures. In the north-east, between the Zambezi and Limpopo, are the Shona. In the south-east, south of the Limpopo, are the South-Eastern Bantu, comprising the Sotho-Tswana of the plateau, the Nguni of the coastlands, and the Tonga-Tsonga of southern Mozambique. Straddling the Limpopo boundary between north and south is the complex of Venda-Lovedu and related peoples, whose ruling groups trace their origin to north of the Limpopo, but who have been heavily Sothoized in recent centuries, so that today they are classified as South-Eastern Bantu. Though the last migration of Venda may have occurred after 1600, their forerunners were probably among the earliest inhabitants of the north-eastern Transvaal.

Throughout the eastern part of southern Africa the period AD 1000 to 1600 saw the gradual emergence of the culture groups and subgroups of today. These emerged out of the disparate and scattered communities of the Early Iron Age, and probably more by the natural processes of local differentiation than by the influence of fresh migrations from the outside. The growth in population, and the development of increased contacts and conflicts between separate small societies, led on the one hand to the disappearance of earlier differences, and on the other to the emergence of broad distinctions between the modern cultural groupings of today. It would be unwise to emphasize any regional homogeneity at the beginning of the period, but by its end many of the salient cultural features of the Shona, Nguni and Sotho-Tswana clusters were probably in evidence.

The emergence of wider groupings may have been partly caused by the growth of new economic relationships as trade developed on an increasing scale, and as new means of production spread from the agricultural and pastoral peoples to their hunter-gatherer neighbours. This affected agricultural and pastoral production, domestic and monumental architecture, the making of metal tools and utensils, skills in pottery and creative art, as well as other specialized crafts and everyday pursuits. It was paralleled by a growth in social organization. In some areas the small, loosely organized societies were supplanted by complex chiefdoms and even states. North of the Limpopo sophisticated and far-reaching religious systems are also known to have developed. The establishment of important and regular links between south-eastern Africa and the outside world added stimulus to many of these developments. The external contacts arose firstly as part of the Indian Ocean monsoon trading system and later through Portuguese maritime expansion.

Despite southern Africa's openness to the north, there were still peoples throughout the period whose history was much more one of continuity than of change. They remained rooted in the past, and the wide range of cultural innovations grouped under the term Early Iron Age had, for a variety of reasons, left them untouched. Late Stone Age tools were still in widespread use on sites adjacent to those of Iron Age peoples. Some of these Stone Age sites reveal pottery, an indication that the occupants were in trading contact with their iron-using neighbours. Other stone-using peoples were beginning to make their own pottery, or to adopt the pastoral and agricultural pursuits of their neighbours and to become gradually absorbed by them. By 1600 there were probably only a few surviving pockets of Late Stone Age peoples in the Zambezi–Limpopo region. Further south, and particularly in the south-west and in the extreme south, such peoples still continued their way of life at least until the arrival of British and Dutch ships at Table Bay in the last decade of the sixteenth century.

THE NORTH-EAST

The north-eastern part of southern Africa, between the Zambezi and Limpopo rivers, is historically divided among three cultural traditions. The first was the Leopard's Kopje tradition, mainly located on the central and south-western parts of the plateau of southern Rhodesia.[1] In this zone a primarily cattle-oriented people discovered that their territory contained numerous reefs of gold-bearing ore. They gradually began to exploit this gold for export and so acquired an entirely new form of wealth. The second cultural zone of this region was the coastland and lowland of central Mozambique. Here a series of small merchant-states developed, which were economically and culturally linked to the medieval states of the East African coast. A proportion of the urban population became Muslim and prospered from its participation in the monsoon trade to Asia. In the sixteenth century the Muslim traders from East Africa were joined by the Christian traders from Portugal and Portuguese India. The third cultural tradition emerged between the mining areas of the open plateau and the merchant ports of the coastal lowland, in a highland zone occupied by several groups of Shona-speaking agriculturalists. From about the thirteenth century onwards these Shona peoples built a chain of kingdoms between the miners and the merchants. These included Zimbabwe, Uteve, Barwe, Manyika and Mutapa. Some of these states, notably Manyika, produced gold from their own domestic mines. In the main, however, these states were not producers of gold but were brokers in the international trade of south-eastern Africa. They bought Indian textiles from the coastal communities and resold them in the highland region for gold, as well as for ivory and other raw materials. The profits were concentrated in the hands of kings, who used this new wealth to enhance their prestige, their authority, and their territorial hold of the middle ground between the plateau and the coast through which trade passed.

By the fifteenth and sixteenth centuries the new political culture of the Shona was spreading beyond the frontier line between plateau and

[1] The term 'Leopard's Kopje' has altered its meaning in recent years. Formerly the Early Iron Age Zhizo culture of this area was associated with the Leopard's Kopje tradition and given the name Leopard's Kopje I. This association is no longer considered valid and so 'early Leopard's Kopje' now refers to the former LK II and 'later Leopard's Kopje' to what was formerly known as LK III.

coast. The first direction of spread was towards the east, as the lowland became more closely invested by Shona kingdoms such as Uteve. Coastal merchants who were unable to travel up-country from the port of Sofala began to seek new routes to the interior, and in particular gained access to the Zambezi valley. A second and even more significant development than the Shona drive towards the sea was their spread to the west and the establishment of Shona kingdoms on the central and western parts of the plateau, in the heart of the gold-producing regions. These new states drew their cultural heritage both from the old stone-built capital city of Great Zimbabwe, and from the newer political systems of the Mutapa empire. By the seventeenth century a new capital town was emerging at Dhlodhlo, as the seat of a Rozwi dynasty (see p. 596), which was to dominate much of the cultural zone of the old Leopard's Kopje tradition.

The Leopard's Kopje tradition represents the Later Iron Age culture of a large southern part of Rhodesia and distinguishes the south very markedly from the northern half of the country. This tradition grew out of, or superseded, the Stamped Ware tradition of the Early Iron Age, from about the tenth century onwards. The Early Leopard's Kopje tradition, formerly known as Leopard's Kopje II, is represented so far by three known variants, Bambandyanalo in the south, Mambo in the west (at the Leopard's Kopje site itself), and Lower Zimbabwe (or Zimbabwe II) in the east.[1] From the thirteenth century these cultures evolved into the Later Leopard's Kopje tradition, or Leopard's Kopje III. The three variants of this later period are principally exemplified by the sites at Mapungubwe in the south, Woolandale in the west and Zimbabwe III in the east.[2] The Later Leopard's Kopje cultures saw the development of large-scale stone-building, which flourished initially from the thirteenth to the fifteenth centuries. Out of this early stone-building tradition there arose a later stone-working tradition exemplified by the site at Khami, which belongs mainly to the seventeenth century, and is noted for the variety of its walling styles.[3]

In the six centuries or so which preceded the development of the Early Leopard's Kopje cultures the southern peoples of Rhodesia,

[1] A new reassessment of the Leopard's Kopje material by T. N. Huffman was not available at the time of writing.

[2] Zimbabwe III was formerly divided into Zimbabwe III and Zimbabwe IV but this no longer seems justifiable.

[3] P. S. Garlake, 'Rhodesian ruins – a preliminary assessment of their styles and chronology', *Journal of African History*, 1970, **11**, 495–513; T. N. Huffman, 'The rise and fall of Zimbabwe', ibid. 1972, **13**, 353–66, and his chart of the Rhodesian Iron Age sequence in 'The linguistic affinities of the Iron Age in Rhodesia', *Arnoldia*, 1974, **7**, 7, 2.

both indigenous and immigrant, had adopted a whole range of Early Iron Age cultural and economic innovations connected with iron-using, pottery-making, agriculture and stock-raising. Although the majority of the population was concerned with planned food-producing, the old skills of hunting and gathering remained important everywhere, and there was no complete polarization between gatherers and farmers. Most settlements were still fairly mobile, and few sites were sufficiently fertile to support long periods of continuous occupation. When the distinctive Leopard's Kopje materials begin to appear on archaeological sites in the Bulawayo area, there are indications that important changes in economic activity were occurring. In particular, cattle-owning was becoming more widespread.

The change of material culture associated with the beginning of the Early Leopard's Kopje tradition is primarily identified by pottery. The styles become more flamboyant, comb-stamping gives way to incised markings, and black and red colourings cease to be used for decoration. There was no great increase in the use of iron and copper at this time, but foreign glass beads became a slightly more common form of personal decoration. On the basis of the latest evidence available, archaeologists are inclining to the view that a sharp break occurred between the culture of the Early Iron Age tradition and the Mambo culture of the Leopard's Kopje Later Iron Age tradition. This break in cultural continuity contrasts sharply with the more continuous nature of the development of Iron Age traditions in the rest of Rhodesia. The abrupt change would seem to indicate an influx of new peoples, with influential new ideas. Such an influx does raise problems as to its origin. So far, no possible alien source for the peoples or cultures of the Leopard's Kopje tradition has been convincingly identified. Speculation has turned to the unknown rather than to the known areas for sources of inspiration, as Garlake makes clear in a cautious recent assessment:

About the ninth or tenth century new immigrants entered the dry *Acacia* sand veld of south-west Matabeleland introducing what is known as the Leopard's Kopje culture. Their pottery shows such a marked typological break with Early Iron Age wares, that, in this instance, there can be little doubt that these people were immigrants who had no direct cultural relationship with the previous inhabitants. No antecedents are apparent in the archaeology of Zambia or Rhodesia, leading to the rather risky supposition (for it is based on ignorance rather than on knowledge) that the new group may have entered Matabeleland from the rich grasslands of northern Botswana and Angola – archaeologically unknown areas.[1]

[1] P. S. Garlake, *Great Zimbabwe* (London, 1973), 155–6.

The double caution with which Garlake proposes his thesis of a break in continuity caused by new peoples coming from an unknown area should be noted. Historians of Rhodesia have been rather prone to facile explanations of change in terms of large-scale migration. In this case, however, it would not be surprising if the blend of local innovation and hitherto alien features had been caused by some immigration of primarily pastoral people. The south-western border of Rhodesia is an open grassland through which cattle-keepers can, and do, drift in search of the best grazing. Wherever they came from, however, it is certain that the immigrants attached great importance to their cattle. In an area only marginally suited to agriculture this gave them advantage over their Early Iron Age predecessors, for whom cattle were probably less plentiful and less economically important, although not unknown.[1] In early Leopard's Kopje settlements cattle had apparently achieved a degree of political, social and ritual importance; small cult figurines were made of clay, showing the symbolic significance of cattle in the society.

The development of an advanced herding economy in south-western Rhodesia probably went hand in hand with increased and improved agriculture. It is shown in chapter 9 of this volume (pp. 626–9, 640, 645–6, 650–1) that pastoralists and farmers, far from being incompatible competitors, could on occasion co-operate most effectively in extending land usage. Such co-operation probably occurred within the Leopard's Kopje economy. On the agricultural side, seeds of millet, cowpea, sorghum and bean have been discovered that date from the early period. Later, during the late twelfth and thirteenth centuries, Leopard's Kopje mixed farming gained a new impetus. Extensive new farmland was brought under cultivation, and more permanent occupation sites began to be used. Advanced agricultural communities apparently attracted more of the Early Iron Age peoples to their settlements, thus increasing their population. At the same time the relative importance of hunting and gathering declined still further. One of the striking features of the intensified agricultural development was the use of terraces on land that was fertile but steep. This hillside farming was able to catch what rain there was, and the terraces prevented the

[1] Seventh-century bones excavated at Makuru have been tentatively identified as those of domestic cattle; see T. N. Huffman, 'Test excavations at Makuru, Rhodesia', *Arnoldia*, 1973, 5, 39. Linguistic evidence suggests that some cattle could conceivably have been herded south of the Zambezi by Central Sudanic speakers even before Bantu languages became spoken in the area; see C. Ehret, 'Patterns of Bantu and Central Sudanic settlement in Central and Southern Africa, *c.* 1000 BC–AD 500', *Transafrican Journal of History*, 1974, **4**, 1, 1–27.

excessive erosion of top-soil. In the west the growth of later Leopard's Kopje farming is demonstrated at Woolandale, near Bulawayo. Some of the most spectacular terracing of the period is found in the southern Leopard's Kopje area, down in the Limpopo basin. At Mapela a hill about 90 metres in height was entirely terraced with walls of rough stone. In addition to gardens, some terraces were built for defensive purposes, or to provide level building sites. The creation of such an extensive complex may have required an organized labour force. Garlake's interpretation of the site suggests that a hierarchical division of the society can be identified. At the summit of the hill, huts were built of solid daga, with thick floors and walls with moulded decorations. These were the houses of the rulers, and the rest of the population lived around the nucleus in much scantier daub-and-wattle houses. The scale on which glass beads are found suggests that the prosperity of Mapela was not only due to its highly organized agriculture. It was also connected with the growing inter-regional trade of south-eastern Africa.[1]

The most striking feature of the later Leopard's Kopje cultures was the development of gold-mining. This created a new economic dynamism which affected a wide area of Rhodesia. Gold is found in a diagonal belt which runs from the Botswana border, south of Bulawayo, to the Zambezi escarpment north-east of Salisbury. By the thirteenth century the southern end of this belt was being mined with increasing intensity. The mines were small, one-man shafts dug out with hand tools, but some of them went very deep, down to around thirty metres and more. There was no system of water-pumping, so when the water table was met excavation had to cease. It is possible that the ore-bearing rock may have been broken underground by heating it with fire and then dousing it with cold water. On the surface, the ore was crushed with pestles in mortars cut into the surface granite, and the powder was then washed for gold dust. Obtaining gold was only the first of the mining industry's problems. Marketing it was an equally difficult operation. Gold was of only limited value to producers unless they could sell it for goods of greater practical or scarcity value. The Leopard's Kopje miners developed three main sets of trading partners through whom they sold their gold. The most shadowy were the little-known southern traders to whom Mapela chiefs owed their glass beads. The most spectacular trading system, but also perhaps the shortest lived, was the Zimbabwe network in the east. The latest and most

[1] Garlake, *Great Zimbabwe*, 156–7.

lasting traders were the northern set, who traded with the Zambezi valley, particularly from the fifteenth century.

The most prosperous southern site was Mapungubwe. This is a steep rocky hill in the Limpopo valley. The area below the hill, known as Bambandyanalo or 'K2', had been occupied since the eleventh century by peoples using Leopard's Kopje-style pottery. Cattle enclosures, cattle burials and cattle figurines demonstrate the importance of pastoralism on this site; agriculture was probably also practised, although this is not yet certain. The cattle culture, the lugged pottery, and the human skeletal material which physical anthropologists described as 'non-negroid' or 'large Khoisan' led Gardner, the excavator of the area, to describe the inhabitants as Khoi or Hottentot pastoralists. In the light of subsequent knowledge about the Iron Age of southern Africa it seems more likely that the inhabitants of Bambandyanalo were Bantu-speaking. It would, however, be unwise to be dogmatic about either the physical characteristics or the language of the eleventh- to fourteenth-century Iron Age peoples of this area. It will be seen later that further south, in the Transvaal, Khoi peoples had already adopted pastoralism over a wide area.

Whoever occupied Bambandyanalo, it was primarily a village of cattle-owners living at a fairly simple level of subsistence. The site at Mapungubwe belongs to the fourteenth and fifteenth centuries and is very much richer. The surrounding valley contains numerous agricultural terraces, and sorghum and cowpeas were among the crops certainly grown. Cattle and small stock were both common, and the midden bones suggest that domestic animals were more important than wild game as a source of meat for the wealthy people of Mapungubwe. Superimposed on the agricultural economy was an exchange economy based on the local raw materials. Copper, probably from the Messina region, and ivory from the elephants of the Limpopo valley were accumulated for commercial purposes. The resources were also worked for local consumption, and personal ornaments of copper and ivory were made. The Mapungubwe area was apparently ruled by a wealthy aristocracy or priesthood, which lived on the hilltop. They built elaborate daga houses and possessed a full range of Later Iron Age tools. The wealth of Mapungubwe can best be seen in a few ostentatious burials of rich men. They were adorned with imported gold beads and local copper bangles. Gold was also imported for other ornamental purposes. Although the wealth of Mapungubwe may have largely derived from the internal trade of the Limpopo basin and adjacent areas, it did not completely exclude longer-range contacts, which brought foreign imports such as glass beads and Ming celadon from China. More important still, cloth was imported at Mapungubwe, and from this an indigenous spinning and weaving industry seems to have evolved.[1]

Evidence for trade between the middle Limpopo and the coast is scant, and any reconstruction must await archaeological knowledge. The valley could have provided the most practical access from the coast to the north-eastern Transvaal as well. In the mid sixteenth century Portuguese merchants traded at Inhambane, approximately 320 kilometres south of Sofala, and at Delagoa Bay, just below the Limpopo mouth. At Inhambane they seem to have met, and co-operated with, earlier Muslim traders. The nature of the traffic is not known, though caravans carrying cloth and beads might have travelled inland in search of gold, ivory and, perhaps, slaves. At Delagoa Bay sixteenth-century traders were offered copper as well as ivory. This copper could have come from small local deposits, though it might equally have come from inland and have been brought to the coast to pay for foreign imports. In the second half of the sixteenth century the Portuguese sent an annual shipload of merchandise to Delagoa Bay; this suggests that the supply of commodities was organized on a regular basis, and that trade was not wholly dependent on occasional local exchanges of used materials such as copper bangles.[2]

The cultural and economic similarities between Mapungubwe and Leopard's Kopje III must lead one to suppose that the Leopard's Kopje mines of Matabeleland were the source of Mapungubwe gold. But Mapungubwe was probably not the major gateway through which Rhodesian gold was exported. Much more important was Great Zimbabwe.[3] The history of Great Zimbabwe begins on a spectacular hilltop in the Early Iron Age. An imposing outcrop of granite rises some ninety metres out of the surrounding countryside. The site was easily protected against attack, and in the valley below typical Early Iron Age small farming settlements could live comfortably. The area also had better rainfall than many of the neighbouring regions. Despite these apparent advantages, the early occupation of the Zimbabwe area was neither continuous nor long-lived. For whatever

[1] The most accessible summaries and interpretations of Mapungubwe are in B. M. Fagan, *Southern Africa during the Iron Age* (London, 1965), and his 'The Greefswald Sequence: Bambandyanalo and Mapungubwe', *Journal of African History*, 1964, **5**, 3, 337–61.

[2] A. K. Smith, 'The struggle for control of southern Mozambique, 1720–1835', Ph.D. thesis (University of California, Los Angeles, 1970), ch. 1.

[3] Garlake, *Great Zimbabwe*, is the latest and most comprehensive history of this site.

reasons, the early sites were abandoned and the area not reoccupied until the eleventh century, when Later Iron Age peoples again made use of it. The new Period II settlers of Zimbabwe used pottery which was fairly similar to that of Leopard's Kopje in Period II. There is no sign at Zimbabwe of any of the last Stamped Ware potteries, or any transitional styles between Early and Later Iron Age. If the hill was reoccupied by local peoples, their cultural transformation must have taken place off the site. On the other hand, the new occupants may have been immigrants to the region coming from Leopard's Kopje regions to the west, or they may have formed part of the same wider migration as the Leopard's Kopje people. Details of cultural contact and population spread are not yet available, but the process does seem to have been rapid, and the new occupants of Zimbabwe, like those of Bambandyanalo, brought or adopted not only the domestic pottery styles similar to those at Leopard's Kopje, but also the figurine art associated with a cattle economy.

The reoccupation of Great Zimbabwe in the eleventh century was followed by 400 years of continuous settlement. The continuity is demonstrated by the uninterrupted evolution of the domestic pottery styles. At first Zimbabwe pots, although of similar shape and style to those of Leopard's Kopje, were less highly decorated. Later Zimbabwe pottery developed a better finish, and a distinctive style of hatched triangular decorations on the shoulders of the pots. Some styles went out of existence as unfashionable or unserviceable. The later wares were often given a burnished graphite finish which was unknown at Leopard's Kopje.

Although the Zimbabwe pottery demonstrates a continuity of culture among the population of the area, the architecture of the site shows that there were two distinct phases of growth. During the first, known as Period II, people lived in daub-and-wattle style houses constructed of poles and coated with daga. From the thirteenth century a new style of house-building in solid daga began to develop among the more influential people of Great Zimbabwe. This transition from Zimbabwe Period II to Zimbabwe Period III involved more than new house-building techniques. It also saw a flourishing of stone-building skills. Early stone building had been of a fairly functional kind. Stone walls were built for fortification, stone terraces were built for hillside gardening, and cattle-kraals and field boundaries were made of stone. In the later period stone building came to be used for much more ostentatious prestige purposes. Courtyards which had previously been surrounded, one supposes, by hedges or fences were now surrounded by stone walls. These walls were free-standing, unlike the earlier terrace walls. At first there was little skill available for building such unsupported walls, but gradually masons learnt how to choose their materials with greater care and to lay their granite blocks in even courses. One very distinctive complex of stone buildings at Zimbabwe is the Hill Ruin, sometimes known as the Acropolis, where numerous walls and natural boulders are linked in a network of enclosures on the summit of a precipice. In the valley below numerous other stone buildings were erected; the most imposing, the Elliptical Building or Temple, which was probably the main royal residence. Here the earliest buildings consist of a clover-leaf pattern of adjoining circular enclosures, with house-sites situated in the gateways between one and another. There are the remains of an early circumference wall, probably intended to enclose the whole complex, though never in fact completed. The last two structures to be built, showing a greatly superior standard of masonry to the rest, were a solid conical tower of unknown significance and, finally, a magnificent surrounding wall, approximately 240 metres in circumference, and much of it more than nine metres in height Though built without mortar, the outer courses are of trimmed stone and perfectly regular, with a slight inward batter for stability. Parts of this wall are approximately five metres thick at the base and are fitted with drainage culverts from the inner floor surface to the outside. The main gateway of the outer enclosure faces straight towards the Acropolis hill, where it is thought that the royal ancestors were buried and their cult maintained. To the east of the 'royal enclosure', a large area of less spectacular ruins, as yet imperfectly investigated, was perhaps the site of the capital town.

The monumental architecture of Zimbabwe raises many questions which historians have been rather slow to answer convincingly. This is partly because the answers depend almost entirely on archaeological data, and much of this data was disturbed by inexpert excavators and treasure-hunters during the late nineteenth century. It is, however, abundantly clear that Great Zimbabwe was the capital of a kingdom. In a community such as this, which was based on subsistence agriculture, considerable authority would have been needed to mobilize the labour necessary to break and carry such enormous quantities of stone. It is also clear that royal patronage would have been needed to train and maintain skilled masons. Since there is no sign that the later

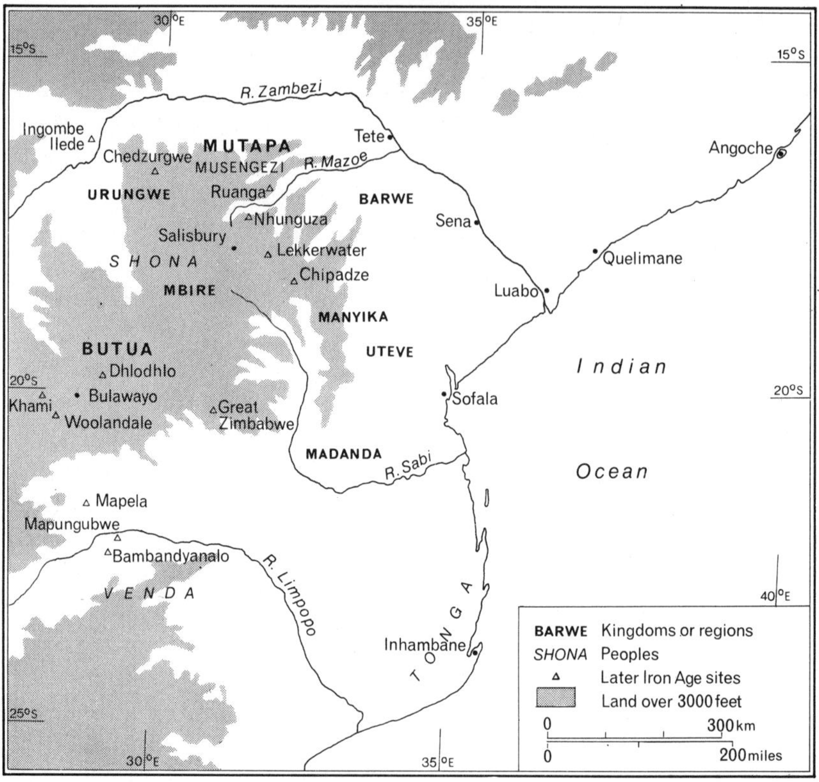

15 Between the Zambezi and the Limpopo

Zimbabwe buildings served any defensive purpose, they were presumably built to enhance the glory of the king and his entourage. This interpretation of Zimbabwe as the hub of a kingdom is strengthened by the results of the growing study of other stone ruins in a similar style. Although Great Zimbabwe is far larger than any other similar site, it is not unique in style, but is one of a hundred or so evenly built stone ruins scattered through the granite country of eastern Rhodesia. At Chipadze, for instance, approximately 240 kilometres north-east of Zimbabwe, an old walled site had a new wall added to it, in classical Zimbabwe style, in the fourteenth or fifteenth century. At a similar or slightly later period a hill-top at Lekkerwater near Salisbury was surmounted by an enclosure of beautiful, evenly built stone walls. Inside the enclosure strong huts of solid daga were built and decorated with moulded motifs. It is strongly suspected that such fine craftsmanship did not evolve locally but was supplied from Zimbabwe, possibly to build a provincial court and establish a governor to represent the central power.

One of the furthest outlying stone enclosures of Zimbabwe's fourteenth-century 'empire' was at Nhunguza, near the upper Mazoe river. Here it has been possible to reconstruct the internal plan of the enclosure in a way that is not possible at Zimbabwe itself. The main hut appears to have been seven and a half metres across and about two and a half metres tall at the centre. The roof was supported on a dozen or more poles. The building's function was probably ceremonial. A small inner sanctum had a raised platform of granite plastered with daga on which religious relics might have been laid. It was reached by a small room with a seat, where the priest may have sat. Finally a large outer hallway with a rough floor could have provided space for a large number of supplicants who had come to the 'shrine' or 'court'. This main hut is surrounded by seven dwelling huts which form a single extended family unit. Political or religious domination over the surrounding people must be assumed in order to explain the very large scale of the building work involved. One curious domestic feature of the archaeological remains is that, although drinking vessels and storage pots typical of the Zimbabwe style have been found, there are no cooking-pots on the site, perhaps emphasizing its ritual rather than its domestic importance.[1]

The architectural evidence from Great Zimbabwe points to the existence of a strong kingdom on the eastern edge of the plateau and immediately west of the Sabi river basin and the Manyika highlands. An extensive political and religious centre would have required a strong economic base. The guardianship of royal graves and shrines and the awesome consultation of spirit media probably required a body of priests who were freed from subsistence farming. The erection of royal buildings would have required the mobilization of hundreds of workmen each season. The agricultural methods used at Zimbabwe were probably not capable of creating adequate food surpluses unaided. Even cattle-keeping by client peoples could not have created an adequate concentration of royal wealth. The special wealth which made the building of Great Zimbabwe possible was doubtless derived from external long-distance trade.

The most substantial evidence of Zimbabwe's commercial importance is to be found in the foreign ceramics which were used by the

[1] Garlake, 'Excavations at the Nhunguza and Ruanga ruins in northern Mashonaland', *South African Archaeological Bulletin*, 1973, **27**, 107–43.

court at the height of its prosperity. These ceramics consist, first of all, of Chinese celadon. Some of these celadon dishes are speckled blue-grey wares, and others have a sea-green crackled glaze over incised floral designs. All are probably of very early Ming manufacture and belong to the fourteenth century. Another rich import to Zimbabwe which has been recovered was a piece of highly glazed Persian faience, probably of the thirteenth century. Further Persian imports included fourteenth- and fifteenth-century blue glazed earthenware. One striking fact about these ceramics is that no comparable finds have been made anywhere else in this region of south-eastern Africa. Similar high-quality wares are confined to places such as Mogadishu and Kilwa on the East African coast. This suggests that, for the time being, we must assume that Zimbabwe alone among interior capitals had an adequate wealth in gold to buy the finest Persian and Chinese wares.[1]

One striking feature of the luxury trade of Great Zimbabwe is that, although it flourished in the thirteenth and fourteenth centuries, it ceased abruptly in the fifteenth century. The Rhodesian gold-trade continued into the sixteenth century and beyond, but none of the exotic ceramics which it then bought are to be found at Zimbabwe. Thus the wealth of Zimbabwe flourished for about two centuries only, after which fundamental changes took place in south-eastern Africa and Zimbabwe was abandoned. The time-span is exactly the same as the time-span of Kilwa's greatest prosperity, and the link between the two seems almost certain. Before turning to the history of the coastland which linked these two great commercial entrepôts, one should ask two last questions about how the gold trade of Great Zimbabwe began and why it so suddenly declined.

It would be possible to ask whether the Rhodesian gold-trade was an alien enterprise conducted by foreign colonists. All the archaeological evidence suggests that it was not. The evolution of the local Zimbabwe culture is continuous through Periods II and III, and there is no sign of a foreign trading quarter near Great Zimbabwe such as those found in the east coast cities or in the market empires of West Africa. The foreign ceramics betoken the greatest luxury; they are the eating vessels of a wealthy king, not the everyday utensils of a Muslim merchant. If the gold trade was not introduced by aliens, it must have grown from the domestic commercial system of the region. Specific evidence about the domestic trade of the southern Shona is still scant,

[1] Garlake, 'The value of imported ceramics in the dating and interpretation of the Rhodesian Iron Age', *Journal of African History*, 1968, 9, 13–33.

but no Iron Age communities were ever entirely self-sufficient, and some exchange of both raw and manufactured materials certainly occurred. The interlocking networks of local trade could also be used for the slow, but far-ranging, dissemination of more valuable items of material wealth. In the local trade salt was obviously a scarce resource, and oral traditions refer to the search for salt, although no serious attempt has yet been made to plot the Shona salt supplies and salt tracks. Pottery was probably also traded, despite its weight, bulk and fragility, and this trade increased the spread of new designs and decorations among local potters. As iron became increasingly important, there was a growing demand for the richest iron ores, the best-worked raw iron and the most proficient iron tools, implements and ornaments. One iron object of particular interest found at Great Zimbabwe is a double gong or bell. A similar pair of bells has been found at Ingombe Ilede on the Zambezi, and double bells were a well-known symbol of royal authority in Zaïre. The Zimbabwe bells may have been relayed by trade from Zambia or Zaïre, or alternatively the necessary welding skills may have been transmitted from one blacksmith fraternity to the next, so that by the fourteenth century Shona smiths were capable of welding iron bells. It seems likely that they were made, or bought, because of their symbolic association with kingship.

Within this framework of Iron Age trade it became possible for gold to be relayed and sold. The earliest mining of gold began about AD 1000, but the trade took on new vigour from the thirteenth century, when Zimbabwe passed from Period II to Period III, and stone building came into prominence. Although there was no mining around Zimbabwe, trade was apparently funnelled that way from the plateau to the coast, between the Sabi valley and the Manyika highlands. Control of this trade channel, either by state participation in the traffic or by the imposition of commercial taxes, could have financed the construction of Zimbabwe's monumental architecture. As the king's wealth increased, so his prestige attracted people to the royal settlement. The process of growth in this wealthy trading state continued until the abrupt decline set in during the fifteenth century. The currently favoured explanation for this reversal suggests that the ecological environment had become over-exploited. The agricultural capacity of the region could have been reached by even quite a small total population of perhaps two thousand or so. Once this limit had been reached there were no reserves to carry the state through an attack of pestilence, drought or famine. In addition to food and land scarcity, there may have developed a shortage of wood fuel, which had been consumed in huge quantities for rock-breaking. In an Iron Age economy, accustomed to very sparse populations, even a small excess may also have led to the over-grazing of stock land and even to the over-hunting of wild game. People were therefore forced to move away, and the political system, now large and highly structured, could not adapt to change but could only crumble. Most people presumably reverted to unspecialized subsistence, but a few moved west, to the Khami area, where the architectural and artistic traditions of Zimbabwe later revived to flourish in adapted stone and pottery styles. Other people moved north to the Zambezi escarpment, where the new empire of the *mwene mutapa* apparently maintained some of the Zimbabwe political traditions.[1]

The main trading partner of Zimbabwe was the port of Sofala. The Sofala coast was known to Indian Ocean sailors by the tenth century, when the name probably applied to most of northern Mozambique. It was generally considered a dangerous and hostile coast, at the end of the known world. Native hostility was increased by the treachery of early sailors, who sometimes captured shore-dwellers as hostages or slaves. Already by the tenth century, however, al-Masʿūdī was reporting that gold could be obtained along the Sofala coast, and increasing numbers of merchants ventured there. They were able to buy not only gold, but also slaves, ivory and, according to al-Idrīsī, in the twelfth century, good quality iron, which was smelted in the Sofala mountains and later sold in India.[2] The problem of this trade was that even the northern end of the Sofala coast could not be reached from Asia in a single monsoon voyage. It was necessary to winter on the East African coast, and make the trip south in the second year. This is how Kilwa developed its commercial importance, and how Kilwa merchants came to establish permanent entrepôts along the trading beaches of Mozambique.

The old town of Sofala was washed away early in this century by maritime erosion,[3] so we have no archaeological means of knowing when it was founded, and when concentration of trade on the coast occurred. It is likely, however, to have been around 1300. At this time

[1] Garlake, *Great Zimbabwe*, is the main source of information on the history of Zimbabwe; but see also Huffman, 'Rise and fall of Zimbabwe', 356–61, for a recent discussion.

[2] Cited in E. E. Burke, 'Some aspects of Arab contact in S.E. Africa', in *Proceedings of the Leverhulme Historical Conference* (Salisbury, 1960), 10.

[3] This is the hypothesis put forward in M. D. D. Newitt, *Portuguese settlement on the Zambesi* (London, 1973), 204.

a new dynasty gained power in Kilwa and the city's wealth increased rapidly. Political envoys from Kilwa became the rulers of Sofala and began to monopolize the trade on the coast. This development was exactly contemporary with the monopolization of the plateau trade which occurred at Great Zimbabwe. A specific indication of the link between the two was found at Zimbabwe in the shape of a Kilwa coin minted in the reign of al-Hasan b. Sulaymān (*c.* 1320–33).[1] It was also during this reign that Ibn Baṭṭūṭa visited Kilwa and described the trade in gold dust which came from a country one month's journey inland from the Sofala coast. The Muslim governors of Sofala established a narrow coastal domain in which they made themselves very comfortable. The Portuguese friar João dos Santos, who visited Sofala in the sixteenth century, marvelled at the range of exotic plants and fruits that grew in the gardens of Muslim households scattered among the coastal palm groves. The traders travelled at least some distance up the local river, and Portuguese travellers found abandoned citrus groves at the old settlement sites. The majority of the Muslim traders were black Africans, but it is not known how many were Swahili immigrants, and how many were local people who had adopted the international trading culture of Muslim townsfolk. Whether local or foreign, however, the urban population was clearly distinguished by the Portuguese from the 'woolly-haired heathens' of the neighbouring countryside. Soon after leaving the coast one entered independent Africa.

The hinterland of Sofala was ruled in the sixteenth century, and probably before then also, by the king of Uteve. Dos Santos had much to say about this king, and although his description belongs to the late sixteenth century, it provides valuable insight into the workings of Shona kingship. The king was the overlord of a large territory. He combined the supernatural attributes of a national god with the human attributes of a reigning king. On the human side the king had a court where his people came to prostrate themselves before him. Foreign visitors entered barefoot and were received in public audience and given local beer. The palace guard consisted of 200 heavily armed men, who were greatly feared. When the king went on progress, he was accompanied by his praise-singers, who rang bells, beat drums and invented extravagant songs about his prowess. He also employed court musicians who played magnificent xylophones and small, well-tuned thumb-pianos with iron keys. His royal attendants served not only as

[1] Huffman, 'Rise and fall of Zimbabwe', 351–66.

courtiers, but also as couriers and ambassadors who carried the king's word within and without the realm. The king also had judicial functions, such as administering poison ordeals. So long as he remained in good health, the king was extremely powerful. As soon as he began to fail, however, he was vulnerable, and the royal clan began intense political activity to select a capable successor among his eligible kinsfolk.

The king's spiritual responsibilities were equal to his political ones. Once a year he left his *zimbabwe* (court) and went to the summit of a high mountain to commune with his ancestors. One of his entourage would become possessed with the spirit of the king's father. Dos Santos describes the scene graphically:

When the king has feasted for eight days, he begins his lamentation for the dead who are buried there, and all join in continual lamentation for two or three days, until the devil enters into one of the Kaffirs of the assembly, saying that he is the soul of the dead king, father of him who is engaged in these ceremonies, come to converse with his son. The demoniac becomes as one into whose body the devil has entered, stretched on the ground, disfigured, deformed, and out of his senses, and while he is in this state the devil speaks through his mouth in all the foreign tongues of other Kaffir nations, which are understood by many of those present. Besides this, he begins to cough and speak like the dead king whom he represents, in such a manner that it seems to be his very self, both in voice and movements, by which signs the Kaffirs recognise the soul of the dead king has come as they expected. The king who is performing the ceremonies, being informed of this, comes accompanied by all his nobles to the place where the demoniac is, and all prostrate themselves before him, showing him great honour. Then all withdraw, leaving the king alone with the demoniac, with whom he converses amicably as if with his dead father, asking him if there will be war, and if he will triumph over his enemies, and if there will be famine or misfortunes in his kingdom, and everything else which he wishes to know. The devil answers all these questions, and counsels him as to what he is to do . . . After this conference the devil goes out of the man's body, leaving the negro very exhausted and broken down, and still disfigured.[1]

The emphasis which dos Santos places on the religious powers and responsibilities of Shona kings is undoubtedly justified. But the Teve king also filled an important economic role. His influence may have extended to the domestic trades of smithing and weaving and to the issue of local squares of cotton *machira* cloth which circulated freely as a means of exchange. He certainly brought the external trade of Uteve

[1] Joao dos Santos, *Ethiopia oriental*, cited in G. M. Theal, ed., *Records of south-eastern Africa* (Cape Town, 1898–1903; reprinted 1964), VII, 197–8.

under close royal supervision. Foreign merchants, both Karanga from the plateau and Muslims or Christians from the coast, were obliged to present themselves at court with suitable gifts before the king would grant them permission to trade. The Teve king was capable of closing all foreign markets for long periods when this suited his interests. Such a closure was effected by Nyamunda in the 1520s, and caused the new Portuguese trade at Sofala to decline very sharply. Later in the century the Portuguese agreed to pay the Teve king an annual tribute of 200 pieces of cloth in return for a licence to trade.[1] The value of such a cloth tax probably amounted to approximately 740 grams of gold. This would suggest that the Teve trade had dwindled to very small proportions. The late fifteenth and early sixteenth centuries had seen some major changes in south-eastern Africa. One of these had been the arrival of Portuguese vessels in the Indian Ocean.

When the Portuguese captured the port of Sofala in 1505, their chief aim had been to penetrate the Indian spice market. They hoped to participate in the local monsoon trade, and then use their profits from East Africa to buy spices in Asia. In the Atlantic Portugal had captured the long-distance ocean-carrying trade by means of its superior navigational skills and shipbuilding technology. In the Indian Ocean conditions were different, and large-scale ocean trading was already well developed. In order to participate in the existing Asian traffic in beads and textiles, Portugal had to use naval and military power. She therefore captured and garrisoned Kilwa and built a fortified factory at Sofala. The intention was to compel traders on the Sofala coast, Muslim and non-Muslim, to buy their Indian trade cloth at the Portuguese factory in return for payments in gold at Portuguese prices. The plan failed on several counts. The military protection of the intended monopoly was inefficient and expensive, and the management of the trade was corrupt. Coastal navigation was difficult and unsuited to the larger European vessels. Many goods had to be trans-shipped at Mozambique island, causing losses and delays. The Portuguese method of buying gold was a mixture of commercial bargaining and counterfeit weighing. The same system of dual weights was used as at São Jorge da Mina, in West Africa, and the instructions to the factors, issued in 1530, specified that they were to buy gold 'weighed in the scales with as great an increase in weight as they can manage by any means, without the said merchants perceiving what they have been subjected to, lest

[1] Dos Santos, in Theal, *Records*, VII, 220. See also the records relating to Teve foreign relations in the seven-volume *Documents on the Portuguese in Mozambique and Central Africa* (Lisbon, 1962).

they take offence thereby'. As soon as the gold-traders had left the premises, the factor was required to reweigh his gold accurately and to credit the gain to the treasury account.[1] Such fraudulent methods did not help the Portuguese to compete with Swahili traders. Neither did their attempts to recruit allies among the Teve chiefly estate. In the 1510s they apparently supplied the Teve king with muskets, which they were themselves just beginning to adopt in place of the cross-bow. Their hope of creating an ally was sorely disappointed.[2]

The sixteenth-century failure of Sofala was due to more than commercial malpractice and political ineptitude. In the fifteenth century a wholesale shift in the pattern of south-eastern Africa's trade occurred, and Sofala was gradually cut out from the commercial mainstream. It was being replaced by a new port, or ports, on the Angoche coast, north of the mouths of the Zambezi. The new Swahili traders were probably independent merchants operating in breach of the Kilwa monopoly. Late in the fifteenth century Angoche was visited by refugees from Kilwa, who founded a new sultanate, the trade of which grew as the Sofala–Kilwa axis collapsed. A few years later commercial power shifted again, as Angoche was gradually replaced by the Portuguese establishments of Mozambique island, north of it, and Quelimane, south of it. The gradual shift from Kilwa to Angoche, Quelimane and the other northern ports was a sign that from the fifteenth century the Zambezi valley had become the major trade artery of the region and replaced the routes inland from Sofala.

The Zambezi is a difficult river to navigate. Its delta is shallow and changing, and its upper reaches have impassable rapids at Cabora Bassa. Fluvial navigation could, nevertheless, provide enormous savings in transport costs, and by the fifteenth century Angoche traders penetrated the Luabo and other mouths of the delta and trans-shipped their goods into river canoes. These canoes could carry loads of several tons and saved the work of many dozens of porters. The opening of river traffic led to the creation of a market town at Sena, 160 kilometres upstream. A few households of Muslim merchants were established there and began to attract local trade. The first area to be affected was Manyika. Manyika is the easternmost area of gold production in Rhodesia, and its surface reefs were intensively exploited. The traditional outlet for Manyika gold had probably been Sofala, but Sena was close enough to attract the trade. As it did so, a new kingdom

[1] Regimentos de Sofala, 20/5/1530, cited in *Documents*, VI, 387.
[2] Newitt, *Portuguese settlement*, 330.

called Barwe developed between Manyika and Sena. Its relationship to the Sena traders was rather similar to Uteve's relationship to Sofala, and it acted alternately as an agent or as an impediment to the free flow of trade.[1]

Barwe was founded in the late fifteenth or early sixteenth century. Because it survived into the twentieth century, it has been possible to recover in some detail oral traditions describing the kingdom's structure and operation. These royal traditions claim that the king's ancestor, Kabundu Kagoro, came from north of the Mazoe, where the Mutapa empire was beginning to emerge, and was the first man to settle in Barwe. This historical charter ignores the historical claims of all Sena, Tonga and Tavara peoples who had previously occupied the area but were subsequently absorbed into the new kingdom. When Kabundu Kagoro died, his *mhondoro* spirit became the national guardian, the senior spirit of the kingdom. Unlike Mwari, the high god of the Shona, the *mhondoro* was amenable to intercession and gave guidance to his people from his mountain shrine. When the *mhondoro* had no human spokesman he was embodied in a lion, but when he wished to speak he took possession of a human being, who then became the life-long guardian of the shrine. The spirit of the first king provided a strong bond of unity in the kingdom. A second important political bond was the ritual of the 'royal fire', which was also practised in other Shona kingdoms. In Barwe, on the occasion of the new year sacrifices, all fires in the country had to be extinguished. New fire was then given to the king by the spirit medium. The king in his turn gave brands of fire to his followers, with which they could relight fires of loyalty in their home villages. The king's fire represented royal power, and any failure to attend the rekindling ceremony was treasonable. Fire from any other source did not protect villages with the same magical efficacy.

Although Barwe possessed the institutions and ideology of a strong kingdom, it also possessed a weakness in its method of royal succession, which was common to other Shona kingdoms. A twin process of inheritance and selection determined the transfer of authority, but there was ample room for civil dispute and widespread instability. Brothers of the older generation commonly inherited before sons and nephews of the younger generation. Royal councillors were expected to weigh up the genealogical status of the many claimants against their

[1] A. Isaacman, 'Madzi-Manga, Mhondoro and the use of oral traditions – a chapter in Barue religious and political history', *Journal of African History*, 1973, 14, 395–409.

proven political skills and following. The final announcement of the succession, which was intended to stop all argument, was entrusted to the *mhondoro*. When the *mhondoro* had no spokesman, a long and perilous interregnum could occur while advisers of the late king tried to rule the country. When the king was finally chosen, all factions attended his investiture, and the king was seen to drink a special potion of *madzi manga* which fortified his powers. In many ways this kingdom of Barwe bore striking similarities to the much larger neighbouring kingdom of the *mwene mutapa*.

The Mutapa empire developed in a rather different historical environment from that which underlay the Zimbabwe empire. The northern half of Rhodesia was not affected by the Leopard's Kopje tradition of the Later Iron Age. Instead a more gradual pattern of change occurred in the early centuries of this millennium. The Later Iron Age cultures had their roots in the varied styles of the Stamped Ware tradition. There is a much clearer continuity of pottery styles between the Early and the Later Iron Age in the north, and a tendency for the varied later cultures to be rather localized.

The best known of these northern cultures is that of the Musengezi people. On their pottery finely elaborated decorations were added to the old stamped motifs. An early archaeological site which gives information about the material possessions of the Musengezi peoples, in the thirteenth and fourteenth centuries, is the Monk's Kop burial cave. At Monk's Kop, funerary offerings were presented in ornate vessels, unlike the simple pots used for everyday cooking. Cloth was made out of strips of beaten bark which were sewn together to make clothing and shrouds. Straw and palm leaves were plaited and woven into patterned mats, and fibre rings were made as head pads to carry pots and gourds and other vessels. No foreign trade cloth had apparently reached this area, but ornamental beads of glass and sea shell were available. They must have been relayed either directly from the coast, or from one of the developing long-distance markets of the Rhodesian south. Other personal ornaments such as copper beads and bangles were traded on a more local scale. The most distinctive styles were in bracelets and anklets of fine copper wire.[1]

The Musengezi are known not only from a burial site but also from a living site excavated at Ruanga near the middle Mazoe river. They lived in rather slight pole-and-daga huts without solid floors. Metal ornaments of the kind found in graves were scarce at Ruanga, but metal

[1] J. R. Crawford, 'The Monk's Kop ossuary', *Journal of African History*, 1967, **8**, 373–82.

tools were in use, and a few glass beads were discovered. The simpler pottery styles of Ruanga may be explained by a difference between domestic use and funerary use, or they may simply represent an earlier twelfth-century style. By the fifteenth century, Ruanga village was occupied by people from Great Zimbabwe who built walled enclosures and solid daga huts. The new occupants possessed an array of gold and copper ornaments and used Zimbabwe-style pottery in preference to the Musengezi pots of their neighbours and predecessors. The Zimbabwe-type enclosure at Ruanga was quite small, and Musengezi peoples maintained their own way of life around it. The enclosure was too small to be economically independent or to have housed an effective military force. It was probably the home of a political or religious chief, appointed from Zimbabwe but maintained by the surrounding Musengezi population. The alien chiefs at Ruanga may have been the first southerners to settle in the north, but according to Shona oral tradition others came later. Meanwhile, however, the north was developing its own small centre of prosperity.[1]

The people who lived to the west of the Musengezi river, in the far north-west of Rhodesia, built up a considerable mineral wealth alongside their subsistence agriculture. The district of Urungwe was well endowed with small deposits of copper. By the thirteenth and fourteenth centuries this copper was being systematically exploited. The ore was smelted and cast into moulds, which created a very distinctive cross-shaped ingot with raised rims. A typical ingot was about thirty centimetres long and weighed roughly three kilograms. Urungwe copper had a high degree of metallurgical purity, and was resold to wire-and bracelet- makers. The major commercial site connected with Urungwe was at Ingombe Ilede in the Zambezi valley. Although mining was important, the miners continued to maintain a mixed food-producing economy which included both hunting and cattle-rearing as well as farming and small stock-raising. The mining settlement of Chedzurgwe used pottery of the Ingombe Ilede tradition. It was finely fired and had comb-stamped decorations of unusual precision and sophistication. Ivory was also carved at Chedzurgwe, but no other craft was as specialized as wire drawing. The quality of the copper wire was so fine that some bracelets were wound with fifty coils to each inch. Although this copper was so fine, there is no sign that Urungwe copper was ever traded directly for foreign goods, even in the fifteenth century. The coppersmiths obtained some beads and shells

[1] Garlake, 'Excavations at the Nhunguza and Ruanga ruins', 107–43.

but not the greater foreign wealth which was reaching the gold-miners by this date. There is not much evidence about local copper-trading, but it is not improbable that Zimbabwe might have been in trading contact with Urungwe, though the suggestion that Urungwe copper could have drawn fleeing Zimbabwe leaders northwards is still mere speculation.[1]

The history of the Urungwe copper industry can be supplemented by two non-archaeological pieces of information. In the Zambezi valley the Tonga remember that the Mbara on the plateau were once metal-working specialists. When they were defeated by invaders from the south-east they stopped trading with the valley, and the local people of Chedzurgwe, at least, no longer have any memory of the industry. The second external source is the written account of the Zambezi interior produced by Antonio Fernandes in 1512. He says that the kingdom of Mubara, seven days beyond the capital of the *mwene mutapa*, produced copper. The ingots, 'shaped like windmill sails', were also known to the Portuguese factor at Sofala, who thought that if the Portuguese could obtain such copper, it would enhance their trade prospects. No further references to the Mbara occur in the literature, and it may be suspected that they were conquered by the new Mutapa empire.[2]

The oral traditions of the Mutapa empire suggest that it was founded in the fifteenth century by Shona-speaking immigrants from the southern part of the Rhodesian plateau. These traditions have been preserved through many generations by *mhondoro* shrine-guardians and religious historians who survived the collapse of the Mutapa state and still live around the old capital of the empire overlooking the northward bend of the Zambezi. The traditions, which are symbolic rather than historic, say that a Shona king sent his son Nyatsimba Mutota out to search for salt. Mutota's servants found good salt in the lands of the Tavara, at the Zambezi bend. They also reported that the Zambezi valley was thinly peopled but full of elephants and game. Mutota thereupon moved to the Zambezi escarpment, and established a new kingdom within range of the salt supplies. He was succeeded in the later fifteenth century by his son, Nyanhehwe Matope, who extended the empire by conquering his neighbours. During his campaigns he captured herds of cattle which he lent to his vassals on the southern

[1] Garlake, 'Iron Age sites in the Urungwe district of Rhodesia', *South African Archaeological Bulletin*, 1971, **25**, 25–44.

[2] Cited in ibid.

plateau. One powerful vassal, Changamire, succeeded in capturing the kingship for himself, but the ruling clan was later restored. Soon after this interlude Portuguese travellers began visiting the empire and the symbolic traditions of origin can be supplemented by outside historical evidence.[1]

The early Portuguese reports on the Mutapa empire have been summarized in the chronicles of de Barros, dos Santos and Bocarro.[2] The royal capital of Mutapa was surrounded by a wooden fence. There was no suitable stone for wall-building, so the *mwene mutapa* could not imitate the enclosures of Great Zimbabwe. De Barros was nevertheless convinced that the Shona had formerly been ruled from there. Although he wrote his description about a hundred years after the fall of Zimbabwe, it is very circumstantial. The ancient mines, he said, were in a plain, in the midst of which there was a fortress,

> built of stones of marvellous size, and there appears to be no mortar joining them. The wall is twenty-five spans in width . . . This edifice is almost surrounded by hills, upon which are others resembling it in the fashion of the stone and the absence of mortar, and one of them is a tower more than twelve fathoms high . . . It is guarded by a nobleman . . . as we should say keeper of the *symbaoe* [zimbabwe] and there are always some of the Benomotapa's [*mwene mutapa*'s] wives therein . . . In the opinion of the Moors who saw it, it is very ancient, and was built to keep possession of the mines, which are very old, and no gold has been extracted from them for years.[3]

De Barros's suggestion that the Mutapa empire gained its political system from the Zimbabwe empire fits well into the known chronology. More substantial support derives from the material possessions archaeologically recovered from both capital districts. The utensils, weapons, tools and trinkets are the same. The difference is that, whereas the material culture of Great Zimbabwe evolved out of the surrounding Leopard's Kopje culture, that of the *mwene mutapa* was an alien court culture confined to the king's entourage and brought in from outside, just as the oral traditions claim. In this case we can assume that the historical charter which underpins the Mutapa dynasty has some basis in historical fact.

The new Shona court of the north, with its pole-and-daga buildings and its wooden palisade, was divided into three sectors around the

[1] D. P. Abraham, 'The early political history of the kingdom of the Mwene Mutapa (850–1589)', in *Historians in tropical Africa* (Salisbury, 1962), 62–6.

[2] João de Barros, *Da Asia*, cited in Theal, *Records*, VI; Antonio Bocarro, *Livro do Estado da India*, cited in Theal, *Records*, III; João dos Santos, *Ethiopia*, cited in Theal, *Records*, VII.

[3] De Barros, *Da Asia*, cited in Theal, *Records*, VI, 267–8.

great courtyard. One contained the king's apartments. Another was the queens' quarter, into which no man could enter. The third part of the court was reserved for the royal pages. These were unmarried young noblemen of fifteen to twenty years, who came to serve the king before becoming warriors. They were sent by the great provincial families of the empire to serve at court, partly in order that they might learn royal customs, and partly to show the loyalty of their clans towards the king. In times of conflict the royal pages presumably became hostages, and the king's hold on his subject chiefs was ensured by having their sons resident at court. The royal pages prepared and served the king's food and waited on his person. When they had completed their term of service, they were, so Bocarro alleges, rewarded with grants of land and the administration of provinces.

In addition to the young body-servants, the royal household had many senior office-holders such as the army commander, the captain of the vanguard, the king's apothecary, the chief musician and the royal door-keeper. But the bureaucratic system revolved around nine office-holders who were known as the 'king's wives'. Only the third of these, the *Nabuiza*, was a real queen who lived in the royal compound. The others were functionaries, or ministers of state, who were related to the crown by fictional marriage ties, but who were not necessarily even women, let alone true wives of the king. Each of the nine wives-of-state had her own houses and estates, and ruled over her own vassals, who paid taxes to maintain the queenly court. Each had judicial responsibilities which included the imposition of the death penalty when required. The maids of the queens' households were probably representatives of the leading clans of the kingdom, like the court pages, and the most privileged of these maids were invited to serve as the king's concubines. The senior wife-of-state, the *mazarira*, was always a sister of the reigning king, and was appointed by a senior court official. She was responsible, among other things, for all dealings with Portuguese visitors to the kingdom. The second wife was minister for Muslim affairs.[1]

The fundamental question as to why this new court flourished so lavishly in the north still has to be answered. The traditional folk answer, that the north was better endowed with salt, may be no more than a late, and rather stereotyped, rationalization. In a nation which was predominantly agricultural one might expect to find explanations connected with basic food production. But the nation as a whole did

[1] A. Bocarro, *Livro*, cited in Theal, *Records*, III, 356–8.

not move northwards; it was only a ruling élite which died out or declined in the south, and was revived or replaced a generation later in the north. This élite, although dependent on farmers for daily living, was more directly concerned with the country's marginal commercial and craft industries. It can be suggested that the Urungwe and Ingombe Ilede copper industry might have been a factor which attracted attention to the north. It does seem that the new empire succeeded in conquering at least part of the copper-producing region, and causing the old market of Ingombe Ilede to die out in the fifteenth century.[1] Another possible factor in Mutapa's genesis may have been the ivory trade. As the cattle economy of the south developed, the wild lands available for elephants were reduced. The decline gained momentum as ivory-hunting techniques improved and the foreign market grew. The major reserves of elephants became confined to the tsetse-infested lowlands of the Zambezi valley, and beyond. At one stage Mwene Mutapa Matope attempted rather abortively to cross the Zambezi and conquer the north bank.[2] He failed to do so, and the northern ivory trade which developed there, in the seventeenth century, was controlled by Maravi and Yao and Bisa peoples, rather than by the Shona. Although all these factors may have been significant in explaining the northern expansion of Shona political power, the most important explanation concerns the extension of gold prospecting.

The gold of the north was partly obtained by alluvial washing. The rivers which flow into the Zambezi, and its south-bank tributaries, carried large quantities of gold which could be panned in the early part of the wet season, before the water rose too high. The discovery of these alluvial deposits may have been made by the Swahili traders who penetrated the Zambezi. Alternatively, their discovery by Shona prospectors may have attracted traders from Sena up the river to found a new trading post at Tete. By the time the *mwene mutapa* conquered the area, there were probably both stone-built outposts of the Zimbabwe empire at Nhunguza and Ruanga on the plateau, and Swahili outposts of the coastal settlements in the valley below. It has been suggested that Ruanga belonged to the *mwene mutapa*, but since he was unable to build in stone at his own central capital, it is unlikely that his provincial quarters should have been stone walled. It must remain an open question whether the valley traders attracted the northern plateau miners, or whether the northern plateau miners attracted the valley

[1] D. W. Phillipson and B. M. Fagan, 'The date of the Ingombe Ilede burials', *Journal of African History*, 1969, 10, 199–204.

[2] Abraham, 'Early political history', 64.

traders. Both developed in the middle and later fifteenth century, at the same time that the Kilwa-Sofala gold monopoly was declining, and the Angoche-Mozambique trade was rising. Once the *mwene mutapa* was established, he did much more than just control the alluvial gold and riverside emporia. He also conquered the northern end of the Rhodesian gold-belt where mined gold was still plentiful. If any Mutapa subject discovered gold while working in his fields, he immediately called in witnesses to show that he had not touched it. He then cut branches to mark the spot and left the area immediately lest he be arrested for illegally working the king's mines.[1]

The manner in which the *mwene mutapa* organized the gold-mining industry was mixed. In part it was an extension of the tribute system. In addition to paying him their dues in foodstuffs, in local cotton cloth, in household goods, and in metal wares, subject peoples paid gold. Gold was of limited internal value, but the *mwene mutapa* could sell it for luxury imports, especially of cloth and clothing in which to dress his courtiers or reward his provincial vassals. Some of the gold was also brought for sale from fringe areas, or foreign regions, where the political authority of the *mwene mutapa* was not strong enough to exact tribute. Payment for gold could be made in foreign luxuries, but was also probably made in cattle, which remained the major traditional form of wealth, at least among chiefs. The third source of gold derived from a corvée, or labour duty, imposed on peasants in gold-bearing regions. Some kind of agricultural corvée may have been traditional, and in the south heavy labour duties must have been imposed for building works, but gold-mining greatly increased the burden.

The most recent assessment of the economic consequences of gold-mining among the northern Shona has been made by Garlake:

> The exchange network that had been established by payments of tribute doubtless served as the channel through which imports and exports passed: imported luxuries flowed from the Mwene Mutapa to officials in provincial courts, in indirect return for tribute passing in the opposite direction. The imports, fine dyed and embroidered cottons, silks and glass beads were luxuries that only reached the small wealthy class to satisfy artificial desires created by the coastal traders. Thus external trade affected the basic mode of life of the villages only marginally. It did not stimulate the development of crafts, industries, a market economy, a currency or new and more efficient modes of exchange, but served instead to reinforce the tribute system and the Mwene Mutapa's authority and thus ensure cohesion in his empire. Instead copper, which was in great demand, and traded widely within the empire

[1] Dos Santos, *Ethiopia*, in Theal, *Records*, VII, 280.

and not subject to the same degree of control as gold, stimulated specializations in mining, working and trading to the extent that a standardized unit of exchange was evolved that was almost a currency.[1]

The full extent of the *mwene mutapa*'s territories at the height of his power cannot be very accurately assessed. In the east Mutapa probably conquered, or at least strongly influenced, both Manyika and Uteve, but the domination was not long lasting. By the later sixteenth century the control of the coastal outlets was not really necessary to Mutapa strategy. Most of the gold trade travelled down the Mazoe valley to the old trading fair of Tete, which had developed greatly under the Portuguese from the 1560s. So long as the *mwene mutapa* controlled the head of the Mazoe trade-route, and maintained an efficient co-operation with the Portuguese, he was master of the gold traffic.

The Portuguese had penetrated the Zambezi to Sena by the 1530s to gain a share of the Manyika trade, but they still faced stiff Muslim competition. They occasionally tried to overcome their rivals by violent means, for instance by burning down the port of Angoche, but this had little effect.[2] On the whole Christian and Muslim traders preferred to co-operate rather than fight. During the first half of the sixteenth century the leading coastal traders of the interior were about half Muslim and half Christian. Each had large 'families' of African retainers to support them, and leased land settlements worked by slave labour.

Tension between the two trading communities heightened in the 1560s, after the Portuguese had tried to increase their influence over the *mwene mutapa* by converting him to Christianity. The Jesuit in charge of the Christian missionary expedition, Father Gonçalo da Silveira, was murdered, and Muslim instigation was suspected. The Portuguese decided in 1571 to invade the Zambezi lowlands. A large colonial army led by Francisco Barreto met insuperable resistance, disease and death. As an act of desperation, Barreto decided to massacre the unsuspecting Muslim traders. This coup, together with the growth of Portuguese influence at Quelimane, reduced Muslim trade and increased the Portuguese share of the traffic.

The relationship between the Portuguese traders and the *mwene mutapa* was organized through a chain of trade fairs stretching along the Mazoe valley. The most important was Massapa, only a few days from

[1] Garlake, *Great Zimbabwe*, 177–8.
[2] Newitt, *Portuguese settlement*, 34.

the palisaded royal *zimbabwe*. The chief Portuguese merchant was recognized by the *mwene mutapa*, and given jurisdiction over the traders throughout the kingdom. He was known as the 'captain of the gates', and no trader could pass without his authority. His judicial power was jointly derived from the Shona king and from the Portuguese governor of Mozambique island. He could settle all commercial lawsuits at the fair, and for the duration of his tenure he became one of the *mwene mutapa*'s great wives-of-state. His value to the *mwene mutapa* was as a tax-collector who was able to levy five per cent customs duty on all Christian and Muslim cloth entering the country. In exchange traders were given unimpeded access to the Shona markets.[1]

The widespread peace and security which the *mwene mutapa* organized lasted until the end of the sixteenth century. Only in the seventeenth century was there a severe challenge to his paramountcy and a decline in his prestige and in the scope of his empire. As the power of the king weakened, so the Portuguese began to fortify their trade fairs, and provide traders with their own armed protection in place of the crumbling *pax mutapa*.

For more than a hundred years the Mutapa rulers governed the main outlets of the Rhodesian goldfields with skill and success. They were, however, much less able to gain access to the central and western parts of the plateau, and control all the gold-mines for themselves. This area was dominated by the rival kingdom of Butua (or Guruhuswa) with which the *mwene mutapa* was often at war. The Butua people, like the earlier Leopard's Kopje people, were primarily cattle keepers, but they also produced gold, and eventually, in the eighteenth century, Butua outlived Mutapa as a major gold producer, and developed its own outlet to the Zambezi at Zumbo, in the north-west. In its southern regions Butua saw the emergence of a wealthy culture which carried on the traditions of Great Zimbabwe. This was the Khami culture, in which stone terraces were built on a large scale with very fine decorative work. At the end of the seventeenth century this area was conquered by a chief called Changamire, who created the new dynasty of the Rozwi. The new capital was at Dhlodhlo, but the stone enclosure was of inferior workmanship, and showed that the Shona had lost much of their skill as stone masons. Material wealth flourished in other directions, however, and blue and white Chinese porcelain was imported from the Portuguese trade forts of Luanze and Dambarare in the south of the old Mutapa dominion.

[1] Dos Santos, *Ethiopia*, in Theal, *Records*, VII, 271.

There remains a great deal to discover about the history of the Shona. For instance, in the region between Mutapa and Manyika, there developed the little known Inyanga culture. Inyanga lies in mountainous country where rainfall can vary greatly from valley to valley. The region had been occupied by Early Iron Age farmers who made Ziwa stamped pottery. Later Iron Age farmers used the land more extensively by building agricultural terraces to retain soil and moisture. These do not appear to have been irrigated, although some water furrows were made. In flattish, dry country the retaining walls were only one or two courses high, but they prevented a rapid run-off of the scarce rainfall. Elsewhere the walls were nearly a metre high. The Inyanga people also built large and very substantial stone enclosures in which they probably kept livestock. On steep land these enclosures could be sunken pits, with tunnelled entrances and gates closed by heavy beams slotted into the masonry. Several of the more substantial structures were hilltop fortifications, where boulders and cliffs were joined by walls with narrow entrance passages. Inside, hut platforms, and even agricultural terraces, were built onto the hillside. Many of the Inyanga terraces are very different from other Rhodesian buildings, in that they are built of rounded dolerite stones rather than squarish granite ones. The Inyanga terraces were a necessary part of the daily struggle for survival, the joint effort of a mountain people, not the work of an élite corps of royal craftsmen.[1]

The dates of the Inyanga culture are not securely established, but the occupation almost certainly overlapped the period of growing external trade in the neighbourhood. Despite this, the Inyanga people do not seem to have acquired many foreign goods such as shells and glass beads. The archaeological investigations have failed so far to find any spindle whorls or other sign of spinning and weaving. The area seems to have been an isolated one, which was affected neither by the miners on the open plateau, nor by the traders down in the lowlands. It is a useful testimonial to the fact that food-producing was the primary concern of most Later Iron Age peoples, despite the emphasis which foreign observers, and latter-day historians, place on the glittering compounds of kings.

SOUTH OF THE LIMPOPO

Thanks to the Portuguese accounts, our knowledge of the kingdom of Mutapa and of the kingdoms of southern Mozambique can be filled

[1] R. Summers, *Inyanga* (Cambridge, 1958).

out in considerable detail, and, taken together with oral tradition and sophisticated archaeological data, they enable us also to see the history of the dynasties of the Rhodesian plateau with some clarity. Further south the picture is far less clear. Not only do we lack any documentary evidence for most of the interior until the nineteenth century; with a few noteworthy exceptions our knowledge of the archaeological evidence is based on random finds and isolated excavations rather than on either broadly based regional surveys or carefully selected sample digs. For the period AD 1000 to 1600, moreover, the available collections of oral traditions are not particularly helpful, not only because they have not been systematically gathered or scientifically analysed, but also because in general this period lies beyond the limits of their effectiveness. For a few areas, most notably amongst the Tswana and the Cape Nguni, genealogies do stretch back twenty generations and more, and their beginnings relate to the period before 1600. But the mere existence of chiefly genealogies unfortunately tells us little of the actual history of the period beyond the simple fact of the existence of an alleged continuous link between the contemporary population and its ruling group so many generations back. Nor can we always be certain that the links between generations are as straightforward as would appear in the royal genealogies; many are the product of contemporary interest and associations.

Perhaps an even more important limiting factor is that while, on the whole, the traditions of peoples who were important in the nineteenth century, when traditional evidence was first recorded by a number of gifted amateurs, have received a fair amount of attention, peoples who may well have been of far greater significance in earlier times had by then already lost their political power and were therefore largely ignored. Very often it is only the odd fragment which points to the earlier role of these submerged groups. The very terms we use to refer to the peoples of South Africa – Sotho-Tswana and Nguni – obscure the crucial question which we are concerned to ask about this period: What were the processes of migration, absorption and local evolution which gave rise to the homogeneous cultural blocs of people which exist today?

South of the Limpopo, the centuries between AD 1000 and 1600 witnessed the spread and proliferation of earlier Iron Age communities, which were to cover, by the end of the period, most of the areas where they were to be found before the devastating wars of the *Mfecane* totally changed the demographic configuration of southern Africa. The first penetration of the area south of the Limpopo by Iron Age farmers in the first millennium AD would appear to have come from a number of directions. As elsewhere in Africa in the Early Iron Age, a number of related but none the less distinct pottery traditions co-existed in the Transvaal, spread thinly over a wide area. Many of the earlier settlements tended to concentrate near the drainage systems of the major rivers and water courses, where these were not too choked by forest and bush; the moist woodland of the north-eastern Transvaal lowveld may well have attracted Early Iron Age cultivators. By the end of this millennium, these had spread south-eastwards into Natal, reaching at least as far as the vicinity of Durban by the tenth century; and into southern Mozambique as well, for some of the early Bantu-speaking inhabitants of these coastlands may also have originated in the north-eastern Transvaal.[1]

Further west, the first millennium saw the establishment of a number of variants of the Early Iron Age tradition, with Gokomere type settlements along the Limpopo valley, and other Early Iron Age settlements reaching as far as the Hartbeespoort dam, near Pretoria, by the fifth century AD.[2] As yet we have no very clear idea of the variety of Early Iron Age traditions in South Africa, or of their precise limits. Nevertheless, the Early Iron Age does not appear to have penetrated beyond the Transvaal and central Natal by the end of the first millennium. By the middle of the present millennium, however, Iron Age farmers had populated most of the well-watered lands in the eastern half of the sub-continent, reaching as far as the Kei river in the south-east, and north-east of an approximate line corresponding to the frontier between the area receiving approximately 50 to 60 centimetres rainfall per annum and the drier lands to the west.[3] By the end of the period covered by this chapter, Iron Age farmers had acquired many of the basic characteristics of the present-day Bantu-speaking population of South Africa. The social divisions between the peoples of the Sotho-Tswana highveld and the Nguni of the south-eastern coast were already in evidence, though equally clearly there were still a number of groups only partially absorbed in these major clusters.

[1] A. Smith, 'The peoples of southern Mozambique: an historical survey', *Journal of African History*, 1973, **14**, 4, 570.

[2] R. J. Mason, et al., 'The Early Iron Age settlements of Southern Africa. The first Early Iron Age settlement in South Africa: Broederstroom 24/73 Brits. District, Transvaal', *South African Journal of Science*, 1973, **69**, 324.

[3] T. M. O'C. Maggs, 'Early farming communities on the southern highveld: a survey of Iron Age settlement', Ph.D. thesis (University of Cape Town, 1974, 2 vols.), I, 31.

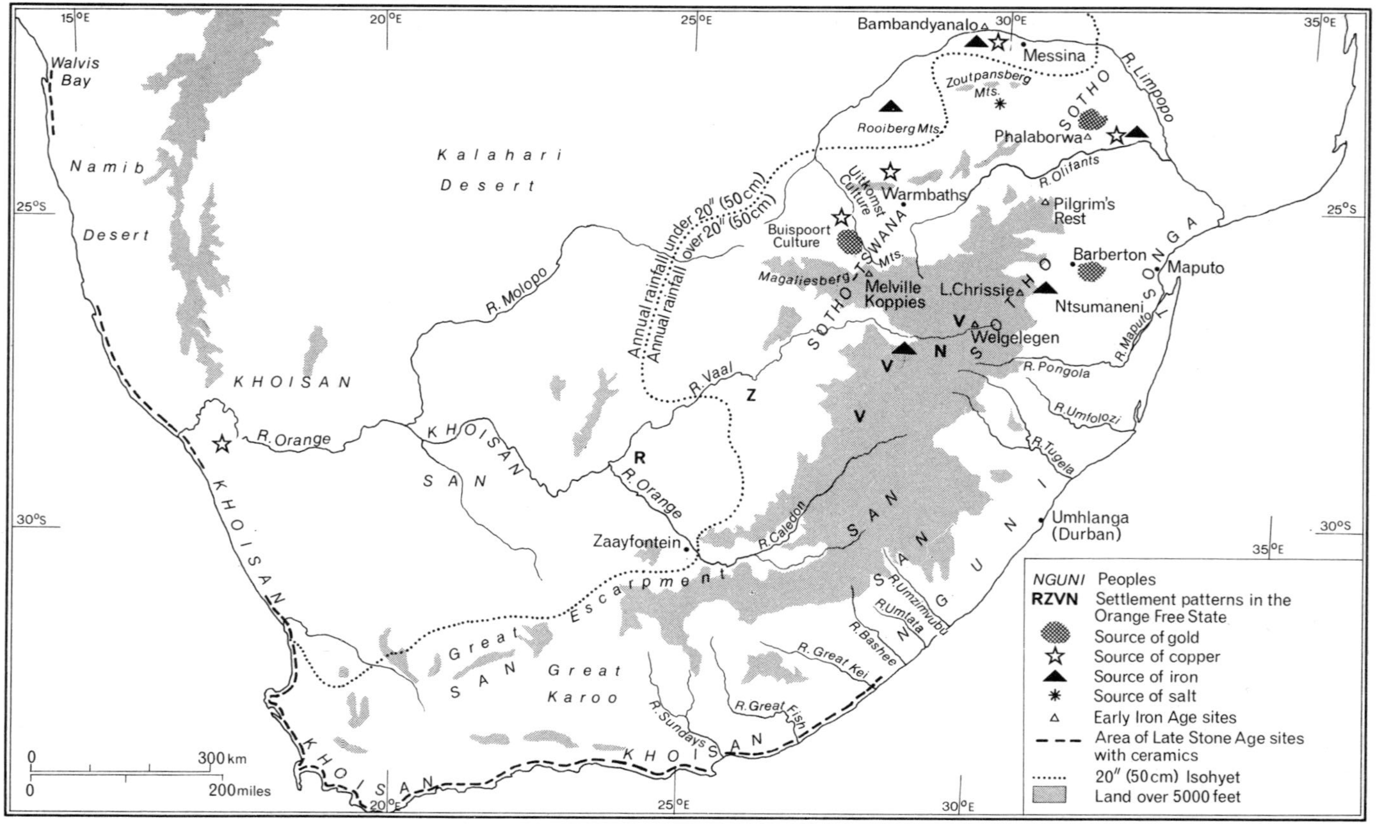

16 South of the Limpopo

At present we have no precise evidence of how this came about, although, as will be shown, possibly the most important development in this period was the spread of more specialized and larger scale cattle keeping, which enabled patrilineal polygynous lineages to expand at the expense of the Early Iron Age farmers on the one hand, and of the Late Stone Age hunter-gatherers who still occupied considerable areas in South Africa in this period, on the other.[1]

In the Transvaal, at least four clearly definable areas of Iron Age settlement can be distinguished in this period. As we have already seen, the northernmost zone between the Zoutpansberg and the Limpopo probably belongs to the Rhodesian cultures of Leopard's Kopje II and Zimbabwe II to the north, and reached its greatest period of development with the heyday of Mapungubwe in the fourteenth and fifteenth centuries. The eastern Transvaal lowveld, between the escarpment on the west and the Lebombo mountains in the east, with its complex and heterogeneous population, formed a second area. A third consisted of the central Transvaal, between the Zoutpansberg and the plateau basin, with sites like Brodie's Hill, Makapansgat and Rooiberg, where the relationships are as yet relatively unknown, but where it is clear that iron, tin and copper, as well as salt, were probably being exploited already in this period. Finally, and best known archaeologically, is the southern Transvaal, and especially the Magaliesberg valley. Here there is evidence of well-constructed daga villages, built around cattle enclosures, and also of agriculture and extensive iron-working, dated to AD 1000–1500. By about the mid sixteenth century, these were probably being replaced by the thousands of stone-walled settlements which have long attracted attention to this area.[2]

On the present evidence, the eastern zone appears to have been an early and important dispersal point into south-eastern Africa, with closely contemporary dates (third–fifth centuries) and a comparable pottery tradition from Early Iron Age sites in the Zoutpansberg, and from Tzaneen, Castle Cavern (Swaziland) and Lydenburg.[3] Apart from the dates, however, relatively little has been published as yet on the cultural affinities of these sites, and there has been almost no Iron Age

[1] M. Wilson, 'Changes in social structure in Southern Africa', in L. Thompson, ed., *African societies in Southern Africa: historical studies* (London, 1969), 79.

[2] R. J. Mason, 'Background to the Transvaal Iron Age – new discoveries at Oliefantspoort and Broederstroom', *Journal of the South African Institute of Mining and Metallurgy*, 1974, **74**, 6, 211–16.

[3] M. Klapwyk, 'The Early Iron Age settlement of Southern Africa. An Early Iron Age site near Tzaneen in the North-Eastern Transvaal', *South African Journal of Science*, 1973, **69**, 324.

excavation in the crucial area of southern Mozambique. Until this is done, the direction of movement in the eastern Transvaal lowveld must remain difficult to interpret. Nevertheless, the lowveld, situated as it is between the cold, bleak and treeless peaks of the Drakensberg and the highveld on the one hand, and the tsetse belt and the swampy ground of southern Mozambique on the other, appears to have served as a corridor of movement in almost every direction. Not only have there been movements into it during the past three or four centuries from the north and west, which are well authenticated in tradition; but from an early stage there have also been movements from the south and the east, as is suggested by the many peoples in the region who trace their origins to *bolaudi* – 'in the South' – a location perhaps not to be defined with too great geographical precision, as it has been variously placed in Swaziland, Pilgrim's Rest or Phalaborwa, depending on the present position of the informant.[1]

With its high rainfall and good climate, but hilly and afforested terrain,[2] the lowveld seems to have provided areas for pockets of settlement, particularly along the watercourses, for numbers of diverse peoples who are today lumped together as 'Sotho'. Within it are to be found Roka (or Ronga), Tokwa (or Ntungwa) and Kone (Nguni) groups, all now heavily Sothoized, as their names suggest, as well as 'ancient Sotho' peoples themselves.[3] Perhaps because of the coexistence of these fragments of almost all the peoples who today make up the South-Eastern Bantu as a group, it has been suggested on linguistic evidence that this was indeed the focal area for the development of the South-Eastern Bantu languages.[4]

Yet the picture is far from clear. Although it is an area of ancient settlement, as the early Iron Age dates and the continuity of its pottery traditions attest, the lowveld has also seen a relatively recent influx of its dominant Venda, Lovedu, Phalaborwa and Pedi ruling groups, who all have well-authenticated traditions of having arrived in the north-eastern Transvaal within the last three or four centuries, two

[1] J. D. Krige, 'Traditional origins and tribal relationships of the Sotho of the northern Transvaal', *Bantu Studies*, 1937, **11**, 323–4, 326–7, 340, 346.

[2] Cf. J. P. N. Acocks, 'Veld types of South Africa', *Botanical Survey of South Africa*, Memoir 28 (Pretoria, 1953), map 1. Today much of this woodland has been converted to sourveld.

[3] N. J. van Warmelo, *A preliminary survey of the native tribes of South Africa*, Native Affairs Dept., Ethnological Publications, **5** (Pretoria, 1935), 45, 50, 52, 54–5; H. O. Mönnig, 'The Baroka ba Nkwana', *African Studies*, 1963, **22**, 170–5; Krige, 'Traditional origins', 329.

[4] C. Ehret et al., 'Outlining Southern African history: a reconsideration, 100–1500 AD', *Ufuhamu*, 1972, **3**, 1, 9–27.

of them from north of the Limpopo. Perhaps for this reason, there are clear traditions of earlier, submerged population groups in the north-eastern Transvaal. Thus the ruling lineages of the Venda, Lovedu and Phalaborwa, for example, all maintain that they found, on their arrival south of the Limpopo, earlier dark black inhabitants, who knew not the use of fire and had no chiefs. Some of these, indeed, were said to be so primitive that they had no weapons. Thus, the Venda tell this tale of the Ngona, the Lovedu of the Kêoga, and the Phalaborwa of the Salane; in addition the Lovedu still fear ruins in their territory which they attribute to the Ngona.[1] Yet the subjugated groups are, today at any rate, virtually indistinguishable from their Bantu-speaking neighbours. Given the relatively late provenance of the ruling lineages in this area, it would appear that we have here a number of myths which justify and try to explain and legitimize their hegemony over the previous inhabitants.

It may well be that some of the tales refer to negroid Stone Age hunter-gatherers, like the Bantu-speaking Kwissie of Angola or the Nama-speaking Bergdama of South-West Africa, a view given force by the continued survival of partly negroid 'Bushmen' at Lake Chrissie in the eastern Transvaal to the present day. From the recently excavated Iron Age site at Welgelegen on the Vaal river near Ermelo in the south-eastern Transvaal, it appears that Late Stone Age hunter-gatherers were living in close symbiotic relationship with Iron Age farmers, based on 'ties of kinship and economics', as late as the thirteenth century AD.[2]

Similar hunting groups may have continued in existence relatively late in the north-eastern Transvaal, which still had rich game resources when the first whites arrived in the nineteenth century. Much of the area is, and was, unsuited to large-scale cattle herding because of the tsetse fly, and the soil is not uniformly suited to agriculture, so that it is probable that a considerable proportion of an Iron Age farmer's food came from hunting, and that this region remained relatively untouched by the spread of more specialized pastoralism in the rest of South Africa.

[1] E. Westphal, 'The linguistic prehistory of Southern Africa: Bush, Kwadi, Hottentot and Bantu linguistic relationships' *Africa*, 1963, **33**, 3, 260–1; H. A. Stayt, *The Bavenda* (London, 1968), 11; E. J. Krige, 'Notes on the Phalaborwa and their Morula complex', *Bantu Studies*, 1937, **11**, 357; E. J. & J. D. Krige, *The realm of a rain queen* (London, 1943), 6; Krige, 'Traditional origins', 325, 336.

[2] P. Beaumont and M. Schoonraad, 'The Welgelegen site', in Schoonraad, ed., *Rock paintings of Southern Africa*, Special Publications no. 2, supplement to *South African Journal of Science*, 1971, 68.

In the case of the Ngona and some of the others, it would seem that the earlier people were not unrelated to the new conquerors, though their political organization may have been somewhat different. And the later conquerors appear to owe much of their culture to their earlier forebears. Thus Lovedu-Venda affinities today may be in part ascribable to this earlier population layer of the Ngona. These earlier peoples may well be related to the earliest layers of Iron Age population in southern Central Africa as a whole, as their veneration for the spirits of the water suggest. With their unique cult of the sacred *komani* drums and their initiation ceremonies, they have made an important contribution to the culture of the area.[1] Amongst the Phalaborwa too, although the ruling lineage asserts its relatively recent arrival from *bolaudi*, the archaeological evidence suggests that the basal stock is far older. Iron was being mined at Phalaborwa in the ninth century, and the pottery tradition is also continuous from then.[2] The contention by anthropologists, made on the basis of ethnographic and traditional evidence, that 'the Phalaborwa are undoubtedly a people among whom many of the complex problems and relationships of the old Sotho population in Swaziland might with advantage be examined', would seem to reflect both this recent arrival of a ruling group from the Swazi area, and the essentially similar substratum of population through most of the north-eastern Transvaal and Swaziland.[3]

It may also be that in earlier, as in later, times the readily accessible mineral resources of the area, in particular iron, salt and copper, proved an attraction to small groups of specialized metal-workers. Their proximity to an abundance of timber in earlier times would have further facilitated the exploitation of these resources. Van Warmelo records the search of the Messina people for suitable copper-mines, and the search for mineral deposits recurs also in the other traditions of the north-eastern Transvaal, pre-eminently in those of the people of Phalaborwa, 'where the hammer is heard, the lowing of cattle is not there, the hammer resounds'.[4] Significantly, too, it is the people of the northern sector of this area who have the closest links with the great

[1] J. R. Gray, 'Ruins and traditions of the Ngona and Mbedzi among the Venda of the northern Transvaal', unpubl. paper, African history seminar, Institute of Commonwealth Studies (London, 1969), 1, 10–11; Krige, 'Traditional origins', 325–6.

[2] M. Stuiver and N. J. van der Merwe, 'Radiocarbon chronology of the Iron Age in sub-Saharan Africa', *Current Anthropology*, 1968, **9**, 1, 56.

[3] Krige, 'Traditional origins', 338.

[4] N. J. van Warmelo, *The copper miners of Musina and the early history of the Zoutpansberg*, Native Affairs Dept., Ethnological Publications, **8** (Pretoria, 1940), p. x.

empires of Rhodesia, those of the *mwene mutapa* and the Rozwi, which had such a strong tradition of mineral extraction. And though the Lovedu and Venda ruling lineages probably arrived only at the end of this period, they were by no means the first miners in the area.

Iron above all was of importance, and was mined at Tshimbupfe in the Zoutpansberg from very early on, but also at Ntsumaneni, south-east of Malelane, and at Ngwenya in Swaziland. At Phalaborwa hundreds of iron-smelting furnaces have been found; and though Phalaborwa was to become more famous as a source of the copper of the area, it is probable that it first attracted Iron Age mineral prospectors by virtue of its iron resources. In addition, a certain amount of alluvial gold was mined on the Olifants at Pilgrim's Rest, in northern Middleburg, in Lydenburg and in the Barberton area, while salt, more humdrum but more vital to the subsistence farmers of the area, was extracted both in the Zoutpansberg and at Letaba, where soapstone bowls have been found which were used in its evaporation.[1]

Trade was clearly of considerable significance in this area, with iron hoes and copper ingots being used instead of cattle for *lobola* (marriage payments). The thirteenth-century site at Welgelegen already shows evidence of widespread trade. Haematite came from Ngwenya, about 95 kilometres to its east. Cowrie shells were brought all the way from the Indian Ocean, roughly 250 kilometres away, while the copper hairpin found in its rich Iron Age assemblage is considered to have come from Phalaborwa, around 300 kilometres to its north-east. Throughout the area, red haematite and specularite were avidly sought as cosmetics.[2] When in 1498 the Portuguese arrived at the mouth of the Limpopo, they called it the Copper river from the quantity of the metal the explorers found there; and it seems that most of this copper came from sites in the north-eastern Transvaal.

Despite its mineral resources, however, the north-eastern Transvaal has always been an area of relatively limited and fragmented settlement, a corridor for movement rather than a focal point for the development of large settled communities. Further south, both westwards on the highveld and eastwards into Natal and the eastern Cape, the picture changes considerably in this period, with the growth of more settled communities, who now combined agriculture with cattle-herding on a considerable scale. In recorded historical times, certainly, most South-

[1] R. J. Mason, *The prehistory of the Transvaal* (Johannesburg, 1962), 415; J. F. Schofield, 'Ancient workings of south-east Africa', *NADA*, 1925, **3**, 10; C. W. Bates, 'Archaeological sites on the Groot Letaba River', *South African Journal of Science*, 1947, **43**, 365–75.

[2] Beaumont and Schoonraad, 'Welgelegen site', 68.

Eastern Bantu, whether Sotho or Nguni, set great store by their herds of cattle. Economically, until comparatively recently both groups were equally dependent on the crops produced by their women, but herding was the prestigious occupation of men. Although cattle were rarely slaughtered for their meat, milk, whether fresh or curdled, was central to their diet, while the use of cattle dung both as fertilizer and fuel was of significance for the economy as a whole. Social and political relationships were determined by a man's wealth in cattle. *Lobola* was paid in cattle, and both the Sotho-Tswana and Nguni had praise-songs honouring their favourite cattle and an extensive and highly specialized descriptive vocabulary devoted to the subject. Both groups today studiously avoid eating fish – a taboo which is associated with cattle-keepers in many parts of eastern and southern Africa. Although the emphasis which Bantu-speaking groups in South Africa place on cattle husbandry varies, this variation cuts across the present-day Sotho-Tswana and Nguni divide. Ethnographic and linguistic data suggest that the South-Eastern Bantu received cattle and much of their cattle culture from a common source, and the differences between their practices relate to ecology, rather than to any innate cultural division.[1]

Cattle-keeping is so important a feature of both Sotho-Tswana and Nguni society, that it is somewhat surprising to find that the words for cattle, sheep and milk in all the South-Eastern Bantu languages (except for Venda and Lovedu, which were late arrivals) derive either from Khoisan or from a source common to both, and that much of the descriptive vocabulary also comes from Khoisan. It would seem, moreover, that at the beginning of this period, knowledge of cattle-keeping and milking amongst Bantu-speakers south of the Limpopo may have been limited. In the south-western Transvaal early groups like the Fokeng and the Kgalagadi, who are said to have preceded the dominant Kwena, Kgatla and Rolong clans, appear to have had relatively few cattle originally, and their traditions tell of extensive intermarriage with Bush or San women.

At Broederstroom, the Early Iron Age site on the Hartbeespoort dam, some teeth of sheep or goats and cattle have been identified, but these are relatively sparse. Although the scarcity of animal remains may be attributable to the acidity of the soil at the site,[2] at the tenth-

[1] C. Ehret, 'Cattle-keeping and milking in Eastern and Southern African history: the linguistic evidence', *Journal of African History*, 1967, **8**, 1, 1–17; Westphal, 'Linguistic prehistory', 253–6; Ehret, 'Patterns of Bantu and central Sudanic settlement'.

[2] R. G. Welbourne, 'The Early Iron Age settlement of Southern Africa: identification of animal remains', *South African Journal of Science*, 1973, **69**, 326.

century settlement recently excavated at Blackburn, near the Umhlanga lagoon not far from Durban, there is similarly no clear evidence of cattle-keeping. The huts here resemble contemporary Nguni beehive-shaped dwellings, and there is an abundance of shellfish on the site, a feature of other Natal coastal sites.[1] At the thirteenth-century Welgelegen site at Ermelo in the south-eastern Transvaal, an area which is quite suitable for extensive cattle-farming, only one ox molar was found amidst a number of other animal bones.[2]

It is therefore likely that this period saw an increased emphasis on cattle-keeping in South Africa, and its source is one of the most crucial problems which needs to be resolved. As has already been shown, it is now held that Rhodesia received a major new influx of pastoral people at this time, associated with the sites at Leopard's Kopje II, Zimbabwe II and Bambandyanalo (see pp. 571–3). It is tempting to think of the increased pastoralism further south as part of the same movement, although in both cases we know little of its origin. Apart from the site at Bambandyanalo, however, there are as yet no other equivalent sites in the Transvaal which might enable us to answer the many questions posed, and to produce a general theory.

In Rhodesia it is clear that the Early Iron Age and the Later Iron Age are separated by a distinct break in the pottery traditions, and that there have thus been at least two separate migrations of peoples into the area. This does not, however, appear to have been the case south of the Limpopo, at least on present evidence. Here there seems to have been a far greater continuity between the Early and Late Iron Age cultures, and there is little evidence of a fresh influx of specialized pastoralists at this time. It is possible that the increased emphasis on cattle-keeping to the south of the Limpopo arose on the one hand from the natural build-up of herds in the healthy grazing lands of the western highveld, and on the other from the spread from the north of new ways of combining more intensive animal husbandry and agriculture.

Further west, where the lower rainfall prohibited the development of agriculture, purely pastoral economies developed both among groups of Late Stone Age people, who became known as the historical Hottentots or Khoi, and indeed, probably later, amongst the Herero – the only specialized pastoralists among Bantu-speakers. As yet we are unable to date the spread of cattle-keeping to Late Stone Age peoples in this area with any precision. Although sheep bones and pottery

[1] O. Davies, 'Excavations at Blackburn', *South African Archaeological Bulletin*, 1971, **26**, Parts 3 and 4, nos. 103 and 104, 165–78.

[2] Beaumont and Schoonraad, 'Welgelegen site', 68.

found on Late Stone Age sites along the south-west and southern Cape coast have been dated to the very beginning of the first millennium AD, the evidence of cattle bones is as yet too sparse to be in any way conclusive. There is, however, considerable support for the view that cattle may have been introduced to this area relatively late: towards the end of the first millennium or even in the first centuries of the second.[1]

It has recently been cogently argued from a variety of linguistic, ethnographic and traditional evidence, that the historical Hottentots or Khoi cattle-herders are probably derived from Central Bushman speakers who dwelt near the present-day area of the Central Bushman group from north-eastern South-West Africa across northern Botswana and into Rhodesia, and who acquired cattle from early farmers in their neighbourhood, or perhaps in the Zambia–Angola borderlands. This seems to have led to their very rapid dispersion in search of fresh water and grazing, and thus accounts for the spread of the relatively homogeneous Khoi languages over much of South-West Africa, the western Cape and Botswana.[2]

On linguistic evidence it seems probable that Khoi speakers (or Central Bushman) were once far more widespread than is indicated by their known distribution in historical times. Thus, according to Westphal,

> A strictly linguistic examination . . . does not by itself produce evidence for a much wider distribution of languages than we already know. It does however produce evidence for very much wider contacts between Bantu and Hottentot [Central Bushman] languages . . . and a massive replacement of Hottentot languages by Bantu languages in areas hitherto not known to have been Hottentot.[3]

It seems at least plausible to argue that some Khoi also trekked with their cattle into the excellent grazing land of the Transvaal highveld and bushveld. While, however, they were able to retain their identity in the drier, more westerly regions of South Africa which never attracted a large Iron Age population, this was more difficult once they spread into areas where they had to compete with the expanding Bantu-speaking farmers. The absorption of Khoisan people which we know of from the later documentary evidence in the eastern Cape and

[1] R. H. Elphick, 'The Cape Khoi and the first phase of South African race relations', Doctoral thesis (Yale University, 1972), 33.

[2] O. Köhler, 'Observations on the central Khoisan languages group', *Journal of African Languages*, 1963, **2**, 3, 227–34; R. Elphick, 'Cape Khoi', 24ff.; Ehret, 'Patterns of Bantu and central Sudanic Settlement', 13.

[3] Westphal, 'Linguistic prehistory', 256.

Natal may well have had its counterpart further north on the highveld in the absorption of Central Bushman people from a relatively early date, but continuing right through this period. As has been shown, the grounds which led Gardner to argue a purely Khoi origin for Bambandyanalo appear inadequate (see p. 574), but it may be equally misguided to deny the possibility of a considerable Late Stone Age contribution both at this site and to South-Eastern Bantu culture in general.

Unfortunately there is nothing in the archaeological record in the south-western Transvaal, or indeed elsewhere south of the Limpopo, which would enable us to identify this contribution with any certainty. We know relatively little about the exact relationships of Iron Age communities and the Late Stone Age people in the early part of this period, though there are some important clues in the latest archaeological evidence. Thus at Oliefantspoort, in the Transvaal, which is related very closely to one of the major Transvaal Later Iron Age traditions of this period, the Iron Age remains contain nonetheless a very large lithic content – although, unlike other sites where this is the case, there is no sign here of a prior Late Stone Age settlement underlying it. Although Oliefantspoort was settled later than the period covered here, it would well represent part of a much wider picture whereby Late Stone Age people became incorporated into and absorbed by the Iron Age communities.[1] It is possible that the great population expansion in the central and southern Transvaal which seems to have occurred at the end of this period was in part the result of the absorption of these groups and their incorporation into a more fully food-producing economy.

Probably the most densely populated area of South Africa in Iron Age times was the southern Transvaal, between the plateau basin and the Vaal river, with its well-watered grasslands suitable both for stock-raising and fairly extensive agriculture, and its rich iron resources. In the Magaliesberg, lateritic reefs provided shelter against the cold of the highveld winter evenings, and the climate was healthy for both man and beast – unlike the malaria and tsetse-ridden lowveld and Limpopo valley. The thousands of stone ruins in this area attest to its former population, although, given that the ruins are the product of hundreds

[1] R. J. Mason, 'Iron Age Stone artefacts from Oliefantspoort, Rustenburg district, and Kaditshwene, Zeerust district', *South African Journal of Science*, 1969, **65**, 2, 41–4; and R. J. Mason and others, 'Prehistoric man at Melville Koppies Nature Reserve, Johannesburg', *Occasional Papers*, **6**, Archaeology Department, University of Witwatersrand (1971), 47–8, 61–2.

of years or so of building and rebuilding, it is impossible to estimate from them what the population density might have been at any one time. The majority of the stone buildings now appear to date from the sixteenth century on, but the first few centuries of the second millennium AD do seem to have been a period of relatively swift population build up in this well-favoured area.

Conventionally, two major Iron Age cultures have been described for this area, named after their type-sites at Uitkomst cave and at Buispoort. Both would appear to have originated in this period, but their overall definition and dating is far from satisafactory. Though the Buispoort culture is as yet undated, both cultures would appear to have been broadly contemporaneous. It is clear that both are quite separate from the Early Iron Age traditions of the Transvaal. A smelting furnace at Melville Koppies on the Witwatersrand, part of the Uitkomst culture, has been carbon-dated to AD 1060 ± 50, while the type-site at Uitkomst cave has a seventeenth-century date. Both may have continued relatively unchanged until the nineteenth century, and both appear to reflect societies based on simple agriculture and animal husbandry, although mining, particularly of iron, was also important.

The Buispoort culture is said to have had its centre in the Magaliesberg, from whence it spread both westwards and southwards. The Uitkomst culture, which, though closely related, has a more ornate pottery style and a slightly different tradition of stone buildings, stretches from the area of present-day Pretoria eastwards and perhaps as far north as Warmbaths. Both cultures are associated with numerous iron furnaces, and the material culture included fibre mats, string, wooden objects and shell ornaments. Neither can be directly connected with the contemporary Leopard's Kopje sites further north. They are, however, both unmistakably linked with the contemporary Sotho-Tswana peoples of the south-western Transvaal and Botswana.[1]

Nevertheless, the archaeological picture in the southern Transvaal may ultimately prove more complex than this simple twofold division suggests. Although so far this does not seem to be clearly reflected in the archaeological record, Tswana traditions maintain that this area was populated in a series of three distinct migrations. Whatever the reality of these 'migrations' – and the notion of 'waves of migration' is probably misleading – different groupings of people represented in the traditions may well have developed somewhat different cultural patterns within the southern and central Transvaal, eastern Botswana

[1] Mason, *Prehistory of the Transvaal*, 385ff.

and the Orange Free State, which may ultimately be discerned in somewhat different architecture and pottery traditions. Unlike the situation in the north-eastern Transvaal, none of these 'migrations' involved substantial movements from across the Limpopo. In so far as the traditions tell of movements, they are movements over relatively short distances within the south-western Transvaal and its immediate environs. Primarily, however, the traditions are concerned with the genealogical connections between dominant lineages, and their subdivision.

According to tradition, the earliest Bantu-speaking people in the south-western Transvaal were the unrelated Kgalagadi and the Fokeng peoples, who today share in the very widespread and homogeneous 'Sotho-Tswana' culture. They may in fact have represented a rather different substratum of population. Thus the Kgalagadi, a heterogeneous group of people who are today dispersed over much of Botswana and into the Kalahari desert, formerly lived much further to the east. For long regarded simply as part of the 'Tswana' group, they are now known to have a distinct dialect of their own, which has affinities with 'ancient Sotho'. It seems that originally they had some cattle, although once they were displaced from the better-watered lands of the south-western Transvaal and eastern Botswana they lost most of their stock.[1]

It was, however, members of the second and third 'wave' of migration who came to dominate the area by the end of this period. Three lineage clusters in particular, the Rolong, the Kgatla and Kwena, had, by the end of the sixteenth century, begun to proliferate and send their offshoots in every direction. Indeed so great has their predominance become, that it is difficult to get behind it and discern the earlier situation – or indeed to establish the precise reasons for their dominance. On a broad level, however, it seems plausible that polygynous, patrilineal Iron Age cattle-keepers who exchanged cattle rather than kin for women would expand, at least in those areas suitable for mixed farming, both at the expense of Early Iron Age farmers, and of Late Stone Age hunter-gatherers and herders.

These factors could account for the expansion of the Tswana as a group – but not for the success of specific lineages within the group. Here the role of the individual leader or of very local factors may have been crucial. Unfortunately, the traditions do not take us so far back

[1] I. Schapera and F. van der Merwe, 'Notes on the tribal groupings, history and customs of the Kgalagadi', *Communications from the School of African Studies, University of Cape Town*, 1945, **2**, no. 13.

into the past. We can only suggest that certain groups may have owed their dominance to their favourable access to particular resources. The Kgatla and Rolong, for example, are remembered in tradition as iron-workers *par excellence*, and their settlements are known to have been near rich iron deposits. Other groups may have had especially good grazing or agricultural lands: this certainly appears to have been the case amongst the Kwena and Hurutshe.

Much of the movement of Iron Age farmers from the south-western Transvaal, both southwards and eastwards, may have been the result of the growth in population and cattle herds. The improvements in cattle-keeping and agriculture in this area may well have led to demographic changes towards the end of the period which were to people the Orange Free State with offshoots of the Fokeng and Kwena lineage-clusters, apparently from the south-western Transvaal. Thus according to the traditions of the Kwena, who expanded into the Orange Free State probably in the late fifteenth or sixteenth century, they were preceded in this area by the Fokeng, a people who had already intermarried extensively with the earlier hunter-gatherer population, and who had dispersed as far afield as the eastern Cape and Natal. Although they were still numerous and relatively powerful at the beginning of the nineteenth century, the Fokeng were so scattered during the *Mfecane* that we have no reliable account of their tradition. Ellenberger remarks of them, however: 'great honour has been invariably paid by all these tribes [south and east of the Limpopo and the Vaal] to them by reason of their antiquity and seniority over all the others which has been freely acknowledged'. The senior Fokeng group still in the southern Transvaal has a geneaology stretching back in time before the dominant chiefdoms of today.[1]

Yet the attempt by previous authors to associate the Fokeng with a trail of similar pottery sherds from Buispoort in the south-western Transvaal through the Orange Free State into Natal and the eastern Cape has foundered on the increasingly detailed archaeological picture that is building up, particularly in the Orange Free State. There is no simple relationship between the Fokeng and the settlements in the Orange Free State, and no great similarity between the Buispoort sherds and those found on the Free State sites. For the present it is wiser not to attempt to attach too precise a tribal name to any of the known archaeological traditions. The overall descriptions of Iron

[1] J. Walton, 'Early Bafokeng settlement in South Africa', *African Studies*, 1956, **15**, 1, 37–40; D. F. Ellenberger and J. C. MacGregor, *A history of the Basotho, ancient and modern* (London, 1912), 15–16, 17. Maggs, 'Early farming communities', 1, 212.

Age pottery in South Africa are still too general to be entirely satisfactory, and in many cases assemblages which have been excavated in the last ten or twelve years have not yet been fully described. On present evidence, the spillover of Iron Age farmers into the Orange Free State does not appear to have occurred much before the fifteenth century, and appears to have stabilized fairly rapidly where soils, climate and vegetation were suited to their way of life. There, too, rainfall needs established a natural frontier between Bantu-speaking farmers and Khoisan herders and hunters to their south.

Although it is as yet not possible to distinguish the precise tribal groupings responsible for all the archaeological evidence in the Orange Free State, it is clear that by the end of this period there were at least four distinguishable settlement patterns in the Free State, Botswana and Lesotho, and these have been labelled types N, V, Z and R by their excavator, Tim Maggs. In the case of the south-western settlement types in the Orange Free State (types R and Z), more precise identification does seem possible. According to Maggs, the type Z settlement patterns show clear features in common with the present-day highveld settlement patterns, and by drawing on the earliest accounts of the area in written sources he is able to show convincingly that these must belong to the Tlhaping-Rolong group of Tswana peoples. Significantly, in view of the later accounts which suggest that the Tlhaping acquired their iron from the Hurutshe in the north, Maggs has found very little iron on his type Z settlements, though bone points and tools are abundant.[1]

Further south, in the area of sparser rainfall and poorer soils along the Riet river, the stone-built settlements appear to be associated with Khoisan people, who herded cattle and made their own crude pottery, but appear to have had no agriculture. This particular settlement, which represents one of the many ways in which Khoisan communities were being affected by the neighbouring Iron Age cultures, is dated to the seventeenth and eighteenth centuries, a period beyond the scope of this discussion.[2] On the middle Orange river, however, pottery was being traded by Late Stone Age hunter-gatherers as early as the twelfth century, while a couple of hundred years later they were making their own pottery.[3]

[1] T. M. O'C. Maggs, 'The Iron Age of the Orange Free State', in *VIe congrès pan-africain de préhistoire*, ed. H. J. Hugot (Chambéry, 1972), 175–81.

[2] T. M. O'C. Maggs, 'Pastoral settlements on the Riet river', *South African Archaeological Bulletin*, 1971, **26**, parts 1 and 2, nos. 101 and 102, 56.

[3] C. G. Sampson, 'The Orange river scheme and aspects of the Stone Age in South Africa', *Annals of the National Museum of Bloemfontein*, 1972, **6**, 199.

By far the most widespread settlement pattern in the Orange Free State is type V, which occurs in a dense corridor from the upper reaches of the Vaal south-eastwards as far south as Ladybrand. There are also type V settlements in the south-eastern Transvaal as far north as Bethel and Ermelo. These settlement units consist of a group of stone enclosures linked to form a large central enclosure, which may have served as a central cattle kraal. Especially in the north, type V, and the closely associated but less common type N settlements, are generally associated with corbelled stone huts. In general also the settlements are at a height of between approximately 1,500 and 2,000 metres, and avoid river banks. Maggs calls them 'a true highveld expression of the Iron Age'.[1] The pottery on these sites shows similarities to the pottery of the south-eastern Transvaal and to pottery of the NC2 type in Natal.[2] It may thus be that these settlements in the north-eastern Orange Free State reflect in some way the first movements of people from the Natal area across the great escarpment, which divides the inland plateau from the coastlands of southern Africa. These may have been the Zizi and related people, who were traditionally among the first inhabitants of Lesotho. Van Warmelo has suggested that the Zizi were of ancient Sotho stock, related to the peoples who inhabited the Swaziland escarpment before the dramatic changes of the nineteenth century.[3]

Unlike the type Z settlements in the north-western Orange Free State and south-western Transvaal as well as in neighbouring Botswana, the N-type settlements appear to have had an abundance of iron. This again may tie in with the traditions of the Zizi people, who had the reputation of being skilled iron-workers. Like the Fokeng, the Zizi had a reputation of former greatness. G. W. Stow remarks of them at the end of the nineteenth century that:

> Not only the Zizi themselves but later authorities belonging to other tribes assert that the Amazizi are the direct descendants of the main or original stem from which both branches of the great Bantu families [i.e. Nguni and Sotho] . . . have descended. For many generations it is said that their chiefs and people were said to represent the paramount tribe, whose prestige and supremacy were acknowledged by all others.[4]

[1] Maggs, 'Early farming communities', I, 49.

[2] Ibid. II, 484.

[3] A. T. Bryant, *Olden times in Zululand and Natal* (London, 1929), 248, 348; Ellenberger and MacGregor, *History of the Basotho*, 21–6; van Warmelo, *Preliminary survey*, part 3, 98, 111.

[4] G. W. Stow, 'The intrusion of the stronger races', Unpubl. Ms, South African Public Library, Cape Town (n.d.), 178–9.

Given the ambiguity in so much of the evidence at this stage, it is probably best not to attach the labels 'Nguni' and 'Sotho' to peoples who were still at this time in course of evolution, and had not yet become the homogeneous groups they were to become in the nineteenth century. By the nineteenth century the Sotho-speaking peoples, whether in the Transvaal, Orange Free State, Lesotho or Botswana, were clearly distinguished from the Nguni-speaking people of the south-east coastlands, both by their large and densely populated settlements, with their well-organized ward structure and intricate devolution of authority, and by their preference for marrying close relatives. Around these settlements, which in some ways resemble pre-industrial towns, lay their agricultural fields, while at some distance were the pastures for large herds of cattle. Though men spent almost half the year in the pastures with their cattle, for both political and social reasons they were expected to return regularly to the political centre, where they could be kept under the eye of the chief.[1] The people of the south-eastern coastlands by contrast had strict rules of lineage exogamy, and this in turn was facilitated by their settlement pattern of small scattered homesteads, usually inhabited by a man and his immediate kin. Until the growth of the larger kingdoms at the beginning of the nineteenth century, political units were in general smaller in scale, though amongst the Tsonga in south Mozambique and the people on their borders, larger-scale kingdoms may have developed rather earlier. There were lesser differences between the two groups as well: differences of dress, hut architecture and ritual. Nevertheless we have no way of knowing at what point these distinguishing traits emerged, whether it was in South Africa or before the arrival of the South-Eastern Bantu south of the Limpopo. What is clear is that the present-day uniformity of these two major groupings masks a situation of very considerable earlier diversity, although already by the end of the sixteenth century some of these distinctive patterns are in evidence. Thus, from Maggs's work in the type Z settlements of the Orange Free State, it would appear that the ward structure of the southernmost Tswana groupings, the Tlhaping and the Rolong, was already well defined in the seventeenth century, and may well have been so earlier.[2]

[1] A. Kuper, 'The social structure of the Sotho-speaking peoples of Southern Africa', Part 2, *Africa*, 1975, **45**, 2, 144–5; I am grateful to Dr Kuper for allowing me to see this before publication. M. Wilson, 'The Sotho-Tswana', in *Oxford History*, I.

[2] T. M. O'C. Maggs, 'Bilobial dwellings: a persistent feature of Southern Tswana settlements', South African Archaeological Society, Goodwin Series, **1**, *The interpretation of evidence* (1972), 63–4; I. Schapera 'The social structure of a Tswana ward', *Bantu Studies*, 1935, **9**, 3, 203–24.

Whatever the factors were which led to the emergence of this form of settlement – and long-distance internal trade may have been a significant factor – they were probably in evidence at least by the end of the sixteenth century.

Along the south-east coast too, it was probably during this period that the contemporary 'Nguni' population acquired many of its salient characteristics, and in particular its emphasis on cattle-keeping. By the sixteenth century, when the first Portuguese sailors were shipwrecked along the treacherous south-eastern coast, they encountered Nguni-speaking people who planted millet, herded cattle, lived in beehive-shaped huts in scattered homesteads and were ruled over by chiefs whom they called *inkosi*. Although it would appear that the people between the Umzimvubu and the Tugela rivers, in Natal 'proper', probably laid a heavier stress on agriculture than did those either to the north or south of them, and although there were differences from area to area in dialect and minor details of dress, already by this time there was a surprising degree of broad similarity in the region as far south as the Kei river. Whereas in the treeless highveld Iron Age communities expressed their identity in the pattern of their stone building and settlement, in the coastlands of Natal and the eastern Cape this was not possible. In this period the area was heavily wooded, and this meant that the expansion of cattle-herding was probably relatively slow. The forest had to be burnt prior to occupation; Vasco da Gama, rounding the continent at the end of the fifteenth century, called the eastern Cape 'the land of the fires' – perhaps evidence of this process of tree-burning.[1] Nor did men have to build in stone in this area. Thus the huts at the tenth-century Iron Age settlement at Blackburn Ridge near Umhlanga Rocks would appear to have been beehive shaped – like the corbelled huts of the Orange Free State, but with walls of grass or matting on a light frame of sticks tied to a central post, similar to historical Nguni huts. This also, unfortunately, makes the archaeological record far more difficult to discern.

Moreover, if one postulates the peopling of this area by Bantu-speakers as extending over about a millennium, as the archaeological evidence now certainly appears to warrant, it is clear that the traditions we have of the area are only those of the more recent past. Thus, amongst the thousand or so clans and sub-clans which Bryant, the most important compiler of Nguni tradition, lists at the back of his work as 'Nguni', some two hundred have no parent clan or grouping in terms

[1] Cited in Acocks, 'Veld types', 13.

of his threefold classification of the peoples of the area. Conceivably this is because these chiefdoms and their traditions were wiped out during the Shakan wars at the beginning of the nineteenth century. Alternatively, however, these may well represent the earlier Bantu-speaking peoples of the coastlands, who were unrelated to the later parent clans.

As in the interior of South Africa, this was an era in which there was close interaction between the incoming Bantu-speakers and the Late Stone Age inhabitants of the area. Traces of these pre-Bantu inhabitants of south-eastern Africa are found in their shell middens all along the coast as well as in the cave paintings in the mountains – although by the sixteenth century the pastoral Khoi do not appear to have lived further east than the Kei river, and by the ninteenth century the hunter-gatherers, who seem to have been responsible for most of the cave paintings, had been driven from most of their original hunting-grounds into the fastnesses of the Drakensberg. Part of this picture may be distorted, however, by the very considerable intermarriage between the Khoisan people and the incoming Bantu speakers; large numbers of the Late Stone Age people may well have disappeared through assimilation, as it has been suggested happened on the highveld.

The 'clicks' in the Nguni language are a well-known indication of the close contact between the two peoples, although they pose a number of problems. On the whole, linguists tend to think that they came into Zulu and Xhosa from Khoi or Central Bushman rather than from any of the other Bushmen languages. Yet, while we have evidence of intensive contact between the Khoi and the Xhosa in the eastern Cape, we have no such evidence of contact between the Khoi or other Central Bushman speakers and the Zulu further north. Moreover, though cognates in Zulu and Xhosa are high (eighty per cent on two separate test lists), of the 2,400 click words in Xhosa only 375 have cognates in Zulu and there are some notable semantic differences between them: this, despite the fact that clicks occur in about one-sixth of the Xhosa vocabulary and one-fifth of Zulu.[1] Thus the evidence suggests that the two languages acquired the click words, or the bulk of them, after their divergence from a common stock. It still leaves open the question of where the Zulu acquired them. If Zulu clicks are indeed from the Khoi language, one has either to posit the presence of this language much further along the coast than the known distribution

[1] L. W. Lanham, 'The proliferation and extension of Bantu phonemic systems influenced by Bushman and Hottentot', *Proceedings of the Ninth International Congress of Linguistics, Camb. Mass., 1962* (The Hague, 1964), 383–4.

at any rate of Khoi herders, and their complete absorption by the incoming Bantu speakers, or their similar presence in an earlier home of the Natal Nguni, which they could only have shared for a short time, if at all, with the Xhosa. Given the strong possibility of a migration of some Bantu speakers into Natal from the Transvaal along the tributaries of the Vaal and perhaps through the passes in the Drakensberg, it is just conceivable that this contact then was somewhere in the southern Transvaal: this might afford another clue to the origin of the Nguni 'cattle culture'.

Contact between the Bantu speakers of Natal and the hunter-gatherer population is better documented. Some evidence of this is the custom called *ndiki*, cutting off the final joint of the little finger, which certain Bantu-speaking groups known to have been in close contact with the San have adopted. It is practised by at least a section of the Thembu in the Cape, and by the Bomvu, Lata, Belesi, Tuli and Ncanu peoples in Natal. Like the archaeological evidence, this is evidence of the much wider spread of hunter-gatherers in earlier days. At Durban Bluff, for example, two types of pottery associated with the Iron Age, NC2 and NC3, have been found closely associated with Late Stone Age samples, while a similar association has been found at Blackburn Ridge. Though the process of absorption of Late Stone Age people by the Bantu speakers had gone a long way by the end of this period, it is clear that when the Portuguese rounded the Cape at the end of the fifteenth century there were still non-Bantu click-speaking people between latitudes 28° and 33° S, and there were many enclaves of both pure and hybrid groups.[1]

Essentially, then, a crucial theme of these centuries is that of interaction between incoming Bantu speakers and Late Stone Age hunter-gatherers and pastoralists of southern Africa. Yet our efforts to understand the Iron Age are bedevilled by the lack of a clear understanding of this phase of the Late Stone Age in South Africa, and in particular the spread of pottery, sheep and cattle amongst the Khoisan people.[2] By the beginning of the first millennium AD, however, all these cultural attributes were present amongst the Khoi peoples in the south-western half of South Africa, although they may not have arrived simultaneously. Thus from the beginning of the Christian era it would appear that people along the south-western coast from Swakopmund in South-West Africa to Plettenberg Bay in the southern Cape were

[1] J. D. Clark, 'A note on the early river-craft and fishing practices of South-East Africa', *South African Archaeological Bulletin*, 1960, **15**, 59, 77–9.

[2] Ehret, 'Patterns of Bantu and Central Sudanic settlement', 13.

making the distinctive pointed-base pottery with internally reinforced lugs, and fine, well-fired fabric, which is found with shell middens along the coast as well as along the Orange river (in particular between the Augrabies Falls and Prieska), an area which seems to have seen prolonged and flourishing activity on the part of Khoisan potters. It has been suggested on linguistic grounds also that this area may have been an important dispersal route for Khoi herders both westwards into South-West Africa and southwards into the Cape province.[1]

The first migration of Central Bushmen speakers southwards may well have been of 'strandlopers' or 'beach rangers', people who lived off the abundant shellfish along the coast, though they may in later times have had a limited number of cattle. Throughout historic times all the Strandlopers appear to have spoken a language closely related to, if not indistinguishable from, Khoi. Racially too they would appear to have been indistinguishable from the 'Hottentots' whom the Dutch met when they arrived at the Cape peninsula in the seventeenth century: indeed the first inhabitants of the Cape encountered by the Dutch were an impoverished and cattle-less group who were at that time living off shellfish and begging from ships which called at the Bay. The speed with which these people were able to acquire herds of cattle by manipulating the trade suggests that the shift from hunting-gathering and fishing and back again was a relatively flexible one.

By the beginning of this period, Khoi people had acquired herds both of cattle and of fat-tailed sheep. It would seem possible, however, that the route that sheep followed into the western Cape was different from that followed by cattle: whereas sheep occur in cave paintings in a distinct trail from north-eastern Rhodesia, northern Botswana, South-West Africa and the western Cape, skirting the mopani belt and the desert land of the Kalahari,[2] there are no cattle in the rock paintings of South-West Africa and the western Cape.[3] Here one is not necessarily positing vast migrations of people; it would seem possible for the knowledge of sheep- and cattle-keeping to be diffused with only very minor population movements.

Knowledge of metals among the Khoisan people appears to have been fairly restricted. Indeed, even among some Bantu-speaking groups

[1] J. Rudner, 'Strandloper pottery from South and South-West Africa', *Annals of the South African Museum*, 1968, **49**, 2, 595.

[2] C. K. Cooke, 'Evidence of human migrations from the rock art of southern Rhodesia', *Africa*, 1965, **35**, 3, 263–85; see also R. R. Inskeep, 'The archaeological background', in *Oxford History*, I, 23.

[3] A. R. Willcox, 'Domestic cattle in Africa: a rock art mystery', in M. Schoonraad, ed., *Rock paintings of Southern Africa*, 44–8.

there was a paucity of iron. This is true both of the NC2 settlements in Natal and of the type Z settlement sites in the Orange Free State, though both of these traditions belong to the Later Iron Age. As late as the sixteenth century fire-hardened pikes were being used around the Umtata, though some were tipped with iron. About sixty years later, the Bantu-speaking people in the area were well armed with iron.

To establish the history of purely hunter-gatherer groups in this period with any kind of precision is virtually impossible. We do get fleeting glimpses of the San in process of change at the Cape colony in the seventeenth- and eighteenth-century records, but to push this back further into the past is extremely difficult. Here again we may be in part the victims of our terminology. Recent linguistic evidence is beginning to suggest that the term San should only be applied to that group of hunter-gatherers who were in close association with the Khoi herders and who spoke a closely related language.[1] Though we have some idea of their history, this tells us little or nothing about these groups of hunter-gatherers elsewhere in southern Africa, some of whom, as has been shown, may not even have shared their physical characteristics. Thus, we probably need to think in this period in terms of several Late Stone Age communities whose precise way of life differed and whose relationships with one another are unknown: hunter-gatherers, shellfish gatherers, pastoralists – categories which at times overlap, for Late Stone Age man has been called 'the great opportunist'. Despite the miraculous record Late Stone Age peoples have left in their rock art, until we have some kind of chronology for this, unfortunately it cannot be used for historical purposes. Nevertheless, together with their vivid mythology, it should act as a warning against our thinking of the life of hunter-gatherers as stunted and impoverished as well as unchanging throughout the long centuries of the Late Stone Age.

[1] For a useful discussion of the term 'San' and its pitfalls, see Elphick, 'Cape Khoi', 60ff.

CHAPTER 9

THE EAST AFRICAN INTERIOR

The third chapter of this volume has already shown how little connection there was between the brilliant medieval civilization of the East African coast and most of the vast interior which lay behind it. The Waqwaq of the tenth-century Arabic geographer al-Mas'ūdī might be the Makua of northern Mozambique. The Matamandalin of the Kilwa Chronicle might be the Matambwe of southern Tanzania. The sixteenth-century Portuguese identified by name three small ethnic groups living in the immediate hinterland of Malindi and Mombasa. There is one late medieval reference to people from the interior arriving at Mombasa carrying ivory tusks and skins on their heads. But there is no record of any penetration of the interior by Arabs or Swahili before the eighteenth century, and the only notable overland journey carried out by a Portuguese to the north of the Zambezi was that of Gaspar Bocarro from Tete to Kilwa in 1616. No significant collection of imported objects has yet been found at any interior site north of the Zambezi dating to the period before 1600.

The reasons for this strange disjunction between coast and interior are certainly in large measure geographical. Behind the narrow coastal plain, the land rises towards the great central plateau, in shelf after shelf of dry thorn scrub, hard to inhabit and difficult to cross. Much of the plateau stands at approximately 1,200 metres above sea level, and its eastern rim rises in places much higher. The Iringa highlands, the Ngulu mountains, the Usambara and Pare hills all rise above a height of 1,800 metres. Further north, Kilimanjaro, Mt Kenya and the Nyandarua range (formerly the Aberdares) soar to more than twice that height, creating a series of micro-climates where high rainfall, often combined with volcanic soil, has enabled pockets of dense agricultural population to develop once the forest has been cleared. Beyond the rim of the plateau, aridity once again supervenes. Over most of its central part rainfall is less than 80 centimetres. It is only within and beyond the crescent formed by the great lakes – Victoria, Tanganyika and Malawi – that conditions for agricultural existence are often favourable, with well-distributed rainfall patterns of approximately 130 to 180 centimetres a year. During Iron Age times at least, then, the focal area for human development into dense populations and larger societies has lain in the centre of the subcontinent, 1,300 kilometres or more from the sea.

The East African interior as treated in this chapter covers parts of seven modern states, including all or most of Uganda, Rwanda, Burundi, Tanzania and Kenya, together with the southern part of the Sudan and the part of Zaïre to the east of the Congo forest. During Iron Age times, which are all that we need to consider, it is clear enough that most of the southern two-thirds of the region was occupied by Bantu-speaking peoples. To the north of the Bantu, four other language groupings were represented – in the north-west, Central Sudanic; in the north centre, Nilotic and Paranilotic; in the north-east, Cushitic. Viewed in a time-scale of several millennia, it is likely that the first three of these groupings were related, while the fourth, the Cushitic, represented a completely separate language family. However, it may be assumed that, long before the beginning of the present millennium, each of the four groupings had established its identity within a core territory, which remained fairly stable. Within our period changes were confined to gains and losses at the peripheries, some of which were nevertheless quite considerable. In particular, it is likely that in the north-centre of the East African interior, Paranilotic advanced at the expense of Cushitic, and that in the north-west Nilotic advanced at the expense of Central Sudanic and of Bantu.

The origins of the Iron Age belong properly to the second volume of this series, where it is shown that right across the Bantu-speaking part of East Africa, from Lake Albert in the north west to Kalambo Falls at the southern corner of Lake Tanganyika, and from there to the Pare hills and Mombasa, Early Iron Age sites have been dated to the first half of the first millennium AD. Throughout this area, and indeed throughout a much larger area comprising central and southern Africa, Angola and southern Zaïre, Early Iron Age pottery shows a family resemblance which, coinciding so largely with the area of Bantu speech, suggests that the Bantu were the pioneers of Iron Age farming in most of eastern and southern Africa. This pottery breaks down into several provincial traditions, of which the best known and the most wide-spread extends from the western shores of Lake Kivu, across Burundi and Rwanda, north-western Tanzania, southern Uganda and western Kenya. It was at first termed 'Dimple-based ware', but is nowadays usually called 'Urewe ware', after the site in western Kenya where the first examples were discovered. Wherever this pottery has been found as part of a stratified sequence, it has been in association with the first evidence of iron-working. Some fifty sites are known so far, and their distribution shows a marked preference for moist areas rather than arid ones. They occur in the areas of high rainfall around the western and northern shores (and on the islands) of Lake Victoria, and in the Rwanda and Burundi highlands they occur in the moister areas which were probably forested at the time of occupation. The most northerly site known at present is near the Kabalega (Murchison) Falls, where the Somerset Nile drops towards Lake Albert. Only one site has been found in the drier belt of western Uganda, and that one, significantly, in the Kagera valley. All in all, it would appear that these were the settlement sites of people who fished even more intensively than they hunted, and who planted fruits and vegetables in preference to sowing cereal crops. Sorghum they certainly knew, but bananas were probably already their staple in many areas. Cattle they may have possessed in small numbers, but pastoralists they were not. For preference they chose a different environment both from the hunter-gatherers who preceded them and probably continued to live alongside them in the drier lands, and from pastoralists and mixed farmers who were later to infiltrate their midst. It is therefore difficult not to conclude that in the makers of Urewe pottery we see the main progenitors of the interlacustrine Bantu – of the Shi, the Rundi, the Rwanda, the Haya, the Ganda, the Nyoro, the Soga and the Luyia. At the beginning of our period ethnic and linguistic differentiation was probably only slightly manifested. By the end of it, distinct local cultures were no doubt fairly well established, and were reflecting, besides the factors of distance and limited communication, the emergence of new political formations and the differential impact of non-Bantu influences upon Bantu communities.

Immediately to the east of the interlacustrine province, in the western highlands of Kenya, no Early Iron Age tradition has yet been identified. Here, it seems likely that the pattern of Stone Age food production established, presumably by Cushitic-speakers, during the first millennium. BC, continued through the first millennium AD. To the east again, however, in central and eastern Kenya and north-eastern Tanzania, another Early Iron Age provincial tradition is beginning to be discernible, based around the pottery first identified at the type-site of Kwale, in the Digo hills behind Mombasa. Kwale overlooks the coastal plain, and the Giryama language spoken in the area today is the language most closely related to the ancestral Kiswahili spoken along the coast north and south of Mombasa before its later spread as the *lingua franca* of the whole coastal region. Though archaeological evidence is still lacking, it is almost inconceivable that the Early Iron Age tradition practised at Kwale did not extend to the coast. Further Kwale-ware sites have been discovered on the slopes of the Pare and Usambara mountains, at levels which were probably forested at the time of occupation and which also enjoyed the advantage of deep escarpment soils. So long as Kwale-ware sites number only a tenth of Urewe-ware sites, conclusions have to be correspondingly provisional, but it may well be that here we have evidence of agricultural penetration and settlement by the ancestors of the North-Eastern Bantu – the Shambaa and the Pare, the Chaga and the Teita, the Giryama and the Digo, perhaps also of the Kamba and the Kikuyu – at a period comparable with the earliest settlements of the interlacustrine Bantu. The terrain of this north-eastern province was, of course, more varied and more broken than that of the interlacustrine region. Fishing would have been a major industry at the coast, and along the rivers from the Pangani to the Tana. Conditions favourable to banana cultivation would have been found only in the well-watered mountain valleys, where the heavy forest cover would have required centuries of clearance before dense populations could develop.

South of the interlacustrine and north-eastern provinces, the Early Iron Age map of East Africa is still almost a blank, This is certainly due more to lack of research than to lack of evidence, for in Malawi and Zambia, where Iron Age archaeologists have been active during recent years, the outlines of a picture already exist. Here, the two groups of sites most relevant to the situation in central and southern Tanzania are those around Mwavarambo in northern Malawi, where an Early Iron Age tradition is said to have affinities with that of Kwale, and those around Kalambo Falls at the southern point of Lake Tanganyika, where the tradition is more reminiscent of Urewe. The broad distinction may therefore be between a western group of traditions and an eastern group of traditions divided by the wedge of arid country running southwards through central Kenya and central Tanzania, which was probably the least attractive environment for Early Iron Age farmers. It is perhaps not surprising that the only Early Iron Age pottery so far found in this dry belt – a surface collection from Lelesu, near Kondoa, in central Tanzania – appears to stand midway between the Urewe and Kwale traditions.

THE LATER IRON AGE

Nothing, of course, could be more natural than that, with the passage of time and the growth of population, the provincial traditions of Early Iron Age potters should have broken down still further into a large number of more localized forms. Such would have been merely one reflection of emerging ethnicity, in which dense local communities cultivating a ridge or a valley, or the area enclosed by a system of large swamps, would have tended increasingly to develop their existence from generation to generation within fixed territories, meeting members of neighbouring communities only to trade, to exchange brides or to fight. While it is theoretically not beyond the powers of archaeologists to document this process of differentiation, it is in practice too costly in manpower and resources. Only when there is a total change in the tradition does a fresh process of exploration and generalization begin. And rightly. For a major change in a very domestic industry like potting often betokens a substantial change in the way of life, involving considerable disturbance of population, of women as well as men, very different from the effect produced by the appearance of limited groups of migrants or conquerors. This process has recently been tested in relation to nineteenth-century Zambia, where, in the south-west, the massive invasion and settlement of southern Bulozi by the Rotse fundamentally changed the ceramic tradition, whereas the snowballing passage and sporadic settlement of Ngoni warrior bands had practically no effect on the activities of potters in north-eastern Zambia.[1]

There is not the slightest doubt that, at sometime around the beginning of our period, the Early Iron Age pottery tradition of the entire interlacustrine province was totally replaced by another tradition, or set of traditions. It was not a case of the replacement of an inferior technology by a superior one, because, in pottery at least, the new technology was in some ways inferior to the old. In place of the well-fired Urewe ware, with its superbly forceful bevelled rims and grooved decoration, there came a series of thick, coarse-fired wares, the main decorative feature of which was a monotonous rouletted pattern executed with a string of knotted grass. Moreover, the new pottery tradition established itself not only in the moister districts already occupied by the makers of Urewe ware, but also in the drier lands left

[1] D. W. Phillipson, 'Iron Age history and archaeology in Zambia', *Journal of African History*, 1974, 15, 1, 1–26.

conspicuously empty by the Early Iron Age people. In parts of the region, therefore, the new pottery was certainly the work of immigrants some of whom were able to live mainly by pastoralism on land that was only marginally suited to agriculture. These may have included the ancestors of the Hima and Tutsi people, who became the specialized pastoralists of southern Uganda, Rwanda and Burundi. But the immigrants must also have included cereal farmers capable of settling in massive numbers on the lands already occupied by the Early Iron Age people. We do not know the exact period of the infiltration, because only a handful of the Later Iron Age sites have been dated by radiocarbon. We do not know the exact provenance, because Iron Age archaeology in northern Uganda and the southern Sudan has scarcely begun to be practised. We do know, from surface collections, that the infiltration must have come from the north, where coarse-fired rouletted wares are the only Iron Age potteries known in most areas. The process of infiltration may have been a very slow one, extending over several centuries. But there can be little doubt that the striking revolution in pottery forms reflected a corresponding transformation of society and culture in the interlacustrine region and other areas to the south of it.

While a great many options must be left open pending the inception of Iron Age archaeology in northern Uganda and the southern Sudan, some discussion of the various possibilities must be attempted. It is clear in the first place that the appearance of rouletted pottery in the interlacustrine province must have been due to the meeting of two entirely separate Iron Age traditions, one from the north and the other from the south. The southern one we have linked with some confidence with the settlement of the interlacustrine region by Bantu-speaking peoples during the first half of the first millennium AD. The northern one, whenever and wherever it originated, is most likely to have reached north-western East Africa from the Central Sudanic sphere, and the rest of East Africa from the Paranilotic sphere. Crazzolara has shown convincingly that the basic Iron Age population of northern Uganda was Central Sudanic-speaking.[1] This population, as will be shown, was later overlaid by Nilotic-speaking Luo from still further north, some of whom moved right through the Central Sudanic-speaking area into the northern part of the Bantu sphere. But almost certainly, the Nilotic movement came later, some centuries after the introduction of the Later Iron Age. Ehret, in a discussion of the

[1] J. P. Crazzolara, *The Lwoo*, III, *Clans* (Verona, 1954).

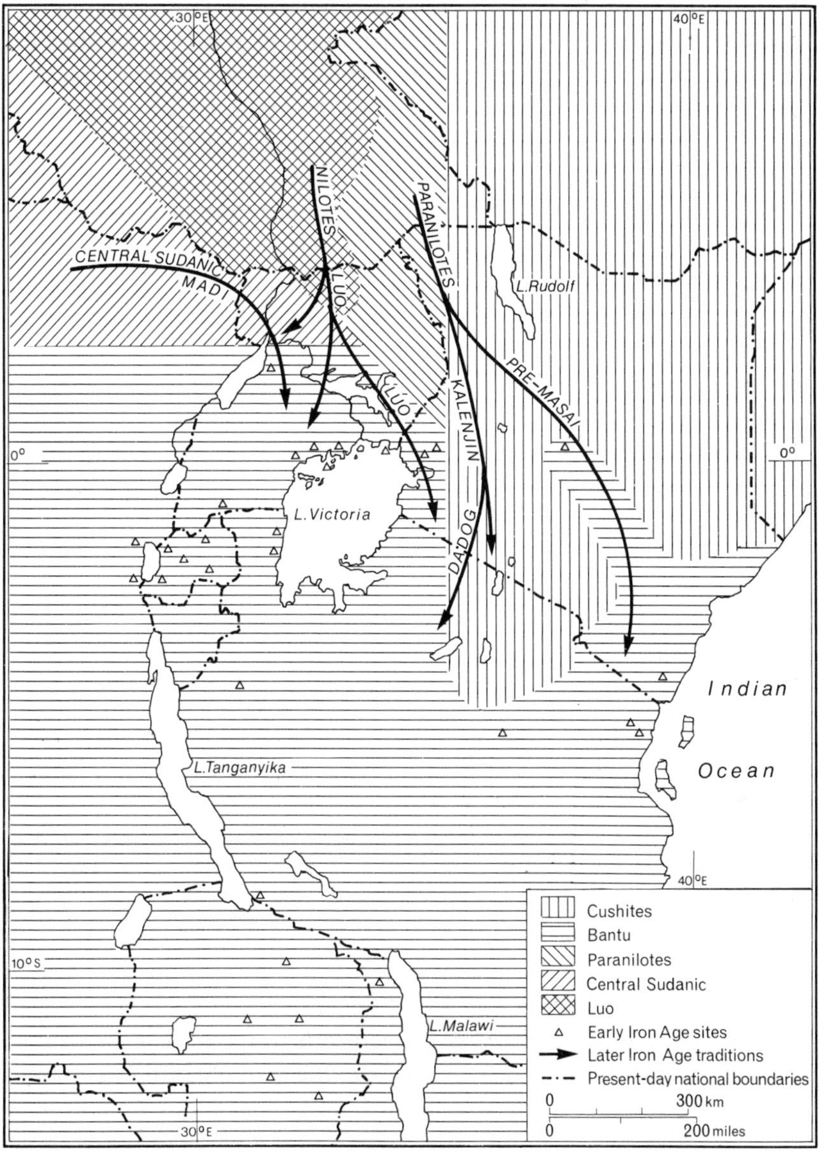

17 The Later Iron Age intrusion

linguistic evidence regarding the spread of cattle-keeping and milking in eastern and southern Africa, has shown that among most of the interlacustrine Bantu an older and much more general Bantu word-root for cattle (*-ngombe*) was displaced by a Central Sudanic root (*-ti* or *-te*), the older form having survived either as an archaism or with a more specialized meaning (e.g. Ganda: *engombe*, 'horn'). The root for cattle in the relevant Nilotic languages (Acholi, Alur, Luo) is quite different.[1] The implication would seem to be that the Central Sudanic influence preceded the Nilotic one, and that in respect to cattle-keeping it was the Central Sudanic influence that was decisive.

It may be that we have here an idea of considerable significance, not only for the interlacustrine province, but also for the whole large region immediately to the south of it. Looking at the map of Early Iron Age sites, one cannot fail to be struck by the very narrow range of environments that were exploited. While neither cattle nor cereals were absolutely ruled out, the emphasis was clearly on fishing and vegeculture. Very large areas remained apparently unexploited by any kind of food production, and these areas must have constituted a standing invitation to Iron Age farmers specializing in cattle, goats and the lighter kinds of millet cereals, especially eleusine. It may be that the forest clearance effected by the Early Iron Age people opened the door to the stock-keeping farmers of the north. Alternatively, it may be that climatic deterioration in the north forced the northerners to shift slowly south. Either way, the enrichment of food production in the equatorial belt may have been quite striking, not only in the exploitation of land hitherto used mainly for hunting, but also by the combination of agriculture and cattle-keeping, especially in the manuring of poorer soils. It may be that we have here the answer to the apparent contradiction posed by the fact that, while it is clear that the major tide of Bantu settlement reached East Africa from the west or the south-west, the earliest layers of oral tradition appear to describe extensive migrations from the north. Given the sporadic and specialized nature of the Early Iron Age occupation, the early intrusions from the north do not have to be seen in terms of long-distance movements or

[1] C. Ehret, 'Cattle-keeping and milking in eastern and southern African history: the linguistic evidence', *Journal of African History*, 1967, 7, 1, 1–17; cf. D. W. Cohen, *The historical tradition of Busoga* (Oxford, 1972), 76–7. More recently (in 'Patterns of Bantu and Central Sudanic settlement in Central and Southern Africa, *c.* 1000 BC–500 AD', *Trans-african Journal of History*, 1974, 4, 1–25), Ehret has suggested that the *-ngombe* root is itself ultimately of Central Sudanic origin, and is derived from a much earlier, Late Stone Age dispersal of Central Sudanic speakers into the central parts of sub-equatorial Africa. The significance of this is discussed in Volume 2, ch. 6.

sudden conquests, but rather as a steady, prolonged infiltration by practitioners of a different kind of Iron Age food production into the gaps and interstices hitherto left vacant. This would be consistent with the adoption of Bantu speech by the migrants, even though in pottery traditions, and no doubt in other aspects of material culture, victory went to the newcomers.

Eastwards of the Central Sudanic-speakers, before the southward movement of the Nilotic Luo, there lay the sphere of the Paranilotes – the ancestors of the Bari and the Lotuko, the Dodos and the Karimojong, the Turkana and the Masai, the Suk and the Pokot, the Nandi, the Kipsigis and the Dadog. Like the Central Sudanic-speakers, the Paranilotes belonged to the northern Iron Age tradition, and Ehret has demonstrated that their southward dispersion across the highlands between Lake Victoria and the Kenya Rift occurred only after they had developed a common vocabulary of special terms relating to an iron-working technology. So far, there are no dated sites demonstrating the presence of such a technology earlier than the sixteenth century, but this must be attributed to the paucity of radiocarbon sampling. However, Ehret is surely in error in dating this dispersion as far back as the early first millennium on the grounds that this period saw the introduction of iron-working in the rest of East Africa.[1] The limited evidence at present available indicates that in this central region of northern East Africa, iron-working came exceptionally late, and that it was linked with the spread of the northern iron-working tradition, for which the earliest dates elsewhere in East Africa fall around the twelfth century. It is likely that, prior to this, the western highlands of Kenya will prove to have been part of the sphere of Stone Age food production established by the Southern Cushites, whose remnant peoples – the Iraqw, the Goroa, the Burungi and the Alagwa – still inhabit the southern extremities of the Rift Valley region. Nevertheless, the Southern Paranilotes, as Were and Ogot have shown,[2] were certainly in occupation of the highlands between Mt Elgon and the Mau well before the arrival of the first Luo in the Nyanza district, and they were in fact the eastern neighbours of the Bantu Luyia at the earliest period remembered in Luyia traditions. Therefore the possibility cannot be ruled out that, just as the north-western frontier of the interlacustrine region may have been infiltrated by Central Sudanic-speakers, so its

[1] C. Ehret, *Southern Nilotic history* (Evanston, 1971), 29.

[2] G. S. Were, 'The Abaluyia of western Kenya and their neighbours: their history down to 1930', Ph.D. thesis (University of Wales, Bangor, 1966), 45; B. A. Ogot, *History of the southern Luo* (Nairobi, 1967), I, 137.

north-eastern frontier may have been infiltrated by Paranilotes. The earliest, semi-mythical layers of Soga and Ganda traditions are in fact dominated by stories of a cultural hero called Kintu, who is depicted as leading bands of migrants from the direction of Mt Elgon, and settling them, by agreement with the local clan-heads, in a series of small centralized polities stretching across southern Busoga and central Buganda. If Kintu and his followers were in any sense historical figures, they may have been either Paranilotes or else Bantu frontiersmen reacting to Paranilotic pressure.

THE INTERLACUSTRINE REGION

As Cohen has shown in an outstanding study of the clan traditions of the northern peripheries of Lake Victoria,[1] it was in the process of contact and interpenetration between peoples of different cultures and antecedents – Bantu, Central Sudanic, Paranilotic and possibly also Cushitic – that the earliest discernible political systems of the interlacustrine region emerged. These were systems in which clan sections of diverse origins agreed to share power within a given small territory. Within each territory a ruling clan was recognized, which supplied the dynasty; but the dynasty made itself acceptable by taking wives and appointing office-holders from all or most of the clan sections inhabiting the territory. Thus there emerged the nucleus of a court, or capital, at which the interests of all the clans were represented, in which power was balanced and family honour satisfied. Genealogy, henceforward, became the key to status, and despite all the human propensity to forget, distort and invent, some fragments of continuous tradition began to be transmitted to later generations. Cohen's estimate of the chronological value of his massive collections is modest enough. He places the origins of ruling dynasties between twenty and thirty generations back. He assigns a notional starting date for the process at AD 1250, with a margin of error of 150 years in either direction. More significantly, he shows that, even in the north-eastern corner of the region, many of the participating Bantu clan sections came from the far west, and not only from the fall-out of the Kintu migration from the north-east. The Kintu episode is to be seen as a catalyst, though probably only one of several, in a process that was affecting the whole of the interlacustrine region at approximately the same period.

One part of the region where political accommodation between

[1] D. W. Cohen, *The historical tradition of Busoga: Mukama and Kintu* (Oxford, 1972).

groups of differing culture would have been especially necessary was, of course, the west, where, midway between Lake Victoria and the lakes of the Western Rift, broken areas of downland covered with short grass and low bush extend from the Somerset Nile deep into eastern Rwanda. These are the natural pasture-lands of western Uganda, dividing the humid banana country of Buganda and southern Busoga from the well-watered mountains and high valleys adjoining the Western Rift. Here, in between, specialized pastoralists could pursue an almost totally different way of life from their agricultural neighbours to the east and west, providing only that relations and exchanges between the two groups could be regulated at the fringes. In colonial times there grew up the myth of a ruling race of pastoralists who had everywhere subjugated their agricultural neighbours and turned them into tribute-paying serfs. Today, it is doubted by many whether there is any greater physical diversity between the pastoralists and the cultivators than could be accounted for by differences of diet and life style within largely endogamous occupational groups. Moreover, thanks largely to the fine study by Karugire of Nkore society,[1] the crude notion of pastoral dominance is seen to have been largely an illusion. Not all, or even most, of the dynasties which flourished in these grasslands were drawn from the clans specially associated with pastoralism. Typically, the dynasty was seen as neutral between the two ways of life, and the chief's court as the place where pastoralists and cultivators met to exchange their products and work out their common interests. Iron-working, including the manufacture of weapons, was a monopoly of the cultivators, and many of the great warriors remembered in popular tradition were men from the cultivating class.

It is in this context that the evidence has to be considered for the emergence in the western grasslands of a state somewhat larger in size than those indicated by the legends of the Kintu period. Some of this evidence is archaeological, and it centres around the great earthwork site at Bigo, which was partially excavated by Shinnie in 1957 and more extensively by Posnansky in 1960.[2] There is no doubt that Bigo was a capital site, with a nucleus similar in layout to those built by the Hinda kings of Nkore during the seventeenth and eighteenth centuries. It is set in an obviously defensible position, in the angle between the Katonga river and its tributary, the Kakinga. It consists of a series of interconnected living enclosures, attached to one larger 'public'

[1] S. K. Karugire, *A history of the kingdom of Nkore in western Uganda to 1896* (Oxford, 1971).

[2] M. Posnansky, 'Bigo bya Mugenyi', *Uganda Journal*, 1969, **2**, 33, 125–50.

enclosure, the outer side of which was originally flanked by a crescent-shaped embankment some one and a half metres high. Perhaps because there was no timber in the area, the enclosures were divided from each other by deep trenches instead of by palisades, and the same form of defensive protection was employed for an outer boundary, approximately seven kilometres in length, closing the arc of open country between the two river valleys. This was clearly a system for the protection of cattle, since the trenches were broken about every hundred metres by broad gateways, so that cattle grazing in the plains outside could be quickly driven within the perimeter. Large as it is, it is unlikely that the whole site was ever occupied by more than a few hundred people and by a few thousand cattle. There is nothing at Bigo which even invites comparison with the earthwork defences of the 'walled towns' of the Hausa or the Yoruba, and the dwellings within them were certainly of the simplest kind. Nevertheless, in East Africa the earthworks at Bigo are unique in scale, and the site is linked, both in the use of trenches and by the presence of a roughly painted variant of the common rouletted pottery, with half a dozen other sites scattered over the grassland country from central Bunyoro to northern Nkore. In purely archaeological terms, all these features taken together do suggest a concentration of political power which perhaps encompassed several thousand square miles and several hundred thousand people, at a period which has been determined by the radiocarbon dating of charcoal samples from beneath the Bigo embankment as lying somewhere between the late thirteenth and the late sixteenth century. Genealogically articulated oral tradition, which probably provides a somewhat more accurate guide to dates of this order, would indicate a period squarely within the limits of those obtained by radiocarbon.

The oral traditions of the region link the earthworks with a comparatively short-lived dynasty belonging to the Chwezi clan, which ruled for only two or three generations, approximately nineteen to twenty-one generations ago, from successive capitals at Mubende and Bigo. Many of these traditions, recorded only during the period of British rule, are heavily laced with colonial analogies, and even by a subtle streak of anti-colonial propaganda. In 1949 one informant gravely told the present writer that the Chwezi were a wonderful people, fair of skin and with piercing eyes, who carried lamps at night and could kill animals at a distance. But, though undoubtedly skilled in the arts of government, their rule was oppressive to their subjects. Chwezi, though few in number, always stood together. In their courts

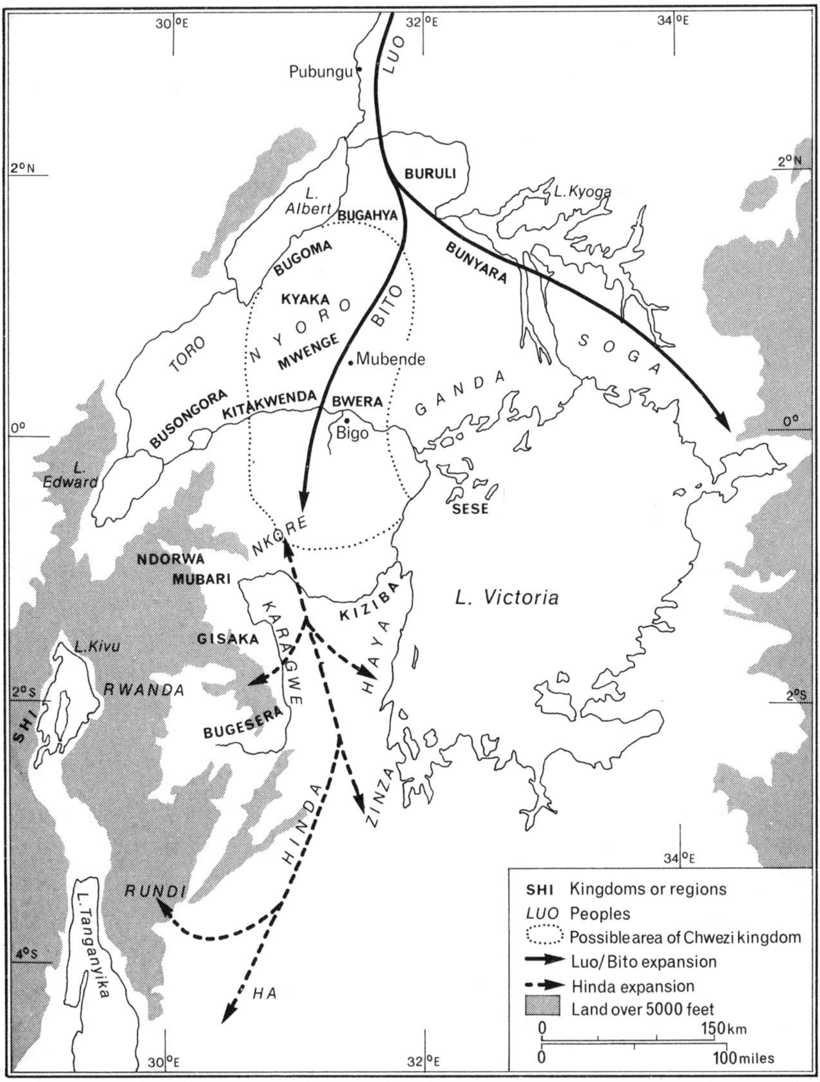

18 The interlacustrine region

there was one law for the rulers and another for the ruled. Taxation was heavy and there were labour corvées. So that, when invasion eventually threatened, the subjects deserted their rulers, who were forced to leave the country. Some traditions, especially those emanating from the court of Bunyoro, made the Chwezi into imperial conquerors on the grand scale, who conducted military expeditions all round Lake Victoria and deep into the Congo basin. Somewhat more credible than these obvious accretions is the list of districts over which the Chwezi are said to have ruled – Bunyara, Buruli, Bugahya, Bugoma, Mwenge, Kyaka, Toro, Busongora, Bwera, Sese – all except the last are in the grasslands between the Somerset Nile and the Katonga, between the foothills of Ruwenzori and the swamp-defended peneplain of central Buganda. There is no inherent unlikelihood about the emergence of a temporary, tribute-imposing overlordship over a series of small chieftainships in such an ecologically coherent area. The distribution of earthwork sites is not quite so extensive, but provides confirmatory evidence of the existence of some considerable organizational power at the period claimed.

Although not remotely on the scale of the states existing in Ethiopia and the Sudanic belt of Africa at this period, nor even of the state based around Great Zimbabwe, which was at this time reaching the peak of its power and prosperity on the Rhodesian plateau, the Chwezi state seems to have been a unique phenomenon in the East Africa of the fifteenth century. It was surrounded on all sides by hundreds, indeed thousands, of tiny chiefdoms, including perhaps forty or fifty situated within the confines of modern Buganda, a hundred or more in Busoga and Kavirondo, and hundreds more in the mountain valleys adjoining the Western Rift. In the grass country of eastern Rwanda and north-western Tanzania, we know the names and ruling clans of twenty or thirty little states, headed by Mubari, Ndorwa, Gisaka and Bugesera, where Tutsi pastoralists were beginning to establish relationships based upon the loan of cattle to the local cultivators. In the rest of Rwanda, Burundi, Bushi and Buha, chieftainships comprised the agricultural populations of one or two hills apiece. It was only in the succeeding, post-Chwezi period, extending over the late fifteenth and sixteenth centuries, that there began to emerge the nuclei of the more important of the pre-colonial states of the interlacustrine region whose growth is described in the next volume of this series.

There can be no doubt that during the final century of our period the pre-eminent one among these larger states was a successor to that of the Chwezi, the Bito kingdom of Bunyoro. The Bito dynasty was of Nilotic origin, and to understand its advent upon the interlacustrine scene, we have to extend our horizon northwards almost to the junction of the White and Blue Niles at modern Khartoum. The core territory of the Nilotic-speaking peoples lies to the north of that of the Central Sudanic-speakers and the Paranilotes, in the swampy country of the southern Sudan, where the Nuer and Dinka peoples have from time immemorial practised an economy based on fishing and cattle-herding, building their villages on the natural elevations, and in the dry season pasturing their herds upon the half-inundated plains around. The Nuer and the Dinka have no traditions of ancient migrations or contacts with other peoples. Protected by their native marshes, they have never needed to build states or armies to defend themselves against their neighbours. A shallow genealogical framework extending over about twelve generations has sufficed to explain to their living members the main facts of their collective existence since the day of creation when their first ancestors emerged from the ground, together with the progenitors of their herds. It is the third group of Nilotes, the Luo, who have an eventful history, the outline of which is written, first and foremost, on the map of their geographical dispersion. The Luo language is only a little more differentiated than the various dialects of Dinka and Nuer, yet it is spoken from Fashoda in the north to Kisumu in the south, a distance of more than 1,500 kilometres. Speakers of Luo, in fact, form an almost complete circle round the Nuer–Dinka nucleus, with the Luo of Wau to the south-west, the Bor to the west, the Shilluk to the north, the Anuak to the south-east, and the Pari, Acholi, Alur, Lango, Jopadhola and Kenya Luo all to the south. From their wide geographical distribution combined with their linguistic propinquity, it is clear that a formerly cohesive population group has been shattered into fragments within comparatively recent times.

We do not know the cause of the Luo dispersion, nor the precise location of the homeland from which it took place. Linguistic evidence demands that it should have been from some area adjacent to the Nuer–Dinka nucleus, and since the great majority of Luo are now found to the south of that nucleus, it is logical to suppose that it was located within the Equatorial or Bahr al-Ghazal provinces of the modern Sudan. In the past many writers have tended to favour a military explanation, whereby the Luo would have been driven from their homeland by the catastrophic invasion of a neighbouring people. Today we are more conscious of the far-reaching effects of cyclical movements of the monsoon rainbelt in the sub-Saharan latitudes of Africa, and we realize that the Nilotic dispersion has to be seen alongside the undoubted evidence for a southward drift by Central Sudanic and Paranilotic peoples at about the same time. In so far as the main thrust of the Nilotic movement went southward, it may have merely followed that of the neighbouring peoples in a slow process occupying several centuries. At the same time, the Luo dispersion seems at some stages to have developed a military momentum reminiscent of the great dispersion of Nguni peoples northwards from Zululand during the nineteenth century. Not all of the Luo bands went south. At the northern end of the sphere, the Shilluk remember the occupation of their present territory as a process of conquest, in which they had to drive out an earlier population known as the ap-Funy: these were perhaps the Fung, who formed a ruling dynasty over the central part of the Sudan from the early sixteenth century until the Egyptian conquest of 1821. Again, towards the south, the traditions of the Acholi, the Alur, the Jopadhola and the Kenya Luo all retain the memory of a great military camp at Pubungu, some 100 kilometres down the White Nile from Lake Albert, from which raiding parties were sent in all directions and sometimes developed into autonomous movements of conquest and settlement.

It was one of these movements, occurring sometime during the late fifteenth or early sixteenth century, which penetrated deep into the Bantu sphere and established a Luo clan, the Jo-Bito, in control of some, or most, of the territory formerly ruled by the Chwezi, known henceforward as Bunyoro. Bito tradition explicitly claims continuity with the Chwezi, to the point of asserting that the first Bito king, Rukidi, moved straight into the capital of his Chwezi predecessor at Bigo, where two of the royal wives stayed behind to receive him and to initiate him into the pastoral rituals of the old dynasty. And, for what it is worth, it is certainly a fact that the central enclosure at Bigo bears unmistakable signs of a second occupation, marked by the breaking down of most of the original crescent-shaped embankment and the use of the spoil to make a large hemispherical mound in its place. From this beginning until the dynasty was abolished by President Obote in 1967, the Bito traditions claim that eighteen generations of kings followed each other in an unbroken line. At twenty-seven years to the generation, which seems to be a well-attested average for this type of succession, the starting-point could have been around AD 1480.

The evidence for the system of chronology based upon dynastic generations, which has come to be accepted by most professional historians of the interlacustrine region, is too complex to be discussed in detail here.[1] It should certainly not be thought of as immaculate.

[1] The best exposition of the problem is that by D. W. Cohen, 'A survey of interlacustrine chronology', *Journal of African History*, 1970, 11, 2, 177–94. A more pessimistic view is expressed by D. P. Henige, 'Reflections on early interlacustrine chronology', ibid. 1974, 15, 1, 27–46.

Irregularities of succession, and even changes of dynasty may have been concealed in the surviving traditions. It is even possible that here and there a whole generation has been forgotten or a spurious one invented. Nevertheless, it should be understood that the genealogy of the main Bito dynasty of Bunyoro is supported over most of its length by those of several other Bito dynasties and by those of Hinda dynasties ruling in southern Uganda and north-western Tanzania, which also claim continuity with the preceding Chwezi dynasty. It is also supported in its general outline by the genealogy of the ruling house of Buganda, which, whatever its precise relationship to the Bito dynasty, had its apparent origin at about the same time, or perhaps a little earlier. The system is a rough one, which is liable to many kinds of errors, due to the inaccuracies of tradition and its deliberate distortion, to irregularities in succession, to the accidents of premature death and exceptional longevity among individual rulers. It cannot be pressed too hard, and, in the view of this writer, certainly not to the extent of adding to the hazards by dubious identifications of possible references to solar eclipses in the attempt to attach absolute dates to the earliest parts of genealogies, which are by definition the least reliable. Nevertheless, with these cautions, the system is useful as a means of comparing the trend of events in different parts of the region, and we are helped to a better understanding of the final century and a half of our period if we think of it as the period comprising the nineteenth to the fourteenth generations of dynastic tradition, reckoning backwards from a notional present around the middle of the twentieth century.

Seen in this light, the later fifteenth and the sixteenth century was a period when, around several different nuclei in the region, local chiefdoms were being amalgamated into larger states, and the key to this development is probably to be sought in the progressive integration of pastoral communities with the neighbouring cultivators. Even if the Bito did begin by occupying the former capital site at Bigo, it is clear that they did not simply become assimilated to the Hima clans of the central grasslands. In Bunyoro the clans of Luo origin, easily recognizable by their names, did not form an endogamous group, but intermarried freely with Bantu clans, whether those of pastoralists or those of cultivators. The Bito court, like those of other Luo chiefs to the north of the Somerset Nile, no doubt started as a war camp, collecting cattle and slaves, first as booty and later as tribute. Booty was taken with the spear. Tribute was guaranteed by hostages, girls and young men taken from every clan to serve as wives and pages, herdsmen and warriors, potters and basket-makers, hunters and iron-workers. The royal camp thus became the centre of a large population, which had to be supplied with beer and grain, bananas and game-meat, honey and building materials brought in from the surrounding districts. The central grasslands were obviously quite unsuitable for such concentrations, and the first Bito ruler is said to have moved his capital quickly northwards to the hilly area north of Mubende, where agriculture and pastoralism could be carried on side by side.

What is most difficult at this period is to discern the outlines of any system of provincial administration whereby people living more than a few days' walk from the capital could be brought under regular control. Presumably, as in later times, the Bito kings planted out their henchmen in miniature versions of the royal camp, and these centres acted as the foci of outlying districts, maintaining a fairly regular tributary relation with the capital. What we can see is that, beyond the core region of the state, there was a circle of smaller dynasties, claimed in Nyoro tradition as subordinate to the main Bito house. These claims should, no doubt, be viewed with considerable scepticism. Since many of the dynasties concerned were Bito, it may probably be assumed that they were established as a result of Bito raids during the early generations of the Luo hegemony. Subsequent relations probably went no further than a certain feeling of pious respect. Still, one of these small states lay as far afield as Kiziba, on the frontiers of north-western Tanzania, and its dynastic genealogy extends backwards through seventeen generations to a grandson of the first Nyoro king. This is an impressive testimony to the range of early Bito military operations, but it would not justify the conclusions that a Bito empire once stretched in an unbroken line from the Somerset Nile to the Kagera. Other early Bito dynasties are reported along the western fringes of the grasslands, in Kyaka and Kitakwenda: these areas may have been continuous with those of the central state. Bito dynasties were also probably established in Buruli and Bugerere, along the southern shores of Lake Kyoga: these would have been adjacent to Luo-speaking territory and close to the main stream of Luo migration and settlement which has been depicted by the researches of Cohen and Ogot as flowing slowly eastward across northern Busoga during the sixteenth and seventeenth centuries.[1]

Finally, to the east of the grasslands, Nyoro traditions have long claimed that the ruling house of Buganda was a Bito foundation, of

[1] Cohen, *Historical tradition*, 156–7; Ogot, *History*, I, 71–3.

which the first ruler, Kimera, was a twin brother of the first Nyoro king, Rukidi. Since Ganda traditions also relate that Kimera came to Buganda from Bunyoro, it is hardly surprising that the Nyoro claim has been accepted by most writers. Lately, however, Kiwanuka has argued persuasively that Kimera must in fact have antedated the Bito founder by at least one, possibly two, generations, and that for a number of reasons he and his followers should more probably be seen as eastward migrants from the territory of the Chwezi kingdom. Kiwanuka thus perceives three main layers of settlement in the population of central Buganda – the 'pre-Kintu clans' with their main base along the shores of Lake Victoria and on the adjacent Sese islands, the 'Kintu clans' with their main settlements a little further inland and strongest on the northern side, and the 'Kimera clans' with their centre of gravity to the west, in the modern countries of Gomba and Singo.[1] On this showing, contact with the Bito did not occur until the middle of the sixteenth century, sixteen and fifteen dynastic generations ago, when two successive Bito kings, Winyi I and Olimi I, invaded Buganda, defeating and killing the Ganda kings, Kaima and Nakibinge. Following these disasters, much Ganda territory was occupied by Bunyoro, and the kingdom had virtually to be rebuilt from its foundations, re-emerging as a powerful state only in the late seventeenth century.

One effect of Kiwanuka's re-evaluation is certainly to diminish considerably our estimate of the initial impact of the Luo in the region as a whole. So long as Buganda appeared to be a Bito foundation, dating from the earliest years of the Luo conquest, the role of Luo statecraft had necessarily to appear to be very dynamic. But if the Buganda of Kimera and his immediate successors evolved its political institutions from a pre-Luo base in the neighbourhood of the Chwezi kingdom, then it would seem likely that the Bito, too, were in large measure the heirs of a pre-existing institutional pattern taken over from their predecessors. And, if so, then certainly there is no need at all to seek a Luo origin for the larger states which emerged around the southern end of the grasslands, in Nkore, Rwanda and north-western Tanzania.[2] Even the more widely held theory that, following the Luo conquest of the northern grasslands, Chwezi forces withdrew and re-grouped themselves to the south, becomes somewhat suspect. If Buganda could emerge from a pre-Luo situation, so could states to the south.

[1] M. S. M. Kiwanuka, *A history of Buganda from the foundation of the kingdom to 1900* (New York, 1972), 41.

[2] e.g. L. de Heusch, *Le Rwanda et la civilisation interlacustre* (Brussels, 1966), 40.

The regroupment theory is strongest in relation to the great family of Hinda dynasties, which claims to have originated nineteen generations ago in Karagwe, the pleasant downland area situated within the great bend of the Kagera river. Ruhinda, the eponymous ancestor of the clan, is said to have been a son of the last Chwezi ruler, Wamara, by a slave-girl in his compound. After gaining possession of the royal drums of the Chwezi, he moved with his herds into Karagwe, from which base he and his descendants established a series of principalities among the Haya and Zinza of north-western Tanzania and the Nkore of southern Uganda. Particularly when seen from the Tanzanian side, it is clear that the secret of Hinda dominance lay in the management of cattle in relation to the needs of cultivators. Karagwe was a grassland area suited to the breeding of cattle, and there existed there a small class of specialized pastoralists, the Nyambo, corresponding to the Hima of Nkore. But the Hinda were not thought of as Nyambo, and their achievement consisted in dispersing the surplus cattle of Karagwe in small groups among the Haya and Zinza agriculturalists living between Karagwe and Lake Victoria. Here rainfall was less than in Buganda and soils were uniformly poor. Haya traditions recall that before the coming of the Hinda it was difficult to grow bananas, and laboriously-cultivated grain-crops formed the staple diet. The manure from the Hinda chiefs' cattle, farmed out in twos and threes to peasant families, made possible the change to bananas and to a much more leisurely way of life. The chief's court was the source of cattle to his loyal subjects, who came to it bearing their gifts of bananas and beer. As in Buganda, the chiefs assigned special duties to every clan. 'This practice', say Cory and Hartnoll, 'was of advantage both to the chief and to the clans. To the chief because he had a large body of his subjects living permanently at his court who could defend him in case of necessity, to the clans because these duties placed the well-being of the chief to a great extent in their hands.'[1]

Seen from the Haya end, there is thus no very visible connection between the proliferation of Hinda states and the advent of the Bito further north. There is the alleged descent of Ruhinda from the Chwezi, and the theft or fabrication of a royal drum, both of which, if not fictitious, could have occurred in pre-Luo times. It is only with the creation of the Hinda state in Nkore that we come a little nearer to the realities of Bito power. The core of this state was undoubtedly Isingiro, the group of hills rising to approximately 1,800 metres which separates

[1] H. Cory and M. M. Hartnoll, *Customary law of the Haya tribe* (London, 1945), 259–68.

the Kagera valley from the Masha plain and the valley of the Katonga. This is agricultural as much as pastoral country, broken by steep valleys where bananas cover the upper slopes, while the bottoms are sometimes forested – as at Ishanje, where the bodies of the Hinda kings were taken for decomposition. Once again, the picture is one of interaction between pastoralists and cultivators, with the dynasty acting as broker between the two. As Karugire has shown,[1] the kingdom of Nkore was probably founded by a son of Ruhinda, Nkuba, who moved north from Karagwe and spent the whole of his reign consolidating his conquest. Nkuba's son, Nyaika, finally 'brought peace to the land', and it was only in the next generation, the sixteenth back from the present, that the Nyoro appeared on the Nkore scene, led by the same king, Olimi I, who had previously invaded the Buganda of Nakibinge. According to Nkore tradition, the Nyoro captured and drove off all the cattle in the country, so that this reign, that of Nyabugaro, is remembered as one in which even bridewealth had to be paid in berries from the *enyonza* bush.

The departure of the Nyoro raiders from Nkore is linked in some traditions with accounts of a celestial occurrence, which *might* have been a total eclipse of the sun, which in turn *might* have been the eclipse known on astronomical grounds to have taken place in this region in 1520. If so, we should have the inestimable advantage of at least one absolute date linking the dynastic traditions of Bunyoro, Buganda and Nkore. But the accounts are at best ambiguous and the astronomical identification doubtful,[2] and in the circumstances it is best to stick to the genealogical evidence. What we must say, particularly in the light of recent work, is that, of the several streams of tradition which have been studied, the early part of the Nyoro stream has proved the least reliable. The initial impact of the Bito dynasty has been greatly exaggerated. The Bito claim of a genetic link with the Chwezi has been rejected as fictitious by all professional historians. It may be that the Bito should not even be regarded as the main political heirs of the Chwezi, for the Bito occupation of Bigo has not been conclusively proved. It may be that the first two generations of Bito kings ruled only in northern Bunyoro, on the fringes of the Luo-speaking area. Nevertheless, using only non-Nyoro traditions, there would seem to be ample evidence that, by about the sixteenth generation from the present, Nyoro armies were threatening much of southern Uganda. The Bito

[1] Karugire, *History of the kingdom of Nkore*, 143–50.
[2] J. R. Gray, 'Eclipse maps', *Journal of African History*, 1965, **6**, 3, 261.

kingdom of Kiziba goes back seventeen generations in its own line to its foundation by a Nyoro ruler standing in the fifteenth generation of the Nyoro line. The invasion of Buganda dates from the sixteenth Ganda generation, which corresponds to the fifteenth of Bunyoro. The great raid on Nkore belongs to the sixteenth Nkore generation, which corresponds with the fourteenth of Bunyoro. It is with these conclusions in mind that we have to assess the evidence about Rwanda.

Rwanda, as we know, was to develop into the largest of the pre-colonial states in eastern Africa, ruling a population of perhaps two million and comprising most of the territory included within its modern boundaries. By the end of the pre-colonial period Rwanda had also developed the most stratified political system to be found anywhere in Africa, in which prestige, power and wealth were nearly monopolized by a Tutsi caste of pastoralist descent, which numbered less than one-tenth of the whole population. In the countryside there was hardly a peasant cultivator who was not the dependant of a Tutsi lord. In the elaborate military system only Tutsi were trained as warriors. In the administrative hierarchy a very few peasant Hutu were chiefs of hills, but most of these posts and all of the higher ones were held by Tutsi. At the court and the provincial capitals there prevailed an education and an oral culture of story, song and recitation remarkable for its wit and delicacy of expression, which served to build up the value system of a ruling class which was normally open only to those of Tutsi birth. Looked at from the viewpoint of one twentieth-century anthropologist, Jacques Maquet, it appeared that the Tutsi had entered Rwanda as conquerors:

> Even if their arrival into the country inhabited by Hutu looked rather like a peaceful infiltration, it was nevertheless a conquest. They wanted to settle in the country and they built a permanent system of economic and political relations with the Hutu whereby they established themselves definitely as masters and exploiters. That is to say, a caste society evolved from their will to stabilise the conquest situation with all its advantages.[1]

Maquet himself suggests the analogy with communities of conquering Europeans living among conquered African populations in southern Africa.

And yet the lesson of early Rwanda traditions, as reinterpreted by Vansina and d'Hertevelt,[2] is a very different one. It is not merely that

[1] J. J. Maquet, *The premise of inequality in Ruanda* (Oxford, 1961), 170.

[2] J. Vansina, *L'évolution du royaume Rwanda des origines à 1900* (Brussels, 1961); N. d'Hertevelt, *Les clans du Rwanda ancien* (Brussels, 1971).

the kingdom of Rwanda grew from very small beginnings, and for a long time very slowly, its great territorial expansion belonging only to the eighteenth and nineteenth centuries. It is also that many of the most fundamental institutions of the Rwanda state – the divine kingship, the sacred fire, the royal drums, the agricultural rituals, the royal burial customs – were taken over from the little kingdoms of Hutu cultivators situated in the districts of Bumbogo and Rukoma at the comparatively late stage when one of several pastoral dynasties ruling in the north-eastern grasslands started to expand into the hilly country of the central watershed, where pastoralism and agriculture had from sheer geographical necessity to be carried on side by side. The great central institution of the *abiru*, the corporation of high ritual office-holders responsible for transmitting the esoteric constitutional and religious traditions of the kingdom, has all the appearance of a classic compromise between invaders and autochthones. The infiltrators, though inferior in numbers, had the military predominance with which to impose their own dynasty, but only at the price of according large constitutional powers to the pre-existing authorities. To judge from their clans and the location of their clan lands, the early *abiru* were mainly Hutu. It was only in the course of their assimilation into a single ruling class that they acquired the status of Tutsi. Likewise, the early settlement pattern was probably based more on economic occupations than on political dominance. The pastoralists settled the hilltops left empty by the cultivators. It was only at a later stage that the cultivators of the lower slopes entered into feudal (*ubuhake*) relationships with the lords of the hill-tops, relationships based on the exchange of cattle in usufruct for supplies and services, which left the Tutsi cattle-owners in the position of a leisured ruling class.

The most ancient layer of Rwanda tradition is that introduced by the early *abiru* into the foundation charter of the Rwanda state. It is clearly of a mythical rather than a historical character, and it corresponds most closely to the Kintu mythology of Buganda and Busoga. The Kintu figure of Rwanda is called Gihanga – the founder. He is seen as the ancestral priest-king of numerous states, both Hutu and Tutsi, stretching from Mubari in the north-east to Bushi on the western shores of Lake Kivu. Gihanga is the archetypal hunter, herder and blacksmith. But he is also and essentially the founder of ruling clans, the lighter of sacred fires, the carver of royal drums, the initiator of the *ubwiru* code. Among the ruling clans that he sired was that of the Renge, with whom are associated in popular tradition the earliest rouletted pottery wares that succeeded the Early Iron Age (Urewe) ware of Rwanda and Burundi. While any interpretation must be speculative, it is tempting to associate the Gihanga traditions with the same northern influences of Central Sudanic or Paranilotic origin which gave rise to the Later Iron Age tradition of the rest of the interlacustrine region.

The Gihanga period of Rwanda tradition is undatable by genealogical means, though it may be that radiocarbon dating of the levels containing 'Renge' pottery in stratified sites where it overlies deposits of Urewe ware may one day supply an approximate answer. For the time being, the roughly datable period of Rwanda history begins with the emergence of the Tutsi dynasty which began the occupation of the central region. This may perhaps be placed around the twenty-first or twenty-second generation back, at a time when the territory of the state was confined to the eastern grasslands, and when the dynasty was probably an offshoot of the neighbouring grassland state of Bugesera. The infiltration of the easternmost of the agricultural Hutu states perhaps began in the eighteenth generation back. Some more systematic control, culminating in the incorporation of the *abiru*, may be placed with some confidence in the sixteenth generation back. Both of the reigns which occurred in this generation, those of the brothers Mukobanyi and Mutabazi, were disturbed by incursions of Nyoro raiders, operating from bases in Nkore and Ndorwa. In view of the genealogical coincidence, it is very probable that the first of these invasions should be equated with that conducted by the Nyoro king Olimi I, which left the Nkore of Nyabugaro bare of cattle in the 'time of the *enyonza* berries'. It is by no means impossible that the presence of the Nyoro in the grasslands was one of the factors leading Mukobanya to his westward conquests and to his compact with the *abiru* of the Bumbogo and Rukoma districts.

The second Nyoro invasion was an even more serious affair. Not only the grasslands but also parts of the central region were attacked, and Mutabazi was temporarily driven from his kingdom. Rwanda traditions retain the most vivid accounts of the ferocity of the invaders who marched through the country, driving before them not only the cattle but also the women and children whom they had captured. The Nyoro were led by their king, whose name is remembered in Rwanda as Chwa. This gives rise to one of the most intractable problems of interlacustrine chronology. In Nyoro tradition Chwa was indeed the throne-name of Olimi's immediate successor, but this king is not remembered for wars in the south. Probably it is once again the Nyoro tradition that is at fault. From Rwanda tradition we can, however, be fairly sure that the Nyoro activity which we have already seen at work in Buganda, Nkore and Kiziba at this mid-sixteenth-century period, extended also to Rwanda. The effects of it, here, were to hasten a process which had already begun – the infiltration of pastoralists into agricultural areas, and the dispersion of herds on a usufruct basis among hoe cultivators in exchange for loyalty and services. Naturally, such an infiltration was not achieved without provoking resistance, and the two generations following Mutabazi were occupied with much campaigning, not all of it successful. In the thirteenth generation back, at the very end of our period, therefore, a thoroughly confused and chaotic situation seems to have been brought under control by a conqueror from Karagwe, Ruganzu Ndori, very likely of Hinda rather than Tutsi origin, under whose successors the Rwanda state climbed slowly to a position of predominant power in the area as a whole. From this time onwards Rwanda was a state based firmly in the central highlands, where a minority of pastoralists lived interspersed among a large majority of cultivators, and it was in these circumstances that the political and military institutions designed to maintain the predominance of the minority were gradually developed.

Southwards from Rwanda, the emergence of the last great state of the interlacustrine region, that of Burundi, which likewise incorporated nearly two million people by the end of the pre-colonial period, lies mostly outside the scope of this volume. Here, as in Rwanda, an Early Iron Age tradition characterized by Urewe pottery was succeeded by a 'Renge' tradition of rouletted ware, made by a dense agricultural population which kept some cattle but lived mainly by cultivating sorghum and peas, and perhaps also bananas, in the well-watered highlands falling away to the east from the Nile–Congo watershed. The high crests of this range are still forested, and it can be clearly seen today how the expansion of population has gone hand in hand with forest clearance. The graves of the eighteenth- and nineteenth-century kings of Burundi were placed in what was then the forest margin, but cultivation has since spread up past them, leaving them now as isolated thickets, a thousand or two thousand feet below the present forest line. In Burundi, as in Rwanda, the infiltration of pastoralists among the cultivators has been a large factor both in agricultural prosperity and in political centralization. In this case the pastoralists, as we know from their clan affiliations, came from two different directions. From the north came Tutsi, not so much from the kingdom of Rwanda as from the still independent states of Gisaka and Bugesera immediately to the west of the upper Kagera, which were conquered by Rwanda only in the late eighteenth century. From the east and south-east came 'Hima' clan sections, deriving ultimately from the Hinda dispersion from Karagwe, which had worked their way up the eastern side of the Kagera valley, founding principalities among the Subi and the Ha before entering the Burundi highlands. As in Rwanda, the pastoral infiltrators seem to have found a multitude of small 'Renge' states already in existence at the time of their arrival. According to tradition, the first relations were established on the basis of the *ubuhake* contract, here known as *umugabire*. Piecemeal conquest followed, by many different groups of immigrants. The final military invasion, which united most of the highland area under the rule of the Nganwa dynasty, came only at the beginning of the eighteenth century, and it came from the south-east, from Buha. It is thus significant that neither in Rwanda nor in Burundi did the great centralizing dynasties come from Tutsi clans.

THE CENTRAL TANZANIAN REGION

With Burundi and Buha we reach the southern periphery of the interlacustrine world, or at least of the region which seems to have had a certain unity during the latter part of our period – a unity deriving from the interaction of the pastoral peoples of the central grassland area with the much more numerous agricultural peoples inhabiting the areas of high rainfall to the east and west of it. The southern boundary of the interlacustrine region is perhaps best marked by the Malagarasi river, and by its tributary streams which rise near the south-west corner of Lake Victoria, in Buzinza, and flow through tsetse-infested *miombo* woodlands to fall into Lake Tanganyika just to the south of Ujiji. South and east of this line we enter upon another huge region, as large in area as the interlacustrine, stretching from Lake Tanganyika to the eastern Rift Valley, but occupied today, and perhaps in our period also, by about one-fifth as many people as the interlacustrine region. Here were no well-watered highlands rising above the general level of the plateau. Here were no great river valleys lined with forest galleries, like those of the tributaries of the Congo and Zambezi. Here, apart from the steeply rising sides of the Tanganyika rift, and the driest, south-eastern shores of Lake Victoria, there was only a great, arid plateau, receiving 65 to 75 centimetres of rainfall a year, and covered with a vegetation of dry bush that was suitable only to cereal agriculture of a marginal kind, involving the frequent movement of farming sites. Throughout the western part of it tsetse fly was widely prevalent, so that even cattle-keeping was hazardous.

Clearly, there would have been little in such an environment to satisfy the highly selective requirements exhibited by the Early Iron Age people of the interlacustrine region. In so far as there was Early Iron Age settlement, it must have resembled that of the Zambian plateau, with a fragile basis of cereal agriculture and a strong emphasis on hunting. In fact, only three Early Iron Age sites have so far been found in the whole of this vast area. There is the site at Kalambo Falls, near the south-east corner of Lake Tanganyika, which shows features reminiscent both of the Zambian and of the interlacustrine Early Iron Age provinces. The same is true of the site at the saline springs near Uvinza on the lower Malagarasi. The third site is that at Lelesu, near the eastern edge of the area, which produced nothing more than an undated, surface collection of Early Iron Age pottery, transitional between Urewe and Kwale ware. It is also relevant that in the northern part of the region, between the southern shores of Lake Victoria and Lake Eyasi, there have been some finds of what appears to be a Stone Age pottery form known as Kansyore ware. This is still undated, but it may well prove to be contemporary with the Early Iron Age in other areas. If so, it will strengthen the supposition that in much of central Tanzania, Early Iron Age communities were very sparse, and that the main build-up of food-producing populations there dates from the Later Iron Age. From the archaeological point of view, little more can be said on this subject until much more evidence is available. However, it may be noted that, whereas at the Kalambo Falls site the Early Iron Age pottery tradition continued undisturbed until about the fourteenth century, at the Ivuna salt-pans near the southern end of Lake Rukwa pottery of a quite different tradition was being made by about the thirteenth century, while at the Uvinza salt springs Early Iron Age pottery was succeeded as early as the twelfth century by a coarse-fired rouletted ware comparable, though not identical, with the 'Renge' and Bigo wares of the interlacustrine region.[1]

Unfortunately, the oral traditions of central Tanzania are scarcely more enlightening for our period than the evidence from archaeology.

[1] B. M. Fagan and J. E. Yellan, 'Ivuna: ancient salt-working in southern Tanzania', *Azania*, 1968, **3**, 1–43; J. E. G. Sutton and A. D. Roberts, 'Uvinza and its salt industry', ibid. 45–86.

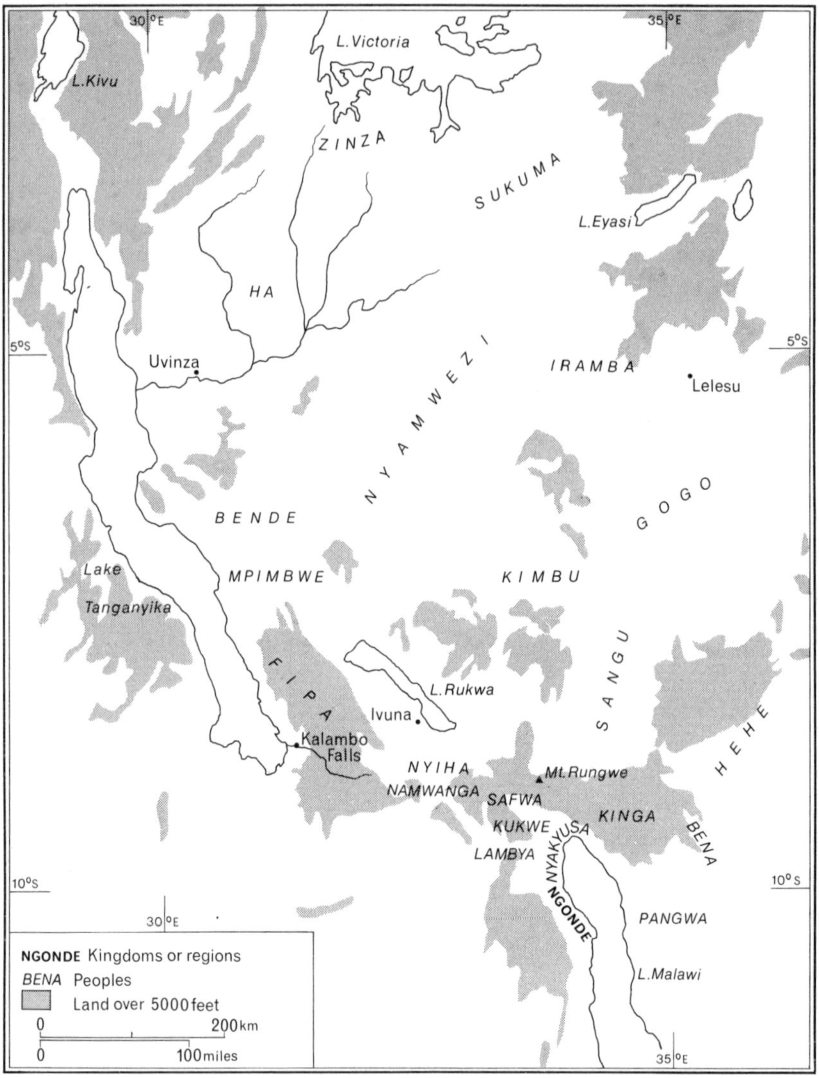

19 The central Tanzanian region

The central population of the region today are the Nyamwezi, with the Sukuma to the north-east of them, the Iramba and Gogo to the east, the Hehe and Sangu to the south-east, the Kimbu to the south, and the Fipa, Mpimbwe and Bende to the south-west. Until the eve of the colonial period, none of these peoples (except the Fipa – see Volume 4, pp. 500–1) developed the centralized political institutions conducive to the handing down of long traditions within the context of a genealogically articulated framework of reference. Political units remained very small, varying in size from a few hundred to a few thousand persons. The circumstances of the environment dictated that when communities grew in size they would split, groups of colonists moving away to open up new areas of land, sometimes at a considerable distance from that of the parent group. To trace such kaleidoscopic gyrations is a delicate task, and one which has so far been performed in the necessary detail only by Shorter in respect of the Kimbu; and even then the results still do not reach back into our period.[1] What they do show, at least in relation to this part of the central Tanzanian region, is that there was no overall trend in the setting up of small states, whether from north to south or from west to east. Of thirty-two ruling clans among the Kimbu, some came from the north, some from the north-east, some from the east and others from the south-east. The picture is one of an unattractive environment, penetrated late in time by the least successful elements from the surrounding lands.

This conclusion has the ring of truth, and it must be taken, for the time being, as having superseded an earlier view which saw the central Tanzanian region primarily as a zone of transition through which early versions of interlacustrine political systems were transmitted southwards. The logic behind the old view was that central Tanzanian chiefship exhibited, though on a miniature scale, the same basic ideas as did interlacustrine chiefship. The Nyamwezi chief of five thousand people was a divine king, with a sacred fire and special insignia, who fulfilled ritual functions and had to be buried in a special way, often to the accompaniment of human sacrifice. The obvious parallels seemed to lie in the north rather than elsewhere. As Cory put it,

> While the part of the Lacustrians living west and north of Lake Victoria has for many years formed and retained a number of kingdoms – the part living south of Lake Victoria has never built an empire. But the immigrants from the north, mainly from Bunyoro, being well acquainted with the idea of powerful and extensive kingdoms, fundamentally influenced the political structure of the area. The immigrating families established authority over sections of the existing population and came to rule over them. The Hamitic element has been wholly absorbed, however, and only faint tradition remains of the historical events of the invasion.[2]

Today such a judgement must be discarded. It may well be that there was some flow of people, including some cattle-owning, therefore

[1] A. Shorter, *Chiefship in western Tanzania* (Oxford, 1972).

[2] H. Cory, *The Ntemi: traditional rites of a Sukuma chief in Tanganyika* (London, 1951), 1–2.

wealthy, and therefore potentially chiefly, families into the central Tanzanian region from the north-west. But it is, for example, remarkable that the long-horned *sanga* cattle, which were the pride of the interlacustrine pastoralists, are rarely found to the south of the Malagarasi frontier; and this is likely to mean that any significant migration from the north-west should be attributed to the pre-Hinda period. However, the real trend of recent research is to see the central Tanzanian region as a kind of sump or backwater, which collected people and influences from all the surrounding areas, and probably as much from the east as from the west.

Indeed the only area adjoining the central Tanzanian plateau where population movements resembling those of the interlacustrine region can be traced to the later part of our period is along the line of highlands which forms its southern rim. And here the catalytic migrations which resulted in the formation of states seem to have come mainly from the north-east. The geographical centre of this area is the Rungwe massif, which rises to a height of nearly 3,000 metres behind the northern shores of Lake Malawi, and from there extends westwards to Lake Tanganyika and north-eastwards to the Iringa highlands. It is an area which provides every variety of scenery and vegetation, from the treeless downlands of Iringa to the forested summits of Mt Rungwe and the Livingstone range, which descend on their southern side through nearly eight thousand feet of lush, well-watered valleys and foothills to the floor of the Malawi Rift. The population is hardly less varied, with the densely settled Nyakyusa cultivating their banana groves on the southern escarpment of the Rungwe massif, the Nyiha and the Safwa, the Lambwa and the Namwanga sowing cereals on the higher land to the north-west, and the Hehe, the Sangu, the Bena and the Pangwa pasturing large herds as well as cultivating eleusine and other cereals on the drier northern and eastern slopes of the great watershed. Both of the Early Iron Age sites known so far lie in the Karonga plain, in river valleys suited to a combination of fishing and banana planting. Here as elsewhere, we have to imagine centuries of forest clearance by growing populations slowly climbing up the hills and the mountain escarpments behind the lakeshores, with hunters retreating upwards within the diminishing forests. Iron is abundant in the Rungwe massif, and the mountain peoples, especially the Kinga and the Nyiha, became the smiths of the surrounding areas. As the higher level forests were cleared, pastoralists from the drier northern and eastern slopes moved in to exploit the new grasslands, and gradually it became clear to both pastoralists and cultivators that each would be enriched by interaction with the other. Here there was apparently no equivalent to the *ubuhake* relationship of the interlacustrine region. But cattle-owners were favoured as chiefs, because they could 'feed' their people, through the milk and manure of the cattle lent out to cultivators of the land. Cereal farmers valued especially the milk, banana planters the manure, which was piled up in small mounds around the young shoots. Except in the Ngonde plain, principalities remained small, dividing and re-dividing like those of the central Tanzanian plateau.

Such a slow dispersal of cattle owners from the north-eastern end of the highland area towards the west and the south would seem to be implied by traditions concerning the origins of perhaps 150 small chieftainships among the Kinga, the Nyakyusa, the Kukwe, the Safwa, the Nyiha, the Namwanga, the Lambya, the Ndali, the Sukwa and the Ngonde. The ostensible point of origin of all these traditions is Bukinga, the small ethnic area situated on the north-eastern crest of the watershed. But this was clearly only a corridor leading from the wider pasture lands further to the north-east. The traditions of the Kinga ruling families themselves point north-eastwards to the high plateau between Iringa and Njombe, which was also a dispersal point of chiefly families among the Hehe, the Sangu, the Bena and the Pangwa. The chronological evidence for the dispersal must be considered to be very tentative. Its strongest link is in Bunyakyusa, where Monica Wilson was able to reconstruct a common genealogy for twenty-nine royal houses from a founding ancestor in the twentieth generation back.[1] Since Nyakyusa chieftainship has a peculiar system of succession, whereby generations succeed each other at fixed intervals of thirty years, irrespective of the life-span of individual chiefs, this should theoretically take us back to the fourteenth or fifteenth centuries. Other chiefly lines, ruling further from the Kinga dispersal centre, have much shorter genealogies. That of the Namwanga chiefs shows sixteen generations, that of the Ngonde *kyungus* only nine or ten. Treated as very rough guides to what was obviously a long drawn-out process, the variation in the genealogical evidence need not be unduly disturbing.

The special interest of the highland region to the south of central Tanzania for the period as a whole is that it is in the gap between Lake Tanganyika and Lake Malawi that we should expect to find the main

[1] M. Wilson, *Communal rituals of the Nyakyusa* (London, 1959), chart 1.

corridor for the passage of pastoral influences from East to Central Africa. The chain of highlands to the west of Lake Tanganyika does indeed present a possible alternative route, though it is not free of obstacles at its southern end. But the Tanganyika–Malawi corridor is in every way more favourable, and the geography of the dispersal through Bukinga does provide one clear example of a route leading into north-eastern Zambia, not from the central Tanzanian plateau immediately to the north, but rather from the Iringa highlands, which lie close to the centre of East African pastoralism in the valley of the Eastern Rift. While we know that cattle-keeping was practised in the Rift Valley region of East Africa from the first millennium BC, it does not seem that cattle were of great importance in most of Bantu Africa during the Early Iron Age. It was only with the coming of the Later Iron Age, around the turn of the present millennium, that many of the drier parts of Bantu Africa began to be occupied by people who were obviously more specialized in pastoralism than the cattle-keepers of the Early Iron Age. Such specialization probably developed from the spread of milking, which enabled people to live in areas which were too arid for much cultivation. But this specialization led, in turn, to interaction between pastoralists and cultivators of the kind we have just been observing. From traditional evidence we can only see the very end of the process, but even that is a useful pointer to what must have gone before.

THE RIFT VALLEY REGION

On its eastern and north-eastern sides the great plateau of central Tanzania borders on a third great region, which may be characterized by its most important geographical feature, the eastern Rift Valley, which cleaves right through it from Lake Rudolf in the north to Lake Manyara and beyond in the south. However, the Rift Valley region essentially includes the highland areas to the east and the west of it. And not only the highlands, but also the dry grazing lands to the east again – the Northern Frontier Province of Kenya, the Athi plain and the Masai Steppe. From the historical point of view, the outstanding fact about this region, and that which gives it a basic unity, is that over nine-tenths of its area the languages spoken are either Paranilotic or Cushitic. Bantu-speaking areas enclose it to the west, the east and the south. Only in central Kenya does a significant island of Bantu speech exist within its confines.

Although there is very little direct traditional or written evidence relating to our period, the basic outlines of the historical situation in the Rift Valley region are fairly well understood both by archaeologists and linguists. Archaeology has shown that early in the first millennium BC a food-producing population established itself in the central part of the Rift Valley and in the highlands to the west of it, a population which lived by hunting and by pastoralism, making good pottery and basketry and carving stone bowls and platters, grindstones and pestles for pounding wild vegetable foods. Skeletal evidence shows that these people were tall and slender, and the distribution of cairn burials from northern Somalia through southern Ethiopia to the southern end of the Masai steppe suggest that they came to East Africa from the north. Seeing that the Rift Valley region represents, ecologically, a protrusion into East Africa of the Ethiopian highland scene, this conclusion is a natural one. Linguistically, Ethiopia and Somalia are, of course, the centre of the Cushitic language area, and the survival at the southern end of the Rift Valley region of a sub-group of strongly differentiated languages known as Southern Cushitic provides ample evidence that most of the region must formerly have been occupied by Cushitic-speaking people. Over most of the Northern Province of Kenya, from Lake Rudolf to Somalia, languages of the Eastern Cushitic sub-group are still spoken by the Galla and Somali who pasture their cattle and their camels in these dry grasslands.

What we do not yet know is the period at which these Cushitic speakers, and particularly those of the southern sub-group, added cereal agriculture and an Iron Age technology to their original hunting and pastoral pursuits. Only towards the southern end of the Rift Valley, at Engaruka, a distance of approximately fifty kilometres to the south of Lake Natron, is there an Iron Age site with dates running well back into the first millennium AD which has strong claims to be associated with a Southern Cushitic population. Here, where a perennial stream from the Ngorongoro hills drops suddenly down the steep western wall of the Rift, the hillside for nearly a mile on each side of the torrent has been terraced with dry-stone walling, to make platforms for house sites and irrigated terraces for gardens. Paths and irrigation channels lead outwards from the stream to some five hundred dwelling plots ranged in dense tiers along the hillside, while the flat floor of the valley below is marked out with lines of large stones in what seem to be field systems covering an area of nearly thirteen square kilometres. This flat area is dotted with stone circles, each some two metres high and about nine metres across, which were clearly pens for stock.

The hillside terraces were excavated in 1964 and 1966 by Sassoon,[1] who established beyond doubt that they were used both for agriculture and for dwelling sites. The middens included cattle bones and grains of sorghum, as well as plain, grooved pottery of a type so far unknown elsewhere. One of the living sites on the hillside showed traces of an iron forge and slag. Two radiocarbon samples taken from the terraces yielded dates around the fourth and eighth centuries AD. It is thought that the hillside terraces were occupied for a long period, the later dwelling sites lying further away from the stream. The walled enclosures on the valley floor are the latest buildings of all, yielding radiocarbon dates around the fifteenth century, and a style of pottery different from that on the hillside, though equally unknown elsewhere. While the identification of Engaruka with the Southern Cushites must be regarded for the present as tentative, the fact that the site adjoins the main surviving pocket of Southern Cushitic speakers is very telling. The first millennium dates are indeed surprisingly early, but mainly perhaps because the accompanying pottery cannot be clearly identified either with the Early Iron Age wares already known in the Bantu-occupied areas to the east and the west, or with the Later Iron Age wares of the rest of the Rift Valley region. The most likely interpretation of the present evidence would seem to be that the hillside occupation does indeed go back to some time in the first millennium, and that it does offer some indication of the period at which some of the Southern Cushites passed from the Stone to the Iron Age, whether through contact with neighbouring Bantu peoples or as the recipients of some northern Early Iron Age tradition as yet unidentified.

The matter is of some importance since, for the period covered here, the overriding problem is to visualize the situation in the Rift Valley region before the advent of the Masai. These militarized and highly specialized pastoralists from the eastern group of Paranilotes emerged from the Lake Rudolf basin only in the seventeenth century, and in the course of a hundred years established a virtual monopoly of the Rift Valley grasslands all the way from the Uasin Gishu plateau in north-western Kenya to the Masai steppe in north-central Tanzania, a distance of approximately 970 kilometres. Sutton has shown convincingly how, in the north-western half of this area, the Masai predominance drove back and fundamentally changed the way of life of the older established Southern Paranilotic group of Kalenjin peoples,

[1] H. Sassoon, 'New views on Engaruka, northern Tanzania', *Journal of African History*, 1967, **8**, 2, 201–17.

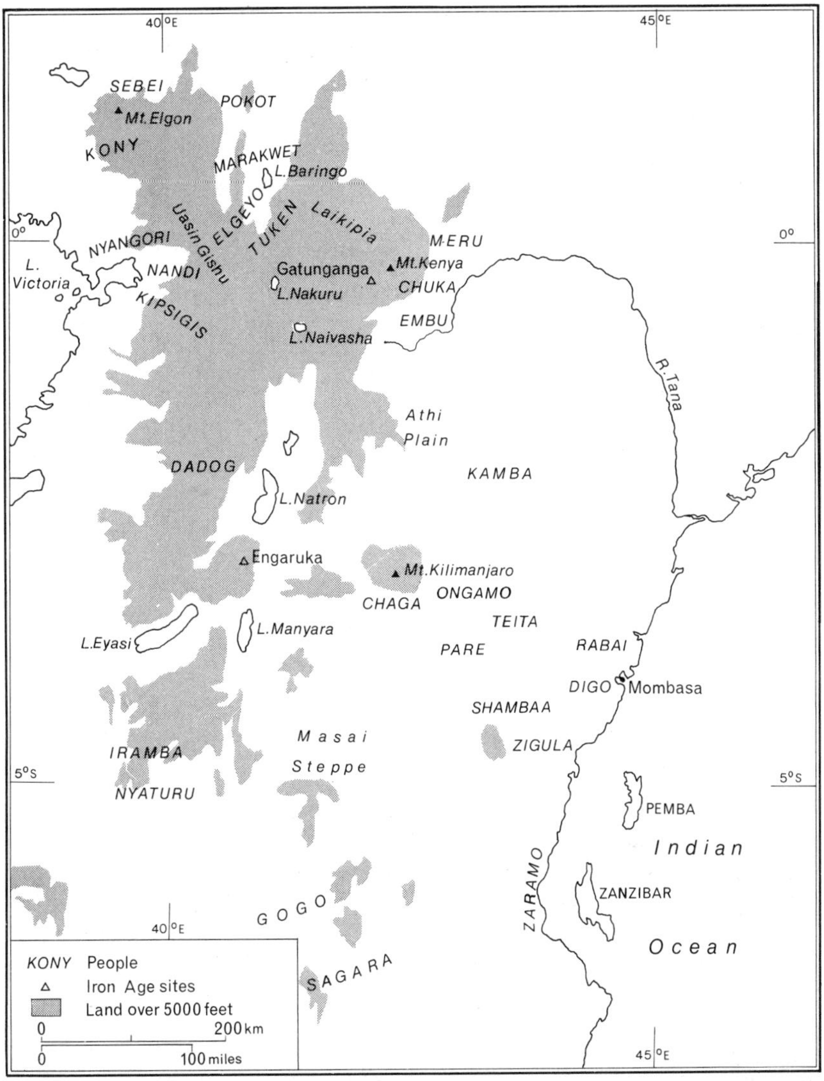

20 The Rift Valley region

whose descendants – the Kipsigis and the Nandi, the Nyangori, Kony and Sebei, the Pokot and the Marakwet, the Elgeyo and the Tuken – now inhabit only the peripheries of the Uasin Gishu grasslands. During our period the Kalenjin were, in fact, the main population of the highlands to the west of the Rift Valley. They were iron-workers of the later, northern tradition, who made rouletted pottery and practised a mixed farming economy, tilling the high and formerly forested areas with the greatest rainfall and the richest soils, and sending out their young men and boys to pasture their herds on the open grasslands of the Uasin Gishu and down into the central section of the Rift Valley itself. They left clear traces of their presence in the so-called 'Sirikwa Holes', which were artificial pits or hollows made for the penning and protection of cattle and smaller stock, sometimes lined with dry stone walling, always with a ramped entrance on the lower side, and with a house site attached to but not within the enclosure. There are thousands of these hollows scattered across the highlands of western Kenya, sometimes in groups of up to a hundred upon a single hillside, and their distribution coincides, more or less, with the area enclosed by the ring of modern Kalenjin homelands. They were abandoned only with the coming of the Masai. As Sutton remarks, 'In order to argue that the Sirikwa in the western highlands were any other than the Kalenjin themselves, one has to postulate a complete linguistic displacement through virtually the whole region only two centuries ago.'[1] This is surely conclusive.

The Kalenjin apart, the only other significant group of Southern Paranilotes were the Dadog, whose descendants today live scattered among a dozen Bantu peoples from the south-eastern shores of Lake Victoria to the southern end of the Rift Valley. We know very little about these people, except that their language shows a considerable differentiation from Kalenjin, and in particular it is much less influenced than Kalenjin by borrowings from Southern Cushitic. The same appears to be true of their social organization, which does not have the age differentiation system adopted by the Kalenjin from their Southern Cushitic predecessors in the Kenya highlands. The brief conclusion would seem to be that here in north-central Tanzania the Southern Paranilotes impinged directly upon the Bantu. The Dadog were, in fact, very likely the introducers of the Later Iron Age tradition of mixed farming into the north-eastern part of the central Tanzanian region. If so, this could have been an important feature of our period, affecting the ancestors of such Bantu peoples as the Kuria and the Zanaki, the Sukuma, the Iramba, the Nyaturu and the Gogo. Indeed, with the fast-disappearing Dadog, now mostly Bantuized as Tatoga, we may have a clearer paradigm than any other of the process of Later Iron Age infiltration into the interlacustrine region which has been obscured by the comparative wealth of its later history.

[1] J. E. G. Sutton, *The archaeology of the western highlands of Kenya* (Nairobi, 1973), 31.

We are still left, however, with the problem of how the Later Iron Age tradition was introduced to the lands east of the Rift Valley, including both the high mountain massifs of the Nyandarua range, Mt Kenya, Kilimanjaro and Mt Meru, and the far more extensive areas of plateau grassland which encompasses them and stretches on southwards across the Masai steppe. The Kalenjin, to judge from their language, absorbed a pre-existing population of Southern Cushites, presumably still Stone Age people, in the highlands of western Kenya. To judge from the distribution of their characteristic cattle-pens, they descended into the central section of the Rift around modern Nakuru, but they did not ascend its eastern wall. South of them, the Dadog did not reach the Rift: indeed, the main surviving pockets of southern Cushites are to be found in the Mbulu highlands between Lake Eyasi and Lake Manyara. East of the Rift, it is today the Masai who dominate the grasslands from the Laikipia plateau north of Mt Kenya to the southern end of the Masai steppe; but they reached most of this area only in the eighteenth century. The question is who preceded them.

In the light of present knowledge any answer must be extremely tentative, but the most likely proposition put forward so far is that they were preceded by earlier waves of Eastern Paranilotes, which passed to the east of the Kalenjin occupied areas, emerging from the Rudolf basin by the Laikipia escarpment and keeping to the eastern side of the Rift. The edges of the Masai steppe are littered with small groups of Masai-like peoples, often known collectively as Kwavi, and the difficulty is to distinguish those which are of recent and genuinely Masai origin – groups which had lost their cattle and were forced to settle as cultivators in the lands of their Bantu neighbours – from older groups descending from pre-Masai layers of settlement. One such older group would, however, seem to be identifiable in the Ongamo (or Ngassa), now living close to the Chaga in the eastern foothills of Kilimanjaro. The Ongamo are associated with the earliest traditions of the Chaga, which must be older by several centuries than the coming of the Masai. They speak a language which is closely related to Masai, and yet much more distinct from it than the Masai spoken by most Kwavi groups (see Volume 4, p. 495). Probably, they are only one of several groups which took part in a movement through the eastern highlands of Kenya parallel with that of the Kalenjin peoples to the west. As in the western highlands, these Eastern Paranilotes must have interpenetrated and absorbed much of the earlier Southern Cushitic population, although some small groups, such as the Magogodo on the northern side of Mt Kenya, have survived in pockets. Other Southern Cushites seem to have retreated southwards before these movements, such as the Mbugwe, now living to the east and west of the Masai steppe, who preserve the tradition of a southward migration all the way from the Laikipia plateau.[1]

Like the Kalenjin between Mt Elgon and the Kavirondo Gulf, and like the Dadog between the southern half of Lake Victoria and the eastern Rift, the Eastern Paranilotes of the pre-Masai dispersion must at an early stage have rubbed shoulders with their Bantu neighbours on their eastern side. Among the first areas where they might have done so would have been the fertile, well-watered foothills of the Nyandarua range and Mt Kenya, where the Kikuyu and related peoples, including the Meru, Embu, Tharaka, Chuka and Mbere, today support a population of nearly two million. Kikuyu traditions of origin appear to describe very clearly a migration into the highlands from the north-east, which came into a still forest-clad country previously inhabited on the one hand by Athi hunters, who were in the view of the immigrants people of normal size, and on the other hand by Gumba, who were very small in stature, yet excellent iron-workers, who taught the newcomers how to work iron, or, perhaps more likely, the places where the ore could be mined. The Athi are fairly clearly identified with the ancestors of the modern Dorobo, or Okiek – which is, as Sutton points out,[2] an imprecise term which is applied to various small hunting bands in Kalenjin country, in the eastern highlands and far out on the Masai steppe; but at any rate its associations are all with Paranilotic people. The Gumba, on the other hand, despite their dwarfishness, are regarded by at least some Kikuyu as being among their own ancestors.[3] At all events, the Gumba disappeared, which means that they were absorbed by the migrants, or perhaps that they absorbed them, whereas some at least of the Athi remained hunters and retreated higher into the forests. The Kikuyu penetration, as seen in the traditions, is one in which the pioneer immigrants were hunters and stock-keepers, who, on learning the iron-working techniques of the Gumba turned increasingly to agriculture, cutting back the forests and multiplying rapidly in numbers. It has usually been taken as an event which occurred fairly late in time, perhaps only during the last century or two of our period – partly because the remembered sequence of ruling

[1] S. Feierman, *The Shambaa kingdom* (Madison, 1974), 74–5.
[2] Sutton, *Archaeology*, 9.
[3] G. Muriuki, *A history of the Kikuyu, 1500–1900* (Nairobi, 1974), 43.

generation groups would account only for a period of about four and a half centuries, and partly because the traditions relating to Kikuyu land settlement show that much of the area has only been cleared for agriculture during the past two centuries, so that the nuclear area of intensive settlement must before then have been very small.

Recently, however, new light has been thrown on the situation in northern Kikuyuland at a much earlier date than that apparently described in the traditions. At Gatunganga, a few kilometres south of Nyeri, in the foothills between Mt Kenya and the Nyandaruas, a long-occupied smelting and iron-working site, discovered by Muriuki and excavated in 1971 by Siiriäinen,[1] strongly suggests that Bantu people were living in the area by about the eleventh or twelfth century, for sherds of Kwale-ware pottery were found sealed beneath thick layers of slag dated by radiocarbon to the period between about 1100 and 1350. The pottery of the period of intensive iron-working is, in contrast, a coarse ware with markedly different vessel shapes to the Kwale ware, much of it decorated with 'rocked zigzag' lines made by walking a two-pronged instrument over the surface. This pottery is known from several other sites, so far undated, from Kikuyuland south-eastwards to the Pare hills. In addition, the later layers at Gatunganga yielded three quite different vessels, presumably imported from neighbouring areas, one with rouletted decoration and two with incised geometric designs, indicating contemporaneity and contact with other Later Iron Age traditions. Assuming, as we must, the general correctness of the identification of Kwale ware with the Bantu, there can be little doubt that Bantu people related to those of the Digo and Pare hills were in occupation of this part of Kikuyuland before the twelfth century. Some iron-working is likely at this period, although blade tools made of obsidian were still in use for some purposes. Food production is unattested, but this is perhaps only to be expected if vegetable foods such as bananas were the staples. To judge from the pottery of the later period of intensive iron-working, this should also be associated with comparable developments away from the Kwale base among the ancestors of people like the Kamba and the Pare living in highland areas to the east of the Rift Valley. The main problem of the Gatunganga site at this period is that, whereas the bones of domestic cattle are plentiful, there is still no sign of cereals. On the other hand, intensive

[1] A. Siiriäinen, 'The Iron Age site at Gatung'ang'a, central Kenya', *Azania*, 1971, **6**, 199–232.

iron-working is unlikely to have been practised in the absence of agriculture of some kind. The problem will doubtless be solved by further excavations at comparable sites.

Meantime, while holding on to the precious evidence that some Bantu occupation of Kikuyuland goes back to Early Iron Age times, it is best to return to the picture painted by Kikuyu traditions of later immigrants finding two very different populations living in the area side by side. If the Athi were Paranilotes and the Gumba were Bantu, this could perhaps explain the obviously ancient Paranilotic influences in the social and ritual systems of the Kikuyu and their Bantu neighbours. As Muriuki points out, the system of age differentiation practised by all these peoples can be proved to be much older than their contacts with the Masai, and male and female circumcision practices are likely to have been so as well.[1] At the same time, the question which must be asked in the light of the Gatunganga evidence, even if it cannot be answered, is whether the Kikuyu migration tradition might not refer, not to a Bantu movement as has usually been supposed, but to a movement of pre-Masai Paranilotes from the Athi plains into the Kikuyu highlands. The migration is said to have come from the north-east, up the valley of the Thagana river. The pioneer migrants are thought to have been hunters and pastoralists, who considered that the Athi were men like themselves, but that the Gumba were undersized and alien. The system of ruling generation groups is thought to date from their arrival, and this is clearly a Paranilotic rather than a Bantu institution. All through East African history, we have learned to see that migrations, even by quite small groups over quite short distances, are highly memorable events which tend to dominate and distort a people's view of the past. This writer once demonstrated how the traditions of origin of the Konjo, the mountain dwellers of the Ruwenzori range, had been dominated by memories of a migration from Buganda, which in fact had been that of a tiny group of refugees which had fled from the Buganda court during the late eighteenth century.[2] In the eastern highlands of Kenya there occurred at least one rather similar case, concerning a group of refugees from the offshore island of Manda, who fled from their Muslim rulers around the beginning of the eighteenth century and trekked up the Tana and its tributaries until they reached the eastern foothills of Mt Kenya. The tale of their experiences was so remarkable that it was adopted as a tradition of origin

[1] Muriuki, *History*, 39–40.

[2] R. Oliver, 'The Baganda and the Bakonjo', *Uganda Journal*, 1954, **18**, 1, 31–3.

by the Meru and Theraka peoples among whom they settled.[1] The Kikuyu migration tradition, however, does not claim any distant point of origin. It can be interpreted as a piecemeal drift from the plains into the hills, which was dramatic for those who took part mainly because it involved a change in the way of life from hunting and herding to forest clearance and intensive planting. In a time of drought those suffering on the plains would see the cloud-caps encircling the mountain-tops and decide that the time had come for them to try out a new environment, inhabited no doubt by wild and dwarfish men cultivating strange and unpalatable crops, but where at least there would be water.

Unlike the rather standardized traditions of origin of the Kikuyu and their immediate neighbours, those of the other mountain peoples to the east of the Rift Valley region, such as the Chaga and the Teita, the Pare and the Shambaa, abound in stories of migration from almost every point of the compass. The classic case is that of the Chaga, among whom Dundas collected particulars of 732 clan segments and found that 113 claimed descent from the Kamba, 106 from the Teita, 101 from the Masai, 31 from the Pare, 22 from the Shambaa, 16 from the Kahe and Arush, 6 from the Kwavi and 2 from the Dorobo. He added the rather revealing comment that 'Of the remainder of the clans the great majority gave some other locality on Kilimanjaro as their place of origin, which I take to be an indication of the fact that they are offshoots of other clans'.[2] Dundas had decided that the Bantu were the newcomers to the mountain, having been preceded by a Pygmy people, the Konyingo, and perhaps by the Paranilotic Ongamo. At the very least, however, his evidence must be taken as a powerful reminder of the role of the great mountain with its running water, as a place of refuge from drought-stricken plains where the pressure of cattle upon limited grazing lands constantly pushed men to warfare and extrusion.

Kilimanjaro is archaeologically still very little known, the only two dated Iron Age sites belonging to about the fifteenth century. In the Pare and Usambara mountains, however, the Early Iron Age base is well attested, thanks to the important archaeological surveys undertaken by Soper.[3] Half a dozen sites with Kwale-ware pottery have been identified, one of them dating to as early as the third century. From here on, the picture seems to be one of the diversification and localization of pottery traditions, with at least three wares distinct to the South

[1] J. A. Fadiman, 'Early history of the Meru of Mt Kenya', *Journal of African History*, 1973, **14**, 1, 9–29.

[2] C. C. F. Dundas, *Kilimanjaro and its people* (London, 1924), 43–4.

[3] R. C. Soper, 'Iron Age sites in north-eastern Tanzania', *Azania*, 1967, **2**, 19–36.

Pare district and two more to the Usambaras. Only two of these wares have been dated, both to around the ninth century. There is here apparent no abrupt transition from Early to Later Iron Age pottery traditions such as seems to have affected so much of the rest of East Africa. Indeed, the interaction of Bantu and non-Bantu peoples is known to us mainly by inference from linguistic and ethnographic data. We know that the Ongamo, speaking a Masai-related Eastern Paranilotic language, lived close to the ancestors of the Bantu-speaking Chaga and Teita. We know that sections of the Mbugu, speaking a Southern Cushitic language, settled among the Pare and the Shambaa. We know that, like the Kikuyu and their neighbours, the Chaga and the Kamba, the Teita and the Pare all in various measures practised customs of initiation and age differentiation which indicate a long co-existence with the non-Bantu peoples of the region. And we have learned, above all from Feierman, that although ethnicity in these highland areas developed around the intensive exploitation of particular, often very local, environments, neighbouring peoples, especially those living at different altitudes above sea level, deliberately practised complementarity – the banana planters of the intermediate levels cultivating relationships both with the hunters of the forested heights and with the cereal farmers and herders of the plains below.

In one respect, the Bantu-speaking peoples of the Rift Valley region from Kilimanjaro southwards differed from those to the north, in that even within our period there are some signs of the emergence of states and chiefly dynasties. This was a feature quite foreign to the Paranilotic and Cushitic peoples of both the western and the eastern highlands, and it completely failed to emerge among the Kikuyu and their immediate neighbours. Its presence further south can perhaps be taken to indicate a diminution of Paranilotic influence. On Kilimanjaro chieftainship may have been a late development. At the beginning of the colonial period the Chaga were organized in twenty-eight kingdoms, of which only one was estimated to have more than 20,000 subjects; and the genealogies of chiefly dynasties do not appear to extend backwards into our period. In North Pare, however, they certainly do so. Kimambo in a careful study has here identified the first centre of government with an iron-working site, where a line of blacksmiths had built up such prestige that people came to them not only to buy tools and weapons but also to have their cases judged and their children initiated.[1] This probably common pattern of local rulership was

[1] I. N. Kimambo, *A political history of Pare* (Nairobi, 1969).

transformed by a coup d'état by the leaders of the Suyia clan, who succeeded in creating the centralized state of Ugweno, covering the whole of the North Pare plateau. Clan elders were organized into a hierarchy of councils. Clan initiation rites were transformed into national ones. Princes from the new ruling clan were posted to rule over outlying districts and became the nucleus of a corps of centrally appointed officials. These events took place in the sixteenth and fifteenth generations back, probably therefore during the last century of our period. In Usambara, the creation of another centralized state was to follow only in the eighteenth century, superseding another local dynasty of blacksmith chiefs which had held power 'because God gave them the gift of iron-working and skill in war'.[1]

The part of the Rift Valley region about which we most need to know more than we do is its southern periphery, where the Masai steppe merges into the desiccated bushland of Ugogo. For it is here that we should expect to find some of the important strands of continuity leading on into the southern parts of the central Tanzanian region, and on from there into Central and Southern Africa. These threads should concern, above all, the developing practice of pastoralism – not merely the keeping of cattle, but also the milking of cattle and the interaction of pastoralism with hoe agriculture. For it was probably somewhere in this area that the Stone Age pastoralism of the Southern Cushites had its southern limit. From there southwards cattle appear only in the Iron Age record, and even then not at first in a predominant economic role. It would seem likely that the Southern Cushites did not milk, or at least that their pastoralism was not of so specialized a kind that it drove them to overcome barriers of terrain and tsetse fly in the effort to find fresh grasslands to feed growing herds. To have survived for so long in such a confined area, they must have found and maintained an ecological balance within their chosen environment. Even when the Early Iron Age Bantu farmers moved into the agricultural lands around the edges of their pastures, it would seem that they did not greatly change their way of life. In the western highlands of Kenya, certainly, and probably in most of the rest of the region also, they lived on through the first millennium AD as Stone Age food producers. It is only at Engaruka that we may have a late exception. In general, it was the Paranilotes who were the Iron Age pastoralists of the Rift Valley region. Having absorbed most of the earlier Cushitic populations, they came among the Early Iron Age Bantu as the practitioners of an Iron

[1] 'Habari za Wakilindi' [R. Allen, tr.], *Tanganyika Notes and Records*, 1936, **2**, 86.

Age way of life that was superior because it was adaptable to more varied conditions. They were milkers, and therefore they could live better in the lands that were only marginally suited to agriculture. Probably they had cereals, such as eleusine, that needed less rain than did sorghum. Probably they had better weapons both for hunting and for warfare. Yet, somewhere around the southern edges of the Rift Valley region they encountered a situation in which Bantu societies were sufficiently established to absorb them. If, like the Dadog, they went further, they became Bantuized in the process.

It is this process of the Bantuization of the Later Iron Age that we should like to be able to see in the traditions of people like the Gogo and the Hehe, the Bena and the Sangu, who live just to the south of the Rift Valley region, in the upper valley of the Great Ruaha and in the Iringa highlands beyond. Unfortunately, we cannot do so, for the only genealogically articulated traditions which survive from this area are those of small chiefly dynasties, most of which seem to have been established only during the eighteenth century (see Volume 4, p. 508). The only memories carried forward from earlier times come from Ugogo, where it is said that the western part of the district was occupied by people of small stature, the Mankala, who lived mainly by hunting and gathering, keeping goats and sheep, but not cattle, whereas the eastern part was inhabited by cattle-keepers, reddish in colour, who dug dew-ponds and lived in houses made of clay fired into dagga, like pottery.[1] From Hehe, Bena and Sangu country we have nothing relevant to our period. There is probably no area of East Africa where an Iron Age archaeological survey is more needed.

THE COASTAL HINTERLAND

There is, of course, a fourth region of East Africa, comprising all the country which falls away from the eastern rim of the great central plateau to the Indian Ocean coast. Geographically, it is a vast area, as large as the other three. At the northern end, behind the Lamu archipelago, nearly 320 kilometres of semi-desert separate the coast from the beginnings of the highland plateau around Kitui. Behind Mombasa and Tanga, the tract of *nyika* lowland, mostly covered with dry thorn scrub, encompasses an area as little as eighty to one hundred kilometres wide. Further south, however, the lowlands broaden out

[1] H. Claus, *Die Wagogo* (Leipzig, 1911); T. Schaegelen, 'La tribu des Wagogo', *Anthropos*, 1938, 33, 195–217.

again, extending for more than 150 kilometres behind Dar es Salaam, while the Rufiji and its main tributaries, the Kilombero and the Great Ruaha, flow through more than 320 kilometres of low and torrid bushland on their way to the sea. Large areas flanking the Rovuma valley are scarcely less desolate. Even today, the population of this coastal hinterland is very sparse. If that of the coastal towns is subtracted, it probably numbers less than a million. During our period it can have amounted only to a small fraction of that number.

It is hardly surprising that little is known of these scattered peoples from their own traditions, and less so when it is remembered that two-thirds of them belong to chiefless, matrilineal societies, living in dispersed homesteads with no political authority wider than that of the head of a household. So long as there was plenty of land and few other resources to attract an aggressor, such people had no need of wider organization or a framework of history to support it. What is much more surprising is that, even by the end of our period, the sophisticated islamized societies living in the midst of these people had nothing whatever to say about them. For there can be no real doubt that from the Rovuma north to the Pangani, the easternmost of the matrilineal peoples – the ancestors of the Makua, the Mwera, the Rufiji, the Zaramo and the Zigula – all reached to the coast, where they fished in the sea and built canoes with outriggers, copied from those of earlier Indonesian migrants, to steady them in rough water. These peoples must have looked across the narrow waters to Songo Mnara and Kilwa and Mafia and Zanzibar and Pemba, with their medieval settlements of Arabs and Persians and 'Swahili' Africans from further up the coast. These people must have supplied the slaves and the ivory and the hippopotamus teeth, and perhaps even the food supplies of the offshore settler communities. If there were trading caravans passing even a hundred miles into the interior, to peoples like the Ngindo and the Pogoro and the Luguru and the Sagara, these native dwellers of the coastlands must have organized them. During the eighteenth century some of these peoples living on the edge of the interior plateau, especially the Sagara (see Volume 4, p. 505), would rise into prominence as the trade-routes began to penetrate still further inland. But of their earlier history we know, as yet, nothing.

In fact, the only part of the coastal hinterland in which a connection can be perceived with developments in the interior during our period is the third of it lying to the north of the Pangani river. Here the Nyika peoples – the Segeju, the Digo, the Duruma, the Rabai, the Giryama and some other smaller groups – show in their social organization the same signs of penetration by non-Bantu influence as do the Bantu peoples of the north-eastern part of the Rift Valley region, such as the Teita, the Kamba and the Kikuyu. All these societies are chiefless, the predominant organization being age-sets (*rika*), composed of persons circumcised at the same time, and generation sets (*kambi*), composed of groups of age-sets, changing at intervals of approximately forty to forty-five years.[1] That the Nyika formerly included groups living as fairly specialized pastoralists is known from the fact that during the late sixteenth century the Segeju were living close to the Portuguese settlement at Mombasa, where the Jesuit Monclaro, writing in 1571, distinguished them from the other coastal peoples as a strong and warlike tribe, which lived by cattle-breeding and whose main food consisted of milk mixed with warm blood drawn from the veins of living animals. When in 1585 Mombasa was attacked by the famous horde of Zimba warriors from the area north of the Zambezi (see Volume 4, pp. 514–28), the invaders were destroyed by a force of 3,000 Segeju warriors who came to the aid of the Portuguese. Dos Santos, writing in 1609, again reported upon them, explicitly differentiating them from the Galla, who were by this time well known to the Portuguese in the regions further north. According to their own traditions, recorded in the early twentieth century (by which time they had been long Bantuized and sedentarized as one of the Nyika tribes), the Segeju claim an origin on the interior plateau, near Mt Kenya.[2] From the known dates of their residence at the coast, they could not have been Masai, with whom their customs have usually been compared. It looks, therefore, as though the Segeju, and the whole element in Nyika life for which they stood, was, like that of the Ongamo near Kilimanjaro, a product of the pre-Masai dispersion of Eastern Paranilotes which we have postulated for the Rift Valley region.

According to one rather common interpretation, the rest of the Nyika migrated into their present positions only during the seventeenth century, having been driven southwards from a former homeland called Shungwaya, situated in the coastal region north of the Lamu archipelago, by the attacks of the Eastern Cushitic Galla (see pp. 230–1). It is true that the *Mosungalos*, whom the Portuguese later came to identify as Nyika, were first reported in the neighbourhood of Mombasa only

[1] A. H. J. Prins, *The coastal tribes of the north-eastern Bantu* (London, 1952), 71–2.

[2] Cf. J. Strandes, *The Portuguese period in East Africa*, J. S. Kirkman, ed., J. F. Wallwork, tr. (Nairobi, 1961), 159–62.

in 1610. It is also true that the oral traditions of a wide region are dominated by the theme of a migration from Shungwaya. The story is found not only throughout Nyikaland, but also among the Pokomo on the banks of the Tana, and among the Teita, the Pare, the Chaga and the Shambaa. Early European reports of the Meru tradition of a migration from Manda island (see p. 660) linked this, too, with Shungwaya, and, since the Kikuyu traditions of origin described a migration from the same direction as the Meru, these were added by many authors to the Shungwaya collection.[1] Thus, at a time when the spread of the Bantu peoples was thought to have proceeded from north to south in relatively recent times, Shungwaya was frequently described as the 'dispersal centre' of the North-Eastern Bantu. Even now that the modern accretions have been identified, some of the mystique of the Shungwaya legend lingers on. However, while there can be no doubt that some reality must underlie a tale so widely told, a modern interpretation must be that these traditions are likely to be those of widely dispersed minorities, whose progenitors may not in origin have even been Bantu. Certainly, with the type-site of the Early Iron Age Kwaleware province situated in the territory of the Digo, it would be rash to identify the main Bantu occupation of the area with a north-to-south migration of the late sixteenth or early seventeenth century. Probably we should assume that in the mid eleventh century the inhabitants of the Nyika hills were indistinguishable from the 'Swahili' mentioned by Ibn Baṭṭūṭa in the early fourteenth century as those who supplied the inhabitants of Mombasa island with their grain. Later, and perhaps not so long before the Segeju appeared in the Portuguese records in their guise of militant pastoralists, the coastal hills seem to have been invaded by cattle-keepers from the interior plateau on a sufficient scale to give the Nyika their characteristic social organization of age-sets and generation groups. Except for the transitory episode of the Zimba horde, it is the only case we can point to where the history of the coast and that of the interior may be said to have met and overlapped.

Essentially, then, the history of the East African interior during the period covered by this volume would seem to be concerned with the changes brought about by the meeting and interaction of two Iron Age traditions. Of these, one had been present in the region for several

[1] J. F. Munro, 'Migrations of the Bantu-speaking peoples of the eastern Kenya highlands: a reappraisal', *Journal of African History*, 1967, **8**, 1, 25–8.

centuries before the beginning of our period and was almost certainly associated with the dispersion of Bantu-speaking people, widely though also selectively, throughout most of the country south of the Somerset Nile, Mt Elgon and Mt Kenya. It was the tradition of people who had developed great social and cultural dynamism by adding not only an iron technology but also some kinds of agricultural food production to the older occupations of hunting and gathering. This enabled them to live a more sedentary existence in larger communities, which gradually absorbed, linguistically and culturally, the descendants of the older hunting and gathering peoples of the region. The Early Iron Age tradition, however, was one which still left many ecological areas unfilled by effective food production. In general, it was strongest in the humid areas and weakest in the arid ones. It was, above all, these gaps which were exploited by the Later Iron Age traditions which spread through the region from north to south during the course of our period. These later traditions were adapted to cereal agriculture in conditions drier than the earlier ones. They also included the effective use of cattle both for milking and manuring. The original practitioners of these traditions came from three linguistic groupings – the Central Sudanic, the Nilotic and the Paranilotic – all of which were probably related in their remoter history. The spread of the new traditions certainly involved some southward movement by these northern peoples. In general, however, the newcomers became linguistically acculturated when settling among peoples who were already in the Iron Age. Only when they settled among Stone Age communities, as the Kalenjin did among the Southern Cushites of the Kenya highlands, did the language of the invaders prevail. Also, of course, the newcomers transmitted their skills. There is no need to look for a Central Sudanic or Paranilotic potter behind every roulette-decorated pot. The dense agricultural populations that built up in the interlacustrine highland areas and to the north of Lake Malawi were Bantu populations. So, no doubt, were the herders upon whom their economy in part depended.

Political centralization was in large measure a result of population density, although some dense populations found a viable alternative in the systems of age differentiation adopted by the Paranilotes from the Southern Cushites and transmitted by them to some of the Bantu. Throughout most of East Africa, however, the dominant political idea was that of a kingdom, ruled by a hereditary dynasty which acted as the vehicle for supernatural powers. Such kingdoms could be very small, and every big state that we know of grew from small beginnings, adding to the number of civil, military and ritual officers as the need arose, and in the most successful cases substituting appointive for hereditary officials as the momentum of expansion developed. Even by the end of the sixteenth century, few kingdoms had progressed to this last and vital stage. But in the interlacustrine region at least, the foundations of several successful polities had been firmly laid, which were to grow and endure until the end of the pre-colonial period, and beyond.

BIBLIOGRAPHICAL ESSAYS

I. EGYPT, NUBIA AND THE EASTERN DESERTS

Among works of reference, an indispensable instrument for all aspects of Islam and the Arabic world remains the five-volume *The Encyclopaedia of Islam*, 1st edn (1913–38). The standard introduction and bibliography is Cahen, *Jean Sauvaget's introduction to the history of the Muslim East* (1965), which gives a systematic regional and thematic arrangement of the available source material. For continuous acquaintance with the periodical literature, the student should follow either Pearson, *Index Islamicus* (1958, and supplements 1962, 1967, 1972), or *Abstracta Islamica*, a supplement to the *Revue des Études Islamiques* (since 1927), which contains short evaluations and registers work done in Arabic.

Unlike other parts of the Arab world (or for that matter of the Middle East and of the rest of Africa), Egypt is in the privileged position of possessing a quantity of primary archival material for its history before the fifteenth century. For the period before the tenth and eleventh centuries there are a number of papyri dealing with administrative, juristic and even private matters. The richest collection is that of the Egyptian Library, cf. Grohmann (1934–62 and 1954). A limited quantity of other primary material (deeds, state correspondence, decrees etc.) is preserved from the Fatimid period, e.g. the letters of the caliph al-Mustanṣir, ed. Magid (1954), and the Fatimid Decrees in Stern (1964). The Ayyubid and Mamluk epochs seem to be rich in this material, but so far only some parts have been made accessible or catalogued; useful introductions to these materials are Atiya (1955), for Ayyubid official documents, and Ernst (1960), for those of the Mamluk sultans.

For the period between *c.* 1000 and 1250 there is the unique collection of the so-called *Geniza* material found in the Old Cairo synagogue. It contains thousands of private letters and documents, which throw interesting light on economic, commercial and private life in Egypt and on the trade relations with other parts of the Muslim world as far as India. A systematic analysis with an attempt at synthesis is provided by Goitein (1967), of which two more volumes are expected. It should, however, be borne in mind that the Jewish communities were not in every respect representative of the whole Arab–Islamic social framework.

For the numismatics we have two catalogues (one of the most complete is Lane-Poole (1875–90), of which vol. IV deals with Egypt), and studies like those of Miles (1951) and P. Balog (1964). Epigraphic material is easily accessible either in the monumental *Corpus Inscriptionum Arabicarum* (CIA), of which the first part deals with Egypt, and was edited by van Berchem (1894–1903) and Wiet (1929–30), or in the more manageable *Répertoire chronologique d'épigraphie arabe*, edited by Combe, Sauvaget and Wiet, in 15 vols. (1931–57), which runs till 1346.

The various periods of Egyptian history under review are unevenly covered by the accessible contemporary narrative sources. The best situation obtains for the Ayyubids and the Burji Mamluks, whereas no early Fatimid chronicle has come down to us in a direct way. For a long time the history of the Bahri Mamluks was known largely through the medium of historians of the Burji period, a situation not without pitfalls; in recent years it has begun to improve through systematic study and publication of the relevant chronicles.

Even so, the list of published chronicles is very impressive, and the historian cannot complain about lack of information on various aspects of Egyptian political and cultural development. To chronicles and administrative manuals must be added the accounts of travellers who visited Egypt at various times, especially the narratives of Nāṣir-e Khosraw, translated by Schefer (1896); of Ibn Jubayr, by Broadhurst (1952); of Abd al-Laṭīf al-Baghdādī, by S. de Sacy (1810); and of Ibn Baṭṭūṭa, by Gibb (1962).

The following survey is restricted to the most important authors; the interested reader can find more information in Cahen (1965). Covering the whole period is al-Maqrīzī's *al-Khiṭaṭ*, a topographical and archaeological work containing a meticulous description of Egypt; unfortunately it has not yet been translated in its entirety into any European language, and the complete Arabic editions (1853, 1906) are mediocre and without indexes. Of importance among universal histories that include Egypt is the work of Ibn al-Athīr (d. 1234), not always accurate in detail but with a truly historical outlook; the edition by Tornberg (1851–76) is not among the best. The compilation of Abu'l-Fidā (d. 1331), although shorter than that of Ibn al-Athīr, has the advantage of using many unpublished sources and of being translated into Latin, by Reiske (1778).

As stated above, no early Fatimid chronicle has survived directly, but much material has come down in later compilations. The best of these is al-Maqrīzī's *Itti'āẓ al-ḥunafā'bi-akhbār al-a'imma al-fāṭimiyyin al-khulafā'*, edited by G. al-Shayyal (1967, not complete), or the sixth volume of the great *Chronicle* of Ibn al-Dawādarī (d. 1313), edited by S. al-Munajjid (1961), both written from the Sunni point of view.

As the late Fatimid period and that of the Ayyubids coincides largely with the Crusades, they are much better provided with published or translated source material. Extracts from Arabic chronicles are accessible in the *Recueil des historiens des Croisades: historiens orientaux* (1872–1906); this edition has many defects and has to be used with caution. Excellent, even if shorter and presented only in translations, is Gabrieli, *Arab historians of the Crusades* (1969). The majority of contemporary sources deal more with Palestine and Syria; Egypt itself is not neglected, but is treated rather perfunctorily. The same applies to the biographies of Ṣalāḥ al-Dīn, mentioned in the text, and to other chronicles written mostly by Syrians. A remarkable account of Egyptian financial and economic systems is Ibn al-Mammātī (d. 1209), *Kitāb qawānīn ad-dawānīn* ('Book of chancery rules'), edited by Atiya (1943). Not without interest are the contemporary autobiographies such as the *Memoirs of an Arab-Syrian gentleman* by Usāma ibn Munkidh (d. 1188), translated by Hitti (1929), or that of 'Umarā of Yemen, edited and translated by Dérenbourg (1897–1904).

As indicated, the Mamluk epoch abounds in rich and accurate historiographical writing, but until lately the Burji period has been better provided with editions than has that of the Bahris. In recent years this situation has begun to change, and much attention is paid to the thirteenth- and fourteenth-century chroniclers. Besides Ashtor's study, 'Some unpublished sources for the Baḥrī period', in Heyd (1961), there are important works on this subject by Little (1970), Haarman (1970), and Schäfer (1971). It is to be expected that many important chronicles will soon be published. A start was made by Roemer's model edition of the ninth volume of Ibn al-Dawādarī's *Chronicle* (1960), dealing with the time of al-Malik al-Nāṣir.

Among the works already published should be mentioned: Ibn 'Abd al-Ẓāhir's biography of Baybars, translated by Sadeque (1956), and that of Khalīl, edited with a Swedish translation by Moberg (1902); also, the anonymous chronicle of the years 1291–1340, published by Zetterstéen (1919), and last but not least the chronicle of the Christian writer Mufaḍḍal ibn Abī'l-Faḍā'il (*fl.* 1358), which was edited and translated (not very well) by Blochet in *Patrologia Orientalis* (1919–28).

For the whole Mamluk period the student has a large number of excellent sources at his disposal. There is again the indefatigable al-Maqrīzī, with his *Kitāb al-sulūk li-ma'rifat duwal al-mulūk*, a chronicle running till 1440; apart from the ancient and partial (covering 1250–1308) but still useful translation with commentary by Quatremère (1837–45), there is a very good edition by Ziyada (1934–58). Similarly indispensable is the monumental work of Ibn Taghrībirdī (d. 1470) called *Al-nujūm al-ẓāhira*, which covers Egyptian history from the Arab conquest until 1467 and is specially important for the Burji period. A full edition (1929–50) is now accessible, and also a partial one, by Popper (1919–36). The same American scholar translated parts of it under the title *History of Egypt 1382–1469 AD* (1952–8). The last decades of Mamluk rule and the beginning of the Ottoman domination are described in detail by Ibn Iyās (d. 1524); Wiet translated these parts of his chronicle under the title *Journal d'un bourgeois du Caire* (1955–60).

The Mamluk period was rich in various kinds of administrative, chancery and financial manuals. Al-'Umarī's work, *Masālik al-abṣār* (unsatisfactory edition, 1924), has not as yet been fully exploited for Egypt proper. The classical representative of this genre remains al-Qalqashandī's *Ṣubḥ al-A'shā* (a good Cairene edition in 14 vols., 1913–19); it is a real mine of documents and information about all aspects of Egyptian history in the fourteenth and fifteenth centuries. A good introduction to this manual is given in Björkmann (1928). *Zubdat kashf al-mamālik* by Khalīl al-Ẓāhirī (d. 1486) presents a very interesting picture of the whole Mamluk state and army; it was edited by Ravaisse (1894), and there exists also a translation by Venture de Paradis (1950). Of the first importance for feudal and fiscal conditions is Ibn al-Ji'ān's *Kitāb al-tuḥfa al-sānīyya*, edited by Moritz (1898), a sort of cadastral survey from the end of the fifteenth century.

The modern historical literature is uneven both in quantity and quality. There is, of course, a large amount of general or more detailed work in Arabic by Egyptian scholars, but for obvious reasons this survey will be confined only to works written in European languages.

No history of medieval Egypt corresponding to modern requirements exists. The book by Lane-Poole, *A history of Egypt in the Middle Ages* (1901, often reprinted), is a solid work on political history, reliable in chronology but inadequate in all other aspects. Wiet's *L'Egypte arabe*, which forms vol. IV of Hanotaux, ed., *Histoire de la nation Egyptienne* (1937), is the only good general survey of the period, despite the fact that it was published prior to several noteworthy sources and studies. Less penetrating, but with excellent chapters on art and architecture, is the same author's *L'Egypte byzantine et musulmane*, which forms vol. II of the *Précis de l'histoire d'Egypte* (1932).

No better is the situation with regard to dynastic histories: for the Fatimids, apart from the obsolete book by Wüstenfeld (1881), only the rather popularized work by O'Leary de Lacy (1923) can be mentioned. In contrast, two books by Lewis, *The origins of Isma'ilism* (1940) and *The Assassins* (1967), even if focussed more on sectarian history, throw much new light on the political and social aspects of the period. Becker's *Beiträge zur Geschichte Ägyptens unter dem Islam* (1902–3) is a stimulating work, notwithstanding the tendency of the author to modernize the historical process.

As could be expected, the epoch of the Crusades has found numerous historians, but the majority of them treat it from a Eurocentric view. A more balanced exposition is given in Setton et al. (eds.), *A history of the Crusades* (1955, 1962), which contains excellent chapters about the Muslim Near East by Lewis, Cahen, Gibb and Mustafa Ziyada. Atiya's *Crusade, commerce and culture* (1962) is a broad picture of mutual influences that could serve as a supplement to the predominantly political approach of the two Setton volumes. The main protagonists did not fail to find their biographers, although Ṣalāḥ al-Dīn still awaits a large scale monograph; Lane-Poole's book on Saladin (1898) is today obsolete and should be read with caution, whereas the new biography by Ehrenkreutz (1972) is rather too concise. More critical and fully documented are the biographies of Nūr al-Dīn by Elisséeff (1967) and of *Al-Malik al-Kāmil*, by Gottschalk (1958). There is still no overall modern history of the Ayyubids.

The same is true for the Mamluk period, although various aspects have been discussed in a number of monographs. Weil's *Geschichte der Chalifen*, vols. IV and V (1860–2), is a pedestrian narrative of political events, obsolete and useful only for the chronological sequence. Some modern biographies treat the epoch of their heroes in a wider context; for example, Schregle's life of Sağarat ad-Durr (1961), or Sadeque's life of Baybars I (1956); the best among them is Darrag's study of Egypt during the reign of Barsbay (1961).

In recent decades research in social and economic history has made great progress. Although many of the author's conclusions have to be accepted with caution, *Feudalism in Egypt, Syria, Palestine and the Lebanon*, by Poliak (1939), together with his numerous articles, remains a pioneer study, with valuable source material. On a much higher theoretical level and more penetrating are many studies by Cahen on social and economic development; one of the most important is his 'L'évolution de l'iqṭa' du IXe au XIIIe siècle' (1953). An attempt at Marxist interpretation is Semenova's work on Ṣālāḥ al-Dīn and the Mamluks in Egypt (1966), the merit of which lies mainly in the painstaking study of the changes in the landholding system, with their impact on economic and social relations. Not so ambitious, but nevertheless very useful, is Popper's *Egypt and Syria under the Circassian Sultans* (1955–7), which contains systematic notes on geography, political administration, fiefs, prices, salaries etc. Financial and monetary history under the Ayyubids was studied in a number of articles by Ehrenkreutz, mainly in *BSOAS* (1953–4), *JAOS* (1954–6) and *JESHO* (1959). Ashtor's *Histoire des prix et des salaires dans l'Orient mediéval* (1969) summarizes previous studies in a synthetical way and throws new light on many sides of the internal history.

Studies in trade and commercial relations, having a longer tradition than those dealing with social history, have the advantage of treating Egyptian history in a wider context. Two older books by Heyd (1885, 1923) and Schaube (1906) are indispensable for their wealth of material, whereas *Medieval trade in the Mediterranean world*, edited by Lopez and Raymond (1955), is more thematic and treats the subject from a wider perspective. The best economic history so far is Labib's *Handelsgeschichte Ägyptens im Spätmittelalter, 1171–1517* (1965), an exhaustive study which combines detailed analysis with an attempt at synthetic treatment. The *Kārimi* merchants have been the objects of many studies, the best among them being an article by Fischel (1937), and Wiet's *Les marchands d'épices sous les Mamluks* (1955).

There is a series of studies about the structure of the Mamluk army by Ayalon (1953–4), as well as his book about the status of slaves (1951). The challenge of the gunpowder revolution to the Mamluk society and its consequences are analysed by the same author in an important study *Gunpowder and firearms in the Mamluk Kingdom* (1956), which is supplemented by his *The Mamluks and naval power* (1965). Several other aspects of the Mamluk period are dealt with by Sauvaget, *La poste aux chevaux dans l'empire des Mamlouks* (1941), which combines narrative sources with archaeological material, Wiet's 'Le traité des famines de Maqrīzī' (1962), and Clerget, *Le Caire, étude de géographie urbain et d'histoire économique* (1934).

So far there is no general study on Egyptian relations with other parts of Africa; the material is dispersed in works on trade and commerce or in studies on separate documents. For Ethiopia there is a very useful paper by Wiet, 'Les relations égypto-abyssines sous les Mamluks' (1938). Of importance is the recent book of Rotter, *Die Stellung des Negers in der islamisch-arabischen Gesellschaft bis zum 16. Jhdt* (1967), which surveys attitudes towards black Africans in the entire Middle East, including Egypt.

For the history of art, Creswell's monumental *Muslim Architecture of Egypt* (1952–9) is indispensable. Locally restricted, but full of important material, is Hautecoeur and Wiet, *Les mosquées du Caire* (1932). Mayer's *Saracenic heraldry* (1933) and *Mamluk costume* (1952) have detailed material for the study of minor arts.

In contrast to Egypt, the source material for Nubia and the Sudan is scarce and dispersed. A survey of the major Arabic sources for the history of the Sudan in the Middle Ages is given as an appendix to Hasan's *The Arabs and the Sudan* (1967).

The best history of Christian Nubia is still that by Monneret de Villard (1938), although written before the period of the systematic archaeological campaigns in the north since 1945. Arkell's *A history of the Sudan from the earliest times to 1821* (1955) concerns mainly the history before the advent of the Arabs and is not free in its medieval parts from some strange hypotheses. MacMichael (1922) is a huge collection of Arabic classical and tribal source material, and as such indispensable, but it lacks the necessary synthesis. The first attempt to give a coherent picture of the Arab and Islamic penetration is Trimingham (1949); though now superseded by Hasan (1967), it gives a clear and penetrating study of all aspects of the arabization of the northern Sudan. The Beja were the object of a mediocre study by Paul (1954).

2. ETHIOPIA, THE RED SEA AND THE HORN

In terms of the bibliographical material, it may be useful to consider this chapter as consisting of two periods with the fourteenth century as an important dividing line. The first of these periods is characterized by the predominance of foreign Arabic sources. Contemporary historical references to the Ethiopian region prior to about 1300 can be gleaned from the works of the major Arab geographers and historians from the end of the ninth century onwards. But, in almost all cases, these references are very brief and often present serious difficulties of interpretation, and the placenames and peoples cited cannot always be definitively identified. Nevertheless, handled with care, and compared, whenever this is possible, with local traditions and other material, they have been most useful in providing a meaningful picture of the history of the area. Three outstanding studies covering the whole area which have been able to make excellent use of the sources in this regard are Conti Rossini's *Storia d'Etiopia* (1928), Kammerer's *La Mer rouge, l'Abyssinie et l'Arabie depuis l'antiquité* (especially vol. 1, 1929), and Cerulli's *Somalia, scritti vari editi ed inediti* (especially vol. 1, 1957).

Conti Rossini has looked into the most significant and relevant Arabic documents and, with his absolute command of the historical traditions of Ethiopia, has left us a very careful critical analysis of Ethiopian history until AD 1270. For the period with which we are concerned here, his views will have to remain the standard interpretation except on some minor issues which have been raised in the text of this chapter. But it is difficult for the student to use and to follow up this work because it does not have annotations or a bibliography; and even the index of the book has only recently been prepared by Ullendorff (1962). A complete re-edition of the whole book in a more accessible language like English seems to be long overdue. The first volume of Kammerer's major work also follows the known Arabic writers, whom he uses for the study of the long interaction among the countries on either side of the Red Sea down to the sixteenth century. But in his general treatment of the period he reflects the emphases of his Arabic sources, for the authors of which Arabia was of course of much greater concern; and the coverage of the African side of the story tends to be peripheral. In all these cases, it will be helpful to make direct use of the sources, among which the most useful and easily accessible are Umarā's *Yaman, its early medieval history* (1892), and al-Khazraji's *History of the Resuli dynasty of Yemen* (1907). For a closer look at local developments on the African coast and interior, the studies made by Basset (1893), Pansera (1945), and Schneider (1967) on the Arabic inscriptions from the Dahlak islands and from Qiha in Tigre are essential. Cerulli's 'Il sultanato dello Scioa' (1941) should also be read with these local Arabic documents. Another set of valuable sources for the first part of this chapter comes from the Coptic Church. The most useful in this category are the *History of the patriarchs of Alexandria*, which refers to

Ethiopia from time to time, and Abū Ṣāliḥ's *Churches and monasteries* (1895). However, just like their Muslim counterparts, the chroniclers of the Egyptian Church display a rather superficial knowledge of Ethiopian affairs and, sometimes, they even confuse Christian Nubia and Ethiopia. Most of the historical traditions transmitted by the Christian Egyptian sources have been rendered into Ge'ez and have become integral parts of the Ethiopian *Synaxarium*, of which Budge has made an English translation in *The book of the saints* (1928). These Ge'ez translations were obviously made under the auspices of the Egyptian bishops to Ethiopia, and they often distort the Arabic original whenever it was felt necessary to place the patriarchate in a better historical light as well as to perpetuate Egyptian supremacy in the relations between the two churches. Except for the Arabic documents cited above, reliable historical sources from the Ethiopian region itself are very few for this period. The highly self-contradictory king-lists of both Aksumite and Zagwe days, the memorials of some early land grants, and the stereotyped historical traditions about the most significant monastic communities and individual monarchs provide us with only the barest skeletal framework and, just like the foreign Arab documents, they also present considerable problems of interpretation and dating. The extent of the difficulty may be seen, for instance, in Budge's *History of Ethiopia* (1928) and in the recent book by the Ethiopian historian Sergew Hable-Sellassie, *Ancient and medieval Ethiopian history to 1270* (1972).

The first volume of Cerulli's *Somalia* is actually a compilation of separate articles mostly published earlier, and they all reflect the very high standard of scholarship which always marks his writings. Foreign Arabic references to the Somali coast and the Horn, inscriptions from Mogadishu and other settlements on the Benadir coast, relevant Ethiopian Christian sources, and the rich historical traditions of the Somali people have all been studied carefully and in detail. One major drawback has been his view that, ever since the thirteenth century, the expansion of the Somali in the interior of the Horn has been mainly at the expense of the Galla, who, he believes, preceded them in the occupancy of the area. From their original habitat between Tajura and Cape Guardafui in the immediate hinterland of the Gulf, Cerulli believes, the early Somali fought the Galla, pushing them ever southwards out of the interior of northern, central and southern Somalia. Although no tangible evidence is presented for this Somali–Galla confrontation in the area prior to the sixteenth century, this assertion litters all his writings on the Horn; and he has been followed in this by most later writers. However, Fleming's 'Baiso and Rendille' (1964) and Lewis's 'The origins of the Galla and Somali' (1966) have placed the issue in its right perspective and it will be useful to read them in connection with Cerulli's *Somalia.* Robert Hetzron's *Ethiopian Semitic* (1972) is of significance for the new light which it sheds on the early history of the speakers of the Semitic languages of northern and central Ethiopia.

For the period after about 1300, local historical sources clearly dominate the scene, particularly in the Christian empire. The major royal chronicles have been edited and translated into French and Italian, respectively, by Perruchon (1889, 1893, 1894) and Conti Rossini (1894). Huntingford's *Glorious victories* (1965) is a new English rendering of the chronicle of Amda-Siyon (1314–44), but his long introduction should be read with much caution, particularly as regards the proposed identification of placenames. Other free translations of the chronicles into English may be found in vol. II of James Bruce's *Travels* (1790) and Budge's *History of Ethiopia* (1928). The few published land grants may be seen in Conti Rossini's *Liber Axumae* (1910), Huntingford's *The land charters of northern Ethiopia* (1965) and Tamrat's 'The abbots of Debre Hayq' (1970). By far the most important documents for this period are the Ethiopian hagiographies, some of which have been edited and translated by the leading European scholars on Ethiopia, but they are too numerous to be discussed severally here. The writer has attempted to make some use of them in his *Church and state* (1972), where they are all listed together with other still unpublished ones. Of the foreign Arabic sources the section on Ethiopia in al-'Umari's *Masālik* (1927), Maqrīzī's narrative as edited and translated by Rinck in *Historia* (1970), and Cerulli's 'L'Etiopia medievale in alcuni brani di scrittori arabi' (1943) are the most accessible; but there are also many other isolated references in the chronicles of the Mamluk rulers of Egypt. Two important local Arabic documents are Arab-Faqih's *Futūḥ al Ḥabasha* as edited and translated by Basset, *Histoire de la conquête* (1897–1901), and Cerulli's 'Documenti arabi per la storia dell'Etiopia' (1931). Very good use of all these has been made in Trimingham's brief discussion of the period covered in this chapter in his *Islam in Ethiopia* (1952). This second period is also noted for the existence of some European documents on Ethiopia. The most important of these may be seen in Cerulli's most valuable *Etiopi in Palestina* (1943–7), de la Roncière's *La découverte de l'Afrique* (1924–7) and

Crawford's *Ethiopian itineraries* (1958). For the last fifty years of the period two very useful additional readings are the early chapters of Merid Wolde-Aregay's excellent Ph.D. thesis, 'Southern Ethiopia and the Christian Kingdom, 1508–1708' (1971) and *The question of the union of the churches in Luso-Ethiopian relations, 1500–1632* (1964), which he wrote jointly with Girmah Beshah.

3. THE EAST COAST, MADAGASCAR AND THE INDIAN OCEAN

The early written sources can be conveniently considered in two categories, 'external sources' written by people living outside East Africa and those set down by authors living on the coast itself, here referred to as 'internal sources'.

After the time when Ptolemy's *Geography* reached its final form, there is a long period during which practically nothing is to be learnt about East Africa from external sources. The earliest of the Arab geographers to provide us with information is al-Jāḥiẓ, in the ninth century. His writings contain a little of value on the social organization of the Zanj. They are amplified by the much fuller accounts by al-Mas'ūdī, who wrote in the middle of the tenth century, but whose information refers largely to a rather earlier date. His work is far and away the most important for this period, and the more valuable because he himself visited the coast, or at least the island of *Qanbalū* (Pemba) on two or more occasions, so that some of what he writes is based on personal observation. His work is supplemented by that of a near contemporary, Buzurg b. Shahriyār (1966). In 1154 al-Idrīsī finished his work *Nuzhat al-mushtāq* (1866). This description of the world is based on second-hand information, and so far as East Africa is concerned identification of the numerous placenames, which probably extend down as far as the region of the Limpopo, is in most cases very problematical. Idrīsī's work is supplemented by Ibn Sa'īd, writing a century later, who incorporates new material concerning Africa from a lost book by Ibn Fāṭima; he gives valuable information relating to the Indonesian immigration to Madagascar. Yāqūt's geographical dictionary, *Mu'jam al-buldān* (1866), written between 1212 and 1229, has information about Mogadishu, some of which at least we know from the observations of Ibn Baṭṭūṭa to be accurate; he also provides information about Pemba which he states to be derived from a named eyewitness. The author of the *Tārīkh al-Mustabṣīr* (1919), written in 1232, reputed to be Ibn al-Mujāwir, appears to have been critical about his informants, and provides information about the Indonesians and the voyage to Madagascar.

The great traveller Ibn Baṭṭūṭa visited the coast, probably in 1332; his account of his voyages (1922), though precious, was dictated many years after his visit. His information is confined to the towns of Mogadishu and Kilwa, with a brief reference to Mombasa.

The most complete and recent redaction of Arabic writers relevant to Africa is in Russian, with Arabic text, edited by Kubbel and Matveyev (1960, 1965); this work is of uneven quality, but contains valuable annotated indices. In other languages the works of Ferrand (1891–1902, 1913–14, 1919) remain valuable for their presentation of early sources. There are translations of most of the relevant Arabic documents in Guillain's (1845, 1848) works, which, however, are most valuable for the information they provide about Madagascar and the coast in the 1840s, and the traditions then remembered by the inhabitants.

The Chinese, from the ninth century onwards, wrote quite extensively about *Barabara* and *Zangibar*, but their work is based entirely on second-hand information, derived from Arab and Persian merchants. Their writings add little to what we learn from the Arabs; where they do, the information is sometimes patently inaccurate, which leads one to question the accuracy of the remainder. Relevant extracts are set out by Duyvendak (1949) and Filesi (1972).

A great many Portuguese documents contemporary with the events they describe survive, as well as formal histories. The descriptions of the cities as they found them on their first voyages are most valuable for filling in our picture of the coastal civilization. There is heavy emphasis on Mozambique, and on Mombasa and towns north thereof. A valuable compendium of Portuguese documents is provided in Theal's *Records of south-eastern Africa* (1964); some are reproduced more handily in Freeman-Grenville's *East African coast* (1962), which gives translations of most of the relevant passages of the Arab authors as well. An exhaustive collection of documents (in Portuguese with English translations) from this source is in course of publication under the title *Documents on the Portuguese in Mozambique and Central Africa* (ed. da Silva Rego and Baxter); the first seven volumes cover the period 1497–1560. These include much detailed material covering the administration of Kilwa and Sofala, lists of personnel and the like. It is planned that the work will eventually extend up to 1840. A detailed account of the expansion of the Portuguese in Mozambique up to 1530 is given in three volumes of Lobato's (1954–60) book. Attention is also called to the works of Eric Axelson (1940, 1960). Strandes' work, translated as *The Portuguese period in East Africa* (1968), remains the best general survey of the Portuguese period.

The second, 'internal' group of sources consists of documents written on the coast in Arabic, or in Swahili in Arabic script. Most are chronicles of individual towns or city-states, and profess to give an account of events, and in particular the succession of rulers, over some centuries. They have been accepted until recently at much too near their face value.

Much the earliest, and by far the most valuable of these internal sources, are the Kilwa chronicles. Of these chronicles, one version is in Arabic, originally written about 1520 or 1530; it survives only in a copy made in Zanzibar in 1877 (published by Strong, 1895). The other is preserved by the Portuguese historian João de Barros in his *Da Asia* (1552–1613). Translations of the texts of these are set out in Freeman-Grenville's *Medieval history* (1962), together with a commentary.

Most of the rest of the internal sources were set down only recently, and none can be traced back beyond the second half of the eighteenth century. They include the various versions of the 'Chronicle of Pate', the 'Chronicle of Lamu', and that of Mombasa; there are also a number of lesser documents dealing with Zanzibar and Pemba. The most remarkable of these works is the *Kitāb al-Zanūj*, or *Book of the Zanj*. The two surviving versions date from after 1900, and appear to have been a compendium of more than one earlier source. This work alone has accounts of pre-Islamic settlement of the coast from south Arabia, but these accounts are wholly without confirmation. Traditions of settlement under the Umayyads appear both in this work and also in the Chronicles of Pate; these traditions are very suspect. The *Book of the Zanj* is most valuable for the traditions it transmits about the region of Shungwaya, the Bantu-speaking *Kashūr* who inhabited it, and their relations with Muslim immigrants. In respect of the first two of these there is considerable confirmation in the oral traditions of the present-day Miji Kenda, or Nyika tribes of the hinterland of the Kenya coast.

The historical sources are supplemented by the evidence of archaeology. Serious work in this field was begun by J. S. Kirkman on the Kenya coast at the end of the 1940s, and was extended through the establishment of the British Institute in Eastern Africa in 1960. Archaeological work has been undertaken at numerous sites, and large-scale excavations carried out at Gedi, near Malindi, and at Kilwa. The work at the latter, combined with a re-examination of the versions of the Kilwa Chronicle, has led the writer to put forward new views on the chronology and other aspects of the early history of the coast, set out in 'The "Shirazi" colonization of the East African coast' (1965). His *Kilwa* (2 vols., 1974) gives a detailed description of the monuments, excavations and finds at the town site. The various versions of the Pate Chronicle, and archaeological evidence bearing thereon, are examined by the writer in 'A new look at the history of Pate' (1969), and 'Discoveries in the Lamu archipelago' (1967); the latter also gives a preliminary account of the early site of Manda. The most promising sites for further excavation are probably in Pemba and at Unguja Ukuu in Zanzibar.

Kirkman's *Men and monuments on the East African coast* (1964) provides a conspectus of the relics of the coastal towns; his other works are detailed reports on excavations. The early architecture of the coast is examined in Garlake's (1966) work on the subject.

The ethnography of most of the region with which we are concerned is covered by volumes in the Ethnographic Survey of Africa, notably those by Prins (1967) and Lewis (1955). The collected essays in Cerulli's *Somalia* (1957) are also important, and include a redaction of the *Kitāb al-Zunūj*, with translation in Italian. Grottanelli's *Pescatori dell'oceano Indiano* (1955) gives an extended account of the Bajun. Whiteley's *Swahili* (1969) is the best general work on the language with a brief account of its origins.

For Madagascar, Deschamps' *Histoire de Madagascar* (1961) is the most useful general work, now supplemented by the work of Kent (1970), some of whose views are open to dispute. The ethnography of the island is dealt with at length in A. and G. Grandidier's (1908–28) work on the subject. Their *Collections des ouvrages anciens concernant Madagascar* (1903–20), and G. Grandidier's *Histoire politique et coloniale* (1942–58) may also be consulted. Dahl (1951) and Dez (1963) have written recently on the question of linguistic origins. Early work on the archaeology of Madagascar – chiefly on the Vohémar tombs, by Gaudebout and Vernier (1941) – is being greatly amplified and corrected by P. Vérin, whose thesis *Les échelles anciennes du commerce sur les côtes nord de Madagascar* provides an up-to-date and exhaustive survey.

4. THE EASTERN MAGHRIB AND THE CENTRAL SUDAN

The sources for the history of the central Sahara and Sudan during the period AD 1050 to 1600 are rather similar to, and in many cases identical with, those discussed for the seventeenth and eighteenth centuries (see Volume 4, pp. 626–9). Of the two bibliographies, the one here is the fuller and more up to date, but the two may usefully be consulted together. Very extensive bibliographies for some parts of the area have recently been published, for example Schlüter (1972) for Libya, and Moreau and Stordeur (1970) for Tchad.

Contemporary written accounts survive from each stage, even the earliest, of the period. Many of these are external, the work of geographers and scholars outside the area. The Arabic sources of this kind, too numerous to list individually here, receive useful and detailed discussion in Lewicki (1969; see also Wansbrough, 1970), and many are reproduced in Youssouf Kamal (1926–51). The work of discovering material relevant for black Africa, but tucked away in relatively obscure Arabic sources, continues gradually, and is far from complete: Sartain (1971), using among other things unpublished biographies from sixteenth-century Cairo, provides a good example of what may be done. Turkish materials appear on the scene rather late, but Martin (1962, 1972) well illustrates the potential value and interest of these. European sources are by contrast very few, though those which do exist may provide valuable information (e.g. Lange, 1972). Leo Africanus bridges the Arabic and European worlds, being a North African writing in Italy; and he is of exceptional importance to us since his account is one of the fullest, and is apparently based to a considerable extent on his own observations, for he visited the Sudan countries probably early in the second decade of the sixteenth century. Leo has appeared recently in an excellent modern French translation (by Épaulard and others, 1956); but, alas, grave uncertainty still attends any attempt accurately to assess his information about the Sudan, at least east of Timbuktu. Mauny (1954) discusses the evidence in favour of Leo as an accurate Sudan traveller, perhaps a little too respectfully; for a specific example of the difficulties, see the current controversy over the location of Leo's Gaoga, with Kalck (1972) and O'Fahey and Spaulding (1973) advocating radically opposed views.

Among documents written within the central Sudan, two works are of outstanding importance, the Kano Chronicle, and the incomplete biography which Aḥmad b. Fartuwa wrote of his patron, Mai Idrīs

Aloma, who ruled Bornu at the end of the sixteenth century. Of the two, the Kano Chronicle covers a far wider time span, while Ibn Fartuwa has the advantage of being a contemporary, often an eyewitness, of the events which he describes. To Palmer we are indebted for English translations of both, and recent reprints (Palmer, 1967 and 1970) make these translations far more widely available. Critical editions, however, are still lacking. There are a number of shorter documents as well; a wide variety appears in Palmer (1936). Of special importance are the *maḥrams*, or letters granting some special privilege (such as exemption from taxation), and *girgams*, or king-lists. Palmer (1912–13) has published such lists; two more are included in Palmer (1970), and Barth (1965) and Nachtigal (1967) give similar information. The lists do not all agree; Urvoy (1941) and Cohen ('Lists', 1966) discuss some of the problems involved. Cohen proposes a tentative reconciliation of the various versions, not attempting specific dates but only periods.

The arrival of Europeans in the nineteenth century, first as travellers, later as rulers, led to the creation of an important new dimension to our sources. Among the travellers, Barth and Nachtigal are pre-eminent; the former is already well known, and with the gradual progress of an English translation of the latter he should become increasingly, and deservedly, familiar to African and other scholars concerned with the central Sahara and Sudan. Some of the raw material gathered in the European colonial period has become more widely available with the recent reprint of the northern Nigerian gazetteers (Kirk-Greene, 1972); Hogben and Kirk-Greene (1966) offer an historical survey based in considerable measure upon such information.

Linguistic evidence has for some time been recognized as a possible source of historical enlightenment: Palmer, for example, attempted this in his *Sudanese memoirs* (1967). But it is only recently that a strict scientific appraisal has begun. Greenberg (1964) explains some of the pitfalls into which earlier scholars have fallen. Abdullahi Smith (in Ajayi and Crowder, 1971) points the way ahead most interestingly for the central Sudan; and a number of articles, sometimes at odds with one another – e.g. Greenberg (1947) and Hiskett ('The historical background', 1965) – argue particular points. Skinner (1968), for instance, suggests that linguistic similarities between Hausa and Songhay seem to lend weight to the view that the Songhay conquest of Hausaland at the beginning of the sixteenth century had a profound influence, a view which, as has been shown (pp. 298–9), is on other grounds rather suspect. The very name, 'Hausa', Skinner derives from the Songhay word for 'east'.

The archaeology of the central Sudan will undoubtedly teach us a great deal; but at the moment even the information which has been collected and published is widely scattered, and still waits for a master hand to marshal it all. There are numerous articles, some of them very brief (e.g. Binet, 1952, and Bivar and Shinnie, 1962); two which deserve particular mention, since they give not only archaeological information but also essential bibliographical directions, are Connah (1971) and Shaw (1969). The work of the Lebeufs also contains much of archaeological interest.

Increasing attention has recently been paid to the value of oral tradition in reconstructing the African past. Low (1972) in particular has attempted this for the central Sudan, and has paid close attention to the methodological problems involved. But the reliance which may be placed upon oral tradition for events of between three and nine centuries ago must be slight. That some value does survive, however, is clear from some songs and poetry which have been published (e.g. Hiskett, 1964–5, and Patterson, 1926). Anthropology, like oral tradition, operates at a disadvantage over such a long time-span, although it may help us to reconstruct the life-styles of earlier times. Some examples (e.g. Nadel, 1942, and Nicolaisen, 1964) have been included; there are, of course, others.

North Africa has a much more highly developed historiographical tradition. This received its classic expression in Julien (1970, first published in 1931); Abun-Nasr (1971), writing more recently, supplies a good survey of North African history, while still standing essentially in the old tradition. Precisely because this tradition exists, the task of re-evaluating the historical evidence and the hitherto received interpretations has been more urgent. The phrase, *décoloniser l'histoire*, 'to de-colonize history', accurately summarizes the ideals of the new school. Wansbrough (1968) briefly discusses some of the major issues involved. Poncet (1967) and Brett (1970) explore one particular episode, that of the arrival of the Banū Hilāl, in depth. Laroui (1970) attempts, in a stimulating way, to survey the new perspectives on a wider stage. In the Sudan, too, it is clear that the rise of nationalism and the coming of independence have likewise been reflected in historiography as in other spheres. Armstrong (1960) and Smith (1970) address themselves directly to the task of such revision; the same trend is clear in Ajayi and Crowder (1971). The new views undoubtedly contribute to a more complete understanding of African history, especially by their emphasis upon the importance of the local, indigenous heritage; whether they in themselves offer a complete understanding, or whether the pendulum must some day swing back a little from present exuberance, is a question the future will resolve.

5. THE WESTERN MAGHRIB AND SUDAN

In the ninth and tenth centuries most of the Arabic sources bearing on the history of the western Sudan were written in the eastern parts of the Muslim world, and mainly by authors of Iranian origin. From the eleventh century onwards most of our sources were written in the Muslim West, by historians, geographers and travellers from Spain and the Maghrib. With improved communications across the Sahara, some of these authors had reliable information recorded from traders who visited the Sudan and from Sudanese pilgrims who visited the Maghrib. Still, for the first eyewitness report we have to wait until the mid fourteenth century for Ibn-Baṭṭūṭa's journey to Mali.

Al-Bakrī, writing in 1067/8, is our principal source for the western Sudan on the eve of the Almoravid conquest. The twelfth-century authors (al-Idrīsī, al-Ẓuhrī and Abū Ḥāmid al-Andalusī) provide some incoherent information about the consequences of the Almoravid intervention in the Sudan. Contemporary evidence in the thirteenth century is of lesser value, because writers of that century (Ibn al-Athīr, Ibn Sa'īd, Yāqūt and al-Qazwīnī) derive much of their information from earlier sources. The fourteenth century, the apogee of Mali, is the best-documented period, with the accounts of al-'Umarī, based mainly on information recorded from Mansa Mūsā in Mali, the report of Ibn Baṭṭūṭa, who visited Mali in 1352–3, and the chronicle of Ibn Khaldūn, based on oral traditions. A late-sixteenth-century historian, al-Maqqarī, provided valuable information on the thirteenth century, based on archival records of his own family. A collection of these Arabic sources in English translation by J. F. P. Hopkins and N. Levtzion is forthcoming.

The decline of medieval Arab geography and historiography in the fifteenth century coincided with the exploration of the African coast by the Portuguese. The discovery of Africa by the Europeans is best documented by de la Roncière (1924–7). Whereas Arab authors viewed the western Sudan from across the Sahara, the Portuguese offered a different perspective from the coast. Zurara (1453; transl. by Bourdon,

1960) and V. Fernandes (1506–10; transl. by de Cenival et al., 1938, 1951) used other travellers' accounts for their compilations, while Cadamosto (1455–7; transl. by Schefer, 1895, Crone, 1937), Diogo Gomes (late fifteenth century; transl. by Monod et al., 1959) and Pacheco Pereira (*c.* 1508; transl. by Mauny, 1956), among others, reported their own personal experiences on the Atlantic coast of Africa. A unique combination of a Muslim's experience (across the Sahara) with an Italian Renaissance quest for knowledge is provided by Leo Africanus, who visited the Sudan *c.* 1512 as a Muslim and wrote his book as a Christian in 1526 (transl. by Épaulard, 1956).

During the fifteenth and sixteenth centuries Europeans were present along the Moroccan coasts both as aggressive invaders and as traders. Their reports are a mine of information, much of which was assembled in the monumental collection of archival sources by de Castries (1934–51).

A local tradition of historiography developed in the Maghrib under the Marinid dynasty in the fourteenth century. Ibn Abī Zar' (ed. by Tornberg, 1843–66), Ibn 'Idhārī (ed. by Dozy, 1848–51), and the anonymous authors of *Mafākhir al-Barbar* and *al-Ḥulal al-Mawshiya* recorded the history of the Maghrib in past centuries. There was a revival of Moroccan historiography under the Sharifian dynasties. Al-Fishtālī (d. 1621–2), a court official of al-Manṣūr, provided a favourable account of the Sa'dids (ed. by Ganun, 1964), which is balanced by the hostile *Chronique anonyme de la dynastie Sa'adienne* (ed. by Colin, 1934). The most important chronicle for the Sa'did dynasty was that of al-Ifrānī, written in 1738–9 (transl. by Houdas, 1888). A collection of letters from the chancellery of the Sa'dids has been edited by A. Ganun (1954).

In his brilliant analysis of Moroccan historiography under the Sharifian dynasties, Lévi-Provençal (1923) distinguished two principal categories of sources – namely, biographies and chronicles. It is significant that these two categories are found also in the historiography of Timbuktu between the sixteenth and eighteenth centuries, which was very probably influenced by historical writings in Morocco. The bibliographical literature of Timbuktu is represented by the *Nayl al-ibtihāj* of Aḥmad Bābā (1596). The two chronicles of Timbuktu, *Ta'rīkh al-Sūdān* (transl. by Houdas, 1900) by al-Sa'dī and *Ta'rīkh al-Fattāsh* (ed. by Houdas and Delafosse, 1913), by Ibn al-Mukhtār, were written in 1645 and 1655, respectively. (On the date and authorship of the latter, see Levtzion, *BSOAS*, 1971.) These chronicles provide detailed and reliable information about the Songhay empire in the sixteenth century.

A recent analytical bibliography of the Maghrib was prepared by Stewart, as an updating of the bibliography of C. A. Julien (1970). A translation of this work into English appeared at the same time as did the first comprehensive history of the Maghrib in English, by Abun-Nasr (1971), and with the book-length historical essay by A. Laroui (1970), a Moroccan historian and sociologist. The history of Morocco by Terrasse (1949) is still indispensable, and so is the religious history of the Maghrib by Bel (1938). For the study of Berber society and politics one must refer to the works of Montagne (1930, 1931; and in English translation, 1972), and of E. Gellner (1969, and many articles).

There are monographic studies of dynasties, such as the Almohads (by Huici-Miranda, 1956–7 and Le Tourneau, 1969), the Wattasids (by Cour, 1920), and the rise of the Sa'dids (Cour, 1904). Cities which were closely related to the rise and fall of dynasties have been treated in special studies: Tlemcen (Abbé Bargès, 1859; Marçais, 1951), Fez (Le Tourneau, 1961) and Marrakesh (Deverdun, 1952).

The Maghrib in the context of Mediterranean history has been brilliantly studied by Braudel (1960, English translation, 1972). Mas Latrie (1886) and Masson (1903) analysed in great detail the growth of European involvement in the Maghrib. Catalan relations with the Mediterranean coast were looked at by Dufourcq (1966), whereas Ricard (1955, and articles) was concerned with the Portuguese on the Atlantic coast of Morocco. Portuguese expansion and their trade along the coasts of Morocco and Africa were analysed in the monumental work of Magalhaes-Godinho (1969). Among the more important studies of the trans-Saharan trade are the works of Pérès (1937), Bovill (1968), Malowist (1966, 1968), and Devisse (1972).

The history of the western Sudan before 1500 as presented in this chapter is largely abstracted from Levtzion (1973). There are quite a few important studies of the empire of Mali in French, such as those by Delafosse, Monteil, Mauny, Niane, Cissoko, Person, Meillassoux, Dieterlen, Cissé and Lhote. Rouch (1953) pioneered the analytical study of the history of Songhay, but there is still a need for a new definitive history of that empire based on a critical reading of the chronicles of Timbuktu. The articles already published by Hunwick (1962–73) will, it is hoped, be followed by his book on Songhay.

A collection of traditions on the history of Futa Toro written in

Arabic by Siré Abbas Soh (1913) was translated into French and annotated by Gaden and Delafosse. Some Wolof traditions were edited by Monteil (1966). Walo is the only Wolof state the history of which has so far been studied in detail (Barry, 1972). Boulègue's doctoral dissertation (1968) on the Senegambia between the fifteenth and seventeenth centuries has broken new ground, but we still wait for its publication. Several papers on the Malinke state of Kabu on the Gambia will appear in the forthcoming two volumes of *Manding Studies* (Dalby, 1975). Farther to the south, the emergence of the Mossi-Dagomba group of states was studied by Fage (1964), Wilks (1971), Levtzion (1968), Izard (1970) and Benzing (1971).

The spread of Islam in West Africa has been surveyed and analysed by Trimingham (1962), Monteil (1964), Levtzion (1971), Stepniewska (1971) and Triaud (1973). Wilks (1968) has studied the transmission of Islamic learning in this area. Hunwick (1966) and Cissoko (1969) have written about the growth of Islamic scholarship in Timbuktu and the role of this town in the Songhay empire. Other aspects of the history of Timbuktu have been dealt with by Norris (1967), M'Baye (1972) and Batrān (1973).

Students of the history of the western Sudan from the eleventh to the sixteenth century have, therefore, a variety of Arabic and Portuguese contemporary sources. There is also an impressive number of modern studies of that period in French, whereas studies in English have only recently been added.

6. UPPER AND LOWER GUINEA

As is probably sufficiently evident from the discussion in the first section of the chapter, the period between the middle of the eleventh and the end of the sixteenth centuries in the history of Guinea is something of a *terra incognita* lying between the frontiers of archaeological and of historical enquiry. There is a further problem in that Guinea has been essentially partitioned between British and French traditions of scholarship, which have not always proceeded in quite the same directions; which, when they have so proceeded, often have not always moved at the same pace; and between which there has sometimes been alarmingly little co-operation.

In these circumstances, it is hardly surprising that there is really no wholly satisfactory general treatment of the period. From the historian's side of the frontier, the major achievement is undoubtedly the first volume of *The history of West Africa*, edited by Ajayi and Crowder, and first published in 1971. Unfortunately, however, these editors seem to have decided that the effective frontier of endeavour by historians for the Guinea region lay in the sixteenth century. Their relevant contributors, Alagoa and Suret-Canale, Akinjogbin and Wilks (the unexpected death of Robert Bradbury left a lacuna for Yorubaland and Benin, though this will be remedied in the second edition now in progress), do often trespass across this frontier, but there is no coherent historical treatment of earlier times. These are left for a useful, though dated archaeological essay by Shaw (written in 1966), and an interesting essay on stateless societies by Horton. On the archaeological side, Davies's *West Africa before the Europeans* (1967), also now somewhat dated, is concerned mainly with the Stone Age, and says little about the important work which has been done in Nigeria. (Luckily this can be remedied through the publications of the Faggs, Shaw, Willett, Connah etc., a selection of which are given in the bibliography.) A better general perspective can probably be gained from the last chapter of Clark's *The prehistory of Africa* (1970), and for Nigeria and Ghana by the chapters, by Willett and Ozanne, respectively, in Shinnie (ed.), *The African Iron Age* (1971). The significance of Willett's *Ife in the history of West African sculpture* (1967) is very much greater than its title may suggest. Finally, among the general works, there will always be an honoured place for Mauny's *Tableau géographique de l'ouest africain au moyen âge, d'après les sources écrites, la tradition et l'archéologie* (1961). As the title may indicate, this is not in the strictest sense a historical work at all (i.e. it is not primarily concerned with the chronological march of cause and effect). But, setting out as it does an immense corpus of information for what Mauny calls 'the middle ages' – between the birth of Islam and the arrival of the Europeans – within a schematic framework, it is a marvellous quarry for historians to mine. Inevitably, however, there is less information for Guinea than there is for the Sudan.

For the period up to the coming of the Europeans, the task of the historian is to try and assemble coherent patterns of cause and effect which join data from archaeology at one end of the scale and from social anthropology and kindred subjects at the other end, in such a way that they are not inconsistent with such historical data as have survived for the period or which may be inferred for it from traditions formulated in, or historical data pertaining to, later times. (Some of the problems involved here may be seen from the collection of essays edited by Biobaku, *Sources of Yoruba history* (1973).) This is necessarily a hazardous and speculative task, and by and large the considerable body of historians now working on Guinea history have been very reluctant to engage in it. It is notable that the vast bulk of the articles in, for example, the excellent *Transactions of the Historical Society of Ghana* and *The Journal of the Historical Society of Nigeria* deal with the period after 1600, indeed with that after 1800. Authors writing for *The Journal of African History* have been rather more bold, however, and many of the journal articles cited in the bibliography come from it.

Articles, for the most part of a speculative character, form the bulk of the material used for section two of the chapter; of particular value are the articles by Alagoa (1966, 1970) on the Niger delta region, by Boston (1969) on the Igala, by Law (1973) and Smith (1965) on the Yoruba, by Northrup (1972) on early Ibo trade, and the collection of essays by many hands on Akan history in *Ghana Notes and Queries* (1966). Early attempts at reconstructing aspects of this period of history at book length, for example by Meyerowitz (1952, 1958, 1960) for the Akan, must now be treated with caution. However, there are good books on Yoruba history by Smith (1969), on Benin history by the late Robert Bradbury (1957, 1973) and by Ryder (1969), and on Igala history by Boston (1968). It will be noted that all these relate to modern Nigeria, which has also produced two classic accounts of oral tradition, that for Yoruba by S. Johnson (1921) and for Benin by Egharevba (1960). Nigeria has also been the subject of two good general histories, Crowder's *The story of Nigeria* (1962), and Hodgkin's *Nigerian perspectives* (2nd ed., 1975), the introduction to which makes it very much more than an anthology.

Other regions have been less fortunate, though Deschamps's *Le Sénégal et la Gambie* (1964) and Flint's *Nigeria and Ghana* (1967) are two short syntheses of considerable merit. However, Wilks's booklet, *The northern factor in Ashanti history* (1961), is one of the few works which addresses itself directly to a major problem of the period, namely the Dyula expansion towards modern Ghana, while Levtzion's *Muslims and chiefs in West Africa* (1968), a study of Islam in the middle Volta basin, is also of considerable value. In default of major studies of much of the history of the period, particular attention needs often to be paid to the early chapters of books dealing with somewhat later times. In this connection, the following are perhaps especially rewarding: Daaku's *Trade and politics in the Gold Coast* (1970), Latham's *Old Calabar* (1973), Newbury's *The western Slave Coast and its rulers* (1961), and Rodney's *A history of the Upper Guinea Coast* (1970).

From the fifteenth century onwards, some documentation becomes available. The Timbuktu *ta'rīkhs*, of course, are concerned essentially with the middle Niger valley, but also contain important clues for territories further south, as does Leo Africanus. Blake's *Europeans in West Africa* (1941) prints a selection of contemporary documents from the European side, and also offers a useful introduction to the Europeans' coming. Relevant sections of Cadamosto and de Barros are printed by Crone (1937). Finally, the beginning and the end of the sixteenth century are marked by two major descriptive works, Pacheco Pereira's *Esmeraldo de situ orbis* (*c.* 1505) admirably edited by Mauny (1956) and Pieter de Marees's *Description and historicall declaration of the Golden Kingdom of Guinea* (1602). The latter deals essentially only with the Gold Coast, though it has a supplementary chapter on Benin by 'D.R.' (Dierrick Ruyters?); unfortunately it is available in English only in a contemporary abridgement (1905), and there is great need of a modern edition of the text.

7. CENTRAL AFRICA FROM CAMEROUN TO THE ZAMBEZI

Evidence for the history of the Later Iron Age in Central Africa comes from archaeology, from oral material and from written documents; but the distribution of these different kinds of data is still extremely patchy. The only part of the region that is archaeologically well known is Zambia and adjacent regions of Zaïre, Malawi and Rhodesia, but even here the Early Iron Age has been more thoroughly studied than the Later Iron Age. New findings usually appear in the *Journal of African History* and in *Azania*, and recent articles by Phillipson (1968–74) should be consulted in particular. The *Journal of African History* regularly publishes and comments on the latest radiocarbon dates. For the important site of Ingombe Ilede it is also necessary to consult work on the Urungwe district of Rhodesia, particularly that by Garlake (1971). The Ingombe Ilede materials themselves can be studied in Fagan et al. (1969), and the revised dating is in Phillipson and Fagan (1969).

Research based on oral evidence in Central Africa is for the most part very new, and is primarily concerned with the history of the last few centuries. There is, however, a growing realization that religious and other beliefs are often rooted in a more distant past. New work on Malawi by Matthew Schofeleers is referred to both in Pachai (1972) and in Ranger (1973). Less is known about the early religious and political history of Zambian peoples, but in southern Zaïre numerous investigators of the colonial period recorded myths and traditions which are now available for historical evaluation and for supplementation by new findings. Among the most outstanding works are those by Verhulpen (1936) and Planquaert (1932 and 1971). Several famous nineteenth-century explorers visited the court of the *mwata yamvo* of Lunda, and their diaries often include historical material, as in Henrique Dias de Carvalho (1890).

In the equatorial forest of northern Central Africa the small-scale societies have been much less well served by both nineteenth-century travellers and twentieth-century scholars. Perhaps they do not have cultures whose historical roots are as readily discernible as those of the savanna, but future ethnographic and linguistic research should help to improve our understanding of the area. Many of the materials available, though often of dubious value, are listed in the bibliographical sections of Vansina (1966).

The most remarkable materials, by African standards, are the written records which relate to Portuguese activities on the west coast of Central Africa from the 1480s. Most of the archival material so far known for the early period has been published in Brasio (1952–), the first four volumes of which bring the story up to 1600. There is, however, still much room for assessing and interpreting both these documents and the major chronicles of the period, which need to be placed against a much surer ethnographic background than has hitherto been available. A notable piece of scholarly editing was done by Bal (1963) in his edition of Pigafetta and Lopez. More recently Leite de Faria (1966) has studied the writing of Rui de Pina, but there is yet no modern edition of João de Barros's *Da Asia*. English and Dutch visitors only reached western Central Africa very late in the sixteenth century; but Ravenstein's edition of *The strange adventures of Andrew Battell* (1901) contains much useful first-hand information. Also useful is the second-hand evidence of several important seventeenth-century writers who collected both information about traditional history and accounts of European activities. The two most important works in this class are Cavazzi, *Istorica descrittione de' tre regni Congo Matamba et Angola* (1965), and Cadornega, *História geral das guerras Angolanas* (1940–2).

Among modern works of scholarship the nearest approximation to an historical survey is Vansina (1965), which covers the region from Kongo to Luba. The most important Portuguese survey is Delgado (1948–55; vols. 1–3 recently (*c.* 1972–4) reprinted), which is useful despite its shortage of bibliographical references. Two surveys of

Kongo, by Randles (1968) and Sigbert Axelson (1971), contain extensive bibliographies in which reference will be found not only to the primary evidence, but also to the earlier secondary authorities, such as Ihle (1929). Birmingham (1966) and Martin (1972) both contain chapters on the period before the Atlantic slave-trade became the dominant theme of the region's history. Finally, Miller's *Kings and kinsmen* (1976) is a major contribution not only to the history of the area, but also to the methods by which current oral information about past societies of central Africa can be linked to the earliest European documentary data.

8. SOUTHERN AFRICA

The source materials for southern African history in the period AD 1000 to 1600 are heavily archaeological, although documentary evidence adds considerably to our knowledge in the north-eastern sector, between the Limpopo and Zambezi rivers. The first archaeological account of Rhodesia's ruins was Bent (1893), but a more thorough investigation was published in Randall MacIver (1906). The two most extensive archaeological campaigns conducted at Great Zimbabwe were those of 1929, published in Caton-Thompson (1931), and of 1958 published in Summers, Robinson and Whitty (1961). All of this work, and more, has recently been thoroughly assessed and placed both in historical context and in geographical setting in Garlake (1973). Garlake's own original contribution to the understanding of Great Zimbabwe was previously presented in two important articles, 'The value of imported ceramics in the dating and interpretation of the Rhodesian Iron Age' (1968) and 'Rhodesian ruins – a preliminary assessment of their styles and chronology' (1970). Some archaeological information on the rest of Rhodesia is contained in three monographs, on *Inyanga* by Summers (1958), *Khami Ruins* by Robinson (1959), and *Ancient Mining in Rhodesia* by Summers (1969), but the more important recent finds and interpretations have been published in article form. Among them are Huffman, 'The rise and fall of Zimbabwe' (1972), Garlake, 'Excavations at the Nhunguza and Ruanga ruins in Northern Mashonaland' (1973), the same author's 'Iron Age sites in the Urungwe district of Rhodesia' (1970), Phillipson and Fagan, 'The date of the Ingombe Ilede burials' (1969), and Crawford, 'The Monk's Kop ossuary' (1967). Recent work by Huffman on the Leopard's Kopje culture was not available at the time of writing.

South of the Limpopo, our knowledge is almost entirely dependent on archaeological data. At the time of the major advances in archaeology in Rhodesia during the fifties and sixties, archaeological work south of the Limpopo, particularly on the Iron Age, lagged behind. Apart from Schofield's pioneering *Primitive pottery* (1948) and the first volume on Mapungubwe edited by Fouché (1937), work on Iron Age sites in South Africa consisted of a handful of reports on sites on the highveld or the top levels of shell middens along the coast, which were, in general, poorly described and undated. Gardner's reports on his excavations at Mapungubwe and the neighbouring Bambandyanalo site (carried out during and just after the war, but only published in 1963) were inadequate both in methodology and interpretation, as Fagan pointed out in an important article in the *Journal of African History* in 1964. The first indication of a renewed interest in South Africa in Iron Age studies was the final section of Revil Mason's *Prehistory of the Transvaal* (1962), which surveyed the known evidence on the Iron Age and in the Transvaal, and particularly the stone building sites in the southern Transvaal. Since then, Mason's own work on the Iron Age in the Transvaal has been presented in a number of short reports published in the *South African Archaeological Bulletin*, *South African Journal of Science*, and Occasional Papers of the Department of Archaeology at Witwatersrand University, and elsewhere.

Since the late sixties considerably more work has been done, particularly on the Iron Age in the Transvaal, some of it under the direction of Mason. Unfortunately, apart from a number of important carbon dates, neither this, nor the work of N. van der Merwe on Phalaborwa, has been fully published. For the Iron Age in the Orange Free State we are almost totally dependent on the articles by Maggs in the *South African Archaeological Bulletin* (1971, 1972) and his recently completed Ph.D. thesis for the University of Cape Town, 'Early farming communities on the southern Highveld' (1971). His are the most fully documented set of excavations for the Iron Age in South Africa to date. Although the earliest of the sites in the Orange Free State relate to the sixteenth century, both Maggs's analysis and conclusions are of considerable relevance for the whole of this period. The final section of Sampson's (1972) work on the Stone Age in the middle Orange river is of relevance to this period, but his broader syntheses are not accepted by a number of other archaeologists. In Natal, new dates and a certain amount of descriptive material has come from the work of Davies (1971), though here, and to an even greater extent in the Cape Province, serious archaeological work on the Iron Age has barely begun. This is equally true of Botswana and South-West Africa.

In the Cape, however, there has been a welcome departure in Late Stone Age studies from the older emphasis on tool typology and the dichotomy between Smithfield and Wilton cultures; the new work of Deacon (1972), Parkington (1971, 1972), Schweitzer (1970) and others has not only broken down this simplified distinction, but also attempts to use the archaeological evidence from Late Stone Age sites to interpret the complex nature of man's adaptation to his environment. Most of this work naturally relates to an earlier period than that of this volume, but the final stages of the Late Stone Age continue well into the second millennium. Though this research is still at an early stage, it should ultimately open up a new area of dialogue between the historian and archaeologist, which should be of particular importance for this period. The new work in progress makes it difficult to rely on such syntheses as Fagan's *Southern Africa* (1965) or the essays by Inskeep in the *Oxford History* (1969) and Fagan in Thompson's *African societies in southern Africa* (1969).

The documentary evidence relating to the Sofala coast and the Rhodesian trade goes back to the Middle Ages. The earliest Arabic records are cited by Burke in *Historians in tropical Africa* (1962), and in Freeman-Grenville (1962). The Kilwa link is discussed by Chittick in Shinnie (1971), and by Sutton (1973). The more plentiful Portuguese documentation has been partially collected in Theal (1964) and in *Documents on the Portuguese in Mozambique and Central Africa*. Much of this documentation is concerned with petty trading accounts and with day-to-day administration in the forts and factories, but several writers gave detailed information on Shona history. Friar João dos Santos wrote an intelligent and sometimes well-informed account of *Ethiopia Oriental* (in Theal, 1964) after an extended stay in Zambezia at the end of the sixteenth century. João de Barros wrote his *Da Asia* (1552–1613; extracts in Theal, 1964) half a century earlier, from secondary information of variable reliability. Antonio Bocarro wrote his *Livro do Estado da India* (extracts in Theal, 1964) in the seventeenth century, at a time when the Portuguese enclaves in Mozambique were still administered by Portuguese India. The latest, and best, modern history of Portuguese relations with the Shona is Newitt, *Portuguese settlement on the Zambesi* (1973).

The Portuguese chroniclers, such as dos Santos and Bocarro, gained their historical evidence primarily by talking to experienced Shona informants, or less directly from old established Swahili merchants who knew the Shona well. In the twentieth century historians have been slow to return to the oral sources, or even to the secondary accounts of oral history published by early settlers and administrators with an amateur taste for history. One early attempt to outline Shona history in this fashion was made in Abraham, 'The early political history of the kingdom of the Mwene Mutapa' (1962), and in several other articles. More recent research, particularly by Beach (1972), is still awaiting publication. Isaacman, in addition to collecting oral data on eighteenth-century *prazos*, collected evidence for an article on Barwe (1973). There is still much room for new local initiatives among Shona historians themselves.

The documentary evidence for South Africa south of the Limpopo is very slight for this period. The records of Portuguese mariners shipwrecked along the treacherous south-east coast, collected and translated by Theal (1898–1903; reprinted 1964), and more recently edited by Boxer (1959), enabled Wilson in a major article (1959) to reconstruct the early history of the Transkei and Ciskei, and to establish the presence of Bantu-speaking Iron Age farmers along the coast in roughly their present configuration by the sixteenth century at latest. For the Bantu-speaking people of the interior, however, there are no documentary sources until the nineteenth century, and our records of oral tradition are equally late. Thus, in the main, both documentary and oral sources refer to a period later than the end of the seventeenth century. At times, however, references in tradition to earlier inhabitants enable us to glimpse earlier developments. Marks and Legassick, in Thompson (1969), have attempted to sift the traditions in this fashion for the Nguni and Sotho-Tswana respectively, but a great deal remains to be done. (For detailed comment on the compilations of oral tradition see the bibliographical essay on Southern Africa in *CHA*, vol. 4.) Ethnographic and linguistic evidence provide some clues for this period, but have to be handled with caution. The latest, and indeed the only comprehensive attempt to deal with the precolonial history of the Bantu-speaking peoples of South Africa, is in Wilson's chapters in the *Oxford history of South Africa* (1969). Unfortunately, however, these fail to establish an adequate chronology of change for the area over more than a thousand years of development.

For the Khoisan peoples, at least in the immediate environs of the Cape, documentary sources exist from the beginning of the seventeenth century, and have been usefully compiled and translated by Raven-Hart (1967). The documentary, linguistic, anthropological and archaeological evidence for this early period of Khoisan history has been examined recently and most cogently in the opening section of Elphick's 'The Cape Khoi and the first phase of South African race relations' (1972), though new archaeological work is already modifying some of his conclusions.

9. THE EAST AFRICAN INTERIOR

Archaeological evidence is of fundamental importance for the whole period, and especially for the first half of it. Nevertheless, it should be realized that work on the Iron Age, and particularly on the Later Iron Age, has so far only been attempted by a handful of scholars. Large parts of the region are still quite unexplored, including the whole of southern Tanzania and the northern parts of Uganda and Kenya. We know nothing at all about the origins of the Iron Age in the southern Sudan or southern Ethiopia.

The main comprehensive work on East African prehistory, that by Cole (1964), is only marginally concerned with the Iron Age, and in that respect is largely outdated. Useful summaries of research on the Iron Age in the interior of East Africa and the neighbouring regions of Rwanda, Burundi and eastern Zaïre by Posnansky and Nenquin are to be found in Bishop and Clark (1967), and an overall synthesis is attempted by Sutton in Shinnie (1971). Sutton (1973) is an important monograph on the Iron Age in western Kenya, as is that by Hiernaux and Maquet (1957–9) on Rwanda, Burundi and Kivu. Posnansky (1969) describes the main excavation at Bigo, and Sassoon (1967) that at Engaruka. Most of the other surveys and site reports used in this chapter, including the important contributions of Soper (1967–71) and Siiriäinen (1971), are to be found in *Azania*, the journal of the British Institute in Eastern Africa (1966–). The results of radiocarbon dating for the Iron Age have been regularly summarized in the *Journal of African History* since 1961.

In contrast with the meagre publications on Iron Age archaeology, there is now an extensive literature concerned with the traditional history of the peoples of the region. The collection and recording of this data was begun by European missionaries, such as Roscoe (1911), Gorju (1920), Pagès (1933), Cézard (1937) and Crazzolara (1950–4); by administrators, such as Rehse (1910), Dundas (1924), Ford and

Hall (1947) and Lambert (1950); and by the early generations of literate East Africans, such as Kagwa (1901 and 1927), Nyakatura (1947), and Katate and Kamugungunu (1955). More recently, this work has been carried on by a number of professional historians committed to specialization in African history, such as Vansina (1961, 1972), Ogot (1967), Kimambo (1969), Were (1966), Karugire (1971), Cohen (1972), Kiwanuka (1972), Feierman (1974) and Muriuki (1974). This generation of scholars had the advantage of studying the methodology outlined for this branch of inquiry by Vansina, *De la tradition orale* (1961), and of being able easily to keep in touch with the work of other specialists throughout the continent. Although the earlier writers often had access to a wider circle of living informants, the later ones were able to pursue their researches more systematically and to bring a more sophisticated critical apparatus to bear upon their interpretation. As an example, one need only cite the revolution brought about in the interpretation of Rwanda traditions by Vansina (1961), despite the immense and careful work of collection carried out by predecessors as respectable as Pagès and Kagame.

In general, it is only in the interlacustrine region of East Africa that genealogically articulated traditions bear in detail upon the period covered in this volume, and even there only from about the fourteenth century onwards. Elsewhere in East Africa, the threshold of continuous tradition, whether expressed in dynastic generations or in age-groups and generation-sets as among the Paranilotic peoples, comes much later – at the very end of, or even beyond, our period. Earlier layers of tradition are notoriously difficult to interpret, and have to be studied in conjunction with archaeological, ethnographic and linguistic data. A good example of these difficulties is provided by the suggestion (on pp. 659–61), arising from Siiriäinen's excavations at Gatunganga, that what have hitherto been accepted as the traditions of origin of the Kikuyu may in fact be those of Paranilotic immigrants into an area long occupied by Bantu cultivators. A similar fundamental inversion seems to be necessary in respect of the traditions of origin of most of the north-eastern Bantu peoples.

The synthesis presented here differs in some fairly important respects from that attempted by the same author in Oliver and Mathew (1963) for the period from 1500 to 1840. It is now seen that the Nilotic dispersion, which then seemed of paramount importance, represented only the last phase of a prolonged southward drift of Central Sudanic, Paranilotic and Nilotic peoples, which affected western and central

Kenya and central Tanzania, no less than Uganda, Rwanda, Burundi and western Tanzania. It is also seen that the process of state formation was much more complex than that previously proposed, originating in a vast multitude of tiny units, of which only a few met the challenges necessary to produce a significant increase of scale.

BIBLIOGRAPHY

GENERAL

The following bibliographic and reference works are of value to the study of the period covered by this volume as a whole. Space permits only a very selective list, which does not purport to be comprehensive.

The most complete guide to the literature of African studies available is P. Duignan's *Guide to research and reference works on sub-Saharan Africa*, Stanford, 1971. This most valuable work should be consulted for further information.

General bibliographies

Attal, R. *Les Juifs d'Afrique du nord: bibliographie*. Leiden, 1973.

Cahen, C. *Jean Sauvaget's introduction to the history of the Muslim East*. Berkeley, 1965.

Cox, E. G. *Reference guide to the literature of travel*, vol. 1, *Old world*. [Africa, pp. 354–401.] Seattle, 1965.

Duignan, P. ed. *Guide to research and reference works on sub-Saharan Africa*. Stanford, 1971.

Garling, A. *Bibliography of African bibliographies*. Cambridge, 1968.

Guides to materials for West African history in European archives (series). London, 1962 onwards.

International Council on Archives. *Guide to the sources of African history outside of Africa* (series). Zug, 1970 onwards.

Mauny, R. 'Contribution à la bibliographie de l'histoire de l'Afrique noire des origines à 1850', *Bulletin de l'IFAN*, 1966, **28**, 927–65.

Meyer-Heiselberg, R. *Bibliographi over Afrikansk historie: nyere litteratur orn syd for Sahara*. Copenhagen, 1963.

Pearson, J. D. ed. *A guide to documents and manuscripts in the British Isles relating to Africa*, compiled by N. Matthews and M. D. Wainwright. London, 1970.

Playfair, R. L. and others. *The bibliography of the Barbary States*. 1888–98; reprinted London, 1971. [Bibliographies of Morocco, Tunisia, Algeria, Tripoli and Cyrenaica by Playfair, Ashbee and Brown.]

Sørbø, Gunnar. *Sudan sources I: Petermanns Mitteilungen*. Occasional paper no. 3, Programme for Middle-Eastern and African Studies, University of Bergen, Norway, 1974.

Stewart, C. C. 'Bibliography of the Maghrib', in C.-A. Julien, *History of North Africa*. London, 1970.

Thomas, D. H. and Case, L. M. eds. *Guide to the diplomatic archives of Western Europe*. Philadelphia, 1959.

General works

Abun-Nasr, J. M. *A history of the Maghrib*. Cambridge, 1971.

Ajayi, J. F. A. and Crowder, M. eds. *History of West Africa*, vol. 1. London, 1971.

Cornevin, R. *Histoire des peuples de l'Afrique noire*. Paris, 1960.
Dalby, D. *Language and history in Africa*. London, 1970.
Davidson, B. *Africa in history*, rev. ed. London, 1974.
Deschamps, H. *Histoire générale de l'Afrique noire*, vol. 1, *Des origines à 1800*. Paris, 1970.
Fage, J. D. *An atlas of African history*. London, 1966.
Greenberg, J. H. *Languages of Africa*, rev. ed. Bloomington, 1966.
Julien, C.-A. *History of North Africa: Tunisia, Algeria, Morocco; from the Arab conquest to 1830*, tr. J. Petrie, ed. C. C. Stewart. London, 1970.
Kamal, Y. *Monumenta Cartographica Africae et Aegypti*. Cairo and Leiden, 1926–51. 16 vols.
Lewis, I. M. ed. *History and social anthropology*. London, 1968.
Mauny, R. *Tableau géographique de l'ouest africain au moyen âge, d'après les sources écrites, la tradition et l'archéologie. Mémoire de l'IFAN* no. 61. Dakar, 1961.
Murdock, G. P. *Africa, its peoples and their culture history*. New York, 1959.
Oliver, Roland and Fage, J. D. *A short history of Africa*. New York, 1963; 5th edn., Harmondsworth, 1975.
Oliver, Roland and Mathew, G. *History of East Africa*, vol. 1. Oxford, 1963.
Vansina, J. *De la tradition orale: essai de méthode historique*. Tervuren, 1961; English ed., *Oral tradition, a study in historical methodology*. London, 1965.
Vansina, J., Mauny, R. and Thomas, L. V. eds. *The historian in tropical Africa*. Oxford, 1964.
Wachsmann, Klaus, P. ed. *Essays on music and history in Africa*. Evanston, 1971.
Westermann, D. *Geschichte Afrikas: Staatenbildungen südlich der Sahara*. Cologne, 1952.
Wilson, M. and Thompson, L. M. eds. *The Oxford history of South Africa*, vol. 1, *South Africa to 1870*. Oxford, 1969.

Archaeology

Bishop, W. W. and Clark, J. D. eds. *Background to evolution in Africa*. Chicago, 1967.
Clark, J. D. *The prehistory of Africa*. London, 1970.
Fage, J. D. and Oliver, Roland, eds. *Papers in African prehistory*. Cambridge, 1970.
Oliver, Roland and Fagan, Brian M. *Africa in the Iron Age*. Cambridge, 1975.
Shinnie, P. L. ed. *The African Iron Age*. Oxford, 1971.

Radiocarbon dates

Beaumont, P. and Schoonraad, M., in M. Stuiver, 'Yale national C14 measurements IX', *Radiocarbon*, 1969, **11**, 645–6.
Fagan, Brian M. 'Radiocarbon dates for sub-Saharan Africa' (parts 1–6), *Journal of African History*: 1961, **2**, 137–9; 1963, **4**, 127–8; 1965, **6**, 107–16; 1966, **7**, 495–506; 1967, **8**, 513–27; 1969, **10**, 149–69.
Flight, C. 'A survey of recent results in the radiocarbon chronology of northern and western Africa', *JAH*, 1973, **14**, 4, 531–4.

Phillipson, D. W. 'Notes on the later prehistoric radiocarbon chronology of eastern and southern Africa', *JAH*, 1970, **11**, 1–15.

Stuiver, M. and Merwe, N. J. van der. 'Radiocarbon chronology of the Iron Age in sub-Saharan Africa', *Current anthropology*, 1968, **9**, 1.

Sutton, J. E. G. 'New radiocarbon dates for eastern and southern Africa', *Journal of African History*, 1972, **13**, 1–24.

Willett, F. 'A survey of recent results in the radiocarbon chronology of western and northern Africa', *JAH*, 1971, **12**, 3, 339–70.

Islamic and Arabic

Abstracta Islamica. Supplement to *Revue des études Islamiques*, 1927 onwards.

Cambridge history of Islam, ed. P. M. Holt, A. K. S. Lambton and Bernard Lewis. Cambridge, 1970. 2 vols.

Encyclopaedia of Islam. Leiden, 1913–32; 2nd ed. [letters A–K] in progress since 1954.

Pearson, J. D. *Index Islamicus, 1950–5.* Cambridge, 1958. *Supplements*, 1956–60, 1961–5, 1966–70; Cambridge, 1962, 1967, 1972.

Arabic writers

Abu'l-Fidā. [Works.] ed. and tr. [into Latin], J. J. Reiske. Leipzig, 1778. French transl. [Aboulfeda], *Géographie*, tr. M. Reinaud. Paris, 1848.

al-Bakrī. *Kitāb al-masālik wa'l mamālik*, ed. M. G. de Slane. Algiers, 1911. French transl., *Description de l'Afrique septentrionale*, tr. M. G. de Slane. Paris, 1913. *See also* 'Routier de l'Afrique blanche et noire du nord-ouest: al-Bakrī (Cordue 1068)', *Bulletin de l'IFAN*, 1968, **30**, 39–116.

Ibn Baṭṭūṭa. *Tuḥfat al-nuẓẓār fī gharā'ib al-amṣār wa-'ajā'ib al-asfār* [*Voyages*] ed. and tr. C. Defrémery and B. R. Sanguinetti. Paris, 1922. Engl. transl., *Travels of Ibn Baṭṭūṭa*, tr. H. A. R. Gibb. Vols. I–III, London, 1958–71.

Ibn Ḥawqal. *Kitāb al-masālik wa'l mamālik* (*Kitāb ṣūrat al-arḍ*). French transl. [Ibn Ḥauḳal], *Configuration de la terre*, tr. J. H. Kramers and G. Wiet. Paris, 1964.

Ibn Sa'īd. *Kitāb basṭ al-arḍ fi'l ṭūl wa'l-'arḍ*, ed. J. V. Gines. Tetuan, 1958.

al-Idrīsī. *Nuẓhat al-mushtāq fī ikhtirāq al-āfāk*, ed. R. Dozy and M. J. de Goeje. Leiden, 1866. French transl., *Description de l'Afrique et de l'Espagne*, tr. R. Dozy and M. J. de Goeje, Leiden, 1966; *Géographie*, tr. A. Jaubert, Paris, 1837.

Leo Africanus [Jean Léon l'Africain]. *Description de l'Afrique*, tr. A. Épaulard, with notes by A. Épaulard, T. Monod, H. Lhote and R. Mauny. Paris, 1956. 2 vols. *See also* R. Mauny, 'Notes sur les "Grands voyages" de Léon l'Africain', *Hespéris*, 1954, **41**, 379–94.

al-Maqrīzī. *Kitāb al-sulūk li-ma'rifat duwal al-mulūk*, ed. M. M. Ziyada. Cairo, 1934–58. 5 vols. French transl., *Histoire des sultans mamlouks*, tr. E. Quatremère. Paris, 1837–45. 2 vols.

al-Maqrīzī. *Ittī'āẓ al-ḥunafā'bi-akhbār al a'imma al fāṭimiyyin al-khulafā*, ed. G. al-Shayyal. Cairo, 1967.

al-Maqrīzī. *al-Khiṭaṭ*. Bulaq, 1853; Cairo, 1906.

al-Mas'ūdī. *Murūj al-dhahab*. French transl., *Les prairies d'or*, ed. and tr. C. Pellat. Paris, 1962–71; [al-Maçoudi] *Les prairies d'or*, ed. and tr. C. Barbier de Meynard and P. de Courteille. Paris, 1864–77.

al-'Umarī. *Masālik al-abṣār fī mamālik al-amṣār*. Ms. no. 5868, Bibliothèque Nationale, Paris.

al-Ya'qūbī. *Historiae*, ed. T. Houtsma. Leiden, 1883.

Yāqūt. *Mu'jam al-buldān*, ed. F. Wüstenfeld. Leipzig, 1866.

al-Zuhrī. *Kitāb al-Ja'rafiyya*, ed. Hadj-Sadok. *Bulletin d'études orientales* [Damascus] 1968, **21**.

Cuoq, J. M. *Recueil des sources arabes concernant l'Afrique occidentale du VIIIe au XVIe siècle (Bilād al-Sūdān)*. Paris, 1975.

Hopkins, J. F. P. and Levtzion, N. *Translations from Arabic sources* [forthcoming].

Kubbel, L. E. and Matveyev, V. V. eds. *Drevniye i Srednyevekoviye Istochniki po Etnografii i Istorii Narodov Afriki Yozhnyeye Sachari*, vol. I, *VII–X Vekov*; vol. II, *X–XII Vekov*. Moscow–Leningrad, 1960, 1965.

Lewicki, T. *Arabic external sources for the history of Africa south of Sahara*. Wroclaw, 1969.

Palmer, H. R. ed. and tr. *Sudanese memoirs: being mainly translations of a number of Arabic manuscripts relating to the central and western Sudan*. Lagos, 1928; reprinted London, 1967.

European sources

Barros, J. de. *Da Asia*. 4 vols: Lisbon, 1552–1613; vol. I, edition a Coimbra, 1932. [Extracts in G. M. Theal, *Records*.] *Da Asia*, vol. I, *Decadas da India*. Nuremberg, 1841. [Extract in Crone, *Cadamosto*.]

Brásio, A. *Monumenta missionaria Africana*. Lisbon, 1952 onwards. 11 vols.

Cadamosto. *Relations des voyages à la côte occidentale d'Afrique*, tr. C. Schefer. Paris, 1895. Engl. transl., *The voyages of Cadamosto, and other documents on western Africa in the second half of the fifteenth century*, ed. and tr. G. R. Crone. London, 1937.

Dapper, O. *Naukeurige Beschrijvinge der Afrikaensche Gewesten*. Amsterdam, 1668.

Fernandes, V. *Description de la côte occidentale d'Afrique*, tr. P. de Cenival and T. Monod. Paris, 1938; *Description de la côte occidentale d'Afrique (Sénégal au Cap de Monte, Archipels)*, tr. P. de Cenival and T. Monod, ed. T. Monod, A. Teixeira da Mota and R. Mauny. Bissau, 1951.

Freeman-Grenville, G. S. P. *The East African Coast – selected documents from the first to the earlier nineteenth century*. Oxford, 1962.

La Roncière, C. de. *La découverte de l'Afrique au moyen âge*. Cairo, 1924–7.

Marmol-Carvajal. *L'Afrique de Marmol*, tr. Perrot d'Ablancourt. Paris, 1867.

Pacheco Pereira. *Esmeraldo de situ orbis (Côte occidentale d'Afrique du sud marocain au Gabon)*, ed. and tr. R. Mauny. *Memorias*, 19, Centro de Estudos da Guiné Portuguesa. Bissau, 1956.

Rego, A. da Silva and Baxter, T. W. eds. *Documents on the Portuguese in Moçambique and Central Africa 1497–1840*. Lisbon, 1962–6. 7 vols.

Theal, G. M. ed. *Records of south-eastern Africa*. 9 vols: Cape Town, 1898–1903; reprinted 1964. [Includes extracts from de Barros, de Couto, Cabral, Barbosa, Correa, Bocarro, de Goes, dos Santos, etc.]

Vasco da Gama. *Journal of the first voyage of Vasco da Gama*, tr. E. G. Ravenstein. London, 1898; *The three voyages of Vasco da Gama*, tr. E. J. Stanley from G. Correa, *Lendas da India*. London, 1869.

Zurara. *Chronique de Guinée*, tr. L. Bourdon. Dakar, 1960.

I. EGYPT, NUBIA AND THE EASTERN DESERTS

'Abd al-Laṭīf al-Baghdādī. '*Relation de l'Egypte*, ed. and tr S. de Sacy. Paris, 1810.

Abū Shāma. *Kitāb al-Rawḍatayn*. Cairo, 1871.

Allen, C. and Johnson, R. W. eds. *African perspectives*. Cambridge, 1970.

Arkell, A. J. 'The history of Darfur, AD 1200–1700', *Sudan Notes and Records*, 1951, **32** and 1952, **33**.

Arkell, A. J. *A history of the Sudan from the earliest times to 1821*. London, 1955.

Ashtor, E. *Histoire des prix et des salaires dans l'Orient mediévale*. Paris, 1969.

Atiya, A. S. *The Arabic manuscripts of Mt Sinai*. Baltimore, 1955.

Atiya, A. S. *Crusade, commerce and culture*. Bloomington, 1962.

Ayalon, D. *L'esclavage des mamlouks*. Jerusalem, 1951.

Ayalon, D. *Gunpowder and firearms in the Mamluk Kingdom*. London, 1956.

Ayalon, D. *The Mamluks and naval power*. Jerusalem, 1965.

Ayalon, D. 'Studies on the structure of the Mamluk army', pts. I–III, *Bulletin of the School of Oriental and African Studies*, 1953, **15**, 203–28, 448–76; 1954, **16**, 57–90.

Balog, P. *The coinage of the Mamluk sultans of Egypt and Syria*. New York, 1964.

Becker, C. H. *Beiträge zur Geschichte Ägyptens unter dem Islam*. Strasburg, 1902–3.

Björkmann, W. *Beiträge zur Geschichte der Staatskanzlei im islamischen Ägypten*. Hamburg, 1928.

Blau, O. 'Chronik der Sulṭâne von Bornu', *Zeitschrift der Deutsche Morgenland Gesellschaft*, 1852, **6**, 305–30.

Blochet, E. *See* Mufaḍḍal ibn Abī'l-Faḍā'il.

Braudel, F. *La Méditerranée*. *See* p. 726.

Cahen, C. 'L'evolution de l'iqṭa' du IXe au XIIIe siècle', *Annales/ESC*, 1953, **8** (1).

Clerget, M. *Le Caire, étude de géographie urbain et d'histoire économique*. Cairo, 1934. 2 vols.

Combe, E., Sauvaget, J. and Wiet, G. eds. *Répertoire chronologique d'épigraphie arabe*. Cairo, 1931–57. 15 vols.

Corpus Inscriptionum Arabicorum, First part, Egypt I, ed. M. van Berchem. Cairo, 1894–1903. *First part, Egypt II*, ed. G. Wiet. Cairo, 1929–30.

Cresswell, K. A. C. *Muslim architecture of Egypt*. Oxford, 1952, 1959. 2 vols.

Darrag, A. *L'Égypte sous le règne de Barsbay, 825–841/1422–1438*. Damascus, 1961.

Ehrenkreutz, A. S. 'Extracts from the technical manual on the Ayyūbid mint in Cairo', *Bulletin of SOAS*, 1953, **15**, 423–47.

Ehrenkreutz, A. S. 'Contributions to the knowledge of the fiscal administration of Egypt in the Middle Ages'. *Bulletin of SOAS*, 1954, **16**, 502–14.

Ehrenkreutz, A. S. 'The standard fineness of gold coins circulating in Egypt at the time of the Crusades', *Journal of the American Oriental Society*, 1954, **74**, 162–6.

Ehrenkreutz, A. S. 'The place of Saladin in the naval history of the Mediterranean', *JAOS*, 1955, **75**, 100–16.

Ehrenkreutz, A. S. 'The crisis of the dinar in the Egypt of Saladin', *JAOS*, 1956, **76**, 178–84.

Ehrenkreutz, A. S. *Saladin*. New York, 1972.

Elisséeff, N. *Nūr al-Dīn: un grand prince musulman aux temps des Croisades*. Damascus, 1967.

Ernst, H. *Die mamlukischen Sultanenurkunden des Sinai-Klosters*. Wiesbaden, 1960.

Fischel, L. 'Uber die Gruppe der Karimi', *Analecta Orientalia*, Rome, 1937.

Gabrieli, F. *Arab historians of the Crusades*. London, 1969.

Gibb, H. A. R. 'The achievement of Saladin', *Bulletin of the John Rylands Library*, 1952–3, **35**, 44–60.

Goitein, S. D. *A Mediterranean society: the Jewish community in the Arab world as portrayed in the documents of the Cairo Geniza*, vol. I, Economic foundations. Berkeley and Los Angeles, 1967.

Gottschalk, H. L. *Al-Malik al-Kāmil und seine Zeit*. Wiesbaden, 1958.

Grohmann, A. *Arabic papyri in the Egyptian library*. Cairo, 1934–62. 6 vols.

Grohmann, A. *Einführung und Chrestomathie zur arabischen Papyruskunde*. Prague, 1954.

Haarman, U. *Quellenstudien zur frühen Mamlukenzeit*. Freiburg, 1970.

Hanotaux, G. ed. *Histoire de la nation Égyptienne*. Paris, 1931.

Ḥasan, Y. F. *The Arabs and the Sudan*. Edinburgh, 1967.

Hautecoeur, L. and Wiet, G. *Les mosquées du Caire*. Paris, 1932. 2 vols.

Heyd, U. ed. *Studies in Islamic history and civilisation*. Jerusalem, 1961.

Heyd, W. *Histoire du commerce du Levant au moyen-âge*. Leipzig, 1885, 1923. 2 vols.

Holt, P. M. *The Mahdist state in the Sudan*. Oxford, 1958.

Holt, P. M. *A modern history of the Sudan*, 2nd ed. London, 1963.

Hunwick, J. 'Notes on a late-fifteenth-century document concerning "al-Takrūr"', in *African perspectives*, ed. Allen and Johnson.

Ibn 'Abd al-Ẓāhir. *Biographi over Sultan el-Malik el-Ashraf Halīl*, ed. and tr. into Swedish, A. Moberg. Lund, 1902.

Ibn al-Athīr. *Kitāb al-Kāmil fi'l-ta'rīkh*, ed. C. J. Tornberg. Leiden, 1851–76.

Ibn al-Athīr. *Annales du Maghrib et de l'Espagne*, tr. E. Fagnan. Algiers, 1901.

Ibn al-Dawādarī. *Chronicle*, vol. VI, ed. S. al-Munajjid. Cairo, 1961; vol. IX, ed. H. R. Roemer. Cairo, 1960.

Ibn Īyās. *See* Wiet, *Journal d'un bourgeois*.

Ibn al-Ji'ān. *Kitāb al-tuḥfa al-sāniyya*, ed. B. Moritz. Cairo, 1898.
Ibn Jubayr [Muḥammad b. Aḥmad]. *The travels of Ibn Jubayr*, tr. R. J. C. Broadhurst. London, 1952.
Ibn Khaldūn. *Kitāb al-'ibar*. Beirut 1956–61. [*See also* under ch. 5.]
Ibn al-Mammātī. *Kitāb qawānīn al-dawānīn*, ed. A. S. Atiya. Cairo, 1943.
Ibn Taghrībirdī. *Al-nujūm al-ẓāhira*. Cairo, 1929–50. 11 vols: vols. 5–7 [years 1345–1467] ed. W. Popper. Berkeley, 1919–36.
Ibn Taghrībirdī. *History of Egypt, 1384–1469 AD*, tr. W. Popper. Berkeley, 1952–8. 4 pts. *See also* Popper, W.
Labib, S. Y. *Handelsgeschichte Aegyptens im Spätmittelalter, 1171–1517*. Wiesbaden, 1965.
Lane, F. C. 'The Mediterranean spice trade', *Amer. Hist. Review*, 1940, **45**, 581ff.
Lane-Poole, S. *Catalogue of oriental coins in the British Museum*. London, 1875–90. 10 vols. [vol. IV deals with Egypt].
Lane-Poole, S. *Saladin and the fall of the Kingdom of Jerusalem*. New York–London, 1898.
Lane-Poole, S. *History of Egypt in the Middle Ages*, 2nd ed. London, 1914.
Leur, J. van. *Indonesian trade and society*. The Hague, 1955.
Lewis, B. *The origins of Isma'ilism*. London, 1940.
Lewis, B. *The Arabs in history*. London, 1958.
Lewis, B. *The Assassins*. London, 1967.
Little, D. P. *An introduction to Mamluk historiography*. Wiesbaden, 1970.
Lopez, R. S. and Raymond, I. W. eds. *Mediaeval trade in the Mediterranean world*. New York, 1955.
MacMichael, H. A. *A history of the Arabs in the Sudan*. Cambridge, 1922. 2 vols.
Magid, A. M. *See* al-Mustanṣir.
al-Maqrīzī. *Historia regnum islamiticorum in Abissinia*, ed. and tr. F. T. Rinck. Leiden, 1790.
Mayer, L. *Saracenic heraldry*. Jerusalem, 1933.
Mayer, L. *Mamluk costume*. Geneva, 1952.
Meilink-Roelofsz, M. A. P. *Asian trade and European influence in the Indonesian archipelago between 1500 and about 1630*. The Hague, 1962.
Miles, G. C. *The Fatimid coins in the collection of the University Museum, Philadelphia, and the American Numismatic Society*. New York, 1951.
Moberg, A. *See* Ibn 'Abd al-Ẓāhir.
Monneret de Villard, U. *Storia della Nubia Cristiana*. Rome, 1938.
Mufaḍḍal ibn Abī'l-Faḍā'il. 'Histoire des sultans mamlouks', ed. and tr. E. Blochet, in *Patriologia Orientalis*, vols. 12 [1919], 14 [1920], 20 [1928].
Muir, W. *The Mamluke or slave dynasty of Egypt, 1260–1517*. London, 1896.
Munier, H. and Wiet, G. *L'Égypte byzantine et musulmane*, vol. II of *Précis de l'histoire d'Egypte*. Cairo, 1932.
al-Mustanṣir, Caliph. *Al-Sijillat al-Mustanṣiriyya*, ed. A. M. Magid. Cairo, 1954.
Nāṣir-i Khosraw. *Sefer Nāme*, ed. and tr. C. Schefer. Paris, 1896.
O'Leary, de Lacy. *A short history of the Fatimid Khalifate*. London, 1923.
Oliver, Roland and Mathew, G. eds. *History of East Africa*, vol. I. Oxford, 1963.

Paul, A. *History of the Beja tribes of the Sudan.* Cambridge, 1954.

Pires, Tomé. *Suma Oriental,* in G. S. P. Freeman-Grenville, *The East African coast.*

Poliak, A. N. *Feudalism in Egypt, Syria, Palestine and the Lebanon 1250–1900.* London, 1939.

Popper, W. *Egypt and Syria under the Circassian sultans, 1382–1468. Systematic notes to Taghrī Birdī's Chronicles of Egypt,* pts. 1, 2. Berkeley–Los Angeles, 1955, 1957.

al-Qalqashandī. *Ṣubḥ al-a'shā.* Cairo, 1913–19. 14 vols.

Recueil des historiens des Croisades: historiens orientaux. Paris, 1872–1906. 5 vols.

Rotter, G. *Die Stellung des Negers in der islamisch-arabischen Gesellschaft bis zum 16. Jhdt.* Bonn, 1967.

Sadeque, S. F. *Baybars I of Egypt.* Dacca, 1956.

Sauvaget, J. *La poste aux chevaux dans l'empire des Mamlouks.* Paris, 1941.

Schäfer, B. *Beiträge zur mamlukischen Historiographie nach dem Tode al-Malik an-Nāṣirs.* Freiburg, 1971.

Schaube, A. *Handelsgeschichte der romanischen Völker des Mittelmeergebiets bis zum Ende der Kreuzzüge.* Munich, 1906.

Schregle, G. *Die Sultanin von Aegypten Sağarat ad-Durr.* Wiesbaden, 1961.

Semenova, L. A. *Salakh ad-Din i mamluki v Egipte* [*Ṣālaḥ al-Dīn and the Mamluks in Egypt*]. Moscow, 1966.

Semenova, L. A. *Iz istorii fatimidskogo Egipta* [From the history of Fatimid Egypt]. Moscow, 1974.

Setton, K. M. and others, eds. *A history of the Crusades,* vols. I, II. Philadelphia, 1955, 1962.

Stern, S. M. *Fāṭimid decrees.* London, 1964.

Trimingham, J. S. *Islam in the Sudan.* Oxford, 1949.

Trimingham, J. S. *Islam in East Africa.* Oxford, 1964.

'Umarā of Yemen. *Oumâra du Yemen, sa vie et son oeuvre,* ed. and tr. H. Derenbourg. Paris, 1897–1904. 3 vols.

Usāma b. Munkidh. *Memoirs of an Arab-Syrian gentleman,* tr. P. K. Hitti. New York, 1929; reprinted Beirut, 1964.

Weil, G. *Geschichte der Chalifen.* Mannheim–Stuttgart, 1846–62. 5 vols.

Wiet, G. *L'Égypte byzantine et musulmane,* vol. II of *Précis de l'histoire de' Égypte.* Cairo, 1932.

Wiet, G. *L'Égypte arabe,* vol. IV of G. Hanotaux ed. *Histoire de la nation Égyptienne.* Paris, 1937.

Wiet, G. 'Les relations égypto-abyssines sous les sultans mamelouks', *Bulletin de la Société d'Archéologie Copte,* 1938, **4**.

Wiet, G. *Les marchands d'épices sous les sultans mamelouks.* Cairo, 1955.

Wiet, G. tr. *Journal d'un bourgeois du Caire, Chronique d'Ibn Iyâs.* Paris, 1955–60. 2 vols.

Wiet, G. 'Le traité des famines de Maqrīzī', *JEHSO,* 1962, **5**, pt. 1.

Wüstenfeld, F. *Geschichte der Fatimidenchalifen.* Göttingen, 1881.

al-Ẓāhirī, Khālil. *Zubdat kashf al-mamālik,* ed. P. Ravaisse. Paris, 1894; tr. Venture de Paradis, Damascus, 1950.

Zetterstéen, K. V. tr. Anonymous chronicle, 1281–1340, in *Beiträge zur Geschichte der Mamlukensultane.* Leiden, 1919.

2. ETHIOPIA, THE RED SEA AND THE HORN

Abū Ṣāliḥ. *The churches and monasteries of Egypt and some neighbouring countries*, tr. B. R. A. Evetts. Oxford, 1895.

Alvarez, F. *The Prester John of the Indies*, tr. C. F. Beckingham and G. W. B. Huntingford. Cambridge, 1961. 2 vols.

Arab-Faqih. *Histoire de la conquête de l'Abyssinie*, tr. René Basset. Paris, 1897–1901.

Aregay, M. W. 'Southern Ethiopia and the Christian Kingdom, 1508–1708'. Doctoral thesis, University of London, 1971; in course of publication by Heinemann.

Aregay, M. W. and Beshah, G. *The question of the union of the churches in Luso-Ethiopian relations, 1500–1632*. Lisbon, 1964.

Azaïs, R. P. and Chambord, R. *Cinq années de recherches archéologiques en Ethiopie*. Paris, 1931.

Basset, R. 'Études sur l'histoire d'Ethiopie', *Journal Asiatique*, 1881, **17**, 315–434; 1882, **18**, 93–183, 285–389.

Basset, R. 'Les inscriptions de l'île de Dahlak', *Journal Asiatique*, 1893, **1**, 77–111.

Bender, M. L. 'The languages of Ethiopia: a new lexicostatistical classification and some problems of diffusion', *Anthropological Linguistics*, 1971, **13**, 5, 165–288.

Bezold, C. *Kebra Nagast*. Munich, 1909.

Bruce, J. *Travels to discover the source of the Nile*. Edinburgh, 1790. 5 vols.

Budge, E. A. W. *The lives of Meba-Siyon and Gabra-Kristos*. London, 1898.

Budge, E. A. W. *The life and miracles of Takla Haymanot*. London, 1906.

Budge, E. A. W. *The book of the Saints of the Ethiopian Church: a translation of the Ethiopian synaxrion made from the manuscripts Oriental 660 and 661 in the British Museum*. Cambridge, 1928.

Budge, E. A. W. *History of Ethiopia, Nubia and Abyssinia*. London, 1928.

Buxton, D. *Abyssinia*. London, 1970.

Cerulli, E. 'Documenti arabi per la storia dell'Etiopia', *Memoria della Reale Accademia dei Lincei* (Classe di scienze morali, storiche e filologiche), 1931, **4**, 37–101.

Cerulli, E. 'L'Etiopia del secolo XV in nuovi documenti storici', *Africa Italiana*, 1933, **5**, 57–112.

Cerulli, E. 'Il sultanato dello Scioa nel secolo XIII secondo un nuovo documento storico', *Rassegna di studi Etiopici*, 1941, **1**, 5–14.

Cerulli, E. 'L'Etiopia medievale in alcuni brani di scrittori arabi', ibid. 1943, **3**, 272–94.

Cerulli, E. *Il libro etiopico dei miracoli di Maria e le sue fonti nella letteratura del medio evo latino*. Rome, 1943.

Cerulli, E. *Etiopi in Palestina*. Rome, 1943–7. 2 vols.

Cerulli, E. *Storia della letteratura etiopica*. Rome, 1956.

Cerulli, E. *Somalia, scritti vari editi ed inediti*. Rome, 1957, 1959, 1964. 3 vols.

Conti Rossini, C. 'La storia di Lebna Dengel re d'Etiopia', *Rendiconti della*

Reale Accademia dei Lincei (Classe di scienze morali, storiche e filologiche), 1894, **3**, 617–40.

Conti Rossini, C. 'Sulla dinastia Zague', *L'Oriente*, 1897. **2**, 144–59.

Conti Rossini, C. 'L'evangelo d'oro di Dabra Libanos', *Rendiconti della Reale Accademia dei Lincei* (Classe di scienze morali, storiche e filologiche), 1901, **10**, 177–219.

Conti Rossini, C. 'Les listes des rois d'Aksum', *Journal Asiatique*, 1909, **14**, 263–320.

Conti Rossini, C. *Liber Axumae*. Paris, 1910. Repr. Louvain, 1954.

Conti Rossini, C. 'Il libro delle leggende e tradizioni abissine dell'ecciaghie Filpos', *Rendiconti della Reale Accademia dei Lincei* (Classe di scienze morali, storiche e filologiche), 1917, **26**, 699–717.

Conti Rossini, C. *Storia d'Etiopia*, vol. I, Bergamo, 1928.

Conti Rossini, C. 'Necropoli musulmane ed antica chiesa Christiana presso Uugri Hariba nell'Enderta', *Rivista degli Studi Orientali*, 1938, **17**, 339–408.

Conzelman, W. E. *La Chronique de Galawdewos, roi d'Ethiopie*. Paris, 1895.

Crawford, O. G. S. *Ethiopian itineraries, c. 1400–1524*. London, 1958.

Creone, F. 'La politica orientale di Alphonso di Aragone', *Archivio storico per le provencie napolitane*, 1902, **27**, 1–93; 1903, **28**, 154–202.

Fleming, H. G. 'Baiso and Rendille: Somali outliers', *Rassegna di studi Etiopici*, 1964, **20**, 35–96.

Fleming, H. G. 'Ethiopic language history: testing linguistic hypotheses in an archaeological and documentary context', *Ethno-History*, 1968, **15**, 353–88.

Hetzron, R. *Ethiopian Semitic: studies in classification*. London, 1972.

Hingeston, F. C. *Royal and historical letters during the reign of Henry IV, King of England and of France, and Lord of Ireland*, vol. I. London, 1860.

Huntingford, G. W. B. *The land charters of northern Ethiopia*. London, 1965.

Huntingford, G. W. B. *The glorious victories of Amda Seyon, king of Ethiopia*. Oxford, 1965.

Johnson, A. R. *Sacral kingship in ancient Israel*. Cardiff, 1955.

Kammerer, A. *La Mer rouge, l'Abyssinie et l'Arabie depuis l'antiquité. Essai d'histoire et de géographie historique*, vol. I. Cairo, 1929.

al-Khazraji. *History of the Resuli dynasty of Yemen*, tr. J. W. Redhouse. E. J. W. Gibb Memorial Series, III, pt. 2. London, 1907.

Leslau, Wolf. *Falasha anthology*. New Haven, 1951.

Leslau, Wolf. 'Is there a Proto-Gurage?', *Proceedings of the International Conference on Semitic studies*. Jerusalem, 1965, 1–20.

Leslau, Wolf, 'A short chronicle on the Gafat', *Rivista di Studi Orientali*, 1966, **41**, 189–98.

Leslau, Wolf. 'Toward a classification of the Gurage dialects', *Journal of Semitic Studies*, 1969, **14**, 96–109.

Lewis, H. S. 'The origins of the Galla and Somali', *Journal of African History*, 1966, **7**, 27–46.

Lewis, I. M. 'The Galla in northern Somaliland', *Rassegna di Studi Etiopici*, 1959, **15**, 21–38.

Lewis, I. M. *A pastoral democracy*. London, 1965.
al-Maqrīzī. *Historia regnum* . . . *See* under ch. 1.
Mufazzal. 'Histoire des sultans mamelouks'. *See* under Mufaḍḍal ch. 1.
Pansera, C. 'Quattro stele musulmane presso Uogher Hariba nell Enderta', in C. Conti Rossini, ed. *Studia Etiopici*. Rome, 1945.
Pereira, F. M. E. *Historia de Minas, rei de Ethiopia*. Lisbon, 1887–8.
Pereira, F. M. E. *Chronica de Susenyos, rei de Ethiopia*. Lisbon, 1892–1900.
Perruchon, J. 'Histoire des guerres d'Amda Seyon, roi d'Ethiopie', *Journal Asiatique*, 1889, **14**, 271–363, 381–493.
Perruchon, J. *Vie de Lalibela, roi d'Ethiopie*. Paris, 1892.
Perruchon, J. *Les Chroniques de Zar'a Ya'eqob et de Ba'eda Maryam*. Paris, 1893.
Perruchon, J. 'Histoire d'Eskender, d'Amda Seyon II et de Naod, rois d'Ethiopie', *Journal Asiatique*, 1894, **3**, 319–66.
Perruchon, J. 'Extrait de la vie d'Abba Jean, 74e patriarche d'Alexandrie, relatif à l'Abyssinie', *Revue Sémitique*, 1898, **6**, 267–71, 365–72; 1899, **7**, 76–85.
Quatremère, E. *Mémoires géographiques et historiques sur l'Egypte et sur quelques contrées voisines*. Paris, 1811. 2 vols.
Renaudot, E. *Historia patriarcharum Alexandronum*. Paris, 1717.
Sanceau, E. *Portugal in quest of Prester John*. London, 1943.
Sawirus, Ibn al-Mukaffa. *History of the patriarchs of the Egyptian Church*, vol. I [to AD 849], tr. B. T. A. Evetts, in *Patrologia Orientalis*. Paris, 1904–15, **1**, **5**, **10**, **11**.
Sawirus, Ibn al-Mukaffa. *History of the patriarchs of the Egyptian Church*, vol. II [AD 849–1102], tr. Yassa 'abd al-Masih, Aziz Sural Atiya and O. H. E. Burmester. Cairo, 1943–59.
Schneider, M. 'Stèles funéraires arabes de Quiha', *Annales d'Ethiopie*, 1967, **7**, 107–22.
Schoff, W. H. *The Periplus of the Erythrean Sea*. London, 1912.
Sergew Hable-Sellassie. *Ancient and medieval Ethiopian history to 1270*. Addis Ababa, 1972.
Simon, G. *L'Éthiopie*. Paris, 1885.
Taddesse Tamrat. 'Some notes on the fifteenth century Stephanite "heresy" in the Ethiopian Church', *Rassegna di Studi Etiopici*, 1968, **22**, 103–15.
Taddesse Tamrat. 'The abbots of Debre Hayq, 1248–1535', *Journal of Ethiopian Studies*, 1970, **8**, 1, 87–117.
Taddesse Tamrat. *Church and state in Ethiopia, 1270–1527*. Oxford, 1972.
Taddesse Tamrat. 'A short note on the traditions of pagan resistance to the Ethiopian Church (14th and 15th centuries)', *Journal of Ethiopian Studies*, 1972, **10**, 137–50.
Taddesse Tamrat. 'Problems of royal succession in fifteenth century Ethiopia', *Proceedings of the Fourth International Congress of Ethiopian Studies, Rome, 1972* [in press].
Tewolde Medhin, Joseph. 'Introduction générale aux églises monolithes du Tigrai', *Proceedings of the Third International Congress of Ethiopian Studies*, Addis Ababa, 1969, **1**, 83–98.
Trimingham, J. S. *Islam in Ethiopia*. London, 1952.

Turaiev, B. *Acta S. Aronis et S. Philippi* (Corpus Christ. Orient.), vols. 30–1. Louvain, 1955, 1961 (reprints).
Turaiev, B. *Acta S. Eustathii.* Petropoli, 1905 (text); Corpus Christ. Orient., vol. 32, Rome, 1906 (transl.).
Ullendorff, E. 'Gurage notes', *Africa*, 1950, **20**, 335–44
Ullendorff, E. *The Semitic languages of Ethiopia.* London, 1955.
Ullendorff, E. 'Hebraic-Jewish elements in Abyssinian (Monophysite) Christianity', *Journal of Semitic Studies*, 1956, **1**, 216–56.
Ullendorff, E. 'Index to Conti Rossini's *Storia d'Etiopia*', *Rassegna di Studi Etiopici,* 1962, **18**, 97–141.
Umarā. *Yaman, its early medieval history*, tr. H. C. Kay. London, 1892.
Whiteway, R. S. *The Portuguese expedition to Abyssinia.* London, 1902.
Wiet, G. 'Les relations égypto-abyssines'. See under ch. 1.
Wiet, G. 'Roitelets de Dahlak', *Bulletin de l'Institut d'Egypte*, 1951–2, **34**, 85–95.
Zara-Ya'qob. *Meshafe-Milad*, ed. and tr. K. Wendt (Corpus Scriptorum Christianorum Orientalium: Scriptores Aethiopici), vols. 41–4. Louvain, 1962.
Zara-Ya'qob. *Meshafe Birhan*, ed. and tr. C. Conti Rossini and L. Ricci. Ibid. vols. 47–8, 51–2. Louvain, 1964, 1965.

3. THE EAST COAST, MADAGASCAR AND THE INDIAN OCEAN

Abraham, D. P. 'The ethno-history of the empire of Mutapa: problems and methods', in Vansina and others, *The historian in tropical Africa*, 104–26.
Axelson, E. *South-East Africa, 1488–1530.* Johannesburg, 1940.
Axelson, E. *Portuguese in South-East Africa, 1600–1700.* Johannesburg, 1960.
Badger, G. P. ed. *History of the Imams and Seyyids of Oman by Salīl ibn Razīk.* London, 1871.
Baumann, O. *Die Insel Mafia und ihre kleineren Nachbarinseln.* Leipzig, 1896.
Baumann, O. *Die Insel Sansibar und ihre kleineren Nachbarinseln.* Leipzig, 1897.
Baxter, H. C. 'Pangani: the trade centre of ancient history', *Tanganyika Notes and Records*, 1944, **17**, 55–7.
Burton, R. *Zanzibar: city, island and coast.* London, 1872. 2 vols.
Buzurg b. Shahriyār. *See* Lith, P.
Cahen, C. 'Le commerce musulman dans l'Océan Indien au Moyen Age', *Sociétés et Compagnies de commerce en Orient et dans l'Océan Indien* (Paris), 1970, 180–93.
Cerulli, E. *Somalia, scritti vari. See under* ch. 2.
Chittick, H. N. *Annual reports of the Department of Antiquities, 1958–61* (annually), Dar es Salaam.
Chittick, H. N. *Kisimani Mafia: excavations at an Islamic settlement on the East African coast.* Antiquities Division Occasional Paper no. 1. Dar es Salaam, 1961.
Chittick, H. N. 'Kilwa and the Arab settlement of the East African coast', *Journal of African History*, 1963, **4**, 2, 179–90; reprinted in J. D. Fage and Roland Oliver, eds. *Papers in African prehistory.*

Chittick, H. N. 'Kilwa, a preliminary report', *Azania*, 1966, **1**, 1–36.
Chittick, H. N. 'Discoveries in the Lamu archipelago', *Azania*, 1967, **2**, 46–67.
Chittick, H. N. 'Two traditions about the early history of Kilwa', *Azania*, 1968, **3**, 197–200.
Chittick, H. N. 'A new look at the history of Pate', *Journal of African History*, 1969, **10**, 3, 375–91.
Chittick, H. N. 'The "Shirazi" colonization of East Africa', *Journal of African History*, 1965, **6**, 3, 275–94; reprinted in Fage and Oliver, *Papers in African prehistory*.
Chittick, H. N. 'On the chronology and coinage of the sultans of Kilwa', *Numismatic Chronicle*, 1973, **13**.
Chittick, H. N. *Kilwa: an Islamic trading city on the East African coast*. Nairobi, 1974. 2 vols.
Chittick, H. N. ed. 'The early history of Kilwa Kivinje', *Azania*, 1969, **4**, 153–9. *See also* [translation with comments] C. Velten, *Prosa und Poesie der Suaheli*.
Chittick, H. N. and Rotberg, R. I. eds. *East Africa and the Orient*. New York, 1975.
Correa, G. *Lendas da India*. Lisbon, 1858–66. 4 vols.
Dahl, O. C. *Malgache et Maanjan, une comparaison linguistique*. Oslo, 1951.
Dale, Archdeacon G. *The peoples of Zanzibar – their customs and their religious beliefs*. London, 1920.
Dames, M. L. ed. *The book of Duarte Barbosa*. London, 1918–21. 2 vols.
Datoo, B. A. 'Rhapta: the location and importance of East Africa's first port', *Azania*, 1970, **5**, 65–75.
Decken, C. C. van der. *Reisen in Ost Afrika*, ed. O. Kersten. Leipzig and Heidelberg, 1869.
Deschamps, H. *Histoire de Madagascar*. Paris, 1961.
Devic, L. M. *See* Lith, P.
Dez, J. 'Aperçus pour une dialectologie du langue malgache', *Bulletin de Madagascar*, 1963, **206**, 600ff.
Duyvendak, J. J. L. *China's discovery of Africa*. London, 1949.
Faria y Sousa, M. de *Asia Portugueza*. Lisbon, 1666–74. [Extracts in Theal, *Records*.]
Ferrand, G. *Les Musulmans à Madagascar et aux Iles Comores*. Paris, 1891–1902. 2 vols.
Ferrand, G. 'Généalogies et légendes arabico-malgaches d'après le manuscrit 13 de la Bibliothèque Nationale', *Revue Madagascar*, May 1902, 392–416.
Ferrand, G. 'Madagascar et les Iles Uaq-Uaq', *Journal Asiatique*, 1904, 489–509.
Ferrand, G. 'Les îles Rammy, Lamery, Wakwak, Komor des Géographes arabes et Madagascar', *Journal Asiatique*, 1907, **10**, 433–500.
Ferrand, G. *Relation de voyages et textes géographiques arabes, persans et turcs*. Paris, 1913–14. 2 vols. [Includes translations of most passages concerned with the East African coast.]
Ferrand, G. 'Le k'ouen-louen et les anciennes navigations inter-océaniques dans les mers du sud', *Journal Asiatique*, 11th series, 1919, **13**, 473–9.

Filesi, T. *Le relazioni della Cina con l'Africa nel Medio-Evo*. Milan, 1962; English ed. (Cass), 1972.

Fontoynont, M. and Raomandahy, E. 'Le grande Comore', *Mémoires de l'Académie malgache*, 1937, **23**, 12.

Freeman-Grenville, G. S. P. 'Historiography of the East African coast', *Tanganyika Notes and Records*, 1960, **55**, 279–89.

Freeman-Grenville, G. S. P. *The medieval history of the coast of Tanganyika*. London, 1962. *See also* Schacht, J. [review of the above in *Bibliotheca Orientalis*, 1964, **21**, 111].

Freeman-Grenville, G. S. P. 'Coin finds and their significance for eastern African chronology', *Numismatic Chronicle*, 1971, **11**, 283–301. *See also* Chittick, H. N. ['Chronology and coinage'].

Garlake, P. S. *The early Islamic architecture of the East African coast*. British Institute in Eastern Africa, Memoir no. 1, London and Nairobi, 1966.

Gaudebout, P. and Vernier, E. 'Notes de la suite d'une enquête sur les objets en pierre de la région de Vohémar', *Bulletin de l'Académie Malgache*, 1941, **24**, 91–9.

Gaudebout, P. and Vernier, E. 'Notes sur une campagne de fouilles à Vohémar, Mission Rasikajy, 1941', *Bulletin de l'Académie Malgache*, 1941, **24**, 100–14.

Grandidier, A. 'Souvenirs de voyages (1865–1870) d'après son manuscrit inédit de 1916', *Documents anciens sur Madagascar* (Tananarive), 1971, **6**.

Grandidier, A. and G. *Ethnographie de Madagascar*. Paris, 1908–28. 5 vols.

Grandidier, A. and G. eds. *Collection des ouvrages anciens concernant Madagascar*. Paris, 1903–20. 9 vols.

Grandidier, G. *Histoire politique et coloniale de Madagascar*, vol. v, pt. 1, Paris, 1942; pt. 2, Tananarive, 1956; pt. 3 [with Decary, R.], Tananarive, 1958.

Gray, Sir J. 'Rezende's description of East Africa in 1634', *Tanganyika Notes and Records*, 1947, **23**, 2.

Gray, Sir J. 'A journey from Tete to Kilwa in 1616', *TNR*, 1948, **25**, 37–47.

Gray, Sir J. 'A history of Kilwa', *TNR*, pt. 1, 1951, **31**, 1–24; pt. 2, 1952, **32**, 11–37.

Gray, Sir J. 'The Wadebuli and the Wadiba', *TNR*, 1954, **36**, 22–42.

Gray, Sir J. 'Early Portuguese visitors to Kilwa', *TNR*, 1959, **52**, 117–28.

Gray, Sir J. 'Commercial intercourse between Angola and Kilwa in the sixteenth century', *TNR*, 1961, **57**, 173–4.

Greenlee, W. B. *The voyage of Pedro Alvares Cabral to Brazil and India*. London, 1938.

Grosset-Grange, H. 'La côte africaine dans les routiers nautiques arabes au moment des grandes découvertes', *Azania* (forthcoming).

Grottanelli, V. L. *Pescatori dell'oceano Indiano*. Rome, 1955.

Guillain, M. *Documents sur le commerce et la géographie de la partie occidentale de Madagascar*. Paris, 1845. 3 vols.

Guillain, M. *Documents sur l'histoire, la géographie et le commerce de l'Afrique orientale*. Paris, 1848, 3 vols.

Herbert, J. C. 'Notes sur les Vazimba du Betsiriry', *Bulletin du Madagascar*, 1971, **304**, 721–33.

Hornell, F. 'Indonesian influences on East African culture', *Journal of the Royal Anthropological Institute*, 1934, **37**, 305–32.

Hourani, F. *Arab seafaring in the Indian Ocean*. Princeton, 1951.

Hrbek, I. 'The chronology of Ibn Battuta's travels', *Archiv orientální*, 1962, **30**, 409–86.

Hudūd al-'ālam: a Persian geography, tr. V. Minorsky, 2nd ed. London, 1970.

Ibn al-Mujāwir. *Tārīkh al-Mustabṣīr*, in Ferrand, 'Le k'ouen-louen'.

al-Jāḥiz. *Kitāb Fakhr as-Sudan 'ala'l Bīḍān*, in *Tria opuscula*, ed. G. van Vloten. Leiden, 1903.

Jones, A. 'The influence of Indonesia: the musicological evidence reconsidered', *Azania*, 1969, **4**, 131–45.

Kent, R. K. *Early kingdoms in Madagascar, 1500–1700*. New York, 1970.

Kirkman, J. S. 'The excavations at Kilepwa', *Antiquaries Journal*, 1952, **32**, 168–84.

Kirkman, J. S. *The Arab city of Gedi: excavations at the Great Mosque, architecture and finds*. Oxford, 1954.

Kirkman, J. S. 'Excavations at Ras Mkumbuu on the island of Pemba', *Tanganyika Notes and Records*, 1959, **53**, 161–78.

Kirkman, J. S. *The tomb of the dated inscription at Gedi*. Royal Anthropological Institute Occasional Paper no. 14, London, 1960.

Kirkman, J. S. *Gedi, the palace*, vol. I of *Studies in African history*. The Hague, 1963.

Kirkman, J. S. *Men and monuments on the East African coast*. London, 1964.

Kirkman, J. S. *Ungwana on the Tana*, vol. IV of *Studies in African history*. The Hague, 1966.

Kirkman, J. S. 'The coast of Kenya as a factor in the trade and culture of the Indian Ocean', *Sociétés et Compagnies de commerce en Orient et dans l'Océan Indien* (Paris), 1970, 247–53.

Kitāb al-Zunūj. *See* Cerulli, *Somalia* (under ch. 2).

Krapf, J. L. *Reisen in Ostafrika*. 1850; reprinted Stuttgart, 1964.

Krapf, J. L. *Travels, researches and missionary labours during an eighteen years' residence in eastern Africa*. 1860; reprinted (Cass) 1968.

Lewis, I. M. *Peoples of the Horn of Africa, Somali, Afar and Saho*, in part I, *North-eastern Africa*, of *Ethnographic survey of Africa*, ed. D. Forde. London, 1955.

Lith, P. van der, ed. and Devic, L. M. tr. *Livre des merveilles de l'Inde par le Capitaine Bozorg fils du Chahriyar de Ramhormuz*. Leiden, 1883–6; reprinted Teheran, 1966.

Lobato, A. *A expansão portuguesa em Moçambique de 1498 a 1530* . República Portuguesa, Ministerio do Ultramar, Estudes Moçambicanos. Lisbon, 1954–60. 3 vols.

Mauny, R. 'Le Périple de la mer Erythrée et le problème de commerce romain en Afrique au Sud du Limes', *Journal de la Société des Africanistes*, 1938, **38**, 1, 19–34.

Miles, S. B. *The country and tribes of the Persian Gulf*, 2nd ed. London, 1966.

Millot, J. 'Considérations sur le commerce dans l'Océan Indien au Moyen Age et au pré-Moyen Age à propos des perles du Zenaga', *Mémoires I.R.S.M.*, 1952, **2**, 2 (sér. C), 153–65.

Pearce, F. B. *Zanzibar, the island metropolis of Eastern Africa.* London, 1920.

Picard, R., Kerneis, J. P. and Bruneau, Y. *La campagnie de Indes, routes de la porcelaine.* Paris, 1966.

Pigott, D. W. I. 'History of Mafia', *Tanganyika Notes and Records*, 1941, **11**, 35–40.

Pigott, D. W. I. tr. 'Mafia, history and traditions collected by Kadhi Amur Omari Saadi', *TNR*, 1941, **12**, 23–5.

Poirier, J. 'Données écologiques et démographiques de la mise en place des Proto-Malagaches', *Taloha*, 1965, **1**, 61–82.

Prins, A. H. J. *The Swahili-speaking peoples of Zanzibar and the East African coast (Arabs, Shirazi and Swahili)*, in pt. XII, *East Central Africa*, of *Ethnographic survey of Africa*, ed. D. Forde. London, 1967.

Revington, T. M. 'Some notes on the Mafia island group', *Tanganyika Notes and Records*, 1936, **1**, 33–7.

Robineau, C. 'L'Islam aux Comores, une étude d'histoire culturelle de l'île d'Anjouan', in *Arabes et Islamisés à Madagascar*, ed. P. Vérin.

Robinson, A. E. 'Some historical notes on East Africa', *Tanganyika Notes and Records*, 1936, **2**, 21–43.

Robinson, A. E. 'The Shirazi colonizations of East Africa', *TNR*, 1937, **3**, 40–81.

Sacleux, P. *Dictionnaire Swahili–Français.* Paris, 1939.

Sanceau, E. *Portugal in quest of Prester John. See under* ch. 2.

Santos, J. dos. *Ethiopia oriental.* Lisbon, 1891.

Serjeant, R. B. *The Portuguese in the Persian Gulf.* Oxford, 1963.

Serjeant, R. B. *The Portuguese off the South Arabian coast.* Oxford, 1963.

Southall, Aidan. 'The problem of Malagasy origins', in *East Africa and the Orient*, ed. Chittick and Rotberg.

Stigand, C. H. *The land of Zinj.* 1913; reprinted London, 1966.

Storbeck, F. 'Die Berichte der Arabischen Geographen des Mittelalters über Ost Afrika', *Mitteilungen des Seminars für orientalische Sprachen zu Berlin*, 1914, **17**.

Strandes, J. *Die Portugiesenzeit von Deutsch- und Englisch Ostafrika.* Berlin, 1899; also in English [without plates], tr. J. F. Wallwork, ed. J. S. Kirkman. *The Portuguese period in East Africa*, 2nd ed. Nairobi, 1968.

Strong, S. A. 'History of Kilwa', *Journal of the Royal Asiatic Society*, 1895, **20**, 385–430. [Text of the Arabic version of the Kilwa Chronicle and English summary.]

Summers, R., Robinson, K. R. and Whitty, A. *Zimbabwe excavations, 1958.* Occasional papers, National Museum of Southern Rhodesia, no. 23A, 1961.

Vansina, J., Mauny, R. and Thomas, L. V. eds. *The historian in tropical Africa.* Oxford, 1964.

Velten, C. *Prosa und Poesie der Suaheli*. Berlin, 1907. [Includes historical traditions recorded at beginning of twentieth century of Kilwa and other towns, 243–64.]

Vérin, P. 'Les recherches archéologiques à Madagascar', *Azania*, 1966, **1**, 124–37.

Vérin, P. ed. *Arabes et Islamisés à Madagascar et dans l'Océan Indien*. Tananarive, 1967.

Vérin, P. *Les échelles anciennes du commerce sur les côtes nord de Madagascar*. Doctoral thesis, University of Paris, n.d.

Vérin, P. *Histoire ancienne du nord-ouest de Madagascar*. Tananarive, 1972.

Vernier, E. and Millot, J. *Archéologie Malgache – comptoirs musulmans*. Catalogue du Musée de l'Homme, sér. F. I, Paris, 1971.

Vloten, G. van. *Tria opuscula auctore Abu Othman Amr Ibn Bahr al-Djahiz Basrensi*, ed. E. J. Brill. Reprinted Leiden, 1968.

Voeltzkow, A. *Reise in Ostafrika in den Jahren 1903–1905*. Stuttgart, 1923.

Whitehouse, D. 'Excavations at Siraf' [interim reports in] *Iran*, 1968–72, **6–10**.

Whiteley, W. H. *Swahili, the rise of a national language*. London, 1969.

4. THE EASTERN MAGHRIB AND THE CENTRAL SUDAN

Abadie, M. *La colonie du Niger*. Paris, 1927.

Abbo, H., Lebeuf, J.-P. and Rodinson, M. 'Coutumes du Mandara', *Bulletin de l'IFAN*, 1949, **11**, 471–90.

Abun-Nasr, J. M. *A history of the Maghrib*. Cambridge, 1971; 2nd ed. 1975.

Adamu, M. 'The Hausa factor in West African history'. Doctoral thesis, University of Birmingham, 1974.

Ahmadu Bello University and Ibadan University. *Northern history research scheme* (first interim report, 1966; second, 1967). Zaria, mimeo.

Anania, G. L. *See* Lange, D.

Armstrong, R. G. 'The development of kingdoms in Negro Africa', *Journal of the Historical Society of Nigeria*, 1960, **2**, 1, 27–39.

Arnett, E. J. tr. 'A Hausa chronicle', *Journal of the African Society*, 1909–10, **9**, 161–7.

Arnett, E. J. *The rise of the Sokoto Fulani: being a paraphrase and in some parts a translation of the Infaku'l Maisuri of Sultan Mohammed Bello*. n.p., n.d. [1922?].

Attal, Robert, *Les Juifs d'Afrique du nord: bibliographie*. Leiden, 1973.

Baldwin, T. H. tr. *The obligations of princes: an essay on Moslem kingship by Shekh Mohammad al-Maghili of Tlemsen*. Beirut, 1932.

Barbour, N. *A survey of north-west Africa*. London, 1959.

Barth, H. *Travels and discoveries in north and central Africa*. London, 1857–8. 5 vols. 3-vol. ed. New York, 1857; reprinted London, 1965.

Batrān, 'Abd-al-'Azīz 'Abd-Allāh. 'A contribution to the biography of Shaikh Muḥammad . . . al-Maghīlī', *Journal of African History*, 1973, **14**, 3, 381–94.

Bel, Alfred. *Les Benou Ghânya: derniers représentants de l'empire almoravide et leur lutte contre l'empire almohade*. Paris, 1903.

Benton, P. A. *The languages and peoples of Bornu: being a collection of the writings of* . . . [intro. by A. H. M. Kirk-Greene]. London, 1968. 2 vols.

Bernus, E. and S. *Du sel et des dattes: introduction à l'étude de la communauté d'In Gall et de Tegidda-n-tesemt*, *Études nigériennes*, Niamey, 1972, no. 31.

Bernus, E. *Les Illabakan (Niger)*... Paris, 1974.

Binet, Capt. 'Notes sur les ruines de Garouméle (Niger)', *Notes africaines*, 1952, **53**, 1–2.

Bivar, A. D. H. and Hiskett M. 'The Arabic literature of Nigeria to 1804: a provisional account', *Bulletin of the School of Oriental and African Studies*, 1962, **25**, 1, 104–48.

Bivar, A. D. H. and Shinnie, P. L. 'Old Kanuri capitals', *Journal of African History*, 1962, **3**, 1, 1–10.

Blau, O. 'Chronik der Sulṭâne von Bornu', *Zeitschrift der Deutschen morgenländerischen Gesellschaft*, 1852, **6**, 305–30.

Boulnois, J. 'La migration des Sao du Tchad', *Bulletin de l'IFAN*, 1943, **5**, 80–121.

Bovill, E. W. *The golden trade of the Moors*. London, 1958; 2nd ed. [revised by R. Hallett]. London, 1968.

Bovill, E. W. ed. *Missions to the Niger*. London, 1964–6. 4 vols. [Includes relevant writings of Hornemann, Laing, Oudney, Denham and Clapperton.]

Brett, M. 'Ifrīqiya as a market for Saharan trade from the tenth to the twelfth century AD', *Journal of African History*, 1969, **10**, 3, 347–64.

Brett, M. 'Fitnat al-Qayrawān: a study of traditional Arabic historiography'. Doctoral thesis, University of London, 1970. 2 vols.

Briggs, L. C. *Tribes of the Sahara*. London and Cambridge, Mass., 1960.

Brunschvig, R. *La Berbérie orientale sous les Hafsids des origines à la fin du XVe siècle*. Paris, 1940, 1947. 2 vols.

Burdon, J. A. *Northern Nigeria: historical notes on certain emirates and tribes*. London, 1909; reprinted 1972.

Carbou, H. *La région du Tchad et du Ouadai*. Paris, 1912. 2 vols.

de Castries, H. 'La conquête du Soudan par El-Mansour, 1591', *Hespéris*, 1923, **3**, 733–88.

Çelebi. *See* Ciecierska-Chlapowa *and* Habraszewski.

Chapelle, J. *Nomades noirs du Sahara*. Paris, 1957.

Chopard, L. and Villiers, A. eds. *Contribution à l'étude de l'Air*. *Mémoires de l'IFAN*, no. 10, Paris, 1950.

Ciecierska-Chlapowa, T. 'Extraits de fragments du Siyahatname d'Evliya Celebi concernant l'Afrique noire', *Folia Orientalia* [Cracow], 1964, **6**, 239–44.

Clapperton, H. *Journal of a second expedition into the interior of Africa* . . . London, 1829; reprinted 1966.

Cohen, R. 'The Just-so So: a spurious tribal grouping in Western Sudanic culture', *Man*, 1962, **62**, 153–4.

Cohen, R. 'The Bornu king lists', *Boston University Papers on Africa*, no. 2 [ed. J. Butler], Boston, 1966, 39–84.

Cohen, R. 'The dynamics of feudalism in Bornu', ibid. 85–106.

Cohen, R. *The Kanuri of Bornu*. New York, 1967.

Connah, G. 'Recent contributions to Bornu chronology', *West African Journal of Archaeology*, 1971, **1**, 55–60. [Contains useful bibliography of Connah's writings.]

Creswell, K. A. C. *A short account of early Muslim architecture*. London, 1958. [Contains valuable material on Qayrawān.]

David, N. 'The archaeological background of Cameroonian history' [mimeo. to] Colloque International du CNRS, *Contribution de la recherche ethnologique à l'histoire des civilisations du Cameroun*. Paris, 1972.

Duisburg, A. von. *Im Lande des Cheghu von Bornu: Despoten und Völker südlich des Tschad*. Berlin, 1942.

Duisberg, A. von. 'Zur Geschichte der Sultanate Bornu und Wándala (Mándara)', *Anthropos*, 1927, **22**, 187–96.

Epstein, H. *The origin of the domestic animals of Africa*. New York, 1971. 2 vols.

Fisher, A. G. B. and Fisher, H. J. *Slavery and Muslim society in Africa*. London, 1970.

Fisher, H. J. '"He swalloweth the ground with fierceness and rage": the horse in the Central Sudan', *Journal of African History*, 1972, **13**, 3, 367–88 and 1973, **14**, 3, 355–79.

Fortier, J. *Le mythe et les contes de Sou en pays Mbaï-Moïssala*. Bruges, 1967.

Fremantle, J. M. 'A history of the region comprising the Katagum division of Kano province', *Journal of the African Society*, 1911, **10**, 34, 198–319. [Subsequent sections of this article relate to later periods.]

Fuchs, P. *Kult und Autorität: die Religion der Hadjerai*. Berlin, 1970.

Fuchs, P. 'Bagirmi und Kenga: zur Geschichte einer Zentralsudanesischen Staatsgründung', *Paideuma: Mitteilung zur Kulturkunde*, 1973–4, **19–20**, 258–79. [Special issue entitled *Festschrift zum 100. Geburtstag von Leo Frobenius*; contains also J.-P. Lebeuf, 'Ethnologie et archéologie'.]

Goody, J. ed. *Literacy in traditional societies*. Cambridge, 1968.

Greenberg, J. H. 'Arabic loan-words in Hausa', *Word*, 1947, **3**, 85–97.

Greenberg, J. H. 'Linguistic evidence for the influence of the Kanuri on the Hausa', *Journal of African History*, 1960, **1**, 2, 205–12.

Greenberg, J. H. 'Historical inferences from linguistic research in sub-Saharan Africa', in *Boston University Papers in African History*, no. 1 [ed. J. Butler], Boston, 1964, 3–15.

Gwarzo, H. I. 'The life and teachings of al-Maghili, with particular reference to the Saharan Jewish community'. Doctoral thesis, University of London, 1972.

Habraszewski, T. 'Kanuri – language and people – in the "Travel-Book" (Siyahetname) of Evliya Çelebi', *Africana Bulletin* [Warsaw], 1967, no. 6, 59–66.

Hair, P. E. H. 'Early Kanuri vocabularies', *Journal of West African Languages*, 1969, **6**, 1, 27–9.

al-Hajj, M. A. 'A seventeenth century chronicle on the origins and missionary activities of the Wangarawa', *Kano Studies*, 1968, **1**, 4, 7–42.

Hallam, W. K. R. 'The Bayajida legend in Hausa folklore', *Journal of African History*, 1966, **7**, 1, 47–60.

Hassan, Alhaji and Shuaibu, Mallam Na'ibi. *A chronicle of Abuja*, tr. F. Heath. Lagos, 1962.

Hirschberg, H. Z. *A history of the Jews in North Africa: from antiquity to our time*. Jerusalem, 1965. [In Hebrew; translation forthcoming, from Brill.]

Hiskett, M. 'An Islamic tradition of reform in the Western Sudan from the sixteenth to the eighteenth century', *Bulletin of the School of Oriental and African Studies*, 1962, **25**, 3, 577–96.

Hiskett, M. 'The "Song of Bagauda": a Hausa king list and homily in verse', *BSOAS*, 1964, **27**, 3, 540–67, and 1965, **28**, 1, 112–35, and **2**, 363–85.

Hiskett, M. 'The historical background to the naturalization of Arabic loanwords in Hausa', *African Language Studies*, 1965, **6**, 18–26.

Hiskett, M. 'Materials relating to the cowry currency of the Western Sudan', *BSOAS*, 1966, **29**, 1, 122–42, and 2, 339–66.

Hogben, S. J. and Kirk-Greene, A. H. M. *The emirates of Northern Nigeria*. London, 1966.

Hornemann, F. 'Journal', in *Proceedings of the Association for promoting the discovery of the interior parts of Africa*, vol. II. London, 1810; reprinted London, 1967. [*See also* Bovill, 1964–6, vol. I.]

Huard, P. 'Introduction et diffusion du fer au Tchad', *Journal of African History*, 1966, **7**, 3, 377–404.

Hunwick, J. O. 'A little-known diplomatic episode in the history of Kebbi (*c.* 1594)', *Journal of the Historical Society of Nigeria*, 1971, **5**, 4, 575–81.

Hunwick, J. O. 'The dynastic chronologies of the central Sudan in the sixteenth century: some reinterpretations', *Kano studies*, N.S., 1973, **1**, 1, 35–55.

Hunwick, J. O. 'Al-Maghīlī's replies to the questions of Askia al-Ḥājj Muḥammad, edited and translated with an introduction on the history of Islam in the Niger bend to 1500'. Doctoral thesis, University of London, 1974.

Ibiraa, Sarkin Makada. *Histoire du Dawra*, tr. Issaka Dankoussou. Niamey, Niger, 1970.

Ibn Fartuwa. *See* Palmer, H. R. (1970) *and* Redhouse, J. W.

Idris, H. R. *La berbérie orientale sous les Zīrīdes, Xe–XIIe siècles*. Paris, 1962.

IFAN. *Contribution à l'étude de l'Aïr. Memoires de l'IFAN* no. 10, Paris, 1950. [Mainly natural sciences.]

Institut National Tchadien pour les Sciences Humaines. *Atlas pratique du Tchad*. Fort Lamy, 1972

Julien, C.-A. *History of North Africa: Tunisia, Algeria, Morocco: from the Arab conquest to 1830*, tr. J. Petrie, ed. C. C. Stewart. London, 1970.

Kalck, Pierre. 'Pour une localisation du royaume de Gaoga', *Journal of African History*, 1972, **13**, 4, 529–48.

Kano Chronicle. See Palmer, H. R. (1909).
al-Khuwārizmī. *Kitāb Ṣūrat al-arḍ*, ed. H. v. Mžik; *Das Kitāb Ṣūrat al-arḍ des Abū Ǧaʿfar . . . al-Huwārizmī.* Leipzig, 1926. *See also* Lewicki, *Arabic external sources.*
Kirk-Greene, A. H. M. ed. *Gazetteers of the northern provinces of Nigeria.* London, 1972 (reprint of vols. orig. publ. 1920–34). [The gazetteers are listed individually in the corresponding bibliography in *CHA*, vol. 4; the reprinted set is likely to be more accessible.]
Lange, D. 'L'intérieur de l'Afrique occidentale d'après Giovanni Lorenzo Anania (XVIe siècle)', *Journal of World History*, 1972, **14**, 2, 299–351.
Lange, D. 'Contribution à l'histoire dynastique du Kānem-Bornū', Thesis, 3rd cycle, Paris I, 1974.
Laroui, A. *L'histoire du Maghreb: un essai de synthèse.* Paris, 1970.
Lavers, J. E. 'Islam in the Bornu caliphate', *Odu*, 1971, **5**, 27–53.
Lebeuf, A. M.-D. *Les populations du Tchad.* Paris, 1959.
Lebeuf, A. M.-D. 'Boum Massénia, capitale de l'ancien royaume du Baguirmi', *Journal de la Société des Africanistes*, 1937, **37**, 1, 215–44.
Lebeuf, A. M.-D. *Les principautés Kotoko: essai sur le caractère sacré de l'autorité.* Paris, 1969.
Lebeuf, J.-P. *Archéologie tchadienne: les Sao du Cameroun et du Tchad.* Paris, 1962.
Lebeuf, J.-P. *Carte archéologique des abords du lac Tchad.* Paris, 1969. 2 vols.
Lebeuf, J.-P. and Detourbet, A. M. *La civilisation du Tchad.* Paris, 1950.
Le Coeur, C. and M. *Grammaire et textes Téda-Daza. Mémoires de l'IFAN* no. 46, Dakar, 1956.
Lembezat, B. *Les populations païennes du Nord-Cameroun et de l'Adamaoua.* Paris, 1961.
Le Rouvreur, A. *Sahéliens et Sahariens du Tchad.* Paris, 1962.
Lethem, G. J. *Colloquial Arabic: Shuwa dialect of Bornu, Nigeria and of the region of Lake Chad.* London, 1920.
Lethielleux, J. *Le Fezzan, ses jardins, ses palmiers....* Tunis, 1948.
Le Tourneau, R. *The Almohad movement in North Africa in the twelfth and thirteenth centuries.* Princeton, 1969.
Lewicki, T. 'A propos du nom de l'oasis de Koufra chez les géographes arabes du XIe et XIIe siècles', *Journal of African History*, 1965, **6**, 3, 295–306.
Lewicki, T. 'The Ibádites in Arabia and Africa', *Cahiers d'histoire mondiale/Journal of World History*, 1971, **13**, 1, 51–130.
Lewicki, T. *West African food in the middle ages.* Cambridge, 1974.
Lézine, A. *Deux villes d'Ifriqiya: études d'archéologie, d'urbanisme, de démographie: Sousse, Tunis.* Paris, 1971.
Lhote, H. 'Le cheval et le chameau days les peintures et gravures rupestres du Sahara', *Bulletin de l'IFAN*, 1953, **15** (sér. B), 1138–1228.
Lhote, H. 'Recherches sur Takedda, ville décrite par le voyageur Ibn Battouta et située en Aïr', *Bulletin de l'IFAN*, 1972, **34** (sér. B), 3, 429–70.
Lovejoy, Paul E. 'The Kambarin Beriberi: the formation of a specialised group of Hausa kola traders in the nineteenth century', *Journal of African History*, 1973, **14**, 4, 633–51.

Lovejoy, P. E. 'The Wangara impact on Kano', in *Kano Studies*, forthcoming.

Low, V. N. *Three Nigerian emirates: a study in oral history*. Evanston, 1972.

Lukas, J. 'The linguistic situation in the Lake Chad area in Central Africa', *Africa*, 1936, **9**, 332–49.

Lukas, J. 'Linguistic research between the Nile and Lake Chad', *Africa*, 1939, **12**, 335–49.

Lukas, R. *Nicht-islamische Ethnien im Südlichen Tschadraum*. Wiesbaden, 1973.

al-Maghili of Tlemsen. *The obligations of princes: an essay on Moslem Kingship by Shekh Mohammed al-Maghili of Tlemsen*, tr. T. H. Baldwin. Beirut, 1932.

Martin, B. G. 'Five letters from the Tripoli archives', *Journal of the Historical Society of Nigeria*, 1962, **3**, 2, 350–72.

Martin, B. G. 'Kanem, Bornu and the Fazzān: notes on the political history of a trade route', *Journal of African History*, 1969, **10**, 1, 15–27.

Martin, B. G. 'Maî Idrîs of Bornu and the Ottoman Turks, 1576–78', *International Journal of Middle East Studies*, 1972, **3**, 470–90.

Mason, M. 'The Nupe kingdom in the nineteenth century: a political history'. Doctoral thesis, University of Birmingham, 1970.

Mauny, R. 'Notes sur les "grands voyages" de Léon l'Africain', *Hespéris*, 1954, **41**, 379–94.

Meek, C. K. *A Sudanese kingdom: an ethnographical study of the Jukun-speaking peoples of Nigeria*. London, 1931.

Meek, C. K. *Tribal studies in Northern Nigeria*. London, 1931. 2 vols.

Mischlich, A. and Lippert, J. 'Beiträge zur Geschichte der Haussastaaten', *Mitteilungen des Seminars für Orientalische Sprachen zu Berlin*, 1903, **6**, *Afrikanische Studien*.

Moreau, J. and Stordeur, D. *Bibliographie du Tchad (sciences humaines)*, 2nd ed. Fort-Lamy, 1970.

Motylinski, A. de C. *Le dialecte berbère de R'edamès*. Paris, 1904.

Nachtigal, G. *Sahara und Sudan*. Berlin, 1879, 1881, Leipzig, 1889. 3 vols. Complete reprint Graz, 1967. [Of the complete English translation, by A. G. B. and H. J. Fisher, vol. IV, on Wadai and Darfur, and vol. I, on Fezzan and Tibesti, have appeared (London, 1971, 1974).]

Nadel, S. F. *A black Byzantium: the kingdom of Nupe in Nigeria*. London, 1942.

Nadel, S. F. 'The *gani* ritual of Nupe: a study in social symbiosis', *Africa*, 1949, **19**, 3, 177–86.

al-Naqar, 'Umar. *The pilgrimage tradition in West Africa*. Khartoum, 1972.

Newman, P. and Ma, R. 'Comparative Chadic: phonology and lexicon', *Journal of African Languages*, 1966, **5**, 218–51.

Nicolaisen, J. *Ecology and culture of the pastoral Tuareg* (Copenhagen, 1964).

Norris, H. T. *The Tuaregs: their Islamic legacy and its diffusion in the Sahel*. Warminster, 1975.

O'Fahey, R. S. and Spaulding, J. L. 'Comment: the geographic location of Gaoga' [with reply from P. Kalck], *Journal of African History*, 1973, **14**, 3, 505–8.

Palmer, H. R. ed. 'The Kano Chronicle', *Journal of the Anthropological Institute*, 1909, **38**, 58–98.

Palmer, H. R. 'Notes on some Asben records', *Journal of the African Society*, 1909–10, **9**, 388–400.

Palmer, H. R. 'Notes on the Korôrofawa and Jukoñ', *JAS*, 1912, **11**, 44, 401–15.

Palmer, H. R. 'The Bornu girgam', *JAS*, 1912–13, **12**, 45, 71–83.

Palmer, H. R. 'Western Sudan history: the Raudthât' ul Afkãri', *JAS*, 1915–16, **15**, 261–73.

Palmer, H. R. 'History of Katsena', *JAS*, 1927, **26**, 103, 216–36.

Palmer, H. R. 'A Muslim divine of the Sudan in the fifteenth century', *Africa*, 1930, **3**, 203–16.

Palmer, H. R. *The Bornu, Sahara and Sudan*. London, 1936.

Palmer, H. R. *Sudanese memoirs*. *See under* 'general' section, Arabic writers.

Palmer, H. R. tr. and ed. *History of the first twelve years of the reign of Mai Idris Alooma of Bornu* [by his Imam, Ahmed Ibn Fartua, together with the 'Diwan of the Sultans of Bornu' and 'Girgam' of the Magumi]. Lagos, 1926; reprinted London, 1970.

Pâques, V. 'Origine et caractères du pouvoir royal au Baguirmi', *Journal de la Société des Africanistes*, 1967, **37**, 1, 183–214.

Patterson, J. R. *Kanuri songs*. Lagos, 1926.

Patterson, J. R. *Stories of Abu Zeid*. London, 1930.

Pitcher, D. E. *An historical geography of the Ottoman Empire from the earliest times to the end of the sixteenth century*. Leiden, 1972.

Poncet, J. P. 'Le mythe de la "catastrophe" hilalienne', *Annales: économies, sociétés, civilisations*, 1967, **22**, 1099–120.

Rattray, R. S. *Hausa folk-lore, customs, proverbs*. Oxford, 1913. 2 vols.

Raymond, A. *Artisans et commerçants au Caire au XVIII siècle*. Damascus, 1973–4. 2 vols.

Redhouse, J. W. tr. 'History of Journal of the events . . . during seven expeditions . . . against the tribes of Bulala', *Journal of the Royal Asiatic Society*, 1862, **19**, 43–123. [Another translation of Ibn Fartuwa's *Kanem Wars*, to compare with that in the first volume of *Sudanese memoirs*.]

Richter, Lore. *Islands of the Sahara: through the oases of Libya*. Leipzig, 1960. [Mostly illustrations.]

Rodd, F. *People of the veil: being an account of the . . . wandering Tuareg . . . in the Central Sahara*. London, 1926.

Rodinson, M. and Lebeuf, J.-P. 'L'origin et les souverains du Mandara', *Bulletin de l'IFAN*, 1956, **18** (sér. B), 227–55.

Sartain, E. M. 'Jalāl ad-Dīn as-Suyūṭī's relations with the people of Takrūr', *Journal of Semitic Studies*, 1971, **16**, 193–8.

Sartain, E. M. *Jalāl al-dīn al-Suyūṭī*. Cambridge, 1975. 2 vols.

Sayous, A.-E. *Le commerce des européens à Tunis depuis le XIIe siècle jusqu'à la fin du XVIe*. Paris, 1929.

Schacht, J. 'Sur la diffusion des formes d'architecture religieuse musulmane à travers le Sahara', *Travaux de l'Institut de Recherches Sahariennes*, 1954, **11**, 11–27.

Schiffers, H. ed. *Die Sahara und ihre Randgebeite*. Munich, 1971–3. 3 vols. (Physiogeographie, Humangeographie, Regionalgeographie).

Schiffers, H. ed. *Dürren in Afrika: Faktoren-Analyse aus dem Sudan-Sahel.* Munich, 1974.

Schlüter, H. *Index Libycus: bibliography of Liyba, 1957–69: with supplementary material, 1915–56.* Boston, 1972.

Schneider, J. L. 'Evolution du dernier lacustre et peuplements préhistoriques aux Pays-Bas du Tchad', *Bulletin de Liaison* (Association sénégalaise pour l'étude du Quaternaire de l'ouest africain), 1967, **14–15**, 18–23.

Schön, J. F. *Magana Hausa: native literature, or proverbs, tales, fables and historical fragments in the Hausa language, to which is added a translation in English.* London, 1885.

Schultze, A. *The sultanate of Bornu*, tr. and ed. P. A. Benton. 1913; reprinted London, 1968.

Sebag, Paul. *The great mosque of Kairouan*, tr. R. Howard. New York, 1965. [Excellent illustrations.]

Sebag, P. *Une relation inédite sur la prise de Tunis par les Turcs en 1574: 'Sopra la desolatione della Goletta e forte di Tunisie' de Bartholomeo Ruffino* [Introduction, text and annotated translation]. Tunis, 1971.

Seliquer, Capitaine. 'Elements d'une étude archéologique des pays bas du Tchad', *Bulletin de l'IFAN*, 1954, **7**, 191–209.

Shaw, C. T. 'Archaeology in Nigeria', *Antiquity*, 1969, **43**, 187–99.

Skinner, N. 'The origin of the name "Hausa"', *Africa*, 1968, **38**, 253–7.

Skinner, N. *Hausa tales and traditions: an English translation of Tatsuniyoyi na hausa, originally compiled by Frank Edgar.* London, 1969. [Two further vols. promised.]

Slavin, K. and J. *The Tuareg.* London, 1973. [Many illustrations.]

Smith, Abdullahi, 'Some considerations relating to the formation of states in Hausaland', *Journal of the Historical Society of Nigeria*, 1970, **5**, 3, 329–46.

Smith, M. G. 'The beginnings of Hausa society', in *The historian in tropical Africa*, ed. Vansina and others.

Sørbø, G. *Sudan sources I: Petermann's Mitteilungen.* Occasional Paper no. 3, Programme for Middle-Eastern and African Studies, University of Bergen, Norway, 1974. [53 pp., index of travellers' names. A useful list of titles of articles and maps appearing in the *Mitteilungen*, 1855–1900.]

Temple, O. *Notes on the tribes, provinces, emirates and states of the northern provinces of Nigeria*, 2nd ed. 1922, reprinted London, 1965.

Tremearne, A. J. N. *Hausa superstitions and customs.* London, 1913.

Trimingham, J. S. *A history of Islam in West Africa.* London, 1962.

Tubiana, M.-J. 'Un document inédit sur les sultans du Waddāy', *Cahiers d'études africaines*, 1960, **1**, 2, 49–112.

Tubiana, M.-J. *Survivances pré-islamiques en pays zaghawa.* Paris, 1964.

al-Tūnusī, Muḥammad b. 'Umar. *Voyage au Ouadây*, tr. Dr Perron. Paris, 1851.

Urvoy, Y. 'Chroniques d'Agadès', *Journal de la Société des Africanistes*, 1934, **4**, 145–77.

Urvoy, Y. *Histoire des populations du Soudan central.* Paris, 1936.

Urvoy, Y. 'Chronologie du Bornou', *Journal de la Société des Africanistes*, 1941, **11**, 21–32.

Urvoy, Y. *Histoire de l'empire du Bornou. Mémoires de l'IFAN* no. 7, Paris, 1949; reprinted Amsterdam, 1968.
Wansbrough, J. 'The decolonization of North African history', *Journal of African History*, 1968, **9**, 4, 643–50.
Wansbrough, J. 'Africa and the Arab geographers', in Dalby, *Language and history in Africa*.
Yahya, D. 'The making of an independent foreign policy: Sa'di Morocco up to the death of Aḥmad al-Manṣūr (1509–1603)'. Doctoral thesis, University of Birmingham, 1975.
Zeltner, J.-C. 'Histoire des Arabes sur les rives du lac Tchad', *Annales de l'Université d'Abidjan*, 1970, **2** (sér. F), 2, 109–237.

5. THE WESTERN MAGHRIB AND SUDAN

Abun-Nasr. *History of the Maghrib. See under* ch. 4.
Aḥmad Bābā. *Nayl al-ibtihāj bi-taṭrīz al-dibāj.* Cairo, 1596.
Anonyme espagnol. *See* de Castries, 'La conquête', under ch. 4.
Bargès, Abbé. *Tlemcen, ancienne capitale du royaume de ce nom.* Paris, 1859.
Barry, Boubacar. *Le royaume du Waalo.* Paris, 1972.
Bathily, I. A. 'Notices socio-historiques sur l'ancien royaume Soninké du Jadiaga', *Bulletin de l'IFAN*, 1969, **31**, 31–105.
Batrān, 'Abd-al-'Aziz 'Abd-Allāh. '. . . al-Maghīlī'. *See under* ch. 4.
Bel, A. *Les Benou Ghânya. See under* ch. 4.
Bel, A. *Religion musulmane en Berbérie.* Paris, 1938.
Benzing, B. *Die Geschichte und das Herrschaftssystem der Dagomba.* Meisenheim am Glan, 1971.
Boulègue, J. 'La Sénégambie du milieu du 15e siècle au début du 17e siècle'. Doctoral thesis, University of Paris, 1968.
Bovill, E. W. *The golden trade. See under* ch. 4.
Boyer, I. G. *Un peuple de l'ouest soudanais: les Diawara.* Dakar, 1953.
Braudel, F. *La Méditerranée et le monde méditerranéen à l'époque de Philippe II*, 2nd ed. Paris, 1960; English transl. New York, 1972.
de Castries, H. 'La conquête'. *See under* ch. 4.
de Castries, H. and others. *Sources inédites de l'histoire du Maroc.* Paris, 1934–51.
Chronique anonyme de la dynastie Sa'adienne, ed. G. S. Colin. Rabat, 1934.
Cissé, Y. 'Notes sur les sociétés de chasseurs Malinkes', *Journal de la Société des Africanistes*, 1964, **34**, 175–226.
Cissoko, S. M. 'Civilisation Wolofo-Sérère', *Présence Africaine*, 1967, **62**, 121–45.
Cissoko, S. M. 'L'intelligentsia de Tombouctou aux 15e et 16e siècles', *Présence Africaine*, 1969, **72**, 48–72.
Cour, A. *L'établissement des dynasties des chérifs au Maroc et leur rivalité avec les Turcs de la Régence d'Alger, 1509–1830.* Paris, 1904.
Cour, A. *La dynastie marocaine des Beni Wattas (1420–1544).* Constantine, 1920.
Dalby, D. ed. *Manding Studies: papers presented to the Conference on Manding Studies.* London, 1975.
Delafosse, M. *Haut-Sénégal-Niger (Soudan français).* Paris, 1912. 3 vols.

Delafosse, M. 'Les relations du Maroc avec le Soudan à travers les âges', *Hespéris*, 1924, 153–74.
Deverdun, G. *Marrakech des origines à 1912*. Rabat, 1952.
Devisse, J. 'Routes de commerce et échanges en Afrique occidentale en relation avec la Méditerranée. Un essai sur le commerce africain médiéval du 11e au 16e siècle', *Revue d'Histoire Économique et Sociale*, 1972, **50**, 42–73 and 357–97.
Dieterlen, G. 'The Mande creation myth', *Africa*, 1957, **27**, 124–38.
Dufourcq, C. E. *L'Espagne catalane et le Maghrib aux 13e et 14e siècles*. Paris, 1966.
Fage, J. D. 'Ancient Ghana: a review of the evidence', *Transactions of the Historical Society of Ghana*, 1957, **3**, 77–98.
Fage, J. D. 'Reflections on the early history of the Mossi-Dagomba group of states', in *The historian in tropical Africa*, ed. Vansina and others.
Fage, J. D. 'Some thoughts on state formation in the Western Sudan before the seventeenth century', in *Boston University papers in African History* no. 1, ed. J. Butler. Boston, 1964, 17–34.
Filipowiak, W. 'Expédition archéologique polono-guinéenne à Niani (Guinée)', *Africana Bulletin*, 1966, **4**, 116–27; 1970, **11**, 107–17.
Fisher, G. A. *Barbary legends: war, trade and piracy in North Africa, 1417–1830*. Oxford, 1957.
al-Fishtālī. *Manāhil al-Safā*, ed. A. Ganun. Rabat, 1964.
Ganun, A. ed. *Rasā'il Sa'diyya*. Tetuan, 1954.
Gellner, E. A. *Saints of the Atlas*. London, 1969.
Gomes, D. *De la première découverte de la Guinée*, tr. T. Monod, R. Mauny and G. Duval. Bissau, 1959.
Goody, J. 'Ethno-history and the Akan of Ghana', *Africa*, 1959, **29**, 67–81.
Hama, Boubou. *Histoire des Songhay*. Paris, 1968.
Hazard, H. W. *The numismatic history of late mediaeval North Africa*. New York, 1952.
Hirschberg, H. Z. 'The problem of the Judaized Berbers', *Journal of African History*, 1963, **4**, 313–39.
Hirschberg, H. Z. *Jews in North Africa*. *See under* ch. 4.
Hiskett, M. 'Materials . . . cowry currency'. *See under* ch. 4.
Houis, M. 'Mouvements historiques et communités linguistiques dans l'ouest africain', *L'Homme*, 1961, **1**, 72–92.
Huici-Miranda, H. *Historia politica del Imperio Almohade*. Tetuan, 1956–7.
al-Ḥulal al-mawshiyya fī dhikr al-akhbār al-Marrākushiyya, ed. I. S. Allouche. Rabat, 1936.
Hunwick, J. O. 'Ahmad Baba and the Moroccan invasion of the Sudan (1591)', *Journal of the Historical Society of Nigeria*, 1962, **2**, 311–28.
Hunwick, J. O. 'Further light on Aḥmad Bābā al-Tinbuktī', *Research Bulletin*, Centre of Arabic Documentation, Ibadan, 1966, **2**, 2, 19–31.
Hunwick, J. O. 'Religion and state in the Songhay empire, 1464–1591', in *Islam in tropical Africa*, ed. Lewis. London, 1966, 296–317.
Hunwick, J. O. '. . . document concerning "al-Takrūr"'. *See under* ch. 1.

Hunwick, J. O. 'Songhay, Bornu and Hausaland in the sixteenth century', in *History of West Africa*, 1, ed. Ajayi and Crowder.

Hunwick, J. O. 'The mid-fourteenth century capital of Mali', *Journal of African History*, 1973, **14**, 195–206.

Ibn Abī Zar'. *Al-anīs al-muṭrib bi-rawḍ al-qirṭās fi akhbār mulūk al-maghrib wa-ta'rīkh madīnat Fās*, ed. C. J. Tornberg. Uppsala, 1843–66.

Ibn al-Athīr. *Kitāb al-Kāmil fi'l-ta'rīkh*, ed. D. J. Tornberg. Leiden, 1851–76.

Ibn al-Athir. *Annales du Maghrib et de l'Espagne*, tr. E. Fagnan. Algiers, 1901.

Ibn 'Idhārī al-Marrākushī. *Al-bayān al-maghrib fī akhbār al-Andalus wa'l-Maghrib*, ed. R. Dozy. Leiden, 1848–51.

Ibn 'Idhārī al-Marrākushī. 'Un fragmente inedite de Ibn Idhari sobre los Almoràvides', ed. A. Huici-Miranda. *Hespéris-Tamuda*, 1961, **2**, 43-111.

Ibn Khaldūn. *Kitāb ta'rīkh al-duwal al-Islāmiya bi'l-Maghrib min Kitāb al-'Ibar*, ed. M. G. de Slane. Paris, 1847; French tr. M. G. de Slane, *Histoire des Berbères et des dynasties musulmanes de l'Afrique septentrionale*. Paris, 1925–56.

Ibn al-Mukhtār. *Ta'rīkh al-Fattāsh*, ed. and tr. O. Houdas and M. Delafosse. Paris, 1913.

al-Ifrānī. *Nuzhat al-hādī bi-akhbār mulūk al-qarn al-ḥadī*; French translation, *Histoire de la dynastie Sa'adienne au Maroc, 1511–1760*, ed. and tr. O. Houdas. Paris, 1888.

Izard, M. *Introduction à l'histoire des royaumes Mossi*. Paris, 1970. 2 vols.

Jobson, R. *The golden trade*. London, 1932.

Johnson, M. 'The cowrie currencies of West Africa', *Journal of African History*, 1970, **11**, 1, 17–49; 3, 331–53.

Julien, C.-A. *History of North Africa*. *See under* ch. 4.

al-Kati, Muḥammad. *See under* Ibn al-Mukhtār.

Koubbel, L. E. 'On the history of social relations in the West Sudan in the 8th to the 16th centuries', in *Africa in Soviet Studies*. Moscow, 1968, 109–28.

Koubbel, L. E. 'Le problème de l'apparition des structures étatiques au Soudan occidental', *Congrès International des Africanistes*. Paris, 1972, 37–46.

La Chapelle, F. de. 'Esquisse d'une histoire du Sahara occidental', *Hespéris*, 1930, **11**, 35–95.

La Roncière, C. de. *La découverte de l'Afrique*... *See under* 'general' section, European sources.

Laroui, A. *L'histoire du Maghreb*. *See under* ch. 4.

Le Tourneau, R. *Fez in the age of the Marinides*, tr. B. A. Clement. Norman, Oklahoma, 1961.

Le Tourneau, R. *The Almohad movement*. *See under* ch. 4.

Lévi-Provençal, E. *Les historiens des Chorfa*. Paris, 1923.

Levtzion, N. *Muslims and chiefs in West Africa: a study of Islam in the middle Volta basin in the pre-colonial period*. London, 1968.

Levtzion, N. 'Patterns of islamization in West Africa', *Boston University Papers on African History*, **5**, ed. D. F. McCall and N. R. Bennett. Boston, 1971, 31–9.

Levtzion, N. 'A seventeenth century chronicle by Ibn al-Mukhtār: a critical study of Ta'rīkh al-Fattāsh', *Bulletin of the School of Oriental and African Studies*, 1971, **34**, 571–93.
Levtzion, N. *Ancient Ghana and Mali*. London, 1973.
Lewicki, T. 'Animal husbandry among mediaeval agricultural peoples of western and middle Sudan', *Acta Ethnographica Academicae Scientiarum Hungaricae*, 1965, 14, 165–78.
Lewicki, T. 'Un état soudanais mediéval inconnu: le royaume de Zāfūn(u)', *Cahiers d'Études Africaines*, 1971, **11**, 4, 501–25.
Lhote, H. 'Contribution à l'histoire des Touaregs soudanais', *Bulletin de l'IFAN*, 1955, **17**, 334–70; 1956, **18**, 391–407.
Magalhaes-Godinho, V. *L'économie de l'empire portugais aux 15e et 16e siècles*. Paris, 1969.
Malowist, M. 'Le commerce d'or et d'esclaves au Soudan occidental', *Africana Bulletin*, 1966, **4**, 49–72.
Malowist, M. 'Les fondaments de l'expansion européenne en Afrique au 15e siècle: Europe, Maghrib et Soudan Occidental', *Acta Poloniae Historica*, 1968, **18**, 156–79.
al-Maqqarī. *The history of the Mohammedan dynasties in Spain* [Extracts], tr. Pascual de Gayangos. London, 1840–3.
al-Maqqari. *Kitāb nafḥ al-ṭīb*, ed. M. M. 'Abd al-Ḥamīd. Cairo, 1949; French transl., *Analectes sur l'histoire et la littérature des Arabes d'Espagne*, ed. R. Dozy, G. Dugat, L. Krehl and W. Wright. Leiden, 1855–61.
Marçais, G. *Les Arabes en Berbérie du 11e au 14e siècle*. Paris, 1913.
Marçais, G. *Tlemcen*. Paris, 1951.
Martin, A. G. P. *Les oases sahariennes*. Algiers, 1908.
Mas Latrie, J. M. J. L. de. *Relations et commerce de l'Afrique septentrionale au Maghrib avec les nations chrétiennes*. Paris, 1886.
Massignon, L. *Le Maroc dans les premières années du 16 siècle; tableau géographique d'après Léon l'Africain*. Algiers, 1906.
Masson, P. *Histoire des établissements et du commerce français dans l'Afrique barbaresque (1560–1793)*. Paris, 1903.
Mauny, R. 'L'expédition marocaine d'Ouadane (Mauritanie) vers 1543–4', *Bulletin de l'IFAN*, 1949, **11**, 129–40.
Mauny, R. 'Le Judaisme, les Juifs de l'Afrique occidentale', *Bulletin de l'IFAN*, 1949, **11**, 354–78.
Mauny, R. *Les siècles obscurs de l'Afrique noire: histoire et archéologie*. Paris, 1970.
M'Baye, El-Hadj Rawane. 'Un aperçu de l'Islam Songhai ou résponses d'al-Maghīlī aux questions posées par Askiya El-Hadj Muḥammad, Empereur de Gao', *Bulletin de l'IFAN*, 1972, **34**, 237–67.
Meillassoux, C. 'Les cérémonies septennales du Kambalon de Kaaba (Mali)', *Journal de la Société des Africanistes*, 1968, **38**, 173–83.
Meillassoux, C. 'L'itinéraire d'Ibn Battuta de Walata à Mali', *Journal of African History*, 1972, **13**, 389–96.
Meyerowitz, E. L. R. *The sacred state of the Akan*. London, 1951.
Montagne, R. *Les Berbères et le Makhzen dans le sud du Maroc*. Paris, 1930.

Montagne, R. *La vie sociale et la vie politique des Berbères.* Paris, 1931; English transl. D. Seddon, *The Berbers: their social and political organisation.* London, 1972.

Monteil, C. 'Les empires du Mali. Étude d'histoire et de sociologie soudanais', *Bulletin du Comité d'Études Historiques et Scientifiques de l'AOF*, 1929, **12**, 291–447.

Monteil, C. *Une cité soudanaise: Djenné, métropole du delta central du Niger.* Paris, 1932; reprinted Paris and London, 1971.

Monteil, C. 'Problèmes du Soudan occidental: Juifs et Judaisés', *Hespéris.* 1951, **38**, 265–98.

Monteil, V. *L'Islam noir.* Paris, 1964.

Monteil, V. *Esquisses sénégalaises.* Dakar, 1966.

Niane, D. T. 'Recherches sur l'empire du Mali en moyen âge', *Recherches Africaines: Études Guinéenes*, 1959, 36–46; 1960, 31–51.

Niane, D. T. *Sundiata: an epic of old Mali*, tr. G. D. Pickett. London, 1965.

Niane, D. T. 'Koly Tenguella et le Tekrour', *Congrès International des Africanistes 1967.* Paris, 1972, 61–76.

Norris, H. T. 'Sanhaja scholars of Timbuctoo', *Bulletin of the School of Oriental and African Studies*, 1967, **30**, 634–40.

Palmer, H. R. 'Kano Chronicle'. *See under* ch. 4.

Pérès, H. 'Relation entre le Tafilet et le Soudan à travers le Sahara, du 12e au 14e siècles', *Mélanges de Géographie et d'Orientalisme offerts à E. F. Gautier.* Tours, 1937, 409–14.

Person, Y. 'Le moyen Niger au 15e siècle d'après des documents européens', *Notes africains*, 1958, **78**, 45–7.

Person, Y. *Samori, une révolution Dyula.* Dakar, 1968–76.

Person, Y. 'Nyani Mansa Mamudu et la fin de l'empire du Mali', unpubl. paper, *Conference on Manding Studies*, London, 1972.

Pianel, G. 'Les préliminaires de la conquête du Soudan par Maulāy Aḥmad al-Manṣūr', *Hespéris*, 1953, **40**, 185–97.

Ricard, R. 'Le commerce de Berbérie et l'organisation économique de l'empire portugais aux 15e et 16e siècles', *Annales de l'Institut d'Études Orientales*, 1936, **2**, 266–85.

Ricard, R. *Études sur l'histoire des Portugais au Maroc.* Coimbra, 1955.

Robert, D. S. and Devisse, J. *Tegdaoust, I: recherches sur Audaghost.* Paris, 1970.

Robson, J. A. 'The Catalan fleet and the Moorish sea-power (1337–1344)', *English Historical Review*, 1959, **74**, 386–408.

Rodney, W. *A history of the Upper Guinea coast, 1545–1800.* Oxford, 1970.

Rouch, J. *Contribution à l'histoire des Songhay* [*Memoirs de l'IFAN*]. Dakar, 1953.

Rouch, J. *La religion et la magie Songhay.* Paris, 1960.

al-Sa'dī. *Ta'rīkh es-Sūdān*, ed. and tr. O. Houdas. Paris, 1900.

Sauvaget, J. 'Les épitaphes royales de Gao', *Bulletin de l'IFAN*, 1950, **12**, 419–29.

Shinnie, P. L. and Ozanne, P. 'Excavations at Yendi-Dabari', *Transactions of the Historical Society of Ghana*, 1963, **6**, 87–118.

Soh, Siré Abbas. *Chroniques des Fouta Sénégalais*, tr. M. Delafosse with H. Gaden. Paris, 1913.

Stepniewska, B. 'Portée sociale de l'Islam au Soudan occidental aux 14e–16é siècles', *Africana Bulletin*, 1971, **14**, 35–58.

Ta'rīkh al-Fattāsh. *See* Ibn al-Mukhtār.

Teixeira da Mota, A. 'The Mande trade in Costa da Mina according to Portuguese documents until the mid-sixteenth century'. Unpublished paper, *Conference on Manding Studies*, London, 1972.

Terrasse, H. *Histoire du Maroc*. Casablanca, 1949.

Triaud, J. L. *Islam et sociétés soudanaises au moyen âge*. Paris, Ouagadougou, 1973.

Trimingham, J. S. *Islam in West Africa*. *See under* ch. 4.

Tymowski, M. 'Le Niger, voie de communication des grands états du Soudan occidental jusqu'au fin du 16e siècle', *Africana Bulletin*, 1967, **6**, 73–95.

Verlinden, C. 'Esclavage noir en France méridionale et courants de traite en Afrique', *Annales du Midi*, 1966, **78**, 335–43.

Wilks, I. 'A medieval trade route from the Niger to the Gulf of Guinea', *Journal of African History*, 1962, **3**, 2, 337–41.

Wilks, I. 'The transmission of Islamic learning in the Western Sudan', in J. R. Goody, ed. *Literacy in traditional societies*. Cambridge, 1968.

Wilks, I. 'The Mossi and Akan states, 1500–1800', in *History of West Africa*, ed. Ajayi and Crowder.

Zurara. *Chronique*... *See under* 'general' section, European sources.

6. UPPER AND LOWER GUINEA

Akinjogbin, I. A. *Dahomey and its neighbours, 1708–1818*. Cambridge, 1967.

Alagoa, E. J. 'Oral tradition among the Ijo of the Niger delta', *Journal of African History*, 1966, **7**, 3, 405–19.

Alagoa, E. J. 'Long distance trade and states in the Niger delta', *JAH*, 1970, **11**, 3, 319–29.

Alagoa, E. J. 'The development of institutions in the states of the eastern Niger delta', *JAH*, 1971, **12**, 2, 269–78.

Biobaku, S. O. ed. *Sources of Yoruba history*. Oxford, 1973.

Blake, J. W. ed. *Europeans in West Africa, 1450–1560*. London, 1941. 2 vols.

Boston, J. S. *The kingdom of the Igala*. Oxford, 1968.

Boston, J. S. 'Oral tradition and the history of Igala', *Journal of African History*, 1969, **10**, 1, 29–43.

Bradbury, R. E. *The Benin kingdom and the Edo-speaking peoples of south-western Nigeria*. pt. XIII, *Western Africa. Ethnographic Survey of Africa*, ed. Daryll Forde. London, 1957.

Bradbury, R. E. 'Chronological problems in the study of Benin history', *Journal of the Historical Society of Nigeria*, 1959, **1**, 4, 263–87.

Bradbury, R. E. 'The historical uses of comparative ethnography with special reference to Benin and the Yoruba', in *The historian in tropical Africa*, ed. Vansina and others.

Bradbury, R. E. *Benin studies*. London, 1973.
Bravmann, R. A. and Mathewson, R. D. 'A note on the history and archeology of "Old Bima"', *African Historical Studies*, 1970, **3**, 133–49.
Brigaud, F. *Histoire traditionelle du Sénégal*, no. 9 of *Études Sénégalaises*. St Louis, 1962.
Connah, G. 'Archaeological research in Benin City, 1961–1964', *Journal of the Historical Society of Nigeria*, 1963, **2**, 4, 465–77.
Connah, G. 'New light on the Benin city walls', *JHSN*, 1967, **3**, 4, 593–609.
Connah, G. 'Radiocarbon dates for Benin City and further dates for Daima', *JHSN*, 1968, **4**, 2, 313–20.
Connah, G. 'Settlement mounds of the *firki*: the reconstruction of a lost society', *Ibadan*, 1969, **26**, 48–62.
Connah, G. 'Archaeology in Benin', *Journal of African History*, 1972, **13**, 1, 25–38.
Connah, G. *The archaeology of Benin*. Oxford, 1975.
Correia, A. Mendes. *Raças do Imperio*. Lisbon, 1943.
Coursey, D. G. *Yams in West Africa*. Legon, 1965.
Coursey, D. G. *Yams*. London, 1968.
Crowder, M. *The story of Nigeria*. London, 1962.
Cultru, P. *Histoire du Sénégal du XVe siècle* à *1870*. Paris, 1910.
Daaku, K. Y. *Trade and politics on the Gold Coast, 1600–1720*. Oxford, 1970.
Davies, O. *West Africa before the Europeans*. London, 1967.
Delafosse, M. and Gaden, H. *Chronique du Fouta sénégalais, d'après deux manuscrits arabes*. Paris, 1913.
Deschamps, H. *Le Sénégal et la Gambie*. Paris, 1964.
Egharevba, J. U. *A short history of Benin*, 3rd ed. Ibadan, 1960.
Fage, J. D. *Ghana: a historical interpretation*. Madison, 1959.
Fage, J. D. 'Some remarks on beads and trade in lower Guinea in the sixteenth and seventeenth centuries', *Journal of African History*, 1962, **3**, 2, 343–47.
Fage, J. D. 'Mossi-Dagomba . . . states'. *See under* ch. 5.
Fage, J. D. *A history of West Africa*, 4th ed. Cambridge, 1969.
Fagg, B. E. B. 'Recent work in West Africa: new light on the Nok culture', *World Archaeology*, 1969, **1**, 41–50.
Fagg, W. *Nigerian images*. London, 1963.
Filipowiak, W., Jasnosz, S. and Wolaeiewicz, R. 'Les recherches archéologiques polonoguinéennes à Niani en 1968', *Materialy Zachodniopomorskie*, 1970, **14**, 575–648.
Flight, C. 'The chronology of the kings and queen-mothers of Bono-Mansu: a revaluation of the evidence', *Journal of African History*, 1970, **11**, 2, 259–68.
Flint, J. E. *Nigeria and Ghana*. Englewood Cliffs, N.J., 1967.
Frobenius, L. *The voice of Africa*, tr. R. Blind. London, 1913. 2 vols.
Garrard, T. F. 'Studies in Akan gold-weights', *Transactions of the Historical Society of Ghana*, 1972, **13**, 1, 1–20.
Ghana Notes and Queries [Legon], special number: 'The Akan of Ghana', 1966, **9**.

Goody, J. 'The Mande and the Akan hinterland', in *The historian in tropical Africa*, ed. Vansina and others.

Hair, P. E. H. 'Ethnolinguistic continuity on the Guinea coast', *Journal of African History*, 1967, **8**, 2, 247–68.

Henige, D. P. 'The problem of feedback in oral tradition: four examples from the Fante coastlands', *Journal of African History*, 1973, **14**, 2, 223–35.

Herbert, E. W. 'Aspects of the use of copper in pre-colonial West Africa', *JAH*, 179–94.

Hodgkin, T. *Nigerian perspectives: a historical anthology*, 2nd ed. London, 1975.

Hunwick, J. O. '. . . capital of Mali'. *See under* ch. 5.

Izard, M. . . . *royaumes Mossi*. *See under* ch. 5.

Johnson, M. 'Cowrie currencies'. *See under* ch. 5.

Johnson, S. *The history of the Yorubas*. Lagos, 1921.

Jones, D. H. 'Jakpa and the foundation of Gonja', *Transactions of the Historical Society of Ghana*, 1962, **6**, 1–29.

Ka'ti, Maḥmūd. *Ta'rīkh al-Fattāsh*. *See under* Ibn al-Mukhtār, ch. 5.

Kea, R. A. 'Trade, state formation and warfare on the Gold Coast, 1600–1826'. Doctoral thesis, University of London, 1974.

Kropp Dakubu, M. F. 'Linguistic prehistory and historical reconstruction: the Ga-Adangme migration', *Transactions of the Historical Society of Ghana*, 1972, **13**, 1, 87–111.

Latham, A. J. H. 'Currency, credit and capitalism on the Cross river in the pre-colonial era', *Journal of African History*, 1971, **12**, 4, 599–605.

Latham, A. J. H. *Old Calabar, 1600–1891*. Oxford, 1973.

Law, R. C. C. 'The Oyo empire: the history of a Yoruba state, principally in the period *c.* 1600–*c.* 1836'. Doctoral thesis, University of Birmingham, 1971.

Law, R. C. C. 'The heritage of Oduduwa: traditional history and political propaganda among the Yoruba', *Journal of African History*, 1973, **14**, 2, 207–22.

Lawal, B. 'Dating problems at Igbo-Ukwu', *JAH*, 1, 1–8.

Lawrence, A. W. *Trade castles and forts of West Africa*. London, 1963.

Lebeuf, J.-P. *Archéologie tchadienne*. Paris, 1962.

Levtzion, N. *Muslims and chiefs*. *See under* ch. 5.

Lloyd, P. C. 'Sacred kingship and government among the Yoruba', *Africa*, 1960, **30**, 3, 221–37.

Lucas, J. O. *The religion of the Yorubas*. Lagos, 1948.

Marees, P. de. *A description and historicall declaration of the Golden Kingdom of Guinea* (1602). [Abridged English transl. in *Purchas his pilgrims* (Glasgow, 1905) VI, 247–366; original Dutch in ed. by S. P. l'Honoré Naber (The Hague, 1909).]

Mathews, A. B. 'The Kisra legend', *African Studies*, 1950, **9**, 144–7.

Mauny, R. *Les siècles obscurs*. *See under* ch. 5.

Meyerowitz, E. L. R. *Akan traditions of origin*. London, 1952.

Meyerowitz, E. L. R. *The Akan of Ghana: their ancient beliefs*. London, 1958.

Meyerowitz, E. L. R. *The divine kingship in Ghana and ancient Egypt*. London, 1960.
Miracle, M. P. 'The introduction and spread of maize in Africa', *Journal of African History*, 1965, **6**, 1, 39–55.
Monteil, C. . . . *Djenné*. *See under* ch. 5.
Monteil, V. *Esquisses sénégalaises*. *See under* ch. 5.
Newbury, C. W. *The western slave coast and its rulers*. Oxford, 1961.
Niane, D. T. 'Koly Tenguella'. *See under* ch. 5.
Nketia, J. H. 'Historical evidence in Ga religious music', in *The historian in tropical Africa*, ed. Vansina and others.
Northrup, D. 'The growth of trade among the Igbo before 1800', *Journal of African History*, 1972, **13**, 2, 217–36.
Ozanne, P. 'Notes on the early historic archaeology of Accra', *Transactions of the Historical Society of Ghana*, 1972, **6**, 51–70.
Ozanne, P. 'Ghana', in *The African Iron Age*, ed. Shinnie.
Painter, C., 'The Guang and West African historical reconstruction', *Ghana Notes and Queries*, 1966, **9**, 58–65.
Posnansky, M. 'Ghana and the origins of West African trade', *Africa Quarterly*, 1971, **11**, 110–25.
Posnansky, M. 'Archaeology, technology and Akan civilization', *Journal of African Studies*, 1975, **2**, 1, 25–28.
Reindorf, C. C. *The history of the Gold Coast and Asante*, 1st ed. Basel, 1895; 2nd ed. Basel, n.d. [1951?].
Richard-Molard, J. *Afrique Occidentale Française*, 2nd ed. Paris, 1952.
Rodney, W. 'A reconsideration of the Mane invasions of Sierra Leone', *Journal of African History*, 1967, **8**, 2, 219–46.
Rodney, W. . . . *Upper Guinea coast*. *See under* ch. 5.
Ryder, A. F. C. 'A reconsideration of the Ife–Benin relationship', *Journal of African History*, 1965, **6**, 1, 25–37.
Ryder, A. F. C. *Benin and the Europeans, 1485–1897*. London 1969.
al-Sa'dī. *Ta'rīkh es-Sūdān*. *See under* ch. 5.
Shaw, C. T. 'Finds at the Iwo Eleru rock shelter, western Nigeria', in *Actes du Congrès pan-africain de préhistoire*. Dakar, 1967.
Shaw, C. T. *Igbo-Ukwu: an account of archaeological discoveries in eastern Nigeria*. London, 1970. 2 vols.
Shaw, C. T. ed. *Lectures on Nigerian prehistory and archaeology*. Ibadan, 1969.
Smith, R. S. 'The Alafin in exile: a study of the Igboho period in Oyo history', *Journal of African History*, 1965, **6**, 1, 57–77.
Smith, R. S. *Kingdoms of the Yoruba*. London, 1969.
Tauxier, L. *Le Noir de Bondoukou*. Paris, 1921.
Teixeira da Mota, A. *Guiné Portuguesa*. Lisbon, 1954.
Ward, W. E. F. *A history of the Gold Coast*. London, 1948.
Warren, D. M. 'A re-appraisal of Mrs Eva Meyerowitz's work on the Brong', *Research Review* [Legon], 1970, **7**, 1, 53–76.
Westermann, D. *Die Glidyi-Ewe*. Berlin, 1932.
Wilks, I. 'The rise of the Akwamu empire, 1650–1710', *Transactions of the Historical Society of Ghana*, 1957, **3**, 2, 99–136.

Wilks, I. 'A note on Twifo and Akwamu', *THSG*, 1958, **3**, 3, 215–17.
Wilks, I. 'The northern factor in Ashanti history: Begho and the Mande', *Journal of African History*, 1961, **2**, 1, 25–34. [Equivalent to ch. 1 in *The northern factor . . . (below)* but more accessible.]
Wilks, I. *The northern factor in Ashanti history*. Legon, 1961.
Wilks, I. 'A medieval trade route'. *See under* ch. 5.
Wilks, I. 'The Mossi and Akan states'. *See under* ch. 5.
Willett, F. 'Investigations at Old Oyo, 1956–57; an interim report', *Journal of the Historical Society of Nigeria*, 1961, **2**, 1, 59–77.
Willett, F. 'The introduction of maize into West Africa: an assessment of recent evidence', *Africa*, 1962, **32**, 1, 1–13.
Willett, F. *Ife in the history of West African sculpture*. London, 1967.
Willett, F. 'Nigeria', in *The African Iron Age*, ed. Shinnie.
Williams, D. *Icon and Image: a study of sacred forms and secular forms of African classical art*. London, 1974.
Wood, W. R. 'An archaeological appraisal of early European settlements in the Senegambia', *Journal of African History*, 1967, **8**, 1, 39–64.

7. CENTRAL AFRICA FROM CAMEROUN TO THE ZAMBEZI

Abreu e Brito. *Un inquerito à vida administrativa e económica do Angola e do Brasil* [1591]. Coimbra, 1931.
Ardener, E. 'Documentary and linguistic evidence for the rise of trading polities between the Rio del Rey and the Cameroons, 1500–1650', in *History and social anthropology*, ed. Lewis.
Arquivos de Angola [periodical]. Luanda. 1933 onwards.
Axelson, E. *Congo to Cape*. London, 1973.
Axelson, S. *Culture confrontation in the lower Congo*. Uppsala, 1971.
Bal, W. *Le royaume du Congo aux XVe et XVIe siècles*. Leopoldville, 1963.
Bal, W. ed. *Description du royaume de Congo et des contrées environnnantes par Filippo Pigafetta et Duarte Lopez* [1591]. Paris, 1963.
Balandier, G. *La vie quotidienne au royaume du Congo*. Paris, 1965; English ed. 1968.
Bastin, M.-L. *L'art décoratif Tschokwe*. Lisbon, 1961.
Bastin, M.-L. *Tschibinda Ilunga: héros civilisateur* [mimeograph]. Brussels, 1966. 2 vols.
Battell, A. *See* Ravenstein, E. G.
Biebuyck, D. 'Fondement de l'organisation politique des Lunda du Mwaantayaav en territoire de Kapanga', *Zaïre*, 1957, **11**, 8, 787–817.
Biographie coloniale belge. Brussels, 1948–56. 5 vols.
Birmingham, D. 'The date and significance of the Imbangala invasion of Angola', *Journal of African History*, 1965, **6**, 143–52.
Birmingham, D. *Trade and conflict in Angola*. Oxford, 1966.
Birmingham, D. 'Early African trade in Angola and its hinterland', in *Pre-colonial African trade*, ed. Gray and Birmingham.
Birmingham, D. tr. *A conquista portuguesa de Angola*. Lisbon, 1974.

Bocarro, A. *Estado da India*. Nova Goa, 1938.
Boone, O. *Carte ethnique du Congo*. Tervuren, 1961.
Borchardt, P. *Bibliographie de l'Angola*. Brussels, 1912.
Bouchaud, J. *La côte du Cameroun*. Duala, 1952.
Bouveignes, O. de. *Les anciens rois de Congo*. Namur, 1948.
Boxer, C. R. *The Portuguese seaborne empire*. London, 1969.
Brásio, A. *See under* 'general' section, European sources.
Burton, W. F. *Luba religion and magic in custom and belief*. Tervuren, 1961.
Cadornega, A. de O. de. *História geral das guerras Angolanas* [1680]. Lisbon, 1940–2. 3 vols.
Cardoso, J. C. F. *Memórias contendo, a história dos goverodores e capitaens generaes de Angola*. Paris, 1825.
Carvalho, H. D. de. *Ethnographia e história tradicional dos povos da Lunda*. Lisbon, 1890.
Carvalho, H. D. de. *Expedicão ao Muatiânvua 1884–1888*. Lisbon, 1890. 4 vols.
Carvalho, H. D. de. *O Jagado de Cassange*. Lisbon, 1898.
Cavazzi, G. A. *Istorica descrittione de' tre regni Congo, Matamba et Angola*. Bologna, 1678; annotated Portuguese ed. Lisbon, 1965.
Childs, G. M. *Umbundu kinship and character*. London, 1949.
Colle, R. P. *Les Baluba*. Brussels, 1913.
Cordeiro, L. *Questões histórico-coloniais*. Lisbon, 1936.
Correia, E. A. da Silva. *Historia de Angola*. Lisbon, 1937. 2 vols. [Correia is variously spelt.]
Cunnison, I. *History on the Luapula*. Cape Town, 1951.
Cuvelier, J. *L'ancien royaume de Congo*. Bruges, 1946.
Cuvelier, J. and Jadin, L. *L'ancien Congo d'après les archives romaines*. Brussels, 1954.
Davidson, B. *Black mother*. London, 1961.
Delgado, R. *História de Angola*. Benguela and Lobito, 1948–55. 4 vols. [vols. 1–3 recently reprinted, n.d.]
Delhaise, Cdt. *Les Warega*. Brussels, 1909.
Denis, J. *Les Yaka du Kwango*. Tervuren, 1964.
Duysters, L. 'Histoire des Aluunda', *Problèmes d'Afrique Centrale*, 1958, **40**, 75–98.
Fagan, B. M. and others. *Iron Age cultures in Zambia*. London, 1967, 1969. 2 vols.
Faria, F. L. de. ed. *Uma relacão de Rui de Pino sobre o Congo escrita em 1492*. Lisbon, 1966.
Felner, A. A. *Angola*. Coimbra, 1933.
Garlake, P. S. 'Iron Age sites in the Urungwe district of Rhodesia', *South African Archaeological Bulletin*, 1971, **25**, 25–44.
Gaud, F. and Overbergh, C. van. *Les Mandja*. Brussels, 1911.
Gray, J. R. and Birmingham, D. *Pre-colonial African trade*. London, 1970.
Guerreiro, F. *Relações Annuais* [Jesuit reports], 2nd ed. Coimbra, 1930–42. 3 vols.
Haveaux, G. L. *La tradition historique des Bapende orientaux*. Brussels, 1954.

Hiernaux, J., Longrée, E. de. and Buyst, J. de. *Fouilles archéologiques dans la vallée du Haut-Lualaba: I, Sanga (1958)*. Tervuren, 1971.
Hutereau, A. *Histoire des peuplades de l'Uele et l'Ubangi*. Brussels, 1922.
Ihle, A. *Das alte Königreich Kongo*. Leipzig, 1929.
Jacobson, A. *Marriage and money*. Lund, 1967.
Jonghe, E. de and Simar, T. *Archives Congolaises*. Brussels, 1919.
Kalck, P. '. . . royaume de Gaoga'. *See under* ch. 4.
Kerken, G. van der. *L'ethnie Mongo*. Brussels, 1944. 2 vols.
Laman, K. *The Kongo*. Uppsala, 1953–63. 3 vols.
Lopes de Lima, J. J. *Ensaios sobre a statistica das possessões Portuguezas*, vol. III. Lisbon, 1846.
Martin, P. M. *The external trade of the Loango coast, 1576–1870*. Oxford, 1972.
Miller, J. C. 'Requiem for the Jaga', *Cahiers d'études Africaines*, 1973, **49**, 121–49.
Miller, J. C. *Kings and kinsmen: early Mbundu states in Angola*. Oxford, 1976.
Moeller, A. *Les grandes lignes des migrations des Bantous de la province orientale du Congo Belge*. Brussels, 1936.
Mveng, E. *Histoire du Cameroun*. Paris, 1961.
Nenquin, J. 'Notes on some early pottery cultures in northern Katanga', *Journal of African History*, 1963, **4**, 19–32.
Nenquin, J. *Excavations at Sanga*. Tervuren, 1963.
Neves, A. R. *Memorias da expedição ao Cassange en 1850*. Lisbon, 1854.
Overbergh, C. van. *Les Basonge*. Brussels, 1908.
Overbergh, C. van and Jonghe, J. de. *Les Mangbetu*. Brussels, 1909.
Pachai, B. ed. *The early history of Malawi*. London, 1972.
Paiva Manso, Viscount. *História do Congo*. Lisbon, 1877.
Phillipson, D. W. 'The Early Iron Age in Zambia', *Journal of African History*, 1968, **9**, 191–211.
Phillipson, D. W. 'Excavations at Twickenham Road, Lusaka', *Azania*, 1970, **5**, 77–118.
Phillipson, D. W. 'The prehistoric succession in eastern Zambia', *Azania*, 1973, **8**, 3–24.
Phillipson, D. W. 'Iron Age history and archaeology in Zambia', *Journal of African History*, 1974, **15**, 1, 1–25.
Phillipson, D. W. and Fagan, B. M. 'The date of the Ingombe Ilede burials', *JAH*, 1969, **10**, 199–204.
Pigafetta, F. and Lopez, D. . . . *Royaume de Congo*. *See* Bal, W. ed.
Pino, Rui de. *See* Faria, F. L. de.
Planquaert, M. *Les Jaga et les Bayaka du Kwango*. Brussels, 1932.
Planquaert, M. *Les Yaka: essai d'histoire*. Tervuren, 1971.
Randles, W. G. L. *L'ancien royaume du Congo*. Paris, 1968.
Ranger, T. O. 'Territorial cults in the history of Central Africa', *Journal of African History*, 1973, **14**, 581–97.
Ravenstein, E. G. ed. *The strange adventures of Andrew Battell*. London, 1901.
Rego, A. da Silva. *Portuguese colonization in the sixteenth century*. Johannesburg, 1959.

Scudder, T. *Gathering among African woodland savanna cultivators.* Lusaka, 1971.
Streit, R. and Dindinger, J. *Bibliotheca Missionum*, vol. 15. Fribourg, 1951.
Teixeira da Mota, A. *A cartografia antiga do Africa Central.* Lourenço Marques, 1964.
Tervuren Museum. *Miscellanea ethnographica.* Tervuren, 1963.
Turnbull, C. M. *The forest people.* New York, 1961.
Vansina, J. 'Note sur l'origine du royaume du Congo', *Journal of African History*, 1963, **4**, 33–8.
Vansina, J. 'The foundation of the kingdom of Kasanje', *Journal of African History*, 1963, **4**, 355–74.
Vansina, J. *Geschiedenis van de Kuba.* Tervuren, 1963.
Vansina, J. *Kingdoms of the savanna.* Madison, 1965.
Vansina, J. 'More on the invasions of Kongo and Angola by the Jaga and the Lunda', *Journal of African History*, 1966, **7**, 421–9.
Vansina, J. *Introduction à l'ethnographie du Congo.* Kinshasha, 1966.
Vansina, J. 'The bells of kings', *Journal of African History*, 1969, **10**, 187–97.
Vansina, J. *The Tio kingdom of the middle Congo.* London, 1973.
Verhulpen, E. *Baluba et Balubaïsés.* Antwerp, 1936.
Wing, J. van. *Études Bakongo*, 2nd ed. Brussels, 1959.

8. SOUTHERN AFRICA

The north-east

Abraham, D. P. 'The Monomotapa dynasty', *NADA*, 1959, **36**, 59–84.
Abraham, D. P. 'Maramuca: an exercise in the combined uses of Portuguese records and oral tradition', *Journal of African History*, 1961, **2**, 211–25.
Abraham, D. P. 'The early political history of the kingdom of the Mwene Mutapa (850–1589)', in *Historians in tropical Africa.* Salisbury, 1962.
Abraham, D. P. 'The ethno-history of . . . Mutapa'. *See under* ch. 3.
Abraham, D. P. 'The roles of "Chaminuka" and the *mhondoro*-cults in Shona political history', in *The Zambesian past*, ed. E. Stokes and R. Brown.
Alpers, E. A. 'The Mutapa and Malawi political systems', in *Aspects of Central African history*, ed. T. O. Ranger.
Axelson, E. *South-East Africa. See under* ch. 3.
Axelson, E. *Portuguese in South-East Africa. See under* ch. 3.
Beach, D. N. 'Historians and the Shona empires'. Mimeo, Henderson Seminar Paper no. 20. Salisbury, 1972.
Bent, J. T. *The ruined cities of Mashonaland.* London, 1893.
Bocarro, A. *Estado da India. See under* ch. 7.
Burke, E. E. 'Some aspects of Arab contact in South-East Africa', in *Historians in tropical Africa.* Salisbury, 1962.
Burke, E. E. ed. *The journals of Carl Mauch.* Salisbury, 1969.
Caton-Thompson, G. *The Zimbabwe culture.* Oxford, 1931.

Chittick, H. N. 'Kilwa, a preliminary report'. *See under* ch. 3.
Chittick, H. N. 'The coast of East Africa', in *African Iron Age*, ed. P. L. Shinnie.
Crawford, J. R. 'The Monk's Kop ossuary', *Journal of African History*, 1967, **8**, 373–82.
Documents on the Portuguese in Mozambique and Central Africa. Lisbon, 1962–71. 7 vols.
Fagan, B. M. *Southern Africa during the Iron Age*. London, 1965.
Garlake, P. S. 'Test excavations at Mapela Hill, near the Shashi river, Rhodesia', *Arnoldia*, 1968, **3**, no. 34.
Garlake, P. S. 'The value of imported ceramics in the dating and interpretation of the Rhodesian Iron Age', *Journal of African History*, 1968, **9**, 13–33.
Garlake, P. S. 'Rhodesian ruins – a preliminary assessment of their styles and chronology', *Journal of African History*, 1970, **11**, 495–513.
Garlake, P. S. 'Iron Age sites in the Urungwe district'. *See under* ch. 7.
Garlake, R. S. 'Excavations at Nhunguza and Ruanga ruins in northern Mashonaland', *South African Archaeological Bulletin*, 1973, **27**, 107–43.
Garlake, P. S. *Great Zimbabwe*. London, 1973.
Hall, R. N. *Great Zimbabwe*. London, 1905.
Hall, R. N. *Prehistoric Rhodesia*. London, 1909.
Hall, R. N. and Neal, W. G. *The ancient ruins of Rhodesia*. London, 1902.
Huffman, T. N. 'The early Iron Age of the Urungwe district', *Rhodesian Prehistory*, 1972, **8**, 12–16.
Huffman, T. N. 'The rise and fall of Zimbabwe', *Journal of African History*, 1972, **13**, 353–66.
Huffman, T. N. 'Test excavations at Makuru, Rhodesia', *Arnoldia*, 1973, **5**, no. 39.
Huffman, T. N. 'The linguistic affinities of the Iron Age in Rhodesia', *Arnoldia*, 1974, **7**, no. 7.
Huffman, T. N. *The Leopard's Kopje tradition*. Salisbury, in press.
Isaacman, A. 'Madzi-Manga, Mhondoro and the use of oral traditions – a chapter in Barue religious and political history', *Journal of African History*, 1973, **14**, 395–409.
Jaffey, A. J. E. 'A reappraisal of the Rhodesian Iron Age up to the 15th century', *Journal of African History*, 1966, **7**, 189–95.
Lobato, A. *A expansão portuguesa em Moçambique de 1498 a 1530*. Lisbon, 1954–60. 3 vols.
Matos, L. C. de. *Origens do povo Chope segundo a tradição oral*. [Memória no. 10, I.I.C.A.] Lourenço Marques, 1973.
Newitt, M. D. D. *Portuguese settlement on the Zambesi*. London, 1973.
Phillipson, D. W. and Fagan, B. M. 'The date of the Ingombe Ilede burials'. *See under* ch. 7.
Randall MacIver, D. *Mediaeval Rhodesia*. London, 1906.
Ranger, T. O. 'Territorial cults'. *See under* ch. 7.
Ranger, T. O. ed. *Aspects of Central African history*. London, 1968.
Robinson, K. R. *Khami ruins*. Cambridge, 1959.

Rudd, S. 'Preliminary report of excavations, 1953–66, at Lekkerwater ruins', *Proceedings and Transactions of the Rhodesian Scientific Association*, 1969, **52**.

Santos, J. dos. *Ethiopia oriental*, in Theal, *Records*, VII.

Smith, A. K. 'The struggle for control of southern Mozambique, 1720–1835'. Doctoral thesis, University of California, Los Angeles, 1970.

Stokes, E. and Brown, R. eds. *The Zambesian past: studies in central African history*. Manchester, 1966.

Summers, R. *Inyanga*. Cambridge, 1958.

Summers, R. *Zimbabwe. A Rhodesian mystery*. Johannesburg, 1963.

Summers, R. *Ancient mining in Rhodesia*. Salisbury, 1969.

Summers, R., Robinson, K. R. and Whitty, A. *Zimbabwe excavations, 1958*. Salisbury, 1961.

Sutton, J. E. G. *Early trade in Eastern Africa*. Dar es Salaam, 1973.

Tracy, H. *Antonio Fernandes, descobridor do Monomotapa*. Lisbon, 1940.

Wieschoff, H. A. *The Zimbabwe-Monomotapa culture in South-East Africa*. Menasha, Wis., 1941.

South of the Limpopo

Acocks, J. P. N. 'Veld types of South Africa', *Botanical survey of South Africa*, Memoir 28. Pretoria, 1953.

Bates, C. W. 'Archaeological sites on the Groot Letaba river', *South African Journal of Science*, 1947, **43**, 365–75.

Beaumont, P. and Schoonraad, M. 'The Welgelegen site', in M. Schoonraad, ed., *Rock paintings of southern Africa*.

Boxer, C. R. ed. *The tragic history of the sea, 1589–1622*. Cambridge, 1959.

Bryant, A. T. *Olden times in Zululand and Natal*. London, 1929.

Carter, P. L. 'Late Stone Age exploitation patterns in Southern Natal', *South African Archaeological Bulletin*, 1970, **25**, part 2, no. 98, 55–8.

Clark, J. D. *The prehistory of Southern Africa*. Harmondsworth, 1959.

Clark, J. D. 'A note on early river-craft and fishing practices in South-East Africa', *South African Archaeological Bulletin*, 1960, **15**, 59, 77–9.

Cooke, C. K. 'Evidence of human migrations from the rock art of southern Rhodesia', *Africa*, 1965, **35**, 3, 263–85.

Curson, H. H. and Thornton, R. W. 'A contribution to the study of African native cattle', *Onderstepoort Journal of Veterinary Science and Animal Husbandry*, 1936, **7**, 613–739.

Davies, O. 'Excavations at Blackburn', *South African Archaeological Bulletin*, 1971, **26**, parts 3 and 4, nos. 103 and 104, 165–78.

Deacon, J. 'Wilton: an assessment after fifty years', *S.A. Arch. Bull.*, 1972, **37**, parts 1 and 2, nos. 105 and 106, 10–47.

Derricourt, R. M. 'Archaeological survey of the Transkei and Ciskei', Interim reports for 1971 and 1972. *Fort Hare Papers*, 1972, **5**, 3, and 1973, **5**, 4.

Ehret, C. 'Cattle-keeping and milking in eastern and southern African history: the linguistic evidence', *Journal of African History*, 1967, **8**, 1, 1–17.

Ehret, C. 'Sheep and Central Sudanic peoples in Southern Africa', *JAH*, 1968, **9**, 213–21.

Ehret, C. and others. 'Outlining Southern African history: a reconsideration, 100–1500 AD', *Ufuhamu*, 1972, **3**, 1, 9–27.

Ehret, C. 'Patterns of Bantu and Central Sudanic settlement in Central and Southern Africa, *c.* 1000 BC–500 AD', *Transafrican Journal of History*, 1974, **4**, 1, 1–27.

Ellenberger, D. F. and MacGregor, J. C. *A history of the Basotho, ancient and modern*. London, 1912.

Elphick, R. H. 'The Cape Khoi and the first phase of South African race relations'. Doctoral thesis, Yale University, 1972.

Evers, T. M. 'Iron Age research in the Eastern Transvaal, South Africa, 1971', *Current Anthropology*, 1973, **14**, 4, 487–9.

Fagan, B. M. 'The Greefswald sequence: Bambandyanalo and Mapungubwe', *Journal of African History*, 1964, **5**, 3, 337–61.

Fouché, L. ed. *Mapungubwe, ancient Bantu civilization*. Cambridge, 1937.

Galloway, A. *The skeletal remains of Bambandyanalo*. Johannesburg, 1959.

Gardner, G. A. *Mapungubwe*, vol. II. Pretoria, 1963.

Goodwin, A. J. H. and van Riet Lowe, C. 'Stone Age cultures of South Africa'. *Annals of South African Museum*, 1927, **27**.

Gray, J. R. 'Ruins and traditions of the Ngona and Mbedzi among the Venda of the northern Transvaal'. Unpubl. paper, African history seminar, Institute of Commonwealth Studies, London, 1969.

Huffman, T. N. 'Excavations at Leopard's Kopje main kraal: a preliminary report', *South African Archaeological Bulletin*, 1971, **36**, parts 1 and 2, nos. 101 and 102, 85–8.

Inskeep, R. R. 'The Late Stone Age in Southern Africa', in *Background to evolution in Africa*, ed. Bishop and Clark.

Inskeep, R. R. 'The archaeological background', *Oxford history of South Africa*, vol. I, ed. Wilson and Thompson.

Junod, H. A. 'The condition of natives of South-East Africa in the sixteenth century according to the early Portuguese documents', *Report of the 11th annual meeting of the South African Association for the Advancement of Science*. Lourenço Marques, 1913.

Klapwyk, M. 'The Early Iron Age settlement of Southern Africa. An Early Iron Age site near Tzaneen in the north-eastern Transvaal', *South African Journal of Science*, 1973, **69**, 324.

Köhler, O. 'Observations on the central Khoisan language group', *Journal of African Languages*, 1963, **2**, 3, 227–34.

Krige, E. J. 'Notes on the Phalaborwa and their Morula complex', *Bantu Studies*, 1937, **11**, 357–67.

Krige, E. J. 'The place of the North-Eastern Transvaal Sotho in the South Bantu complex', *Africa*, 1938, **11** 265–93.

Krige, E. J. and J. D. *The realm of a rain queen*. London, 1943.

Krige, J. D. 'Traditional origins and tribal relationships of the Sotho of the northern Transvaal', *Bantu Studies*, 1937, **11**, 321–56.

Kuper, A. 'The social structure of the Sotho-speaking people of Southern Africa'. In 2 parts; *Africa*, 1975, **45**, 67–81 and 139–49.

Lanham, L. W. 'The proliferation and extension of Bantu phonemic systems influenced by Bushman and Hottentot', *Proceedings of the Ninth International Congress of Linguistics, Cambridge, Mass. 1962*. The Hague, 1964.

Lawton, A. C. 'Bantu pottery of southern Africa', *Annals of the South African Museum*, 1967, **49**, part 1.

Maggs, T. M. O'C. 'Pastoral settlements on the Riet river', *South African Archaeological Bulletin*, 1971, **26**, parts 1 and 2, nos. 101 and 102, 37–63.

Maggs, T. M. O'C. 'Bilobial dwellings: a persistent feature of southern Tswana settlements', in The South African Archaeological Society, Goodwin Series, **1**, *The interpretation of evidence*, 1972, 54–65.

Maggs, T. M. O'C. 'The Iron Age of the Orange Free State', in *VIe congrès panafricain de préhistoire*, ed. H. J. Hugot. Chambéry, 1972.

Maggs, T. M. O'C. 'Early farming communities on the southern Highveld: a survey of Iron Age settlement'. Doctoral thesis, University of Cape Town, 1974. 2 vols.

Mason, R. J. *The prehistory of the Transvaal*. Johannesburg, 1962.

Mason, R. J. 'Transvaal and Natal Iron Age settlement revealed by aerial photography and excavation', *African Studies*, 1968, **27**, 4, 167–80.

Mason, R. J. 'Iron Age stone artefacts from Oliefantspoort, Rustenberg district, and Kaditshwene, Zeerust district', *South African Journal of Science*, 1969, **65**, 2, 41–4.

Mason R. J. 'Iron Age research in the Western Transvaal South Africa, 1971–2', *Current Anthropology*, 1973, **14**, 4, 485–7.

Mason, R. J. 'Background to the Transvaal Iron Age – new discoveries at Oliefantspoort and Broederstroom', *Journal of the South African Institute of Mining and Metallurgy*, 1974, **74**, 6, 211–16.

Mason, R. J. and others. 'Prehistoric man at Melville Koppies Nature Reserve, Johannesburg'. *Occasional Papers*, **6**, Archaeology Department, University of Witwatersrand, 1971.

Mason, R. J. and others. 'The Early Iron Age settlement of Southern Africa', *South African Journal of Science*, 1973, **69**, 324–7.

Mönnig, H. O. 'The Baroka ba Nkwana', *African studies*, 1963, **22**, 170–5.

Parkington, J. E. 'Seasonal mobility in the Late Stone Age', *African Studies*, 1972, **31**, 223–43.

Parkington, J. E. and Poggenpoel, C. 'Excavations at De Hangen, 1968', *South African Archaeological Bulletin*, 1971, **36**, parts 1 and 2, nos. 101 and 102, 1–36.

Potgieter, E. F. *The disappearing Bushmen of Lake Chrissie*. Pretoria, 1955.

Raven-Hart, A. *Before van Riebeeck; callers at the Cape from 1488 to 1652*. Cape Town, 1967.

Riet Lowe, C. van and Dart, R. A. 'A preliminary report on the stone huts of Vechtkop', *Journal of the Royal Anthropological Institute*, 1927, **57**, 217–33.

Rudner, J. 'Strandloper pottery from South and South-West Africa', *Annals of the South African Museum*, 1968, **49**, part 2.

Rudner, J. and I. *The hunter and his art: a survey of rock-art in Southern Africa.* Cape Town, 1970.

Sampson, C. G. 'The Orange river scheme and aspects of the Stone Age in South Africa', *Annals of the National Museum of Bloemfontein*, 1972, **6**.

Sampson, C. G. *The Stone Age archaeology of Southern Africa.* New York and London, 1974.

Schapera, I. *The Khoisan peoples of South Africa.* London, 1930.

Schapera, I. 'The social structure of a Tswana ward', *Bantu Studies*, 1935, **9**, 3, 203–24.

Schapera, I. *The Bantu-speaking tribes of South Africa.* London, 1937.

Schapera, I. *The Tswana.* London, 1953.

Schapera, I. and van der Merwe, F. 'Notes on the tribal groupings, history and customs of the Kgalagadi', *Communications from the School of African Studies, University of Cape Town*, 1945, **2**, 13.

Schofield, J. F. 'Ancient workings of south-east Africa', *NADA*, 1925, **3**, 5–11.

Schofield, J. F. 'Natal coastal pottery from the Durban district: a preliminary survey', *South African Journal of Science.* 1935, **32**, 509–27; 1936, **33**, 993–1009.

Schofield, J. F. *Primitive pottery.* Cape Town, 1948.

Schoonraad, M. ed. *Rock paintings of Southern Africa.* Special Publication no. 2, supplement to *South African Journal of Science*, 1971, 62–9.

Schweitzer, F. R. 'A preliminary report of excavations of a new cave at Die Kelders', *South African Archaeological Bulletin*, 1970, **35**, parts 3 and 4, nos. 99 and 100, 136–8.

Shaw, E. M. and van Warmelo, N. J. 'The material culture of the Cape Nguni, part 1: settlement', *Annals of the South African Museum*, 1972, **58**, 1.

Smith, A. 'The peoples of southern Mozambique: an historical survey', *Journal of African History*, 1973, **14**, 4, 565–80.

Stayt, H. A. *The Bavenda.* Reprinted London, 1968.

Stow, G. W. 'The intrusion of the stronger races'. Unpubl. Ms, South African public Library, Cape Town, n.d.

Stow, G. W. *The native races of South Africa.* London, 1905.

Stow, G. W. *Early Ghoya settlement in the Orange Free State*, ed. J. Walton. Researches of the National Museum of Bloemfontein, Memoir 2, 1956.

Sydow, W. 'The pre-European pottery of south-west Africa', *Cimbebasia*, memoir 1. Windhoek, 1967.

Thompson, L. M. ed. *African societies in southern Africa: historical studies.* London, 1969.

Tobias, P. V. 'Physical anthropology and the somatic origins of the Hottentots', *African Studies*, 1955, **14**, 1, 1–15.

Walton, J. 'Corbelled stone huts in Southern Africa', *Man*, 1951, **51**, 45–8.

Walton, J. 'Early Bafokeng settlement in South Africa', *African Studies*, 1956, **15**, 1, 37–43.

Warmelo, N. J. van *A preliminary survey of the native tribes of South Africa*. Native Affairs Department, Ethnological Publications, **5**. Pretoria, 1935.

Warmelo, N. J. van. *The copper miners of Musina and the early history of the Zoutpansberg*. Native Affairs Department, Ethnological Publications, 8. Pretoria, 1940.

Welbourne, R. C. 'The Early Iron Age settlement of Southern Africa: identification of animal remains', *South African Journal of Science*, 1973, **69**, 325.

Westphal, E. 'A reclassification of southern African non-Bantu languages', *Journal of African Languages*, 1962, **1**, 1–8.

Westphal, E. 'The linguistic prehistory of Southern Africa: Bush, Kwadi, Hottentot and Bantu linguistic relationships', *Africa*, 1963, **33**, 3, 237–65.

Willcox, A. R. 'Domestic cattle in Africa: a rock art mystery', in '*Rock paintings of Southern Africa*', ed. Schoonraad.

Wilson, M. 'The early history of the Transkei and Ciskei', *African Studies*, 1959, **18**, 4, 167–79.

Wilson, M. 'The hunters and herders', 'The Nguni people' and 'The Sotho, Venda and Tsonga', in *Oxford history of South Africa*, 1, ed. Wilson and Thompson.

9. THE EAST AFRICAN INTERIOR

Allen, R. tr. 'The story of Mbega, by Abdallah bin Hemedi bin Ali Linjemmi [Habari za Wakilindi]', *Tanganyika Notes and Records*, 1936, **1**, 38–51; 80–98.

d'Arianoff, A. *Histoire des Bagesera, souverains du Gisaka*. Brussels, 1952.

Beidelman, T. O. *The matrilineal peoples of eastern Tanzania*. London, 1967.

Cézard, E. 'Le Muhaya', *Anthropos*, 1937, **32**, 32–57.

Claus, H. *Die Wagogo*. Leipzig, 1911.

Cohen, D. W. 'A survey of interlacustrine chronology', *Journal of African History*, 1970, **11**, 2, 177–94.

Cohen, D. W. *The historical tradition of Busoga: Mukama and Kintu*. Oxford, 1972.

Cole, S. *The prehistory of East Africa*, 2nd ed. London, 1964.

Cory, H. *The Ntemi: traditional rites of a Sukuma chief in Tanganyika*. London, 1951.

Cory, H. *History of Bukoba District*. Dar es Salaam, 1958.

Cory, H. and Hartnoll, M. M. *Customary law of the Haya tribe*. London, 1945.

Crazzolara, J. P. *The Lwoo*. Verona, 1950–4. 3 vols.

Dundas, C. C. F. *Kilimanjaro and its people*. London, 1924.

Ehret, C. 'Cattle-keeping and milking'. *See under* ch. 8.

Ehret, C. *Southern Nilotic history: linguistic approaches to the study of the past*. Evanston, 1971.

Fadiman, J. A. 'Early history of the Meru of Mt Kenya', *Journal of African History*, 1973, **14**, 1, 9–29.

Fagan, B. M. and Yellan, J. E. 'Ivuna: ancient salt-working in southern Tanzania', *Azania*, 1968, **3**, 1–43.

Feierman, S. *The Shambaa kingdom*. Madison, 1974.

Ford, J. and Hall, R. de Z. 'The history of Karagwe', *Tanganyika Notes and Records*, 1947, **24**, 3–27.

Fülleborn, F. *Das deutsche Njassa und Ruwumagebeit*. Berlin, 1906.

Gorju, J. *Entre le Victoria, l'Albert et l'Edouard*. Rennes, 1920.

Gorju, J. *Face au royaume hamite du Ruanda, le royaume frère de l'Urundi*. Brussels, 1938.

Gray, J. R. 'Eclipse maps', *Journal of African History*. 1965, **6**, 3, 251–62.

Gulliver, P. and Gulliver, P. H. *The central Nilo-Hamites*. London, 1953.

Henige, D. P. 'Reflections on early interlacustrine chronology', *Journal of African History*, 1974, **15**, 1, 27–46.

d'Hertefelt, M. *Les clans du Rwanda ancien*. Brussels, 1971.

d'Hertefelt, M., Trouwborst, A. R. and Scherer, J. H. *Les anciens royaumes de la zone interlacustre méridionale, Rwanda, Burundi, Buha*. Tervuren, 1962.

Heusch, L. de. *Le Rwanda et la civilisation interlacustre*. Brussels, 1966.

Hiernaux, J. and Maquet, E. *Cultures préhistoriques de l'âge des métaux au Ruanda-Urundi et au Kivu (Congo-Belge)*. Brussels, 1957, 1959. 2 vols.

Huntingford, G. W. B. *The northern Nilo-Hamites. Ethnographic Survey of Africa*, ed. Daryll Forde. London, 1953.

Huntingford, G. W. B. *The southern Nilo-Hamites. Ethnographic Survey of Africa*, ed. Daryll Forde. London, 1953.

K. W. 'Abakama ba Bunyoro-Kitara', *Uganda Journal*, 1953, **3**, 155–60; 1936, **4**, 75–83; 1937, **5**, 53–68.

Kagame, A. 'Le code ésotérique de la dynastie du Ruanda', *Zaïre*, 1947, 363–86.

Kagame, A. *Le code des institutions politiques du Rwanda précolonial*. Brussels, 1952.

Kagame, A. *Histoire du Rwanda*. Leverville, 1958.

Kagame, A. *La notion de génération appliquée à la généalogie dynastique et à l'histoire du Rwanda des Xe–XIe siècles à nos jours*. Brussels, 1959.

Kagwa, A. *Basekabaka be Buganda, Bunyoro, Toro, Ankole ne Koki*, 3rd ed. Kampala, 1927.

Karugire, S. K. *A history of the kingdom of Nkore in western Uganda to 1896*. Oxford, 1971.

Katate, A. G. and Kamugungunu, L. *Abagabe b'Ankole*. Kampala, 1955. 2 vols.

Kimambo, I. N. *A political history of Pare*. Nairobi, 1969.

Kiwanuka, M. S. M. *A history of Buganda from the foundation of the kingdom to 1900*. New York, 1972.

Lacger, J. de. *Le Ruanda: 1, le Ruanda ancien*. Namur, 1939.

Lambert, H. E. *Systems of land tenure in the Kikuyu land unit*, part 1, *History of the tribal occupation of the land*. Cape Town, 1950.

Leakey, M. D., Leakey, L. S. B. and Owen, W. E. 'Dimple-based pottery from Central Kavirondo', *Occasional papers of the Coryndon Museum*, **2**, Nairobi, 1948.
Maquet, J. J. *The premise of inequality in Ruanda*. Oxford, 1961.
Middleton, J. *The Kikuyu and Kamba of Kenya*. London, 1953.
Munro, J. F. 'Migrations of the Bantu-speaking peoples of the eastern Kenya highlands: a reappraisal', *Journal of African History*, 1968, **7**, 1, 25–8.
Muriuki, G. *A history of the Kikuyu, 1500–1900*. Nairobi, 1974.
Nigmann, E. *Die Wahehe*. Berlin, 1908.
Nyakatura, J. W. *Abakama ba Bunyoro-Kitara*. St Justin, 1947.
Ogot, B. A. *History of the southern Luo*, vol. 1, *Migration and settlement, 1500–1900*. Nairobi, 1967.
Ogot, B. A. and Kieran, J. A. *Zamani: a survey of East African history*. Nairobi, 1968.
Oliver R. 'The Baganda and the Bakonjo', *Uganda Journal*, 1954, **18**, 1, 31–3.
Oliver, R. 'The traditional histories of Buganda, Bunyoro and Ankole', *Journal of the Royal Anthropological Institute*, 1955, **85**, 111–17.
Pagès, A. *Un royaume hamite au centre de l'Afrique*. Brussels, 1933.
Phillipson, D. W. 'Iron Age history'. *See under* ch. 7.
Posnansky, M. 'Pottery types from archaeological sites in East Africa', *Journal of African History*, 1961, **2**, 177–98.
Posnansky, M. 'The Iron Age in East Africa', in *Background to evolution in Africa*, ed. W. W. Bishop and J. D. Clark. Chicago, 1967.
Posnansky, M. 'Bigo bya Mugenyi', *Uganda Journal*, 1969, **2**, 33, 125–50.
Prins, A. H. J. *The coastal tribes of the North-Eastern Bantu*. London, 1952.
Prins, A. H. J. 'The Shungwaya problem', *Anthropos*, 1972, **67**, 9–35.
Reche, O. *Zur Ethnographie des abflusslosen Gebietes Deutsch-Ostafrikas*. Hamburg, 1914.
Rehse, H. *Kiziba, Land und Leute*. Stuttgart, 1910.
Roberts, A. D. ed. *Tanzania before 1900: seven area histories*. Nairobi, 1968.
Robinson, K. R. 'A preliminary report on the recent archaeology of Ngonde, northern Malawi', *Journal of African History*, 1966, **7**, 2, 169–88.
Roscoe, J. *The Baganda*. London, 1911.
Sassoon, H. 'New views on Engaruka, northern Tanzania', *Journal of African History*, 1967, **8**, 2, 201–17.
Schaegelen, T. 'La tribu des Wagogo', *Anthropos*, 1938, **33**, 195–217.
Shorter, A. *Chiefship in western Tanzania: a political history of the Kimbu*. Oxford, 1972.
Siiriäinen, A. 'The Iron Age site at Gatung'ang'a, central Kenya', *Azania*, 1971, **6**, 199–232.
Soper, R. C. 'Kwale: an Early Iron Age site in south-eastern Kenya', *Azania*, 1967, **2**, 1–17.
Soper, R. C. 'Iron Age sites in north-eastern Tanzania', *Azania*, 1967, **2**, 19–36.
Soper, R. C. 'Early Iron Age pottery types from East Africa: comparative analysis', *Azania*, 1971, **6**, 39–52.

Strandes, J. *The Portuguese period. See under* ch. 3.
Sutton, J. E. G. 'The interior of East Africa', in *African Iron Age*, ed. Shinnie.
Sutton, J. E. G. *The archaeology of the western highlands of Kenya*. Nairobi, 1973
Sutton, J. E. G. and Roberts, A. D. 'Uvinza and its salt industry', *Azania*, 1968, **3**, 45–86.
Vansina, J. *L'évolution du royaume de Rwanda des origines à 1900*. Brussels, 1961.
Vansina, J. *La légende du passé: traditions orales du Burundi*. Tervuren, 1972.
Were, G. S. 'The Abaluyia of western Kenya and their neighbours: their history down to 1930'. Doctoral thesis, University of Wales (Bangor), 1966.
Wilson, G. McL. 'The Tatoga of Tanganyika', *Tanganyika Notes and Records*, 1952, **33**, 34–47.
Wilson, M. *The peoples of the Nyasa–Tanganyika corridor*. Cape Town, 1958.
Wilson, M. *Communal rituals of the Nyakyusa*. London, 1959.

INDEX

Page numbers in italic indicate substantive references

Abyan (Yemen) 196
Abzin (= Asben) 88, 91, 263, 264
Acacia commiphora bush 186 *see also* scrub
'Accany', 'Acanistiens' 494
Accra 443, 509, 511, 513, 514
acculturation 235, 460, 493
acephalous societies *see* chiefless societies
Acholi 635, 636
Acocks, J. P. N. 602n., 616n.
Acre 17, 19, 31, 35, 45
Adal 83, 145, 146, 147, 149, 150, 153, 154, 155, 156, 164, 166–180
Adam, William, archbishop of Sulṭāniyya 179
Adamawa 263, 485
Adangbe 464, 493
Adansi 494, 495, 496
Addis Ababa 117
Adefa 114, 115, 117
Aden: and East Africa and Madagascar 183, 196, 206, 207, 217, 220, 223; and Egypt 19, 29, 57, 63, 75, 84, 152; and Yemen 118, 119, 122, 131, 151
  Gulf of: coastal settlements 103, 104, 105, 134, 136, 139, 151, 180; hinterland 103, 118, 142, 149, 151
al-'Āḍid 25, 26, 269
al-'Ādil, brother of Ṣalāḥ al-Dīn 32–4
al-Ādil II 36
administration: Egypt 11, 28, 47, 94; Ethiopia 84, 147, 175; North Africa 250, 337, 406; Portuguese 231; Sudan and Fezzan 94, 263, 387, 444; provincial, provincial governors 26, 364, 387, 545, 547, 551, 560, 566, 638
administrative manuals 671, 673
administrators 12, 66, 492, 642, 669, 698, 700
Adrar 349, 450
Adrar of the Iforas 381
Afar 146
al-Afḍal, vizier al-Malik 18, 23, 24
Aftel (= *Awdal* = Zeila) 175
Afughal 399, 400, 401
Afutu 493
Agades 92, 264, 265, 266, 278, 286, 294, 295, 430, 433
Agadir (Santa Cruz de Aguer) 398, 401, 402, 405, 453, 454
Agaw 108, 111, 112, 117, 124, 129, 131, 172, 176; Agaw monks, monastic officials 124, 129
Agawmeder 111
agba, head of Janissaries 404
age differentiation, systems of 656, 660, 662, 668; *see also* age-sets; generation groups
age-sets 666, 667, 700
Aghlabids 247
agriculture: in Central Africa 519, 520, 521, 522, 524, 525, 527, 537, 538, 540, 544, 557, Central Africa (northern) 558, 562, 564, 565; in central Sudan 239, 287, 289, 293, 474, 478, 487; in East Africa (coast and hinterland) 187, 188, 189, 208, East African interior 621, 623, 626, 629, 638, 639, 640, 654, 656, 658, 663, 668; in Guinea 467, 479, 483, 484, 485; in Madagascar 220; in North Africa 340, 343; in Nubia 78; in Somalia 185; in southern Africa (north-eastern part) 571, *572–3*, 574, 575, 577, 579, 581, 589, 592–3, 597, southern Africa (south of the Limpopo) 597, 599, 601, 603, 606, 609, 610, 611, 612, 613, 615, 698; in western Sudan 387
  agricultural corvée 594; fiefs 28; revenue 51, 56; settlement, white 544, 554; technology 388, 483
'Agusale' 497
ahl Songhay ('people of Songhay') 445
Aḥmad, brother of 'Abdallāh al-Ghālib 408
Aḥmad al-A'raj b. Muḥammad al-Qā'im 399, 400, 401, 402, 407, 410, 411
Aḥmad Bābā 92, 417, 418 and n., 420n., 688
Aḥmad al-Badāwi 32
Aḥmad b. 'Alī b.Sabredin 148
Aḥmad b. Ibrāhīm al-Ghāzī, *imām* (*Gragn*) 101, 134, 168–9, 171–7, 181, 182
Aḥmad al-Ḥājj (father of Bābā) 419
Aḥmadīyya (or Badāwiyya) 32
Aḥmad al-Ma'qūr 303, 304
Aḥmad al-Waṭṭāsī 401, 405
Al-Aḥsā 136, 199, 200
Aïr: as source of copper 475; as trading centre 262, 433; expeditions 266, 292, 298; horses, 310; Islam 312; people 240, 260; region 264, 281, 293; routes 91, 238, 375; sultan, sultanate 264, 266, 289, 310, 325, 326; al-Suyūṭī's questions 265, 274; *zāwiya* 268
Aisa (Bornu) 317
Aja states, people 502, 514
Ajayi, J. F. A. and Crowder, M. 686, 690
ajnād al-ḥalqa (locally recruited soldiers) 41
Ajuran 155–6, 230
Akan forest 5, 369, 374, 381, 493–4, 511; goldfields 375, 452, 459; gold-trade 489, 491, 494, 510, 514; people 464, 466, 491, 492, 493, 516; states 479, 495–6, 498, 513; traditions 413, 465
Akani 495, 514; Akani/Twifo region 495, 496
Akilu 416, 425
Akilu-ag-Malwal 421–2
Akinjobin, I. A. 691

languages (*cont.*)
Persian 68; Portuguese 517; Pygmy (lost) 559; Saho-Afar 135; Semitic 107, 125, 176, 679; spread of 111, 112; Serer 485; Shona 590; Somali 135, 189; Songhay 266, 433; Sotho 614; Spanish 409; Swahili 185, 187, 207, 218, 225, 623, 683; Teda/Daza 233, 240; Tuareg 262; Tukolor 485; Turkish 68, 409; Twi 493, 494; Voltaic 461; West Atlantic 482, 483, 509; Zaghawa 240; 'Zanj' 192
Langworthy, H. W. 532n.
Lanham, L. W. 617
al-Laqānī 418
Laqqūt 334
Larache 399, 451
La Roncière, C. de 449, 450, 679, 687
Laroui, A. 242n., 253n., 686, 689
Las Navas de Tolosa, battle 344, 354
Lasta 98, 108, 111, 114, 117, 125, 143, 175, 176
Lata people 618
Later Iron Age: Central Africa 519, 520, 522, 527, *528–30*, 531, 532, 534, 537 540, 542, 566; East Africa *625–30*, 627 (map), 644, 647, 652, 654, 656, 657, 659, 662, 664, 668; southern Africa 570, 571, 576, 588, 597, 607, 609, 620, 693, 694
Late Stone Age peoples 521, 567, 568, 601, 603, 607, 608, 609, 611, 613, 616, 618, 620, 697
Latham, A. J. H. 692
Latin states 25, 29, 31, 33, 35, 41, 43, 247; *see also* Jerusalem, Latin kingdom
law: Chwezi 633; Islamic see *sharī'a* (Muslim law); Wadai 303
Law, R. C. C. 503, 692
Lawal, B. 474
Lawāta Berbers 17, 244
lead 475, 555
leather 255, 305, 347, 356, 369, 472; leather workers 388
Lebanon 16
Lebeuf, J.-P. and A. M.-D. 474, 686
Lebna-Dengel, emperor 167, 170, 171, 172, 173, 176, 177, 180, 181
Lebombo mts 601
legends of origin 477, 478
Lekkerwater 578
Lelesu 624, 647
lemons 218
Leite de Faria, Francisco 546
Lengola 564
Leo Africanus: Agades, Aïr 265, 266, 286, 433 and n.; Gaoga 276, 279, 291, 304, 311–12, 314, 368; North Africa and desert 261, 262, 376, 399 and n.; Sudan 272, 275, 277 and n., 298, 449 and n., 454 and n., 488, 684, 688; Timbuktu 92n., 281, 374, 392, 428 and n., 432 and n., 448n., 450n.
leopard, panther skins 192, 220
Leopard's Kopje 569 and n., 570 and n., 571, 572, 573, 575, 576, 588, 591, 596, 601, 607, 610, 695; Leopard's Kopje mines 575
Lepanto, battle 258
Lesotho 613, 614, 615
Letaba 605
Le Tourneau, R. 689
Leur, J. van 64n.
Lévy-Provençal, E. 688
Levtzion, N. 379, 425n., 688, 689, 690, 692
Lewicki, T. 287n., 684
Lewis, B. 674
Lewis, H. S. 135, 679
Lewis, I. M. 138, 153 and n., 170n., 423n., 683
Lézine, A. 242n.
Lhote, H. 310, 689
Liberia 280, 465, 472, 479, 481, 482, 486, 488, 490, 509; area north-west 483; Liberia/Guinea boundary 486
Libya 232, 235, 250, 258, 684; Libyan desert 237, 238, 261
licence, Portuguese royal 506
Libolo 535, 536, 537
lifidi (quilted armour) 94–5, 96
lime plaster 212
Līmiyyīn 300
Limpopo: area 190, 680; area north of 7, 567, 568, 569, 586, 603; area south of 597–620, 600 (map), 609, 612, 615; basin 573, 574, 575, 611; mouth 605
lineage 530, 535, 536, 539, 541
linguistic acculturation, change 95, 668; diversity 662; origins 683
linguistic evidence: Central Africa 518, 624; East Africa 653, 656, 662, 700; Ethiopia 127–8; Guinea 464, 508; southern Africa 572n., 606 and n., 608, 617, 620, 698, 699; Sudan 240, 241, 292, 324, 685
Linschoten, J. H. 199 and n.
Lisbon 177, 453, 457, 511, 544; *see also* Portugal
litanies (Sufi) 316
literacy 3, 67, 219, 226, 234, 316, 423, 448, 463; and Islam 320–2
literature 21, 67, 115, 219, 361, 418; folk 67
lithām (veil) 337
Little, D. P. 672
Little Armenia 45, 47

traders, merchants, Sudan (*cont.*) 452; Dyula 6, 369, 375, 450, 459, 472, 488, 490, 493, 495, 510; Hausa 6, 495, 510; Mande 5, 6, 473, 485, 486, 489, 490, 491, 507, 510; Malinke 450; Marka 375; Soninke 374, 375; Takedda 279; Tuareg 411, 412, 432; Wangara 375, 472; Yarse 459
trading: agents 254; centre, emporium 289, 529; class 548; communities 366–7, 490, 491; contact, connection 475–6, 478; empire, state 547, 563
network, system: North Africa/desert 356, 368, 452; Sudan/Guinea 6, 374, 388, 452, 453, 459, 473, 475, 487, 488; Rhodesia 573, 574
settlement 507, 529
traditional heritage 440, 446
Traditions of the Prophet (*ḥadīth*) 323, 338, 339, 346, 417
Traghen 263, 290
Transcaucasia 54
Transkei 698
transport: animal 265, 467; ocean 183; river 16, 36, 72, 561, 566
trans-Saharan communications, travel 1, 232, 318
Transvaal 599, 601, 615, 618, 696; central 610; eastern 603; north-eastern 567, 575, 599, 602, 603, 604, 605, 611; south-eastern 603, 614; southern 609, 610, 618, 696; south-western 6, 610, 611, 612, 614
travellers, long-distance 1, 2, 687
treaties 34, 35; commercial 35, 37, 45, 51, 228, 253, 255
treehouses 272
Tremearne, A. J. N. 328n.
Triaud, J. L. 690
tribute: Central Africa 536, 545, 547, 553, 555; East Africa 216, 229, 631, 634, 637, 638; Egypt 12, 26, 56; Ethiopia 100, 112, 170; North Africa and Sahara 262, 323, 334, 354, 358, 397, 406, 449; southern Africa 585, 594; Sudan: central 234, 239, 266, 271, 282, 293, 298–9, 303, 308, western 381, 387, 421, 432, 433, 442; West Africa 5, 487
Trimingham, J. S. 85n., 100 and n., 107 and n., 123 and n., 670, 679, 690
Tripoli (North Africa): control 46, 243, 246, 251, 257, 258; European capture 245, 257, 403; Ottomans 415; relations with Sudan 292; trade, trade-routes 237, 263, 279, 283, 347, 433, 447–8
Tripoli (Syria) 24, 31, 45
Tripolitania 95, 235, 237, 241, 250, 258, 259
truce 30, 31, 33, 258, 401
tsetse 186, 467, 525, 535, 593, 602, 603, 609, 646, 663
Tshimbupfe 605
Tsoede 299, 300, 302, 502, 503
Tsonga 615
Tsumburburai (spirit of Dala hill) 293, 294
Tswana 598, 610, 611, 613, 615
Tuareg: Aïr 240, 264, 265, 293, 433; desert 238; Songhay 422, 425, 432, 435, 436, 440, 442, 449; Timbuktu 383, 392, 393, 416, 421, 422; traders, trade-routes 279, 411, 412, 433, 449
Tuat: brotherhoods 399; control 357, 412, 454; Jews 449–50; al-Maghīlī 295, 418, 449, 450; scholars 416; trade, trade-routes 91, 366, 373, 376, 411, 449, 451
Tubu 238, 240, 260, 263, 280, 287, 289, 309, 310, 313, 323
tubungu (elders) 538
Tugela r. 616
Ṭughrul Beg, sultan 15
Tuken 655
Tukolor ('people of Takrur') 354, 482, 485, 486
Tuli people 618
Tulunid dynasty 22, 269
Ṭūmān Bay 65
Tumbata 195
Tumbuka 532
Tumur (= Somali) 154
Tunis: control 246, 247, 248, 250, 357, 358; Crusade 249; Ibn Khaldūn 255; Ottomans 271, 323, 403 (*see also* Turks); Spanish conquest 258; trade 251, 252, 253, 254, 255, 258, 279, 347, 449; tradition of origin from 303
Tunisia 1, 11, 80, 233, 235, 237, 241, 244, 250, 258, 259, 403; Tunisian seamen 87
Tunjur 79, 80, 303, 320
tunkara (royal title) 378, 444
Tunsam 305
al-Tūnusī, Muḥammad b. 'Umar 270n., 284 and n.
Tūrān-Shāh, brother of Ṣalaḥ al-Dīn 29, 30, 74
Tūrān-Shāh, sultan 37, 39
Ture 427; Ture clan 427
Turkana 629
Turkey 67, 447
Turks: in North Africa 259, 263, 292, 403; in Red Sea 229; *see also* Ottoman intrusion
Turkish/Mongol hordes (Timūr Lenk) 54
Turkish sources 684
Turkish troops: *amīrs*, generals 13 14; army instructors 510; cavalry 12, 17,